D0218898

The Routledge
Handbook of Syntax

The study of syntax over the last half century has seen a remarkable expansion of the boundaries of human knowledge about the structure of natural language. *The Routledge Handbook of Syntax* presents a comprehensive survey of the major theoretical and empirical advances in the dynamically evolving field of syntax from a variety of perspectives, both within the dominant generative paradigm and between syntacticians working within generative grammar and those working in functionalist and related approaches.

The *Handbook* covers key issues within the field that include:

- core areas of syntactic empirical investigation,
- contemporary approaches to syntactic theory,
- interfaces of syntax with other components of the human language system,
- experimental and computational approaches to syntax.

Bringing together renowned linguistic scientists and cutting-edge scholars from across the discipline and providing a balanced yet comprehensive overview of the field, *The Routledge Handbook of Syntax* is essential reading for researchers and postgraduate students working in syntactic theory.

Andrew Carnie is Professor of Linguistics and Dean of the Graduate College at the University of Arizona, USA.

Yosuke Sato is Associate Professor of Linguistics at the Department of English Language and Literature of the National University of Singapore.

Daniel Siddiqi is an Associate Professor of Linguistics, Cognitive Science, and English at Carleton University in Ottawa, Canada.

Routledge Handbooks in Linguistics

Routledge Handbooks in Linguistics provide overviews of a whole subject area or sub-discipline in linguistics, and survey the state of the discipline, including emerging and cutting edge areas. Edited by leading scholars, these volumes include contributions from key academics from around the world and are essential reading for both advanced undergraduate and postgraduate students.

The Routledge Handbook of Syntax
Edited by Andrew Carnie, Yosuke Sato and Daniel Siddiqi

The Routledge Handbook of Historical Linguistics
Edited by Claire Bowern and Bethwyn Evans

The Routledge Handbook of Language and Culture
Edited by Farzad Sharifian

The Routledge Handbook of Linguistics
Edited by Keith Allan

The Routledge Handbook of Semantics
Edited by Nick Riemer

The Routledge Handbook of Linguistic Anthropology
Edited by Nancy Bonvillain

The Routledge Handbook of the English Writing System
Edited by Vivian Cook and Des Ryan

The Routledge Handbook of Metaphor and Language
Edited by Elena Semino and Zsófia Demjén

The Routledge Handbook of Systemic Functional Linguistics
Edited by Tom Bartlett, Gerard O'Grady

The Routledge Handbook of Heritage Language Education
From Innovation to Program Building
Edited by Olga E. Kagan, Maria M. Carreira and Claire Hitchins Chik

The Routledge Handbook of Language and Humor
Edited by Salvatore Attardo

Further titles in this series can be found online at www.routledge.com/series/RHIL

Praise for this volume:

"The *Handbook* brings together thoughtful and judicious essays by outstanding scholars, covering the many aspects of syntax that have been explored and developed extensively in recent years. It is sure to be of great value to a wide range of users, from students to those engaged in advanced research, as well as to others who want to gain some sense of current ideas about the nature of language. A very welcome and impressive contribution."

Noam Chomsky, *Massachusetts Institute of Technology, USA*

"This is an excellent book, both rich in detail and beautifully clear and accessible. The most important phenomena and theoretical issues in generative grammar are discussed in an even-handed and interesting way. I especially appreciate the sections that situate syntactic theory in its various contexts: interfaces with other structural aspects of language, relations to language change, acquisition and processing, and the rich range of theoretical approaches currently being pursued. The combination of historical perspective, theoretical and methodological breadth, and up-to-date insights makes it a must-read for graduate students, and a valuable resource for specialists."

Elizabeth Cowper, *University of Toronto, Canada*

"This comprehensive handbook presents in an impressively clear way the current issues on the central topics of the rapidly advancing field. It is a valuable resource for researchers and is useful especially for graduate students as each chapter includes a concise introduction of a research area and illustrates the recent developments step by step, leading up to ongoing research."

Mamoru Saito, *Department of Anthropology and Philosophy, Nanzan University, Japan*

The Routledge
Handbook of Syntax

Edited by Andrew Carnie,
Yosuke Sato, and Daniel Siddiqi

LONDON AND NEW YORK

First published in paperback 2018
First published 2014
by Routledge
2 Park Square, Milton Park, Abingdon, Oxon OX14 4RN

and by Routledge
711 Third Avenue, New York, NY 10017

*Routledge is an imprint of the Taylor & Francis Group, an informa
business*

©2014, 2018 selection and editorial matter, Andrew Carnie, Dan Siddiqi
and Yosuke Sato; individual chapters, the contributors

The right of Andrew Carnie, Dan Siddiqi and Yosuke Sato to be
identified to be identified as the authors of the editorial matter, and of the
authors for their individual chapters, has been asserted in accordance
with sections 77 and 78 of the Copyright, Designs and Patents Act 1988.

All rights reserved. No part of this book may be reprinted or reproduced
or utilised in any form or by any electronic, mechanical, or other means,
now known or hereafter invented, including photocopying and
recording, or in any information storage or retrieval system, without
permission in writing from the publishers.

Trademark notice: Product or corporate names may be trademarks
or registered trademarks, and are used only for identification and
explanation without intent to infringe.

British Library Cataloguing-in-Publication Data
A catalogue record for this book is available from the British Library

Library of Congress Cataloging-in-Publication Data
The Routledge handbook of syntax / edited by Andrew Carnie, Yosuke
Sato and Daniel Siddiqi.
      pages cm – (Routledge handbooks in linguistics)
   "Simultaneously published in the USA and Canada by Routledge."
   Includes index.
   1. Grammar, Comparative and general–Syntax–Handbooks, manuals,
   etc. 2. Generative grammar–Handbooks, manuals, etc. I. Carnie,
   Andrew, 1969- editor of compilation. II. Sato, Yosuke, 1978- editor of
   compilation. III. Siddiqi, Daniel, editor of compilation. IV. Title:
   Handbook of syntax.
   P291.R68 2014
   415–dc23

ISBN: 978-0-415-53394-2 (hbk)
ISBN: 978-1-138-48058-2 (pbk)
ISBN: 978-1-315-79660-4 (ebk)

Typeset in Times New Roman
by Sunrise Setting Ltd, Paignton, UK

Contents

List of contributors   x
Acknowledgments   xvi
Editors' introduction   xvii

PART I
Constituency, categories, and structure   1

  1 Merge, labeling, and projection   3
    Naoki Fukui and Hiroki Narita

  2 Argument structure   24
    Jaume Mateu

  3 The integration, proliferation, and expansion of
    functional categories: an overview   42
    Lisa deMena Travis

  4 Functional structure inside nominal phrases   65
    Jeffrey Punske

  5 The syntax of adjectives   89
    Artemis Alexiadou

  6 The syntax of adverbs   108
    Thomas Ernst

PART II
Syntactic phenomena   131

  7 Head movement   133
    Michael Barrie and Éric Mathieu

  8 Case and grammatical relations   150
    Maria Polinsky and Omer Preminger

Contents

9   A-bar movement   167
    Norvin Richards

10 The syntax of ellipsis and related phenomena   192
    Masaya Yoshida, Chizuru Nakao, and Iván Ortega-Santos

11 Binding theory   214
    Robert Truswell

12 Minimalism and control   239
    Norbert Hornstein and Jairo Nunes

13 Scrambling   264
    Yosuke Sato and Nobu Goto

14 Noun incorporation, nonconfigurationality, and polysynthesis   283
    Kumiko Murasugi

PART III
Syntactic interfaces   **305**

15 The syntax–semantics/pragmatics interface   307
    Sylvia L.R. Schreiner

16 The syntax–lexicon interface   322
    Peter Ackema

17 The morphology–syntax interface   345
    Daniel Siddiqi

18 Prosodic domains and the syntax–phonology interface   365
    Yoshihito Dobashi

PART IV
Syntax in context   **389**

19 Syntactic change   391
    Ian Roberts

20 Syntax in forward and in reverse: form, memory,
    and language processing   409
    Matthew W. Wagers

21 Major theories in acquisition of syntax research   426
    Susannah Kirby

22 The evolutionary origins of syntax   446
    Maggie Tallerman

PART V
Theoretical approaches to syntax   **463**

23 The history of syntax   465
    Peter W. Culicover

24 Comparative syntax   490
    Martin Haspelmath

25 Principles and Parameters/Minimalism   509
    Terje Lohndal and Juan Uriagereka

26 Head-driven Phrase Structure Grammar   526
    Felix Bildhauer

27 Lexical-functional Grammar   556
    George Aaron Broadwell

28 Role and Reference Grammar   579
    Robert D. Van Valin, Jr.

29 Dependency Grammar   604
    Timothy Osborne

30 Morphosyntax in Functional Discourse Grammar   627
    J. Lachlan Mackenzie

31 Construction Grammar   647
    Seizi Iwata

32 Categorial Grammar   670
    Mark Steedman

Index   702

Contributors

Peter Ackema obtained his PhD in Linguistics from Utrecht University (the Netherlands) in 1995. He worked at a number of universities in the Netherlands before moving to the University of Edinburgh (UK) in 2004, where he is currently a Reader in the department of Linguistics and English Language. His research interests lie in the area of theoretical syntax and morphology and in particular topics that concern the interaction between these two modules of grammar. He is the author of *Issues in Morphosyntax* (John Benjamins, 1999) and co-author (with Ad Neeleman) of *Beyond Morphology* (OUP, 2004).

Artemis Alexiadou is Professor of Theoretical and English Linguistics at the University of Stuttgart. She received her PhD in Linguistics in 1994 from the University of Potsdam. Her research interests lie in theoretical and comparative syntax, morphology, and, most importantly, in the interface between syntax, morphology, the lexicon, and interpretation. Her publications include books on the noun phrase (*Functional Structure in Nominals*: John Benjamins, 2011; *Noun Phrase in the Generative Perspective* with Liliane Haegeman and Melita Stavrou, Mouton de Gruyter, 2007) as well as several journal articles and chapters in edited volumes on nominal structure.

Michael Barrie is an Assistant Professor of Linguistics at Sogang University. His specialization is Syntax and Field Linguistics. His main theoretical interests are noun incorporation and *wh*-movement, and his main empirical interests are Northern Iroquoian, Romance, and Chinese.

Felix Bildhauer studied Romance Linguistics at the Universities of Göttingen and Barcelona. He received his doctorate from the University of Bremen in 2008 with a dissertation on representing information structure in a Head-Driven Phrase Structure Grammar of Spanish. Since 2007 he has been working as a research assistant at Freie University, Berlin, focusing on corpus-based approaches to information structure in German and various Romance languages. His research interests also include the compilation of corpora from the Web to overcome the lack of large available corpora in some of the languages on which he is working. He has taught courses on a variety of subjects, including syntax, phonology, semantics, Corpus Linguistics, and Computational Linguistics.

George Aaron Broadwell (PhD 1990 UCLA) is a Professor in the Department of Anthropology and the Program in Linguistics and Cognitive Science at University at Albany, SUNY. His research focuses on endangered languages of the Americas, and he works in both theoretical syntax and language documentation. He has worked on the Choctaw language for the last thirty years, and his more recent work has focused on the Zapotec and Copala Triqui languages of Oaxaca, Mexico.

Andrew Carnie is Professor of Linguistics and Dean of the Graduate College at University of Arizona. He received his PhD from MIT in 1995. His research focuses on constituent structure, hierarchies, case, and word order. He has an emphasis on the syntax of the Celtic languages and does research on the sound systems of these languages as well. His thirteen volumes include *Syntax: A Generative Introduction* (3rd edn, Wiley, 2013), *Modern Syntax: A Coursebook* (Cambridge University Press, 2011), *Constituent Structure* (Oxford University Press, 2010), and *Irish Nouns* (Oxford University Press, 2008).

Peter W. Culicover is Humanities Distinguished Professor in the Department of Linguistics at Ohio State University and a Fellow of the American Academy of Arts and Sciences and of the Linguistic Society of America. He received his PhD in Linguistics from MIT in 1971. His research has been concerned with explaining why grammars are the way they are. He has worked in recent years on grammar and complexity, the theory of constructions ("syntactic nuts"), the history of the core constructions of English, and ellipsis. Recent major publications include *Grammar and Complexity* (Oxford, 2013) and *Simpler Syntax* (with Ray Jackendoff: Oxford, 2005).

Yoshihito Dobashi is an Associate Professor in the Faculty of Humanities at Niigata University, Japan. He received his PhD in Linguistics in 2003 from Cornell University, Ithaca, New York. His research interests are in syntactic theory and syntax–phonology interface.

Thomas Ernst is a Visiting Scholar at the University of Massachusetts, Amherst, and has taught at a number of institutions, such as Indiana University, the University of Delaware, the University of Connecticut, and Dartmouth College. His research has always revolved around the syntax and semantics of adverbial adjuncts, with forays into such related areas as negation, questions, and polarity phenomena.

Naoki Fukui is Professor of Linguistics and Chair of the Linguistics Department at Sophia University, Tokyo. He is the author of several books, including *Theoretical Comparative Syntax* (Routledge, 2006) and *Linguistics as a Natural Science* (new paperback edition, Chikuma Math & Science, 2012), and has been an editorial board member of various international journals. His research interests include syntax, biolinguistics, philosophy of linguistics, and the brain science of language.

Nobu Goto received his PhD in Literature from Tohoku Gakuin University, Sendai, Japan. He is currently Specially Appointed Lecturer of the Liberal Arts Center at Mie University. He works on Japanese, English, and European languages and specializes in syntactic theory and comparative syntax. He has published his research in journals such as *English Linguistics* and *Tohoku Review of English Literature.*

Martin Haspelmath is Senior Scientist at the Max Planck Institute for Evolutionary Anthropology and Honorary Professor at the University of Leipzig. He received his PhD from Freie University, Berlin after studies in Vienna, Cologne, Buffalo, and Moscow. His research interests are primarily in the area of broadly comparative and diachronic morphosyntax (*Indefinite Pronouns*, 1997; *From Space to Time*, 1997; *Understanding Morphology*,

2002) and in language contact (*Loanwords in the World's Languages*, co-edited with Uri Tadmor, 2009; *Atlas of Pidgin and Creole Language Structures*, co-edited with Susanne Maria Michaelis *et al.*, 2013). He is perhaps best known as one of the editors of the *World Atlas of Language Structures* (2005).

Norbert Hornstein is Professor of Linguistics at the University of Maryland, College Park. Recent publications include *A Theory of Syntax and Control as Movement* (with C. Boeckx and J. Nunes).

Seizi Iwata is currently a Professor at Osaka City University, Japan. He received his PhD from the University of Tsukuba in 1996. His major research interest lies with lexical semantics and pragmatics. He is the author of *Locative Alternation: A Lexical-Constructional Approach* (John Benjamins, 2008) and has published articles in such journals as *Linguistics*, *Journal of Linguistics*, *Linguistics and Philosophy*, *English Language and Linguistics*, *Language Sciences*, and *Cognitive Linguistics*.

Susannah Kirby holds a BA in Psychology and a PhD in Linguistics from the University of North Carolina at Chapel Hill (UNC-CH), and has previously held appointments at UNC-CH, the University of British Columbia (UBC), and Simon Fraser University (SFU). She is currently working towards a degree in Computer Science with a focus on artificial intelligence and cognitive neuropsychology. Despite a winding career trajectory encompassing mental health care, academic research, higher education, and now IT, Susannah has always been fascinated by how brains work.

Terje Lohndal is an Associate Professor of English Linguistics at the Norwegian University of Science and Technology. He mostly works on syntax and the syntax–semantics interface.

J. Lachlan Mackenzie is Professor of Functional Linguistics at VU University Amsterdam, the Netherlands, and a researcher at ILTEC, Lisbon, Portugal. He collaborates with Kees Hengeveld on the development of Functional Discourse Grammar and is editor of the international journal *Functions of Language*.

Jaume Mateu is Associate Professor of Catalan Language and Linguistics at the Universitat Autònoma de Barcelona (UAB). He is the current Director of the Centre de Lingüística Teòrica (Center for Theoretical Linguistics) at UAB. Most of his recent work is on the syntax of argument structure in Romance and Germanic languages.

Éric Mathieu is an Associate Professor of Linguistics at the University of Ottawa. He specializes in syntax and works on French and Algonquian languages. He has published on *wh*-in situ, the count/mass distinction, noun incorporation, and other topics related to the noun phrase.

Kumiko Murasugi is an Assistant Professor of Linguistics in the School of Linguistics and Language Studies at Carleton University, Ottawa, Canada. Her research focus is the morphology, syntax, and sociolinguistics of Inuktitut, the language of the Canadian Inuit.

Chizuru Nakao is a Lecturer/Assistant Professor at Daito Bunka University, Japan. He received his PhD in Linguistics from the University of Maryland, College Park, in 2009.

His main research interest lies in comparative syntax, with a particular focus on elliptical constructions in Japanese and English.

Hiroki Narita is Assistant Professor of Linguistics at Waseda University/Waseda Institute for Advanced Study (WIAS), Tokyo, and has published extensively on various issues concerning endocentricity and labeling in bare phrase structure. He is the author of *Endocentric Structuring of Projection-free Syntax* (John Benjamins).

Jairo Nunes is Professor of Linguistics at the University of São Paulo. He is the author of *Linearization of Chains and Sideward Movement* (MIT Press, 2004) and co-author of *Understanding Minimalism* (Cambridge University Press, 2005) and *Control as Movement* (Cambridge University Press, 2010).

Timothy Osborne received his PhD in German (with a specialization in linguistics) from Pennsylvania State University in 2004. At the time of writing, he was an independent researcher living in the Seattle area. His research and publications focus on areas of syntax, such as coordination and ellipsis, whereby the analyses are couched in a dependency-based model. He is the primary translator (French to English) of Lucien Tesnière's *Éléments de syntaxe structurale* (1959), the translation being due to appear with Benjamins in 2014.

Maria Polinsky is Professor of Linguistics and Director of the Language Science Lab at Harvard University. She received her PhD from the Russian Academy of Sciences in 1986. She has done primary research on Austronesian languages, languages of the Caucasus, Bantu languages, and Chukchi. She has also worked extensively in the field of heritage languages. Her main interests are in syntactic theory and its intersections with information structure and processing.

Omer Preminger is Assistant Professor of Linguistics at Syracuse University. He received his PhD from the Massachusetts Institute of Technology (2011). He has done research on the morphology and syntax of various languages, including Basque; Hebrew; Kaqchikel, Q'anjob'al and Chol (Mayan); Sakha (Turkic); and others. Topics he has worked on include predicate-argument agreement, case, ergativity and split ergativity, and the mapping between argument structure and syntax. His work has appeared in *Linguistic Inquiry* and *Natural Language and Linguistic Theory*, among others.

Jeffrey Punske currently teaches theoretic linguistics and composition in the English Department at the Kutztown University of Pennsylvania. Previously he taught in the department of Modern Languages, Literatures and Linguistics at the University of Oklahoma. He earned his PhD in Linguistics from the University of Arizona in 2012.

Norvin Richards is a Professor of Linguistics at MIT. Much of his work centers on *wh*-movement, and on the investigation of lesser-studied and endangered languages.

Ian Roberts received his Ph.D. in linguistics from the University of Southern California. He has worked as a professor at the University of Geneva, the University of Wales in Bangor where he was also the department head, at the University of Stuttgart and now at the University of Cambridge. He has published six monographs and two textbooks, and has edited several collections of articles. He was also Joint Editor of the *Journal of Linguistics*.

He was president of Generative Linguistics of the Old World (GLOW) from 1993–2001 and was president of the Societas Linguistica Europaea in 2012–13. His work has always been on the application of current syntactic theory to comparative and historical syntax. He is currently working on a project funded by the European Research Council called "Rethinking Comparative Syntax".

Iván Ortega-Santos is an Assistant Professor at the University of Memphis. He completed his doctoral work in Linguistics at the University of Maryland, College Park, in 2008. His research focuses on focalization and ellipsis with an emphasis on Romance languages.

Yosuke Sato received his PhD in Linguistics from the University of Arizona, Tucson, USA. He is currently Assistant Professor of Linguistics at the National University of Singapore. He works on Indonesian, Javanese, Japanese, and Singapore English and specializes in syntactic theory and linguistic interfaces. He has published his research in journals such as *Linguistic Inquiry*, *Journal of Linguistics*, *Journal of East Asian Linguistics* and *Studia Linguistica*.

Sylvia L. R. Schreiner (who has previously appeared as Sylvia L. Reed) is currently a Mellon Post-Doctoral Fellow in Linguistics at Wheaton College in Massachusetts. Her research focuses primarily on the semantics and morphosyntax of temporal and spatial aspects of the grammar, especially tense/aspect phenomena and prepositional notions.

Daniel Siddiqi is an Assistant Professor of Linguistics, Cognitive Science, and English at Carleton University in Ottawa. His research record includes a focus on the morphology–syntax interface especially as it relates to realizational theories, particularly Distributed Morphology. Other research interests include non-standard English morphosyntactic phenomena and morphological metatheory. He is an editor of this volume as well as the forthcoming *Morphological Metatheory* with Heidi Harley.

Mark Steedman is the Professor of Cognitive Science in the School of Informatics at the University of Edinburgh. He was trained as a psychologist and a computer scientist. He is a Fellow of the British Academy, the American Association for Artificial Intelligence, and the Association for Computational Linguistics. He has also held research positions and taught at the Universities of Sussex, Warwick, Texas, and Pennsylvania, and his research covers a wide range of issues in theoretical and computational linguistics, including syntax, semantics, spoken intonation, knowledge representation, and robust wide-coverage natural language processing.

Maggie Tallerman is Professor of Linguistics at Newcastle University, UK. She has worked extensively on Welsh (morpho)syntax, but started researching into evolutionary linguistics in case a guy on a train asks her where language came from. Her books include *Language Origins: Perspectives on Evolution* (2005), *Understanding Syntax* (2011), *The Syntax of Welsh* (with Borsley and Willis, 2007), and *The Oxford Handbook of Language Evolution* (2012).

Lisa deMena Travis received her PhD from MIT in 1984. Since then she has been a Professor in the Department of Linguistics at McGill University in Montreal, Quebec.

Robert Truswell is Assistant Professor of Syntax at the University of Ottawa. He has published research on event structure, locality theory, connectivity, the structure of noun phrases, and the diachrony of relative clauses, and is the author of *Events, Phrases, and Questions* (Oxford University Press).

Juan Uriagereka is Associate Provost for Faculty Affairs and Professor of Linguistics at the University of Maryland, College Park. Though his work is focused on syntax, his interests range from comparative grammar to the neurobiological bases of language.

Robert D. Van Valin, Jr. received his PhD in Linguistics at the University of California, Berkeley, in 1977. He has taught at the University of Arizona, Temple University, the University of California, Davis, and the University at Buffalo, the State University of New York. He is currently on leave from the University at Buffalo and is the Professor of General Linguistics at the Heinrich Heine University in Düsseldorf, Germany. In 2006 he received the Research Award for Outstanding Scholars from Outside of Germany from the Alexander von Humboldt Foundation. In 2008 he was awarded a Max Planck Fellowship from the Max Planck Society. His research is focused on theoretical linguistics, especially syntactic theory and theories of the acquisition of syntax and the role of syntactic theory in models of sentence processing. He is the primary developer of the theory of Role and Reference Grammar.

Matthew W. Wagers is an Assistant Professor in the Department of Linguistics at the University of California, Santa Cruz. He received his PhD in Linguistics from the University of Maryland, College Park, in 2008 and was a research scientist in the Department of Psychology at New York University before moving to Santa Cruz in 2009. His research and teaching concerns questions about the mental data structures of syntactic representation and the interface between language and memory. In addition, he does research on incremental language processing in psycholinguistically understudied languages, particularly Chamorro.

Masaya Yoshida is an Assistant Professor at Northwestern University. He received his PhD in Linguistics from the University of Maryland, College Park. The main focus of his research is syntax and real-time sentence comprehension.

Acknowledgments

A number of people have helped us to get this volume together. First, we would like to thank the editorial staff at Routledge and their contractors: Nadia Seemungal, Sophie Jaques, Rachel Daw, Sarah Harrison, and Katharine Bartlett. The contributors to the volume have been fantastic to work with and have made putting this volume together a pleasure. Our colleagues and students have supported us in our professional activities and our families have supported us at home. Our deepest thanks thus go to Ash Asudeh, Zhiming Bao, Tom Bever, Maria Biezma, Lev Blumenfeld, Cynthia Bjerk-Plocke, Fiona Carnie, Jean Carnie, Morag Carnie, Pangur Carnie, Qizhong Chang, Michael Hammond, Heidi Harley, Mie Hiramoto, Dianne Horgan, Deepthi Kamawar, Chonghyuck Kim, Simin Karimi, Alicia Lopez, Mark MacLeod, Kumiko Murasugi, Diane Ohala, Massimo Piatelli-Palmarini, Yoichiro Shafiq Sato, Charlie Siddiqi, Julianna Siddiqi, Jack Siddiqi, Raj Singh, Ida Toivonen, Dorian Voorhees, Zechy Wong, Jianrong Yu, and Dwi Hesti Yuliani.

Editors' introduction

The description and analysis of the syntactic patterns of language have been a central focus of linguistics since the mid 1950s. Our understanding of the complex nature of the relationships between words and among phrases has increased dramatically in that time. Our knowledge of the range of grammatical variation among languages, and the apparent restrictions thereon, is significantly advanced and we have made serious ventures into questions of how syntactic knowledge changes, and is structured, used, acquired, and applied.

The study of syntax has been rife with controversy both within the dominant generative paradigm and among those working in functionalist and related approaches. These lively debates have fostered an empirically rich body of knowledge about the syntactic structures of language.

This handbook brings together experts from all walks of the discipline to write about the state of the art in syntax. It includes chapters on all the major areas of empirical investigation and articles on most of the modern approaches to syntactic theory. It also includes chapters on each of the areas where syntax interfaces with other parts of the human language system.

One unique aspect of this handbook is that we have attempted to include not only established linguists in the field but also some of the young scholars that are doing the most exciting and innovative work in the field. We hope that our mix of senior scholars, with their breadth of experience, with more junior colleagues means that the articles in this handbook will have a fresh feel.

The handbook is presented in five parts, each of which covers a different major focus of syntactic research. Part I, titled *Constituency, categories, and structure*, investigates the nature of the atomic units of phrases and sentences and principles of syntactic derivation, including constituent structure, phrase structure, projection, labelling, functional structure both for nominal and verbal projections, the nature of modification through adjectives and adverbs. Chapter 1, *Merge, labeling, and projection*, lays out the scaffolding for the discussion of constituency by providing a brief historical review of the theory of phrase structure and describing the major contemporary issues currently under investigation. The remaining chapters of Part I break the overall structure of a syntactic structure into smaller, more manageable topics and detail historical and contemporary research into each topic.

The chapters of Part II, *Syntactic phenomena*, provide an overview of the major phenomena that form the empirical foundation of formal syntactic research. Part III, Syntactic interfaces, surveys the major interfaces of other grammatical modules with the syntactic module. Various issues that arise in syntax with semantics/pragmatics, the lexicon, morphology, and phonology are covered. Part IV, *Syntax in context*, surveys four major topics in syntax as a part of grammar that is employed by humans, giving context to the grammar. Chapters focus on syntactic change, processing, acquisition, and the evolution of syntax. Part V, *Theoretical approaches to syntax*, contains brief descriptions of several dominant models of syntax. Two introductory chapters cover the history of syntactic theory and comparative syntax. Following these, chapters are dedicated to each of the following major contemporary theories of syntax: Chomskyan Minimalism, Head-Driven Phrase Structure Grammar, Lexical-Functional Grammar, Role and Reference Grammar, Dependency Grammar, Functional Discourse Grammar, Construction Grammar, and Categorial Grammar.

We have seen the expansion of the boundaries of knowledge of natural language syntax in all possible directions in the last fifty years. The exponential growth in the findings achieved in modern syntax, backed up by an increasing number of publication venues (peer-reviewed journals, book chapters, books, conference proceedings and handbooks) and conferences, is itself an encouraging sign that our field is quite lively. However, this also means that it has become very difficult, if not impossible, to catch up with all major strands of research even within a single framework. The goal of this handbook, therefore, is to provide the reader with a glimpse of the dynamic field of syntax through chapter-length introductions to major theoretical and empirical issues in contemporary syntactic theory. For advanced syntacticians, this handbook should be very useful in reorganizing and reconstructing the enormous volume of accumulated knowledge. On the other hand, novice researchers will find this volume helpful in learning what exactly the current issues are and venturing into the exciting discipline of syntax.

Part I

Constituency, categories, and structure

1

Merge, labeling, and projection

Naoki Fukui and Hiroki Narita

1 Introduction[*]

Thousands of years of language study share the belief, commonly ascribed to Aristotle, that the grammar of human language is in essence a system of pairing "sound" (or "signs") and "meaning." The enterprise of generative grammar initiated by Chomsky (1955/1975; 1957) is just a recent addition to this long tradition, but it brought a couple of important insights into the nature of human language, which have massively revolutionized our perspective from which to study language. At the core of this "Chomskyan revolution" lies an old observation, essentially due to Descartes and other rationalists, that the capacity to pair sounds and meanings in human language exhibits unbounded creativity: humans can produce and understand an infinitude of expressions, many of which are previously unheard of or too long and/or senseless to be produced. This Cartesian observation specifically led Chomsky to suppose that the grammar of human language must be essentially "generative" and "transformational" in the following sense, setting the basis for sixty years of contemporary linguistic research:

(1) The grammar of human language is "generative" in the sense that it is a system that uses a finite number of basic operations to yield "discrete infinity" (i.e., the infinity created by combinations of discrete units) of linguistic expressions.

(2) Further, it is "transformational" in the sense that it has the property of mapping an abstract representation to another representation.

For example, any linguistic expression – say, *the boy read the book* – can be infinitely expanded by adding optional adjuncts of various types (3), coordinating its constituents (4), or embedding it into another expression (5), yielding various sorts of discrete infinity.

[*] Part of this research is supported by a grant from Japan Science and Technology Agency (JST, CREST) and a grant from Japan Society for the Promotion of Science (Grant-in-Aid for Scientific Research, Scientific Research (A) #23242025, and Challenging Exploratory Research #25580095). We would like to thank Noam Chomsky, Bridget Samuels, and Yosuke Sato for their detailed written comments and suggestions on earlier versions of this paper.

(3) Adjunction:
   a. the boy (often) (eagerly) read the book (carefully) (quickly) (at the station) (at 2pm) (last week) …
   b. the (smart) (young) (handsome) … boy (who was twelve years old) (who Mary liked) (whose mother was sick) … read the book.

(4) Coordination:
   a. the boy read the book (and/or/but) the girl drank coffee (and/or/but) …
   b. [the boy (and/or/but not) the girl (and/or)…] read the book.

(5) Embedding:
   a. I know that [the girl believes that [it is certain that…[the boy read the book]…]]
   b. The boy [(that/who) the girl [(that/who) the cat […] bit] liked] read the book.

Moreover, the same sentence can be "transformationally related" to many other sentences of different types, yielding the massive expressive potential of human language:

(6) Passive:
   The book was read (by the boy).

(7) Interrogatives:
   a. Did the boy read the book?
   b. {Which book/what} did the boy read?
   c. {Which boy/who} read the book?

(8) Topicalization/Fronting:
   a. The book, the boy read (last week).
   b. Read the book, the boy did (last week).

The recognition of the generative and transformational aspects of human language led Chomsky to conclude that structural linguistics was fundamentally inadequate in that it restricted its research focus to the techniques of sorting finite linguistic corpora (see, e.g., Harris 1951). Linguists were instead urged to shift their focus of study from an arbitrarily chosen set of observable utterances to the mind-internal mechanism that generates that set and infinitely many other expressions (i.e., "I-language" in the sense of Chomsky 1986b). This shift of focus effectively exorcised the empiricist/behaviorist doctrine that attributes the knowledge of language in its entirety to reinforcement of finite experience, resurrecting the rationalist/mentalist approach to the human mind and its innate mechanism (the topic of *Universal Grammar* (UG)). It further came to be recognized in subsequent years that (1)–(2) (or specifically the recursive property attributable to the operations underlying (1)–(2)) are unique properties of human language and apparently shared by no other species (Hauser *et al.* 2002; Fitch *et al.* 2005). The recognition of (1)–(2) as a species-specific trait (an "autapomorphy" in cladistical terms) stirred the interest of evolutionary biologists and comparative ethologists, leading to a lively discussion on the human-uniqueness of language and its evolutionary origins (although the other themes of domain-specificity and theory-internal complexity largely prevented generative linguists from addressing the question of evolution for several decades).

The history of generative linguistics can be understood in significant part by the development of theories of the generative and transformational aspects of human language (1)–(2). The purpose of this chapter is to provide a brief overview of this development, which will be organized as follows. We will first see in §2 how sixty years of generative research has emerged as a system of phrase structure rules and transformations and converged on the framework of "bare phrase structure" (BPS) (Chomsky 1995a; 1995b, *et seq.*). We will see how this framework incorporates major insights of earlier approaches, and how a single operation hypothesized therein, called *Merge*, provides an arguably minimal but sufficient account of (1)–(2). Some possible refinement of Chomsky's (1995a; 1995b) theory of Merge will be suggested in §3, and further research questions will be addressed in §4.

2 An historical overview

2.1 *Phrase structure rules and transformations: Grammar as a rule-system*

In the earliest tradition of transformational generative grammar initiated by Chomsky (1955/1975; 1957) it was assumed that the syntax of natural language at its core is a bifurcated system of *phrase structure rules* (PSRs) and *transformational rules* (*grammatical transformations*). According to this conception, the skeletal structure of a sentence is initially generated by a finite set of PSRs, each of which maps a nonterminal symbol to its ordered constituents. PSRs are illustrated by (9), which represents the basic structure of English sentences.

(9) a. S′ → COMP S
     b. S → NP Infl VP
     c. Infl → Present, Past, will, …
     d. VP → V NP
     e. VP → V S′
     f. NP → (D) N
     g. D → the, a, …
     h. N → boy, mother, student, book, apple, …
     i. V → read, see, eat, make, open, touch, …

Starting with a designated initial symbol (S′ in (9)), each PSR converts a nonterminal symbol to a sequence of its internal constituents. Applied one by one, the PSRs in (9) generate phrase-markers such as the one in (10).

(10)

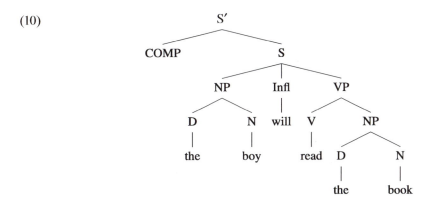

The phrase-marker (10) indicates, for example, that the largest constituent is an S′ comprising COMP (Complementizer) and S (Sentence), lined up in this order; that S is made up of a constituent NP (Noun Phrase), Infl(ection), and VP (Verb Phrase) in this order; and so forth. In this manner, each PSR encapsulates three kinds of information about phrase-markers, namely the constituent structure, "label" symbol of a phrase, and left-to-right ordering of internal constituents:

(11) a. Constituent structure: the hierarchical and combinatorial organization of linguistic elements ("constituents")
      b. Labeling: the nonterminal symbol ("label") associated with each constituent
      c. Linear order: the left-to-right order of the constituents

The part of transformational grammar that generates phrase-markers such as (10) by means of PSRs is referred to as the *phrase structure component.*

Structures generated by the phrase structure component are then mapped to the corresponding derived structures by the *transformational component,* which is characterized by a finite sequence of transformations or conversion rules by which a phrase-marker is mapped to (transformed into) another phrase-marker. For example, (12) is a transformation (called *wh*-movement) by which a *wh*-phrase is deleted at its original position and inserted at COMP, with *t* representing a trace assigned an index *i* identical to the *wh*-phrase. Applied to S′ in (13a), (12) maps this phrase-marker to another phrase-marker in (13b), representing the underlying structure of (*Guess*) [*what the boy will read*].

(12)   *wh*-movement:
          structural analysis (SA): $X — COMP — Y — NP_{[+wh]} — Z$
     →   structural change (SC): $X — NP_{[+wh]i} — Y — t_i \quad — Z$

(13)

Another example of transformations is Coordination (14), which conflates two sentences into one by conjoining two constituents of the same category with *and* and reducing overlapping parts of the sentences. (15) represents some illustrations of its application.

(14) Coordination:

      SA of S'_1: $X — W_1 — Y$
         of S'_2: $X — W_2 — Y$ (where W_1 and W_2 are of the same category)
      SC: $X — W_1$ and $W_2 — Y$

(15) a. S_1': the boy will read [$_{NP1}$ the book]
   S_2': the boy will read [$_{NP2}$ the magazine]
   → the boy will read [$_{NP1}$ the book] and [$_{NP2}$ the magazine]
   b. S_1': the boy will [$_{V1}$ buy] the book
   S_2': the boy will [$_{V2}$ read] the book
   → the boy will [$_{V1}$ buy] and [$_{V2}$ read] the book
   c. S_1': the boy will [$_{VP1}$ read the book]
   S_2': the boy will [$_{VP2}$ drink coffee]
   → the boy will [$_{VP1}$ read the book] and [$_{VP2}$ drink coffee]

The first type of transformation, exemplified by *wh*-movement (12), is referred to as the category of *singulary transformations*, in that they take a single phrase-marker as their input: Passivization, Topicalization, Auxiliary Inversion, Heavy NP-Shift, and a number of other rules have been proposed as instances of singulary transformations (see Chomsky 1955/1975; 1957 and many others). On the other hand, Coordination (14) represents another type of transformation, referred to as *generalized transformations*, which take more than one phrase-marker (say two S's) as their input and conflate them into a unified phrase-marker: Relative Clause Formation and Nominalization are other instances of generalized transformations. See Chomsky (1955/1975) and others for details.

In this sort of traditional generative grammar, the generative and transformational aspects of language (1)–(2) are characterized by the interplay of PSRs and transformations: first of all, the transformational capacity of language (2) is straightforwardly ascribed to the set of transformations such as (12) and (14). Moreover, discrete infinity naturally results, for example, from an indefinite application of generalized transformations. For example, Coordination may expand a sentence to an unlimited length, say *the boy will read [the book and the magazine and the report and …]*. Chomsky (1965) further notices that PSRs can also be devised to yield discrete infinity once we allow the initial symbol S′ to appear on the right hand side of PSRs, as in rule (9e) = VP → V S′, whose application results in embedding of an S′ within another S′, as in (16):

(16)

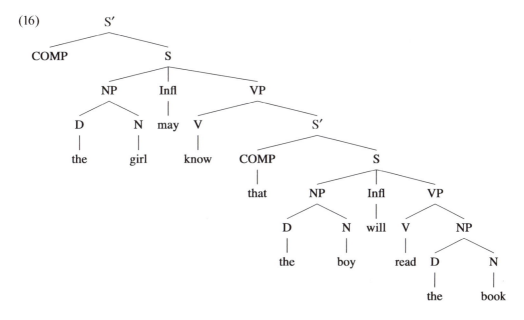

(16) or any other S′ of an arbitrary size may be further embedded into another sentence by means of rule (9e) over and over again, thus yielding discrete infinity.

2.2 X-bar Theory and Move-α: The emergence of principles and parameters

As described in the previous subsection, the theory of transformational generative grammar (Chomsky 1955/1975; 1957) held that human language is essentially a complex system of conversion rules. The rules posited in this framework were, as we have seen, quite abstract as well as language- and construction-specific, and, therefore, linguists were led to face the problem of language acquisition (also called "Plato's problem"): how can the child learn the correct set of highly complex rules from limited experience? In order to address this question, it was necessary for linguists of the day to set the following two tasks for their inquiry (see Chomsky 1965: Ch. 1):

(17) a. To reduce, as much as possible, the complexity and language-specificity (i.e., properties specific to particular languages) of rules that the child is supposed to learn without sacrificing descriptive adequacy of the proposed rule system.
  b. To enrich the power of the innately endowed language acquisition device (*Universal Grammar, UG*) so that it can reduce the burden of the child's language learning.

Though challenging, the research agenda in (17) turned out to be valuable as a heuristic, yielding a number of novel insights into the architecture of UG. By the early 1980s, research oriented by these goals converged on what we now call the *Principles-and-Parameters* (P&P) framework. According to this model of UG, the body of adults' linguistic knowledge is characterized in significant part by a finite set of innately endowed *principles*, which are invariant and universal across languages, and *parameters*, whose values are open to being set by a child learner with the help of linguistic experience, allowing certain forms of linguistic variation. In this conception of linguistic knowledge, what the child has to learn from experience reduces to the values for the parameters and the set of lexical entries in the lexicon, a radical simplification of the problem of language acquisition.

Specifically, serious efforts to achieve the goals in (17) in the domain of phrase structure resulted in the crystallization of *X-bar theory* (Chomsky 1970, *et seq.*). Historically, this UG principle was put forward as a way to remedy one of the fundamental inadequacies of earlier PSRs, pointed out by Lyons (1968). Lyons correctly argued that the system of PSRs is inadequate or insufficient in that it fails to capture the fact that each XP always dominates a unique X (NP dominates N, VP dominates V, etc.). That is to say, nothing in the formalism of PSRs excludes rules of the following sort, which are unattested and presumed to be impossible in human language but formally comparable to the rules in, say, (9), in that one symbol is rewritten (converted) into a sequence of symbols in each rule.

(18) a. NP → VP PP
  b. PP → D S Infl V
  c. AP → COMP NP

X-bar theory was put forward by Chomsky (1970) essentially to overcome this inadequacy of PSRs, and has been explored in much subsequent work. X-bar theory holds that the class of possible PSRs can be radically reduced by postulating the following two general schemata, where an atomic category X (X^0) is necessarily dominated by an intermediate category X′, which in turn is necessarily dominated by the maximal category X″ (XP) (see also Jackendoff's 1977 tripartite X-bar structure).

(19) *X-bar schemata*:
    a. X′ = X (Y″) or (Y″) X   (where Y″ is called the *Complement* of X)
    b. X″ = (Z″) X'   (where Z″ is called the *Spec(ifier)* of X)

For example, the X-bar schemata yield the following phrase-marker from the same set of terminal elements as those in (10), assuming the DP-analysis of nominals (Brame 1981; 1982; Fukui and Speas 1986; Fukui 1986/1995; Abney 1987) and the head-initial linear order in (19a) (X (Y″)) for English:

(20)

Note that, in (20), S′ and S from earlier theories were replaced by C″ and I″, respectively (Chomsky 1986a). This move is motivated by X-bar theory's fundamental hypothesis that phrasal nodes are obtained essentially by projecting the lexical features of X and attaching bar-level indices (′ or ″) to them. In this theory, there is a strong sense in which all phrasal nodes, X′ and X″, are "projections" of some X: N′ and N″ are projections of N, V′ and V″ are projections of V, and so on. We may refer to this consequence of X-bar theory as "labeling by projection."

(21) *Labeling by Projection*:

Each phrasal constituent is a projection of a lexical item (LI, X^0) it contains.

The class of possible constituent structures is hence restricted to those "endocentric" projections, while "exocentric" (non-headed) structures like (18), together with traditional S′ and S, are ruled out as a matter of principle. Lyons's criticism is thus naturally overcome as a result of (21). However, it is worth noting that Chomsky (1970) first put forward the X-bar schemata in such a way that they could be interpreted not as strict formats for PSRs but as a kind of evaluation measure that merely sets a preference for (unmarked) X-bar-theoretic projections, leaving open the possibility of (marked) exocentric structures such as S′ and S. The C″ analysis of S′ and the I″ analysis of S were introduced only later by Chomsky (1986a). See also Carnie (this volume) for other empirical motivations for X′- and X″-structures.

X-bar theory is so strong a generalization over the possible forms of PSRs that idiosyncratic PSRs of the sort exemplified in (9) can be entirely eliminated (with the help of other "modules" of grammar), a highly desirable result acknowledged by Stowell (1981) and Chomsky (1986a), among others. This is not only a considerable simplification of the child's acquisition task, but also constitutes an indispensable building block of the emergent P&P framework: according to the P&P model of UG, the grammar of human language is essentially "ruleless" and conversion rules such as PSRs and transformations play no role in the account of the human linguistic capacity. Elimination of PSRs in favor of the X-bar schemata was a real step toward embodying this radical conceptual shift.

Furthermore, X-bar theory also takes part in reducing the class of transformations, essentially by providing the structural notion of *Spec(ifier)* (19b). Thanks to the X-bar schemata, Spec positions are distributed throughout the clausal architecture, with each of these Specs being further assumed to hold some special relation to the head (so-called "Spec-head agreement;" Chomsky 1986a), so they can serve as the target of various movement transformations: *wh*-movement targets Spec-C in order for the *wh*-phrase to be licensed under Spec-head agreement with C, a subject NP moves to Spec-I in order to receive Nominative Case under Spec-head agreement with I, and so on. More generally, the notion of Spec allows us to characterize various movement transformations as serving Spec-head relations in which categories have to participate. Pushing this line of approach to its limit, then, we may generalize various movement transformations into a single, highly underspecified transformation schema (called *Move-α*), which can be utilized for establishing various Spec-head relations:

(22) *Move-α* (Chomsky 1981):

Move anything anywhere.

If we can indeed reformulate all language- and construction-specific transformations in the form of Move-α, serving different Spec-head relations at different times, then we may envisage the complete picture of "ruleless grammar," eliminating all PSRs and specific transformations in favor of X-bar theory and Move-α interacting with various other modules of UG. This is indeed the shift generative linguistics has taken to solve the problem of language acquisition (17), setting the stage for the full-blown P&P research program, which has turned out to be remarkably successful in a number of research domains (comparative grammar, language acquisition, and so on).

2.3   Merge: Unifying the phrase structure and transformational components

In the original conception of transformational generative grammar (summarized in §2.1), the phrase structure component generates the class of underlying structures by means of PSRs and the transformational component maps those structures to various transformed structures (S-structures, LF, etc. in standard and extended standard theories) by means of transformations. The separation of these two components was then assumed to be a necessary device to capture the generative and transformational aspects of human language (1)–(2). However, we saw in §2.2 that the P&P framework paves the way for eliminating PSRs and specific transformational rules as a matter of principle. Thus, it is interesting to ask if the distinction between the phrase structure and transformational components has any ground within the P&P framework.

This problem is addressed by Chomsky (1993; 1995a; 1995b), who eventually proposes the replacement of the relevant distinction with the notion of *Merge*. According to Chomsky, UG is endowed with an elementary operation, Merge, whose function is to recursively combine two syntactic objects (SOs) α, β and form another SO, which is just a set of α and β with one of them projected as the label γ (23a). (23b) visualizes the relevant set-theoretic object using a familiar tree-diagram, but it should be understood that, unlike traditional PSRs and X-bar theory, linear order between α and β is not specified by Merge, since $\{\alpha, \beta\}$ is defined as an unordered set.

(23) Merge$(\alpha, \beta) =$ a. $\{\gamma, \{\alpha, \beta\}\}$, where the label $\gamma =$ the label of α or β.

b.

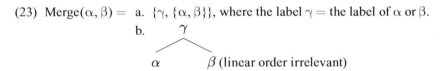

Chomsky argues that, once recursive Merge constitutes an inborn property of UG, its unconstrained application immediately derives the basic effects of X-bar theory and Move-α in a unified fashion, as we will see below.

Consider first the case where Merge applies to two lexical items (LIs) drawn from the lexicon: say, *the* and *book*, as in (24). It yields an SO comprising a determiner *the* and a noun *book*, with the former projected (for the DP-analysis of nominals, see Brame 1981; 1982; Fukui and Speas 1986; Fukui 1986/1995; Abney 1987).

(24) Merge(the, book) $=$ a.   {the, {the, book}}

b.   the

the   book

This SO can constitute another input to Merge, as in (25), for example, where it is combined with a verb *read*, projecting the latter.

(25) Merge(*read*, {*the*, {*the*, *book*}}) $=$ a.   {*read*, {*read*, {*the*, {*the*, *book*}}}}

b.

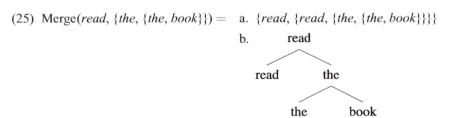

SOs such as (24)–(25) can provide minimal but sufficient information about constituent structure and labeling: (25) is a phrasal SO that is labeled "verbal" by *read*; it contains (or "dominates" in earlier terms) a subconstituent SO (24) labeled "nominal" by *the*; and so on. Recursive application of Merge can generate SOs of an arbitrary size in a bottom-up fashion, including sentential SOs such as (26) that can be further subjected to Merge, yielding discrete infinity.

(26)

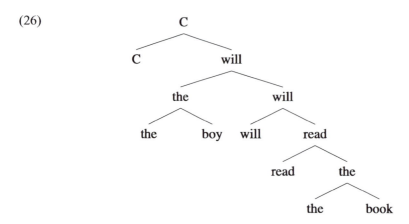

In articulating a Merge-based theory of phrase-markers, Chomsky (1995a; 1995b) capitalizes on Muysken's (1982) proposal that the notions of minimal and maximal projections are relational properties of categories and not inherently marked by additional devices such as bar-level indices (see also Fukui 1986/1995; 1988; Fukui and Speas 1986; and Speas 1990 for their relational approaches to X-bar theory). Chomsky's relational definition of maximal and minimal projections is stated in (27):

(27) *Relational definition of projection* (Chomsky 1995a: 61):

Given a phrase-marker, a category that does not project any further is a maximal projection X^{max} (XP), and one that is not a projection at all is a minimal projection X^{min} (X^0); any other is an X', invisible for computation.

For example, the SO in (24) embedded within (25) or (26) counts as a maximal projection X^{max} of *the*, given that it does not project any further in those phrase-markers, and its immediate constituent *the* is a minimal projection X^{min} since it is an LI and not a projection at all. In this manner, Merge supplemented by the relational definition of projection (27) can derive the effects of X-bar theory. In particular, Merge as defined in (23) incorporates the basic insight of X-bar theory, namely that each phrase is a projection of an LI (labeling by projection (21)).

   In the above cases, the two operands of Merge, α and β, are distinct from, or external to, each other. This type of Merge represents what Chomsky calls *External Merge* (EM). Chomsky further notes that, if Merge applies freely, it should also be able to apply to α and β, one of which is *internal* to the other. This case represents the second type of Merge, called *Internal Merge* (IM). For example, if there is an $SO_i = \{the, \{the, book\}\}$ (23) and some other SO that contains SO_i – for example, (25) – Merge applying to the two SOs yields an $SO_j = \{SO_i, \{\ldots SO_i \ldots\}\}$ with two copies of SO_i.

(28)

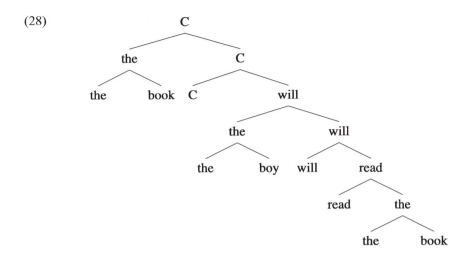

Chomsky (1993) proposes that the excessively powerful operation of Move-α may be eliminated in favor of IM, with traces in earlier theories replaced by copies created by IM (compare (28) with, for example, the trace-based conception of *wh*-movement in (12)). This consequence is called the "copy theory of movement" and has proven to be highly advantageous for the account of various properties of movement transformations, such as reconstruction (see Chomsky 1993). If we follow this line of approach, then we may regard (28) as the representation of a sentence with Topicalization, *the book, the boy will read*, with the lower copy of SO$_i$ unpronounced at its phonetic form. If this reductionist approach to movement proves to be successful, then the whole spectrum of movement transformations, which was once reduced to Move-α, can be further reformulated as an aspect of the basic operation Merge.

Without any stipulation, then, the ubiquity of discrete infinity and movement with copy-formation (Chomsky 1993; 1995a; 1995b) becomes an automatic consequence of the unbounded character of Merge. This simple device immediately yields the bifurcation of EM and IM, and these two types of Merge incorporate a significant part of X-bar theory and Move-α. It thus naturally unifies the theories of the phrase structure component and the transformational component.

These considerations suggest that the theory of Merge-based syntax, called the framework of *bare phrase structure* (BPS) (Chomsky 1995a; 1995b), arguably provides a minimal explanation of the generative and transformational aspects of human language (1)–(2). This completes our historical review of how the theory of transformational generative grammar converged on the current BPS framework.

3   Towards the "barest" phrase structure

In the previous section, we saw that the theory of phrase structure evolved into the simple theory of Merge by critically examining the technical devices proposed earlier and reducing them to a conceptual minimum that can still satisfy their target functions. Such an endeavor of reductionist simplification is sometimes termed the "Minimalist Program" (MP) (Chomsky 1993; 1995a; 1995b, *et seq.*), but it just exemplifies an ordinary practice of science, persistent throughout the history of generative linguistics, which seeks the best account of empirical data with a minimal set of assumptions.

In this section, we will turn to the discussion of how we may advance further simplification of Merge-based syntax, even more radically departing from earlier theories of conversion rules and X-bar theory.

3.1   The labeling algorithm and projection-free syntax

Consider again the formulation of Merge (23) advocated by Chomsky (1995a; 1995b). We saw that this operation is a simple device to incorporate the major insight of X-bar theory, namely labeling by projection (21). However, the open choice of the label γ in (23) is admittedly too unrestricted. It is typically specified either as the label of α or β, but then nothing in (23) precludes, for example, D of the object from projecting over VP, instead of V, as in (29).

(29)   Merge(read, {the, {the, book}}) =   a.   {the, {read, {the, {the, book}}}}

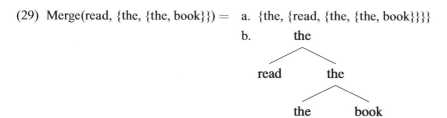

This sort of "wrong choice" would make a number of ill-advised predictions: for example, that this SO can act as a DP and can be merged with another V (*the boy will touch [read the book]). Therefore, there must be some mechanism that determines the "correct" label/head for each Merge-output. Following the standard convention, we may refer to this mechanism as the *labeling algorithm* (LA).

The exact nature of the LA is one of the major research topics in the current literature, and, indeed, a great variety of proposals have been advanced, with more in press. For example, Chomsky (1995b; 2000) hypothesizes that determining the label of a set-theoretic object {α, β} correlates with a selectional or agreement dependency between α and β, an idea followed by a number of researchers:

(30)   LA (Chomsky 1995b; 2000):

The output of Merge(α, β) is labeled by α if
a.   α selects β as its semantic argument, or
b.   α agrees with β: that is, β is attracted by α for the purpose of Spec-head agreement (feature-checking).

This LA excludes the wrong choice in (29) by (30a), since it is the V *read* that selects/theta-marks DP, not the converse. Moreover, the merger of the subject DP to the edge of I(nfl) (or, as it is more recently called, T(ense)) results in projection of the latter, given that it agrees with the DP in person, number, and gender (these agreement features are also called "φ-features"). As intended, (30) closely keeps to the basic result of X-bar theory. However, recourse to such external relations as (semantic) selection and agreement may be regarded as a potentially worrisome complication of the LA. As a possible reformulation of the LA, Chomsky (2008: 145, (2)–(3)) puts forward another algorithm in (31).

(31) LA (Chomsky 2008: 145):
 The output of Merge(α, β) is labeled by α if
 a. α is an LI, or
 b. β is internally merged to α.

According to this version of the LA, the output of Merge(V, DP) is labeled V by virtue of V being an LI, and movement of subject DP to Spec-I/T lets the latter element (I/T) be the label, by virtue of the merger being an instance of IM. Chomsky (2013) further suggests eliminating (31b) from the LA, reducing it to minimal search for an LI for each phrase (31a), a proposal to which we will return (see also Narita 2012; forthcoming; Ott 2012; Lohndal 2012; Narita and Fukui 2012 for various explorations).

(32) LA (Chomsky 2013):
 The label/head of an SO Σ is the most prominent LI within Σ.

See also Boeckx (2008; 2009; forthcoming), Narita (2009; forthcoming), Hornstein (2009), Fukui (2011) and many others for different approaches to labeling.

Incidentally, it should be noted that once we decide to let UG incorporate a LA in addition to Merge, it becomes questionable whether Merge itself has any role to play in labeling/projection at all. In particular, the specification of the label γ in (23) becomes superfluous, because the choice of the label is independently determined by the LA. As redundancies are disfavored in scientific theories, Chomsky (2000) proposes further simplification of the definition of Merge, as in (33):

(33) Merge(α, β) = a. $\{\alpha, \beta\}$.

 b.
 α β (linear order irrelevant)

In this simpler theory, Merge reduces to an elementary set-formation operation, and SOs generated thereby are all "bare" sets. That is, such SOs are associated with no nonterminal symbols such as projections, while the reduced notion of "label," which now amounts to nothing more than the syntactically or interpretively relevant "head" of a phrase, is determined independently by the LA. Indeed, any version of the LA in (30)–(32) can be understood as a mere search mechanism for head-detection, free from additional steps of projection. In this manner, theories of labeling can render BPS really "bare": that is, completely projection-free (see Collins 2002; Chomsky 2007; 2013; Narita 2012; forthcoming).

It is instructive to recall that nonterminal symbols such as S, VP, NP, etc., used to constitute necessary input to and/or output of conversion rules in the earlier system of PSRs: cf., for example, S → NP Infl VP (9b). However, the BPS framework now invites us to ask if there is any strong empirical evidence that requires an extraneous mechanism of nonterminal symbol-assignment or projection, in addition to the simplest means of constituent structuring (i.e., Merge). See Collins (2002), Chomsky (2007; 2008; 2013), Fukui (2011), Narita (2012; forthcoming), Narita and Fukui (2012) for a variety of explorations along these lines.

3.2   *Linearization as part of post-syntactic externalization*

Recall that PSRs embody the following three kinds of information regarding phrase-markers (11): constituent structure, labeling, and linear order. For example, PSR (9d), VP → V NP, represents that a phrase is labeled VP, that VP immediately dominates V and NP, and that V precedes NP. We saw that Merge takes over the role of constituent structuring while eliminating labeling. Moreover, as Merge creates unordered sets, it is also ineffective in determining the linear order of its constituents. Therefore, BPS bears the burden of providing an independent account of linear order. Conventionally, this hypothesized mechanism of linear order-assignment is referred to as *linearization*, for which a variety of proposals have been made in the growing literature.

It is obvious that linear order appears at the "sound"-side of linguistic expressions. However, observations in the literature suggest that linear order plays little role in the "meaning"-side of linguistic computation: for example, there is no evidence that linear order is relevant to core syntactic–semantic properties such as predicate-argument structure or theta-role assignment. Reinhart (1976; 1983), among others, further points out that purely hierarchically determined relations such as c-command are sufficient to encode the conditions on binding, scope, and other discourse-related properties as well. This strongly suggests that linear order may not be a core property of phrase-markers that persists throughout the derivation, as the system of PSRs predicts, but rather may be assigned relatively "late" in linguistic computation, probably post-syntactically. Obviously, the less relevant linear order is shown to be to syntactic computation, the less necessary, desirable, or even plausible it becomes to encapsulate linear order into the core of structure-generation. These considerations strongly suggest that linear order should not belong to syntax or its mapping to the syntax–semantics interface (called SEM). Given that linear order must be assigned before SOs get "pronounced" at the syntax-phonetics interface (called PHON), we conjecture that linearization may most plausibly be a part of the syntax-PHON mapping, or what is sometimes called *externalization* (Chomsky 2013).

(34)   Linear order is only a peripheral part of human language, related solely to externalization (the syntax-PHON mapping).

Various attempts are currently being made to approach the theory of linearization under the working hypothesis in (34). However, see, for example, Kayne (1994; 2011), Fukui (1993), and Saito and Fukui (1998) for indications that linear order may play some role in syntax.

We would like to deepen our understanding of linearization, whether it is located in the core of syntax or only at externalization. It seems that various competing theories of linearization proposed in the literature more or less share the goal of reformulating the basic results of X-bar theory (19), namely:

(35)   a. the variability of head-complement word order (cf. "directionality parameter" in (19a))
       b. the apparent universal "specifier-left" generalization (cf. (19b))

See Saito and Fukui (1998), Epstein *et al.* (1998), Richards (2004; 2007), and Narita (forthcoming) for various attempts to reformulate the directionality parameter in BPS. In this context, it is worth noting that some researchers attempt to provide a parameter-free account of word order by advocating a single universal word order template. By far the most influential account of this sort is Kayne's (1994) "antisymmetry," which proposes a universal Spec-Head-Complement word order and typically analyzes apparent head-final, Spec-Complement-Head order as being derived from the movement of the Complement to some intermediate Spec-position (for various implementations, see Kayne 1994; 2009; 2011; Chomsky 1995a; 1995b; Epstein *et al.* 1998; Uriagereka 1999; and Moro 2000, to name just a few). The Kaynean approach can be contrasted with Takano (1996) and Fukui and Takano's (1998) hypothesis that the universal template is rather Spec-Complement-Head (see also Gell-Mann and Ruhlen 2011), while apparent Spec-Head-Complement order is derived by moving the Head to some intermediate position. Attractive though it seems, imposing a particular word order template appears to be generally costly, in that it invites a number of technical stipulations to explain cases of disharmonic word order, as pointed out by Richards (2004) and Narita (2010; forthcoming).

It is interesting to note that most of the previous theories of linearization make crucial recourse to projection, as is expected since they aim to recapture the basic results of X-bar theory (35). Exceptions are Kayne (2011) and Narita (forthcoming), who approach linearization from a truly projection-free perspective, but they still rest on the notion of "head" (LA) and involve complications in some other domains (Kayne reformulates Merge as ordered-pair formation; Narita relies on a specific formulation of cyclic Spell-Out). Thus, it is a curious open question whether linearization necessitates projection or how linearization relates to the LA.

3.3 Summary: A modular approach to constituent structure, labeling, and linearization

We saw that the treatment of three kinds of information (constituent structure, labeling, and linear order) was once encapsulated into PSR-schemata. However, the theory of Merge holds that they should rather be fully modularized into different components of UG (or even a third factor which governs the functioning of UG): constituent structuring is fully taken care of by unbounded Merge; the identification of the head/label of each SO is carried out by some version of the LA (30)–(32) or others; and the mechanism of linearization may be properly relegated to post-syntactic externalization (34).

4 Questions for future research

The BPS theory is at a very initial stage of inquiry, leaving a number of important problems for future research. The following were already mentioned above.

[1] *Is BPS free from nonterminal symbols/projection? Cf. §3.1.*
[2] *What is the exact nature of the LA? In particular, does it involve projection? Cf. §3.1.*
[3] *Does linear order play any role in syntax or SEM, or is it only a property of externalization? Cf. §3.2.*
[4] *What is the exact nature of linearization? In particular, does it make recourse to projection or the notion "head?" Cf. §3.2.*

And we will review some others in the rest of this section. First, let us consider an open question about Merge:

[5] *How is unbounded Merge constrained?*

As we saw above, we would like to keep the application of Merge unbounded, if only to provide a principled account of discrete infinity and movement with copy-formation (Chomsky 1993; 1995a; 1995b). However, it is of course not true that any random application of Merge yields a legible output. Therefore, there must be some constraints on Merge-application that limit the space of interface-legible outputs of Merge.

It is quite likely that the relevant constraints on Merge include proper theories of labeling and linearization. Moreover, many proposals have been made regarding "economy" conditions on IM/Move, such as the principle of "Last Resort" (Chomsky 1986b) ("Move only when necessary"), a variant of which is the idea that an application of IM is contingent on the presence of "Agree(ment)" (feature-checking, or more recently "probe-goal" relations; see Chomsky 2000, *et seq.*). Further, current research provides interesting pieces of evidence for the view that the Merge-based computation is demarcated into several well-defined cycles of derivation, called *phases*: see Chomsky (2000; 2001; 2004; 2007; 2008; 2013), Uriagereka (1999), Boeckx (2009; forthcoming), Gallego (2010; 2012), and Narita (forthcoming), among others, for various explorations of phase theory. See also Fukui (2011) and Narita and Fukui (2012), who argue, on different grounds, that Merge-based computation is fundamentally driven by the need for symmetric {XP, YP} structures (or what Narita and Fukui call "feature equilibrium").

[6]   *Is the notion of label/head relevant to narrowly syntactic computation, or does it appear only at SEM (and linearization)?*

We saw that the notion of "label" is now reduced to nothing more than the computationally or interpretively relevant "head" of each SO, detected by the LA, and that it may well be free from the now-superfluous notion of projection. Clearly, at least some aspect of the syntax–semantics interface (SEM) is dependent on the notion of label/head: the semantics of VP is prototypically configured by the head V, and the same obviously applies to NP-N, AP-A, CP-C, etc., as well. Therefore, it seems reasonable to assume that the LA feeds information to SEM. Questions remain regarding where, or at which point of linguistic computation, the LA applies. Does it apply at each and every point of Merge-application, just as in Chomsky's (1995a; 1995b) earlier theory of Merge, or only at particular points in a syntactic derivation, say at the level of each phase, as hypothesized in Chomsky (2008; 2013) and Ott (2012), or only post-syntactically at SEM, as suggested by Narita (forthcoming)? These possibilities relate to question [2], and depending on the answer, they may also invite particular answers to [4] as well.

It is worth recalling in this connection that virtually all the past theories of linearization make crucial recourse to the concept of label/head (see references cited in §3.2). Thus, the LA appears to feed information not only to SEM but also to linearization. Under the conception of syntax as *the* mechanism of "sound"–"meaning" pairing, a natural conclusion from this observation seems to be that the LA should be regarded as an operation internal to narrow syntax, applying before the computation branches off into the semantic and phonological components (this argument was put forward by Narita 2009).

What remains curious in this approach is the fact that there is actually less and less evidence for the relevance of labeling/headedness to narrowly syntactic computation under minimalist assumptions. C(ategorial)-selection/subcategorization used to constitute a *bona fide* instance of a label-dependent operation, but it is often assumed in the modern framework that c-selection is reducible to s(emantic)-selection applying at SEM (Pesetsky 1982), and that selection (categorial or semantic) plays virtually no role in narrow syntax (Chomsky 2004: 112–113).

However, consider also Chomsky's (2013) hypothesis that the LA reduces to minimal search for the most prominent LI for each SO (32). He further suggests that the minimality property of the LA can be regarded as a reflection of the laws of nature, specifically the principle of computational efficiency in this case, i.e., that minimal search is attributable to the so-called "third factor" of language design (see Chomsky 2007; 2008). Third-factor principles are by definition domain-general and, thus, they may be simultaneously applicable to any aspect of linguistic computation, be it narrowly syntactic computation or post-syntactic mapping to SEM and PHON. It may turn out that further inquiry into the LA provides some empirical support for this "LA-as-third-factor" hypothesis, a possibility left for future research.

[7]   *Is every SO endocentric: that is, headed by an LI?*

The earlier PSR-based conception of phrase-markers holds that each phrase is associated with nonterminal symbols, and X-bar theory further maintains that phrases are all projections of head LIs (labeling by projection, (21)). Under the assumption that projection imposes headedness, the X-bar-theoretic approach in effect subscribes to the "Universal Endocentricity" hypothesis:

(36) *Universal Endocentricity*:
      Every phrase is headed by an LI.

(36) has become a standard assumption since the advent of X-bar theory, followed by the majority of subsequent theories in the generative framework. However, it should be noted that, once X-bar theory is replaced with the theory of Merge, universal labeling by projection can be correspondingly eliminated from the BPS framework. (36) thus loses its theorem-like status, and it becomes open to scrutiny. Does (36) receive real support from empirical data, or should it be regarded as an unwarranted residue of X-bar theory that is to be discarded as well?

In fact, (36) becomes less obvious when we seek to reduce the LA to a bare minimum. For example, while Chomsky's (2013) LA in (32) is able to determine the head LI H in {H, XP}, it is not clear whether it is effective at all in determining the label/head of SOs with two phrasal constituents, {XP, YP}, where no LI immediately stands as the most prominent. In the earlier X-bar-theoretic approach, such SOs are generally characterized as involving one of the two phrases, say XP, being the "specifier" of the other, YP, thereby letting the latter project. But this projection-based characterization of Spec and universal endocentricity becomes unavailable in the approach based on (32). Chomsky (2013) argues that this result is indeed desirable, and that there should be room for certain non-endocentric structures appearing at SEM (see also Narita forthcoming).

X-bar theory was originally proposed to replace earlier idiosyncratic PSRs. This was a real step toward the simplification of UG, setting the basis for the later P&P framework, but, in hindsight, it also effectively brought the stipulation of universal endocentricity (36) into the theory of phrase structure. However, now that X-bar theory has been eliminated in favor of projection-free Merge (33), any {XP, YP} structures, regardless of whether they are created by EM or IM, are open to non-endocentric characterizations. Inquiry into the nature of non-endocentric structures appears to be a potentially fruitful research topic. See, in this connection, Narita and Fukui (2012), who put forward the hypothesis that endocentric (asymmetric) structures {H, XP}, typically created by EM, are generally in need of

19

being mapped to "symmetric," non-endocentric {XP, YP} structures via IM, exploring the significance of symmetry/non-endocentricity in BPS (see also Fukui 2011).

The above discussion also raises the following question:

[8]   *Is the notion of Spec(ifier) relevant to linguistic computation?*

The radical thesis put forward by Chomsky (2012a; 2013) is that the notion of specifier is an illegitimate residue of X-bar theory and has no place in BPS – that is, projection-free syntax. See Chomsky (2012a; 2013), Narita (2009; 2012; forthcoming), Lohndal (2012), and Narita and Fukui (2012) for various explorations of Spec-free syntax.

[9]   *Is Merge always restricted to binary set-formation?*

So far, we have restricted our attention to cases where Merge is limited to a binary set-formation: (33). This was partly because linguistic structures are generally assumed to involve binary branching in almost every case (see Kayne's (1981) influential work on "unambiguous paths"). Indeed, considerations of binding, quantifier scope, coordination, and various other phenomena seem to lend support to the universal binary branching hypothesis. However, we do not know why human language is structured that way. Binarity is a nontrivial constraint on Merge and, if possible, we would like to remove this constraint, generalizing the Merge operation to the simplest conception of *n-ary* set-formation:

(37) $\text{Merge}(SO_1, \ldots, SO_n) = \{SO_1, \ldots, SO_n\}$

What is the factor that almost always restricts n to two? Again, it is likely that theories of labeling and linearization play major roles in this binarity restriction. Moreover, the relevance of third-factor principles of efficient computation has been suggested at times, though arguments are inconclusive (Collins 1997; Chomsky 2008; Narita forthcoming).

[10]   *What is the nature of adjunction?*

Finally, we would briefly like to mention another case that has been put aside so far, namely *adjunction*. In any natural language there are classes of adjectives, adverbials, and other modifiers that can be optionally adjoined, indefinitely many times, to relevant constituents (Harris 1965). Multiple adjunction, as in (3), may expand a sentence to an unlimited length, yielding another type of discrete infinity. Curiously, the presence of those optional adjuncts does not affect the core architecture of the sentence, a distinct property of adjunction that has to be captured in some way or another in the BPS framework.

It is desirable if the theory of adjunction can be devised to make no recourse to projection. One such proposal is actually made by Chomsky (2004), who proposes that Merge has two varieties, one being the usual set-formation Merge (called *set-Merge*, producing {α, β}) and the other being an operation that creates an ordered pair of constituents (called *pair-Merge*, producing <α, β>). Chomsky proposes that adjunction in general can be reformulated as instances of pair-Merge, where the head–nonhead asymmetry is built in the asymmetry of order. Another approach originates from Lebeaux (1991), among others, who holds that, while usual instances of Merge apply cyclically from the bottom up, adjuncts are introduced to the structure only after the main clausal structure is constructed in the derivation (this operation is called "late-Merge"). Still another approach is to eliminate the notion of adjunction as a distinct mechanism and assimilate adjuncts to the class of Specs. This approach is most notably carried out by Kayne (1994 *et seq.*) and other proponents of antisymmetry (see §3.2). All these possibilities are open to future inquiry.

Further reading

Readers may find it useful to consult Fukui (2001; 2011) as supplementary reading to this chapter. After reading this chapter, which provides a general background in the theory of phrase structure, readers are referred to more technical and advanced works on this topic, such as the papers collected in Chomsky (1995b; 2012b), among many others. See also Narita (forthcoming), which explores various empirical consequences of a truly projection-free approach to labeling, linearization, and universal endocentricity.

References

Abney, Steven Paul. 1987. The English noun phrase in its sentential aspect. Doctoral dissertation, MIT.

Boeckx, Cedric. 2008. *Bare syntax.* Oxford: Oxford University Press.

Boeckx, Cedric. 2009. On the locus of asymmetry in UG. *Catalan Journal of Linguistics* 8: 41–53.

Boeckx, Cedric. ed. 2011. *The Oxford handbook of linguistic minimalism.* Oxford: Oxford University Press.

Boeckx, Cedric. forthcoming. *Elementary syntactic structures.* Cambridge: Cambridge University Press.

Brame, Michael. 1981. The general theory of binding and fusion. *Linguistic Analysis* 7.3:277–325.

Brame, Michael. 1982. The head-selector theory of lexical specifications and the nonexistence of coarse categories. *Linguistic Analysis* 10.4:321–325.

Cable, Seth. 2010. *The grammar of Q.* Oxford: Oxford University Press.

Chomsky, Noam. 1955/1975. *The logical structure of linguistic theory.* Ms. Harvard University, 1955. Published in part in 1975, New York: Plenum.

Chomsky, Noam. 1957. *Syntactic structures.* The Hague: Mouton. 2nd edn (2002).

Chomsky, Noam. 1965. *Aspects of the theory of syntax.* Cambridge, MA: MIT Press.

Chomsky, Noam. 1970. Remarks on nominalization. In *Readings in English transformational grammar*, ed. Roderick A. Jacobs and Peter S. Rosenbaum, 184–221. Waltham, MA: Ginn.

Chomsky, Noam. 1975. *Reflections on language.* New York: Pantheon Books.

Chomsky, Noam. 1981. *Lectures on government and binding.* Dordrecht: Foris.

Chomsky, Noam. 1986a. *Barriers.* Cambridge, MA: MIT Press.

Chomsky, Noam. 1986b. *Knowledge of language.* New York: Praeger.

Chomsky, Noam. 1993. A minimalist program for linguistic theory. In *The view from Building 20: Essays in linguistics in honor of Sylvain Bromberger*, ed. Ken Hale and Samuel J. Keyser, 1–52. Cambridge, MA: MIT Press.

Chomsky, Noam. 1995a. Bare phrase structure. In *Evolution and revolution in linguistic theory: Essays in honor of Carlos Otero*, ed. Héctor Ramiro Campos, Paula Marie Kempchinsky, 51–109. Washington D.C.: Georgetown University Press.

Chomsky, Noam. 1995b. *The minimalist program.* Cambridge, MA: MIT Press.

Chomsky, Noam. 2000. Minimalist inquiries. In *Step by step: Essays on minimalist syntax in honor of Howard Lasnik*, ed. Roger Martin, David Michaels, and Juan Uriagereka, 89–155. Cambridge, MA: MIT Press.

Chomsky, Noam. 2001. Derivation by phase. In *Ken Hale: A life in language*, ed. Michael Kenstowicz, 1–52. Cambridge, MA: MIT Press.

Chomsky, Noam. 2004. Beyond explanatory adequacy. In *Structures and beyond: The cartography of syntactic structures*, ed. Adriana Belletti, volume 3, 104–131. New York: Oxford University Press.

Chomsky, Noam. 2007. Approaching UG from below. In *Interfaces + recursion = language?: Chomsky's minimalism and the view from semantics*, ed. U. Sauerland and H.-M. Gärtner, 1–29. Berlin and New York: Mouton de Gruyter.

Chomsky, Noam. 2008. On phases. In *Foundational issues in linguistic theory: Essays in honor of Jean-Roger Vergnaud*, ed. Robert Freidin, Carlos Otero, and Maria Luisa Zubizarreta, 133–166. Cambridge, MA: MIT Press.

Chomsky, Noam. 2012a. Introduction. In Noam Chomsky, ed. and trans. by Naoki Fukui, *Gengokisoronshu* [*Foundations of biolinguistics: Selected writings*], 17–26. Tokyo: Iwanami Shoten.

Chomsky, Noam. 2012b. *Chomsky's linguistics*. Cambridge, MA: MITWPL.

Chomsky, Noam. 2013. Problems of projection. *Lingua* 130:33–49.

Collins, Chris. 1997. *Local economy*. Cambridge, MA: MIT Press.

Collins, Chris. 2002. Eliminating labels. In *Derivation and explanation in the minimalist program*, ed. Samuel David Epstein and T. Daniel Seely, 42–64. Oxford: Blackwell.

Epstein, Samuel David, Erich M. Groat, Ruriko Kawashima, and Hisatsugu Kitahra. 1998. *A derivational approach to syntactic relations*. Oxford: Oxford University Press.

Fitch, W. Tecumseh, Marc D. Hauser, and Noam Chomsky. 2005. The evolution of the language faculty: Clarifications and implications. *Cognition* 97:179–210.

Fukui, Naoki. 1986/1995. A theory of category projection and its applications. Doctoral dissertation, MIT. Published in 1995 with revisions as *Theory of projection in syntax*, Kurosio Publishers and CSLI publications.

Fukui, Naoki. 1988. Deriving the differences between English and Japanese: A case study in parametric syntax. *English Linguistics* 5:249–270.

Fukui, Naoki. 1993. Parameters and optionality. *Linguistic Inquiry* 24:399–420. Reprinted in Fukui (2006).

Fukui, Naoki. 2001. Phrase structure. In *The handbook of contemporary syntactic theory*, ed. Mark Baltin and Chris Collins, 374–406. Oxford: Blackwell. Reprinted in Fukui (2006).

Fukui, Naoki. 2006. *Theoretical comparative syntax*. London/New York: Routledge.

Fukui, Naoki. 2011. Merge and bare phrase structure. In Boeckx, ed. (2011), 73–95.

Fukui, Naoki, and Margaret Speas. 1986. Specifiers and projection. *MIT Working Papers in Linguistics* 8:128–172. Reprinted in Fukui (2006).

Fukui, Naoki, and Yuji Takano. 1998. Symmetry in syntax: Merge and demerge. *Journal of East Asian Linguistics* 7:27–86. Reprinted in Fukui (2006).

Gallego, Ángel J. 2010. *Phase theory*. Amsterdam: John Benjamins.

Gallego, Ángel J., ed. 2012. *Phases: Developing the framework*. Berlin: Mouton de Gruyter.

Gell-Mann, Murray, and Merritt Ruhlen. 2011. The origin and evolution of word order. *Proceedings of the National Academy of Sciences* 108(42):17290–17295.

Harris, Zellig S. 1951. *Methods in structural linguistics*. Chicago: University of Chicago Press.

Harris, Zellig S. 1965. Transformational theory. *Language* 41(3):363–401.

Hauser, Marc D., Noam Chomsky, and W. Tecumseh Fitch. 2002. The Faculty of Language: What is it, who has it, and how did it evolve? *Science* 298(5598):1569–1579.

Hornstein, Norbert. 2009. *A theory of syntax*. Cambridge: Cambridge University Press.

Jackendoff, Ray. 1977. *X'-syntax*. Cambridge, MA: MIT Press.

Kayne, Richard S. 1981. Unambiguous paths. In *Levels of syntactic representation*, ed. R. May and J. Koster, 143–183. Reidel.

Kayne, Richard S. 1994. *The antisymmetry of syntax*. Cambridge, MA: MIT Press.

Kayne, Richard S. 2009. Antisymmetry and the lexicon. *Linguistic Variation Yearbook* 8:1–31.

Kayne, Richard S. 2011. Why are there no directionality parameters? In *Proceedings of WCCFL 28*, 1–23. Somerville, MA: Cascadilla Proceedings Project.

Lebeaux, David. 1991. Relative clauses, licensing, and the nature of the derivation. In *Perspectives on phrase structure: Heads and licensing*, ed. Susan Rothstein, 209–239. New York: Academic Press.

Lohndal, Terje. 2012. Without specifiers: Phrase structure and events. Doctoral dissertation, University of Maryland, College Park.

Lyons, John. 1968. *Introduction to theoretical linguistics*. Cambridge: Cambridge University Press.

Moro, Andrea. 2000. *Dynamic antisymmetry*. Cambridge, MA: MIT Press.

Muysken, Pieter. 1982. Parametrizing the notion 'head'. *Journal of Linguistic Research* 2:57–75.

Narita, Hiroki. 2009. Full interpretation of optimal labeling. *Biolinguistics* 3:213–254.

Narita, Hiroki. 2010. The tension between explanatory and biological adequacy: Review of Fukui (2006). *Lingua* 120:1313–1323.

Narita, Hiroki. 2012. Phase cycles in service of projection-free syntax. In Gallego, ed. (2012), 125–172.

Narita, Hiroki. forthcoming. *Endocentric structuring of projection-free syntax*. Amsterdam: John Benjamins.

Narita, Hiroki, and Naoki Fukui. 2012. Merge and (a)symmetry. Ms. Waseda Institute for Advanced Study and Sophia University.

Ott, Dennis. 2012. *Local instability*. Berlin/New York: Walter De Gruyter.

Pesetsky, David. 1982. Paths and categories. Doctoral dissertation, MIT.

Reinhart, Tanya. 1976. Syntacic domain of anaphora. Doctoral dissertation, MIT.

Reinhart, Tanya. 1983. *Anaphora and semantic interpretation*. London: Croom Helm.

Richards, Marc D. 2004. Object shift, scrambling, and symmetrical syntax. Doctoral dissertation, University of Cambridge.

Richards, Marc D. 2007. Dynamic linearization and the shape of phases. *Linguistic Analysis* 33: 209–237.

Saito, Mamoru, and Naoki Fukui. 1998. Order in phrase structure and movement. *Linguistic Inquiry* 29:439–474. Reprinted in Fukui (2006).

Speas, Margaret J. 1990. *Phrase structure in natural language*. Dordrecht: Kluwer Academic.

Stowell, Tim. 1981. Origins of phrase structure. Doctoral dissertation, MIT.

Takano, Yuji. 1996. Movement and parametric variation in syntax. Doctoral dissertation, University of California, Irvine.

Uriagereka, Juan. 1999. Multiple spell-out. In *Working minimalism*, ed. Samuel David Epstein and Norbert Hornstein, 251–282. Cambridge, MA: MIT Press.

2

Argument structure*

Jaume Mateu

---

1 Introduction

Argument structure can be defined from semantic or syntactic perspectives; it has two faces. As a semantic notion, argument structure is a representation of the central participants in the eventuality (event or state) expressed by the predicate. As a syntactic notion, argument structure is a hierarchical representation of the arguments required by the predicate determining how they are expressed in the syntax.

The semantic face of argument structure is often understood in terms of thematic roles, which are said to be selected in the lexical entries of the predicates. The list of thematic roles often includes agent, causer, patient, theme, experiencer, source, goal, location, beneficiary, instrument, and comitative, among others (see Gruber (1965/1976) or Fillmore (1968; 1977) for classic works on the topic). It is not an easy task to provide a finite list or precise definition of these roles. For example, a biargumental predicate such as *break* s(emantically)-selects two thematic roles: causer and theme. In the simplified lexical entry in (1), the causer is assigned to the external argument (i.e., the argument that is projected external to VP [and as such it does not appear in SYN in (1)]), whereas the theme is assigned to the direct internal argument (see the NP argument in (1), which is projected internally to the VP). Notice that causer and theme are lexical-*semantic* notions, whereas the distinction between external vs. internal arguments is a lexical-*syntactic* one.

(1)

$$\begin{bmatrix} \text{PHON: } \textit{break} \\ \text{SYN: } [\underline{\quad}_v \text{ NP}] \\ \text{SEM: } \{\underline{\text{causer}}, \text{theme}\} \\ \text{some encyclopedic notion of what } \textit{break} \text{ means} \end{bmatrix}$$

---

*I acknowledge the funding of grants FFI2010-20634 and FFI2011-23356 (Spanish *Ministerio de Ciencia e Innovación*) and 2009SGR1079 (*Generalitat de Catalunya*). I am very grateful to the editors for their constructive comments, suggestions, and editorial assistance.

According to the classic Theta Theory (e.g., see Chomsky 1981), universal principles such as the Theta Criterion (i.e., "every theta role that a verb can assign must be realized by some argument, and each argument may bear only a single theta role") and the Projection Principle (i.e., "lexical structure must be represented categorically at every syntactic level") would filter out ill-formed syntactic structures, ensuring that the predicate *break* could not appear in a sentence with fewer arguments than required (2a) or with more than required (2b).

(2) a. John broke *(the table).
     b. John broke the table (*to Peter) (cf. *John gave the table to Peter*).

Argument structure alternations such as those exemplified in (3)–(7) have become central in the literature on the lexicon-syntax interface (for example, Levin (1993), Hale and Keyser (2002), Reinhart (2002), Levin and Rappaport Hovav (2005), and Ramchand (2008), among many others). These alternations do not simply involve individual lexical items. Rather, each alternation seems to be productively available for a wide class of verbs in each case. A much debated question is how to capture the relevant regularity in each case (e.g., either via lexical rules or via syntactic ones: to be discussed in §2).

(3) *The causative-inchoative alternation*
     a. John broke the table.
     b. The table broke.

(4) *The locative alternation*
     a. John sprayed paint on the table.
     b. John sprayed the table with paint.

(5) *The dative alternation*
     a. John gave the table to Mary.
     b. John gave Mary the table.

(6) *The conative alternation*
     a. John wiped the table.
     b. John wiped at the table.

(7) *The active-passive alternation*
     a. John broke the table.
     b. The table was broken (by John).

Related to argument structure alternations is the *elasticity* of verb meaning, exemplified in (8) with the verb *dance* (see Goldberg (1995), Levin and Rappaport Hovav (2005), and Ramchand (2008)), where a single verb takes on a range of lexical meanings depending upon which kinds of argument it appears with.[1] One claim about this phenomenon is that the syntax and semantics of argument structure are not projected exclusively from the lexical specifications of the verb. For example, consider (8g): it does not seem to make any sense to claim that there exists a special sense of *dance* that involves three arguments – that is, an agent (*John*), a theme (*the puppet*), and a goal (*across the stage*). Rather, the direct object and the obligatory oblique object (cf. **John danced the puppet*) are not directly licensed as arguments of the verb *dance* but by the particular transitive/causative argument structure. Such a proposal is that lexically unfilled argument structures exist independently of the particular lexical verbs which instantiate them.

(8) a. John danced.
    b. John danced {a beautiful dance/a polka}.
    c. John danced into the room.
    d. John danced away.
    e. John outdanced Mary.
    f. John danced the night away.
    g. John danced the puppet across the stage.
    h. John danced his debts off.
    i. John danced himself tired.
    j. John danced his way into a wonderful world.
    …

In this chapter, I concentrate on some of the most relevant theoretical and empirical issues where argument structure has been shown to play an important role. Below, I address the question of to what extent (verbal) argument structures are projected from lexical-semantic structures or are constructed outside of the lexicon. In doing so, I review the recent debate between projectionist and neo-constructionist approaches to argument structure. In this context, some special attention is also devoted to some syntactic approaches to argument structure, such as Hale and Keyser's (1993; 2002) configurational theory, which has been very influential for many syntacticians interested in analyzing argument structure from a minimalist perspective.

2   Argument structure: two views

The role of argument structure in the lexicon-syntax interface has been studied from two different perspectives: the projectionist view and the constructivist/(neo)constructionist one. In §2.1, we see that the syntax of argument structure can been argued to be projected from the lexical meaning of the (verbal) predicate. In §2.2, we see that proponents of the constructivist/ (neo)constructionist approach argue that argument structures are (i) provided with a config-urational meaning that is independent from the conceptual contribution of the verb and (ii) constructed out of the lexical entry of the verb. The notion of "mapping" from the lexicon to syntax or the "linking" of arguments has no meaning in this second approach; instead, the syntax narrows down possible semantic interpretations of predicates and arguments.

2.1   Argument structure at the lexicon-syntax interface: the projectionist account

As a starting point, one can assume that argument structure is determined by the *lexical* (typically, semantic) properties of the predicate, which have been expressed in terms of thematic roles, in terms of proto-roles (see §2.1.1), or in terms of lexical decompositions of the predicate (see §§2.1.2 and 2.1.3).

2.1.1   Thematic proto-roles and argument selection

Dowty (1991) provides one of the most well-known critiques of theta theory. He expresses a skepticism of the usefulness of thematic roles in linguistic theory and claims that their best use is in explaining argument selection. In particular, according to him, there are only two syntactically relevant "proto-roles": Proto-agent and Proto-patient (cf. also Foley and Van Valin's (1984) macro-roles: *Actor* and *Undergoer*), which are conceived of as generalizations on lexical meaning and are associated with the following properties in (9) and (10), respectively.

(9) *Proto-Agent*:
  a. Volitional involvement in the event or state
  b. Sentience (and/or perception)
  c. Causing an event or change of state in another participant
  d. Movement (relative to the position of another participant)
  e. Exists independently of the event named by the verb

(10) *Proto-Patient*:
  a. Undergoes change of state
  b. Incremental theme
  c. Causally affected by another participant
  d. Stationary relative to movement of another participant
  e. Does not exist independently of the verb

Proto-roles are related to argument selection through the *Argument Selection Principle* in (11). The clustering of semantic properties such as those above provides a ranking according to which the arguments of a verb compete with one another for subjecthood and objecthood. For example, the subject of a transitive verb such as *build* corresponds to the argument for which the properties of volition, sentience, and causation are entailed, while its direct object argument is generally understood to be an incremental theme, causally affected, and undergoing a change of state.

(11) *Argument Selection Principle* (Dowty 1991)
  The argument of a predicate having the greatest number of Proto-agent properties entailed by the meaning of the predicate will, all else being equal, be lexicalized as the subject of the predicate; the argument having the greatest number of Proto-patient properties will, all else being equal, be lexicalized as the direct object of the predicate.

Dowty also argues for the two corollaries in (12), which are associated to the principle in (11).

(12) a. *Corollary 1*: If two arguments of a relation have (approximately) equal numbers of entailed Proto-agent and Proto-patient properties, then either may be lexicalized as the subject (and similarly for objects).
  b. *Corollary 2*: With a three-place predicate, the non-subject argument having the greater number of entailed Proto-patient properties will be lexicalized as the direct object, the non-subject argument having fewer entailed Proto-patient properties will be lexicalized as an oblique or prepositional object (and if two non-subject arguments have approximately equal entailed Proto-patient properties, either may be lexicalized as direct object).

For example, Corollary 2 in (12b) applies to the locative alternation examples in (13):

(13) a. John loaded hay into the wagon.
  b. John loaded the wagon with hay.

The choice of the direct object in (13) mostly depends on which argument has the property of being an *incremental theme* – that is, the element involved in defining a homomorphism from properties of an argument to properties of the event it participates in. For example, *hay* is the incremental theme in (13a), since the progress of the loading event is reflected in the amount of hay that is put into the wagon. Similarly, *the wagon* is the incremental theme in (13b), since the progress of the loading event is reflected in the part of the wagon that is being covered: that is, when the wagon is half-loaded, the event is half done; when the wagon is two-thirds loaded, the event is two-thirds done; and so on (see also Tenny (1994) for related discussion).

As pointed out by Dowty (1991), another typical case where the determination of grammatical relations can be somewhat subtle is that of psychological verbs such as *like* and *please* (see also *fear* and *frighten*), where the syntactic realization of the Experiencer and Stimulus arguments differ in spite of similarities in meaning.

(14) a. I like Latin.
      b. Latin pleases me.

Dowty observes that, with respect to properties which promote proto-agentivity (e.g., volition, sentience, or causation), either the stimulus or experiencer role can be realized as a subject. The predicate *like* in (14a) entails that the experiencer has some perception of the stimulus – that is, the experiencer is entailed to be sentient/perceiving – hence it becomes the subject. In contrast, the predicate *please* in (14b) entails that the stimulus causes some emotional reaction in the experiencer (the latter becomes causally affected), whereby in this case it is the stimulus that is selected as subject.

Dowty's principle in (11) and the associated corollaries in (12) are in tune with the claim that argument structure generalizations lie outside of the grammar proper. In the rest of the chapter, I deal with the opposite approach: that is, the idea that the existence of argument structure generalizations tells us something important about the way that linguistic representations are structured.

2.1.2 Lexical decomposition and argument structure I: From lexical semantics to syntax

Another alternative to the thematic role approach is the view that verbal predicates are decomposed into smaller event structure primitives (see Levin and Rappaport Hovav (1995; 2005), among others after Dowty (1979)). For example, the structural semantics of the verb *break* might be lexically decomposed as depicted in (15): that is, *the action of x causes y to become broken*.

(15) [[X ACT] CAUSE [Y BECOME <*BROKEN*>]]

In (15) the angular brackets contain the constant *BROKEN*, which encodes the idiosyncratic meaning. The variable x is associated to the external argument, while the variable y is associated to the direct internal argument. Levin and Rappaport Hovav (1995; 2005) claim that event structure is a lexical-*semantic* level. Argument structure, by contrast, is a lexical-*syntactic* level. The former provides a structural semantic decomposition of lexical meaning, whereas the latter accounts for (i) the number of arguments selected by a predicate and (ii) the hierarchy that can be established among them: for example, external argument vs. internal argument(s); direct internal argument vs. indirect internal argument. For instance, the minimal syntactic information contained in the argument structure of a biargumental verbal predicate such as *break* is the following one: $<x <y>>$, where x is the external argument and Y is the direct internal argument. (16) depicts the lexical entry of *break* under such an approach:

(16)
$$\left[\begin{array}{l} \textit{break} \\ [\ \underline{\quad}_v \text{ NP}] \\ <\text{x} <\text{y}>> \\ [[\text{x ACT}] \text{ CAUSE } [\text{y BECOME } <\textit{BROKEN}>]] \\ \text{some encyclopedic/conceptual notion of what \textit{break} means} \end{array}\right]$$

Sadler and Spencer (2001) argue for the distinction between two different levels of lexical representation (i.e., the *semantic* event structure and the *syntactic* argument structure) on the basis of a distinction between "morphosemantic operations", which alter the semantics of the predicate, and "morphosyntactic operations", which are meaning-preserving operations that alter the syntactic manifestation of a given semantic representation, particularly the way it is mapped on to grammatical relations. To put it in Levin and Rappaport Hovav's (2001; 2005) terms, the morphosemantic operations involve distinct event structure patterns that are related via a constant/root, whereas the morphosyntactic operations involve the very same event structure pattern but a different mapping between argument structure and syntax. Consider the argument structure alternations in (17) and (18).

(17) a. John loaded hay into the wagon.
      b. John loaded the wagon with hay.

(18) a. Tom broke the vase.
      b. The vase was broken (by Tom).

According to Levin and Rappaport Hovav (2001), the locative alternation exemplified in (17) involves different semantic representations that are related by the same constant/root. (19a) expresses a caused change of location (*John put hay into the wagon*), whereas (19b) expresses a caused change of state (*John filled the wagon with hay*).

(19) a. $[[\text{x ACT}_{<LOAD>}] \text{ CAUSE } [\text{y BECOME P}_{LOC} \text{ z}]]$
      b. $[[\text{x ACT}_{<LOAD>}] \text{ CAUSE } [\text{z BECOME } [_{STATE}\ ] \text{ WITH-RESPECT-TO Y}]]$

By contrast, the active–passive alternation exemplified in (18) is analyzed by Sadler and Spencer (2001) as depicted in (20). In the passive representation in (20b), the suppression of the external argument is notated by means of parentheses: *(x)*. This suppressed external argument can be expressed in the syntax with an adjunct PP (*by Tom*).

(20) a. $[[\text{x ACT}] \text{ CAUSE } [\text{y BECOME } <\textit{BROKEN}>]]$: lexical-semantic structure (event str.)

          $<\text{x} <\text{y}>>$: lexical-syntactic structure (arg. str.)

          Tom broke   the vase
          SUBJECT   OBJECT   : syntax

b. [[X ACT] CAUSE [Y BECOME <*BROKEN*>]]   : lexical-semantic structure
                                             (event str.)

<(x) <Y>>   : lexical-syntactic structure
                                             (arg. str.)

The vase was broken   (by Tom)
SUBJECT   OBLIQUE   : syntax

Adopting a more syntactocentric perspective, Baker (1997) argues that lexical-syntactic representations or argument structures such as the ones exemplified in (16) and (20) are not necessary. For example, according to Baker, the abstract syntactic structure in (21b) can be claimed to be a *direct* projection of a lexical-semantic representation like the one in (21a). Given this, argument structure representations such as $<x <y>>$ (e.g., *x shelved y; x broke y*) or $<x <y, prep-z>>$ (e.g., *x put y on z*) are redundant and should be eliminated.

(21) a. [X CAUSE [Y GO on shelf]]

b.

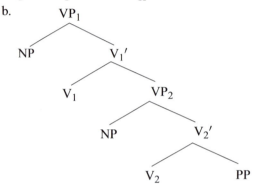

Following earlier proposals by Larson (1988), Baker (1997) argues that there is a more complex structure in the VP than meets the eye. In particular, he argues that syntactically relevant thematic roles can be associated to an abstract syntactic decomposition of VP:[2] for example, according to Baker's (1997: 120–121) syntactic representation in (21b), Agent/Causer is the specifier of the higher VP of a Larsonian structure (see Chomsky's (1995) little *v*), Theme is the specifier of the lower VP, and Goal/Location is the complement of the lower VP.[3] Indeed, by looking at the two representations in (21), the question arises as to what extent both structures are needed. According to Hale and Keyser (1993), the syntax of (21b) is *not* a projection of the lexical-semantic structure in (21a). Rather, their claim is that the structural/configurational meaning of (21a) can be read off from the complex syntactic structure in (21b). In the following section, special attention is given to their syntactic approach (see also Harley (2011) for a detailed review).

2.1.3 Lexical decomposition and argument structure II: the l(exical)-syntactic approach

One of the most important insights that can be found in Hale and Keyser's (1993; 2002) l-syntactic theory of argument structure is that two apparently different questions such as (22a) and (22b) have the very same answer (see Hale and Keyser 1993: 65–66 and Mateu 2002).

(22) a. Why are there so few (syntactically relevant) thematic roles?
      b. Why are there so few l(exical)-syntactic categories?

Essentially, Hale and Keyser's answer is that (syntactically relevant) thematic roles are limited in number because the number of specifier and complement positions of the abstract syntax of l(exical)-syntactic structures is also quite reduced. This paucity of structural positions is related to the reduced number of l-syntactic categories of the abstract syntax of argument structure. Hale and Keyser conceive of argument structure as the syntactic configuration projected by a lexical item. Argument structure is the system of structural relations holding between heads (nuclei) and the arguments linked to them and is defined by reference to the head-complement relation and the head-specifier relation. A given head may enter into the structural combinations in (23). According to Hale and Keyser (2002), the prototypical or unmarked morphosyntactic realizations of the head (x) in English are the following ones: verb in (23a), preposition in (23b), adjective in (23c), and noun in (23d).

(23)

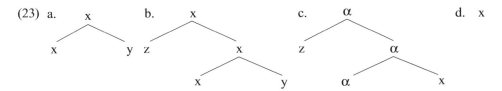

The main empirical domain on which their hypotheses have been tested includes unergative creation verbs such as *laugh*, transitive location verbs such as *shelve* or transitive locatum verbs such as *saddle*, and (anti)causative verbs such as *clear*. Unergative verbs are hidden transitives in the sense that they involve merging a non-relational element (typically, a noun) with a verbal head (24a); both transitive location verbs such as *shelve* and transitive locatum verbs such as *saddle* involve merging the structural combination in (23b) with the one in (23a): (24b). Core unaccusative verbs involve the structural combination in (23c). Finally, causative verbs involve two structures: (23c) is combined with (23a): (24c). Hale and Keyser (2002) also provide arguments for distinguishing causative constructions such as (24c) from transitive ones such as (24b): only the former enter into the causative alternation owing to their having a double verbal shell (24c).

(24)

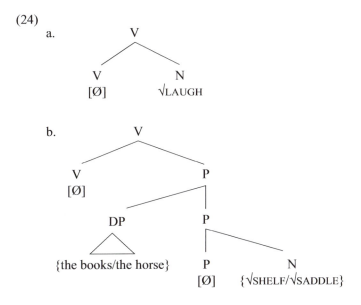

c.

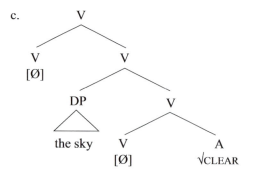

A crucial insight of Hale and Keyser's (1993; 2002) work is their claim that verbs always take a complement. Another important claim of their approach is that the structural semantics of argument structure can be claimed to be read off from the syntactic structures. Four theta roles can be read off from the basic syntactic argument structures (see Mateu 2002 and Harley 2005; 2011): *Originator* is the specifier of the relevant functional projection that introduces the external argument; *Figure* is the specifier of the inner predicate, headed by P or Adj; *Ground* is the complement of P; and *Incremental Theme* is the nominal complement of V.[4] Concerning the semantic functions associated to the eventive element (i.e., V), DO can be read off from the unergative V,[5] CAUSE can be read off from the V that subcategorizes for an inner predicative complement, and CHANGE can be read off from the unaccusative V.[6]

Let us see how the syntactic argument structures depicted in (24) turn to be lexicalized into the surface verbs. Applying the incorporation operation to (24a) involves copying the full phonological matrix of the nominal root *laugh* into the empty one corresponding to the verb. Applying it to (24b) involves two steps: the full phonological matrix of the noun {*shelf*/*saddle*} is first copied into the empty one corresponding to the preposition. Since the phonological matrix corresponding to the verb is also empty, the incorporation operation applies again from the saturated phonological matrix of the preposition to the unsaturated matrix of the verb. Finally, applying incorporation to (24c) involves two steps as well. The full phonological matrix of the adjectival root *clear* is first copied into the empty one corresponding to the internal unaccusative verb. Since the phonological matrix corresponding to the upper causative verb is also empty, the incorporation applies again from the saturated phonological matrix of the inner verb to the unsaturated matrix of the outer verb.

It is crucial in Hale and Keyser's (1993) theory of argument structure that specifiers cannot incorporate in their l(exical)-syntax: only complements can (cf. Baker (1988)). The ill-formed examples in (25) involve illicit incorporation from a specifier position: *sky* and *book* occupy an inner specifier position.[7]

(25) a. *The strong winds skied clear (cf. *The strong winds made [the sky clear]*)
     b. *John booked on the shelf (cf. *John put [a book on the shelf]*)

As predicted, external arguments cannot incorporate since they occupy a specifier position. The ill-formed example in (26a) involves the incorporation of *cow*, which occupies a spec position. In contrast, the incorporation in (26b) is licit since it involves incorporation from a complement position.

(26) a. *It **cow**ed a calf (cf. *A **cow** [had a calf]*)
     b. A cow **calv**ed (cf. *A cow [had **calf**]*)

Hale and Keyser (1993; 2002) argue that the external argument (i.e., the Originator/Initiator) is truly external to argument structure configurations. Unaccusative structures can be causativized, while unergatives ones cannot (e.g., *Mary laughed John; cf. Mary made John laugh) for precisely this reason. Accordingly, the external argument occupies the specifier position of a functional projection in so-called "s(entential)-syntax" (Kratzer 1996; Pylkkännen 2008; Harley 2013). Hale and Keyser's s-syntax refers to the syntactic structure that involves both the lexical item and its arguments and also its "extended projection" (Grimshaw 1991/2005), and including, therefore, the full range of functional categories.[8]

Hale and Keyser (1993; 2002) discussed only two verb classes: those verbs that have a nominal complement (e.g., unergatives) and those ones that have a sort of propositional complement, sometimes called a small clause (or SC) (Hoekstra 1988; 2004 among others), whose members are characterized by the appearance of an internal predication and therefore an internal subject (e.g., the steadfastly transitive locative verbs and the alternating deadjectival causative/inchoative verbs). They claim that all descriptive verb types can be reduced to these two basic ones: the ones that consist of V plus a nominal (N) complement and the ones that consist of V plus a predicative (P or Adj) complement.[9]

One important advantage of Hale and Keyser's program is that it sheds light on the syntactic commonalities that can be found in apparently distinct lexical semantic classes of verbs: for example, creation verbs (27a) and consumption verbs (27b) are assigned the unergative structure in (24a).[10] Since these verbs incorporate their complement, it is predicted that their object can be null, as shown in (27a–b). In contrast, the inner subject/specifier of change of {location/state} verbs cannot be easily omitted: see (27c–d). Accordingly, a crucial syntactic difference can be established between Incremental Theme (i.e., the complement of an unergative structure) and Figure (i.e., the subject/specifier of an inner locative (preposition) or stative (adjective) predication).

(27) a. John sang (a beautiful song).
　　 b. John ate (a pizza).
　　 c. John shelved/saddled *({the books/the horse}).
　　 d. The strong winds cleared *(the sky).

Hale and Keyser (2002: 37f) stick to the very restrictive system sketched out above and, for example, analyze agentive atelic verbs (e.g., impact verbs such as *push* or *kick*) as involving a transitive structure like the one assigned to locative verbs – that is, (24b): for example, *push the cart* is analyzed as $[_V$ PROVIDE $[_P$ the cart WITH >PUSH$]]$.[11] Perhaps more controversially, Hale and Keyser (2002: 214–221) claim that stative verbs such as *cost* or *weigh* are analyzed as having the same unaccusative configuration associated with *be* or *become*: $[_V$ This bull weighs one ton$]$ and $[_V$ This bull is brave$]$.

In the next section, I review the constructivist or neo-constructionist approach to argument structure, which is deeply influenced by Hale and Keyser's syntactic proposals. The main difference between the two approaches has to do with whether argument structure is encoded in the lexical entry of the verbal predicate or built in the syntax proper. According to the latter approach (e.g., see Marantz 2005; Ramchand 2008; Acedo-Matellán 2010; Harley 2011), the distinction between l(exical)-syntactic operations and s(entential)-syntactic ones does not seem to be fully congruent with the minimalist program. As pointed out by Harley (2011: 430), "argument-structure alternations can be, and should be, treated entirely within the syntactic component, via the same Merge and Move operations which construct any syntactic constituent".

2.2 Argument structure out of the lexical entry of the verb: the neo-constructionist approach

Before reviewing the neo-constructionist approach to argument structure, an important caveat is in order: one needs to distinguish generative constructivist or neo-constructionist approaches (Borer 2005; Marantz 1997; 2005; Ramchand 2008; Acedo-Matellán 2010) from cognitive constructionist approaches (Goldberg 1995 or Croft 2001). According to the former, the reason syntactic argument structures have meaning is because they are systematically constructed as part of a generative system that has predictable meaning correlates. In contrast, cognitive grammarians claim that no such generative system exists in our mind and argument structures are rather directly associated with our general cognitive system.

Unlike proponents of classical projectionism, such as Levin and Rappaport Hovav (1995), both cognitive constructionists and generative constructivists claim that argument structure has a structural meaning that is independent from the one provided by lexical items. Marantz (1997), however, claims that generative constructivists and neo-constructionists deny the major assumption of Goldberg's (1995) Construction Grammar that the constructional meaning may be structure-specific. According to Marantz, the "constructional" meaning is structured universally (i.e., it is restricted by UG) and is constructed by syntax rather than by our general conceptual system. To exemplify both cognitive and generative (neo-)constructionist approaches, consider the example in (28).

(28) John broke the eggs into the bowl.

Note the distinction between the constructional meaning – the caused change of location meaning – and the lexical meaning of the verbal predicate in (29). In Goldberg's approach the *argument roles* are associated to the constructional meaning, whereas the *participant roles* are provided by the verbal meaning. In the Goldbergian representation in (29) the argument roles *agent* and *theme* can be unified with the participant roles of the verb (*breaker* and *breakee*), whereas the argument role *goal* is brought about only by the construction (clearly, *into the bowl* is not selected by the verbal predicate *break*).

(29)
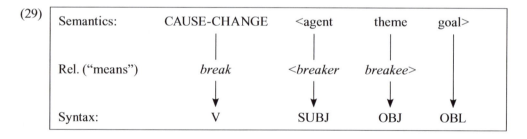

By contrast, proponents of generative neo-constructionist approaches such as Marantz (2005) or Acedo-Matellán (2010) claim that the structural (or "constructional") meaning of the argument structure of (28) can be read off the syntactic structure in (30). The null causative light verb (i.e., Chomsky's (1995) little *v*) subcategorizes for a small clause (SC) whose inner predicate is the telic PP *into the bowl* and whose internal subject is *the eggs*.[12] The idiosyncratic or encyclopedic meaning is the one provided by the root √BREAK, which is adjoined to or *conflated* with the null light verb, providing it with phonological content.[13]

(30) [$_{vP}$ John [$_v$ √BREAK-CAUSE] [$_{SC}$ the eggs into the bowl]].

Ramchand (2008) is a generative constructivist who claims that a much more explicit event semantics can be expressed in a syntactic decompositon of VP (or vP). Syntactic combinatoric primitives correlate with structural semantic combinatoric primitives. Indeed, she claims that there is no way to make a principled modular difference between the core syntactic computation and structural semantic effects (see also Borer 2005). In particular, she attempts to decompose verbs into three syntactic heads: Init(iation), Proc(ess), and Res(ult), each of which projects a syntactic phrase. A verb may consist of all three heads (as, for example, *break*, as in (31)) or may have some subset of them, with its arguments projected as specifiers of the three syntactic heads. The three eventive heads in (31) are defined by Ramchand as follows: *Init* denotes an initial state that causally implicates another eventuality, and its subject is the initiator of that eventuality; *Proc* is a dynamic event, and its subject is an undergoer of the process; and *Res* is a final state that is causally implicated by the process event, and its subject is a resultee, something that attains a final state.

(31)

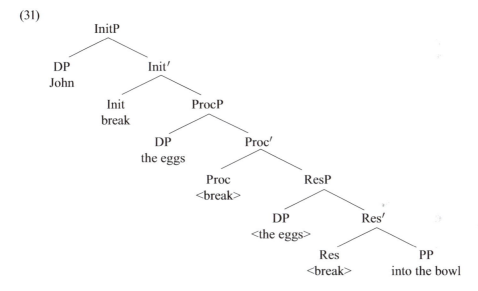

Ramchand (2008) argues against the classical principle of Theta-Criterion, whereby each argument bears only one theta-role, and each theta-role is assigned to one and only one argument.[14] For example, in (31) *the eggs* have two roles: Undergoer (or subject of process, which occupies the specifier position of the dynamic subevent, i.e., Process) and Resultee (or subject of result, which occupies the specifier position of the final state subevent, i.e., Result). In contrast, *John* only has one semantic role in (31): Initiator (or subject of initiation).

Unlike radical neo-constructionists such as Borer (2005), Ramchand (2008) claims that the explanation of contrasts such as those exemplified in (32) and (33) cannot be relegated to the functioning of our general conceptual system (cf. Borer 2005).[15] As shown by Levin and Rappaport-Hovav (2005), *manner* verbs such as *wipe*, and more generally verbs that express an activity, such as *eat*, are allowed to enter into unselected object constructions such as (32b)–(33b), whereas *result* verbs such as *break* (and more generally verbs that express a transition) do not enter into these constructions. Accordingly, it is a linguistic fact that verbal predicates such as *eat* or *wipe* are more "elastic" than the causative change of

Jaume Mateu

state predicate *break* (however, see McIntyre (2004) and Mateu and Acedo-Matellán (2012) for some relevant qualifications). According to Ramchand, the relevant difference at issue here is that *break* already contains the *res*(ult) feature in its lexical entry, whereas such a feature is absent from the lexical entries of *eat* or *wipe*, which accounts for their 'elasticity'.

(32) a. *The naughty child broke the cupboard bare.
          (meaning: The child broke the dishes so that the cupboard ended up bare)
      b. The naughty child ate the cupboard bare.

(33) a. *Kelly broke the dishes off the table.
          (meaning: Kelly removed the dishes from the table by breaking the table)
      b. Kelly wiped the crumbs off the table (cf. *Kelly wiped {*the crumbs/ᵒᵏthe table}*).

The resultative formation process exemplified in (32b) and (33b) is a well-known example of "argument structure extension", which has been argued by neo-constructionists or constructivists to take place in the syntax and not in the lexicon (as argued by Levin and Rappaport Hovav (2005); i.e., their template augmentation operation).

The leading idea of proponents of syntactic constructivism or neo-constructionism is that argument structures are not constructed in the lexicon but are systematically constructed as part of a generative system (i.e., syntax) that has predictable meaning correlates.

3 Conclusions

Early approaches to argument structure link it to the lexical-semantic properties of the predicate: for example, it is expressed in terms of thematic roles or in terms of lexical-semantic decompositions of the predicates. Departing from this tradition, Hale and Keyser (1993; 2002) claimed that semantics does *not* determine the syntax of argument structure. If anything, it is the other way around: that is, the structural meaning associated with event structure and (syntactically relevant) thematic roles can be read off from the l(exical)-syntactic configurations of argument structure. Different syntactic argument structures (e.g., unergative, unaccusative, transitive, and causative structures) are associated with different abstract structural meanings, which are separated from the conceptual/encyclopedic meanings provided by the roots. This insight is realized in more recent terms by deriving the formation of argument structures and argument structure alternations within the syntax proper (Harley 2011: 430).

Notes

1 As shown by Talmy (1985; 2000), such a variability is quite typical of English and other Germanic languages (for the lack of it in Romance languages, see Mateu (2002), Mateu and Rigau (2002), Zubizarreta and Oh (2007), Acedo-Matellán (2010), and Real-Puigdollers (2013), among others).
2 Some well-known proponents of non-syntactocentric approaches to argument structure and event structure (e.g., Jackendoff 1997; 2002) have said that positing complex structural representations like the one in (21b) suffers from the same problems that Generative Semantics had (see Lakoff (1971) and McCawley (1973), among others; but see Hale and Keyser (1992), Mateu (2002: Ch. 1), and Harley (2012), for a rebuttal of this comparison). According to Jackendoff, complex/layered VP structures like the one in (21b) are not necessary since this task is not to be assigned to syntax but to a semantic/conceptual component. As a result, a simpler VP is assumed (i.e., no VP-shell hypothesis is assumed) but, instead, a much more complex syntax-semantics interface module is posited. Furthermore, no generalized uniformity between syntax and structural

semantics is assumed: for example, Culicover and Jackendoff's (2005) proposal of "Simpler Syntax" rejects Baker's (1988; 1997) *Uniformity of Theta Assignment Hypothesis* (UTAH), whereby identical thematic relationships between items are represented by identical structural relationships between those items at the first level of syntactic representation. In Jackendoff's (1990) or Bresnan's (2001) approaches the linking between thematic roles and grammatical structure is not carried out via UTAH but rather via relative ranking systems like, for example, the so-called *thematic hierarchy* (see Levin and Rappaport Hovav (2005), for a complete review). As a result, the syntax of VP is quite simple and even flat.

3 It is worth noting that Baker (1997) establishes an interesting connection between his syntactic proposal of three *macro-roles* and Dowty's (1991) semantic theory of two *proto-roles*. Baker argues that only three "macro-roles" (Agent/Causer, Patient/Theme, and Goal/Location) are necessary for most syntactic purposes. For example, being inspired by Dowty (1991), Baker (1997) concludes that the experiencer role is not necessary in linguistic theory (see also Bouchard (1995) for a similar proposal). Structurally speaking, he claims that the experiencer role that *John* has in *John fears dogs* can be conflated with the Agent role. In particular, following Dowty (1991), he claims that "*John* is the subject of a predicate like *fear* by the usual agent-to-subject rule, but the term 'agent' is now understood as a fuzzy, prototype notion rather than a categorical one … Indeed, it is a property of John's psychological make-up – though not necessarily his will – that causes him to respond in a particular way to dogs." As a result, it is expected that *fear* behaves like an ordinary transitive verb in most respects, and this seems to be the case (see Belletti and Rizzi 1988; Grimshaw 1990; Bouchard 1995; Pesetsky 1995; Landau 2010, etc. for further discussion on experiencer predicates).

4 The Figure, in Talmy's (1985; 2000) terms, is the entity which is located or moving with respect to some other entity, which is the Ground. In the change of state domain, the relation between Figure and Ground can be metaphorical in terms of the predication of some property: the Figure is an entity to which some property, encoded by the Ground, is ascribed. See Mateu (2002) and Acedo-Matellán (2010) for further discussion on a localistic approach to argument structure.

5 See Hale and Keyser (1993; 2002) for the claim that unergative verbs typically express creation or production (i.e., [DO SOMETHING]).

6 See also Marantz (2005: 5) for the claim that one does not have to posit "*cause, become* or *be* heads in the syntax …. Under the strong constraints of the theoretical framework, whatever meanings are represented via syntactic heads and relations must be so constructed and represented, these meanings should always arise structurally."

7 Kiparsky (1997) points out that Hale and Keyser's (1993) syntactic theory predicts that an example like the one in (i) should be well-formed, contrary to fact.
   (i) *I housed a coat of paint (cf. *I put [$_{PP}$ a coat of paint ON house]*)
   However, Espinal and Mateu (2011) show that Kiparsky's criticism is flawed since the ungrammaticality of **I **housed** a coat of paint* (on the reading *I PROVIDED [$_{SC/PP}$ **house** WITH a coat of paint]*) should be kept apart from the unacceptability of *#I **housed** a coat of paint* (on the reading *I PUT [$_{SC/PP}$ a coat of paint ON **house**]*). Espinal and Mateu (2011) make it clear that Kiparsky's (1997) *Canonical Use Constraint* (CUC) in (ii) cannot account for the ungrammaticality of **I **housed** a coat of paint* (on the relevant reading above: i.e., *I PROVIDED [$_{SC/PP}$ **house** WITH a coat of paint]*). At most, the CUC can only be claimed to account for its unacceptability (on the relevant reading above: i.e., *I PUT [$_{SC/PP}$ a coat of paint ON **house**]*).
   (ii) Location verbs: putting x in y is a canonical use of y; Locatum verbs: putting x in y is a canonical use of x.
       "Therefore, the reason we do not … *house paint* is that … it is not a canonical use of houses to put paint on them (whereas it is of course a canonical use of … paint to put it on houses)."
       Kiparsky (1997: 482–483)

8 Hale and Keyser do not discuss the status of adjuncts, since these constituents are not to be encoded in l-syntactic structures like the ones in (24) (cf. Gallego 2010).

9 The latter disjunction could in fact be eliminated assuming Mateu's (2002) and Kayne's (2009) proposal that adjectives are not a primitive category but are the result of incorporating a noun into an adpositional marker. Similarly, following Hale and Keyser's program, Erteschik-Shir and Rapoport (2007: 17–18) point out that "the restricted inventory of meaning components that comprise verbal meanings includes (as in much lexical research) Manner (=means/manner/instrument) (M), State (S), Location (L) and, as far as we are able to tell, not much else" (p. 17). "Each such

semantic morpheme has categorical properties … MANNERS project N, STATES project A and LOCA-
TIONS project P … The restricted inventory of verbal components parallels the restricted inventory of lexical categories, restricting verb types and consequently possible interpretations,
following Hale and Keyser" (p. 18).

10 See Volpe (2004) for empirical evidence that consumption verbs are unergative.

11 A different analysis for agentive atelic verbs is pursued by Harley (2005), who assumes the
non-trivial claim that roots (non-relational elements) can take complements (vs. cf. Mateu (2002)
and Kayne (2009)). Accordingly, *push*-verbs are, for example, analyzed by Harley (2005: 52, e.g.
(25)) as in (i), where the root of *push* is claimed to take *the cart* as complement.

    (i)   Sue pushed the cart: [$_{vP}$ Sue [$_v$ DO [$_{\sqrt{P}}$ push the cart]]]

    Interestingly, Harley's syntactic distinction between structural arguments (i.e., introduced
by relational elements) and "non-structural" arguments (e.g., complements of root) can be
said to have a nice parallel in Levin and Rappaport Hovav's (2005) semantic distinction
between event structure arguments vs. mere constant/root participants.

12 See Hoekstra (1988; 2004) for the claim that *the eggs into the bowl* in (30) forms a small clause
result where *the eggs* can be considered the subject of the result predication expressed by *into the
bowl*.

13 See Haugen (2009) and Mateu (2010; 2012) for the important distinction between those syntactic
argument structures that are formed via *incorporation* and those ones formed via *conflation*.
According to Haugen (2009: 260), "*Incorporation* is conceived of as head-movement (as in Baker
(1988) and Hale and Keyser (1993)), and is instantiated through the syntactic operation of Copy,
whereas *Conflation* is instantiated directly through Merge (compounding)." In incorporation
cases, the verb is formed via *copying* the relevant set of features of the complement into the null
light verb: see (i). In contrast, in those cases that involve conflation the verb is formed via *compounding* a root with the null light verb: see (ii). From a minimalist perspective, no primitive
theoretical status can be attributed to these two formal operations since they can be claimed
to follow from the distinction between Internal Merge ($\rightarrow$ incorporation) and External Merge
($\rightarrow$ conflation).

    (i) a. Beth smiled
        a'. [$_{vP}$ [$_{DP}$ Beth] [$_v$ [$_v$ SMILE] [$\sqrt{\text{SMILE}}$]]]
        b. John flattened the metal (with a hammer).
        b'. [$_{vP}$ [$_{DP}$ John] [$_v$ [$_v$ FLAT-en] [$_{sc}$ the metal $\sqrt{\text{FLAT}}$]]]
    (ii) a. Beth smiled her thanks.
        a'. [$_{vP}$ [$_{DP}$ Beth] [$_v$ [$_v$ $\sqrt{\text{SMILE}}$ v] [$_{DP}$ her thanks]]]
        b. John hammered the metal flat.
        b'. [$_{vP}$ [$_{DP}$ John] [$_v$ [$_v$ $\sqrt{\text{HAMMER}}$ v][$_{sc}$ the metal flat]]]

14 See also Hornstein (2001) for a different criticism of the classic Theta Criterion. In his feature-
based approach to thematic roles, the representations where a single DP checks more than one
theta-role are the classical ones of obligatory control and anaphor binding. Theta-roles are then
features of predicates, checked by DPs: a DP may merge with a predicate, checking its theta-
feature, and subsequently undergo Move (Copy and re-Merge) to check the theta-feature of
another predicate.

15 The contrasts in (32) to (33) are taken from Levin and Rappaport-Hovav (2005: 226; (61–63)).

Further reading

Baker, Mark. 1997. Thematic roles and syntactic structure. In *Elements of grammar*, ed. Liliane
    Haegeman, 73–137. Dordrecht: Kluwer.

In this chapter Baker argues for a strict one-to-one mapping from thematic roles to syntactic
positions. He accomplishes this by positing fairly coarse-grained thematic roles and abstract
syntactic representations.

Hale, Kenneth L., and Samuel Jay Keyser. 2002. *Prolegomenon to a theory of argument structure*.
    Cambridge, MA: MIT Press.

The best-developed example of how the Larsonian *VP-shell hypothesis* can be useful for argument structure. The authors identify a small number of major semantic classes and assume that

the verbs in each class are lexically associated with a particular l-syntactic structure that configurationally encodes the semantic relations between a verb of that type and its arguments.

Harley, Heidi. 2011. A Minimalist Approach to Argument Structure. In *The handbook of linguistic minimalism*, ed. Cedric Boeckx, 427–448. Oxford and New York: Oxford University Press.

In this excellent chapter Harley puts forward some important theoretical and empirical issues that should be addressed by linguists interested in approaching argument structure from a minimalist perspective.

Levin, Beth, and Rappaport Hovav, Malka. 2005. *Argument realization*. Cambridge: Cambridge University Press.

This comprehensive survey provides an up-to-date overview of the current research on the relationship between lexical semantics and argument structure. In particular, this work reviews many interesting issues in the relationship between verbs and their arguments and explores how a verb's semantics can determine the morphosyntactic realization of its arguments.

References

Acedo-Matellán, Víctor. 2010. Argument structure and the syntax-morphology interface. A case study in Latin and other languages. Doctoral dissertation. Universitat de Barcelona. http://hdl.handle.net/10803/21788 (accessed 31 January 2014).

Baker, Mark. 1988. *Incorporation: A theory of grammatical function changing*. Chicago: University of Chicago Press.

Baker, Mark. 1997. Thematic roles and syntactic structure. In *Elements of grammar*, ed. Liliane Haegeman, 73–137. Dordrecht: Kluwer.

Belletti, Adriana, and Luigi Rizzi. 1988. Psych-Verbs and Θ-theory. *Natural Language and Linguistic Theory* 6:291–352.

Borer, Hagit. 2005. *Structuring sense II: The normal course of events*. Oxford: Oxford University Press.

Bouchard, Denis. 1995. *The semantics of syntax. A minimalist approach to grammar*. Chicago: The University of Chicago Press.

Bresnan, Joan. 2001. *Lexical-functional syntax*. Malden, MA: Wiley, Blackwell.

Chomsky, Noam. 1981. *Lectures on government and binding*. Dordrecht: Foris.

Chomsky, Noam. 1995. *The minimalist program*. Cambridge, MA: MIT Press.

Croft, William. 2001. *Radical construction grammar. Syntactic theory in typological perspective*. Oxford and New York: Oxford University Press.

Culicover, Peter, and Ray Jackendoff. 2005. *Simpler syntax*. Oxford and New York: Oxford University Press.

Dowty, David. 1979. *Word meaning and Montague grammar*. Dordrecht: Reidel.

Dowty, David. 1991. Thematic proto-roles and argument selection. *Language* 67(3):547–619.

Erteschik-Shir, Nomi, and Tova Rapoport. 2007. Projecting argument structure. The grammar of hitting and breaking revisited. In *Argument structure*, ed. Eric Reuland, Tanmoy Bhattacharya, and Giorgos Spathas, 17–35. Amsterdam: John Benjamins.

Espinal, M. Teresa, and Jaume Mateu. 2011. Bare nominals and argument structure in Catalan and Spanish. *The Linguistic Review* 28:1–39.

Fillmore, Charles. 1968. The case for case. In *Universals in linguistic theory*, ed. Emmon Bach and Robert T. Harms, 1–88. New York: Holt, Rinehart and Winston.

Fillmore, Charles. 1977. The case for case reopened. In *Syntax and semantics* 8: *Grammatical relations*, ed. Peter Cole and Jerrold Sadock, 59–81. Academic Press Inc.

Fillmore, Charles. 1985. Frames and the semantics of understanding. *Quaderni di Semantica* 6(2):222–254.

Foley, William, and Robert Van Valin. 1984. *Functional syntax and universal grammar*. Cambridge: Cambridge University Press.

Gallego, Ángel J. 2010. An l-syntax for adjuncts. In *Argument structure and syntactic relations*, ed. Maia Duguine, Susana Huidobro, and Nerea Madariaga, 183–202. Amsterdam and Philadelphia: John Benjamins.

Goldberg, Adele. 1995. *Constructions. A construction grammar approach to argument structure.* Chicago and London: The University of Chicago Press.

Grimshaw, Jane. 1990. *Argument structure.* Cambridge, MA: MIT Press.

Grimshaw, Jane. 1991. Extended projection. Ms. Brandeis University [revised version in Jane Grimshaw. 2005. *Words and structure,* 1–71. Stanford, CA: CSLI Publications].

Gruber, Jeffrey. 1965. *Studies in lexical relations.* Cambridge, MA: MIT dissertation. Published as Gruber, Jeffrey. 1976. *Lexical structures in syntax and semantics.* Amsterdam and New York: North Holland.

Hale, Kenneth L., and Samuel Jay Keyser. 1992. The syntactic character of thematic structure. In *Thematic structure: Its role in grammar,* ed. Iggy M. Roca, 107–144. Berlin and New York: Foris.

Hale, Kenneth L., and Samuel Jay Keyser. 1993. On argument structure and the lexical expression of syntactic relations. In *The view from Building 20: Essays in linguistics in honor of Sylvain Bromberger,* ed. Kenneth L. Hale and Samuel Jay Keyser, 53–109. Cambridge, MA: MIT Press.

Hale, Kenneth L., and Samuel Jay Keyser. 2002. *Prolegomenon to a theory of argument structure.* Cambridge, MA: MIT Press.

Harley, Heidi. 2005. How do verbs get their names? Denominal verbs, manner incorporation, and the ontology of verb roots in English. In *The syntax of aspect. Deriving thematic and aspectual interpretation,* ed. Nomi Erteschik-Shir and Tova Rapoport, 42–64. Oxford and New York: Oxford University Press.

Harley, Heidi. 2011. A minimalist approach to argument structure. In *The handbook of linguistic minimalism,* ed. Cedric Boeckx, 427–448. Oxford and New York: Oxford University Press.

Harley, Heidi. 2012. Lexical decomposition in modern syntactic theory. In *The Oxford handbook of compositionality,* ed. Markus Werning, Wolfram Hinzen, and Edouard Machery, 328–350. Oxford: Oxford University Press.

Harley, Heidi. 2013. External arguments and the mirror principle: On the distinctness of voice and v. *Lingua* 125:34–57.

Haugen, Jason D. 2009. Hyponymous objects and late insertion. *Lingua* 119:242–262.

Hoekstra, Teun. 1988. Small clause results. *Lingua* 74:101–139.

Hoekstra, Teun. 2004. Small clauses everywhere. In *Arguments and structure,* ed. Rint Sybesma Sjef Barbiers, Marcel den Dikken, Jenny Doetjes, Gertjan Postma, and Guido Vanden Wyngaerd, 319–390. Berlin and New York: Mouton de Gruyter.

Hornstein, Norbert. 2001. *Move! A minimalist theory of construal.* Malden and Oxford: Blackwell.

Jackendoff, Ray. 1990. *Semantic structures.* Cambridge, MA: MIT Press.

Jackendoff, Ray. 1997. *The architecture of the language faculty.* Cambridge, MA: MIT Press.

Jackendoff, Ray. 2002. *Foundations of language. Brain, meaning, grammar, evolution.* Oxford: Oxford University Press.

Kayne, Richard. 2009. Antisymmetry and the lexicon. *Linguistic Variation Yearbook* 8(1):1–31.

Kiparsky, Paul. 1997. Remarks on denominal verbs. In *Complex predicates,* ed. Àlex Alsina, J. Bresnan, and P. Sells, 473–499. Stanford, CA: CSLI Publications.

Kratzer, Angelika. 1996. Severing the external argument from its verb. In *Phrase structure and the lexicon,* ed. Johan Rooryck and Laurie Zaring, 109–137. Dordrecht: Kluwer.

Lakoff, George. 1971. On generative semantics. In *Semantics. An interdisciplinary reader,* ed. Danny Steinberg and Leon Jakobovits, 232–296. New York: Cambridge University Press.

Landau, Idan. 2010. *The locative syntax of experiencers.* Cambridge, MA: MIT Press.

Larson, Richard. 1988. On the double object construction. *Linguistic Inquiry* 19:335–391.

Levin, Beth. 1993. *English verb classes and alternations: A preliminary investigation.* Chicago and London: The Chicago University Press.

Levin, Beth, and Malka Rappaport Hovav. 1995. *Unaccusativity. At the syntax-lexical semantics interface.* Cambridge, MA: MIT Press.

Levin, Beth, and Malka Rappaport Hovav. 2001. Morphology and lexical semantics. In *The handbook of morphology,* ed. Andrew Spencer and Arnold Zwicky, 248–271. Oxford/Malden: Blackwell.

Levin, Beth, and Malka Rappaport Hovav. 2005. *Argument realization.* Cambridge: Cambridge University Press.

McCawley, James. 1973. Syntactic and logical arguments for semantic structures. In *Three dimensions in linguistic theory,* ed. Osamu Fujimura, 259–376. Tokyo: TEC Corp.

McIntyre, Andrew. 2004. Event paths, conflation, argument structure, and VP shells. *Linguistics* 42(3):523–571.

Marantz, Alec. 1997. No escape from syntax: Don't try morphological analysis in the privacy of your own lexicon. *University of Pennsylvania Working Papers in Linguistics* 4(2):201–225.

Marantz, Alec. 2005. Objects out of the lexicon: Argument structure in the syntax! Ms. MIT. Downloadable at http://web.mit.edu/marantz/Public/UConn/UConnHOApr05.pdf (accessed 31 January 2014).

Mateu, Jaume. 2002. *Argument structure. Relational construal at the syntax-semantics interface*. Bellaterra: Universitat Autònoma de Barcelona dissertation. Downloadable at http://www. tesisenxarxa.net/TDX-1021103-173806/ (accessed 31 January 2014).

Mateu, Jaume. 2010. On the lexical syntax of manner and causation. In *Argument structure and syntactic relations*, ed. Maia Duguine, Susana Huidobro and Nerea Madariaga, 89–112. Amsterdam and Philadelphia: John Benjamins.

Mateu, Jaume. 2012. Conflation and incorporation processes in resultative constructions. In *Telicity, change, and state. A cross-categorial view of event structure*, ed. Violeta Demonte and Louise McNally, 252–278. Oxford and New York: Oxford University Press.

Mateu, Jaume, and Gemma Rigau. 2002. A minimalist account of conflation processes: Parametric variation at the lexicon-syntax interface. In *Theoretical approaches to universals*, ed. Artemis Alexiadou, 211–236. Amsterdam and Philadelphia: John Benjamins.

Mateu, Jaume, and M. Teresa Espinal. 2007. Argument structure and compositionality in idiomatic constructions. *The Linguistic Review* 24:33–59.

Mateu, Jaume, and Víctor Acedo-Matellán. 2012. The manner/result complementarity revisited: A syntactic approach. In *The end of argument structure? (Syntax and Semantics, Volume 38)*, ed. María Cristina Cuervo and Yves Roberge, 209–228. Bingley: Emerald.

Pesetsky, David. 1995. *Zero syntax. Experiencers and cascades*. Cambridge, MA: The MIT Press.

Pinker, Steven. 1989. *Learnability and cognition. The acquisition of argument structure*. Cambridge, MA: The MIT Press.

Pylkkänen, Liina. 2008. *Introducing arguments*. Cambridge, MA: MIT Press.

Ramchand, Gillian. 2008. *Verb meaning and the lexicon. A first phase syntax*. Cambridge: Cambridge University Press.

Real-Puigdollers, Cristina. 2013. *Lexicalization by phase: The role of prepositions in argument structure and its cross-linguistic variation*. Bellaterra: Universitat Autònoma de Barcelona dissertation.

Reinhart, Tanya. 2002. The theta system: An overview. *Theoretical Linguistics* 28:229–290.

Sadler, Louise, and Andrew Spencer. 2001. Morphology and argument structure. In *The handbook of morphology*, ed. Andrew Spencer and Arnold Zwicky, 206–236. Oxford/Malden: Blackwell.

Talmy, Leonard. 1985. Lexicalization patterns: Semantic structure in lexical forms. In *Language typology and syntactic description* (vol. 3), ed. Timothy Shopen, 57–149. Cambridge: Cambridge University Press.

Talmy, Leonard. 2000. *Toward a cognitive semantics. Typology and process in concept structuring*. Cambridge, MA: MIT Press.

Tenny, Carol. 1994. *Aspectual roles and the syntax-semantics interface*. Dordrecht: Kluwer.

Volpe, Mark. 2004. Affected object unergatives. *Snippets* 8:12–13.

Zubizarreta, María Luisa, and Eunjeong Oh. 2007. *On the syntactic composition of manner and motion*. Cambridge, MA: MIT Press.

3

The integration, proliferation, and expansion of functional categories

An overview

Lisa deMena Travis

1   Introduction

In early transformational grammar (e.g. Chomsky 1957, 1965) functional categories[1] such as Det(erminer), Aux(iliary) had a rather peripheral function in the phrase stucture system. This minor role was reflected in the terminology where functional categories were labeled "minor lexical categories" (see Jackendoff 1977: 32). In the past sixty years, however, functional categories have come to take a major role. I describe this ascent in three stages – integration, proliferation, and then expansion. First I show how functional categories became structurally equal to the "major" lexical categories such as N(ouns), V(erbs), and A(djectives). At this point, categories such as D and Infl(ection) (an updated version of Aux)[2] become normalized, and new functional categories are added to this group such as Comp(lementizer), Num(ber), K(ase). Soon after this structural shift, the inventory of categories expanded first slowly and then, with the advent of Cinque (1999), explosively. Also, during this period where the structures of functional categories come to resemble those of lexical categories (formerly known as major categories), efforts are made to keep functional categories as a distinct class of category with specific properties. The current state of functional categories can be seen as the extreme end of a pendulum swing. Lexical categories themselves are being put under the microscope and, in some sense, they have become minor or perhaps nonexistent. In this chapter I give a brief description of minor categories, and then track the development of functional categories within X'-theory, their proliferation, and their distinct characteristics. Later I give a glimpse of the far end of the pendulum swing, followed by some concluding remarks.

2   Minor categories

Functional categories for decades had the role of the chorus in syntactic theory. They were important but relegated to the background – considered "minor categories" to be distinguished from "major categories" such as N(oun), V(erb), A(djective).[3] In *Aspects of the Theory of Syntax* (Chomsky 1965), the structure of the clause places all of the inflectional material that appears between the subject and the verb phrase in one (sometimes branching) node dominated by S, as shown in the tree below.[4]

(1)   AUX in Chomsky (1965)

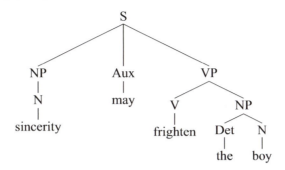

The material that appeared in AUX comprises a set of inflectional elements as characterized by the phrase structure rule in (2) below.

(2)   Aux → Tense (M) (Aspect) (Chomsky 1965: 107)

In the discussion of the structure in (1), Chomsky divides the elements into category symbols (N, V, etc.) and formatives (*the, boy*, etc.). The formatives he further subdivides into lexical items (*sincerity, boy*, etc.) and grammatical items (*Perfect, Progressive, the*, etc.). Jackendoff, in *X'-syntax: a Study of Phrase Structure* (Jackendoff 1977), citing Chomsky (1970) as a forerunner, divides categories into two types through a system of features. He proposes that what distinguishes functional (minor) categories from lexical (major) categories is the ability of the latter to take a complement, a property that is represented by the feature [±Comp]. He begins the discussion by distinguishing Adjective and Preposition ([+Comp]) from Adverbial and Particle ([-Comp]) respectively, but continues the discussion to include modals (with respect to verbs), articles and quantifiers (with respect to nouns), and degree words (with respect to adjectives). He thereby creates a system where every lexical [+Comp] category is linked to a set of functional [-Comp] categories as shown in the following table.

(3)   Jackendoff's features (1977: 32)

	Subj	Obj	Comp	Det
V	+	+	+	
M	+	+	−	
P	−	+	+	
Prt	−	+	−	
N	+	−	+	
Art	+	−	−	+
Q	+	−	−	−
A	−	−	+	
Deg	−	−	−	+
Adv	−	−	−	−

At this point, functional categories begin to be part of the larger phrase structural system in that they are part of the featural system that Jackendoff created. They are not, however, part of the X'-theory of projection. The minor categories remain minor in the creation of trees, mainly appearing in specifier positions either as lexical items (e.g. *have, en* in (4)) sometimes with category labels (e.g. *pres* in (4)) or as maximal projections (X''') with no internal complexity (e.g. Art in (5)).

(4)   Jackendoff (1977: 40)

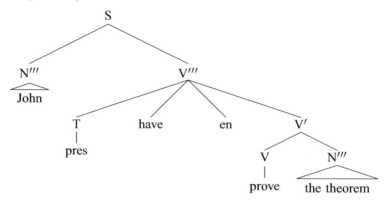

(5)   Jackendoff (1977: 59)

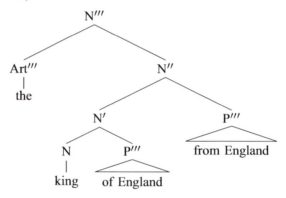

Jackendoff proposes that there are parallel systems within the projections of the lexical categories – N, V, A, and P. The minor categories that appear in the specifier positions of the four lexical categories are seen to share properties across the systems. Not only do the complex specifiers such as N''' subjects in the verbal system and N''' possessors in the nominal system share characteristics, but so do specifiers such as Aux, Det and Degree across the three systems of V, N, and A. He acknowledges, however, that specifiers (as opposed to complements) are difficult to study as a class given their relatively small numbers, their idiosyncrasies, and their skewed distribution across the different projections. Many of the themes set up in Jackendoff are taken up in later work on functional categories, as we will see in subsequent sections.

3 Stage I: Equal but distinct

The first important step in the development of a theory of functional categories involves giving them a place in the phrase structure system. It is shown that they behave mechanically much the same way as lexical categories such as nouns, verbs, and adjectives – projecting structure, taking complements and specifiers, acting as launching and landing sites of movement. However, they still have a distinct function – not introducing arguments but rather contributing particular feature based semantic content. This section is an overview of the regularization of the structure of functional categories, the establishment of their (distinct) properties, and the additions to their inventory.

3.1 Functional categories and X′-theory

In Stowell's important PhD thesis, *Origins of Phrase Structure* (Stowell 1981), minor categories join the family of categories structurally. In the earlier versions of X′-theory (Chomsky 1970; Jackendoff 1977), only the major (lexical) categories can be the head of a phrase. The head V projects to S, S projects to S′ (Bresnan 1976). Aux is a specifier of VP, Comp is specifier of S′, Determiner is a specifier of DP. Stowell (1981: 68), however, proposes that Aux (now labeled Infl) is the head of S, making S now I″ (or IP). He further proposes (Stowell 1981: 388ff.) that Comp is the head of S′ (CP). These two proposals change the sentential phrase structure quite dramatically, as can be seen in (6) and (7) below. In (6) the functional categories are truly minor but in (7) the functional categories C and Infl behave like their lexical counterparts, projecting to a phrasal level along the spine of the tree.

(6)   Minor categories

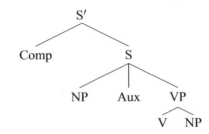

(7)   Functional categories project

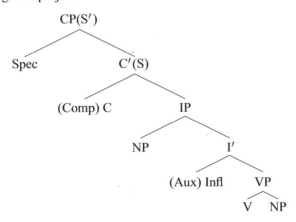

It is important to note at this point the type of argumentation that Stowell uses to support his claim that, for example, Comp is a head.[5] He observes that verbs specify what type of clausal complement they require, (i.e. ± wh). If one assumes that this sort of selection must be local (i.e. a head may only specify the properties of its complement or the head of this complement), both selecting elements and selected elements will be identified as projecting heads.[6] If a verb can specify whether it selects a [–wh] clausal complement (with *that* or *for*) or a [+wh] complement (with *whether* or *if*), then these lexical items must head the complement of the verb.

(8)   a. The children believe **that/*whether** it will snow.
        b. The children prefer **for** it to snow.
        c. The children wonder **whether/*that** it will snow.

The same sort of argument can be used to support Stowell's proposal for Infl as the head of IP (S). The complementizer *that* selects for a +finite complement, while the complementizer *for* selects for a [–finite] complement, as the examples above show. This suggests not only that the selectors *that* and *for* are heads but also that the items that are being selected, [+finite] Infl or [–finite] Infl, are also heads.

Stowell's thesis, by integrating functional categories into the formal phrase structure system, sets the stage for serious research on these categories. This research takes a variety of directions that are discussed below.

3.2   The nominal system

Abney's thesis, *The English Noun Phrase in its Sentential Aspect* (Abney 1987), represents an important further step in the development of functional categories.[7] Just as Stowell argues that Aux is not the specifier of VP but is the head of its own projection along the clausal spine, Abney, extending proposals of Brame (1981, 1982), argues that Determiner is not the specifier of NP but is a head of its own projection along the nominal spine.[8]

Abney shows that Det is a selector (the way that we saw above that Comp is a selector). Determiners, like verbs, can take a complement obligatorily (*The children wore *(costumes).*) or take a complement optionally (*The children sang (a song).*). We can see below that the Det *the* must have a complement while the Det *that* optionally takes a complement.

(9)   a. The *(child) was tired.
        b. That (song) amused the children.

A further test for the head status of the determiner comes from head movement. If it can be assumed that heads may only move into the heads that select them (see the Head Movement Constraint of Travis 1984: 131), then evidence of head movement *into* a position or *from* a position can be used to argue that the landing site or the launching site of the movement, respectively, is a head. Abney uses the following paradigm to argue that Det is a head. First we see in (10a) and (10b) that bare adjectives generally cannot follow the N head in English. However, with forms like *someone* (in (10c)) or *everything* (in (10d)), these adjectives can appear in the final position of the phrase (data from Abney 1987: 287).

(10)   a. a (clever) man (*clever)
        b. a (good) person (*good)
        c. someone clever
        d. everything good

According to Abney, *one* and *thing* are generated in N and undergo head movement from N to D, resulting in this otherwise unexpected word order.

(11) Head movement to D

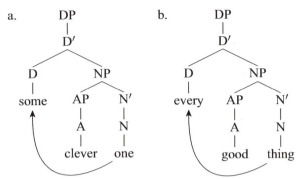

Abney's work is important in the development of functional categories not only because he proposes a nominal structure which contains a functional head Det that parallels the functional head Infl in the verbal domain, but also because he outlines a set of criteria that distinguish functional elements from lexical elements (what he terms "thematic elements").[9] He argues that functional categories form a natural class with the following characteristics (adapted from Abney 1987: 54–68).[10]

(12) Properties of functional categories
   a. Functional elements f(unctionally)-select their complement.
   b. Functional categories select a unique element.
   c. Functional elements are a closed class.
   d. Functional elements are morphologically weaker than lexical elements (often dependent, affixes, clitics, and sometimes null).
   e. Functional elements are generally not separable from their complement.
   f. Functional elements lack "descriptive content", contributing to the interpretation of their complement often through grammatical or relational features.

At this point in the history of functional categories, they have been incorporated into phrase structure and X'-theory, heading projections along the phrase structure spine in the same way as (major) lexical categories. However, they are still recognized as having distinct characteristics. For Abney, the crucial distinction is that functional categories do not take arguments. In terms of Government Binding Theory (Chomsky 1981), this means that lexical categories can assign theta-roles while functional categories cannot. The functional categories f(unctionally)-select their (single) complements rather than setting up a structure that allows theta-assignment to take place.

3.3   Parallel structures and extended projections

Abney's thesis begins to outline the grammatical contribution that functional categories make to syntactic structure. Further work develops and refines this. Ken Hale in class lectures in the 1980s presented a view of phrase structure where Ns and Vs set up parallel systems with parallel domains, in a way reminiscent of Jackendoff's earlier work discussed in Section 2. Both projections contain a lexical domain (VP and NP) where lexical selection and theta-assignment occur. Above this domain is an inflectional domain (Infl and Det) which gives reference to the descriptive content of the lexical projection (event or item) and locates it in time and space. The structural layer above this inflectional domain has a purely grammatical function – to provide a formal connection to the rest of the utterance. This layer contains the Comp in the verbal domain and Case (K) in the nominal domain.[11]

Grimshaw (1991, 2000) also outlines a general view of the phrase structure architecture, introducing the notion of extended projections. As in Hale's work, she describes the general pattern whereby a lexical head is topped by a complex functional category shell.[12] As Abney points out, in some sense the functional categories that make up this shell pass on the descriptive content of the most deeply embedded complement. Grimshaw captures this continuity by having one feature shared from the bottom of this projection to the top. In the tree in (13) we see that the V, the I, and the C all share the categorial feature [verbal]. Where they vary is in the level of the F feature. The verbal head that asymmetrically c-commands the other verbal heads in the tree is labeled F2, while the sole verbal head that selects no other verbal head is labeled F0. An extended projection is a projection that shares a categorial feature. Grimshaw labels the more traditional notion of projection a *perfect projection*. Perfect projections share not only categorial features but also have the same {F} value. CP is the perfect projection of C and the extended projection of V.

(13) Extended projections

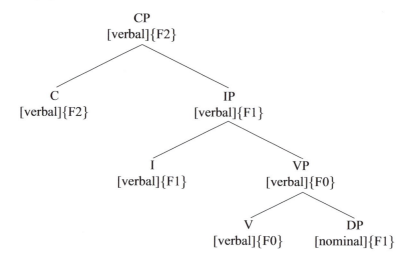

Note that an l-head (lexical head) will never be part of the extended projection of its complement since it will either be selecting a projection with a different categorial feature, or it will select a complement with a higher {F} value, as would be the case if V, {F0}, selects CP, {F2}, or both as is the case in (13).

The importance of Grimshaw's contribution is that she can capture why, for some processes, C acts as the head of CP and sometimes a lower head appears to be visible to processes outside of CP. As an example, we can look at selection. While we have used the locality of selection as an argument for the head status of C in Section 3.1, we can see in (14) below that selection sometimes appears not to be local. Grimshaw calls this semantic selection and posits that the N is being selected.[13]

(14)   a. They merged the files/#the file.   Grimshaw (2000): (10)
       b. They amalgamated the files/#the file.
       c. They combined the files/#the file.

If features are allowed to percolate through an extended projection, this apparent counter-example to selection and locality can be accounted for.

3.4   Functional categories as a distinct class

We have seen in the previous section that the functional shells that dominate the projection of the lexical category are different in their content and selectional properties. Now we will look at ways that these differences affect other parts of the grammatical model – in particular, how the distinction between functional categories and lexical categories affects projection and movement, and how this distinction interacts with parameterization.

3.4.1   Projection: Fukui (1986)

Fukui (1986) introduces the term *functional category* and presents one of the first views of functional categories that treats them as a natural class of category, distinguished from lexical categories in principled ways. According to Fukui, the members of the class of functional categories are similar to lexical categories in that they head a projection that appears along the spine of the tree. He argues, however, that the exact mechanism of this projection differs from that of lexical categories. Among the list of differences articulated in Abney (1987),[14] Fukui proposes that only functional categories can project true specifier positions. He argues that positions within lexical categories are determined by the argument structure of the head (the theta-grid or lexical conceptual structure) and that while this might include external arguments (the VP-internal subject hypothesis of Fukui and Speas 1986, among others), the generation of these positions depends on semantic rather than syntactic considerations. One way of thinking of this in current terms is that the "specifier" position of a lexical head is always created through EXTERNAL MERGE (see Chomsky 2004), that is, through base generation of an element in this position.[15] In contrast, specifiers of functional categories, according to Fukui, were always filled by a moved constituent (INTERNAL MERGE of Chomsky 2004). This distinction foreshadows a distinction made in the Minimalist Program, which will be discussed in Section 5.1, where functional categories consist of formal features, including features that trigger movement.

3.4.2   Movement: Li (1990)

We have seen in Section 3.2 above how head movement has been used to argue that a particular element is a head along the spinal projection of the structure. However, not all head movements are possible. We look at one case of impossible head movement here that highlights a distinction between lexical and functional categories. In Li (1990), a parallel is drawn between head movement and XP movement, and a crucial distinction is made between functional and lexical categories.[16] He investigates the structure of morphologically complex verbal formation using proposals of Baker (1988). In Baker's analysis of productive verb incorporation structures, the higher verb selects for a sentential complement, CP. For example, a typical causative structure with the relevant movement is shown below. The structure and movement for the data in (15) would be as in (16) (Swahili example taken from Li 1990: 399 and credited to Vitale 1981).

(15)　Musa a-li-m-pik-ish-a　　　　　　mke　wake　chakula
　　　　Musa he-past-her-cook-cause-ind　wife　his　　food
　　　　"Musa made his wife cook some food."

(16)　Head movement in causatives 1

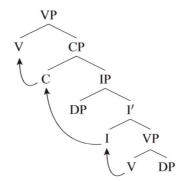

Li notes, however, that in spite of the movement of the lower V through two functional categories, I and C, material typically found in I and in C is not found within morphologically complex verbal structures. He argues that morphologically complex causatives, in fact, have a simpler structure where the causative V directly selects a VP. The structure for (15), then, should be as shown in (17) rather than as we have seen in (16).

(17)　Head movement in causatives 2

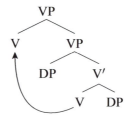

Li nevertheless acknowledges that structures of the type in (16) do exist. The example that he gives is presented below where it is clear that the embedded complement selected by the higher verb contains inflectional material and a complementizer (Swahili example taken from Li 1990: 400 and credited to Vitale 1981).

(18)　Na-ju-a　　　kama Hamisi a-na-ogop-a　　giza.
　　　　I-know-ind that　Hamisi he-pres-fear-ind darkness
　　　　"I know that Hamisi is afraid of the dark."

Li claims, however, that the sort of structure given in (18) would never allow head movement. Basically, movement of a lexical category through a functional category back to a lexical category is ruled out for principled reasons – in particular, this movement would violate Binding Theory. He characterizes functional categories as being the head equivalent of A′-positions and lexical categories being the head equivalent of A-positions. Movement from a lexical category to a functional category to a lexical category would be similar to movement from an A-position to an A′-position back to an A-position, improper movement, constituting a Principle C violation.

An example of improper movement of an XP is given below.

(19) *John seems that it is [VP t' [VP considered [t to be intelligent]]]

John has undergone movement from an A-position (the subject position of the most deeply embedded clause) to an A'-position (adjoined to VP) to an A-position (the subject position of the matrix clause). This sort of movement produces an ungrammatical string and one way of accounting for the ungrammaticality is through Binding Theory. An empty category that is A'-bound (e.g. the trace in the lowest subject position) is an R-expression (Chomsky 1981) and R-expressions must be A-free. In this construction, however, this R-expression will be A-bound by *John* in the matrix Spec, TP incurring a Principle C violation.

If lexical heads are similar to A-positions and functional heads similar to A'-positions, we can now see why movement of the sort shown in (16) would create the same violation as that in (19). Just as the trace in the embedded subject position in (19) is locally A'-bound, making it a variable, the trace in the embedded V in (16) is locally A'-bound (by the coindexed material in I), making it the head equivalent of a variable. However, this variable will be A-bound by the coindexed material in the matrix V position, in violation of (the head equivalent of) Principle C.

Li's contribution, and others like it (e.g. Baker and Hale 1990), are important to the development of functional categories because they confirm not only the existence of these categories, but also their distinctiveness, in modules of the grammar other than phrase structure.

3.4.3   Parameters: Borer (1984) and Ouhalla (1991)

Functional categories begin to take a major role in the grammar in Borer's (1984) work on parameters.[17] Before this work, it is not clear how exactly the grammar encodes parameters such as the pro-drop parameter or the choice of bounding nodes. Borer (1984: 29), however, argues that "all interlanguage variation [can be reduced to] properties of the inflectional system". She claims that grammatical formatives and their idiosyncratic properties are learned the way other vocabulary is learned. Since this learning includes inflectional properties of these formatives, learning these properties is equivalent to acquiring parameters. Borer's proposal not only changes the view of where parameters are encoded but also gives a central role to functional categories since functional categories are the repository of inflectional information.

Borer concentrates on variation seen in clitic constructions, agreement properties and case assigning properties, but the encoding of parameters in functional categories extends easily to other instances of language variation. While there are many examples of this, I briefly present one of the earliest ones here.[18]

Ouhalla (1991) extends the range of properties by which functional categories can vary to include the order in which these categories are introduced into the syntactic tree. He looks particularly at variation in word order and ascribes these differences to the selectional properties of functional categories. Since selection determines the order of elements on the phrase structure spine, different selectional properties can vary this order and thereby affect the overall word order of a language. Looking at the differences between SVO and VSO languages, he argues that SVO languages generate Agr above Tense while in VSO Agr is below Tense. The hierarchical order of the functional heads can be seen in the order of the relevant morphemes. In (20) we see an example from Berber, a VSO language where Tense precedes Agr. In (21) we see an example from Chichewa, an SVO language where Agr precedes Tense.

(20)   ad-y-segh   Moha ijn teddart   Tense>Agr: VSO
       fut(TNS)-3ms(AGR)-buy Moha one house
       "Moha will buy a house."

(21)   Mtsuko   u-na-gw-a.   Agr>Tense: SVO
       waterpot SP(AGR)-past(TNS)-fall-ASP
       "The waterpot fell."

He examines other languages as well, such as Italian and French (both SVO languages) and
Arabic and Chamorro (both VSO languages), to support his claims.

   The work of Fukui and Li shows how early in the development of functional categories,
they came to be seen as a distinct class. The work of Borer and Ouhalla gave this distinct
class a central role in explaining language variation. Next we turn to the explosion of the
inventory of functional categories.

4   Stage II: Proliferation

With the regularization of the status of functional categories comes a flurry of interest in
both the inflectional (T, D) domain and the grammatical domain (C, K) in both the verbal
and nominal extended projections. The sorts of tests that we have seen in previous sections
as well as others are employed to uncover additional functional categories. We can highlight five different tests that have been used to test for the presence of a functional head.[19]

(22)   Tests for presence of a (functional) head
       a. The presence of a lexical item
       b. The presence of a morpheme
       c. The landing site of head movement
       d. The presence of a specifier
       e. The presence of semantic material or features

While each of these will be fleshed out with examples below, I note here the important work
of Baker (1985, 1988). Baker (1985) points out the tight relationship between morphology
and syntax, which can be interpreted as a tight relationship between morphology and the
heads along the spine of the phrase structure. Baker (1988) solidifies this relationship with
the process of incorporation, or head movement, accounting for why morphology so closely
tracks the relative order of syntactic heads. This allows not only the presence of a lexical
item (test (22a)) but also the presence of a morpheme (test (22b)) to indicate the presence
of a functional head. We will see below how several of these tests may be put to use.[20]

4.1   Articulation of Infl: Pollock (1989)

Pollock's work (Pollock 1989) on the articulation of the verbal inflectional domain can be
seen as the beginning of a general dissection of these domains that before appeared peripheral
to phrase structure – relegated to the morphological component of the grammar. Pollock
uses head movement (see test (22c)) of verbs in nonfinite clauses in French to show that the
verb can appear in a position that is neither V (the launching site of the head movement) nor
Infl (the landing site of head movement of the V in finite clauses). The important data are
given below, starting with the relevant template. Pollock shows that the negation marker

pas and adverbs such as *à peine* "hardly" or *souvent* "often" appear on either side of this intermediate landing site and serve as signposts as to whether the verb appears in its merged position (below both: LOW), in the intermediate position (above the adverb but below negation: MID) or in Infl (above both: HIGH).

(23) [$_{Infl}$HIGH] NEG [MID] ADVERB [$_V$ LOW]

As was already well known (Emonds 1978), when the verb is finite in French, it moves to the high position above NEG and the adverb – a position which is assumed to be Infl.[21]

(24) a. Jean n'*aime*   **pas** Marie.
          Jean NEG.like NEG Marie
          "Jean doesn't like Marie."
      b. Jean *embrasse* **souvent** Marie.
          Jean kiss   often   Marie
          "Jean often kisses Marie."

Pollock shows, however, that when the verb is nonfinite, it moves above the adverb (shown in (25a)) but must remain below negation (shown in (25b) vs. (25c)).

(25) a. *Parler* **à peine** l'italien …
          to.speak hardly   Italian
          "To hardly speak Italian …"
      b. *Ne   parler   **pas** l'italien …
          NEG to.speak NEG Italian
          "Not to speak   Italian …"
      c. Ne **pas** parler   l'italien …
          NEG NEG to.speak Italian
          "Not to speak Italian …"

In this way, Pollock uses head movement of the verb in French to argue for an additional functional category in the verbal inflectional domain between NEG and V.[22] He labels the new category Agr – a labeling that is slightly speculative. Infl at the time was encoding both Tense and Agreement – features of very different types – suggesting that perhaps they should appear in different heads (see test (22e) which specifies that the presence of distinct features can be used to argue for a separate head). Since Pollock connects the difference in the use of this intermediate position to the presence of rich agreement morphology in French and not in English, he labels the intermediate position Agr. While his intention is that this Agr head be used for subject agreement, given that the difference between English and French shows up in subject agreement, the order of morphemes crosslinguistically suggests that subject agreement is outside of tense.[23] In a slightly different view of the expansion of Infl, the high position is AGRS – subject agreement – and the intermediate one is T (see Belletti 1990). Another possibility, and the one that becomes fairly standard for a decade, is to have two Agr heads – one above T (AGRS) and one below T (AGRO) (see Chomsky 1991). At this point, inflectional heads begin to proliferate for a variety of reasons. Pollock proposes a new head to account for a landing site of head movement (test (22c)). The presence of both object agreement and subject agreement on verbs suggests two additional functional heads (see test (22b)).[24]

(26) Articulation of Infl

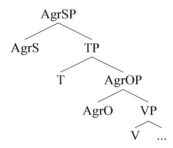

This articulation of Infl sets the stage for an explosion in the number of functional categories over the next 20 years, two of the best known examples of this being cartography and nano-syntax.

4.2 Cartography: Cinque (1999)

Cartographic syntax is a research program which seeks to map out the details of the functional phrase structure spine using crosslinguistic data (see Belletti 2004; Cinque 2002; Shlonsky 2010; Rizzi 2004). The assumption is that there is a universal template or map.[25] As one of the pioneers of this research program, Cinque (1999), using several of the tests seen in (22), argues for one of the most articulated versions of the verbal spine.[26] What is particularly impressive is the range of evidence brought to bear on his proposals and the number of languages considered. The discussion below only gives a brief overview of this study.

The first type of evidence that Cinque uses, and the one that is best known, is his proposed universal hierarchy of adverbs. He argues that adverbs in many languages appear in specifier positions that are paired with heads that are sometimes unrealized (see test (22d)) and that the arrangement of the specifiers, and therefore the heads, is consistent crosslinguistically. Using adverb ordering from a variety of languages, he fleshes out the details of the hierarchy. Below I have given the relative order for the lower adverbs in Italian and French (other languages discussed by Cinque are English, Norwegian, Bosnian/Serbo-Croatian, Hebrew, Chinese, Albanian, Malagasy).

(27) Relative ordering of "lower" adverbs in Italian and French (Cinque 1999: 11)
   a. solitamente > mica > già > più > sempre > completamente > tutto > bene
   b. généralement > pas > déjà > plus > toujours > complètement > tout > bien

To argue that these adverbs are in specifier positions rather than head positions, he shows that verb movement can place a verb between the adverbs. More specifically, he shows that the past participle may be placed in a variety of positions relative to the lower adverbs in Italian. Given the example below, the past participle *rimesso* may appear in all of the positions marked by X (Cinque 1999: 45).

(28) Da allora, non hanno X di solito X mica X più X sempre X completamente *rimesso* tutto bene in ordine.
   "Since then, they haven't usually not any longer always put everything well in order."

Assuming that each position represents a possible landing site for head movement, we have arguments for six head positions above the VP (test (22c)).

Using two more traditional tests, the order of lexical items (test (22a)) and the order of morphemes (test (22b)), Cinque continues to both confirm and fine-tune his proposals concerning a highly articulated universal hierarchy of functional categories. Below I give an illustrative example of each. In (29b), we see a case of complex morphology from Korean (Cinque 1999: 53, credited to Sohn 1994: 354) and in (29a) we see a sequence of particles from Guyanese (Cinque 1999: 59, credited to Gibson 1986: 585).

(29) a. ku   say-ka   cwuk-ess-keyss-kwun-a!
          that bird-NOM die-ANT-EPISTEM-EVALUAT-DECL
          "That bird must have died!"
     b. Jaan shuda   bin kyaan get fu gu
          J.   MOD$_{epistemic}$ PAST MOD$_R$ MOD$_r$ go
          "J. should not have been allowed to go."

By lining up relative orders of adverbial elements (arguably appearing in specifier positions), morphemes, and free-standing functional heads, Cinque constructs the very articulated hierarchy given below (Cinque 1999: 106).

(30) [*frankly* Mood$_{speechact}$ [*fortunately* Mood$_{evaluative}$ [*allegedly* Mood$_{evidential}$ [*probably* Mod$_{epistemic}$ [*once* T(Past) [*then* T(Future) [*perhaps* Mood$_{irrealis}$ [*necessarily* Mod$_{necessity}$ [*possibly* Mod$_{possibilty}$ [*usually* Asp$_{habitual}$ [*again* Asp$_{repetitive(I)}$ [*often* Asp$_{frequentative(I)}$ [*intentionally* Mod$_{volitional}$ [*quickly* Asp$_{celerative(I)}$ [*already* T(Ant) [*no longer* Asp$_{terminative}$ [*still* Asp$_{continuative}$ [*always* Asp$_{perfect(?)}$ [*just* Asp$_{retrospective}$ [*soon* Asp$_{proximative}$ [*briefly* Asp$_{durative}$ [*characteristically(?)* Asp$_{generic/progressive}$ [*almost* Asp$_{prospective}$ [*completely* Asp$_{SgCompletive(I)}$ [*tutto* Asp$_{PlCompletive}$ [*well* Voice [*fast/early* Asp$_{celerative(II)}$ [*again* Asp$_{repetitive(II)}$ [*often* Asp$_{frequentative(II)}$ [*completely* Asp$_{SgCompletive(II)}$

While this view of the extended projection of the verb may seem extreme, it is, in fact, followed by proposals for still further articulation of the functional spine.

4.3   Nano-syntax: Starke (2009) and Caha (2009)

Nano-syntax (see Starke 2009, and references cited therein) is the extreme of proliferation where syntactic heads do not represent lexical items or even morphemes, but rather single features. We have already seen something like this in Pollock's work. Pollock gives evidence through head movement for an extra head in the verbal inflectional domain and he labels that head Agr. His reason for the label comes from the fact that Infl previously housed two unrelated features, T and Agr. Rather than having two unrelated features in one head, he assigns each feature a separate head. One can further support this move by showing that Tense and Agr are often represented by separate morphemes (*-ez* in French indicates 2pl Agr while other morphemes – *0, -i, -er* – indicate Tense and/or Aspect). Nano-syntax proposes that there is a universal one-feature/one-head mapping. These heads are often sub-morphemic and lexical items often span several heads.

Here I show how nano-syntax leads to a proliferation of heads within the representation of case (for other uses of nano-syntax, see Pantcheva 2011 and Taraldsen 2010). While Travis and Lamontagne (1992) propose that case is a separate head in the syntax (K parallel to C in the verbal projection), Caha (2009) argues that Case has its own feature geometry and that this feature geometry is represented in syntax by separate syntactic heads, expanding K into six distinct heads. One of the generalizations that this hierarchy is created to explain is the pattern of syncretism – only contiguous heads can be realized by the same forms. Below is a table provided by Caha which shows what sort of syncretism is possible given a case hierarchy of NOM > ACC > GEN > DAT where shaded cells indicate for which cases the same forms are used.

(31) Table of case contiguity (Caha 2009: 8)

	NOM	ACC	GEN	DAT
possible				
possible				
possible				
possible				
possible				
possible				
not possible				
not possible				
not possible				
not possible				
not possible				

Using data from a variety of languages, he investigates crosslinguistic patterns of syncretism in case forms and creates the following hierarchy, where Nominative is the least complex case and Comitative is the most complex (containing all of the other cases that it dominates).

(32) Caha's split K

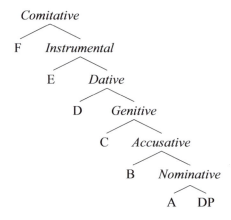

Morphology realizes subtrees of the spine, so, for example, Accusative case is represented by the constituent that immediately dominates B and *Nominative*, etc. (see Starke 2009 and Caha 2009 for details).

   This is necessarily a very brief overview of nano-syntax, and a full understanding requires much more than this introduction, but what is clear is that this follows from a natural progression of what preceded it. Minor categories such as Determiners became projecting heads in their own right. Since some languages represent these same notions through affixation, it is logical to give affixes the same status, including those that encode Number and Case. And finally, since functional heads are seen as encoding values of binary features, it is logical to see functional categories as being features rather than lexical items. Syntax, then, represents an architecture of features rather than an arrangement of lexical items. As a final step in the argumentation, if some notions, such as Case, can be characterized by a system of features with hierarchical dependencies, these features too can be represented in the phrase structure.

4.4 Summary

At this point, while the functional domains along the spine of the tree become progressively complex, one can still maintain the functional/lexical divide. The very complex functional sequences (f_{seq}) in Starke above the lexical projections still are separate domains. Below we will see, however, that the dividing line between the functional domain and the lexical domain can become easily blurred.

5 Stage III: The expansion

As functional domains of Infl and Comp are articulated, so are the domains of the lexical categories. Larson (1988) argues for VP shells, dividing the verb into different heads in order to create a structure that accounts for the hierarchical relationships of elements internal to the VP (e.g. the asymmetric c-command relationship between that the first object has over the second object of a double object construction) while maintaining a binary branching structure (his Single Complement Hypothesis). As the heads are proliferated within what is known as the lexical domain of the phrase structure (e.g. Grimshaw 1991, 2000), it is no longer clear where the lexical/functional divide occurs. For some, the external argument within the predicate is introduced by a V (e.g. Larson 1988), most likely a lexical category. For some it is introduced by a head that is more arguably functional – for example, Pred (Bowers 1993), Voice (Kratzer 1996), ExtArg (Pylkkänen 2008), The question, then, is where the divide should be between lexical and functional within a projection of a semantic head.

In terms of looking at the phrase structural system, along the lines of Jackendoff (1977) or Grimshaw (1991), one might want to keep just one lexical category at the bottom of every projection. Every subsequent category along the spine of the projection, then, would be functional. However, now there is a mismatch between argument domains and lexical domains. With the advent of VP-internal subjects (e.g. Fukui and Speas 1986; Kitagawa 1986; Koopman and Sportiche 1991), there is a clean divide between thematic domains (VP/NP) and inflectional domains (TP/DP and CP/KP) that coincides with the divide between lexical and functional domains. With the articulation of the VP and the introduction of a new head that introduces only the external argument, one either has to give up the assumption that there is only one lexical head per projection or revise one's notion of what functional categories are capable of and where the division between the functional domain and the lexical domain can be drawn. This shift in the division between the functional domain and the lexical domain is described in more detail below.

5.1 Chomsky (1995)

Chomsky's Minimalist Program (Chomsky 1995), while still viewing the distinction between functional (nonsubstantive) and lexical (substantive) categories as being an important one, begins to shift the concept of what counts as a functional category. Parts of the structure that might earlier have been considered lexical categories now are considered to be functional categories according to the criteria that distinguish the two.

Lisa deMena Travis

In the early Minimalist Program, it is clear that functional categories are central to the theory of movement. Movement is triggered by (strong) features on a head and strong features can only be hosted by nonsubstantive (functional) categories (Chomsky 1995: 232).[27]

(33) If F is strong, then F is a feature of a nonsubstantive category and F is checked by a categorial feature.

Examples of functional categories with strong features are T in French where a strong V feature forces (overt) V-movement to T, T in English where a strong D feature forces (overt) movement of DP to Spec, TP. C might have a strong feature forcing T to C movement or movement of a *wh*-phrase to Spec, CP, and D might have a strong feature forcing either head movement of N to D or XP movement of the possessor to Spec, DP. All of these movements involve categories that are uncontroversially functional (T, C, D).

With the introduction of *v* (little v), the distinction is less clear. This category was assumed to be the highest head within the now articulated predicate phrase (VP). In this position, it was assumed to introduce the external argument into the phrase structure – a.k.a. Pred (Bowers 1993), Voice (Kratzer 1996), ExtArg (Pylkkänen 2008). But the question is whether it is a functional category. The predecessors of *v* – Larson's (1988) VP shell and Hale and Keyser's (1993) "causative" V – might have appeared lexical. Using Abney's criteria given in (12) to determine whether *v* is lexical or functional, we get results which are mixed, but tending towards functional. For some, including Chomsky, this head introduces an external argument making it look like a lexical category, since functional categories may only functionally select. For Abney, this test was the most important (see Section 3.2). However, *v* passes all of the other tests for being a functional category. It may have only one complement.[28] In languages where it has an overt manifestation such as Japanese (see Harley 1995) or Malagasy (see Travis 2000), it is a closed category, it is morphologically weak, and it is generally not separable from its complement.[29] Further, its contribution to the semantic content of the predicate can be seen to be grammatical or relational, suggesting that it is a functional category. For Chomsky (1995) it is crucial that this head be a functional head as it is the possible host of a strong feature which triggers movement of the object to the edge of vP.

If *v* is now seen as functional, we have shifted where the functional and lexical divide is within the verbal projection. Below we can see that, in a less articulated system (34), the domain divide falls above the external argument, while in an articulated VP structure (35), the divide falls below the external argument.

(34) Thematic vs. inflectional domain = lexical vs. functional domain

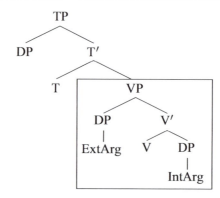

(35) Thematic vs. inflectional domain ≠ lexical vs. functional domain

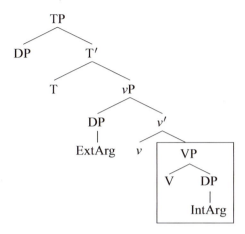

5.2   Marantz (1997)

The encroachment of functional categories into the thematic domain becomes even more marked in versions of phrase structure where lexical categories themselves are viewed being encoded by functional category, that is, where the verb *destroy* is comprised of a root √*DESTRUCT–* plus a functional category, *v*.[30]

Marantz (1997), for example, revives and expands on a proposal that lexical items are, in fact, without category. This idea was central in Chomsky (1970) where lexical items like the verb *destroy* and the noun *destruction* are derived from the same categoriless root DESTRUCT. It may, then, be the case that the VP is even more articulated and may not contain any Vs at all, only *v*s, and the functional/lexical divide falls even lower within the predicate.[31]

(36) Categoriless roots

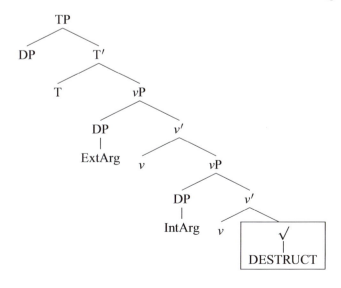

In a system such as this, it is no longer clear that there are any truly lexical categories, and if no truly lexical categories remain, it is not clear whether the types of distinctions that are laid out in, for example, Jackendoff (1977), Abney (1987), Borer (1984), Li (1990), and Chomsky (1995) have any validity. In other words, it is not clear there is any place in the current theoretical framework where the distinction between lexical and functional categories is relevant.

6 Conclusion

Since the birth of generative grammar 60 years ago, functional categories have gone from having an important supportive role to being the machinery that drives the grammar. Becoming a full-fledged member of X'-theory is the first step in this progression. At this point, while functional categories remain distinct from lexical categories, most notably having a different sort of relationship to the material in their complement and specifier positions, they nevertheless have the status of projecting heads – heads that can place selectional restrictions on the content of their complements and can act as launching and landing sites for head movement.

As the particular characteristics of functional categories become more understood, additional functional categories are uncovered. If a functional category has a particular meaning, and that meaning is represented in one language by a separate word and in another by an affix, it is a small step to assume that additional affixes indicate additional functional categories. If functional categories can be shown to represent small bits of meaning, perhaps binary features, then additional features can be seen to indicate additional functional categories.

Gradually more and more of phrase structure becomes part of the functional domain of an extended projection. In the end, functional categories have gone from being a niggling detail in syntactic structure to being the defining material of syntactic structure. In an extreme view, all syntactic heads are functional except for the lowest head which is a root.

The central role of functional categories is evident in the syntactically well-formed "Colorless green ideas sleep furiously". The functional skeleton of the tree, the inflectional heads and the category heads, obey the rules of English syntax. The lexical choice for the adjective ("bright" vs. "colorless") or for the noun ("ideas" vs "goblins") etc., while producing semantic mismatches, has no effect on the syntactic machinery. In the end, a view of syntactic structure that is comprised mostly of functional categories is appropriate in that it more accurately represents the formal features that are the tools of syntax and the interest of syntacticians.

Notes

1 This terminology, to my knowledge, first appeared in Fukui (1986). For other works that look at the status of functional categories in more depth, see, for example, van Gelderen (1993) and Muysken (2008). See Hudson (1999) for a critique of the notion that functional words comprise a distinct class. He, however, distinguishes functional word classes from functional position categories. In other work (Hudson 1995) he discusses particular functional position categories.

2 Aux will take on various labels in the course of this paper such as Infl, I, and T.

3 P(repositions) sit on the fence between major/minor or lexical/functional categories in many theories. I leave the discussion of P aside for most of this paper.

4 Abbreviations: ACC = accusative; Agr = agreement; ANT = anterior; art = article; DAT = dative; DECL = declarative; EPISTEM = epistemic; EVALUAT = evaluative; ExtArg = external argument;

GEN = genitive; ind = Indicative; Infl(I) = inflectional head; IntArg = internal argument; K = case head; MOD = modal; MOD$_r$ = root modal; NEG = negation; NOM = nominative; pres = present; prt = particle; sg = singular; SP = subject agreement; suf = suffix; TNS = tense; 2sS = 2nd person singular subject; 3pS = 3rd person plural subject.

5 We will see later in Section 4.2 other arguments for proposing new functional structure.

6 Care has to be taken with this test, as Abney (1987: 268ff) shows, since there are times when it is a nonlocal head that can be selected. This is discussed again in Section 3.3.

7 Kornfilt 1984 had already proposed a projecting functional category within the nominal projection in her analysis of nominals in Turkish – an Agr projection that only appears in nominals that contain a possessor.

8 Note that the distinction between subjects of sentences and subjects of nominals that is pointed out by Stowell becomes less obvious in Abney's system.

9 Abney chooses to label the major lexical categories "thematic elements" to avoid the problem of having a **lexical** item such as "will" be a **functional** category and not a **lexical** category. I will continue to use the more common labels "functional category" and "lexical category".

10 Abney is careful to point out that (12a) is definitional, (12b) follows from (12a), while the others are observations of commonly occurring properties. (12a) is not unlike Jackendoff's proposal of the [–COMP] feature for minor categories indicating that they do not select arguments.

11 This notion of domains is found in much current work such as that of Grohmann and Etxepare (2003) and Wiltschko (forthcoming).

12 Grimshaw proposes that P is the highest head in the extended projection of the nominal constituent, parallel to C in the verbal constituent. Others, such as Baker and Hale (1990), crucially divide Ps into functional Ps and lexical Ps. I do not discuss this further.

13 With a more articulated DP, we might now posit that the functional head Number (see Ritter 1992) is being selected.

14 These differences had already appeared in manuscript form (Abney 1985). Fukui and Abney were investigating similar issues at the same time in the same graduate program.

15 Part of Fukui's proposal is that "specifiers" of lexical categories can iterate unlike the true specifiers of functional categories. Fukui and Narita (this volume) in more recent work raise questions concerning the role of Specifier in linguistic computation. See their chapter for a relevant discussion.

16 Baker and Hale (1990) also discuss a restriction on head movement that involves distinguishing lexical and functional categories. They use the distinction within a fine-tuned application of Relativized Minimality (Rizzi 1990).

17 Fukui proposes a different sort of parameter involving functional categories – namely whether a language has functional categories or not. He argues that Japanese does not have functional categories such as Det or Infl and therefore does not have true specifiers (see Section 3.4.1). This is very different, however, from claiming that functional categories encode parameters.

18 A more recent view of parameterization within the domain of functional categories is outlined in Ritter and Wiltschko (2009). They propose that the semantic content of the functional category (i.e. the flavor of a functional category) may be be language specific. For example, a language may choose tense, location, or person as a way to connect the described event to the utterance.

19 We have seen earlier tests, like selection, that are used to determine that a particular lexical item projects. The tests in (22) may be used to determine that a functional category exists.

20 I give examples mainly from the proliferation of functional categories in the verbal projection, which is the domain where this sort of research often begins. There is, however, parallel research in the domain of the nominal projection. See e.g. Kornfilt (1984) for Agr in the nominal projection; Ritter (1992) for Number; Travis and Lamontagne (1992) for K(ase). See also Punske (this volume) for a discussion of the phrase structure within the nominal system.

21 It is the *pas* part of negation that is important for this argument. As is clear from the English translations, English lexical verbs (as opposed to auxiliaries) do not move to Infl.

22 See Iatridou (1990) for a different account of these facts that does not involve positing an additional head.

23 Though see the discussion in the Section 3.4.3 where Ouhalla shows that the order of these two heads might vary.

24 Agr heads did not have a long shelf-life. See Chomsky (1995: 349–355) for conceptual arguments against the existence of Agr heads.

25 We have seen that Ouhalla argues that order of functional categories might be parameterized; however, it could be that this is restricted to certain functional categories such as Agreement.

26 Rizzi (1997) has done similar work on the articulation of the CP domain.

27 This is reminiscent of Fukui's observation that the specifiers of functional categories may only be filled by INTERNAL MERGE. Chomsky's view differs, however, since he allows the same head to have a specifier filled by EXTERNAL MERGE and then a second specifier filled by INTERNAL MERGE as is the case with *v*.

28 This may follow from the condition that all structure is binary branching, however (see Kayne 1984).

29 Arguably serial verb constructions have a *v* that is not weak and that can be separated from the head of its complement. See, for example, Travis (2010).

30 This *v* is not the same as the *v* that introduces the external argument. This one represents the categorial signature of the root.

31 Others also have a view of phrase structure comprised mostly of functional categories (Kayne 2011; Borer 2003).

Further reading

See Abney (1987), Cinque (1999), Grimshaw (2000), Muysken (2008), and Wiltschko (forthcoming).

References

Abney, S. 1985. Functor theory and licensing: toward the elimination of the base component. Unpublished manuscript, Massachusetts Institute of Technology.

Abney, S. 1987. The English noun phrase in its sentential aspect. PhD thesis, Massachusetts Institute of Technology.

Baker, M. 1985. The Mirror Principle and morphosyntactic explanation. *Linguistic Inquiry*, 16: 373–416.

Baker, M. 1988. *Incorporation*. University of Chicago Press, Chicago.

Baker, M. and Hale, K. 1990. Relativized Minimality and pronoun incorporation. *Linguistic Inquiry*, 21:289–297.

Belletti, A. 1990. *Generalized Verb Movement*. Rosenberg & Sellier, Turin.

Belletti, A., editor 2004. *Structures and Beyond. The Cartography of Syntactic Structures, Volume 3*. Oxford University Press, New York.

Borer, H. 1984. *Parametric Syntax*. Foris Publications, Dordrecht.

Borer, H. 2003. Exo-skeletal vs. endo-skeletal explanations: Syntactic projections and the lexicon. In Polinsky, M. and Moore, J., editors, *Explanation in Linguistic Theory*. CSLI Publications, Stanford, CA.

Bowers, J. 1993. The syntax of predication. *Linguistic Inquiry*, 24:591–656.

Brame, M. 1981. The general theory of binding and fusion. *Linguistic Analysis*, 7:277–325.

Brame, M. 1982. The head-selector theory of lexical specifications of the nonexistence of coarse categories. *Linguistic Analysis*, 10:321–325.

Bresnan, J. 1976. Nonarguments for raising. *Linguistic Inquiry*, 7:485–501.

Caha, P. 2009. The nanosyntax of case. PhD thesis, University of Tromsø.

Chomsky, N. 1957. *Syntactic Structures*. Mouton, The Hague.

Chomsky, N. 1965. *Aspects of the Theory of Syntax*. MIT Press, Cambridge, MA.

Chomsky, N. 1970. Remarks on nominalization. In Jacobs, J. and Rosenbaum, P., editors, *Readings in English Transformational Grammar*, pages 184–221. Ginn, Waltham, MA.

Chomsky, N. 1981. *Lectures on Government and Binding*. Foris Publications, Dordrecht.

Chomsky, N. 1991. Some notes on economy of derivation and representation. In Freidin, R., editor, *Principles and Parameters in Comparative Grammar*, pages 417–454. MIT Press, Cambridge, MA.

Chomsky, N. 1995. *The Minimalist Program*. MIT Press, Cambridge, MA.

Chomsky, N. 2004. Beyond explanatory adequacy. In Belletti, A., editor, *Structures and Beyond: The Cartography of Syntactic Structures, Volume 3*, pages 104–131. Oxford University Press, Oxford.

Cinque, G. 1999. *Adverbs and Functional Heads: A Cross-linguistic Perspective*. Oxford University Press, New York.

Cinque, G., editor 2002. *Functional Structure in DP and IP. The Cartography of Syntactic Structures, Volume 1*. Oxford University Press, New York.

Emonds, J. 1978. The verbal complex V'-V in French. *Linguistic Inquiry*, 9:151–175.

Fukui, N. 1986. *A Theory of Category Projection and its Application*. PhD thesis, Massachusetts Institute of Technology.

Fukui, N. and Speas, M. 1986. Specifiers and projection. In Fukui, N., Rapoport, T. R., and Sagey, E., editors, *MIT Working Papers in Linguistics, Volume 8*, pages 128–172. Massachusetts Institute of Technology, Cambridge, MA.

Gibson, K. 1986. The ordering of auxiliary notions in Guyanese Creole. *Language*, 62:571–586.

Grimshaw, J. 1991. Extended projection. Unpublished manuscript, Brandeis University.

Grimshaw, J. 2000. Locality and extended projection. In Coopmans, P., Everaert, M., and Grimshaw, J., editors, *Lexical Specification and Insertion*, pages 115–134. John Benjamins Publishing Company, Philadelphia.

Grohmann, K. K. and Etxepare, R. 2003. Root infinitives: A comparative view. *Probus*, 15: 201–236.

Hale, K. and Keyser, S. J. 1993. On argument structure and the lexical expression of syntactic relations. In Hale, K. and Keyser, S. J., editors, *The View from Building 20*, pages 53–110. MIT Press, Cambridge, MA.

Harley, H. 1995. Subjects, events and licensing. PhD thesis, Massachusetts Institute of Technology.

Hudson, R. 1995. Competence without comp? In Aarts, B. and Meyer, C. F., editors, *The Verb in Contemporary English: Theory and Description*, pages 40–53. Cambridge University Press, Cambridge.

Hudson, R. 1999. Grammar without functional categories. In Borsley, R. D., editor, *The Nature and Function of Syntactic Categories (Syntax and Semantics, Volume 32)*, pages 7–35. Emerald Group Publishing, Bingley, W. Yorks.

Iatridou, S. 1990. About Agr(P). *Linguistic Inquiry*, 21:551–576.

Jackendoff, R. 1977. *X' Syntax*. MIT Press, Cambridge, MA.

Kayne, R. 1984. *Connectedness and Binary Branching*. Foris Publications, Dordrecht.

Kayne, R. 2011. Antisymmetry and the lexicon. In di Sciullo, A.-M., and Boeckx, Cedric, editors, *The Biolinguistic Enterprise: New Perspectives on the Evolution and Nature of the Human Language Faculty*, pages 329–353. Oxford University Press, London.

Kitagawa, Y. 1986. Subjects in Japanese and English. PhD thesis, University of Massachusetts, Amherst.

Koopman, H. and Sportiche, D. 1991. The position of subjects. *Lingua*, 85:211–258.

Kornfilt, J. 1984. Case marking, agreement, and empty categories in Turkish. PhD thesis, Harvard University, Cambridge, MA.

Kratzer, A. 1996. Severing the external argument from its verb. In Rooryck, J. and Zaring, L., editors, *Phrase Structure and the Lexicon*, pages 109–137. Kluwer Academic Publishers, Dordrecht.

Larson, R. 1988. On the double object construction. *Linguistic Inquiry*, 19:335–392.

Li, Y. 1990. X°-binding and verb incorporation. *Linguistic Inquiry*, 21:399–426.

Marantz, A. 1997. No escape from syntax: Don't try morphological analysis in the privacy of your own lexicon. In Dimitriadis, A., Siegel, L., Surek-Clark, C., and Williams, A., editors, *University of Pennsylvania Working Papers in Linguistics vol. 4.2*, pages 201–225. University of Pennsylvania.

Muysken, P. 2008. *Functional Categories*. Cambridge University Press, Cambridge.

Ouhalla, J. 1991. *Functional Categories and Parametric Variation*. Routledge, London.

Pantcheva, M. 2011. The nanosyntax of directional expressions. PhD thesis, University of Tromsø.

Pollock, J.-Y. 1989. Verb movement, UG and the structure of IP. *Linguistic Inquiry*, 20:365–424.

Pylkkänen, L. 2008. *Introducing Arguments*. MIT Press, Cambridge, MA.

Ritter, E. 1992. Cross-linguistic evidence for Number Phrase. *Canadian Journal of Linguistics*, 37:197–218.

Ritter, E. and Wiltschko, M. 2009. Varieties of INFL: TENSE, LOCATION, and PERSON. In Craenenbroeck, J. v., editor, *Alternatives to Cartography*, pages 153–202. De Gruyter, Berlin.

Rizzi, L. 1990. *Relativized Minimality*. MIT Press, Cambridge, MA.

Rizzi, L. 1997. The fine structure of the left periphery. In Haegeman, L., editor, *Elements of Grammar*, pages 281–337. Kluwer Academic Publishers, Dordrecht.

Rizzi, L. 2004. On the cartography of syntactic structures. In Rizzi, L., editor, *The Structure of CP and IP*, pages 3–15. Oxford University Press, Oxford.

Shlonsky, U. 2010. The cartographic enterprise in syntax. *Language and Linguistic Compass*, 4:417–429.

Sohn, H.-M. 1994. *Korean*. Routledge, London.

Starke, M. 2009. Nanosyntax: A short primer to a new approach to language. In Svenonius, P., Ramchand, G., Starke, M., and Taraldsen, K. T., editors, *Nordlyd 36.1, special issue on Nanosyntax*, pages 1– 6. CASTL, Tromsø.

Stowell, T. 1981. Origins of phrase structure. PhD thesis, Massachusetts Institute of Technology.

Taraldsen, T. 2010. The nanosyntax of Nguni noun class prefixes and concords. *Lingua*, 120: 1522–1548.

Travis, L. d. 1984. Parameters and effects of word order variation. PhD thesis, Massachusetts Institute of Technology.

Travis, L. d. 2000. The L-syntax/S-syntax boundary: Evidence from Austronesian. In Paul, I., Phillips, V., and Travis, L., editors, *Formal Issues in Austronesian Linguistics*, pages 167–194. Kluwer Academic Publishers, Dordrecht.

Travis, L. d. 2010. *Inner Aspect: The Articulation of VP*. Springer, Dordrecht.

Travis, L. d. and Lamontagne, G. 1992. The Case Filter and licensing of empty K. *Canadian Journal of Linguistics*, 37:157–174.

van Gelderen, E. 1993. *The Rise of Functional Categories*. John Benjamins, Amsterdam and Philadelphia.

Vitale, A. J. 1981. *Swahili Syntax*. Foris Publications, Dordrecht.

Wiltschko, M. forthcoming. *The Universal Structure of Categories: Towards a Formal Typology.* Cambridge University Press, Cambridge.

4

Functional structure inside nominal phrases

Jeffrey Punske

1 Introduction

The goal of this chapter is to discuss the theoretic development (within generative grammar) of the functional structure within nominal projections, with special attention to the DP-hypothesis (Abney 1987). The chapter focuses primarily on the determiner and determiner-like elements, though other potential functional categories are also addressed.

In this chapter I address the theoretic development of the DP; the DP's potential limitations cross-linguistically; the semantic contributions of determiners; and proposals of other functional categories within nominals. Much of this work touches on issues which are still under robust debate and empirical investigation; I try to avoid advocacy when there is no consensus.

One of the major ongoing controversies in studies on nominal syntax is the universality of functional structure. To avoid confusion, I use the term *nominal phrase* throughout this chapter when referring to the syntactic phrase that is often colloquially referred to as "the noun phrase". This term allows me to avoid making specific claims about the highest functional head/label of nominal constructions when such claims would be confusing, unnecessary, or inappropriate; this use is also found when the status of the highest functional projection is the object of study (for example, see Trenkic 2004). My use of the term *nominal phrase* more or less captures the spirit of Grimshaw's (1991) Extended Projection. An extended projection is defined as the lexical head (in this case, N) and all functional heads associated with it and projected above it (i.e., D, Num, etc.). A similar definition of *nominal phrase* is found in Chatman (1960: 83): "any endocentric phrase [(Bloomfield 1933)] whose center is nominal". Regardless of the particular definition chosen, the use of the term *nominal phrase* throughout this work is designed to capture the core insight that regardless of what functional structure sits on top of the noun, the noun remains the most fundamental defining element of a nominal.

I reserve the term *Noun Phrase* (NP) for discussion of claims that have the noun as the label or maximal projection of the nominal phrase. I use the term *Determiner Phrase* (DP) for discussion of claims that have the determiner (or other related functional item such as quantifiers) as the label or maximal projection.

The chapter is organized as follows: Section 2, 'Development of the DP', discusses the historic development of the DP-hypothesis, and Section 3, 'Cross-linguistic variation', looks at the DP-hypothesis from a cross-linguistic perspective. Proposed functional projections other than determiners are addressed in Section 4, 'Non-D functional items'. The chapter concludes with an outlook on future research.

2   Development of the DP

This section discusses the theoretic development of the DP-hypothesis through the different Chomskyan generative approaches. This discussion includes: Phrase Structure Rule (PSR)-based approaches to nominal syntax; the emergence of X′-Theory; Abney's (1987) DP hypothesis; Cartographic approaches to the DP; and the modern reassertion of the noun as the syntactic core of the nominal phrase. Because this discussion spans so many different programmatic approaches to syntactic theory, particular theoretic assumptions are sometimes elided in favor of a clear discussion of the issues as they relate to nominal syntax.

The primary interest of this section is the distribution and relationships of determiner-like elements. These elements include determiners (e.g., *the*), possessor phrases (e.g., *Scott's*), and quantifiers (e.g., *every, few*). Finer distinctions between some of these elements as well as discussion of other functional items is found in the section 'Non-D functional items'. This section focuses almost exclusively on the determiner and its greater role in syntactic theory.

In generative frameworks developed before the emergence of X′-theory (Chomsky 1970; Jackendoff 1977), D-elements (determiners, numerals, quantifiers, etc.) are constituents of an n-branching NP determined by a PSR. Determiners lack any phrase structure of their own and are dominated by the NP projection.

(1)   Determiners in early generative structure

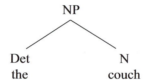

Under this view of the nominal, there is no real internal hierarchical structure within the phrase. The noun is considered the semantic and syntactic core of the nominal. Because of the flat structure and impoverished approach to modification there is little discussion of the relationship between functional elements and lexical elements. The emergence of interest in these functional elements and the study of the hierarchical organization of the internal structure of nominals drive most of the major empirical and conceptual innovations discussed in this chapter.

Starting with Chomsky (1970), PSRs associated with particular lexical categories are abandoned for a generalized set of rules – the X′-schema. Jackendoff (1977) first fully develops X′-theory with the following proposal for the structure of nominals.

(2)   Jackendoff's (1977) NP structure

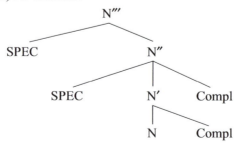

There are several important things to note about this structure. Unlike many future proposals, N is the maximal projection in Jackendoff's structure. The NP in Jackendoff's structure also contains two SPEC positions which is not part of a standard X′-schema. For Jackendoff, the different SPECs are filled by different classes of items. The higher SPEC is where possessors and determiners are located. The lower SPEC contains quantifiers, numerals, measure phrases, and group nouns[1] (we return to several of these categories in Section 4). The presence of multiple SPECs can explain why elements previously treated as category Det can co-occur:

(3)   Jen's every move…   [Possessor + Quantifier]

(4)   The few men…   [Determiner + Quantifier]

(5)   The two men   [Determiner + Numeral]

Abney (1987) questions the need for multiple specifiers within a single phrase. Abney agrees with Jackendoff that there are two separate SPEC positions within a nominal phrase; however, for Abney they are part of two distinct phrases (DP and NP). Abney (1987) develops this proposal based on parallels between POSS-ing constructions (gerunds) and main clauses:

(6)   The werewolf's destroying the city

(7)   The werewolf destroyed the city

This contrasted with other nominals which could not directly assign Case to direct objects:

(8)   *The werewolf's destruction the city

Within the X′-theoretic/GB framework of the time, the apparent parallels were mysterious. Nominals were generally assumed to be unable to assign Case. This would require that *destroying* be category V, not N, in examples such as (6), so that it could assign Case to *the city*; however, gerunds, like *the werewolf's destroying*, behave like nominals within sentences. Thus, we have a non-nominal that needs to project as a nominal. This leads to a problematic unheaded structure such as (9):

(9)   Illegitimate Gerund Structure

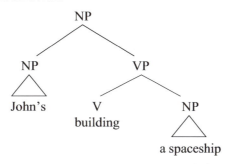

(adapted from Abney 1987: 15)

A structure such as (9) is problematic because the maximal projection (NP) has no head – it is simply a label tacked onto another maximal projection, VP. Under standard GB approaches to phrase-structure, such a structure should be impossible – phrases require heads. The highest NP in (9) is unheaded. Abney argues that a functional head akin to I^2 (i.e., D) is present in gerunds and other nominal constructions.

(10) Gerund with DP structure

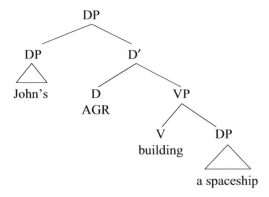

The above structure, avoids the problem of having an unheaded maximal projection simply tacked onto another structure. In (10), a functional category (D) embeds a lexical category (V). This structure is in line with standard GB approaches to phrase-structure and further explains the internal verbal properties of the phrase along with its nominal distribution in sentential syntax.

Similarly, Abney's proposal provided a simple account of the distribution of possessives in English. Abney places possessive phrases in the specifier of DP, which accounts for their high structural position.

(11) Abney-style possessive DP structure

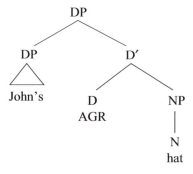

In the above structure, the possessive clitic 's does not occupy the D position. The proposal where the possessive marker/genitive marker 's is located within the D-head is often misattributed to Abney (1987). While Abney (1986) advocates for such a proposal, Abney (1987)

argues for an agreement marker within D and the base-generation of a genitive marked DP in SPEC$_{DP}$ (see Coene and D'hulst (2003) for more discussion).

We can schematize Abney's proposal into the following structure:

(12) Abney-style DP structure

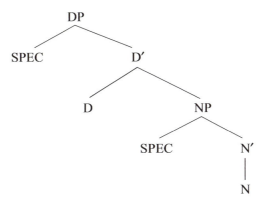

This analysis captures the same fundamental insights as Jackendoff's earlier approach to nominals which contained two distinct specifier positions. While Jackendoff's proposal violated the general X'-schema, Abney's proposal derives the two needed specifier positions while following the X'-schema. Further, it allows Abney to address Jackendoff's evidence for a two-specifier structure with a couple of different structural proposals. For the [determiner + quantifier] examples, Abney argues that the lower quantifier occupies SPEC$_{NP}$ while the determiner is in D^0. For [possessor + determiner] constructions the possessor is in SPEC$_{DP}$ while the determiner is in D^0. With these two proposals Abney correctly predicts that all three elements can occur, while Jackendoff would incorrectly predict that they cannot:

(13) Jen's every few moves [were monitored by the FBI].

(14)

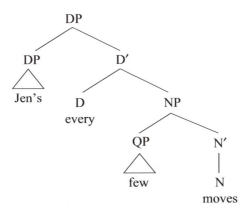

Following Abney, numerous functional heads were proposed to exist between the DP and the embedded NP. I discuss the most significant of these in 4. Here, I discuss only the general trends in DP-related structure as related to D itself. The discussion is by no means an exhaustive examination of proposed structures related to the DP; rather, it is meant as a representative sample of such proposals.

Rizzi's (1997) work on the expanded left periphery of the CP and the emergence of functional projections associated with that proposal lead to proposals of CP-DP parallelism such as this expanded DP-structure from Alexiadou *et al.* (2007):

(15) Expanded DP

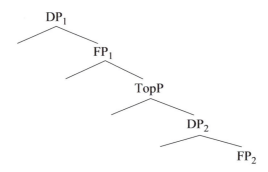

In the above structure, the FP projections correspond to FinP and ForceP from Rizzi's expanded CP. The highest DP encodes discourse and pragmatic information while the lower DP is the locus of (in)definiteness.

Cartographic approaches to syntax have greatly expanded the number of proposed functional heads in both the CP and DP. As such, examples such as (15) represent a relatively impoverished functional structure compared with other related approaches.

Cinque and Rizzi (2010) estimate that there are, sententially, 400+ functional heads which are all universally ordered. Proposals for the DP vary, but a reduced example from Guardiano (2009) has twelve functional heads independent of D or N – though the actual number of heads is greater.

Recently there has been some push back against the notion that D is the maximal category/label for nominal phrases. Modern objections to the DP-hypothesis are largely on conceptual grounds – that the noun should be the most fundamental element in nominal phrases. Chomsky (2007) argues that unlabeled (indefinite) nominal phrases and labeled (definite) nominal phrases should both bear a nominal label (in his terms n*). In this analysis, D, when present, is the derived visible head akin to V in verbal projections.

> …the head is now n* (analogous to v*) with the complement [X (YP)]. In this case X = D. D inherits the features of n*, so YP raises to its SPEC, and D raises to n*, exactly parallel to v*P. Therefore, the structure is a nominal phrase headed by n*, not a determiner phrase headed by D, which is what we intuitively always wanted to say…

> (Chomsky 2007: 26)

(16) Chomsky-style *n*P

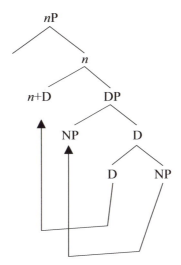

This proposal is obviously quite tentative but it reflects one of the two major programmatic approaches in current studies on nominals. On one hand, we have the Cartographic approaches to the DP, with an ever-expanding array of functional heads above the noun; and, on the other, we have the Chomsky-style approach with reduced functional structure and reassertion of the noun as the central part of the nominal phrase.

Overall, there is broad consensus that something like the DP-Hypothesis is correct, at least for languages with overt DPs. The location of DP within the nominal structure, however, is somewhat unsettled. The DP embedding the NP is the most common structural assumption, though there may be conceptual reasons to object to this. Further, the universality of the position is unclear.

3 Cross-linguistic variation

Beyond the theoretic/conceptual issues surrounding the DP hypothesis, there are also questions about the universality of D-like elements. Not all languages have overt lexical items that are typically associated with the functional category D (though demonstratives are universal, as discussed in Section 4. Even in languages with overt determiners, not all nominals necessarily contain one. The relevant issues discussed in this section are: whether DP-structure is universal; what it would mean for a language to lack DP-structure; and whether languages can vary internally with respect to the presence or absence of DP structure. Fundamentally, these questions can be traced back to a single unifying question: what syntactic (or semantic) differences (if any) can be traced to the presence or absence of a determiner.

Setting aside demonstratives for now, it is an undisputed fact that there are languages that lack *overt* determiners defined by any reasonable, standard semantic definition of the category. The question is whether or not this lexical absence also reflects the syntactic absence of functional structure associated with D. We examine this problem in two ways: the semantic consequences of the lack of this structure and the syntactic consequences.

3.1 The semantics of DP-structure

Chierchia (1998) argues that languages may differ with respect to the featural make-up of their nominals in a way that either requires determiners or deems them unnecessary. This set of features is termed the *Nominal Mapping Parameter*. Nominals across languages can be marked [+/−arg] (for argument) or [+/−pred] (for predicate).

Languages that are [+arg] allow bare nouns to be arguments in the syntax – and these nominals are treated as kind terms (see Carlson 1977). Languages that are [−arg] do not allow bare nouns in the syntax. Languages that are [+pred] can treat nominals as predicates (which may be individuated) while languages that are [−pred] cannot.

Japanese and Chinese are prototypical examples of [+arg]/[−pred] languages. They allow bare nominals as arguments. These nominals are interpreted as kind terms which leads to the development of a generalized classifier system and the lack of plural morphology (because "the property corresponding to a kind comes out as being mass" (Chierchia 1998: 351)).

A [−arg]/[+pred] language disallows bare nouns as arguments. Such a language will also have a morphological plural/singular distinction. French and Italian are prototypical examples of such a language.

Languages that are [+arg]/[+pred] exhibit properties of both of the aforementioned classes. Such languages do allow bare nouns in argument position (and they are treated as kind terms) but also have a morphological plural/singular distinction and determiners. Because this group can individuate, a generalized classifier system is not developed. Germanic languages, including English, are members of this group.

There is a special set of languages that is argued to be [+arg]/[+pred]: Slavic. Slavic languages, with the exception of Bulgarian, lack overt determiners. Yet in all respects associated with Chierchia's typology they appear to behave like Germanic languages. They lack a generalized quantifier system; they have a morphological singular/plural distinction; but they do not have overt determiners. We will return to the Slavic problem shortly.

In both [−arg]/[+pred] and [+arg]/[+pred] languages determiners take predicates (in this case, count nouns) and convert them into arguments. As such, determiners are an essential ingredient to [+pred] languages.

Languages with the feature make-up [−arg]/[−pred] are not included in Chierchia's typology. All of the potential featural specifications are summed up in (17).

(17) Chierchia's Nominal Mapping Parameter

	[+arg], [−pred]	*[−arg], [+pred]*	*[+arg], [+pred]*	*[−arg], [−pred]*
Example languages	Japanese and Chinese	French	Germanic and Slavic	
Bare nouns in argument position	Yes	No	Yes	
Morphological singular/plural distinction	No	Yes	Yes	
Generalized classifiers?	Yes	No	No	

With the Nominal Mapping Parameter we have a potential diagnostic for the presence or absence of DP functional structure within languages that lack overt Ds. Using this as a diagnostic we would have two distinct types of languages without overt Ds. Languages such as Japanese and Chinese appear to lack the semantic properties associated with D and thus potentially the functional structure. Slavic behaves in a manner similar to languages with overt Ds, so could arguably have a DP projection despite the lack of overt Ds – however, we will re-examine this point. Chierchia's analysis does not claim that Slavic has covert Ds or D-functional structure.

3.2   Functional versus lexical categories

Languages such as Japanese, Polish and possibly Mohawk (among many others) are argued to lack the category entirely. Each of these languages behaves rather differently with respect to behaviors which are arguably associated with D. This section examines these behaviors.

There need not necessarily be any formal connection between the functional category D and the lexical category of determiner. "Functional heads correspond to grammatical or semantic categories rather than to word classes" (Lyons 1999: 298(f)).

This means that the absence of a given lexical category (for our purposes, the absence of determiners/articles) in a given language is insufficient evidence for the absence of the functional projection. For Slavic-type and Japanese-type languages that means that while the lexical category D is apparently absent, the presence of functional D structure is not ruled out.

Looking first at languages that uncontroversially have lexical determiners, we can see arguments for functional structure in the absence of lexical content. As discussed earlier, English allows surface bare-nominals in argument positions:

(18)   Jen bought pears.

(19)   Jen bought the pear. / #Jen bought pear.

Under Chierchia's approach the argument *pears* in (18) is a true bare NP with no functional DP structure. For Chierchia, the absence of lexical determiners means the absence of functional structure (however, nothing would necessarily rule out lexically specified null determiners). Longobardi (1994, *et seq.*) argues for the existence of a null determiner in examples such as (18), while Progovac (1998) and Abraham *et al.* (2007) argue for the presence of the functional structure without any lexical content.

(20)   Structure of *pears* in a Longobardi-style analysis

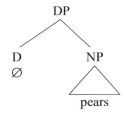

(21) Structure of *pears* in no-lexical-content-style analysis

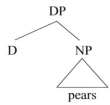

While the presence or absence of a null-lexical item in a functional projection may seem like a trivial matter, these two styles of analysis do make different predications about the behavior of D. Distinguishing between all three approaches is obviously an empirical matter.

Under a Longobardi-style approach phonetically null, but lexically specified, determiners should behave exactly like other lexical items, meaning that they should exhibit arbitrary behavior. A functional-structure-only approach would not expect any arbitrary behavior. However, such structure would necessarily be constrained to universal syntactic/semantic effects.

In contrast, a bare-NP approach should predict different syntactic behaviors for nominals that have overt determiners and those that do not while also not predicting any arbitrary behaviors associated with lexically specified, null functional items. We have already discussed potential semantic differences between bare NPs and corresponding DPs.

Longobardi (1994) provides evidence from Italian for the presence of (at least) D-functional structure even when no overt lexical determiner is present. Longobardi claims that the presence of D is necessary for a nominal to be an argument (in line with Chierchia's claims about Italian). In Italian proper names provide evidence for the presence of determiner structure even when no determiner is present.

First, note that in Italian overt determiners are optional when used with a singular proper name:

(22) Gianni mi ha telefonato.
      Gianni me has called
      'Gianni called me up.'

(23) Il Gianni mi ha telefonato.
      the Gianni me has called
      'The Gianni called me up.'

(23 and 24 adapted from Longobardi 1994: 622)

Longobardi notes an interaction between the presence and absence of overt determiners with proper names and the ordering of the name with possessive adjectives. When a determiner is present possessive adjectives can occur pre- or post-nominally. When they occur post-nominally, they are "interpreted with contrastive reference" (Longobardi 1994: 623).

(24) Il mio Gianni ha finalmente telefonato.
      the my Gianni has finally   called

(25) Il Gianni mio ha finalmente telefonato.
      The Gianni my has finally   called

(24 and 25 from Longobardi 1994: 623)

When the determiner is not present, the possessive adjective is obligatorily post-nominal without the contrastive reference interpretation.

(26) *Mio Gianni ha finalmente telefonato.
    my Gianni has finally   called

(27) Gianni mio ha finalmente telefonato.
    Gianni my has finally   called

(26 and 27 from Longobardi 1994: 623)

Longobardi notes that similar effects are found with non-possessive adjectives, pronouns, and, occasionally, common nouns. He argues that the reason that the pre-nominal adjectives are ungrammatical in cases such as (27) is that the noun is obligatorily raising into D.

However, identical facts are not found universally – a fact Longobardi was well aware of (see Longobardi (1994) for his treatment of English). Looking again at English (a language with unambiguous overt determiners), we do not find Italian-like effects when there is no overt determiner: proper names do not occur to the left of adjectives.

(28) Big John

(29) *John big

This does not necessarily imply that languages such as English lack D-structure when an overt determiner is not present (Longobardi argues for LF movement). However, if we recall Chierchia's respective analyses of Italian and English, that is certainly a possible outcome. Regardless, Longobardi's evidence does not prove that DP-structure is universally present. However, it does appear certain that D-structure can be present in the absence of overt Ds.

3.3 Potential syntactic consequences of DP-less structure

The lack of lexical determiners alone is insufficient evidence to rule out determiner structure in such languages. What is required is predictable syntactic (and semantic) consequences for the lack of DP-structure. This subsection addresses such potential consequences, both internal and external to the nominal phrase.

3.3.1 Nominal phrase internal consequences

Slavic-type languages and Japanese-type languages present data that may be suggestive of a lack of functional D-structure in these languages. Looking first at Slavic, we see two types of evidence that may be suggestive of a lack of DP: (1) Slavic languages generally allow Left Branch Extraction (LBE); (2) Slavic languages do not exhibit some of Longobardi's Italian-style effects.

Slavic-type languages also allow extraction of NP-internal constituents (determiners, adjectives, possessors), which is banned in numerous other languages. Ross (1967) terms the phenomena the Left Branch Condition because, in the terminology of the day, it involved extraction from the leftmost branch of an NP projection:

(30)   Which boy's guardian's employer did we elect president?

(31)   *Which boy's guardian's did we elect employer president?

(32)   *Which boy's did we elect guardian's employer president?

(30–32 from Ross 1967: 211)

(33) *Whose$_i$ did you see [t$_i$ father]?

(34) *Which$_i$ did you buy [t$_i$ car]?

(35) *That$_i$ he saw [t$_i$ car].

(36) *Beautiful$_i$ he saw [t$_i$ houses].

(37) *How much$_i$ did she earn [t$_i$ money]?

(33–37 from Bošković 2005a: 14)

In Slavic-type languages, such extraction (termed Left Branch Extraction (LBE)) is permitted, as seen in this data from Serbo-Croatian:

(38) Čijeg$_i$ si   video   [t$_i$ oca]?
      whose   are   seen   father
      'Whose father did you see?'

(39) Kakva$_i$ si   kupio   [t$_i$ kola]?
      what-kind-of   are   bought   car
      'What kind of car did you buy?'

(40) Ta$_i$ je video [t$_i$ kola]
      that   is seen   car
      'That car, he saw.'

(41) Lijepe$_i$ je video [t$_i$ kuće]
      beautiful   is seen   houses
      'Beautiful houses, he saw.'

(38–41 from Bošković 2005a: 15)

Bošković (2005a; 2005b) claims that the availability of LBE is due to the absence of DP structure in these languages. Bošković notes a correlation between the presence of LBE within a language and the lack of overt determiners. Simplifying the analysis for this limited discussion, the main distinction between an English-type language and a Slavic-type language is the presence of a phase boundary (see Chomsky 2001) in English because of the presence of the DP and no such phase boundary in Slavic-type languages because NP is not a phase.

   Willim (2000) provides arguments from the distribution of morphological elements in Polish nominals for the lack of DP-structure. In Polish (which lacks overt determiners), adjectives and demonstratives have the same gender/case makers. Willim argues that this suggests that Polish demonstratives are not in a head position. Willim (2000) also notes that, unlike in Italian, Polish proper names do not undergo N-to-D movement (see via the relative order of attributive adjectives and the proper name):

(42) mały Kowalski
      young Kowalski
      'the young/little Kowalski'

(43) *Kowalski mały
      Kowalski young

(42–43 from Willim 2000: 330)

However, it is worth noting that English also does not have Italian-style N-to-D raising for proper names, but does unambiguously have determiners.

(44) young John

(45) *John young

Drawing too many conclusions from the absence of N-to-D movement would be a mistake. Nonetheless, there is a compelling circumstantial case that Slavic-type languages lack a DP-projection.

However, Progovac (1998) does provide arguments for the existence of DP-structure even in Slavic-type languages based on noun/pronoun asymmetries in Serbo-Croatian. In Serbo-Croatian, adjectives that can co-occur with pronouns must follow the pronoun, which is opposite to the pattern found with full nouns.

(46) I   **samu Mariju** to   nervira.
      and alone   Mary   that   irritates
      'That irritates even Mary.'

(47) ?*I   **Mariju samu** to   nervira.
      and Mary   alone   that   irritates

(48) I   **nju/mene samu** to   nervira.
      and her/me   alone that   irritates
      'That irritates even her/me.'

(49) ?*I   **samu   nju/mene** to   nervira.
      and alone   her/me   that   irritates

(46–49 from Progovac 1998: 167)

Progovac argues that this order is a by-product of pronouns surfacing in D^0, which is similar to results from Longobardi (1994) for Italian pronouns.

3.3.2 DP-external Consequences

Bošković (2004), extending an analysis of Japanese by Bošković and Takahashi (1998), argues that the lack of DP-structure is associated with a language's ability to scramble (which for Bošković includes LF-reconstructing word order phenomena). In particular, Bošković argues that the difference between DP-languages and NP-languages is "that DPs, but not necessarily NPs, must establish a θ-relation as soon as possible, namely, in over syntax" (2004: 632). For Bošković, NP-languages "scramble" because they are free to merge into non-θ-positions and receive their θ-roles at LF.

Noun incorporation is another syntactic property argued to be associated with the presence or absence of DP-structure. Noun incorporation involves the combination of a bare nominal and a verb which results in a loss of transitivity (or distransitivity). This is argued to be a lexical process (see Rosen 1989) or a syntactic process (see Baker 1988). Leaving aside the particulars, noun incorporation and other properties associated with polysynthesis are argued to be associated with the lack of determiners within the relevant language.

(50) Summary of syntactic properties associated with the presence or absence of overt determiners cross-linguistically (based on Bošković (2009: 199)).

	Overt D	No Overt D
Allow LBE	No	Yes
Allow scrambling	No	Yes
Can be polysynthetic	No	Yes
Allow negative raising	Yes	No
Superiority effects with multiple *wh*-fronting	Yes	No
Allow adjunct extraction from "traditional noun phrase"	No	Yes
Allow transitive nominals with two non-lexical genitives	Yes	No
Allow the majority superlative reading	Yes	No
Island sensitivity in head internal relatives	No	Yes

3.4 Outlook for universality

3.5 Semantics of D

Within generative theories of syntax, the most common analysis of English determiners is that of a definite/indefinite distinction (see Heim 1988). Whether or not definiteness is a primary feature or a derived one is something of an open question. Ghomeshi *et al.* note that "definiteness may be derivable in different ways and thus be subject to variation within and across languages" (2009: 12).

The determiner system in English displays a clear definite/indefinite distinction:

(51) Jen bought **the** pear.   (definite)

(52) Jen bought **a** pear.   (indefinite)

However, this distinction is not the only one found (see Lyons 1999). In languages such as Niuean (Seiter 1980; but see Massam *et al.* 2006 for counter arguments) determiner-like elements are argued to bear specificity (see Enç 1991). Cambell (1996) argues that specific nominals have DP-structure while non-specific ones do not. Karimi (1999) argues that specificity effects are structural (at least in Persian). For Karimi, D-elements (numerals, quantifiers) may be base generated in either D^0 or $SPEC_{DP}$. When they are generated in D^0 the nominal is non-specific; in $SPEC_{DP}$, it is specific. Gillon (2006; 2009) argues that Skwxwú7mesh determiners do not encode definiteness, specificity, or uniqueness. The universal semantics of D, if any, is a far from settled manner.

4 Non-D functional items

Moving away from determiners, this section discusses several other functional categories that may be found within nominals. In particular, demonstratives, quantifiers, number and gender are discussed.

4.1 Quantifiers

The separation of quantifiers and determiners is not a universally adopted position. Barwise and Cooper's (1981) groundbreaking work on quantification grouped quantifiers and determiners into the same class: Generalized Quantifiers. Distributional evidence from English may also be suggestive of a single syntactic category for quantifiers and determiners:

(53) every boy

(54) *every the boy

However, in other languages the presence of both the quantifier and a determiner is required in analogous quantificational phrases. This is seen in the following examples from St'át'imcets (Matthewson 2001: 150):

(55) léxlex   [**tákem**   **i**   smelhumúlhats-**a**].
      intelligent **all**   DET-PL   woman(PL)-DET]
      'All (of the) women are intelligent.'

(56) *léxlex   [**tákem**   smelhumúlhats].
      intelligent **all**   woman(PL)
      'All women are intelligent.'

These facts suggest that QP is in fact a higher functional projection than DP. Such a structure would be as follows (see Demirdache *et al.* 1994; Matthewson and Davis 1995; Matthewson 2001).

(57) Quantificational Phrases

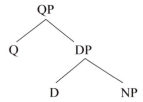

Some English quantifiers appear below the determiner and pose an apparent problem for this analysis:

(58) The many wolves…

(59) The few vampires…

Recall that such examples were critical elements of Jackendoff's (1977) and Abney's (1987) proposals for the structure of nominal phrases. For Jackendoff, the lower quantifier-like element occupied the lower of two specifier positions.

(60) Determiners and Quantifiers in Jackendoff's (1977)

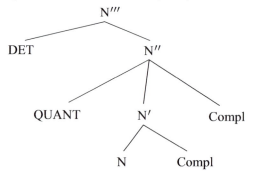

Abney (1987) treated the lower quantifier as its own XP found in the specifier of NP:

(61) Determiners and Quantifiers in Abney (1987)

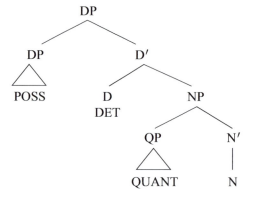

If, following Abney, English QPs are in a lower structural position than DP, the QP hypothesis would require modification. However, Partee (1987) argues that quantifiers such as *few* and *many* from the examples above are in fact adjectives. As such, they would not occupy Q^0 and thus pose no threat to the QP analysis. However, it is worth noting that many modern accounts of quantifiers follow Barwise and Cooper's (1981) account of quantifiers and determiners and assume that they are the same element.

4.2   Demonstratives

"All languages have at least two demonstratives that are deictically contrastive" (Diessel 1999: 2). However, there is a great deal of variation in both morphological form and semantic function of demonstratives cross-linguistically (see Diessel 1999 for full discussion).

For generative approaches to nominal structure, the evidence suggests two possible analyses of the structural position of demonstratives: (i) demonstratives are located in SPEC$_{DP}$; (ii) demonstratives occupy a lower structural position (see discussion in Alexiadou *et al.* 2007).

Evidence for the SPEC$_{DP}$ analysis comes from the distribution of demonstratives and determiners in languages where both items can occur in a single nominal phrase. In languages such as Hungarian, Javanese, and Greek the demonstrative precedes the determiner.

(62) ez   a   haz   (Hungarian)
     this the   house

(63) ika   n   anak   (Javanese)
     this the   baby

(64) afto to   vivlio   (Greek)
     this the   book

(62–64 from Alexiadou *et al.* 2007: 106)

(65) Demonstratives in SPEC$_{DP}$

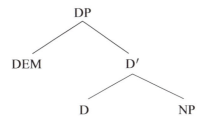

However, Alexiadou *et al.* (2007) note that SPEC$_{DP}$ may be a derived position for demonstratives. Indeed, numerous scholars (see Giusti 1997; Brugè 2002; and many others) argue that demonstratives start the derivation in a lower position and sometimes raise into SPEC$_{DP}$. Evidence for these proposals comes from languages which allow demonstratives before the determiner/nominal or post-nominally:

(66) este hombre   (Spanish)
     this man

(67) el   hombre este   (Spanish)
     the   man   this

(68) afto   to   vivlio   (Greek)
     this   the   book

(69) to   vivlio afto   (Greek)
     the   book   this

(66–69 from Alexiadou et al. 2007: 110)

These facts suggest that demonstratives start lower in the structure and may raise to SPEC_{DP}. There are semantic differences between a low demonstrative and a high demonstrative, but they are beyond the scope of this paper (see Alexiadou *et al.* 2007).

4.3   Number

Ritter (1993; but also see Ritter 1988) proposes a DP internal functional projection NumP which is the complement of D based on data from Modern Hebrew construct states. Construct states are "a type of noun phrase containing a bare genitive phrase immediately following the head noun" (Ritter 1991: 38). Determiners, when they occur, may never surface initially:

(70) beyt   ha-mora
     house   the-teacher
     'the teacher's house'

(71) *ha-beyt   ha-mora
      the-house   the-teacher

(72) *ha-beyt   mora
      the-house   teacher

(73) ha-bayit
     the-house
     'the house'

(70–73 from Ritter 1991: 40)

Ritter notes that these constructions can easily be analyzed as N-to-D movement (around the possessor in SPEC_{NP}). However, such an analysis cannot handle the free genitive construction, which appears similar but does have an initial determiner.

(74) ha –axila   ha-menumest   ʃel dan   et   ha-uga.
     the-eating   the-polite   of Dan   ACC   the cake
     'Dan's polite eating of the cake.'

(Ritter 1991: 45)

To solve this puzzle Ritter argues that the N is actually raising to an intermediate position (Num) in the free genitives. In construct states, movement to Num is intermediate to movement to D.

(75) Structure of Hebrew Free Genitive

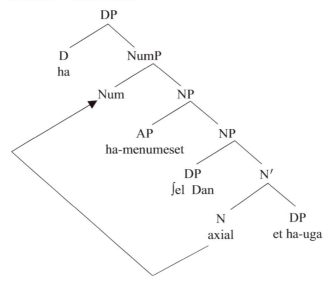

Ritter argues that Num is the locus of plural/singular interpretations for the nominal as well as the site of a class of quantifiers.

Other similar analyses of DP-internal NumP come from Carstens (1991; Yapese) and Delfitto and Schroten (1991; Spanish and Italian) (see Coene and D'hulst (2003) for a summary of these works).

4.4 K(ase)P

Lamontagne and Travis (1987) propose a level of functional structure, KP, above DP, which is analogous to CP (see also Loebel 1994). KP is the source of Case for nominals – or, more accurately, K is Case.

(76) Nominal Structure with KP

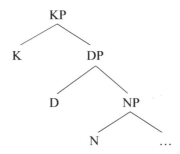

(Lamontagne and Travis 1987: 177)

Lamontagne and Travis (1987) propose that the phenomena of optional case marking in languages such as Turkish and Japanese and the optionality of embedded complementizers in languages such as English are fundamentally linked. According to their analysis, complementizers and overt morphological case can be dropped only when these elements appear adjacent to the verb, as seen in the paradigms below.

(77) John believes (that) Mary will win.

(78) John believes wholeheartedly ?*(that) Mary will win.

(79) That Mary will win, John believes with all his heart.

(80) *Mary will win, John believes with all his heart.

(77–80 from Lamontagne and Travis 1987: 175)

The examples above show that the complementizer *that* is optional only when the CP and the verb (which licenses the CP) are adjacent. *That* may be unpronounced in (77) because there are no intervening elements or movement, but it is required in all other examples. Lamontagne and Travis note that this fact is analogous to optional Case marking, as seen in the data below, originally from Kornfilt (1984):

(81) Hasan   dün   (bu) pasta-(yi)   ye-di.
      Hasan   yesterday   this case-ACC   eat-PST
      'Hasan ate (this) cake yesterday.'

(82) Hasan *(bu) pasta-*(yi) dün ye-di.

(81–82 from Lamontagne and Travis 1987: 174)

In (81), the realization of Case is optional because the nominal is adjacent to the verb; in (82), the realization of Case is required because the nominal is not adjacent. The full details of this analysis require a technical discussion of Government and Binding theory which is beyond the scope of this short chapter. For an updated view of KP, argued from a Distributed Morphology approach, see McFadden (2004).

4.5   Gender

Bernstein (1993) proposes that gender (i.e., word class) has its own functional head above the noun but below all other functional structure (DP, NumP, etc.). Alexiadou (2004) argues against this position based on evidence from Greek which suggests that gender is inherent to the noun and is not an independent projection. Di Domenico (1997) argues that the interpretable gender feature is located within the Num projection and the uninterpretable feature is inherent to the noun. Ritter (1993) argues that gender is not its own functional projection and varies in location cross-linguistically; in Romance it is with Num and in Hebrew it is with the N.

4.6   Ordering

The surface order of some functional and lexical items within nominals is also subject to universals. Greenberg (1963) discusses the relative order of demonstratives, numerals, descriptive adjectives, and nouns: "[w]hen any or all of the items (demonstrative, numeral, and descriptive adjective) precede the noun, they are always found in that order. If they follow, the order is either the same or its exact opposite" (Greenberg 1963: 87).

Cinque (2005) and Abels and Neeleman (2009) update the generalization, showing that some predicted orders are not found, while other non-predicted orders are found. These findings are summarized in (83) (from Medeiros 2012: 5):

(83) Medeiros (2012) summary table of universal nominal orderings

D = demonstrative, M = numeral, A = adjective, N = noun
shaded = unattested orders, non-shaded = attested orders

DMAN	DMNA	DNMA	NDMA
MDAN	MDNA	MNDA◊	NMDA
ADMN	ADNM	ANDM	NADM[†]
DAMN	DANM	DNAM	NDAM[†]
MADN	MAND	MNAD	NMAD[†]
AMDN	AMND	ANMD	NAMD

◊: Order predicted by Greenberg (1963) but unattested
†: Order not predicted by Greenberg (1963) but attested

Universal ordering restrictions like the one seen in (84) could certainly be suggestive of some form of universal underlyingly ordered functional structure (see Cinque 2005). However, ordering restrictions may also be derived through other syntactic processes not directly related to universal ordering.

4.7 Other functional projections

There are numerous other proposals for functional structure within nominal phrases that I have not been able to address. Functional projections hosting particular adjectives have been proposed and are discussed in Chapter 7 of this volume. Functional projections for Case agreement (see Cornilescu 1993) and possession (see Valois 1991), along with a multitude of projections from Cartographic perspectives, have been posited for nominals.

5 Conclusions

The structural configuration of the nominal projection is far from a settled matter. The dominant hypothesis for the last several decades is that nominals are dominated by functional structure of some form (the DP-hypothesis and its offshoots). During this period an enormous body of work clarifying, motivating, and expanding this functional structure has been produced.

However, there are several challenges to this line of inquiry. As discussed in Section 2, Chomsky (2007) raises conceptual issues surrounding DP-hypothesis since it is ultimately the nominal itself that is selected for. Section 3 outlined a number of cross-linguistic challenges as well, suggesting that even if the DP-hypothesis is correct it might not be universal.

The universality question raises some very deep questions about the nature of syntax. We could ask to what extent the notion of universality is undercut if languages can lack syntactic projections based on the lack of lexical items. Conversely, if DP-structure is universally found, why do so many languages lack lexical content for the position? Further, do any intermediate languages exist (languages that sometimes have DP and sometimes NP)? If not, why not? There are obviously no easy answers to these questions. However, nominal phrases may provide a unique Petri dish for the interaction of the lexicon and syntactic projections that may not be easily found elsewhere.

Notes

1 I do not discuss measure phrases or group nouns here.
2 Also INFL (inflection); roughly equivalent to T(ense) in many modern approaches.

Further reading

Abney, Steven. 1987. The English noun phrase in its sentential aspect. PhD dissertation, MIT, Cambridge, MA.

Alexiadou, Artemis, Liliane Haegeman, and Melita Stravou. 2007. *Noun Phrase in the Generative Perspective*. Berlin/New York: Mouton de Gruyter.

Coene, Martine, and Yves D'hulst (eds). 2003. *From NP to DP Volumes I & II*. Amsterdam/Philadelphia: John Benjamins Publishing Company.

Ghomeshi, Jila, Ileana Paul, and Martina Wiltschko (eds). 2009. *Determiners: Universals and Variation*. Amsterdam/Philadelphia: John Benjamins Publishing Company.

References

Abels, Klaus, and Ad Neeleman. 2009. Universal 20 without the LCA. In *Merging Features: Computation, Interpretation and Acquisition*, ed. Josep M. Brucart, Anna Gavarró, and Jaume Solà, 60–80. Oxford: Oxford University Press.

Abney, Steven. 1986. Functional elements and licensing. Paper presented at GLOW 1986. Gerona, Spain.

Abney, Steven. 1987. The English noun phrase in its sentential aspect. PhD dissertation, MIT, Cambridge, MA.

Abraham, Werner, Elizabeth Stark, and Elizabeth Leiss. 2007. Introduction. In *Nominal Determination. Typology, Context Constraints, and Historical Emergence. Typological Studies in Language 79*, ed. Elizabeth Stark, Elizabeth Leiss, and Werner Abraham, 1–20. Amsterdam: John Benjamins.

Alexiadou, Artemis. 2004. Inflection class, gender and DP internal structure. In *Exploration in Nominal Inflection*, ed. Gereon Müller, Lutz Gunkel, and Gisela Zifonun, 21–50. Berlin/New York: Mouton de Gruyter.

Alexiadou, Artemis, Liliane Haegeman, and Melita Stravou. 2007. *Noun Phrase in the Generative Perspective*. Berlin/New York: Mouton de Gruyter.

Baker, Mark. 1988. *Incorporation: A Theory of Grammatical Function Changing*. Chicago: University of Chicago Press.

Baker, Mark. 1995. Lexical and nonlexical noun incorporation. In *Lexical Knowledge in the Organization of Language*, ed. Urs Egli, Peter E. Pause, Christoph Schwarze, Arnim von Stechow, Götz Wienold, 3–34. Amsterdam/Philadelphia: John Benjamins Publishing Co.

Barwise, Jon, and Robin Cooper. 1981. Generalized quantifiers and natural language. *Linguistics and Philosophy* 4:159–219.

Bernstein, Judy. 1993. Topics in syntax of nominal structure across Romance. PhD dissertation, City University of New York.

Bloomfield, Leonard. 1933. *Language*. New York: Holt, Rinehart and Winston.

Bošković, Zeljko. 2004. Topicalization, focalization, lexical insertion, and scrambling. *Linguistic Inquiry* 35:613–638.

Bošković, Zeljko. 2005a. Left branch extraction, structure of NP, and scrambling. In *The Free Word Order Phenomenon: Its Syntactic Sources and Diversity*, ed. Joachim Sabel and Mamoru Saito, 13–73. Berlin: Mouton de Gruyter.

Bošković, Zeljko. 2005b. On the locality of left branch extraction and the structure of NP. *Studia Linguistica* 59:1–45.

Bošković, Zeljko. 2009. More on the no-DP analysis of article-less languages. *Studia Linguistica* 63:187–203.

Bošković, Zeljko, and Diako Takahashi. 1998. Scrambling and last resort. *Linguistic Inquiry* 29: 347–366.

Brugè, Laura. 2002. The position of demonstratives in the extended nominal projection. In *Functional Structure in DP and IP*, ed. Guglielmo Cinque, 15–53. New York/Oxford: Oxford University Press.

Campbell, Richard. 1996. Specificity operators in SpecDP. *Studia Linguistica* 50:161–188.

Carlson, Gregory. 1977. Reference to kinds in English. PhD dissertation, University of Massachusetts, Amherst.

Carstens, Vicki. 1991. The morphology and syntax of determiner phrases in Kiswahili. PhD dissertation, University of California.

Chatman, Seymour. 1960. Pre-adjectivals in the English nominal phrase. *American Speech* 2:83–100.

Chierchia, Gennaro. 1998. Reference to kinds across languages. *Natural Language Semantics* 6:339–405.

Chomsky, Noam. 1970. Remarks on nominalization. In *Readings in English Transformational Grammar*, ed. Roderick Jacobs and Peter Rosebaum, 184–221. Waltham, MA: Ginn & Co.

Chomsky, Noam. 2001. Derivation by phase. In *Ken Hale – a Life in Language*, ed. Michael Kenstowicz, 1–52. Cambridge, MA: MIT Press.

Chomsky, Noam. 2007. Approaching UG from below. In *Interfaces + Recursion = Language?*, ed. Uli Sauerland and Hans-Martin Gärtner, 1–31. Berlin: Mouton de Gruyter.

Cinque, Guglielmo. 2005. Deriving Greenberg's Universal 20 and its exceptions. *Linguistic Inquiry* 36:315–332.

Cinque, Guglielmo, and Luigi Rizzi. 2010. *Mapping Spatial PPs. The Cartography of Syntactic Structures, Vol. 6*. Oxford/New York: Oxford University Press.

Coene, Martine, and Yves D'hulst (eds). 2003. Introduction: The syntax and semantics of noun phrases. In *From NP to DP Volume I: The Syntax and Semantics of Noun Phrases*, ed. Martine Coene and Yves D'hulst, 1–35. Amsterdam/Philadelphia: John Benjamins Publishing Company.

Cornilescu, Alexandra. 1993. Notes on the structure of the Romanian DP and the assignment of genitive case. *Venice Working Papers in Linguistics* 3:107–133.

Delfitto, Dennis, and Jan Schroten. 1991. Bare plurals and the number affix in DP. *Probus* 3:155–185.

Demirdache, Hamida, Dwight Gardiner, Peter Jacobs, and Lisa Matthewson. 1994. The case for D-quantification in Salish: 'All' in St'át'imcets, Squamish and Secwepemctsín. In *Papers for the 29th International Conference on Salish and Neighboring Languages*, 145–203. Salish Kootenai College, Pablo, Montana.

Di Domenico, Elisa. 1997. *Per una Teoria del Genere Grammaticale*. Padova: Unipress.

Diessel, Holger. 1999. *Demonstratives: Form, Function and Grammaticalization*. Amsterdam: John Benjamins Publishing co.

Enç, Murvet. 1991. Semantics of specificity. *Linguistic Inquiry* 22:1–25.

Ghomeshi, Jila, Ileana Paul, and Martina Wiltschko. 2009. Determiners: universals and variation. In *Determiners: Universals and Variation*, ed. Ghomeshi, Jila, Ileana Paul, and Martina Wiltschko, 1–24. Amsterdam/Philadelphia: John Benjamins Publishing Company.

Gillon, Carrie. 2006. The semantics of determiners: Domain restriction in Skwxwú7mesh. PhD dissertation, University of British Columbia.

Gillon, Carrie. 2009. The semantic core of determiners. In *Determiners: Universals and Variation*, ed. Ghomeshi, Jila, Ileana Paul and Martina Wiltschko, 177–214. Amsterdam/Philadelphia: John Benjamins Publishing Company.

Giusti, Giuliana. 1997. The categorical status of determiners. In *The New Comparative Syntax*, ed. Liliane Haegeman, 95–124. London: Longman.

Greenberg, Joseph. 1963. Some universal of grammar with particular reference to the order of meaningful elements. In *Universals of Language*, ed. Joseph Greenberg, 73–113. Cambridge, MA: MIT Press.

Grimshaw, Jane. 1991. Extended Projection. Ms. Brandeis University.

Guardiano, Cristina. 2009. The syntax of demonstratives: A parametric approach. Slides from a presentation at CCG 19. Available here: http://cdm.unimo.it/home/dipslc/guardiano.cristina/GuardianoDem.pdf (accessed 31 January 2014).

Heim, Irene. 1988. *The Semantics of Definite and Indefinite Noun Phrases*. New York: Garland Publications.

Jackendoff, Ray. 1977. *X'-Syntax. A Study of Phrase Structure*. Cambridge, MA: MIT Press.

Jelinek, Eloise. 1995. Quantification in Straits Salish. In *Quantification in Natural Languages*, ed. Emmon Bach, Eloise Jelinek, Angelika Kratzer, and Barbara Partee, 487–540. Norwell, MA/Dordrecht: Kluwer Academic Publishers.

Jelinek, Eloise, and Richard Demers. 1994. Predicates and pronominal arguments in Straits Salish. *Language* 70(4):697–736.

Karimi, Simin. 1999. Specificity Effect: Evidence from Persian. *Linguistic Review* 16:125–141.

Kornfilt, Jaklin. 1984. Case marking, agreement, and empty categories in Turkish. PhD dissertation, Harvard University.

Lamontagne, Greg, and Lisa Travis. 1987. The syntax of adjacency. In *Proceedings of WCCFL*, ed. Megan Crowhurst, 173–186. Stanford, CA: CSLI Publications.

Loebel, Elisabeth. 1994. KP/DP-Syntax: Interaction of case-marking with referential and nominal features. *Theoretical Linguistics* 20:38–70.

Longobardi, Giuseppe. 1994. Reference and proper names: A theory of N-movement in syntax and logical form. *Linguistics Inquiry* 25:609–665.

Lyons, Christopher. 1999. *Definiteness*. Cambridge: Cambridge University Press.

McFadden, Thomas. 2004. The position of morphological case in the derivation. PhD dissertation, University of Pennsylvania, Philadelphia, PA.

Massam, Diane, Colin Gorrie, and Alexandra Kellner. 2006. Niuean determiner: Everywhere and nowhere. In *Proceedings of the 2006 Canadian Linguistics Association Annual Conference*, ed. Claire Gurski and Milica Radisic, 16 pages. Available at: http://westernlinguistics.ca/Publications/CLA2006/Massam.pdf (accessed 31 January 2014).

Matthewson, Lisa. 2001. Quantification and the nature of cross-linguistic variation. *Natural Language Semantics* 9:145–189.

Matthewson, Lisa, and Henry Davis. 1995. The structure of DP in St'át'imcets (Lillooet Salish). In *Papers for the 30th International Conference on Salish and Neighboring Languages*, 54–68. University of Victoria.

Medeiros, David. 2012. Movement as tree-balancing: an account of Greenberg's Universal 20. Handout from presentation at 86th annual meeting of the Linguistic Society of America.

Partee, Barbara. 1987. Noun phrase interpretation and type shifting principles. In *Studies in Discourse Representation Theory and the Theory of Generalized Quantifiers*, ed. Jeroen Groenendijk and Martin Stokhof, 115–143. Dordrecht: Forus.

Progovac, Ljiljana. 1998. Determiner phrase in a language without determiners. *Journal of Linguistics* 34:165–179.

Ritter, Elizabeth. 1988. A head-movement approach to construct-state noun phrases. *Linguistics* 26:909–929.

Ritter, Elizabeth. 1991. Two functional categories in noun phrases: Evidence from Modern Hebrew. In *Syntax and Semantics 25: Perspectives on Phrase Structure: Heads and Licensing*, ed. Susan Rothstein, 37–62. San Diego, CA: Academic Press.

Ritter, Elizabeth. 1993. Where's gender? *Linguistic Inquiry* 24:795–803.

Rizzi, Luigi. 1997. The fine structure of the left periphery. In *Elements of Grammar: A Handbook of Generative Syntax*, ed. Liliane Haegeman, 281–337. Dordrecht: Kluwer.

Rosen, Sara. 1989. Two types of noun incorporation: A lexical analysis. *Language* 65:294–317.

Ross, John. 1967. Constraints of variables in syntax. PhD dissertation, MIT.

Seiter, William. 1980. *Studies in Niuean Syntax*. New York: Garland Press.

Stanley, Jason. 2002. Nominal restriction. In *Logical Form and Language*, ed. Gerhard Preyer and Georg Peter, 365–388. Oxford: Oxford University Press.

Trenkic, Danijela. 2004. Definiteness in Serbian/Croatian/Bosnian and some implications for the general structure of the nominal phrase. *Lingua* 114:1401–1427.

Valois, Daniel. 1991. The internal syntax of DP. PhD dissertation, University of California Los Angeles.

Willim, Ewa. 2000. On the grammar of Polish nominals. In *Step by step: Essays on Minimalism in Honor of Howard Lasnik*, ed. Roger Martin, David Michaels, and Juan Uriagereka, 319–346. Cambridge, MA: MIT Press.

The syntax of adjectives

Artemis Alexiadou

1 Introduction/definitions

By now there is a relatively rich literature on adjectives, which contributes to our better understanding of what adjectives are and how they should be introduced into syntactic structure. However, several issues of controversy remain. This chapter offers a survey thereof, and references for the reader to follow up on the ongoing discussion.

From a typological perspective, it is rather questionable whether adjectives belong to the universal set of lexical categories. For instance, Dixon (2004) points out that the category of adjectives does not exist in the same way in all languages (see also Croft 1991; Beck 1999). Beck shows that languages with few or no adjectives are a typological commonplace and that, therefore, there is something marked about the adjective class compared with noun or verbs.

At the very core of the controversy surrounding adjectives is the issue of providing a definition of what an adjective actually is. Criteria that work for one language prove ineffective for other languages regardless of whether they are syntactic (distribution), morphological (inflection and agreement), or semantic (gradability and quality-denoting); see Beck (1999) for an overview of the different definitions of adjectives.

Traditional grammars take the fact that adjectives modify nouns directly – that is, in attributive modification – to be their most obvious distinctive feature. While this holds for cases such as (1a–b), (2a–b) show that there are adjectives that cannot be used as attributive modifiers, but can only function as predicates.

(1)   a. a proud student, a shiny coin
      b. the student is proud, the coin is shiny

(2)   a. *the asleep dog
      b. the dog is asleep

Croft (1991) signals that, while the attributive modification is the most common use of adjectives, predicative modification is not uncommon.

Attempts have been made to offer a categorial specification of adjectives in terms of binary features ($\pm$N/V) (Chomsky 1970). Recently, Baker (2003) argued that adjectives can be defined as a category: that is, -N, -V. This approach is distinct from what is proposed in, for example, Croft (1991), who sees adjectives as being by definition the prototypical modifiers of natural languages. It is also distinct from approaches in formal semantics, such as that of Kamp (1975), which characterize adjectives as inherently gradable predicates. Support for the view that a definition of adjectives cannot rely on their function as modifiers comes from the fact that other constituents can have a modificatory role, such as participial forms of verbs, *the shining light*.

Turning to the uses of adjectives, we can say that adjectives have three main uses: they may be used as the complement of a copula (1b), they may be used as pre-nominal modifiers of a noun (1a), and they may be used in postnominal modifiers of a noun (3).

(3)   a student proud of his work

At first sight, the interpretation of the adjectives is rather similar: in all these examples, the adjectives denote a property associated with an entity denoted by a noun or by the nominal constituent. Given that the adjectives in the three sets of examples seem to have some degree of commonality, the following questions arise, to which I will turn shortly. Are pre-nominal adjectives syntactically related to postnominal adjectives? Are both related to the postcopular adjectives? In other words, could we argue that the different patterns in (1) and (3) are simply variants of each other? Does the different distribution of the adjectives correlate with any difference in interpretation?

2   Historical perspectives

The patterns illustrated above have provoked a large amount of controversy in the literature. Throughout the history of generative grammar, claims have been made both in favour and against derivationally relating the attributive and predicative use of adjectives. We can recognize two main trends (see the detailed discussion in Alexiadou *et al.* 2007): (a) a 'reductionism' approach (Jacobs and Rosenbaum 1968; Kayne 1994; among others) and (b) a 'separationism' approach (Cinque 1993; Sproat and Shih 1988; among others)). According to (a), the two uses of the adjectives share an underlying structure; according to (b), the two patterns are fundamentally distinct.

Let me briefly summarize these positions here. Beginning with the reductionist approach, the main idea is as follows: the fact that DP-internal adjectives have attributive and predicative interpretations should not be taken as evidence against adopting a unified analysis of all adnominal adjectives. From this perspective, it is assumed that an adjective is a one-place predicate that is true of things (e.g. *interesting*(x)). The same observation holds of bare nouns – they too are predicates that are true of things (e.g. *student*(x)). For the interpretation of the sequence adjective + noun in examples such as (4) these two predicates are conjoined:

(4)   a. an interesting student   *interesting*(x) & *student*(x)
      b. a very kind student   *very kind*(x) & *student*(x)

Thus the interpretation of (4a) is as in (6):

(5)   Mary is an interesting student.

(6)   Mary is a student and Mary is interesting.

Adjectival modification can thus be viewed as a conjunction of properties, and see Higginbotham (1985) for a particular implementation of this idea. Conjunction of properties as illustrated in (4) is also called 'intersectivity': the set of the entities denoted by the noun and the set of properties denoted by the adjective intersect. The complex nominal expression 'interesting student' is found at the intersection of the set (or denotation) of STUDENT and INTERESTING. This is why adjectives such as *red, wooden, kind* are usually also termed intersective. Below, I will offer a more formal definition of intersectivity.

From the reductionist perspective, pre-nominal attributive modifiers like those in (4) are derived from postnominal predicative modifiers, like those in (5), by a fronting operation (Chomsky 1965; Jacobs and Rosenbaum 1968; and Kayne 1994 for the same basic idea implemented in different ways). In particular, pre-nominal attributive adjectives were ana-lyzed in the older generative tradition as resulting from leftward movement of adjectives which are generated to the right of the N. (7) is a schematic representation of this process:

(7)   a [[$_{AP_i}$ very proud]   student t$_i$]
      ◄───────────────

Assuming that postnominal adjectives are in essence predicative, a general application of the derivation in (7) to all pre-nominal adjectives would analyse all pre-nominal adjectives as fronted predicative adjectives. In arguing in favour of such a link between predicative (5) and the pre-nominal attributive adjective in (4), the postnominal position of the adjective can be considered as providing an intermediate derivational step between the predicative relative clause (8) and the pre-nominal position (4). In other words, the examples with postnominal adjectives (5) could be paraphrased as in (8), containing a relative clause with the verb *be* in which the adjective is predicated of the head noun. In these paraphrases the postnominal APs of (5) function as predicative APs on a par with those in (4):

(8)   a student proud of her work
      = a student [$_{CP}$ who is proud of her work]

There are several steps involved in the derivation. Taking (9a) as the input structure, the next step is a relative clause reduction, followed by predicate fronting:

(9)   a.   the student who is proud
    ⇒ b.   the student proud
    ⇒ c.   the proud student

However, while it is the case that many adjectives that appear before the noun can be para-phrased by means of a *be*-relative clause, there are also many adjectives for which this analysis, which is based on the integration of the notions of predicativity and attribution, cannot be maintained. Adjectives such as *former, present, fake, alleged*, but also, and more importantly, *good* in *good tax payer*, and *nuclear* in *nuclear energy*, are not predicative adjectives and neither are they intersective. See the discussion in §3.5. for arguments as to why adjectives such as *former* and *good* are not intersective.

According to the separationism approach (Lamarche 1991; Cinque 1993), pre-nominal and post-nominal adjectives are distinct entities. Specifically, Lamarche argued on the basis of French data that pre-nominal adjectives are zero-level entities and together with the noun they form an N^0. Postnominal adjectives are maximal projections and come out as daughters of N′. (10), from Lamarche (1991: 227), illustrates the difference:

(10) a.   N^0 b.   N$'$

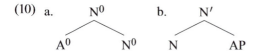

      A^0 N^0 N   AP

For the sake of completeness, let me point out that several other researchers have been pursuing a mixed approach, whereby some APs are base-generated pre-nominally and others are moved there from a postnominal position. From this perspective, pre-nominal adjectives may have two sources: either they are moved to the pre-nominal position by the operation of predicate-fronting that fronts the predicate of a reduced relative; or they are base generated, as heads or maximal projections, in such a position: see Alexiadou *et al.* (2007) for details.

3 Critical issues and topics

While the debate among the three lines of thought introduced in §2 is still going on, in this section I turn to some other issues that have been critically discussed in the literature.

3.1 Adjective placement and N-movement

The first issue concerns the observation that languages differ as far as the position of the adjective with respect to the noun it modifies is concerned (see Abney 1987; Bernstein 1993; Bouchard 1998; Cinque 1993; 2010; Kamp 1975; Lamarche 1991; Sproat and Shih 1988; Valois 1991). While in English (as in Greek and German) adjectives precede the noun, in Romance languages, illustrated below with a French example, adjectives occur primarily post-nominally, though certain classes of adjectives such as *mere* or *former* occur strictly in pre-nominal position.

(11)   a.   the   red book
       b.   le   livre rouge   *French*
           the   book red

However, English is not identical to German and Greek, as certain adjectives can appear in postnominal position in this language. Specifically, in English adjectives that can appear in post-nominal position are those which are either morphologically derived from verbs by means of the suffix -*a/ible* – e.g., *the stars visible/the visible stars* – or which are participles used as adjectives; in addition, adjectives formed with the aspectual prefix *a-* – e.g., *alive, asleep* (1b) – behave alike. On the other hand, post-nominal placement in German and Greek is impossible. In Greek, in fact, it is permitted only if the adjective is preceded by a determiner and is limited to a specific group of adjectives (see §4, and Alexiadou *et al.* (2007) for details and references).

Let me begin with a discussion of the pattern in (11). In principle, there are two possible analyses of (11). One could argue that adjectives adjoin to the right of the noun in French, while they adjoin to the left in English. According to this hypothesis, the difference in word order between the English A+N order and the French N+A order can also be explained in terms of a difference in the base position of the adjectives. Specifically, attributive adjectives in English (and in Germanic in general) are always inserted pre-nominally, while in languages such as French (and Romance languages in general) attributive adjectives can be inserted both pre-nominally or post-nominally. For instance, adopting an adjunction approach, this would implicate assuming both right and left adjunction. (12) offers a schematic representation:

(12) a. English $[_{DP}$ D $[_{NP}$ AP $[_{NP}$ AP $[_{NP}$ N ...]]]]
      b. French $[_{DP}$ D $[_{NP}$ $[_{NP}$ $[_{NP}$ N ...] AP] AP]]

However, several problems arise. First of all, there is the theoretical problem that, according to some strict views on X-bar, adjunction is a problematic operation, and as such it should be excluded or severely restricted. I will come back to this issue. Second, it is not clear how to account for the observed ordering constraints on adjectives under the adjunction hypothesis. As has been noted, when more than one adjective is present there are clear restrictions as to which adjective precedes the other(s) (see §3.3). Consider (13):

(13) a. nice red dress (*red nice dress)
      b. an ugly big table (*a big ugly table)
      c. large red Chinese vase (*Chinese large red vase) (?large Chinese red vase)
                                                        (Sproat and Shih 1988)

According to Sproat and Shih (1988), non-absolute (speaker-oriented or evaluative) adjectives precede absolute ones. In addition, among the absolute adjectives, adjectives denoting size precede adjectives denoting shape, which in turn precede adjectives denoting colour, which precede adjectives denoting nationality or material. It is normally assumed that there is no ordering constraint on constituents adjoined to a single node.

An alternative hypothesis would be to assume that attributive adjectives are universally inserted in a pre-nominal position and, in those languages in which it is attested, the surface order noun–adjective is derived by (cyclic) leftward movement of the noun to a higher functional head (e.g. Number, Gender) in the nominal domain (Valois 1991; Cinque 1993; Bernstein 1993; and many others; see Alexiadou *et al.* 2007 for further discussion and references). As (14) illustrates, the APs stay in place and it is the noun that raises cyclically passing by one (or, depending on the language, more than one) adjective.

(14) a. English $[_{DP}$ D $[_{FP}$ AP F $[_{FP}$ AP F $[_{NP}$ N ...]]]]
      b. French $[_{DP}$ D $[_{FP}$ AP $[_{F}$ N_n] $[_{FP}$ AP $[_{F}$ t_n] $[_{NP}$ t_n...]]]]

There are two underlying hypotheses for such an account. The hypothesis that the noun moves leftwards past one or more adjectives is based on the prior assumption that the adjective(s) is (are) generated to the left of the noun as NP-adjunct(s) or as specifier(s) of dedicated functional projections, as illustrated in (15a–b):

(15) a. $[_{DP}$ D $[_{NP}$ AP $[_{NP}$ AP $[_{NP}$ N ...]]]]
      b. $[_{DP}$ D $[_{FP}$ AP F $[_{FP}$ AP F $[_{NP}$ N ...]]]]

Since the N-movement analysis treats pre-nominal adjectives as being adjoined to the NP or to functional projections higher than the NP, this also entails, of course, that there must be additional heads between N and D. If there were no intervening projections, there would be no landing site for the moved N. I will come to this discussion in §4.

3.2   Adjective placement and interpretation

Researchers seem to agree that when two different positions are possible for adjective–noun combinations, the position the adjective occupies relative to the noun it modifies will have a reflex on the way it is interpreted. This has been argued to be the case with examples such as *the visible stars/the stars visible*: when post-nominal the adjective appears to attribute a temporary property to the individuals denoted by N. In pre-nominal position, however, it can have this temporary property, but it can also refer to the stars whose intrinsic brightness renders them detectable to the unaided eye. Thus, while the adjective is ambiguous in pre-nominal position, it is unambiguous in postnominal position. Consider (16) below:

(16)   the (visible) stars visible
      the (explorable) rivers explorable
      the (stolen) jewels stolen
      the (present) cats present

Bolinger (1967) suggests that the directionality in the positioning of adjectives with respect to the noun they modify correlates with a basic interpretational difference: in pre-nominal position the adjective attributes a permanent, enduring, or characteristic property of the entity denoted by the noun, whereas in post-nominal position the adjective refers to a transient, temporary, and certainly not typical property of the denotation of the noun; it modifies the *referent* (or extension) of the noun 'river' at a given point as a whole. Bolinger argues that the pre-nominal adjective *navigable* modifies the *reference* of the noun. This is why the temporary or occasional navigability of river X falsifies the content of the whole sentence involving permanently navigable rivers. Evidence for this comes from the following example (see Larson and Marušič 2004: 274). In (17a) the continuation that necessarily makes reference to rivers that generally can be used for trade or not is not felicitous:

(17)   a   #List all the rivers navigable whether they can be used for trade or not.
      b.   List all the navigable rivers whether they can be used for trade or not.

The distinction reference modification vs. referent modification – or, synonymously, permanent/temporary property – has been re-stated by Larson (1998) in terms of the Individual-Level vs. Stage-Level contrast, in the sense that the permanent or salient property assigned by a (pre-nominal) adjective applies on the individual-level, whereas the temporary or transitory property assigned by a (pre-nominal or post-nominal) adjective is a stage-level property.
    Larson (1998), however, shows that this semantic difference is not one of directionality of adjective placement (i.e., whether an adjective is pre- or post-nominal) but rather of relative closeness of the adjective to N. Consider (18a–b):

(18)   a.   The *visible* stars *visible* include Capella.
      b.   The *visible visible* stars include Capella.

(18a) is understood as meaning that the inherently visible stars (those whose brightness makes them visible to the unaided eye) that happen to be visible at the moment include Capella. The same is true for (18b). The adjective *visible* that is found closest to the noun in (18b) is the individual-level one and the one found farther from it is the stage-level one. However, as shown by (18a), pre-nominal occurrence can have the individual-level reading, while the post-nominal adjective is strictly stage-level. See also the discussion in §4.2.

3.3 Adjective placement and semantic classification

Semantic properties seem to have a reflex on hierarchical order in cases where more than one adjective modifies a single noun. As has been observed, multiple adjectival modifiers of a noun typically observe strict ordering restrictions. Pre-nominal adjectives in English and in other languages follow an ordering which is often stated in terms of hierarchically organized semantic classes of adjectives (19a) (Sproat and Shih 1988).

(19) a. QUANTIFICATION < QUALITY < SIZE < SHAPE/COLOUR < PROVENANCE
　　　b. numerous/three beautiful big grey Persian cats

These hierarchical effects were taken as evidence for Cinque (1993) to analyse adjectives as unique specifiers of designated functional heads instead of adjuncts to NP. This led to the postulation of a number of functional projections within the DP that host adjectives (see (20)). This, then, in conjunction with the idea that nouns undergo head movement in Romance languages but not in English, suggests that the following structures can be assumed for the two language groups:

(20) a. Germanic $[_{DP} D [_{F1P} AP [_{F1P} F [_{F2P} AP [_{F2P} F [_{NP} N \dots]]]]]]$
　　　b. Romance $[_{DP} D [_{F1P} AP [_{F1P} [_{F} N_n] [_{F2P} AP [_{F2P} [_{F} t_n] [_{NP} t_n..]]]]]]$

(20a) illustrates how such an account would work for Germanic languages. For the Romance languages the proposal is that N-movement targets the intermediate heads (20b). This is not the case in Germanic languages; hence, we introduce the N-movement parameter.

3.4 Categorial status

The analysis of adjectives as specifiers and the N-parameter are further viewed in connection with the head vs. XP status of the adjectives. Some researchers, following crucially Abney (1987), analyse adjectives as heading their own APs, while others, such as Bernstein (1993), claim that adjectives split into two categories, those that have a head status and those that function as a maximal projection. The debate remains unresolved.

Let me, however, briefly summarize the arguments in favour of and those against the head status of the adjective. A first argument that adjectives are heads is provided in Delsing (1993). This is based on Danish data. In this language, the suffixed article may be attached to the noun:

(21) hus-et
　　　house-the

However, in the presence of a pre-nominal adjective, the article has to be spelled out independently by a free morpheme (*det* in (22)). The Spell-Out as an affix is not available (22b):

(22) a. det　gamle　hus
　　　　　this　old　　house
　　　b. *gamle huset

Delsing (1993) proposes that the adjective *gamle* ('old') in (22a) heads an AP projection, and that it takes the NP headed by *hus* as its complement. He assumes that the order Noun+determiner-affix in (21) is derived by movement of N to D. He proposes that the intervention of the adjective in (22a) blocks N to D movement because it would lead to a violation of the head movement constraint. One head, N, would cross an intervening head, A, on its way to a higher head, D.

The head analysis predicts that pre-nominal adjectives will not be able to take complements since they already have a phrasal projection of the N–D extended projection as their complement. This is the case in English; hence, it could be safely concluded that adjectives are heads (Abney 1987) (23). However, there are languages – for instance, Greek and German – where phrasal APs appear normally in pre-nominal position (24).

(23) a. *the proud of her son mother
      b. the mother proud of her son

(24) i [periphani ja   to jo tis] mitera   Greek
      the proud   for the son her   mother

One of the most convincing arguments against the head analysis of adjectives is offered in Svenonius (1994). This concerns the interpretation of pre-adjectival modifiers within the noun phrase. Consider (25):

(25) some barely hot black coffee

As Svenonius points out, in (25) the degree adverb *barely* modifies the adjective *hot*. The degree adverbial does not bear on the adjective *black*. The coffee may be completely black, it is not necessarily 'barely' black. Assuming a restrictive X'-theory, *barely* must be associated with a maximal projection. Under the head analysis, *barely* will be associated with an AP dominating the projection *hot black coffee*. This structure, in which *barely* c-commands *hot black coffee* will incorrectly lead to the prediction that *barely* takes scope over *hot black coffee*.

The arguments against the generalized head analysis of adjectives cannot be extended to all pre-nominal adjectives. In particular, we cannot use the arguments with respect to modifiers of the *alleged, former, nuclear* type, which cannot be modified (see Bernstein 1993). Thus, it might be possible to maintain the head analysis for these types of modifiers, which behave as zero-level categories.

Two further issues have been discussed in the literature on adjectives: the argument structure of adjectives and the inflectional properties of adjectives. I will not discuss these here (see, e.g., Higginbotham 1985 on the first issue).

3.5   Intersectivity

It has been argued that there exists a strong correlation between semantic classification and the syntax of adjectives. The literature on the semantics of adjectives has focused on the question of the appropriate characterization of adjectives in terms of the intersective vs. predicate modifier distinction, along the lines of (26) (see Kamp 1975; Kamp and Partee 1995).

(26) The intersectivity hypothesis, Kamp and Partee (1995):

Given the syntactic configuration [$_{CNP}$ Adj CNP], the semantic interpretation of the whole is $\| \text{Adj} \| \cap \| \text{CNP} \|$ (set intersection, predicate conjunction)

On the basis of (26), adjectives fall into two classes: the class of intersective adjectives – e.g., *carnivorous* – and the class of non-intersective adjective. The latter group of adjectives comprises a number of sub-types, including (i) Subsective such as *good* (John is a good lawyer $\neq$ John is good and John is a lawyer, but $=$ John is good as a lawyer); (ii) Non-subsective plain such as *former* (John is a former senator, $\neq$ John is former and John is a senator, but $=$ John was formerly a senator); (iii) Non-subsective privative such as *fake* (fake pistol $\neq$ this is fake and this is a pistol).

Importantly, several adjectives are ambiguous between intersective and non-intersective readings.

(27) Peter is an old friend
    a. Peter is old
    b. The friendship is old

In order to treat such and other similar patterns, some researchers assume a dual category Adjective (Siegel 1976). Others focus on the internal structure of the noun phrase (Larson 1998). I will summarize this debate briefly here. Before doing that, let me point out, however, that from the perspective of the head vs. XP analysis it seems to be the case that non-intersective modifiers are amenable to a head analysis while intersective ones are amenable to an XP analysis.

Consider the data in (28), where the adjective is used as a modifier of a deverbal noun: that is, a noun which is morphologically related to a verb. In (28a) the adjective *beautiful* may either indicate a property attributed directly to Olga (21b) or refer to a property attributed to Olga in her capacities as a dancer (28c) (see Larson 1998 and references therein):

(28) a. Olga is a beautiful dancer.
    b. Olga is a dancer and [Olga] is beautiful.
    c. Olga is beautiful as a dancer.

In the first reading the adjective is intersective. Here the adjective *beautiful* is ultimately predicated of the referent of the (proper) noun – that is, of Olga. Olga herself is beautiful, even if her dancing may be awkward. In the second reading the adjective is non-intersective. Here, the adjective *beautiful* applies to Olga *qua* dancer. Olga's dancing is beautiful even if she herself may be unattractive. The majority of adjectives that appear in combination with a deverbal noun can have either an intersective or a non-intersective reading. To account for these two interpretations, Larson (1998) proposes that a noun such as *dancer* includes in its semantic structure two arguments:

(a) an event argument (e) which ranges over events and states;
(b) an argument (x) which is a variable ranging over entities.

This way, the semantics of a common noun (*dancer*) is relativized to events. With respect to the noun *dancer* (28a), (e) is the event 'dancing' and (x) is Olga. The adjective *beautiful* – a predicate – can be predicated either of the event argument (e), in which case we obtain the non-intersective reading, or of the external argument (x), in which case the intersective reading is ensured. Crucially, for Larson, the intersective/non-intersective ambiguity arises not from the semantics of the adjective itself but from the semantic structure of the noun. (27) is one more example that illustrates this contrast. The semantic representation of (27a) is given in (29b) and that of (27b) is given in (29b):

(29) a. ∃e[friendship(e) & Theme(Peter, e) & old(Peter)]
      b. ∃e[friendship(e) & Theme(Peter, e) & old(e)]

Larson developed this analysis in contrast to Siegel's, which assumed that the ambiguity observed is related to the fact that adjectives belong to two syntactically and semantically distinct classes. The first class is that which Larson calls predicative adjectives. These occur underlyingly as predicates, although surface syntax may disguise this. When they combine with a noun, the semantic result is predicate conjunction. This is the source of the intersective reading. An example of the predicative class is *aged*. The second class is that of attributives. These occur underlyingly as nominal modifiers, although, again, surface syntax may disguise this to some extent. They combine with their nominal as function to argument and, so, they invoke intensions. This is the source of the non-intersective reading. An example of the attributive class is *former*. The issue with *beautiful* is, according to Siegel, that it can be a member of both classes at the same time, thus giving rise to ambiguity.

4   Current issues and research

4.1   *Two types of modification*

In §3, I briefly discussed the N-movement parameter. More recent analyses (Alexiadou 2001; Cinque 2010; Shlonsky 2004; Laenzlinger 2005 among others) argue against the N-raising parameter, mainly on the basis of adjectival ambiguity. These researchers put forward a generalized XP analysis, which naturally pre-supposes an analysis of adjectives in terms of (reduced) relative clauses.

From the perspective of Alexiadou and Wilder (1998), Alexiadou (2001), and, most notably, Cinque (2010), there are two types of modification across languages. Following Sproat and Shih (1988), these are identified as in (30):

(30) *Direct modification*
      permits intersective and non-intersective modifiers
      Indirect modification
      permits intersective modifiers only

Sproat and Shih propose that, syntactically, direct modifiers are simply bare APs adjoined to a projection of N, while indirect modifiers are reduced relative clauses that may be adjoined outside the scope of 'specifiers of N' (in terms of the DP-hypothesis, adjoined higher than NP within DP). The authors discuss the syntactic reflexes of the direct/indirect distinction with respect to Mandarin Chinese. In this language, bare adjectives modifying nouns (direct modification) must obey ordering restrictions. Multiple APs violate hierarchical ordering restrictions only when accompanied by a particle (*de*). Interestingly, this particle is also a relative clause marker, supporting the suggestion that indirect modification is modification by (reduced) relative clauses. *De*-modifiers are further constrained in that they may only contain predicative adjectives:

(31) a. xiaǒ-de   lüde   hua-ping
         small-DE green-DE vase
         'a small green vase'
     b. a xiaǒ lü   hua-ping
         small green vase
         'a small green vase'

A further reflex of this distinction is the availability of long vs. short adjectives in Bosnian/Serbian/Croatian, data from Cinque (2010):

(32) a. nov   kaput
         new (short form) coat
         'a new coat'
     b. novi   kaput
         new (long form) coat
         'the/a new coat'

Adjectives that cannot be used predicatively do not even possess a short form; they only have the long form:

(33) a. navodni/*navodan komunista
         An/the alleged (long form)/(*short form) communist
     b. budući/*buduć predsjednik
         a/the future (long form)/(*short form) president

A further case where the two types of modification are morphosyntactically distinct is determiner spreading in Greek. In this language, normally all adjectives precede the noun. However, it is also possible for certain adjectives to be introduced by their own determiner, yielding what has been labelled by Androutsopoulou (1995) Determiner Spreading. In (34b), the Det-Adj string can precede or follow the Det+Noun sequence:

(34) a. to   kokino   vivlio
         the   red   book
     b. to   kokino   to   vivlio/ to   vivlio   to   kokino   *Determiner Spreading*
         the   red   the   book/   the   book   the   red

The articled adjective in Determiner Spreading is always interpreted restrictively with respect to the noun it modifies, whereas adjectives in non-Determiner Spreading DPs can be either restrictive or non-restrictive, as in English. Consider (35), from Kolliakou (1995):

(35) a. O   diefthindis dilose   oti   i   ikani   erevnites
         The   director   declared that   the   efficient researchers
         tha   apolithun.   (monadic)
         will   be fired
     b. O   diefthindis dilose   oti   i   ikani   i   erevnites
         The   director   declared that   the   efficient the   researchers
         (i   erevnites   i   ikani) tha   apolithun.
         (the   researchers the   efficient) will be-fired
         'The director declared that the efficient researchers will be fired.'

The construction in (35a) is ambiguous between what Kolliakou calls an 'insane reading' and a 'life is tough' reading. In the 'insane' reading, out of the set of researchers, only the efficient researchers will be fired. In the 'life is tough' reading, a set of researchers will be fired and the efficient researchers happen to be part of that larger group that will be fired. While (35a) is ambiguous between these two readings, (35b) is not. It only has the 'insane' reading: that is, the reading that, out of the set of researchers, only those researchers that are efficient will be fired.

The restrictive function of the articled adjective can explain the ungrammaticality of the examples in (36). Adjectives that cannot be interpreted restrictively cannot appear in Determiner Spreading:

(36) a. *O   monos   tu   o   erotas   ine   i   dulja   tu.
         The only   his the love   is   the work   his
         'His only love is his work.'
     b. *o   dithen   o   antagonismos
          the alleged   the competition
          'the alleged competition'

Alexiadou and Wilder (1998) analyzed determiner spreading as a case of indirect modification (see also Cinque 2010). The consensus reached is that the syntax of indirect modification is captured under the relative clause analysis of modifiers, briefly discussed in §2, (see Alexiadou and Wilder 1998; Cinque 2010, building on Kayne 1994). Thus, indirect modifiers, which are intersective, are introduced as predicates in relative clauses. Direct modifiers are introduced otherwise, and here researchers have not reached a consensus.

(37) illustrates the syntax for indirect modification, building on Kayne (1994):

(37) a.   *Base structure*

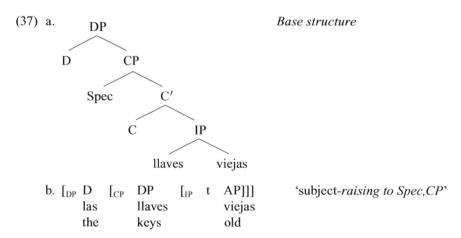

     b. [DP D   [CP DP   [IP t   AP]]]   'subject-*raising to Spec,CP*'
           las   llaves   viejas
           the   keys   old

In (37), the head of the relative clause raises from within the relative clause to the specifier position of CP and ends up as adjacent to the external determiner. This analysis differs from that in Cinque (2010), to which I turn below.

In contrast, direct modifiers are generated as specifiers of functional projections within the extended projection of the noun (see Cinque 2010; Alexiadou and Wilder 1998):

(38) [DP [FP **AP** [NP]]]

4.2 Arguments against N-movement

But what are the reasons to abandon the N-movement parameter idea? A detailed discussion of this is given in Alexiadou (2001) and Cinque (2010), but I will mention two problematic areas here (see also Alexiadou *et al.* 2007 for details).

Lamarche (1991) was the first to point out a series of problems with the N-movement analysis. One empirical prediction of the N-movement analysis is that the order of DP-internal adjectives should remain constant cross-linguistically and that only the position of the head N varies. This prediction is indeed borne out by French examples such as those in (39a): the pre- and post-nominal adjectives in French display the same ordering as their English pre-nominal counterparts. The sequencing of the three adjectives, *joli/beautiful*, *gros/big*, *rouge/red*, remains constant.

(39) a. un joli gros ballon rouge French
   a beautiful big ball red
 b. une énorme maison magnifique
   a big house beautiful
 c. un fruit orange énorme
   an fruit orange enormous
 d. un poulet froid délicieux
   a chicken cold delicious
 e. une voiture rouillé blanche
   a car rusty white
 f. une bière blonde froide
   a beer pale cold

However, it is by no means always the case that the sequencing of post-nominal adjectives in French corresponds to that of pre-nominal adjectives in English. This is shown by (39b), in which the linear order of the underlined French adjectives, two pre-nominal and one post-nominal, is the opposite of the linear order of the corresponding English pre-nominal adjectives (from Cinque 1993: 102). The same is observed in (39c–e), where both adjectives are post-nominal (c–d from Cinque 1993: 102, e–f from Bernstein 1993: 47).

Svenonius (1994) shows that the problem of relative scope of modifiers also raises a problem for the N-movement analysis. This problem was first noticed by Lamarche (1991). The spec analysis combined with the N-movement analysis makes the incorrect prediction that the relative scope of adjectives should be from left to right both in the Germanic languages, such as English, Dutch and German, and in the Romance languages, such as Italian and French. Consider the noun phrases in (40):

(40) a. chopped frozen chicken
 b. frozen chopped chicken

The DPs in (40a) refer to chicken that was first frozen, then chopped, while the DPs in (40b) refer to the chicken that was first chopped, then frozen. The higher adjectives (those to the left) modify the entire constituent that they combine with. In other words, *chopped* has scope over *frozen chicken* in (40a). These effects follow from the Spec approach: AP1 in (41) c-commands and has scope over AP2.

(41) $[_{DP}$ D $[_{FP}$ AP1 F $[_{FP}$ AP2 F $[_{NP}$ N ...]]]]

In the light of the spec analysis combined with the N-movement analysis (Bernstein 1993; Cinque 1993), post-nominal adjectives in Romance should have the same scope properties as pre-nominal adjectives in English: adjectives to the right of the head noun should be within the scope of the adjectives to their left.

(42) $[_{DP}$ D $[_{FP}$ $[_{F}$ N] $[_{F1P}$ AP1 F $[_{F2P}$ AP2 F $[_{NP}$ N ...]]]]]

However, this prediction does not seem to be correct. (42a–b) below are from Lamarche (1991: his ex. 18):

(42) a. une personne agée   handicappée   French
          a   person   elderly handicapped
      b. une personne handicappée agée
          a   person   handicapped elderly

Quite unexpectedly, an adjective to the right seems to take scope over an adjective to its left (see Bernstein 1993: 48). This contrast between the French data in (42a) and their English counterparts in (43) below is unexpected if adjectives are specifiers of specialized projections and post-nominal positions of adjectives are derived by leftward N-movement.

(43) a. a handicapped elderly person
      b. an elderly handicapped person

In (42a) the adjective *agée* in the specifier of F1P would be expected to c-command *handicappée* in Spec,F2P, as shown in (44a). In (43b) *handicappée* in Spec,F1P should c-command *agée* in Spec,F2P, as shown in (44b). If anything, we would thus expect the inverse scope relations.

(44) a. $[_{DP}$ D $[_{FP}$ $[_{F}$ personne] $[_{F1P}$ agée F $[_{F2P}$ handicappée F $[_{NP}$ N ...]]]]]
      b. $[_{DP}$ D $[_{FP}$ $[_{F}$ personne] $[_{F1P}$ handicappée F $[_{F2P}$ agée F $[_{NP}$ N ...]]]]]

In sum, with respect to scope relations, the Romance post-nominal adjectives manifest the mirror image of their English counterparts. This led to the abandoning of the idea of an N-movement parameter.

4.3 Cinque (2010)

Cinque (2010) offers a very systematic study of patterns of adjectival modification across languages, focussing on some important differences between Germanic vs. Romance adjectival placement and interpretation. Consider the data in (45). In Italian only the post-nominal position of the adjective gives rise to an ambiguity, while the pre-nominal position is strictly associated with a non-intersective reading (45a–b). In English, on the other hand, it is the pre-nominal position that is ambiguous, while the post-nominal position is strictly associated with an intersective reading (see the discussion in §3.2 above).

(45) a. Un **buon** attaccante non farebbe mai una cosa del genere   **(unambiguous)**
         a good forward player neg do never a thing this kind
         1. 'a person good at playing forward would never do such a thing' *non-intersective*
         2. #'A good-hearted forward would never do such a thing' *intersective*
      b. Un attaccante **buono** non farebbe mai una cosa del genere   **(ambiguous)**
         a forward player good neg do never one thing this kind
         1. 'a person good at playing forward would never do such a thing' *non-intersective*
         2. 'A good-hearted forward would never do such a thing' *intersective*

For Cinque, the individual-level vs. stage-level (*visible stars vs. stars visible*), restrictive vs. non-restrictive (*acts unsuitable vs. unsuitable acts*), specific vs. non-specific (*nearby house vs. house nearby*), and modal vs. implicit (*every possible candidate vs. every candidate possible*) readings of adjectives are taken to pattern like *buon* above.

In addition, as Cinque (2010) notes, building on Sproat and Shih (1988), there is a hierarchical organization available for the different readings of adjectives, shown in (46):

(46)

	Indirect modification		Direct modification	
Det	stage level	<	individual level	N
Det	restrictive	<	non-restrictive	N
Det	implicit	<	modal	N
Det	non-specific	<	specific	N
Det	intersective	<	non-intersective	N
Det	relative	<	absolute	N

To account for this, Cinque (2010) adopts the idea that there exist two sources for adjectival modification, one in terms of relative clauses and one in terms of pure adjectives (see also Alexiadou and Wilder 1998; Alexiadou 2001). Unlike what is suggested in these works, Cinque proposes the following structure for the two types of modifiers:

(47)

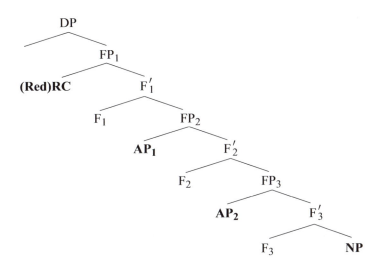

In (47) both indirect and direct modifiers precede the head noun, and indirect modifiers are placed higher than direct modifiers. On this analysis, N-raising plays no role, only XP raising does. As Cinque argues in detail, the word order facts observed across languages can be accounted as follows. In English, and in Germanic more generally, no raising takes place. In Romance, however, direct modifiers precede indirect modifiers. This suggests that in Romance AP direct modifiers move higher than indirect modifiers via XP raising. Consider (48):

(48)

			dir. mod.		indir. mod.	
Maria	ha intervistato	ogni	personaggio	politico	possibile	della sua città
Mary	has interviewed	every	potential	politician	possible	of her city

The direct modifier *potential* precedes both the head and the indirect modifier *possible*. In addition, the head noun intervenes between the two types of modifiers. In order for this word order to be generated, Cinque proposes that the string [$_{FP2}$ direct modification APs NP] raises around an indirect modification AP. Cinque argues that such an analysis is rendered plausible by the fact that Romance allows no reduced relative clauses to precede the N (as opposed to Germanic) (see (49)):

(49) a. The recently arrived letters
     b. *Le recentemente arrivate lettere

But, since (most) direct modification APs also follow N, this implies that NP also raises around direct modification APs internally to [$_{FP2}$ direct modification APs NP] (as the order of post-nominal direct modification APs is the mirror image of that of English, the raising must be of the roll-up kind).

As Cinque points out, a series of facts follow from this analysis. I briefly summarize those here, and see Cinque (2010) for details.

First, the observed word order generalizations follow: the APs which have a reduced relative clause source, and which precede the direct modification APs in pre-nominal position in English (Germanic), are found in post-nominal position in Romance, following the direct modification APs.

Second, the mirror image orders between English and Romance also follow (owing to the two types of rolling-up movements in Romance). Consider (50–51), examples illustrating the mirror image order effect in the two language groups:

		indir.mod.	dir.mod.	
(50)	a. The	*American*	*musical* comedy of the '50s	
	b. The only	*possible*	*Italian* invasion of Albania	
	c. She interviewed every	*possible potential*	candidate for President	

		dir.mod.	indir.mod.	
(51)	a. La commedia	*musicale*	*americana*	degli Anni '50
	b. La sola invasione	*italiana*	*possibile*	dell'Albania
	c. Ha intervistato ogni candidato	*potenziale possibile*	alla presidenza	

Third, the existence of unexpected scope effects mentioned above also follows:

		dir.mod.	indir.mod.	
(52)	a. E' un [*giovane* scrittore]	*assai noto* di romanzi gialli	(assai noto > giovane)	
	b. He is a very well-known young writer of detective stories			

Fourth, pre-nominal APs in Romance are unambiguous because they can have only a direct modification source since (reduced) relative clauses obligatorily end up post-nominally in Romance (whence their syntactic and interpretive properties).

Fifth, some direct modification adjectives can only be pre-nominal (*vecchio* 'aged; of long standing'; *povero* 'pitiable'; etc.). According to Cinque, this suggests that they are high in the hierarchy of direct modification APs and the NP does not roll-up past them.

On the other hand, post-nominal APs in Romance are instead ambiguous because they can arise either from a direct modification source or from an indirect modification source.

4.4 Linkers

Den Dikken (2006) presents a different take on adjectival modification, according to which this is best understood as predication. The core idea is that "all predication relationships are syntactically represented in terms of a structure in which the constituent denoting the subject and the predicate are dependents of a connective or Relator that establishes the connection, both the syntactic link and the semantic one between the two constituents" (den Dikken 2006: 11). This is illustrated in (53), which corresponds to the representation of all predication relationships, which are not taken to be directional. This means that in (53) the predicate can also be generated in Spec,RelatorP, with the subject being the complement of the relator:

(53)

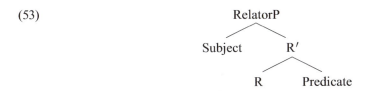

Consider now the treatment of adjectives that are ambiguous between intersective and non-intersective readings from this perspective, discussed in §3.2 and in the previous section.

(54) a. Olga is a beautiful dancer
      b. [$_{RP}$ Olga [Relator = be [[$_{RP}$ [$_{AP}$ beautiful] [Relator [$_{NP}$ dancer]]]]]]

For den Dikken, *dancer* originates in the complement position of the relator. There is a two-way relationship between *dancer* and *beautiful* in (54b) above. The AP is predicated of the noun phrase thanks to the fact that it is connected to the extended noun phrase via the relator, and at the same time the extended noun phrase restricts the adjective owing to the fact that the noun phrase is the complement of the relator head.

Further reading

The following sources are recommended for further reading.

C. Kennedy and L. McNally (eds). 2008. *Adjectives and adverbs: syntax, semantics, and discourse.* Oxford University Press.

This volume presents new work on the semantics and pragmatics of adjectives and adverbs, and their interfaces with syntax. Its concerns include the semantics of gradability; the relationship between adjectival scales and verbal aspect; the relationship between meaning and the positions of adjectives and adverbs in nominal and verbal projections; and the fine-grained semantics of different subclasses of adverbs and adverbs.

P. Cabredo Hofherr and O. Matushansky (eds). 2010. *Adjectives: formal analyses in syntax and semantics*. John Benjamins.

The volume contains four contributions that investigate the syntax of adjectives in English, French, Mandarin Chinese, Modern Hebrew, Russian, Spanish, and Serbocroatian. The theoretical issues explored include: the syntax of attributive and predicative adjectives, the syntax of nominalized adjectives, and the identification of adjectives as a distinct lexical category in Mandarin Chinese. A further four contributions examine different aspects in the semantics of adjectives in English, French, and Spanish, dealing with superlatives, comparatives, and aspect in adjectives.

References

Abney, S. 1987. The English noun phrase in its sentential aspect. PhD dissertation, MIT.

Alexiadou, A. 2001. Adjective syntax and noun raising: word order asymmetries in the DP as the result of adjective distribution. *Studia Linguistica* 55:217–248.

Alexiadou, A., and C. Wilder. 1998. Adjectival modification and multiple determiners. In *Possessors, predicates and movement in the DP*, ed. A. Alexiadou and C. Wilder, 303–332. Amsterdam: John Benjamins.

Alexiadou, A., L. Haegeman, and M. Stavrou. 2007. *Noun phrase in the generative perspective*. Berlin and New York: Mouton de Gruyter.

Androutsopoulou, A. 1995. The licensing of adjectival modification. *Proceedings of West Coast Conference on Formal Linguistics* 14:17–31.

Baker, M. 2003. *Lexical categories: verbs, nouns and adjectives*. Cambridge: Cambridge University Press.

Beck, D. 1999. The typology of parts of speech: the markedness of adjectives. PhD dissertation, University of Toronto.

Bernstein, J. 1993. Topics in the syntax of nominal structure across Romance. PhD dissertation, CUNY.

Bolinger, D. 1967. Adjectives in English: attribution and predication. *Lingua* 18:1–34.

Bouchard, D. 1998. The distribution and interpretation of adjectives in French: a consequence of bare phrase structure. *Probus* 10:139–183.

Cabredo Hofherr, P. and O. Matushansky (eds). 2010. *Adjectives: formal analyses in syntax and semantics*. John Benjamins.

Chomsky, N. 1965. *Aspects of the theory of syntax*. Cambridge, MA: MIT Press.

Chomsky, N. 1970. Remarks on Nominalization. In *Readings in English transformational grammar*, ed. R. Jacobs and P. Rosenbaum Ginn, 184–221. Waltham, MA.

Cinque, G. 1993. On the evidence for partial N-movement in the Romance DP. *University of Venice Working Papers in Linguistics* 3(2):21–40.

Cinque, G. 2010. *The syntax of adjectives*. Cambridge, MA: MIT Press.

Croft, W. 1991. *Syntactic categories and grammatical relations*. Chicago, IL: University of Chicago Press.

Delsing, H.O. 1993. The internal structure of noun phrases in Scandinavian languages: a comparative study. PhD dissertation, University of Lund.

den Dikken, M. 2006. *Relators and linkers: the syntax of predication, predication inversion, and copulas*. Cambridge, MA: MIT Press.

Dixon, R.M.W. 1982. *Where have all the adjectives gone?* Berlin: Mouton Publishers.

Dixon, R.M.W. 2004. *Adjective classes: a cross-linguistic typology*. Oxford: Oxford University Press.

Higginbotham, J. 1985. On semantics. *Linguistic Inquiry* 16(4):547–594.

Jacobs, R.A. and P.S. Rosenbaum. 1968. *English transformational grammar*. Waltham, MA: Blaisdell.

Kamp, H. 1975. Two theories about adjectives. In *Formal semantics of natural language*, ed. E. Keenan, 123–155. Cambridge: Cambridge University Press.

Kamp, H., and B. Partee. 1995. Prototype theory and compositionality. *Cognition* 57:129–191.

Kayne, R. 1994. *The antisymmetry of syntax*. Linguistic Monograph series. Cambridge, MA: MIT Press.

Kennedy, C., and L. McNally (eds). 2008. *Adjectives and adverbs: syntax, semantics, and discourse.* Oxford: Oxford University Press.

Kolliakou, D. 1995. Definites and possessives in Modern Greek: an HPSG syntax for noun phrases. PhD dissertation, University of Edinburgh.

Kolliakou, D. 2004. Monadic definites and polydefinites: their form meaning and use. *Journal of Linguistics* 40:263–333.

Laenzlinger, C. 2005. Some notes on DP-internal movement. *GGG* 4:227–260.

Lamarche, J. 1991. Problems for N-movement to NumP. *Probus* 3(2):215–316.

Larson, R. 1998. Events and modification in nominals. In *Proceedings from Semantics and Linguistic Theory (SALT) VIII*, ed. D. Strolovitch and A. Lawson. Ithaca, NY: Cornell University.

Larson, R., and F. Marušič. 2004. Indefinite pronoun structures with APs. *Linguistic Inquiry* 35: 268–287.

Shlonsky, U. 2004. The form of Semitic nominals. *Lingua* 114(12):1465–1526.

Siegel, M. 1976. Capturing the adjective. PhD dissertation, University of Massachusetts.

Sproat, R., and C. Shih. 1988. Pre-nominal adjectival ordering in English and Mandarin. *Proceeding of NELS* 12:465–489.

Svenonius, P. 1994. On the structural location of the attributive adjective. *Proceedings of the West Coast Conference on Formal Linguistics* 12:439–454.

Valois, D. 1991. The syntax of DP. PhD dissertation, UCLA.

6

The syntax of adverbs

Thomas Ernst

1 Introduction

If the study of adverbs once represented a "swamp", as was sometimes remarked forty years ago, it is perhaps now low-lying marshy ground, messy and prone to flooding, but with a few solid paths meandering though it. If nothing else, there is a consensus that the ordering of adverbs is very consistent across languages, with a significant amount of this being sequences of rigidly ordered adverbs. There is also agreement that the semantics of individual adverbs is an important determinant – perhaps the main determinant – of their ordering. And there are now at least two fairly well-defined approaches to adverb syntax to provide, if not final answers, then some first results and a set of useful questions with which to work toward definitive answers.

The modern study of adverb syntax within the generative tradition essentially began with Jackendoff (1972), whose framework was picked up and extended by Ernst (1984; 2002; 2009), Haider (1998; 2000; 2004) and others. This has been termed the "scopal" approach. The work of Cinque (1999) inaugurated a second approach to adverb data, in what has become known as the "cartographic" research program; it has been elaborated in Alexiadou (1997), Laenzlinger (2004), and Haumann (2007). Though there have been other proposals – perhaps most notably Frey and Pittner (1998; 1999) – the Jackendoff and Cinque lineages seem to be the main ones in the field.

The most important empirical syntactic issue is linear order: how can the distribution of a given adverb be explained? Perhaps the main theoretical issues are (a) the extent to which semantics is a major and direct determinant of adverb syntax, and (b) whether phrase structure conforms to some version of the Linear Correspondence Axiom of Kayne (1994), or is closer to a more traditional conception, with directionality parameters and/or right adjunction. The scopal camp claims that adverbs mostly adjoin freely as far as syntax is concerned, with impossible orders and positions ruled out when there is some violation of selection or some broader semantic (or occasionally morphological) principle. The cartographic view is that semantics is encoded in a long string of functional heads, each one licensing a semantic subclass of adverbs in its specifier position, with the order of these heads fixed by Universal Grammar (UG). Positions or orders that deviate from this initial structure are derived by various movements.

The bulk of this chapter is dedicated to sketching how these issues play out in the two approaches: how is linear order to be accounted for, how direct is the effect of adverb semantics on syntax, and what is the nature of phrase structure (and, secondarily, movement) that underlies the proper explanation of adverb distribution?

A quick note about terminology and coverage is in order. It is becoming increasingly standard to distinguish *adjuncts, adverbials,* and *adverbs.* The first of these comprises any nonhead that is not an argument. *Adverbials* refers to those adjuncts that modify verbs or other predicates (eventualities), or whole sentences (propositions); adverbs are those adverbials with the syntactic category Adverb – for example, not DPs functioning adverbially (e.g. *yesterday*) or PPs such as *on the beach* or *with a spoon.* Nevertheless, in this chapter I will include such DPs and PPs in the discussion, since they seem to be governed by a common set of principles and have often been treated along with adverbs in the literature.[1]

2 Survey of types: distributions and semantic bases

The major adverbials (aside from adverbial CP clauses) can conveniently be divided into three types: predicational adverbs, functional adverbs, and participant adverbials (PPs and DPs): each will be discussed in turn in this section. In considering them, we must abstract away from parentheticals, including sentence-final afterthoughts, since these seem to be much freer than non-parentheticals and do not obey the normal constraints on scope (this is standard in the literature on adverbials). Thus, for example, while *probably* is impossible in either of the positions indicated in 1a, it is fine if set off prosodically in 1b, where it takes scope over *not*:

(1)   a.   *The athletes have not (probably) been tested for drugs (probably).
      b.   The athletes have not (, probably,) been tested (, probably,) for drugs (, probably).

We also abstract away from small cross-linguistic differences in linear order and concentrate on generalizations that seem to hold for all languages that have been looked at seriously up to now. Examples come mostly from English, but to a large extent the patterns hold for other well-studied languages.

2.1   Predicational adverbs

Predicational adverbs are those based on gradable content predicates; in English and the other well-known European languages they are largely derived from adjectives.[2] They are ordered according to the template in (2). All but the manner class may be grouped together as clausal (or sentential) adverbs, while manner (and degree) adverbs can be termed *verb-oriented* or *verb-modifying.*

(2)   Discourse-Oriented > Evaluative > Epistemic > Subject-Oriented (> Neg) > Manner[3]

Discourse-oriented adverbs, sometimes known as "pragmatic" or "speech act" adverbs, include (on one of their readings) *frankly, honestly,* and *briefly.* They commonly occur in clause-initial position, though they may sometimes crop up in the other normal positions for sentential adverbs, just before or after the finite auxiliary, depending on the adverb and the construction:

Thomas Ernst

(3) a. Frankly, she (frankly) would (frankly) never be caught dead in an SUV.
     b. Briefly, their solution (?briefly) was (*briefly) to tighten the frame and readjust the
        cylinder.
     c. Honestly, why would (*honestly) the management try to do such a thing?

These adverbs always precede other predicationals, as in (4) (where *honestly* has the discourse reading):

(4) a. Honestly, she has {unfortunately/bravely} stopped worrying about advancing her
         career.
     b. *{Unfortunately/Bravely}, she has honestly stopped worrying about advancing her
         career.

Adverbs of this class are discourse-oriented in that they indicate the speaker's manner of expression; (3a), for example, could be paraphrased as "I say frankly that she would never be caught dead in an SUV."
   Examples of epistemic and evaluative adverbs are given in (5):

(5) a. Epistemic:
         (i) modal: *probably, certainly, possibly, maybe, definitely, necessarily, perhaps*
         (ii) evidential: *obviously, clearly, evidently, allegedly*
     b. Evaluative: *(un)fortunately, mysteriously, tragically, appropriately, significantly*

This group (usually along with discourse-oriented adverbs) constitutes the speaker-oriented class, defined as those making reference to the speaker's attitude toward the associated proposition. Epistemic adverbs are concerned with the truth of that proposition, either the degree to which the speaker subscribes to its truth (for the modal subclass), or how, or how easily, the proposition can be known (evidentials). Evaluatives express the speaker's evaluation of the proposition in context, in being fortunate, significant, mysterious, and so on. (2) shows their normal relative ordering (occasionally other orders are possible; see Ernst 2009), which is exemplified in (6):

(6) a. Albert unfortunately has probably/obviously bought defective batteries.
     b. *Albert probably/obviously has unfortunately bought defective batteries.

All of these speaker-oriented adverbs must precede subject-oriented adverbs (see (7)):

(7) a. Marcia {luckily/definitely/clearly} will wisely open all the packages with extreme
         care.
     b. *Marcia wisely will {luckily/definitely/clearly} open all the packages with extreme
         care.

Subject-oriented adverbs indicate either the speaker's evaluation of some quality of the subject referent (s/he is brave, wise, clever, stupid, and so on: the agent-oriented subclass), or describe the subject's mental attitude (the mental-attitude subclass):

(8) Subject-oriented adverbs
     a. Agent-oriented: *wisely, intelligently, bravely, stupidly, …*
     b. Mental-attitude: *calmly, willingly, enthusiastically, …*

Agent-oriented adverbs can only be used felicitously when the subject has some sort of control over her/his participation in the event or state, in the sense that s/he could choose not to do it. In (9), for example, there is necessarily the sense that the fugitive could have avoided falling:

(9) The fugitive cleverly fell five stories.

As noted, subject-oriented adverbs always follow speaker-oriented adverbs. Normally they precede negation (see (10)), but in marked contexts they may follow (as in (11)):

(10) a. The winners of the competition {cleverly, bravely, stupidly} didn't use ropes.
      b. *The winners of the competition didn't {cleverly, bravely, stupidly} use ropes.

(11) From year to year, the winners didn't (always) {cleverly, bravely, stupidly} use ropes.

Crucially, although the adverbs in (11) may have a manner reading, they also can be clausal, as shown by the possibility of paraphrases (e.g. "It is not the case that the winners always were clever to use ropes").

Exocomparative adverbs include *accordingly*, *similarly*, *differently*, and *alternatively*; they refer to some sort of matching or contrast between propositions, events, or manners, as illustrated in (12a–c), respectively:

(12) a. Fred bought a red Maserati at age 40. Similarly, Janice bought purple shoes after she got divorced.
      b. The corporation is now accordingly insisting on following the letter of the law.
      c. I normally see things differently from my brother.

Exocomparatives have somewhat more freedom of position than other predicational adverbs, as (13) exemplifies (excluding manner readings):

(13) (Similarly,) some applicants (similarly) must (similarly) have been (similarly) providing counsel.

All of the clausal adverbs described above modify either a proposition or an eventuality "unrestrictively" – in effect, taking that entity as an argument of predicates such as PROBABLE, FORTUNATE, WISE, and so on. By contrast, manner adverbs are restrictive, picking out a subset of eventualities represented by the verb. So, in (14a), for example, *loudly* circumscribes just the events of playing music at a higher decibel level than normal:

(14) a. This orchestra plays even the soft sections loudly.
      b. The committee arranged all of our affairs appropriately.
      c. She faced her fears bravely.

Many manner adverbs have homonyms among clausal adverbs: discourse-oriented adverbs (*honestly*, *frankly*), evaluatives and evidentials (*oddly*, *clearly*), and all agent-oriented adverbs (*cleverly*, *politely*).[4] As noted earlier, all adverbs with manner readings follow all clausal adverbs:

(15) a. Karen {unfortunately/stupidly/obviously} tightly gripped the knife in her wrong hand.
      b. *Karen tightly {unfortunately/stupidly/obviously} gripped the knife in her wrong hand.

Thomas Ernst

There are two types of verb-oriented adverbs that are sometimes lumped in with manner adverbs and sometimes taken as separate: result adverbs (as in 16a) and method adverbs (16b), which are homophonous with domain adverbs:

(16) a. The peasants loaded the cart heavily.
     b. The assistant analyzed the sediments chemically.

In SVO languages such as English, among the predicationals only manner adverbs may occur postverbally (though they may also occur in an immediately preverbal position):

(17) a. Karen {unfortunately/stupidly/obviously/tightly} gripped the knife.
     b. *Karen gripped the knife {unfortunately/stupidly/obviously}.
     c. Karen gripped the knife tightly.

2.2 Participant-oriented PPs (PPPs)

Participant PPs (PPPs) are those like *on the mantlepiece, with a blowgun, for his favorite cat*, or *from the cellar*, which serve to introduce an extra entity – usually a participant – relating to the event: a location, an instrument, a beneficiary, or the like.[5] They tend to be positioned where the unmarked manner-adverb position is, so that in English and similar languages they occur after the verb and any argument(s):

(18) Maria will (*with a rake) prop open the door (with a rake).

When several PPPs co-occur they generally may occur in any order, though there may be differences of emphasis; three of the possible six orders for three PPs are shown in (19).

(19) a. The celebrants raised a flag with a rope on the hill for the soldiers' honor.
     b. The celebrants raised a flag on the hill with a rope for the soldiers' honor.
     c. The celebrants raised a flag on the hill for the soldiers' honor with a rope.

2.3 Functional adverbials

At the core of the diverse group of functional adverbials are the notions of time, quantity, and information structure, though other functional notions may be expressed as well, and there may be overlaps among these categories. Time-related adverbials include point-time expressions (many of them DPs or PPs) such as *now, yesterday, on a Friday*, or *next week*, relative-time adverbials such as *previously* and *afterwards*, aspectual adverbs such as *already* and *still*, and duration expressions such as *for five minutes*. To some extent, their positioning depends on whether they are "lighter" (adverbs) or "heavier" (DPs/PPs), with both groups allowed after the verb in SVO languages, but only the former also showing up easily before the verb:

(20) a. She has bought bagels {now/previously/already/on a Friday/today}.
     b. She has {now/previously/already/*on a Friday/*today} bought bagels.

Some time-related adverbs may have different positions in a sentence, corresponding to different scopes:

112

(21) a. (Previously,) she cleverly had (previously) prepared a sumptuous meal.
   b. We (already) are almost certainly (already) out of contention for the prize.
   c. (For a year,) George has not been home (for a year).

Quantity-related adverbs include frequency, iterative, habitual, and degree/intensifier adverbs, illustrated in (22a–d), respectively:

(22) a. My brother {always/sometimes/occasionally/rarely} can resist a new video game.
   b. Danny once again has failed to come home on time.
   c. Francine {generally/habitually} buys her coffee whole-bean.
   d. The committee {very much/really/so} appreciates what you've done.

Functional adverbs with a quantitative component also typically allow different scopes corresponding to different positions:

(23) a. Jay (often) doesn't (often) go out of his way to buy organic food.
   b. (Occasionally,) they willingly have (occasionally) been paying for catering help (occasionally).
   c. Kendra (again) must (again) close the door (again).

Though the distinctions are sometimes subtle, each distinct position of an adverbial in (23a–c) takes a different scope (see Ernst 2007 for discussion; for the special case of *again*, see Stechow 1996).

Degree/measure adverbs typically modify adjectives, other adverbs, or verbs; in the latter case, they pattern just like manner adverbs – that is, occurring either immediately before the verb or in postverbal positions close to the verb:

(24) a. The voters will (*slightly) be (slightly) leaning (slightly) toward conservative candidates (slightly).
   b. The judges (*partially) have (partially) reversed their decision (partially).

Adverbs related to information structure include at least the focusing and discourse-oriented types. The former, such as *even* and *only*, allow focusing on one constituent within their c-command domain, often picked out with prosodic emphasis. Thus in (25) any of *buys*, *sushi*, or *restaurants* may be stressed:

(25) Maggie only buys sushi at restaurants.

They also have other attachment options aside from the usual VP (or predicate) and IP (or sentence) points; they standardly also occur at the edge of DPs, PPs, APs, and so on:

(26) a. Only members are admitted.
   b. They buy newspapers only on Sundays.
   c. She could have been even quieter than she was.
   d. Sam has even tried to find water with a dowsing rod.

In (26a), the subject constituent is *only members*, as shown by a number of standard constituency tests; in (26b) *only on Sundays* is a constituent, and similarly in (26c–d) (see Ernst 2002: 218ff. for discussion).

Discourse adverbs include the examples such as *frankly* and *honestly* discussed above, but also more functional items such as *however, yet/still* (on one of their uses), and *thus/ therefore*:

(27) a. Marie is tired; {yet/still,} she will persevere.
      b. George has thus failed in his main task.

I leave aside a grab-bag of other, less prominent functional adverbs, such as the emphatic *so* and the exocomparative *otherwise* in (28):

(28) a. She did **so** study Uzbek!
      b. Otherwise, we have no incentive to invest.

2.4   Domain

Domain expressions invoke a real-life domain of endeavor, knowledge, or the like, and can be PPs or adverbs:

(29) a. This company has been declining, {reputation-wise/in terms of its reputation}.
      b. Wilma is very strong physically.
      c. Economically, their proposal is doomed to fail.

Although they share having a content-adjective base with predicational adverbs, they differ in not being gradable (compare (29c) with (30)) and they have considerably more distributional freedom (compare (31) with the predicational examples above):

(30) *Very economically, their proposal is doomed to fail.

(31) (Physically,) she (physically) might (?physically) have (?physically) been (physically) strong (physically).

Domain adverbs are somewhat unusual also in being able to occur within DPs in English such as the bracketed one in (32):

(32) [The major influence on prices globally at the moment] is oversupply.

2.5   Some generalizations

Aside from the basic distributions of single adverbs and PPPs which were given above, one can make several generalizations about adverb behavior overall. The first generalization concerns what have been called *concentric phenomena*: that is, those where there is some sort of hierarchy extending progressively away from the verb (possibly its base position) in both directions. Thus, for scope, the further an adverbial is from the main verb – whether to its left or to its right – the wider scope it has. This is easiest to illustrate for preverbal modifiers (since clausal predicational adverbs are restricted postverbally and multiple scope-taking adverbs are sometimes disfavored) as in (33), but it can still be shown for postverbal modifiers (see (34)):

(33) Amazingly, George has probably also willingly been gently retired from his position.

(34) Gina is eating muffins often again quite willingly.

(In (34), imagine someone who had mostly avoided muffins for a while, but now is very happy to go back to eating them frequently.) In (33), the proposition-modifying *amazingly* takes scope over *probably*, and both take wide scope over the event-modifier *willingly* and the manner adverb *gently*; this represents normal scope relationships among propositions, events, and manners. In (34), *quite willingly* has scope over *again*, which has scope over *often*. In a similar way, constituent structure is concentric, as shown by ellipses and pro-forms. Thus for a sentence such as (34), the interpretation of *do so* in (35) shows a concentric layering of constituents:

(35) a. ..., but Emilio is doing so very reluctantly.   (*doing so* = eating muffins often again)
     b. ..., but Emilio is doing so for the first time.   (*doing so* = eating muffins often)
     c. ..., but Emilio is doing so occasionally.   (*doing so* = eating muffins)

A second generalization covers the broadest patterns of word order according to adverb classes: among predicational adverbs, the discourse adverbs come first, then speaker-oriented adverbs, subject-oriented adverbs, and verb-oriented adverbs in that order (as in (2), where "manner" is verb-oriented); functional adverbs also line up in a parallel way, with sentence-modifiers high in the clause, event-modifiers lower down (closer to the verb). Semantically, this corresponds at least roughly to modification of propositions, (nonrestrictive) modification of (whole) events, and (restrictive) modification of events ("processes" or "specified events"): that is, Manner as given in (36):

(36) PROPOSITION > EVENT > MANNER

Thus there is wide recognition that adverbials can be grouped into "zones" or "fields", the most basic distinction being clausal (or sentential) vs. verb-modifying, but with further differences usually included. (37) shows how a number of proposals have referred to these zones, with (very rough) indications of commonly assumed attachment points in clausal structure:

(37)

	CP	IP	*v*P?	VP
a. Jackendoff (1972)	— Speaker-Oriented —		Sbj-Oriented	Manner
b. Quirk *et al.* (1972)	Conjunct	— Disjunct —		Process Adjunct
c. McConnell-Ginet (1982)	— Ad-S —		Ad-VP	Ad-V
d. Frey and Pittner (1999)	Frame	Proposition	Event	Process
e. Ernst (2002)	Speech-Act	Proposition	Event	Specified Event

The third generalization concerns predicational adverbs, which in English and other languages display the ambiguity between clausal and manner readings (with some subtypes excepted) noted above:

(38) a. {Clearly/oddly/cleverly}, she answered the questions.
     b. She answered the questions {clearly/oddly/cleverly}.

While (38a) would be paraphrased with *It is clear/odd that...* or *She is clever to...*, indicating clausal readings, (38b) represent manner readings (*She answered in a clear/odd/clever manner*). This ambiguity shows up systematically in English and French, but less so in many languages. Some may use different morphological markings for the two readings, at least in some cases (as in German); others typically employ an adverbial for manner readings, but encode (most) equivalents of (25a) as a predicate taking a sentential complement, equivalent to (e.g.) *It is clear that S*.

Fourth, there are cross-linguistic word order generalizations to account for: VO languages typically allow adverbials on either side of the verb, while OV languages tend strongly to restrict them to preverbal positions (see Ernst 2002 and 2003 for further data and discussion):

(39) a. Elle a certainement préparé des plats pareils fréquemment l'année dernière.
      she has certainly   prepared some dishes similar frequently   the year last
      "She certainly prepared such dishes frequently last year."   (French)

   b. Mi wnaeth o yfed cwrw am awr ar bwrpas.
      art did   drink beer for hour on purpose
      "He drank beer for an hour on purpose."   (Welsh)

(40) a. (Kanojo-wa) tokidoki   mizukara lunch-o   nuita   (*tokidoki/*mizukara).
      she-TOP   occasionally willingly lunch-ACC skip.PAST
      "She has occasionally willingly given up her lunch hour."   (Japanese)

   b. Raam-ne zaruur   vah kitaab dhyaan se paRhii   thii (*zaruur/*dhyaan se).
      Ram$_{ERG}$ certainly that book care   with read$_{PERF-fem}$ be$_{PST-fem}$
      "Ram certainly read that book carefully."   (Hindi)

Fifth, adverbs partake of the usual preposing processes for focused or topicalized elements, yet with certain restrictions. (41) shows that adverbs with non-initial presumed base positions can be sentence-initial with pauses – including the manner adverb *clumsily* – and this is widely assumed to be a result of movement:

(41) {Wisely/Clumsily/Willingly}, she answered the questions.

However, manner adverbs cannot be topicalized over elements such as modals or other adverbs, as shown in (42):

(42) a. *Clumsily, she might answer the questions.
   b. *Clumsily, she obviously answered the questions.

Other types of adverbs have slightly different restrictions, or can be preposed over intervening elements via other types of processes, such as *wh*-movement and focalization in (43) (see Li *et al.* 2012):

(43) a. How skillfully would Albert presumably mow his lawn?
   b. Albert just mowed the lawn quietly.
      No, NOISILY Albert just mowed the lawn.

3   Two main approaches

3.1   Cartographic theories

In current Principles-and-Parameters (P&P) theorizing there are two main approaches to the syntax of adverbials, with a focus on adverbs. The first, advanced primarily by Cinque (1999), puts all adverbs in Spec positions, licensed by a semantically appropriate head (which is often phonologically empty), in a rigid sequence of heads mandated by UG. Each head licenses one and only one semantic type of adverb. The great advantage of (and motivation for) this is that many sequences of adverbs are in fact rigidly ordered, cross-linguistically. Thus the obligatory ordering represented in (2), part of which is represented by (44a), is predicted because UG requires a universal set of functional heads including the partial sequence in (44b); each of the heads licenses one of the adverbs in its Spec position:

(44) a. Fortunately, Carol probably has wisely not spoken openly about her problems.
      b. Eval - Epist - SubjOr - Neg - Man

Since there are fine gradations in ordering, and each distinct adverb type must have its own unique licenser, Cinque (1999: 106) proposes a large number of heads, a subset of which is given in (45), with the adverbs they license:

(45) ...Mood$_{Sp.Act}$ - Mood$_{Eval}$ - Mood$_{Evid}$ - Mood$_{Epist}$ - T(Past) - T(Future) -...
      frankly   fortunately allegedly probably once   then

      Asp$_{Repetitive(I)}$ - Asp$_{Frequentative (I)}$ - Mod$_{Volitional}$ - Asp$_{Celerative(I)}$ - T(Anterior) -...
      again   often   intentionally quickly   already

Since other syntactic elements, such as auxiliary verbs, are also rigidly ordered, this theory predicts rigid ordering among adverbs and these elements as well in base structure.

In order to account for alternate surface orders, the cartographic approach adopts (at least) three kinds of movement. One is shared with other current approaches: preposing of adverbs to clause-initial positions, as illustrated earlier; this is relatively uncontroversial, and goes along with the assumption – also widely shared among theoretical approaches – that movement of adverbs themselves can only be topicalization, focalization, and other general, pragmatically based processes. The second is head movement, which, although shared with other theories, is deployed more extensively in the cartographic approach. Thus, while simple movements as in (46) are well established in the P&P literature (especially since *could* takes narrow scope with respect to *obviously not*, and so needs to be interpreted in its base position, indicated by *t*), a sentence such as (47) seems to require multiple and longer-distance movements:

(46) Esther could$_i$ obviously not t$_i$ have meant what she said.

(47) Paulette will have been wisely getting involved in other pursuits.

Given the logic of the cartographic theory, for (47) *wisely* must have a base position above the modal *will* (Ernst 2002: 117ff.) on the grounds of sentences such as (48):

(48) Paulette wisely will have been getting involved in other pursuits.

Therefore, all three of the auxiliaries *could*, *have*, and *be* must successively raise over the adverb via head movement.

The third type of movement is somewhat more complex, since cartographic theories subscribe to some version of the Linear Correspondence Axiom (LCA: Kayne 1994), by which all structure "goes down to the right" – that is, there is no right-adjunction, since precedence (X before Y) requires c-command (X c-commands Y). This restriction has two implications for sentences like (34) in cartographic theories of adverbs. First, on the most common analysis, the base order of the adverbs must be the reverse of what is seen in (34) (i.e. *willingly > again > often*), given the relative scope and the cross-linguistic generalizations justified on the basis of (the more common) preverbal orders. Second, as a result of this base order, some sort of "roll-up" (also known as "intraposition" or "snowballing") movements must derive the correct surface order along with the correct constituent structure, which in this case has *eats muffins often* as the lowest phrase, then *eats muffins often again*, then the whole VP (see Cinque 2004 for a representative analysis). Typically, the cartographic analysis therefore takes the base order to be that in (49) (where the categorial labels are irrelevant to the immediate problem, and subjects are omitted for convenience):

(49)

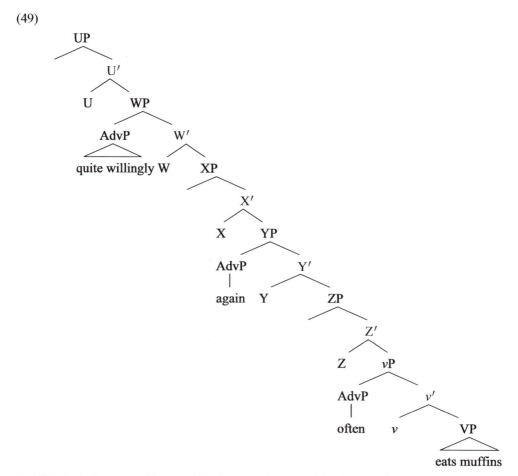

In (49), the VP *eats muffins* would raise to a Spec position in ZP (licensed by an empty functional head Z); the resulting *eats muffins often* would similarly raise to Spec,XP, and the resulting *eats muffins often again* would then raise to Spec,UP in a similar manner to derive (34).

It is clear from Cinque (1999) and subsequent literature that the approach just described is standard for postverbal adverbs. The proper analysis of PPPs is somewhat less clear, given their rather different semantics, the fact that typically they are normally postverbal in SVO languages, and their relatively free ordering. One solution is to treat PPPs like adverbs by licensing them via ordered functional heads associated with specific adverbial meanings (Cinque 2004; Schweikert 2005). On this analysis there are subsequent roll-up movements, though these must occur more freely than in the case of adverbs, so as to account for the greater flexibility in possible surface orders. A second solution (Haumann 2007: 89, 143, 148) would be to place each PP within one of a succession of descending postverbal VPs in the correct surface order, thus requiring no movements, but licensing them with respect to a sequence of preverbal *pro*'s representing the normal hierarchical scope relationships. For example, for a postverbal sequence of locative, instrumental, and benefactive PPs, each PP would be placed within one postverbal VP in (49′); in the upper part of the clause, a *pro* in the specifier position of semantically active Locative, Instrumental, and Benefactive heads would license the PP in the lower part of the clause:

(49′) ... Loc - Inst - Ben - ... - V - VP - VP - VP

Cartographic theories of adverbs have certain theoretical and empirical advantages. First of all, they directly account for the large number of cases of rigid ordering between two or more adverbs. Second, at least for the approach to PPPs described above (assuming the LCA), it is possible to handle a number of effects that depend on c-command. In particular, this theory can account for the so-called "Barss–Lasnik effects" such as NPI licensing, anaphor binding, and variable binding (Barss and Lasnik 1986). In (50a–b), for example, if the first PP c-commands the second PP, with some sort of "shell" projection after the verb hosting the PPs (or two projections, each of which hosts one PP), then the negative polarity item *any* and bound-variable pronoun *his* are properly licensed:[6]

(50) a. Frederika reads novels on no weekday with any electronic device.
      b. They performed the chant in honor of every soldier on his birthday.

On the other hand, there are a number of problems with the cartographic adverb theory. First, by positing a UG-mandated sequence of functional heads to license specific semantic notions, it seems to miss certain generalizations. One of these is that it has nothing to predict the several well-defined "zones" of adverbs; for example, the sequence in Cinque (1999) has most modal heads preceding aspectual heads, and both of these preceding the heads that license manner and degree adverbs, yet this is not derived from anything more fundamental, and so might be expected to line up in a different way. Also, for adverbs that allow alternate positions fairly easily, such as *often* or *politically* (see (23a), (31)), the theory is forced to posit as many different functional heads. Where these positions have different readings, as for *often*, the cartographic theory can and must posit distinct heads that in effect encode different scopes; however, since this must be done separately for each adverb subclass, simple generalizations are missed about scope behavior that should fall out from the normal interpretation of quantification. Thus the theory implicitly claims that very general scope differences are individual lexical matters. Where there is no difference in meaning, as is common for frequency and domain adverbs, this approach must either relax its principle that every adverb-licensing head must have a different meaning, or else resort to movement (though this option is not always plausible; see Ernst 2007 for discussion). Similarly, in the cartographic approach the fact that PPPs are fairly free in their surface order is not (pending a fuller analysis) derived from any semantic fact underlying their licensing, yet could easily be related to the fact that they do not take scope in any obvious way, while more rigidly ordered adverbs do (Ernst 2002: Ch. 7).

A second set of problems centers on roll-up movements. As pointed out by Bobaljik (2002), Ernst (2002), and others, it is not clear that they can derive the required structures without a great loss of restrictiveness. For one thing, the movements must be triggered by arbitrary features on empty functional heads having no purpose other than to provide landing sites (U, X, and Z in (49), for example); unlike well-known A'-movements such as *wh*-movement or topicalization, the movements have no clear functional correlate. Moreover, roll-up movements (i) complicate anaphor-licensing and scope relationships, such that these phenomena often must be "locked in" at base structure or some intermediate stage of a derivation (see, e.g. Cinque 2004; Hinterhölzl 2009), requiring further stipulations;[7] and (ii) may complicate a principled account of extraction, since the rolled-up constituents, by moving into Spec positions, ought to become opaque to extraction, yet are not (Haider 2004).

3.2 Scopal theories

The major alternative to the cartographic approach to adverbs is known as the scopal (or "adjunction", or "semantically-based adjunction") theory. Its core idea is that adverbials are generally adjoined in phrase structure (with possibly a few exceptional cases, such as negative adverbs like *not* in Spec positions), and that otherwise their distribution is accounted for by semantic and "morphological" principles. Thus adverbials of all types may adjoin freely as far as syntax is concerned, with the scope (or semantic selectional) requirements and "weight" of a given adverbial modifier accounting for its possible positions.

Though right-adjunction is not a core property of scopal theories, it fits easily in the theory and is common in scopal analyses. Thus, in contrast to (49) above, a possible traditional, right-adjunction analysis of (34) is shown in (51) (omitting the subject *Gina* and assuming verb movement to *v*):

(51)

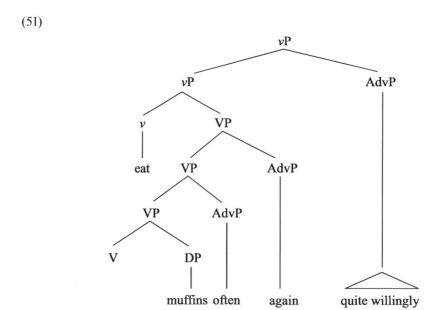

Whatever constraints apply to the syntax-semantics mapping ought to be very general, such as one that requires all event-modifiers (such as *cleverly*) to combine with predicates before all proposition-modifiers (such as *luckily*), as part of some larger principle establishing the well-recognized "zones" of adverbial modification. Haider (2000) proposes the three-level mapping in (52a), while Ernst (2002) makes further distinctions as in (51b), his "FEO Calculus" (though Ernst (2009) suggests that something closer to (52a) may be right, with FACT eliminated):

(52) a. PROPOSITION > EVENT > PROCESS
     b. SPEECH ACT > FACT > PROPOSITION > EVENT > SPECIFIED EVENT

The idea behind (52) is that all verb-oriented modifiers (= "process" or "specified event") must combine with verbs before moving on to any subject-oriented or other event-modifiers, and that only when this stage is finished are propositional modifiers possible. This accounts for many cases of rigid ordering by establishing zones of different adverb types, yet allows for alternative ordering, at least in principle, for two adverbs that may occur in the same zone (e.g. *willingly* and *occasionally* in (23b)). While there are some problems and exceptions, and no further formalization as yet, something along the lines of (52) is accepted within the scopal theory.

The relevant "morphological" (PF) principles are also very general, involving factors such as prosody and length. One such principle, presumably, is some version of the idea that heavier elements are more peripheral – thus more likely to go to the right when after the verb in head-initial languages, for example – than lighter elements. For cases of reorderable postverbal elements, there is therefore some freedom, but also a tendency for the heaviest constituents to go to the right; (53) shows perhaps the most comfortable orders of two sentences where the three adverbials have the same semantic function in each case, but reversed linear order:

(53) a. We left yesterday in my brother's car as quickly as we could gather our things.
     b. We left quickly in my brother's car on a day when we were finally able to get out of town.

Some scopal analyses also use weight considerations to account for restrictions like those in (54), where "light" adverbs are often barred from peripheral positions in a clause, and "heavy" ones are disfavored between the subject and the verb:

(54) a. (*Even) Cal Tech (even) won a basketball game.
     b. Sally has always (*on Saturday) rested (on Saturday).

In (54), *even* is to be taken as taking scope over the whole sentence, expressing that Cal Tech's victory was the oddest thing that could have happened, for example, in the news of the year; see Anderson (1972) for discussion. While details of a Weight Theory are not well worked out, scopal theories tend to take adverbial distribution as responding to these morphological/PF principles as well as semantic ones (see Ernst 2002; Haider 2004; Kiss 2009 for some discussion).

Perhaps the only important purely syntactic mechanism that specifically mentions adverbials would be an extension of the head-direction parameter to adjuncts. One such account (Ernst 2002; 2003) allows adverbials in either direction in which a complement or specifier is allowed, thus predicting that adverbials are uniformly preverbal in base structure in OV languages, but may be on either side of the verb in VO languages. Another, in Haider (2004), treats all adverbials as preverbal in narrow syntax, but allows some postposing in VO languages in the PF component. Other syntactic mechanisms may affect adverbs but only as part of a general process – for example, head movement in simple cases such as (46) or preposing (as in (41)) as part of A'-movement for discourse purposes. Finally, most versions of the scopal theories allow right adjunction, so that the word order, concentric scope, and concentric constituency of sentences such as (33–34) are accounted for directly in base structure, without movements. As noted, limited rightward movement is often allowed as well, which permits noncanonical orders of adverbials, or (as for Haider) normal word orders in VO languages.

Possibly the most important advantage of scopal theories is in being able to capture many generalizations about adverbials' distribution directly from their semantic properties, without movements, associated extra projections and features, or stipulated exceptions to general principles governing movement. Two examples will illustrate this point with respect to rigid orderings of adverbs. Speaker-oriented adverbs such as *unfortunately* and *possibly* are positive polarity items, as shown in Nilsen (2004). As a result, they normally must precede negation, as (55a) demonstrates; however, the fact that they may follow negation in special cases where independent evidence shows the polarity semantics to be suspended, as in the rhetorical question in (55b), shows that this ordering is a semantic matter, not a syntactic one (Ernst 2009):

(55) a. Marcia (probably) hasn't (*probably) bought that new house she had her eye on.
      b. Hasn't Marcia probably bought that new house she had her eye on (by now)?

(56) (Honestly,) they unfortunately have (*honestly) gotten a raw deal.

In a similar way, the fact that discourse-oriented adverbs such as *honestly* and *frankly* must precede evaluative and epistemic adverbs, as in (56), falls out if the former type modifies an utterance in some sense – perhaps realized via some speech-act operator or covert verb SAY – and the latter types modify a proposition. If we assume some general constraint requiring propositions to be "inside utterances", and a mapping to structure such that propositional modifiers are "inside" and thus structurally lower than those associated with utterances (however this is to be captured), the pattern shown in (56) is accounted for.

The scopal theory treats the difference between rigid and more flexible orderings in the same, mostly semantic way: by saying that alternative orderings result when there are no relevant violations of scope constraints, selectional requirements, or other semantic effects, as there were in (55–56). For example, adverbs shown in (23a–c) have no requirements violated in these sentences, either by the presence of the others or by more general considerations, although different positions induce different readings for the sentences. The same dynamic also predicts why PPPs and domain adverbs generally allow alternative orders freely, while predicational and (to a lesser extent) functional adverbs are more restricted. It is commonly assumed that PPPs take an event argument in a NeoDavidsonian representation such as (57) (for the VP in (19)); the three adjunct PPs can be placed in any order because they do not interact semantically, and so no order causes problems for the semantic representation.

(57) ∃e [Raise (e) & Agt (e, celebrants) & Theme (e, flag) & Inst (e, rope) & Loc (e, hill) & Ben(e, honor)]

Predicational adverbs, on the other hand, most often do create such problems, such as when an event-taking adverb tries to occur above a proposition-taking adverb, when a positive polarity item's requirements are not met, or the like, as noted above.[8]

Finally, scopal theories that countenance right adjunction handle constituency facts in a straightforward (and traditional) manner. Returning to (34), standard constituency tests such as VP proforms (in (35)) reveal concentric constituents, and right adjunction predicts this directly, given a structure like (51).

(34) Gina is eating muffins often again quite willingly.

(35) a. ..., but Emilio is doing so very reluctantly.   (*doing so* = eating muffins often again)
   b. ..., but Emilio is doing so for the first time.   (*doing so* = eating muffins often)
   c. ..., but Emilio is doing so occasionally.   (*doing so* = eating muffins)

The layered VP constituent structure that allows these three *do so* substitutions is the regular base structure for right-adjoined adverbs, so no movement or extra stipulations are necessary.

None of this is to say that the scopal theory is without blemish. Perhaps the most important problem is that many of the relevant semantic selectional and/or scope specifications needed to induce rigid ordering have not been worked out in detail. While studies have shown clear semantic motivations in some cases, other effects, such as why subject-oriented adverbs precede negation in unmarked contexts (as in (11)), are less clear. Nor (as noted earlier) is there a precise account of why the major adverbial "zones" – especially the clausal/propositional versus the verb-oriented/eventive – are derived beyond (52), even if everyone agrees that there is some intuitive sense to (52), on iconic grounds. Second, while allowing right-adjunction accounts directly for word orders, concentric scope relationships, and constituency facts, it also requires weakening the classic structural conditions for Barss–Lasnik effects, probably by means of some loosened formulation of c-command plus precedence (see Barss and Lasnik 1986; Jackendoff 1990; Ernst 1994). This is necessary for sentences such as (50a–b) since, if the first PP is structurally lower than the second one, the wrong predictions are made with traditional c-command (assuming, at any rate, that the latter is at least loosened to allow c-command out of PPs).

A third difficulty is a grab-bag of linear order restrictions (which in fact neither major theory can handle in a principled way). Among these are a ban in some languages on adverbs between subjects and finite verbs (see (58)), restrictions on some adverbs that "should" on semantic grounds appear in a given position but do not (such as *well* in (59)), and the general ban on postverbal clausal predicationals (as in (60)):

(58)   Jean (*apparemment)   veut   (apparemment) démissionner.   (French)
       John apparently   want apparently   resign
       "John apparently wants to resign."

(59) Karen can (*well) play chess (well).

(60) (Luckily), the game (luckily) will (luckily) be rescheduled (*luckily).

Currently, there does not seem to be strong consensus in the field of formal linguistics as a whole as to which of the two theories, cartographic or scopal, is to be preferred. In practice, of course, the former is assumed in cartographically oriented syntactic works; the latter seems preferred in research with a semantic orientation. Perhaps the best summation is the following. The cartographic theory offers more precision at present, since each micro-class of adverbs can be located in a specific position with respect to any other element, and movements necessary to derive surface order can all be specified as well; on the other hand, it seems to miss many broad generalizations and, in its present form is rather unconstrained, since it has few accepted limits on movement triggers, numbers of duplicate nodes, exceptions to well-known constraints, and the like. The scopal theory is less precise, in particular lacking developed analyses for many cases of rigid ordering among adverbs; by contrast, it offers the chance to derive a number of generalizations about adverbials from independently needed semantics, and to construct a more highly constrained theory – the final verdict depending on how each answers the many questions raised above. (For further comparison of these two approaches, see Ernst (2002) and Haumann (2007).)

4   Theoretical issues

4.1   How direct is the semantic basis for adverb distribution?

The sketch of the two major theories above reveals perhaps the most important underlying difference between them. On the one hand, they agree that adverbial syntax is determined in an important way by the semantics of individual adverbial modifiers. On the other, they differ in their visions of how syntax and semantics are related in the case of adverbials. The scopal theory takes the relationship as very direct, and holds that given that, in general, adverbials adjoin freely to phrase structure and that scope is represented by c-command, then the basics of adverbial distribution and ordering can be accounted with only a few, and relatively minor, additional syntactic mechanisms, once the scopal/selectional requirements are properly understood. The cartographic theory is based on the idea that the semantic input to syntax is more indirect than this, and must be realized as a set of ordered functional heads to license adverb micro-classes. Once the sequence is adopted, the theory then requires a number of head movements and roll-up movements to account for linear orders, which increases the role of syntax.

4.2   Pesetsky's Paradox

Perhaps the thorniest issue is *Pesetsky's Paradox* (after Pesetsky 1995), centering on the proper treatment of multiple postverbal adverbials in SVO languages. There is a tension between scope and constituency tests, which support the traditional right-adjoined phrase structure (each additional rightward adverbial being adjoined higher in the tree), and tests involving the Barss–Lasnik effects, which support a "down to the right" structure for adverbials, each rightward element being situated in the Spec position of (or possibly adjoined to) a successively lower projection, the complement of the head of the previous one. Thus for the VP in (34) the scopal theory would posit (51), while the cartographic theory usually posits either (49) or (61) (where category labels are again irrelevant):

(61)

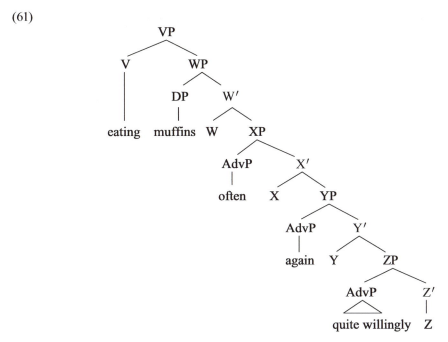

Neither approach seems to have a very satisfying solution for the problems they face. The cartographic theories require either additional roll-up movements for (49) to derive the correct surface order (with the attendant problems noted earlier), or, for (61), some additional mechanism to account for scope relations, for which this structure makes the exactly wrong prediction (given a simple c-command condition on scope). Scopal theories with right-adjunction, where they address the problem at all, advocate weakening the c-command condition on Barss–Lasnik effects.

4.3 Word order typology

Little has been written about the major cross-linguistic word order patterns of adverbs in terms of head-initial and head-final languages, aside from a few mentions in the functional-typological literature. However, there is one fairly strong generalization: as noted above for (39–40), head-final languages tend to disallow or strongly disfavor postverbal positions (aside from afterthoughts, as usual), while head-initial languages normally allow them on either side of the verb. There are at least three approaches to this generalization in the current literature, not mutually exclusive: (a) an extension of traditional left-right parameterization to adjuncts, (b) verb-raising, and (c) phrasal movements, either roll-ups or extrapositions. The first of these can say that the head-initial parameter value implies nothing for adjuncts (allowing free ordering, left or right of a head in principle), but that head-finality applies additionally to adverbials as well as to complements (Ernst 2003). A scopal theory with adjunction, as is traditional, can also use a mix of verb- and phrasal-movement, as in Haider (2004), who posits traditional head-direction parameterization for complements, but with all adjunct base positions on left branches (some of these may be within "shell" constituents below V). For postverbal adverbials in VO languages, he then posits a combination of verb-raising (leaving some adverbial base positions to the right of the verb) and extrapositions of adverbials.

Cartographic approaches have at least two options. If some base positions are to the right of (below) the verb in a basic SVO order, roll-up movements are employed to derive the proper order in SOV languages; this was sketched above in (49). Alternatively, if all adverbial positions are higher than the verb's base positions, then the verb will raise high enough to put some adverbials to its right. This option, similar to (61), is shown in (62) (where *eat* would raise to *v*):

(62)

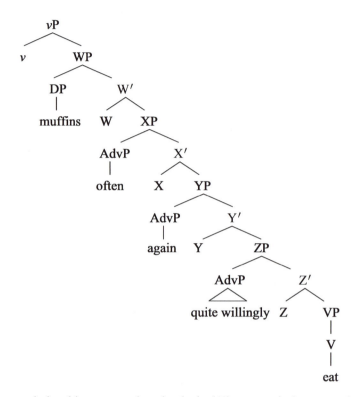

As in (61), the scope relationships among the adverbs in (62) are precisely reversed from the correct pattern, given normal assumptions about c-command as a condition on scope. Thus some further movements, focus-interpretation mechanisms (Larson 2004), special additional structures allowing reversed scope interpretation (Haumann 2007), or different assumptions about scope representation (Haider 2004; Phillips 2003) are necessary on this hypothesis.

4.4 Further issues

I have so far ignored several issues concerning adverbs that have had a high profile in P&P theory in the last few decades, but which have ended up being somewhat peripheral more recently. Still, they deserve a mention.

The first – a central one for government-binding theory – is that of argument-adjunct asymmetries. (63) illustrates that an object (*what*) can be moved out of a *wh*-island more easily than an adjunct (*how*), and (64) shows that extraction out of a complement clause is better than extraction out of an adjunct clause:

(63) a. ?What did they wonder how to fix?
    b. *How did they wonder what to fix?

(64) a. What did she think Tim bought?
     b. *What did she sleep after buying?

In classical GB theory (e.g. Chomsky 1986), the distinction in (63) is a matter of arguments being theta-marked – essentially, having the function of arguments – while adjuncts are not; that in (64) ultimately results from adjuncts being adjoined in structure, while arguments are not. In more recent Minimalist theory, things are somewhat less clear. (For discussion of the asymmetry in (64), see Truswell 2011 and references cited there.)

A second issue is that of adverbs used as diagnostics for VP structure, head positions, or the like, most classically in Pollock (1989), where adverbs such as *often* and its French equivalent *souvent* are assumed to mark the edge of VP in sentences such as (65a–b) (providing an argument for head movement):

(65) a. Patrick (often) sees (*often) his mother.
     b. Patrick (*souvent) voit (souvent) sa mère.
        Patrick (often) sees (often) his mother

Another well-known case, used to justify object shift in Scandinavian languages, likewise depends on taking adverbs as being at the left edge of VP (see Holmberg 1986). The point is little remarked upon, but after some twenty years of progress in adverb theorizing, the assumptions underlying these arguments can no longer be taken for granted (see also Thráinsson 2003). The possibility of multiple positions for adverbs such as these means that such tests can work only if the position is specifically determined (e.g., as at the edge of VP) by other factors in a given case. Moreover, given the explosion of functional categories – and, in the cartographic theory, the multiple heads for different occurrences and massive head movements – it is simply not clear what traditional constituent(s) can be determined by adverbs.

5 Conclusion

An initial burst of work on adverbs in formal syntax in the late 1960s and early 1970s led to a long period of perhaps twenty-five years when one read of adverbs almost exclusively in terms of the words *why* and *how*. But the last two decades have seen the development of the first coherent theories of adverbial distribution and have led both to useful descriptive discoveries and to a fruitful debate with implications for phrase structure theory, constraints on movement, issues of economy, and especially the proper balance of and relationship between syntax and semantics. One hopes that continued, if not more focused, investigation of these issues will answer some of the questions raised here and lead us to new data and deeper questions.

Notes

1 I leave aside several adverbials with somewhat more complex structure, mostly because they are less relevant to adverbs per se, including CP adverbials as in (i) and present participial adjuncts as in (ii); I also ignore depictives (as in (iii)).
   (i) Because she ordered supplies way in advance, she had less trouble running the meeting.
   (ii) They drove him crazy trying to fix that broken table.
   (iii) Adele always eats carrots raw.
2 Some languages use adjectives adverbially, at least some of the time; as one example, see the discussion of this in German in Schäfer (2005).

Thomas Ernst

3 I leave exocomparative adverbs such as *accordingly* out of (2), as their ordering is freer; see later in this section for discussion.
4 Some mental-attitude adverbs, such as *intentionally* and *unwillingly*, seem not to partake of this homonymy, or at least not in an obvious way. Some writers do not consider them to be manner adverbs even when they seem, intuitively, to be verb-modifiers, e.g. Maienborn and Schäfer (2011).
5 The traditional term *circumstantial* is similar but often (depending on the writer) does not include exactly the same items: the latter also may include time expressions like *(on) Tuesday*, and some writers also include manner PPs. We include point-time PPs in the following discussion since they often pattern with PPPs.
6 This assumes some mechanism to allow apparent c-command out of PPs; see Pesetsky (1995), Cinque (2004), and Hinterhölzl (2009) for proposals along these lines.
7 Sentences (i)–(ii) illustrate why it is necessary to find some way to constrain the points in a derivation at which licensing principles apply; we must generate (i) but exclude (ii):
    (i)   She wrapped no gift on any boy$_i$'s bed on his$_i$ birthday.
    (ii) *She wrapped his$_i$ gift on any boy's bed on no boy$_i$'s birthday.
Given a preverbal base order of Time – Locative – Theme, raising of these phrases, and subsequent remnant movements of what remains, both of these sentences can be derived. (ii) Appears to violate variable-binding and NPI licensing conditions, but the correct structural configuration for each type of licensing holds at some point of the derivation. One possibility, suggested by Guglielmo Cinque (personal communication) is that variable-binding and NPI licensing would be constrained by whether items are in Merge A-positions or derived A-positions. But since such analyses have not been worked out in detail, the exact nature of these stipulations remains unclear.
8 Predicational adverbs combine with events and propositions in a different way from PPPs; generally speaking, they represent event operators or propositional operators, which build up event-descriptions or proposition-descriptions in a "layered" manner. Thus, for example, in (i), PROB(ably) takes the proposition "She has resigned" and builds "Probably she has resigned"; then UNF(ortunately) builds the final proposition from that.
    (i)   She unfortunately has probably resigned.
    (ii) [UNF [PROB [she has resigned]]]
See Ernst (2002), Maienborn and Schäfer (2011) and references therein for discussion.

Further reading

The foundations of the two major approaches discussed here are Cinque (1999) for the cartographic approach and Ernst (2002) for the scopal approach. Both provide fairly detailed descriptions of the theories as well as copious data; as one might expect, Ernst delves more deeply into the semantics of adverb classes and how this underlies their syntax, while Cinque uses a wealth of cross-linguistic data to justify the detailed clausal sequence of adverbs. The references they give make a useful starting point for delving into more specific descriptions and theorizing.

Three anthologies provide a variety of articles that, taken together, constitute a good overview of the field in the early 2000s. The first two, Lang *et al.* (2003) and Austin *et al.* (2004), lay out a rich mix of articles on adverb syntax and semantics, touching on many auxiliary issues, such as the argument-adjunct distinction, event-based adverb semantics, and issues of left-right linear order. The last, a special issue of *Lingua* (No. 114, 2004), has more general, theoretically oriented works, including follow-up articles by Ernst and Cinque. All three of these have useful introductory overviews by the editors.

References

Alexiadou, Artemis. 1997. *Adverb Placement*. Amsterdam: John Benjamins.
Anderson, Stephen. 1972. How to Get Even. *Language* 48:893–906.
Austin, Jennifer R., Stefan Engelberg, and Gisa Rauh (eds). 2004. *Adverbials*. Amsterdam: John Benjamins.
Barss, Andrew, and Howard Lasnik. 1986. A Note on Anaphora and Double Objects. *Linguistic Inquiry* 17:347–354.

Bobaljik, Jonathan. 2002. A-Chains at the PF Interface: Copies and Covert Movement. *Natural Language and Linguistic Theory* 20:197–267.

Chomsky, Noam. 1986. *Barriers*. Cambridge, MA: MIT Press.

Cinque, Guglielmo. 1999. *Adverbs and Functional Heads: A Cross-Linguistic Perspective*. Oxford: Oxford University Press.

Cinque, Gugielmo. 2004. Issues in Adverbial Syntax. *Lingua* 114:683–710.

Ernst, Thomas. 1984. *Towards an Integrated Theory of Adverb Position in English*. Bloomington, IN: IULC.

Ernst, Thomas. 1994. M-Command and Precedence. *Linguistic Inquiry* 25:327–335.

Ernst, Thomas. 2002. *The Syntax of Adjuncts*. Cambridge: Cambridge University Press.

Ernst, Thomas. 2003. Adjuncts and Word Order Typology in East Asian Languages. In *Functional Structure(s), Form and Interpretation*, ed. Audrey Li and Andrew Simpson, 241–261. London: Routledge Curzon.

Ernst, Thomas. 2004. Principles of Adverbial Distribution in the Lower Clause. *Lingua* 114:755–777.

Ernst, Thomas. 2007. On the Role of Semantics in a Theory of Adverb Syntax. *Lingua* 117:1008–1033.

Ernst, Thomas. 2009. Speaker-Oriented Adverbs. *Natural Language and Linguistic Theory* 27:497–544.

Frey, Werner, and Karin Pittner. 1998. Zur Positionierung der Adverbiale im deutschen Mittelfeld (On the Positioning of Adverbials in the German Middle Field). *Linguistische Berichte* 176:489–534.

Frey, Werner, and Karin Pittner. 1999. Adverbialpositionen im Deutsch-Englischen Vergleich. In *Schprachspezifische Aspekte der Informationsverteilung*, ed. M. Doherty. Berlin.

Haider, Hubert. 1998. Adverbials at the Syntax-Semantics Interface. Ms. University of Salzburg.

Haider, Hubert. 2000. Adverb Placement – Convergence of Structure and Licensing. *Theoretical Linguistics* 26:95–134.

Haider, Hubert. 2004. Pre- and Postverbal Adverbials in OV and VO. *Lingua* 114:779–807.

Haumann, Dagmar. 2007. *Adverb Licensing and Clause Structure in English*. Amsterdam: Benjamins.

Hinterhölzl, Roland. 2009. A Phase-Based Comparative Approach to Modification and Word Order in Germanic. *Syntax* 12:242–284.

Holmberg, Anders. 1986. Word Order and Syntactic Features in the Scandinavian Languages and in English. University of Stockholm.

Jackendoff, Ray. 1972. *Semantic Interpretation in Generative Grammar*. Cambridge, MA: MIT Press.

Jackendoff, Ray. 1990. On Larson's Treatment of the Double Object Construction. *Linguistic Inquiry* 21:427–456.

Kayne, Richard. 1994. *The Antisymmetry of Syntax*. Cambridge, MA: MIT Press.

Kiss, Katalin, É. 2009. Syntactic, Semantic, and Prosodic Factors Determining the Position of Adverbial Adjuncts. In *Adverbs and Adverbial Adjuncts at the Interfaces*, ed. Katalin É. Kiss, 21–8. Berlin: Mouton de Gruyter.

Laenzlinger, Christopher. 2004. A Feature-Based Theory of Adverb Syntax. In *Adverbials: The Interplay Between Meaning, Context, and Syntactic Structure*, ed. Jennifer R. Austin, Stefan Engelberg, and Gisa Rauh, 205–252. Amsterdam: John Benjamins.

Lang, Ewald, Claudia Maienborn, and Cathrine Fabricius-Hansen (eds). 2003. *Modifying Adjuncts*. Berlin: Mouton de Gruyter.

Larson, Richard. 2004. Sentence-Final Adverbs and "Scope". In *Proceedings of NELS 34*, ed. Matthew Wolf and Keir Moulton, 23–43. Amherst, MA: GLSA.

Li, Yafei, Rebecca Shields, and Vivian Lin. 2012. Adverb Classes and the Nature of Minimality. *Natural Language and Linguistic Theory* 30:217–260.

McConnell-Ginet, Sally. 1982. Adverbs and Logical Form: A Linguistically Realistic Theory. *Language* 58:144–184.

Maienborn, Claudia, and Martin Schäfer. 2011. Adverbs and Adverbials. In *Semantics: An International Handbook of Natural Language Meaning*, Vol. 2, ed. Claudia Maienborn, Klaus von Heusinger, and Paul Portner, 1390–1420. Berlin: Mouton de Gruyter.

Nilsen, Øystein. 2004. Domains for Adverbs. *Lingua* 114:809–847.

Pesetsky, David. 1995. *Zero Syntax*. Cambridge, MA: MIT Press.

Phillips, Colin. 2003. Linear Order and Constituency. *Linguistic Inquiry* 34:37–90.

Pollock, Jean-Yves. 1989. Verb Movement, Universal Grammar, and the Structure of IP. *Linguistic Inquiry* 20:365–525.

Quirk, Randolph, Sydney Greenbaum, Geoffrey Leech, and Jan Svartvik. 1972. *A Grammar of Contemporary English*. London: Longman.

Schäfer, Martin. 2005. *German Adverbial Adjectives: Syntactic Position and Semantic Interpretation*. Doctoral dissertation, Universität Leipzig.

Schweikert, Walter. 2005. *The Order of Prepositional Phrases in the Structure of the Clause*. Amsterdam: John Benjamins.

Stechow, Arnim von. 1996. The Different Readings of *Wieder* 'Again': A Structural Account. *Journal of Semantics* 13:87–138.

Thráinsson, Hüskuldur. 2003. Object Shift and Scrambling. In *Handbook of Contemporary Syntactic Theory*, ed. Mark Baltin and Chris Collins, 148–202. Malden, MA: Blackwell.

Truswell, Robert. 2011. *Events, Phrases, and Questions*. Oxford: Oxford University Press.

Part II
Syntactic phenomena

7

Head movement

Michael Barrie and Éric Mathieu

1 Introduction

This chapter discusses head movement (HM) as a distinct syntactic operation, as well as the empirical facts argued to be covered by such. We start with a brief history of the development of HM in the Government and Binding era and then go on to discuss how HM was enriched through to the beginning of Minimalism. It was at this point that HM began to be seriously questioned. We discuss the problems that HM raises for Bare Phrase Structure (BPS) and the solutions that have been proposed in the literature. Then we run through the current status of HM and some of its technical aspects. Finally, we discuss how HM is affected in patients with aphasia. We restrict ourselves principally to a discussion of HM within the Principles and Parameters framework (notably Minimalism and Government & Binding Theory, though we do not focus on the mechanics of the latter). HM, as a derivational process, does not play a role in representational theories such as Head-Driven Phrase Structure Grammar (HPSG) or Role and Reference Grammar (RRG), so we do not discuss these here. See Kiss and Wesche (1991), however, for a discussion of how to treat verb movement in an HSPG and Combinatory Categorial Grammar (CCG) framework.

The remainder of this chapter is structured as follows. Section 2 discusses the early inceptions of HM as it arose from Standard Theory and its successors. Section 3 discusses how HM changed in the wake of discussions on the Lexicalist Hypothesis and its role in these discussions. Section 4 presents HM in light of Minimalism and BPS. Specifically, it discusses problematic aspects of HM and how these were addressed. Section 5 presents the current status of HM, in particular, we highlight the lack of consensus of HM in current syntactic theory. Section 6 presents some current research on the comprehension of HM in aphasic individuals and briefly discusses how this is related to our current theoretical understanding of HM. Section 7 is a brief summary.

2 The birth of head movement

HM as a distinct operation was made explicit by Government and Binding Theory (Chomsky 1981). Previously movement operations in Revised Extended Standard Theory

Michael Barrie and Éric Mathieu

and its predecessors were accomplished by language-specific operations targeting strings of specified lengths without regard as to whether the element moved was a single item or a whole phrase. Specifically, it was the implementation of X-Bar Theory that led to the distinction between HM and XP-movement (Chomsky 1970; Jackendoff 1977).

In X-Bar Theory, HM is accomplished by the terminal from one head detaching and raising to the terminal of the immediately c-commanding head. Unlike XP movement, which can target a c-commanding landing site at a distance, HM is constrained in this extremely local fashion under what came to be known as the Head Movement Constraint (HMC) (Travis 1984).

(1)

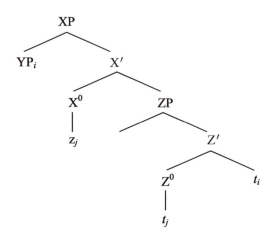

The HMC can be illustrated by the following pair of examples. In order to license a polarity question in English, an auxiliary or modal must raise to C. The following data show that only the higher head can raise (2a). It is not possible for the lower head to raise, skipping the intermediate head (2b).

(2) a. Will John *t* have eaten?
     b. *Have John will *t* eaten?

Head movement as a distinct operation was given considerable cross-linguistic thrust by Koopman's (1984) landmark study on verb movement in the Kru languages of Africa, underscoring the universality of this operation.

The operation of HM served as a diagnostic for syntactic structure, especially in the derivation of V2 order in German and verb-initial order in Irish. V2 order in German is found only in matrix clauses. Embedded clauses typically always contain a complementizer and the verb appears at the right edge of the clause. Recall that HM operates mechanically on the terminals under the head nodes. The terminal raises to an immediately c-commanding empty head node. If this head node already contains a terminal, then head movement is blocked. Consider the following German data.

(3) a. Er   hat   den   Apfel   gegessen.
         he   has   the   apple   eaten
         'He has eaten the apple.'

134

b. ...dass er den Apfel gegessen hat.
   ...that he the apple eaten has
   '...that he ate the apple.'

Example (3a) illustrates the phenomenon of V2 in Germanic. The highest tensed head appears in "second" position – that is, immediately after the first constituent. This property of the highest tensed head appearing in this position is argued to arise by the contents of T^0 raising to C^0 (Thiersch 1978; den Besten 1977; 1983). The evidence for this analysis resides in the failure of V2 to hold in embedded clauses when an overt complementizer is present (3b). This kind of diagnostic was used repeatedly in the early to mid GB era to argue for particular clausal structures of a number of languages. The axiomatic foundation for this line of argumentation resides strongly in the notion that a head can undergo HM only to the next highest head, and only if that head is empty. We will revisit this second point later on in §3.

A major alteration to the theory of HM was made by a series of papers introducing Long Head Movement (LHM) (Lema and Rivero 1990a; 1990b; Rivero 1994; 1993). LHM appears to involve violations of the HMC presented above. Consider the following example.

(4) Ver -te -ei   [Portuguese]
    see -you -3.SG.FUT
    'I will see you.'

The future and conditional forms in Portuguese (as in Romance languages in general) is formed with the infinitive as a base to which is attached various agreement markers based on the verb 'have'. In the future and conditional forms of modern literary Portuguese, however, the infinitival form of the verb is interrupted by clitics, as shown in (4). This was a pervasive feature of several older varieties of Romance languages but has since disappeared except in Portuguese, where it is found only in very formal speech today. Since the verbal base and the agreement marker are separated by a clitic, we have evidence that this structure is clearly formed in the syntax. The verbal base, however, originates low in the structure, below agreement. Thus, we have the following rough derivation.

(5) $[_{CP} ... [_{C^0} \text{ver}_i] [_{TP} [_{T^0} \text{ei}] [_{VP} [_V t_i]]]]$

What's noteworthy here, of course, is that the verb has raised to T^0, across an intervening head in an apparent violation of the HMC. As mentioned, movement of this type was commonplace in older varieties of Romance, but is also found in some Slavic languages. Rivero's original solution to this problem is as follows. She argues that the verb forms an agreement chain with T^0 as well as a movement chain with C^0. Thus, there is a set of chains linking these three heads. This view requires us to understand the HMC as a condition on representations rather than as a condition on derivations.

To conclude this section, we have introduced the first discussions of HM in GB Theory, firmly couched within an X-Bar theoretic framework. HM proceeds by a head targeting an immediately c-commanding vacant head position. This extremely local movement is captured under the HMC. Finally, we saw that violations of the HMC are found in so-called LHM in Romance and Slavic languages. The next section discusses some further advances in the mechanism of HM at the dawn of early Minimalism as GB Theory was declining.

3   Expanding the role of head movement

A major shift in the role of HM in generative grammar came in the 1980s, when HM started to play a larger role in word formation. To appreciate the issues discussed in this section we need to understand the Lexicalist Hypothesis (Di Sciullo and Williams 1987). This hypothesis holds that the atoms of syntax are words, which possibly possess internal morphological complexity. This internal structure is not visible to the syntax. Crucially, this hypothesis posits a pre-syntactic word-formation module. Theories such as Distributed Morphology reject the Lexicalist Hypothesis by claiming that there is no such module (Marantz 1997). Rather, words are put together in the syntax (or additionally, in the case of DM, in a post-syntactic morphological module). The notion that words can be put together in the syntax is not new (Lees 1960; Chomsky 1970); however, it was the pioneering works of Baker (1985; 1988) and Pollock (1989) that set the stage for this development in HM.

The concept of building words by HM in the syntax was spurred primarily by the Mirror Principle of Baker (1985). Baker's observation was that the order of affixes in a word mirrors the order of functional projections. Thus, if the order of the affixes in a verbal complex is Verb-X-Y-Z, then the order of functional projections is ZP > YP > XP > VP. Consider the following Bembe (Niger Congo) example.

(6)   a.   Naa-   mon   -an   -ya   [Mwape na Mutumba]
           1sgS-   see   -RECIP   -CAUS   Mwape and Mutumba
           'I made Mwape and Mutumba see each other.'
      b.   [Mwape na Chilufya]   baa-   mon   -eshy   -ana   Mutumba
           [Mwape and Chilufya]   3pS-   see   -CAUS   -RECIP   Mutumba.
           'Mwape and Chilufya made each other see Mutumba.'

In (6a) the causative suffix appears to the right of the reciprocal suffix. Thus, the causative scopes over the reciprocal marker, as indicated in the translation. In (6b), on the other hand, the reciprocal suffix appears to the right of the causative suffix. Here, the reciprocal takes scope outside the causative, giving rise to the reading indicated. This correlation between affix order and the functional hierarchy has been replicated in subsequent works (Julien 2002; Cinque 1999). The explanation for this phenomenon is simple. HM, restricted by the HMC, goes up the tree head by head, picking up affixes in order on the way. The proposal given above offers an attractive account of the strong correlation between the order of suffixes in the verbal complex and the order of functional projections; however, it is difficult to extend to prefixes. Harley (2011) proposes simply that affixes vary cross-linguistically as to whether they attach as prefixes or as suffixes (see also Wojdak 2008). See the Further Reading section for more comments on this point.

Pollock's (1989) discussion of verb movement in English and French offers a further illustration of word formation by HM. Pollock was chiefly concerned with verb movement and the structure of Infl, which he split into a tense phrase (TP) and an agreement phrase (AgrP). His proposal for verb movement accounts for the difference in word order in the following English and French sentences.

(7)   a.   John often kisses Mary.
      b.   *John kisses often Mary.

(8) a. Jean embrasse souvent Marie.
         John kisses   often   Mary
         'John often kisses Mary.'
     b. *Jean souvent embrasse Marie.
         Jean   often   kisses   Mary
         ('John often kisses Mary.')

Assuming that the adverb *often/souvent* consistently adjoins to VP, Pollock argued that the difference in word order can be captured by assuming that French has V-to-T movement, but English does not, as shown in the following bracketed illustrations.

(9) a. [$_{CP}$ [$_{TP}$ John T [$_{VP}$ often [$_{VP}$ kisses Mary]]]].   [English]
     b. [$_{CP}$ [$_{TP}$ Jean [$_{T}$ embrasse$_i$] [$_{VP}$ souvent [$_{VP}$ t_i Marie]]]].   [French]

Additional evidence for V-to-T raising in French and its absence in English comes from negation and yes/no question formation. We do not present these here for reasons of space. These diagnostics have become standard in syntactic theorizing. See, for instance, Adger's (2003) textbook for a clear discussion and illustration of these diagnostics in various languages.

Based on the order of the morphemes in Romance verbs, Belletti (1990) proposed that the order of the functional heads is AgrP > TP. Consider the following Italian verb form.

(10) legg-eva-no
      see-IMP-3.PL
      'They were reading.'

Note that the tense/aspect morphology is closer to the root than the agreement marking. The proposed structure is as follows.

(11)

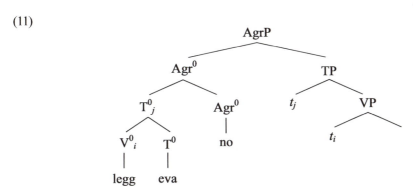

Here, the verb raises to T^0, picking up the tense/aspect affix. This complex head undergoes further HM to Agr^0, picking up the agreement affix. Successive HM in this manner creates a larger and larger complex head.

Let us now turn to Baker (1988), who develops a comprehensive theory of incorporation involving word formation via HM. Baker considered noun incorporation, causativization, applicativization, and restructuring. We will demonstrate the case of noun incorporation here, as this phenomenon plays an important role in later discussions of HM (Barrie and Mathieu 2012; Roberts 2010; Baker 2009). Consider the following example.

(12) Wa'-   ke-   nákt-   a-   hnínu   -'
      FACT- 1sS- bed-   EPEN- buy   -PUNC
      'I bought the/a bed.'

Here, the root *nakt* ('bed') appears inside the verbal complex. Note that the epenthetic vowel (EPEN) is not a morpheme, but rather is added phonologically to break up an illicit consonant cluster. Baker's proposal for a syntactic treatment of noun incorporation is quite simple. The head noun of the NP undergoes HM to V^0.

(13)

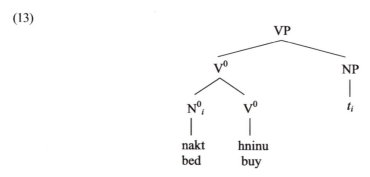

We end this section with a discussion on excorporation, illustrated in (14). Here, a head, Z^0, has raised to Y^0, and has then detached off, or excorporated, and raised to X^0.

(14)

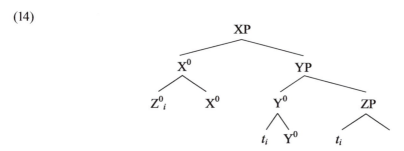

First, it is important to note that XP movement allows a phrase to raise to a given position, and then to continue to raise, such as with long-distance *wh*-movement. An obvious question comes to mind: Is there an equivalent operation for HM? To answer this question, we need to understand two structure building operations from GB theory: adjunction and substitution. Adjunction is still a familiar operation today. Substitution referred to movement to a specifier position, but the term is no longer in general use. It had always been unclear whether HM proceeds by adjunction or by substitution. Roberts (1991) proposes that HM can proceed either by substitution or by adjunction. Substitution involves the satisfaction of some property of a head by the element that moves to its specifier. Likewise, Roberts proposes that HM that satisfies some property of the head targeted by HM is a kind of substitution. A typical case is subcategorization: for example, an I^0 head subcategorizes for a V^0. Thus, V-to-I movement is an instance of substitution. However, if HM does not involve selection of any kind, then such HM proceeds by adjunction. Working under a Barriers framework, Roberts showed that a head to which substitution HM has taken place acts as a barrier, while a head to which adjunction HM has taken place does not. Thus, excorporation can happen only with adjunction HM. The cases Roberts discusses involve clitic climbing and V2 effects in Dutch. We illustrate the first here with the following Italian example.

(15) La$_i$ volevo t_i chiamare t_i ieri
      her   I-wanted to-call   yesterday
      'Yesterday, I wanted to call her up.'

Roberts assumes that clitic movement is an HM operation. It is not selected, however, so it proceeds by adjunction. In non-finite clauses, the clitic can raise up to the higher, tensed verb. Roberts argues that this is excorporation, as illustrated above, made possible by virtue of the mechanism of adjunction HM.

To sum up, we have seen that HM firmly implanted itself as a fundamental operation vital to the role of syntax during the GB era. In particular, HM was shown to underpin word formation in a variety of situations, such as noun incorporation, causativization, and the formation of morphologically complex verb forms in Romance. Of course, many other empirical illustrations were discussed during this time and continue to be discussed in relation to the role of HM in word formation. Finally, we illustrated the possibility of excorporation with clitic climbing.

4 Head movement and the minimalist program

As GB Theory and X-Bar Theory were becoming fraught with more and more empirical and theory internal problems, Chomsky started developing what became known as the Minimalist Program (Chomsky 1993) and Bare Phrase Structure (BPS) (Chomsky 1994). BPS consists of a single operation, Merge, which takes two syntactic objects, α and β, and forms a single syntactic object as follows:

(16) Merge $(\alpha, \beta) \rightarrow \{\gamma, \{\alpha, \beta\}\}$

The resulting structure is an XP with a label, γ.

Several problems with HM came to light in the early 2000s (Mahajan 2003; Fanselow 2003). As noted by several authors, HM is unformulable in BPS (there were, in fact, also numerous problems within the X-bar theory/GB paradigm, so much so that Rizzi (1990: 117 n. 19), for example, decides that head movement must be substitution). The single operation, Merge, can only form an XP. Unless modifications or enrichments are made to BPS there is no set-theoretic way to distinguish a complex head from an XP. Another problem is that HM violates the Extension Condition. That is, HM does not target the root projection, but rather targets an embedded node. Finally, depending on how c-command is defined, a moved head does not c-command its trace. Several solutions have been advanced to some or all of these problems, and we take these up here. First, we examine those proposals in which HM is slightly altered to address these issues. Then we examine those proposals which radically alter HM by making it a PF operation or replacing it with XP movement.

4.1 Adjustments to head movement

An early solution to the problem of the Extension Condition violations (and that pre-dates the commonly cited papers that discuss the problems with HM) is that of Bobaljik and

Brown (1997). Bobaljik and Brown exploit the concept of parallel derivations taking place in the same workspace and sideward movement. Here is how they derive V-to-T movement (we ignore *v* here for simplicity). Once the VP has been formed, T^0 is selected and placed into the workspace (17a). V^0 is copied and merged to T^0. At this point, T^0 is a root node because it is not yet attached to VP (17b). This complex T^0 head then merges with the VP and projects a TP (17c). Notice that at no point is the Extension Condition violated.

(17)

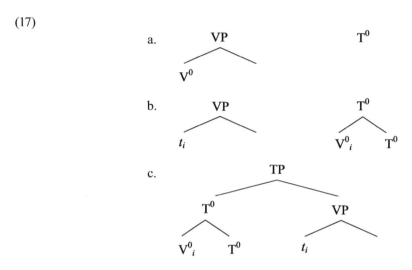

Although this proposal solves the problem of the violation of the Extension Condition, it does not solve the problem of c-command, nor does it address the fact that HM is incompatible with BPS.

With the shackles of X-Bar Theory gone, researchers were free to explore alternative conceptions of movement. Toyoshima (2000) develops a model of Head to Spec movement to account for a range of phenomena related to Economy. It is exactly this kind of movement that solves many of the problems related to HM discussed above (in BPS nothing bars head movement to a specifier position). Matushansky (2006) develops just such an analysis. She acknowledges the problems of HM discussed above, in particular the acute problem of the counter-cyclic aspect of HM. She invokes the mechanism of morphological merger in addition to Head-to-Spec movement. Morphological merger is an operation proposed under the framework of DM. It is a post-syntactic operation which locally dislocates a syntactic object with another string-adjacent syntactic object. Thus, as far as syntax is concerned, the Extension Condition and the requirement that a moved element c-command its trace are satisfied. Also, since the head moves to the specifier position, Matushansky's conception of HM is compatible with BPS.

Finally, we mention "reprojection" analyses that also propose to keep head movement in the syntax (Bury 2003; 2007; Donati 2006; Koeneman 2000; Surányi 2005; 2007). The idea is to treat head movement as arising from a different set of conditions from XP-movement. Whereas Chomsky (1995: 256–60) argues that where a new category γ is formed by movement of α to β, γ must always project the target of movement, leading to a situation where, for example, DP-movement attracted by T will always create a new projection of T or *wh*-movement attracted by C will always create a new projection of C, the alternative is to suggest that this may not always be the case, and that "reprojective" movement may arise. In "reprojection" the moving category gives its label to the new category formed by movement. This analysis has been applied to free relatives and related constructions as well as to V2 phenomena.

4.2   Removing Head Movement from Syntax

Boeckx and Stjepanovic (2001) argue from the analysis of pseudo-gapping that head movement is best viewed as a PF phenomenon. Their evidence is based on Lasnik's (1995) analysis of pseudo-gapping, exemplified in (18) where the object *emagazines* escapes the VP and undergoes object shift to the Spec of an Agr projection so that the rest of the VP can be deleted (namely, the verb *buy*).

(18)   Although I wouldn't buy ebooks, I would __emagazines ~~buy~~.

The question that immediately arises is why the verb does not raise in pseudo-gapping constructions, given that in non-elliptical sentences it must, as shown in the following example.

(19)   *John will emagazines$_i$ buy t_i.   (vs. John will buy$_i$ emagazines$_j$ t_i t_j)

Lasnik observes that if V fails to raise, and no relevant process takes place, the strong feature that is not checked overtly causes a crash at PF. But if the VP containing V is deleted in the PF component, then, patently, the strong feature cannot cause a PF crash, since the category containing the feature will be gone at that level. However, in Lasnik's system nothing stops the verb to raise and the object to stay put, as in (20). Since this sentence is clearly ungrammatical, the conclusion is that head movement is optional, but XP movement is not.

(20)   *John bought ebooks, and Mary bought ~~ebooks~~ too.

Boeckx and Stjepanović believe that a solution to both problems – stipulating obligatory/optional movement, and the syntactic-feature-triggered head movement – is to assume that head movement (in this case, V-movement) takes place after Spell-Out, in the phonological component. They assume that XP-movement, like object shift, is syntactic (driven by the checking of some feature): it necessarily takes place in the syntax. They further argue that if head movement is a PF (post-Spell-Out) phenomenon, it necessarily follows all syntactic movement operations and could be "superseded" by an ellipsis rule: not being syntactically driven, head movement and ellipsis (both PF operations) compete.

In other words, if head movement is a PF phenomenon, we have an answer to Lasnik's puzzle as to why V need not raise in the pseudogapping cases. Suppose ellipsis is a PF operation. Then head movement and ellipsis become competing operations: V either moves or is deleted. In short, not only does the view of head movement as a PF operation remove any look-ahead and extrinsic ordering from the computational system, it also avoids the question of which head has the inadequacy that forces movement.

The advantage that this analysis and other similar ones have is that we can now understand why head movement has no effect on interpretation as argued by Chomsky (2000; 2001). Whether the verb moves to T, as in French, or whether it does not, as in English, makes no difference for the semantics, since the relevant sentences have the same truth conditions. The idea that head movement is a PF phenomenon explains this kind of semantic weight: PF movement, unlike syntactic movement (i.e., XP movement), has no bearing on interpretation.

However, it must be noted that the idea that HM has no effect on interpretation is not uncontroversial. A few researchers have attempted to demonstrate that HM is necessarily a syntactic operation needed to account for changes in interpretations cross-linguistically (Benedicto 1998; Lechner 2006; 2007; Kishimoto 2007; 2008). According to Matushansky (2006), the reason why head movement has no LF effect is due to an independent factor (for her there is a syntactic side to head movement, in that the head moves to a specifier in the syntax): it lies in the very nature of the items moved by head movement. Most of them are predicates of some sort: verbs, nouns, most affixes, and so on.

While many claim head movement is a PF phenomenon, often the specifics of the PF operation are not spelled out. Harley (2004) is an exception. She proposes that the Conflation mechanism proposed in Hale and Keyser (2002) is a good candidate for the mechanism behind head movement *à la* PF. Conflation is a concomitant of Merge. It is an operation that occurs when a head X merges with a maximal constituent YP whose label is H(Y). The label of Y, by assumption, contains all the features of Y°, including a copy of its phonological features that Hale and Keyser call a *p-signature* (p-sig for short). If X's p-sig is defective, Y's p-sig is conflated into X's when X and Y Merge, meaning that X is now pronounced with Y's phonological features. When X projects, the label of the whole constituent, H(X), will now contain Y's phonological features. This can be applied to noun incorporation, for example, but also, as argued by Harley, to V2 cases and other such head movement phenomena. As pointed out by Harley (2004), the conflation mechanism allows us implement the idea that head-movement is "phonological" while simultaneously ensuring that it is local.

A more radical proposal is that of Brody (1997; 2000) and his Mirror Theory. In allowing the projection of complementation structure directly from the lexical information encapsulated in the structure of words, Brody's Mirror Theory makes it possible to abandon head movement completely. While in traditional syntax the information pertaining to the structure of words is expressed both word-internally (i.e., X^0-internally) and by the (inverse) structure of complementation (the Mirror Principle: Baker 1988), Brody suggests that the information carried by words can be directly projected in the syntax without the recourse of any additional matching/movement. This avoids redundancy in the system. Traditionally, redundancies are frowned upon, and Brody takes the example of the earlier coexistence of both Phrase Structure Rules (PSR) and the Projection Principle that led to a reappraisal and the abandonment of PSR.

In Brody's view, lexical items have projection lines (PLs) and words correspond to these projection lines. They are created pre-syntactically (either in the Lexicon or prior to the point of insertion). To illustrate, a word of the form V-Ptcpl-Aux-T will have the structure in (21). All the information that has to do with the spell out of the word as the mirror image of that sequence is contained in the lowest element: that is, V.

(21)

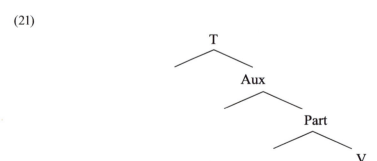

In this view, objects – that is, complements of verbs – are necessarily specifiers (like subjects). They never occur on the right side of the head: they are always projected on the left side.

This theory has a clear advantage over other theories in that it makes no distinction between words and phrases: both are created in the syntax. At the same time, it is a lexicalist theory, in that all the information about words (including morphophonological information) is contained in those words.

The theory has an appealing result: there is no need to explain why excorporation is generally not possible, why a moved head does not c-command its trace and why HM should be local. Excorporation is not possible, because there was no movement involved in the first place. The c-command problem does not arise, since nothing moved. Finally, locality is captured inside the word, since there is no possibility of a head raising and skipping another head.

Another radical way of dispensing with HM is to adopt a remnant movement approach to HM. In this view, syntax simply makes no reference to information related to heads. Remnant movement was originally proposed to handle topicalization of incomplete VPs, as in (22). Only the verb in this case moves to Spec-CP and the object remains below after having raised to a higher object position (AgroP or external specifier of v). For this structure to be possible in a given language, scrambling of objects must be an available option in the grammar.

(22) [t_i Gelesen]$_j$ hat   Hans [das   Buch]$_i$ t_j nicht
          read   has   Hans   the   book   not
      'Hans has not read the book.'

Since the mid-nineties it has been suggested (most notably by Kayne 1998) that remnant movement can be extended to many other domains. For example, Koopman and Szabolcsi (2000) propose that in Hungarian, Dutch, and German, the verb raises via XP movement generally. The need to appeal to HM becomes obsolete.

5   Head movement today

Roberts (2010) provides the most recent, thoroughly worked-out analysis of HM within the Minimalist Program, so we will cover his proposal in more detail here. Roberts recasts HM as a reflex of Agree between a Probe and a defective Goal, bringing it in line with mainstream Minimalist syntax. He takes a defective goal to be one whose features are a proper subset of the Probe. Following Roberts, we illustrate the operation with Romance clitics. Roberts assumes that an active, transitive v^* has an interpretable V-feature, [iV] (to categorize the lexical root) and [$u\varphi$]. Following Cardinaletti and Starke (1999) and Déchaine and Wiltschko (2002), he further assumes that a clitic is a bare φP devoid of Case features – in other words, a bundle of interpretable φ-features, [$i\varphi$]. When the V-v^* complex enters into an Agree relation with the clitic, the [$u\varphi$] feature set on v^* is valued by the clitic (Roberts 2010: ex (30)).

(23) a. *Trigger for Agree*
         v^* [Pers:____, Num:____] φ[Pers:a, Num :b]
      b. *Outcome of Agree*
         v^* **[Pers:a, Num:b]**   (φ[Pers:a, Num :b])

Michael Barrie and Éric Mathieu

Roberts argues that there is no formal difference between, on the one hand, Agree that exhausts all the features of the Goal and, on the other, Move/Internal Merge of the Goal to the Probe. In other words, the outcome of (23b), Agree(v^*, φ) is indistinguishable from Merge(v^*,φ) precisely because the set of features on φ is a subset of the features of v^*. Contrast the two structures below. In both cases exactly the same set of features appears on v^* after either Agree or Move.

(24) a. [$_{vP}$ v^* [**Pers:*a*, Num:*b***]   [$_{φP}$ φ [Pers:*a*, Num :*b*]]] - outcome of Agree
     b. [$_{vP}$ [$_{v*}$ φ [Pers:*a*, Num :*b*]$_i$ v^*]   [$_{φP}$ t_i]]   - outcome of Move

Finally, HM fails with a full DP object because it contains features that are not part of v^* (such as D and Case).

Since the technical aspects of Roberts' proposal are quite different from that of standard HM, we will go over the derivation in more detail here. First, let us examine a structure containing a verb and a clitic.

(25) Pierre   le   voit
      Pierre   it.CL.3.SG   sees
      'Pierre sees it.'

The final structure for the v^* head we will derive is shown in (26). As with Roberts, we assume that the underlying order of projections is $vP > VP > DP$.

(26)   (Roberts 2010: 50)

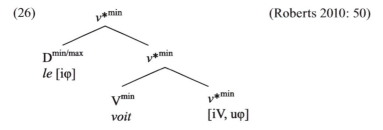

There are two important points to consider here. First, both V and D have undergone HM to v^*: thus, they must be featurally non-distinct from v^*. Second, Roberts must ensure that V raises to v^* before D. It is easy to see in (26) that the features of D are a subset of the features of v^*. Roberts makes the reasonable assumption that a pronominal clitic is simply a bundle of phi-features, devoid of Case features. A full DP, of course, does have Case features, and so is not a subset of the features of the Probe, v^*. Roberts also assumes that lexical roots must raise to a category-defining head in the sense of Marantz (2001). In order to derive the correct surface order of heads, Roberts restates Strict Cyclicity in terms of "prominence". Given the order projections, we expect the clitic to raise first (because it is more deeply embedded), followed by the verb, giving the incorrect order *verb-clitic-v. Roberts proposes the following definitions, where *merger* refers to the element that does not project upon Merge, and *mergee* refers to the element that does project (Roberts 2010: 52).

(27) α is more prominent than β if either:
     (i) α is a merger for β (i.e., β projects the label of {α, β}, or
     (ii) there is a category γ, γ a mergee for β, such that δ (reflexively) dominates γ, and
          α is a merger for δ.

This formulation gives rise to the following three scenarios. In all three cases, α is more prominent than β, and so must raise first if both α and β are targeted by the same Probe. (In fact, the definition above refers to any configuration akin to (28c) where α and β are separated by any number of projections.

(28)

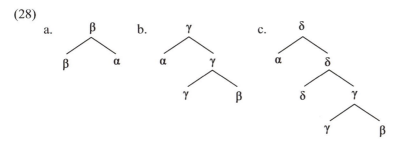

Of course, for Roberts' proposal to work, he must show that a wide range of HM phenomena are amenable to this account. Specifically, he must show that the set of features of the 'moved' head is always a subset of those of the landing site. Indeed, he shows this with a wide range of phenomena, including second position clitics, clitic climbing, V-to-T movement, long head movement, verb second, and verb incorporation. He also suggests that noun incorporation may be handled under his approach (but see Barrie and Mathieu (2012) for an alternative view).

6   Head movement and aphasia

In this last section we make a few brief remarks on some current research on HM and Broca's aphasia. Broca's aphasia is usually characterized as slow, laboured speech which frequently omits function words. Van der Meulen (2004) summarizes previous research on comprehension deficits with movement in individuals with Broca's aphasia in addition to presenting her own research. We mention just two previous studies here before describing van der Meulen's research.

Pioneering research by Grodzinsky and Finkel (1998) indicates a significant difference in Broca's patients' understanding of HM versus XP movement. Their discussion centres on the following paradigm.

(29) a.   It seems likely that John will win.
     b.   John$_i$ seems likely t_i to win.
     c.   *John$_i$ seems that it is likely t_i to win.

(30) a.   They could have left town.
     b.   Could they t_i have left town?
     c.   *Have$_i$ they could t_i left town?

Both sets of data contain an ungrammatical sentence. In (29c), the DP *John* has undergone superraising, a phenomenon usually handled by Case Theory. In (30c), the auxiliary *have* has raised above the modal *could*, in violation of the HMC. What the researchers found was that Broca's patients were able to detect the ungrammaticality in (29c), the case involving XP movement, far more easily than in (30c), the case involving HM. Grodzinsky and Finkel take these results to mean that comprehension in Broca's patients is not affected by HM.

Whatever the explanation, these results indicate a fundamental difference between XP movement and HM. More recently, Friedmann *et al.* (2006) have examined the comprehension of verb movement in Hebrew in aphasic patients. Their results indicate that aphasics *are* sensitive to comprehension of verb movement, in direct contrast to the previous experiment. Van der Meulen examined the comprehension of HM in French *wh*-questions, but the question as to whether HM affects comprehension in Broca's aphasia patients was not able to be conclusively answered, although she does ultimately conclude (on the basis of other experiments reported in her dissertation) that XP movement does affect comprehension more than does HM in individuals with Broca's aphasia.

We have just scratched the surface with respect to the relationship between HM and aphasia. What is clear from the discussion above is that more research into the neurological processing of HM versus XP movement is necessary. Important research such as this has the potential to address many of the issues related to HM discussed above. Recall that several proposals have been put forth to amend HM, including minor alterations keeping HM basically intact, relegating HM to PF, and recasting HM as remnant XP movement. It is entirely possible that more than one of these mechanisms is at play. That is, some instances of HM are really PF movement, while other instances of HM are really remnant XP movement. In this light, we do not expect uniform experimental results in the examination of HM and aphasia. Thus, we tentatively end this section with the suggestion that the contradictory experimental results above arise from differences in how HM manifests in the languages under consideration.

7 Conclusion

In this chapter we have surveyed the rise of HM from its earliest incarnations in GB Theory to our most recent understanding of it within a Minimalist perspective. Throughout the GB era, the operation of HM began to play a larger and larger role in syntax. Specifically, early work by Baker and Pollock led to an enormous research program on deriving word structure syntactically – a research program that remains active to this day. The empirical underpinning of this line of research was the realization that morphological structure within a word and syntactic structure bear too many striking similarities to be a mere accident. As the properties of HM were being investigated, a clear property came to light that still figures in syntactic theorizing. The Head Movement Constraint of Travis states that HM is confined to targeting the immediately c-commanding head. Long Head Movement was shown to be a counter-example to this generalization, prompting a re-thinking of the HMC.

Minimalism adopts Bare Phrase Structure, which does not provide any formal mechanism for HM. Furthermore, several other problems with HM were identified early on by researchers, leading to numerous discussions and reformulations of this operation. These include the following: (i) relegating HM to the PF component, (ii) recasting HM as massive remnant movement, and (iii) reprojection. We discussed the theoretical and empirical underpinnings of these three approaches. Despite the theory-internal problems with HM, many researchers to this day eschew discussions on this matter and simply assume there is some technical solution that makes HM available as an overt syntactic operation. We then presented Roberts' current proposal on HM within a Minimalist framework. As the most worked-out proposal on HM, we have presented, we hope, enough of the core details of his mechanism to allow the reader to apply these to other instances of HM.

In the final section we reviewed briefly some current research on how HM is affected in patients with aphasia. As the research presented indicates, there is a lack of consensus on the effect of aphasia on HM. We suggested tentatively that some of the observed variation in how HM is affected may be due to the lack of a uniform operation of HM. Although an elegant solution to the problems of HM is certainly desired, the studies on alternatives to HM (PF movement, remnant XP movement, and reprojection) suggest that HM may not be a unitary operation, but that some of instances of HM may indeed be better understood as one of these other kinds of movement, crucially with a difference in how they are affected by aphasia. In brief, the issue of HM is far from settled. How it is to be understood and whether it should be treated as a single operation remain open questions.

Further reading

An excellent discussion of the empirical issues of HM in Germanic, Romance, and Celtic can be found in Roberts (2001), along with a general discussion on the properties of HM. Contemporary discussions on the properties of HM may be found in Harley (2011 and 2013). Finally, a recent survey that compares the empirical strengths of recent alternatives to HM (HM at PF, remnant XP movement, and reprojection) can be found in Roberts (2011).

References

Adger, D. 2003. *Core Syntax*. Oxford: Oxford University Press.

Baker, M.C. 1985. The mirror principle and morphosyntactic explanation. *Linguistic Inquiry* 16:373–416.

Baker, M.C. 1988. *Incorporation: A Theory of Grammatical Function Changing*. Chicago, IL: University of Chicago Press.

Baker, M.C. 2009. Is head movement still needed for noun incorporation? *Lingua* 119:148–165.

Barrie, M., and E. Mathieu. 2012. Head movement and noun incorporation. *Linguistic Inquiry* 43:133–142.

Belletti, A. 1990. *Generalized Verb Movement: Aspects of Verb Syntax*. Turin: Rosenberg and Sellier.

Benedicto, E.E. 1998. Verb movement and its effects on determinerless plural subjects. In *Romance Linguistics: Theoretical Perpectives*, ed. A. Schwegler, B. Tranel, and M. Uribe-Etxebarria, 25–40. Amsterdam/Philadelphia: John Benjamins.

Bobaljik, J.D., and S. Brown. 1997. Interarboreal operations: Head movement and the extension requirement. *Linguistic Inquiry* 28:345–356.

Boeckx, C. and S. Stjepanovic. 2001. Head-ing towards PF. *Linguistic Inquiry* 32:345–355.

Brody, M. 1997. Mirror theory. *UCL Working Papers in Linguistics* 9:179–122.

Brody, M. 2000. Mirror theory: Syntactic representation in perfect syntax. *Linguistic Inquiry* 31: 29–56.

Bury, D. 2003. Phrase structure and derived heads. PhD dissertation, University College London.

Bury, D. 2007. Verb movement and VSO-VOS alternations. *UCL Working Papers in Linguistics* 19:77–91.

Cardinaletti, A., and M. Starke. 1999. The typology of structural deficiency: On the three grammatical classes. In *Clitics in the Languages of Europe*, ed. H. van Riemsdijk, 145–233. Berlin: Mouton de Gruyter.

Chomsky, N. 1970. Remarks on nominalization. In *Readings in English Transformational Grammar*, ed. R. Jacobs and P. Rosenbaum, 184–221. Washington: Georgetown University Press.

Chomsky, N. 1981. *Lectures on Government and Binding*. Dordrecht: Foris.

Chomsky, N. 1993. A minimalist program for linguistic theory. In *The View from Building 20: Essays in Linguistics in Honor of Sylvain Bromberger*, ed. K. Hale and S.J. Keyser, 1–52. Cambridge, MA: MIT Press.

Chomsky, N. 1994. *Bare Phrase Structure*. MIT Occasional Papers in Linguistics, 5.

Chomsky, N. 1995. *The Minimalist Program*. Cambridge, MA: MIT Press.

Chomsky, N. 2000. Minimalist inquiries: The framework. In *Step by Step: Essays on Minimalist Syntax in Honor of Howard Lasnik*, ed. R. Martin, D. Michaels, and J. Uriagereka, 89–156. Cambridge, MA: MIT Press.

Chomsky, N. 2001. Derivation by phase. In *Ken Hale: A Life in Language*, ed. M. Kenstowicz, 1–52. Cambridge, MA: MIT Press.

Cinque, G. 1999. *Adverbs and Functional Heads: A Cross-linguistic Perspective*. New York, NY: Oxford University Press.

Déchaine, R.M., and M. Wiltschko. 2002. Decomposing pronouns. *Linguistic Inquiry* 33:409–442.

Den Besten, H. 1977. On the interaction of root transformations and lexical deletive rules. MIT and University of Amsterdam.

Den Besten, H. 1983. On the interaction of root transformations and lexical deletive rules. In *On the Formal Syntax of the Westgermania*, ed. W. Abraham, 47–131. Amsterdam: John Benjamins.

Di Sciullo, A.M., and E. Williams. 1987. *On the Definition of Word*. Cambridge, MA: MIT Press.

Donati, C. 2006. On Wh-head movement. In *Wh-movement: Moving On*, ed. L. Cheng and N. Corver, 21–46. Cambridge, MA: MIT Press.

Fanselow, G. 2003. Münchhausen-style head movement and the analysis of verb second. *UCLA Working Papers in Linguistics* 13:40–76.

Friedmann, N., A. Gvion, M. Biran, and R. Novogrodsky. 2006. Do people with agrammatic aphasic understand verb movement? *Aphasiology* 20:136–153.

Grodzinsky, Y., and L. Finkel. 1998. The neurology of empty categories. *Journal of Cognitive Neuroscience* 10:281–292.

Hale, K.L., and S.J. Keyser. 2002. *Prolegomenon to a Theory of Argument Structure*. Cambridge, MA: MIT Press.

Harley, H. 2004. Merge, conflation and head movement: The first sister principle revisited. In *NELS 34*, ed. K. Moulton and M. Wolf, 239–254. Amherst, MA: GLSA.

Harley, H. 2011. Affixation and the mirror principle. In *Interfaces in Linguistics*, ed. R. Folli and C. Ulbrich, 166–186. Oxford: Oxford University Press.

Harley, H. 2013. Getting morphemes in order: Merger, affixation and head-movement. In *Diagnosing Syntax*, ed. L. Cheng and N. Corver, 44–74. Oxford: Oxford University Press.

Jackendoff, R. 1977. *X-bar Syntax: A Study of Phrase Structure*. Cambridge, MA: MIT Press.

Julien, M. 2002. *Syntactic Heads and Word Formation*. Oxford: Oxford University Press.

Kayne, R. 1998. Overt vs. covert movements. *Syntax* 1:128–191.

Kishimoto, H. 2007. Negative scope and head raising in Japanese. *Lingua* 117:247–288.

Kishimoto, H. 2008. On the variability of negative scope in Japanese. *Journal of Linguistics* 44: 379–435.

Kiss, T., and B. Wesche. 1991. Verb order and head movement. In *Text Understanding in LILOG*, ed. H. Otthein and R. Claus-Reiner, 216–240. Dordrecht: Springer.

Koeneman, O. 2000. *The Flexible Nature of Verb Movement*. Utrecht University.

Koopman, H. 1984. *The Syntax of Verbs: From Verb Movement Rules in the Kru Languages to Universal Grammar*. Dordrecht: Foris.

Koopman, H., and A. Szabolcsi. 2000. *Verbal Complexes*. Cambridge, MA: MIT Press.

Lasnik, H. 1995. A note on pseudogapping. In *MIT Working Papers in Linguistics 27: Papers in Minimalist Syntax*, 143–163. Cambridge, MA: MITPLS, Department of Linguistics and Philosophy, MIT.

Lechner, W. 2006. An interpretive effect of head movement. In *Phases of Interpretation*, ed. M. Frascarelli, 45–71. Berlin: Mouton de Gruyter.

Lechner, W. 2007. Interpretive effects of head movement. *LingBuzz*. Downloadable at http://ling.auf.net/lingbuzz/000178

Lees, R. 1960. *The Grammar of English Nominalizations*. The Hague: Mouton.

Lema, J., and M.-L. Rivero. 1990a. Long head movement: ECP vs. HMC. *Cahiers Linguistiques d'Ottawa* 18:61–78.

Lema, J., and M.-L. Rivero. 1990b. Long head-movement: ECO vs. HMC. In *NELS 20*, ed. J. Carter, R.-M. Déchaine, W. Philip, and T. Sherer, 333–347. Amherst, MA: University of Massachusetts, GLSA.

Mahajan, A. 2003. Word order and (remnant) VP movement. In *Word Order and Scrambling*, ed. S. Karimi, 217–237. Malden, MA: Blackwell Publishers.

Marantz, A. 1997. No escape from syntax: Don't try morphological analysis in the privacy of your own lexicon. *University of Pennsylvania Working Papers in Linguistics* 4:201–225.

Marantz, A. 2001. Words. In *20th West Coast Conference on Formal Linguistics*. University of Southern California.

Matushansky, O. 2006. Head movement in linguistic theory. *Linguistic Inquiry* 37:69–109.

Pollock, J.-Y. 1989. Verb movement, universal grammar, and the structure of IP. *Linguistic Inquiry* 20:356–424.

Rivero, M.-L. 1993. Long head movement vs V2 and null subjects in Old Romance. *Lingua* 89: 217–245.

Rivero, M.-L. 1994. Clause structure and V-movement in the languages of the Balkans. *Natural Language & Linguistic Theory* 12:63–120.

Rizzi, L. 1990. *Relativized Minimality*. Cambridge, MA: MIT Press.

Roberts, I. 1991. Excorporation and minimality. *Linguistic Inquiry* 22:209–218.

Roberts, I. 2001. Head movement. In *The Handbook of Contemporary Syntactic Theory*, ed, M. Baltin and C. Collins, 113–147. Oxford: Blackwell.

Roberts, I. 2010. *Agreement and Head Movement: Clitics, Incorporation, and Defective Goals*. Cambridge, MA: MIT Press.

Roberts, I. 2011. Head-movement and the minimalist program. In *The Oxford Handbook of Linguistic Minimalism*, ed. C. Boeckx, 195–219. Oxford: Oxford University Press.

Surányi, B. 2005. Head movement and reprojection. In *Annales Universitatis Scientiarum Budapestinensis de Rolando Eötvös Nominatae. Sectio Linguistica. Tomus XXVI*, 313–342. Budapest: ELTE.

Surányi, B. 2007. On phase extension and head movement. *Theoretical Linguistics* 33:121–132.

Thiersch, C. 1978. Topics in German syntax. PhD dissertation, MIT.

Toyoshima, T. 2000. Head-to-spec movement and dynamic economy. PhD dissertation, Cornell University.

Travis, L.D.M. 1984. Parameters and effects of word order variation. PhD dissertation, MIT.

Van der Meulen, A.C. 2004. Syntactic movement and comprehension deficits in Broca's aphasia. PhD dissertation, Universiteit Leiden.

Wojdak, R. 2008. *The Linearization of Affixes: Evidence from Nuu-Chah-Nulth*. New York, NY/ Berlin: Springer.

8

Case and grammatical relations

Maria Polinsky and Omer Preminger

1 Morphological case, Abstract Case, and the need for Case Theory

Certain constituents in clause structure are known to determine the form and/or position of other clausal constituents. In particular, verbs and adpositions determine the morphological form of their associated nouns. For example, in the Latin (1a–b), the form of the noun 'eyes' depends on the preposition that it appears with, varying between accusative and ablative:

(1) a. ante   ocul-ōs   *Latin*
         before   eye-ACC.PL
     b. de   ocul-is
         from   eye-ABL.PL

The alternation in the form of a nominal or adjectival constituent based on its function is captured under the label "case". Generative grammar and related formalisms recognize two kinds of case: morphological and abstract. We will explore each of these notions in turn. Although the two versions of case are quite distinct, they both appeal to the basic insight that nominals occurring in particular forms (cases) should be identified with distinct phrase-structural configurations.

Morphological case is a category that reflects the relationship between a head and its dependent noun(s), or between different nouns in a clause. Taken to the next level of abstraction, the position/form exhibited by a nominal constituent in a clause is determined by its syntactic configuration. Traditional grammars appeal to a one-to-one mapping from case to function: from nominative case to the grammatical function of sentential subject, from accusative case to the grammatical function of direct object, etc. This one-to-one mapping (abstracting away, for the moment, from certain empirical inadequacies it faces) can be more accurately expressed as a correspondence between the grammatical function of a nominal constituent and its morphological marking.

The apparent empirical variation in morphological case can be constrained along at least three dimensions: variation in the expression of core arguments; overt vs. covert expression of case; and a distinction between argument and adjunct cases.

Cross-linguistic accounts of the variation in case marking among core arguments employ three argument-structural primitives: S – the sole argument of a one-place verb; A – the agent or most agent-like argument of a two-place verb; and P – the theme (patient) or most patient-like argument of a two-place verb (Comrie 1978; 1989; Dixon 1994 among others). The three most common morphological case systems are "accusative", "ergative", and "neutral". Case systems where S and A are marked alike and contrast with P are known as "accusative"; such systems are well known from Latin, Greek, and the Balto-Slavic languages. This system is illustrated in (2), for Russian, and (3), for the Cushitic language Harar Oromo. The Russian example illustrates the cross-linguistically typical nominative-accusative pattern; Harar Oromo instantiates a morphologically less frequent pattern where the nominative is overtly marked, but the accusative is not.

(2) a. starušk-a   odnaždy s   bazar-a   prišla   *Russian*
          old_woman-NOM once   from market-GEN came
          'The old woman once came back from the market.'
     b. kot   zametil   starušk-u
          cat.NOM noticed old_woman-ACC
          'The cat noticed the old woman.'

(3) a. níitíi-n   magaláa xéesá meesháa   *Harar Oromo*
          woman-NOM market inside things.ACC
          náa-f   gurgur-t-e
          me-DAT   sold-FEM-TENSE
          'The woman inside the market sold goods for me.' (Owens 1985: 86)
     b. níitíi-n   magaláa deeme
          woman-NOM market went
          'The woman went to the market.' (Owens 1985: 56)
     c. *pro* níitíi   taná arke
               woman.ACC this saw
          'He saw this woman.' (Owens 1985: 225)

Case systems where S and P are marked alike and contrast with A are known as "ergative"; morphologically ergative languages include Basque, Georgian, Tongan, or Chukchi, illustrated in (4).

(4) a. keyŋ-e ətlʔəg-ən təm-nen   *Chukchi*
          bear-ERG man-ABS kill-AOR.3SG:3SG
          'The bear killed the man.'
     b. ətlʔəg-ən ret-gʔe
          man-ABS arrive-AOR.3SG
          'The man arrived.'

In a "neutral" case system, the overt marking does not distinguish between S, A, and P: the surface form of a noun does not change depending on whether it is, for example, a subject or an object (this is the case for English outside of the pronominal system). Overt case marking is absent in Mandarin, Thai, Vietnamese, and all or most creole languages. In derivational approaches to grammar, the presence or absence of surface case marking is considered a matter of parametric variation (see Ouhalla 1991).[1] However, beyond isolating morphology, it is not yet clear what other features of language design correlate with the absence of overt case marking.

Finally, "tripartite" or "contrastive" systems are those where S, A, and P all have different case marking, as in Antekerrepenhe (Arandic; Central Australia):

(5) a. **arengke-le** aye-nhe ke-ke *Antekerrepenhe*
         dog-**A** me-**P** bite-PAST
         'The dog bit me.'
     b. athe **arengke-nhe** we-ke
         me:**A** dog-**P** strike-PAST
         'I hit the dog.'
     c. **arengke-ø** nterre-ke
         dog-**S** run-PAST
         'The dog ran.' (Bittner and Hale 1996: 4)

The accusative, ergative, neutral, and tripartite case systems are often referred to as different *alignments*, and have received significant attention in the typological literature (Silverstein 1976; Comrie 1989, among others). Much of the theoretical interest surrounding alignment systems has to do with the correlation between case and agreement (see §3), the notion of splits (see Coon 2013a; 2013b and references therein), and the differences in abstract Case assignment between accusative and ergative systems (Aldridge 2004; Legate 2002; 2008).

The number of distinct overt cases in a single language may vary significantly; one extreme is represented by languages with no morphological case marking whatsoever, while, at the other extreme, one finds languages with extremely rich case systems, such as Uralic, Dravidian, or Nakh-Dagestanian. Iggesen (2013) finds the distribution of morphological cases shown in Table 8.1 in his language sample.

The Nakh-Dagestanian languages represent perhaps the furthest extreme among rich case systems; some languages in this family appear to have fifty cases or more (Comrie and Polinsky 1998). However, even in such case-rich languages, the number of argument cases is predictably small: the case(s) of subject, object, possessor, and indirect object (Blake 2001). The majority of other forms are represented by locative (adjunct) cases, which encode location and direction (Comrie and Polinsky 1998). Setting such adjunct cases aside, we can describe the availability of morphological cases within a given language by the following implicational hierarchy (cf. Blake 2001 for a similar formulation):

(6) subject case/object case > possessor (genitive) case > indirect object (dative) case

Linguistic theory has gone beyond viewing case as a purely morphological phenomenon by extending the idea of dependency in a more general way. The notion of *abstract Case* can

Table 8.1. Surface case marking across languages

No morphological case marking	100 languages
2 cases	23 languages
3 cases	9 languages
4 cases	9 languages
5–7 cases	39 languages
8–9 cases	23 languages
10 or more cases	24 languages

be used to predict the distribution of both overt and non-overt nominal forms, and may thus be thought of as one of the fundamental abstract syntactic relations in the mental grammar. Vergnaud's conjecture, expressed in his 1977 letter to Chomsky advocating the principle of abstract Case, was an important step in the development of the idea. As summarized by Lasnik,

> Vergnaud's now very familiar basic idea was that even languages like English with very little case morphology pattern with richly inflected languages in providing characteristic positions in which NPs with particular cases occur.
>
> (Lasnik 2008: 18)

We defer the discussion of the actual modeling of Case assignment to §3; in §2, we address the main motivations for positing abstract Case.

2 Abstract Case

Abstract Case (which we will refer to simply as Case,[2] below) is a primitive feature that reflects a relationship between an argument and its syntactic context; in other words, the assignment of abstract Case is determined by syntactic structure. The principles of Case assignment were grouped under the rubric of Case Theory, which included the following components:

(7) *Case Uniqueness Principle*: A lexical NP may receive only one Case.

(8) *Case Filter*: Every lexical NP must be assigned Case (Chomsky and Lasnik 1977; Vergnaud 1977/2008).

(9) *Principle of Case licensing*: Every instance of Case must be properly licensed.

The Uniqueness Principle (7) correctly rules out such forms as English **my's*, where the form *my* receives the inherent lexical genitive, and is then assigned the genitive again via *'s*,[3] but incorrectly rules out the case stacking such as the stacking of dative and accusative in Korean, illustrated in (10c).

(10) a. haksayng-tul-i   ton-i   philyohata   *Korean*
       student-PL-NOM   money-NOM   need
   b. haksayng-tul-eykey   ton-i   philyohata
       student-PL-DAT   money-NOM   need
   c. haksayng-tul-eykey-ka   ton-i   philyohata
       student-PL-DAT-NOM   money-NOM   need
       'Students need money.' (Gerdts and Youn 1988: 160; Schütze 2001: 194)

The condition in (7) remains controversial and a number of researchers have argued that it may need to be relaxed (see, e.g., McCreight Young 1988; Bejar and Massam 2002; Richards 2013, among others); we will not discuss the more complex issues of multiple case assignment (or "case-stacking") here.

The Case Filter (8) accounts for the ill-formedness of examples such as (11), where the nominals *book* and *editor* have not received the appropriate genitive case:

(11) *[[the book] editor] insistence on completing the work

To understand the Case Filter better, we need to recognize two types of positions where nominals can occur: Cased and Caseless positions. The contrast between these two types of positions is correlated with the contrast between lexical DPs, on the one hand, and all other complements (sentential complements and empty categories) on the other.[4] Lexical DPs can appear only in Cased positions; Caseless DPs, therefore, have to move to a position where they can receive Case. To see an application of the Case Filter, consider the following examples, where *expect* can take either a nominal or a sentential complement:

(12) Everybody expected this rough patch.

(13) Everybody expected that this rough patch was going to come.

Both types of complements can appear as subjects of the corresponding passive clauses:

(14) This rough patch$_i$ was generally expected t$_i$.

(15) [That this rough patch was going to come]$_i$ was generally expected t$_i$.

However, only sentential complements are possible in the impersonal passive (with the expletive *it*):

(16) *It was generally expected this rough patch.

(17) It was generally expected [that this rough patch was going to come].

The contrast between (16) and (17) is explained in terms of Case. Sentential complements do not receive Case and can therefore appear in Caseless positions. In contrast, the DP *a rough patch* has to receive Case; the addition of the passive morphology to *expect* renders its complement position Caseless, so leaving *a rough patch* in this position violates the Case Filter.

   Like passive verbs, predicative adjectives that take sentential complements are unable to Case-mark their complements. This means that their DP complements are Caseless and result in ill-formed structures (19). Such a structure can be rescued if the DP *a victory* moves to the subject position to receive Case (20):

(18) It is unlikely [that we will win].

(19) *It is unlikely [a victory].

(20) [A victory]$_i$ is unlikely t$_i$.

A strong argument in favor of the Case Filter comes from the conditions on lexical/overt subjects of infinitival clauses.[5] In English, lexical subjects of infinitivals can be assigned Case in situ by the complementizer *for*:

(21) a. [For him/*he to admit such a thing] is impossible.
     b. It is impossible [for him/*he to admit such a thing].

The complementizer *for* assigns objective Case, as shown by the form of the pronoun in (21a–b). The presence in (21a–b) of objective case marking on what is clearly a subject illustrates the sort of problem one encounters when seeking a precise one-to-one mapping between grammatical functions (e.g. SUBJECT, OBJECT) and case markings (e.g. nominative, accusative/objective). In practice, these alignments are often imperfect.

While (21) exhibits an overt prepositional complementizer, in many other languages null complementizers may assign objective Case to infinitival subjects as well. Consider the following Russian sentence, in which the silent interrogative complementizer assigns dative Case to the subject of the infinitive:

(22) [Comp INTERR   Maš-e/*Maš-a   [prixodit' segodnja]]?   *Russian*
                    Masha-DAT/*Masha-NOM come.INF   today
     'Should Masha come today?'

Without the complementizer, an overt infinitival subject is impossible:[6]

(23) *It is impossible [him to admit this]

(24) *Maš-e   prixodit'   segodnja   *Russian*
      Masha-DAT come.INF   today
     ('Masha should come today.' – declarative)

Recall that the Case Filter (8) applies to lexical DPs, but not to empty categories. Thus, in the following examples, the infinitival clause is licit with a non-lexical subject, PRO:

(25) [PRO to admit such a thing] is impossible.

(26) It is impossible [PRO to admit such a thing].

As the only item not subject to the Case Filter, PRO is in near-complementary distribution with overt subjects (see, e.g., Radford 2004).[7] Furthermore, since it is not able to receive objective Case, PRO is incompatible with the Case-assigning complementizer *for* (although see, for example, Bobaljik and Landau (2009) and references therein for empirical challenges to this approach):[8]

(27) *It is impossible [for PRO to admit such a thing]

In some contexts, however, lexical/overt subjects of infinitival complements are able to occur in either the presence or absence of *for*:

(28) They want [for him to succeed]

(29) They want [him to succeed]

Case in (28) is assigned by the complementizer *for*, and the derivation is straightforward, with the Case Filter observed. However, Case on *him* in (29) has to be assigned in some other way. A correlate of this difference is that in (29), unlike in (28), the verb *want* cannot be separated from *him* by intervening lexical material (Postal 1974):

(30) I have wanted all my life for him to succeed

(31) *I have wanted all my life him to succeed

The obligatory adjacency between *want* and *him* indicates that the latter can receive Case from *want* only under special conditions, namely when there is no separation between the two. If an adverbial phrase intervenes, as in (31), such Case assignment is blocked; at the same time, the lexical DP cannot receive Case from within the infinitival clause, and the result is ungrammatical (29). The Case assignment configuration illustrated in (29) is known as Exceptional Case Marking (ECM). The subset of English verbs that allows this configuration is referred to as ECM predicates (e.g., *want, expect, find, prove, judge*). The phenomenon of exceptional Case assignment across an infinitival clause boundary is closely related to the *accusativus cum infinitivo* construction found in classical languages such as Latin:

(32) hodie   necesse   est   te   solum   ambulare   *Latin*
      today   necessary is   2SG.ACC   alone.ACC   walk.INF
      'It is necessary for you today to walk alone.'

Certain questions on the topic of Case theory, concerning both the range of categories that can assign Case and the manner in which Case is assigned, remain to be addressed. We have already observed that both C heads (such as English *for*) and certain prepositions may have Case-assigning properties; we have also tacitly assumed that verbal and inflectional heads can act as Case assigners (verbs assign Case to their complements; inflectional heads assign Case to clausal subjects). One of the most intriguing aspects of Case Theory concerns the general principles that regulate the situations in which Case assignment is and is not possible. What prevents particular lexical items from assigning Case? What is the relationship between Case and agreement? Are the rules of Case assignment the same across different alignment systems? We take up these issues in the next section.

3   Explanations

3.1   *Case assigners*

An ongoing issue in discussion of Case has been the distinction between Case-assigning and non-Case-assigning heads. In the preceding sections, we alluded to several such distinctions: between verbal predicates (which can, in some cases, assign Case to their complements) and adjectival predicates (which cannot); between finite inflectional heads (which can assign Case to their clausal subjects) and non-finite ones (which cannot); and between active transitive verbs (which can assign Case to their complements) and passives (which cannot).

There have been attempts in the theoretical literature to derive at least some of these distinctions from deeper principles. Chomsky's (1981) dual binary-feature system, shown in Table 8.2, was one such attempt. In this account, the [−N] feature was the crucial property that allowed a category to be, in principle, an assigner of abstract Case. This explanation had the desirable effect of ruling in verbs and prepositions as Case assigners, and ruling out nouns and adjectives; however, it also faced many challenges. For instance, the status of inflectional categories such as finite tense as Case assigners, despite their absence from the typology in Table 8.2, was problematic; equally inexplicable was the contrast between adjectives, which apparently universally fail to assign Case, and nouns, which assign genitive Case under certain circumstances. Essentially, it turned out that lexical

Table 8.2 Featural decomposition of lexical categories (Chomsky 1981)

	+N	−N
+V	adjective	verb
−V	noun	preposition

categories were not fine-grained enough to capture both the necessary and sufficient conditions for the status of a head as a Case assigner (compare finite vs. non-finite tense, active vs. passive verbs, etc.).

Another important attempt to predict the distribution of Case assigners grew out of the Split VP Hypothesis – the idea that there is a functional head (often labeled v^0), distinct from the lexical verb, that is responsible for introducing the external argument, assigning accusative Case to the object, and, perhaps, "verbalizing" the category-less lexical root (see Chomsky 1995; Hale and Keyser 1993; Kratzer 1996; Marantz 1997 among others). This hypothesis located the Case-assigning capacity of verbs away from the verb itself, in v^0. The move allowed alternations such as the passive or the (anti-)causative to be viewed as variations in the verbal functional head; given that accusative Case assignment was a property of this verbalizing head, it was natural that adjectives would lack this capacity.

These newer approaches, however, still treated Case itself as a sui generis syntactic feature. As noted in §2, such attempts to reduce case to grammatical function (e.g., SUBJECT) run into significant empirical problems. More recently, Pesetsky and Torrego (2001; 2004; 2007) have proposed that Case features are simply the uninterpretable counterparts of tense/aspect features, much as phi-features (person, number, gender) on tense/aspect/mood (TAM) markers or finite verbs are understood as the uninterpretable counterparts of phi-features on nominal projections.

3.2   Case and agreement: a brief history of co-occurrence and causality

One of the central empirical issues which has pervaded the literature on case is the relationship between case and agreement.[9] Pre-theoretically, the most clear illustration of this relationship comes from the subjects of finite clauses: in a great many languages, such subjects obligatorily bear nominative case and also obligatorily determine agreement on the finite verb or tense/aspect-marker. For example, in Latvian:

(33) Bērn-s   zīmē   veikal-u   *Latvian*
       child-NOM   draw.3SG.PRES   store-ACC
       'The child is drawing a store.'

Within generative linguistics, this observation has been captured in different ways at different times. The Government & Binding framework was able to capture the relationship between nominative case and finite agreement by ascribing a dual role to the I(nfl)^0 node (Chomsky 1986; Mohanan 1982; Ouhalla 1991; Reuland 1983; Rizzi 1982; Stowell 1981 among others). Government by I^0 was considered to be responsible for the assignment of nominative Case, which (in at least a subset of nominative-accusative languages) was coupled with movement of the governed phrase to the specifier position of the inflectional projection.

(34)

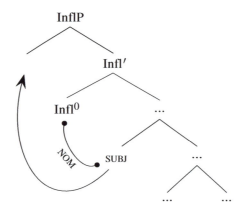

Additionally, the structural relationship between a head and its specifier – or *spec-head*, for short – was afforded a special status, in that it could give rise to the sharing (or checking) of values between the phrase in specifier position and the head of the entire projection.

(35)

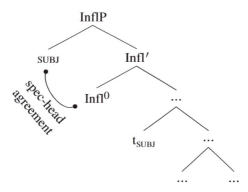

This dual role of I^0 captured the observed coupling of nominative case and finite agreement.

Notice that, at this stage of theoretical development, no *causal* relationship between case and agreement was assumed; the phrase governed by I^0 simply happened to be the one to move to [Spec, IP], which in turn determined finite agreement on I^0. Thus, it was perfectly possible to have other sources of Case assignment – for example, inherent Case assignment by *of* in English – that were associated with no agreement whatsoever.

The advent of the Minimalist Program (Chomsky 1995, *et seq.*) resulted in a subtle but important change in the logic of the case–agreement relationship. An increased interest in what "drove" certain syntactic operations led to the hypothesis that agreement was a fundamental *need* of the finite verb or tense/aspect-marker; this idea was reflected in the introduction of "uninterpretable features", elements of the derivation that would cause ill-formedness unless tended to by a particular syntactic operation. Agreement was construed as a response to the syntactic system's need to neutralize these uninterpretable features on the finite verb or tense/aspect-marker. This change in the theoretical treatment of agreement came with a concomitant change in the theory of case: the Case Filter was recast as an uninterpretable feature in its own right, which resided on noun phrases; it was assumed that this feature got "checked" precisely when the noun phrase in question entered into a full-fledged agreement relation with some syntactic head.[10]

(36)

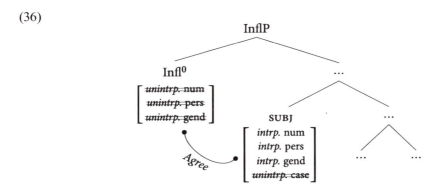

The choice of Case assignment was understood to be fundamentally linked to the identity of the head with which the noun phrase entered its agreement relationship (nominative for I^0, accusative for V/v^0, and so forth).

These changes brought on by Minimalism created a much tighter coupling between case and agreement than had existed before. Consider the fate of a noun phrase that is *not* the subject of a finite clause. Under the GB treatment, this noun phrase needed to satisfy the Case Filter, and did so if it stood in the appropriate structural relation (i.e., government) with an appropriate head – for example, a preposition, or a verb capable of assigning accusative Case. There was no requirement that this noun phrase enter an agreement relationship with any other syntactic element (although this was of course possible if the language in question had agreeing prepositions and/or object-agreement). Under the MP treatment, however, no Case assignment could exist without agreement: Case assignment was now a "side effect" of a noun phrase entering into a full-fledged agreement relationship with a given head. Every overt noun phrase now needed an agreement relationship – observed or hypothesized – to explain how it could satisfy this new implementation of the Case Filter.

This path was not the only conceivable one that could have been taken. Indeed, an alternative view was articulated almost concurrently with the publication of Chomsky's (1995) "Minimalist Program":[11]

> [By] virtue of being licensed in situ by Case binders that are or contain functional heads, ergative and accusative arguments may agree with those heads.
>
> (Bittner and Hale 1996: 3)

The view espoused by Bittner and Hale holds that it is the assignment of Case to (at least some) noun phrases that allows those noun phrases to control agreement, and not the other way around. About a decade later, this same view on agreement was defended in greater detail within an entirely different view of case assignment. Bobaljik (2008) revived a set of typological observations made by Moravcsik (1974; 1978) concerning the set of arguments that are eligible to be targeted for agreement in a given language. But, while Moravcsik's observations were phrased in terms of grammatical functions ("subject", "object", "indirect object", "adverb"), Bobaljik demonstrated that the empirical coverage of those observations could be extended to cover ergative-absolutive languages and languages with 'quirky subjects', if the observations were phrased in terms of case marking rather than grammatical functions.

The particular implementation adopted by Bobaljik cannot be properly illustrated without first discussing Marantz's (1991) configurational theory of case (see §3.3); however, the crucial observation is that, in a given language, the case marking borne by a DP is a better predictor of that DP's agreement pattern than its grammatical function is. Left as is, this observation – much like the previously discussed correlation between nominative case and finite agreement – would amount to a statement about correlation rather than causation. However, Bobaljik demonstrated that, although bearing the "correct" case marking is a necessary condition for agreement with a given noun phrase, it is not a *sufficient* condition; the agreement target must also be, structurally, the highest DP among those whose case qualifies them for agreement; furthermore, the agreement target must be sufficiently local to the head that agrees with it.

The observation that correct case marking is a necessary but insufficient condition for agreement crucially supports the view that assignment of case is a pre-condition to the calculus of agreement. This, of course, means that the MP view of case as a "side effect" of agreement is untenable; however, that view was in trouble independently of Bobaljik's observation (see, e.g., Preminger (2011) for a demonstration that absolutive in Basque does not arise via agreement, overt or otherwise).

Of course, for this new view of the interaction between case and agreement to be viable, there needs to be a theory of case assignment where case arises independently of (and prior to) agreement. Fortunately, this is provided by configurational approaches to case assignment, to which we turn next.

3.3 The structural determination of case: head-centered vs. configurational approaches

Since agreement has canonically been viewed as a relationship between a head and a phrase, the view of case as a by-product of agreement necessarily commits its proponents to the view that case likewise depends on the same structural relation. But, in actuality, it is possible to ponder the structural conditions on case and agreement separately. Specifically, we might reject the MP-style causal link between agreement and case while maintaining an MP-style structural condition on case assignment, consisting of (i) a c-command relation obtaining between a designated head and the relevant noun phrase and (ii) the absence of an intervening phase boundary or DP between the two.

This approach can be contrasted with what is known as a configurational system of case assignment, in which noun phrases are assigned case by virtue of their structural position relative to certain lexical heads and, more importantly, to other noun phrases in the clause. Implementations of configurational case assignment differ (see Bittner and Hale 1996; Marantz 1991; Yip *et al.* 1987, among others), but all these approaches share the insight that accusative and ergative (see §1) can be given a unified treatment as dependent cases. While this insight is not entirely new, configurational approaches to case assignment take seriously the fact that both accusative and ergative are cases that typically depend on the presence of another, case-marked noun phrase in their local vicinity (see also Bobaljik 1993; Laka 1993). Configurational approaches allow these cases to arise directly by virtue of the presence of this other noun phrase; the difference between accusative and ergative alignments then reduces to a question of the direction of dependent case assignment (i.e., whether the dependent case is assigned to the higher or lower of the two relevant noun phrases).

Another crucial virtue of configurational approaches to case assignment is their ability to account for so-called 'quirky case' languages. In Icelandic, the normal nominative-accusative pattern of case assignment in the clause is disrupted under certain circumstances – specifically, when the particular predicate chosen idiosyncratically selects a subject with non-nominative case (e.g., dative, genitive, or accusative; see Zaenen *et al.* 1985 and much subsequent literature for arguments that, despite being non-nominative, these arguments are indeed grammatical subjects). Interestingly, selection of a quirky subject inhibits the appearance of accusative on the direct object; the direct object surfaces with nominative case in these instances.

(37) Henni   líkuðu   hestarnir/*hestana.   *Icelandic*
      she.DAT liked.PL horses-the.NOM.PL/*horses-the.ACC.PL
      'She liked the horses.' (Thráinsson 2007: 172)

Approaches to case that locate the ability to assign case in the functional infrastructure of the clause have difficulty accounting for the disappearance of the accusative; configurational approaches, on the other hand, handle these facts with ease.

3.4   Case in ergative languages

Case assignment in ergative languages, where the morphological case of the intransitive subject aligns with that of the transitive object, has posed particular challenges for Case Theory. Currently, there are several families of approaches to this pattern of case assignment, which we survey below.

The first family of approaches is configurational (see also §3.3). Under these approaches, the assignment (or "discharging") of ergative case is assumed to depend on some intrinsic morphosyntactic property of the clause in which the ergative case arises. In one variant of this approach, the Obligatory Case Parameter (Bobaljik 1993; Laka 1993), ergative case emerges only when the absolutive has already been discharged within the same clause. On this view, the distinction between ergative alignment and accusative alignment arises from a parameter which requires the obligatory discharging of either "subject case" or "object case" (the former setting giving rise to an accusative alignment, the latter to an ergative one). In another variant of the configurational approach, Marantz's (1991) theory of dependent case, the emergence of ergative case depends not on the discharge of the absolutive, but on the presence of a non-oblique nominal which is distinct from, and syntactically lower than, the ergative nominal.[12] In this view, the parameter setting determines whether dependent case is assigned to the lower or higher of two distinct nominals (again, the former setting results in an accusative alignment and the latter in an ergative one).

The second family of analyses views the ergative as an inherent case. It is virtually uncontroversial that certain lexical heads in a given language place idiosyncratic requirements on the case borne by their arguments (e.g. different cases assigned by different prepositions, as, for example, in German). If we take seriously the status of v^0 as a lexical head introducing the external argument (see discussion and references in §3.1), then it is entirely possible that, in a given language, this lexeme would place the same sort of idiosyncratic case requirements upon the argument it introduces (i.e., the external argument). The result would be a particular case marking associated with the transitive subject, but not with the transitive object or the intransitive subject. The proposal that the ergative is assigned as an inherent case relies on two main types of evidence. First, in a number of ergative languages, the link between ergative case and the thematically agentive event participant seems quite strong; at least, it is stronger than the link between nominative case and the agent role. For instance, Laka (2006) argues for a strong connection between case and theta roles in Basque, which in turn favors the inherent-case approach to the ergative.[13] The second argument in favor of treating the ergative as an inherent case comes from case preservation under raising (see Woolford (2006) for discussion and examples).[14]

Inherent Case can be assigned to a DP directly by a verbal head, as suggested by Laka (2006), Legate (2008), and Aldridge (2004; 2008), among others. On the other hand, Markman and Graschenkov (2012) and Polinsky (2013) argue that the thematic role of the agent is assigned to the subject not by a verbal projection but by a morphologically dependent adposition; the PP, in its entirety, is located in the specifier of the highest v^0, which accounts for the subject properties of the ergative expression. Assuming that adpositions assign inherent case (cf. Landau 2010),[15] this brings the latter approach closer to that of Laka, Legate, and Aldridge. One of the challenges for the proposal that ergative is an inherent case lies in accounting for agreement patterns observed across ergative languages, which are far from uniform. Another dimension along which ergative languages differ has to do with the accessibility of the ergative expression to A-bar extraction under relativization, *wh*-question formation, or topicalization. Some ergative languages disallow such extraction for the ergative, but invariably permit it for the absolutive – a phenomenon known as "syntactic ergativity" (Manning 1996). Such differences in agreement and extraction patterns have led to the idea that the ergative languages do not constitute a uniform class. A number of recent approaches, most notably those of Legate (2008) and Aldridge (2004; 2008), pursue the idea that ergative languages fall into two distinct subtypes. In the first subtype, the absolutive corresponds to the nominative case and is assigned to the intransitive subject and the direct object by T; the ergative is treated as an inherent case. In these languages, only intransitive subjects can appear in control infinitives, the ergative is not accessible to A-bar movement, and agreement is determined by the absolutive DP. Examples of such languages include Seediq, Inuit, and Chukchi. In the second subtype, absolutive case is seen as a morphological default, inserted when a dedicated morphological realization is unavailable for a given abstract Case. Intransitive subjects receive nominative Case and direct objects receive accusative Case, but the morphology of these Cases is identical and its surface form is what we have come to call 'absolutive'. These languages use only the absolutive for DPs without dedicated abstract Case (e.g., hanging topics); and since the morphological absolutive can appear on DPs marked with abstract Cases other than absolutive (lacking a distinct morphological form of their own), multiple absolutives can appear in a single clause. Finally, subject agreement in these languages may be triggered by all subjects, by the intransitive subject alone, or by the highest DP with structural Case (this last pattern is sometimes known as absolutive agreement). This subclass of ergative languages does not manifest syntactic ergativity – for example, it does not impose extraction restrictions on the ergative argument.

4 Summary

In this chapter, we have presented and discussed the notions of morphological (surface) case and abstract Case, showing the empirical and theoretical motivation for each. The discussion of morphological case presented the dimensions of cross-linguistic variation found in this domain and surveyed main tendencies in the expression of case. Although significant variation is found in the expression of morphological case, this variation is constrained by certain limitations and tendencies, which we have attempted to outline. The notion of abstract Case is used to predict the distribution of overt and non-overt nominal forms, and is considered one of the fundamental abstract syntactic relations in linguistic theory. The main role of abstract Case is in constraining the distribution of various types of nominals. Accordingly, the formalization of abstract Case has been an important task for modern linguistic theory.

Notes

1 We take the notion of *parametric variation* to include variation in lexical properties of functional categories. There is a stronger position, found in the generative literature, that takes all parametric variation to be lexically determined in this fashion (this position is sometimes referred to as the *Borer–Chomsky conjecture*; see, e.g., Baker 2008).
2 Distinguished from morphological case marking by the initial capital C.
3 One could argue that the inner DP in *my's is in fact genitive even before the possessive *'s*, which can be seen from examples such as *a car of yours/hers/theirs*. Then one could contend that *my's exists in English, but as an irregular form: *mine*.
4 Throughout this chapter, we use the label "DP" (Determiner Phrase) to refer to the maximal projection of a nominal, except when quoting directly from sources that use a different label. As far as we can tell, though, nothing stated here hinges on this particular choice.
5 In what follows we will concentrate on English, but see Szabolcsi (2009), who shows that, in Hungarian, infinitival complements of subject control verbs and subject raising verbs can host overt nominative subjects.
6 Russian does allow declarative sentences with dative subjects, but not with the meaning intended in (24); such root infinitive constructions require the interpretation that the event is beyond the main participant's control. See Moore and Perlmutter (2000), Sigurðsson (2002), and references therein.
7 The complementarity between PRO and lexical/overt DPs is incomplete because of instances such as (i), where neither PRO nor any other DP can appear in the underlined position (without *of*):
   (i)   Kim is fond _____
   Within the Government & Binding framework, this imperfect complementarity was handled by subjecting PRO not to the precise inverse of the Case Filter but to the *PRO Theorem*, which stated that PRO cannot tolerate syntactic government in general (even government by non-Case-assigners).
8 Note, however, that some English dialects, most notably Belfast English (Henry 1995: Ch. 1, 4), seem to have reanalyzed *for* as a complementizer that cliticizes to the infinitival marker *to*. Accordingly, Belfast English allows constructions such as (i) and (ii):
   (i)   For to stay here would be just as expensive.
   (ii) I don't like the children for to be late.
9 The term *agreement* should be understood here in the narrow sense, as morphophonologically overt co-variance between two morphosyntactic elements in one or more features of the set *{number, person, gender/noun-class}*.
10 The qualifier *full-fledged* here is meant to distinguish agreement relations involving the full set of nominal features with relations involving only a subset of those features. This distinction is not crucial at the current juncture (although see below); for the purposes of the current discussion, it is sufficient to know that agreement between a finite verb or tense/aspect-marker and the subject is considered full-fledged.
11 The opposition established in the text below is a very circumscribed one, pertaining to the causal relation between (some) case markings and (some) agreement relations; this should not be taken as an indication that Bittner and Hale (1996) were opposed to the Minimalist Program more generally. As the paper in question makes clear, these authors were working decidedly within the general framework espoused by Chomsky (1995).
12 The term *distinct* here is meant to preclude positions occupied by a moved nominal in the course of the syntactic derivation from counting as separate operands for the calculation of dependent case.
13 This analysis of Basque is not shared by all researchers – see Režać *et al.* (in press) for the proposal that the Basque ergative is a structural case.
14 However, Artiagoitia (2001) and Režać *et al.* (in press) show that under raising, the ergative in Basque patterns as a structural case.
15 This assumption is not uncontroversial, but for reasons of space, we will not expand on it here.

Further reading (ordered chronologically)

Jakobson, Roman. 1936. Beitrag zur allgemeinen Kasuslehre: Gesamtbedeutung der russischen Kasus. Reprinted in: Roman Jakobson. 1971. *Selected writings: Word and language*, II, vol. 2, 23–71. Berlin: Mouton de Gruyter.

Fillmore, Charles. 1968. The case for case. In *Universals in linguistic theory*, ed. Emmon Bach and Robert T. Harms, 1–88. New York: Holt, Rinehart, and Winston.

Williams, Edwin. 1994. *Thematic structure in syntax*. Cambridge, MA: MIT Press.

Bobaljik, Jonathan David, and Susi Wurmbrand. 2008. Case in GB/Minimalism. In *Oxford handbook of case*, ed. Andrej Malchukov and Andrew Spencer, 44–58. Oxford: Oxford University Press.

Sigurðsson, Halldór Ármann. 2012. Minimalist C/case. *Linguistic Inquiry* 43:191–227.

References

Aldridge, Edith. 2004. Ergativity and word order in Austronesian languages. PhD dissertation, Cornell University.

Aldridge, Edith. 2008. Generative approaches to ergativity. *Language and Linguistics Compass* 5:966–995.

Artiagoitia, Xabier. 2001. Seemingly ergative and ergatively seeming. In *Features and interfaces in Romance: Essays in honor of Heles Contreras*, ed. Julia Herschensohn, Enrique Mallen, and Karen Zagona, 1–22. Amsterdam: John Benjamins.

Baker, Mark C. 2008. *The syntax of agreement and concord*. Cambridge: Cambridge University Press.

Bejar, Susana, and Diane Massam. 2002. Multiple case checking. *Syntax* 2:65–79.

Bittner, Maria, and Kenneth Hale. 1996. The structural determination of case and agreement. *Linguistic Inquiry* 27:1–68.

Blake, Barry. 2001. *Case*. 2nd edn. Cambridge: Cambridge University Press.

Bobaljik, Jonathan. 1993. On ergativity and ergative unergatives. *MIT Working Papers in Linguistics* 19:45–88.

Bobaljik, Jonathan. 2008. Where's phi? Agreement as a post-syntactic operation. In *Phi-Theory: Phi features across interfaces and modules*, ed. Daniel Harbour, David Adger, and Susana Bejar, 295–328. Oxford: Oxford University Press.

Bobaljik, Jonathan David, and Idan Landau. 2009. Icelandic control is not A-movement: the case from case. *Linguistic Inquiry* 40:113–132, doi: 10.1162/ling.2009.40.1.113.

Chomsky, Noam. 1981. *Lectures on government and binding*. Dordrecht: Foris.

Chomsky, Noam. 1986. *Knowledge of language: Its nature, origins, and use*. New York: Praeger.

Chomsky, Noam. 1995. *The Minimalist Program*. Cambridge, MA: MIT Press.

Chomsky, Noam, and Howard Lasnik. 1977. Filters and control. *Linguistic Inquiry* 8:425–504.

Comrie, Bernard. 1978. Ergativity. In *Syntactic typology: Studies in the phenomenology of language*, ed. Winifred Lehmann, 329–394. Austin: University of Texas Press.

Comrie, Bernard. 1989. *Language universals and linguistic typology*. 2nd edn. Chicago, IL: University of Chicago Press.

Comrie, Bernard, and Maria Polinsky. 1998. The great Dagestanian case hoax. In *Case, typology, and grammar*, ed. Anna Siewierska and Jae Jung Song, 95–114. Amsterdam: John Benjamins.

Coon, Jessica. 2013a. TAM split ergativity. Part I. *Language and Linguistics Compass* 7:171–190.

Coon, Jessica. 2013b. TAM split ergativity. Part II. *Language and Linguistics Compass* 7:191–200.

Dixon, R.M.W. 1994. *Ergativity*. Cambridge: Cambridge University Press.

Gerdts, Donna, and Cheong Youn. 1988. Korean psych constructions: Advancement or retreat? In *Papers from the 24th Annual Regional Meeting of the Chicago Linguistic Society, Part One: The General Session*, ed. Lynn MacLeod, Gary Larson, and Diane Brentari, 155–175. Chicago: Chicago Linguistic Society.

Hale, Kenneth, and Samuel Jay Keyser. 1993. On argument structure and the lexical expression of syntactic relations. In *The view from Building 20: Essays in linguistics in honor of Sylvain Bromberger*, ed. Kenneth Hale and Samuel Jay Keyser, 53–110. Cambridge, MA: MIT Press.

Henry, Alison. 1995. *Belfast English and Standard English*. Oxford: Oxford University Press.

Iggesen, Oliver. 2013. Number of cases. In *World atlas of language structures online*, ed. Matthew S. Dryer and Martin Haspelmath, Leipzig: Max Plank Institute for Evolutionary Anthropology Available online at http://wals.info/chapter/49 (accessed 31 January 2014).

Kratzer, Angelika. 1996. Severing the external argument from its verb. In *Phrase structure and the lexicon*, ed. Johan Rooryck and Laurie Zaring, 169–196. Dordrecht: Kluwer.

Laka, Itziar. 1993. Unergatives that assign ergative and unaccusatives that assign accusative. In *Papers on case and agreement* I, ed. Jonathan Bobaljik and Colin Phillips, 149–172. (*MITWPL* 18).

Laka, Itziar. 2006. On the nature of case in Basque: structural or inherent? In *Organizing grammar: Linguistic studies in honor of Henk van Riemsdijk*, ed. Hans Broekhuis, Norbert Corver, Riny Huybregts, Ursula Kleinhenz, and Jan Koster, 374–382. Berlin/New York: Mouton de Gruyter.

Landau, Idan. 2010. *The locative syntax of experiencers*. Cambridge, MA: MIT Press.

Lasnik, Howard. 2008. On the development of case theory: Triumphs and challenges. In *Foundational issues in linguistic theory: Essays in honor of Jean-Roger Vergnaud*, ed. Robert Freidin, Carlos P. Otero, and Maria Luisa Zubizarreta, 17–41. Cambridge, MA: MIT Press.

Legate, Julie A. 2002. Warlpiri: Theoretical implications. PhD dissertation, MIT.

Legate, Julie A. 2008. Morphological and abstract case. *Linguistic Inquiry* 39:55–101.

McCreight Young, Katherine. 1988. Multiple case assignments. PhD dissertation, MIT.

Manning, Christopher. 1996. *Ergativity*. Stanford, CA: CSLI.

Marantz, Alec. 1991. Case and licensing. In *Eastern States Conference on Linguistics*, ed. Germán Westphal, Benjamin Ao, and Hee-Rahk Chae, 234–253. Ithaca, NY: Cornell University, Cornell Linguistics Club.

Marantz, Alec. 1997. No escape from syntax: Don't try morphological analysis in the privacy of your own lexicon. In *Proceedings of the 21st Penn Linguistics Colloquium (PLC 21)*, ed. Alexis Dimitriadis, Laura Siegen, Clarissa Surek-Clark, and Alexander Williams, 201–225, vol. 4.2, University of Pennsylvania Working Papers in Linguistics. Philadelphia, PA: Penn Linguistics Club.

Markman, Vita, and Pavel Graschenkov. 2012. On the adpositional nature of ergative subjects. *Lingua* 122:257–266.

Mohanan, K.P. 1982. Infinitival subjects, government, and abstract case. *Linguistic Inquiry* 13: 323–327.

Moore, John, and David Perlmutter. 2000. What does it take to be a dative subject? *Natural Language and Linguistic Theory* 18:373–416.

Moravcsik, Edith A. 1974. Object-verb agreement. *Working Papers on Language Universals*, 15: 25–140.

Moravcsik, Edith A. 1978. Agreement. In *Universals of human language IV: Syntax*, ed. Joseph H. Greenberg, 331–374. Stanford, CA: Stanford University Press.

Ouhalla, Jamal. 1991. *Functional categories and parametric variation*. London: Routledge.

Owens, Jonathan. 1985. *A grammar of Harar Oromo (Northeastern Ethiopia): Including a text and a glossary*. Hamburg: Buske Verlag.

Pesetsky, David, and Esther Torrego. 2001. T-to-C movement: causes and consequences. In *Ken Hale: A life in language*, ed. Michael Kenstowicz, 355–426. Cambridge, MA: MIT Press.

Pesetsky, David, and Esther Torrego. 2004. Tense, case, and the nature of syntactic categories. In *The Syntax of time*, ed. Jacqueline Gueron and Jacqueline Lecarme, 495–537. Cambridge, MA: MIT Press.

Pesetsky, David, and Esther Torrego. 2007. The syntax of valuation and the interpretability of features. In *Phrasal and clausal architecture: syntactic derivation and interpretation, in honor of Joseph E. Emonds*, ed. Simin Karimi, Vida Samiian, and Wendy Wilkins, 262–294. Amsterdam: John Benjamins.

Polinsky, Maria. 2013. A tale of two ergatives. Ms. Harvard University.

Postal, Paul. 1974. *On raising: One rule of English grammar and its theoretical implications*. Cambridge, MA: MIT Press.

Preminger, Omer. 2011. Asymmetries between person and number in syntax: A commentary on Baker's SCOPA. *Natural Language and Linguistic Theory* 29:917–937.

Radford, Andrew. 2004. *English syntax: An introduction*. Cambridge: Cambridge University Press.

Reuland, Eric. 1983. Governing -ing. *Linguistic Inquiry* 14:101–136.

Režać, Milan, Pablo Albizu, and Ricardo Etxepare. forthcoming. The structural ergative of Basque and the theory of case. *Natural Language* and *Linguistic Theory*.

Richards, Norvin. 2013. Lardil "case stacking" and the timing of case assignment. *Syntax* 16:42–76.

Rizzi, Luigi. 1982. *Issues in Italian syntax*. Dordrecht: Foris.

Schütze, Carson. 2001. On Korean "Case stacking": The varied functions of the particles *ka* and *lul*. *The Linguistic Review* 18:193–232.

Sigurðsson, Halldór A. 2002. To be an oblique subject: Russian vs. Icelandic. *Natural Language and Linguistic Theory* 20:691–724.

Silverstein, Michael. 1976. Hierarchy of features and ergativity. In *Grammatical categories in Australian languages*, ed. R.M.W. Dixon, 112–171. Canberra: Australian National University Press.

Stowell, Timothy. 1981. Origins of phrase structure. PhD dissertation, MIT.

Szabolcsi, Anna. 2009. Overt nominative subjects in infinitival complements in Hungarian. In *Approaches to Hungarian*, vol. 11: *Papers from the 2007 New York Conference*, ed. Marcel den Dikken and Robert Vago, 251–276. Amsterdam: John Benjamins.

Thráinsson, Höskuldur. 2007. *The syntax of Icelandic*. Cambridge: Cambridge University Press.

Vergnaud, Jean-Roger. 1977. Letter to Noam Chomsky and Howard Lasnik on "Filters and control". Reprinted in 2008 *Foundational issues in linguistic theory: Essays in honor of Jean-Roger Vergnaud*, ed. Robert Freidin, Carlos P. Otero, and Maria Luisa Zubizarreta, 3–15. Cambridge, MA: MIT Press.

Woolford, Ellen. 2006. Lexical case, inherent case, and argument structure. *Linguistic Inquiry* 37:111–130.

Yip, Moira, Joan Maling, and Ray Jackendoff. 1987. Case in tiers. *Language* 63:217–250.

Zaenen, Annie, Joan Maling, and Höskuldur Thráinsson. 1985. Case and grammatical functions: The Icelandic passive. *Natural Language* and *Linguistic Theory* 3:441–483.

9

A-bar movement

Norvin Richards

1 Introduction

Chomsky (1977) identifies several movement operations that have come to be known as instances of A-bar movement:

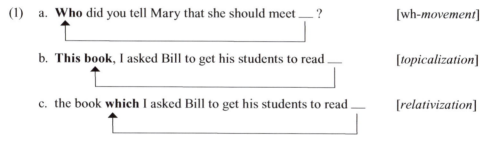

(1) a. **Who** did you tell Mary that she should meet ___ ?   [wh-*movement*]

     b. **This book**, I asked Bill to get his students to read ___   [*topicalization*]

     c. the book **which** I asked Bill to get his students to read ___   [*relativization*]

Subsequent work has expanded Chomsky's original list; movement to initial position in V2 clauses, for example, appears to be A-bar movement, as are certain kinds of scrambling:

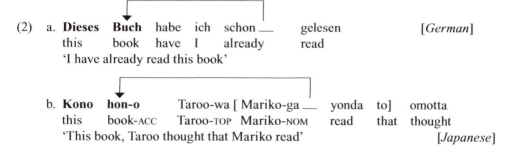

(2) a. **Dieses Buch** habe ich schon ___ gelesen   [*German*]
         this book have I already read
         'I have already read this book'

     b. **Kono hon-o** Taroo-wa [Mariko-ga ___ yonda to] omotta
         this book-ACC Taroo-TOP Mariko-NOM read that thought
         'This book, Taroo thought that Mariko read'   [*Japanese*]

A-bar movement is generally taken to be one of the two major types of phrasal movement (the other being A-movement[1]). Predicting whether a particular instance of movement will be A-movement or A-bar movement has proven difficult, but the two have generally been taken to differ in a number of ways.

First, A-movement is typically unable to cross tensed clause boundaries, while A-bar movement typically can:[2]

(3) a. *__John__ seems [__ will win]
     b. __Who__ do you think [__ will win]?

Second, A-movement allows the moved phrase to bind anaphors that it could not previously bind, while A-bar movement does not:

(4) a. **[John and Mary]**$_i$ seem to [each other$_i$'s parents] __ to be smart.
     b. *__[Which children]__$_i$ does it seem to [each other$_i$'s parents]
            that the teacher should praise __ ?

A third, similar distinction involves pronominal variables, which can be bound from A-positions but not (always[3]) from A-bar positions (the ill-formedness of examples such as (5b) is known as *Weak crossover*; Postal 1971):

(5) a. **[Every priest]**$_i$ seems to [his$_i$ parishioners] __ to be smart.
     b. *__[Which priest]__$_i$ does it seem to [his$_i$ parishioners]
            that the bishop should praise __ ?

Fourth, A-bar movement obligatorily reconstructs (e.g., for purposes of binding of R-expressions inside the moved phrase), while A-movement is not required to do so (Lebeaux 1988; 2009; Chomsky 1993; 1995; Fox 1999; Takahashi and Hulsey 2009):

(6) a. *__[Which argument that John__$_i$ __is a genius]__ did he$_i$ believe __?
     b. **[Every argument that John**$_i$ **is a genius]** seems to him$_i$ __ to be flawless.

Fifth, A-movement may be restricted to non-Case-marked DPs, while A-bar movement typically shows no such restriction:

(7) a. *__[To John]__ was said __ [that it is raining]
     b. **[To whom]** did you say __ [that it is raining]?

Sixth, A-bar movement can license parasitic gaps, while A-movement cannot:

(8) a. *__John__ was hired __ [without talking to __]
     b. __Who__ did you hire __ [without talking to __]?

A seventh asymmetry between the two types of movement has to do with the relation between them: A-movement can feed A-bar movement, but A-bar movement cannot feed A-movement (an observation known as the ban on *Improper Movement*):

(9) a. __Who__ do you think [__ will be told __]?
     b. *__Who__ is known [__ [it will be told __].

(9b) involves A-bar movement of *who* to the specifier of the embedded CP, where it takes scope, followed by A-movement to the specifier of matrix TP. The ban on Improper

Movement is one way of preventing this derivation from yielding a structure with a meaning like that of (10):

(10) It is known [who will be told].

Finally, Fitzpatrick (2006) argues for an eighth asymmetry between A-movement and A-bar movement, involving quantifier float. A-bar movement, he points out, can strand quantifiers in theta-positions, while A-movement cannot. In the West Ulster dialect of English discussed by McCloskey (2000), for example, quantifiers may be stranded in theta-positions by A-movement, as (11a) shows, but quantifiers related to A-moved phrases cannot be, as we see in (11b):

(11) a. **Who** did Officer Smith (*all) arrest (all) __?   [*West Ulster English*]
      b. **The suspects** have (all) been arrested (*all) __.

Fitzpatrick (2006) argues that quantifiers may literally be stranded by A-bar movement, but not by A-movement (in his analysis, A-movement relates DPs to quantifiers base-generated in adverbial positions).[4]

One important issue is how the properties discussed above (along with their exceptions) are related to each other. This question is surely related to a previously mentioned one: what determines whether a particular movement will be A-movement or A-bar movement? Chomsky (1981) proposed that A-movement is movement to positions in which arguments could potentially get theta-roles; passivization, in this account, is A-movement because it lands in "subject position". The discovery of the Internal Subject Hypothesis made this proposal untenable, since movements such as passivization are no longer taken to move nominals into the same positions in which subjects get their theta-roles. A-movements are often related to case and agreement phenomena, but there are well-known difficulties with this definition as well. For example, there are instances of scrambling that behave like A-movement, despite having no effects on case or agreement. There may also be A-bar movements that do affect case and agreement (Richards 1999; Rackowski 2002; van Urk 2013).

Section 2, below, discusses the participants in A-bar movement. Section 3 turns to the conditions on where such movement lands. Section 4 concerns island effects and other conditions on movement.

2   What participates in A-bar movement?

Here I concentrate on two puzzles concerning the phrases that undergo A-bar movement. The first is the general problem of so-called "pied-piping". The second has to do with relative clauses, which have been analyzed as involving A-bar movement either of the head of the relative clause itself or of an operator associated with the head.

2.1   Pied-piping

Wh-movement can move a constituent that is larger than a *wh*-word (Ross 1967). This is known as "pied-piping":

(12) a. **What** did he buy?
      b. [**Whose** car] did he buy?
      c. [**Whose** parents' car] did he buy?

The extent of pied-piping is a point of cross-linguistic variation. For example, English is cross-linguistically unusual in allowing movement of objects of prepositions without pied-piping the PP:

(13) **Who** did you talk [to __]?

In many languages, pied-piping of the entire PP is obligatory:

(14) [S **kem**] vy razgovorival-i __ ? [*Russian*]
      to whom you.PL talked-PL
      'Who did you talk to?'

Recent work on pied-piping includes Heck (2004; 2009) and Cable (2007; 2010). For Heck, pied-piping is the consequence of a family of constraints on Agree and movement relations, which interact with each other in an Optimality-theoretic fashion. The constraints include a general one requiring that pied-piping be minimal, and others that force pied-piping under specific circumstances. Cable's work centers on the distribution, in Tlingit *wh*-questions, of a particle he calls Q (see Hagstrom 1998 and Kishimoto 2005 for discussion of similar particles in Sinhala, Ryukyuan, and premodern Japanese):

(15) a. [Daa] **sá** i éesh al'óon? [*Tlingit*: Cable 2007]
        what Q your father he.hunts.it
        'What is your father hunting?'
     b. [Aadóo yaagu] **sá** ysiteen?
        who boat Q you.saw.it
        'Whose boat did you see?'
     c. [Aadóo teen] **sá** yigoot?
        who with Q you.went
        'Who did you go with?'
     d. [Wáa kwligeyi xáat] **sá** i tuwáa sigóo?
        how it.is.big.REL fish Q your spirit it.is.happy
        '[A fish that is how big] do you want?'

The Q particle *sá* always follows the fronted *wh*-phrase in Tlingit. Cable proposes that Q heads a projection QP which dominates the moved phrase in all of the examples in (15); more generally, his idea is that "*wh*-movement" is actually always movement of a projection of Q. The apparently mysterious nature of pied piping, in this view, is due to the fact that Q is null in many languages, leading us to think of *wh*-questions as simply involving a relation between C and a *wh*-word; if Cable is right, the relevant relation actually involves C, the *wh*-word, and Q, and the phrase that moves is simply a QP. Solving the problem of pied-piping, in this view, is a matter of developing an account of the distribution of Q (which will involve, among other things, a theory about the relation between Q and *wh*-words, and the conditions on that relation).

2.2 Relative clauses

Relativization offers another kind of case in which it is not straightforward to identify the phrase that A-bar moves:

(16) John saw the book that Mary wrote

One type of derivation generates the head *book* outside the relative clause and moves an operator to the specifier of the relative CP. In another type of derivation, known as "raising", the phrase that A-bar moves is some subpart of the head itself.

Arguments for the raising analysis include connectivity effects, which seem to demonstrate that the head of the relative clause begins the derivation inside it:

(17)   John was impressed by the headway that Mary made on the problem

If the idiom *make headway* must be a structural unit at some point (perhaps at LF), then (17) represents an argument for generating the head of the relative clause inside the clause.

The distribution of these two types of derivation is still a topic of debate; one proposal is that both derivations are possible, perhaps under different structural circumstances (e.g., Carlson 1977; Hulsey and Sauerland 2006). See also Kayne (1994), Sauerland (1998), Bianchi (1999), Bhatt (2002), and Henderson (2007).

3.   Where does A-bar movement land?

An important concern in the literature on A-bar movement has been to determine the landing sites occupied by such movement, both in its final position and along its path.

3.1   Final landing sites

The earliest work on *wh*-movement distinguished two possible positions for *wh*-phrases; they could be moved to the specifier of CP, or remain in situ:

(18)   a.   **What** did John buy __?
       b.   Taroo-wa   **nani**-o   kaimasita   ka?   [*Japanese*]
            Taroo-TOP   what-ACC   bought   Q
            'What did Taroo buy?'

There are also languages in which *wh*-phrases may be either moved or *in situ*:

(19)   a.   Tu   as   vu   **qui**?   [*French*]
            you   have   seen who
            'Who did you see?'
       b.   **Qui**   tu   as   vu?
            who   you   have   seen

(20)   a.   Yàar   cí   **ŋó**   ɣòoc   [*Dinka*]
            Yaar   PRF   what   buy.TR
            'What did Yaar buy?'
       b.   **Ye-ŋó**   cíi   Yâar   ɣòoc
            Q-what   PRF.NS   Yaar.GEN   buy.TR

Approaches to *wh*-in-situ include theories that posit unseen *wh*-movement (Huang 1982; Richards 1997; 2001; Pesetsky 2000; Kotek and Erlewine 2013; Kotek forthcoming) and those which do not (Baker 1970; Tsai 1994; Shimoyama 2008). A central deciding factor in choosing between these approaches has been the effects of islands on *wh*-in-situ. Adjunct *wh*-in-situ seems to be subject to the CED[5] (Huang 1982):

(21) a. *Mary [zai John **weishenme** mai shu yihou] shengqi le?[*Mandarin*]
        Mary   at   John   why   buy book after   get.angry ASP
        'What's the reason X such that Mary got angry after John, for X, bought a book?'
     b. *__Why__ did Mary get angry [after John bought a book __]

Similarly, Nishigauchi (1986) and Watanabe (1992) claim that Japanese exhibits *wh*-island effects:[6]

(22) a. *John- wa [Mary-ga **nani** -o katta ka dooka] siritagatteiru no[*Japanese*]
        John   TOP Mary NOM what ACC bought whether   wants.to.know Q
        'What does John want to know whether Mary bought __?'
     b. John- wa [Mary-ga **nani** -o katta ka dooka] omotteiru no?
        John   TOP Mary NOM what ACC bought whether   thinks   Q
        'What does John think that Mary bought __?'

However, there are other island effects that seem to be reliably absent for *wh*-in-situ:

(23) a. Mary [zai John mai **sheme** yihou] shengqi   le?   [*Mandarin*]
        Mary   at   John buy what   after get.angry ASP
        'What did Mary get angry [after John bought __]?'
     b. Mary-wa [John-ga **nani**-o katta ato de] okotta   no?   [*Japanese*]
        Mary TOP John NOM what ACC bought after   got.angry Q
        'What did Mary get angry [after John bought __]?'
     c. *__What__ did Mary get angry [after John bought __]?

For some discussion of these issues, see Richards (2008) and Shimoyama (2008).
   Some languages require *wh*-phrases to be immediately preverbal:

(24) a. Mirenek **séin**   ikusi   rau?   [*Ondarroa Basque*: Arregi 2002]
        Miren-ERG who-ABS see.PRF   AUX
        'Who has Miren seen?'
     b. *__Séin__   Mirenek ikusi   rau?
        who-ABS   Miren-ERG see.PRF AUX
     c. Jon   **señek** ikusi   rau?
        Jon-ABS who-ERG see.PRF AUX
        'Who saw Jon?'
     d. *__Señek__ Jon   ikusi   rau?
        who-ERG Jon-ABS see.PRF AUX

(25) a. nin-ne **aarə** talli?   [*Malayalam*: Jayaseelan 2004]
        you-ACC who   beat
        'Who beat you?'
     b. *__aarə__ nin-ne talli?

Another group of languages has been described as having an immediately postverbal position for *wh*-phrases:

(26) a. bvú ↓tí mɔ̀ zí **kwɔ̀** né (à)   [*Aghem*: Hyman and Polinsky 2009]
      dogs D P₂ eat what today QM
      'What did the dogs eat?'

   b. à mɔ̀ zì **ndúghɔ̀** ↓bɛ́ ↓kɔ́ né (à)
      ES P₁ eat who fufu D.OBL today QM
      'Who ate fufu today?'

   c. tí-bvú tì-bìghà mɔ̂ zì **zín** bɛ́ ↓kɔ́ (á)
      dogs two P₁ eat when fufu D.OBL QM
      'When did the two dogs eat fufu?'

(27) a. úm-fá:na ú-yí-nikezê:-**ni** ín-tómbazâ:ne? [*Zulu*: Cheng and Downing 2012]
      1-boy 1SUBJ-9OBJ-give-what 9-girl
      'What did the boy give to the girl?'

   b. ú-Síph' ú-yí-phékê: **nì:n'** ín-kúkh' émzini wa:kho
      1-Sipho 1SUBJ-9OBJ-cook when 9-chicken LOC.3.house 3.your
      'When did Sipho cook chicken at your house?'

   c. u-wa-thwéle **ngâ:n'** amá-tha:nga?
      you-6OBJ-carry how 6-pumpkin
      'How are you carrying the pumpkins?'

Two major approaches to these kinds of languages have arisen. One (Ortiz de Urbina 1989; Jayaseelan 2004) posits dedicated syntactic positions for *wh*-movement. Another regards these languages as exhibiting *wh*-in-situ, appealing to non-syntactic requirements (stress, prosody, focus placement) as filters to force *wh*-phrases to surface in the correct positions (Arregi 2002; Hyman and Polinsky 2009; Buell 2009; Richards 2010; Cheng and Downing 2012).

We also find languages that use biclausal structures, arguably a form of pseudocleft, to form some or all of their *wh*-questions (Potsdam 2009):

(28) a. **Ano** ang inilagay mo sa lamesa?   [*Tagalog*]
      what ANG OBL-put NG.2SG DAT table
      'What did you put on the table?'

   b. **Saan** mo inilagay ang libro?
      where NG.2SG OBL-put ANG book
      'Where did you put the book?'

Tagalog uses clefts for DP *wh*-questions (such as 26a), but not for non-DPs (such as 26b).

Perhaps just as striking as the existence of this language variation is the absence of certain imaginable but apparently unavailable variations. It is not clear, for example, that there are any genuine cases of *wh*-movement to the right, at least in spoken languages. There are languages that require *wh*-phrases to be right-peripheral in the clause:

(29) λ'ə-r Ø-q'a-z-šx̂wə-aɣ-r **x̂ət-r** Ø [*Kabardian*: Colarusso 1992]
      meat-ABS 3-HOR-WHO-eat-PAST-GER who-ABS be
      'Who ate the meat?'

However, Kabardian uses an in-situ version of the clefting strategy just discussed; a more literal translation of (29) would be '[The one who ate the meat] is who?'[7] Literal *wh*-movement to the right, then, may be unattested in spoken languages. Kayne's (1994) Antisymmetry theory is one account of the absence of such languages. The existence of languages such as Kabardian is evidence against the most straightforward imaginable processing-based account; the requirement is apparently not that *wh*-expressions must linearly precede their gaps, for example. Many signed languages have been argued to have *wh*-movement to the right (Neidle *et al.* 1998; Cecchetto *et al.* 2009), though there are other accounts on the market (Petronio and Lillo-Martin 1997).

3.2 Multiple wh-movement

Another point of cross-linguistic variation involves multiple questions. There are languages in which such questions are banned (McCloskey 1979; Calabrese 1984; Stoyanova 2008):

(30) a. *Cé   a^L   rinne   caidé?   [*Irish*: McCloskey 1979]
        who c   did   what
        'Who did what?'
     b. *Chi ha   scritto   che   cosa?   [*Italian*: Calabrese 1984]
        who has   written   what   thing
        'Who wrote what?'

In a second type of language, one *wh*-phrase moves and others remain in situ:

(31) **What** did John give **to whom when**?

A third kind of multiple *wh*-question is found in languages such as Bulgarian, Serbian, and Croatian:

(32) a. **Kakvo   na   kogo**   e   dal   Ivan?   [*Bulgarian*]
        what   to   whom   AUX   given   Ivan
        'What did Ivan give to whom?'
     b. **Ko**   je   **koga**   vidio?   [*Serbian*]
        who   AUX   whom   seen
        'Who saw whom?'

Within this last group, we find a split, discovered by Rudin (1988), between languages of the Bulgarian type, in which the order of fronted *wh*-phrases tends to be rigid, and languages of the Serbian/Croatian type, in which it tends to be free:

(33) a. ***Na   kogo   kakvo**   e   dal   Ivan?   [*Bulgarian*]
        to   whom   what   AUX   given   Ivan
        'What did Ivan give to whom?'
     b. **Koga**   je   **ko**   vidio?   [*Serbian*]
        whom   AUX   who   seen
        'Who saw whom?'

Literature on multiple *wh*-movement includes Billings and Rudin (1996), Bošković (1997; 1999; 2002), Citko (1997), Richards (1997; 2001), Pesetsky (2000), Grewendorf (2001), Müller (2001), Grebenyova (2004), Jaeger (2004), Krapova and Cinque (2005), Bailyn (2011), and Scott (2012).[8]

A popular approach to apparent word order freedom appeals to information structure as a motivator of movements, the idea being that *wh*-order is determined not only by c-command relations between the *wh*-phrases but also by considerations of topic and focus, which distinguish among the various *wh*-phrases (in some theories, moving some of the *wh*-phrases to dedicated information-structural positions) (Rudin (1988, 476), Billings and Rudin (1996), Jaeger (2004), Krapova and Cinque (2005), Scott (2012)).

To the extent that (modulo factors just mentioned) some languages can be described as having their *wh*-phrases in a rigid order, the logical question of how to derive the order arises. A widely held conclusion about such languages is that their *wh*-phrases appear in an order determined by the underlying c-command relations among them. One class of accounts of this fact invokes Optimality-theoretic constraints that reward preservation of underlying c-command relations (Billings and Rudin 1996; Müller 2001). A second approach posits adjunction of *wh*-phrases to each other (Rudin 1988; Grewendorf 2001):

(34)

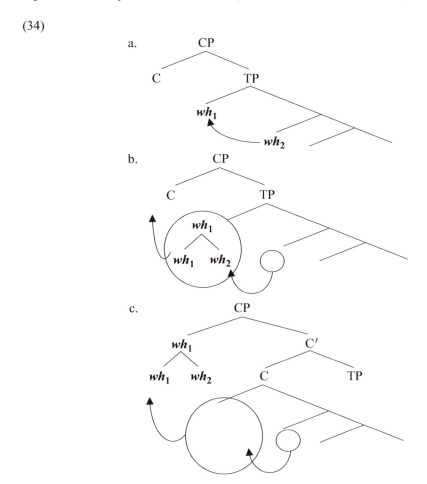

The order of *wh*-phrases can be derived by requiring *wh*-phrases to follow the phrases to which they adjoin, as long as adjunction must take place cyclically. A third approach (known as *tucking in*) takes advantage of Chomsky's (1995) rejection of the Extension Condition and derives the ordering of *wh*-phrases from locality conditions (Mulders 1997;

Richards 1997; 2001); the highest *wh*-phrase must move first to a specifier of CP, since this is the shortest move available, and subsequent *wh*-movements must land in specifiers below the existing one(s), again to make movements maximally short (assuming that higher specifiers are relevantly structurally higher than lower ones):

(35)

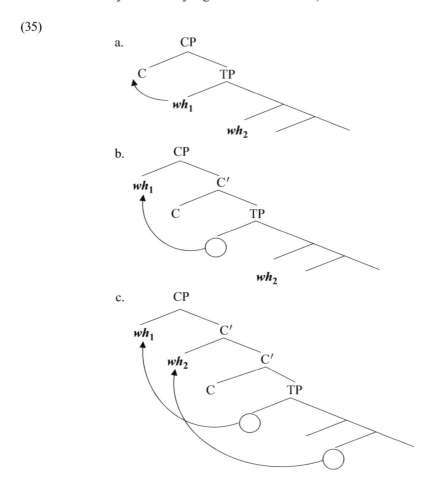

In multiple *wh*-movement, we again find constrained variation. There are, for example, languages that move all of their *wh*-phrases (e.g., Bulgarian), and languages that move one (e.g., English), but no languages that move two. We find languages with multiple overt *wh*-movement in which the word order of the *wh*-phrases is fixed, and reflects the underlying c-command relations between the *wh*-phrases (e.g., Bulgarian); we find no languages in which this order is reversed.

3.3 Intermediate landing sites

The previous two sections have concentrated on the final landing sites of *wh*-movement. We also have evidence that A-bar moved phrases land in intermediate positions on their way up the tree – that is, that movement is *successive-cyclic*.

McCloskey (2000), for example, discusses quantifier float in West Ulster English; quantifiers left behind by *wh*-movement may appear in theta-positions or at the beginnings of clauses exited by movement (though not in just any position along the path of *wh*-movement, as (36d) shows):

(36) a. What **all** did he tell him [that he wanted __]?
   b. What did he tell him [that he wanted __ **all**]?
   c. What did he tell him [**all** that he wanted __]?
   d. *What did he tell **all** him [that he wanted __]?

Since quantifiers cannot simply appear anywhere, the facts require some explanation; the fact that quantifiers can appear in theta-position supports the idea that the quantifiers appear in positions that the moved phrase has occupied. This idea can be extended to examples such as (36c), in which a quantifier is left at the beginning of the embedded clause, if we are willing to posit successive-cyclic movement through clause-initial position. Other work on successive-cyclicity includes Torrego (1984), Lebeaux (1990; 2009), Henry (1995), Chung (1998), Fox (2000), Nissenbaum (2000), McCloskey (2002), Abels (2003), Rackowski and Richards (2005), den Dikken (2009; 2012a; 2012b), and van Urk and Richards (2013).

We can then ask why grammar should work in this way. One level of proposed answer invokes locality conditions on movement, guaranteeing that most *wh*-phrases will begin too far from their final landing sites to be able to reach them in a single move. Such theories include Chomsky (1986) and Takahashi (1994), as well as current work on phases (e.g., Chomsky 2001; 2008). Another strand of literature is concerned with reconciling the existence of successive-cyclic movement with the Minimalist idea that movement is always related to feature-checking. What distinguishes, for example, a declarative complementizer that triggers an intermediate step of successive-cyclic movement from one that does not? Are there features that are optionally present on such complementizers just when successive-cyclic movement takes place past them? Or should we re-examine our assumptions about the relation of feature-checking with movement? Relevant work pursuing this second idea includes Stroik (1999), Heck and Müller (2000), Bošković (2007), and Preminger (2008).

4 When does A-bar movement fail?

Ross (1967) discovered a number of structures out of which movement is impossible ('islands'). Subsequent work has discovered others; at least one work (Chomsky 1986) proposes that islandhood is the default state for any phrase, seeking to explain the distribution of phrases that are not islands.

4.1 Wh-*interactions*

Much current work posits a constraint requiring movement paths to be maximally short (Shortest Move (Chomsky 1993), Attract Closest (Chomsky 1995), the Minimal Link Condition (Chomsky 1995), all of which can be viewed as descendants of Rizzi's (1990) Relativized Minimality).[9] Two phenomena attributable to such a condition are Superiority and *wh*-island effects:

(37) a. **Who** __ bought **what**?   [*Superiority*]
   b. ***What** did **who** buy __ ?

(38) a. **Where** do you think [that Bill put the book __]?   [Wh-*islands*]
   b. ***Where** did you ask [**what** Bill put __ __]?

In (37), the grammar must move the higher of the two *wh*-phrases to Spec CP, making the resulting path as short as possible. In (38), movement of *where* past *what* creates an excessively long path in (potentially) two ways: *where* has moved past a landing site (namely, the embedded Spec CP) and past another *wh*-phrase that could in principle have moved (namely, *what*). The *wh*-island case illustrates the necessity for a precise definition of 'maximally short'; in this case, it would not actually be possible to move *what*, perhaps because it is the only *wh*-phrase in the specifier of an interrogative CP.

Kitahara (1997) points out that the Minimal Link Condition, together with a ban on movement that would deprive interrogative C of its only *wh*-specifier, and a cyclic bottom-up derivation, can derive the effects of the Path Containment Condition of Pesetsky (1982):

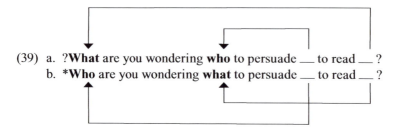

(39) a. ?**What** are you wondering **who** to persuade __ to read __ ?
     b. ***Who** are you wondering **what** to persuade __ to read __ ?

Both of the examples in (39) are *wh*-island violations; the *wh*-phrase that moves into the matrix clause passes another *wh*-phrase in the specifier of the embedded CP. As Pesetsky (1982) discusses, however, the examples do not have the same status; (39a), in which the intersecting *wh*-movement paths are nested, is preferable to (39b), in which they cross. What distinguishes (39a), in Kitahara's theory, is the fact that the first move (that of *who*) obeys the Minimal Link Condition (as opposed to (39b), where the first move is of *what*). Richards (1997; 2001) extends this reasoning to languages such as Bulgarian and Japanese, correctly predicting that these languages will prefer crossed paths to nested paths.

4.2   Movement from within moving phrases

One special case of interaction between *wh*-paths involves a *wh*-phrase that contains another *wh*-phrase:

(40) a. *[**What**] are you wondering [[**how many pictures of** __] John bought __]
     b. *[**How many pictures of** __] are you wondering [[**what**] John bought __]

Both of the questions in (40) involve a *wh*-phrase *how many pictures of what*, which is disassembled by movement of *what* and of *how many pictures of* __ to different Spec,CP positions. Both examples are ill-formed, though (40b) seems worse than (40a). Sauerland (1996) refers to the two derivations in (40) as *surfing* and *diving* respectively; the second type of derivation is also called *remnant movement*.

Surfing and diving are often discussed together: see Wexler and Culicover (1980), Takano (1994; 2000), Sauerland (1996), Müller (1996; 1998), Kitahara (1997), Abels (2007), and Hunter (2010). Wexler and Culicover (1980) propose a general ban on surfing derivations such as (40a). This ban has appeared in much work since, including work on subject islands, to be discussed in the next section.

The diving/remnant movement derivation in (40b) has been ruled out in several ways, including a general requirement that moved phrases c-command the positions in which they are originally Merged (the Proper Binding Condition of Fiengo (1977)). Such a condition apparently cannot hold of all kinds of movement, however, since there are well-formed derivations that produce representations that violate it:

(41) [**How likely** __ **to win**] does **John** seem to be?

In (41), *John* A-moves out of a *wh*-fronted constituent. One proposal (Takano 1994; Müller 1996; Kitahara 1997) argues that remnant movement is only possible when the two movements involved are of different kinds. (40b) is therefore ill-formed, because the two movements are both *wh*-movement.

4.3   Condition on extraction domain (CED)

Huang's (1982) CED bans extraction out of subjects and adjuncts:

(42) a. *__Who__ does [a pictures of __] hang on the wall?
      b. *__Who__ did Mary cry [after John hit __]?

Work on the CED includes Takahashi (1994), Toyoshima (1997), Nunes and Uriagereka (2000), Stepanov (2001; 2007), Johnson (2002), Boeckx (2003), Rackowski and Richards (2005), Truswell (2007; 2011), Chomsky (2008), Müller (2010), Lohndal (2011), and van Urk and Richards (2013).

One class of proposals tries to derive CED effects from the way that trees are constructed; examples include Toyoshima (1997), Nunes and Uriagereka (2000), Stepanov (2001; 2007), Johnson (2002), and Müller (2010). For Nunes and Uriagereka (2000), Spellout makes the offending structures opaque (and Spellout is forced to apply to complex specifiers and adjuncts, following Uriagereka (1999), in order to make the resulting structures linearizable by a modified form of Kayne's (1994) LCA). For Stepanov (2001; 2007), adjuncts are opaque to extraction because they are Merged into the structure late, after extraction would take place; similarly, Müller (2010) posits a condition on feature checking that guarantees that, by the time adjuncts are Merged, the features that would trigger extraction out of them have already been checked. For Johnson (2002), adjuncts and subjects have had some of their phonological properties fixed by the time extraction is possible; Johnson links the island effects with conditions on focus projection.

Another set of proposals seeks to reduce the CED to other locality conditions. Takahashi (1994), for example, posits locality conditions that determine that movement must adjoin to every XP along the path, along with a condition on adjunction that makes adjunction to any moved XP impossible. Rackowski and Richards (2005) and van Urk and Richards (2013) posit locality conditions that guarantee that if an XP α moves successive-cyclically to the specifier of some YP, YP will be a potential Goal for higher Probes seeking to move α further. Higher Probes must therefore first Agree with YP before they can Agree with α. Thus, CP, for example, is transparent for probing by v just when it is Agreed with by v; that is, when CP is a complement, and not when it is an adjunct or a subject.

Truswell (2007; 2011) offers a semantic characterization of part of the CED, concentrating on contrasts like the one in (43):

(43) a.   What did John arrive [whistling __]?
      b. *What does John work [whistling __]?

Truswell's *Single Event Condition* prevents extraction out of structures that do not denote a single event.

Stepanov (2001; 2007) casts doubt on the idea that extraction from subjects and extraction from adjuncts should be banned by a single condition, noting that there are languages in which extraction from subjects is acceptable, while extraction from adjuncts is blocked:

(44) a. **S   kem**   by   ty   xotel   [*Russian*: Stepanov 2007]
         with whom SUBJ you wanted
         čtoby [govorit' __] bylo by   odno udovol'stvie?
         that-SUBJ to.speak   was SUBJ one   pleasure
         'With whom would you want that [to speak __] were sheer pleasure?'
     b. *S   **kem**   Ivan   rasserdilsja [potomučto   Petr   vstretilsja __]?
         with whom   Ivan   got.angry   because   Peter   met
         'With whom did Ivan get angry [because Peter met __]?

Some subsequent work takes up this challenge (Chomsky 2008; Polinsky *et al.* 2014). Some of this work seems to uphold the generalization that at least some subject positions are (perhaps universally) opaque, with cross-linguistic variation coming from differences in the position of subjects.

4.4   Coordinate Structure Constraint

Ross (1967) posits the Coordinate Structure Constraint (CSC), which bans extraction out of coordinated phrases (including extraction of the coordinated phrases themselves):

(45) a. ***What** did you buy [a book] and [__] ?
      b. ***What** did you [buy a book] and [eat __] ?

As Ross notes, extraction out of both conjuncts is permitted (*across-the-board movement*):

(46) **What** did you [eat __] and [drink __] ?

Another type of permissible CSC violation is exemplified in (47) (Goldsmith 1985; Culicover and Jackendoff 1997):

(47) a. **What** did you [go to the store] and [buy __]?
      b. **How much** can you [drink __] and [still stay sober]?
      c. That's the stuff that the guys in the Caucasus [drink __] and [live to be a hundred]

Examples such as (47) involve *asymmetric coordination*, in which the semantics of *and* is not obviously that of simple conjunction (Postal 1998; Bjorkman 2010).

Ruys (1992) discusses another permissible CSC violation. He notes (following May 1985) that the CSC constrains covert movements as well as overt ones:

(48) Someone is [publishing every book] and [writing a check]

In (48), *every book* cannot take wide scope over *someone*; Ruys analyses this as a CSC effect on QR, preventing *every book* from moving high enough to take wide scope. He contrasts (48) with (49):

(49) Someone is [publishing every book$_i$] and [writing its$_i$ author a check]

In (49), Ruys says, *every book* can take wide scope. He concludes that the CSC should be understood representationally; the requirement is that if a moved phrase binds a variable in one conjunct, it must also bind a variable in the other conjunct (and it is possible that, as in (49), one variable is a gap left behind by movement, while the other is a pronominal variable).

4.5 Intervention effects

In many cases, *wh*-in-situ cannot be c-commanded by certain kinds of quantificational or focused elements:

(50) a. *Minsu-<u>man</u>   **nuku-lûl**   po-ass-ni?   [*Korean*: Beck and Kim 1997]
       Minsu-only   who-ACC   see-PAST-Q
       'Who did only Minsu see?'
    b. **Nuku-lûl**   Minsu-<u>man</u>   po-ass-ni?
       who-ACC   Minsu-only   see-PAST-Q

(51) a. *Wen   hat   <u>niemand</u>   **wo**   gesehen?   [*German*: Beck and Kim 1997]
       who   has   nobody   where   seen
       'Who did nobody see where?'
    b. Wen   hat   **wo**   <u>niemand</u>   gesehen?
       who   has   where   nobody   seen

In (50a), for example, *Minsu-man* 'only Minsu' c-commands *nuku-lûl* 'who-ACC', intervening between the *wh*-phrase and C, and the result is ill-formed. In (50b), intervention has been avoided by scrambling the *wh*-phrase past the offending intervener. Relevant literature includes Beck (1996; 2006), Beck and Kim (1997), Tanaka (1997; 2003), Hagstrom (1998), Pesetsky (2000), Mayr (2010), and Kotek (forthcoming).

4.6 Special properties of subjects

In the section 'Movement from within moving phrases', above, we discussed the special status of subjects as islands. Subjects have also been argued to be uniquely sensitive to certain types of island effects. Here I will concentrate on two instances: complementizer-trace phenomena, and extraction of ergative subjects.

4.6.1 Complementizer-trace phenomena

Extraction of subjects from subordinate clauses is often sensitive to the form of the complementizer of the clause from which extraction takes place. The classic instance of this is the *that*-trace effect in English (Perlmutter 1971):

(52) **Who** do you think [(*that) __ ate the orange]?

This effect holds for many (but not all: Sobin 1987) dialects of English, and comparable effects have been found in many (but not all) languages. Certain adverbs can eliminate the effect (Bresnan 1977; Culicover 1993):

(53) Who do you think [that [after years and years of cheating death] __ finally died]?

The effect is not limited to declarative complementizers; subjects seem to be more sensitive to a variety of island constraints than, for example, direct objects, in a way that we might attribute to properties of elements in the C domain:

(54) a. ***Who** are you wondering [whether __ ate the orange]?
     b. ??**What** are you wondering [whether she ate __]?

(55) a. ***Who** will you be mad [if __ eats an orange]?
     b. ??**What** will you be mad [if he eats __]?

Literature on complementizer-trace phenomena includes Pesetsky and Torrego (2001), Ishii (2004), and Bošković (2011). For Pesetsky and Torrego (2001) and Ishii (2004), the relevant property of subjects is their failure to trigger movement of T to C:

(56) a. **Who** (*did) leave?
     b. **What** *(did) you buy?

In (56a), *do*-support, seen here as a reflex of T-to-C movement, is impossible without special emphasis, while in (56b) it is obligatory. Pesetsky and Torrego relate this fact to the *that*-trace effect, regarding *that* as the result of a kind of T-to-C movement (and offering an account of why such movement should be blocked in subject extraction).

4.6.2 Extraction of ergative subjects

Some ergative languages have a ban on extraction of ergatives (Dixon 1994; Manning 1996; Aldridge 2008; Coon *et al.* 2011; Assmann *et al.* 2013; Erlewine 2013):

(57) a. *angut   [__ aallaat tigu-sima-sa-a]   [*West Greenlandic*: Manning 1996]
        man.ABS   gun.ABS take-PERF-REL.TR-3S
        'the man who took the gun'
     b. nanuq   [Piita-p   __   tuqu-ta-a]
        polar.bear.ABS Piita-ERG   kill-TR.PART-3S
        'a polar bear that Piita killed'
     c. miiraq [__   kamat-tuq]
        child   angry-REL.INTR
        'the child that is angry'

(58) a. *Maktxel max-Ø   y-il-a'   __   ix   ix?   [*Q'anjob'al*: Coon *et al.* 2011]
        who   ASP-ABS3 ERG3-see-TV   CL   woman
        'Who saw the woman?'
     b. Maktxel max-Ø   y-il-a'   naq   winaq __?
        who   ASP-ABS3 ERG3-see-TV CL   man
        'Who did the man see?'
     c. Maktxel max-Ø   way-i __?
        who   ASP-ABS3   sleep-ITV
        'Who slept?'

(57a) and (58a) above involve extraction of a transitive (ergative) subject, and are ill-formed; the other examples are extractions of absolutives (transitive objects or intransitive subjects), and are acceptable.

Not all morphologically ergative languages ban extraction of ergatives:

(59) Maxki tyi y-il-ä   jiñi wiñik   [*Chol*: Coon *et al.* 2011]
      who   ASP ERG3-see-TV DET   man
      'Who saw the man?'/'Who did the man see?'

The ambiguity in (59) demonstrates that extraction here may be either of the absolutive or of the ergative.

4.7 Parasitic gaps

A-bar movement can license parasitic gaps (Engdahl 1983; Kayne 1983; Chomsky 1986; Nunes 1995; 2001; Nissenbaum 2000; Culicover and Postal 2001):

(60) a. What did John file __ [without reading __]?
      b. Who did you talk to __ [about friends of __]?

The *wh*-phrases in (60) bind two gaps; the 'parasitic gap' is the one in the bracketed constituent. This constituent must be along the path of an A-bar movement (that is, it must be c-commanded by the head of that movement, and c-command the tail):

(61) *What __ was filed __ [without reading __]?

The constituent containing the parasitic gap can be an island ((60a)), though it need not be ((60b)). It cannot, however, contain islands that contain the parasitic gap:

(62) a.   What did John file __ [without knowing [that Mary hadn't read __]]
      b. *What did John file __ [without getting angry [because Mary hadn't read __]]

In both of the examples in (62), the parasitic gap is contained in an adjunct island, headed by *without*. (62b) is ill-formed because of a second adjunct island contained within the first.

One approach to parasitic gaps posits a null operator, which moves to the periphery of the constituent along the path of the 'real' gap (Chomsky 1986; Nissenbaum 2000). Another approach posits 'sideward movement', moving a *wh*-phrase from the position of the parasitic gap directly to the position of the 'real' gap (Nunes 1995; 2001).

4.8 Improper movement

In (63), A-movement is fed by A-bar movement:

(63) *[$_{TP}$ Who is known [$_{CP}$ __ it was told __]]

Here, *who* A-bar moves to the specifier of the embedded (interrogative) CP, and then A-moves to the specifier of the matrix TP. In so doing, the moved phrase participates in both of the kinds of movement that it needs to be fully licensed.

One way of ruling out such derivations is a ban on 'improper movement', which prevents A-bar movement from feeding A-movement; see Chomsky (1973; 1981), Fukui (1993), Williams (2003), Abels (2007), and Obata and Epstein (2011). A question about improper movement has to do with the apparent asymmetry between A-movement and A-bar movement; improper movement is standardly taken to be a ban on feeding of A-bar movement by A-movement, and crucially not on the reverse:

(64) Who do you think [__ was told __]?

Several of the theories above take this asymmetry as an explanandum. Another attested approach is to deny that examples such as (64) involve feeding of A-bar movement by A-movement. A popular proposal is that such examples really involve two chains, both with the position for the internal theta-role of *told* as their tail: one chain has its head in the matrix Spec CP and the other has its head in the embedded Spec TP. In this view, there is no movement relation between Spec TP and Spec CP and thus no feeding of A-bar movement by A-movement (Holmberg and Hróarsdóttir 2003; Fitzpatrick 2006; Chomsky 2008).[10]

Another way in which theories of improper movement vary is in how absolutely improper movement is to be banned. One candidate for a well-formed instance of improper movement is *tough*-movement (Postal 1971; Chomsky 1977; 1981; Hicks 2003; Hartman 2009):

(65) John is tough [to talk to __]

Evidence that *tough*-movement involves an A-bar movement step in the bracketed constituent includes the availability of parasitic gaps, which can only be licensed by A-bar movement:

(66) John is tough [to talk to __ [without insulting __]]

Hartman (2009) offers an argument from locality effects that *tough*-movement also has an A-movement step in the matrix clause. If he is right, *tough*-movement is a form of improper movement, raising the challenge of how to distinguish between acceptable and unacceptable versions of improper movement.

4.9 More mysteries

Space considerations prevent me from covering island phenomena any further. I have omitted many island effects, perhaps most egregiously the Complex NP Constraint of Ross (1967). This constraint, classically paired with the *wh*-island effect as an instance of Subjacency (Chomsky 1973), bans extraction from clauses dominated by NP:

(67) *__**What** did Mary believe [the rumor [that Bill was eating __]]?

I have also failed to discuss some factors affecting the strength of islands. For example, various islands are stronger when tensed:

(68) a. ?**What** are you wondering [whether to buy __]?
      b. *__**What** are you wondering [whether you should buy __]?

We saw in §4.6 that subjects are particularly difficult to extract in some contexts; similarly, adjuncts have long been noted to be especially sensitive to islands (a fact classically captured by the ECP):

(69) a. *__**What** are you wondering [whether you should buy __]?
      b. **__**Why** are you wondering [whether you should buy it __]?

Finally, many languages, including English, permit the use of resumptive pronouns, which take the place of gaps in contexts in which extraction would violate an island:

(70) a. *__Who__ are you wondering [whether __ should resign]?
     b. ?__Who__ are you wondering [whether *he* should resign]?

Some languages make wider use of resumptive pronouns than English does (McCloskey 1990; Aoun *et al.* 2001; Boeckx 2003; Imanishi 2012)

(71) an   scríbhneoir   a^N molann   na   mic léinn   é   [*Irish*: McCloskey 1979]
     the   writer   C   praise   the   students   him
     'the writer that the students praise'

5   Conclusion

A-bar movement has been a fruitful probe into the nature of the derivation and the representation. Since it is comparatively free to move over long distances, it is particularly useful for studying limitations on movement and the effects of movement on binding. Several types of it (e.g., *wh*-movement, relativization) are comfortably associated with a particular semantics, which make them comparatively easy to isolate and study cross-linguistically (though, as we have seen, the cross-linguistic syntactic unity of these constructions has been questioned).

Notes

1 See Polinsky and Preminger (this volume) for discussion.
2 However, see Carstens and Diercks (2013) on "hyper-raising", which may be A-movement out of tensed clauses; conversely, *wh*-movement is apparently unable to escape tensed clauses in some languages (e.g., Russian: Williams 2003: 70).
3 Lasnik and Stowell (1991) argue that some instances of A-bar movement lack weak crossover.
4 Johnson (1996) argues for a ninth asymmetry between A-movement and A-bar movement: A-bar movement, but not A-movement, is subject to the Coordinate Structure Constraint (the argument is related to his theory of Gapping). Lin (2002) argues against Johnson's proposal, attempting to show that the CSC applies in the same way to A-movement and A-bar movement.
5 See subsection 'Condition on Extraction Domain (CED)' below.
6 See subsection '*Wh*-interactions' below.
7 Thanks to Sasha Podobryaev (pers. comm.) for discussion.
8 Consider another type of question with multiple *wh*-phrases:
   (i)   Where and when did he die?
   For further discussion of questions with coordinated *wh*-phrases, see Lipták (2003), Gračanin Yuksek (2007), Gribanova (2009), and Citko and Gračanin Yuksek (2013).
9 Another literature posits a ban on movement which is excessively short (*anti-locality*): Pesetsky and Torrego (2001); Abels (2003); Grohmann (2003); Erlewine (2013).
10 Another instance where A-movement and A-bar movement have been argued not to be in a feeding relation is (i):
    (i)   Who left?
    Much work explores the claim that *wh*-movement does not occur in examples such as (i), an idea known as the *Vacuous Movement Hypothesis* (George 1980; Chung and McCloskey 1983; Chomsky 1986; Lasnik and Saito 1992; Agbayani 2000), which states that string-vacuous movement does not occur.

Further reading

Cable (2012; 2013) is a good overview of work on pied-piping. Cinque (1990), Postal (1998), and Szabolcsi (2002) all contain overviews of the literature on islands. Richards (2008) and Shimoyama (2008) both summarize literature on (Japanese) *wh*-in-situ; Cheng (1991), Bruening (2007), and Richards (2010) discuss factors that might determine the distribution of overt *wh*-movement.

References

Abels, Klaus. 2003. Successive cyclicity, anti-locality, and adposition stranding. Doctoral dissertation, University of Connecticut.

Abels, Klaus. 2007. Towards a restrictive theory of (remnant) movement. *Linguistic Variation Yearbook* 7:57–120.

Agbayani, Brian. 2000. *Wh*-subjects in English and the Vacuous Movement Hypothesis. *Linguistic Inquiry* 31:703–730.

Aldridge, Edith. 2008. Generative approaches to ergativity. *Language and Linguistic Compass: Syntax and Morphology* 2:966–995.

Aoun, Joseph, Lina Choueiri, and Norbert Hornstein. 2001. Resumption, movement, and derivational economy. *Linguistic Inquiry* 32:371–403.

Arregi, Karlos. 2002. Focus on Basque movements. Doctoral dissertation, MIT.

Assmann, Anke, Doreen Georgi, Fabian Heck, Gereon Müller, and Philipp Weisser. 2013. Ergatives move too early: on an instance of opacity in syntax. In *Linguistische Arbeitsberichte 90: Rule Interaction in Grammar*, ed. Anke Assmann and Fabian Heck, 363–412. Institut für Linguistik, Universität Leipzig.

Bailyn, John. 2011. *The syntax of Russian.* Cambridge: Cambridge University Press.

Baker, Carl Lee. 1970. Notes on the description of English questions: the role of an abstract Q morpheme. *Foundations of Language* 6:197–219.

Beck, Sigrid. 1996. Quantified structures as barriers for LF movement. *Natural Language Semantics* 4:1–56.

Beck, Sigrid. 2006. Intervention effects follow from focus interpretation. *Natural Language Semantics* 14:1–56.

Beck, Sigrid, and Shin-Sook Kim. 1997. On *wh*- and operator scope in Korean. *Journal of East Asian Linguistics* 6:339–384.

Bhatt, Rajesh. 2002. The raising analysis of relative clauses: evidence from adjectival modification. *Natural Language Semantics* 10:43–90.

Bianchi, Valentina. 1999. *Consequences of antisymmetry: headed relative clauses.* Berlin: Mouton de Gruyter.

Billings, Loren, and Catherine Rudin. 1996. Optimality and superiority: a new approach to overt multiple-*wh* ordering. In *Proceedings of the Third Symposium on Formal Approaches to Slavic Linguistics*, ed. Jindřich Toman, 35–60. Ann Arbor: Michigan Slavic Publications.

Bjorkman, Bronwyn. 2010. A syntactic correlate of a semantic asymmetry. Paper presented at NELS 41.

Boeckx, Cedric. 2003. *Islands and chains: resumption as stranding.* Amsterdam: John Benjamins.

Bošković, Željko. 1997. Superiority effects and multiple *wh*-fronting in Serbo-Croatian. *Lingua* 12:1–20.

Bošković, Željko. 1999. On multiple feature checking: multiple WH fronting and multiple head movement. In *Working Minimalism*, ed. Sam Epstein and Norbert Hornstein, 159–188. Cambridge, MA: MIT Press.

Bošković, Željko. 2002. Multiple *wh*-fronting. *Linguistic Inquiry* 33:351–383.

Bošković, Željko. 2007. On the locality and motivation of move and agree: an even more minimal theory. *Linguistic Inquiry* 38:589–644.

Bošković, Željko. 2011. Rescue by PF-deletion, traces as (non)interveners, and the *that*-trace effect. *Linguistic Inquiry* 42:1–44.

Bresnan, Joan. 1977. Variables in the theory of transformations. In *Formal syntax*, ed. Peter Culicover, Thomas Wasow, and Adrian Akmajian, 157–196. New York: Academic Press.

Bruening, Benjamin. 2007. *Wh*-in-situ does not correlate with *wh*-indefinites or question particles. *Linguistic Inquiry* 38:139–166.

Buell, Leston. 2009. Evaluating the immediate postverbal position as a focus position in Zulu. In *Selected Proceedings of the 38th Annual Conference on African Linguistics*, ed. Masangu Matondo, Fiona McLaughlin, and Eric Potsdam, 166–172. Somerville, MA: Cascadilla Proceedings Project.

Cable, Seth. 2007. The grammar of Q: Q-particles and the nature of *wh*-fronting, as revealed by the *wh*-questions of Tlingit. Doctoral dissertation, MIT.

Cable, Seth. 2010. Against the existence of pied-piping: evidence from Tlingit. *Linguistic Inquiry* 41:563–594.

Cable, Seth. 2012. Pied-piping: introducing two recent approaches. *Language and Linguistics Compass* 6(12):816–832.

Cable, Seth. 2013. Pied-piping: comparing two recent approaches. *Language and Linguistics Compass* 7(2):123–140.

Calabrese, Andrea. 1984. Multiple questions and focus in Italian. In *Sentential complementation*, ed. Wim de Geest and Yvan Putseys, 67–74. Dordrecht: Foris.

Carlson, Greg. 1977. Amount relatives. *Language* 53:520–542.

Carstens, Vicki, and Michael Diercks. 2013. Parameterizing case and activity: hyper-raising in Bantu. In *Proceedings of NELS 40*, ed. Seda Kan, Claire Moore-Cantwell, and Robert Staubs, 99–118. Amherst, MA: GLSA.

Cecchetto, Carlo, Carlo Geraci, and Sandro Zucchi. 2009. Another way to mark syntactic dependencies: the case for right-peripheral specifiers in sign languages. *Language* 85:278–320.

Cheng, Lisa L.-S. 1991. On the typology of *wh*-questions. Doctoral dissertation, MIT.

Cheng, Lisa L.-S., and Laura Downing. 2012. Against FocusP: evidence from Durban Zulu. In *Contrasts and positions in information structure*, ed. Ivona Kučerová and Ad Neeleman, 247–266. Cambridge: Cambridge University Press.

Chomsky, Noam. 1973. Conditions on transformations. In *A Festschrift for Morris Halle*, ed. Steven Anderson and Paul Kiparsky, 232–285. New York: Holt, Rinehart, and Winston.

Chomsky, Noam. 1977. On *wh*-movement. In *Formal syntax*, ed. Peter Culicover, Thomas Wasow, and Adrian Akmajian, 71–132. New York: Academic Press.

Chomsky, Noam. 1981. *Lectures on government and binding*. Dordrecht: Foris.

Chomsky, Noam. 1986. *Barriers*. Cambridge, MA: MIT Press.

Chomsky, Noam. 1993. A minimalist program for linguistic theory. In *The view from Building 20: essays in linguistics in honor of Sylvain Bromberger*, ed. Kenneth Hale and Samuel Jay Keyser, 1–52. Cambridge, MA: MIT Press.

Chomsky, Noam. 1995. *The Minimalist Program*. Cambridge, MA: MIT Press.

Chomsky, Noam. 2001. Derivation by phase. In *Ken Hale: a life in language*, ed. Michael Kenstowicz, 1–52. Cambridge, MA: MIT Press.

Chomsky, Noam. 2008. On phases. In *Foundational issues in linguistic theory: essays in honor of Jean-Roger Vergnaud*, ed. Robert Freidin, Carlos Otero, and Maria-Luisa Zubizaretta, 133–166. Cambridge, MA: MIT Press.

Chung, Sandy. 1998. *The design of agreement: evidence from Chamorro*. Chicago, IL: University of Chicago Press.

Chung, Sandy, and James McCloskey. 1983. On the interpretation of certain island facts in GPSG. *Linguistic Inquiry* 14:704–713.

Cinque, Guglielmo. 1990. *Types of A'-dependencies*. Cambridge, MA: MIT Press.

Citko, Barbara. 1997. On multiple *wh*-movement in Slavic. In *Proceedings of formal approaches to Slavic linguistics VI*, ed. Željko Bošković, Stephen Franks, and William Snyder, 97–113. Ann Arbor: Michigan Slavic Publications.

Citko, Barbara, and Martina Gračanin Yuksek. 2013. Towards a new typology of coordinated *wh*-questions. *Journal of Linguistics* 49:1–32.

Colarusso, John. 1992. *A grammar of the Kabardian language*. Calgary: University of Calgary Press.

Coon, Jessica, Pedro Mateo Pedro, and Omer Preminger. 2011. *The role of case in A-bar extraction asymmetries: evidence from Mayan*. ms, McGill, Harvard, and MIT.

Culicover, Peter. 1993. Evidence against ECP accounts of the *that-t* effect. *Linguistic Inquiry* 24:557–561.

Culicover, Peter, and Paul Postal. 2001. *Parasitic gaps*. Cambridge, MA: MIT Press.

Culicover, Peter, and Ray Jackendoff. 1997. Semantic subordination despite syntactic coordination. *Linguistic Inquiry* 28:195–217.

den Dikken, Marcel. 2009. Arguments for successive-cyclic movement through Spec-CP: a critical review. *Linguistic Variation Yearbook* 9:89–126.

den Dikken, Marcel. 2012a. The phase impenetrability condition and successive cyclicity: a reconsideration. Paper presented at CLS 48, University of Chicago.

den Dikken, Marcel. 2012b. On the strategies for forming long A'-dependencies: evidence from Hungarian. Ms. CUNY.

Dixon, Robert M.W. 1994. *Ergativity*. Cambridge University Press.

Engdahl, Elisabet. 1983. Parasitic gaps. *Linguistics and Philosophy* 6:5–34.

Erlewine, Michael Yoshitaka. 2013. Anti-locality and optimality in Kaqchikel Agent Focus. Ms. MIT.

Fiengo, Robert. 1977. On trace theory. *Linguistic Inquiry* 8:35–61.

Fitzpatrick, Justin. 2006. The syntactic and semantic roots of floating quantification. Doctoral dissertation, MIT.

Fox, Danny. 1999. Reconstruction, binding theory, and the interpretation of chains. *Linguistic Inquiry* 30:157–196.

Fox, Danny. 2000. *Economy and semantic interpretation*. Cambridge, MA: MIT Press.

Fukui, Naoki. 1993. A note on improper movement. *The Linguistic Review* 10:111–126.

George, Leland. 1980. Analogical generalization in natural language syntax. Doctoral dissertation, MIT.

Goldsmith, John. 1985. A principled exception to the coordinate structure constraint. In *Papers from the Twenty-first Annual Regional Meeting of the Chicago Lingustic Society*. Chicago: Chicago Linguistic Society.

Gračanin Yuksek, Martina. 2007. About sharing. Doctoral dissertation, MIT.

Grebenyova, Lydia. 2004. Interpretation of Slavic multiple *wh*-questions. In *Annual Workshop on Formal Approaches to Slavic Linguistics (FASL) 12: the Ottawa meeting*, ed. Olga Arnaudova, Wayles Browne, Maria Luisa Rivero, and Danijela Stojanovic, 169–186. Ann Arbor: Michigan Slavic Publications.

Grewendorf, Günther. 2001. Multiple *wh*-fronting. *Linguistic Inquiry* 32:87–122.

Gribanova, Vera. 2009. Structural adjacency and the typology of interrogative interpretations. *Linguistic Inquiry* 40:133–154.

Grohmann, Kleanthes. 2003. *Prolific domains*. Amsterdam: John Benjamins.

Hagstrom, Paul. 1998. Decomposing questions. Doctoral dissertation, MIT.

Hartman, Jeremy. 2009. Intervention in tough-constructions. In *Proceedings of the 39th Annual Meeting of the North East Linguistic Society*, ed. Suzi Lima, Kevin Mullin, and Brian Smith, 387–398. Amherst, MA: GLSA.

Heck, Fabian. 2004. A theory of pied-piping. Doctoral dissertation, Universität Tübingen.

Heck, Fabian. 2009. On certain properties of pied-piping. *Linguistic Inquiry* 40:75–111.

Heck, Fabian, and Gereon Müller. 2000. Successive cyclicity, long-distance superiority, and local optimization. In *Proceedings of the 19th West Coast Conference on Formal Linguistics*, ed. Roger Billerey and Brook Danielle Lillehaugen, 218–231. Somerville, MA: Cascadilla Press.

Henderson, Brent. 2007. Matching and raising unified. *Lingua* 117:202–220.

Henry, Alison. 1995. *Belfast English and Standard English: dialect variation and parameter setting*. Oxford: Oxford University Press.

Hicks, Glyn. 2003. So easy to look at, so hard to define: tough movement in the minimalist framework. MA thesis, University of York.

Holmberg, Anders, and Thorbjörg Hróarsdóttir. 2003. Agreement and movement in Icelandic raising constructions. *Lingua* 113:997–1019.

Huang, C.-T. James. 1982. Logical relations in Chinese and the theory of grammar. Doctoral dissertation, MIT.

Hulsey, Sarah, and Uli Sauerland. 2006. Sorting out relative clauses. *Natural Language Semantics* 14:111–137.

Hunter, Timothy. 2010. Relating movement and adjunction in syntax and semantics. Doctoral dissertation, University of Maryland.

Hyman, Larry, and Masha Polinsky. 2009. Focus in Aghem. In *Information structure*, ed. Malte Zimmermann and Caroline Féry, 206–233. Oxford: Oxford University Press.

Imanishi, Yusuke. 2012. Null resumption in Kaqchikel and its theoretical implications. Ms. MIT.

Ishii, Toru. 2004. The phase impenetrability condition, the vacuous movement hypothesis, and *that*-t effect. *Lingua* 114:183–215.

Jaeger, T. Florian. 2004. Topicality and superiority in Bulgarian *wh*-questions. In *Annual Workshop on Formal Approaches to Slavic Linguistics (FASL) 12: the Ottawa meeting*, ed. Olga Arnaudova, Wayles Browne, Maria Luisa Rivero, and Danijela Stojanovic, 207–228. Ann Arbor: Michigan Slavic Publications.

Jayaseelan, K.A. 2004. Question movement in some SOV languages and the theory of feature checking. *Language and Linguistics* 5:5–27.

Johnson, Kyle. 1996. In search of the English middle field. Ms. University of Massachusetts, Amherst.

Johnson, Kyle. 2002. Towards an etiology of adjunct islands. Ms. University of Massachusetts, Amherst.

Kayne, Richard. 1983. Connectedness. *Linguistic Inquiry* 24:223–249.

Kayne, Richard. 1994. *The antisymmetry of syntax*. Cambridge, MA: MIT Press.

Kishimoto, Hideki. 2005. *Wh*-in-situ and movement in Sinhala questions. *Natural Language and Linguistic Theory* 23:1–51.

Kitahara, Hisatsugu. 1997. *Elementary operations and optimal derivations*. Cambridge, MA: MIT Press.

Kotek, Hadas. forthcoming. *Wh*-fronting in a two-probe system. *Natural Language and Linguistic Theory*.

Kotek, Hadas, and Michael Yoshitaka Erlewine. 2013. Covert pied piping in English multiple-*wh* questions. Ms. MIT.

Krapova, Iliyana, and Guglielmo Cinque. 2005. On the order of *wh*-phrases in Bulgarian multiple-*wh* fronting. *University of Venice working papers in linguistics* 15:171–196.

Lasnik, Howard, and Mamoru Saito. 1992. *Move α: conditions on its application and output*. Cambridge, MA: MIT Press.

Lasnik, Howard, and Tim Stowell. 1991. Weakest crossover. *Linguistic Inquiry* 22:687–720.

Lebeaux, David. 1988. Language acquisition and the form of grammar. Doctoral dissertation, University of Massachusetts, Amherst.

Lebeaux, David. 1990. Relative clauses, licensing and the nature of the derivation. In *Proceedings of NELS 20*, 318–332. Amherst, MA: GLSA.

Lebeaux, David. 2009. *Where does binding theory apply?* Cambridge, MA: MIT Press.

Lin, Vivian. 2002. Coordination and sharing at the interfaces. Doctoral dissertation, MIT.

Lipták, Anikó. 2003. Conjoined questions in Hungarian. In *Multiple-wh fronting*, ed. Cedric Boeckx and Kleanthes Grohmann, 141–160. Philadelphia, PA: Benjamins.

Lohndal, Terje. 2011. Freezing effects and objects. *Journal of Linguistics* 47:163–199.

McCloskey, James. 1979. *Transformational grammar and model theoretic semantics*. Dordrecht: Reidel.

McCloskey, James. 1990. Resumptive pronouns, Ā-binding and levels of representation in Irish. In *Syntax and Semantics 23: the syntax of the modern Celtic languages*, ed. Randall Hendrick, 199–248. New York: Academic Press.

McCloskey, James. 2000. Quantifier float and *wh*-movement in an Irish English. *Linguistic Inquiry* 31:57–84.

McCloskey, James. 2002. Resumption, successive cyclicity, and the locality of operations. In *Derivation and explanation in the Minimalist Program*, ed. Samuel Epstein and T. Daniel Seely, 184–226. Blackwell Publishers, Oxford.

Manning, Christopher. 1996. *Ergativity: argument structure and grammatical relations*. Stanford, CA: CSLI.

May, Robert. 1985. *Logical form*. Cambridge, MA: MIT Press.

Mayr, Clemens. 2010. The role of alternatives and strength in grammar. Doctoral dissertation, Harvard University.

Mulders, Iris. 1997. Mirrored specifiers. In *Linguistics in the Netherlands 1997*, ed. Helen de Hoop and Jane Coerts, 135–146. Amsterdam: John Benjamins.

Müller, Gereon. 1996. A constraint on remnant movement. *Natural Language and Linguistic Theory* 14:355–407.

Müller, Gereon. 1998. *Incomplete category fronting: a derivational approach to remnant movement in German*. Dordrecht: Kluwer.

Müller, Gereon. 2001. Order preservation, parallel movement, and the emergence of the unmarked. In *Optimality-theoretic syntax*, ed. Géraldine Legendre, Jane Grimshaw, and Sten Vikner, 279–313. Cambridge, MA: MIT Press.

Müller, Gereon. 2010. On deriving CED effects from the PIC. *Linguistic Inquiry* 41:35–82.

Neidle, Carol, Dawn MacLaughlin, Robert Lee, Benjamin Bahan, and Judy Kegel. 1998. The rightward analysis of *wh*-movement in ASL: a reply to Petronio and Lillo-Martin. *Language* 74:819–831.

Nishigauchi, Taisuke. 1986. Quantification in syntax. Doctoral dissertation, University of Massachusetts, Amherst.

Nissenbaum, Jon. 2000. Investigations of covert phrase movement. Doctoral dissertation, MIT.

Nunes, Jairo. 1995. The copy theory of movement and linearization of chains in the minimalist program. Doctoral dissertation, University of Maryland.

Nunes, Jairo. 2001. Sideward movement. *Linguistic Inquiry* 32:303–344.

Nunes, Jairo, and Juan Uriagereka. 2000. Cyclicity and extraction domains. *Syntax* 3:20–43.

Obata, Miki, and Samuel David Epstein. 2011. Feature-splitting internal merge: improper movement, intervention, and the A/A' distinction. *Syntax* 14:122–147.

Ortiz de Urbina, Jon. 1989. *Parameters in the grammar of Basque*. Dordrecht: Foris.

Perlmutter, David. 1971. *Deep and surface structure constraints in syntax*. Holt, Rinehart, and Winston, New York.

Pesetsky, David. 1982. Paths and categories. Doctoral dissertation, MIT.

Pesetsky, David. 2000. *Phrasal movement and its kin*. Cambridge, MA: MIT Press.

Pesetsky, David, and Esther Torrego. 2001. T-to-C movement: causes and consequences. In *Ken Hale: a life in language*, ed. Michael Kenstowicz, 355–426. Cambridge, MA: MIT Press.

Petronio, Karen, and Diane Lillo-Martin. 1997. *Wh*-movement and the position Spec-CP: evidence from American Sign Language. *Language* 73:18–57.

Polinsky, Maria, and Larry Hyman. 2009. Focus in Aghem. In *Information structure: theoretical, typological, and experimental perspectives*, ed. Malte Zimmermann and Caroline Féry, 206–233. Oxford: Oxford University Press.

Polinsky, Maria, Carlos Gomez Gallo, Peter Graff, Ekaterina Kravtchenko, Adam M. Morgan, and Anne Sturgeon. 2014. Subject islands are different. In *Experimental syntax and island effects*, ed. Jon Sprouse and Norbert Hornstein, 286–309. Cambridge: Cambridge University Press.

Postal, Paul. 1971. *Cross-over phenomena*. New York: Holt, Rinehart, and Winston.

Postal, Paul. 1998. *Three investigations of extraction*. Cambridge, MA: MIT Press.

Potsdam, Eric. 2009. Austronesian verb-initial languages and *wh*-question strategies. *Natural Language and Linguistic Theory* 27:737–771.

Preminger, Omer. 2008. (Im)perfect domains: yet another theory of syntactic movement. In *Proceedings of the 26th West Coast Conference on Formal Linguistics*, ed. Charles Chang and Hannah Haynie, 402–410. Somerville, MA: Cascadilla Proceedings Project.

Rackowski, Andrea. 2002. The syntax and morphology of specificity. Doctoral dissertation, MIT.

Rackowski, Andrea, and Norvin Richards. 2005. Phase edge and extraction: a Tagalog case study. *Linguistic Inquiry* 36:565–599.

Richards, Norvin. 1997. What moves where when in which language? Doctoral dissertation, MIT.

Richards, Norvin. 1999. Another look at Tagalog subjects. In *Formal issues in Austronesian linguistics*, ed. Ileana Paul, Vivanne Phillips, and Lisa Travis, 105–116. Dordrecht: Kluwer.

Richards, Norvin. 2001. *Movement in language: interactions and architectures*. Oxford: Oxford University Press.

Richards, Norvin. 2008. *Wh*-questions. In *The Oxford handbook of Japanese linguistics*, ed. Shigeru Miyagawa and Mamoru Saito, 348–371. Oxford: Oxford University Press.

Richards, Norvin. 2010. *Uttering trees*. Cambridge, MA: MIT Press.

Rizzi, Luigi. 1990. *Relativized minimality*. Cambridge, MA: MIT Press.

Ross, John Robert. 1967. Constraints on variables in syntax. Doctoral dissertation, MIT.

Rudin, Catherine. 1988. On multiple questions and multiple *wh*-fronting. *Natural Language and Linguistic Theory* 6:445–501.

Ruys, Eddie. 1992. The scope of indefinites. Doctoral dissertation, Utrecht University.

Sauerland, Uli. 1996. The interpretability of scrambling. In *MITWPL 29: Formal approaches to Japanese linguistics 2*, ed. Masatoshi Koizumi, Masayuki Oishi, and Uli Sauerland, 213–234. Cambridge, MA: MIT Working Papers in Linguistics.

Sauerland, Uli. 1998. The meaning of chains. Doctoral dissertation, MIT.

Scott, Tatyana. 2012. Whoever doesn't HOP must be superior: the Russian left-periphery and the emergence of superiority. Doctoral dissertation, Stony Brook University.

Shimoyama, Junko. 2008. Indeterminate pronouns. In *The Oxford handbook of Japanese linguistics*, ed. Shigeru Miyagawa and Mamoru Saito, 372–393. Oxford: Oxford University Press.

Sobin, Nicholas. 1987. The variable status of comp-trace phenomena. *Natural Language and Linguistic Theory* 5:33–60.

Stepanov, Artur. 2001. Cyclic domains in syntactic theory. Doctoral dissertation, University of Connecticut.

Stepanov, Artur. 2007. The end of CED? Minimalism and extraction domains. *Syntax* 10:80–126.

Stoyanova, Marina. 2008. *Unique focus: languages without multiple* wh-*questions*. Amsterdam: John Benjamins.

Stroik, Thomas. 1999. The survive principle. *Linguistic Analysis* 29:278–303.

Szabolcsi, Anna. 2002. Strong vs. weak islands. Ms. NYU. [https://files.nyu.edu/as109/public/szabolcsi_strong_and_weak_islands.htm: accessed 16 July 2013].

Takahashi, Daiko. 1994. Minimality of movement. Doctoral dissertation, University of Connecticut.

Takahashi, Shoichi, and Sarah Hulsey. 2009. Wholesale late merger: beyond the A/A′-distinction. *Linguistic Inquiry* 40:387–426.

Takano, Yuji. 1994. Unbound traces and indeterminacy of derivation. In *Current topics in English and Japanese*, ed. Masaru Nakamura, 229–253. Tokyo: Hituzi Syobo.

Takano, Yuji. 2000. Illicit remnant movement: an argument for feature-driven movement. *Linguistic Inquiry* 31:141–156.

Tanaka, Hidekazu. 1997. Invisible movement in *sika-nai* and the linear crossing constraint. *Journal of East Asian Linguistics* 6:143–188.

Tanaka, Hidekazu. 2003. Remarks on Beck's effects: linearity in syntax. *Linguistic Inquiry* 34:314–323.

Torrego, Esther. 1984. On inversion in Spanish and some of its effects. *Linguistic Inquiry* 15:103–129.

Toyoshima, Takashi. 1997. Derivational CED: a consequence of the bottom-up parallel-process of merge and attract. In *Proceedings of the West Coast Conference on Formal Linguistics 15*, ed. Brian Agbayani and Sze-Wing Tang, 505–519. Stanford, CA: CSLI Publications.

Truswell, Robert. 2007. Extraction from adjuncts and the structure of events. *Lingua* 117:1355–1377.

Truswell, Robert. 2011. *Events, phrases, and questions*. Oxford: Oxford University Press.

Tsai, Wei-Tien Dylan. 1994. On economizing the theory of A-bar dependencies. Doctoral dissertation, MIT.

Uriagereka, Juan. 1999. Multiple spell-out. In *Working minimalism*, ed. Sam Epstein and Norbert Hornstein, 251–282. Cambridge, MA: MIT Press.

van Urk, Coppe. 2013. How to get a case alternation: voice in Dinka. Ms. MIT.

van Urk, Coppe, and Norvin Richards. 2013. Two components of long-distance extraction: successive cyclicity in Dinka. Ms. MIT.

Watanabe, Akira. 1992. Subjacency and S-structure movement of *wh*-in-situ. *Journal of East Asian Linguistics* 1:255–291.

Wexler, Ken, and Peter Culicover. 1980. *Formal principles of language acquisition*. Cambridge, MA: MIT Press.

Williams, Edwin. 2003. *Representation theory*. Cambridge, MA: MIT Press.

10

The syntax of ellipsis and related phenomena

Masaya Yoshida, Chizuru Nakao, and Iván Ortega-Santos

1 Introduction

A variety of linguistic expressions can appear in what looks like incomplete utterances. For example, in (1a), a verb (= the head of a verb phrase (VP)) is omitted, in (1b) a noun and its complement (= a noun phrase (NP)) are omitted, and in (1c) the whole clause (= a Tense Phrase (TP)) is omitted, leaving a *wh*-element behind.

(1) a. John ate bananas and Mary, ~~ate~~ caviar.
     b. John read Sapir's book on philosophy, and Mary read Chomsky's ~~book on philosophy~~.
     c. John ate something, but I don't know what ~~John ate~~.

The omission of linguistic expressions, *ellipsis*, has long attracted the attentions of linguists. Upon reading or hearing these sentences, native speakers can easily interpret the sentence and tell what the content of the elided portion of the sentence is. The question is how native speakers can tell what is elided, and what process makes it possible.

Some important observations can give us clues to answer these questions. For example, ellipsis is possible when some type of "antecedent" is available, in the form of either linguistic expressions or non-linguistic expressions. In (1a), the content of the elided part of the sentence (i.e., the verb *eat*) is available in the first conjunct. In the same way, the missing information in (1b) and (1c) is also linguistically found in the first conjunct. In other words, the interpretation of the elided portions in (1) is not arbitrary but somehow constrained by the information available in the first conjunct. For example, (1a) cannot mean **John ate apples and Mary, ~~sold~~ caviar*. Thus, it seems to be the case that the interpretation of the ellipsis is somehow dependent on the information carried in the antecedent of ellipsis. One of the central goals of the study of ellipsis is therefore to understand this relation between ellipsis and its antecedent. In this respect, there are roughly two major approaches. The first is the so-called syntactic/structural analysis (Ross 1969; Chung *et al.* 1995; Merchant 2001, among others). Under the syntactic/structural analysis, ellipsis has an invisible/inaudible syntactic structure that holds a certain parallelism with the antecedent. Under the second approach, the interpretive analysis, ellipsis is not associated with full-fledged syntactic structures. It is argued that the content of the ellipsis is constrained by semantic and pragmatic principles (van Riemsdijk 1978; Ginzburg 1992).

There have been many important observations and arguments for both kinds of account. Excellent survey pieces on the general problem of ellipsis have recently been produced (Craenenbroeck and Merchant 2013; Merchant 2013b; forthcoming) and it is impossible to explore all the important issues on ellipsis within the limited space available here. Therefore, this chapter concentrates on a rather narrow range of phenomena that can give us important clues to the syntax of ellipsis. We mostly discuss clausal ellipsis and primarily draw crucial data from English. More specifically, this chapter touches on the following questions: What is elided? What can remain when ellipsis takes place? What process is responsible for the ellipsis (or ellipsis-like) constructions? This work is structured as follows: Section 2 presents and reviews the main approaches to ellipsis found in the literature; and Section 3 focuses on the identity requirements between an ellipsis site and the antecedent. While Sections 2 and 3 have an emphasis on two specific ellipsis structures – namely, Sluicing and Stripping – Section 4 presents a survey of other clausal ellipsis constructions recently discussed in the literature.

2   What is elided?

One of the long-standing controversies in the study of ellipsis in modern linguistics is what structure is associated with ellipsis. The major question has been whether ellipsis has a full-fledged syntactic structure that holds structural parallelism with the antecedent or not. In the generative transformational framework, it has been traditionally argued that the ellipsis has a syntactic structure paralleling its antecedent (Chomsky 1972; Fiengo and May 1994; Ross 1967; 1969; Sag 1976 among many others). However, this assumption has been challenged by observations that show that ellipsis and its antecedent can be structurally mismatched. In the domain of VP-ellipsis (VPE), it has long been noticed that the ellipsis site and its antecedent can be mismatched in voice (Arregui *et al.* 2006; Dalrymple *et al.* 1991; Hardt 1993; Johnson 2001; Kehler 2002; Kim *et al.* 2011; Sag 1976 among many others). Structural mismatch has also been noted in the domain of clausal ellipsis such as Sluicing. It has been noted that structural constraints such as islands can be violated under Sluicing (Chomsky 1972; Chung *et al.* 1995; Erteschik-Shir 1977; Lasnik 2001a; Merchant 2001; Ross 1969), which is not expected if ellipsis and its antecedent hold strict syntactic parallelism. Against this background, in this section we discuss some studies that may suggest to what extent the structural mismatch is tolerated in the ellipsis context, and see what argument can be made for the structure within ellipsis.

2.1   Argument for the syntactic structure in ellipsis: In terms of Sluicing

Let us illustrate the debate on the syntactic versus interpretive analyses of ellipsis using examples of Sluicing such as (1c), repeated here.

(1)   c.   John ate something, but I don't know what ~~John ate~~.

Sluicing is a construction where a *wh*-phrase shows up as a fragment. The syntactic analyses assume that (1c) has the same CP-structure as that in (2), although only the *wh*-phrase is pronounced and the TP is elided.

(2)   John ate something, but I don't know [$_{CP}$ what$_1$ [$_{TP}$ ~~John ate t$_1$~~]].

The syntactic analyses can be further classified into two subtypes: The PF-deletion analysis (Ross 1969; Merchant 2001, among others) and the LF-copying analysis (Chung *et al.* 1995). The PF-deletion analysis assumes that the structure (2) is constructed in overt syntax and the TP is deleted at PF, yielding the PF form in (1c). The LF-copying analysis claims that only the *wh*-phrase is base-generated in overt syntax and the sentential structure in (2) is 'copied' from the antecedent clause, as the antecedent clause after QR is identical to that of the elided clause, as shown in (3).

(3)   [$_{CP}$ something$_2$ [$_{TP}$ **John ate t$_2$**]], but I don't know [$_{CP}$ what$_1$ [$_{TP}$ **John ate t$_1$**]].

The second line of analysis is an interpretive analysis (van Riemsdijk 1978; Ginzburg 1992). Under this analysis, the fragment *wh*-phrase in Sluicing is a fragment DP in syntax (4) and the sentential structure under the *wh*-phrase is not constructed. However, this DP is interpreted in the same way as the sentence in (2) because of an interpretive rule.

(4)   I don't know [$_{DP}$ **who$_1$**].

Below, we will survey some arguments for both analyses and show that evidence for the syntactic analysis has more validity.

2.1.1   Argument for syntactic analyses

Ross (1969) gives some arguments to show that Sluicing has an underlying clausal structure, some of which we will survey here. First, Sluicing shows Case-matching effect, as shown in the German example (5).

(5)   a.   Er will   jemandem   schmeicheln, aber Sie wissen nicht {wem/*wen}
           He wants-to someone$_{(Dat)}$ flatter   but they know   not   {whom$_{(Dat)}$/
                                                                          *whom$_{(Acc)}$}
           "He wants to flatter someone, but they don't know who."
      b.   Er will   jemanden   loben, aber Sie wissen nicht {*wem /wen}
           He wants-to someone$_{(Acc)}$ praise but they know   not   {*whom$_{(Dat)}$/whom$_{(Acc)}$}
           "He wants to praise someone, but they don't know who."

(Ross 1969: 253)

The verb 'flatter' in (5a) is a Dative-assigning verb, while the verb 'praise' in (5b) is an Accusative-assigning verb. The Case of the *wh*-phrase in Sluicing matches the Case that the NP *someone* gets inside the antecedent clause. This is straightforwardly accounted for under the syntactic analysis, given that the same verb as the antecedent clause exists inside the elided clause, as shown in (6).

(6)   a.   but they know not [$_{CP}$ **whom$_{1(DAT)}$** [$_{TP}$ he wants to flatter t$_1$]]
      b.   but they know not [$_{CP}$ **whom$_{1(ACC)}$** [$_{TP}$ he wants to praise t$_1$]]

Second, Sluicing shows number agreement in the cases where the sluiced clause is the subject of a bigger sentence, as shown in (7).

(7)   He's going to give us some old problems for the test, but which problems **isn't/*aren't** clear.

(revised from Ross 1969: 256)

If the sluiced *wh*-phrase *which problems* is simply a DP, the copular verb should show plural agreement, contrary to fact. If Sluicing involves a clausal structure, on the other hand, the singular agreement is expected because a clausal subject shows singular agreement (e.g., *That the linguists left is/*are tragic*).

The above arguments provide evidence for the existence of clausal structure in Sluicing. Ross further points out that the possibility of pied-piping and P-stranding in Sluicing correlates with that of *wh*-movement; when the pied-piping of a preposition is prohibited in *wh*-movement, Sluicing of such a pied-piped PP is also impossible, as shown in (8) and (9). This serves as an argument that Sluicing involves *wh*-movement.

(8) a. **Who$_1$** are you going to do away with **t$_1$**?
     b. *[$_{PP}$ **With whom**]$_1$ are you going to do away **t$_1$**?

(9) a. Bill's planning on doing away with one of his inlaws, but I don't know **which**.
     b. *Bill's planning on doing away with one of his inlaws, but I don't know **with which**.

Similarly, Merchant (2001) argues that in languages such as German, where *wh*-movement does not allow P-stranding, Sluicing also resists P-stranding, as illustrated in (10).[1]

(10) a. *Wem hat sie mit gesprochen?
         Who has she with spoken?
         "Who has she spoken with?" (Merchant 2001: 94)
     b. Anna hat mit jemandem gesprochen, aber ich weiß nicht, *(mit) wem.
         Anna has with someone   spoken   but I   know not   with who
         "Anna has spoken with someone, but I don't know with whom."

2.1.2   Argument for the interpretive analysis

Van Riemsdijk (1978) argues for the interpretive analysis and against the syntactic analyses, based on the fact that Sluicing is licensed by a non-linguistic antecedent. (11) shows that matrix Sluicing is possible when there is no linguistic antecedent. According to Hankamer and Sag's (1976) diagnostics, the possibility of ellipsis with a non-linguistic antecedent is evidence for base-generation of an anaphoric expression (which they call Deep Anaphora), which is distinct from an anaphoric relation generated via a deletion operation (which they call Surface Anaphora).

(11) [Hankamer, standing in front of a table-tennis table, a second bat in his hand looking at the bystanders]   Who?

(Van Riemsdijk 1978: 234)

As van Riemsdijk admits, however, this property does not extend to embedded Sluicing, as shown in (12). Based on this, Hankamer and Sag's original analysis actually treats Sluicing as an instance of deletion (Surface Anaphora in their term).

(12) [Hankamer, standing in front of a table-tennis table, a second bat in his hand looking at the bystsanders]   *I wonder who.

(Van Riemsdijk 1978: 235)

Therefore, it is unclear whether this argument favors the interpretive analysis over the deletion analysis.

Also, van Riemsdijk (1978) claims that the lack of island effects under Sluicing, which is exemplified in (13), favors the interpretive analysis. Let us take an example of Left-Branch Extraction (LBE) violations. Violating these islands in the non-ellipsis context gives rise to a severe unacceptability, as in (13a) (an LBE violation). However, when the structure violating these islands is within the ellipsis site, such unacceptability does not arise (13b). If Sluicing involves *wh*-movement, it should obey island constraints in the same way as regular *wh*-movement.

(13) a. *I don't know *how big*₁ she bought [NP a t₁ car]
       b. She bought a big car, but I don't know *how big*₁ ~~she bought [NP a t₁ car]~~.

Merchant (2001) gives an analysis that accounts for the lack of island effects under the PF-deletion analysis. Some cases of island violations are PF phenomena, and island violations caused by overt *wh*-movement are 'repaired' by the PF-deletion of TP involved in Sluicing (see §3.1 for further discussion of the relation between islands and ellipsis).

As shown above, the arguments for the interpretive analysis are not necessarily threatening for the syntactic analyses. Below, we will assume the syntactic analyses of Sluicing.

2.2   An instance of movement in ellipsis: Stripping

In ellipsis constructions some elements survive ellipsis – that is to say, they remain outside the scope of ellipsis. For example, in case of Sluicing in (1c), the *wh*-phrase, *what* (let us call it a remnant: Reinhart 1991), which corresponds to an indefinite phrase, *something* (let us call it a correlate: Reinhart 1991), in the antecedent clause is left unelided. One of the major questions in the study of ellipsis is how the remnant escapes ellipsis. For example, in Sluicing the remnant is a *wh*-phrase: Therefore, it is expected that the *wh*-remnant undergoes wh-movement to [Spec,CP] as shown in (2), and thus does not undergo the ellipsis that targets TP. However, not all the ellipsis structures can receive such a straightforward analysis. In a typical example of Stripping or Bare Argument ellipsis, as in (14a), the second conjunct in a coordinate construction is stripped from most of its elements except for a non-*wh*-remnant and one more element, such as *not* or *only* (Depiante 2000; Fiengo and May 1994; Hankamer and Sag 1976; Kim 1998; Lobeck 1995; May 1991; McCawley 1988; Merchant 2004; Reinhart 1991; Ross 1969, among many others). The fragmental phrase *sushi* gets a contrastive focus interpretation against other possible food candidates. (14a) receives the same interpretation as (14b).

(14) a. John ate sashimi, but <u>not</u> *sushi*.
       b. John ate sashimi, but John did <u>not</u> eat *sushi*.

How can the remnant escape the ellipsis in these cases? The syntactic analyses of ellipsis standardly assume that non-constituents cannot be elided (see n. 5 for evidence against the deletion of non-constituents in situ). Within this view, the Stripping remnant cannot be in situ as shown in (15b), as it forces non-constituent ellipsis of "John ate"; instead, the remnant must move out of the sentence to escape the sentential ellipsis as shown in (15a).[2]

(15) a. John ate sashimi, but not [XP *sushi*ₓ [TP ~~John ate tₓ~~]].
       b. John ate sashimi, but not [TP ~~John ate~~ *sushi*.]

As a consequence, an analysis in terms of focus movement plus ellipsis has been put forward (Depiante 2000), mimicking the syntactic analyses of Sluicing ((2)).

Furthermore, the fact that the unelided counterpart of (15a) (which is shown in (16)), is uacceptable shows that ellipsis is obligatory.

(16) *John ate sashimi, but not [$_{XP}$ **sushi**$_1$ [$_{TP}$ John ate **t**$_1$]].

Arguably, this movement is focus movement to [Spec,FP] (Depiante 2000, among others), given the fact that the Stripping remnant (e.g., *sushi*) is new/focused information, while the rest of the sentence is old/given information, identical to the already mentioned portion in the antecedent clause. (See the widely accepted view that Focus is quantificational and that focused elements move to the left-periphery to bind a variable: Rizzi 1997, among others.) Under the Copy Theory of Movement (Chomsky 1993; 1995, among others), this can be interpreted as follows (Nakao 2009): In English focus movement, the lower copy is usually pronounced and thus the phrase with a focused interpretation (i.e., *sushi*) does not move overtly in the non-elliptical sentence in (14b). This is illustrated in (17a), where < > indicates an unpronounced copy.

(17) a.   John ate sashimi, but not [$_{FP}$ < **sushi**> [$_{TP}$ John ate **sushi**]].
      b.   *John ate a lot, but not [$_{FP}$ **sushi** [$_{TP}$ ~~John ate~~ <**sushi**>]].

On the other hand, when there is TP-ellipsis the higher copy must be pronounced as shown in (17b); otherwise the focused phrase is not pronounced at all and the focused information is not available anywhere in the discourse (see Pesetsky's 1997 recoverability condition). This account captures the fact that overt focus movement can be licensed only under ellipsis.

Arguments for the syntactic analysis include Case-matching effects and the P-stranding generalization, which are parallel to that of Sluicing reviewed in §2.1.1. The German example (18), which is parallel to the Sluicing example in (5), shows that the remnant of Stripping (e.g., *the boss*) must have the same Case as the correlating phrase (e.g., *the secretary*). This indicates that the elided structure includes the same verb as its antecedent clause, which assigns Case to the remnant.

(18) a.   Peter will   der   Sekretaerin gefallen, aber nicht dem/*den   Chef.
            Peter wants the$_{(Dat)}$ secretary   please, but not the$_{(Dat)}$/*the$_{(Acc)}$ boss.
            "Peter wants to please the secretary, but not the boss."
      b.   Peter will   die   Sekretaerin loben, aber nicht *dem/den   Chef.
            Peter wants the$_{(Acc)}$ secretary   praise, but not *the$_{(Dat)}$/the$_{(Acc)}$ boss
            "Peter wants to praise the secretary, but not the boss."

(19) shows that the preposition on the remnant can be omitted in P-stranding languages such as English, while the remnant obligatorily comes with a preposition in non-P-stranding languages such as Spanish (Depiante 2000; though see n. 1 for additional discussion). This shows that Stripping also involves movement in the same way as Sluicing ((9), (10)).

(19) a.   John talked about Mary, and (about) Susan, too.   *English*
      b.   Juan escribe para Clarín y   *(para) La Nación también. *Spanish*
            Juan writes   for Clarin and *(for) La Nacion too

Also, the fact that Stripping is sensitive to at least some kinds of islands (Depiante 2000; May 1991; Reinhart 1991, among others) provides further evidence for movement in Stripping. (20) shows that when the correlate of Stripping (e.g., *some politician*) is included inside the sentential subject island, Stripping is unacceptable. This supports the analysis where the Stripping remnant (e.g. *the defense minister*) undergoes movement out of the parallel structure to its antecedent.

(20) *[The fact that some politician has resigned] got much publicity, but not the defense minister.

In this respect, Sluicing and Stripping are not parallel; Sluicing shows island-repair, as we have seen in (13). Fragment answers (Merchant 2004) behave the same way as Stripping in this respect. For accounts of such an asymmetry between Sluicing and other ellipsis, see Merchant (2004), Park (2005), Nakao (2009), and Griffiths and Lipták (forthcoming); see also §3.1.

In summary, the syntactic analyses of ellipsis are sometimes forced to posit movement that is not observed in non-elliptical sentences, as the discussion of Stripping shows.

3 Problem of identity

Though previous sections have reviewed the syntactic analyses of ellipsis, there are observations that are problematic for those approaches. One of these cases involves the mismatch in terms of the syntactic structure of the ellipsis site and the antecedent site. Taking examples from clausal ellipsis, we discuss the problem of identity and its possible solutions.

3.1 Islands under clausal ellipsis

One of the biggest challenges to the syntactic approaches to clausal ellipsis is the so-called island-repair phenomenon. While overt movement in non-elliptical context is ungrammatical (see (21a) and (21b) for the Complex NP Constraint and the LBE), the effect of island violations is somehow neutralized when the island is within the scope of ellipsis, (22b). (See Ross 1969).

(21) a. *I don't remember *which*$_1$ (Balkan language) they want to hire [$_{NP}$ someone [$_{CP}$ who speaks t$_1$]]
b. *I don't know *how big*$_1$ she bought [$_{NP}$ a t$_1$ car]

(22) a. They want to hire someone who speaks a Balkan language, but I don't remember *which*$_1$ (Balkan language) ~~they want to hire [$_{NP}$ someone [$_{CP}$ who speaks t$_1$]]~~.
b. She bought a big car, but I don't know *how big*$_1$ ~~she bought [$_{NP}$ a t$_1$ car]~~.

Under the syntactic analyses, island effects are expected in the ellipsis context in the same way as in the non-ellipsis context. Thus, these island-repair effects of Sluicing raise a challenge to syntactic analyses of ellipsis in general (see Barker 2012; Culicover and Jackendoff 2005; Ginzburg and Sag 2000, among others for details).

Merchant (2001), who brings up various important arguments for the syntactic analyses of Sluicing (see §2.1.1, above), evades the problem in the following way. He classifies islands into two subtypes: Propositional islands such as CNPC, and PF-islands such as LBE. He argues that the apparent 'repair'-examples of propositional islands such as (22a) actually does not violate island constraints in the first place. He suggests that there is non-island violating source structure available for these cases. On the other hand, he argues that PF-islands are constraints on PF-representation; thus PF-deletion operation such as ellipsis can erase the problematic PF-representation.

For the analysis of propositional islands, Merchant suggests that the ellipsis site is associated with the "short extraction" source structure shown in (23), which includes just a simple clause with a E-type pronoun subject *he* (See Evans 1980 for discussions on E-type pronouns) and no island.

(23) They want to hire someone who speaks a Balkan language, but I don't remember *which*$_1$ (Balkan language) [$_{CP}$ ~~he$^{E\text{-type}}$ speaks t$_1$~~]

This type of "alternative source" analyses has been advanced in the more recent studies. Some of the recent studies argue for the analysis in which the "island-violating" Sluicing is associated with the (truncated) cleft/copular source (Abels 2011; Barros forthcoming; Craenenbroeck 2010b). Thus the structure in the ellipsis site is as follows:

(24) They want to hire someone who speaks a Balkan language, but I don't remember *which*$_1$(Balkan language) [$_{CP}$ ~~it was~~].

Contrary to the alternative source analyses, Yoshida *et al.* (2012) point out that there are cases in which the ellipsis site unambiguously involves a violation of propositional island. They argue that parasitic gaps (PGs) (Culicover 2001; Engdahl 1983) are licensed in the Sluicing context. They cite the following example, in which a PG is hosted in the *wh*-remnant of Sluicing.

(25) The editor told me which book I have to review __$_{RG}$, but I don't remember [how soon after receiving __$_{PG}$].

They cite various pieces of evidence that suggest that the gap in the *wh*-remnant is indeed a PG. For example, this gap is not licensed if the antecedent clause does not involve overt *wh*-movement and thus does not involve the licensing gap (or real gap: RG), or if the RG is generated in the subject position.

(26) a. *The editor told me who reviews which book, but I don't remember [how soon after receiving __$_{PG}$].
b. *The editor told me which book must be reviewed __$_{RG}$ by me, but I don't remember [how soon after he receives __$_{PG}$.]

The contrast between (25) and (26) indicates that the gap in the *wh*-remnant obeys restrictions on PGs such as the licensing of PGs (in English) by an overt A-bar movement and the failure to license a PG if the RG c-commands the PG (see Culicover 2001 for a recent survey of the licensing conditions on PGs).

The fact that PGs are licensed in the Sluicing context strongly suggests that the ellipsis site in Sluicing must have a full-fledged syntactic structure that involves overt *wh*-movement and corresponding RG, which licenses PGs, and consequently that this structure contains a *wh*-island violation.

(27) … but I don't remember [how soon after receiving __~PG~] ~he told me [~CP~ which book I~ ~have to review __~RG~]~.

Any other type of structure, such as short extraction structures and truncated copular structures, cannot license PGs, as they do not have the structure involving an overt A-bar movement and RG. Therefore, the PG examples suggest that ellipsis can indeed violate propositional islands such as *wh*-islands, and also suggest that a full-fledged syntactic structure is associated with the ellipsis site. As Kennedy (2003) argues, the same logic can be extended to the other type of ellipsis constructions: That is, if PGs are licensed by the element inside ellipsis, it means that the ellipsis site must have the syntactic structure necessary to license PGs.

3.2   Voice mismatch

While the matching effects between ellipsis and its antecedent (e.g., Case-matching effects in (5)) is an argument for the syntactic analysis, the mismatch in terms of syntactic structure (the syntactic mismatch, hereafter) between them makes a strong argument against the position that ellipsis sites contain syntactic structure that structurally parallels the antecedent site. For example, VPE exhibits voice mismatch as shown in (28a); the antecedent clause is active, while the elided clause is passive. Importantly, however, clausal ellipsis does not tolerate such a mismatch (28b).

(28) a. The janitor must remove the trash whenever it is apparent that it should be ~removed~.
      b. Someone must remove the trash, but it is not clear *(by) who.

This observation suggests that the syntactic mismatch is not generally observed but only some types of ellipsis allow syntactic mismatch. The fact that VPE tolerates syntactic mismatch but Sluicing does not suggests that the size of the constituent that undergoes ellipsis seems to be an important independent factor (Merchant 2008; 2013). Merchant (2008) observes that there is an asymmetry between VPE and Pseudogapping in terms of the possibility of voice mismatch. Unlike VPE, Pseudogapping, which has sometimes been analyzed as a variety of VPE (Johnson 2009; Lasnik 1995; 1997; 1999a; 1999b; 2001b among others), does not tolerate voice mismatch.[3]

(29) *Roses were brought by some, and others did ~bring~ lilies.

Merchant (2013a) further observes that the type of syntactic mismatch that is tolerated under VPE is restricted to voice mismatch. Specifically, Merchant points out that, unlike voice mismatch, syntactic mismatches in terms of argument structure alternations are not allowed under VPE. When the antecedent clause involves the transitive verb *melt*, the intransitive verb *melt* cannot be elided even in VPE, as shown in (30), although the transitive/intransitive uses of *melt* are semantically equivalent.

(30) a.   Bill melted the copper vase, and the magnesium vase melted, too.
      b. *Bill melted the copper vase, and the magnesium vase did, too.

Based on these observations, Merchant argues that the syntactic mismatches under ellipsis are structurally constrained. First he assumes the following structure of verbal projections:[4]

(31)

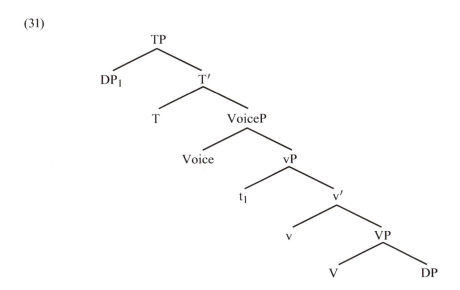

When the verbal projection undergoes ellipsis, there are two types of ellipsis. The scope of ellipsis can cover the lower projection (vP) or a higher projection (TP/VoiceP). Assuming syntactic identity restrictions on ellipsis, Merchant argues that when the scope of ellipsis contains only the lower projection, and excludes the VoiceP, the voice mismatch is tolerated. This is so because the voice projection is not within the ellipsis and, therefore, it is not subject to syntactic identity requirement. On the other hand, when the VoiceP is contained within the scope of ellipsis (as in Sluicing and Pseudogapping), the voice mismatch is not tolerated owing to the syntactic identity requirement: That is, the ellipsis must be syntactically identical to the antecedent. If this line of argument is correct, then the voice mismatch under VPE does not necessarily argue against the structural/syntactic analyses of ellipsis.

3.3   Ellipsis size mismatch

Merchant (2001) makes a very interesting and important argument for a semantic identity approach to ellipsis. If the identity condition on ellipsis is stated semantically, it is expected that the syntactic structure of the ellipsis site and the antecedent site can be mismatched. Among other cases, Merchant (2001; 2002) argues that VP can be the antecedent for TP-ellipsis in some cases of Sluicing. If this type of mismatch between the antecedent and ellipsis is possible, it can provide a strong argument for semantic identity approaches to ellipsis, as VP and TP are clearly not identical syntactically, but they may have similar semantics. There are two cases where Merchant suggests that VP serves as the antecedent for TP-ellipsis. One is Sluicing in VP-coordination (Merchant 2001: 223–226), exemplified in (32). Merchant argues that the structure of ellipsis is (32a) rather than (32b).

(32)   Fiona [$_{VP}$ [$_{VP}$ ate dinner] and [$_{VP}$ saw <u>a movie</u>]] that night, but she didn't say which.
    a.   …which she^{E-type} ~~saw t~~$_{which}$ ~~that night~~.
    b.   …which ~~she ate dinner and saw t~~$_{which}$ ~~that night~~.

Merchant's argument is as follows. First, he assumes that propositional islands, including VP-coordination, are LF-islands and PF-deletion cannot repair the violation of these islands. Thus (32) should have a short extraction structure. Under the semantic identity approach proposed in Merchant (2001), VP in the antecedent clause, which includes the trace of the subject that is understood as an E-type pronoun, can hold certain semantic parallelism with the TP in the ellipsis site, as in (32a). Thus, by means of taking VP as the antecedent of the TP-ellipsis, (32) can have an non-island-violating structure. Note, however, that if we are to reject the E-type pronoun analysis of island-violating Sluicing (Yoshida *et al.* 2012; see §3.1.), we cannot endorse this account as it is.

The second case of this type of mismatch is Swiping (Merchant 2002), as illustrated in (33). In Swiping, the *wh*-phrase and the preposition are inverted. Such *Wh*-P inversion is possible in some restricted environments (see Craenenbroeck 2010a; Hartmann 2007; Merchant 2002 for details).

(33)   Peter went to the movies, but I don't know who with.

Normally, Swiping is licensed in the so-called Sprouting environment. Sprouting is a type of Sluicing where the *wh*-remnant does not have a correlating indefinite phrase (e.g. *something* in (1c)) in the antecedent clause. In such a Sprouting environment, the swiped phrase *who with* constitutes 'new information' not present in the antecedent clause. Merchant (2002) explains this in terms of a GIVENness condition that states that a swiped preposition must not be GIVEN in the context. (Here, GIVEN roughly means existing as an old information; he takes this notion from Schwarzschild (1999)). If the preposition is not contained in the antecedent, as in (33), it can satisfy the GIVENness condition.

Some speakers accept Swiping with an explicit antecedent (three native speakers of English in our sample), but only when the *wh*-phrase and its antecedent are adjuncts ((34); Merchant 2002; Rosen 1976). The PP *to someone* in (34a) is a complement of the verb *talk*, while the instrumental PP *with something* in (34b) is an adjunct. Swiping is possible only with the latter example.

(34)   a.   *John talked **to someone**, but I don't know who to.
       b.   John fixed it **with something**, but I don't know what with.

The Swiped preposition *with* in (34b) apparently does not satisfy the GIVENness condition, because it is already GIVEN in the antecedent clause. Merchant evades this problem by arguing that TP-ellipsis in Swiping can take a VP segment, rather than the whole TP, as its antecedent. In (34b), for example, the antecedent of TP-ellipsis in Swiping is the lower VP-segment, VP$_2$, which does not include the preposition *with*. If the adjunct PP *with something* counts as absent (= not GIVEN) in the antecedent it satisfies the GIVENness requirement, and can license Swiping.

(35)

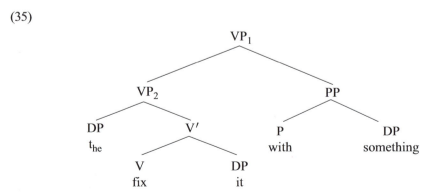

In line with Merchant (2001; 2002), Yoshida (2010) points out another environment where VP serves as the antecedent of TP-ellipsis, namely the Sluicing in Adjunct (*SiA*) construction, as in (36).

(36) a. John must [$_{VP}$[$_{VP}$ select a color] [$_{PP}$ without knowing [$_{CP}$ which one]]].
     b. John cannot [$_{VP}$[$_{VP}$ select a color] [$_{PP}$ without knowing [$_{CP}$ which one]]].

Yoshida points out two properties of *SiA*. First, the modals and negation are not interpreted in the ellipsis site; (36a) and (36b) have the interpretation (37a) and (38a), respectively, and the interpretation (37b) and (38b) are unavailable.

(37) a.   John must select a color without knowing which one he selects.
     b. # John must select a color without knowing which one he must select.

(38) a.   John cannot select a color without knowing which one he selects.
     b. # John cannot select a color without knowing which one he cannot select.

Second, the structure of *SiA* in which the *without*-clause is adjoined to the matrix VP gives rise to an infinite regress problem, even though the examples of *SiA* are totally acceptable. Yoshida argues that these two properties of *SiA* follow straightforwardly, if TP-ellipsis in *SiA* takes a lower VP-segment as its antecedent, excluding the PP, similarly to VP-coordination and Swiping cases. Assuming the VP internal subject hypothesis (the subject *John* originates inside the VP), the structure of (36a) is the one illustrated in (39).

(39) John must [$_{VP}$[$_{VP}$ t$_{John}$ **select a color**] [$_{PP}$ without knowing [$_{CP}$ which one ~~[$_{VP}$ (John)~~
     ~~select a color]~~]]].

Under this structure, the unavailability of (37b) and (38b) is natural, because the ellipsis site does not contain the modal or the negation. Also, the infinite regress does not arise, as the ellipsis site does not contain the PP.

    Yoshida (2010) suggests that the mismatch is possible as a last resort. (See Frazier and Yoshida (2012) for a similar line of argument.) Thus, these mismatch cases do not necessarily argue against the syntactic analysis of ellipsis.

4 Controversial cases

The previous sections discussed constructions that are analyzed as sentential ellipsis. The following subsections deal with other phenomena that are potentially analyzed in terms of ellipsis. In some of these cases there is still an ongoing debate concerning the adequacy of the ellipsis vs. non-ellipsis analyses or the content of the ellipsis site.

4.1 Multiple Sluicing and Sluice Stripping

Under the syntactic analyses of Sluicing and Stripping, the remnants escape ellipsis via *wh*- and focus movement, respectively. Still, other options have been put forward for Multiple Sluicing (e.g., (40)) and *Wh*-Stripping (e.g., (41)); Yoshida *et al.* (2012) call ellipsis with *wh*- and non-*wh*-remnants 'Sluice-Stripping' (because it is similar to both Sluicing and Stripping); among Sluice-Stripping, they refer to the examples where the first remnant is a *wh*-element other than *why* as '*Wh*-Stripping' (e.g., (41)) (examples where the first element is *why* are distinguished as 'Why-Stripping': See below).

(40) Peter read something with someone, but I don't know what with whom.

(41) Peter studied syntax, but I wonder who phonology. (= who studied phonology)

All these structures show properties such as Case-matching effects and thus we can assume that a full-fledged syntactic structure underlies the ellipsis site. Arguably, the non-*wh*-remnant of *Wh*-Stripping (e.g., *phonology* in (41)) undergoes rightward movement rather than leftward movement in order to escape ellipsis (Nevins 2008). Multiple Sluicing also arguably instantiates rightward movement of the second *wh*-element (Lasnik 2014). These constructions indicate that not only leftward movement but also rightward movement is a strategy for a remnant to escape ellipsis.

Crucially, the rightward movement approach has been argued for on the basis of the following properties: Rightward movement neither allows for P-stranding (Ross 1967; van Riemsdijk 1978; Jayaseelan 1990; Pesetsky 1995; Lasnik 1999a; Drummond *et al.* 2011) (42) nor for long-distance movement (Ross 1967; Baltin 1978; Grosu 1972) (43):

(42) a. John counted *on* **a total stranger** for support.
      b. John counted for support **on a total stranger**.
      c. *John counted *on* for support **a total stranger**.   (Jayaseelan 1990: 66)

(43) a. I expect t_{NP} to arrive, [$_{NP}$ my good friend John].
      b. *I expect (that) t_{NP} will have arrived, [$_{NP}$ my good friend John].
                                                                        (Stowell 1981: 234)

Those properties are found in both Multiple Sluicing and *Wh*-Stripping. With regard to Multiple Sluicing, (44) illustrates the unavailability of P-stranding for the second *wh*-remnant (even though P-stranding is known to be allowed under regular *wh*-movement, as seen for the first remnant) whereas (45) shows that a clausal boundary may not intervene between both *wh*-elements:[5]

(44) Peter talked about something to somebody, but I can't remember (about) what *(to) whom. (Rodrigues *et al.* 2009: 180)

(45) a. One of the students spoke to one of the professors, but I don't know which student to which professor.
      b. *One of the students said that Mary spoke to one of the professors, but I don't know which student to which professor.

In turn, (46) illustrates the ban on P-drop of the non-*wh*-remnant as opposed to the *wh*-remnant in *Wh*-Stripping, whereas (47) illustrates the clause-mate requirement between both remnants (see Nevins 2008):

(46) A: Lou talked to Mary about syntax. B: And (to) whom *(about) phonology?

(47) *No phonetician$_1$ thought that a syntactician talked about his$_1$ paper, but I wish I could remember who ~~no phonetician$_1$ thought that t$_{who}$ talked~~ about his$_1$ presentation.

Based on these facts, Lasnik (2014) argues for leftward *wh*-movement of the first remnant and rightward movement of the second remnant for Multiple Sluicing, whereas Nevins (2008) and Yoshida *et al.* (2012) do so for *Wh*-Stripping.

Wh-Stripping contrasts with another type of Sluice-Stripping, namely Why-Stripping, a construction licensed in a wide variety of languages ranging from Romance to Japanese or English (see Yoshida *et al.* forthcoming). Here, the *wh*-element is restricted to *why* (and for some speakers *how come*) and the non-*wh*-remnant is repeated from the antecedent clause and is contrasted to other alternatives (*other food*); (see Merchant 2006 for discussion of the *why not* construction):

(48) a. John was eating natto.
     b. Why/*Where/*When/*Who NATTO (but not other food)?

English does not allow for overt focus movement in contexts other than ellipsis, even though the non-*wh*-remnant shows a number of connectivity effects. Thus, a PF-deletion approach is in order:

(49) [CP1 Why [CP2 NATTO1 [TP ~~he was eating t1~~]]]

Interestingly, in spite of the close resemblance between *Wh*-Stripping and Why-Stripping (e.g., in both cases the non-*wh*-remnant survives ellipsis owing to its being a focused element, whereas the elided portion constitutes old information), the latter structure shows none of the hallmarks of rightward movement: It allows for P-drop and it is not clause-bound:

(50) A: Lou will ask Doris about syntax.   B: Why (about) syntax?

(51) No linguist1 believes that NLLT would publish his1 best papers, but I don't see why his1 best paper.

Based on this and other properties of Why-Stripping, Yoshida *et al.* (forthoming) argue for base-generation of *why* (Rizzi 1997, among others) and leftward focus movement of the non-*wh*-remnant.

4.2 Gapping: ATB movement and ellipsis

There are now an increasing number of studies on the Gapping construction illustrated in (52) (Coppock 2001; Jackendoff 1971; Johnson 1994; 2006; 2009; Repp 2009; Ross 1970; Siegel 1984, among many others).

(52) John ate apples and Mary ~~ate~~ bananas.

Gapping has long been proved to be problematic in syntactic theories because of its unique properties. Among others, the following two properties have been debated in the study of Gapping (for a survey of the property of Gapping, see Johnson 1994). First, Gapping can be applied over coordinating connectives, but not subordinating connectives (the so-called coordination constraint).

(53) John ate apples [ok]and/[ok]or/[ok]but *while/*because/*if/*although Mary ~~ate~~ bananas.

Masaya Yoshida, Chizuru Nakao, and Iván Ortega-Santos

Second, Gapping shows the properties of the coordination of VP rather than the larger constituents such as TP or CP. In Gapping, the TP-level element such as modals, negation, and the subject DP can scope over the whole coordinated structure. For example, *or* is interpreted conjunctively when Gapping involves negation (54a), and the subject DP in the first clause can bind the subject DP in the second clause (54b).

(54) a.   John hasn't seen Harry or Bill, Sue.
         = John has not seen Harry and /[??]or Bill has not seen Sue.
     b.   Not every girl₁ ate a green banana, and her₁ mother ate a ripe one.

As Johnson (1996) shows, these properties are not seen in other ellipsis constructions, and any study of Gapping must be able to capture these properties.

   Johnson (1996) argues that these properties all follow if Gapping involves Across-the-Board (ATB) movement of the verb-head, rather than ellipsis. (55) illustrates the (simplified) derivation of Gapping in ATB analysis.

(55)

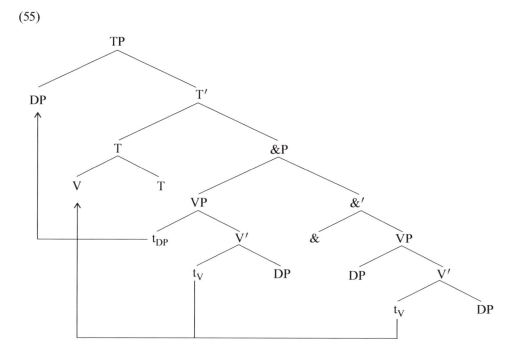

First, the head-movement normally cannot go across the finite clause boundary. Therefore, ATB Head-movement analysis explains why Gapping is restricted to the Coordination environment (e.g., (53)). Second, the verb movement cannot go across the auxiliary verbs owing to the Head Movement Constraint (Baker 1988; Travis 1984); in the examples where the modals/negation precede the verb in the first conjunct and the verb is missing in the second conjunct, as in (54), the only possible structure is the coordination of VP. Thus, ATB head-movement analysis explains why the modals/negation scope over the whole coordination (e.g., (54a)). Finally, if the size of the conjuncts is VP then there is only one [Spec,TP] available for the subject DP. Thus, the subject DP in the first conjunct occupies

[Spec,TP] and the one in the second conjunct must stay in [Spec,VP]. This is why the first subject binds, thus c-commands, the second subject (e.g., (54b)).[6]

Various ellipsis analyses have also been proposed. Coppock (2001), for example, gives an example where Gapping omits more than just a verb and thus should not be treated as a mere instance of verb movement. She claims that, in (56), *too weak* undergoes movement and the LBE violation is repaired under ellipsis in the same way as Sluicing.

(56) John made too strong an espresso, Mary too weak ~~made t~~$_{too weak}$ ~~an espresso~~.

Coppock further argues that Gapping has the same focus structure as Sluicing, and thus Gapping is to be analyzed as ellipsis (see Kennedy 2001; Repp 2009 among others for recent discussion on ellipsis analyses of Gapping). However, ellipsis analyses still have not succeeded in explaining the coordination constraint and other generalizations that Gapping shows. Thus, it is fair to say that some version of the ATB-movement analysis is still the most successful explanation of the generalizations of Gapping (see Repp 2009; Vicente 2010, among others for problems of the ATB-movement analysis).

Besides the regular Gapping construction seen in the clausal domain, Gapping-like constructions can also be seen in other constituents. For example, Gapping-like head omission is possible in DP, the so-called Nominal Gapping (NG) (Chaves 2005; Jackendoff 1971; Lobeck 2006; Postal 2004; Yoshida *et al.* 2012, among others).

(57) John read Mary's book of music and David's ~~book~~ of poems.

An obvious question is whether NG shows the signature properties of Gapping in the clausal domain (Verbal Gapping: VG). Yoshida *et al.* (2012) directly tackle this question. They point out that the distribution of NG is different from that of VG. Specifically, the coordination constraint is not respected by NG, as (58) suggests. In (58), NG is applied across subordinating connectives.

(58) John's book of music will be published [because/if Mary's ~~book~~ of poems is successful].

Yoshida *et al.* (2012) investigated the distribution of NG in detail and found that NG obeys the same licensing condition as NP-ellipsis (NPE: e.g., (59)) obeys. Therefore, when NPE is not licensed, NG is not licensed either, and when NPE is possible, NG is possible.

(59) a. The books are new, and all ~~books~~ (of music) are on sale.
 b. Mary likes those books of poems, but I like these ~~books~~ (of music).
 c. *John read the/a/every book of music and Mary read the /a /every ~~book~~ (of poems).
 d. *John read Mary's long book of poems and Bill's short ~~book~~ (of music).

These observations led Yoshida *et al.* (2012) to conclude that NG is a variant of NPE and the ATB-movement derivation is not responsible for NG.

This conclusion raises an interesting question. What differentiates NG and VG? In other words, if ATB-analysis is correct, why is it not true with NG? At least, they look superficially very similar: In both NG and VG, it looks like only the head is omitted.

4.3   Argument ellipsis in Japanese

East Asian languages allow for a productive use of empty arguments. Among others, the analysis of empty objects in Japanese has long been a point of contention (Oku 1998; Otani and Whitman 1991; Saito 2007; Takahashi 2008, among many others). Since Kuroda (1965), the empty object, indicated by ___ in examples such as (60), has been analyzed as an empty pronominal, *pro*.

(60)   Taroo-wa zibun-no hahaoya-o   sonkeisiteiru.
      T-top   self-gen mother-acc respect
      "Taroo respects his mother."
      Hanako-mo ___ kanojo-o sonekeisiteiru.
      H-also ___/her-acc   respect
      "Hanako also respects ___ (=T's mother/H's mother)/ her (T's mother/*H's mother)."

As (60) indicates, however, the empty object exhibits both strict reading and sloppy readings, unlike an overt pronoun, which allows only for the strict reading (Otani and Whitman 1991). This indicates that the empty object in (60) is not an empty pronominal. Based on this observation, Otani and Whitman argue that the empty object is actually a product of VP ellipsis. They argue that Japanese has V-to-T movement and, thus, V can evacuate from VP. The ellipsis process targets the VP from which the verb is moved out, and a string such as (60) surfaces.

(61)   [$_{TP}$ H-mo[$_{VP}$ ~~zibun-no hahaoya-o~~ t$_V$] [$_T$[$_V$ sonkeisite][$_T$ -iru]]]

The sloppy reading naturally follows from the VP-ellipsis approach, as ellipsis typically exhibits the sloppy reading.

Despite its advantage over the *pro* analysis, the VP-ellipsis analysis also has some problems. Most notably, a similar sloppy reading is also possible with empty subjects, which are, arguably, generated outside of the VP (Oku 1998).

(62)   Taroo-wa [zibun-no teian-ga saiyousareru-to] omotteiru.
      T-top self-gen proposal-nom accepted-be-that think
      "Taroo thinks that his proposal will be accepted"
      Hanako-mo [___ saiyousareru-to] omotteiru.
      H-also accepted-be-that think
      "Hanako also thinks that ___ (=T's proposal/H's proposal) will be accepted."

To resolve this problem, an alternative analysis has recently been proposed: The null object is indeed the product of ellipsis, but what is elided is not VP but the argument itself (Oku 1998; Saito 2007; Takahashi 2008 among many others).

(63)   H-mo[$_{VP}$ [$_{DP}$ ~~zibun-no hahaoya-o~~] sonkeisiteiru]

In recent studies, the debate is over whether or not the empty object is really the product of ellipsis. At this point, an argument for ellipsis is based on the possibility of sloppy readings and it is still not clear whether the null object shows other properties of ellipsis (for recent development, see Kim 1999; Şener and Takahashi 2010; Takahashi 2008; Takita 2008, among others).

5 Conclusion

Whether ellipsis is associated with a full-fledged syntactic structure or not has been a long-standing problem in syntax. In this chapter we have summarized various cases that support the syntactic analysis of ellipsis. In spite of the increase in the number of studies supporting that line of analysis, there are various compelling arguments against it as well (Barker 2012; Culicover and Jackendoff 2005; Ginzburg and Sag 2000 among others): That is, there is a lot to study in the domain of ellipsis and a wide variety of perspectives is required.

Acknowledgments

We would like to thank Norbert Hornstein, Howard Lasnik, Jason Merchant and Yosuke Sato for their valuable comments and discussion. This work has been supported in part by a grant to Masaya Yoshida from the National Science Foundation (BCS-1323245).

Notes

1   Note that a number of recent studies include possible counterexamples to the P-stranding gener-
    alization. Therefore, it is not clear how strong this correlation is (see Almeida and Yoshida 2007;
    Rodrigues *et al.* 2009; Stjepanovic 2008; Vicente 2008, among others).
2   Depiante (2000) assumes that the negation *not* forms a constituent with the remnant. See Nakao
    (2009) for an argument that *not* in Stripping is base-generated in the sentence-initial position.
3   Note that Tanaka (2011) casts a doubt on voice mismatch asymmetry between VPE and Pseu-
    dogapping. Tanaka observes the cases where Pseudogapping tolerates voice mismatch. More
    detailed empirical testing is necessary in this domain.
4   Note that this is a simplified structure. There has been a discussion on where the Voice feature
    should be attributed to. In Merchant (2008) the Voice feature is attributed to the v head, but it
    is possible to assume that there is an independent Voice projection as in (31) (see Merchant
    2013a).
5   An in situ approach that allows for the deletion of non-constituents à la López (2009), by contrast,
    does not predict the existence of those asymmetries between Why-Stripping and *Wh*-Stripping
    and, thus, is not able to account for them in a principled way. Note that the mechanism underlying
    Multiple Sluicing in Multiple *Wh*-Movement languages is different from the one explored in this
    paper, in that Multiple Sluicing in those languages is not subject to the clause-mate restriction
    (Lasnik 2014).
6   This derivation violates Coordination Structure Constraint (CSC). However, it is pointed out in
    the literature that A-movement can indeed violate CSC (Johnson 1994; Lin 2000; 2001).

Further reading

Chung, Sandra, William A. Ladusaw, and James McCloskey. 1995. Sluicing and Logical Form. *Natural Language Semantics* 3:239–282.

> Chung *et al.* investigate the syntax and semantics of sluicing in detail. To account for scope prop-
> erties, island (in)sensitivity and other major properties of sluicing, they propose an LF-copying
> approach to sluicing. The difference between Sprouting-type sluicing and Merger-type sluicing
> has been documented in this work.

Lobeck, Anne. 1995. *Ellipsis: Functional Heads, Licensing, and Identification*. New York: Oxford University Press.

> Lobeck offers a theory of identity and licensing condition on ellipsis. She argues that ellipsis is
> licensed by functional heads that show strong agreement with the ellipsis site.

Merchant, Jason. 2001. *The Syntax of Silence: Sluicing, Islands, and the Theory of Ellipsis: Oxford Studies in Theoretical Linguistics*. Oxford: Oxford University Press.

Merchant argues that properties of ellipsis constructions follow from a semantic identity condition. He argues that the syntactic mismatch between the antecedent and the ellipsis site follows if the identity condition is stated semantically not syntactically. He also presents evidence for a full-fledged syntactic structure under ellipsis.

Ross, John Robert. 1969. Guess Who? In *Papers from the 5th Regional Meeting of the Chicago Linguistic Society*, ed. Robert I. Binnick, A. Davison, Georgia M. Green, and James L. Morgan, 252–286. Chicago: Chicago Linguistic Society.

Ross shows that sluicing and non-elliptical *wh*-interrogatives exhibit parallel properties and thus concludes that sluicing is associated with a full-fledged syntactic structure. Island amelioration effects of sluicing have been originally documented in this paper.

References

Abels, Klaus. 2011. Don't Repair That Island! It Ain't Broke. Ms. University College London, London.

Almeida, Diogo, and Masaya Yoshida. 2007. A Problem for the Preposition Stranding Generalization. *Linguistic Inquiry* 38:349–362.

Arregui, Ana, Charles Clifton Jr., Lyn Frazier, and Keir Moulton. 2006. Processing Elided Verb Phrases with Flawed Antecedents: The Recycling Hypothesis. *Journal of Memory and Language* 55:232–246.

Baker, Mark. 1988. *Incorporation: A Theory of Grammatical Function Changing*. Chicago and London: The University of Chicago Press.

Baltin, Mark. 1978. *Toward a Theory of Movement Rules*. PhD Dissertation, Massachusetts Institute of Technology.

Barker, Chris. 2012. Scopability and Sluicing. Ms. New York University.

Barros, Matthew. forthcoming. Arguments against Island Repair: Evidence from Contrastive TP Ellipsis. In *The 48th Annual Meeting of the Chicago Linguistic Society (CLS 48)*. Chicago, IL: Chicago Linguistic Society.

Chaves, Rui P. 2005. A Linearization-Based Approach to Gapping. In *The Proceedings of the 10th Conference on Formal Grammar and the 9th Meeting on Mathematics of Language*, 1–14. Stanford, CA: CSLI.

Chomsky, Noam. 1972. Some Empirical Issues in the Theory of Transformational Grammar. In *Goals of Linguistic Theory*, ed. Paul Stanley Peters, 63–130. Englewood Cliffs, NJ: Prentice-Hall.

Chomsky, Noam. 1993. A Minimalist Program for Linguistic Theory. *The View from Building 20*, ed. Kenneth Hale and Samuel Keyser, 1–52. Cambridge, MA: MIT Press.

Chomsky, Noam. 1995. *The Minimalist Program*. Cambridge, MA: MIT Press.

Chung, Sandra, William A. Ladusaw, and James McCloskey. 1995. Sluicing and Logical Form. *Natural Language Semantics* 3:239–282.

Coppock, Elizabeth. 2001. Gapping: In Defense of Deletion. *CLS* 37:133–147.

Craenenbroeck, Jeroen van. 2010a. *The Syntax of Ellipsis*. Oxford: Oxford University Press.

Craenenbroeck, Jeroen van. 2010b. Invisible Last Resort: A Note on Clefts as the Underlying Source for Sluicing. *Lingua* 120:1714–1726.

Craenenbroeck, Jeroen van, and Jason Merchant. 2013. Ellipsis Phenomena. In *Cambridge Handbook of Generative Syntax*, ed. Marcel den Dikken, 701–745. Cambridge: Cambridge University Press.

Culicover, Peter W. 2001. Parasitic Gaps: A History. In *Parasitic Gaps*, ed. Peter W. Culicover and Paul M. Postal, 3–68. Cambridge, MA: MIT Press.

Culicover, Peter W., and Ray Jackendoff. 2005. *Simpler Syntax*. Oxford: Oxford University Press.

Dalrymple, Mary, Stuart M. Shieber, and Fernando C.N. Pereira. 1991. Ellipsis and Higher-Order Unification. *Linguistics and Philosophy* 14:399–452.

Depiante, Marcela A. 2000. The Syntax of Deep and Surface Anaphora: A Study of Null Complement Anaphora and Stripping/Bare Argument Ellipsis. PhD dissertation, University of Connecticut.

Drummond, Alex, Norbert Hornstein, and Howard Lasnik. 2011. A Puzzle About P-Stranding and a Possible Solution. *Linguistic Inquiry* 41:689–692.

Engdahl, Elisabet. 1983. Parasitic Gaps. *Linguistics and Philosophy* 6:5–34.

Erteschik-Shir, Nomi. 1977. *On the Nature of Island Constraints*. Bloomington, IN: Indiana University Linguistics Club.

Evans, Garreth. 1980. Pronouns. *Linguistic Inquiry* 11(2):337–362.

Fiengo, Robert, and Robert May. 1994. *Indices and Identity*. Linguistic Inquiry Monographs 24. Cambridge, MA: MIT Press.

Frazier, Michael, and Masaya Yoshida. 2012. When Can VP be the Antecedent for TP-ellipsis? A Study on Syntactic Mismatch between Clausal Ellipsis and its Antecedent. Ms. Northwestern University.

Ginzburg, Jonathan. 1992. Questions, Queries, and Facts: A Semantics and Pragmatics for Interrogatives. PhD dissertation, Stanford University.

Ginzburg, Jonathan, and Ivan A. Sag. 2000. *Interrogative Investigations*. Stanford, CA: CSLI Publications.

Griffiths, James, and Anikó Lipták. forthcoming. Contrast and Island-sensitivity in Clausal Ellipsis. *Syntax*.

Grosu, Alexander. 1972. *The Strategic Content of Island Constraints*. PhD dissertation, The Ohio State University.

Hankamer, Jorge, and Ivan A. Sag. 1976. Deep and Surface Anaphora. *Linguistic Inquiry* 7:391–426.

Hardt, Daniel. 1993. Verb Phrase Ellipsis: Form Meaning and Processing. PhD dissertation, University of Pennsylvania, Philadelphia.

Hartmann, Jeremy. 2007. Focus, Deletion, and Identity: Investigations of Ellipsis in English. BA thesis, Harvard University.

Jackendoff, Ray. 1971. Gapping and Related Rules. *Linguistic Inquiry* 2:21–36.

Jayaseelan, Karattuparambil A. 1990. Incomplete Vp Deletion and Gapping. *Linguistic Analysis* 20:64–81.

Johnson, Kyle. 1994. Bridging the Gap. Ms. University of Massachusetts at Amherst.

Johnson, Kyle. 1996. In Search of the English Middle Field. Ms. University of Massachusetts, Amherst.

Johnson, Kyle. 2001. What VP-Ellipsis Can Do, What It Can't, but Not Why. In *The Handbook of Contemporary Syntactic Theory*, ed. Mark Baltin and Chris Collins, 439–479. Malden, MA: Blackwell.

Johnson, Kyle. 2006. Gapping. In *The Blackwell Companion to Syntax*, ed. Martin Everaert and Henk van Riemsdijk, 407–435. Cambridge: Blackwell.

Johnson, Kyle. 2009. Gapping Is Not (VP-) Ellipsis. *Linguistic Inquiry* 40:289–328.

Kehler, Andrew. 2002. *Coherence, Reference and the Theory of Grammar*. Stanford, CA: CSLI Publications.

Kennedy, Christopher. 2001. In Search of Unpronounceable Structure. Ms. University of Chicago.

Kennedy, Christopher. 2003. Ellipsis and Syntactic Representation. In *The Interfaces: Deriving and Interpreting Omitted Structure*, ed. Kerstin Schwabe and Susanne Winkler, 29–53. Amsterdam: John Benjamins.

Kim, Christina, Gregory Kobele, Jeffrey Runner, and John T. Hale. 2011. The Acceptability Cline in VP Ellipsis. *Syntax* 14:318–354.

Kim, Jeong-Seok. 1998. *Syntactic Focus Movement and Ellipsis: A Minimalist Approach*. Ann Arbor: UMI.

Kim, Soowon. 1999. Sloppy/Strict Identity, Empty Objects, and NP Ellipsis. *Journal of East Asian Linguistics* 8:255–284.

Kuroda, Shige-Yuki. 1965. Generative Grammatical Studies in the Japanese Language. PhD dissertation, Massachusetts Institute of Technology.

Lasnik, Howard. 1995. A Note on Pseudogapping. In *Papers on Minimalist Syntax, MIT Working Papers in Linguistics 27*, ed. R. Pensalfini and H. Ura, 143–163.

Lasnik, Howard. 1997. A Gap in an Ellipsis Paradigm: Some Theoretical Implications. *Linguistic Analysis* 27:166–185.

Lasnik, Howard. 1999a. Pseudogapping Puzzles. In *Fragments: Studies in Ellipsis and Gapping*, ed. Shalom Lappin and Elabbas Benmamoun, 141–174. New York: Oxford University Press.

Lasnik, Howard. 1999b. On Feature Strength: Three Minimalist Approaches to Overt Movement. *Linguistic Inquiry* 30:197–217.

Lasnik, Howard. 2001a. When Can You Save a Structure by Destroying It? In *Proceedings of the North East Linguistics Society 31*, ed. M. Kim and U. Strauss, 301–320. Amherst, MA: University of Massachusetts: GLSA.

Lasnik, Howard. 2001b. Derivation and Representation in Modern Transformational Syntax. In *The Handbook of Contemporary Syntactic Theory*, ed. Mark Baltin and Chris Collins, 62–88. Oxford: Blackwell.

Lasnik, Howard. 2014. Multiple Sluicing in English? *Syntax* 171:1–20.

Lin, Vivian. 2000. Determiner Sharing. In *Proceedings of WCCFL* 19, ed. R. Billerey and B. D. Lillehaugen, 274–287. Somerville, MA: Cascadilla Press.

Lin, Vivian. 2001. A Way to Undo a-Movement. In *Proceedings of WCCFL 20*, ed. K. Megerdoomian and L.A. Barel, 358–371. Somerville, MA: Cascadilla Press.

Lobeck, Anne C. 1995. *Ellipsis: Functional Heads, Licensing, and Identification*. New York: Oxford University Press.

Lobeck, Anne. 2006. Ellipsis in DP. In *The Blackwell Companion to Syntax*, ed. Martin Everaert, Henk van Riemsdijk, Rob Goedemans, and Bart Hollebrandse, 145–173. Malden, MA: Blackwell.

López, Luis. 2009. *A Derivational Syntax for Information Structure*. Oxford: Oxford University Press.

McCawley, James D. 1988. *The Syntactic Phenomena of English*. Chicago, IL: University of Chicago Press.

May, Robert. 1991. Syntax, Semantics, and Logical Form. In *The Chomskyan Turn*, ed. Asa Kasher, 334–359. Oxford: Blackwell.

Merchant, Jason. 2001. *The Syntax of Silence: Sluicing, Islands, and the Theory of Ellipsis*. Oxford Studies in Theoretical Linguistics. Oxford: Oxford University Press.

Merchant, Jason. 2002. Swiping in Germanic. In *Studies in Comparative Germanic Syntax: Proceedings from the 15th Workshop on Comparative Germanic Syntax*, ed. C. Jan-Wouter Zwart and Werner Abraham, 289–315. Amsterdam: John Benjamins Publishing Company.

Merchant, Jason. 2004. Fragments and Ellipsis. *Linguistics and Philosophy* 27:661–738.

Merchant, Jason. 2006. Why No(t)? *Style* 40:20–23.

Merchant, Jason. 2008. An Asymmetry in Voice Mismatch in VP-Ellipsis and Pseudogapping. *Linguistic Inquiry* 39:169–179.

Merchant, Jason. 2013a. Voice and Ellipsis. *Linguistic Inquiry* 44:77–108.

Merchant, Jason. 2013b. Diagnosing Ellipsis. In *Diagnosing Syntax*, ed. Lisa L.S. Cheng and Norbert Cover, 537–542. Oxford: Oxford University Press.

Merchant, Jason. forthcoming. Ellipsis. In *Syntax: An International Handbook*, 2nd edn, ed. Artemis Alexiadou and Tibor Kiss. Berlin: Mouton de Gruyter.

Nakao, Chizuru. 2009. Island Repair and Non-repair by PF-Strategies. PhD dissertation, University of Maryland, College Park.

Nevins, Andrew. 2008 Sluicing ≠ Stripping: Evidence from P-Stranding. Ms. Harvard University.

Oku, Satoshi. 1998. A Theory of Selection and Reconstruction in the Minimalist Perspective. PhD dissertation, University of Connecticut.

Otani, Kazuyo, and John B. Whitman. 1991. V-Raising and VP-Ellipsis. *Linguistic Inquiry* 22:345–358.

Park, Bum-Sik. 2005. Locality and Identity in Ellipsis. PhD dissertation, University of Connecticut, Storrs.

Pesetsky, David. 1995. *Zero Syntax : Experiencers and Cascades*. Cambridge, MA: MIT Press.

Pesetsky, David. 1997. Some Optimality Principles of Sentence Pronounciation. In *Is the Best Good Enough*, ed. Pilar Barbosa, Danny Fox, Paul Hagstrom, Martha Mcginnis and David Pesetsky, 337–383. Cambridge, MA: MIT Press.

Postal, Paul M. 2004. *Skeptical Linguistic Essays*. Oxford: Oxford University Press.

Reinhart, Tanya. 1991. Elliptic Conjunctions – Non-Quantificational LF. In *The Chomskyan Turn*, ed. Asa Kasher, 360–384. Oxford: Blackwell.

Repp, Sophie. 2009. *Negation in Gapping*. Oxford: Oxford University Press.

Riemsdijk, Henk van. 1978. *A Case Study in Syntactic Markedness: The Binding Nature of Prepositional Phrases*. Dordrecht: Foris.

Rizzi, Luigi. 1997. The Fine Structure of the Left Periphery. In *Elements of Grammar: Handbook in Generative Syntax*, ed. L. Haegeman, 281–337. Dordrecht: Kluwer.

Rodrigues, Cilene, Andrew Nevins, and Luis Vicente. 2009. Cleaving the Interactions between Sluicing and P-Stranding. In *Romance Languages and Linguistic Theory 2006*, ed. Danièle Torck and Leo. W. Wetzels, 245–270. Amsterdam: John Benjamins.

Rosen, Carol. 1976. Guess What About? In *Papers from the 6th Meeting of the North Eastern Linguistic Society*, ed. Alan Ford, John Reighard, and Rajendra Singh, 205–211. Montreal: Montreal Working Papers in Linguistics.

Ross, John Robert. 1967. Constraints on Variables in Syntax. PhD Dissertation, Massachusetts Institute of Technology.

Ross, John Robert. 1969. Guess Who? In *Papers from the 5th Regional Meeting of the Chicago Linguistic Society*, ed. Robert I. Binnick, A. Davison, Georgia M. Green, and James L. Morgan, 252–286. Chicago: Chicago Linguistic Society.

Ross, John Robert. 1970. Gapping and the Order of Constituents. In *Progress in Linguistics*, ed. Manfred Bierwisch and K.E. Heidolph, 249–259. The Hague: Mouton.

Sag, Ivan A. 1976. Deletion and Logical Form. PhD dissertation, Massachusetts Institute of Technology.

Saito, Mamoru. 2007. Notes on East Asian Argument Ellipsis. *Language Research* 43:203–227.

Salzmann, Martin. 2012. A Derivational Ellipsis Approach to ATB-movement. *The Linguistic Review* 29:397–438.

Schwarzschild, Roger. 1999. Givenness, Avoid-F, and Other Constraints on the Placement of Accent. *Natural Language Semantics* 7:141–177.

Şener, Serkan, and Daiko Takahashi. 2010. Argument Ellipsis in Japanese and Turkish. *MIT Working Papers in Linguistics* 61:325–339.

Siegel, Muffy E.A. 1984. Gapping and Interpretation. *Linguistic Inquiry* 15:523–530.

Stjepanovic, Sandra. 2008. P-Stranding under Sluicing in a Non-P-Stranding Language? *Linguistic Inquiry* 39:179–190.

Stowell, Timothy. 1981. Origins of Phrase Structure. PhD dissertation, Massachusetts Institute of Technology.

Takahashi, Daiko. 2008. Quantificational Null Objects and Argument Ellipsis. *Linguistic Inquiry* 39:307–326.

Takita, Kensuke. 2008. An Argument for Argument Ellipsis from -Sika NPIs. In *Proceedings of the Thirty-Ninth Annual Meeting of the North East Linguistic Society*, ed. Suzi Lima, Kevin Mullin and Brian Smith, 771–784. Amherst, MA: GLSA.

Tanaka, Hidekazu. 2011. Voice Mismatch and Syntactic Identity. *Linguistic Inquiry* 42:470–490.

Travis, Lisa. 1984. Parameters and Effects of Word Order Variation. PhD dissertation, Massachusetts Institute of Technology.

Vicente, Luis. 2008. On the Availability of Copular Clauses as Sources for Clausal Ellipsis. Ms. The Talk given at the 44th Chicago Linguistics Society (CLS 44), at University of Chicago, Chicago, IL, USA.

Vicente, Luis. 2010. A Note on the Movement Analysis of Gapping. *Linguistic Inquiry* 41:509–517.

Yoshida, Masaya. 2010. "Antecedent Contained" Sluicing. *Linguistic Inquiry* 42:348–356.

Yoshida, Masaya, Honglei Wang, and David Potter. 2012. Remarks on "Gapping" in DP. *Linguistic Inquiry* 43:475–494.

Yoshida, Masaya, Chizuru Nakao, and Iván Ortega-Santos. forthcoming. On the Syntax of Why-Stripping. *Natural Language and Linguistic Theory*.

Yoshida, Masaya, Tim Hunter, and Michael Frazier. 2012. Parasitic Gaps Licensed under Sluicing. Ms. Northwestern University.

11
Binding theory

Robert Truswell

1 Introduction

This chapter discusses the distribution of NPs such as the following:[1]

1. **Reflexives** such as *herself* and **reciprocals** such as *each other* are referentially dependent on another nominal (an **antecedent**).
2. **Pronouns** such as *her* lack descriptive content. They can be, but are not necessarily, referentially dependent.
3. **Full NPs** (**R-expressions** in Chomsky 1981) such as *the actress* are typically referentially independent, and descriptively richer than reflexives, reciprocals, or pronouns.

Unsurprisingly, these classes have different distributions. For example, because reflexives and reciprocals require antecedents, (1a–b) are well-formed (with *himself* referentially dependent on *John* and *each other* dependent on *the boys*), but (1c–d) are ungrammatical, either because the potential antecedent is mismatched in ϕ-features (1c), or because there are no potential antecedents (1d).

(1) a. *John* injured *himself.*
    b. *The boys* injured *each other.*
    c. *Susan injured himself.
    d. *Himself was injured.

The relation between *John* and *himself* in (1a), or between *the boys* and *each other* in (1b), is one of **anaphora**, or referential dependence. Where possible, I indicate anaphoric relations with italics.

Other distributional restrictions on anaphora are less trivial. For example, in (2a), *John* cannot antecede *himself*, because it is embedded within a larger NP; no anaphoric relation is possible in (2b) because *John* is too remote from *himself* (perhaps because the clause boundary or the subject *Susan* intervenes); while in (2c), *John*, no relation can be established, because *himself* c-commands *John*.[2]

(2) a. *[[*John*]'s mother] injured *himself.*
     b. * *John* believed [that Susan injured *himself*].
     c. (i) *Himself* injured *John*.
         (ii) *Susan showed *himself* to *John*.

There are other constraints on anaphoric relations. Assume that *John* denotes some individual *j*. Countless other NPs, in the right circumstances, can denote *j*, including *himself, him*, and *that guy*. All the variants in (3a) could mean that Bill injured John, and all those in (3-b) could mean that John injured Bill.

(3) a. Bill injured him/John/that guy.
     b. He/John/That guy injured Bill.

However, to express the proposition *injure'(j,j)*, we cannot freely choose among these NPs, as (4) shows.

(4) *He/John/that guy* injured *him/John/that guy.*

These sentences are well-formed, but they cannot mean what (1-a) means, despite the fact that *him, he, John*, and *that guy* can denote *j*. This is an example of **obviation**: the two NPs in (4) cannot both denote *j*.

The contrast between (1a) and (2) shows that **locality** effects constrain the distribution of reflexives and pronouns. Because of this, binding theory is intertwined with locality theory. Indeed, a major goal of the Extended Standard Theory (Chomsky 1973, 1976; Fiengo 1974; Reinhart 1976) was a unified theory of the locality of movement and binding. The crowning achievement of this period is the binding theory of Chomsky (1981). Chomsky proposed three simple binding principles, which also constrained the distribution of control and movement relations. Almost every nontrivial aspect of this theory has subsequently been challenged, but the *LGB* binding theory remains a landmark. We summarize it in a slightly modified form in Section 2. Following this, Sections 3 and 4 discuss the scope of the binding theory, distinguishing referential dependencies like that of *himself* from "**accidental**" coreference. Next, Section 5 discusses **long-distance anaphors**, which problematize the tripartition suggested above; and then Section 6 scrutinizes the claim, implicit in Chomsky (1981), that reflexives and pronouns are in complementary distribution. The penultimate section, Section 7, discusses the interaction of movement and binding, focusing on **connectivity** effects, where the binding theory applies to a moved element as if that element were still in its trace position. Finally, Section 8 concludes.

Given the breadth of binding-theoretic research, many key topics cannot be addressed in this chapter. We will adopt a narrowly syntactic focus on binding theory here, and largely ignore the morphology and semantics of pronominals and anaphora. Binding theory, by definition, straddles the syntax–semantics interface, and there is a rich semantic literature on anaphora (see Evans 1980 for foundational work, and Büring 2005: Ch. 7–11 for a recent introduction). Finally, there will be no discussion here of the acquisition of binding principles, despite its implications for our conception of the binding principles in adult as well as child grammar. See Chien and Wexler (1990), Grodzinsky and Reinhart (1993), and Thornton and Wexler (1999).

2 The GB binding theory

Our starting point is the **GB binding theory**, essentially as in Chomsky (1981).[3] We will approach this theory incrementally, to understand why it has the (quite abstruse) form it does.

The GB binding theory inherits from the earliest generative work on anaphora (Lees and Klima 1963) the assumption that reflexives and pronouns are in **complementary distribution**. Still following Lees and Klima, we guarantee this by defining an environment in which reflexives must occur and pronouns are barred.

More precisely, we say that X **binds** Y iff Y is anaphorically related to X and X c-commands Y, and Y is **free** (within domain D) if nothing within D binds Y. We then state two **binding principles**:

A: Reflexives are bound within a **binding domain**.
B: Pronouns are free within a **binding domain**.

Next, we define *binding domain*. (2b) suggests that binding domains might be clauses. This would predict contrasts like (5).

(5)   a.   [*John* adores *himself/*him*].
      b.   *John* said that [Susan adores *him/*himself*].
      c.   [[[*John*]'s mother] adores *him/*himself*].

In (5a), there is a binder within the clause, so Principle A allows *himself* and Principle B forbids *him*. In (5b), the opposite is true: the pronominal is **locally free** (unbound within the clause), so *him* is chosen over *himself*. Finally, in (5c) there is no binder, as the antecedent *John* does not c-command the pronominal, and binding requires c-command. Again, then, *himself* is barred.

However, binding domains are not identical to clauses. Firstly, exceptionally case marked (ECM) subjects with an antecedent in the immediately superordinate clause are realized as reflexives rather than pronouns.

(6)   [*Susan* believes [*herself/*her* to be adorable]].

Only ECM subjects can be thus bound: the subordinate clause remains a binding domain for objects.

(7)   [*Susan* expects [John to adore *her/*herself*]].

ECM subjects are distinguished by being assigned case across a clause boundary. This suggests that an NP's binding domain must include its case-assigner.

Next, consider binding within nominals. We correctly predict that (8) requires a reflexive rather than a pronoun: the smallest clause containing *herself* and a case-assigner is the matrix clause, which also contains the antecedent *Susan*.

(8)   [*Susan* heard [stories about *herself/*her*]].

However, we also predict, incorrectly, that (9) requires a reflexive.[4]

(9) [*Susan* heard [my stories about *her/*herself*]].

The contrast between (8) and (9) is predicted if binding domains can be either TP or NP, but must contain a subject (where possessors are construed as subjects of NP). The contrast then follows: the binding domain is then TP in (8), but NP in (9), as only in (9) does NP contain a subject.

Finally, consider anaphoric elements *within* ECM subjects. Here, we find the same contrast as in (8)–(9).

(10) a. [*Susan* expects [[stories about *herself/*her*] to be flattering]].
      b. [*Susan* expects [[my stories about *her/*herself*] to be flattering]].

However, at present, we predict both of these to require a pronoun: the binding domain in (10b) is *my stories about her(self)*, exactly parallel to (9), while in (10a) it is *stories about her(self) to be flattering*, the minimal TP containing *her(self)*, a case-assigner (*about*), and a subject (*stories about her(self)*). Neither domain contains the binder, *Susan*, so the pronominal is locally free, and must be realized as *her*.

We therefore refine the notion of "subject" pertinent to binding domains. We ignore *stories about her(self)* when calculating the binding domain for *her(self)*, because *her(self)* is part of *stories about her(self)* (Chomsky's **i-within-i filter**). If we ignore *stories about her(self)*, the local subject in (10a) is *Susan*, in the matrix clause. This derives the contrast in (10): the matrix clause (including *Susan*) is the binding domain for *her(self)* in (10a), but in (10b) the binding domain is just the NP *my stories about her(self)*, excluding *Susan*.

This gives the following characterization of binding domains.[5]

(11) The **binding domain** for X is the minimal NP/TP containing:
      (i) X;
      (ii) X's case-assigner;
      (iii) a subject which does not contain X.

Full NPs, our third nominal class, occur in a proper subset of the environments which allow pronouns. Substituting *Susan* for *her* in (5)–(10) is typically impossible. The sole exception is (5c), where substituting *John* for *him* is marginally acceptable.

(12) ?[[[*John*]'s mother] adores *John*].

This is the only example in which neither instance of *John* c-commands the other, so neither NP is bound. This suggests the following.

    C: Full NPs are globally free.

This completes the GB binding theory, summarized below.

(13) **Binding:**
      a. X binds Y (within domain D) iff X c-commands Y and Y is anaphorically related to X.
      b. Y is free (within domain D) iff there is no X within D that binds Y.

(14) **Binding Domain:** The binding domain for X is the minimal NP or TP containing:
    (i) X;
    (ii) X's case-assigner;
    (iii) a subject which does not contain X.

(15) Binding Principles:

    A: Reflexives are bound within their binding domain.
    B: Pronouns are free within their binding domain.
    C: Full NPs are globally free.

This theory uses three binding principles to regulate three NP classes. These classes can be distinguished using two binary features, as in Table 11.1.

In fact, Chomsky proposed that each of these feature combinations also corresponds to an empty category, as in Table 11.2. The same principles that constrain overt nominals then determine the distribution of empty categories.

This implicates binding theory in the locality of movement and control. For example, A-traces, being anaphors, must be bound within their binding domain. Therefore, A-movement cannot cross a subject (a prohibition on **superraising**), because subjects delimit binding domains.

(16) **Susan* seems that Bill adores *t*.

On this approach, binding principles also constrain the distribution of PRO.[6] PRO is anaphoric *and* pronominal. It is therefore subject to Principles A and B. Therefore, it is both bound and free within its binding domain, a contradiction if PRO has a binding domain. Therefore, PRO cannot have a binding domain. This is known as the **PRO-theorem**, largely responsible in Chomsky (1981) for restricting the distribution of PRO to a subset of nonfinite subject positions.

(17) **PRO-theorem**: PRO lacks a binding domain.

This is a hugely ambitious and conceptually attractive theory: not just a nuanced statement of the distribution of anaphoric NPs, but also the culmination of the programme of situating binding at the heart of a theory of nonlocal dependencies. Ultimately, its merits depend on the reality of the similarities between these syntactic phenomena. We will return to this question in the conclusion to this chapter.

Table 11.1 Features of three nominal classes

	+anaphoric	**−anaphoric**
+pronominal	—	pronoun
−pronominal	reflexive	full NP

Table 11.2 Features of four covert NPs

	+anaphoric	**−anaphoric**
+pronominal	PRO	*pro*
−pronominal	A-trace	A'-trace

3   Binding and coreference

Reflexives are **dependent** elements: they need a binder and they know where to find one. Full NPs are free, **independent** elements. Pronouns, though, are more complex. Principle B says that they are locally free. Indeed, they are sometimes globally free. However, they are sometimes locally free but nonlocally bound.

To identify nonlocally bound pronouns, we must first distinguish between two types of anaphoric relation. **Variable binding** (also referred to below as *semantic binding*, to distinguish it from *syntactic binding*, defined in Section 2) occurs when a pronominal is interpreted as a variable, bound by an NP which has scope over it. The NP need not be referential: the clearest cases of variable binding involve **quantifiers** like *no boy* in (18).

(18)   a.   *No boy* loves *himself/*him*.
        b.   *No boy* thinks that Richard loves *him/*himself*.

However, variable binding is structurally constrained because the binder must take scope over the variable. Assume, minimally, that binders cannot take scope across sentence boundaries. This explains the impossibility of variable binding in (19b).

(19)   a.   *No boy* [left because *he* felt dejected].
        b.   **No boy* [left]. *He* felt dejected.

The intersentential relationship between *Susan* and *she* in (20) cannot therefore be one of variable binding.

(20)   *Susan* went to sleep. *She* was exhausted.

We call such nonlocal anaphoric relations **coreference**: the assumption is that *Susan* and *she* refer to the same individual without any mediation from syntactic or semantic structure.

In sum, variable binding and coreference can be doubly dissociated. Variable binding must be local, but can involve nonreferential NPs. Coreference can be nonlocal, but must involve referential NPs.

Within the *LGB* binding theory, it is natural to assume that NPs can bind variables that they c-command at LF. In fact, though, Barker (2012) has argued convincingly that the structural configuration which determines variable binding is more inclusive than c-command. For instance, if X c-commands Y, then X can bind Y, but so can [Spec, X], [Spec,[Spec, X]], and so on.

(21)   a.   [[*Every boy*]'s mother] worries about *him*.
        b.   [[[*Every cat*]'s owner]'s furniture] is covered with *its* hair.

Although (21) could conceivably be analysed in terms of c-command at LF following local quantifier raising of the universal quantifier, other examples from Barker (2012) such as (22), where the quantifier is more deeply embedded in the subject, are not amenable to such an analysis.

(22)   a.   [A friend [of *each contestant*]] stood behind *her*.
        b.   [The grade [that [*each student* receives]]] is recorded in *his* file.

We conclude, with Barker, that, although there is surely some structural constraint on variable binding, that constraint is not stated in terms of c-command. We will not attempt to define this more inclusive relation here. Instead, we will simply call it **almost-c-command** (following Hornstein 1995), and enumerate cases of almost-c-command.

(23) a. *X* **almost-c-commands** *Y* **iff**:
    (i) *X* c-commands *Y*;
    (ii) *X* is [Spec,*Z*], where *Z* almost-c-commands *Y*;
    (iii) other configurations not discussed here.
  b. X can **sem-bind** *Y* only if *X* almost-c-commands *Y*.

The dissociation between variable binding and coreference can then be stated as follows: Variable binding requires that the binder almost-c-command the variable; coreference requires that both NPs be referential.

VP-ellipsis provides further evidence for this distinction. A pronoun within an elided VP often leads to ambiguity, as in (24).

(24) John loves his shoes, and Bill does too.

If the first conjunct means that John loves John's shoes, the second conjunct can mean either that Bill loves John's shoes (the **strict** reading) or that Bill, like John, loves his own shoes (the **sloppy** reading). It cannot mean that Bill loves someone else's shoes. If the first conjunct means that John loves someone else's shoes (say, Terry's), the second must mean that Bill loves Terry's shoes too, not his own shoes, and not, say, Martin's. This gives four grammatical readings.[7]

(25) a. John$_i$ loves his$_i$ shoes, and Bill$_j$ does ⟨loves his$_{i/j/*k}$ shoes⟩ too.
  b. John$_i$ loves his$_j$ shoes, and Bill$_j$ does ⟨loves his$_{*i/j/*k}$ shoes⟩ too.
  c. John$_i$ loves his$_k$ shoes, and Bill$_j$ does ⟨loves his$_{*i/*j/k/*l}$ shoes⟩ too.

Suppose that the elided constituent must be semantically identical to the antecedent VP (a **parallelism** condition). This explains (25b–c), where *loves his$_{j/k}$ shoes* is interpretively identical in both conjuncts. However, the proposition that John$_i$ loves his$_i$ shoes (25a) can be generated in two ways: via binding or coreference. This difference is often represented as in (26).

(26) a. John$_i$[λx.x loves his$_i$ shoes].   (coreference)
  b. John$_i$[λx.x loves *x*'s shoes].   (binding)

The second conjunct can then be interpreted in the following ways.

(27) a. John$_i$[λx.x loves his$_i$ shoes] and Bill$_j$[λx.x loves his$_i$ shoes]. (strict)
  b. John$_i$[λ.x.x loves *x*'s$_i$ shoes] and Bill$_j$[λx.x loves *x*'s$_i$ shoes]. (sloppy)

This exhausts the interpretive options: none of the ungrammatical interpretations in (25) can be generated without violating parallelism. The distinction between coreference and binding therefore provides an account of the strict/sloppy ambiguity under VP-ellipsis.

Table 11.3 Properties of noun classes

Class	Binding properties	Referential properties
Reflexives	Locally bound	Nonreferential
Pronouns	{Locally free / May be nonlocally bound}	Referential when free
Referential NPs[8]	Free	Referential
Quantifiers	Free	Nonreferential

We can similarly explain an ambiguity in the interpretation of pronouns under focus, still following Reinhart (1983). (28) has three distinct interpretations.

(28) I said that only Popeye should eat his spinach.
  (i) I said that Popeye should eat Popeye's spinach and no one else should eat Popeye's spinach.
  (ii) I said that Popeye should eat Popeye's spinach and for no other individual x should x eat x's spinach.
  (iii) I said that Popeye should eat some other individual y's spinach and no one else should eat y's spinach.

Should eat his spinach can be interpreted with *his* coreferential with *Popeye* (i), bound by *Popeye* (ii), or distinct from *Popeye* (iii). Given a standard semantics for *only*, where *only P* is true iff *P* is true and every proposition not entailed by *P* in *P*'s alternative set is false, the three readings for (28) fall out automatically.

We therefore distinguish variable binding (structurally constrained referential dependence) from coreference, where two NPs independently denote the same individual. Variable binding requires almost-c-command, while coreference is constrained by Principles B and C. Table 11.3 summarizes the properties of different nominal classes.

4 Obviation

The distinction between binding and coreference forces us to sharpen Principles B and C, the **obviation principles** which prohibit binding in certain configurations. As Reinhart (1983) noted, these principles rule out certain cases of binding, but something must prohibit coreference in the same configurations. For instance, Principle B states that *John* cannot bind *him* in (29), but we must also ensure that *John* and *him* do not corefer.

(29) * *John* admires *him.*

Relatedly, Principles B and C have several counterexamples, including the following (Grodzinsky and Reinhart 1993; Heim 1998).

(30) Everyone hates Lucifer. Only *he himself* pities *him.*

(31) *He* is *Colonel Weisskopf.*

(32) I dreamt that I was Brigitte Bardot and *I* kissed *me.*

In all these examples, an NP's referent is considered from multiple perspectives. In (30), Lucifer is both a focus of hatred and a self-pitier. (31) does not mean that Colonel Weisskopf is himself, but rather reveals the identity of the person under discussion. Finally, (32) distinguishes George *qua* Brigitte from George *qua* George. Principles B and C are apparently suspended, then, if the two NPs in question refer to the same individual under different **guises**.

We cannot straightforwardly represent these meanings using variable binding. While *John is himself* could be given truth-conditionally identical representations using coreference (33a) or binding (33b), *he is John* can only be represented with coreference (34a): variable binding would render the sentence indistinguishable from *John is himself* (34b).

(33) a. $j[\lambda x.x = j]$
      b. $j[\lambda x.x = x]$

(34) a. $x_1[\lambda x.x = j]$
      b. $\#x_1/j[\lambda x.x = x]$

Similarly, (30) means that only Lucifer pities Lucifer, not that Lucifer is the only self-pitier. And (32) means that Brigitte Bardot, George's dreamworld counterpart, kissed George-in-the-real-world, not that George kissed George or Brigitte kissed Brigitte. We cannot use binding to represent these meanings, then. This suggests that NP_1 and NP_2 may occur in a configuration violating an obviative binding condition only if the resulting interpretation cannot be represented with NP_1 a variable bound by NP_2 (or vice versa).

If this is accurate, a syntactic constraint fails to apply in certain semantically defined circumstances. Reinhart (1983) took this as evidence that obviation was not, in fact, a syntactic phenomenon, but reflects a preference for variable binding over coreference, formulated as follows.

(35) *Rule I: Intrasentential Coreference*
      NP A cannot corefer with NP B if replacing A with C, C a variable A-bound by B, yields an indistinguishable interpretation (Grodzinsky and Reinhart 1993: 79).

Rule I is a transderivational economy principle rather than a strictly syntactic constraint. It mostly has similar effects to Principles B and C. For example, Principle C blocks (36), because *John* must be free.

(36) a. *He* worships *John*.
      b. *He* thinks Sally worships *John*.

Similarly, Principle B blocks (37), because *him* must be locally free.

(37) *He* worships *him*.

Rule I also prohibits (36)–(37), because an identical interpretation is available using the appropriate bound form.

(38) a. *He/John* worships *himself.*
      b. *He* thinks Sally worships *him*.

Rule I allows coreference in two cases. One, discussed in Section 3 and also covered by Principles B and C, is where absence of c-command precludes binding.

(39) [[Problems with *his* visa] mean [that *John* cannot come on tour]].

The other is where the bound interpretation and coreferential interpretation are distinct, as in (30)–(32). If the two interpretations are distinct, Rule I does not choose between them.

This leads to the natural suspicion that Principles B and C are unnecessary. However, it turns out that Rule I cannot replace Principles B and C: Principles B and C are concerned with syntactic binding (and so sensitive to c-command), while Rule I is concerned with semantic binding (and so sensitive to almost-c-command). It appears that we need conditions that are sensitive to both relations.

The evidence for this comes from patterns of variable binding involving **epithets**, a class of referentially dependent full NPs, like *the bastard* in (40).

(40) I asked *my boss* for a raise, but *the bastard* refused.

The relationship between *my boss* and *the bastard* in (40) must be one of coreference, because the two NPs are not in an appropriate configuration for variable binding. As predicted by Principle C, if *my boss* c-commands the epithet (which, as a full NP, cannot be syntactically bound), *the bastard* cannot be interpreted anaphorically.

(41) *My boss* said that *he/*the bastard* can't give me a raise.

The interest comes in cases where a quantified NP binds an epithet. The logic of Rule I implies that it is concerned with the possibility of variable binding, and so is sensitive to almost-c-command rather than c-command. In contrast, Principle C constrains syntactic binding, and so is sensitive to c-command. Because of the discrepancy between c-command and almost-c-command, syntactic binding occurs in fewer configurations than variable binding. Principle C and Rule I therefore jointly make a subtle prediction: an NP cannot bind an epithet which it c-commands, but it can bind an epithet which it *almost*-c-commands. Rule I alone cannot match this prediction, because it does not distinguish c-command from almost-c-command.

This prediction is accurate (see Haïk 1984 for early discussion). (42a) shows that an epithet cannot be bound by a c-commanding NP, while (42b) shows that an epithet *can* be bound by an almost c-commanding NP.

(42) a. **Every boy* thinks *the little angel* deserves more pocket money.
     b. *Every boy*'s mother wishes *the little brat* would clean his room.

A syntactic Principle C, sensitive to c-command, must therefore exist independently of Rule I. However, we cannot abandon Rule I: it is our only explanation for (30)–(32). We must therefore keep both principles. Principle C guarantees that a full NP is syntactically free, while Rule I enforces variable binding wherever possible. Similarly, Rule I selects a reflexive over a pronoun whenever binding requires a reflexive, but Principles A and B are still needed to determine the configurations in which reflexives are bound and pronouns are free.

Rule I is therefore logically separate from the binding principles, which determine the distribution of syntactically bound forms. By way of a summary, we state a binding theory compatible with these considerations.

(43) *X* may **sem-bind** *Y* only if *Y* is interpreted as a variable and *X* almost-c-commands *Y*.

(44) a. *X* **syn-binds** *Y* iff *X* sem-binds *Y* and *X* c-commands *Y*.
    b. *Y* is **syn-free** iff nothing **syn-binds** *Y*.

(45) **Binding Principles:**

    A: Reflexives are syn-bound within their binding domain.
    B: Pronouns are syn-free within their binding domain.
    C: Full NPs are syn-free.

(46) **Rule I**
    A cannot corefer with B if there is a well-formed syntactic representation that yields an indistinguishable interpretation with A replaced by a variable sem-bound by B.

5 How many distinctions?

This section discusses two related empirical challenges to the form of the binding principles. Firstly, many pronominals behave like both reflexives and pronouns. For example, English possessive pronouns can be locally bound, as in (47a), or locally free, as in (47b).

(47) a. [*Bill* loathes [*his* shoes]].
    b. *Bill* says that [Rachel loathes [*his* shoes]].

Under the GB binding theory, this entails that *his* is lexically ambiguous between a reflexive and a pronoun. However, English lacks forms such as *himself's*, so it intuitively must use *his*. The challenge, following Safir (2004), is to make sense of this intuition.

A complementary challenge comes from forms which are sensitive to different binding domains, such as ZICH-**forms**, monomorphemic forms deficient in ϕ-features like Dutch *zich*, Norwegian *seg*, and Icelandic *sig* (we concentrate on Dutch here: see Koster 1985; Everaert 1986; Koster and Reuland 1991b; Reinhart and Reuland 1993; Reuland 2001, 2011; Rooryck and Vanden Wyngaerd 2011). Dutch has a reflexive SELF-**form**, *zichzelf*, which mainly behaves like the similarly bimorphemic English *himself*: it can be locally bound (48), but not nonlocally bound (49).[9]

(48) a. *John* haat *zichzelf*
      John hates *zichzelf*
      "John hates himself".
    b. *John* schoot op *zichzelf*
      John shot   at *zichzelf*
      "John shot at himself".

(49) a. **Mary* liet [Peter op *zichzelf* schieten]
      Mary let   Peter at *zichzelf* shoot
      "Mary let Peter shoot at herself"

b. **Mary* acht   [Peter verliefd   op   *zichzelf*]
    Mary considers Peter in love   with   *zichzelf*
    "Mary considers Peter to be in love with herself".

Meanwhile, *zich* must be bound, but typically cannot occur where *zichzelf* can, with certain counterexamples discussed in Section 6. Instead, *zich* is used when the reflexive is more remote from its antecedent, for example across nonfinite subordinate clause boundaries, or as the complement of an unselected preposition.

(50) a. [*Peter* zag [Mary naar *zich(*zelf)* toe komen]]
      Peter saw   Mary to   *zich*   to come
      "Peter saw Mary coming towards him".
   b. [*John* zag de slang [naast *zich(*zelf)*]]
      John   saw the snake near   *zich*
      "John saw the snake near him".

It seems, then, that *zich* is free within a domain, but bound within a larger domain. If the antecedent is outside even this larger domain, both *zich* and *zichzelf* become impossible, and a pronoun *hem/haar* must be used instead.

(51)   *Mieke* zag dat ik **zich/*zichzelf/haar* schilderde
      Mieke saw that I   *zich/zichzelf*/her   painted
      "Mieke saw that I painted her".

(Everaert 1986: 1)

Zich, then, is a "middle-distance" anaphor:[10]

(52) a. *Zichzelf* is very locally bound (where subjects delimit very local domains).
   b. *Zich* is locally, but not very locally, bound (where tense delimits local domains).
   c. *Hem/haar* is locally free.

This suggests that binding domains come in different sizes. In turn, Principles A and B might be families of constraints, where "A-type" constraints insist that an element is bound within a certain domain, and "B-type" constraints insist that an element is free within a certain domain. *Zich* is even simultaneously subject to an A-type constraint within one domain and a B-type constraint within a smaller domain. Following Büring (2005), Principle C is reducible to a B-type constraint: full NPs are free within a domain corresponding to the root clause.

    These ideas sparked two typologically oriented research projects. One concerns the enumeration of binding domains (see Koster and Reuland 1991b), because these domains, together with the conjunction of A-type and B-type constraints, imply a typology of anaphors. The other concerns the relationship between an NP's form and its binding domain. Morphologically complex *zichzelf*, like morphologically complex *himself* in English, requires local binding, while simplex *zich* requires nonlocal binding. Pica (1985, 1987) suggests that this is no accident: monomorphemic anaphors have larger binding domains than bimorphemic anaphors. It is common to see this, broadly speaking, as a combination of a general prohibition on identity among coarguments (enforcing disjoint reference in *John hates him*), and a notion of *-self* as a "shield", somehow obviating that general prohibition. See Reuland (2011) for a recent take on this idea.

Moreover, Pica claims, **long-distance reflexives** like *zich* are subject-orientated. (50b) showed that *zich* in the PP *naast zich* is bound within the local tensed clause. In (53), then, either *Jan* or *Peter* could bind *zich* in principle, but only *Jan* is actually available.

(53) Jan$_i$ raadde   Peter$_j$ de   vrouw   naast zich$_{i/*j}$ aan
     Jan recommended Peter   the   woman   near   *zich*   PRT
     Jan recommended the woman near him to Peter.

(Koster 1987: 329)

It is common, still following Pica (1987), to explain this by positing an association between finite T and *zich*. Subject-orientation then follows from the fact that the subject position is the only A-position locally c-commanding finite T. However, there is no generally accepted explanation of Pica's generalizations: it is widely accepted that the morphological composition of anaphors largely determines their syntactic and semantic behaviour, but no real consensus as to how this occurs. See Safir (2004), Reuland (2011), and Rooryck and Vanden Wyngaerd (2011) for different approaches.

6   Complementarity and noncomplementarity

Where English has three noun classes, Dutch has five: *zich*, pronouns like *hem* and *haar*, *zichzelf*, a further class of reflexives like *hem/haarzelf* not discussed here, and full NPs. This could lead us to replace Principles A–C with Dutch-friendly Principles A–E. However, this would multiply apparent lexical ambiguities. Sometimes *him* translates as *zich*, and sometimes as *hem*. So *him* would share a class with *zich*, and also with *hem*, making *him* lexically ambiguous.

Instead, it seems natural that *him* has a wider distribution than *hem* or *zich* precisely because English has a tripartition where Dutch has a quinquepartition. English has just locally bound reflexives, and a class of pronouns which occur elsewhere. Dutch has more forms to cover the same configurations, so some forms have narrower distributions.

This suggests a competition-based analysis, as recently pursued by Safir (2004). We specify constraints like (54), alongside a general **blocking principle**, that we pick the most specific form available.[11]

(54)   a.   English reflexives are bound within their binding domain.
      b.   Pronouns need not be bound.

The blocking principle then ensures that pronouns are not bound within their binding domain: a reflexive could be used there instead, so pronouns are blocked.

This approach generalizes to the more complex Dutch system.

(55)   a.   *Zichzelf* is bound within the minimal domain containing a subject.
      b.   *Zich* is bound by a subject within the minimal domain containing tense [blocked by *zichzelf*].
      c.   Pronouns need not be bound [blocked by *zich* and *zichzelf*].

A strength of this approach is that a form's apparently disjunctive behaviour does not imply lexical ambiguity. For example, *his* in (47) can be analysed as an unambiguous pronoun, which can encroach on the locally bound territory of reflexives because English does not have possessive reflexives.

A competition-based theory makes two general predictions. First, provided there is an elsewhere variant, a pronominal form is always available (that is, there is no **ineffability**). Second, pronominal forms are in **complementary distribution**. Unfortunately, both of these predictions have apparent counterexamples. For example, both reflexives and pronominals are possible in **picture-NPs**, discussed in Jackendoff (1968) (see also Pollard and Sag 1992; Reinhart and Reuland 1993). It is classically assumed that NP-internal subjects delimit a reflexive's binding domain (56b). If, however, an NP does not contain a subject, it can contain a pronoun or a reflexive.[12]

(56) a. *Sally* saw a picture of *her(self)*.
　　 b. *Sally* saw Peter's picture of *her(*self)*.

Following Huang (1982), such noncomplementarity suggests that the domain in which pronouns are free is smaller than that in which reflexives are bound. This is the basis of an ambitious reworking of the binding theory in Reinhart and Reuland (1993) (henceforth R&R). R&R proposed that binding theory is at heart about the relationship between the reflexivity of a predicate (one argument filling two argument positions) and the marking of a predicate as reflexive. A simplified version of their theory states that a predicate is reflexive-marked (by some reflexive form) iff it is reflexive.

This simplified version predicts complementarity: reflexives would be bound by coarguments, and pronouns would be used elsewhere. The noncomplementarity in R&R's theory comes from their use of two different definitions of *predicate*. A **syntactic predicate** contains a head P, everything case- or θ-marked by P, and a subject. A **semantic predicate** is a functor and all its arguments in some semantic representation.

On these definitions, a syntactic predicate is typically bigger than a semantic predicate: the arguments in a semantic predicate are typically θ-marked, and so included within a syntactic predicate, but a syntactic predicate contains material excluded from semantic predicates, such as ECM subjects (which are case-marked by P but not semantic arguments of P) or material between P and the locally c-commanding subject. This is the factor deriving noncomplementarity: if Principle B requires that pronouns be free within semantic predicates, and Principle A requires that reflexives be bound within larger syntactic predicates, either form is possible when a dependency is contained within a syntactic predicate but not a semantic predicate.

R&R formulated the binding principles as follows.

(57) **Binding Principles (Reinhart and Reuland 1993):**
　　 A: A reflexive-marked syntactic predicate is reflexive.
　　 B: A reflexive semantic predicate is reflexive-marked.

Reflexive-marking canonically involves use of a reflexive form like *herself*. (58a) is acceptable because the semantic predicate is reflexive, and *herself* provides the reflexive-marking. (58b), though, violates Principle A: *himself* reflexive-marks the subordinate clause, but it is not reflexive.

(58) a. *Julie* adores *herself.*
　　 b. **John* said that [*Julie* adores *himself*].

Of course, (59) is both reflexive and reflexive-marked.

(59) **Herself* adores *Julie*.

R&R rule this out using their chain condition, which states that **dependent** elements (SELF-forms, ZICH-forms, and NP-trace) are always bound from an A-position, while **independent** elements (pronouns and full NPs) never are. This separates the parts of the binding theory concerning the general, asymmetric notion of dependency (handled by the chain condition) from a symmetrical, binding-specific residue consisting of well-formedness conditions on reflexive predicates (Principles A and B).

As for standard Principle B violations, (60a) is reflexive, but not reflexive-marked, so Principle B rules it out. In (60b), in contrast, *John* and *him* are arguments of different semantic predicates, so Principle B does not require reflexive-marking and the sentence is grammatical.

(60) a. *_John_ adores _him_.
      b. _John_ thinks that [no one adores _him_].

R&R therefore predict complementarity in the basic cases. However, they also predict non-complementarity when a pronominal and its antecedent are within the same syntactic predicate but different semantic predicates. When that obtains, neither semantic predicate is reflexive, so Principle B does not require reflexive-marking. However, the syntactic predicate is reflexive, so Principle A is satisfied if an argument is reflexive-marked.

This configuration can arise because semantic predicates are delimited only by functors, while syntactic predicates, like binding domains in the GB binding theory, must contain other material, in particular subjects. So NP is both a syntactic and semantic predicate in (61b), but in (61a) _Julie_ and _her(self)_ are arguments of the same syntactic predicate, but not the same semantic predicate. Principle B therefore does not require reflexive-marking (the semantic predicates are nonreflexive), while Principle A is compatible with reflexive-marking (the syntactic predicate is reflexive).[13]

(61) a. _Julie_ adores pictures of _her(self)_.
      b. _Julie_ adores [John's pictures of _her(*self)_].

A second example of noncomplementarity involves _zich_ and _zichzelf_ in ECM subjects. _Zich_ is a dependent element (like _zichzelf_) which does not reflexive-mark a predicate (unlike _zichzelf_). Because _zich_ does not reflexive-mark a predicate, it always satisfies Principle A. Its distribution is rather regulated by Principle B for R&R, following similar proposals by Koster (1985) and Everaert (1986).

Because of Principle B, _zich_'s antecedent is typically not within the same semantic predicate: the predicate would be reflexive, but not reflexive-marked, illegitimately.

(62) *_John_ haat   _zich_
      John hates _zich_
      "John hates himself".

When _zich_'s antecedent is not a semantic coargument, Principle B is satisfied and the sentence is well-formed. This correctly predicts noncomplementarity in Dutch ECM subjects.

(63) _Max_ hoorde _zich(zelf)_ zingen
      Max heard   _zich(zelf)_ sing
      "Max heard himself sing".

(63) contains two semantic predicates: *zich(zelf) zingen* and *Max hoorde [zich(zelf) zingen]*. Crucially, *Max* and *zich(zelf)* are not semantic coarguments. Therefore, there is no reflexive semantic predicate, and Principle B is vacuously satisfied. Moreover, the whole sentence is a reflexive syntactic predicate. Therefore, even if the pronominal is reflexive, Principle A is satisfied.[14]

R&R also claim that their theory predicts cases of ineffability, the second challenge to competition-based theories. Lasnik (1989) claimed that neither a reflexive nor pronominal object is possible if the referent of that object is properly included in the referent of the antecedent subject.

(64) *We voted for me/myself.

However, R&R show that this ineffability only holds with distributive predicates. Collective predicates allow pronouns in this configuration.

(65) We elected me/*myself.

The impossibility of *myself* follows from Principle A: *myself* reflexive-marks the syntactic predicate, but it has no antecedent. As for Principle B, the acceptability of (65) follows along similar lines: so long as *me* is distinct from *we* at the relevant level of representation, the predicate is not reflexive and Principle B is vacuously satisfied. In (64), in contrast, *vote for* is arguably distributive: *we voted for me* iff *I voted for me* and *X voted for me*, for some $X \neq$ "*I*". Of these conjuncts, *I voted for me* is reflexive, without reflexive-marking. If Principle B is evaluated at a level which is sensitive to distributivity, then, R&R's theory can capture this contrast.[15]

None of these failures of complementarity fit naturally with a competition-based theory like that of Safir (2004). However, they are not incompatible with such theories if competition is sometimes suspended. For example, the optionality in Dutch ECM subjects (63) could reflect an interpretive difference noted by R&R and many subsequent authors. The *zich*-variant of (66) means that Munchhausen extracted himself from the swamp by pulling on something, while the *zichzelf*-variant means that Munchhausen extracts himself by pulling his own hair.

(66) *Munchhausen trok   zich(zelf) uit   het moraas*
       Munchhausen pulled *zich(zelf)* from the swamp
       "Munchhausen pulled himself out of the swamp".

(Reinhart and Reuland 1993: 710)

This is surely related to the fact that the **statue readings** of Jackendoff (1992) require a *self*-reflexive. (67a) is naturally interpreted in such a way that flesh-and-blood Ringo falls on the waxwork of Ringo, while (67b) is more resistant of an interpretation where the waxwork of Ringo falls on flesh-and-blood Ringo.

(67) The other day I was strolling through the wax museum with Ringo Starr, and we
       came upon the statues of the Beatles, and…
       a. ?… all of a sudden Ringo stumbled and fell on himself.
       b. *… all of a sudden I accidentally bumped into the statues, and Ringo toppled over
          and fell on himself.

(Jackendoff 1992: 4–5)

As first discussed by Reuland (2001), Dutch translations of these statue readings, where the reflexive's referent is nonidentical to the full NP's referent, require *zichzelf* rather than *zich*, even in syntactic environments where both forms are normally available. This is useful for competition-based theories like Safir's, because if the two forms mean different things, it may be possible to explain noncomplementarity on the grounds that the two forms are not competing anyway. Likewise, Safir may attempt to account for cases of ineffability ((64)– (65)) if an elsewhere variant is sometimes exceptionally unavailable.

The complementarity debate is therefore central to global binding-theoretic concerns. Safir's theory is very elegant: intricate binding patterns are explained by the interaction of simply specified binding domains, a general blocking principle, and general syntactic and interpretive conditions. R&R's theory, in contrast, is quite inelegant: one condition is stated over syntactic domains, another over semantic domains, and a third condition constrains the form of A-dependencies. Moreover, R&R deploy three principles to capture the distribution of three categories (ZELF-forms, ZICH-forms, and pronouns), and more classes would require more principles.[16] In contrast, Safir's theory generalizes to arbitrarily complex pronominal systems.

Which of these routes is to be preferred is substantially dependent on one's treatment of complementarity. Safir sees it as pervasive, so he built a system to capture it. R&R see it as essentially accidental, as do Rooryck and Vanden Wyngaerd (2011), in their otherwise very different take on binding theory. For R&R, complementarity is widespread because syntactic and semantic predicates tend to align, but noncomplementarity may arise when these domains diverge.

7 Connectivity

In (68), *herself* is bound by a non-c-commanding antecedent, in apparent violation of Principle A.

(68) a. [Which picture of *herself*] does [*no girl* want to see ___]?
     b. (She likes her family, but) *herself,* [*Susan* just adores ___].

This is apparently related to movement of *herself,* either on its own (68b), or as part of a larger NP (68a): (68) would be unremarkable if *herself* were interpreted in its base position. Cases where movement does not affect binding relations are known as **reconstruction** or **connectivity** effects. The predominant theory of connectivity is currently Chomsky's (1993) copy theory. In that theory, movement phenomena arise when multiple copies of the same constituent are merged, and connectivity effects arise when the copy that is interpreted is not the last to be merged.

Here, we discuss binding data like (68) and their implications for theories of connectivity in general, with a view to evaluating the empirical basis of those theories. Of course, one's theory of connectivity depends on one's theory of binding. (68) is surprising under the standard GB binding theory, but the foregoing has demonstrated a number of independent problems with that theory. We must therefore ask whether (68) is really indicative of connectivity.

Similar concerns extend to (69).

(69) Which picture of *himself* does [*John* think ___ [Mary likes ___]]?

If *himself* were bound in its base position, *Mary* would be the only local potential antecedent, so (69) should be ungrammatical. Instead, *himself* seems to be locally bound by *John* in the intermediate trace position.

Sentences like (69) therefore assumed a deal of theoretical significance, because they apparently demonstrated binding into intermediate trace positions. However, this conclusion is called into question by the independent existence of a class of cases, known, following Pollard and Sag (1992), as **exempt anaphora**, where a reflexive appears without a locally c-commanding antecedent. Two environments which tolerate exempt anaphora are coordinate structures (70a) and unselected PPs (70b); many researchers, including Pollard and Sag, also include *picture*-NPs like (61a).

(70) a. *Max* boasted that the queen invited [Lucie and *him(self)*] for a drink. (Reinhart and Reuland 1993: 670)
   b. *Lucie* counted five tourists in the room [apart from *her(self)*]. (Reinhart and Reuland 1993: 661)

Without aiming to construct a theory of why exempt anaphora exist, or their distribution or interpretation,[17] the immediate worry is that, if the reflexives in (70) are interpreted *in situ* without a locally c-commanding antecedent, perhaps the same holds for the reflexive in (69), and so that example is not in fact indicative of interpretation of a moved element in an intermediate trace position.

This alternative is supported by the fact that such binding configurations are acceptable even at *wh*-island boundaries, where no intermediate trace site is typically assumed.[18]

(71) a. Which picture of *himself* did [*John* ask [whether Mary liked ___]]?
   b. Which picture of *himself* is [*John* wondering [what Mary should say about ___]]?

Moreover, as Büring (2005) points out, in German, which lacks exempt anaphors, an A′-moved reflexive must be interpreted in its base position. (72) is therefore acceptable, while (73) is not, as the reflexive would have to be interpreted in its surface position to be bound by *Hans*.

(72) Wieviele Gedichte   über *sich* wird Schulze noch schreiben?!
     How many poems   about *zich* will Schulze still write
     "How many more poems about himself is Schulze going to write?!".
                                                      (Büring 2005: 247)

(73) *Hans fragte welche Bilder   von *sich* ich gesehen hatte
     Hans asked which pictures of *zich* I   seen   had
     "Hans asked which pictures of him(self) I had seen".
                                                      (Büring 2005: 255)

We conclude, with Büring, that Principle A connectivity is real, but must target a constituent's base position. Apparent counterexamples are actually exempt anaphors.

Specificational pseudoclefts illustrate further surprising properties of connectivity.

(74) a. [[What$_i$ *John* likes t_i] is *himself*].
   b. *[[What$_i$ *John* likes t_i] is *him*].
   c. *[[What$_i$ *he* likes t_i] is *John*].

Neither NP c-commands the other in (74), but if the postcopular NP were interpreted in the trace position, the judgements would follow automatically. This suggests a connectivity effect.

In fact, (74b–c) suggest not only that Principle B and C connectivity *exists*, but also that it is *obligatory* (see also Lebeaux 2009). If it were optional, we would predict (74b–c) to be grammatical, provided connectivity was not established. We will return to this shortly.

Higgins (1973) claimed that pseudocleft connectivity demonstrated that connectivity is independent of movement. Movement targets c-commanding positions, but the postcopular NP in (74) does not c-command the trace. Moreover, the trace is bound by A′-moved *what*. The postcopular NP therefore cannot have moved from the trace position.

To handle this in the standard GB approach, we must re-create something with the form of *John likes himself* from (74a), *John likes him* from (74b), and *he likes John* from (74c). There are several ways of doing this: we could associate the postcopular NP with the gap position, either at LF (Bošković 1997), or at a post-LF representation (Heycock and Kroch 1999). Alternatively, we could treat (74) as derived by ellipsis from colloquial sentences like (75) (Ross 1972; Schlenker 2003).

(75) a. [[What John likes ___] is [*John* likes *himself*]].
     b. *[[What John likes ___] is [*John* likes *him*]].
     c. *[[What he likes ___] is [*he* likes *John*]].

The binding principles would then be evaluated within the (possibly elided) postcopular material.

Reinhart and Reuland's binding theory handles (74b–c) more straightforwardly. For R&R, Principle B operates over semantic predicates, regardless of the syntactic realization of those predicates. If all of the examples in (74) contain a semantic predicate like $\lambda x.like$ $(x, x))(j)$, then they are all reflexive. Principle B requires that that predicate be reflexive-marked. Only (74a) satisfies that requirement.

The grammaticality of (74a) is *not* directly predicted by that theory, though: *John* and *himself* are not syntactic coarguments, so we have reflexive-marking without reflexivity, in violation of R&R's Principle A. Some account of Principle A connectivity is still needed, then.

Unifying the insights from German and from specificational pseudoclefts, we could generalize that binding connectivity effects arise when a moved XP is interpreted in a θ-position with which it is associated. Reflexives within a moved XP are bound in XP's θ-position or are interpreted as exempt anaphors; pronouns must be locally free in XP's θ-position; and full NPs must be free in XP's θ-position.

This generalization is surprising on standard formulations of the copy theory, which tie connectivity effects to movement rather than to θ-positions. However, possible support for the copy theory comes from the distribution of Principle C effects in A′-movement constructions, discussed by Lebeaux (1988). For many speakers, (76) is ungrammatical, as predicted.[19]

(76) *[[Which picture of *John*] does [*he* like ___]]?

A more nuanced pattern emerges, though, with (77).

(77) a. *[Whose claim [that *John* is nice]] did *he* believe ___?
     b. [Which story [that *John* wrote]] did *he* like ___?

(Lebeaux 1988: 103)

Early discussions like that of van Riemsdijk and Williams (1981) assumed that such distinctions were gradient, related to depth of embedding of *John* within the *wh*-phrase. However, Lebeaux proposed a discrete distinction, which we will call **Lebeaux's generalization**: if NP is A′-moved, Principle C connectivity effects obtain within complements of the moved N (77a), but not within adjuncts adjoined to NP (77b). This distinction reduces to the projection principle: complements must be merged in base positions, but unselected adjuncts can be merged after movement, obviating the connectivity effect. Copy-theoretically, the distinction is as follows.

(78) a. *[Whose claim that *John* is nice] did [*he* believe [~~whose~~ claim that *John* is nice]].
      b. [Which story that *John* wrote] did [*he* like [~~which~~ story]].

Only in (78a) is an instance of *John* c-commanded by *he*, so only (78a) violates Principle C. This is potentially a major argument in favour of copy theory: it provides a natural account of Lebeaux's generalization, relying only on independently motivated principles like the projection principle.

However, we briefly explore here an alternative, based on Kuno (1997). Lebeaux's argument–adjunct distinction is independently predicted in a proper subset of A′-movement cases. Rule I, which requires the use of bound forms wherever possible, dictates that examples like (79) are possible iff corresponding examples like (80) are impossible.

(79) a. ?*Which pictures of *John* did *he* destroy ___?
      b. Which pictures near *John* did *he* destroy ___?

(Lebeaux 1988: 103)

(80) a. Which pictures of *himself* did *John* destroy ___?
      b. *Which pictures near *himself* did *John* destroy ___?

This explains the apparent adjunct–complement distinction in (79), without reference to connectivity.[20] However, this explanation cannot extend to (77), as nominative reflexives are universally ungrammatical.

(81) a. *Whose claim that *himself* is nice did *John* believe ___?
      b. *Which story that *himself* wrote did *John* like ___?

If the contrast in (77) is robust and general, then, it supports Lebeaux's generalization. However, these data are in fact highly variable. Kuno writes that most speakers find (82) unacceptable "only under the interpretation whereby *which claim that John was asleep* is paraphraseable as 'which of the claims that John made to the effect that he was asleep'. To those speakers, the sentence is acceptable if other people's claims that John was asleep are under discussion" (p.16).

(82) *Which claim that *John* was asleep was *he* willing to discuss? (Chomsky 1993, Chomsky's judgement)

Kuno attributes this effect to his **logophoric NP constraint** (see also Büring 2005), which predicts Principle C connectivity effects in configurations like (82) only if the CP describes the feelings, thoughts, or speech of *John* or communicated to *John*.

This approach splits Lebeaux's generalization in two. One part follows Lebeaux's predictions, but with independent justification. The other part replaces Lebeaux's argument–adjunct distinction with an orthogonal distinction related to logophoricity. Although Lebeaux's generalization seems too variable to form the basis of a solid argument about the architecture of the grammar, this alternative has received little critical attention, and effects related to logophoricity are poorly understood.

As a matter of priority, the empirical facts must be determined. At least four different factors have been claimed to influence Principle C connectivity: depth of embedding (van Riemsdijk and Williams 1981), the argument–adjunct distinction (Lebeaux 1988), competition with reflexive forms (Kuno 1997 as reinterpreted above), and logophoricity (Kuno 1997). Given that Lebeaux's generalization directly supports Chomsky's fine-grained copy-theoretic proposals, it is vital to current syntactic theory that the impact of these multiple factors be assessed systematically. However, this has not yet been carried out, to my knowledge.

8   Summary, and future directions

After fifty years of binding-theoretic research, and over thirty years after Chomsky (1981), we are still far from a definitive binding theory. However, progress has been substantial. The initial phase of binding-theoretic research, leading to *LGB* and Reinhart (1983), was characterized by discovery of fundamental distinctions in English anaphora like that between binding and coreference, and increasingly subtle statements of the locality constraints on binding. Three major subsequent developments have occurred: the empirical base has broadened to include extensive data from Romance, Germanic, East Asian languages, and beyond, which have demonstrated that Chomsky's tripartition of nominals is insufficient. In parallel, nontrivial exceptions have been discovered to the complementarity implicit in the classical Principles A and B. Finally, connectivity effects have increasingly occupied researchers.

These trends have pulled researchers in different directions. A competition-based theory like Safir (2004) has the virtue of scalability: the general principle requiring the use of the most dependent available form applies regardless of how many anaphors a language has. However, complementarity inheres in the architecture of such a theory, and apparent exceptions to complementarity certainly exist.

In contrast, Reinhart and Reuland (1993) and subsequent research is designed to accommodate noncomplementarity, because their Principles A and B are stated over different domains. Competition in Reinhart's binding theory is extrinsic to the binding principles, in a separate, interpretation-sensitive principle (Rule I, Grodzinsky and Reinhart 1993).

Just as this theory is strong where Safir's appears weakest, this theory lacks Safir's main strength. The ratio of nominal classes to regulatory principles in R&R's theory is 1:1. There is therefore no reason to expect this theory to handle anaphors with other distributions, especially elsewhere-type distributions, as neatly as Safir's.

This suggests a critical question for future binding-theoretic research:

• What is the status of exceptions to complementarity among the nominal classes? When is a binding theory based on competition and complementarity appropriate?

A second question concerns connectivity effects. As we have seen, it is hard to spot a genuine connectivity effect, given the uncertainty about the basic nature of the binding theory.

However, the distribution of genuine connectivity effects is vital to the construction not only of more accurate theories of binding, but also of the architecture of the grammar, as demonstrated by Lebeaux (1988) and Chomsky (1993). We therefore ask:

- What constitutes a genuine connectivity effect? Where do we find them, and what do they imply about theories of the syntax–semantics interface?

This brings us back to the extraordinary scope of Chomsky's (1981) binding theory, intended not just as a theory of the distribution of anaphors, but as a major constraint on nonlocal dependencies. That project has been largely abandoned. Within Chomskyan theories in particular, the distinction of four empty categories (NP-trace, *wh*-trace, PRO, and *pro*) has collapsed. The two traces are no longer construed as primitives within the copy theory (but see Neeleman and van de Koot 2002), while it is now common to distinguish reflexive-like obligatory control PRO from pronominal PRO in non-obligatory control constructions (Hornstein 1999).

Of the original four empty categories, then, only *pro* remains more or less unscathed. Moreover, despite attempts to unify the locality of movement and binding (Chomsky 1986; Rizzi 1990b; Cinque 1990), a residual distinction between the two classes always remained, weakening the original basis for the unification of binding and movement.

And yet the underlying idea remains compelling, and attempts to conflate aspects of movement and binding remain widespread. For example, subject-oriented anaphors have been analysed in terms of movement to T combined with a requirement that the antecedent locally c-command the anaphor (Pica 1987); and locality of NP-movement has been analysed using a lexicalized NP-trace that behaves like a null reflexive (Williams 1994; Neeleman and van de Koot 2002). This suggests a third major question.

- How similar are binding and movement? How should any similarities be captured?

Such questions are daunting, but that is why research in this area retains its vitality. Indeed, it is remarkable that we began with the modest aim of describing the distribution of forms like *herself* and *her*, and progressed via a series of increasingly rich theories to a point, fifty years later, where those questions directly inform fundamental theories of the architecture of the grammar.

Notes

Thanks go to Dan Siddiqi and Françoise Moreau-Johnson for comments on an earlier draft.

1 I use the term *reflexive* rather than Chomsky's (1981) term *anaphor*, because *anaphor* is also used to describe any referentially dependent constituent. However, I adopt Chomsky's restricted sense of *pronoun*, and reserve the term *pronominal* as a general term for overt nominals other than full NPs.
2 We largely ignore reciprocals from now on. As the reader can verify, the distribution of *each other* is largely identical to that of *himself*. However, complex semantic issues arise with reciprocals (see Dalrymple *et al.* 1998): *The delegates greeted each other* typically means that each delegate greeted all the other delegates, while *the chairs are stacked on top of each other* typically means that each table is either on top of, or underneath, some other table. These semantic subtleties are beyond the scope of this chapter.
3 The major difference between what follows and Chomsky (1981) is that we assume Reinhart's (1976) definition of c-command: *A* c-commands *B* iff *A* does not dominate *B* and *A*'s mother dominates *B*. Chomsky used a more inclusive relation sometimes called *m-command* instead. I believe the theory presented here is the normal understanding of the GB binding theory, m-command having fallen by the wayside.

4 How degraded (9) is is a matter of debate, being addressed by experimental research (see Kaiser *et al.* 2009 and references therein).

5 (11) incorrectly predicts that (i) is acceptable, with the matrix clause as a binding domain.

    (i) **Susan* thinks that *herself* is adorable.

This led Chomsky to state that finite agreement is a subject distinct from *herself* for the determination of binding domains (see also Rizzi 1990a). Finite clauses are then always binding domains.

6 The other two empty categories, A′-trace and *pro*, are beyond the scope of this chapter.

7 I represent multiple anaphoric relations with coindexation. This does not imply a commitment to an indexing-based treatment of anaphora.

8 We define **referential NPs** as nonquantified full NPs. With minor exceptions, any full NP is a referential NP or a quantifier.

9 All Dutch examples are from Koster (1985) unless otherwise stated.

10 This approach, based on variation in the size of locality domains, was pioneered by Koster (1985, 1987) and Koster and Reuland (1991a), and endorsed by Büring (2005). The text ignores locally bound uses of *zich* occurring as an argument of an inherently reflexive predicate (e.g. *Jan schaamt zich* "Jan is ashamed of himself"). See Reinhart and Reuland (1993) and much subsequent work for discussion.

11 "Most specific" can be understood, following Reinhart (1983), as "compatible with the narrowest range of structural binding configurations", the idea being that this would leave the hearer less work to identify the intended antecedent. If we assume, along the lines of Reuland (2011), that discourse-based coreference relations are less deterministic than variable binding relations, which in turn are less deterministic than syntactically mediated binding relations, then the preference for binding over coreference described by Rule I becomes a special case of this more general preference for tightly constrained binding relations.

12 Picture-NPs feature prominently in the literature on **backwards binding**, in which a reflexive c-commands its antecedent (see (i)).

    (i) [Pictures of *him(self)*] frighten *John*.

It is assumed, following Belletti and Rizzi (1988), that the possibility of backwards binding is related to the thematic role of the subject NP: (ii) is only acceptable if the subject is interpreted nonagentively, while (iii) is typically taken to be ungrammatical.

    (ii) [Clones of *himself*] (*deliberately) frighten *John*.
    (iii) *[Clones of *himself*] fear *John*.

This means that backwards binding can be assimilated to the discussion of connectivity effects in Section 7 below, if we assume, with Belletti and Rizzi, that the *frighten* construction is a form of unaccusative, in which *John* c-commands the θ-position of *clones of himself*.

13 These predictions are actually only partially verified. Although the reflexive in (61b) is dispreferred in comparison to that in (61a), Kaiser *et al.* (2009) demonstrate that it is considered online as an antecedent.

14 In fact, *zichzelf* in (63) is a syntactic argument of both *hoorde* and *zingen*, being case-marked by *hoorde* and θ-marked by *zingen*. *Zichzelf zingen* in (63) is therefore a reflexive-marked but nonreflexive syntactic predicate, in apparent violation of Principle A. This led R&R to postulate head-raising of *zingen* to *hoorde*, creating one big syntactic predicate. However, this in turn overgenerates, predicting that (i) is acceptable: the whole sentence is a reflexive, and reflexive-marked, syntactic predicate.

    (i) *John* heard Susan criticize *himself*.

See further discussion in Reuland (2011).

15 In fact, many people find *We voted for me* acceptable. The more specific prediction of R&R's approach is that *We voted for me* should be as acceptable as *I voted for me*. This seems to conform better to the empirical facts. A full discussion would take us too far into the semantics of anaphora, but it appears that *I voted for me* is acceptable only if it involves reference to the speaker under two different guises, similar to *I kissed me* in the Brigitte Bardot example (32). Thanks to Lyra Magloughlin for discussion of this and related issues.

16 This concern disappears if atttempts, like that of Reuland (2011), to ground many of these principles in lexical properties of the anaphors in question should prove successful.

17 To my knowledge, no comprehensive theory of exempt anaphora currently exists. However, their interpretation is standardly related to notions of point of view (e.g. Kuno 1987), and there is a tantalizing similarity between the domains which allow exempt anaphora and islands for *wh*-movement.

18 The examples in (71) are slightly degraded because of subjacency violations, but no more than any other subjacency violation.

19 Judgements in this passage are as reported in the literature. There is substantial variability in judgements in this area, to which we return briefly below.

20 In the interests of academic hygiene, note that Kuno does not mention competition. This passage is a reformulation of Kuno's analysis in the light of Reinhart and Safir's insights.

Further reading

- Büring (2005) is an excellent textbook-length introduction to the syntax and semantics of binding, with copious references to core primary literature.
- Book-length comprehensive treatments of the binding theory are currently appearing at a rate of roughly one per year: the ideas summarized here are developed much further in Safir (2004), Reuland (2011), and Rooryck and Vanden Wyngaerd (2011). These works also all develop theories of the relationship between the morphological form and syntactic behaviour of pronominals.
- Although this chapter has aimed to highlight issues in the syntax of binding, the semantics of binding is equally interesting. Büring (2005) is again an excellent starting point, with papers such as Evans (1980), Sells (1987), Jackendoff (1992), and Holmberg (2010) providing an indication of the wealth of empirical challenges in this area.

References

Barker, C. 2012. Quantificational binding does not require c-command. *Linguistic Inquiry*, *43*, 614–633.

Belletti, A. and Rizzi, L. 1988. Psych-verbs and θ-theory. *Natural Language and Linguistic Theory*, *6*, 291–352.

Bošković, Ž. 1997. Pseudoclefts. *Studia Linguistica*, *51*, 235–277.

Büring, D. 2005. *Binding Theory*. Cambridge: Cambridge University Press.

Chien, Y.-C. and Wexler, K. 1990. Children's knowledge of locality conditions in binding as evidence for the modularity of syntax and pragmatics. *Language Acquisition*, *1*, 225–295.

Chomsky, N. 1973. Conditions on transformations. In S. Anderson and P. Kiparsky (eds), *A Festschrift for Morris Halle* (pp. 232–286). New York: Holt, Rinehart and Winston.

Chomsky, N. 1976. Conditions on rules of grammar. *Linguistic Analysis*, *2*, 303–351.

Chomsky, N. 1981. *Lectures on Government and Binding*. Dordrecht: Foris.

Chomsky, N. 1986. *Barriers*. Cambridge, MA: MIT Press.

Chomsky, N. 1993. A minimalist program for linguistic theory. In K. Hale and S. J. Keyser (eds), *The View from Building 20: Essays in Honor of Sylvain Bromberger* (pp. 1–52). Cambridge, MA: MIT Press.

Cinque, G. 1990. *Types of Ā-dependencies*. Cambridge, MA: MIT Press.

Dalrymple, M., Kanazawa, M., Kim, Y., Mchombo, S., and Peters, S. 1998. Reciprocal expressions and the concept of reciprocity. *Linguistics and Philosophy*, *21*, 159–210.

Evans, G. 1980. Pronouns. *Linguistic Inquiry*, *11*, 337–362.

Everaert, M. 1986. *The Syntax of Reflexivization*. Dordrecht: Foris.

Fiengo, R. 1974. *Semantic Conditions on Surface Structure*. PhD thesis, MIT.

Grodzinsky, Y. and Reinhart, T. 1993. The innateness of binding and coreference. *Linguistic Inquiry*, *24*, 69–101.

Haïk, I. 1984. Indirect binding. *Linguistic Inquiry*, *15*, 185–223.

Heim, I. 1998. Anaphora and semantic interpretation: A reinterpretation of Reinhart's approach. In U. Sauerland and O. Percus (eds), *The Interpretive Tract* (pp. 205–246). Cambridge, MA: MIT Working Papers in Linguistics.

Robert Truswell

Heycock, C. and Kroch, A. 1999. Pseudocleft connectedness: Implications for the LF interface level. *Linguistic Inquiry, 30*, 365–397.

Higgins, F. R. 1973. *The Pseudo-cleft Construction in English*. PhD thesis, MIT.

Holmberg, A. 2010. How to refer to yourself when talking to yourself. In *Newcastle Working Papers in Linguistics 16*, (pp. 57–65).

Hornstein, N. 1995. *Logical Form: From GB to Minimalism*. Oxford: Blackwell.

Hornstein, N. 1999. Movement and control. *Linguistic Inquiry, 30*, 69–96.

Huang, C.-T. J. 1982. *Logical Relations in Chinese and the Theory of Grammar*. PhD thesis, MIT.

Jackendoff, R. 1968. An interpretive theory of pronouns and reflexives. Distributed by Indiana University Linguistics Club.

Jackendoff, R. 1992. Mme. Tussaud meets the binding theory. *Natural Language and Linguistic Theory, 10*, 1–31.

Kaiser, E., Runner, J., Sussman, R., and Tanenhaus, M. 2009. Structural and semantic constraints on the resolution of pronouns and reflexives. *Cognition, 112*, 55–80.

Koster, J. 1985. Reflexives in Dutch. In J. Guéron, H.-G. Obenauer, and J.-Y. Pollock (eds), *Grammatical Representation* (pp. 141–167). Dordrecht: Foris.

Koster, J. 1987. *Domains and Dynasties: The Radical Autonomy of Syntax*. Dordrecht: Foris.

Koster, J. and Reuland, E. 1991a. *Long-distance Anaphora*. Cambridge: Cambridge University Press.

Koster, J. and Reuland, E. 1991b. Long-distance anaphora: An overview. In J. Koster and E. Reuland (eds), *Long-distance Anaphora* (pp. 1–25). Cambridge: Cambridge University Press.

Kuno, S. 1987. *Functional Syntax: Anaphora, Discourse, and Empathy*. Chicago: University of Chicago Press.

Kuno, S. 1997. Binding theory in the minimalist program. Manuscript, Harvard University.

Lasnik, H. 1989. *Essays on Anaphora*. Dordrecht: Kluwer.

Lebeaux, D. 1988. *Language Acquisition and the Form of the Grammar*. PhD thesis, University of Massachusetts, Amherst, MA.

Lebeaux, D. 2009. *Where Does Binding Theory Apply?* Cambridge, MA: MIT Press.

Lees, R. and Klima, E. 1963. Rules for English pronominalization. *Language, 39*, 17–28.

Neeleman, A. and van de Koot, H. 2002. The configurational matrix. *Linguistic Inquiry, 33*, 529–574.

Pica, P. 1985. Subject, tense, and truth: Towards a modular approach to binding. In J. Guéron, H.-G. Obenauer, and J.-Y. Pollock (eds), *Grammatical Representation* (pp. 259–291). Dordrecht: Foris.

Pica, P. 1987. On the nature of the reflexivization cycle. In J. McDonough and B. Plunkett (eds), *Proceedings of NELS 17* (pp. 483–500). Amherst, MA: GLSA.

Pollard, C. and Sag, I. 1992. Anaphors in English and the scope of the binding theory. *Linguistic Inquiry, 23*, 261–305.

Reinhart, T. 1976. *The Syntactic Domain of Anaphora*. PhD thesis, MIT.

Reinhart, T. 1983. *Anaphora and Semantic Interpretation*. London: Croon Helm.

Reinhart, T. and Reuland, E. 1993. Reflexivity. *Linguistic Inquiry, 24*, 657–720.

Reuland, E. 2001. Primitives of binding. *Linguistic Inquiry, 32*, 439–492.

Reuland, E. 2011. *Anaphora and Language Design*. Cambridge, MA: MIT Press.

Rizzi, L. 1990a. On the anaphor-agreement effect. *Rivista di Linguistica, 2*, 27–42.

Rizzi, L. 1990b. *Relativized Minimality*. Cambridge, MA: MIT Press.

Rooryck, J. and Vanden Wyngaerd, G. 2011. *Dissolving Binding Theory*. Oxford: Oxford University Press.

Ross, J. R. 1972. Act. In D. Davidson and G. Harman (eds), *Semantics of Natural Language* (pp. 70–126). Dordrecht: Reidel.

Safir, K. 2004. *The Syntax of Anaphora*. Oxford: Oxford University Press.

Schlenker, P. 2003. Clausal equations: A note on the connectivity problem. *Natural Language and Linguistic Theory, 21*, 157–214.

Sells, P. 1987. Aspects of logophoricity. *Linguistic Inquiry, 18*, 445–479.

Thornton, R. and Wexler, K. 1999. *Principle B, VP Ellipsis, and Interpretation in Child Grammar*. Cambridge, MA: MIT Press.

van Riemsdijk, H. and Williams, E. 1981. NP-structure. *Linguistic Review, 1*, 171–217.

Williams, E. 1994. *Thematic Structure in Syntax*. Cambridge, MA: MIT Press.

12

Minimalism and control[1]

Norbert Hornstein and Jairo Nunes

1 Introduction

This chapter discusses what properties a minimalist theory of control should have and how close extant proposals are to meeting these desiderata. In particular, we concentrate on movement and PRO-based approaches to control, taking Hornstein (1999; 2001) and Boeckx *et al.* (2010) to be representative of the former, and Landau (2000; 2004), the latter.[2] Though the review is intended to be dispassionate, the reader should be familiar with the biases of the authors. We are of the vociferous opinion that a minimalistically respectable account of control will necessarily have some version of the Movement Theory of Control (MTC) at its core. Thus, in what follows the star is the MTC, the PRO-based approaches exploited as a useful foil (think Holmes and Watson).

Before getting down to some detail, we would like to outline the form of the argument in what follows. It has three steps. First, we show that many of the salient properties of obligatory control follow if we assume that it involves A-movement of the controller from the position of "PRO".[3] Second, we show how the MTC heavily relies on central minimalist assumptions. Third, we argue that standard PRO-based accounts of control violate one or another minimalist stricture. The conclusion is that if minimalism is on the right track, then some version of the MTC must be correct.

2 What any theory of control should account for

Any adequate theory of control should meet at least four desiderata. First, it must specify the kinds of control structures that are made available by UG and explain how and why they differ.

Assuming, for instance, that obligatory control (OC) and non-obligatory control (NOC) are different, their differences should be reduced to more basic properties of the system.

Second, the theory must specify the nature of the controllee: what is its place among the inventory of null expressions provided by UG? Is it a formative special to control construction or is it something that is independently attested?

Third, the theory must correctly describe the configurational properties of control, accounting for the positions that the controller and the controllee can occupy. In addition, it should provide an account as to why the controller and the controllee are so configured. Assuming, for instance, that the controllee can only appear in a subset of possible positions (e.g., ungoverned subjects), why are controllees so restricted?

Finally, the theory must account for the interpretation of the controllee, explaining how the antecedent of the controllee is determined and specifying what kind of anaphoric relation obtains between the controllee and its antecedent (in both OC and NOC constructions) and why these relations obtain and not others. For instance, assuming that controllers must locally bind controllees in OC constructions, why is the control relation so restricted in these cases?

As mentioned above, these desiderata hold of any approach – be it minimalist or not – that aims to *explain* the central features of control, rather than simply listing or stipulating them. Of course, additional strictures also come into place once these goals are explored against a minimalist setting. In the sections that follow we will discuss how the MTC and PRO-based accounts fare with respect to the four tenets listed above, once the mechanisms they rely on are examined using minimalist guidelines.

3 Control and the Duck Principle

The starting point of our discussion will be the useful methodological maxim expressed in (1):

(1) *The Duck Principle*: If something walks, talks and defecates like a duck, the default position is that it is a duck: that is, if constructions α and β have the same properties, the grammar should generate them in the same way.

3.1 Warming up

Bearing the Duck Principle in mind, let us consider the data in (2)–(7) for starters:

(2) a. *[It$_i$ was expected [t$_k$ to shave himself$_k$]]
     b. *[It$_i$ was hoped [PRO$_k$ to shave himself$_k$]]

(3) a. *[[John$_1$'s sister] was hired t$_1$]
     b. *[John$_1$'s campaign hopes [PRO$_1$ to shave himself]]

(4) a. *[John$_1$ seems [that it was likely [t$_1$ to shave himself]]]
     b. [John$_k$ convinced Mary$_i$ [PRO$_{i/*k}$ to leave]]

(5) a. *[John$_1$ seems [(that) t$_1$ will travel tomorrow]]
     b. *[John$_1$ said [(that) PRO$_1$ will travel tomorrow]]

(6) a. John seems to be cooperative and Bill does too
     b. [John$_1$ wants [PRO$_1$ to win]] and [Bill does too]
         ('… and Bill wants himself to win'/*'… and Bill wants John to win')

(7) a. *[John$_1$ strikes Bill$_2$ [t$_{1+2}$ as jealous of each other]]
     b. *[John$_1$ asked Bill$_2$ [PRO$_{1+2}$ to shave themselves/each other]]

Given that the expletive is not a suitable antecedent for the anaphor in (2a), its ungrammaticality shows that A-traces cannot simply pick up their antecedent in discourse, but rather require a syntactic antecedent. In turn, (3a) shows that such syntactic antecedent must be in c-commanding position. (4a) further shows that minimality also matters: there can be no proper interveners between an A-trace and its (c-commanding) antecedent. (5a) shows that an A-trace (in English) cannot occupy the subject position of a finite clause. Finally, (6a) and (7a) respectively show that an A-trace receives sloppy interpretation under ellipsis and cannot take split antecedents.

The *a*-sentences in (2)–(7) are textbook illustrations of configurational and interpretive properties ascribed to A-traces. What is crucial for our discussion is that the same properties describe OC PRO. Thus, (2b), (3b), and (4b) jointly show that OC PRO also requires a local c-commanding antecedent; (5b), that OC PRO cannot be the subject of a finite clause (in English); and (6b) and (7b), that OC PRO also triggers sloppy interpretation under ellipsis and cannot be licensed by split antecedents.

The *b*-sentences in (2)–(7) illustrate some of the general properties of OC,[4] but in no way depict all of the empirical diversity associated with OC. For instance, the property illustrated in (5b) is not universal. In Brazilian Portuguese, for example, the embedded null subject of a finite (indicative) clause has the same interpretive properties as OC PRO.[5] The sentence in (8) (below), for instance, shows that the empty category in the embedded subject position cannot freely pick up an antedecent in the discourse (indicated by the *w*-index), but must be interpreted as co-indexed with a local c-commanding DP. Hence, it must be interpreted as the *m*-indexed phrase *[o irmão d[o João$_k$]]$_m$*; not as *[o Pedro]$_i$* because it is not local and not as *João$_k$* because it is not in a c-commanding position.

(8) *Brazilian Portuguese:*
 [[o   Pedro]$_i$ disse [que [o   irmão   d[o   João$_k$]]$_m$ estava achando
  the Pedro   said   that the brother of-the João   was   thinking
 [que *ec*$_{m/*i/*k/*w}$ deveria ganhar uma medalha]]]
  that   should receive a   medal
 'Pedro said that [João's brother]$_m$ was thinking that he$_m$ should get a medal.'

The interesting thing to point out is that languages that admit sentences like (5b) also allow sentences analogous to (5a). In other words, once "PRO" is permitted in the subject position of a finite clause in Brazilian Portuguese, so is an A-trace. Thus, hyper-raising sentences such as (9) are also possible in Brazilian Portuguese:[6]

(9) *Brazilian Portuguese:*
 [osestudantes]$_i$**parecem/acabaram**   que *t*$_i$**viajaram**   mais cedo
 thestudents   seem.3PL/finished.3PL   that traveled.3PL   more early
 'The students seem to have traveled earlier.'/'The students ended up traveling earlier.'

If we examine the data in (2)–(9) in light of the Duck Principle, the conclusion is inescapable: the grammatical mechanisms involved in generating A-movement are also involved in generating OC.[7,8] It should be noted that this conclusion is by no means new or intrinsically related to minimalism. Already in Chomsky (1977: 82), for instance, we find the remark that "trace and PRO are the same element; they differ only in the way the index is assigned – as a residue of a movement rule in one case, and by a rule of control in the other". So, the task before us now is to investigate which mechanisms available in our minimalist arsenal can be resorted to in order to capture the phenomena that fall under these two rubrics in a unifying way. For the MTC, the answer is straightforward: OC is simply A-movement. Exploring (a version of) Chomsky's (2000; 2001) Agree operation, Landau (2000; 2004) in turn takes OC to be the output of an agreement relation triggered by PRO's feature under-specification.

Given that Agree is taken to be a subcomponent of Move in many minimalist approaches to movement (see, e.g., Chomsky 2001), it is not surprising that, by and large, the two competing approaches cover the same empirical terrain and, in particular, account for (2)–(9) with a comparable degree of success. Thus, both the MTC and Landau's PRO-based approach to control rely on c-command, minimality, some version of Chomsky's (2000) Activation Condition, and the Parallelism Requirement, for instance. Take the contrast between English and Brazilian Portuguese, for example. Suppose for the sake of the argument that finite T in Brazilian Portuguese may be ϕ-defective.[9] If so, finite clauses may define "porous" domains for *both* A-movement and Agree. In other words, contrasts such as (5) and (8)/(9) in themselves do not provide evidence for one approach over the other, for each approach can equally well incorporate comparable provisos to handle special cases such as (8)/(9).

It is very important to stress this point, for departures from standard cases are often taken to invidiously distinguish PRO-based accounts from the MTC, the exceptions taken as being problematic for the latter but not the former. The control differences between *convince* (see (4b)) and *promise* (see (10a) below), between *ask* (see (7b)) and *propose* (see (10b)), and the phenomenon of control shift illustrated in (11) are emblematic in this regard. However, *if* both movement and Agree are subject to minimality, then, as a point of logic, both accounts should in principle be empirically equal as regards controller selection in such cases. The theories do not diverge in their conceptions of minimality or in their assumption that the control relation is syntactically mediated by an operation subject to minimality. Thus a problem for either is a problem for both and a remedy for one is likely to heal the other.[10]

(10) a. [John$_k$ promised Mary$_i$ [PRO$_{k/*i}$ to leave]]
    b. [John$_1$ proposed to Bill$_2$ [PRO$_{1+2}$ to help each other]]

(11) a. [John$_k$ begged Mary$_i$ [PRO$_{i/*k}$ to leave the party early]]
    b. [John$_k$ begged Mary$_i$ [PRO$_{k/*i}$ to be allowed to leave the party early]]

A phenomenon that is taken to favor PRO-based theories over the MTC in a less trivial way is partial control, illustrated in (12) below. The ungrammaticality of (12a) is due to the fact that *gather* requires a semantically plural subject. In turn, the grammaticality of the OC control structure in (12b) indicates that the plurality requirement of *gather* is somehow met in the embedded clause, for the antecedent of PRO is singular. Thus, the mismatch in number between controller and controllee in (12b) appears to show that the controllee cannot be the same as the controller, which would be problematic for the MTC, but may be accommodated in PRO-based theories.

(12) a. *The chair gathered at three.
    b. The chair hoped [PRO to gather at three]]

In his in-depth study of partial control, Landau (2000; 2004) notes that only a subset of control structures support partial control. The complement of implicative verbs such as *manage*, for instance, does not allow it, as exemplified in (13) below. This leads Landau to propose that tense is what is relevant in the licensing of partial control, only tensed infinitives such as the complement of desiderative verbs such as *hope* (see (12b)) being able to do it.

(13)   *The chair managed [PRO to gather at three]]

Putting aside technical problems with Landau's implementation of this licensing of a plural PRO by tense,[11] it is not at all clear that partial control is dependent on tensed infinitival T heads or, more broadly, that it is even a control phenomenon. As observed by Rodrigues (2007), one also finds "partial control" effects where no infinitival complements are involved, as illustrated in (14b) and (15b) below, which have predicates that require semantically plural subjects (see (14a) and (15a)). Rodrigues's conclusion is that what is relevant in the licensing of plurality in (12b), (14b), and (15b) is not tense, but modality.

(14)   a.   *The chair met at 6.
       b.   The chair can only meet tomorrow.

(15)   a.   *The chair applied together for the grant.
       b.   The chair cannot apply together for the grant.

What matters for our current discussion is that, under the predicate internal subject hypothesis, the sentences in (14b) and (15b) are to be represented as in (16).

(16)   a.   [The chair]$_i$ can only [t$_i$ meet tomorrow]
       b.   [The chair]$_i$ cannot [t$_i$ apply together for the grant]

Thus, when we compare (12) with (14) and (15), we have a Duck Principle effect before us again, as OC PRO and A-traces are behaving alike. So, whatever accounts for the plurality interpretation in (16) should in principle be extended to (12b). Based on the fact that the plurality requirement at stake may also be satisfied via a commitative structure, as illustrated in (17) below, Boeckx *et al.* (2010) in fact propose that "partial control" effects involve the licensing of a null commitative complement (perhaps by a modal element along the lines of Rodrigues' proposal), as sketched in (18).[12] Notice, in particular, that in (18a) there is no mismatch between PRO and its antecedent, which makes it perfectly possible to analyze PRO as an A-trace.

(17)   a.   The chair gathered **with Bill** at three
       b.   The chair met **with Bill** yesterday]
       c.   The chair applied together for the grant **with Bill**

(18)   a.   [The chair]$_i$ hoped [PRO$_i$ to gather ***pro***$_{commitative}$ at three]]
       b.   [The chair]$_i$ can only [t$_i$ meet ***pro***$_{commitative}$ tomorrow]
       c.   [The chair]$_i$ cannot [t$_i$ apply together for the grant ***pro***$_{commitative}$]

Regardless of whether Boeckx *et al.*'s proposal is on the right track, the important point to emphasize here is that if the MTC has to say something special about partial control in (12b), so do PRO-based accounts with respect to "partial control" effects in monoclausal structures (see (14b)/(15b)). Moreover, as PRO-based accounts and the MTC need comparable provisos in terms of tense/mood licensing in order to account for partial control, they are on equal footing in this regard.[13]

Let us then discuss some cases where the Duck Principle may indeed distinguish the MTC from PRO-based approaches.

3.2 Case issues

We may start by examining Duck Principle effects in the domain of Case and morphophological computations.

It has long been observed that the application of some sandhi rules may be blocked by certain syntactic empty categories, the most well-known example of such being *wanna*-contraction in English. As illustrated in (19) below, *want* and *to* may contract across an intervening PRO, but not across an intervening A′-trace. Curiously, A-traces also allow similar contraction, as shown in (20).[14]

(19) a. Who$_1$ do you **want PRO to** banish t$_1$ from the room $\rightarrow$
       Who do you **wanna** banish from the room?
    b. ho$_1$ do you **want t$_1$ to** vanish from the room $\rightarrow$
       *Who do you **wanna** vanish from the room?

(20) a. John$_1$ **has t$_1$ to** kiss Mary $\rightarrow$ John hasta kiss Mary
    b. John$_1$ **used t$_1$** to kiss Mary $\rightarrow$ John usta kiss Mary
    c. John$_1$ is **going t$_1$ to** kiss Mary $\rightarrow$ John usta kiss Mary

Given that one of the standard differences between A-traces and A′-traces is that the former is Caseless while the latter is Case-marked, it is very reasonable to assume that this difference is ultimately responsible for contrasts such as the one between (19b) and (20).[15] That being so, PRO in (19a) should be Caseless, which is in consonance with the MTC and GB accounts of control,[16] but not with the major PRO-based accounts within minimalism.[17] Under the approach proposed by Chomsky and Lasnik (1993) and developed by Martin (2001), for instance, PRO is assigned null Case, whereas for Landau (2004) PRO receives regular Case, like any other DP. Both approaches face problems of their own. The former has to explain why only PRO can bear null Case, while the latter fails to account for why PRO cannot be phonetically realized like other DPs marked with regular Case.[18] These problems already hint that the special properties ascribed to PRO in PRO-based accounts may *track* some properties of OC by coding the properties to be accounted for in terms of lexical features, but do not *explain* them. But even if we put these problems aside, what is relevant for our current discussion is that in (19a) we again see that OC PRO walks and talks like a (Caseless) A-trace.

If PRO is a lexical element that receives structural Case (be it null or regular), one might expect it to function like A′-traces rather than A-traces with respect to *wanna*-contraction. As the data above indicate, this is incorrect. At the very least PRO-based accounts will have to explain why PRO, though Case-marked, functions like an A-trace and not as an A′-trace. As PRO-based accounts currently stipulate the distributional properties of OC PRO, these data indicate that a rather articulated stipulation will be required.[19]

The conclusion is that here the Duck Principle does tease apart the MTC from PRO-based accounts within minimalism. It is not the case, as we saw in the subsection 'Warming up', above, that the special provisos required by PRO-based accounts can be incorporated by the MTC. The MTC simply doesn't need them! Thus, the Duck Principle in tandem with Occam's Razor implicates the MTC.

3.3 Adjunct control

Let us now consider adjunct control. Of course, adjunct control involves adjuncts and adjuncts are perennial troublemakers. They always challenge attempts towards unification as there are many different types, which require different heights for merge, etc. Our aim here is not to explore adjuncts in depth, but to consider a subset of adjuncts, the ones which trigger OC. Take the data in (21), for example.

(21) a. $John_i$ said [that [$Mary_k$'s brother]$_m$ left [after $PRO_{m/*i/*k/*w}$ eating a bagel]]
      b. *$John_i$ watched TV [while PRO_i ate a bagel]
      c. $John_i$ left before PRO_i singing and $Bill_k$ did too
          '… and $Bill_k$ left before $he_{k/*John_i}$ sang'
      d. *$John_i$ called $Mary_k$ after [PRO_{i+k} criticizing each other]

(21a) shows that PRO in this configuration requires a local c-commanding antecedent, (21b) that PRO cannot sit in the subject position of a finite adjunct (in English), (21c) that PRO inside the adjunct triggers a sloppy reading under ellipsis, and (21d) that PRO does not permit a split antecedent. All of these properties, the reader may recall, describe both OC PRO in complement control *and A-traces* (see (2)–(7)).[20] In other words, in adjunct control configurations OC PRO also quacks like an A-trace.

It should be noted that the similarities go beyond the orthodox cases. As mentioned in the subsection 'Warming up', Brazilian Portuguese allows both an A-trace (see (9)) and an OC PRO (see (8)) in the subject position of a finite complement clause. Unsurprisingly, in adjunct control configurations in Brazilian Portuguese, the null subject of a finite adjunct clause behaves like OC PRO, as illustrated in (22).[21]

(22) *Brazilian Portuguese*

[O	pai	do	João$_i$]$_k$	cumprimentou o	Pedro$_m$	[quando $ec_{k/*i/*m/*w}$	entrou
the	*father*	*of-the João*		*greeted*	*the Pedro*	*when*	*entered*
						na	sala]
						in-the	*room*

'[$John_i$'s father]$_k$ greeted Pedro$_m$ when $he_{k/*i/*m/*w}$ entered the room.'

Another telling pattern is found in instances of interclausal epicene agreement in Romance, as discussed by Rodrigues (2004; 2007).[22] The word for 'victim' in Italian, for instance, is invariably [+feminine] regardless of whether it refers to males or females. Accordingly, in raising constructions such as (23), for instance, the adjectival predicate takes the feminine form even in the context where a man has been hurt.

(23) *Italian* (Rodrigues 2004):

La	vittima	sembra	essere	**ferita/*ferito**
the	*victim*	*seems*	*be*	*injured-FEM/injured-MASC*

'The victim seems to be injured.'

Interestingly, the agreement seen in (23) is replicated in both complement and adjunct control, as shown in (24), but, crucially, not in NOC, as shown in (25).

(24) *Italian* (Rodrigues 2004):

    a. La vittima ha cercato di essere **trasferita/??trasferito**
       the victim had tried of be transferred-FEM/transferred-MASC
       alla stazione di polizia di College Park.
       to-the station of police of College Park
       'The victim tried to be transferred to the police station at College Park.'

    b. La vittima mori' dopo essere **stata trasportata /??stato**
       the victim died after be been.FEM brought.FEM been.MASC
       trasportato all' ospedale.
       brought.MASC to-the hospital
       'The victim died after being brought to the hospital.'

(25) *Italian* (Rodrigues 2004):

    La vittima ha detto che essere ***portata/portato*** alla stazione
    The victim has said that be brought-FEM/brought-MASC to-the station
    di polizia non era una buona idea.
    of police not was a good idea
    'The victim said that being brought to the police station was not a good idea.'

As Rodrigues reasons, if the null subject inside the infinitival in (24) is an A-trace, it must pattern with the A-trace in the embedded subject position of the raising constructions in (23) and the agreement morphology on the embedded predicate must match the gender feature of the antecedent of the embedded subject. Again, this should be so independently of the specific analysis one assumes for inter-clausal agreement in standard raising constructions. (25), on the other hand, cannot be analyzed as involving an A-trace in the subject of the infinitival clause, as the infinitival is a subject island. Once (25) cannot be analyzed in terms of an A-trace, inter-clausal agreement is blocked and the embedded predicate takes an (arguably default) masculine form.

The data above pose very serious problems for PRO-based analyses that rely on Agree, such as Landau's (2000; 2004). Crucially, subjects are CED islands and whatever accounts for CED effects should prevent inter-clausal agreement to license OC PRO. This is a good result in the case of the subject island in (25), for example, but not in cases of adjunct control such as (21a), (21c), (22), and (24b). To deny that these sentences involve OC because they do not instantiate an Agree configuration (see, e.g., Landau 2000: section 5.1) raises the mystifying question of why the grammar should require additional mechanisms that yield the same effects as the ones related to PROs of complement control *and A-traces*. Ignoring the Duck Principle in the face of similarities between OC PROs in adjunct control and A-traces such as the ones illustrated above comes, we believe, at a considerable cost.

At first sight, the same kind of problem faced by Agree-based analyses of OC PRO with respect to adjunct control should also haunt the MTC. After all, adjuncts are islands for movement and therefore movement out of the adjunct island in adjunct control constructions should also yield a CED violation. This is actually true if we are referring to GB-style grammars, but not to grammars with a *minimalist* architecture. Let's consider why.

Within GB, D-Structure provides the computational system with a unique root tree and all the syntactic computations after D-Structure must operate within this single rooted syntactic object. Thus, if we find an adjunct island between a trace and its antecedent, the movement that gives rise to this configuration must have incurred a CED violation. So, within the GB model incorporating the CED there is no way to generate adjunct control via movement.

Minimalist theories, on the other hand, dispense with D-structure (as it is not an interface level) and syntactic trees are constructed in a step-by-step fashion through (possibly) interleaved applications of Merge and Move.[23] Furthermore, Chomsky (1995) has argued that the computational complexity of syntactic derivations can be substantially reduced if we assume the Extension Condition, which requires that projecting operations work at the root node. Thus, whereas in GB the structure *[$_{VP}$ [$_{DP}$ the boy] [$_{V'}$ saw her]]*, for example, is generated in one fell swoop as part of the D-Structure corresponding to the whole sentence, in minimalism it is built from the (simplified) numeration N in (26a) through several applications of Select and Merge, as sketched in (26b–h).

(26) a. N = {the$_1$, boy$_1$, saw$_1$, her$_1$}
  b. *Select:* N$'$ = {the$_1$, boy$_1$, **saw$_0$**, her$_1$}
       K = **saw**
  c. *Select:* N$''$ = {the$_1$, boy$_1$, saw$_0$, **her$_0$**}
       K = saw
       L = **her**
  d. *Merge:* M = [saw her]
  e. *Select:* N$'''$ = {the$_1$, **boy$_0$**, saw$_0$, her$_0$}
       M = [saw her]
       O = **boy**
  f. *Select:* N$''''$ = {**the$_0$**, boy$_0$, saw$_0$, her$_0$}
       M = [saw her]
       O = boy
       P = **the**
  g. *Merge:* M = [saw her]
       Q = [the boy]
  h. *Merge:* VP = [[the boy] [saw her]]

Although the final result is the same in both the one-fell-swoop and the step-by-step derivations, there is a crucial difference in how this result is obtained: in the derivation sketched in (26) the computational system must be able to handle more than one root syntactic object at a time. This is in fact trivially true for the first steps of any syntactic derivation. Take the derivational step in (26c), for instance. Before *saw* and *her* merge, they are independent root syntactic objects. Moreover, given the Extension Condition, the derivation of complex subjects and complex adjuncts invariably demands that the computational system deal with more than one root syntactic object at a time. For instance, the Extension Condition prevents an alternative continuation of (26e) where *boy* first merges with *[saw her]*, yielding *[boy [saw her]]*, and later *the* merges with *boy* in a noncyclic manner; hence, *the* must be selected and merged with *boy* so that the resulting structure merges with *[saw her]* (cf. (26e–h)). Interestingly, in the derivational step in (26f) there are three different root syntactic objects available to the computational system.

Another relevant difference between GB and minimalism is the copy theory of movement, which reinterprets Move as the output of the interaction between the more basic operations Copy and Merge.[24] Under the copy theory, the derivation of a sentence such as (27) below, for instance, proceeds along the lines of (28), where the computational system creates a copy of *John*, merges it with the previously assembled TP, and deletes the lower copy in the phonological component. Again, notice that in a system that has Copy as a basic operation, the computational system must be able to handle more than one root syntactic

object, namely, the copy newly created and the root syntactic object containing the replicated material (cf. (28b)).

(27) John was arrested.

(28) a. K = [$_{TP}$ was arrested John]
     b. *Copy:*   K = [$_{TP}$ was arrested **John^i**]
                  L = **John^i**
     c. *Merge:* M = [$_{TP}$ John^i was arrested John^i]
     d. *Delete:* P = [$_{TP}$ John^i was arrested ~~John^i~~]

What is relevant for our discussion is that if the computational system can operate with
more than one root syntactic object at a time and if movement is understood as the interaction between the basic operations of Copy and Merge, "sideward movement" becomes a
logical possibility within the system. That is, given two root syntactic objects K and L in
(29), the computational system may copy α from K and merge it with L.[25]

(29) a. K = [… α…]
             L = […]
     b. *Copy*:   K = [… $\boldsymbol{\alpha^i}$…]
                  L = […]
                  M = $\boldsymbol{\alpha^i}$
     c. *Merge*: K = [… α^i…]
                  P = [α^i [$_L$ …]]

Terminological metaphors aside, note that there is no intrinsic difference between the "upward"
movement seen in (28), for instance, and the "sideward" movement sketched in (30) with
respect to the computational tools employed. In both cases, we have trivial applications of
movement viewed as Copy plus Merge. Sideward movement is therefore *not* a novel operation
or a new species of movement.[26] This point is worth emphasizing, as it has been consistently
misunderstood. The fact that α in (29) does not merge with the structure that contains the
"source" of the copy, as opposed to *John* in (28), may have independent explanations. First,
(28) differs from (29) in an obvious way: the copy of *John* in (28) has only one syntactic object
to merge with, whereas the copy of α in (29) has two. But, more importantly, it may be the case
that Last Resort licenses merger of the copy of α in (29) with L but not with K.[27]

Bearing these differences between GB and minimalism in mind, the derivation of an
adjunct construction such as (30) under a sideward movement approach should proceed
along the lines of (31).[28]

(30) John$_i$ saw Mary after [PRO$_i$ eating lunch]

(31)
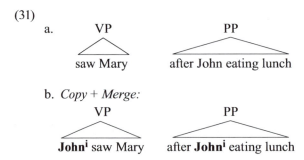
  a.   VP   PP
        saw Mary   after John eating lunch

  b. *Copy + Merge:*
          VP   PP
     John^i saw Mary   after **John^i** eating lunch

c. *Merge:*

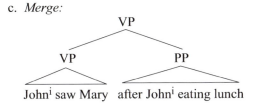

Johnⁱ saw Mary   after Johnⁱ eating lunch

d. *Copy + Merge:*

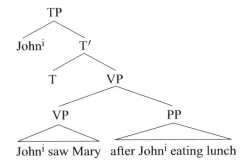

Johnⁱ saw Mary   after Johnⁱ eating lunch

e. *Delete:*   [$_{TP}$ Johnⁱ [$_{T'}$ T [$_{VP}$ [$_{VP}$ ~~**John**~~ⁱ saw Mary] [$_{PP}$ after ~~**John**~~ⁱ eating lunch]]]]

Once VP and PP in (31a) are assembled, the computational system makes a copy of *John* from PP and merges it with VP (cf. (31b)), an instance of sideward movement that allows the external θ-role of the matrix clause to be discharged. After PP adjoins to VP (cf. (31c)) and the subject moves to [Spec,TP] (cf. (31d)), the lower copies of *John* are deleted in the phonological component (cf. (31e)) and the structure surfaces as (30).

Notice now that at the derivational step where *John* moves from PP to VP (cf. (31a–b)), PP is *not* an adjunct. Crucially, *adjunct* is not an absolute, but a relational notion: a given expression is an *adjunct of* another. In (31a) PP is just a root syntactic object. Assuming that syntactic computations operate in a local fashion, the fact that later on PP will become an adjunct is irrelevant *at the derivational step where movement takes place*.[29] In other words, there is no island configuration in (31a) that would prevent copying. In fact, the copying and merger seen in (31a–b) is no different from the copying and merger found in licit instances of "upward movement" (cf. (28b–c)): in both circumstances, copying proceeds from a configuration that is not an island.

This approach correctly distinguishes licit cases of adjunct control such as (30) from standard CED violations such as (32) below, for instance. Given that the Extension Condition bars late adjunction, it must be the case that the PP in (32) merges with the matrix VP before the derivation builds the matrix TP. This being so, by the time the interrogative complementizer Q is merged, as sketched in (33), *which book* cannot move to check the strong feature of Q, as it is within an adjunct; hence the ungrammaticality of (32).

(32)   *[[which book]$_i$ did [John [$_{VP}$ [$_{VP}$ call Mary] [$_{PP}$ after he read t_i]]]]

(33)   [$_{CP}$ did+**Q** [John [$_{VP}$ [$_{VP}$ call Mary] [$_{PP}$ after he read **[which book]**]]]]

Similar considerations apply to the illicit adjunct control construction in (34) below, with PRO taking the matrix subject as its antecedent. Under the relevant reading indicated by the brackets in (34), the PP headed by *without* is an adjunct of the VP headed by *answered*. The Extension Condition requires that these two constituents be merged before they become part of a larger structure. Thus, by the time the VP *left the room* is built, *John* is unable to undergo sideward movement to reach the matrix predicate, for it is inside an adjunct, as illustrated in (35).

(34) *[John$_i$ left the room [after Mary answered the questions without PRO$_i$ understanding them]]

(35)

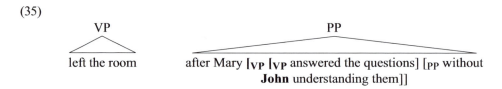

$$\text{VP}$$
left the room

$$\text{PP}$$
after Mary [$_{VP}$ [$_{VP}$ answered the questions] [$_{PP}$ without **John** understanding them]]

Before exiting this subsection, let us briefly consider how to account for a very distinctive property of adjunct control: namely, that PRO must be controlled by the subject and not the object of the next higher clause, as illustrated in (36).

(36) John$_i$ saw Mary$_k$ after PRO$_{i/*k}$ eating lunch

Hornstein (1999; 2001) has argued that this subject–object asymmetry follows from economy computations. Consider the derivational step sketched in (37), for instance.

(37) N = {John$_0$, saw$_0$, Mary$_1$, after$_1$, eating$_0$, lunch$_0$}
 K = [John eating lunch]
 L = saw

In (37), *saw* must assign its internal θ-role and there are two potential candidates to receive it: *Mary*, which is still in the numeration, and *John*, in the subject position of the gerundive clause. If *Mary* is selected and merged with *saw*, the derivation results in a subject control structure, after *John* undergoes sideward movement to [Spec,VP] (cf. (31a–b)). On the other hand, if *John* is copied and merged with *saw*, the derivation should give rise to an object control structure after *Mary* is plugged in as the external argument. Under the assumption that Merge is more economical than Move (see Chomsky 1995), the first option is enforced, yielding the subject–object asymmetry observed in (36). In sum, if economy independently restricts movement and sideward movement is just an instance of Move, then the restriction to subject control into adjuncts is what we expect (and find).[30]

To conclude, once we note that PROs in adjunct control configurations also behave like A-traces, the Duck Principle invites us to analyze them as members of the same species. However, this guiding principle leads to a dead end if we have in mind a GB-style grammar, for movement out of an adjunct structure that is part of the bigger D-Structure representation that feeds the computation necessarily results in a CED violation. Another dead end is met if the interpretation of OC PRO is to be licensed by an Agree operation, as in Landau's (2000; 2004) PRO-based account. Given that an intervening adjunct island should bar an application of Agree, the only way out is to say that adjunct control PRO walks and talks like complement control PRO, but this is due to something else. Of course, Occam's Razor disfavors this route. In contrast, by relying on the combination of some key aspects of the Minimalist Program – namely, the abandonment of D-Structure, cyclicity as deter-mined by the Extension Condition, and the copy theory of movement – the MTC is able to analyze adjunct control PROs as A-traces, like their complement control cousins. Cru-cially, by exploring the possibility of sideward movement made available by these minimal-ist architectural properties, the MTC manages to capture the fact that adjunct control PRO is also a residue of movement without incorrectly ruling in standard adjunct island violations.

The result of comparing PRO-based accounts and the MTC with respect to the Duck Principle is much stronger here than the one regarding *wanna*-contraction. As mentioned in Section 3.2, PRO-based accounts that assume that OC PRO is Case-marked can always invoke special provisos to account for why OC PRO behaves like Caseless traces. But here there is simply no such escape for PRO-based accounts other than denying that adjunct control involves control. By contrast, adjunct control brings no turbulence to the MTC.

3.4 Phonetic realization

Let us finally examine how the MTC and PRO-based accounts fare with respect to the PF side of the grammar. Consider the (simplified) structure each approach assigns to a control sentence such as (38), for instance:

(38)   John tried to work hard.

(39)   a. *MTC analysis:* [John^i tried [~~John^i~~ to work hard]]
       b. *PRO-based analysis:* [John$_i$ tried [**PRO$_i$** to work hard]]

Both approaches account for the fact that the null subject of the embedded clause is phonet-ically null. However, this by itself does not put them on equal footing. If you ask *why* the embedded subject is null, the nature of the answers offered are completely different. The MTC will respond that this issue reduces to the more general question of why copies are deleted in the phonological component: whatever mechanism is responsible for deleting copies in other instances of movement is also put to work in the case of (39a).[31] In other words, the phonetic nullness of the controllee in (39a) is not a construction-specific prop-erty pertaining to control, but the product of a grammatical process that is shared by stand-ard instances of movement. In turn, the PRO-based account will have to say that it is an irreducible (i.e., non-explainable) lexical property of PRO that it does not have phonetic content. Of course, there is nothing incoherent in stipulating that PRO has no phonetic content, but, all things being equal, we would be a step closer to theoretical nirvana if this followed from deeper features of the system.

Interestingly, the answers the MTC and PRO-based approaches provide to the issue of the phonetic content of OC PRO are not only different on conceptual grounds but also differ in their empirical coverage. An increasing body of literature has been showing that deletion of lower copies (our traditional traces) is not the only possibility found in natural languages. One may find cases where lower copies are pronounced instead of the head of the chain and even cases where more than one copy is phonetically realized.[32] These find-ings are completely orthogonal if we are examining control under PRO-based approaches, but become quite relevant if control is to be analyzed as in the MTC. Our friend the Duck Principle is ready to point out that, if these unusual cases of copy realization exist, we should expect comparable cases in the domain of control. Haddad and Potsdam (2013) discuss this and argue that the full spectrum of options is indeed attested. In addition to the familiar cases of forward control, where the controller (the highest copy) is phonetically realized (cf. (38)/(39a)), there are cases of backward control, where the controllee (a lower copy) is pronounced (see (40)), cases of alternating control, where either the controller or the controllee is pronounced (see (41)), and cases of copy control, where both controller and controllee are phonetically realized (see (42)):[33]

(40) *Tsez (Polinsky and Potsdam 2006):*
kid [**kid**-bā čorpa bod-a] y-oqsi.
girl.ABS girl-ERG soup.ABS make-INF II-began
'The girl began to make soup.'

(41) *Greek (Alexiadou et al. 2010):*
(O Janis) emathe **(o Janis)** na pezi **(o Janis)** kithara **(o Janis)**
John-NOM learn-3SG John-NOM SUBJ play-3SG John-NOM guitar John-NOM
'John learned to play the guitar.'

(42) *San Lucas Quiaviní Zapotec (Lee 2003):*
a. R-càaa'z **Gye'eihlly** g-auh **Gye'eihlly** bxaady.
HAB-want Mike IRR-eat Mike grasshopper
'Mike wants to eat grasshopper.'
b. B-quìi'lly bxuuhahz **Gye'eihlly** ch-iia **Gye'eihlly** scweel.
PERF-persuade priest Mike IRR-go Mike school
'The priest persuaded Mike to go to school'
c. B-ìi'lly-ga' **Gye'eihlly** zi'cygàa' nih cay-uhny **Gye'eihlly** zèèiny.
PERF-sing-also Mike while that PROG-do Mike work
'Mike sang while he worked.'

Moreover, one may even find the same kinds of restrictions that play a role in allowing or precluding unusual outputs of chain realization operating in these less familiar control constructions. Take the contrast in (43) below, for instance. Given that Romanian is a multiple *wh*-fronting language, the expected pattern should be (43a) and not (43b). Bošković (2002) argues that appearances here are misleading and the *wh*-object in (43b) does undergo *wh*-fronting; however, a language-specific PF constraint banning adjacent homophonous *wh*-phrases prevents the higher copy of the moved object from being realized and forces the pronunciation of the lower copy instead, as sketched in (44).

(43) *Romanian* (Bošković 2002)
a. *****Ce** **ce** precede?
what what precedes
b. **Ce** precede **ce**?
what precedes what
'What precedes what?'

(44) [ce **ce**^{i} precede **ce**^{i}]

The same type of reasoning is used by Fujii (2006) to account for the contrast in the object control constructions in (45) below, where the controller is realized with nominative and not with accusative Case. Fujii argues that if the highest copy of the chain headed by *John* were realized, there would arise a violation of the Double-*o* Constraint in Japanese, which bans two instances of accusative marked expressions in the same VP domain; hence, the unacceptability of (45a). In (45b), on the other hand, a lower copy of *John* is realized (as nominative) instead of the head of the chain and the Double-*o* Constraint is circumvented, as sketched in (46).

(45) *Japanese* (Fujii 2006):
     a. ?? Taro-wa **John-o** [siken-ni too-ru-no]-o tetudat-ta
            Taro-TOP John-ACC exam-DAT pass-PRS-C_{NO}]-ACC assisted
     b. Taro-wa **[John-ga** siken-ni too-ru-no]-o tetudat-ta
            Taro-TOP John-NOM exam-DAT pass-PRS-C_{NO}]-ACC assisted
            'Taro assisted John to pass the exam.'

(46) [Taro-wa ~~John^i=o~~ [**John^i-ga** siken-ni too-ru-no]-o tetudat-ta]

As for cases with pronunciation of multiple copies, a common restriction is that the more morphologically complex a given copy is, the less likely it is for it to be pronounced more than once.[34] This is illustrated in (47), for instance, which shows that *wh*-copying constructions in German may allow pronunciation of multiple copies of simplex *wh*-element such as *wen*, but not of full phrases such as *wessen Buch*.

(47) *German* (McDaniel 1986):
     a. ***Wen*** glaubt Hans ***wen*** Jakob gesehen hat?
            whom thinks Hans *wen* Jakob seen has
            'Who does Hans think Jakob saw?'
     b. ****Wessen Buch*** glaubst du ***wessen Buch*** Hans liest?
            whose book think you *whose book* Hans reads
            'Whose book do you think Hans is reading?'

Analogously, languages that allow copy control exhibit similar restrictions on how morphologically encumbered copies can be. Thus, although San Lucas Quiaviní Zapotec allows copy control with only a name (cf. (42)), it rules out copy control constructions such as the ones in (48a), which involves a quantifier phrase, or (48b), which involves an anaphoric possessor.[35]

(48) *San Lucas Quiaviní Zapotec* (Lee 2003):
     a. ***Yra'ta' zhyàa'p** r-càaa'z g-ahcnèe' **yra'ta' zhyàa'p** Lia Paamm.
            every girl HAB-want IRR-help every girl FEM Pam
            'Every girl wants to help Pam.'
     b. *R-e'ihpy Gye'eihlly **behts-ni'** g-a'uh **behts-ni'** bx:àady.
            HAB-tell Mike brother-REFL.POSS IRR-eat brother-REFL.POS grasshopper
            'Mike told his brother to eat grasshoppers.'

In sum, if OC is a residue of movement, as advocated by the MTC, and if movement is to be understood in terms of the copy theory, as minimalism does, the Duck Principle leads us to expect that the full range of options available for copy pronunciation in standard movement operations should also be available in the case of control. Haddad and Potsdam provide substantial evidence that this expectation is realized.[36]

This line of reasoning has one important implication. There is really no way of combining backward control or copy control together with PRO-based accounts. To account for backward control, PRO-based theories would require base generating OC PRO in a position c-commanding its antecedent, as sketched in (49) below. However, this should lead to a violation of Principle C and thus should be impossible.

(49) $[\text{PRO}_1 \text{ V } [\text{DP}_1 \text{ VP}]]$

As for copy control, PRO-based approaches would have to incorporate rules that copy phonological matrices from antecedents to PRO.[37] Such rules are conceivable, but, if not treated gingerly, would appear to collapse into complex versions of MTC under the copy theory. At any rate, as we hope to have made clear, the existence of cases of backward and copy control provides an interesting *novel* kind of evidence for the MTC and against PRO-based accounts.[38]

3.5 Wrapping up

Let us take stock in view of the discussion entertained above. Any adequate theory of control must:

(50) (i) specify the kinds of control structures that are made available by UG and explain how and why they differ;
 (ii) correctly describe the configurational properties of control, accounting for the positions that the controller and the controllee can occupy;
 (iii) account for the interpretation of the controllee, explaining how the antecedent of the controllee is determined and specifying what kind of anaphoric relation obtains between the controllee and its antecedent; and
 (iv) specify what is the place of the controllee among the inventory of grammatical formatives provided by UG.

With respect to (50i), the MTC divides control into those cases parasitic on A-movement (OC) and those that are not (NOC). If "PRO" is a link in a well-formed A-chain, we have OC and "PRO" must have a local c-commanding antecedent, for example (cf. (2)–(4)). Otherwise, we have NOC. In other words, NOC acts like a pronominal relation not subject to the strict restrictions characteristic of A-chains.[39] In (51), below, for instance, we see that NOC PRO may have no antecedent (cf. (51a)), a nonlocal one (see (51b)), or a non c-commanding one (see (51c)). This is what we expect as the PROs in (51) sit within subject islands and so movement is impossible and no chain can relate the PRO within the subject gerund to any position outside it higher up.

(51) a. It is believed that $[\text{PRO}_{\text{arb}}$ washing oneself once a week] is hygienic.
 b. John$_1$ thinks that Mary said that $[\text{PRO}_1$ shaving himself] is vital.
 c. John$_1$'s friends believe that $[\text{PRO}_1$ keeping himself under control] is vital.

The MTC also offers a straightforward answer to (50ii), in particular with respect to the distribution of "PRO." If "PRO" is actually a residue of movement, then we expect it to appear where A-traces (i.e., deleted copies in A-chains) are licit and to exhibit the properties that A-traces generally manifest. In languages such as English, this coincides with caseless positions. Moreover, if minimality regulates movement, then we expect that no c-commanding DP can intervene between links of the OC chain. This implies that in the more familiar cases of forward control, OC "PRO" is phonetically null (being an A-trace), that it must be the highest DP of its clause, and that its antecedent must be the "closest" available DP. In addition, language specific rules may also trigger the pronunciation of a lower copy instead of the head of the chain or pronunciation of more than one copy, yielding backward control and copy control, respectively.

As for (50iii), the MTC provides a precise answer to the issue of identifying which DP can serve as the antecedent of OC PRO:[40] the antecedent is the head of the A-chain of which OC PRO is a link. Given standard requirements on A-chain, this implies that controller selection under the MTC will comply with Rosenbaum's (1970) Principle of Minimal Distance and pick the closest c-commanding DP as the antecedent for PRO. In a subject control construction such as (52), for example, *Mary* must be the antecedent for PRO as it is the closest DP and movement of *John* from the position of PRO across *Mary* violates minimality.

(52) [John$_1$ expects [Mary$_2$ to try [PRO$_{2/*1}$ to wash]]]

Finally, with respect to (50iv), the MTC takes OC PRO to be not a lexical item with idiosyncratic properties but a garden-variety trace of movement. So, whatever properties one may ascribe to PRO, they should be reduced to properties associated with movement operations.

It is worth observing that the MTC is the *only* current approach to control that derives the answers to the issues in (50) from more general grammatical principles. All PRO-based theories end up stipulating the properties to be captured in the guise of lexical features. Take the null Case and the Agree-based accounts, for concreteness. In Chomsky and Lasnik (1993) the distribution of PRO is tied to assignment of null Case. However, null Case is carried exclusively by the T^0 found in control clauses, and it is a Case that only PRO can realize. In turn, in Landau's (2004) approach, the distribution and interpretation of PRO are ultimately related to his assignment of [+R] and [−R] features to functional categories, where [+R] and [−R], when associated with a DP, are meant to indicate whether or not it may support independent reference. To the extent that they succeed, this type of account can *track* the distribution and interpretation of OC PRO, but does not *explain* why OC PRO has this specific distribution and interpretation and not others.[41]

4 Further architectural issues

4.1 The elimination of D-Structure

The MTC rests on one key assumption: namely, that movement into θ-positions is grammatically viable. In other words, the MTC is at odds with D-Structure. D-Structure, recall, is the syntactic level where all and only θ-relations are coded. It is also the input to all transformation processes (e.g., movement). Together, these two properties (i) prohibit movement into θ-positions and (ii) require that all argument DPs begin their derivational lives in θ-positions. The MTC is clearly incompatible with (i) and thus its theoretical viability requires the elimination of D-Structure as a grammatical level. As disposing of D-Structure (a methodologically unwelcome grammar-internal level) is a central architectural feature of the Minimalist Program, there exists a very tight conceptual connection between the Minimalist Program and the MTC. Not only does MTC imply the absence of D-Structure, but the absence of D-Structure is sufficient for the MTC given standard ancillary assumptions. Specifically, once D-Structure is eliminated as a grammatical level, nothing *prohibits* movement into θ-positions. Thus, eliminating D-Structure is both a necessary and sufficient condition for the MTC. Thus, to the extent that the elimination of D-Structure is a central feature of the Minimalist Program, the MTC is quintessentially minimalist. If this is correct, the reader may be asking, why has this not been observed previously?

The main reason is that eliminating D-Structure does not necessarily imply removing all of D-Structure conditions from the grammar. Here's some Whig history: Chomsky's (1993) argument against D-Structure was actually quite narrowly focused. It dealt with only one of its properties: namely, that it is the input to the transformational component, thus preceding all movement operations. Chomsky (1993) describes this property of D-Structure in terms of *Satisfy*, an "all-at-once" operation that selects an array of items from the lexicon, arranges them in the X'-format, and presents the result to the computational system. Chomsky argues that Satisfy must be dispensed with and grammars must adopt generalized transformations that allow derivations to interleave operations akin to lexical insertion with operations akin to movement. This idea has been incorporated into the minimalist doctrine and was in fact the guiding intuition behind sideward movement, as seen in the subsection 'Adjunct control'. Recall that, once generalized operations are resorted to, the system must be able to deal with more than one root syntactic object at a time; furthermore, once lexical insertion and movement are allowed to intersperse, a given expression may move from one root syntactic object to another before further lexical insertion proceeds.

The other defining property of D-Structure – namely, that it is the level where "pure GF-θ" is represented – was actually retained, but took another form. It was converted into the ban on movement into θ-role positions (Chomsky 1995: section 4.6) or the principle stating that "pure Merge in θ-positions is required of (and restricted to) arguments", where "*[p]ure* Merge is Merge that is not part of Move" (Chomsky 2000: 103). However, neither translation of the "base-properties" of D-Structure fits snugly with other theoretical assumptions internal to the Minimalist Program. The most flagrant oddity in this revamping of D-Structure regards Merge. An unavoidable assumption within the system once Satisfy was dropped is that not only merger but also movement is a structuring building operation. In other words, Move must involve Merge as one of its components (cf. Chomsky's 2000 definition of pure Merge cited above) or is just another instantiation of Merge (see Chomsky's 2004 internal and external Merge). Now, if "pure"/"external" Merge is independently able to license θ-relations, why does it lose its powers when it is part of/related to movement? Whichever tack one takes, the prior differentiation between Move and Merge is conceptually difficult to retain and, correspondingly we believe, the prohibition against movement into θ-positions becomes theoretically awkward to enforce. There seems to be no reason *why* this difference should exist if D-Structure does not. Thus, on both methodological and theory-internal grounds, we believe that there is every reason to retain the methodologically superior option (the complete elimination of D-Structure and its properties) that underwrites the MTC.

Before we leave this discussion, it should be observed that the residue of D-Structure clothed as a ban on movement into θ-positions or the requirement that arguments can only receive a θ-role in their first merge has also been put into empirical service in the account of contrasts such as the one in (53).

(53) a. *John expected [t to be [someone in the room]]
      b.   John expected [someone to be [t in the room]]

The EPP-feature of the embedded T is checked after insertion of *John* in (53a) and movement of *someone* in (53b). Given a Merge-over-Move approach, (53a) should trump (53b) *if* they were both convergent. Chomsky (1995) proposes that (53a) does not converge because *John* cannot receive the external θ-role of *expected* by moving to its Spec. Once (53a) crashes, it does not compete for economy purposes with the convergent derivation of (53b), where *John* gets θ-role when it is first merged.

Note, however, that the contrast in (53) can also be derived if *someone* cannot have its Case checked by the matrix verb in (53a) owing to the intervention of the trace of *John* (see Nunes 1995, 2004)[42] or if nonfinite clauses do not have TP specifiers (see Castillo *et al.* 1999 and Epstein and Seely 2006). In other words, it is not obvious that we are forced to resuscitate D-structure restrictions in order to account for data such as (53).

In sum, in Chomsky (1993), the elimination of D-Structure is only partial. The MTC requires that it be complete: not only must Satisfy be rejected, but the segregation of functions between lexical insertion and movement (the first being designated to satisfy θ-relations, the latter to satisfy all the other grammatical dependencies) should be given up as well.

4.2   The nature of PRO

Generative grammar has generally analyzed control properties as grammatical by-products for good reasons. Only in this way are its properties amenable to explanation. For example, in the Standard Theory, PRO is a phonetic gap that results from deletion under Equi. Why in this view is "PRO" phonetically null? Because it is the product of a deletion operation. Why is OC PRO anaphoric? Because deletion here is deletion under identity. Taking "PRO" to be the product of a grammatical deletion operation thus allows for an explanation of its semantic and phonetic properties.

The same holds for the EST conception of PRO as [$_{DP}$ *e*]. This is a permissible grammatical option in a model that distinguishes between phrase structure rules and lexical insertion operations: a "PRO" is what the grammar generates when the DP phrase structure rule applies but is *not* followed by a lexical insertion operation. This analysis also provides an account for PRO's phonetic and semantic properties. It is phonetically null because it has no lexical content and requires an antecedent because, having no content, it has no interpretation of its own. Once again, this analysis of "PRO" reflects the view that control facts (should) directly follow from basic operations and organizing principles of grammars.[43]

So, how is PRO to be described in a minimalist setting? It can be a grammar-internal formative or a primitive lexical item. There is no third alternative. In particular, the Inclusiveness Condition forbids PRO from being a non-lexical expression inserted during the course of the derivation and bare phrase structure eliminates the option of identifying PRO as [$_{XP}$ *e*]. Let us then briefly examine each of the options available.

In consonance with the Duck Principle, the option explored by the MTC takes the similarities between PRO and traces to their logical conclusion: PROs are actually traces! In particular, PRO is what we call the A-trace of an element that has wandered into a θ-position. As copies replace traces in the Minimalist Program, PROs are accordingly reanalyzed as copies, with significant empirical gain, as we saw in the subsection 'Phonetic realization'. What is critical to note here is that within minimalism copies are perfectly well defined in consonance with bare phrase structure: a copy is either a lexical item or a phrase built from lexical items. Moreover, the properties of control structures are expected to derive from general principles of grammar, as control relations – like A-trace dependencies – are grammatical products formed by movement. So, following a venerable tradition, the MTC embodies the assumption that the properties of control configurations derive from (and so directly reflect) the underlying operations and principles of UG.

Under the option of treating PRO as a lexical item, PRO is in turn expected to behave like *the, dog, bring, this*, etc. That is, it lives in the lexicon and it can merge and move, just like any other lexical item or phrase. Notice that there are no problems with bare phrase structure in this conception because PRO functions like any other (nominal) expression drawn from the lexicon. However, it is worth considering for a moment how radical a departure this is from the classical conceptions of control.

Since the early 1980s, generative grammarians have assumed that constructions do not exist as grammatical primitives. The idea is that the fundamental principles of grammar operate independently of the lexical items that they manipulate. For example, relative clauses are islands not because they involve particular lexical heads or contain particular lexical items but because they instantiate particular structural dependencies. Likewise, topicalization, focalization, or relativization obey islands not because they involve topic, focus, or relative heads but because they all involve (A$'$)-movement and movement is subject to island effects. In other words, grammatical operations and restrictions have the properties they do not because of the functional features of the "constructions" in which they apply, but because of the formal properties that these constructions instantiate. It is in this sense that constructions do not exist; they are not the fundamental units of syntactic analysis. The problem with treating "PRO" as a lexical item is that it amounts to analyzing control configurations as constructions: control properties follow from the unique properties (often sets of stipulated features) of the lexical item *PRO*, which defines the construction. In effect, the "control construction" directly reflects the idiosyncratic properties of a distinctive lexical item, rather than the basic operations and organization of the grammar. Landau's (2004) featural specification of PRO is a good example. What drives the requisite operations is PRO's feature make-up. And PRO has the features it does because of the control facts attested. Were the control facts different, all that would be required is a different feature make-up for PRO. So if one asks: why does PRO have these features and not others? The answer is: just because. It is a brute fact about the properties of PRO, not the reflections of the operations of the grammar.

Indeed, many (if not all) of the properties of the "lexical" item PRO cannot even be identified independently of the grammar. PRO needs a local, c-commanding, syntactic antecedent and can only be licensed within (tense- or ϕ-) defective domains. How are these requirements to be stated in purely "lexical" terms? How can they be expressed except by adverting to grammars, their structures, and their basic operations and principles? They cannot be. PRO's requirements are *grammatical* licensing requirements. Postulating PRO makes no sense except in a grammatical context. Its requirements are entirely grammar-internal. Even describing what they are requires reference to principles and operations of the grammar. Consequently, the analysis of PRO as a lexical element is subject to the minimalist antipathy towards constructionism inherited from GB and so renders PRO a suspect element, given minimalist standards. In the end, postulating lexical elements such as PRO to account for the attested properties of control cannot yield explanations of these properties (descriptions yes, explanations no), for a lexical item such as *PRO* codes as part of its content the very properties that are supposed to be explained. This is the (very high) cost of treating PRO as a lexical item.

5   Conclusion

The MTC is unique in unifying PRO's distribution and antecedent selection under a single mechanism. Precisely the same theory that accounts for where OC PRO can appear determines which of the potential DP antecedents controls it. OC PRO is a link in a well-formed A-chain. The head of the chain is PRO's antecedent. That is the theory and it fits the facts, to a very good first approximation. Thus, among the alternatives on offer at present, only the MTC has the capacity to move beyond description to explanation. The reason is that only the MTC evades constructionism and tries to derive the properties of control structures from general principles of grammar rather than from the special licensing conditions of a peculiar lexical item. These theoretical ambitions are thwarted if one assumes that PRO is a primitive lexical item. In this constructionist view, its special licensing requirements are simply lexical quirks.

As discussed above, there is also a very close conceptual connection between the Minimalist Program and the MTC. The elimination of D-Structure, which is one of the central tenets of the Minimalist Program, is also a necessary and sufficient condition for the MTC to be viable:

(54) MTC ↔ no D-Structure

This picture sharply contrasts with what is found with PRO-based approaches to control within minimalism. They do not rely on any distinctive minimalist assumptions and thus, though they might be compatible with the Minimalist Program, their theoretical apparatus (though not the technology used to express control dependencies) is largely independent of it. Moreover, their constructionist bias is quite at odds with the explanatory ideals of the Minimalist Program.

That said, one should not conclude that because the MTC fits well with the Minimalist Program that the MTC is correct. However, it does suggest that those with minimalist aspirations should smile on the MTC and that the burden of proof must be with those that reject it. Furthermore, if the fit between the Minimalist Program and the MTC is as tight as we have suggested, then the evidentiary bar relevant to rejecting the MTC should be quite high. To put things differently, *if minimalism is on the right track*, then some version of the MTC must be correct: that is, from a minimalist perspective, the MTC is everything it's quacked up to be!

Notes

1 We would like to thank the editors of this volume, and especially Yosuke Sato, for comments and suggestions on an earlier version of this paper. We would also like to acknowledge the support received from CNPq (grant 309036/2011–9; second author).
2 Owing to space limitations, we will examine only syntax-centered approaches to control. For detailed criticism of semantic-based accounts see, in particular, Boeckx *et al.* (2010: Chap. 7).
3 We use scare quotes (i.e. "PRO") as the MTC denies that OC PRO exists. Thus, the usage here is purely descriptive.
4 This is a subset of the relevant properties of OC. A fuller description is found in Boeckx *et al.* (2010: Chap 3). We ignore other properties here for reasons of space.
5 For relevant data and discussion, see Ferreira (2000; 2009), Rodrigues (2002; 2004), Nunes (2008; 2010), and Petersen (2011; 2013).
6 See Ferreira (2000; 2009), Martins and Nunes (2005; 2010), and Nunes (2008; 2010).
7 Please note how this statement is worded. It does *not* identify raising and control. It simply indicates that whatever operations underlie raising *qua* A-movement are also operative in OC configurations.
8 The Duck Principle in fact invites us to go further and reanalyze anaphoric binding as species of movement, given that Principle A enforces virtually the same conditions on the relation between antecedent and anaphor that OC does. For reasons of space we will not be able to explore this

issue here. For specific proposals and relevant discussion, see, for example, Lidz and Idsardi (1997), Hornstein (2001), Zwart (2002), and Drummond *et al.* (2011).

9 See, e.g., Ferreira (2000; 2009), Rodrigues (2004), and Nunes (2008).

10 For extensive discussion of the exceptional cases in (8), (10), and (11) and their analyses within the MTC, see Boeckx *et al.* (2010: sections 4.4, 5.5, and 5.6.2 and references therein).

11 See Boeckx *et al.* (2010: sec. 2.5.2) for detailed discussion.

12 There are non-syntactic ways of implementing the commitative analysis. A recent interesting proposal by Pearson (2012) provides a purely semantic version of the analysis, reducing partial control to a temporal containment principle (rather than modality, as in Rodrigues). The paper has three important virtues: (i) it restricts partial control to embedded clauses in a principled way by making it a by-product of a certain kind of anaphoric tense dependency; (ii) (in Pearson's words) "it is compatible with any mechanism whereby PRO inherits φ-features from the controller" (under the MTC this is so as PRO is a trace/copy of the controller); and (iii) it immediately accounts for why partial control PRO cannot license plural anaphors, as does any commitative analysis.

13 That mood properties may interact with control is clearly seen in Japanese, which has three mood particles associated with obligatory control: the "intentive" marker *-(y)oo* with subject control, the "imperative" marker *-e/-ro* with object control, and the "exhortative" marker *-(y)oo* with split control. See Fujii (2006; 2010) for detailed discussion and analysis.

14 See, e.g., Lightfoot (1976).

15 See, e.g., Jaeggli (1980).

16 Recall that in GB must sit in an ungoverned position and Case assignment must take place under government (see Chomsky (1981)); hence, PRO is bound to be Caseless.

17 See Boeckx (2000) on this point.

18 See Boeckx *et al.* (2010: sections 2.5.1 and 5.4).

19 It is worth noting that this parallel between PRO and A-traces and the contrast between both and A′-traces is not tied to how sandhi effects are to be properly analyzed. What is relevant is that *whatever* the etiology, A-traces and PRO are treated similarly and that both are distinguished from A′-traces. For another approach to these "contraction" effects, see Anderson (2005: 72ff).

20 There are several other properties that both complement control and adjunct control display. For fuller discussion, see Boeckx *et al.* (2010: section 4.5.1).

21 See Rodrigues (2004).

22 See also Rodrigues and Hornstein (2013).

23 Or E-merge/I-merge, both applications of the single merge operation.

24 The difference between copies and occurrences is immaterial for present purposes (see Larson and Hornstein 2012 for relevant discussion). For concreteness, we will frame the following discussion in terms of copies, which will be annotated by superscripted indices. We could recast the discussion in terms of E/I-merge but we leave this translation as an exercise for the fastidious.

25 The theoretical option of sideward movement as a licit application of Move/I-Merge was first mooted in Bobaljik (1995), Nunes (1995), Bobaljik and Brown (1997), and Uriagereka (1998). For developments, applications, and detailed discussion on how overgeneration is prevented, see, e.g., Nunes (2001; 2004; 2012), Hornstein (2001), Hornstein and Nunes (2002), and Drummond (2009).

26 As Chomsky is wont to say concerning E/I merge, *preventing* the option of sideward movement requires extra stipulations and hence, significant empirical motivation.

27 Sideward movement is similarly compatible with an E/I-merge account, which dispenses with a Copy operation. Further, this view of things comes with a plausible cost accounting for why sideward movement is less preferred than upward movement and E-merge. Here, however, is not the place to elaborate on these, no doubt, cryptic comments.

28 See Hornstein (1999; 2001) and Boeckx *et al.* (2010).

29 For relevant discussion, see, e.g., Nunes and Uriagereka (2000), Hornstein (2001), Nunes (2001; 2004), and Hornstein and Nunes (2002).

30 The result is actually a bit more robust than this. There are various ways of ensuring preference of merger over movement in these contexts. Under Nunes's (1995; 2001; 2004) system, for instance, the structure underlying (36) that could result in object control is independently excluded because it cannot be linearized, as the two copies of *Mary* do not form a chain and, accordingly, are not subject to deletion under Chain Reduction. For refinements and further discussion, see Nunes (2012: section 5).

31 Say, for instance, Nunes's (1995; 2004) Chain Reduction operation, which is triggered by linearization considerations.

32 See, e.g., Nunes (1999; 2004; 2011), Bošković and Nunes (2007), the collection of papers in Corver and Nunes (2007), and references therein.

33 See Haddad and Potsdam (2013) for additional data, references, and more detailed discussion.

34 See Nunes (1999; 2004) for an account of this restriction.

35 Boeckx *et al.* (2008) for details and further discussion.

36 One more expectation: just as there are cases of backward control and copy control, we should expect to find cases of backward raising and copy raising. As Polinsky and Potsdam (2006; 2012) discuss in detail, this expectation is also met. See their papers for data, arguments, and references.

37 Another option would be to allow the numeration to contain two copies of the controlled expression with some marked dependency between them. The problem then would be to explain why these do not induce a Principle C effect analogous to the ones found in (i):

(i)   a. *John$_i$ managed for John$_i$ to win.
     b. *John$_i$ wants John$_i$ to win.

38 Backward control and copy control are also problematic for Manzini and Roussou's (2000) movement approach, according to which the "controller" is merged where it appears and attracts features of the controlled predicate.

39 We have analyzed NOC PRO as essentially a phonetically null pronoun. Space limitations bar further elaboration. See Boeckx *et al.* (2010: Chap 6) for discussion.

40 Recall that there is no theory of antecedent selection for NOC PRO as it does not require an antecedent.

41 Landau (2004: 842) in fact describes his R-assignment rule as an "honest stipulation" that plays the role of Case in previous models.

42 If *be* in (53a) assigns Case to *someone* (see, e.g., Belletti (1988) and Lasnik (1995)), the comparison with (53b) becomes irrelevant, for in (53b) *someone* could not have undergone A-movement if it had its Case deactivated by *be*. Moreover, if *someone* is Case-licensed by *be* in (53a), *John* can have its Case valued as accusative by the matrix verb while it is in the embedded subject position. But if that happens, *John* cannot undergo any further A-movement, regardless of whether or not the target is a θ-position.

43 See Boeckx *et al.* (2010: sections 2.3 and 2.4) for further discussion.

Further reading

Boeckx, Cedric, Norbert Hornstein, and Jairo Nunes. 2010. *Control as Movement*. Cambridge: Cambridge University Press.

Drummond, Alex, Norbert Hornstein, and Dave Kush. 2011. Minimalist Construal: Two Approaches to A and B. In *The Oxford Handbook of Linguistic Minimalism*, ed. C. Boeckx, 396–426. Oxford: Oxford University Press.

Hornstein, Norbert. 2001. *Move! A Minimalist Theory of Construal*. Oxford: Blackwell.

Hornstein, Norbert, and Maria Polinsky (eds). 2010. *Movement Theory of Control*. Amsterdam/Philadelphia: John Benjamins.

Landau, Idan. 2004. The Scale of Finiteness and the Calculus of Control. *Natural Language and Linguistic Theory* 22:811–877.

References

Alexiadou, Artemis, Elena Anagnostopoulou, Gianina Iordachioiaia, and Mihaela Marchis. 2010. No objection to backward control. In *Movement Theory of Control*, ed. Norbert Hornstein and Maria Polinsky, 89–117. Amsterdam/Philadelphia: John Benjamins.

Anderson, Stephen. 2005. *Aspects of the Theory of Clitics*. Oxford: Oxford University Press.

Belletti, Adriana. 1988. The Case of Unaccusatives. *Linguistic Inquiry* 19:1–34.

Bobaljik, Jonathan. 1995. Morphosyntax: The Syntax of Verbal Inflection. Doctoral dissertation, MIT.

Bobaljik, Jonathan, and Samuel Brown. 1997. Inter-arboreal Operations: Head-movement and the Extension Requirement. *Linguistic Inquiry* 28:345–356.

Boeckx, Cedric. 2000. A Note on Contraction. *Linguistic Inquiry* 31:357–366.

Boeckx, Cedric, Norbert Hornstein, and Jairo Nunes. 2008. Copy-reflexive and Copy-control Constructions: A Movement Analysis. *Linguistic Variation Yearbook* 8:61–99.

Boeckx, Cedric, Norbert Hornstein, and Jairo Nunes. 2010. *Control as Movement*. Cambridge: Cambridge University Press.

Bošković, Željko. 2002. On Multiple *Wh*-Fronting. *Linguistic Inquiry* 33:351–383.

Bošković, Željko, and Jairo Nunes. 2007. The Copy Theory of Movement: A View from PF. In *The Copy Theory of Movement*, ed. N. Corver and J. Nunes, 13–74. Amsterdam/Philadelphia: John Benjamins.

Castillo, Juan Carlos, John Drury, and Kleanthes Grohmann. 1999. Merge over Move and the Extended Projection Principle. *University of Maryland Working Papers in Linguistics* 8:63–103.

Chomsky, Noam. 1977. On *Wh*-movement. In *Formal Syntax*, ed. P.W. Culicover, T. Wasow, and A. Akmajian, 71–132. New York: Academic Press.

Chomsky, Noam. 1981. *Lectures on Government and Binding*. Dordrecht: Foris.

Chomsky, Noam. 1993. A Minimalist Program for Linguistic Theory. In *The View from Building 20: Essays in Linguistics in Honor of Sylvain Bromberger*, ed. Kenneth Hale and Samuel Jay Keyser, 1–52. Cambridge, MA: MIT Press.

Chomsky, Noam. 1995. *The Minimalist Program*. Cambridge, MA: MIT Press.

Chomsky, Noam. 2000. Minimalist Inquiries: The Framework. In *Step by Step: Essays on Minimalist Syntax in Honor of Howard Lasnik*, ed. Roger Martin, David Michaels, and Juan Uriagereka, 89–155. Cambridge, MA: MIT Press.

Chomsky, Noam. 2001. Derivation by Phase. In *Ken Hale: A Life in Language*, ed. Michael Kenstowicz, 1–52. Cambridge, MA: MIT Press.

Chomsky, Noam 2004. Beyond Explanatory Adequacy, in *Structures and Beyond*, ed. A. Belletti, 104–131. Oxford: Oxford University Press.

Chomsky, Noam, and Howard Lasnik. 1993. The Theory of Principles and Parameters. In *Syntax: An International Handbook of Contemporary Research*, ed. by Joachim Jacobs, Arnim von Stechow, Wolfgang Sternefeld, and Theo Vennemann, 506–569. Berlin/New York: Walter de Gruyter.

Corver, Norbert and Jairo Nunes (eds). 2007. *The Copy Theory of Movement*. Amsterdam: John Benjamins.

Drummond, Alex. 2009. How Constrained is Sideward Movement? General's Paper, University of Maryland, College Park.

Drummond, Alex, Norbert Hornstein, and Dave Kush. 2011. Minimalist Construal: Two Approaches to A and B. In *The Oxford Handbook of Linguistic Minimalism*, ed. C. Boeckx, 396–426. Oxford: Oxford University Press.

Epstein, Samuel D., and T. Daniel Seely. 2006. *Derivations in Minimalism*. Cambridge: Cambridge University Press.

Ferreira, Marcelo. 2000. Argumentos Nulos em Português Brasileiro. MA thesis, Universidade Estadual de Campinas.

Ferreira, Marcelo. 2009. Null Subjects and Finite Control in Brazilian Portuguese. In *Minimalist Essays on Brazilian Portuguese Syntax*, ed. Jairo Nunes, 17–49. Amsterdam/Philadephia: John Benjamins.

Fujii, Tomohiro. 2006. Some Theoretical Issues in Japanese Control. Doctoral dissertation, University of Maryland, College Park.

Fujii, Tomohiro. 2010. Split Control and the Principle of Minimal Distance. In *Movement Theory of Control*, ed. Norbert Hornstein and Maria Polinsky, 211–244. Amsterdam/Philadelphia: John Benjamins.

Haddad, Youssef A., and Eric Potsdam. 2013. Linearizing the Control Relation: A Typology. In *Principles of Linearization*, ed. Theresa Biberauer and Ian Roberts, 235–288. Berlin: Mouton de Gruyter.

Hornstein, Norbert. 1999. Movement and Control. *Linguistic Inquiry* 30:69–96.

Hornstein, Norbert. 2001. *Move! A Minimalist Theory of Construal*. Oxford: Blackwell.

Hornstein, Norbert, and Jairo Nunes. 2002. On Asymmetries between Parasitic Gap and Across-the-board Constructions. *Syntax* 5:26–54.

Jaeggli, Osvaldo. 1980. Remarks on *To*-contraction. *Linguistic Inquiry* 11:239–245.

Landau, Idan. 2000. *Elements of Control. Structure and Meaning in Infinitival Constructions*. Dordrecht: Kluwer.

Landau, Idan. 2004. The Scale of Finiteness and the Calculus of Control. *Natural Language and Linguistic Theory* 22:811–877.

Larson, Bradley and Norbert Hornstein. 2012. Copies and Occurrences. Lingbuzz. http://ling.auf. net/lingbuzz/001484.

Lasnik, Howard. 1995. Case and Expletives Revisited. *Linguistic Inquiry* 26:615–633.

Lee, Felicia. 2003. Anaphoric R-expressions as Bound Variables. *Syntax* 6:84–114.

Lidz, Jeff, and William Idsardi. 1997. Chains and Phono-logical Form. *UPenn Working Papers in Linguistics* 8:109–125.

Lightfoot, David. 1976. Trace Theory and Twice-moved NPs. *Linguistic Inquiry* 7:559–582.

McDaniel, Dana. 1986. Conditions on wh-chains. Doctoral dissertation, CUNY.

Manzini, Maria Rita, and Anna Roussou. 2000. A Minimalist Theory of A-movement and Control. *Lingua* 110:409–447.

Martin, Roger. 2001. Null Case and the Distribution of PRO. *Linguistic Inquiry* 32:141–166.

Martins, Ana Maria, and Jairo Nunes. 2005. Raising Issues in Brazilian and European Portuguese. *Journal of Portuguese Linguistics* 4:53–77.

Martins, Ana Maria, and Jairo Nunes. 2010. Apparent Hyper-raising in Brazilian Portuguese: Agreement with Topics across a Finite CP. In *The Complementiser Phase: Subjects and Operators*, ed. Phoevos E. Panagiotidis, 142–163. Oxford: Oxford University Press.

Nunes, Jairo. 1995. The Copy Theory of Movement and Linearization of Chains in the Minimalist Program. Doctoral dissertation, University of Maryland at College Park.

Nunes, Jairo 1999. Linearization of Chains and Phonetic Realization of Chain Links. In *Working Minimalism*, ed. S.D. Epstein and N. Hornstein, 217–249. Cambridge, MA: MIT Press.

Nunes, Jairo. 2001. Sideward Movement. *Linguistic Inquiry* 31:303–344.

Nunes, Jairo. 2004. *Linearization of Chains and Sideward Movement*. Cambridge, MA: MIT Press.

Nunes, Jairo. 2008. Inherent Case as a Licensing Condition for A-movement: The Case of Hyper-raising Constructions in Brazilian Portuguese. *Journal of Portuguese Linguistics* 7:83–108.

Nunes, Jairo. 2010. Relativizing Minimality for A-movement: ϕ- and θ-relations. *Probus* 22:1–25.

Nunes, Jairo. 2011. The Copy Theory. In *The Oxford Handbook of Linguistic Minimalism*, ed. Cedric Boeckx, 143–172. Oxford: Oxford University Press.

Nunes, Jairo. 2012. Sideward Movement: Triggers, Timing, and Outputs. In *Ways of Structure Building*, ed. M. Uribe-Etxebarria and V. Valmala, 114–142. Oxford: Oxford University Press.

Nunes, Jairo, and Juan Uriagereka. 2000. Cyclicity and Extraction Domains. *Syntax* 3:20–43.

Pearson, Hazel. 2012. A Semantic Theory of Partial Control. Presented at NELS 43, CUNY, New York.

Petersen, Maria Carolina. 2011. O licenciamento do sujeito nulo em orações subjuntivas no português brasileiro. M.A. thesis, Universidade de São Paulo, São Paulo.

Polinsky, Maria, and Eric Potsdam. 2006. Expanding the Scope of Control and Raising. *Syntax* 9:171–192.

Polinsky, Maria, and Eric Potsdam. 2012. Backward Raising. *Syntax* 15:75–108.

Rodrigues, Cliene. 2002. Morphology and Null Subjects in Brazilian Portuguese. In *Syntactic Effects of Morphological Change*, ed. D. Lightfoot, 160–178. Oxford: Oxford University Press.

Rodrigues, Cilene. 2004. Impoverished Morphology and A-movement out of Case Domains. Doctoral dissertation, University of Maryland at College Park.

Rodrigues, Cilene. 2007. Agreement and Flotation in Partial and Inverse Partial Control Configurations. In *New Horizons in the Analysis of Control and Raising*, ed. W.D. Davis and S. Dubinsky, 213–229. Dordrecht: Springer.

Rodrigues, Cilene, and Norbert Hornstein. 2013. Epicene Agreement and Inflected Infinitives when the Data is "Under Control": A reply to Modesto (2010). *Syntax* 16(3):292–309.

Rosenbaum, P.S. 1970. A Principle Governing Deletion in English Sentential Complementation. In *Readings in English Transformational Grammar*, ed. R.A. Jacobs and P.S. Rosenbaum, 20–29. Waltham, MA: Ginn and Company.

Uriagereka, Juan. 1998. *Rhyme and Reason: An Introduction to Minimalist Syntax*. Cambridge, MA: MIT Press.

Zwart, C. Jan-Wouter. 2002. Issues Relating to a Derivational Theory of Binding. In *Derivation and Explanation in the Minimalist Program*, ed. S.D. Epstein and T.D. Seely, 269–304. Oxford: Blackwell.

13

Scrambling

Yosuke Sato and Nobu Goto

1   Introduction

The term *scrambling* was coined in the 1960s by Ross (1967), who originally defined it as a truly stylistic rule applying freely in the grammar. This phenomenon is closely correlated with the fundamental issue of "basic word order" in scrambling languages. Hale (1980) was the earliest attempt to explore the availability of this operation within a larger context of the configurational parameter. He claimed that scrambling is available only in non-configurational languages with flat phrase structures, such as Japanese, because there is no structural difference among grammatical functions (such as subjects and objects). Ross's intuition has also been variously reflected in subsequent work in the literature on scrambling in languages such as Japanese (Saito 1985; 1989; Kuroda 1988; Fukui 1986): these claim that this phenomenon is a semantically vacuous movement operation in the syntax which is undone at the level of semantic interpretation. This time-honored conception of scrambling fit well with the Move-α format of the so-called Government-Binding Theory within the Generative Framework (Chomsky 1981; 1986) where any syntactic constituent can move anywhere as long as the resulting outputs meet independently motivated constraints. However, this traditional description of scrambling as a truly optional movement operation has become a central issue in the Minimalist Program (MP) (Chomsky 1995). One of the most important precepts in minimalism is that movement occurs only as Last Resort, driven by morphosyntactic factors such as Case or *wh*-features. This framework, therefore, has effectively eliminated the very concept of optional movement, of which scrambling has hitherto been considered an exemplary case.

There are two strands of research that attempt to accommodate the idea of optional movement with the stringent minimalist guidelines. One (Fukui 1993; Saito and Fukui 1998) has proposed a parametric theory of comparative syntax where optional movement, such as scrambling, can be defined as cost-less operations. The other (Bošković and Takahashi 1998; Miyagawa 1997; 2001) has proposed a new analysis of scrambling as an obligatory syntactic movement driven by independently motivated features (e.g., θ-features, the Extended Projection Principle/EPP-feature, topic, and focus) in conformity with the minimalist guidelines.

While the characterization of scrambling as an instance of Move-α has received compelling support in the 1980s, the central debate has shifted to uncovering the exact syntactic properties of scrambling. In particular, investigations of various scrambling languages such as Japanese (Saito 1992; Tada 1993), Persian (Karimi 1999), and Hindi (Mahajan 1990) have addressed the question of whether scrambling patterns with (1) A-movement, (2) A$'$-movement, (3) both A and A$'$-movement, or actually (4) none of the above.

The purpose of this chapter is to provide a review of the literature on scrambling with particular reference to four central issues raised by this phenomenon: (1) the relation between scrambling and free word order; (2) the exact defining characteristic of scrambling; (3) potential triggers for scrambling; and (4) syntactic properties of scrambling. In addition to these issues, this chapter also discusses two long-standing empirical puzzles relating to Japanese scrambling which have steadfastly resisted a satisfactory explanation: the Proper Binding Condition effect and the difference in the possibility of scrambling out of finite vs. non-finite clauses.

Our discussion of these issues will be based on data from Japanese since this language has been the most extensively studied with respect to this phenomenon, though references to the major works on other scrambling languages such as Hindi, Persian, and German will be made where deemed necessary.

2   Central issues relating to scrambling

There are four central issues relating to scrambling. They are summarized in [a]–[d]:

[a]   What is the basic word order in scrambling languages?
[b]   What is the nature of scrambling as syntactic movement?
[c]   What triggers scrambling?
[d]   What are syntactic properties of scrambling?

In this section we discuss these questions, introducing major representative works in the literature which address them specifically.

2.1   What is the basic word order in scrambling languages?

It is well known that word order is relatively free in languages with scrambling, such as Japanese, Korean, German, Hindi, and Persian. Thus, for a simple transitive sentence in Japanese, for example, both SOV and OSV orders are acceptable, as in (1).[1]

(1)   a.   John-ga   hon-o   katta.
            John-NOM   book-ACC   bought
            'John bought a book.'
      b.   Hon-o   John-ga   katta.
            book-ACC   John-NOM   bought
            'John bought a book.'

This free word order phenomenon was first addressed by Hale (1980): Hale categorized languages into two groups – configurational vs. non-configurational languages – and argued that non-configurational languages are defined by a non-rigid flat phrase structure without VPs. Since there is no VP constituent in this type of language, there is no structural difference between subjects and objects. This flat structure, in turn, yields the free word order phenomenon in languages such as Japanese.

Subsequent work (Saito 1985; Hoji 1985; Whitman 1986), however, has amassed considerable evidence in favor of the configurationality of Japanese phrase structure, contra Hale. Thus, Saito (1985) argued that the OSV order is derived from the basic SOV order by a movement operation called *scrambling*, as shown in (2).

(2)   Saito's (1985) movement analysis

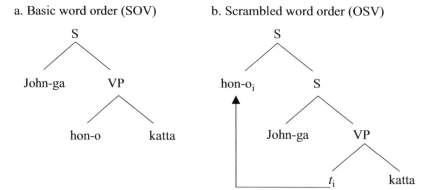

   a. Basic word order (SOV)   b. Scrambled word order (OSV)

Saito provided three arguments for this analysis. The underlying logic behind his arguments is that various structural properties of the OSV order in Japanese (e.g., pronominal coreference, crossover effects, and floating quantifiers) are exactly what we would predict if a movement operation applies to the SOV order to yield the OSV order. Let us first consider English examples in (3).

(3)   a.   *He$_i$ has not read the letter that Mary sent to John$_i$.
  b.   [$_{DP}$ The letter that Mary sent to John$_i$]$_j$, he$_i$ has not read t_j.

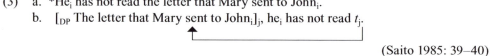

(Saito 1985: 39–40)

(3a) shows that pronominal coreference cannot obtain when the pronoun *he* in the subject position precedes its antecedent *John* within the direct object. (3b), on the other hand, shows that this coreference is possible when the object NP is fronted to the sentence-initial position. Note that such a phenomenon is also found in Japanese:

(4)   a.   *Kare$_i$-ga [$_{NP}$ Mary-ga John$_i$-ni okutta tegami]-o mada yondeinai.
    he-NOM Mary-NOM John-DAT sent letter-ACC yet have.not.read
   '*He$_i$ has not read the letter which Mary had sent to John$_i$.'
  b.   [$_{NP}$ Mary-ga John$_i$-ni okutta tegami]-o kare$_i$-ga mada yondeinai.
    Mary-NOM John-DAT sent letter-ACC he-NOM yet have.not.read
   'Lit. The letter which Mary had sent to John$_i$, he$_i$ has not read.'

(Saito 1985: 39–40)

The contrast between (4a) and (4b) can be accounted for in a way parallel to that between (3a) and (3b) in English if (4b) is derived from (4a) by scrambling.

A similar argument for the movement analysis can be made on the basis of (5)–(6):

(5) a.   John$_i$'s mother loves him$_i$.
     b. ??/?*John$_i$'s mother, he$_i$ loves t_i.

(Saito 1985: 48)

(6) a. John$_i$-no   hahaoya-ga   kare$_i$-o   aisiteiru.
         John-GEN   mother-NOM   he-ACC   love
         'John's mother loves him.'
     b. ?*John$_i$-no   hahaoya-o   kare$_i$-ga   aisiteiru
         John-GEN   mother-ACC   he-NOM   love
         'Lit. John's mother, he loves.'

(Saito 1985: 48)

(5a) shows that pronominal coreference is allowed when the pronoun *him* in the object position is preceded by its antecedent *John*. (5b), however, shows that this reading is impossible when the object NP is fronted to the sentence-initial position. This phenomenon is an example of crossover effect (see §2.4). Note that this effect also obtains in Japanese, as shown in (6b). Again, the contrast between (6a) and (6b) in Japanese falls out straightforwardly from the movement analysis.

The third argument concerns quantifier floating. Consider (7)–(8):

(7) a. San-nin-no   gakusei-ga   sake-o   nonde iru.
         three-CL-GEN   student-NOM   sake-ACC   drinking
         'Three students are drinking sake.'
     b. Gakusei-ga   san-nin   sake-o   nonde iru.
         student-NOM   three-CL   sake-ACC   drinking
         'Three students are drinking sake.'

(Saito 1985: 51)

(8) *Gakusei-ga   sake-o   san-nin   nonde iru.
     student-NOM   sake-ACC   three-CL   drinking
     'Three students are drinking sake.'

(Saito 1985: 52)

(9) Sake-o   John-ga   san-bon   motte kita.
     sake-ACC   John-NOM   three-CL   with-came
     'John came with three bottles of sake.'

(Saito 1985: 52)

In (7b), the quantifier *san-nin* 'three-CL' is floated out of the host NP *gakusei-ga* 'student-NOM' which it is semantically associated with. This quantifier floating, however, comes with a syntactic restriction. Specifically, a floating quantifier cannot be related to its host when another NP intervenes between them, as shown in (8). Interestingly enough, however, this intervention effect is lifted in the OSV order. This point is shown in (9). The lack of the intervention effect is exactly what we predict under the movement analysis under the assumption that the trace of the moved object serves as the appropriate host for the floating quantifier in the manner shown in (10).

(10) [$_S$ sake-o$_i$ [$_S$ John-ga [$_{VP}$ t_i san-bon motte kita]]]

Given the compelling evidence presented above, it has been standard since Saito's (1985) work to assume that Japanese employs scrambling as a syntactic movement operation to yield non-canonical orders such as OSVs for transitive clauses. One of the current major debates in Japanese scrambling is instead concerned with whether there is any "basic word order" with ditransitive constructions which involve two internal arguments – Theme and Goal arguments – as illustrated in (11a–b):

(11) a. John-ga   Mary-ni   hon-o   ageta.   (S-IO-DO-V)
        John-NOM   Mary-DAT   book-ACC   gave
        'John gave a book to Mary.'
   b. John-ga   hon-o   Mary-ni   ageta.   (S-DO-IO-V)
        John-NOM   book-ACC   Mary-DAT   gave
        'John gave a book to Mary.'

Hoji (1985) proposes that the IO–DO order in (11a) is the canonical word order, with the DO–IO order in (11b) being derived by movement, as shown in (12). Miyagawa (1997), on the other hand, argues that both orders in (11a–b) are base-generated in syntax without scrambling, as shown in (13).

(12) Hoji's (1985) movement analysis

      a. Basic word-order (IO–DO)   b. Scrambled word-order (DO–IO)

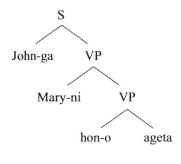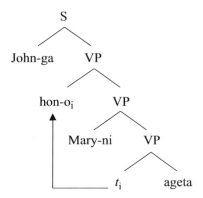

(13) Miyagawa's (1997) non-movement analysis

      a. Basic word-order I (IO–DO)   b. Basic word-order II (DO–IO)

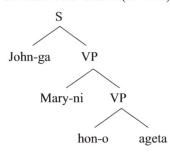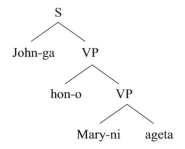

Both analyses are motivated on the basis of scope interpretation (Kuroda 1970; Kuno 1973). To set the stage, consider scope interpretation in a transitive sentence, as in (14).

(14) a. Daremo-ga   dareka-o   aisiteiru.
       Everyone-NOM   someone-ACC   love
       'Everyone loves someone.'   (*∃>∀ ; ∀>∃)
    b. Dareka-o   daremo-ga   aisiteiru.
       someone-ACC   everyone-NOM   love
       'Lit. Someone, everyone loves.'   (∃>∀;∀>∃)

                                                (Hoji 1985: 64)

Kuroda (1970) was the first to observe that Japanese is a rigid scope language in that sur-face order closely mirrors scope interpretation. Thus, in (14a), the only interpretation avail-able is one where the subject takes scope over the object. In (14b), on the other hand, the sentence-initial phrase can take either wide or narrow scope with respect to the subject. The contrast in (14a–b) thus points to a descriptive generalization that scope ambiguity in Japanese obtains only when syntactic movement has taken place.
    With this generalization in mind, consider example (15).

(15) a. Bill-ga   daremo-ni   [John   ka   Mary]-o   syookaisita.
       Bill-NOM   everyone-DAT   John   or   Mary-ACC   introduced
       'Bill introduced John or Mary to everyone.'
    b. Bill-ga   [John   ka   Mary]-o   daremo-ni   syookaisita
       Bill-NOM   John   or   Mary-ACC   everyone-DAT   introduced
       'Bill introduced John or Mary to everyone.'

                                                (Hoji 1985: 66)

Hoji reports that, while the IO-DO order in (15a) has only one interpretation, shown in (16a), the DO-IO order in (15b) allows both interpretations shown in (16a–b).

(16) a. ∀x, x = a person, ∃y, y {John, Mary}, x introduced y
    b. ∃y, y {John, Mary}, ∀x, x = a person, x introduced y.

                                    (adopted from Hoji 1985: 67)

    Takano (1998) also argues for a movement-based analysis of the ditransitive construc-tion in Japanese whereby the DO-IO order is derived from the basic IO-DO order via short scrambling of the DO across the IO. His central argument for this analysis concerns pronominal binding effects, illustrated in (17).

(17) a. John-ga [PP subete-no gakusei-ni] [NP soitu-no   sensei-o]   syookaisita.
       John-NOM   all-GEN   student-DAT   that guy-GEN   teacher-ACC   introduced
       'John introduced his teacher to every student.'
    b. *John-ga [PP soitu-no   sensei-ni] [NP subete-no gakusei-o]   syookaisita.
       John-NOM   that guy-GEN   teacher-ACC   all-GEN   student-ACC   introduced
       'John introduced every student to his teacher.'
    c. John-ga [NP subete-no gakusei-o] [PP soitu-no   sensei-ni]   syookaisita.
       John-NOM   all-GEN   student-DAT   that guy-GEN   teacher-DAT   introduced
       'John introduced every student to his teacher.'

According to Takano, the order in (17a) represents the basic word order in ditransitive constructions. (17b) shows that there is no point in the derivation where the DO is structurally higher than the IO in the IO–DO order. The acceptability of (17c) follows if the DO undergoes local scrambling within the VP over the IO to yield the DO–IO order (see §2.4 for a discussion on syntactic properties of VP-internal scrambling).

On the other hand, Miyagawa (1997) argues for the base-generation analysis of ditransitive constructions based on the following scope fact.

(18) a. Hanako-ga   dareka-o   daremo-ni   syookaisita.
         Hanako-NOM   someone-ACC   everyone-DAT   introduced
         'Hanako introduced someone to everyone.'   (∃>∀;∀>∃)
     b. Hanako-ga   dareka-ni   daremo-o   syookaisita.
         Hanako-NOM   someone-DAT   everyone-ACC   introduced
         'Hanako introduced everyone to someone.'   (∃>∀;(?)∀>∃)

                                                           (Miyagawa 1997: 12)

Miyagawa observes that scope ambiguity arises both in the DO–IO order and in the IO–DO order. He takes this fact as showing that both orders can be base-generated in Japanese. Similarly, Matsuoka (2003) argues that Japanese allows for both orders as underlying orders, but provides considerable evidence showing that which order is canonical crucially depends on the predicate involved; *watasu*-type "to pass" verbs have the base DO–IO order, whereas *miseru*-type "to show" verbs have the base IO–DO order.

Some recent studies address the issue of basic word order in ditransitive sentences from a new perspective of sentence processing (Koizumi and Tamaoka 2004) and L1 language acquisition (Sugisaki and Isobe 2001). Such studies report experimental results which are more compatible with the movement approach rather than with the base-generation approach. However, the scope data presented above is notoriously intricate and subject to considerable inter-speaker variation (Hoji 2003; Ueyama 1998).

2.2 What is the nature of scrambling as syntactic movement?

If scrambling is indeed an instance of movement, as argued for by Hoji (1985) and Saito (1985), the next question is what the nature of this movement operation is.

Saito (1989) hypothesizes that scrambling in Japanese is a semantically vacuous movement which undergoes radical reconstruction at LF. This hypothesis is supported by a certain behavior of scrambled phrases in *wh*-questions. Consider example (19):

(19) a. John-ga   [dare-ga   sono   hon-o   katta]   ka]   siritagatteiru].
         John-NOM   who-NOM   DEM   book-ACC   bought   Q   want.to.know
         'John wants to know who bought that book?'
     b. *Dare-ga   [John-ga   sono   hon-o   katta]   ka]   siritagatteiru].
         who-NOM   John-NOM   DEM   book-ACC   bought   Q   want.to.know
         'Who wants to know John bought that book?'

                                                           (Saito and Fukui 1998: 441)

(19a–b) show that *wh*-phrases in Japanese must be contained within an interrogative clause headed by the Q-marker *ka*. (19a) is grammatical because *dare-ga* 'who-NOM' is within the Q-marked clause; (19b) is ungrammatical because the *wh*-phrase is in a position outside the Q-marked interrogative clause. With this observation in mind, let us consider (20):

(20) a. John-ga [Mary-ga   dono hon-o   yonda   ka]   siritagatteiru.
       John-NOM Mary-NOM which book-ACC read   Q   want-to-know
       'John wants to know which book Mary read.'
   b. ?Dono hon-o$_i$ John-ga   [Mary-ga t_i yonda   ka]   siritagatteiru.
       which book-ACC John-NOM Mary-NOM   read   Q   want-to-know
       'Which book does John want to know Mary read?'

(Saito and Fukui 1998: 441)

Although the *wh*-phrase *dono hon-o* 'which book-ACC' in (20b) is scrambled to a position outside the Q-marked interrogative clause, it does not have the ungrammatical status of (19b). In other words, the *wh*-phrase can take embedded scope even though it is in a position outside the Q-marked interrogative clause. Given examples of this kind, Saito (1989) proposes that long-distance scrambling in Japanese is semantically vacuous. Thus, the scrambled *wh*-phrase in (20b) is literally moved back to its original position when interpretation takes place at LF, as shown in (21).

(21) Saito's (1989) analysis of long-distance scrambling
    ? Dono hon-o$_i$ John-ga   [Mary-ga t_i yonda ka] siritagatteiru.

                                           Scrambling
                                           Radical Reconstruction

This property of scrambling has been called Radical Reconstruction, and has long been taken to be one of the defining properties of Japanese scrambling (see also §2.3).

Takahashi (1993), further considering the interaction between scrambled *wh*-phrases and a Q-marker in Japanese, shows that there are certain cases where what looks like long-distance scrambling of *wh*-phrases counts as *wh*-movement. He supports this possibility from the scope interpretations found in the following examples:

(22) a. John-wa   [Mary-ga nani-o   tabeta   ka]   siritagatteiru   no?
       John-TOP   Mary-NOM what-ACC ate   Q   want.to.know   Q
      i. Does John want to know what Mary ate?
      ii. What does John want to know whether Mary ate?
   b. Nani$_i$-o   John-wa · [Mary-ga t_i tabeta   ka]   siritagatteiru   no?
      what-ACC   John-TOP Mary-NOM   ate   Q   want.to.know   Q
      i. *Does John want to know what Mary ate?
      ii. What does John want to know whether Mary ate?

(Takahashi 1993: 657)

The examples in (22a–b) differ from those in (20a–b) in that the former have a Q-marker *no* in the matrix clause as well as in the embedded clause. (22b) is derived from (22a) by fronting the embedded *wh*-phrase *nani-o* 'what-ACC' to the sentence-initial position. Takahashi observes that the *wh*-phrase in (22a) can have either matrix scope or embedded scope, but the *wh*-phrase in (22b) can have only matrix scope. Takahashi reasons that if radical reconstruction is the defining property of long-distance scrambling in Japanese, then (22b) should be able to have embedded scope, contrary to fact. This observation, therefore, indicates that the movement of a *wh*-phrase to a higher clause headed by the overt Q-marker *no* is *wh*-movement rather than scrambling. Takahashi further supports the *wh*-movement analysis with superiority effects. This effect arises when a *wh*-phrase is moved over another *wh*-phrase, as illustrated by the English examples in (23).

(23) a. Who$_i$ did you persuade t_i to read what?
      b. ?*What$_j$ did you persuade who to read t_j?

The examples in (24) show that superiority effects also exist in Japanese.

(24) a. John-ga   dare-ni [Mary-ga   nani-o   tabeta   to]   itta   no?
          John-NOM who-DAT Mary-NOM   what-ACC   ate   COMP   said   Q
          'Who did John tell that Mary ate what?'
      b. ??Nani$_i$-o John-ga   dare-ni   [Mary-ga t_i tabeta   to]   itta   no?
          what-ACC   John-NOM who-DAT   Mary-NOM   ate   COMP   said   Q
          'Lit. What did John tell who that Mary ate?'

(Takahashi 1993: 664)

In (24b), the *wh*-phrase *nani-o* 'what-ACC' moves to the Q-marked interrogative clause and hence it counts as *wh*-movement under the *wh*-movement analysis. Thus, it is no surprise that (24b) exhibits a superiority effect, just as in (23b).

Miyagawa (1997) suggests a different analysis of scrambling as focus-driven movement. He argues that such movement is necessary to account for the contrast between (25a) and (25b):

(25) a. ??John-ga   isoide   hon-wa   katta.
          John-NOM   quickly   book-TOP bought
          'John quickly bought A BOOK.'
      b. John-ga   hon-wa$_i$ isoide t_i katta.
          John-NOM book-TOP   quickly   bought
          'John quickly bought a BOOK.'

(Miyagawa 1997: 10)

(25a) shows that the contrastive focus-marked phrase *hon-wa* 'book-TOP' cannot be licensed in the VP-internal domain, but once it is moved to a position above the VP, the sentence becomes grammatical, as illustrated in (25b). Miyagawa points out that neither the semantically vacuous movement analysis nor the *wh*-movement analysis can successfully capture this phenomenon. Instead, assuming a focus position between the subject and the VP, Miyagawa concludes that a contrastive focus-marked *wa*-phrase needs to be licensed by focus movement to that position.

In sum, insofar as our current understanding of the identity of scrambling permits, this phenomenon can be defined as either (a) semantically vacuous movement (Saito 1989); (b) *wh*-movement (Takahashi 1993); and/or (c) focus movement (Miyagawa 1997). It may well be that scrambling is simply an umbrella term for all of these processes (see Bošković 2004). We have seen that the structural and interpretive effects of scrambling change radically depending on the presence of discourse markers such as *no* and *wa*, as shown by Takahashi and Miyagawa. Therefore, one fruitful analytical possibility for future research on the exact definition of scrambling would be to investigate it at the discourse-level along the lines of recent work on the left periphery (Rizzi 1997).

2.3 What triggers scrambling?

Once scrambling is identified as a movement operation, the next question is what the trigger is. A related question here is whether this operation is optional or obligatory, as the literature (Fukui 1993) has succinctly put it. The consensus view on this issue until the mid-1990s was that scrambling is an optional movement operation that takes place overtly with no driving force (Fukui 1986; 1993; Hoji 1985; Kuroda 1988; Saito 1985; 1989; 1992; Saito and Fukui 1998; Tada 1993). However, an alternative view emerged around the late 1990s claiming that scrambling is an obligatory movement operation that takes place either overtly or covertly with some driving force within the syntax or information structure (Bošković and Takahashi 1998; Grewendorf and Sabel 1999; Kawamura 2001; Kitahara 1997; 2000; Miyagawa 1997; 2001; Karimi 2005). Therefore, for the advocates of the optional movement analysis, the issues are why scrambling can apply optionally with no driving force and how to rationalize this optionality within the MP. For the advocates of the obligatory movement analysis, on the other hand, the issue is what triggers scrambling. Below, we briefly introduce Fukui (1993) and Bošković and Takahashi (1998) as representative of the two strands of approach.

Fukui (1993) represents an attempt to rationalize the existence of optional movement without any driving force within the Principles-&-Parameters approach and proposes that the cost of a movement operation is determined by the Parameter Value Preservation (PVP) measure, which is defined in (26).

(26) The Parameter Value Preservation (PVP) Measure

> A grammatical operation (Move-α, in particular) that creates a structure that is inconsistent with the value of a given parameter is costly in that language, whereas one that produces a structure consistent with the parameter is costless.
>
> (Fukui 1993: 400)

Fukui assumes that a costly movement operation must apply with some driving force, whereas a costless movement operation can apply optionally with no driving force. As for the measure of "cost", Fukui suggests that the head-parameter determines what he calls the Canonical Precedence Relation (CPR) in a given language and that the CPR is determined on the basis of the precedence of a head and its complement. Thus, the CPRs of a verb (V) and its complements (C) for English and Japanese are as follows (">" means 'precedes'):

(27) a. English: $V^0 > Y^{max}$
      b. Japanese: $Y^{max} > V^0$

(Fukui 1993: 402)

The PVP measure dictates that a leftward movement be costly in English. Thus, *wh*-movement, a leftward movement, must apply obligatorily with some driving force (i.e., the uninterpretable *wh*-feature) in English. On the other hand, the PVP measure requires that a leftward movement be costless in Japanese. It follows, therefore, that scrambling in Japanese can apply optionally with no driving force in Japanese. The PVP measure makes several other correct predictions. For example, although a leftward movement in English is costly and must apply obligatorily with some driving force, rightward movements such as Heavy NP-Shift are costless and hence can apply optionally with no driving force. Likewise, although a leftward movement is costless in Japanese and can apply optionally with no driving force, rightward movements such as right dislocation are costly and must apply

Yosuke Sato and Nobu Goto

obligatorily with some driving force. A number of empirical problems remain, however, with Fukui's parametric theory of cost evaluation. First, even though the majority of scrambling languages do exhibit an SOV order, such as Japanese and Korean, there are also SVO languages which allow scrambling, such as Polish (Haegeman 1995) and Russian (Müller and Sternefeld 1993; Bailyn 1995; 2001). Second, Fukui's hypothesis has nothing to say about scrambling languages such as German and Chinese, which exhibit mixed head-directionality depending on the identity of syntactic heads.

Bošković and Takahashi (1998), on the other hand, advance a radical analysis of scrambling which is compatible with the Last-Resort view of syntactic movement within the guidelines of the MP. They argue that "scrambled" elements are actually base-generated in their surface positions and undergo obligatory LF movement to the position where they receive θ-roles, which they consider to be formal features that license syntactic movement (Hornstein 1999). Thus, Bošković and Takahashi's analysis derives the sentence in (28) by covert LF movement, as shown in (29):

(28) Sono hon-o   John-ga   [Mary-ga   katta   to]   omotteiru.
     DEM book-ACC   John-NOM Mary-NOM   bought   COMP   think
     'John thinks that Mary bought that book.'

(Bošković and Takahashi 1998: 349)

(29) Sono hon-o   John-ga   [Mary-ga   *e*   katta to]   omotteiru.
     | *Obligatory LF movement* ↑   (*e* = θ-position)

Bošković and Takahashi demonstrate that the LF-lowering analysis straightforwardly explains the radical reconstruction property of scrambling (see §2.2) illustrated earlier in (20b). Recall that the problem raised by (20b) was why the *wh*-phrase *dono hon-o* 'which book-ACC' must take embedded scope even if it is located outside the Q-marked interrogative clause. This question receives a straightforward answer under Bošković and Takahashi's analysis; the *wh*-phrase is base-generated in its surface position, but is obligatorily lowered in LF to the position where it receives a θ-role. They also observe that the same analysis can be extended to derive the impossibility of long scrambling of adverbials (Saito 1985), as exemplified by (30):

(30) a. Mary-ga   [John-ga   riyuu-mo   naku   sono setu-o
        Mary-NOM   John-NOM   reason-even without DEM theory-ACC
        sinziteiru to   omotteiru]
        believe COMP think
        'Mary thinks that John believes in that theory without any reason.'
     b. *Riyuu-mo   naku_i   Mary-ga   [John-ga t_i   sono setu-o
        reason-even without   Mary-NOM John-NOM   DEM theory-ACC
        sinziteiru to] omotteiru.
        believe COMP think
        'Mary thinks that John believes in that theory without any reason.'

(Bošković and Takahashi 1998: 355)

Under the movement analysis, (30b) would be derived from (30a) by long scrambling of the reason adjunct *riyuu-mo naku* 'without any reason', which modifies the embedded predicate. The ungrammaticality of (30b), however, remains mysterious under this analysis. This fact is exactly what the lowering analysis of scrambling predicts; given that adjuncts are licensed by being adjoined to semantically contentful categories rather than receiving a θ-role from a predicate, there is no driving force which pushes back the adjunct into some position within the embedded clause.

Bailyn (2001) presents arguments from Russian scrambling against Bošković and Takahashi's analysis of Japanese scrambling. Bošković (2004) objects to Bailyn's arguments by showing that the Russian data used by Bailyn are orthogonal to the question, since Russian scrambling does not exhibit the core defining characteristic of Japanese-style scrambling: namely, radical reconstruction. Bošković also points out a cross-linguistic correlation between the lack of articles and the availability of scrambling. To establish this correlation in minimalist terms, Bošković proposes that functional categories are merged only if the syntactic derivation requires their presence. This proposal serves to ensure that functional items such as D appear in the expected θ-position, as in English, so that they can check their θ-features once they are introduced into the syntactic workspace. If a language has no Ds, however, that language can freely merge NPs in any argument position as long as their θ-features are checked by the LF. This is what happens in Japanese. Though this theory is quite appealing, at least two questions remain. One is whether DPs are universally required for argumenthood or not (Abney 1987; Stowell 1989; Longobardi 1994). If so, Bošković's theory may not be sustained; see Chierchia (1998), though, for an alternative hypothesis that some languages, such as Japanese and Chinese, do not require Ds to lift predicates (of type <e, t>) to saturated arguments (of type <e>). Bošković's theory is also potentially problematic because Japanese has demonstratives and strongly quantified nominals, both of which can undergo scrambling without any loss of grammaticality. The other question is whether there are any languages whose scrambling exhibits the same core distributional properties with Japanese scrambling such as radical reconstruction. If only Japanese shows such a property, then Bošković's theory may lose much of its explanatory potential.

2.4   What are syntactic properties of scrambling?

Scrambling consists of three distinct subclasses: long-distance scrambling, clause-internal scrambling, and VP-internal scrambling. Long-distance scrambling moves an element to sentence-initial position across a clause boundary. Clause-internal scrambling moves an element to sentence-initial position across a subject within the same clause. VP-internal scrambling is permutation of the IO–DO order within the VP-internal domain (see §2.1).

Examples of these three types of scrambling are given below from Japanese:

(31)   VP-internal scrambling
    a.   John-ga   Mary-ni   hon-o   ageta.
        John-NOM Mary-DAT book-ACC gave
        'John gave a book to Mary.'
    b.   John-ga hon-o_i Mary-ni t_i ageta.
        John-NOM book-ACC Mary-DAT   gave
        'John gave a book to Mary.'

(32)   Clause-internal scrambling
    a.   John-ga   hon-o   katta.
        John-NOM book-ACC bought
        'John bought a book.'

b. Hon-o$_i$ John-ga t_i katta.
    book-ACC   John-NOM   bought
    'Lit. A book, John bought.'

(33) Long-distance scrambling
a. Mary-ga   [John-ga   hon-o   katta   to]   omotta.
    Mary-NOM   John-NOM   book-ACC   bought   COMP   thought
    'Mary thought that John bought a book.'
b. Hon-o$_i$ Mary-ga   [John-ga t_i katta   to]   omotta.
    book-ACC   Mary-NOM   John-NOM   bought   COMP   thought
    'Mary thought that John bought a book.'

It is well-known that Japanese scrambling exhibits mixed behavior with respect to the A/A$'$-distinction (Saito 1992; Tada 1993). Specifically, it shows different properties depending on the distance of movement, as summarized in (34).

(34) a. VP-internal scrambling is unambiguously A-movement.
    b. Clause-internal scrambling can be either A- or A$'$-movement.
    c. Long-distance scrambling is unambiguously A$'$-movement.

Before we verify these formal properties of scrambling in Japanese, let us examine some English examples which illustrate the A/A$'$-distinction of movement. It has been widely acknowledged in the literature that syntactic movement is divided into two types: A-movement and A$'$-movement. They exhibit different properties with respect to anaphor-binding and weak crossover (WCO) effects (see §2.1). Examples (35) and (36) illustrate the differences in question:

(35) A-movement
    a. [John and Mary]$_i$ seemed to each other$_i$ to be t_i polite.
    b. Everyone$_i$ seemed to his$_i$ mother to be t_i polite.

(36) A$'$-movement
    a. *Who$_i$ did [each other$_i$'s friends] speak ill of t_i?
    b. ?*Who$_i$ does [his$_i$ mother] love t_i?

In (35), the NP *John and Mary* is moved to the subject position as an instance of A-movement. In (36), on the other hand, the *wh*-phrase *who* is moved to the sentence-initial position, where it takes scope – a typical instance of A$'$-movement. The examples in (35) and (36) illustrate that A-movement creates a new anaphor-binder relation, while A$'$-movement does not. Furthermore, the contrast between (35) and (36) shows that A$'$-movement induces WCO effects but A-movement does not.

    With these observations in mind, let us now see how the three types of scrambling in Japanese play out with respect to the A- vs. A$'$-diagnostics. First, consider examples of VP-internal scrambling in (37):

(37) a. ?*Hanako-ga   [otagai-no   ryoosin]-ni   [Taroo-to   Ziroo]-o
    Hanako-NOM   each other-GEN   parents-DAT   Taro-and   Jiro-ACC
    syookaisita.
    introduced
    'Hanako introduced Taro and Jiro to each other's parents.'

b. Hanako-ga   [Taroo-to Ziroo]-o$_i$ [otagai-no   ryoosin]-ni t_i syookaisita
    Hanako-NOM   Taro-and Jiro-ACC   each other-GEN parents-DAT   introduced
    'Hanako introduced Taro and Jiro to each other's parents.'

(Saito 2003: 511–512)

Assuming Hoji's (1985) analysis, (37a) represents the basic word order of the ditransitive sentence, and (37b) is derived from (37a) by VP-internal scrambling. In (37a), the anaphor *otagai* remains unbound, which results in Condition (A) violation. However, the scrambled variant of (37a) shown in (37b), where VP-internal scrambling takes place, is acceptable. This fact shows that VP-internal scrambling is A-movement. This type of scrambling can be shown not to be A'-movement, as in (38).

(38) a. Maikeru-ga   [Keeto-to   Zyoo]-ni   otagai-o   syookaisita.
      Michael-NOM   Kate-and   Joe-DAT   each other-ACC   introduced
      'Michael introduced Kate and Joe to each other'
   b. *Maikeru-ga   otagai-o$_i$ [Keeto-to Zyoo]-ni t_i syookaisita.
      Michael-NOM   each other-ACC   Kate-and Joe-DAT   introduced
      'Michael introduced Kate and Joe to each other'

(Saito 2003: 512)

The sentence in (38b), in which the anaphor *otagai* moves across the R-expression *Keeto to Zyoo* 'Kate and Joe', is unacceptable. This fact can be explained if this type of scrambling can only ever be A-movement. That is, given that the scrambled anaphor A-binds its antecedent R-expression from the moved position, (38b) is correctly excluded as a violation of Condition (C) effects. If VP-internal scrambling were A'-movement, the R-expression in (38b) would be A-free and the Condition (C) violation would be evaded, contrary to facts. Thus, VP-internal scrambling is unambiguously A-movement.

How about clause-internal scrambling? Consider (39):

(39) a. ?*[Otagai-no   sensei]-ga   karera-o   hihansita.
        each other-GEN teacher-NOM   they-ACC   criticized
      '[Each other's teachers] criticized them'
   b. ?Karera-o$_i$ [otagai-no   sensei]-ga t_i hihansita.
      they-ACC   each other-GEN   teacher-NOM   criticized
      'Lit. Them$_i$, [each other's teachers] criticized t_i'

(Saito 2003: 485)

The sentence in (39a) is ruled out as a Condition (A) violation. However, note that such a violation is evaded in (39b), where the scrambled phrase *karera-o* 'they-ACC' can bind the anaphor within the subject from the moved position. This indicates that clause-internal scrambling is A-movement. However, at the same time, this type of scrambling can behave as A'-movement as well. This point is proved in (40).

(40) Otagai-o$_i$ [Taroo-to Hanako]-ga t_i semeta
    each other-ACC   Taro-and Hanako-NOM   blamed
    'Each other$_i$, Taro and Hanako blamed t_i'

(Saito 2003: 485–486)

The grammaticality of (40) shows that the scrambled anaphor does not induce Condition (C) effects, in contrast to VP-internal scrambling. This fact follows if clause-internal scrambling can also be A′-movement. If the movement in (40) is an instance of A′-movement, the R-expression *Taroo-to Hanako-ga* 'Taro and Hanako' can stay A-free, and hence a Condition (C) violation is circumvented. Therefore, clause-internal scrambling can be either A- or A′-movement.

Let us finally examine long-distance scrambling. Consider (41):

(41) a. *[Otagai-no   sensei]-ga [_CP_ Tanaka-ga   karera-o hihansita] to]   itta].
        each other-GEN teacher-NOM Tanaka-NOM they-ACC criticized COMP said
        '[Each other's teachers] said that Tanaka criticized them'
     b. *Karera-o_i [otagai-no   sensei]-ga   [_CP_ Tanaka-ga t_i hihansita to]   itta.
        they-ACC   each other-GEN teacher-NOM   Tanaka-NOM criticized COMP said
        'Lit. Them_i, [each other's teachers] said that Tanaka criticized t_i'

(Saito 2003: 485–486)

(41b) is derived from (41a) by scrambling of the pronoun *karera-o* 'they-ACC' out of the embedded clause to the sentence-initial position. The unacceptability of (41b) indicates that the scrambled NP cannot serve as the antecedent of the anaphor in the matrix subject *otagai* 'each other.' This is in contrast to the VP-internal and clause-internal cases. This binding pattern, therefore, shows that long-distance scrambling does not create a new A-binder and hence counts uniformly as A′-movement.

Needless to say, the most important question about scrambling discussed here is why the three distinct types of scrambling in Japanese (and other scrambling languages, for that matter) exhibit the particular cluster of movement properties they do, as summarized in (34). For example, why is it that VP-internal scrambling cannot be A′-movement, say, to a VP-internal focus position, whereas long-distance scrambling cannot be A-movement, say, to an argument position in the higher clause? A full resolution of this question will certainly lead to a better understanding of another question raised in §2.2: namely, whether or not scrambling is a syntactic movement forced by some independent feature in the syntactic computation or the discourse structure.

3   Two puzzles about scrambling

This section briefly introduces two specific empirical puzzles that have resisted a satisfactory explanation in the literature on scrambling: the Proper Binding Effect and the contrast between scrambling out of finite and non-finite complements.

Saito (1985; 1989) notes that scrambling in Japanese is constrained by the Proper Binding Condition (PBC) (Fiengo 1977), which states that traces must be bound by their antecedents. To illustrate this PBC effect, consider (42):

(42) a. Taroo-ga [_CP_ Hanako-ga   [_PP_ Sooru-ni] iru to]   omotteiru.
        Taro-NOM   Hanako-NOM   Seoul-LOC is COMP think
        'Taro thinks [that Hanako lives [in Seoul]]'
     b. [_PP_ Sooru-ni]_i Taroo-ga [_CP_ Hanako-ga   t_i iru to]   omotteiru.
        Seoul-LOC   Taro-NOM   Hanako-NOM   is COMP think
        '[In Seoul]_i, Taro thinks [that Hanako lives t_i].'

c. [$_{CP}$ Hanako-ga   [$_{PP}$ Sooru-ni]   iru   to]$_i$ Taroo-ga t_i omotteiru
    Hanako-NOM   Seoul-LOC is COMP Taro-NOM   think
    '[That Hanako lives [in Seoul]]$_i$, Taro thinks t_i.'

d. *[$_{CP}$ Hanako-ga t_i iru   to]$_j$ [$_{PP}$ Sooru-ni]$_i$ Taroo-ga t_j omotteiru
    Hanako-NOM is COMP Seoul-LOC Taro-NOM   think
    '[That Hanako lives t_i]$_j$, [in Seoul]$_i$, Taro thinks t_j.'

(Saito 2003: 498–499)

(42b) is derived from (42a) by long-distance scrambling of the PP *Sooru-ni* 'in Seoul,' and (42c) involves long-distance scrambling of the CP *Hanako-ga Sooru-ni iru to* 'that Hanako lives in Seoul.' Although both the PP and the CP can each be scrambled on their own, the ungrammaticality of (42d) indicates that, once the PP is scrambled, it is no longer possible to further scramble the CP which contains the trace of the scrambled PP.

This PBC-based analysis, however, has become untenable with the advent of the Copy Theory of Movement within the MP (Chomsky 1995), according to which a moved element leaves behind a copy of itself rather than its trace. To capture the ungrammaticality of (42d) within the MP, Saito (2003) reformulates the PBC as a constraint on the application of Merge, as shown in (43):

(43) Constraint on Merge (Saito 2003: 507–508)
    a. α is subject to Merge only if α is a complete constituent.
    b. α is a complete constituent $=_{df}$ (i) α is a term, and (ii) if a position within α is a member of a chain γ, then every position of γ is contained within α.

With details aside, the constraint in (43) essentially states that a constituent that contains a trace cannot be subject to Merge. If scrambling is an instance of syntactic movement, which in turn is an instance of (Internal) Merge (Chomsky 2008; 2013), (42d) is ruled out by (43) because this example involves movement of the CP that contains a trace of the PP. Though Saito's constraint on Merge can capture the empirical facts, it suffers from conceptual problems: why such a constraint exists and how it is derived from independent principles postulated within the MP. That is, it is far from clear why Merge is sensitive to such a constraint. If Merge is unconstrained (Chomsky 2008), then a constraint such as (43) should be entirely eliminated from the grammar. Therefore, the PBC effect remains one of the interesting issues relating to scrambling (see Hiraiwa 2010 for a recent analysis).

Another interesting puzzle relating to scrambling that calls for an explanation is the difference between long-distance scrambling out of a finite clause and long-distance scrambling out of a control complement. Consider (44) and (45):

(44) Long-distance scrambling out of a finite/non-control Clause
    a. Taroo-ga   minna-ni [$_{CP}$ Hanako-ga   sono hon-o   motte-iru to]   itta.
        Taro-NOM   all-DAT   Hanako-NOM DEM   book-ACC have   COMP said
        'Taro said to all [that Hanako has that book]'
    b. Sono hon-o$_i$ Taroo-ga   minna-ni [$_{CP}$ Hanako-ga t_i motte-iru to]   itta.
        DEM   book-ACC Taro-NOM   all-DAT   Hanako-NOM   have   COMP said
        'Lit. That book$_i$, Taro said to all [that Hanako has t_i].'
    c. ??Taroo-ga   sono hon-o$_i$ minna-ni [$_{CP}$ Hanako-ga t_i motte-iru to]   itta.
        Taro-NOM   DEM   book-ACC all-DAT   Hanako-NOM   have   COMP said
        'Taro, that book$_i$, said to all [that Hanako has t_i]'

(Saito 1985: 267)

(45) Long-distance scrambling out of a non-finite/control complement
  a. Taroo-ga   Hanako-ni$_i$ [$_{CP}$ PRO$_i$ sono hon-o   yomuyoo] itta.
     Taro-NOM   Hanako-DAT   DEM book-ACC read.to   said
     'Taro said Hanako [to read that book].'
  b. Sono hon-o$_i$ Taroo-ga   Hanako-ni$_j$ [$_{CP}$ PRO$_j$ t_i yomuyoo] itta.
     DEM book-ACC   Taro-NOM   Hanako-DAT   read.to   said
     'Lit. That book$_i$, Taro said Hanako [to read t_i].'
  c. Taroo-ga   sono hon-o$_i$ Hanako-ni$_j$ [$_{CP}$ PRO$_j$ t_i yomuyoo] itta.
     Taro-NOM   DEM book-ACC   Hanako-DAT   read.to   said
     'Lit. Taro, that book$_i$, said Hanako [to read t_i].'

(Saito 1985: 225)

(44b) is derived from (44a) by long-distance scrambling of the embedded object *sono hon-o* 'that book' to the sentence-initial position. Saito (1985) observes that the sentence is marginal if a phrase that has undergone long-distance scrambling out of a finite clause follows the subject of the higher clause, as in (44c). Interestingly, however, Saito (1985) observes that the subject of the higher clause may precede or follow the phrase which has been scrambled out of a non-finite complement, as shown in (45). (45b) and (45c) are derived from (45a) by long-distance scrambling of the embedded object *sono hon-o* 'that book' to the sentence-initial position and the position between the matrix subject and the indirect object, respectively. Note that unlike (44b) and (44c), both (45b) and (45c) are acceptable. This contrast between (44c) and (45c) thus poses an important puzzle for researchers on Japanese scrambling. See Goto (2013) for one recent analysis of the impossibility of long-distance scrambling in (44c) in terms of the unlabelability of {XP, YP} structures within Chomsky's (2013) theory of labeling.

4 Conclusion

This chapter has reviewed major theoretical issues raised by scrambling by introducing representative works in the literature – free word order, optionality, nature, trigger, and the identity of the landing site of scrambling – with primary reference to data from Japanese, one of the best-studied languages with regard to this phenomenon. Our survey has shown that though the descriptive results regarding the landing site of scrambling as a movement operation seem non-controversial, things are less clear for the basic word order, trigger, and nature of scrambling. As shown in our discussion in §2, the three issues here are closely connected with one another, so that a better understanding of any one of the issues will certainly shed light on the other two. As hinted at §2.2, one might want to investigate scrambling from the perspective of the syntax–pragmatics interface to gain a more balanced holistic understanding of this phenomenon. Furthermore, as discussed at §3, if scrambling is an instance of unconstrained Merge, there remain many other specific puzzles, including the PBC effect and the scrambling out of finite vs. non-finite clauses, which await a principled explanation in future research on scrambling.

Note

1 The following abbreviations are used in the data section of this chapter: ACC, accusative; CL, classifier; COMP, complementizer; DAT, dative; DEM, demonstrative; GEN, genitive; LOC, locative; NOM, nominative; Q, question particle; TOP, topic marker.

Further reading

Karimi, Simin (ed.). 2008. *Word order and scrambling*. Oxford: Blackwell.

Nemoto, Naoko. 1999. Scrambling. In *The handbook of Japanese linguistics*, ed. Natsuko Tsujimura, 121–153. Oxford: Blackwell.

Takano, Yuji. 2008. Ditransitive constructions. In *The handbook of Japanese linguistics*, ed. Shigeru Miyagawa and Saito Mamoru, 423–455. Oxford: Blackwell.

References

Abney, S. 1987. The English noun phrase in its sentential aspect. Doctoral dissertation, MIT.

Bailyn, John F. 1995. Underlying phrase structure and 'short' verb movement in Russian. *Journal of Slavic Linguistics* 3:13–58.

Bailyn, John F. 2001. On scrambling: A reply to Bošković, and Takahashi. *Linguistic Inquiry* 32: 635–658.

Bošković, Željko. 2004. Topicalization, focalization, lexical insertion, and scrambling. *Linguistic Inquiry* 35:613–638.

Bošković, Željko, and Daiko Takahashi. 1998. Scrambling and last resort. *Linguistic Inquiry* 29: 347–366.

Chierchia, Gennaro. 1998. Reference to kinds across languages. *Natural Language Semantics* 6:339–405.

Chomsky, Noam. 1981. *Lectures on government and binding*. Dordrecht: Foris.

Chomsky, Noam. 1986. *Knowledge of language: Its nature, origin, and use*. New York: Praeger.

Chomsky, Noam. 1995. *The minimalist program*. Cambridge, MA: MIT Press.

Chomsky, Noam. 2008. On phases. In *Foundational issues in linguistic theory*, ed. Robert Freidin, Carlos Otero, and Maria Luisa Zubizarreta, 133–166. Cambridge, MA: MIT Press.

Chomsky, Noam. 2013. Problems of projection. *Lingua* 130:33–49.

Fiengo, Robert. 1977. On trace theory. *Linguistic Inquiry* 8:35–61.

Fukui, Naoki. 1986. A theory of category projection and its implications. Doctoral dissertation, MIT.

Fukui, Naoki. 1993. Parameters and optionality. *Linguistic Inquiry* 24:399–420.

Goto, Nobu. 2013. Labeling and scrambling in Japanese. *Tohoku: Essays and studies in English Language and Literature* 46:39–73.

Grewendorf, Günther, and Joachim Sabel. 1999. Scrambling in German and Japanese: Adjunction versus multiple specifiers. *Natural Language and Linguistic Theory* 17:1–65.

Haegeman, Liliane. 1995. *The syntax of negation*. Cambridge: Cambridge University Press.

Hale, Ken. 1980. Remarks on Japanese phrase structure: Comments on the papers on Japanese syntax. In *MIT Working Papers in Linguistics 2: Theoretical issues in Japanese linguistics*, ed. Yukio Otsu and Ann K. Farmer, 185–203. Department of Linguistics and Philosophy, MIT: MITWPL.

Hiraiwa, Ken. 2010. Scrambling to the edge. *Syntax* 13:133–164.

Hoji, Hajime. 1985. Logical form constraints and configurational structures in Japanese. PhD dissertation, University of Washington.

Hoji, Hajime. 2003. Falsifiability and repeatability in generative grammar: A case study of anaphora and scope dependency in Japanese. *Lingua* 113:377–446.

Hornstein, Norbert. 1999. Movement and control. *Linguistic Inquiry* 30:169–196.

Karimi, Simin. 1999. Is scrambling as strange as we think it is? In *MIT Working Papers in Linguistics 33: Papers on morphology and syntax, cycle one*, ed. Karlos Arregi, Benjamin Bruening, Cornelia Krause, and Viviane Lin, 159–190. Department of Linguistics and Philosophy, MIT: MITWPL.

Karimi, Simin. 2005. *A minimalist approach to scrambling: Evidence from Persian*. Berlin: Mouton de Gruyter.

Kawamura, Tomoko. 2001. A feature-checking analysis of Japanese scrambling. MA thesis, Nanzan University.

Kitahara, Hisatsugu. 1997. *Elementary operations and optimal derivations*. Cambridge, MA: MIT Press.

Kitahara, Hisatsugu. 2000. Case and scrambling: A derivational view. Ms. Keio University.

Koizumi, Masatoshi, and Katsuo Tamaoka. 2004. Cognitive processing of Japanese sentences with ditransitive verbs. *Gengo Kenkyu* 125:173–190.

Kuno, Susumu. 1973. *The structure of the Japanese language*. Cambridge, MA: MIT Press.

Kuroda, S.-Y. 1970. Remarks on the notion of subject with reference to words like also, even, or only, Part 1. *Annual Bulletin* 3:111–129. Research Institute of Logopedics and Phoniatrics, University of Tokyo. [Reprinted in *Papers in Japanese Linguistics* 11:98–120. Represented in Kuroda 1992.]

Kuroda, S.-Y. 1988. Whether we agree or not. In *Papers from the Second International Workshop on Japanese Syntax*, ed. William Poser, 103–143. Stanford, CA: CSLI Publications. [Distributed by Cambridge University Press.]

Kuroda, S.-Y. 1992. *Japanese syntax and semantics: Collected papers*. Dordrecht: Kluwer.

Longobardi, Giuseppe. 1994. Reference and proper names: A theory of N-to-D movement in syntax and logical form. *Linguistic Inquiry* 25:609–665.

Mahajan, Anoop. 1990. The A/A′-distinction and movement theory. Doctoral dissertation, MIT.

Matsuoka, Mikinari. 2003. Two types of ditransitive constructions in Japanese. *Journal of East Asian Linguistics* 12:171–203.

Miyagawa, Shigeru. 1997. Against optional scrambling. *Linguistic Inquiry* 28:1–25.

Miyagawa, Shigeru. 2001. EPP, scrambling, and *wh*-in-situ. In *Ken Hale: A life in language*, ed. Michael Kenstowicz, 293–338. Cambridge, MA: MIT Press.

Müller, Gereon, and Wolfgang Sternefeld. 1993. Improper movement and unambiguous binding. *Linguistic Inquiry* 24:461–507.

Rizzi, Luigi. 1997. The fine structure of the left periphery. In *Elements of grammar: A handbook of generative syntax*, ed. Liliane Hageman, 281–337. Dordrecht: Kluwer.

Ross, John R. 1967. Constraints on variables in syntax. Doctoral dissertation, MIT.

Saito, Mamoru. 1985. Some asymmetries in Japanese and their theoretical implications. Doctoral dissertation, MIT.

Saito, Mamoru. 1989. Scrambling as semantically vacuous A′-movement. In *Alternative conceptions of phrase structure*, ed. Mark Baltin and Anthony Kroch, 182–200. Chicago, IL: University of Chicago Press.

Saito, Mamoru. 1992. Long distance scrambling in Japanese. *Journal of East Asian Linguistics* 1:69–118.

Saito, Mamoru. 2003. A derivational approach to the interpretation of scrambling chains. *Lingua* 113:481–518.

Saito, Mamoru, and Naoki Fukui. 1998. Order in phrase structure and movement. *Linguistic Inquiry* 29:439–474.

Stowell, Tim. 1989. Subjects, specifiers, and X′-theory. In *Alternative conceptions of phrase structure*, ed. Mark Baltin and Anthony Kroch, 232–262. Chicago, IL: University of Chicago Press.

Sugisaki, Koji, and Miwa Isobe. 2001. What can child Japanese tell us about the syntax of scrambling. In *Proceedings of WCCFL 20*, ed. Karine Megerdoomian and Leora Anne Bar-el, 538–551. Somerville, MA: Cascadilla Press.

Tada, Hiroaki. 1993. A/A′-partition in derivation. Doctoral dissertation, MIT.

Takahashi, Daiko. 1993. Movement of *wh*-phrases in Japanese. *Natural Language and Linguistic Theory* 11:655–678.

Takano, Yuji. 1998. Object shift and scrambling. *Natural Language and Linguistic Theory* 16:817–889.

Ueyama, Ayumi. 1998. Two types of dependency. Doctoral dissertation, University of Southern California.

Whitman, John. 1986. Configurationality parameters. In *Issues in Japanese linguistics*, ed. Takashi Imai and Mamoru Saito, 351–374. Dordrecht: Foris.

14

Noun incorporation, nonconfigurationality, and polysynthesis

Kumiko Murasugi

1 Introduction

This chapter focuses on three topics typically associated with lesser-known, non-Indo-European languages: noun incorporation, nonconfigurationality, and polysynthesis. All three share the property of describing a wide variety of languages with very different characteristics, making the phenomena difficult to characterize and define. While there is an overlap in the languages that exhibit these phenomena, they differ quite clearly in their research focus. Noun incorporation is concerned with the morphology-syntax relation, nonconfigurationality with arguments and syntactic structure, and polysynthesis with language typology. All three have contributed greatly to syntactic theory by providing insights into languages whose properties could only be discovered through field research.

2 Noun incorporation

Noun incorporation (NI) is a construction in which a noun and a verb stem combine to yield a complex verb (Sapir 1911; Mithun 1984). The incorporated noun is an argument of the verb, normally the object of a transitive verb. Example (1) is from Mohawk (Baker 1996: 12). Sentence (1a) consists of a verb and its direct object, while (1b) contains the incorporated form.[1]

(1)   a. Wa'-k-hnínu-'   ne ka-nákt-a'.
           FACT-1sS-buy-PUNC NE NsS-bed-NSF
           'I bought the/a bed.'
    b. Wa'-ke-nakt-a-hnínu-'.
           FACT-1sS-bed-ø-buy-PUNC
           'I bought the/a bed.'

The study of NI began as a means of characterizing polysynthetic languages (see §4 below), and has since developed into a separate domain of study (Massam 2009). While NI is found in many polysynthetic languages, such as Algonquian, Athabaskan, Caddoan,

Iroquoian, Muskogean, Chukchee, Gunwinggu, and Inuit, it is a property of non-polysynthetic ones as well, such as Turkish, Mayan, Hindi, German, English, and French. It has been difficult to articulate a precise definition of NI given cross-linguistic differences in its implementation. For example, Mithun (1984: 848) defines NI as "compounding ... of a complex lexical item from a combination of two or more stems." While this definition captures the intuitive property of NI, it makes two assumptions that have been widely debated in the literature. The first is that NI involves compounding, a lexical process. Many linguists consider NI to be syntactic, or to involve a type of morphology that allows access to the internal components of words. Secondly, Mithun's definition restricts NI to stems, which excludes incorporation with bound verbs found in Greenlandic and Inuktitut, for example, and bound nominals (lexical suffixes) found in Salish languages. Because NI is not a homogeneous phenomenon, assumptions regarding its component parts and underlying processes differ widely across languages. The following sections present the major issues on this topic, focusing on lesser-known languages.[2]

2.1 Variations on the parts: nouns and verbs

Morphological, syntactic and semantic variations are found in the nouns and verbs that form the derived verbal element. Morphologically, the incorporated noun can be a free morpheme identical in form to the unincorporated noun (see (1) above), or it can be a lexical affix. Lexical affixes, typically found in northwestern Native American languages such as Salish and Wakashan, are bound morphemes that have the semantic content of free-standing nouns but bear no resemblance to them in form (Gerdts 1998; 2003; Bischoff 2011).

Incorporated nouns can vary widely in their syntactic properties. While most structures involve incorporation of the direct object or intransitive non-agentive subject, some languages, such as Koyukon Athapaskan, allow incorporation of transitive nonvolitional agentive subjects (Axelrod 1990). Incorporation of benefactives, locatives, instruments, and possessors have been attested as well (Gerdts 1998; Massam 2009). There is also a range of syntactic forms that the incorporated structure can take: uncategorized root (Wiltschko 2009), N head (Baker 1988; 1996), nP (Mathieu 2009), full NP (Déchaine 1999), and even *wh*-word (Sadock 1991; Davis and Sawai 2001). Languages vary in the extent to which they permit noun modifiers to appear in the empty object position. Some languages allow no modifiers to remain outside the verbal complex, while a language such as Mohawk permits demonstratives, adjectival modifiers, quantifiers, and relative clauses in the original object position (Baker 1995). Another phenomenon found in some languages is the doubling of the incorporated noun by a semantically related noun phrase in object position. Sometimes the free-standing noun is identical in form and meaning to the incorporated noun (Baker 1995: 9), but in most cases it has a more specific meaning. For example, in Mohawk the incorporated noun has the generic meaning of 'fish' while the free-standing object is a particular type of fish (Mithun 1984). Finally, the incorporability of a noun may depend on the type of clause: in Alamblak (Papua New Guinea) a subject, object, or locative can be incorporated in a dependent clause, while only inalienably possessed nouns can be incorporated in a main clause (Bruce 1984).

Semantically, the incorporated noun is normally interpreted as nonreferential and indefinite (e.g., Greenlandic: Sadock 1980), but referential and definite nouns have also been attested (e.g., Mohawk: Baker 1988). Johns (2009) even provides an example of incorporated personal names in Inuktitut. Another semantic difference is whether or not an incorporated noun displays "discourse transparency:" that is, the ability to be referenced by an anaphor in subsequent discourse (Sadock 1980; van Geenhoven 1992; 1998; Farkas and de Swart 2003). One source of semantic variation is the broadening of the definition of NI to include structures that have the semantic but not necessarily the morphological properties of NI.

While the noun can vary widely in its properties, there is much less variation in the properties of the verb. In most languages the verb is identical to its unincorporated form, but in some languages, such as Greenlandic and Inuktitut, it belongs to a closed class of bound morphemes (Sadock 1980; Johns 2007). While Sadock (1980) claims that verbs do not agree with the incorporated object, Johns (2009) claims that in some cases they can.

2.2 Implications of the variation

The extensive variation in NI found among languages has implications for both linguistic description and theory. At the most basic level, the variation makes it difficult to define what the phenomenon is, and thus to determine which languages can be considered noun incorporating. In most cases it seems to depend on the particular definition of individual linguists, who base their assumptions on languages they are familiar with. For example, Sapir (1911) and Mithun (1984) do not consider the Inuit languages to be noun incorporating, since the verb in incorporated structures is a lexical affix rather than a free morpheme. Sadock (1980) and Johns (2007; 2009), on the other hand, have argued that these languages do involve NI, since they share with definitive NI languages the property that "the position of the nominal differs from that of a canonical object DP" (Johns 2007: 537). Similarly, Baker (1988) permits only object incorporation in his characterization of NI, thus excluding languages such as Chipewyan that permit incorporation of other argument types.

One approach to accommodating variation is to classify languages based on their functional properties. In a comprehensive study of NI encompassing typological, functional, and historical perspectives, Mithun (1984) presents four types of NI based on their function. She claims, moreover, that the four types are "not distributed randomly among languages, but appear in an implicational hierarchy: IV > III > II > I" (p. 890).

Type I NI involves lexical compounding, where a noun and a verb combine to form a new intransitive verb. This type of NI occurs to denote unitary, recognizable activities such as coconut-grinding or bread-eating. The incorporated noun loses its individual saliency and appears without markers of definiteness, number, or case. Examples of Type I languages are Mokilese (Austronesian), Mam (Mayan), Nisgha (Tsimshian), and Comanche (Uto-Aztecan). Type II NI is similar to Type I in the properties of the noun and derived verb, but it allows an oblique argument to fill the case position vacated by the incorporated noun. This process, found in languages such as Tupinamba (Tupi-Guarani) and Blackfoot (Algonquian), is a "lexical device for manipulating case relations within clauses" (Mithun 1984: 859). Languages with Type III NI, such as Huahtla Nahuatl (Uzo-Aztecan) and Chukchi (Paleo-Siberian), use the devices of Types I and II to manipulate discourse structure. It is typically found in polysynthetic languages, whose relatively free word order allows word order to be used for pragmatic purposes. Finally, with Type IV classificatory NI, a specific independent noun phrase appears with a derived verb consisting of a related but more general incorporated noun stem. The independent nominals often become classified according to the stem they appear with. For example, in the Caddoan languages of Oklahoma and North Dakota, nouns appearing with the classifier noun 'eye' include 'bead' and 'plum', which are both small, round objects. Mithun's classification appears to be supported by theoretical studies on NI such as Rosen (1989) and Baker *et al.* (2004).

In terms of linguistic theory, it is difficult for one unified theory to encompass all languages considered by one definition or another to be noun incorporating. Proposing such a theory necessarily restricts the class of NI languages to those with the particular properties that fit within the theory, raising the problem of circularity. As an example, Baker (1988) restricts his theory of NI to languages where the incorporating noun is a direct object, has a patient role, allows stranding of modifiers, and exhibits discourse transparency (see §2.3.1 below). Languages that do not fit within the definition are excluded, either by being reinterpreted or by being overlooked. One must keep in mind, though, that Baker's (1988) goal was not to account for every known example of NI, as NI for him was just one type of grammatical-function changing process. The objective of most linguists working on NI is to find an adequate theory for the language(s) they are most familiar with, putting it into the context of a more general class of noun incorporating languages. Baker (2007: 163) notes that "[i]t may well be that most of the NI theorists are correct for the language(s) they know best, and become wrong only if they say or imply that there is a single unified syntax for all the constructions called NI in the languages of the world."

2.3   The process: syntactic or lexical

One of the major questions in the study of NI is whether it is a syntactic or lexical process. Proponents of the syntactic approach assume that the verb and noun originate in distinct structural positions and come together through syntactic means (Sadock 1980; 1986; Baker 1988; 1996; van Geenhoven 1998; 2002; Massam 2001; 2009). The alternative view is that NI structures are derived from word formation rules that apply in the lexicon, similar to compounding (Mithun 1984; 1986; Di Sciullo and Williams 1987; Rosen 1989; Anderson 1992; 2001).[3] As Massam (2009: 1081) observes, "[t]he two opposing positions on the topic … highlight the central linguistic debate regarding the relation between morphology (canonically adding affixes to stems) and syntax (canonically putting words together), and the difficulty of placing processes like compounding and incorporation, which have properties of both, in this dichotomy."

2.3.1   NI as a syntactic process

The first major work on NI in the generative tradition was Baker (1988). For Baker, all incorporation structures (including noun, verb, and preposition incorporation) involve syntactic head movement to a higher head. Specifically, in NI a head noun moves out of object position and adjoins to a governing verb. Evidence for the original position of the incorporated noun comes from the Uniformity of Theta Assignment Hypothesis, which ensures that the incorporated and non-incorporated nouns both originate in the same structural position, as well as evidence from stranded modifiers in the NP (see also Baker 1993). Universal and language-specific instantiations of NI are accounted for by general linguistic principles such as the Empty Category Principle and the Case Filter. Baker's work provided an elegant unified account of the grammatical-function changing processes he investigated, including NI, but could not account for the extensive range of languages included under the various definitions of NI. It did, however, provide a starting point for subsequent syntactic analyses of NI, both with and without head movement.

The first studies consisted mainly of critical analyses of Baker's theory based on data from different languages. While some studies, such as Mellow's (1989) work on Cree, adopted Baker's head movement analysis, others were more critical, pointing out areas that

Baker's analysis could not account for. These included phenomena such as adjunct incorporation in Chukchee (Spencer 1995), non-object incorporation in Northern Athapaskan (Cook and Wilhelm 1998), and morpheme-specific variation in Mohawk incorporation (Mithun and Corbett 1999). More recently, Barrie and Mathieu (2012) discuss Roberts' (2010) reworking of head movement within the Minimalist framework, pointing out problems with his analysis based on additional data from Algonquian and Northern Iroquoian languages.

New syntactic analyses were proposed as well, many within the Minimalist framework. Massam (2001; 2009) explored pseudo noun incorporation in Niuean, claiming that what appears to be NI is actually the syntactic Merging of a base-generated object NP with an adjacent verb, which then undergo predicate raising. In Johns' (2007) study of Inuktitut, NI involves the verb in little v undergoing Merge with a nominal root. Barrie (2010), based on data from Northern Iroquoian, proposed that when a noun and verb Merge in a NI structure, they form "a point of symmetric c-command," violating the Linear Correspondence Axiom (LCA). The noun moves to Spec VP, creating an asymmetric c-command relation that satisfies the LCA (following the Dynamic Asymmetry framework of Moro 2000).

There are studies on NI in other theoretical frameworks as well, such as Allen *et al.* (1984; 1990) and Rosen (1990), who investigate Southern Tiwa within the theory of Relational Grammar. Norcross's (1993) dissertation investigates Shawnee NI from three theoretical perspectives – Government and Binding, Relational Grammar, and LFG – and concludes that LFG can best account for her data.

2.3.2 NI as a lexical process

The alternative to the syntactic approach is the lexicalist view, according to which NI structures, similar to compounds, are built in the lexicon by word-formation rules. Proponents of this view include Mithun (1984; 1986), Di Sciullo and Williams (1987), Rosen (1989), and Anderson (1992; 2001). Both Di Sciullo and Williams (1987: 63–69) and Anderson (2001) challenge Baker's evidence for a head movement analysis and conclude that a lexicalist approach is superior. For example, Di Sciullo and Williams claim that the "NP remnant" left behind in the object position and "copies" of the incorporated noun (e.g., *fish-bullhead*) are independent of incorporation, and that the direct object role of the incorporated noun can be specified in terms of argument structure rather than syntax. Rosen (1989) proposes two types of NI, Compound and Classifier. In Compound NI the incorporated noun satisfies one of the verb's arguments, resulting in an alteration of the verb's argument structure since the complex verb has one fewer argument than the original simple form. In Classifier NI the verb's argument structure remains unchanged, as the incorporated noun is linked to the verb semantically. Rosen claims that her account correctly predicts clusters of properties associated with each type, something that syntactic approaches are unable to do.

2.3.3 Combined approaches

Two relatively new theories, Autolexical Syntax (Sadock 1991) and Distributed Morphology (Halle and Marantz 1993; Harley and Noyer 1999), present an approach to morphosyntactic phenomena that allows integrated access to both syntax and morphology. Sadock's (1985; 1991) studies on West Greenlandic are based on his Autolexical Syntax theory, which posits autonomous levels of information (e.g., morphology, syntax, semantics, discourse, and, possibly, phonology) that assign separate representations to a linguistic expression. Sadock claims that his theory can account for modular mismatches as well as phenomena such as NI in which the same expression can be represented at two different levels (i.e., morphology and syntax). Although in earlier work Sadock argued for a syntactic rather than lexical analysis of NI (e.g., Sadock 1980; 1986), his Autolexical Syntax approach "dissolves the controversy by saying that it is both" (Baker 1997: 848).

In Distributed Morphology (DM) the word formation process is not independent of syntax, but works along with the syntax in the course of a derivation. The syntax manipulates abstract formal features rather than fully formed words; phonological content is added at spellout after all syntactic processes have been completed (Late Insertion). Haugen (2009) analyzes hyponomous objects in Hopi using DM and Chomsky's (1995) Copy Theory, proposing a solution that makes use of DM's abstract syntactic categories and feature spellout.

While this section has focused on the morphology and syntax of NI, the literature on NI also includes important work on semantics. Van Geenhoven's (1998) analysis of NI in West Greenlandic presents a theory of semantic incorporation where incorporated nouns are predicative indefinites that are absorbed by semantically incorporating verbs. Her work addresses many key issues, including the existential force of the incorporated nominal, incorporated nouns and indefinite descriptions, external modification, and discourse transparency (see also van Geenhoven 1992). Other studies on the semantics of NI include Bittner (1994) on West Greenlandic, Farkas and de Swart (2003) on Hungarian, and Dayal (2007) on Hindi. Most of these works focus on the interpretation of structures that have the semantic but not necessarily morphological properties of NI. Finally, the role of pragmatics in the use of NI is explored in Haugen (2009).

3 Nonconfigurationality

3.1 (Non)configurational structure

Nonconfigurationality is a classification for languages that appear to lack a structural distinction between subjects and objects. Most of the languages described by syntactic theory distinguish subjects and objects structurally: the verb and its object form a unit (the VP), while the subject is in a higher position external to the VP. Evidence for this configurational structure comes from word order, constituency tests, and binding asymmetries. In contrast, there is a distinctive class of languages that do not structurally differentiate between the arguments of a verb. It was Hale (1981; 1983) who first proposed that such languages, called nonconfigurational languages, have a flat structure where subjects and objects are not in a hierarchical relation. Hale observed that these languages (for example, Warlpiri) often appear with the following cluster of properties: (i) free word order, (ii) syntactically discontinuous constituents, and (iii) null anaphora – that is, arguments not represented by overt NPs. Nonconfigurationality occurs in most Australian languages, American Indian languages, South American languages, South Asian languages (e.g., Malayalam), Hungarian, Japanese, and perhaps German (Baker 2001).

Shown in (2) are Warlpiri examples from Hale (1983: 6–7). The words in (2a) can appear in any order as long as the Aux is in second position. Sentence (2b) is an example of a discontinuous expression (in bold), and (2c) shows the use of null anaphora.

(2) a. Ngarrka-ngku ka   wawirri   panti-rni.
        man-Erg   Aux kangaroo spear-Nonpast
        'The man is spearing the kangaroo.'

b. **Wawirri** kapi-rna panti-rni **yalumpu**.
 kangaroo Aux spear-Nonpast that
 'I will spear that kangaroo.'

c. Panti-rni ka.
 spear-Nonpast Aux
 'He/she is spearing him/it.'

3.2   A nonconfigurationality parameter

Nonconfigurationality has been investigated more within a theoretical rather than a descriptive framework. This is primarily because the earliest studies, in particular Hale (1981; 1983) and Jelinek (1984), worked within the Principles-and-Parameters framework of Chomsky (1973; 1981), using hierarchical notions such as phrase structure, constituents, and binding to describe the properties of configurational and nonconfigurational languages. The goal of those studies was to find a parameter to account for the differences between the two language types. The parameter also had to account for the fact that even prototypical nonconfigurational languages distinguish subjects from objects in certain constructions such as agreement, control, and reflexives/reciprocals.

Hale's (1981; 1983) parametric difference focused on phrase structure. In his earlier work Hale (1981) proposed two types of phrase structure rules. In languages such as English, the rules "impose a hierarchical or 'configurational' organization upon syntactic expression" (p. 2). The other type, exemplified by Warlpiri, has a very basic phrase structure rule, $X' \rightarrow X'^* X$, that generates only one level of structure and allows lexical insertion of category-neutral elements in any linear order (p. 43). In a subsequent study, following new ideas of that time that phrase structure may be derivatives of independent grammatical principles (e.g., Chomsky 1981; Stowell 1981), and that hierarchical phrasal structure may be predictable from the properties of lexical heads (Bresnan 1982), Hale (1983) explored the relationship between phrase structure (PS) and lexical structure (LS) (i.e., a predicate and its arguments) as a possible source of parametric difference. He proposed a Configurationality Parameter that allowed the Projection Principle to apply differently in the two language types. In configurational languages the Projection Principle applies to the pair (LS, PS), requiring each argument in LS to have a corresponding constituent in PS. In nonconfigurational languages the Projection Principle applies only to LS, where subject-object asymmetries exist, and not to PS, permitting a flat structure in PS. The three nonconfigurational properties listed above follow from this dissociation between LS and PS: free word order and discontinuous constituents are permitted because the order of LS arguments is not constrained by PS rules, and arguments that are present in LS are not required to be present in PS, accounting for the extensive use of null anaphors.

Hale's proposals sparked much theoretical discussion on non-Indo-European, lesser-known languages, as many of them exhibited some form of nonconfigurationality. One of the most influential papers in response to Hale's work was that of Jelinek (1984), who disagreed with the parameterization of the Projection Principle and presented a different view of the difference between configurational and nonconfigurational languages. In this and subsequent papers (e.g., Jelinek and Demers 1994; Jelinek 2006) Jelinek claimed that in nonconfigurational languages such as Warlpiri the arguments of a verb are the clitic pronouns appearing in AUX, and not the full lexical NPs. The NPs are adjuncts coindexed with the pronominal arguments through case-related linking and compatibility rules. To Jelinek (p. 50), the relation between pronominal arguments and NP adjuncts is similar to the NPs in the English sentence *He, the doctor, tells me, the patient, what to do*. This analysis became widely known as the Pronominal Argument Hypothesis (PAH). Jelinek accounted for discontinuous elements in Warlpiri by allowing multiple nominals to be referentially linked to a single argument. Furthermore, since lexical NPs are adjuncts they may appear in any order, without hierarchical structure, accounting for the free word order of Warlpiri and other nonconfigurational languages. Finally, she explained that the so-called hierarchical properties such as reflexive binding and control can equally be described in terms of grammatical function rather than structural positions.

Many papers subsequently appeared discussing the implications of the PAH. As with any new theory, some were supportive while others were critical. In support of Jelinek's analysis were studies such as Speas (1990), Baker (1991; 1996), and Hale (2003). Adopting the PAH, Hale (2003) revised his original head movement analysis of the order of elements in the Navajo verb and proposed a non-movement, phonological account. Many studies adopted the basic ideas of the PAH but modified it to accommodate the particular language they were investigating. For example, Speas (1990) accepted that the agreement clitics in Aux are the arguments of the verb, but claimed that they were originally in syntactic argument positions and were incorporated into the verb. She proposed, furthermore, that lexical NPs are secondary predicates adjoined to the verb in a position lower than that of the pronominal arguments. Baker (1991; 1996), in his study of Mohawk, claimed that the arguments are null pronouns appearing in argument positions in the syntax, which, by his Polysynthesis Parameter (see §4.3 below), are licensed by agreement morphology. For Baker, lexical NPs are clitic left dislocation structures, similar to the NPs in the sentence *The doctor, the patients, she really helped them*.

Other studies were more critical. Davis and Matthewson (2009: 1107–1114) provided an excellent summary of the debate surrounding a PAH analysis of Salish (see Jelinek 2006; Jelinek and Demers 1994) based on works such as Davis (2005; 2006; 2009), Davis and Matthewson (2003), Davis *et al.* (1993), and Gardiner (1993). They noted that the Salish languages exhibit some properties of a Pronominal Argument (PA) language, but have many properties that contradict the predictions of the PAH. These include the existence of unregistered arguments – that is, DPs with no corresponding pronominal affix or clitic – different interpretations (e.g., definiteness) between DPs and their corresponding pronouns, and asymmetries between adjuncts and arguments and between subjects and objects. Given such evidence, they concluded that *"no Salish language is a pronominal argument language"* (p. 1114, their italics): a bold yet well-supported conclusion. Bruening (2001) showed that Passamaquoddy, a language which displays typical nonconfigurational properties, also exhibits configurational properties in ditransitives and discontinuous NPs. He suggested that both the configurational and nonconfigurational properties were the result of movement, but of different types, implying that in Passamaquoddy lexical NPs are arguments and not adjunct clauses. LeSourd (2006), in another study of Maliseet-Passamaquoddy, claimed that the PAH cannot explain certain facts about the inflectional system, the comitative construction, and discontinuous constituents. He concluded that if Maliseet-Passamaquoddy, an ideal candidate for a PA language, could not be appropriately analyzed as one, then "some skepticism may be in order when considering other possible cases of pronominal argument languages" (p. 512).

Such criticisms revealed a major problem with a parametric account of nonconfigurationality: languages do not fall into two types, those that exhibit nonconfigurational properties and those that do not. Nonconfigurational languages, far from being a heterogeneous class, differ in the extent to which they exhibit the properties identified by Hale (1983) and

Jelinek (1984). Given that all the properties do not need to be attested in a language for it to be considered nonconfigurational, it was not clear how nonconfigurationality should be defined. While for Hale (1983) the three nonconfigurational properties were intimately connected to flat structure, it was suggested that these properties were in fact independent of each other, and of flat structures as well (Austin and Bresnan 1996), further supporting the idea that nonconfigurationality is not a unified phenomenon (Tait 1991; Baker 2001).

Such concerns were recognized as early as Hale (1989). Hale accounted for the differences among nonconfigurational languages by suggesting that independent factors may prohibit nonconfigurationality properties from surfacing. He also suggested that nonconfigurationality was "a property of constructions" rather than "a global property of languages," allowing for nonconfigurational constructions in configurational languages, and vice versa (p. 294).

With others coming to the same conclusion about the heterogeneity of nonconfigurational languages, the focus of theoretical studies shifted from the search for one parameter to the investigation of more general grammatical principles as the source of nonconfigurationality. However, as the investigations continued, there was increasing evidence that nonconfigurational languages may in fact be underlyingly configurational. For example, Baker (1991; 1996) assumed that Mohawk was configurational, and proposed a series of parameters and language-specific conditions to account for its classic nonconfigurational properties, including the Polysynthesis Parameter and conditions on Case absorption and adjunct chain relations. Baker (2001) proposed three types of nonconfigurational languages, all with configurational structures but different underlying causes of their nonconfigurational properties.

Most studies, though, were heading in the direction of accounting for nonconfigurationality by universal rather than language-specific principles. Speas (1990) examined the evidence claimed to support the existence of both configurational and nonconfigurational properties in a number of nonconfigurational languages (Japanese, Malayalam, Warlpiri, and Hungarian), and concluded that the data pointed to a configurational rather than nonconfigurational structure in all the languages examined. In particular, she claimed that the surface properties of Warlpiri resulted from "the interaction of parameters having to do with theta relations, direction of Case assignment and lexical properties of the Warlpiri Kase particles" (p. 172). Similarly, Legate (2002) adopted a "microparametric approach" where nonconfigurational parameters result from "a collection of parameter settings" that also apply to configurational languages (p. 124).

Research continues today on finding the appropriate model of (non)configurationality. One paper in the recent Minimalist Program (Chomsky 1995; 2000; 2001) is Kiss (2008), who claims that phase theory is the most suitable framework for explaining the configurational and nonconfigurational properties of Hungarian. Hungarian word order is fixed preverbally but is free postverbally. Kiss claims that when a functional phrase (TP or FocP) headed by the verb is constructed, the copy of the lower V and its projections are deleted, resulting in a flat structure that allows freedom of word order. This is an interesting proposal, as it posits two different sub-structures for configurational and nonconfigurational word order, with both of them appearing in the same clause.

3.3   LFG and dependent-marking languages

The initial challenge of nonconfigurationality for the Principles-and-Parameters framework was that the supposedly universal relation between arguments and structural positions appeared not to hold. Equally prominent in the literature on nonconfigurationality are studies in the syntactic framework of Lexical-Functional Grammar (LFG), which does not make similar assumptions about grammatical function and structure. In fact, Bresnan (2001) states that nonconfigurationality was one of the phenomena that inspired LFG. Studies within the LFG framework include Bresnan (1982; 2001), Mohanan (1982), Simpson (1983; 1991), Kroeger (1993), Austin and Bresnan (1996), and Nordlinger (1998). In the LFG framework grammatical functions are not identified with phrase structure positions. Rather, LFG consists of parallel structures that contain separate information on the structural properties of a language. F(unctional)-structure is where grammatical relations belong, a(rgument)-structure contains information on predicate-argument relations, and c(onstituent)-structure is the surface expression of languages, similar to s-structure in Principles-and-Parameters theory. These parallel independent structures are associated through linking or mapping principles.

While f-structures express universal grammatical relations and thus are similar across languages, c-structures exhibit great cross-linguistic variation. In LFG it is the organization of c-structure that distinguishes configurational and nonconfigurational languages. In configurational languages c-structures are organized endocentrically, represented by hierarchical tree structures similar to those in Principles-and-Parameters theory. In nonconfigurational languages c-structures are organized lexocentrically, consisting of flat structures with all arguments sister to the verb. In such languages grammatical functions are identified by morphology, such as case and agreement. Bresnan (2001: 14) claims that in LFG "words, or lexical elements, are as important as syntactic elements in expressing grammatical information".

One of the main issues addressed by LFG studies on nonconfigurationality is the role of case in the identification of grammatical roles. While much work in Principles-and-Parameters theory, starting with Jelinek's PAH, had been done on languages that associate grammatical functions with verbal agreement (i.e., head-marking languages), few studies had looked at nonconfigurational languages with rich case systems and little or no verbal agreement (i.e., dependent-marking languages). Many of the LFG studies investigate a variety of Australian languages, some of which, such as Warlpiri, are head-marking, while other related ones, such as Jiwarli, are head-dependent. For example, Austin and Bresnan (1996) provide extensive empirical evidence against Jelinek's PAH based on eight Australian languages, including Warlpiri and Jiwarli. They present arguments refuting the idea of lexical NPs being adjuncts, including semantic differences between lexical NPs and clitic pronouns, unregistered arguments, differences in case-marking between lexical NPs and true adjuncts (e.g., temporal nominals), and the absence of bound pronominals in non-finite clauses. They show that Australian languages exhibit great variation in the behavior of bound pronominals in: their presence or absence, the arguments that they encode, the features of the arguments they encode, and split ergativity. Furthermore, they show that languages differ in the nonconfigurational properties they exhibit, and that those properties cannot be predicted by the presence or absence of bound pronominals. They conclude that the PAH, which proposes a unified explanation for nonconfigurational languages such as Warlpiri based on pronominal arguments, is inadequate and inferior to a dual structure LFG analysis.

Nordlinger (1998) presents a formal theory of case-marking (constructive case) to account for the identification of grammatical functions in dependent-marking nonconfigurational languages. She extends the LFG analysis of head-marking nonconfigurational languages, in which grammatical relations are identified through verbal affixes, to those nonconfigurational languages in which grammatical functions are identified through case.

Nordlinger also proposes a typology of (non)configurationality based on how languages identify grammatical functions and their degree of head- or dependent-marking. Fully non-configurational languages identify grammatical relations morphologically through case or agreement, while fully configurational ones identify them syntactically. In between are languages that combine both strategies. This continuum, combined with the degree to which languages exhibit head- or dependent-marking properties, results in the following typological classifications (p. 49): head-marking nonconfigurational (Mohawk, Mayali), dependent-marking nonconfigurational (Jiwarli, Dyirbal), head-marking configurational (Navajo, Chichewa), and dependent-marking configurational (Icelandic, Martuthunira). This typology is claimed to be easily captured within LFG, where information on grammatical relations can come from different places (i.e., verbal morphology, case marking, phrase structure) and then "be unified and identified (in the f-structure) with the structure of the clause as a whole."

4   Polysynthesis

Polysynthetic languages have traditionally been characterized as having a large number of morphemes per word, containing in one word what in other languages would be expressed by an entire sentence. As Boas (2002: 74) observed, "in polysynthetic languages, a large number of distinct ideas are amalgamated by grammatical processes and form a single word, without any morphological distinction between the formal elements in the sentence and the contents of the sentence." Derivational and inflectional morphemes affixed to a verb express grammatical functions, tense/aspect, modifiers, quantification, and adverbial notions. Nouns are often incorporated into the verbal complex as well. Polysynthetic languages are found in North, Central and South America, Australia, Papua New Guinea, Siberia, India, and the Caucasus. Shown in (3) is an example from Central Siberian Yupik.

(3)   Central Siberian Yupik
        negh-yaghtugh-yug-uma-yagh-pet(e)-aa   =llu
        eat-go.to.V-want.to.V-Past-Frustr-Infer-Indic.3s.3s=also
        'Also, it turns out she/he wanted to go eat it, but...'   (de Reuse 2006: 745)

4.1   Polysynthetic properties

While the main property of a polysynthetic language is its complex verbal morphology, attempts have been made to provide a more precise characterization of polysynthesis by listing properties that are common to all languages of this type. The following are some properties of the verb form (see Mithun 1988; Fortescue 1994; 2007; Mattissen 2006): a large inventory of non-root bound morphemes, the possibility of more than one root, many morphological slots, and sentential equivalence. The bound morphemes may represent various semantic categories, including adverbial elements, modality, quantification, core arguments, and tense, aspect, and mode. Additional diagnostic properties not necessarily restricted to polysynthetic languages are head-marking types of inflection, and productive morphophonemics. The problem with such lists is that, while they describe properties found in polysynthetic languages in general, they are neither necessary nor sufficient conditions for a language to be classified as polysynthetic. Mattissen (2004; 2006), after investigating about 75 polysynthetic languages in her search for a "common denominator," concludes that languages display different subsets of polysynthetic properties.

A different approach to characterizing polysynthesis is to find one or two properties that are shared by all polysynthetic languages, such as polypersonalism, noun incorporation, or a particular morpheme. One traditionally definitive property of polysynthesis is polypersonalism, "the idea that the verb form itself picks out, cross-references, incorporates or otherwise specifies the arguments of the verb" (Spencer 2004: 396). This is most commonly realized in the form of bound pronominals (see also Mithun 1988; Kibrik 1992; Fortescue 1994). Polypersonalism allows a verb form to function as a sentence. Yet while polypersonalism is a property of polysynthetic languages, there exist morphologically complex polysynthetic languages such as Haida and Tlingit in which pronominal markers are independent pronouns rather than morphemes on the verb (Boas 2002). Making polypersonalism the defining property is problematic without a clear definition of what counts as argument marking. For example, in Macedonian and Bulgarian person clitics behave similarly to bound morphemes, and many Bantu languages have object markers that appear in certain discourse situations, yet these languages are not considered to be polysynthetic (Spencer 2004).

Another potential defining property is noun incorporation, where object nouns appear in the verbal complex and not as independent words (see §2). Yet there are languages such as Yimas (Papua New Guinea) that are polysynthetic in terms of morphological complexity but do not exhibit noun incorporation (Boas 2002; Drossard 1997; Mattissen 2004). For Drossard (1997; 2002), the minimal condition for polysynthesis is the incorporation of adverbial elements as bound morphemes on the verb form. This criterion has been criticized by Mattissen (2004), who shows that certain languages, such as Russian, Hungarian, and Laz (South Caucasian), have preverbs that fulfill adverbial functions, yet are not considered polysynthetic. Furthermore, she notes that Drossard does not adequately define what constitutes an adverbial, requiring that one "concretize the criterion" or consider it a necessary but not sufficient condition (Mattissen 2004: 193).

In some cases the defining criterion is the existence of a verbal morpheme of a particular form rather than meaning. De Reuse (2006) defines a polysynthetic language as one with a large number of productive noninflectional concatenation (PNC) postbases. PNC postbases have the following properties: they are fully productive, recursive, in most cases concatenative (i.e., linearly ordered), interact with syntax, and can change lexical category. De Reuse proposes a continuum of polysynthesis based on the number of PNC elements found in a language. Dutch, with only a few PNC elements, is non-polysynthetic, mildly polysynthetic languages such as Arawakan and Siouan have more than a dozen PNC elements, solidly polysynthetic ones such as Caddoan and Wakashan have over 100, and extreme polysynthetic languages such as Eskimo contain several hundred PNC elements. Mattissen (2003; 2004; 2006) proposes a similar condition: the existence of at least one non-root bound morpheme in the verb form. Non-root bound morphemes are affixes that would have independent forms in a non-polysynthetic language but never appear as free word forms in polysynthetic ones. While acknowledging that "the richer an inventory of non-root bound morphemes a language manifests, the clearer its case for polysynthesis becomes" (Mattissen 2003: 194), Mattissen sets the minimum number of non-bound morphemes in a polysynthetic language to one, in order to differentiate it from non-polysynthetic agglutinating languages such as Yucatec Maya, Swedish, and Japanese. Greenberg (1960) proposes a quantitative index of synthesis, M(orpheme) per W(ord), to measure the degree of synthesis in a language.

The absence of uncontroversial or uncontested criteria for polysynthesis has led some linguists to classify polysynthetic languages into subclasses based on their properties, rather than to find properties shared by all languages of this type.

4.2 Types of polysynthesis

Polysynthetic languages have been classified along several dimensions: affixal (non-root bound morphemes) vs. compositional (lexical morphemes) (Mattissen 2004; 2006); sentential vs. non-sentential (Drossard 1997); and templatic vs. scope-ordered organization of verb form (Mattissen 2004; 2006).

Mattissen (2003; 2004; 2006) presents a classification of polysynthetic subtypes along two dimensions: the type of word formation process used and the internal organization of the verb form. The first classification is based on whether semantic elements in the complex verb form appear as non-root bound morphemes (affixal) or lexical morphemes (compositional). Mattissen classifies as affixal those languages that allow only one root in the verb complex and whose other semantic elements appear as non-root bound morphemes (e.g., Greenlandic). This contrasts with compositional languages such as Chukchi, in which the verb form consists of more than one lexical root (but at least one non-root bound morpheme, by definition). Structures consisting of multiple lexical roots include noun, adverb, and adjective incorporation, and verb root serialization. Mattissen also proposes two mixed categories between the affixal and compositional classes: those that exhibit noun incorporation but not verb serialization (e.g., Takelma and Blackfoot) and those that have verb serialization but not NI (e.g., Chinook and Awtuw). A similar classification is found in Fortescue (1994), consisting of pure incorporating (Mattissen's compositional), field-affixing, and recursive suffixing types, with combinations of types included as well.

A second classification is based on whether or not the language exhibits polypersonalism, the representation of arguments on the verb. Drossard (1997; 2002) divides languages into sentential and non-sentential classes. Languages with bound pronouns are considered sentential, since the verbal element, containing both subject and object information, represents a grammatical sentence.

The third classification concerns the internal structure of the polysynthetic verb form – that is, the way the morphemes are combined (Mattissen 2006: 293). The elements in the verbal complex can be templatic, with a fixed number of slots appearing in a particular order, or they can be semantically organized by scope (e.g., Athapaskan; see Rice 2000). A third subtype consists of a combination of templatic and scope structures.

The heterogeneous structure of polysynthetic languages makes it difficult to evaluate these classifications, as some languages do not fit into any of them and others appear in several categories simultaneously. While languages are normally classified typologically based on their most salient morphological properties, most languages combine elements of different morphological types. Thus it may be better to describe polysynthetic languages within a continuum of polysynthesis, based on the types of morphological structures that are found in the language.

4.3 The polysynthesis parameter

Any unified explanation of the clusterings of properties that define polysynthesis requires a wide sample of languages as an empirical base with which to determine which properties go together and which ones are independent. "Otherwise the clustering of properties is simply circular, the result of definitionally excluding from consideration any language that fails to meet at least one of the criteria" (Evans and Sasse 2002: 4). This danger of circularity is one of the reasons why polysynthetic languages are challenging for linguistic theory.

Baker (1996) was the first investigation of polysynthesis within the framework of formal Principles-and-Parameters theory (Chomsky 1981; 1986). Baker presented a detailed analysis of one polysynthetic language, Mohawk, and proposed a single parameter to explain the properties of Mohawk and other polysynthetic languages, as well as how they differ from non-polysynthetic ones. His Polysynthesis Parameter, also called the Morphological Visibility Condition (MVC), states that "[e]very argument of a head must be related to a morpheme in the word containing that head" (Baker 1996: 14). This relation, required for theta-role visibility, may be satisfied by agreement or movement (i.e., noun incorporation). By Baker's definition a polysynthetic language is one in which both agreement and noun incorporation can make a phrase visible for theta-role assignment, and thus are "part of the same system for expressing argument relationships" (Baker 1996: 20). However, it is noun incorporation that is the critical element, as Baker claims that every language with robust noun incorporation also has full and obligatory subject and object agreement paradigms. "Robust" noun incorporation is productive, has fully integrated, referentially active noun roots, and has noun and verb roots that can both be used independently.

For Baker, true polysynthetic languages that meet the criteria for noun incorporation include Mohawk and other Northern Iroquoian languages, Tuscarora, Wichita, Kowa, Southern Tiwa, Huauhtla Nahuatl, the Gunwinjguan languages of Northern Australia, Chukchee, and perhaps Classical Ainu. His restrictive definition of polysynthesis excludes languages traditionally considered to be polysynthetic, which he claims may have "quite impressive amounts of morphological complexity [but] may not use that complexity to *systematically* represent *argument* relationships" (Baker 1996: 18). Examples of such languages are Warlpiri, Navajo, and the Algonquian languages, which lack productive noun incorporation. His definition also excludes languages such as Slave, Haisla, Yimas, and the Eskimoan languages, which may have some pronominal affixes and/or incorporation but in which affixation and incorporation are not systematic for all arguments.

Baker's work was the first to provide a framework for a theoretical rather than a descriptive discussion of polysynthetic languages. There was bound to be controversial, as languages traditionally considered to be polysynthetic, such as the Eskimo-Aleut languages, were excluded based on his definition. There were also languages that were considered by Baker to be polysynthetic, but did not exhibit other characteristic properties. For example, Nahuatl has the requisite noun incorporation and verbal agreement, but has relatively fixed word order and true quantifiers (MacSwan 1998). In Machiguenga, a polysynthetic language of Peru, agreement morphemes and incorporated nouns follow the verb root, contradicting Baker's generalization that such elements precede the verb in polysynthetic languages (Lorenzo 1997). Lorenzo argued for an AgrO head attached to the verb at the lexical level, contrary to the elimination of Agr heads in Baker (1996). Evans (2006) provided evidence from Dalabon, a Gunwinyguan language of Australia, for the existence of subordinate clauses, one of the features Baker claimed is absent in polysynthetic languages. Evans showed that Dalabon has many structural options for signaling subordination on the verb, and concludes that claims about the lack of subordination in polysynthetic languages "represent statistical correlations, rather than categorical requirements" (Evans 2006: 31).

The strength of Baker's proposal was its theoretical contribution to the study of polysynthesis, providing a "unified explanation" for many of the properties characteristic of these languages. These include properties found in nonconfigurational languages, such as free word order, omission of noun phrase arguments and discontinuous expressions, and obligatory agreement, as well as lesser discussed properties such as the absence of adpositional phrase arguments, NP reflexives, true quantifiers and infinitival verb forms, and restrictions on incorporation structures (Baker 1996: 498–499). On the other hand, Baker's theory could not avoid the circularity problem, as he "definitionally excludes" those languages that do not satisfy the MVP. As Koenig and Michelson (1998: 130) note: "… B[aker]'s use of polysynthetic does not refer to an independently defined class of languages. In fact, for B[aker] polysynthesis is defined by the polysynthesis parameter." The MVP could equally be applicable to the subset of polysynthetic languages that exhibit both polypersonalism and noun incorporation, such as the sentential languages of Drossard (1997) or those that belong to one of Mattissen's (2004; 2006) classes.

5   General discussion

The study of noun incorporation, nonconfigurationality, and polysynthesis originated from investigations into non-Indo-European, lesser-known languages. While linguists had an intuitive notion of what these topics entailed, it became clear that more precise characterizations of the phenomena were necessary, as they were discovered to occur in many different forms in a wide variety of languages. The goal of theoretical descriptions was to find the best model that could explain the properties associated with each phenomenon while at the same time accommodating the variation found within them. Basic questions were raised – questions that remain central and relevant to research on these topics today.

For noun incorporation, the questions concern what can be combined in an incorporated structure, and the process by which those elements are combined: that is, is it syntactic or lexical? There has been a real divide among the proponents of each view, strengthened by their conviction that their analyses can best account for their particular data. More recent theories, though, such as Autolexical Syntax (Sadock 1991) and Distributed Morphology (Halle and Marantz 1993; Harley and Noyer 1999), propose a more interactive approach to the morphological and syntactic components of the grammar, allowing a more conciliatory perspective on the NI debate.

For nonconfigurationality, the central questions involve the relation between arguments and syntactic structure. It seems that we have come full circle in the characterization of this phenomenon. In the first stage, before Hale (1981; 1983) and Jelinek (1984), all languages were assumed to be configurational. Properties such as free word order, null arguments, and verbal agreement were not perceived to reflect any typological differences, since they all appeared in familiar configurational languages as well. In the second stage, with the works of Hale and Jelinek, came the proposal that there are two types of languages: configurational and nonconfigurational. The distinction between the two types could be (i) binary, best accounted for by a parameter (e.g., Hale 1983; Jelinek 1984), or (ii) a continuum, with configurational and nonconfigurational languages appearing at opposite ends, and with many languages in between exhibiting properties of both (e.g., Nordlinger 1998). We are now heading back to the first stage, with the prevailing view again being that all languages are configurational, with nonconfigurational properties best accounted for at a different level of structure. Nonconfigurationality is one area which is not dominated by Principles-and-Parameters theory but has equal representation in LFG, at least among major works. The advantage of the LFG model is that it can accommodate more easily the absence of asymmetry among arguments. However, given recent views that all nonconfigurational languages are underlyingly configurational, the disadvantage for Principles-and-Parameters is less obvious.

For polysynthetic languages, the questions concern which properties (including verbal elements), and how many of them, are necessary for a language to be classified as polysynthetic. Some have even questioned the basic notion of polysynthesis as a separate morphological type, suggesting that it is just an extreme form of agglutination combining lexical and grammatical morphemes (e.g., Iacobini 2006). One reason for this is that properties identified with polysynthetic languages can be found in non-polysynthetic ones as well. Furthermore, if a polysynthetic language were to be defined in terms of the number rather than type of elements that make up the verbal complex, it seems justifiable to assume that the boundary between agglutinating and polysynthetic languages is a "continuum rather than a dichotomy" (Aikhenvald 2007: 7).

Despite the decades of research into noun incorporation, nonconfigurationality, and polysynthesis, it appears that linguists generally still subscribe to the traditional intuitive definitions of these phenomena. For example, for most linguists the term "nonconfigurationality" still consists of the meaning suggested by Hale (1983). As observed by Baker (2001), in general the term can be used in two ways: in a narrow sense to refer to languages that exhibit the three properties identified by Hale (1983), and in a broader sense to refer to languages in which grammatical functions cannot be distinguished by phrase structure. For linguists investigating nonconfigurational languages, though, the term encompasses much more than that, for, as Baker (2001: 413) observes, nonconfigurationality "is relevant to some of the deepest issues of linguistics, including the questions of how much variation Universal Grammar allows and what are its proper primitives (phrase structure, grammatical functions, or something else)."

The same is true for polysynthesis, which typically describes languages with a large number of morphemes per word, containing in one word what in other languages would be expressed by an entire sentence. A survey of recent articles in the *International Journal of American Linguistics* reveals that "polysynthesis" is used most often as a typological classification rather than in a theoretical sense such as that proposed by Baker (1996). In these articles the descriptive criteria for classifying a language as polysynthetic include the following: the existence of complex verbs (Danielsen 2011; van Gijn 2011; Beavert and Jansen 2011; Petersen de Piñeros 2007), pronominal affixes (Seifart 2012; van Gijn 2011; Jany 2011; Gerdts and Hinkson 2004; Junker 2003), extensive suffixation (Jany 2011; Stenzel 2007; Kroeker 2001), many morphemes per word (Lavie *et al.* 2010), and syntactic phrases (Tonhauser and Colijn 2010; Junker 2003). Even Baker's work, which greatly influenced theoretical research on polysynthesis, has at its core "the very traditional idea that polysynthesis characterizes languages in which words can be sentences, so that predicate-argument relations, which are at the core of the structural make-up of sentences, are defined and satisfied within the word" (Koenig and Michelson 1998: 129). The years of research on polysynthesis, from description to theory, have not resulted in any concrete definitions or defining criteria. Yet, as observed by Fortescue (1994: 2601), "in practice linguists are rarely in doubt as to whether a particular language should be called 'polysynthetic'."

The challenge for researchers investigating phenomena such as polysynthesis, noun incorporation, and nonconfigurationality is to discover what underlies the intuitive descriptions of languages of these types.

Notes

1   The following abbreviations are used in (1): FACT: factual; PUNC: punctual; NSF: noun suffix; 1sS: 1st singular subject.
2   For other overviews of NI see Baker (1993), Gerdts (1998), Aikhenvald (2007), Mathieu (2009), and Massam (2009).

3 It is claimed that this debate started 100 years earlier with Sapir (1911) and Kroeber (1909, 1911). Sapir (1911: 257) defined NI as a lexical process "compounding a noun stem with a verb." He was reacting to Kroeber's (1909) definition that "[n]oun incorporation is the combination into one word of the noun object and the verb functioning as the predicate of the sentence" (cited in Sapir 1911: 254). Sapir objected to the fact that the definition combined a morphological requirement (that the noun and verb form a word) and a syntactic requirement (that the noun be the object of the verb), claiming that it made the definition too restrictive: "Noun incorporation is primarily either a morphologic or syntactic process; the attempt to put it under two rubrics at the same time necessarily leads to a certain amount of artificiality of treatment" (p. 255). In response to Sapir (1911), Kroeber (1911: 578) acknowledged that "[t]his criticism is correct" and claimed that "the basis of the definition was historical rather than logical... This leads to a new conception: incorporation is no longer an essentially objective process... but is non-syntactical in its nature." Thus the "debate" was based more on a need for clarification rather than on two opposing views.

Further reading

Noun incorporation

Baker, M. 1988. *Incorporation: A Theory of Grammatical Function Changing.* Chicago, IL: University of Chicago Press.

An investigation of syntactic incorporation encompassing both grammatical function changing phenomena (e.g. passives and causatives) and the creation of complex predicates.

Mithun, M. 1984. The evolution of NI. *Language* 60:847–894.

A typological, functional and descriptive study of NI across a wide-ranging sample of languages supporting a lexical view of NI.

Nonconfigurationality

Austin, P. and J. Bresnan. 1996. Non-configurationality in Australian Aboriginal languages. *Natural Language and Linguistic Theory* 14:215–268.

A study of several Australian aboriginal languages showing the superiority of an LFG over a PAH analysis of nonconfigurationality.

Hale, K. 1983. Warlpiri and the grammar of non-configurational languages. *Natural Language and Linguistic Theory* 1:5–47.

This first theoretical study of nonconfigurationality proposes a parametric account of the cluster of properties found in nonconfigurational languages such as Warlpiri.

Jelinek, E. 1984. Empty categories, case, and configurationality. *Natural Language and Linguistic Theory* 2:39–76.

This study introduces the Pronominal Argument Hypothesis (PAH), which claims that nominals in nonconfigurational languages are adjuncts to the verbal arguments appearing as clitics in Aux.

Polysynthesis

Baker, M. 1996. *The Polysynthesis Parameter.* New York/Oxford: Oxford University Press.

Study of polysynthesis within a Principles-and-Parameters framework.

References

Aikhenvald, A.Y. 2007. Typological distinctions in word-formation. In *Language Typology and Description, Second Edition. Volume III: Grammatical Categories and the Lexicon*, ed. T. Shopen, 1–65. Cambridge: Cambridge University Press.

Allen, B.J., D.B. Gardiner, and D.G. Frantz. 1984. Noun incorporation in Southern Tiwa. *International Journal of American Linguistics* 50:292–311.

Allen, B.J., D.G. Frantz, D. Gardiner, and J.M. Perlmutter. 1990. Verb agreement, possessor ascension, and multistratal representation in Southern Tiwa. In *Studies in Relational Grammar 3*, ed. D.M. Perlmutter, 321–383. Chicago, IL: University of Chicago Press.

Anderson, S.R. 1992. *A-morphous Morphology*. Cambridge: Cambridge University Press.

Anderson, S.R. 2001. Lexicalism, incorporated (or incorporation, lexicalized). In *CLS 36: The Main Session*, ed. A. Okrent and J.P. Boyle, 13–34. Chicago, IL: Chicago Linguistic Society.

Austin, P., and J. Bresnan. 1996. Non-configurationality in Australian Aboriginal languages. *Natural Language and Linguistic Theory* 14:215–268.

Axelrod, M. 1990. Incorporation in Koyukon Athapaskan. *International Journal of American Linguistics* 56:179–195.

Baker, M. 1988. *Incorporation: A Theory of Grammatical Function Changing*. Chicago, IL: University of Chicago Press.

Baker, M. 1991. On some subject/object asymmetries in Mohawk. *Natural Language and Linguistic Theory* 9:537–576.

Baker, M. 1993. Noun incorporation and the nature of linguistic representation. In *The Role of Theory in Language Description*, ed. W.A. Foley, 13–44. Berlin: Mouton de Gruyter.

Baker, M. 1995. Lexical and nonlexical noun incorporation. In *Lexical Knowledge in the Organization of Language*, ed. U. Egli, P.E. Pause, C. Schwarze, A. von Stechow, and G. Wienold, 3–33. Amsterdam/Philadelphia: John Benjamins.

Baker, M. 1996. *The Polysynthesis Parameter*. New York/Oxford: Oxford University Press.

Baker, M. 1997. Review of *Autolexical Syntax* by J. Sadock. *Language* 73:847–849.

Baker, M. 2001. The natures of nonconfigurationality. In *The Handbook of Contemporary Syntactic Theory*, ed. M. Baltin and C. Collins, 407–438. Malden, MA: Blackwell.

Baker, M. 2007. Is head movement still needed for noun incorporation? *Lingua* 119:148–165.

Baker, M., R. Aranovich, and L.A. Golluscio. 2004. Two types of syntactic noun incorporation: Noun incorporation in Mapudungun and its typological implications. *Language* 81:138–176.

Barrie, M. 2010. Noun incorporation as symmetry breaking. *Canadian Journal of Linguistics* 55:273–301.

Barrie, M., and E. Mathieu. 2012. Head movement and noun incorporation. *Linguistic Inquiry* 43:133–142.

Beavert, V., and J. Jansen. 2011. Yakima Sahaptin bipartite verb stems. *International Journal of American Linguistics* 77:121–149.

Bischoff, S.T. 2011. Lexical affixes, incorporation, and conflation: The case of Coeur d'Alene. *Studia Linguistica* 65:1–31.

Bittner, M. 1994. *Case, Scope, and Binding*. Dordrecht: Kluwer Academic.

Boas, F. 2002; first published 1911. *Handbook of American Indian Languages, Part I*. Thoemmes Press.

Bresnan, J. 1982. Control and complementation. *Linguistic Inquiry* 13:343–434.

Bresnan, J. 2001. *Lexical-Functional Syntax*. Malden, MA: Blackwell.

Bruce, L. 1984. *The Alamblak Language of Papua New Guinea (East Sepik)*. Canberra, ACT: Dept. of Linguistics, Research School of Pacific Studies, Australian National University.

Bruening, B. 2001. Constraints on dependencies in Passamaquoddy. In *Papers of the Twenty-Third Algonquian Conference*, ed. W. Cowan, J.D. Nichols, and A.C. Ogg, 35–60. Ottawa: Carleton University.

Chomsky, N. 1973. Conditions on transformations. In *A Festschrift for Morris Halle*, ed. S. Anderson and P. Kiparsky, 232–286. New York: Holt, Rinehart and Winston.

Chomsky, N. 1981. *Lectures on Government and Binding*. Dordrecht: Foris.

Chomsky, N. 1986. *Knowledge of Language: Its Nature, Origins, and Use*. New York: Praeger.

Chomsky, N. 1995. *The Minimalist Program*. Cambridge, MA: MIT Press.

Chomsky, N. 2000. Minimalist inquiries: The framework. In *Step by Step: Essays on Minimalist Syntax in Honor of Howard Lasnik*, ed. R. Martin, D. Michaels, and J. Uriagereka, 89–155. Cambridge: MIT Press.

Chomsky, N. 2001. Derivation by phase. In *Ken Hale: A Life in Language*, ed. M. Kenstowicz, 1–52. Cambridge, MA: MIT Press.

Cook, E.-D., and A. Wilhelm. 1998. Noun incorporation: New evidence from Athapaskan. *Studies in Language* 22:49–81.

Danielsen, S. 2011. The personal paradigms in Baure and other Southern Arawakan languages. *International Journal of American Linguistics* 77:495–520.

Davis, H. 2005. Constituency and coordination in St'át'imcets (Lillooet Salish). In *Verb First: On the Syntax of Verb Initial Languages*, ed. A. Carnie, S.A. Dooley, and H. Harley, 31–64. Amsterdam: John Benjamins.

Davis, H. 2006. The status of condition C in St'át'imcets. In *Studies in Salishan (MIT Working Papers in Linguistics on Endangered and Less Familiar Languages 7)*, ed. S.T. Bischoff, L. Butler, P. Norquest, and D. Siddiqi, 49–92. Cambridge, MA: MIT.

Davis, H. 2009. Cross-linguistic variation in anaphoric dependencies: Evidence from the Pacific northwest. *Natural Language and Linguistic Theory* 27:1–43.

Davis, H., and L. Matthewson. 2003. Quasi-objects in St'át'imcets: On the (semi)independence of agreement and case. In *Formal Approaches to Function in Grammar: In Honor of Eloise Jelinek*, ed. A. Carnie, H. Harley, and M.A. Willie, 80–106. Amsterdam/Philadelphia: John Benjamins.

Davis, H., and L. Matthewson. 2009. Issues in Salish syntax and semantics. *Language and Linguistics Compass* 3(4):1097–1166.

Davis, H., and N. Sawai. 2001. *Wh*-movement as noun incorporation in Nuu-chah-nulth. In *Proceedings of WCCFL 20*, ed. Karine Megerdoomian and Leora Anne Bar-el, 123–136. Somerville, MA: Cascadilla Press.

Davis, H., D. Gardiner, and L. Matthewson. 1993. A comparative look at *Wh*-questions in northern interior Salish. In *Papers for the 28th International Conference on Salish and Neighboring Languages*, 79–95. Seattle: University of Washington.

Dayal, V. 2007. Hindi pseudo-incorporation. *Natural Language and Linguistic Theory* 29:123–167.

de Reuse, W.J. 2006. Polysynthetic language: Central Siberian Yupik. In *Encyclopedia of Language and Linguistics*, ed. Keith Brown, 745–748. Amsterdam: ScienceDirect.

Déchaine, R.-M. 1999. What Algonquian morphology is really like: Hockett revisited. In *Papers from the Workshop on Structure and Constituency in Native American Languages, MIT Occasional Papers in Linguistics, Vol. 17, MITWPL*, ed. R.-M. Déchaine and C. Reinholtz, 25–72. Cambridge, MA: MIT.

Di Sciullo, A.M., and E. Williams. 1987. *On the Definition of Word*. Cambridge, MA: MIT Press.

Drossard, W. 1997. Polysynthesis and polysynthetic languages in comparative perspective. In *Proceedings of Linguistics and Phonetics 1996*, ed. B. Palek, 251–264. Charles University Press.

Drossard, W. 2002. Ket as a polysynthetic language, with special reference to complex verbs. In *Problems of Polysynthesis*, ed. N. Evans and H.-J. Sasse, 223–256. Berlin: Akademie Verlag.

Evans, N. 2006. Who said polysynthetic languages avoid subordination? Multiple subordination strategies in Dalabon. *Australian Journal of Linguistics* 26:31–58.

Evans, N., and H.-J. Sasse. 2002. Introduction: Problems of polysynthesis. In *Problems of Polysynthesis*, ed. N. Evans and H.-J. Sasse, 1–13. Berlin: Akademie Verlag.

Farkas, D., and H. de Swart. 2003. *The Semantics of Incorporation: From Argument Structure to Discourse Transparency*. Stanford, CA: CSLI.

Fortescue, M. 1994. Polysynthetic morphology. In *Encyclopedia of Language and Linguistics, Volume 5*, ed. R.E. Asher et al., 2600–2602. Oxford: Pergamon Press.

Fortescue, M. 2007. The typological position and theoretical status of polysynthesis. In *Linguistic Typology*, ed. J. Rijkhoff, 1–27. Århus: Statsbiblioteket.

Gardiner, D. 1993. Structural asymmetries and pre-verbal position in Shuswap. PhD dissertation, Simon Fraser University.

Gerdts, D. 1998. Incorporation. In *The Handbook of Morphology*, ed. A. Spencer and A.M. Zwicky, 84–100. Malden, MA: Blackwell.

Gerdts, D. 2003. The morphosyntax of Halkomelem lexical suffixes. *International Journal of American Linguistics* 69:345–356.

Gerdts, D., and M.Q. Hinkson. 2004. The grammaticalization of Halkomelem 'face' into a dative application suffix. *International Journal of American Linguistics* 70:227–250.

Greenberg, J.H. 1960. A quantitative approach to the morphological typology of language. *International Journal of American Linguistics* 26:178–194.

Hale, K. 1981. *On the Position of Walbiri in a Typology of the Base*. Bloomington: Indiana University Press.

Hale, K. 1983. Warlpiri and the grammar of non-configurational languages. *Natural Language and Linguistic Theory* 1:5–47.

Hale, K. 1989. On nonconfigurational structures. In *Configurationality: The Typology of Asymmetries*, ed. L. Marácz and P. Muysken, 293–300. Dordrecht: Foris.

Hale, K. 2003. On the significance of Eloise Jelinek's pronominal argument hypothesis. In *Formal Approaches to Function in Grammar: In Honor of Eloise Jelinik*, ed. A. Carnie, H. Harley, and M.A. Willie, 11–43. Amsterdam/Philadelphia: John Benjamins.

Halle, M., and A. Marantz. 1993. Distributed morphology and the pieces of inflection. In *The View from Building 20*, ed. K. Hale and S.J. Keyser, 111–176. Cambridge, MA: MIT Press.

Harley, H., and R. Noyer. 1999. Distributed morphology. *Glot International* 4:3–9.

Haugen, J.D. 2009. Hyponymous objects and late insertion. *Lingua* 119:242–262.

Iacobini, C. 2006. Morphological typology. *Encyclopedia of Language and Linguistics*, ed. Keith Brown, 278–282. Amsterdam: ScienceDirect.

Jany, C. 2011. Clausal nominalization as relativization strategy in Chimariko. *International Journal of American Linguistics* 77:429–443.

Jelinek, E. 1984. Empty categories, case, and configurationality. *Natural Language and Linguistic Theory* 2:39–76.

Jelinek, E. 2006. The pronominal argument parameter. In *Arguments and Agreement*, ed. P. Ackema, P. Brandt, M. Schoorlemmer, and F. Weerman, 261–288. Oxford: Oxford University Press.

Jelinek, E., and R. Demers. 1994. Predicates and pronominal arguments in Straits Salish. *Language* 20:697–736.

Johns, A. 2007. Restricting noun incorporation: Root movement. *Natural Language and Linguistic Theory* 25:535–576.

Johns, A. 2009. Additional facts about noun incorporation (in Inuktitut). *Lingua* 119:185–198.

Junker, M.-O. 2003. East Cree relational verbs. *International Journal of American Linguistics* 69:307–329.

Kibrik, A.A. 1992. Relativization in polysynthetic languages. *International Journal of American Linguistics* 58:135–157.

Kiss, K.E. 2008. Free word order, (non)configurationality, and phases. *Linguistic Inquiry* 39:441–475.

Koenig, J.-P., and K. Michelson. 1998. Review of *The Polysynthesis Parameter* by M. Baker. *Language* 74:129–136.

Kroeber, A.L. 1909. Noun incorporation in American languages. *XVI Internationaler Amerikanisten-Kongress* 1909:569–576.

Kroeber, A.L. 1911. Incorporation as a linguistic process. *American Anthropologist* 13:577–584.

Kroeger, P. 1993. *Phrase Structure and Grammatical Relations in Taglog*. Stanford, CA: CSLI Publications.

Kroeker, M. 2001. A descriptive grammar of Nambikuara. *International Journal of American Linguistics* 67:1–87.

Lavie, R.-J., A. Lescano, D. Bottineau, and M-A. Mahieu. 2010. The Inuktitut marker *la*. *International Journal of American Linguistics* 76:357–382.

Legate, J.A. 2002. Warlpiri: Theoretical implications. PhD dissertation, MIT.

LeSourd, P.S. 2006. Problems for the pronominal argument hypothesis in Maliseet-Passamaquoddy. *Language* 82:486–514.

Lorenzo, G. 1997. On the exceptional placement of AgrO morphology in Machiguenga: A short note on Baker's polysynthesis parameter. *Linguistics* 35:929–938.

MacSwan, J. 1998. The argument status of NPs in Southeast Puebla Nahuatl: Comments on the polysynthesis parameter. *Southwest Journal of Linguistics* 17:101–114.

Massam, D. 2001. Pseudo noun incorporation in Niuean. *Natural Language and Linguistic Theory* 19:153–197.

Massam, D. 2009. Noun incorporation: Essentials and extensions. *Language and Linguistics Compass* 3(4):1076–1096.

Mathieu, E. 2009. Introduction to special issue on noun incorporation. *Lingua* 119:141–147.

Mattissen, J. 2003. *Dependent-head Synthesis in Nivkh: A Contribution to a Typology of Polysynthesis*. Amsterdam: Benjamins.

Mattissen, J. 2004. A structural typology of polysynthesis. *Word* 55:189–216.

Mattissen, J. 2006. The ontology and diachrony of polysynthesis. In *Advances in the Theory of the Lexicon*, ed. D. Wunderlich, 287–353. Berlin: Mouton de Gruyter.

Mellow, J.D. 1989. A syntactic analysis of noun incorporation in Cree. PhD dissertation, McGill University.

Mithun, M. 1984. The evolution of NI. *Language* 60:847–894.

Mithun, M. 1986. On the nature of noun incorporation. *Language* 62:32–37.

Mithun, M. 1988. System-defining structural properties in polysynthetic languages. *Zeitschrift für Phonetik, Sprachwissenschaft und Kommunikationsforschung* 41:442–452.

Mithun, M., and G. Corbett. 1999. The effect of noun incorporation on argument structure. In *Boundaries of Morphology and Syntax*, ed. L. Mereu, 49–71. Amsterdam: Benjamins.

Mohanan, K.P. 1982. Grammatical relations and clause structure in Malayalam. In *The Mental Representation of Grammatical Relations*, ed. J. Bresnan, 504–589. Cambridge, MA: MIT Press.

Moro, A. 2000. *Dynamic Antisymmetry*. Cambridge, MA: MIT Press.

Norcross, A.B. 1993. Noun incorporation in Shawnee. PhD dissertation, University of South Carolina.

Nordlinger, R. 1998. *Constructive Case: Evidence from Australian Languages*. Stanford, CA: CSLI Publications.

Petersen de Piñeros, G. 2007. Nominal classification in Uitoto. *International Journal of American Linguistics* 73:389–409.

Rice, K. 2000. *Morpheme Order and Semantic Scope: Word Formation in the Athapaskan Verb*. Cambridge: Cambridge University Press.

Roberts, I.G. 2010. *Agreement and Head Movement: Clitics, Incorporation, and Defective Goals*. Cambridge, MA: MIT Press.

Rosen, C. 1990. Rethinking Southern Tiwa: The geometry of a triple-agreement language. *Language* 66:669–713.

Rosen, S.T. 1989. Two types of noun incorporation: A lexical analysis. *Language* 65:297–317.

Sadock, J.M. 1980. Noun incorporation: A case of syntactic word formation. *Language* 56:300–319.

Sadock, J.M. 1985. Autolexical syntax: A proposal for the treatment of noun incorporation and similar phenomena. *Natural Language and Linguistic Theory* 3:379–439.

Sadock, J.M. 1986. Some notes on noun incorporation. *Language* 62:19–31.

Sadock, J.M. 1991. *Autolexical Syntax*. Chicago, IL: Chicago University Press.

Sapir, E. 1911. The problem of noun incorporation in American languages. *American Anthropologist* 13:250–282.

Seifart, F. 2012. Causative marking in Resígaro (Arawakan). *International Journal of American Linguistics* 78:369–384.

Simpson, J. 1983. Aspects of Warlpiri morphology and syntax. PhD dissertation, MIT.

Simpson, J. 1991. *Warlpiri Morpho-Syntax: A Lexicalist Approach*. Dordrecht: Kluwer.

Speas, M. 1990. *Phrase Structure in Natural Language*. Dordrecht: Foris.

Spencer, A. 1995. Incorporation in Chukchi. *Language* 71:439–489.

Spencer, A. 2004. Review of *Problems of Polysynthesis* by Evans, N. and Sasse, H-J., eds. *Linguistic Typology* 8:394–401.

Stenzel, K. 2007. Glottalization and other suprasegmental features in Wanano. *International Journal of American Linguistics* 73:331–366.

Stowell, T. 1981. Origins of phrase structure. PhD dissertation, MIT.

Tait, M. 1991. Review of *Configurationality: The Typology of Asymmetries* by Lázló, M. and Muysken, P., eds. *Journal of Linguistics* 27:283–300.

Tonhauser, J., and E. Colijn. 2010. Word order in Paraguayan Guaraní. *International Journal of American Linguistics* 76:255–288.

van Geenhoven, V. 1992. Noun incorporation from a semantic point of view. In *Proceedings of the Eighteenth Annual Meeting of the Berkeley Linguistics Society: General Session and Parasession on the Place of Morphology in a Grammar*, 453–466.

van Geenhoven, V. 1998. *Semantic Incorporation and Definite Descriptions: Semantic and Syntactic Aspects of Noun Incorporation in West Greenlandic*. Stanford, CA: CSLI.

van Geenhoven, V. 2002. Raised possessors and noun incorporation in West Greenlandic. *Natural Language and Linguistic Theory* 20:759–821.

van Gijn, R. 2011. Subjects and objects: A semantic account of Yurakaré argument structure. *International Journal of American Linguistics* 77:595–621.

Wiltschko, M. 2009. √Root incorporation: Evidence from lexical suffixes in Halkomelem Salish. *Lingua* 119:199–223.

Part III
Syntactic interfaces

15

The syntax–semantics/
pragmatics interface

Sylvia L.R. Schreiner

1 Introduction

A number of phenomena important to our understanding of the structures and meanings of natural language lie at the juncture between the two. This overview considers the major phenomena at the interface between syntax and semantics/pragmatics, as well as the major theoretical questions that have arisen around these phenomena and around the interface itself.

There is only an interface to talk about between syntax and semantics inasmuch as the two are considered to be separate components (as has generally been the case in the generative tradition). We can talk about this "interface" in at least two ways: on the one hand, we can talk about the location in a model of language competence and/or performance where the syntactic and semantic modules meet and interact. On the other hand, we can talk about phenomena that seem to be driven by both syntactic and semantic mechanisms or principles. Both perspectives will be considered here.

Studies of phenomena at the interface seek to answer questions such as the following: Does each part of a syntactic structure play an equal role in determining the meaning? Which parts of the meaning have overt reflexes in the structure? Can the overall meaning be easily deduced from the summed meaning of the parts? And which kinds of meaning are instantiated with a piece of morphosyntax, and which merely have a syntactic effect (i.e., on ordering relations, co-occurrence restrictions, limitations on movement, etc.)? Several approaches to overarching versions of these questions are discussed here.

This chapter is structured as follows: Section 2 presents some of the major issues at the interface between syntax and semantics, with special attention paid to compositionality, theta theory, and functional heads; the final subsection is devoted to phenomena at the interface with pragmatics. Section 3 describes major models of the interface in syntactic and semantic theory, with the last subsection focusing on approaches to the interface(s) with pragmatics. Section 4 concludes and suggests avenues for future work.

2 Issues at the interface of syntax and semantics

Here I present some of the major topics that seem to occur naturally at the syntax–semantics interface, along with examples of work in each area.

2.1 Interpretation and compositionality

The issue that underlies most if not all work at the syntax–semantics interface is how to arrive at the meaning of a structure. Many approaches have come to the same conclusion: that the structure is built first, and the meaning is then obtained from the structure in one way or another. This is the case in the Principles & Parameters framework in general (from Deep Structures, Surface Structures, or Logical Form) and in the Minimalist Program (from LF), but not, for instance, in Muskens' (2001) non-compositional λ-grammar account (in which semantics is strictly parallel to syntax, rather than secondary to it in any way). In Lexical Functional Grammar, as well, syntactic and semantic levels of representation exist in parallel with mappings between them; meaning is read from the semantic representation.

In mainstream generative syntax the basic picture of the grammar has been one in which the syntax is responsible for building structures and the semantics is responsible for assigning interpretations to those structures. In early views (the "Standard Theory"), syntactic Deep Structures were the input to the semantics. (In Generative Semantics, on the other hand, the interpretations were actually generated there.) In the "Extended Standard Theory", semantic interpretation occurred at two points – once at Deep Structure and once at Surface Structure (this was in response to issues with the interpretation of scope, as discussed below). This was followed by the move to an LF-input view. In much current Minimalist thinking, chunks of structure are interpreted piece-by-piece – for example, at phase edges.

Compositionality is the concept of assembling the meaning of a larger constituent from the meaning of its component parts via some principles of combination. A number of pragmatic or discourse-level (context dependent) phenomena present problems even for non-strict interpretations of compositionality; it is difficult, for instance, to see how conversational implicatures or the meaning lent by sarcasm could be computed by the same mechanism that determines the interpretation of verb phrases. At the syntax–semantics interface, there are several levels at which compositionality might be expected to hold: with sentence-level modification such as negation; at clause level, from the composition of the external argument with the verb phrase; within the VP, to account for the composition of the verb with its internal argument; and within (the equivalent of) determiner phrases, adjective phrases, adverb phrases, etc. Depending on one's theory of morphology, the syntax may also be responsible for producing the input to the lexical(-level) semantics – see, for example, Distributed Morphology (Halle and Marantz 1993; Harley 1995, etc.) for a view of morphology where word-building is done in the syntax.

In formal semantics, Frege's concept of semantic composition as the "saturation" of functions (i.e., as functional application) has remained in the fore, with Heim and Kratzer's (1998) work being an important contribution. The concept of composition as functional application has been used in both extensional and intensional semantics. It is based on the idea that the meanings of words (and larger constituents) need to be "completed" with something else. (For example, the meaning of a transitive verb is incomplete without its direct object.) Sentence meanings are arrived at by a series of applications of functions to their arguments (which the functions need in order to be "saturated"). At the sentence level, the output is no longer a function but whatever the theory holds to be the meaning of a sentence – in extensional truth-conditional semantics, a truth value. Early formalisms based on Montague Grammar (Montague 1974) worked from the perspective that each phrase level's syntactic rule had a separate mechanism for semantic interpretation. Klein and Sag (1985) proposed that each constituent needing an interpretation was of a certain basic type; in their theory it was these types that had rules for interpretation rather than the syntactic rules themselves. Klein and Sag used the types of individuals, truth values, and situations to form their higher types; work in event semantics (following Davidson 1967) has also proposed a type for events. Other rules of composition have been introduced, such as predicate modification (e.g., Heim and Kratzer 1998). This allows the meaning of intersective adjective phrases to be computed: it essentially lets us say that the meaning of *brown house* is the same as the meaning of *brown* plus the meaning of *house*. Non-intersective adjectives present some trouble for predicate modification.

In addition to the mechanics of compositionality, theories of semantic interpretation differ in terms of how *homomorphic* they assert the syntax and the semantics to be – that is, how much of the interpretation is allowed outside the confines of the compositional meaning. Sentence meaning in strictly compositional theories (e.g., Montague's 1970 approach) is derived only from the meaning of the syntactic parts and the way they are combined; in non-strictly compositional theories there are also rules that operate on the semantics itself, without a syntactic rule involved (as in some of Partee's work: e.g., Partee and Rooth 1983).

2.2 Theta Theory

The interaction between theta roles (e.g., *external argument*) and their associated thematic roles (e.g., *agent*) sits naturally at the syntax–semantics interface. The aim is to discover the connections between syntactic arguments and the semantic part(s) they play in sentences.

The Theta Criterion has been the focus of much work in Government and Binding theory and its successors. The original formulation (Chomsky 1981) said that each theta role must be realized by one argument and each argument must be assigned one theta role. This was recast in Chomsky (1986) in terms of *chains*. An argument (e.g., a subject noun phrase in a passive) undergoes movement, and the coindexed positions it occupies before and after this movement make up a chain; the chain itself gets the theta role. The formal representation of theta roles also underwent changes – the early "theta grid" represented only the theta roles themselves with an indication of their status as internal or external, while later conceptions (e.g., as laid out in Haegeman's 1991 textbook) also include argument structure information.

Thematic roles and relations themselves have also received much attention. Work on "thematic hierarchies" (e.g., Larson 1988; Grimshaw 1990) attempts to explain the assignment of thematic role participants to their positions in the syntax. Dowty's work (beginning with 1991) on proto-roles (*Proto-Agent* and *Proto-Patient*) was a reaction to the difficulty researchers were having in finding cross-linguistically reliable role categories. A notably different approach to defining roles is seen in Jackendoff's work on *thematic relations*. Jackendoff (e.g., 1983) approaches the task from the semantics (or, rather, "conceptual structure") side only – thematic relations are defined by conceptual structure primitives in different configurations.

A number of researchers have also concerned themselves with the relation between thematic roles, argument structure/selection, and event structure. Krifka (1989) and Verkuyl (e.g., 1989) both propose aspectually specifying features to better account for particular thematic relationships (see Ramchand 1993 for an implementation). More recently, Ramchand (in her 2008 monograph) lays out primitives for decomposing verb meaning. She argues that, in order to discover and understand thematic roles, we must first have the correct features that make up events, "since participants in the event will only be definable via the role they play in the event or subevent" (p. 30).

Sylvia L.R. Schreiner

2.3 Functional heads

Proposals about the nature, number, and location of functional heads have also been integral to the development of our understanding of the syntax–semantics interface. Notable work on parameterization and functional heads came out of the University of Geneva in the late 1980s (see the papers in Belletti and Rizzi 1996). Then, Ramchand's (1993) dissertation on aspect and argument structure draws on data from Scottish Gaelic, investigating the relationship between the verb and its arguments in aspectual terms. Hers is both a semantic and a syntactic account; she argues for a different concept of θ-role-like labels, based on classes defined by event structure and Aktionsart. She motivates Aspect as a functional head in Scottish Gaelic, giving us the idea that the verb and its aspectual features need not be rolled into one complex bundle. Adger's important (1994) dissertation on the relationship between functional heads and the interpretation of arguments focuses on the Agr(eement) head, while also calling for separate Tense and Aspect heads. Svenonius (1996) is concerned with the meaning and function of heads. He argues that lexical projections denote properties while functional projections denote entities; functional heads end up serving to connect the utterance to the discourse.

Cinque (1999) has been highly influential for those concerned with the number and placement of functional projections. His arguments there rest largely on observations about the cross-linguistic requirements on the placement of adverbs in relation to their related functional material. (See also work on adverb placement by Nilsen 1998, *et seq.*) Cinque observes that across languages we see a consistent ordering of classes of adverbs (e.g., temporal, aspectual, etc.); that we also see a consistent ordering of functional material that encodes concepts such as tense, aspect, and mood; and, importantly, that the orderings of adverbs and functional material match each other from left to right. This leads him to suggest that adverb phrases are the specifiers of their corresponding functional projections. Based on these observations, he also suggests a very rich collection of functional projections – one for each adverb class – and proposes that these projections are always present in a language, even if all heads are not pronounced. Work on the inventory, structure, order, and parameterization of functional categories has extended into a research program of its own, Cartography (especially by Cinque, Belletti, and Rizzi; with a series dedicated to it, *The Cartography of Syntactic Structures* – Cinque 2002; Rizzi 2004; Belletti 2004; Cinque 2006; Beninca and Munaro 2010; Cinque and Rizzi 2010; Brugé *et al.* 2012; and Haegeman 2012).

2.4 Events, argument structure, aspect, and type issues

Events and eventhood, lexical aspect, and type assignment lie at the heart of the syntax–semantics interface. Lexical aspect plays an undeniably large role in the semantics of event structure. Notions of durativity (whether an event has duration or is punctual), telicity (whether an event has a natural endpoint or not), and eventiveness vs. stativeness largely define the semantics of events, and often arise as points of contact with the syntax.

Discussions of argument structure beyond the theta theory considerations discussed above also naturally fall at the juncture of syntax and semantics. Grimshaw (1990), for example, argues that the thematic and aspectual information of argument structure should itself be structured in the form of prominence relations. She then proposes a new conception of external arguments, extending into the nominal domain. Levin and Rappaport-Hovav (1995) approach these topics through the phenomenon of unaccusativity. They work to support Perlmutter's hypothesis about the interfacing nature of unaccusativity: that it is represented in the syntax, and as such can affect other syntactic mechanisms; and that it is determined by the semantics: aspects of verb meaning determine whether or not unaccusativity arises. Tenny (1994) is another good example of work on aspect and argument structure that explicitly considers the influence of the syntax on lexical semantics, and vice versa. Tenny argues that the internal semantic properties of the event, which are spatiotemporal in nature, are what determine the syntactic characteristics of the verb describing the event and the verb's arguments.

Partee's (1986/2003) influential work on type-shifting and the interpretation of noun phrases does not make explicit claims about the interface, but nonetheless makes an important contribution to our understanding of it. Motivating semantic types necessarily involves discussing the interaction between the elements involved and the syntax. For instance, Partee is looking to explain how we interpret a particular syntactic piece, the noun phrase. The question of what semantic type that syntactic piece is, and whether/when it shifts types, depends heavily upon evidence from how it interacts syntactically with determiners, quantifiers, etc.

2.5   Quantifiers and Quantifier Raising

The structure of sentences with quantified phrases has been difficult to fit into theories of semantic composition. Quantifiers stymied early generative linguists because it was not clear how they should be treated – they act neither like individuals (proper names) nor like sets of individuals. Generalized Quantifier Theory (Barwise and Cooper 1981) established quantificational phrases as second-order sets; for Heim and Kratzer, quantificational DPs are "functions whose arguments are characteristic functions of sets, and whose values are truth-values" (i.e., type $<<e,t>,t>$) (1998: 141). This works for quantified subjects, but quantified objects result in a type mismatch when composition is attempted. Proposed resolutions to this include type shifting and raising the quantified object out of the VP (Quantifier Raising, proposed in Robert May's dissertation, discussed at length in Heim and Kratzer 1998). This does not solve every problem related to quantifiers, but it does help us explain ambiguous scope readings of sentences with two quantifiers, and similar phenomena.

2.6   (Scalar) implicatures and related phenomena

Scalar implicatures are often considered to be solely in the domain of pragmatics, as they depend on factors outside the sentence or discourse for their meaning. We might reconsider this, however, given their apparent similarities to polarity items, which seem to have real syntactic restrictions. Chierchia (2004) argues that scalar implicatures and negative polarity items are actually remarkably similar in their distribution (i.e., the kind of polarity context they are affected by). He finds that problems arise (e.g., with some quantifiers) for theories that take scalar implicatures to be computed fully after the grammar, and that these problems can be solved if we take implicatures to undergo processing by a kind of pragmatic "component" at multiple stages of the derivation, and not just "after" the grammar. He claims that there is a recursive computation, running parallel to the standard one, that brings in implicatures. This leaves scalar implicatures in the domain of pragmatics, but allows us to understand how they might have restrictions similar to purely "grammatical" phenomena.

2.7 Verbal phenomena

Mood, modality, focus, force, middles, and lexical and grammatical aspect vary greatly from language to language as to whether and how they are instantiated syntactically. This makes for interesting work at the interface, bringing up questions of how compositionality proceeds in similar but distinct instantiations, or how best to structure these categories cross-linguistically.

Zanuttini and Portner (2003) consider the syntax and semantics of exclamatives (e.g., "How big you've gotten!"). They conclude that two syntactic components, a factive and a *Wh*-operator, interact to produce the semantic features carried by exclamatives. Portner (2004) also brings up some important interface questions in his discussion of the semantics of imperatives and force. Comorovski (1996), after considering the structures and interpretations of interrogative phrases in various kinds of constituent questions and with quantifying adverbs, argues that the ability to front interrogative phrases out of questions depends on a factor that is semantic (and pragmatic) in nature: namely, a requirement that questions be answerable.

Ackema and Schoorlemmer (1994) take middle constructions in English and Dutch as evidence for a "pre-syntactic" level of semantic representation that itself interacts with the syntax. They argue that a middle's subject is in fact the external argument, and that the representation of the verb's logical subject is at an earlier semantic level. Steinbach (2002) finds that middles in German share semantic properties with passives but pattern morphosyntactically with actives, and are morphosyntactically identical to transitive reflexives in the language. His account derives the ambiguity in this syntactic form from the syntax–semantics interface; he argues that syntactic derivations of the middle cannot account for either the syntactic ambiguity or the semantic properties of the sentences that are seen. Instead, a combination of independently motivated assumptions from syntax and semantics account for the different interpretations.

2.8 Issues at the interface with pragmatics

Some facets of meaning do seem to fall primarily within the domain of pragmatics. Conversational implicatures, for instance, rely wholly on the discourse in which they are situated to draw their intended meaning. Some phenomena, however, do not fit so neatly into the pragmatic realm. Grice's *conventional* implicatures, for example, were meanings that were not fully determined by context, but that were not fully within the category of truth-conditional semantics, either. The meanings of many functional items also seem to require input both from grammatical meaning and from pragmatics. *And* has several possible complex interpretations, depending on the sentence – in *I hit the ball and ran to first base*, the most felicitous reading is one that includes a notion of ordering between the two conjuncts. In a sentence such as *He left the door open and the cat got out*, there is a notion of causation. These "additional" meanings are held to be pragmatic contributions. Cann *et al.* (2005) discuss the notion of grammaticality versus acceptability by considering the use of resumptive pronouns in English. They give a syntactic account of relative clauses and anaphora construal that leads to the pronouns' generation by the grammar, and then argue that the typical judgment of unacceptability by native speakers (in neutral, non-extended contexts) is due to pragmatic effects – they are used only when the speaker deems them necessary for a particular meaning to be conveyed. They are working within Dynamic Syntax and Relevance Theory, both common approaches at this particular interface.

Some phenomena at the syntax–semantics interface have also been analyzed as interacting significantly with pragmatics. Polarity items (e.g., Chierchia 2004), scalar implicatures (ibid.), scalar quantifiers (e.g., Huang and Snedeker 2009), and clitics in Spanish (e.g., Belloro 2007), for example, have all been approached from a pragmatic standpoint. Work on the syntax–pragmatics interface has also turned up in the literature on bilingual and L2 speakers. Hulk and Müller (2000), for instance, propose that syntactic inter-language influence only occurs at this interface. Rothman (2008), concerned with the distribution of null versus overt subject pronouns, concludes that elements at this interface are more difficult to acquire owing to their complexity. Studies like these bring us to interesting questions about the modularity of pragmatics and its interaction with the grammar, and establish new ways of thinking about whether pragmatics might be governed by the same rules as syntax and the rest of the grammar, or by different ones.

3 Models of the interfaces

The status of the syntax–semantics interface in a given syntactic model, and the phenomena that might be seen to reside there, will differ depending on how that model deals with the modules themselves. Here we briefly look at how the interface has surfaced in various ways in models both within and alongside or outside the generative tradition.

3.1 The Chomskyan Tradition

In early generative grammar (including the "Standard Theory," as set up in Chomsky 1955), the semantics component interpreted Deep Structures, the direct output of the syntax. Later models of the grammar adjusted to this view, trying to make sense of the various scope phenomena affected by transformations that were supposed to happen *after* Deep Structure. In the revised model, the semantic components that dealt with scope instead interpreted the Surface Structures resulting from transformations, rather than the Deep Structures. More issues with scope and passivity (see, e.g., treatment by Lakoff (1971)) led to the creation of a further level of representation, Logical Form. This was first thought to be located after a second set of transformations that followed Surface Structure. In this model, the interface with the semantics was found in two places: part of the semantic component read meaning off of Deep Structures, and part off of Logical Forms. The model eventually developed was the "(inverted) Y-model", with Deep Structure and Surface Structure in their previous positions, but with Logical Form (LF) and Phonetic Form (PF) as branches after Surface Structure. This was what the model looked like when the beginnings of the Minimalist Program (Chomsky 1993) were taking form at the start of the 1990s.

In the Minimalist Program (MP) (Chomsky 1995), Deep Structure and Surface Structure are done away with as syntax-internal levels of representation, while LF and PF remain as levels of representation that interface with the conceptual-intentional and articulatory/perceptual systems, respectively. Spell-Out occurs after the syntax-internal operations of Merge and Move (later, Internal Merge); Spell-Out is the point at which syntactic structures get sent to LF or PF for interpretation. In some more recent minimalist work, including Chomsky's (e.g., 2001) work on phases, there are no "levels of representation" *per se*, where syntactic structures are interpreted as wholes; rather, each step of a syntactic derivation is interpreted by the appropriate systems. This changes things: in these more derivational models there is no longer a place that can be pointed to as "the" interface between structure and meaning. Instead, (partial) structures are interpreted at each spell-out or at the edge of each phase.

3.2 Generative Semantics

A major departure from the patterns of early generative grammar was Generative Semantics (Ross 1967; McCawley 1968; Lakoff 1971). While theories within the Principles & Parameters framework have taken the view that the semantic component *interprets* the syntactic structures input to it, Generative Semantics took the semantic interpretation to be solely the product of (*generated* by) the Deep Structures themselves. While in interpretive theories the syntax and the semantics were left with a particular kind of independence from each other, this was not the case in Generative Semantics. Instead, one set of rules – transformations – applied to Deep Structure meanings to produce the syntactic forms seen on the surface.

An important contribution of Generative Semantics to later theories, including some modern Chomskyan ones, was its approach to lexical decomposition – breaking down the meaning of verbs into component subevents. Decomposition of word (and especially verb) meaning featured in Dowty's (1972, *et seq.*) approach to Montague Semantics, Jackendoff's (1983, *et seq.*) Conceptual Semantics, and Pustejovsky's Event Structure Theory (1988, *et seq.*). This has continued into the work on varieties of little *v* (DO, CAUSE, BECOME, BE, etc.) including Hale and Keyser (1993), Kratzer (1993), Harley (1995), and Distributed Morphology (starting with Halle and Marantz 1993), and extending to more recent work such as Folli and Harley (2005). Wunderlich's (1997, *et seq.*) strictly lexicalist Lexical Decomposition Grammar also grew out of the Generative Semantics tradition, and involves four levels of representation – Conceptual Structure, Semantic Form, Theta Structure, and Morphology/Syntax. In this model, semantic forms determine syntactic structure.

3.3 LFG

Two of the more well-known non-Chomskyan phrase structure grammars are Lexical Functional Grammar (LFG) and Head-Driven Phrase Structure Grammar (HPSG). LFG (Bresnan and Kaplan 1982; see, e.g., Bresnan 2001; Falk 2001) focuses primarily on syntactic relations, analyzing sentences in terms of both constituency (represented in c-structures) and grammatical functions (in f-structures). While the c-structure of a sentence is in the form of a phrase structure marker similar to what one would see in work within Government and Binding theory, the f-structure (or "attribute-value matrix") contains a number of unordered valued features (such as 'TENSE', 'SUBJ[ect]', etc.). These structures exist in parallel, connected by correspondence functions. Because there is more than one syntactic level (c- and f-structures, but also a(rgument)-structure), there is more than one "interface" between syntax and semantics – presumably, there will be a correspondence function between the semantic structure and each level of syntactic structure (see the brief discussion in Falk 2001). Lexical Mapping Theory (LMT) was developed as a proposal about how to map thematic/θ roles to their syntactic realizations. LMT provides a mapping first between a semantic structure ("θ-structure", possibly part of s-structure or another semantic/conceptual level) and a-structure, and then another mapping from a-structure to f-structure. Since f-structure already interfaces with c-structure, argument positions are able to be determined in this way.

Glue semantics (Dalrymple *et al.* 1993) is a theory of semantic composition and interpretation developed for LFG. The theory, which is "deductive" rather than compositional, assigns semantic interpretation to syntactic structures (f-structures) via the principles of linear logic (the "glue"). Since f-structures contain both complement and modifier information and are unordered to help account for flexible- or free word order languages, composition via function application becomes impossible without some extra structure being imposed. Dalrymple *et al.* (1993: 98) introduce "a language of meanings" (any logic will do) and "a language for assembling meanings" (specifically, the tensor fragment of first-order/linear logic). The f-structures and lexical items provide constraints for how to assemble word and phrase meaning ("lexical premises"). Rules in the logic stage combine those premises via "unordered conjunction, and implication" (Dalrymple *et al.* 1993: 98) to yield sentence-level meaning; meanings are simplified via deduction rather than λ-reduction. Postlexical principles apply to map thematic roles to grammatical functions (Dalrymple *et al.* 1993: 99). Glue semantics has been implemented for other syntactic theories as well, including HPSG (Asudeh and Crouch 2001).

3.4   HPSG

HPSG (Pollard and Sag 1994; Sag *et al.* 2003) is the successor to Generalized Phrase Structure Grammar (GPSG, Gazdar *et al.* 1985). GPSG established a system for computing the meaning of a sentence based on semantic tags on the syntactic structures, but otherwise dealt little with the syntax–semantics interface. Central to HPSG is a rich lexicon whose entries have feature structures with phonetic as well as syntactic (SYN) and semantic (SEM) features. This lays a natural groundwork for interface constraints and interactions.

The syntactic part of the structure involves two important features, SPR (specifier) and COMPS (complements). On the semantic side there are three features: MODE (type of phrase), INDEX (links to the situation or individual in question), and RESTR(iction) (an unordered list of conditions that must be met for the meaning to hold). It is through RESTR that thematic-like roles are specified. The entry for *run*, for example, is tagged for a runner while *give* contains a giver, recipient, and gift; each of these roles carries an index that allows it to be linked to something else in the structure. Compositionality proceeds via RESTR; the Semantic Compositionality Principle states that "the mother's RESTR value is the sum of the RESTR values of the daughters" (Sag *et al.* 2003: 143), where summation means taking values in order. In addition, the Semantic Inheritance Principle (Sag *et al.* 2003: 144) ensures that MODE and INDEX values are shared between a mother and its head daughter.

Argument structure and agreement are effected via the feature ARG(ument)-ST(ructure), which is separate from both SYN and SEM. The ARG-ST of a lexical head represents the values of the specifier plus its complements, in order (the "Argument Realization Principle"). Coindexation among SYN, SEM, and ARG-ST features accounts for binding facts, among other things.

3.5   Models from semantic theory

Semantics in the generative tradition has been less overtly concerned with the exact positioning of syntax in the model of the grammar. Heim and Kratzer (1998) assume a phrase structure grammar approach to the syntax, but note that a number of different theories of syntax are compatible with the version of formal semantics they present. Since their approach to interpretation is "type-driven,"

> it's the semantic types of the daughter nodes that determine the procedure for calculating the meaning of the mother node. The semantic interpretation component, then, can

ignore certain features that syntactic phrase structure trees are usually assumed to have. All it has to see are the lexical items and the hierarchical structure in which they are arranged. Syntactic category labels and linear order are irrelevant. (Heim and Kratzer 1998: 44)

Although their phrase structure trees are labeled and linearized, they note that "the only requirement for the syntax is that it provides us with phrase structure trees" (Heim and Kratzer 1998: 45). However, not every kind of syntactic theory is compatible with Heim and Kratzer's semantics; notably, a theory in which meaning is interpreted from both Deep and Surface Structures is incompatible with the semantic picture they present. Such a syntactic model would make the semantics interpret "something like *pairs* of phrase structure trees" (Heim and Kratzer 1998: 47): that is, something uninterpretable in the theory as it stands.

While a little further afield from the mainstream generative tradition, Conceptual Semantics (e.g., Jackendoff 1983, *et seq.*; Pinker 1989) still separates syntactic and semantic components and also addresses the nature of the interface between the two. This approach locates the formulation of meaning in the Conceptual Structure, a level of representation located in Cognition (along with Spatial Structure) rather than in Language proper. The Conceptual Structure in turn interfaces with the syntax and phonology levels in Language. Some semantic frameworks fully outside generative linguistics such as Cognitive Grammar do not include a concept of an interface between form and meaning components. In Cognitive Grammar (see especially Langacker 1987), the syntactic organization is constructed from the meaning itself; there is no autonomous "syntax" that a semantic component could interact with.

Discourse Representation Theory (DRT), introduced in Kamp (1981), is a semantic framework whose first instantiations aimed especially to resolve issues dealing with tense and anaphora across multiple sentences in a discourse. DRT's major innovations are for the most part semantic in nature – in particular, a level of mental representations called *discourse representation structures*; and the inclusion of discourse in the interpretation of meaning. However, DRT is also of interest because it seats these semantic innovations within a representationalist theory. Representations are built via a generative syntax and concomitant set of syntactic rules. If not for this DRT would be a dynamic theory of meaning, since meaning interpretation is seen as being "updated" as one moves through the discourse.

3.6   The interface with pragmatics

Another important question is how, or whether, to distinguish in the theory between the work done by semantics and that done by pragmatics. The generative approach (at least on the syntactic side) has in general clearly separated syntax from the meaning component, but it has not spent much time addressing the question of where pragmatics comes in. The functions of pragmatics are often taken to exist as part of the semantic (or conceptual/intentional) system, or else pragmatics is pushed off on some other system within language or general cognition. In Minimalism, for instance, the interpretation of both semantic and pragmatic meaning is done at LF. In research on pragmatics, however, the interface between semantics and pragmatics has been the topic of a great deal of debate.

The main strategy in this debate has been to take pragmatics as being fully separate from the grammar – the grammar deals with conventional or coded meaning and pragmatics with nonconventional (inferential, contextual, non-coded) meaning. Alternately, the divide is taken to be between truth-conditional meaning (in the semantics/the grammar) and non-truth-conditional meaning (in the pragmatics). "The grammar" here is, in the cognitive view, the linguistic module, containing syntax and semantics and their corresponding rules. This picture of pragmatics as separate originates in Grice's (1957, *et seq.*) pioneering work.

Fodor's (1983) take on modularity removes pragmatics from the language system (which is for him a domain-specific module). Pragmatics is instead "global," part of the general computational system of the mind. For Fodor this is due to the fact that pragmatics requires contextual, domain-general information in order to be processed, rather than just the local information available to the language module.

One important approach to pragmatics in this vein is Relevance Theory (starting with Sperber and Wilson (1981), and much work since then). Relevance Theory takes Grice's work as a jumping-off point, but focuses on the idea that there are certain expectations of relevance when a discourse occurs. Some more recent work in Relevance Theory (Wilson 2005) proposes that pragmatics is actually a sub-module of a mind-reading module (again, non-grammatical in nature). Wilson uses the term *module* in a different sense than Fodor does, embracing a broader definition: "From an evolutionary perspective, the question is not so much whether the processes involved are global or local, but whether they are carried out by general-purpose mechanisms or by autonomous, special-purpose mechanisms attuned to regularities existing only in the domain of intentional behaviour" (Wilson 2005: 1132). In this sense, she claims, mind-reading (i.e., utilizing a theory of mind) is modular. She claims that pragmatics is not just a special application of (generalized) mind-reading, but a sub-module of the specialized mind-reading module.

It is perhaps not surprising that a consensus has not yet been reached as to how to characterize the semantics–pragmatics interface, nor as to exactly which phenomena fall on one side or the other. Even among those who are clear about locating pragmatics somewhere outside the grammar proper there has been a good deal of debate as to what is explicable using the truth-conditional or conventional meanings of semantics, and what requires recourse to context and inference and therefore pragmatics.

4 Conclusion

The interaction between syntax and semantics/pragmatics is necessary to explain a number of phenomena that have been important to the development of theories within and outside the generative enterprise. In this overview, we have looked at several possible approaches to the interface and discussed a number of important issues there, including the ever-present question of compositionality – how to extract meaning from the structures formed by the syntax. Other questions at the interface either seem to be best solved by an appeal to functionality on both sides of the structure/meaning divide, or simply have both syntactic and semantic components.

The other issue discussed was the question of where pragmatics should be located in one's model of language. We saw that a common tactic is to locate the semantics in the language "module", while deriving pragmatic meaning outside that module. Depending on one's theory of the cognitive and linguistic architecture, this might mean that the duties of pragmatics are accomplished in a separate (but not language-specific) module, or accomplished via a combination of domain-general processes.

4.1 Directions for future work

As we move forward, one pattern of data seems particularly likely to lead to further interface phenomena of interest: categories that tend to vary between languages as to whether and how they are instantiated morphosyntactically (e.g., mood/modality/force/voice, as mentioned above).

Comparing data across languages of this type for a particular piece of semantics can lead to insights about how we should be dividing up the semantic distinctions in the first place. For instance, if across languages one particular distinction of mood is instantiated in a manner conspicuously different from that of other moods, we have a strong hint that something is incomplete about our picture of the semantics of mood or our understanding of the interaction between the syntax and the semantics with respect to that category. In the realm of aspect, for example, Coon (2010) observes that the perfective (as opposed to other aspects) has a tendency to be realized non-periphrastically across languages, and theorizes that this is due to the unavailability of a natural language expression for the time relation involved in perfectivity. In Reed (2012) I use the syntactic instantiations of aspectual distinctions in Scottish Gaelic to support a claim about the semantics of grammatical aspect – namely, that we should view the category as a bifurcated one, with (im)perfective-type aspects on one branch and perfect-type aspects on the other. Focus on this particular kind of interaction between syntax and semantics has already led to some very interesting discoveries, and is likely to lead to more.

Further reading

Levin, Beth, and Malka Rappaport-Hovav. 1995. *Unaccusativity: At the Syntax-Lexical Semantics Interface*. Cambridge, MA: MIT Press.

This book focuses on establishing linking rules between syntax and lexical semantics, developing unaccusativity as a diagnostic for phenomena at that interface.

Pelletier, Francis Jeffry. 1994. The principle of semantic compositionality. *Topoi* 13:11–24.

A good summary of various arguments for and against different versions of compositionality, from a semantic perspective. See also the reprint (in S. Davis and B.S. Gillon's 2004 *Semantics: A Reader*, Oxford University Press) for later thoughts on the topic from the author.

Van Valin Jr., Robert D. 2005. *Exploring the Syntax–Semantics Interface*. Cambridge: Cambridge University Press.

This is an updated introduction to Role and Reference Grammar, a model not discussed here but one intimately concerned with the interface, featuring lexical decomposition and its own set of thematic roles.

References

Ackema, Peter, and Maaike Schoorlemmer. 1994. The middle construction and the syntax–semantics interface. *Lingua* 93(1):59–90.
Adger, David. 1994. Functional heads and interpretation. Dissertation, University of Edinburgh.
Asudeh, Ash, and Richard Crouch. 2001. Glue semantics for HPSG. In *Proceedings of the 8th International HPSG Conference*, ed. F. van Eynde, L. Hellan, and D. Beerman, 1–19. Stanford, CA: CSLI Publications.
Barwise, Jon, and Robin Cooper. 1981. Generalized quantifiers and natural language. *Linguistics and Philosophy* 4(2):159–219.
Belletti, Adriana (ed.). 2004. *Structures and Beyond. The Cartography of Syntactic Structures, Vol. 3*. New York: Oxford University Press.

Belletti, Adriana, and Luigi Rizzi (eds). 1996. *Parameters and Functional Heads: Essays in Comparative Syntax*. New York: Oxford University Press.

Belloro, Valeria A. 2007. Spanish clitic doubling: A study of the syntax–pragmatics interface. Dissertation, State University of New York at Buffalo, NY.

Beninca, Paolo, and Nicola Munaro (eds). 2010. *Mapping the Left Periphery. The Cartography of Syntactic Structures, Vol. 5*. New York: Oxford University Press.

Bresnan, Joan. 2001. *Lexical-Functional Syntax*. Oxford: Blackwell.

Bresnan, Joan, and Ronald Kaplan. 1982. Introduction: grammars as mental representations of language. In *The Mental Representation of Grammatical Relations*, ed. Joan Bresnan, xvii–lii. Cambridge, MA: MIT Press.

Brugé, Laura, Anna Cardinaletti, Giuliana Giusti, and Nicola Munaro (eds). 2012. *Functional Heads. The Cartography of Syntactic Structures, Vol. 7*. New York: Oxford University Press.

Cann, Ronnie, Tami Kaplan, and Ruth Kempson. 2005. Data at the grammar-pragmatics interface: the case of resumptive pronouns in English. *Lingua* 115:1551–1577.

Chierchia, Gennaro. 2004. Scalar implicatures, polarity phenomena, and the syntax/pragmatics interface. In *Structures and Beyond: The Cartography of Syntactic Structures, Vol. 3*, ed. Adriana Belletti, 39–103. Oxford: Oxford University Press.

Chomsky, Noam. 1955. The logical structure of linguistic theory. Ms. Harvard/MIT.

Chomsky, Noam. 1981. *Lectures on Government and Binding. Studies in Generative Grammar 9*. Dordrecht: Foris.

Chomsky, Noam. 1986. *Barriers*. Cambridge, MA: MIT Press.

Chomsky, Noam. 1993. A minimalist program for linguistic theory. In *The View from Building 20*, ed. K. Hale and S.J. Keyser, 1–52. Cambridge, MA: MIT Press.

Chomsky, Noam. 1995. *The Minimalist Program*. Cambridge, MA: MIT Press.

Chomsky, Noam. 2001. Derivation by phase. In *Ken Hale: A Life in Language*, ed. M. Kenstowicz, 1–52. Cambridge, MA: MIT Press.

Cinque, Guglielmo. 1999. *Adverbs and Functional Heads: A Cross-linguistic Perspective*. Oxford: Oxford University Press.

Cinque, Guglielmo (ed.). 2002. *Restructuring and Functional Heads. The Cartography of Syntactic Structures, Vol. 4*. New York: Oxford University Press.

Cinque, Guglielmo (ed.). 2006. *Functional Structure in DP and IP. The Cartography of Syntactic Structures, Vol. 1*. New York: Oxford University Press.

Cinque, Guglielmo, and Luigi Rizzi (eds). 2010. *Mapping Spatial PPs. The Cartography of Syntactic Structures, Vol. 6*. New York: Oxford University Press.

Comorovski, Ileana. 1996. *Interrogatives and the Syntax–Semantics Interface*. Dordrecht: Kluwer Academic Publishers.

Coon, Jessica. 2010. Complementation in Chol (Mayan): A theory of split ergativity. Dissertation, MIT, Cambridge, MA.

Dalrymple, Mary (ed.). 1999. *Semantics and Syntax in Lexical Functional Grammar: The Resource Logic Approach*. Cambridge, MA: MIT Press.

Dalrymple, Mary, John Lamping, and Vijay Saraswat. 1993. LFG semantics via constraints. In *Proceedings of the Sixth Meeting of the European ACL*, 97–105. University of Utrecht.

Davidson, Donald. 1967. The logical form of action sentences. In *The Logic of Decision and Action*, ed. Nicholas Rescher, 81–95. Pittsburgh, PA: University of Pittsburgh Press.

Dowty, David R. 1972. Studies in the logic of verb aspect and time reference in English. Dissertation, University of Texas, Austin, TX.

Dowty, David. 1991. Thematic proto-roles and argument selection. *Language* 67(3):547–619.

Falk, Yehuda N. 2001. *Lexical-Functional Grammar: An Introduction to Parallel Constraint-based Syntax*. Stanford, CA: CSLI Publications.

Fodor, Jerry. 1983. *The Modularity of Mind*. Cambridge, MA: MIT Press.

Folli, Raffaella, and Heidi Harley. 2005. Flavors of v. In *Aspectual Inquiries*, ed. P. Kempchinsky and R. Slabakova, 95–120. Dordrecht: Springer.

Gazdar, Gerald, Ewan Klein, Geoffrey K. Pullum, and Ivan A. Sag. 1985. *Generalized Phrase Structure Grammar*. Cambridge, MA: Harvard University Press.

Grice, H. Paul. 1957. Meaning. *Philosophical Review* 66:377–388.

Grimshaw, Jane. 1990. *Argument Structure*. Cambridge, MA: MIT Press.

Haegeman, Liliane. 1991. *Introduction to Government and Binding Theory*. Malden, MA: Blackwell.

Haegeman, Liliane. 2012. *Adverbial Clauses, Main Clause Phenomena, and the Composition of the Left Periphery. The Cartography of Syntactic Structures, Vol. 8.* New York: Oxford University Press.

Hale, Kenneth, and Samuel Jay Keyser. 1993. On argument structure and the lexical expression of syntactic relations. In *The View from Building 20*, ed. Kenneth Hale and Samuel Jay Keyser, 53–109. Cambridge, MA: MIT Press.

Halle, Morris, and Alec Marantz. 1993. Distributed morphology and the pieces of inflection. In *The View from Building 20*, ed. Kenneth Hale and S. Jay Keyser, 111–176. Cambridge, MA: MIT Press.

Halle, Morris, and Alec Marantz. 1994. Some key features of distributed morphology. In *MITWPL 21: Papers on Phonology and Morphology*, ed. Andrew Carnie and Heidi Harley, 275–288. Cambridge, MA: MITWPL.

Harley, Heidi. 1995. Subjects, events, and licensing. Dissertation, MIT, Cambridge, MA.

Heim, Irene, and Angelika Kratzer. 1998. *Semantics in Generative Grammar.* Malden, MA: Blackwell.

Huang, Yi Ting, and Jesse Snedeker. 2009. Online interpretation of scalar quantifiers: Insight into the semantics–pragmatics interface. *Cognitive Psychology* 58(3):376–415.

Hulk, Aafke, and Natascha Müller. 2000. Bilingual first language acquisition at the interface between syntax and pragmatics. *Bilinguilism: Language and Cognition* 3(3):227–244.

Jackendoff, Ray. 1983. *Semantics and Cognition.* Cambridge, MA: MIT Press.

Kamp, Hans. 1981. A theory of truth and semantic representation. In *Formal Methods in the Study of Language*, ed. Jeroen A.G. Groenendijk, T.M.V. Janssen, and Martin B.J. Stokhof, 277–322. Amsterdam: Mathematical Center Tract 135.

Klein, Ewan, and Ivan A. Sag. 1985. Type-driven translation. *Linguistics and Philosophy* 8(2): 163–201.

Kratzer, Angelika. 1993. On external arguments. In *University of Massachusetts Occasional Papers 17: Functional Projections*, ed. Elena Benedicto and Jeff Runner, 103–130. Amherst, MA: GLSA.

Krifka, Manfred. 1989. Nominal reference, temporal constitution and quantification in event semantics. In *Semantics and Contextual Expression*, ed. R. Bartsch, J. van Benthem and P. van Emde Boas, 75–115. Dordrecht: Foris.

Lakoff, George. 1971. On generative semantics. In *Semantics: An Interdisciplinary Reader in Philosophy, Linguistics and Psychology*, ed. D.D. Steinberg and L.A. Jakobovitz, 232–296. Cambridge: Cambridge University Press.

Langacker, Ronald W. 1987. *Foundations of Cognitive Grammar, Volume 1: Theoretical Prerequisites.* Stanford, CA: Stanford University Press.

Larson, Richard K. 1988. On the double object construction. *Linguistic Inquiry* 19:335–391.

Levin, Beth, and Malka Rappaport-Hovav. 1995. *Unaccusativity: At the Syntax-Lexical Semantics Interface.* Cambridge, MA: MIT Press.

McCawley, James D. 1968. Lexical insertion in a transformational grammar without deep structure. In *Papers from the Fourth Regional Meeting of the Chicago Linguistic Society*, ed. B.J. Darden, C.-J.N. Bailey, and A. Davison, 71–80. University of Chicago.

Montague, Richard. 1970. Universal grammar. *Theoria* 36:373–398.

Montague, Richard. 1974. *Formal Philosophy.* Cambridge, MA: MIT Press.

Muskens, Reinhard. 2001. Lambda grammars and the syntax–semantics interface. In *Proceedings of the Thirteenth Amsterdam Colloquium*, ed. R. van Rooy and M. Stokhof, 150–155. Amsterdam: University of Amsterdam.

Nilsen, Øystein. 1998. The syntax of circumstantial adverbials. Ms. University of Tromsø, Hovedoppgave (published in 2000 by Novus, Oslo).

Partee, Barbara H. 1986. Noun phrase interpretation and type-shifting principles. In *Studies in Discourse Representation Theory and the Theory of Generalized Quantifiers*, ed. J. Groenendijk, D. de Jongh, and M. Stokhof, 115–144. Dordrecht: Foris Publications. Republished in P. Portner and B. Partee (2003) *Formal Semantics: The Essential Readings.* Oxford: Blackwell.

Partee, Barbara H., and Mats Rooth. 1983. Generalized conjunction and type ambiguity. In *Meaning, Use, and Interpretation of Language*, ed. R. Bäuerle, C. Schwarze, and A. von Stechow, 361–383. Berlin: Walter de Gruyter.

Pinker, Steven. 1989. *Learnability and Cognition. The Acquisition of Argument Structure.* Cambridge, MA: The MIT Press.

Pollard, Carl, and Ivan A. Sag. 1994. *Head-Driven Phrase Structure Grammar.* Chicago: University of Chicago Press.

Portner, Paul. 2004. The semantics of imperatives within a theory of clause types. In *Proceedings of SALT 14*, ed. K. Watanabe and R.B. Young, 235–252. Ithaca, NY: CLC Publications.

Pustejovsky, James 1988. The geometry of events. In *Studies in Generative Approaches to Aspect*, ed. Carol Tenny, 19–39. Cambridge, MA: The MIT Press.

Ramchand, Gillian. 1993. Aspect and argument structure in Modern Scottish Gaelic. Dissertation, Stanford University, Stanford, CA.

Ramchand, Gillian. 2008. *Verb Meaning and the Lexicon: A First-phase Syntax*. Cambridge: Cambridge University Press.

Reed, Sylvia L. 2012. The semantics of grammatical aspect: Evidence from Scottish Gaelic. Dissertation, University of Arizona, Tucson, AZ.

Rizzi, Luigi (ed.), 2004. *The Structure of IP and CP. The Cartography of Syntactic Structures, Vol. 2*. New York: Oxford University Press.

Ross, John R. 1967. Constraints on variables in syntax. Dissertation, MIT, Cambridge, MA.

Rothman, Jason. 2008. Pragmatic deficits with syntactic consequences?: L2 pronominal subjects and the syntax–pragmatics interface. *Journal of Pragmatics* 41(5):951–973.

Sag, Ivan A., Thomas Wasow, and Emily M. Bender. 2003. *Syntactic Theory: A Formal Introduction*, 2nd edn. Stanford, CA: CLSI Publications.

Sperber, Dan, and Deirdre Wilson. 1981. Irony and the use-mention distinction. In *Radical Pragmatics*, ed. P. Cole, 295–318. New York: Academic Press.

Steinbach, Markus. 2002. *Middle Voice: A Comparative Study in the Syntax–Semantics Interface of German*. Amsterdam: John Benjamins.

Svenonius, Peter. 1996. Predication and functional heads. In *The Proceedings of the Fourteenth West Coast Conference on Formal Linguistics*, ed. Josè Camacho, Lina Choueri, and Maki Watanabe, 493–507. Stanford, CA: CSLI.

Tenny, Carol L. 1994. *Aspectual Roles and the Syntax–Semantics Interface*. Dordrecht: Kluwer Academic Publishers.

Tesnière, Lucien. 1959. *Eléments de Syntaxe Structurale*. Paris: Klincksieck.

Verkuyl, Henk J. 1989. Aspectual classes and aspectual composition. *Linguistics and Philosophy* 12:39–94.

Wilson, Deirdre. 2005. New directions for research on pragmatics and modularity. *Lingua* 115: 1129–1146.

Wunderlich, Dieter. 1997. Cause and the structure of verbs. *Linguistic Inquiry* 28(1):27–68.

Zanuttini, Raffaella, and Paul Portner. 2003. Exclamative clauses: at the syntax–semantics interface. *Lingua* 79(1):39–81.

16

The syntax–lexicon interface

Peter Ackema

1   Introduction: what is the lexicon?

This chapter discusses the interface between the lexicon and the syntactic module of grammar. A proper discussion is only possible, though, if these terms are properly defined first. Although different authors have very different ideas about the kind of notions and analyses that should play a role in accounts of syntax, the notion of what syntax refers to in general is pretty universally accepted: it is the part of grammar that deals with the possibilities and impossibilities of how words can be combined to form larger units, phrases, clauses, and sentences. Unfortunately, the notion lexicon can refer to rather different things in various strands of linguistic work. I will begin, therefore, by outlining how the term is understood in this chapter. It is perhaps clearest to do this by first giving a negative characterisation of how the term will *not* be understood here.

Most importantly, the lexicon is not to be understood as morphology. Of course, the lexicon must contain at least a list of the simplex words of a language, and it may therefore seem attractive to have it deal with the structure of complex words, the subject matter of morphology, as well. This view links in with the view that morphology in general deals with the irregular, unproductive, and unexpected, as opposed to supposedly regular, productive, and transparent syntax.

However, it will keep things clearer if we simply define morphology as those principles that govern the structure of complex words, syntax as those principles that govern the structure of complex phrases and clauses, and keep the interesting debate about to what extent these are the same principles or not away from the lexicon. This is because, despite the traditional view just mentioned, it has been pointed out regularly that it is not possible to equate morphology with irregularity and syntax with regularity in any straightforward way. There are many morphological processes that are productive and transparent (for instance, synthetic compounding in English: see Ackema and Neeleman (2004; 2010) for some discussion). Therefore, as pointed out by Di Sciullo and Williams (1987), it is not possible to equate anything that is a morphologically complex, but syntactically atomic, entity with something that needs to be listed. Conversely, the number of syntactic phrases and sentences that have an irregular, unexpected property (such as idioms) is in fact quite large, as pointed out by Jackendoff (1997), among others. These do need to be listed.

The lexicon, then, is the list of those elements that have a property that does not follow from the regular application of the grammatical rules or principles of the language in question, regardless of whether the rules in question are morphological or syntactic in nature.[1] In the words of Di Sciullo and Williams (1987: 3) "the lexicon is like a prison - it contains only the lawless, and the only thing that its inmates have in common is lawlessness." This would also seem to mean that, as Di Sciullo and Williams also say, "the lexicon is incredibly boring by its very nature." On the other hand, the interaction between the listed properties of a lexical item and the syntactic context in which that item can find itself is not boring at all. That is the topic of this chapter.

2 Argument structure

It may seem that a list of unpredictable things may not be that interesting for syntax, which, after all, tries to capture the regularities in how words can be combined. However, there are several properties a word can have that are not entirely predictable as such, but are highly relevant for syntax. In particular, the selectional restrictions of a word are important.

It is an open question in how far selectional restrictions are unpredictable, but it has been observed that they do not seem to follow entirely from a word's semantics. As Grimshaw (1979) observes, for example, it does not seem to follow from the semantics of the verb *wonder* that it cannot take an NP complement, as the semantically related verb *ask* can:

(1) a. Mary asked what the time was.
     b. Mary asked the time.

(2) a. Mary wondered what the time was.
     b. *Mary wondered the time.

If selectional restrictions cannot be reduced entirely to semantics, they will need to be encoded somehow in the lexicon. Thus, a central concept in the debate about the Syntax–Lexicon interface is that of argument structure. The argument structure of a predicative element is an indication of (i) how many semantic roles, or theta-roles, this element assigns; (ii) what the content of these roles is; and, perhaps most importantly for the interface with syntax, (iii) how the number and content of these roles determines which syntactic arguments the syntactic head that realizes the element will appear with. (These descriptions are in fact not entirely theory-neutral, since there are theories that would formulate the central question in the opposite way: how the syntactic arguments that an element appears with determine the semantic roles that they receive; this is discussed below).

The remainder of the chapter is structured as follows. The issue of the content and number of theta-roles is discussed in §3. Section 4 contains a discussion of the correspondences there can be between types of theta-roles and syntactic arguments. A central question here is to what extent it is predictable that a particular type of theta-role is assigned to an argument with a particular grammatical function. If there were always the same correspondences between theta-roles and syntactic positions, there would not be much else to discuss beyond this. However, there are various grammatical processes that appear to manipulate such correspondences. Such processes, and the various types of analyses proposed for them, are the topic of §5.

3   The content of theta-roles

In the previous section it was mentioned that it needs to be listed in the lexicon which theta-roles a predicative element assigns. Naturally, this raises the issue of which types of theta-role exist and how many an element can assign.

Usually, theta-roles are defined in terms of their semantic content. That is to say, they are given a label that describes the semantic role the relevant argument plays in the event or state expressed by the predicative element. Considering an event, one can describe the possible roles of the participants in it in terms of motion, however abstractly conceived. For example:

(3)   Cause: the person/thing that instigates the motion
       Theme: the person/thing that undergoes the motion
       Goal: the person/thing towards which the motion is directed

It is also possible to focus on how participants in the event affect each other. This leads to labels such as:

(4)   Agent/Actor: the person/thing affecting someone/something else
       Patient: the person/thing being affected

Sentient beings can also be affected by an event mentally rather than physically. Hence we can also distinguish:

(5)   Experiencer: the person experiencing a (mental) event/state/process

There is no strict consistency in the literature in the use of these labels. For example, the label Theme can be used so as to include what I labelled as Patient in (4); sometimes a distinction between affected Themes and non-affected Themes is made, the former then being the equivalent to Patient. Alternatively, it has been argued that both ways of classifying theta-roles in (3) and (4) are necessary, and that an argument can carry a role from (3) and one from (4) simultaneously (compare Jackendoff 1990; Grimshaw 1990 for variants of this basic idea, each with somewhat different terminology from that used here: see below). Such issues are not merely terminological, as it can matter for the syntactic and semantic behaviour of an argument whether it is, for example, an affected Theme (or Patient) or a non-affected one (see, e.g., Anderson 1979; Verkuyl 1993; Tenny 1994; Borer 2005).

Sometimes roles are added that do not indicate the role of a core participant in an event/state, but rather indicate that the bearer of the role expresses the location where the event takes place, or the person to whose benefit the event is, or the place/thing from which the event emanates, or any other information one could care to list about an event. So one could add at least the list in (6) to (3)–(5).

(6)   Location: the place where the event takes place
       Beneficiary: the person/thing to whose benefit the event is
       Source: the person/place/thing from which the event emanates

It is not unreasonable to add, for example, Location to the list of possible theta-roles that an argument can carry. Many prepositions, for example, take an obligatory complement that expresses exactly that role:

(7)   in *(the house), over *(the mountains), beside *(the railway tracks)

However, it does lead to the tricky question of how many, and which, theta-roles a single element can assign. Consider verbs, for example. If roles as in (6) are on a par with roles such as in (3), there does not seem to be a principled limit to how many theta-roles a verb can assign. After all, it is difficult to think of a principled limit on the number of elements that can express information about an event. So the following could be considered theta-roles as well:

(8) Time: the time at which the event took place
Instrument: the thing used to help bring the event about
Reason: the reason why the event was instigated
Simultaneous: the thing that also happened while the event was happening

However, while elements in a verbal clause can have a semantic role like this, it is generally agreed that, at least in many languages and at least usually, the syntactic status of the elements carrying them is different from the syntactic status of the elements carrying roles as in (3)–(5). Thus, the subject, direct object, and indirect object in (9) are said to be syntactic arguments of the verb; in this example they carry the roles of Agent, Theme, and Goal respectively (see §4 for more discussion). The elements carrying the other roles are said to be syntactic adjuncts.

(9) Yesterday evening Joanna gave me a book for my birthday while she was singing.

There are thought to be several syntactic differences between arguments and adjuncts: for example, in terms of their being obligatory or optional and in terms of the kind of constituent they form with the element they combine with. None of these criteria is without complications (see, for instance, Ackema forthcoming for a recent overview of the issues), and it is probably fair to say that there is still no overall consensus about exactly what kind of and how many arguments – that is, theta-role carrying constituents – there can be.

One type of approach to this issue is to assume that theta-roles are not primitives but rather shorthand names for a type of constituent that occurs in a structure representing the lexical semantics of the predicate. There are various accounts of this kind, differing quite radically in how they regard the nature of this representation. The representation is always syntactic in the sense that it contains constituents and combines these into hierarchical structures according to particular rules. However, opinions differ as to whether these structures can be reduced to those known from phrasal syntax or have their own particular nature, belonging to a dedicated module of grammar distinct from the syntactic module.

Jackendoff (1983; 1987; 1990; 1993), for example, holds that there is a distinct component of Lexical Conceptual Structure. This contains two so-called tiers: a thematic tier and an action tier. Both tiers are built from semantic predicates, taking semantic arguments. The thematic tier represents lexical semantic information about spatio-locational and temporal relations. A sentence such as *John ran into the room*, for example, is represented as follows at this tier (Jackendoff 1990: 45):

(10) $[_{\text{EVENT}} \text{GO} ([_{\text{THING}} \text{JOHN}]_A, [_{\text{PATH}} \text{TO} ([_{\text{PLACE}} \text{IN} ([_{\text{THING}} \text{ROOM}]_A)])])]$

Some of the semantic arguments are marked as mapping to syntactic arguments; this is indicated by the subscript A. The thematic tier of Lexical Conceptual Structure thus allows a structural definition of traditional theta-roles such as Theme, Agent, or Goal. For instance,

Agent can be defined as the first argument of a CAUSE function, while Theme is the first argument of a movement function such as GO or STAY.

At the second tier, the action tier, the affectedness relations between the arguments of a predicate are expressed. It uses a general predicate AFFECT, like this:

(11)   AFF [A, B]

By definition, the first argument of this function is Actor, the second either Patient or Beneficiary, depending on whether it is affected negatively or positively. Note the distinction between Agent (a thematic tier role) and Actor (an action tier role) in this model, which in more traditional classifications would probably both fall under the Agent label.

One and the same element may be an argument on both the thematic tier and the action tier. For instance, if there is an Agent this will often also be Actor. However, there are no fixed correspondences in this respect, and it is possible that an argument is both Theme and Actor at the same time, as in (12).

(12)   **John** went for a jog. (thematic tier: Theme; action tier: Actor)

For another proposal in which a dedicated lexical semantic representation of predicates and their arguments is developed, see Lieber (2004). Lieber focuses especially on the effects on argument structure of various types of morphological derivation.

As noted, there is another type of approach to lexical semantics that is like Jackendoff's in assuming that argument structure is derived from an elaborate hierarchical structure in which predicative heads combine with constituents representing their arguments. The difference is that in this approach it is assumed that this representation is subject to the same sort of wellformedness conditions that hold of phrasal syntax.

A particular instance of this latter approach is represented by work by Hale and Keyser (1991; 1993; 2002). The lexical argument structure of the verb *put*, for example, is represented by the structure in (13) (Hale and Keyser 1993: 56). Clearly, this structure conforms to syntactic phrase structural principles.

(13)

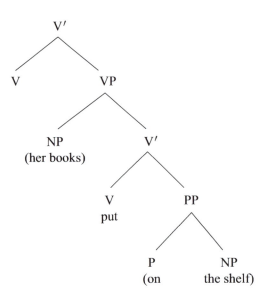

Hale and Keyser argue that, given this conception, the relation between pairs as in (14) can be seen as resulting from regular syntactic processes.

(14) a. She put her books on the shelf.
      b. She shelved her books.

In particular, (14b) derives from a structure that is identical to (13) except for the lower V and P positions being empty. Regular head movement of the noun *shelf* of the NP complement to the P head, followed by head movement to the lower V and the higher V, then gives (14b). An attractive aspect of this proposal is that it may account for the ungrammaticality of examples such as (15a) and (15b) by appealing to independently motivated constraints on head movement. (15a) is ruled out since it violates the Head Movement Constraint: N-to-V movement in (13) has skipped P in this example. (15b) is ruled out because head movement out of a subject NP down to the head of VP is generally impossible (because of general conditions on movement: see Baker 1988a). (Note that in (13) the subject argument is in fact not represented at all; this is not just because it is the single argument external to VP, but because Hale and Keyser assume it is not represented in the verb's lexical argument structure at all; see §4.3 on this issue.)

(15) a. *She shelved the books on.
      b. *It womaned her books on the shelf. (cf. The woman put her books on the shelf)

A more problematic aspect appears to be that the type of stranding of NP material that Baker (1988a; 1996) adduces as evidence that certain types of N-V complex are derived by syntactic incorporation of the N head of an NP complement to V is systematically impossible in these cases:

(16) a. She put her books on large shelves.
      b. *She shelved her books large.

Also, while (15a) is correctly ruled out, something needs to be said about why it is allowable to have an empty preposition in English only if this gets incorporated, and, moreover, why overt prepositions and verbs cannot partake in this process, again in contrast to the incorporation processes Baker discusses:

(17) a. *She on-shelved/shelved-on her books.
      b. *She put-shelved/shelve-put her books.
      c. *She shelve-on-put/put-on-shelved her books.

Such problems may be more serious in accounts in which it is assumed not only that the representation of a verb's argument structure complies with similar principles of well-formedness as syntactic structures do but that this representation simply *is* a structure generated by the syntactic component of grammar. On the plus side, such approaches have the appeal of simplicity, if it is possible to reduce all of the interpretation of predicate-argument relations to independent syntactic principles plus compositional rules of interpretation. Typically, in such an approach, verbs do not come with lexically specified restrictions on how many and what kind of arguments they can take. Rather, in principle any verb can be plugged into a structure containing any specifiers and/or complements, as long as this structure conforms to syntactic wellformedness conditions. Principles that map syntactic structures onto semantic predicate-argument relations (including aspects of this such as whether or not the argument is affected by the action expressed by the predicate: see above) then result in a particular interpretation of this overall structure. The result will be fine as long as the conceptual content of the verb is at all compatible with this interpretation. (It is not for nothing that one book in which such an approach is developed, Borer (2005), is called *Structuring Sense* – the "sense" is provided not by specifying it lexically for each individual verb but by the structural syntactic context in which the verb appears). For instance, in such an approach a sentence such as (18) would be deemed to be deviant not because the verb *laugh* is lexically specified as not taking an internal argument but rather because the concept of laughing is such that there is no way to interpret it in such a way that it acts upon something like a lawn.

(18) *They laughed the lawn.

This general description encompasses approaches that differ in the details of how syntactic structure relates to interpretation in terms of argument structure (for discussion see, for instance, Pylkkänen (2002), Borer (2005), and Ramchand (2008)). A critique of approaching lexical argument structure in terms of structures complying with the rules of the syntactic component of grammar can be found in Culicover and Jackendoff (2005), for example.

Approaches such as the ones just described can be termed decompositional, in the sense that they decompose the lexical semantics of a verb into a series of heads, complements, and specifiers occurring in a syntax-style structure. A different type of decompositional approach to theta-roles decomposes them into sets of atomic features. In such an approach, theta-roles are assumed to derive their content from a combination of primitive features, each contributing a specific meaning component. One such proposal is Reinhart's (2000; 2002) Theta System (for other versions of featural decomposition of theta-roles see, for instance, Ostler (1979) and Rozwadowska (1988)). Reinhart uses two features, [c] for 'cause change' and [m] for 'mental state involved'. Under the assumption that these features are bivalent, and that any combination of them gives rise to a particular type of theta-role, all and only the following roles exist (the name on the right-hand side indicates what the traditional label for the role would be) (see Everaert *et al.* 2012: 6):

(19) feature cluster   traditional label

     a. [+c +m]   Agent
     b. [+c −m]   Instrument
     c. [−c +m]   Experiencer
     d. [−c −m]   Theme (Patient)
     e. [+c]   Cause
     f. [+m]   Sentient
     g. [−m]   Subject matter/target of emotion (typically oblique)
     h. [−c]   Goal/benefactor (typically dative/PP)
     i. [Ø]

Generalisations can be made over, for instance, all roles with a feature cluster containing only +values, or only −values, or mixed values. This plays a role in the principles that determine how theta-roles are distributed across syntactic arguments (discussed in the next section). The role in (19i), consisting of the empty feature set, might perhaps seem a somewhat superfluous artefact of this system. However, Ackema and Marelj (2012) argue that it is instrumental in accounting for the grammatical behaviour of the verb *have* and (other) light verbs, while Siloni (2012) suggests that lexical reciprocal verbs can utilise this empty role.

4 The syntactic realisation of arguments

4.1 The Theta Criterion and its problems

In §3 the possible number and content of theta-roles was discussed. One of the central issues concerning the lexicon–syntax interface is how these roles are distributed across syntactic arguments. Let us start out from the generalisation expressed by the classic Theta Criterion (see Chomsky 1981):

(20) Every argument must receive exactly one theta-role and every theta-role must be assigned to an argument.

It is probably not necessary to regard this as an independent principle of grammar. The observation that arguments need to receive at least one theta-role reduces to the independently necessary principle of Full Interpretation: an argument without such a role could not be interpreted. It is not clear whether the other generalisations expressed by (20) are actually valid; at the least, they are analysis-dependent. These other generalisations are that every theta-role must be assigned to some argument, and that an argument cannot receive more than one such role.

Consider the generalisation that every theta-role must be assigned to some argument. It is evident that many syntactic arguments appear not be obligatorily present:

(21) a. Henry was painting (the shed). (optional Theme)
b. The police gave (the crowd) the order to disperse. (optional Goal)
c. (I) don't know. (optional Agent)

Whether or not the generalisation fails therefore depends on one's analysis of implicit arguments. If every theta-role of a verb must always be assigned, there must be empty arguments present in syntax in all these cases, and a theory of what licenses such empty arguments needs to be developed. Alternatively, (20) may be relaxed, and a theory of when it can be relaxed must be developed. Clearly, in theories of both types, the fact that some unexpressed roles are associated with implicit arguments that do not have a specific reference but have arbitrary content must play a role (see Rizzi 1986). For example, (21a) with the object unexpressed must mean 'Henry was painting something or other' and cannot mean 'Henry was painting it'; something similar holds for (21b). (21c) is different in this respect, as *Don't know* cannot mean 'some people or other don't know'. The restrictions on leaving out sentence-initial subjects in a non-pro-drop language such as English are discussed in Haegeman and Ihsane (1999; 2001) and Weir (2012), among others. Other cases where some theta-role is not assigned to a visible argument involve 'grammatical function changing' processes. These are discussed in §5.

The final generalisation expressed by (20) is that an argument cannot receive more than one theta-role. This, too, encounters apparent problems, though again it depends on one's analysis of the relevant structures in how far it can be maintained. Clauses containing a secondary predicate are one instance where an argument seems to receive more than one theta-role. Consider the following resultative construction, for instance:

(22) The farmer painted the barn red.

Here, it seems as if *the barn* receives both the Patient role of the verb *paint* and the Theme role of the adjectival predicate *red* (just as it does when *red* is the main predicate, as in *the barn is red*). According to one analysis of such constructions, this is only apparently so. This analysis holds that, while it is true that *barn* is the subject of the predicate *red*, it is not the object of the predicate *paint*. Rather it is the combination of *the barn* and *red*, together forming a so-called Small Clause, that functions as this object (see, for instance, Hoekstra (1988); den Dikken (1995)). According to another type of analysis *paint* and *red* form a so-called complex predicate, in which the argument structures of the individual predicates are unified to make up a single argument structure. The object in (22), then, is the object of this complex predicate (see, for instance, Neeleman and Weerman (1993); Neeleman and Van de Koot (2002)). Strictly speaking, the generalisation under discussion is maintained in this view as well, as the object does indeed not receive more than one theta-role. However, this role is the result of the unification of two theta-roles of two distinct predicative elements. So in that sense it would be more accurate to say that the generalisation should be amended to the following (see Williams 1994):

(23) An argument does not receive more than one theta-role *from the same predicate*.

Another proposal according to which the generalisation 'no more than one theta-role for an argument' must be given up is the movement account for control structures proposed by Hornstein (1999; 2001). Hornstein proposes that in structures with a control verb, as in (24b), what we see as the matrix subject is raised out of the subject position of the infinitival complement, just as in cases where the matrix verb is raising verb, as in (24a). The only difference between the two is precisely that in (24b) this subject receives a second theta-role from the matrix verb in addition to the theta-role it received from the embedded infinitive, whereas in (24a) it does not receive an additional role in its derived position, as *seem* does not assign a role to its subject.

(24) a. The passengers seem to leave the plane.
b. The passengers promised to leave the plane.

This account of control is certainly not uncontroversial (see Culicover and Jackendoff 2001; Landau 2003), but for our purposes it is interesting to note that it does still comply with the modified generalisation in (23). The original generalisation, part of the Theta Criterion in (20), was intended to rule out that sentences such as (25) can mean the same thing as 'John admires himself': it is not allowed to assign *John* the Theme role of *admire* in object position, then move it to subject position and assign it the Agent role of this verb there.

(25) John is admired.

This is still ruled out by (23) as well, as here the offending argument receives multiple roles from the same predicate. Of course, if (23) is the correct generalisation, the question remains why that should be so; see Williams (1994) for relevant discussion.

4.2 Correspondences between theta-roles and argument positions

So far, we have considered the issue that an argument should be assigned *some* theta-role. But, of course, the relation between syntax and lexicon goes further than that. If the only demand imposed by this interface would be that arguments must get some theta-role, pairs such as the following would be indistinguishable, which they obviously are not:

(26) a. Mary saw Bill.
　　 b. Bill saw Mary.

The fact that the subject in (26) can only be interpreted as Agent and the object as Theme, rather than the other way around, indicates that there are grammatical principles that regulate which syntactic argument is assigned which theta-role. In syntax, the syntactic arguments appear in positions that are hierarchically ordered with respect to each other. A common assumption is that, on the lexical side, theta-roles, too, stand in a hierarchical order and there are mapping principles between the two hierarchies that basically state that they must be aligned. A typical, but partial, thematic hierarchy is (27).

(27) Agent > Goal > Theme

One question is whether this hierarchy is aligned with the hierarchy of syntactic positions in an absolute sense or a relative one. If the former is the case, a particular syntactic position must always be associated with the same type of theta-role. If the latter is the case, the position to which a theta-role is assigned can depend on whether or not the predicate also assigns another theta-role that is higher on the thematic hierarchy. (Clearly, approaches in which syntactic structure *determines* thematic interpretation are of the former type).

The issue is closely related to the issue of how to deal with cases where the same verb appears with (apparently) different configurations of arguments, as the result of an operation such as passive or (anti-)causativisation. If the relation between syntactic argument positions and thematic roles is entirely constant, the underlying configuration of syntactic arguments must be the same in such cases and the phenomenon in question must be the result of purely syntactic processes of argument displacement and non-spell-out. If more leeway in this relation is accepted this is not necessary. This issue is discussed in §5.

Ignoring this issue for the moment, the most straightforward type of mapping rule would look like this:

(28) a. Agent ↔ Subject
　　 b. Goal ↔ Indirect Object
　　 c. Theme ↔ Direct Object

In theory it is possible that there is cross-linguistic variation in such basic mapping principles. Indeed, if Marantz (1984) is correct, then 'syntactically ergative' languages such as Dyirbal (Dixon 1972) would be accurately characterised by switching the place of Subject and Direct Object in (28). It is not clear that this is really necessary, though (see Van de Visser

(2006) and references cited therein). A different issue is that some languages do not seem to contain syntactic argument positions at all, preferring to realise all their arguments morphologically (see Baker (1996) and Jelinek (2006) for discussion).

In some models the mapping principles will be somewhat more complex than this. In particular, both in models where argument structure is defined as resulting from lexical semantic representations with a complex internal structure and in models where thematic roles are viewed as internally structured feature complexes (see §3), there can be no simple list of atomic theta-roles that can be aligned with syntactic positions.

This may, in fact, have some advantages. Grimshaw (1990), for instance, advances the following argument for the idea that, alongside a hierarchy as in (27), there is a second, aspectually based, hierarchy between the arguments (compare Jackendoff's (1990) distinction between a thematic tier and an action tier mentioned in the previous section). Paraphrasing somewhat, in this second dimension an argument having a 'causer' role is more prominent than an argument having a 'caused' role. To see what the advantage of having two distinct hierarchies can be, consider first the contrast in (29) (from Grimshaw 1990: 16).

(29) a. Flower-arranging by novices
     b. *Novice-arranging of flowers

This contrast, Grimshaw argues, simply follows from the hierarchy in (27). Suppose that arguments can freely be realised not only in syntactic positions (as per (28)) but also in the non-head position of morphological compounds, as long as the hierarchy in (27) is respected in the sense that the position of the more prominent argument must be higher than the position of the less prominent one. Since any position outside the compound is structurally higher than any position within it, (29a) respects the thematic hierarchy: the Agent is structurally higher than the Theme. In (29b) this hierarchy is violated.

Surprisingly, there are cases involving psych-verbs taking an Experiencer and a Theme argument, where any example of the type in (29) is impossible, regardless of the relative positions of the arguments:

(30) a. *A child-frightening storm
     b. *A storm-frightening child

Grimshaw argues that the thematic role Experiencer outranks the role Theme, which rules out (30a) on a par with (29b). Why, then, is (30b) impossible as well? This is because, in the other dimension relevant to argument hierarchy, the aspectual dimension, the Cause *storm* is more prominent than the Causee *child*, and therefore the relative structural positions of the two in (30b) are not in alignment with this hierarchy. This same problem does not occur in (29a), where the Agent > Theme hierarchy gives the same result as the Cause > Causee hierarchy, since the Agent and Cause fall together here.

In a system where theta-roles consist of feature complexes, there are no mapping rules of the type in (28) to begin with. Rather, the mapping rules will refer to the individual features and their values. In Reinhart's (2000; 2002) Theta System (see the discussion around (19)), for example, the relevant rules are the following:

(31) Marking procedures
      a. Mark a [−] cluster with index 2
      b. Mark a [+] cluster with index 1

(32) Merging instructions
   a. When nothing rules this out, merge externally.
   b. An argument realizing a cluster marked 2 merges internally; an argument with a cluster marked 1 merges externally.

The terms external and internal for theta-roles, as used in (32), were introduced by Williams (1981). They reflect the fact that the role for the subject is seen as special, as it is the only role assigned to an argument that is external to the projection of the theta-role assigning head (under the assumption that the subject is external to VP already in the base, pace the VP-internal subject hypothesis). In some theories, an even greater disparity between the thematic roles for objects and subjects is assumed, in that it is hypothesised that the role for the subject is assigned by a functional head distinct from the lexical verb, thus severing a thematic relationship between this verb and the external argument altogether. This hypothesis will be discussed in more detail at the end of this section.

Regarding the other terminology in (31)–(32), a [–] cluster refers to a cluster with exclusively negative values for its features and a [+] cluster to a cluster with exclusively positive values for its features (see the list in (19)). Other clusters, in particular (19b) and (19c), are mixed clusters. The basic correspondences in (28a) and (28c) follow, since the traditional Agent is the [+] cluster in (19a), while the traditional Theme is the [–] cluster in (19d).

The system also captures the fact that a mixed role such as Experiencer ([–c +m]) can sometimes be realised externally, sometimes internally. In particular, it captures that what happens to the Experiencer depends on the other role(s) assigned by the same verb. As observed by Belletti and Rizzi (1988), Pesetsky (1995), and others, there are two classes of psych-verbs. In cases of the 'fear'-type the Experiencer is realised as external argument, while with the 'frighten'-type it is an internal argument:

(33) a. Harry fears storms.
      b. *Storms fear Harry.

(34) a. Storms frighten Harry.
      b. *Harry frightens storms.

The other argument (besides the Experiencer) of *fear* is a [–] cluster ([–m] or possibly [–c –m]), as it represents a Target of emotion or perhaps Theme. Hence, by (31a) and (32b) this must be merged internally. Consequently, the Experiencer [–c +m] is free to merge externally by (32a). The other argument of *frighten*, however, is a Cause [+c], or in case the frightening is done consciously (on purpose), it is an Agent [+c +m]. By (31b) and (32b), this argument must merge externally, leaving no other option for the Experiencer than to merge internally.

4.3   The issue of the external argument

As noted, some authors have argued that an argument being merged externally in fact means that this argument is not thematically related to the lexical verb at all. In this view, subject arguments are not represented in a lexical verb's argument structure. Rather, they are assumed to be the argument of a designated head that takes the VP as its complement. This head is a functional head that is part of the extended verbal projection making up the clause, and is usually designated as v ("little v", to distinguish it from lexical V):

(35)

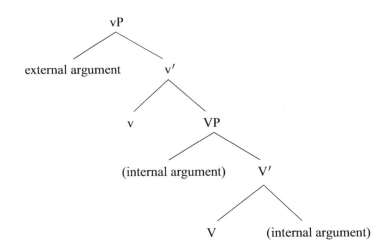

An unaccusative verb (which only assigns internal theta-roles, see Perlmutter and Postal (1984), Burzio (1986)) either lacks the vP-layer, or has a defective/inactive v that assigns neither an external theta-role nor accusative Case (to capture Burzio's generalisation; see Folli and Harley (2004) for discussion).

The arguments for separating the relation between the lexical verb and the external argument date back to Marantz (1984), and are given in some detail in Kratzer (1996), Marantz (1997), and Pylkkänen (2002), among others. A critical re-assessment is provided by Horvath and Siloni (2011; forthcoming); see also Wechsler (2005) and Williams (2007) for discussion. The main arguments put forward in favour of the idea are the following.

First, there seems to be a tighter semantic relation between the verb and its internal argument(s) than between the verb and the external argument. This expresses itself by the facts that (i) there are many cases where a combination of verb and internal argument is interpreted idiomatically, whereas idioms consisting of external argument and verb but excluding the internal argument are claimed to be absent; (ii) choice of internal argument can fix the meaning of a polysemous verb in such a way that the choice of external argument must be compatible with one particular meaning for the verb; again, the claim is that the reverse situation does not occur. Second, in nominalisations derived by particular deverbal affixes, the external argument of the base is not inherited. This can be accounted for by the assumption that the relevant class of affixes do not select vP but VP.

The latter point can be illustrated with an example like (36) (see Marantz 1997).

(36) a. John grows tomatoes.
     b. *John's growth of tomatoes

Marantz argues that the agentive interpretation of the subject argument of *grow* in (36a) relies on the presence of little v rather than on *grow* itself, and that this head is not present in the nominalisation in (36b) – hence its infelicity. Williams (2007) notes that this argument is incomplete as it stands. Genitive phrases in nominalisations have a very wide range of possible semantic relations to the head noun. However, a semantic interpretation that would accidentally be identical to the one that holds between v and its argument must be blocked, but it is not clear how such blocking is achieved.

Consider next the first type of argument to sever the lexical verb from the external argument mentioned above. That the choice of internal argument can have an effect on the precise meaning given to the verb is illustrated by examples such as (37) (cf. Marantz 1984).

(37) a. John took a pen. (*take* ≈ 'grab')
    b. John took a pill. (*take* ≈ 'swallow')
    c. John took a bus. (*take* ≈ 'travel on')

Marantz claims there are no comparable examples where the external argument has this effect. Also, there are many idioms of the type in (38), but not of the type in (39) (where X and Y represent an open place in the idiom: that is, a position where non-idiomatically interpreted material can be inserted).

(38) X kicked the bucket, X broke the ice, X buried the hatchet, X pulled Y's leg

(39) the player kicked X, the axe broke X, the undertaker buried X, the conductor pulled X

The question is whether this indicates that the external argument is really not represented in the verb's argument structure at all. Horvath and Siloni (2011; forthcoming) argue that it does not. They claim that the asymmetries observed by Marantz and others can be accounted for purely by the (fairly standard) assumption that semantic interpretation proceeds bottom up, and therefore first deals with any verb + internal argument combination before the contribution of the external argument is considered. They further argue that certain data indicate that a thematic relationship between lexical verb and external argument must exist. For a start, they point out that examples such as (40) indicate that the observation that idioms of the type in (39) do not exist appears to be incorrect (see also Nunberg *et al.* 1994 and Williams 2007); they just are much rarer than examples of the type in (38).

(40) a. A little bird told X Y.
    b. Lady Luck smiled on X.

Moreover, they point out that a verb can impose selectional restrictions on its external argument just as well as on its internal arguments, as shown by examples such as (41). This is unexpected if this argument is not assigned a thematic role by the verb in the first place. It is, of course, possible to assume that selectional relationships may hold between v and the verb in its VP-complement, but such a move would seem to re-establish a selectional link between verb and external argument, albeit only indirectly.

(41) a. The bees stung/*bit John.
    b. The snake *stung/bit John.

The argument could be extended to the issue of whether a verb has an external argument to begin with. At least to a certain extent, unaccusativity (lack of an external argument) appears to have a semantic basis (for discussion of this issue see, for instance, Levin and Rappaport Hovav (1995) and papers in Alexiadou *et al.* (2004)). If so, the phenomenon in itself is not difficult to accommodate in any theory adopting non-relative correspondences between conceptual semantics/thematic roles and syntactic positions, be this a theory that lets syntactic structure determine interpretation or a theory in which thematic features or roles determine projection as internal vs. external argument. (In contrast, if thematic hierarchies are only relative, meaning the highest available theta-role should be projected to the highest available syntactic position, there can be no syntactic difference between unergatives and unaccusatives). However, consider the phenomenon that the same verb can alternate between an unaccusative inchoative alternant and a causative transitive alternant:

(42) a. The door opened.
     b. They opened the door.

(43) a. The fire ignited.
     b. They ignited the fire.

Clearly, we would not want to say that the verbs in (42a) and (42b) are different verbs, given that they share a core conceptual meaning, so we cannot assume that there are two unrelated verbs *open*, for example, each with its own argument structure. The two, despite having apparently different argument structures, must be related somehow. (This basic assumption is sometimes known as lexicon uniformity: see Reinhart (2000); Rappaport Hovav and Levin (2012); see §5 for discussion of argument structure alternations more generally).

At least at first sight, an approach in which external arguments are introduced by v rather than the lexical verb appears to have a straightforward account for this relationship: the verb, and the VP it projects, are indeed completely identical in the (a) and (b) cases of (42)–(43). The only difference is whether a v has been added to the structure ((b) examples) or not ((a) examples) (or, alternatively, whether the v that is present is defective or not). The problem is that not every verb can undergo the inchoative–causative alternation:

(44) a.   They arrived
     b. *The pilot arrived the plane.

(45) a.   The patient died.
     b. *The assassin died his victim.

If the property of having an external argument or not is not a lexically specified property of the argument structure of the verb, this is unexpected. One solution would be to assume that (44b) and (45b) are not in fact ungrammatical, but that the transitive versions of the verbs in question happen not be lexicalised in English. Perhaps somewhat surprisingly, this would be equivalent to what is assumed in one of the theories that do assume the verb's external argument is represented in its lexical argument structure, namely Reinhart's theory. Reinhart argues that all unaccusatives, not just those with an existing transitive counterpart, are the result of a lexical operation working on argument structure, by which the external role of the verb is reduced (inspired by Chierchia's (2004) semantic account along such lines). She notes that, while an unaccusative such as *come* does not have a transitive counterpart in English, it does in Hebrew, and concludes that the absence of transitive counterparts for unaccusatives in individual languages may simply be a matter of accidental lexical gaps.[2]

The opposite phenomenon, where a transitive verb does not have an unaccusative/inchoative counterpart, occurs as well, and is potentially more problematic for the view that verbs do not have a lexically specified relationship to the external argument. Consider (46)–(47), for example.

(46) a.   The assassin killed his victim.
     b. *The victim killed. (with meaning 'the victim got killed')

(47) a.   The Romans destroyed the city.
   b.   *The city destroyed (meaning 'the city got destroyed').

As indicated, the (b) examples can receive a perfectly plausible inchoative reading (e.g., *the city destroyed* would mean 'the city became destroyed' just like *the door opened* means 'the door became open'). Nevertheless, they are impossible. A straightforward account for that would be to assume that it is a lexical property of a verb such as *destroy* that it must have an external argument. If such a specification is not allowed, the question becomes how we can ensure that the element that does assign the external role, namely v, always accompanies a VP headed by a verb like this, without assuming any selectional relationship between v and particular verbs (which would be tantamount to assuming a selectional relationship between V and the external argument, after all).

5   Argument structure alternations

5.1.   Changing the correspondences between theta-roles and argument positions

The causative–inchoative alternation discussed in the previous section is one of a number of processes in which a verb's argument structure is manipulated, or at least seemingly so. Other ones in English include passivisation, middle formation, and reflexivization.

In passivisation, an argument that is an internal argument in the verb's active guise shows up in subject position, whereas what is the external argument with the active verb does not appear in an argument position at all (but at most in an adjunct *by*-phrase):

(48) a.   active: Flora has fed the tigers.
   b.   passive: The tigers have been fed (by Flora).

A similar alternation is shown by middle formation, some examples of which are given in (49b) and (50b).

(49) a.   active: Barry read this book.
   b.   middle: This book reads well.

(50) a.   active: The mafia bribed the bureaucrats.
   b.   middle: Bureaucrats bribe easily.

Middles differ from passives in a number of respects. For example, the original external argument cannot be expressed optionally through a *by*-phrase in a middle. Passives and middles also differ in their meaning, in that passives can express an event, while middles typically express a property of their subject (i.e., the original internal argument). Moreover, middles can distinguish themselves from passives formally as well. In English, for example, middle formation does not express itself morphologically at all.

Reflexivisation is the process by which the internal argument of some verbs that are otherwise obligatorily transitive can remain syntactically unexpressed if this argument refers to the same entity as the external argument:

(51) a.   John dresses. (can only mean: 'John dresses himself')
   b.   Mary washes. (can only mean 'Mary washes herself')

Many languages have the same or similar operations, although probably none of these processes is universal. Languages that do not have passives, for instance, include Tongan, Samoan, and Hungarian (Siewierska 1984). On the other hand, languages can also have yet other ways of manipulating a verb's argument structure. In a so-called applicative, for example, a phrase that is not usually an argument of the verb, but, for instance, an instrumental modifier, becomes an internal argument. An example from the Bantu language Chingoni is given in (52) (from Ngonyani and Githinji (2006), with the gloss slightly simplified). Various tests show that phrases such as *chipula* 'knife' in (52) indeed function as an object rather than an instrumental modifier (as it would be if the verb had not undergone applicative). For example, such phrases can in turn become the subject of the sentence if the applicative sentence is passivized; for discussion, see Baker (1985; 1988b) and Hyman (2003), among others.

(52) Mijokwani   vidumul-il-a   chipula.
      sugar cane   *cut*-Applicative   *knife*
      'They use the knife to cut the sugar cane with.'

The closest thing in English to an applicative is the so-called spray/load alternation (see, for instance, Levin and Rappaport Hovav 1995). Verbs such as *spray* and *load* can have their Theme argument as internal argument, in line with (28). But, as the (b) sentences in (53) and (54) show, the element expressing Location can also occur as object argument with these verbs, resembling the promotion to argument status of such modifiers in applicatives.

(53) a. They sprayed paint on the wall.
      b. They sprayed the wall with paint.

(54) a. They loaded hay onto the wagon.
      b. They loaded the wagon with hay.

Some verbs taking both a Theme argument and a Goal or Benefactive argument allow similar promotion of the latter argument. In this case, the Theme argument is not introduced by a preposition even in case the other argument behaves like a direct internal argument, the result therefore being a so-called double object construction; compare the (b) examples in (55)–(56) with the (a) examples (also note the obligatory switch in order of the two arguments).

(55) a. Janice sent a letter to Frances.
      b. Janice sent Frances a letter.

(56) a. Gerald baked a cake for Frances.
      b. Gerald baked Frances a cake.

5.2   Possible analyses

Turning now to the question of how to analyse such processes, it will not come as a surprise after §§3 and 4 that, at least roughly speaking, we can distinguish two approaches, one that allows for manipulation of argument structures in the lexicon and another that does not and sees these alternations as the product of purely syntax-internal processes.

The lexical approach assumes that the lexicon contains not only entries for verbs (and other predicative elements) that specify their basic argument structure but also a set of operations that can manipulate this argument structure. One of the earliest such approaches was outlined by Williams (1981), who proposed that there are rules such as Externalise(X) and Internalise(X) where X is some designated argument of the predicate. One problem is that not all externalisation processes, for instance, seem to have the same effect. Both middles and passives involve externalisation of an internal argument, but, at least in some languages, middles behave on a par with unergative verbs while passives behave on a par with unaccusatives, which might indicate that the surface subject does not have the same underlying syntactic position in the two (see Ackema and Schoorlemmer 1994; 1995). Also, the suppressed original external argument is active as an implicit argument in passives but not in middles. For instance, it licenses the presence of agent-oriented adverbs in a passive but not in a middle:

(57) a. The boat was sold on purpose.
      b. Such books sell well (*on purpose).

Hence, the status of the original external argument appears not to be the same either in the two cases. A lexical approach could deal with this by assuming that there are different kinds of rules of argument structure manipulation. Reinhart (2000), for example, proposes that there are not only rules that reduce arguments (such as the external-role-reducing rule discussed in §4) but also rules that existentially bind a role; this rule would apply to the external argument in passives. For discussion see also Spencer and Sadler (1998), Aranovich and Runner (2000), and Reinhart and Siloni (2005).

According to the syntactic approach, lexical manipulation of argument structure is not possible, so the semantic arguments always correspond to syntactic arguments in exactly the same way initially (this is the tenet of Baker's (1988a) Uniformity of Theta Assignment Hypothesis). Argument promotion or demotion processes such as the ones mentioned above are then the result of syntactic operations that can put constituents in a different argument position, in combination with the assumption that syntactic arguments can sometimes be realised by empty elements, or by special morphology such as passive morphology; see, for instance, Baker (1988a), Baker *et al.* (1989), Stroik (1992), and Hoekstra and Roberts (1993). The attractive aspect of this approach is that it allows for simpler correspondences between syntax and lexical semantics, as these correspondences are always the same and not subject to lexical manipulation. The other side of the coin is that syntax itself may need to be complicated in some instances. For example, if in both middles and passives the original external and internal argument of the verb are assigned to subject and direct object position, respectively, some questions arise. For instance, we need to assume that the underlying subject in a middle is an empty category (while in passives it could be the participial morpheme (see Jaeggli (1986); Baker *et al.* (1989)), which is unexpected at least in non-pro-drop languages such as English. Also, if in both cases the surface subject is an underlying object, the question is why middles (but not passives) show unergative behaviour in languages such as Dutch and English, if Ackema and Schoorlemmer (1995) are correct. Of course, analyses that address these questions can be given, but they may involve qualitative extensions of the theory of syntax (for example, Hoekstra and Roberts (1993) explicitly address the question of why a pro subject can be present in an English middle, but they need to extend the theory of how pro can be licensed specifically because of this case). But this does mean that it is not straightforward to base a decision as to what the best approach to (apparent) argument structure alternations is on considerations of simplicity, as such considerations should be applied to the overall resulting grammar, not just one aspect (syntax–semantics correspondences) of it.

It is fair to say that the issue is still very much debated. To some extent, it depends on one's overall theoretical predilections which approach is chosen. Thus, a core tenet of a theory such as LFG is that such alternations must be the result of lexical principles (see Bresnan 2000), while the majority of articles in which a Minimalist approach is adopted appear to favour an all-syntactic approach. It should be noted, however, that it is quite conceivable that not all argument structure changing processes should be analysed in the same way. That is to say, instead of assuming that all such processes are the result of lexical rules that manipulate argument structure, or that they are all the result of syntactic movement and licensing mechanisms, it is possible that some are the result of the former type of rule and some the result of the latter. Such variation can come in two guises: it is possible that within a single language, one type of argument structure alternation is lexical while another is syntactic. It is also possible that what appears to be the same type of argument structure alternation is the result of lexical rules in one language but of syntactic processes in another. To conclude the chapter, let me give some examples of this possibility.

If English and Dutch middles are indeed unlike passives in showing unergative behaviour, this could be accounted for under the assumption that passives involve syntactic A-movement of the object to subject position, while middles involve a lexical process by which the internal argument becomes an external one.[3] That would be an example of language-internal variation. At the same time, it has been observed that in some other languages (e.g., the Romance languages and Greek) middles behave more like passives and so might be better analysed as involving syntactic A-movement. If so, that would be an example of cross-linguistic variation in which middles are formed (lexically in Germanic, syntactically in Romance); for discussion see Authier and Reed (1996), Lekakou (2004), Marelj (2004), and Ackema and Schoorlemmer (2005).

Reinhart (2002) and Reinhart and Siloni (2005) propose to extend such an approach to other processes affecting argument structure as well. Thus, they propose the following general parameter (where thematic arity more or less corresponds to what is termed argument structure here):

(58) *The lex-syn parameter*
      Universal Grammar allows thematic arity operations to apply in the lexicon or in the syntax.

Reinhart and Siloni (2005) argue that the parameter applies to reflexivisation. In English, for example, reflexivisation is the result of lexical reduction of the verb's internal thetarole (compare with the reduction of the external role, resulting in an inchoative, discussed in §4). They argue that it must be a lexical process in this language because a role can only be reduced in this way if it is thematically related to the same predicate that assigns the role that functions as its antecedent, which is lexical information.[4] This is illustrated by (59).

(59) a.   John washes. (meaning 'John washes himself')
      b.   *John considers intelligent. (intended meaning 'John considers himself intelligent')

In other languages, such as French, the equivalent of (59b) is fine (see (60)), which would indicate that these languages opt for the 'syntax' setting for reflexivisation.

(60) Jean se considère intelligent.
      Jean SE *considers intelligent*
      'Jean considers himself intelligent.'

Horvath and Siloni (2011) extend the coverage of (58) to causativisation; see also Horvath and Siloni (forthcoming) for general discussion.

6 Conclusion

The central question about the Syntax–Lexicon interface may be formulated as 'how does the lexical content of a predicate affect the possible syntactic realisations of it and its arguments'? The main conclusion one could draw from the above is that there still is quite a lot of controversy surrounding this question, particularly where it concerns the balance of power between syntax and the lexicon. Are all syntactic realisation possibilities of a predicate-argument complex the result of syntactic principles alone, the lexicon only supplying the conceptual content of the predicate and arguments? Or is it possible to manipulate argument structure lexically, possibly leading to a leaner syntax? While the answer to this is at least partially determined by theoretical preferences, the controversy has led to a lot of fascinating in-depth discussions of many different argument structure alternations, thereby showing that such disagreements can be stimulating rather than aggravating.

Notes

1 In some models, the lexicon is assigned additional power, in that it is enriched with a set of rules that can manipulate some aspect of the lexically listed properties of a predicate (as will be discussed in §5). These rules certainly are intended to capture regularities, not idiosyncracies. Still, they should not be confused with morphological rules – that is, the rules that determine the well-formedness or otherwise of complex words.
2 Another matter is that the transitive and unaccusative counterparts can be realized by distinct morphological forms: compare, for instance, transitive *fell* versus unaccusative *fall* in English. This is not problematic in any 'realisational'/'late spell-out' model of morphology.
3 Throughout here, 'passive' refers to verbal passives rather than adjectival passives. Adjectival passives arguably differ from verbal ones precisely in not involving syntactic A-movement but lexical externalisation: see, for instance, Wasow (1977) for English and Ackema (1999) for Dutch. If so, this is another instance of language-internal variation in the component responsible for the various valency-changing operations.
4 At least, under the assumption that external roles are assigned by the lexical predicate as well, see §4 for discussion.

Further reading

Borer, Hagit. 2005. *Structuring Sense*. Oxford: Oxford University Press.
Everaert, Martin, Marijana Marelj, and Tal Siloni (eds). 2012. *The Theta System*. Oxford: Oxford University Press.
Grimshaw, Jane. 1990. *Argument Structure*. Cambridge, MA: MIT Press.
Hale, Kenneth, and Samuel J. Keyser. 2002. *Prolegomenon to a Theory of Argument Structure*. Cambridge, MA: MIT Press.
Jackendoff, Ray. 1990. *Semantic Structures*. Cambridge, MA: MIT Press.

References

Ackema, Peter. 1999. *Issues in Morphosyntax*. Amsterdam: John Benjamins.
Ackema, Peter. forthcoming. Arguments and Adjuncts. In *Syntax: An International Handbook*, 2nd edn, ed. A. Alexiadou and T. Kiss. Berlin: Mouton de Gruyter.

Ackema, Peter, and Marijana Marelj. 2012. To Have the Empty Theta-Role. In *The Theta System*, ed. M. Everaert, M. Marelj, and T. Siloni, 227–250. Oxford: Oxford University Press.

Ackema, Peter, and Ad Neeleman. 2004. *Beyond Morphology*. Oxford: Oxford University Press.

Ackema, Peter, and Ad Neeleman. 2010. The Role of Syntax and Morphology in Compounding. In *Cross-disciplinary Issues in Compounding*, ed. S. Scalise and I. Vogel, 21–36. Amsterdam: John Benjamins.

Ackema, Peter, and Maaike Schoorlemmer. 1994. The Middle Construction and the Syntax-Semantics Interface. *Lingua* 93:59–90.

Ackema, Peter, and Maaike Schoorlemmer. 1995. Middles and Non-movement. *Linguistic Inquiry* 26:173–197.

Ackema, Peter, and Maaike Schoorlemmer. 2005. Middles. In *The Blackwell Companion to Syntax* vol. III, ed. M. Everaert and H. van Riemsdijk, 131–203. Oxford: Basil Blackwell.

Alexiadou, Artemis, Elena Anagnostopoulou, and Martin Everaert (eds). 2004. *The Unaccusativity Puzzle*. Oxford: Oxford University Press.

Anderson, Mona. 1979. Noun Phrase Structure. PhD dissertation, University of Connecticut.

Aranovich, Raul, and Jeffrey Runner. 2000. Diathesis Alternations and Rule Interaction in the Lexicon. In *Proceedings of WCCFL 20*, ed. K. Meegerdomian and L.A. Bar-el, 15–28. Somerville, MA: Cascadilla Press.

Authier, Jean-Marc, and Lisa Reed. 1996. On the Canadian French Middle. *Linguistic Inquiry* 27:513–523.

Baker, Mark. 1985. The Mirror Principle and Morphosyntactic Explanation. *Linguistic Inquiry* 16:373–416.

Baker, Mark. 1988a. *Incorporation*. Chicago, IL: University of Chicago Press.

Baker, Mark. 1988b. Theta Theory and the Syntax of Applicatives in Chichewa. *Natural Language and Linguistic Theory* 6:353–389.

Baker, Mark. 1996. *The Polysynthesis Parameter*. Oxford: Oxford University Press.

Baker, Mark, Kyle Johnson, and Ian Roberts. 1989. Passive Arguments Raised. *Linguistic Inquiry* 20:219–251.

Belletti, Adriana, and Luigi Rizzi. 1988. Psych-verbs and θ-theory. *Natural Language and Linguistic Theory* 6:291–352.

Borer, Hagit. 2005. *Structuring Sense* vol I: *In Name Only*. Oxford: Oxford University Press.

Bresnan, Joan. 2000. *Lexical-Functional Syntax*. Oxford: Blackwell.

Burzio, Luigi. 1986. *Italian Syntax*. Dordrecht: Reidel.

Chierchia, Gennaro. 2004. A Semantics for Unaccusatives and its Syntactic Consequences. In *The Unaccusativity Puzzle*, ed. A. Alexiadou, E. Anagnostopoulou and M. Everaert, 288–331. Oxford: Oxford university Press.

Chomsky, Noam. 1981. *Lectures on Government and Binding*. Dordrecht: Foris.

Culicover, Peter, and Ray Jackendoff. 2001. Control is not Movement. *Linguistic Inquiry* 32: 493–512.

Culicover, Peter, and Ray Jackendoff. 2005. *Simpler Syntax*. Oxford: Oxford University Press.

den Dikken, Marcel. 1995. *Particles*. Oxford: Oxford University Press.

Di Sciullo, Anna-Maria, and Edwin Williams. 1987. *On the Definition of Word*. Cambridge, MA: MIT Press.

Dixon, R.M.W. 1972. *The Dyirbal Language of North Queensland*. Cambridge: Cambridge University Press.

Everaert, Martin, Marijana Marelj, and Tal Siloni (eds). 2012. *The Theta System*. Oxford: Oxford University Press.

Folli, Raffaella, and Heidi Harley. 2004. Flavours of v: Consuming Results in Italian and English. In *Aspectual Inquiries*, ed. R. Slabakova and P. Kempchinsky, 95–120. Dordrecht: Kluwer.

Grimshaw, Jane. 1979. Complement Selection and the Lexicon. *Linguistic Inquiry* 10:279–326.

Grimshaw, Jane. 1990. *Argument Structure*. Cambridge, MA: MIT Press.

Haegeman, Liliane, and Tabea Ihsane. 1999. Subject Ellipsis in Embedded Clauses in English. *English Language and Linguistics* 3:117–145.

Haegeman, Liliane, and Tabea Ihsane. 2001. Adult Null Subjects in the Non-*pro*-drop Languages: Two Diary Dialects. *Language Acquisition* 9:329–346.

Hale, Kenneth, and Samuel J. Keyser. 1991. *On the Syntax of Argument Structure*. Lexicon Project Working Papers, MIT.

Hale, Kenneth, and Samuel J. Keyser. 1993. On Argument Structure and the Lexical Expression of Syntactic Relations. In *The View from Building 20*, ed. K. Hale and S. J. Keyser, 53–109. Cambridge, MA: MIT Press.

Hale, Kenneth, and Samuel J. Keyser. 2002. *Prolegomenon to a Theory of Argument Structure*. Cambridge, MA: MIT Press.

Hoekstra, Teun. 1988. Small Clause Results. *Lingua* 74:101–139.

Hoekstra, Teun, and Ian Roberts. 1993. The Mapping from the Lexicon to Syntax: Null Arguments. In *Knowledge and Language* vol. II, ed. E. Reuland and W. Abraham, 183–220. Dordrecht: Kluwer.

Hornstein, Norbert. 1999. Movement and Control. *Linguistic Inquiry* 30:69–96.

Hornstein, Norbert. 2001. *Move!* Oxford: Blackwell.

Horvath, Julia, and Tal Siloni. 2011. Causatives across Components. *Natural Language and Linguistic Theory* 29:657–704.

Horvath, Julia, and Tal Siloni. forthcoming. The Thematic Phase and the Architecture of Grammar. In *Concepts, Syntax, and their Interface*, ed. M. Everaert, M. Marelj, E. Reuland, and T. Siloni. Cambridge, MA: MIT Press.

Hyman, Larry. 2003. Suffix Ordering in Bantu: A Morphocentric Approach. In *Yearbook of Morphology 2002*, ed. G. Booij and J. van Marle, 245–281. Dordrecht: Kluwer.

Jackendoff, Ray. 1983. *Semantics and Cognition*. Cambridge, MA: MIT Press.

Jackendoff, Ray. 1987. The Status of Thematic Relations in Linguistic Theory. *Linguistic Inquiry* 18:369–411.

Jackendoff, Ray. 1990. *Semantic Structures*. Cambridge, MA: MIT Press.

Jackendoff, Ray. 1993. On the Role of Conceptual Structure in Argument Selection: A Reply to Emonds. *Natural Language and Linguistic Theory* 11:279–312.

Jackendoff, Ray. 1997. *The Architecture of the Language Faculty*. Cambridge, MA: MIT Press.

Jaeggli, Osvaldo. 1986. Passive. *Linguistic Inquiry* 17:587–622.

Jelinek, Eloise. 2006. The Pronominal Argument Parameter. In *Arguments and Agreement*, ed. P. Ackema, P. Brandt, M. Schoorlemmer, and F. Weerman, 261–288. Oxford: Oxford University Press.

Kratzer, Angelika. 1996. Severing the External Argument from its Verb. In *Phrase Structure and the Lexicon*, ed. J. Rooryck and L. Zaring, 109–137. Dordrecht: Kluwer.

Landau, Idan. 2003. Movement out of Control. *Linguistic Inquiry* 34:471–498.

Lekakou, Marika. 2004. In the Middle, Somewhat Elevated. PhD dissertation, University College London.

Levin, Beth, and Malka Rappaport Hovav. 1995. *Unaccusativity*. Cambridge, MA: MIT Press.

Lieber, Rochelle. 2004. *Morphology and Lexical Semantics*. Cambridge: Cambridge University Press.

Marantz, Alec. 1984. *On the Nature of Grammatical Relations*. Cambridge, MA: MIT Press.

Marantz, Alec. 1997. No Escape from Syntax: Don't Try Morphological Analysis in the Privacy of Your Own Lexicon. *University of Pennsylvania Working Papers in Linguistics* 4:201–225.

Marelj, Marijana. 2004. Middles and Argument Structure across Languages. PhD dissertation, Utrecht University.

Neeleman, Ad, and Hans van de Koot. 2002. Bare Resultatives. *Journal of Comparative Germanic Linguistics* 6:1–52.

Neeleman, Ad, and Fred Weerman. 1993. The Balance between Syntax and Morphology: Dutch Particles and Resultatives. *Natural Language and Linguistic Theory* 11:433–475.

Ngonyani, Deo, and Peter Githinji. 2006. The Asymmetric Nature of Bantu Applicative Constructions. *Lingua* 116:31–63.

Nunberg, Geoffrey, Ivan Sag, and Thomas Wasow. 1994. Idioms. *Language* 70:491–538.

Ostler, Nicholas. 1979. Case-linking: A Theory of Case and Verb Diathesis Applied to Classical Sanskrit. PhD dissertation, MIT.

Perlmutter, David, and Paul Postal. 1984. The 1-Advancement Exclusiveness Law. In *Studies in Relational Grammar 2*, ed. D. Perlmutter and C. Rosen, 81–125. Chicago, IL: University of Chicago Press.

Pesetsky, David. 1995. *Zero Syntax*. Cambridge, MA: MIT Press.

Pylkkänen, Liina. 2002. Introducing Arguments. PhD dissertation, MIT.

Ramchand, Gillian. 2008. *Verb Meaning and the Lexicon: A First Phase Syntax*. Cambridge: Cambridge University Press.

Rappaport Hovav, Malka, and Beth Levin. 2012. Lexicon Uniformity and the Causative Alternation. In *The Theta System*, ed. M. Everaert, M. Marelj, and T. Siloni, 150–176. Oxford: Oxford University Press.

Reinhart, Tanya. 2000. The Theta System: Syntactic Realization of Verbal Concepts. Ms. Utrecht University.

Reinhart, Tanya. 2002. The Theta System: An Overview. *Theoretical Linguistics* 28:229–290.

Reinhart, Tanya, and Tal Siloni. 2005. The Lexicon-Syntax Parameter: Reflexivization and Other Arity Operations. *Linguistic Inquiry* 36:389–436.

Rizzi, Luigi. 1986. Null Objects in Italian and the Theory of Pro. *Linguistic Inquiry* 17:501–557.

Rozwadowska, Bozena. 1988. Thematic Restrictions on Derived Nominals. In *Thematic Relations*, ed. W. Wilkins, 147–165. San Diego: Academic Press.

Siewierska, Anna. 1984. *The Passive*. London: Croom Helm.

Siloni, Tal. 2012. Reciprocal Verbs and Symmetry. *Natural Language and Linguistic Theory* 30:261–320.

Spencer, Andrew, and Louisa Sadler. 1998. Morphology and Argument Structure. In *The Handbook of Morphology*, ed. A. Spencer and A. Zwicky, 206–236. Oxford: Blackwell.

Stroik, Thomas. 1992. Middles and Movement. *Linguistic Inquiry* 23:127–137.

Tenny, Carol. 1994. *Aspectual Roles and the Syntax-Semantics Interface*. Dordrecht: Kluwer.

Van de Visser, Mario. 2006. The Marked Status of Ergativity. PhD dissertation, Utrecht University.

Verkuyl, Henk. 1993. *A Theory of Aspectuality*. Cambridge: Cambridge University Press.

Wasow, Thomas. 1977. Transformations and the Lexicon. In *Formal Syntax*, ed. P. Culicover, A. Akmajian, and T. Wasow, 327–360. New York: Academic Press.

Wechsler, Stephen. 2005. What is Right and Wrong about Little v. In *Grammar and Beyond*, ed. M. Vulchanova and T. Åfarli, 179–195. Oslo: Novus Press.

Weir, Andrew. 2012. Left-edge Deletion in English and Subject Omission in Diaries. *English Language and Linguistics* 16:105–129.

Williams, Edwin. 1981. Argument Structure and Morphology. *The Linguistic Review* 1:81–114.

Williams, Edwin. 1994. *Thematic Structure in Syntax*. Cambridge, MA: MIT Press.

Williams, Edwin. 2007. Dumping Lexicalism. In *The Oxford Handbook of Linguistic Interfaces*, ed. G. Ramchand and C. Reiss, 353–381. Oxford: Oxford University Press.

17

The morphology–syntax interface

Daniel Siddiqi

1 Introduction

The morphology–syntax interface (MSI) has historically been one of the most important and contentious interfaces in formal syntactic theory. This is not because morphology is somehow more important than the other linguistic realms but because the *a priori* assumptions about the nature of the MSI are often foundational to the architecture of the grammar. Historically, while Chomskyan tradition has assumed a clear division between syntactic phenomena and semantic and phonological phenomena since the 1970s and the time of the *Linguistics Wars* (Harris 1995), it has always fully incorporated morphological processes. Indeed, in the beginning of the generative tradition, morphology was not a domain unto itself. Instead, any morphological phenomenon was treated as either a phonological phenomenon or a syntactic one (a view that still persists in some models).

More importantly, whatever the nature of the morphological component, most models of grammar consider it to feed the syntactic component in some way. Since every model of syntax needs to identify some atom that is manipulated by the syntax, the nature of those atoms, and thus the nature of the morphological component, is crucial to the model of the syntax. One of the main reasons that the morphology–syntax interface is so contentious is that the form of what is fed into the syntax is radically different from one model to another. There are at least three distinct major camps on what is fed from the morphology to the syntax: (a) words, (b) morphemes, and (c) any complex structure with unpredictable meaning (idiom chunks).

Despite this feeding, the relative order of syntactic processes and morphological processes is not always clear. For the syntax–semantics interface, an obvious question that has plagued the study of the interface is this: does the meaning of the utterance follow the form or does the form follow the meaning? The MSI has a similar type of question. Language has three different ways of expressing grammatical relations: case, agreement, and word order. Typologically speaking, languages tend to prefer one of these tactics but typically do not exclude the others (Greenberg 1959; 1963). It seems that these three tactics all have the same function. However, while word order are syntactic, case and agreement are morphological. This is where the ordering problem for the MSI is seen: Does the position of a nominal in a sentence trigger case and agreement marking; or does the marking license the position of the nominal? Is a subject nominal marked with nominative case and does it trigger agreement on the verb *because* it is in subject position? Or is the nominal only permitted in subject position because it is marked with nominative case and the verb is marked with the corresponding subject agreement? Does syntactic position determine morphological marking or the other way around?

That there is at least a separate passive component that stores language-specific vocabulary is fairly uncontroversial. The major source of disagreement on the nature of the MSI is whether or not there is a separate *generative* morphological component. There are roughly three classes of syntactic theory along these lines. The first division is over Lexicalism. Lexicalism is the name for the family of models, including Government and Binding Theory (Chomsky 1981), Lexical Functional Grammar (Bresnan and Kaplan 1982), Head-Driven Phrase Structure Grammar (Pollard and Sag 1994), and many others, that posit that the phrase-building component of the grammar and the word-building component are crucially separate generative components. There is also a family of models that take the opposite view: That the lexicon is not generative but is rather just a passive storage device. Models such as Generative Semantics (Lakoff 1971), Distributed Morphology (Halle and Marantz 1993), Construction Grammar (Lakoff 1987), and Nanosyntax (Starke 2009), which I call Anti-Lexicalist, assume that the syntax, in one way or another, is responsible for building complex words as well as phrases.

The picture is further complicated because Lexicalism is divided into two varieties: Strong Lexicalism, which claims that all morphological processes are done by the Lexicon; and Weak Lexicalism, which claims that only derivational morphology is done by the Lexicon. In Weak Lexicalism, inflectional morphology, such as agreement, case, and verbal inflection, is all done by the syntactic component. In contemporary theory, Lexical-Functional Grammar and Head-Driven Phrase Structure Grammar are Strong Lexicalist models of syntax. On the other hand, while some frameworks and theories within the Minimalist Program (Chomsky 1995) are Anti-Lexicalist (notably Distributed Morphology and Nanosyntax), the default position for Minimalism is Weak Lexicalist. Indeed, while Minimalism is the only major model that assumes Weak Lexicalism, its dominance among syntacticians makes Weak Lexicalism the default position in contemporary syntactic theory.

The purpose of this chapter is to showcase such issues within morphological and syntactic theory that define the different perspectives of the MSI. Section 2 provides a brief history of Lexicalism (the perspective that the syntax and the morphology are two separate generative components of the grammar). Section 3 provides a detailed discussion of the inflection/derivation split and its ramifications on Weak Lexicalism. Section 4 provides contemporary arguments in support of Lexicalism. Section 5 provides contemporary arguments against Lexicalism.

2   A brief history of lexicalism

If we mark the beginning of generative syntactic theory with the publication of Chomsky (1957), *Syntactic Structures*, then Lexicalism was certainly not present in the beginning nor would it develop for quite some time. Within Chomskyan tradition from Chomsky (1957) to Chomsky (1965) there was no need for a generative lexicon because the transformational grammar manipulated both morphemes and words and also created complex words through the transformations (see Lees 1960, for example). Allomorphy, or alternate surface forms for the same morpheme, was a result of the phonological component (see Chomsky and Halle 1968, for example). Indeed, the "lexicon" was no more than terminal phrase structure rules that replaced a variable with phonological content. These terminal nodes contained only arbitrary signs with non-compositional, idiomatic meaning. Anything with predictable complex structure (including derived words and compounds) and anything with grammatical relations was composed by the transformational grammar.

Chomsky (1965) changed that view subtly and introduced the first lexicon to Chomskyan tradition, though this lexicon was not generative. With Chomsky (1965), rather than words coming into the syntax as the result of replacement rules, words came from a separate storage component. What this allowed generative grammar to do was remove from the syntax many of the properties of words that were idiosyncratic or did not directly relate to the syntax, thus making the syntax much simpler. In Chomsky (1965) the lexicon was an elaborate subcategorization mechanism that endowed words with specific formal features that affected how they behaved in the syntax. Their features formed complex attribute-value matrices that fulfilled two main jobs: (a) they defined what features the words selected of their arguments (such as [+___NP NP] to indicate a ditransitive verb); and (b) they listed the features that were selected by another word (such as [+/− COUNT]). These matrices drove the morphological processes as much as they drove the syntax. For example, Latinate affixes such as -ity selected for bases with the feature [+LATINATE], etc.

During this time, two problems in the domain of morphology continued to be very difficult for Chomskyan tradition to handle: the variable productivity of derivation and the non-compositionality of compounding. The problem of derivation is that relatively few derivational affixes are completely productive. Rather, many are lexically conditioned (width vs *?heighth vs *coolth), others create idiosyncratic meaning (transmission can mean "car part"), and many trigger stem allomorphy (changing the stem phonology: receive + tion = reception). The problem with compounding is that, while it is completely productive, the semantic relationship between the members of a compound is difficult to predict (cf. nurse shoes vs alligator shoes) or even ambiguous (toy box).[1]

Chomsky (1970) marked a turning point for the MSI and gave rise to Lexicalism. In this work Chomsky directly confronts the problem of derivational morphology's potential limited productivity and idiosyncratic meaning, in particular looking at derived nominalization versus gerunds. For the transformational model to account for syntax, the transformations need to be transparent, regular, semantically predictable, and wholly productive. Derivational morphology often has none of these properties. In the case of nominalizations, Chomsky (1970) identified a difference between gerunds (such as destroying and growing), which are always regular, and "derived nominalization" (such as destruction and growth). Chomsky (1970) claimed that the irregular, less productive, and idiosyncratic morphological transformations must be located elsewhere – that lexical rules derived the irregular behavior of derivational morphology. While Chomsky (1970) did not describe what this generative Lexicon might look like and how it might work, what he established was that there was a separate component that generated word forms, allowing the syntactic grammar to remain regular and 100% productive, and effectively shifting the burden of unproductive morphology out of the syntax.

Halle (1973) was the first to sketch out a model of what a generative lexicon might look like and how it might function. Halle's was a four-piece model containing a passive list of morphemes, a set of generative word-formation rules (WFRs), a passive dictionary that stored completed words, and the most controversial component: the Filter. The WFRs were fed by the list of morphemes as well as by the dictionary and later the syntactic and phonological components, making the WFRs cyclic. The Filter's job was two-fold: (a) it was responsible for blocking (*glory* blocks **gloriosity*) by preventing some possible words; and (b) it gave non-compositional, idiosyncratic meaning to complex words (*divinity* referring to a rich dessert). The Filter's ability to do blocking was crucial. Productive morphological forms are very often blocked by the presence of another form with the same meaning. This is never true of syntax. Thus, Halle's (1973) sketch provided exactly what Lexicalism needed: a model of the morphology that removed the problematic aspects of syntax from the grammar.

Halle (1973) was significant in other ways. Firstly, Halle's (1973) model diverged from Chomsky's (1970) proposal because Halle (1973) proposed that the Lexicon was responsible for *all* morphological processes. Indeed, the original justification for Lexicalism, the difference between *destruction* and *destroying*, was lost in Halle's model. Secondly, it diverged from most previous models of morphology. The generative component of Halle's (1973) model, WFRs, is effectively transformations at the word level. These WFRs are abstract replacement rules. Prior to Halle (1973), formal morphology was mostly done in a concatenation-based, or *Item-and-Arrangement*, model (see Hockett 1954). Halle (1973) is a rule-based or *Item-and-Process* model. *Item-and-Process* morphology, which must be distinct from the concatenative processes in the syntax, is the chief justification for Lexicalism from the morphology theory point of view. Halle's (1973) model was particularly unrestricted, even for a transformation-based model, because the Filter was completely unrestricted in what it could block (see Booij 1977 for discussion) and how it could lexicalize meaning.

Halle (1973) was a sketch of a possible Lexicon, meant to draw attention to what formal Lexical inquiry could look like. Aronoff (1976) was the first completely articulated model of the Lexicon, making it considered by many (see Scalise and Guevara 2005) to be the foundational work in Lexicalism. Some of the main claims of Aronoff (1976) are still debated today and are often assumed as the defaults of the Lexicalist position. He defined productivity as categorical (anything that was idiosyncratic must be stipulated rather than generated by the rules) rather than scalar, introduced many restrictions of WFRs that are still assumed today (such as the Binary Branching Hypothesis and the Righthand Head Rule[2]), and developed a model of blocking. Two features of Aronoff (1976) that are crucial to the MSI are: (a) it is a Weak Lexicalist model (in that it assumes inflection and perhaps compounding are syntactic phenomena) and (b) the model introduced the Word-based Hypothesis, completely rejecting the idea of a morpheme as a unit manipulated by the grammar. The former entails Lexicalism as there must be two different components.

The Weak Lexicalist viewpoint in Aronoff (1976) was in stark contrast to the Strong Lexicalist viewpoint of Halle (1973). Indeed, the two different views have developed along separate paths somewhat independently from each other. The Strong Lexicalist viewpoint eventually becomes the Lexical Integrity Principle (Lapointe 1980), which is typically defined as "no syntactic rule can refer to elements of morphological structure" (Lapointe 1980) or, more contemporarily, "syntactic rules cannot create words or refer to the internal structure of words, and each terminal node is a word" (Falk 2001). The Strong Lexicalist position is assumed by most syntactic models including LFG, HPSG (and GPSG before it), and many practitioners of Minimalism. In the meantime, the Weak Lexicalist viewpoint was also developing. Anderson (1982; 1992) provides a detailed account of a Weak Lexicalist model of a late-insertion grammar (also known as a realizational model: the syntax feeds the MSI rather than the morphology feeding it: Distributed Morphology and Nanosyntax are contemporary realizational models, see below), and Weak Lexicalism is largely adopted by Government and Binding Theory. Also, during this time is the Linguistics Wars and the advent of Generative Semantics (Lakoff 1971), which, among many other things, is different from Transformational Grammar in its rejection of a pre-syntactic, generative lexicon. However, Generative Semantics, while significant, was not nearly as mainstream as the Lexicalist models of syntax, so it is fair to say that Lexicalism dominated syntactic theory throughout the 1970s and 1980s.

This was roughly the state of Lexicalism until the late 1980s and early 1990s, when Lexicalism came under fire from a number of different sources. The first of these was the Mirror Principle. Baker (1985; 1988) developed the Mirror Principle, which states that "morphological derivations must directly reflect syntactic derivations and vice versa". In other words, morpheme order must be explained by syntax (and vice versa). For example, if a syntactic derivation involves causativization followed by passivization, that must be the order of the causative and passive morphology on the verb. While many researchers have since claimed some counter examples to the Mirror Principle (see, for example, Boskovic 1997), it remains an important and ubiquitous generalization which has been supported by other such parallels between syntactic and morphological order (such as a remarkable typological similarity between the order of affixal verbal inflection and the order of auxiliary verbs). It follows from the Mirror Principle that the simplest account for this data is the one where morphology and the syntax are the same component.

Hot on the heels of Baker's Mirror Principle was Lieber's (1992) model of morphology as syntax. She proposed that the X-bar schema could be extended down within the word, thereby showing that most morphology could be accounted for with syntactic principles. To support her ideas, Lieber (1992) showcased what is often considered to be the definitive list of data that disputes the Lexicalist hypothesis (see below). Lieber's (1992) work was quickly followed by Halle and Marantz's (1993) proposal of Distributed Morphology, a framework within the Minimalist Program that rejects the Lexicalist hypothesis completely and laid the architecture for a syntactic model that was completely responsible for word formation as well as phrase structure. Finally, Marantz (1997) declared: "Lexicalism is dead, deceased, demised, no more, passed on. … The underlying suspicion was wrong and the leading idea didn't work out. This failure is not generally known because no one listens to morphologists."

Of course, contrary to Marantz (1997), Lexicalism was not dead, but, throughout the 1990s and early 2000s, Distributed Morphology slowly became the chief competitor to Lexicalist Minimalism, as HPSG and LFG slowly became more obscure. Contemporary Minimalist syntactic theory seems on a whole agnostic to Lexicalism, and Distributed Morphology has become increasingly a dominant syntactic framework. More recently, an even more extreme alternative, Nanosyntax (Starke 2009), has appeared as a competitor to Distributed Morphology and argues that not only is syntax sub-lexical but it is indeed sub-morphemic as well.

3 Weak lexicalism: inflection versus derivation

There is a series of well-known connections between syntax and the three types of inflectional morphology: case, agreement, and verbal inflection (tense, aspect, mood, etc.). Verbal inflection is a direct expression of formal features that are considered by most syntacticians to be syntactic features. Case (head-marking) and agreement (dependent-marking) are two sides of the same coin: they express grammatical relations morphologically,[3] a function that is clearly, and indeed only, syntactic in nature. Dating back at least to Sapir (1921) is the typological generalization that languages have a choice in expressing grammatical

Daniel Siddiqi

relations: use syntax or use morphology. Since this choice seems to be scalar rather than categorical, this typological pattern is normally presented as a continuum called the Index of Synthesis (Comrie 1981). At one end of this scale are isolating languages (e.g., English, Mandarin) which use word order to encode grammatical function. At the other end are synthetic languages (e.g., Latin, Navajo) which use affixation for the same job (see also Greenberg 1959; 1963). Furthermore, the inflectional meanings/features expressed by affixation or word order are also often expressed with syntactic elements as well. For example, in English, the only productive case marking is genitive, which is expressed by a determiner clitic (*'s*) when the genitive argument is left of the head noun and by a case particle (*of*) when the argument is to the right. Also, what is often marked by oblique cases (such as instrumental) in some languages is marked with prepositions in others. Perhaps most convincing, some languages express verbal inflection primarily with auxiliary verbs while other languages express it primarily with affixes. In fact, it is not uncommon for languages to use the combination of affixation and an auxiliary to express a singular inflectional meaning (perfect aspect in English and Latin, for example).

These connections strongly suggest that inflectional morphology is a function of the syntactic component of the grammar. Assuming that the arguments beginning with Chomsky (1970) that exclude derivational morphology from the syntax are compelling, it is logical then to adopt a Weak Lexicalist perspective. It seems odd, then, that this position is overwhelmingly held by syntacticians and only very infrequently by morphologists. This is because this position assumes an easily categorizable dichotomy between derivational and inflectional morphology, an assumption which may not be tenable.

Pre-theoretically, the traditional conceptual definition of derivational morphology is that it derives a new word (i.e., a new lexical entry) from an extant one. Inflectional morphology, on the other hand, changes the form of a word to express morphosyntactic features. In practice, a strict dichotomy is difficult to defend. It has been long acknowledged within the morphological literature that there is no agreed upon definitional distinction that captures the intuition that they are distinct (see Matthews 1972). For example, one of the traditional distinctive features of derivation, perhaps the most important, is that forms created through derivational processes are susceptible to lexicalization (cf. *cat* > *catty*). However, the majority of derived forms do not have idiosyncratic form or meaning and are completely compositionally transparent (*rethink*, *unequip*). Furthermore, some inflected forms can actually lexicalize (*brethren*). Other such definitions include: (a) derivational morphology is typically contentful (though this is not true of many nominalizers, negators, etc.), while inflectional morphology is functional; (b) inflectional morphology is obligatory for grammaticality and derivational is not (again with some exceptions such as nominalizers and the like that are often obligatory); (c) derivational morphology can be iterable (but again, not always); etc. One of the most convincing definitions of inflection is that it is paradigmatic, but even that definition can be unsatisfactory as what features are and are not in a paradigm of opposites is stipulative (for example, *sing/sang/sung* traditionally form a paradigm of opposites, but not *sing/sang/sung/song*).

The three strongest definitional distinctions are (a) inflection is completely productive and derivation is not; (b) derivation changes class and inflection does not; and (c) inflection is relevant to the syntax and derivation is not. The most cogent discussion of these three definitions is Anderson (1982; 1992), which I will summarize here. Anderson (1982; 1992) points out that productivity is insufficient on both accounts. First, inflectional morphology can have gaps in productivity, as evidenced by defective paradigms (where one predicted form is unavailable – for example, in English: *am/are/is* but XX/*aren't/isn't* and *drive/drove/driven* but *dive/dove/*XX). Halle (1973) shows a systematic case of defective paradigms in Russian where an entire verb class disallows present tense with first person singular agreement. On the other hand, there are multiple examples of derivational morphology that are completely productive: in English *-ing* to create gerunds/participles is completely productive without exception, and *-ly* to create adverbs has only a small closed set of exceptions. Anderson (1982; 1992) points out that the class-changing can never be a necessary distinction, because not all derivational affixes change class (e.g. prefixes in English, such as *un-* and *re-*; the only counter-example seems to be *de-*, which is a prefixal verbalizer). Anderson (1982; 1992) argues that we cannot even stipulate a set of features that are inflectional (such as agreement, case, tense, aspect, and mood), because the sets are not the same from language to language (for example, Anderson (1992) argues that the diminutive in Fula is inflectional while in most other languages it is derivational). Settling on "relevance to the syntax" as the definitional distinction, he then claims that inflectional morphology in fact realizes syntactic features (see below). In order to avoid circularity, he defines properties as relevant if they are "assigned to words by principles which make essential reference to larger syntactic structure." This supports the dominant view in syntactic theory, the Split Morphology Hypothesis (Perlmutter 1988; Anderson 1992), that the syntactic component of the grammar is responsible for inflection while the morphological component is responsible for derivation.

It is not the case that Anderson's (1992) claims were iron-clad. Anderson (1982; 1992) explicitly excludes from this definition "connections between distinct (but related) subcategorization frames" (such as causative/inchoative alternations such as *rise/raise*, *lie/lay*, and *fall/fell*). However, such an exclusion may not be warranted. Causativizers (such as Japanese *-sase-*) and other valence changing devices (such as passive voice and applicatives) with morphological reflexes are surely inflectional, as they indeed make reference to larger syntactic structure. Similarly, DiSciullo and Williams (1987) argue that it seems that any morphological process that only changes category (such as English's *-ing*, *-ly*, *-ness*, etc.) is in fact syntactic in the relevant sense. For example, a nominalizer's only job is to license a stem's nominal distribution, which is surely a reference to larger syntactic structure. DiSciullo and Williams (1987) also argue that classical contentful derivation, such as the English prefix *out-*, affects the syntax (in this case it is also a transitivizer). On the other hand, Anderson's (1992) definition is also too narrow (which he acknowledges). Verbal inflection such as tense and aspect have always been uncontroversially considered inflectional morphology, but verbal inflection does *not* make reference to larger syntactic structure at all. Its inclusion in the set of syntax relevant meanings is there because IP is a prominent head in the syntax (which means his definition is circular as it relies on the fact that syntactic theory, in this regard, was already Weak Lexicalist).

In the end, there is no satisfactory definitional distinction between derivation and inflection, which seems to doom the Split Morphology Hypothesis. Alas, it is not only on theoretical grounds that Split Morphology theory has been rejected. In fact, the only distinction that seems to be empirically true is that derivational morphology is always inside of inflectional morphology (Greenberg 1959; 1963), and, even in this case, Booij (1994; 1996; 2005) has shown ample evidence that this distinction is in fact empirically false as well. For example, past participles appear inside of de-adjectivers (*excitedness*) and, in Dutch, plural markers appear inside of nominalizers (*held-en-dom* 'heroism', lit hero+pl+nom, Booij 2005).

Because the *conceptual* categorical distinction is difficult to maintain *theoretically*, it is fairly typical in morphological study to assume one of two competing approaches: either

(a) the two types represent opposite ends of a continuum (Bybee 1985; Dressler 1989) or (b) the distinction is abandoned entirely. That leaves practitioners of Weak Lexicalist models of syntax in a precarious situation: Their model of syntax is dependent on Split Morphology Hypothesis, which is widely rejected by morphologists because it is both theoretically untenable and empirically incorrect. Regardless, Weak Lexicalism remains a dominant model of the MSI in formal syntactic theory, if only because it is the default position of Minimalism.[4]

4 Strong Lexicalism: arguments for a separate morphological component

The arguments in favor of Lexicalism usually revolve around empirical coverage since Lexicalism has more than just concatenative processes available to it, allowing it access to more powerful processes that can account for more data. Two such classes of data I will cover here in this chapter are stem allomorphy and blocking. Though Anti-Lexicalism is typically considered to be the more restricted model, there are some metatheoretical arguments in favor of Lexicalism. One common argument (as typified by DiSciullo and Williams 1987) is that morphological structure and syntactic structure are fundamentally different. For example, headedness in morphology is different from headedness in syntax or syntax displays long-distance dependencies while morphology does not. These types of arguments tend to be overwhelmingly theory sensitive. For example, DiSciullo and Williams (1987) use bracketing paradoxes[5] to argue for Strong Lexicalism while Lieber (1992) uses them as evidence for Anti-Lexicalism. Because of this theory sensitivity, I do not cover many of these types of arguments. In this section, I cover several that are less theory sensitive, including null morphemes, bound forms, and productivity.

4.1 Stem Allomorphy

Probably the most significant of the arguments for Lexicalism is the rule-based approach to morphology. The rule-based model argues that morphological alternations are the outputs of algorithms that replace the input phonology of a word with a new phonological form. On the other hand, the concatenation-based model posits that morphological alternations are the result of only two sources: concatenation of two morphemes and regular phonological processes. The concatenation model is easily compatible with Anti-Lexicalism since syntax, especially from the current Minimalist view, is also reduced to simple concatenation. On the other hand, the rule-based approach is more compatible with Lexicalism from this point of view because therein the Lexicon employs non-concatenative processes.

The distinctions between the rule-based approach and the concatenation approach are too numerous to do justice here, but the crux of the difference is this: Rules, by their very nature, are extremely powerful, giving them great empirical coverage. The problem with rules is how to restrict that power. If a grammar has rules powerful enough to rewrite *good* as *better* or *person* as *people*, there seems to be no way to stop the grammar from rewriting *cat* as *dogs* (Harley and Noyer 2000). On the other hand, concatenation models are much more restricted but sacrifice empirical coverage.

Nowhere is this more evident than in the realm of stem allomorphy and other non-concatenative processes (such as vowel ablaut: *mouse > mice*; stress shift: *PROduce > proDUCE*; and the famous Semitic templatic pattern: Arabic *kitab* 'book', *kattib* 'write perf. act.', *kuttib* 'write perf. pass.', etc., McCarthy 1981). A pure concatenative approach predicts that these processes should not exist; that all morphology ought to be affixal. Attempts to make concatenative approaches compatible with these processes tend to be *ad hoc* and overly complicated (such as suprafixes and transfixes). Rule-based models have no problems with stem allomorphy as rules have no restriction on where and how much phonology is replaced.

In fact, the main problem with stem allomorphy and other non-concatenative processes for the rule-based approach is that it predicts that there ought to be *more* of it! Rule-based models have no means to restrict the non-concatenative rules so they do not generate a proportional amount of base modification. In other words, proportionally speaking, a rule-based model predicts that there ought to be as much non-concatenative morphology as there is concatenative. It has been known since at least Sapir (1921) that this prediction is false. Instead, concatenative morphology makes up the vast majority of the world's morphological processes. Non-concatenative processes are clearly exceptions to the generalization that the world's morphology is concatenative. Concatenation-based models predict this prevalence of concatenation. However, this relative infrequency is easily explained by diachronic reasons: productive base modification is typically the result of a conspiracy of phonological changes, while concatenative morphology is the result of the more frequent process of grammaticalization.

4.2 Blocking

Blocking occurs when a productive word-formation process is ungrammatical only because it would create synonymy with another extant form. Some famous examples from throughout the literature are *gloriosity* being blocked by *glory*, *productiveness* being blocked by *productivity*, *goodly* being blocked by *well*, and *to broom* being blocked by *to sweep*. Blocking cannot be the result of a categorical ban on synonymy as derived synonymy is actually commonplace. Plank (1981) and Rainer (1988) conclude that a word's ability to block synonyms is a function of its frequency, which means that that information must be available to the grammar via stored complex forms, suggesting that the morphological component is word-based (or at least stores complex words). This strongly suggests that the lexicon stores its outputs in some way and that this storage fails when the result would be storing two synonyms (this argument originates with Kiparsky 1982). This suggests that the Lexicon is a separate component from the syntax because this storage of outputs is decidedly not a feature of syntax. Furthermore, one sentence never blocks another no matter how frequent that sentence is. There has been some discussion throughout the literature about words blocking phrases (such as *tomorrow* blocking **the day after today* or *happier* blocking **more happy*), but the apparent consensus of the literature is that these effects are fundamentally different from morphological blocking. For example, *more happy* is not blocked in *I am more happy than relieved* (see Embick and Marantz (2008) for detailed discussion).

4.3 Null morphemes

A theoretical problem with concatenative models that is magnified several-fold in an Anti-Lexicalist model is that of formal features that are not overtly expressed with phonology. This can be seen in cases of unmarked plurals (*fish*, *deer*) and is taken to be the standard account for conversion.[6] In a concatenative model, a morpheme without any phonological expression is affixed to the stem to realize the meaning/features. These zero morphemes litter a derivation, being proposed to be syntactic licensing conditions for innumerable syntactic and morphological phenomena (they are normally taken to license base modification, for example). The existence of a null morpheme is typically *ad hoc* and serves only theoretical considerations. Clearly, the requirement of null morphemes (and in such great quantity) is a significant weakness of concatenative models because they are not only impossible to confirm empirically but also gross violations of Occam's Razor. Again, the single component hypothesis assumes a concatenative model of morphology, so this is a weakness of concatenative models that Anti-Lexicalism inherits.

4.4   Cran morphs and bound roots

When Aronoff (1976) proposed the Word-based Hypothesis, his most forceful arguments were against the existence of morphemes. He argued from this starting point: "A sign is only analyzable into two or more constituents in a grammar if *each* of these constituents can be identified as a sign" (Mulder and Hervey 1972). Basically, Aronoff's argument is that, by being aggressively decompositional in identifying morphemes, we are often left with complex words where the "leftovers" after identifying the morphemes are not linguistic signs. This is clearly a bad position to be in for morpheme-based, concatenative morphology since it leaves us with two options: either *some* complex words are stored (in which case, why not all? Wouldn't that be simpler?) or some morphemes don't mean anything. Aronoff (1976) showed three different places where this was a problem.

Cran morphs get their names from the famous example of berry names. The words *cranberry, boysenberry*, and *huckleberry* are all types of berries and clearly have the morpheme *berry* inside of them, so the impulse is to identify the morpheme *berry* as contributing the meaning 'berry'. If we do that, however, what then do *cran, boysen*, and *huckle* contribute to the meaning and why don't they show up anywhere else? Either the answer is completely circular ("cran" means "cranberry") or the answer is that they mean nothing.

The reverse of that argument comes from the tremendous amount of complex Latinate borrowings in English. There are a host of Latinate stems that never appear in simplex words. They also appear with easily identifiable affixes and have no consistent meaning from word to word. For example, *-struct* in *obstruct, instruct*, and *construct*; *-ceive* in *receive, deceive*, and *conceive*; *illus-* in *illusive, illusory, illusion*; and *-sume* in *resume, presume*, and *consume*. If we do not accept that these complex words are stored whole in the Lexicon and then used as the inputs to morphological processes, we have to assume that the bound stems are what is stored and acted upon by the morphology. These bound stems never surface without affixes, and their variant meaning suggests only two alternatives: (a) that there are several different bound stems that are homophones with each other; or (b) that they that have variant meaning when affixed to predictable prefixes.

The first possibility (homophony) is unsatisfying because the bound stems all undergo the same allomorphy (*ceive > cept*), strongly suggesting that they are the same entity. This is not limited to borrowings, either. In the native words *understand* and *withstand*, the stems are clearly the same morpheme, as both undergo the same past tense allomorphy (*stand > stood*), but neither complex form has any identifiable meaning relationship to the verb *stand* upon which they are built (for that matter, *under* and *with* do not seem to contribute their (synchronic) meanings either). What the theory that posits these bound stems is left with is the rather unsatisfactory stipulation that morphemes, which are defined as minimal correspondences between sound and meaning, can pick out several different meanings depending on environment or none at all. This makes the theoretical entity of morpheme useless and easily abandoned.

On the other hand, these problems do have analogs in the syntax. The individual words in many idiomatic phrases such as *the whole kit and kaboodle* can be claimed to be cran morphs, but Aronoff (1976) claims the crucial difference is that the words in an idiomatic phrase are separable syntactically. DiSciullo and Williams (1987) also argue that the features of bound stems are present at the syntactic level as well in Germanic particle verbs (cf. *throw up, throw out, throw down, throw in*) which are also syntactically separable. I discuss particle verbs and idioms in greater detail below.

4.5   Listedness and productivity

I return now to the two main arguments that Chomsky (1970) used to argue that words are a special domain and warrant their own component of the grammar: listedness and productivity. Listedness (or lexicalization) is the weaker of the two, but is still somewhat compelling. Lexicalization is the commonplace process by which a complex word, ostensibly having been stored in the Lexicon, becomes vulnerable to semantic shift, and then over time takes on a non-compositional meaning. The typical example is *transmission* (Marantz 1997), but examples abound, including native formations (such as *ice cream* and *reader*). If the lexicon were only a storage device of simplex morphemes and the syntax was the only component manipulating those morphemes, the meaning of words should always be compositional. The central claim here is that the syntax is a combinatoric mechanism that only creates transparent compositional meanings. Since complex words are most often the location of non-compositional meaning, word-formation must not be part of the syntax. Furthermore, in order for a complex word to shift in meaning, the complex word must have been stored whole. This suggests that more than just simplex morphemes is stored in the lexicon.

On the other hand, listedness is not necessarily an ironclad argument for Lexicalism. DiSciullo and Williams (1987), in what is, overall, an argument for Lexicalism, reject the argument from listedness because not all words are listed (low frequency, productive, compositional forms such *purpleness* and *blithely* are likely not stored – see much of Harald Baayan's work, starting with Baayan (1989), for discussion) and because listedness exists at every level of the grammar – many complex words are listed, all morphemes are listed, and some phrases and even some sentences are listed (we call them idioms, but they are just listed phrases). DiSciullo and Williams (1987) argue that listing even happens at units smaller than the morpheme, such as in the case of sound symbolism (for example, words for small things have a tendency to have high front vowels, such as in *tweet* and *stick*, while words for big things have a tendency to have low back vowels, as in *roar* and *log*).

However, variable productivity does seem to be limited to the domain of the word. Phonological and syntactic rules are always totally productive given the right environment. Morphological rules, however, vary in productivity. Productivity is how likely an affix is to be applied to a new stem (where it is licensed via categorical or phonological selection) to create a novel word. Some affixes have a very small set of lexically determined stems, such as *-th* (*length, width, girth, growth*) and *-age* (*drainage, frontage, tonnage*), and adding new stems to that set happens only very infrequently (*heighth, ownage*). In other cases, there are sets of affixes that serve the same function that compete for stems (*-ness, -ity, -hood, -dom*), often times with one being the default (*-ness*). This is not limited to derivation either: the plural marker *-en* is completely unproductive in English, being limited to only three stems; the plural marker *-i* can only go on new forms provided the singular is borrowed and ends with the sounds /-us/, regardless of historical source (*octopi, syllabi,* *platypi*). No phenomena exist like this in syntax. Syntactic phenomena tend to be completely productive or not at all.

There is a competing hypothesis that variant productivity is not a grammatical phenomenon but is rather creative (Lieber 1992); the dominant position is that productivity is only in the domain of morphology and therefore justifies excluding morphology from the syntactic grammar.

5 Anti-Lexicalism: arguments for one morphosyntactic module

The primary argument for a combined morphosyntactic model is that it embodies several strengths that are expected of scientific theories: it is economical, restrictive, and elegant. This comes from the fact that there is only one generative process for both the syntax and the morphology: concatenation. Unlike replacement rules, which are overly powerful, concatenation is extremely theoretically limited. This is especially appealing to syntactic theory since the 1990s and the 2000s witnessed a movement from the rule-based transformative grammars to the current Minimalist models of grammar where the only process, even for movement, available to the grammar is Merge (which is simple concatenation).

The arguments for Lexicalism largely revolve around better empirical coverage and the overly restrictive nature of the morpheme-driven, concatenation-based model. Since the cost of this better coverage is generative restriction, the objections to Lexicalism are largely metatheoretical in nature. However, there are also some phenomena that the Lexicalist model is powerful enough to cover but does not effectively explain, many of which I will describe in this section in addition to the metatheoretical arguments.

It is worth taking a moment to state that the "relevance to the syntax" arguments made in favor of the Split Morphology Approach above in §3 on Weak Lexicalism, especially those regarding inflection and valence changing devices such as causatives, applicatives, and nominalizations, also support an Anti-Lexicalist approach, independent of their use to support Weak Lexicalism. The connection between these morphological phenomena and the corresponding syntactic processes is so strong that it convincingly suggests that they are two reflexes of the same mechanism. However, I will not repeat that argumentation in this section.

5.1 Occam's Razor

The most compelling theoretical argument against Lexicalism is Occam's Razor, the principle of parsimony. When selecting between two competing models, Occam's Razor demands that the model with the fewest assumed entities is to be preferred. Bertrand Russell (1985/1924) articulated Occam's Razor as "whenever possible, substitute constructions out of known entities for inferences to unknown entities." In practice, in developing scientific models, Occam's Razor places the burden of proof on the less parsimonious of two competing models to provide greater explanatory adequacy. In the Lexicalism debate, both sides have made claims to being more parsimonious. The Lexicalists argue that the Anti-Lexicalist models posit unnecessarily complicated constituent structures and, by assuming the existence of morphemes, also assume many more entities (especially null morphemes, cran morphs, and bound stems). The Anti-Lexicalist claim to parsimony comes from the fact that they claim to have only one generative process at work (concatenation) and only one module in their model. These are not equal claims to parsimony: separate modules and separate generative mechanisms are the greater violations of parsimony because ultimately greater parsimony is a result of a greater number of consequences arising from a smaller number of causes.

Traditionally, Occam's Razor is only applicable if neither of the two models has greater empirical coverage. Correspondingly, Lexicalists can claim that the Anti-Lexicalist model does not have as much empirical coverage as the Lexicalist model so Occam's Razor does not apply. While this is true, the concern of Occam's Razor is ultimately whether the Lexicalist model has greater explanatory adequacy, not empirical coverage. In fact, most Anti-Lexicalists would argue that Anti-Lexicalism offers an explanation for the many similarities between morphology and syntax and Lexicalism does not. Indeed, Lexicalism sacrifices both parsimony and explanatory adequacy (as well as restrictiveness) for its empirical coverage.

Kaplan (1987) offers an extensive counter-argumentation to parsimony arguments in linguistics. Two of the arguments he supplies are these: (a) linguistics as a field suffers from a severe paucity of data at this time, so any attempts at restrictiveness are misguided until we can be more sure of which generalizations are true and which are not; and (b) modularity of the model does not entail modularity of the actual linguistic faculty – that is, it is the task of linguistic theory not to simulate language (which is likely not modular) but to explain it, and modular grammars with significant mapping mechanisms such as LFG are an effective way of reaching explanations.

5.2 Domain of the word

The Lexical Integrity Principle is built at its core on one claim: that the word is a special domain that is distinct from the syntax. This claim matches an intuition that many, if not most, speakers have about language. However, this pre-theoretical concept of "word" is more orthographic than categorical. Linguistic theory needs to have categorical definition of word and a set of criteria to use to distinguish a complex word from a phrase if we are going to posit that a separate component of the grammar produces words. A host of work throughout the literature (including much of the work on polysynthesis: Baker (1985); Pesetsky (1985); and Lieber (1992) among others) has shown that there appears to be no way to limit the domain "word" such that it is isolatable from the domain "phrase". Anderson (1982; 1992) jokes that the problem of defining a word "is a classic chestnut of traditional grammar".

Marantz (1997) is probably the most cogent set of arguments against the word being a domain of grammar. Marantz argues that there are three main arguments for Lexicalism's granting special status to the word: (a) that the word is a domain for phonological processes, (b) that the word is a domain for special meanings, and (c) that the word is a domain for special structure/meaning correspondences. To the first, Marantz (1997) argues that, while phonologists do have the domain of "prosodic word", there seems to be no claim within phonology that that domain aligns with Lexical Item, as used by syntacticians. For example, phrases with cliticising functional words, such as *an apple* or *by tomorrow*, are definitely two words in syntax, but can be argued to be one prosodic word to the phonology. To the second, Marantz (1997) argues that the domain of idiomatic meaning is indeed every level of the syntax up to, but not including, the agent. This is why idiomatic phrases can be as small as bound morphemes such as *illus-* and as large as idiom phrases such as *kick the bucket*, but cannot contain agents. To the third, Marantz (1997) points out that complex derived words cannot be interpreted as having a simple meaning like a root: just as *cause to die* can't mean *kill* (Fodor 1970), *transmission* can't mean *part*.

There are many more arguments for the definition of "word" than I can do justice to here. In the end, none are satisfactory and none are agreed upon. Indeed, DiSciullo and Williams's (1987) *On the Definition of Word* ultimately argues that there are three distinct theoretical entities that are all called "word": the listed item, the morphological object, and the syntactic atom (DiSciullo and Williams (1987) argue for Strong Lexicalism based on the systematic differences between the latter two). If the domain "word" is indefinable, it is certainly the better scientific position to abandon it as a categorical domain upon which we argue for modularity.

5.3 Turkish and other highly agglutinative languages

Recall from above that a strength of the Lexicalist model is blocking, the most prevalent account for which is the argument that words produced by the lexicon are stored (Kiparsky 1982). Recall also that the storage of the output of the lexicon is also an argument for Lexicalism because it will lead to lexicalization. This argument from stored outputs of the lexicon is also the source of a considerable argument against the lexicon as a separate generative component: agglutinative languages. According to Hankamer (1989), twenty percent of Turkish words contain five concatenated inflectional morphemes and the upward limit on inflectional affixes is over ten. Even accepting that not all affixes can co-occur, this means that there is a gargantuan amount of inflected forms for each stem. Hankamer (1989) (and then later Frauenfelder and Schreuder 1992) argues that the type of lexicon where wholly inflected words are stored is impractical and unlikely and that it is much more computationally efficient to combine the affixes as needed.[7] With a heavily agglutinative language, the computational burden placed on the speaker by a concatenative model is much more cognitively realistic than the memory burden placed on the speaker by a word storage model. Since a combined morphosyntactic model has already bought the computation-load of the syntax, the computation-load of the concatenative morphology comes free (as it is the same mechanism). The only memory-load is the storage of unpredictable form-meaning correspondences, which all models require. On the other hand, the Lexicalist model needs to buy increased computation-load for the non-concatenative rules *and* increased memory-load for the tremendous amount of stored fully inflected forms. This makes the Lexicalist model significantly more cognitively expensive and thus less desirable.

Polysynthetic languages are obviously an extension of this issue. Polysynthetic languages are languages with extraordinarily complex words, so complex that syntactic functions typically fulfilled by free lexical items are affixal in these languages (see Baker 1988). Baker (1988) even argues that the seemingly free word order in these languages is derived from the fact that nominals are adjuncts and agreement marking is actually affixal arguments. Polysynthetic languages have object (or noun) incorporation, the process of creating a compound verb where the object of the verb is the dependent member of the compound, discharging that object's theta role (see Mithun 1984). Typically, the verb cannot have both an incorporated object and a syntactic argument simultaneously. Object incorporation, then, is an obvious overlap of syntactic function and morphological process, suggesting an integrated MSI as opposed to separate components.

5.4 Lieber (1992)'s empirical evidence

Lieber (1992) claims that the division between words and phrases is empirically false: There are several phenomena that just cannot be categorized as either syntactic or lexical or are predicted to not exist if word formation feeds the syntax, four of which I describe here: clitics, phrasal compounds, particle verbs, and sublexical co-reference.

In effect, clitics are affixes that attach to phrases rather than words. In particular, they are terminal nodes in the syntax that are phonologically and prosodically dependent. Anderson (2005) developed a distinction here that is useful: "simple clitics" versus "special clitics". To Anderson (2005) simple clitics are phonologically reduced forms of larger free morphemes, such as English contractions (*I'll, I'd, mustn't*). These types of clitic are like affixes in the sense that they are phonologically dependent, but they are dependent on whatever happens to be next to them. Their phonological reduction and resulting dependence can be treated as a phonological phenomenon. Special clitics, on the other hand, are not reduced forms and have specific selectional requirements of the (potentially phrasal) stems that they attach to.

One famous example is the Spanish and French object pronouns that affix to the left of the verb even though the base-generated position for objects is to the right of the verb (Spanish *No me gusta* 'it doesn't please me'; French *Je le vois* 'I see him'). Another famous example is the English genitive affix *'s* which clearly attaches to noun phrases (*The queen of England's throne*) and not nouns. Similarly, owing to phonological dependence (such as the *a/an* alternation) and the fact that they are often not minimal words in English phonology (i.e., at least two moras), English determiners and prepositions are easily argued to be clitics as well.

These special clitics are important because they behave like affixes in every way save one: they have independent syntactic function in most models of syntax. Clitics are thus very difficult for a Lexicalist model to explain since they must simultaneously head their own syntactic phrase and be phonologically and morphologically dependent.[8] Clitics are strong evidence for a combined morphosyntactic component, as *every* affix takes a phrase as its dependent in such models, so clitics are completely predictable. The Lexical Integrity Hypothesis predicts no morphological processes with phrasal dependents. This prediction seems empirically false.

Another such example of a morphological process with phrasal dependents is so-called phrasal compounds (Hoeksema 1988; Lieber 1992; Harley 2009). A common phenomenon in Germanic languages, phrasal compounds are compounds with a noun as the head and a syntactic phrase as the dependent: *stuff-blowing-up effects, bikini-girls-in-trouble genre* (Harley 2009), *bottom-of-a-birdcage taste, off-the-rack look* (Lieber 1992). In every distinctive way these are compounds and not phrases. For example, they have compound stress not phrasal stress, and they have compound inseparability. Spencer (2005) later described a similar phenomenon in English that was later discussed in Lieber and Scalise (2006) and Harley (2009): derivational affixes attaching to phrases (usually indicated orthographically with quotes or hyphens). Spencer's (2005) example is *a why-does-it-have–to-be-me-ish expression*. Spencer suggests that these might be limited to *-ish* and might be indicative of *-ish* becoming a free morpheme, but Harley (2009) expands the data to include *-y* and *-ness*: a *feeling a bit rainy-day-ish / a bit 'don't bother'-y / the general 'bikini-girls-in-trouble'-ness of it all*. Ackema and Neeleman (2004) also describe an affix in Quechua that nominalizes phrases. Ultimately, both Harley (2009) and Lieber and Scalise (2006) adopt a hypothesis that these are all instances of phrases zero derived into nouns. Again, like the existence of clitics, the existence of phrasal compounds and phrasal affixation shows the predictions of the Lexical Integrity Hypothesis to be empirically false.

The next empirical evidence provided by Lieber (1992) that I will discuss here is particle verbs. A particle verb, such as *take out* or *throw down* is a verb made up of (at least) two parts, typically a verb and a preposition, which combine to have idiosyncratic meaning. Particle verbs act as inputs to morphological processes but are separable by the syntax. The most well-known particle verb constructions are those in English, Dutch, German, and Hungarian. In English, particle verbs are subject to nominalization (*We need to have a sit-down*; *These tires are vulnerable to blow-outs*) but their component parts are required to be separated by any pronominal object (*We will have to sit this out*; **We will have to sit out this*). In Dutch, in the SOV subordinate clauses, particle verbs appear as a verb and a prefix (*dat Hans zijn moeder opbelde* "that Hans his mother up-called", Booij 2002), but in the V2 matrix clauses the particle and the verb are separated by verb raising (*Hans belde zijn moeder op* "Hans called his mother up"). Like phrasal compounds and clitics, these seem to be an empirical challenge to the Lexical Integrity Hypothesis because something that is syntactically complex can be fed into morphological processes.[9]

Finally, Lieber (1992) also discusses sublexical co-reference. If the inside structure of words were truly opaque to the syntax, pronouns should not be able to anaphorically refer to elements embedded within the structure of the word, but for at least some dialects that is perfectly well formed: *I consider myself Californian even though I haven't lived there for years*. This data, Lieber (1992) argues, seems to unequivocally falsify the strongest versions of the Lexical Integrity Hypothesis, as it is clear that the syntax "sees" inside the derivation. Obviously, such data is much easier to account within an Anti-Lexicalist model.

6 Conclusion: realizational theories and the future of the MSI

At the outset of this chapter, I describe the MSI as feeding the syntax, determining the nature of the syntactic atoms. That is not entirely true. In the somewhat recent history of the MSI, many models have begun to propose that the morphological component of the grammar follows the syntactic component – that the syntax feeds the morphology. In these models, such as Anderson's (1992), Distributed Morphology (Halle and Marantz 1993), and Nanosyntax (Starke 2009), the morphology expresses the output of the syntax. The atoms of syntax are purely formal features and the terminal nodes of the syntax are increasingly submorphemic (smaller than morphemes). "Words" in these models are phonological strings that are inserted into the syntax after spellout to realize the features combinations of the syntactic derivation. Correspondingly, these models are called "Late-Insertion" or "Realizational" (Beard 1995). In the context of the discussion contained herein, realizational models come in every variety of lexicalism: Anderson's (1992) model is Weak Lexicalist with a Lexicon that operates in parallel to the syntax. Nanosyntax can be accurately described as Anti-Lexicalist, as there are no non-syntactic operations. Distributed Morphology, while typically described as rejecting Lexicalism (in nearly every description of the framework, including Siddiqi (2010)), actually has significant post-spellout morphological operations. These post-syntactic operations could be called a morphological component of the grammar, and increasingly are being called just that in the modern literature. This morphological component is not strictly speaking a generative lexicon as traditionally articulated, but certainly can be interpreted as a separate grammatical machine that interfaces with the syntax at spellout. Beard (1995), Wunderlich (1996), Stump (2001), and Ackema and Neeleman (2004) are also all realizational models that are traditionally Lexicalist in that they have a separate generative component for word-formation.

Late-Insertion itself is not an articulated theory of syntax and as such does not make any predictions outside of those made by the theories that are themselves realizational. Rather, Late-Insertion is a framework for approaching the MSI. In the last twenty years, Late Insertion has grown in significance to become one of the dominant models of the MSI in contemporary morphological and syntactic discussion and increasingly is becoming the focus of the discussions involving the MSI as exemplified by the current debate regarding the nature of realization (for example, does it target syntactic terminals or entire syntactic structures?), especially regarding phenomena such as portmanteaux, stem allomorphy, and blocking (see Caha 2009; Bye and Svenonius 2012; Embick 2012; Haugen and Siddiqi 2013). After gaining twenty years of increasing traction, it seems to be a safe assumption that realizational approaches to the MSI may likely be the future of investigation into the interface. This is an exciting time for MSI research because realizational models represent such a radical departure from traditional articulations of the MSI and their longevity and persistence in the literature suggest that the realizational approach to the MSI is likely here to stay as a major alternative approach to the MSI.

Notes

1   Lees (1960) had the best account for compounding at the time. His claim was that compounds were derived from sentences via several deletion transformations (*nurse shoes* derives from *shoes made FOR nurses*, while *alligator shoes* derives from *shoes made FROM alligators*). However, deletion transformations are exceptionally unrestricted and powerful, even in a time where transformational syntax was typical. Later, when Chomsky (1965) formulated the constraint on transformations that they need always be recoverable, Lees' (1960) solution to the compounding problem became completely untenable.
2   The Binary Branching Hypothesis is essentially that only one affix is added at a time. The Righthand Head Rule is that the morphological element on the right projects category. Both have counter examples but both are generally accurate generalizations that are still assumed today.
3   Agreement on adjectives and determiners indicates which noun the element is a dependent of. Subject and object agreement on verbs and case marking on nouns indicates the grammatical function (subject or object, etc.) of the nominals in the clause.
4   Minimalism is also compatible with both Strong Lexicalism and Anti-Lexicalism and is indeed practiced from both perspectives.
5   Bracketing Paradoxes are morphological constructions that have two hierarchical structures, both of which must be right. The classic examples are *unhappier* (semantically *unhappy+er*; morphophonologically *un +happier*) and *transformational grammarian* (syntactically *transformational + grammarian*; semantically *transformational grammar + ian*).
6   Also called functional shift or zero derivation, conversion is when a word exists as two different lexical categories, such as *table* in to *table* (v) *a proposal* and *to sit at a table* (n)).
7   Frauenfelder and Schreuder (1992) suggest that extremely frequent combinations of inflection may indeed be stored whole, and Gurel (1999) claims to have confirmed this prediction experimentally.
8   Indeed, introductory textbooks for the Strong Lexicalist models of LFG (Falk 2001) and HPSG (Sag *et al.* 2001) have very interesting and enlightening discussions on *'s*, acknowledging that there is likely no satisfactory analysis for English genitive in a Strong Lexicalist model.
9   This does not mean that particle verbs have not been studied in Lexicalist models. Indeed, LFG has a rich tradition of research into particle verbs (see especially Toivonen 2001) where particles are treated as non-projecting lexical items. In fact, in response to issues like these, Ackerman and LeSourd (1997) revised the Lexical Integrity Hypothesis so that the definition of "word" was no longer "morphologically generated object" but rather "terminal syntactic node", though with that definition it is very difficult to see why Lexicalism still needs a Lexicon, as that would make the Lexical Integrity Hypothesis inviolate in most Anti-Lexicalist models as well. In fact, it seems that such a definition makes the Lexical Integrity Hypothesis tautological.

Further reading

Hockett, Charles. 1954. Two models of grammatical description. *Word* 10:210–234.
Kaplan, Ronald. 1987. Three seductions of computational psycholinguistics. In *Linguistic Theory and Computer Applications*, ed. P. Whitelock *et al.*, 149–188. London: Academic Press.

Lieber, Rochelle, and Sergio Scalise. 2006. The lexical integrity hypothesis in a new theoretical universe. *Lingue e linguaggio* 1:7–37.

Scalise, Sergio, and Emiliano Guevara. 2005. The lexicalist approach to word-formation and the notion of the lexicon. In *Handbook of Word-formation*, ed. P. Stekauer and R. Lieber, 147–187. Dordrecht: Springer.

Spencer, Andrew. 2005. Word-formation and syntax. In *Handbook of Word-Formation*, ed. P. Stekauer and R. Lieber, 73–97. Dordrecht: Springer.

References

Ackema, Peter, and Ad Neeleman. 2004. *Beyond Morphology: Interface Conditions on Word Formation*. Oxford: Oxford University Press.

Ackerman, Farrell, and Philip LeSourd. 1997. Toward a lexical representation of phrasal predicates. In *Complex Predicates*, ed. A. Alsina, J. Bresnan, and P. Sells, 67–106. Stanford, CA: CSLI.

Anderson, Stephen. 1982. Where's morphology? *Linguistic Inquiry* 13:571–612.

Anderson, Stephen. 1992. *A-morphous Morphology*. Cambridge: Cambridge University Press.

Anderson, Stephen. 2005. *Aspects of the Theory of Clitics*. Oxford: Oxford University Press.

Aronoff, Mark. 1976. *Word Formation in Generative Grammar*. Cambridge, MA: MIT Press.

Baayan, Harald. 1989. A corpus-based approach to morphological productivity: Statistical analysis and psycholinguistic interpretation. PhD thesis, Vrije Universiteit, Amsterdam.

Baker, Mark. 1985. The mirror principle and morphosyntactic explanation. *Linguistic Inquiry* 16(3):373–415.

Baker, Mark. 1988. *Incorporation: A Theory of Grammatical Function Changing*. Chicago, IL: University of Chicago Press.

Beard, Robert. 1995. *Lexeme-Morpheme Base Morphology; a General Theory of Inflection and Word Formation*. Albany, NY: SUNY Press.

Bloomfield, Leonard. 1933. *Language*. New York: Holt.

Booij, Geert. 1977. *Dutch Morphology: A Study of Word Formation in Generative Grammar*. Dordrect: Foris.

Booij, Geert. 1994. Against split morphology. In *Yearbook of Morphology 1993*, ed. G. Booij and J. van Marle, 27–50. Dordrecht: Kluwer.

Booij, Geert. 1996 Inherent versus contextual inflection and the split morphology hypothesis. In *Yearbook of Morphology 1995*, ed. G. Booij and J. van Marle, 1–16. Dordrecht: Kluwer.

Booij, Geert. 2002. *The Morphology of Dutch*. Oxford: Oxford University Press.

Booij, Geert. 2005. Context-dependent morphology. *Lingue e Linguaggio* 2:163–178.

Boskovic, Zeljko. 1997. *The Syntax of Nonfinite Complementation: An Economy Approach*. Cambridge, MA: MIT Press.

Bresnan, Joan, and Ronald Kaplan. 1982. Lexical-Functional Grammar: A formal system for grammatical representation. In *The Mental Representation of Grammatical Relations*, ed. J. Bresnan, 173–281. Cambridge, MA: MIT Press.

Bybee, Joan. 1985. *Morphology: A Study of the Relation between Meaning and Form*. Amsterdam: Benjamins.

Bye, Patrik, and Peter Svenonius. 2012 Non-concatenative morphology as epiphenomenon. In *The Morphology and Phonology of Exponence*, ed. Jochen Trommer, 427–498. Oxford: Oxford University Press.

Caha, Pavel. 2009. The nanosyntax of case. PhD dissertation, University of Tromsø.

Chomsky, Noam. 1957. *Syntactic Structures*. Den Haag: Mouton.

Chomsky, Noam. 1965. *Aspects of the Theory of Syntax*. Cambridge, MA: MIT Press.

Chomsky, Noam. 1970. Remarks on nominalization. Reprinted in D. Davidson and G. Harman. 1975. *The Logic of Grammar*. Encino, CA: Dickenson, 262–289.

Chomsky, Noam. 1981. *Lectures on Government and Binding*. Dordrecht: Foris.

Chomsky, Noam. 1995. *The Minimalist Program*. Cambridge, MA: MIT Press.

Chomsky, Noam, and Morris Halle. 1968. *The Sound Pattern of English*. New York: Harper and Row.

Comrie, B. 1981 *Language Universals and Linguistic Typology*. Chicago, IL: University of Chicago Press.

Di Sciullo, Anna Maria, and Edwin Williams. 1987. *On the Definition of Word*. Cambridge, MA: MIT Press.

Dressler, Wolfgang, 1989. Prototypical differences between inflection and derivation. *Zeitschrift für Phonetik, Sprachwissenschaft und Kommunikationsforschung* 42:3–10.

Embick, David. 2000. Features, syntax, and categories in the Latin perfect. *Linguistic Inquiry* 31(2):185–230.

Embick, David. 2012. On the targets of phonological realization. Talk given to the MSPI Workshop at Stanford University, 13 October 2012.

Embick, David, and Alec Marantz. 2008. Architecture and blocking. *Linguistic Inquiry* 39(1):1–53.

Embick, David, and Rolf Noyer. 2007. Distributed morphology and the syntax/morphology interface. In *The Oxford Handbook of Linguistic Interfaces*, ed. Gillian Ramchand and Charles Reiss, 289–324. Oxford: Oxford University Press.

Falk, Yehuda. 2001. *Lexical-Functional Grammar: An Introduction to Parallel Constraint-Based Syntax*. Stanford, CA: CSLI.

Fodor, J. 1970. Three reasons for not deriving 'kill' from 'cause to die'. *Linguistic Inquiry* 1:429–438.

Frauenfelder, U.H., and R. Schreuder. 1992. Constraining psycholinguistic models of morphological processing and representation: the role of productivity. In *Yearbook of Morphology 1991*, ed. G.E. Booij and J. van Marle, 165–183. Dordrecht: Kluwer Academic.

Greenberg, Joseph. 1959. A quantitative approach to morphological typology of language. *International Journal of American Linguistics* 26:198–94.

Greenberg, Joseph. 1963. *Universals of Language*. Cambridge, MA: MIT Press.

Gurel, A. 1999. Decomposition: To what extent? The case of Turkish. *Brain and Language* 68: 218–224.

Halle, Morris. 1973. Prolegomena to a theory of word formation. *Linguistic Inquiry* 4:3–16.

Halle, Morris, and Alec Marantz. 1993. Distributed morphology and the pieces of inflection. In *The View from Building 20: Essays in Linguistics in Honor of Sylvain Bromberger*, ed. Kenneth Hale and Samuel Jay Keyser, 111–176. Cambridge, MA: MIT Press.

Halle, Morris, and Alec Marantz. 1994. Some key features of distributed morphology. In *Papers on Phonology and Morphology*, ed. Andrew Carnie and Heidi Harley, 275–288. Cambridge, MA: MIT Working Papers in Linguistics 21.

Hammond, Michael. 1999. *The Phonology of English. A Prosodic Optimality-theoretic Approach*. Oxford: Oxford University Press.

Hankamer, Jorge. 1989. Morphological parsing and the lexicon. In *Lexical Representation and Process*, ed. W. Marslen-Wilson, 392–408. Cambridge, MA: MIT Press.

Harley, Heidi. 2009. Compounding in distributed morphology. In *The Oxford Handbook of Compounding*, ed. R. Lieber and P. Strekaur, 129–144. Oxford: Oxford University Press.

Harley, Heidi, and Rolf Noyer. 2000. Licensing in the non-lexicalist lexicon. In *The Lexicon/ Encyclopedia Interface*, ed. Bert Peeters, 349–374. Amsterdam: Elsevier Press.

Harris, Randy. 1995. *The Linguistic Wars*. Oxford: Oxford University Press.

Haugen, Jason, and Daniel Siddiqi. 2013. Roots and the derivation. *Linguistic Inquiry* 44(3):493–517.

Hockett, Charles. 1954. Two models of grammatical description. *Word* 10:210–234.

Hoeksema, Jack. 1988. Head types in morphosyntax. In *Yearbook of Morphology 1*, ed. G. Booij, and J. van Marle, 123–138. Dordrecht: Kluwer Academic.

Kaplan, Ronald. 1987. Three seductions of computational psycholinguistics. In *Linguistic Theory and Computer Applications*, ed. P. Whitelock et al., 149–188. London: Academic Press.

Kiparsky, Paul. 1982. Lexical morphology and phonology. In *Linguistics in the Morning Calm: Selected Papers from SICOL 1981*, Linguistic Society of Korea, 3–91. Seoul: Hanshin.

Lakoff, George. 1971. On generative semantics. In *Semantics: An Interdisciplinary Reader in Philosophy, Linguistics and Psychology*, ed. D.D. Steinberg and L.A. Jakobovits, 232–296. Cambridge: Cambridge University Press.

Lakoff, George. 1987. *Women, Fire, and Dangerous Things: What Categories Reveal about the Mind*. Chicago, IL: CSLI.

Lapointe, Steven. 1980. A theory of grammatical agreement. PhD dissertation, UMass Amherst.

Lees, Robert. 1960. *The Grammar of English Nominalization*. Bloomington: Indiana University Press.

Lieber, Rochelle. 1992. *Deconstructing Morphology: Word Formation in Syntactic Theory*. Chicago, IL: University of Chicago Press.

Lieber, Rochelle, and Sergio Scalise. 2006. The lexical integrity hypothesis in a new theoretical universe. *Lingue e linguaggio* 1:7–37.

McCarthy, John. 1981. A prosodic theory of non-concatenative morphology. *Linguistic Inquiry* 12:373–418.

Marantz, Alec. 1997. No escape from syntax: Don't try morphological analysis in the privacy of your own lexicon. *University of Pennsylvania Working Papers in Linguistics* 4:201–225.

Matthews, Peter. 1972. *Inflectional Morphology: A Theoretical Study Based on Aspects of Latin Verb Conjugation.* Cambridge: Cambridge University Press.

Mithun, Marianne. 1984. The evolution of noun incorporation. *Language* 60:847–894.

Mulder, J.W.F., and S.G.J. Hervey. 1972. *Theory of the Linguistic Sign.* Den Haag: Mouton.

Newmeyer, Frederick. 1980. *Linguistic Theory in America: The First Quarter Century of Transformational Generative Grammar.* New York: Academic Press.

Perlmutter, David. 1988. The split morphology hypothesis: Evidence from Yiddish. In *Theoretical Morphology*, ed. Michael Hammond and Michael Noonan, 79–99. San Diego: Academic Press, Inc.

Pesetsky, David. 1985. Morphology and logical form. *Linguistic Inquiry* 16(2):193–246.

Plank, Frank. 1981. *Morphologische (Ir-)Regularitaten.* Tubingen: Nerr.

Pollard, C., and I. Sag. 1994. *Head-driven Phrase Structure Grammar.* Chicago, IL: University of Chicago Press.

Rainer, Franz. 1988. Towards a theory of blocking. Italian and German quality nouns. In *Yearbook of Morphology 1988*, ed. G. Booij and J. van Marle,155–185. Dordrecht: Kluwer Academic.

Russell, Bertrand. 1985; first published 1924. Logical atomism, in *The Philosophy of Logical Atomism*, ed. D.F. Pears, 157–181. La Salle: Open Court.

Sag, Ivan, and Thomas Wasow. 2001. *Syntactic Theory: A Formal Introduction.* Stanford, CA: CSLI Publications.

Sapir, Edward. 1921. *Language.* New York: Harcourt, Brace, Jovanovich.

Scalise, Sergio, and Emiliano Guevara. 2005. The lexicalist approach to word-formation and the notion of the lexicon. In *Handbook of Word-Formation*, ed. P. Stekauer and R. Lieber, 147–187. Dordrecht: Springer.

Siddiqi, Daniel. 2010. Distributed morphology. *Language and Linguistics Compass* 4:524–542.

Spencer, Andrew. 2005. Word-formation and syntax. In *Handbook of Word-formation*, ed. P. Stekauer and R. Lieber, 73–97. Dordrecht: Springer.

Starke, Michael. 2009. Nanosyntax: A short primer on a new approach to language. In *Nordlyd: Tromsø University Working Papers on Language and Linguistics 36*, ed. P. Svenonius, G. Ramchand, M. Starke, and T. Taraldsen, 1–6. Tromsø: University of Tromsø.

Stump, Gregory T. 2001. *Inflectional Morphology.* Cambridge: Cambridge University Press.

Toivonen, Ida. 2001. The phrase structure of non-projecting words. PhD dissertation, Stanford University.

Wunderlich, Dieter. 1996. Minimalist morphology: The role of paradigms. In *Yearbook of Morphology 1995*, ed. G. Booij and J. van Marle, 93–114. Dordrecht: Kluwer.

18

Prosodic domains and the syntax–phonology interface

Yoshihito Dobashi

1 Introduction

In the past three decades or so, a growing body of researches on syntax–phonology interface have been conducted from various theoretical perspectives. The term "syntax–phonology interface" has included a wider range of linguistic study, particularly since the advent of the so-called minimalist program (Chomsky 1995, *et seq.*), which seeks to minimize the theoretical devices in the "narrow syntax" component and attribute to the interfaces what was once taken to be the properties of narrow syntax. Thus the following are often taken to be subsumed under the study of syntax–phonology interface: linearization, ellipsis, "movement" operations such as Heavy NP Shift, head movement and clitic placement, morphological phenomena in general, and phrasal phonology.[1] This chapter, however, is concerned with the syntax–phonology interface in a narrower, or more or less traditional, sense: the prosodic domains that are sensitive to syntax.

Three kinds of phonological rules are generally known to be sensitive to prosodic domains: domain span, domain juncture, and domain limit rules (Selkirk 1980).[2] A domain span rule applies throughout a domain, a domain juncture rule applies between prosodic domains within their superordinate prosodic domain, and a domain limit rule applies at one of the edges of a domain. The following formulations are from Nespor and Vogel (1986: 15):

(1) a. domain span:
     $A \rightarrow B / [\ldots X \_\_ Y \ldots]_{Di}$
   b. domain juncture:
     i. $A \rightarrow B / [\ldots [\ldots X \_\_ Y]_{Dj} [Z \ldots]_{Dj} \ldots]_{Di}$
     ii. $A \rightarrow B / [\ldots [\ldots X]_{Dj} [Y \_\_ Z \ldots]_{Dj} \ldots]_{Di}$
   c. domain limit:
     i. $A \rightarrow B / [\ldots X \_\_ Y]_{Di}$
     ii. $A \rightarrow B / [X \_\_ Y \ldots]_{Di}$

* I would like to thank Lisa Selkirk and the editors of this volume for invaluable comments and suggestions. I would also like to thank Ian Megill for suggesting stylistic improvements. This work is in part supported by JSPS KAKENHI Grant No. 25370545.

One of the central issues we will focus on here pertaining to the area of syntax–phonology interface is how to delimit these prosodic domains in terms of syntactic information.[3] Below are some of the research questions and issues often discussed in this field.

Mismatch. One of the phenomena that motivated the study of syntax–phonology interface is the mismatch between syntactic and phonological structure. Perhaps the best-known example is the following, from Chomsky and Halle (1968: 372), where syntactic structure does not match intonational structure:

(2) syntax: This is [the cat that caught [the rat that stole [the cheese]]]
    phonology: (this is the cat)(that caught the rat)(that stole the cheese)

Two problems emerged: the syntactic boundaries do not match the phonological ones, and syntactic phrase structure is right-branching, while the phonological structure is flat.[4] How do we resolve these syntax–phonology mismatches?

Direct Reference or Indirect Reference. Another issue, which is related to the first one, is the nature of the relationship between syntax and phonology. More specifically, the question is whether or not phonology can directly refer to syntactic information. If it can, what is visible and what is not? If it cannot, then what algorithm do we need in order to relate syntax and phonology?

Cross-linguistic variation. As in syntax, prosodic domains show cross-linguistic variation. For example, a verb is phrased with its direct object in some languages while not in others, and such phrasing is optional in yet others. How do we capture this variation? Does it arise as a result of the mapping algorithms? Is it a matter of phonology? Is it a reflex of syntactic variations? Or is there any other way to explain it?

Prosodic Categories. Several kinds of prosodic domains, such as the intonational phrase and the phonological phrase, have been proposed. What kinds of prosodic categories, and how many of them, do we need? How do we differentiate these categories? How are they organized?

Mapping Direction. Is mapping unidirectional, from syntax to phonology, as often assumed in minimalist syntax literature? Or is phonological structure present in parallel with syntactic structure, as argued for by, for example, Jackendoff (1997)? Also, is it possible for phonology to affect syntax?

Information Structure. Topic and focus often affect prosodic domains. How can such effects be accounted for?

These and other issues have been considered from various theoretical standpoints in the framework of generative grammar.[5] In what follows, I will sketch chronologically some of the important theories that have been proposed over the last few decades in order to provide a general overview of developments in the field of the syntax–phonology interface.[6]

2   The standard theories

This section will briefly recapitulate the two major theories of syntax–phonology mapping: Relation-based Theory (Nespor and Vogel 1986) and End-based Theory (Selkirk 1986, *et seq.*).[7] Although they are not without problems, especially with respect to current theoretical settings, most of the present theoretical and empirical issues have their roots in these two theories, and there is no doubt that these theories have laid the foundations for the many investigations in this area today. We will first start with descriptions of prosodic hierarchy and strict layering, adopted by both theories, and then review these two standard theories, making reference to their approaches to cross-linguistic variation.

2.1 The Prosodic Hierarchy Theory

Although there has been some debate over the number of prosodic categories as well as suitable names for them, the following prosodic categories are often adopted in the study of prosody, and they are assumed to be hierarchically ordered (Nespor and Vogel 1986; Selkirk 1980; 1986):[8]

(3) *Prosodic Hierarchy*:

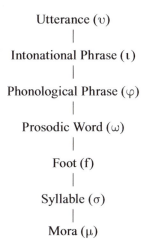

Of these, the four top categories are what Ito and Mester (2012: 281) call *interface categories*, formed in terms of syntax–phonology relations, and the rest below them are called *rhythmic categories*, which are intrinsically defined word-internally. These categories are organised to form a prosodic hierarchy, to accord with the *Strict Layer Hypothesis* that bans recursive structures and level-skipping in this hierarchically ordered set of prosodic categories (Nespor and Vogel 1986; Selkirk 1980; 1984; 1986; Hayes 1989):

(4) Strict Layer Hypothesis (SLH): A constituent of category-level *n* in the prosodic hierarchy immediately dominates only constituents at category-level *n-1*. (Selkirk 2009: 38)

Thus, (5a) is a valid structure while (5b) is not (rhythmic categories are omitted here and below):

(5)

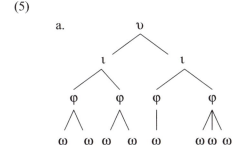
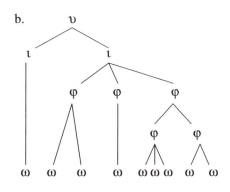

(5b) violates the SLH in two respects: φ is recursive and ι immediately dominates ω, skipping φ. Note that branches can be n-ary, unlike the current prevailing syntactic assumptions.

2.2 Relation-based Theory

Nespor and Vogel (1986), investigating prosodic phenomena in Italian and several other languages, proposed the following rules to define phonological phrases. Note that C in (6) is a Clitic Group, which they define as another prosodic category posited between φ and ω:[9]

(6) Phonological Phrase Formation (Nespor and Vogel 1986: 168)
    a. φ domain
        The domain of φ consists of a C which contains a lexical head (X) and all Cs on its nonrecursive side up to the C that contains another head outside of the maximal projection of X.
    b. φ construction
        Join into an n-ary branching φ all Cs included in a string delimited by the definition of the domain of φ.

Given (6), the syntactic structure in (7a) is mapped to the phonological phrases in (7b):

(7)   a. $[_{IP}$ NP$_{Subj}$ Infl $[_{VP}$ V NP$_{Obj}$]]
      b. (NP$_{Subj}$)$_{\varphi}$ (Infl V)$_{\varphi}$ (NP$_{Obj}$)$_{\varphi}$

Assuming that each of the NPs, the Infl (auxiliary verb), and the V corresponds to a Clitic Group, Infl and V are phrased together since Infl, which is a functional (but not lexical) category, is on the verb's nonrecursive side, while the NP$_{Subj}$ is not phrased with Infl or V since it is a maximal projection containing a lexical head, N, that stays outside of the VP. V is not phrased with NP$_{Obj}$ since it is on the nonrecursive side of the NP$_{Obj}$ as well as outside of the NP$_{Obj}$.

Note that this algorithm maps the layered syntactic structure to the flat organization of phonological phrases, and also that it captures the mismatch between the syntactic and phonological constituents. Thus Infl and V form a single constituent in the phonological component while they do not in the syntactic one.

Although the phrasing in (7b) successfully accounts for basic phrasing facts in Italian, Nespor and Vogel observe that NP$_{Obj}$ may optionally be phrased with V when it is non-branching (i.e., it consists of only one lexical item), resulting in the following phrasing:

(8)   (NP$_{Subj}$)$_{\varphi}$ (Infl V NP$_{Obj}$)$_{\varphi}$

To account for this variation, they propose the following optional rule:

(9)   φ restructuring (Nespor and Vogel 1986: 173)
    A non-branching φ which is the first complement of X on its recursive side is joined into the φ that contains X.

Although it is optional in Italian, they argue that this rule can be extended to account for cross-linguistic variation: Such restructuring is forbidden in French, while it is obligatory in Chimwiini even if the complement is branching.

Below are Nespor and Vogel's definitions of other prosodic categories – that is, prosodic words and intonational phrases – in order to complete the rough outline of Relation-based Theory:

(10) ω domain (Nespor and Vogel 1986: 141)
    A. The domain of ω is Q [= a terminal element of the syntactic tree]

    or

    B. I. The domain of ω consists of
          a. a stem;
          b. any element identified by specific phonological and/or morphological criteria;
          c. any element marked with the diacritic [+W].
      II. Any unattached elements within Q form part of the adjacent ω closest to the stem; if no such ω exists, they form a ω on their own.

(11) Intonational Phrase Formation (Nespor and Vogel 1986: 189)
    I. ι domain
      An ι domain may consist of
      a. all the φs in a string that is not structurally attached to the sentence tree at the level of s-structure, or
      b. any remaining sequence of adjacent φs in a root sentence.
    II. ι construction
      Join into an n-ary branching ι all φs included in a string delimited by the definition of the domain of ι.

Note that the definitions of phonological phrase and intonational phrase take their immediately lower respective prosodic category (φ taking C, and ι taking φ) to form these phrases, incorporating the effects of the SLH.

2.3 End-based Theory

Elaborating on Clements' (1978) study of Ewe and Chen's (1987) study of Xiamen, Selkirk (1986) proposes a general theory of prosodic constituency, the End-based Theory (or Edge-based Theory). Its basic premise is that prosodic words and phonological phrases are defined in terms of the ends or edges of certain syntactic constituents, and the specification of these ends is parameterised:

(12) i. a. $]_{\text{Word}}$ b. $_{\text{Word}}[$
     ii. a. $]_{\text{Xmax}}$ b. $_{\text{Xmax}}[$

(Selkirk 1986: 389)

Here, "Xmax" means a maximal projection in the X-bar Theory. (12i) and (12ii) derive the prosodic word and phonological phrase, respectively, from the syntactic phrase structure. Thus, for the ditransitive VP structure in (13), (12iia) gives the phonological phrasing in (14a) by deriving the right-edges of phonological phrases from the right edges of the VP and the NPs, and (12iib) gives the phrasing in (14b) by referring to the left edges of the syntactic XPs:

(13) [$_{VP}$ V NP NP]

(14) a. (V   NP)$_\varphi$ (NP)$_\varphi$
      b. (V)$_\varphi$ (NP)$_\varphi$ (NP)$_\varphi$

Selkirk shows that (14a) and (14b) are observed in Xiamen and in Ewe, respectively.

As we have seen in §2.2, the branching may affect the phrasing. Following Cowper and Rice (1987), Bickmore (1990) suggests the following parameterization in the framework of End-based Theory:

(15) a.]$_{Xmax-b}$ b. $_{Xmax-b}$[

(Bickmore 1990: 17)

Here, Xmax-b stands for a branching XP. He shows that (15a) and (15b) account for the phrasings in Mende and Kinyambo, respectively.

End-based Theory is in a sense simpler than Relation-based Theory since it is not necessary to mention syntactic notions such as the recursive side or the head/complement distinction. Although End-based Theory, at this early stage of its development, does not explicitly state how intonational phrases are formed, Selkirk (1984: Ch. 5) suggests that it is defined semantically, in terms of the *Sense Unit Condition* (see also Watson and Gibson 2004; see Selkirk 2005).

So far in this section, we have reviewed the two major approaches to the syntax–phonology interface. These two theories are indirect-reference theories: they construct phonological domains within which relevant phonological rules apply. That is, phonological rules do not refer to syntax at all. Note that Kaisse (1985), for example, proposes a direct-reference theory of syntax–phonology interface which refers to c-command (her *domain-c-command*) in syntax (see also Cinque (1993) and Odden (1987; 1990; 1996) for direct-reference; and see Selkirk (1986: 398–400) for criticisms of Kaisse's theory). The debate over the direct vs. indirect reference is not over yet, as we shall see in §3.4.

3 Recent developments

3.1 *Generalized Alignment*

The 1990s saw new developments in the study of grammar: Minimalism in syntax and Optimality Theory in phonology (Chomsky 1995; Prince and Smolensky ([1993] 2004).

The development of Optimality Theory has resulted in End-based Theory being integrated into the Generalized Alignment Theory (McCarthy and Prince 1993; Selkirk 1995; 2000; Truckenbrodt 1995; 1999; 2007; Gussenhoven 2004, among others). Thus the parametric formulation of End-based Theory in (12) is recast in terms of the following constraints:

(16) a. ALIGN(XP, R; φ, R): The right edge of each syntactic XP is aligned with the right
          edge of a phonological phrase φ.

b. ALIGN(XP, L; φ, L): The left edge of each syntactic XP is aligned with the left edge of a phonological phrase φ.

c. *P-PHRASE: Avoid phonological phrases.

*P-PHRASE has the effect of making either (16a) or (16b) inactive. Thus, for the syntactic structure [$_{VP}$ V NP], the ranking ALIGN-XP,R >> *P-PHRASE >> ALIGN-XP,L gives the phrasing (V NP)$_φ$, while the ranking ALIGN-XP,L >> *P-PHRASE >> ALIGN-XP,R gives (V)$_φ$ (NP)$_φ$.

These and other constraints such as the ones prohibiting recursive structures (NONREC(URSIVITY)) and level-skipping in the prosodic constituency (EXHAUSTIVITY) are taken to be universal and violable, and the ranking among them accounts for cross-linguistic variation (Selkirk 1995). One of the interesting consequences of Optimality-Theory approach equipped with violable constraints is that recursive phrasing is allowed to emerge, something strictly prohibited by the SLH. Truckenbrodt (1995; 1999) shows that this is in fact the case in the Bantu language Kimatuumbi. He proposes that the alignment constraints interact with the constraint WRAP-XP, which requires that each XP be contained in a φ.

Based on observations by Odden (1987; 1990; 1996), Truckenbrodt argues that Kimatuumbi has recursive phonological phrasing. First he shows that Vowel Shortening is sensitive to the right edge of phonological phrases while Phrasal Tone Insertion (PTI) is sensitive to their left edge. He then shows that the two complements of a verb are separated by the right edge but not by the left edge of phonological phrases, as schematically shown in (17):

(17) syntax: [V NP NP]$_{VP}$
     phonology: ((V NP)$_φ$ NP)$_φ$

He shows that this recursive phrasing is obtained through the following constraint interaction (Truckenbrodt 1999: 241):[10]

(18) *WRAP-XP and ALIGN-XP,R compel a recursive structure*

[X_1 XP_2 XP_3]$_{XP1}$	ALIGN-XP,R	WRAP-XP	NONREC	*P-PHRASE	ALIGN-XP,L
a. ( )	XP$_2$!			*	XP$_2$ XP$_3$
b. ( )( )		XP$_1$!		**	XP$_2$
c. ☞(( ))			XP$_3$	**	XP$_2$ XP$_3$
d. (( ))			X$_1$! XP$_3$	**	XP$_3$
e. (( )( ))			XP$_3$ X$_1$(!) XP$_2$	***(!)	XP$_2$

Here, WRAP-XP serves to exclude candidate (18b), which would otherwise have been allowed as a valid "flat" structure.

Truckenbrodt further shows that the ranking WRAP-XP = NONREC >> ALIGN-XP,R = *P-PHRASE derives the nonrecursive phonological phrasing (X XP XP)$_φ$ for the syntactic structure [X XP XP] observed in the Bantu language Chichewa (Kanerva 1990). That is, the cross-linguistic variation in phonological phrasing as well as the emergence of recursive phrasing is attributed to differences in constraint ranking.

Note that Optimality-Theory approaches such as Truckenbrodt's or Selkirk's (1995; 2000) assume a fairly traditional, simple theory of syntactic phrase structure such as the one below:

(19) [$_{IP}$ NP$_{Subj}$ Infl [$_{VP}$ V NP$_{Obj}$]]

In the literature on Bantu syntax, for example, it is often assumed that V moves to Infl (the same is also true of Romance languages such as Italian):

(20) [$_{IP}$ NP$_{Subj}$ V-Infl [$_{VP}$ t_V NP$_{Obj}$]:

It is therefore not clear how ALIGN-XP and WRAP-XP apply in Kimatuumbi after V has moved out of VP. Is a VP whose head has been vacated still involved in the alignment constraint? Or does a phonological phrase containing an object NP and the trace of V satisfy WRAP-XP? These questions concerning inconsistencies between syntactic and phonological theories seem to remain open in the Optimality-Theory framework.

3.2 Minimalist syntax and syntax–phonology interface

New theoretical devices in minimalist syntax have also urged significant changes in the study of the syntax–phonology interface. Especially influential is the Multiple Spell-Out Theory proposed by Uriagereka (1999). It was commonly held until the mid-1990s that the syntactic computation splits to Logical Form (LF) and Phonetic Form (PF) at some point in the derivation:

(20)

$$
\text{Lexicon} \diagup\diagdown
\begin{array}{l} \nearrow \text{LF} \\ \searrow \text{PF} \end{array}
$$

In an attempt to give a derivational account of the "induction step" of Kayne's (1994) antisymmetry theory of linearization, Uriagereka proposes that Spell-Out applies in a multiple fashion, independently spelling out a complex "left branch," so that the induction step can be eliminated from the antisymmetry theory:

(21)

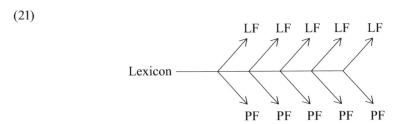

As suggested by Uriagereka, this model not only derives part of the linearization procedure but also provides prosodic domains, as well as syntactic islands and semantic domains.[11]

Another important development in syntactic theory that has had an influence on syntax–phonology relations was an attempt to eliminate labels from the phrase structure. Collins

(2002) argues that labels such as VP and NP can be eliminated from phrase structure theory. Thus the phrase structure of "read the book" will look like (22a) and not (22b):

(22)

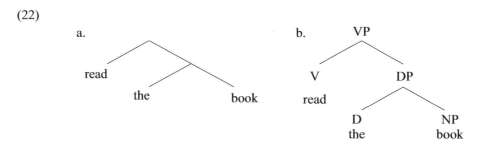

Note that it is impossible to refer to an XP in this label-free theory, so an alignment theory such as the one reviewed in Section 3.1 cannot be maintained. Collins points out that some version of Multiple Spell-Out is required to account for phonological phrasing.[12]

In line with these and many other syntactic investigations, Chomsky (2000; 2001; 2004) has proposed a phase theory of syntactic derivation. He argues that syntactic derivation proceeds cyclically, phase by phase. In the following phrase structure, CP and vP are taken to be (strong) phases, and the sister of a phase head undergoes Spell-Out:

(23) $[_{CP}$ C $[_{TP}$ NP$_{Subj}$ T $[_{vP}$ v $[_{VP}$ V NP$_{Obj}$]]]]

First the vP phase is constructed. The CP phase is then constructed, and at this point the sister of the lower phase, namely VP, is spelled-out. As the derivation goes on, TP, the sister of C, is spelled-out.

It should be pointed out that the domain of Spell-Out does not match the attested phrasing. Applied to the derivation of (23), Spell-Out would give the following prosodic domains, on the commonly held assumption that V moves to v:

(24) (C) (NP$_{Subj}$ T V-v) (t_V NP$_{Obj}$)

However, such phrasing is not usually observed. The following are the phrasings that are attested and also predicted by the standard theories reviewed in the previous section:

(25) a. (NP$_{Subj}$)$_\varphi$ (T V NP$_{Obj}$)$_\varphi$
       b. (NP$_{Subj}$)$_\varphi$ (T V)$_\varphi$ (NP$_{Obj}$)$_\varphi$

As argued by Dobashi (2003; 2009), the linearization procedure among the units of Spell-Out can resolve the mismatch.[13] Notice that the units of Spell-Out shown in (24) are sent to the phonological component separately from each other. Thus, first, (t_V NP$_{Obj}$) is sent to the phonological component, as in (26a), and then (NP$_{Subj}$ T V-v) is sent to the phonological component, as in (26b):

(26) a. (t_V NP$_{Obj}$)
       b. (NP$_{Subj}$ T V-v) (t_V NP$_{Obj}$)

Note that there is no a priori reason to assume that a domain spelled-out later precedes one spelled-out earlier because syntactic information such as c-command upon which linear

Yoshihito Dobashi

order is defined is presumably no longer available in the phonological component. So it would be equally possible to have the following order:

(27) $(t_V \, \mathrm{NP_{Obj}}) (\mathrm{NP_{Subj}} \, \mathrm{T} \, \mathrm{V\text{-}v})$

This problem, called the *Assembly Problem*, can be resolved if we assume that the leftmost element in each unit of Spell-Out is left behind for the next Spell-Out, so the linearization between the units of Spell-Out is possible. That is, when Spell-Out applies to the sister of v, the linear order between t_V and $\mathrm{NP_{Obj}}$ is defined. Then the leftmost element in this domain (i.e., t_V) is left behind until the sister of C is spelled-out, with only $\mathrm{NP_{Obj}}$ being sent to the phonological component, as in (28a) below. When the sister of C is spelled-out, the linear order is defined among $\mathrm{NP_{Subj}}$, T, V-v, and t_V, which has been left behind and is still available for linearization. At this point, t_V (defined to precede $\mathrm{NP_{Obj}}$ and follow V-v) acts as a pivot for linearization, so that the order between the two units of Spell-Out is unambiguously given as in (28b). $\mathrm{NP_{Subj}}$ is left behind for the next Spell-Out, and it is only sent to the phonological component later, resulting in the phrasing in (28c).

(28) a. $(\mathrm{NP_{Obj}})_\varphi$
     b. $(\mathrm{T} \, \mathrm{V})_\varphi \, (\mathrm{NP_{Obj}})_\varphi$
     c. $(\mathrm{NP_{Subj}})_\varphi \, (\mathrm{T} \, \mathrm{V})_\varphi \, (\mathrm{NP_{Obj}})_\varphi$

Within this theory, the typological variation in phonological phrasing is largely attributed to syntactic variation.[14] The object is phrased with the verb in languages such as Kimatuumbi, as in (29a), but phrased separately from the verb in languages such as Italian, as in (29b):

(29) a. $(\mathrm{NP_{Subj}}) \, (\mathrm{V} \, \mathrm{NP_{Obj}})$
     b. $(\mathrm{NP_{Subj}}) \, (\mathrm{V}) (\mathrm{NP_{Obj}})$

Given the analysis of Bantu languages where V raises to T and $\mathrm{NP_{Obj}}$ moves to the Spec of vP, we have the following phrase structure (see, e.g., Seidl 2001):

(30) $[_{CP} \, \mathrm{C} \, [_{TP} \, \mathrm{NP_{Subj}} \, \mathrm{V\text{-}v\text{-}T} \, [_{vP} \, \mathrm{NP_{Obj}} \, t_{V\text{-}v} \, [_{VP} \, t_V \, t_{Obj} \,]]]]$

Spell-Out applying to the sister of (the trace of) v does not give any phonological material since everything has moved out, and Spell-Out applying to the sister of C gives the phrasing where V and $\mathrm{NP_{Obj}}$ are phrased together, as in (29a). In contrast, in the analysis of languages such as Italian where V moves to T and $\mathrm{NP_{Obj}}$ stays in situ, we have the following phrase structure:

(31) $[_{CP} \, \mathrm{C} \, [_{TP} \, \mathrm{NP_{Subj}} \, \mathrm{V\text{-}v\text{-}T} \, [_{vP} \, t_{V\text{-}v} \, [_{VP} \, t_V \, \mathrm{NP_{Obj}}]]]]$

Spell-Out applying to the sister of v gives a phonological phrase containing only the object, and Spell-Out applying to the sister of C gives the phrase containing V on T, with the subject being included in the domain of the next Spell-Out, resulting in the phasing in (29b).

Phase-based or syntactic-cycle-based approaches to prosody include Fuß (2007; 2008), Ishihara (2003; 2005; 2007), Kahnemuyipour (2004; 2009), Kratzer and Selkirk (2007), Marvin (2002), Pak (2008), Samuels (2009; 2011a), Sato (2009), Seidl (2001), Scheer (2012), Shiobara (2009; 2010), and Wagner (2005; 2010), among many others.[15]

3.3 Reassessing prosodic hierarchy and the SLH

The Strict Layer Hypothesis reviewed in §2.1 has been adopted, often without controversy, as a basic assumption in a wide range of investigations. However, it has sometimes been challenged on an empirical basis. Ladd (1986; 1996), for instance, shows that the intonational phrase can in fact be recursive. Thus in sentences of the form *A and B but C* and *A but B and C*, the *but* boundary is stronger:

(32) a. Warren is a stronger campaigner, and Ryan has more popular policies, but Allen has a lot more money.
      b. Warren is a stronger campaigner, but Ryan has more popular policies, and Allen has a lot more money.

(Ladd 1996: 242)

Under the SLH, we would have the following flat intonational phrasing in both of these examples:

(33)

However, the initial peak of the clause after *but* is higher than that after *and*, and the pause before *but* is longer than that before *and*. That is, the same phenomena show up on different scales, depending on where they show up. The following recursive intonational phrasing accounts for the difference in boundary strength in an obvious way:

(34)

a. υ
     ι
 ι ι ι
A and B but C

b. υ
     ι
ι ι ι
A but B and C

More arguments for recursive phrasing in the prosodic hierarchy are presented by, among others, Booij (1996), Ito and Mester (2007; 2009), Kabak and Revithiadou (2009), and Zec (2005) for prosodic words and Gussenhoven (2005) and Truckenbrodt (1999) for phonological phrases.

Given these and other findings, Ito and Mester (2012) lay out a general model for prosodic structure, Recursion-based Subcategories. They adopt three interface categories: the intonational phrase ι, phonological phrase φ, and prosodic word ω, all of which can be recursive. They assume[16] that the utterance υ is in fact the maximal projection of the ι, which accounts for why υ is not recursive:

(35)

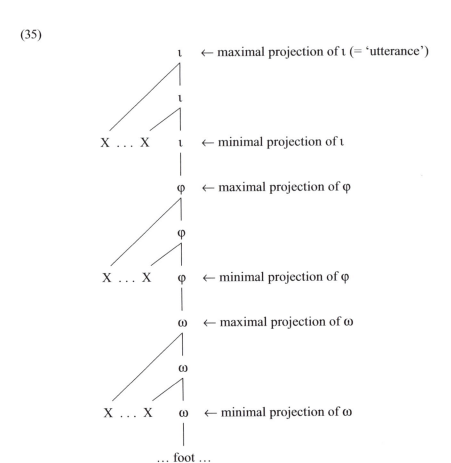

        ι   ← maximal projection of ι (= 'utterance')

        ι

X … X   ι   ← minimal projection of ι

        φ   ← maximal projection of φ

        φ

X … X   φ   ← minimal projection of φ

        ω   ← maximal projection of ω

        ω

X … X   ω   ← minimal projection of ω

        … foot …

Since this recursive model of prosodic hierarchy is radically different from previous theories, a new mapping algorithm is required for matching syntax with the recursive prosodic structure. One such theory is proposed by Selkirk (2009; 2011) and further elaborated by Elfner (2010; 2012).

In the standard Prosodic Hierarchy theory reviewed in §2.1, there is no inherent relationship assumed between prosodic and syntactic categories. Selkirk (2009; 2011) advances the idea that the hierarchical relationship among the interface categories (i.e., ω, φ, and ι) is syntactically grounded (see also Selkirk 2005: Section 5). Specifically, she proposes a *Match Theory* of syntactic-prosodic constituency correspondence:

(36) *Match Theory* (Selkirk 2009: 40; 2011: 439)
    (i) Match Clause
        A clause in syntactic constituent structure must be matched by a constituent of a corresponding prosodic type in phonological representation, call it ι.
   (ii) Match Phrase
        A phrase in syntactic constituent structure must be matched by a constituent of a corresponding prosodic type in phonological representation, call it φ.
  (iii) Match Word
        A word in syntactic constituent structure must be matched by a constituent of a corresponding prosodic type in phonological representation, call it ω.

Note that this is an informal formulation, and it is refined in terms of the Correspondence Theory (McCarthy and Prince 1995), to which we will return later. The notions of clause, phrase, and word are minimally necessary in any theory of morphosyntax, and the theory of syntax–phonology interaction makes use of these syntactic notions, which have correspondents in phonology. In this theory, ω, φ, and ι are not stipulated phonological entities, but rather syntactically motivated categories.

One of the most salient features of this theory is that recursion and level-skipping in the prosodic structure are taken to mirror the recursion in syntax. Thus the prosodic structure in (37b)–(37c) is obtained from the syntactic structure in (37a), where JP and OP are clauses, other XPs are phrases, and each terminal element is a word:

(37)

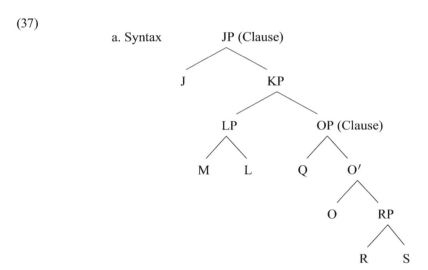

a. Syntax

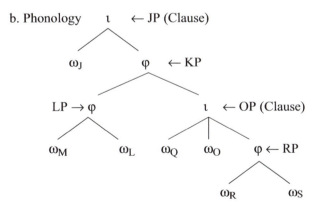

b. Phonology

c. $(\omega_J \ ((\omega_M \ \omega_L)_\varphi \ (\omega_Q \ \omega_O \ (\omega_R \ \omega_S)_\varphi \ )_\iota \ )_\varphi \ )_\iota$

Here the φ that matches KP dominates the φ that matches LP, instantiating a case of recursion. The ι that matches JP dominates ω_J, and the ι that matches OP dominates ω_Q and ω_O, instantiating level-skipping. The intonational phrasing is also recursive in that the ι that matches JP dominates the ι that matches OP, even though it does not immediately dominate it.

Based on Kubo's (2005) analysis of the Fukuoka dialect of Japanese, Selkirk (2009) examines the effects of ι-recursion in terms of the Match Theory, in conjunction with the Multiple Spell-Out theory. In the *wh*-question in this dialect, a H tone spreads rightward from a *wh*-word (H Tone Plateau):

(38) a. da|re-ga   kyoo   biiru   nonda
      who-NOM   today   beer   drank ØCOMP
      'Who drank beer today?'

The H Tone Plateau extends up to the end of the embedded clause when the *wh*-word is in the embedded clause:

(39) [[[da|re-ga kyoo biiru nonda]|ka] sitto |o]
      who-NOM today beer drank   COMP know ØCOMP
      'Do you know who drank beer today?'

If a *wh*-word appears in the matrix clause and another *wh*-word appears in the embedded clause, as in (40), the H of the matrix *wh*-word spreads to the end of the matrix clause:

(40) [[da|re-ga [[dare-ga   biiru nonda] ka]   sittoo]
      who-NOM who-NOM beer drank COMP know ØCOMP
      'Who knows who drank beer?'

On the assumption that a clause is defined as the complement of $Comp^0$, the bottom-up phase-by-phase derivation first creates an intonational phrase, as in (41a), then the next Spell-Out of the complement of (matrix) $Comp^0$ gives the recursive intonational phrasing shown in (41b), within which the H Tone Plateau applies:

(41) a. (dare-ga biiru nonda)$_\iota$
     b. (dare-ga (dare-ga biiru nonda)$_\iota$ ka sittoo)$_\iota$

Presumably the H Tone Plateau would have applied at the derivational stage of (41a), but the H Tone Plateau at the higher, or later, phase of derivation takes precedence over the lower, earlier, application, and its effects carry over to the end of the entire sentence. Note that this analysis is made possible by recursive ι-phrasing coupled with Multiple Spell-Out (see Ishihara 2005; 2007).

As alluded to earlier, the Match Theory is formally recast as a set of violable Match constraints within the framework of the Correspondence Theory. If a markedness constraint is ranked above the Match constraint, we will obtain prosodic domains that do not match the syntactic structure. That is, the Match Theory is an indirect-reference theory, in that we need to have prosodic domains that are independent of syntactic structure. For an illustration, let us examine the phonological phrasing in Xitsonga discussed by Selkirk (2011).

Drawing on Kisseberth's (1994: 157) observations, Selkirk shows that the H Tone Spread in Xitsonga does not apply across the left edge of a branching noun phrase, while it can apply across the left edge of a non-branching noun phrase:

(42) a. vá-súsá [$_{NP}$ n-gúlú:ve]
      'They are removing a pig'

b. vá-súsá [$_{NP}$ n-guluve y$^!$á vo:n$^!$á]
'They are removing their pig'

Here, the subject marker *vá-* has a H tone. It spreads across the left edge of the NP in (42a) while it does not in (42b), where the NP is branching. In the Optimality-Theory formulation of the Match Theory, the phrasing is obtained through the interaction of a syntax-prosody correspondence constraint Match(Phrase, φ) with a prosodic markedness constraint BinMin(φ,ω). The former requires syntactic phrases to correspond to phonological phrases, and the latter requires φ to be minimally binary and to consist of at least two prosodic words (Inkelas and Zec 1995; Selkirk 2000; Zec and Inkelas 1990). In Xitsonga, BinMin(φ,ω) >> Match(Phrase,φ):

(43) i.

[[verb [noun]$_{NP}$]$_{VP}$]$_{clause}$	BinMin(φ,ω)	Match(Phrase,φ)
a. ((verb (noun)$_\varphi$)$_\varphi$)$_\iota$ b. ☞((verb noun)$_\varphi$)$_\iota$	*	*

ii.

[[verb [noun adj]$_{NP}$]$_{VP}$]$_{clause}$	BinMin(φ,ω)	Match(Phrase,φ)
a. ☞((verb (noun adj)$_\varphi$)$_\varphi$)$_\iota$ b. ((verb noun)$_\varphi$ adj)$_\iota$		*

In (43i), where the object is non-branching, (b) is the optimal candidate even though it violates the Match constraint since the higher-ranked markedness constraint BinMin(φ,ω) is satisfied, while candidate (a) that satisfies the Match constraint is excluded in violation of BinMin(φ,ω). In (43ii), where the object is branching, candidate (a) satisfies both of the constraints, mirroring the syntactic constituency and at the same time violating the SLH in the standard theory.[17]

So far we have provided a rough sketch of Match Theory, but it remains unclear exactly how the syntactic notions of clauses, phrases, and words in Match Theory are formally defined. For example, the notion of phrases rests on the labels and projections in syntax, but their status has been reconsidered in recent development of syntactic theory, as we have seen in §3.2 (also see Chomsky 2012).[18]

3.4 Minimalist phonology

The minimalist program is not a theory but rather a program which offers guidelines such as simplicity and efficiency to assist researchers in discovering the "right" theory of grammar. Since minimalist perspectives are not syntax-specific, it is expected that such a rigorous attitude toward theory construction, or its "heuristic and therapeutic value" (Chomsky 2000: 93), would also be applicable to the study of the syntax–phonology interface.[19]

On purely conceptual grounds, Dobashi (2003) suggests that it would be possible to eliminate phonological phrases from a theory of grammar. If phonological rules can apply to a phonological string mapped by Spell-Out as the syntactic derivation proceeds, and if that string becomes inaccessible when another string is spelled-out, we would not need to create a phonological phrase: the phenomena of phonological phrasing could be reduced to the derivational properties of the syntactic cycle. As Samuels (2009: Section 5.4, 2011a: 97) points out, this is the null hypothesis, since it does not require any phonological phrase formation mechanism. The direct-reference theory then is called for, in which phonological rules apply directly to the domain of a syntactic cycle (see Scheer 2012 for further arguments for direct reference theory).

As an illustration of such a null theory of phonological phrasing, let us sketch Pak's (2008) proposals. What follows is a very rough and simplified illustration of her theory, largely abstracting away technical details. She suggests that the linear order among words is defined in two steps: head-level linearisation and phrase-level linearization. In the first step, linear order between overt heads is defined in terms of left-adjacency and c-command in a pairwise fashion. Thus, in the following syntactic structure, where only X, Y, and Z are overt, X is defined as being left-adjacent to Y because X c-commands Y and no other overt head intervenes between them, but Y cannot be defined as being left-adjacent to Z in this first step of the linearization, because Y does not c-command Z.

(44)

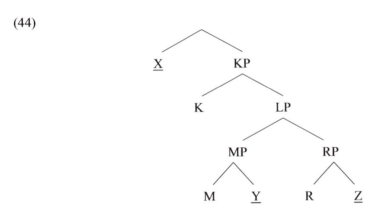

Y is defined as being left-adjacent to Z in the second step of linearization – that is, the phrase-level linearization. Y precedes Z because of their mother nodes: MP dominating Y precedes RP dominating Z. Given this linearization procedure, Pak proposes that different phonological rules apply to different steps of linearization. That is, some rules apply to the structure created by the head-level linearization and others apply to the structure created by the phrase-level linearization.

Under this proposed model of linearization, Pak gives an analysis of prosodic domains in the Bantu language Luganda, using two domain-specific rules. One is a rule of Low Tone Deletion (LTD), which applies between two H_nL_n words, deleting L on the first word and forming a H-Plateau between the two words. Another is a rule of High Tone Anticipation (HTA), which spreads a H leftward onto toneless moras.

(45) a. No LTD between indirect object and direct object: (Pak 2008: 29–30)
     i. bá-lìs-a   kaamukúúkùlu   doodô
        sbj2-feed-ind   la.dove   la.greens
        'They're feeding greens to the dove.'
     ii. → (bálísá káámúkúúkùlù) (dòòdô)

  b. HTA applies throughout double-object structure:
   i. a-lis-a   empologoma   doodô
      sdj1-feed-ind   9.lion   la.greens
      'S/he's feeding greens to the lion.'
   ii. → (àlís' émpólógómá dóódò)

In (45a), LTD applies between the verb and the indirect object, while it does not between the indirect object and the direct object. By contrast, in (45b), which has the same syntactic structure as (45a) but differs only in that the verb and the indirect object are toneless, HTA spreads the H tone of the direct object leftward to the indirect object and the verb. That is, the domain of LTD is smaller than that of HTA.[20]

Pak proposes that LTD is an early rule that applies to the output of the first step of linearization (head-level linearization), and HTA applies later to the output of the second step (phrasal linearization). She assumes the following syntactic structure for double-object constructions:

(46)

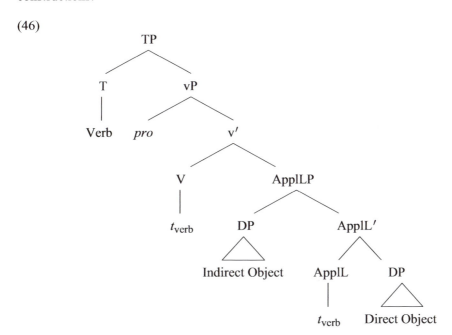

Here ApplLP is a low applicative phrase, and the verb originates as the head of ApplLP and moves up to T through v (see Seidl 2001). She assumes quite naturally that both of the DP objects have their own internal structure. Given this structure, the first step of linearization defines the linear order among overt heads. The verb in T is defined as being left-adjacent to the indirect object, but the indirect object is embedded within DP and cannot be defined as being left-adjacent to the direct object (see (44) above), so the first step just gives the string V-IO. This string serves as the domain for the "early rule" LTD. The next step is the phrasal linearization, which defines the string of V-IO as being left-adjacent to the direct object. At this point, we have the string V-IO-DO, to which the late rule HTA applies.

This is a direct-reference approach, as we do not construct any prosodic domain. Moreover, there is no need to stipulate Prosodic Hierarchy (Pak 2008: 43). The apparent hierarchy is derived from the linearization procedure.

Yoshihito Dobashi

In the debates over direct vs. indirect reference (see, e.g., Selkirk (2009: 64) for related discussion), one of the arguments for indirect reference is the mismatch between phonological and syntactic constituents. However, as the Match Theory reviewed in §3.3 reveals, the discrepancy between recursive syntax and flat phonology in the standard theory is now turning out to be resolved as a case of isomorphism even in the indirect-reference theory. Another argument for indirect reference is the fact that prosodic domains are affected by speech rate and prosodic size, which are irrelevant to any syntactic notion. For example, Nespor and Vogel (1986: 173–174) and Frascarelli (2000: 19, 48) point out that the (optional) restructuring of phonological phrases and intonational phrases can be affected by style, speech rate, and prosodic weight.[21] For example, a verb and a non-branching object tend to be phrased together in fast speech. Moreover, as pointed out by Ghini (1993), the overall prosodic weight distribution may also affect phonological phrasing. It remains to be seen how performance factors such as speech rate and purely prosodic properties such as prosodic weight could come into play in the direct reference theory.

4 Concluding remarks

This chapter has sketched the development of theories of syntax–phonology interface. All the research questions mentioned in §1 are still left unresolved, and one hopes that the theoretical tools and conceptual guidelines seen in §3 will offer new directions for research. Besides that, it seems important to consider the syntax–phonology interface from a broader perspective. Previous approaches to prosodic domains tended to simply look at syntax and phonology, but it seems necessary to consider other factors, such as linearization (e.g., Pak 2008), and various morphological processes (e.g., Fuß 2008), as well as to construct an explicit organization of the "PF branch" in the theory of grammar (e.g., Idsardi and Raimy 2013), in order to understand exactly where prosodic domains fit within the architecture of grammar. Also important would be to conduct systematic cross-linguistic research on prosodic domains, since many previous studies depended on surveys of particular languages, and they have often been carried out independently of one another.

Notes

1 For these topics, see, e.g., papers in Erteschik-Shir and Rochman (2010).
2 Rice (1990) argues that domain juncture rules can be reanalyzed as domain span rules. See also Vogel (2009a).
3 One school of thought assumes that prosodic domains are defined with reference to the surface phonetic form but not the syntactic structure (e.g., Jun 1998; Beckman and Pierrehumbert 1986; Ladd 1996 among many others).
4 See, e.g., Shiobara (2009; 2010) for an approach to the mismatch resolution within a left-to-right derivational framework.
5 For the effects of phonology on syntax, see, e.g., Shiobara (2011) and Zec and Inkelas (1990). For information structure, see, e.g., Dehé *et al.* (2011) and Frascarelli (2000).
6 For earlier approaches, see Bierwisch (1966), Chomsky and Halle (1968), Clements (1978), Downing (1970), Selkirk (1972; 1974). For overviews of the field, see, e.g., Inkelas and Zec (1995), Elordieta (2007), Kager and Zonneveld (1999), Revithiadou and Spyropoulos (2011), and Selkirk (2002).
7 For more papers published around this time, see papers in Inkelas and Zec (1990) and Zwicky and Kaisse (1987), among many others.
8 An earlier proposal on the prosodic organization was made by Halliday (1967).
9 See, e.g., Zec and Inkelas (1991) for critical discussion of the Clitic Group. See, e.g., Vogel (2009b) for arguments for the Clitic Group.
10 Technically, NONREC here is defined as follows:

(i) Any two phonological phrases that are not disjoint in extension are identical in extension (adapted from Truckenbrodt 1999: 240).
This constraint has the effect of choosing (18c) over (18d) since the inner and outer phonological phrases are more similar in the former. See Truckenbrodt (1999) for details.

11 See Revithiadou and Spyropoulos (2009) for a case study of phonological phenomena conducted under Uriagereka's proposal.

12 See Tokizaki (2005) for a theory of syntax–phonology interface that does not require labels.

13 See Fuß (2007; 2008) for another approach to the mismatch within the phase-by-phase Spell-Out framework.

14 See Seidl (2001) for cross-linguistic variation within Bantu languages, and see Samuels (2009; 2011a; 2011b) for the further elaboration of typology and the hybrid approach incorporating Uriagereka's Multiple Spell-Out Theory and Chomsky's phase theory.

15 See Downing (2011) for a mixed approach that combines phase and alignment. See also Chen and Downing (2012) for a criticism of the phase-based approach. For a much earlier cyclic approach, see Bresnan (1971).

16 Following a suggestion made to them by Shigeto Kawahara.

17 Selkirk (2011: 469) notes that the opposite ranking Match(Phrase,φ) >> BinMin(φ,ω) accounts for the phrasing in Chimwiini, German, and so on, where branchingness is irrelevant to phrasing.

18 Thus it could be that the EPP feature of TP distinguishes clauses from phrases.

19 For more on the minimalist view on phonology, see Samuels (2009; 2011a; 2011b) and Scheer (2012).

20 It remains to be seen if this phrasing can be recast in terms of recursive phrasing, or if the recursive phrasing can be recast in Pak's model.

21 See the end of Section 3.3 for prosodic weight. See Tokizaki (2008) for an analysis of the effect of speech rate on phrasing in terms of boundary strength.

Further reading

Nespor, M. and Vogel, I. 1986. *Prosodic Phonology*. Dordrecht: Foris.

A classic volume that motivates all the basic prosodic categories on empirical grounds and introduces the Relation-based Theory. Now available from Mouton de Gruyter.

Samuels, B.D. 2011. *Phonological Architecture: A Biolinguistic Perspective*. Oxford: Oxford University Press.

A comprehensive discussion of the phonological component of grammar within a recent framework of the minimalist program.

Selkirk, E. 1986. On Derived Domains in Sentence Phonology. *Phonology* 3:371–405.

A classic paper that laid the foundation for much subsequent work that has led to the more recent Correspondence Theoretic approach.

Selkirk, E. 2011. The Syntax–Phonology Interface. In *The Handbook of Phonological Theory*, 2nd edn, ed. John Goldsmith, Jason Riggle, and Alan C.L. Yu, 435–484. Oxford: Wiley-Blackwell.

A recent paper by Selkirk that proposes the syntax-grounded Match Theory, incorporating the recursive prosodic structure.

Truckenbrodt, H. 2007. The Syntax–Phonology Interface. In *The Cambridge Handbook of Phonology*, ed. Paul de Lacy, 435–456. Cambridge: Cambridge University Press.

A review of the Edge-alignment Theory that covers the topics not mentioned in this chapter, such as focus, stress, eurhythmic influences, etc.

References

Beckman, M.E., and J.B. Pierrehumbert. 1986. Intonational Structure in Japanese and English. *Phonology Yearbook* 3:225–309.

Bickmore, L. 1990. Branching Nodes and Prosodic Categories: Evidence from Kinyambo. In *The Phonology–Syntax Connection*, ed. S. Inkelas and D. Zec, 1–17. Chicago, IL: University of Chicago Press.

Bierwisch, M. 1966. Regeln für die Intonation deutscher Sätze. In *Studia Grammatica* VII, 99–201. Untersuchungen über Akzent und Intonation im Deutschen. Berlin: Akademie-Verlag.

Booij, G. 1996. Cliticization as Prosodic Integration: The Case of Dutch. *The Linguistic Review* 13:219–242.

Bresnan, J. 1971. Sentence Stress and Syntactic Transformations. *Language* 47:257–281.

Bresnan, J., and S.A. Mchombo. 1987. Topic, Pronoun, and Agreement in Chichewa. *Language* 63: 741–782.

Chen, L.L.-S., and L.J. Downing. 2012. Prosodic Domains Do Not Match Spell-out Domains, *McGill Working Papers in Linguistics* 22(1): available at https://www.mcgill.ca/mcgwpl/archives/volume-221-2012 (accessed 31 January 2014).

Chen, M. 1987. The Syntax of Xiamen Tone Sandhi. *Phonology* 4:109–150.

Chomsky, N. 1995. *The Minimalist Program*. Cambridge, MA: MIT Press.

Chomsky, N. 2000. Minimalist Inquiries: The Framework. In *Step by Step*, ed. R. Martin, D. Michaels, and J. Uriagereka, 89–155. Cambridge, MA: MIT Press.

Chomsky, N. 2001. Derivation by Phase. In *Ken Hale: A Life in Language*, ed. M. Kenstowicz, 1–52. Cambridge, MA: MIT Press.

Chomsky, N. 2004. Beyond Explanatory Adequacy. In *Structure and Beyond*, ed. A. Belletti, 104–131. Oxford: Oxford University Press.

Chomsky, N. 2012. Problems of Projection. Ms. MIT.

Chomsky, Noam, and Morris Halle. 1968. *The Sound Pattern of English*. New York: Harper & Row/Cambridge, MA: MIT Press.

Cinque, G. 1993. A Null Theory of Phrase and Compound Stress. *Linguistic Inquiry* 24:239–297.

Clements, G.N. 1978. Tone and Syntax in Ewe. In *Elements of Tone, Stress, and Intonation*, ed. D.J. Napoli, 21–99. Georgetown University Press.

Collins, C. 2002. Eliminating Labels. In *Derivation and Explanation in the Minimalist Program*, ed. S.D. Epstein and T.D. Seely, 42–64. Oxford: Blackwell Publishing.

Cowper, E.A., and K.D. Rice. 1987. Are Phonosyntactic Rules Necessary? *Phonology Yearbook* 4:185–194.

Dehé, N., I. Feldhausen, and S. Ishihara. 2011. The Prosody-Syntax Interface: Focus, Phrasing, Language Evolution. *Lingua* 121:1863–1869.

Dobashi, Y. 2003. Phonological Phrasing and Syntactic Derivation. PhD thesis, Cornell University: available at http://dspace.lib.niigata-u.ac.jp/dspace/bitstream/10191/19722/1/CU_2003_1–251.pdf (accessed 31 January 2014).

Dobashi, Y. 2009. Multiple Spell-out, Assembly Problem, and Syntax–phonology Mapping. In *Phonological Domains: Universals and Deviations*, ed. Janet Grijzenhout and Baris Kabak, 195–220. Berlin: Mouton de Gruyter.

Downing, B.T. 1970. Syntactic Structure and Phonological Phrasing in English. PhD thesis, the University of Texas at Austin.

Downing, L.J. 2011. The Prosody of 'Dislocation' in Selected Bantu Languages. *Lingua* 121:772–786.

Elfner, E. 2010. Recursivity in Prosodic Phrasing: Evidence from Conamara Irish. To appear in *Proceedings of the 40th Annual Meeting of the North-East Linguistic Society*, ed. Seda Kan, Claire Moore-Cantwell, and Robert Staubs, 191–204. Amherst, MA: GLSA publications.

Elfner, E. 2012. Syntax-Prosody Interactions in Irish. PhD thesis, University of Massachusetts, Amherst.

Elordieta, G. 1999. Phonological Cohesion as a Reflex of Morphosyntactic Feature Chains. In *Proceedings of the Seventeenth West Coast Conference on Formal Linguistics*, ed. K. Shahin, S. Blake, and E. Kim, 175–189. Stanford, CA: Center for the Study of Language and Information.

Elordieta, G. 2007. Segmental Phonology and Syntactic Structure. In *The Oxford Handbook of Linguistic Interfaces*, ed. G. Ramchand and C. Reiss, 125–177. Oxford: Oxford University Press.

Erteschik-Shir, N., and L. Rochman (eds). 2010. *The Sound Patterns of Syntax*. Oxford: Oxford University Press.

Frascarelli, M. 2000. *The Syntax–Phonology Interface in Focus and Topic Constructions in Italian*. Dordrecht: Kluwer.

Fuß, E. 2007. Cyclic Spell-out and the Domain of Post-syntactic Operations: Evidence from Complementizer Agreement. *Linguistic Analysis* 33:267–302.

Fuß, E. 2008. Word Order and Language Change: On the Interface between Syntax and Morphology. Post-graduate thesis, der Johann-Wolfgang-Goethe Universität.

Ghini, M. 1993. Φ-formation in Italian: A New Proposal. *Toronto Working Papers in Linguistics* 12(2): 41–78.

Gussenhoven, C. 2004. *The Phonology of Tone and Intonation*. Cambridge: Cambridge University Press.

Gussenhoven, C. 2005. Procliticized Phonological Phrases in English: Evidence from Rhythm. *Studia Linguistica* 59:174–193.

Halliday, M.A.K. 1967. *Intonation and Grammar in British English*. The Hague: Mouton.

Hayes, B. 1989. The Prosodic Hierarchy in Meter. In *Phonetics and Phonology 1, Rhythm and Meter*, ed. P. Kiparsky and G. Youmans, 201–260. Orlando: Academic Press.

Idsardi, W., and E. Raimy. 2013. Three Types of Linearization and the Temporal Aspects of Speech. In *Challenges to Linearization*, ed. T. Biberauer and I. Roberts, 31–56. Berlin: Mouton de Gruyter.

Inkelas, S., and D. Zec (eds). 1990. *The Phonology–Syntax Connection*. Chicago, IL: University of Chicago Press.

Inkelas, S., and D. Zec. 1995. Syntax–Phonology Interface. In *The Handbook of Phonological Theory*, ed. John. A Goldsmith, 535–549. Oxford: Blackwell.

Ishihara, S. 2003. Intonation and Interface Conditions. PhD thesis, MIT.

Ishihara, S. 2005. Prosody-Scope Match and Mismatch in Tokyo Japanese *Wh*-Questions. *English Linguistics* 22:347–379.

Ishihara, S. 2007. Major Phrase, Focus Intonation, Multiple Spell-out (MaP, FI, MSO). *Linguistic Review* 24:137–167.

Ito, J., and A. Mester. 2007. Prosodic Adjunction in Japanese Compounds. *Formal Approaches to Japanese Linguistics* 4:97–111.

Ito, J., and A. Mester. 2009. The Extended Prosodic Word. In *Phonological Domains: Universals and Deviations*, ed. J. Grijzenhout and B. Kabak, 135–194. Berlin: Mouton de Gruyter.

Ito, J., and A. Mester. 2012. Recursive Prosodic Phrasing in Japanese. In *Prosody Matters: Essays in Honor of Elisabeth Selkirk*, ed. T. Borowsky, S. Kawahara, T. Shinya, and M. Sugahara, 280–303. London: Equinox.

Jackendoff, R. 1997. *The Architecture of the Language Faculty*. Cambridge, MA: MIT Press.

Jun, S.-A. 1998. The Accentual Phrase in the Korean Prosodic Hierarchy. *Phonology* 5:189–226.

Kabak, B., and A. Revithiadou. 2009. An Interface Approach to Prosodic Word Recursion. In *Phonological Domains: Universals and Deviations*, ed. J. Grijzenhout and B. Kabak, 105–133. Berlin: Mouton de Gruyter.

Kager, R., and W. Zonneveld. 1999. Phrasal Phonology: An Introduction. In *Phrasal Phonology*, ed. R. Kager and W. Zonneveld, 1–34. Nijmegen: Nijmegen University Press.

Kahnemuyipour, A. 2004. The Syntax of Sentential Stress. PhD thesis, University of Toronto.

Kahnemuyipour, A. 2009. *The Syntax of Sentential Stress*. Oxford: Oxford University Press.

Kaisse, E.M. 1985. *Connected Speech: The Interaction of Syntax and Phonology*. New York: Academic Press.

Kanerva, J.M. 1990. Focusing on Phonological Phrases in Chichewa. In *The Phonology–Syntax Connection*, ed. S. Inkelas and D. Zec, 145–161. Chicago, IL: University of Chicago Press.

Kayne, R. 1994. *The Antisymmetry of Syntax*. Cambridge, MA: MIT Press.

Kisseberth, C.W. 1994. On Domains. In *Perspective in Phonology*, ed. J. Cole and C. Kisseberth, 133–166. Stanford, CA: CSLI.

Kratzer, A., and E. Selkirk. 2007. Phase Theory and Prosodic Spellout: The Case of Verbs. *The Linguistic Review* 24:93–135.

Kubo, T. 2005. Phonology–Syntax Interfaces in Busan Korean and Fukuoka Japanese. In *Cross-linguistic Studies of Tonal Phenomena: Historical Development, Tone-Syntax Interface, and Descriptive Studies*, ed. S. Kaji, 195–210. Tokyo: Research Institute for Languages and Cultures of Asian and Africa, Tokyo University of Foreign Studies.

Ladd, D.R. 1986. Intonational Phrasing: The Case for Recursive Prosodic Structure. *Phonology Yearbook* 3:311–340.

Ladd, D.R. 1996. *Intonational Phonology*. Cambridge: Cambridge University Press.

McCarthy, J., and A. Prince. 1993. Generalized Alignment. In *Yearbook of Morphology 1993*, ed. G.E. Booij and J. van Marle, 79–153. Dordrecht: Kluwer.

McCarthy, J., and A. Prince. 1995. Faithfullness and Reduplicative Identity. In *Papers in Optimality Theory. University of Massachusetts Occasional Papers in Linguistics 18*, ed. J. Beckman, L.W. Dickey, and S. Urbancxyk, 249–384. Amherst, MA: GLSA.

Marvin, T. 2002. Topics in the Stress and Syntax of Words. PhD thesis, MIT.

Nespor, M., and I. Vogel. 1986. *Prosodic Phonology*. Dordrecht: Foris.

Odden, D. 1987. Kimatuumbi Phrasal Phonology. *Phonology* 4:13–36.

Odden, D. 1990. Syntax, Lexical Rules, and Postlexical Rules in Kimatuumbi. In Inkelas and Zec (eds), 259–278.

Odden, D. 1996. *The Phonology and Morphology of Kimatuumbi*. Oxford: Oxford University Press.

Pak, M. 2008. The Postsyntactic Derivation and its Phonological Reflexes. PhD thesis, University of Pennsylvania.

Prince, A., and P. Smolensky. 1993/2004. *Optimality Theory: Constraint Interaction in Generative Grammar*. Oxford: Blackwell [ms circulated in 1993].

Revithiadou, A., and V. Spyropoulos. 2009. A Dynamic Approach to the Syntax–Phonology Interface: A Case Study from Greek. In *InterPhases: Phase-theoretic Investigations of Linguistic Interfaces*, ed. K.K. Grohmann, 202–233. Oxford: Oxford University Press.

Revithiadou, A., and V. Spyropoulos. 2011. Syntax–Phonology Interface. In *The Continuum Companion to Phonology*, ed. N.C. Kula, B. Botma, and K. Nasukawa, 225–253. London: Continuum.

Rice, K.D. 1990. Predicting Rule Domains in the Phrasal Phonology. In Inkelas and Zec (eds), 289–312.

Samuels, B.D. 2009. The Structure of Phonological Theory. PhD thesis, Harvard University.

Samuels, B.D. 2011a. *Phonological Architecture: A Biolinguistic Perspective*. Oxford: Oxford University Press.

Samuels, B.D. 2011b. A Minimalist Program for Phonology. In *The Oxford Handbook of Linguistic Minimalism*, ed. C. Boeckx, 575–594, Oxford: Oxford University Press.

Sato, Y. 2009. Spelling Out Prosodic Domains: A Multiple Spell-out Account. In *InterPhases: Phase-theoretic Investigations of Linguistic Interfaces*, ed. K.K. Grohmann, 234–259. Oxford: Oxford University Press.

Scheer, T. 2012. *Direct Interface and One-channel Translation: A Non-diacritic Theory of the Morphosyntax–Phonology Interface*. Berlin: Mouton de Gruyter.

Seidl, A. 2001. *Minimal Indirect Reference: A Theory of the Syntax–Phonology Interface*. New York and London: Routledge.

Selkirk, E. 1972. The Phrase Phonology of English and French. PhD thesis, Massachusetts Institute of Technology.

Selkirk, E. 1974. French Liaison and the X' Notation. *Linguistic Inquiry* 5:573–590.

Selkirk, E. 1980. Prosodic Domains in Phonology: Sanskrit Revisited, in *Juncture*, ed. M. Aronoff and M.-L. Kean, 107–129. Saratoga, CA: Anma Libri.

Selkirk, E. 1984. *Phonology and Syntax: The Relation between Sound and Structure*. Cambridge, MA: MIT Press.

Selkirk, E. 1986. On Derived Domains in Sentence Phonology. *Phonology* 3:371–405.

Selkirk, E. 1995. The Prosodic Structure of Function Words. In *University of Massachusetts Occasional Papers in Linguistics*, ed. J. Beckman, L. Walsh-Dickey, and S. Urbanczyk, 439–469. Amherst, MA: GLSA.

Selkirk, E. 2000. The Interaction of Constraints on Prosodic Phrasing. In *Prosody: Theory and Experiment*, ed. M. Horne, 231–261. Dordrecht: Kluwer.

Selkirk, E. 2002. The Syntax–Phonology Interface. In *International Encyclopedia of the Social and Behavioral Sciences*, Section 3.9, Article 23. Elsevier.

Selkirk, E. 2005. Comments on Intonational Phrasing in English. In *Prosodies*, ed. S. Frota, M. Vigário, and M.J. Freitas, 11–58. Berlin: Mouton de Gruyter.

Selkirk, E. 2009. On Clause and Intonational Phrase in Japanese: The Syntactic Grounding of Prosodic Constituent Structure. *Gengo Kenkyu* 136:35–73.

Selkirk, E. 2011. The Syntax–Phonology Interface. In *The Handbook of Phonological Theory, Second Edition*, ed. J. Goldsmith, J. Riggle, and A.C.L. Yu, 435–484. Oxford: Wiley-Blackwell.

Shiobara, K. 2009. A Phonological View of Phases. In *InterPhases: Phase-theoretic Investigations of Linguistic Interfaces*, ed. K.K. Grohmann, 182–201. Oxford: Oxford University Press.

Shiobara, K. 2010. *Derivational Linearization at the Syntax-Prosody Interface*. Tokyo: Hituzi Syobo.

Shiobara, K. 2011. Significance of Linear Information in Prosodically Constrained Syntax. *English Linguistics* 28:258–277.

Tokizaki, H. 2005. Prosody and Phrase Structure without Labels. *English Linguistics* 22:380–405.

Tokizaki, H. 2008. *Syntactic Structure and Silence*. Tokyo: Hituzi Syobo.

Truckenbrodt, Hubert 1995. Phonological Phrases: Their Relation to Syntax, Focus, and Prominence. PhD thesis, MIT.

Truckenbrodt, Hubert. 1999. On the Relation between Syntactic Phrases and Phonological Phrases. *Linguistic Inquiry* 30:219–255.

Truckenbrodt, Hubert. 2007. The Syntax–Phonology Interface. In *The Cambridge Handbook of Phonology*, ed. P. de Lacy, 435–456. Cambridge: Cambridge University Press.

Uriagereka, J. 1999. Multiple Spell-out. In *Working Minimalism*, ed. S. Epstein and N. Hornstein, 251–282. Cambridge, MA: MIT Press.

Vogel, I. 2009a. Universals of Prosodic Structure. In *Universals of Language Today*, ed. S. Scalise, E. Magni, and A. Bisetto, 59–82. Dordrecht: Springer.

Vogel, I. 2009b. The Status of Clitic Group. In *Phonological Domains: Universals and Deviations*, ed. Janet Grijzenhout and Baris Kabak, 15–46. Berlin: Mouton de Gruyter.

Wagner, M. 2005. Prosody and Recursion. PhD thesis, MIT.

Wagner, M. 2010. Prosody and Recursion in Coordinate Structures and Beyond. *Natural Language and Linguistic Theory* 28:183–237.

Watson, D., and E. Gibson. 2004. Making Sense of the Sense Unit Condition. *Linguistic Inquiry* 35:508–517.

Zec, D. 2005. Prosodic Differences among Function Words. *Phonology* 22:77–112.

Zec, D., and S. Inkelas. 1990. Prosodically Constrained Syntax. In *The Phonology–Syntax Connection*, ed. S. Inkelas and D. Zec, 365–378. Chicago, IL: University of Chicago Press.

Zec, D., and S. Inkelas. 1991. The Place of Clitics in the Prosodic Hierarchy. In *Proceedings of WCCFL 10*, ed. D. Bates, 505–519. Stanford: SLA.

Zwicky, A.M., and E.M. Kaisse (eds). 1987. Syntactic Conditions on Phonological Rules. *Phonology Yearbook* 4:1–263.

Part IV

Syntax in context

19

Syntactic change

Ian Roberts

1 Introduction: Universal Grammar, principles and parameters

Work on syntactic change in the context of generative grammar assumes the principles-and-parameters approach to reconciling observed variation among grammatical systems with the postulation of an innate language faculty. The leading idea is aptly summarised in the following quotation from Chomsky (1995: 219):

> A particular language L is an instantiation of the initial state of the cognitive system of the language faculty with options specified.

One way to think of the parameters of Universal Grammar is as the "atoms" of grammatical variation (this idea was introduced and developed in Baker 2001). Consider, for example, the following pairs of Mandarin Chinese and English sentences:

(1) a. What does Zhangsan think Lisi bought?
    b. Zhangsan wonders what Lisi bought.
    c. Zhangsan yiwei   Lisi mai-le   shenme?
      Z.   thinks L.   buy-PST what   (=(1a))
    d. Zhangsan xiang-zhidao Lisi mai-le   shenme
      Z.   wonders   L.   buy-PST what   (=(1b))

Here we see that, where English displays obligatory *wh*-movement to the root in (1a) and to the edge of the subordinate clause selected by *wonder* in (1b), giving rise to a direct and an indirect question respectively, Mandarin Chinese shows no such movement, with the item corresponding to the English *wh*-phrase, *shenme*, remaining in the canonical direct-object position for this language. Nonetheless, (1c) is interpreted as a direct question and (1d) as an indirect question; Huang (1982) argues that this happens in virtue of the different selectional properties of the equivalents of "think" and "wonder" (which in this respect at least are broadly parallel to those of their English counterparts), and implements this insight in terms of the postulation of covert *wh*-movement in Mandarin. Whatever the precise technical details, we observe here a parametric difference between English and Mandarin which has profound implications for the surface form of interrogatives of various kinds in the two languages: English has overt *wh*-movement while Mandarin does not (perhaps having covert movement "instead").

Following the standard view in generative grammar as argued many times by Chomsky (see, in particular, Chomsky 1965; 1975; 1980; 1981; 1986; 1995; 2001), we take Universal Grammar (UG) to be the set of grammatical principles which makes human language possible (and defines a possible human language). UG is usually thought to be at least in part determined by the human genome and, in some way yet to be discovered, to have a physical instantiation in the brain.

More specifically, UG is made of two rather different entities:

(2)   a. invariant principles
      b. associated parameters of variation

The nature of the invariant principles is clear: they do not vary from system to system or individual to individual (except perhaps in cases of gross pathology). The term "parameter" may seem obscure, but, as Baker (2001) points out, it has a sense connected to its mathematical usage. Consider, for example, the two sets specified in (3):

(3)   a. $\{x: x = 2y, y \text{ an integer}\}$ ($\{2, 4, 6, 8 \dots \}$)
      b. $\{x: x = 7y, y \text{ an integer}\}$ ($\{7, 14, 21, 28 \dots \}$)

The set defined in (3a) consists of multiples of 2; the one in (3b) of multiples of 7. The two sets are defined in exactly the same way, except the value of the multiplier of y: this value can be seen as a parameter defining the different sets. We observe that a simple change in the value of that integer, holding all else constant in the intensional definitions of the two sets, gives rise to two sets with very different extensions. This is an important point that the linguistic and mathematical notions of parameter have in common.

So we can say that there is a "*wh*-movement parameter" which gives languages (or, more precisely, grammars), the option of overt *wh*-movement or *wh*-in-situ (lack of overt movement), as follows:

(4)   *Wh*-movement (e.g., English, Italian) vs. *wh*-in-situ (e.g., Chinese, Japanese)

UG principles define what *wh*-elements are (a kind of quantificational determiner, presumably) and the nature of the movement operation (Internal Merge, in current formulations); a parameter such as that in (4) determines whether overt movement takes place.

Parameters tell us what is variant (and by implication what is invariant) in grammars, and as such they:

(5)   a. predict the dimensions of language typology;
      b. predict aspects of language acquisition;
      c. *predict what can change in the diachronic dimension.*

Here, of course, our main concern is with (5c). Before coming to that, however, let us look more closely at the connection between a hypothesised invariant UG and syntactic change.

2   Universal Grammar and the poverty of the stimulus

The principal argument for Universal Grammar is the "argument from the poverty of the stimulus" (for a recent formulation, see Berwick *et al.* (2011)). This argument is well summarised in the following quotations:

> the inherent difficulty of inferring an unknown target from finite resources ... in all such investigations, one concludes that *tabula rasa* learning is not possible. Thus children do not entertain every possible hypothesis that is consistent with the data they receive but only a limited class of hypotheses. This class of grammatical hypotheses H is the class of possible grammars children can conceive and therefore constrains the range of possible languages that humans can invent and speak. It is Universal Grammar in the terminology of generative linguistics.
>
> (Niyogi 2006: 12)

> The astronomical variety of sentences any natural language user can produce and understand has an important implication for language acquisition ... A child is exposed to only a small proportion of the possible sentences in its language, thus limiting its database for constructing a more general version of that language in its own mind/ brain. This point has logical implications for any system that attempts to acquire a natural language on the basis of limited data. It is immediately obvious that given a finite array of data, there are infinitely many theories consistent with it but inconsistent with one another. In the present case, there are in principle infinitely many target systems ... consistent with the data of experience, and unless the search space and acquisition mechanisms are constrained, selection among them is impossible... No known 'general learning mechanism' can acquire a natural language solely on the basis of positive or negative evidence, and the prospects for finding any such domain-independent device seem rather dim. The difficulty of this problem leads to the hypothesis that whatever system is responsible must be biased or constrained in certain ways. Such constraints have historically been termed 'innate dispositions,' with those underlying language referred to as 'universal grammar.'
>
> (Hauser *et al.* 2002: 1576–7)

The argument from the poverty of the stimulus is the main motivation for assuming an innate UG, which therefore must be essentially invariant across the species. First-language acquisition consists in setting parameters on the basis of Primary Linguistic Data (PLD). This scenario has an interesting consequence for diachronic linguistics generally and diachronic syntax in particular. Again, this is best summed up by a quotation, this time from Niyogi and Berwick (1995: 1):

> it is generally assumed that children acquire their ... target ... grammars without error. However, if this were always true, ... grammatical changes within a population would seemingly never occur, since generation after generation of children would have successfully acquired the grammar of their parents.

But of course it is clear that languages change. At the same time, it is clear that, except perhaps under unusual external conditions, acquisition is generally sufficiently close to convergent as to pose no serious problems of intergenerational communication. We could conclude, then, that most of the time most parameter values do not change. This idea has been encapsulated as the Inertia Principle by Keenan (2002: 2) (see also Longobardi 2001):

(6) Things stay as they are unless acted on by an outside force or decay.

Of course, we can think of this as nothing more than the usual case of convergent (or near-convergent) acquisition. We can define the central notions of convergent acquisition and syntactic change as follows:

(7) a. Convergent acquisition: for every $P_{1...n}$, the value $v_{1...m}$ of P_i in the acquirers' grammar converges on that of P_i in the grammar underlying the PLD;
     b. Syntactic change: at least one P in $P_{1...n}$ has value v_i in the acquirers' grammar and value $v_{i \neq j}$ in the grammar underlying the PLD.

Here we see very clearly the tension between convergent acquisition and syntactic change. Given the nature of acquisition, how is syntactic change, however "inertial", possible at all?

3 A dynamical-systems approach to language change

Niyogi and Berwick (1995; 1997) and Niyogi (2006) demonstrate on the basis of simulations of populations of acquirers that language change will arise given the following three things:

(8) a. a learning algorithm A
     b. a probability distribution of linguistic tokens across a population
     c. a restricted class of grammars from which to select (parametrised UG)

Given these three elements in the language-acquisition scenario (which, if one takes the learning algorithm to be a non-language-specific aspect of cognition, correspond closely to the "three factors of language design" of Chomsky 2005), variability will inevitably result *as long as the time allowed for the selection of hypotheses is restricted*. In other words: *the existence of a critical period for language acquisition may be sufficient to guarantee variation in a speech community* (in fact, a strong notion of the critical period is not needed; attainment of the steady state of adult-like competence in finite time is sufficient for the argument to go through, and this clearly happens).

To see more fully how this works, consider the following thought experiment put forward by Niyogi (2006: 14–15):

> imagine a world in which there are just two languages, L_{h1} and L_{h2}. Given a completely homogeneous community where all adults speak L_{h1}, and an infinite number of sentences in the Primary Linguistic Data, the child will always be able to apply a learning algorithm to converge on the language of the adults, and change will never take place.

This is clearly not a desirable or realistic scenario for language change. But consider, on the other hand, the following scenario:

> Now consider the possibility that the child is not exposed to an infinite number of sentences but only to a finite number N after which it matures and its language crystallizes.

Whatever grammatical hypothesis the child has after N sentences, it retains for the rest of its life. Under such a setting, if N is large enough, it might be the case that most children learn L_{h1}, but a small proportion ε end up acquiring L_{h2}. In one generation, a completely homogeneous community has lost its pure character. (Niyogi 2006: 15)

So, let us assume the following three elements:

(9) a. a UG capable of variation (a parametrised UG)
     b. the random distribution of PLD (poverty of the stimulus)
     c. the limited time for learning (critical period for language acquisition)

The result is that language change is inevitable. Note once more the closeness to the "three factors of language design" of Chomsky (2005). Note further that language change and language variation are essentially the same thing, from what one might call this "panchronic" perspective: the variation currently attested among the world's languages, as well as that which has existed at any point in the past back to, if Niyogi's scenario is correct, the second generation of humans to have language, is the result of diachronic change. The idea that change emerges from the interaction of the three factors of language design parallels the idea, actively pursued in Biberauer (2011), Biberauer and Branigan (forthcoming), Biberauer and Roberts (2012), Biberauer *et al.* (forthcoming b), and Roberts (2012) that parametric variation is an emergent property of the interaction of the three factors: UG is not in fact pre-specified for variation in the manner outlined in §1, but, rather, *underspecified*, with parametric variation created by the interaction of that underspecification, the learning algorithm, and the PLD.

This view is also consistent with the following ideas put forward by Niyogi (2006: xv–xiv):

much like phase transitions in physics, … the continuous drift of such frequency effects could lead to discontinuous changes in the stability of languages over time …

… the dynamics of language evolution are typically non-linear.

Finally, these considerations lead Niyogi (2006: 230) to formulate the following diachronic criterion of adequacy for grammatical theories:

[t]he class of grammars G (along with a proposed learning algorithm A) can be reduced to a dynamical system whose evolution must be consistent with that of the true evolution of human languages (as reconstructed from the historical data).

Like most adequacy criteria, this one sets the standard very high, making it difficult to reach. In order to get a sense of the empirical challenges involved, let us now look at some cases of syntactic change.

4 Some examples of syntactic change

As we saw in (7b), we construe syntactic change as change in the value of a parameter over time. More generally, a syntactic change takes place when a population of language acquirers converge on a grammatical system which differs in at least one parameter value from the system internalised by the speakers whose linguistic behaviour provides the input to those acquirers. This is basically the view articulated in Lightfoot (1979), the pioneering work on generative diachronic syntax (which in fact predates the development of the principles-and-parameters model, but the view of change as driven by language acquisition articulated there can be readily assimilated to the parametric approach; see Lightfoot (1991; 1999) and Roberts (2007)).

Furthermore, we take the view here that parametric variation reduces to variation in the formal features of functional categories (see Chomsky 1995); on the "emergentist" view of parametric variation alluded to above this amounts to the claim that these features are underspecified by UG. The "core functional categories" identified by Chomsky (2001) are C, T, and v, illustrated in the simple example in (10):

(10) [$_{CP}$ Who [$_{C'}$ did [$_{TP}$ Lisi [$_{T'}$ (did) [$_{vP}$ (Lisi) [$_{VP}$ see (who)]]]]]] ?

So C, T, and v are the categories whose underspecified features make parametric variation possible. With this much background, we can proceed to some cases.

4.1 Grammaticalisation

This kind of change, much discussed in the functional/typological literature on language change (see, in particular, Heine and Kuteva 2002; Narrog and Heine 2011), was originally identified (or at least the term was coined) by Meillet (1912: 132). He defined it as "the attribution of a grammatical character to a formerly independent word"; another characterisation is as "an evolution whereby linguistic units lose in semantic complexity, pragmatic significance, syntactic freedom, and phonetic substance" (Heine and Reh 1984: 15). Roberts and Roussou (2003) develop a formal approach to grammaticalisation which treats the phenomenon as the categorial reanalysis of a member of a lexical category as a member of a functional category (or from one functional category to another).

One very well-known case of grammaticalisation involves the English modals (see Lightfoot 1979; Roberts 1985; Warner 1993). In Middle English (up to roughly 1500) modals were raising and/or control verbs with infinitive (and other) complements. Some modals could also take direct objects, as shown in (11a), and they generally were able to appear in non-finite forms (although not with epistemic interpretations (11b)):

(11) a. direct objects:
          Wultu kastles and kinedomes? (c1225, Anon; Visser 1963–73: §549)
          "Will you [do you want] castles and kingdoms?"
      b. non-finite forms:
          I shall not konne answere (1386, Chaucer; Roberts 1985: 22)
          "I shall not can [be able to] answer."

By around 1550, modals had become restricted to finite contexts and, with a few exceptions, only show bare VP "complements". Roberts and Roussou suggest that the following structural reanalysis affected the modals, probably at some point in the early sixteenth century:

(12) [$_{TP}$ it [$_{T}$ may [$_{vP}$ (may) [$_{TP}$ (it) happen]]]] >
      [$_{TP}$ it [$_{T}$ may [$_{vP}$ happen]]]

This structural reanalysis involves categorial change: V becomes T; following a standard view of the nature of functional categories we can take this to entail the loss of argument structure of the original V, contributing to what is known as "semantic bleaching" in the functional/typological literature.

Roberts and Roussou further suggest that the cause of the change was loss of infinitive ending on verbs (formerly $-e(n)$), which took place c.1500. Prior to that time, although becoming ever rarer during the fifteenth century, we find forms such as the following:

(13) nat can we se**en** ...
      Not can we see
      "we cannot see"
                (c.1400: Hoccleve *The Letter of Cupid* 299; Gray 1985: 49; Roberts 1993: 261)

Roberts and Roussou suggest that the presence of the infinitival ending triggered the postulation of a non-finite T in the complement to the modal. Once this was lost (presumably due to phonological change), there was no trigger for the non-finite T and hence no bar to the reanalysis in (9), which only has a single T node. If we further assume a general conservative preference on the part of acquirers to postulate the minimal amount of structure consistent with UG and the PLD (this can be seen as a third-factor optimisation strategy; this preference is more explicitly formulated in (29) below), then the reanalysis will be favoured once the infinitive is lost. It is striking that the reanalysis took place within at most fifty years (i.e., roughly two generations) of that loss.

Another possible case of V becoming T is Mandarin aspectual *le* (Sun 1996: 82ff.). This marker of completive aspect derives diachronically from the verb *liao*, "to complete". The change is illustrated by the examples in (14):

(14) a. zuo ci yu liao
          make DEM words complete
          "(One) finished making this statement."
          (10th century (?): *Dunhuang Bianwen*; Sun (1996: 88))
      b. wo chi le   fan le
          I   eat Asp food Asp
          "I have eaten."

Whether *le* is in T or some other clausal functional head in contemporary Chinese is a question that would take us too far afield here. It clearly seems to be a functional head in the contemporary language, and *liao* was clearly a verb at the earlier stage, and so we are witnessing another case of grammaticalisation as characterised by Roberts and Roussou here.

Grammaticalisation seems ubiquitous in the histories of all the languages for which we have reasonable historical attestation. Here are some further examples, from Campbell (1998: 239–40). In each case, I have indicated the plausible categorial reanalysis, although of course many of these require further substantiation (cases (15a, c, f, i) are discussed in detail by Roberts and Roussou):

(15) a. complementiser < "say" (many West African languages):
          V > C

b. copula < positional verbs (e.g., Spanish *estar* < Latin *stare* "to stand"):
V > v/T

c. definite article < demonstrative pronoun (Romance *il/le/el* < Lat *ille*):
A > D

d. direct-object markers < locatives/prepositions (Spanish *a*)

e. existential constructions < "have"/locative (*there is/are*, Fr *il y a*)
V > v/T

f. future < "want", "have", "go" (English *will*, Romance *–ai* forms, English *gonna*)
V > T

g. indefinite article < "one" (Germanic, Romance)
N > D

h. indefinite pronoun < "man" (German *man*, French *on*)
N > D

i. negative < minimisers, indefinites (many languages)
N > Neg/D

The different cases of grammaticalisation listed here also illustrate parametric variation in the realisation of functional heads as free morphemes, affixes, or zero. The future forms in Romance languages can illustrate. Here we take them all to realise T[+future]. Each example means "I will sing":

(16) French: chanter-ai   ("I will sing"; suffix)
Rumanian: voi cînta   (auxiliary)
Southern Italian dialects: canto   (no special form)

So we see how grammaticalisation falls under the general characterisation of parametric change adopted here.

4.2 Word-order change

It is clear that languages differ in the surface order of heads and their complements. English and the Romance languages are essentially head-initial, and so verbs precede their objects and auxiliaries precede their VP complements. Other languages show the opposite, head-final, ordering of most heads and complements. Japanese is a well-known example:

(17) a. Sensei-wa   **Taro-o   sikata**.   – O V
teacher-TOP Taro-ACC scolded
"The teacher scolded Taro"

b. John-ga   Mary-to   renaisite   iru   – V Aux
John-NOM Mary-with in-love   is
"John is in love with Mary."

Where there is synchronic variation, there is diachronic change. Word-order change is in fact attested in the recorded history of English. So, in Old English (OE) subordinate clauses we find a very strong tendency to verb-final order:

(18) a.   ... þæt ic **þas boc** of   Ledenum gereordre to Engliscre spræce **awende**
           ... that I this book from Latin   language to English   tongue translate
           "... that I translate this book from the Latin language to the English tongue."
           (AHTh, I, pref, 6; van Kemenade 1987: 16)
      b.   ... forþon of   Breotone nædran on scippe **lædde wæron**.
           ... because from Britain   adders on ships brought were
           "... because vipers were brought on ships from Britain"

(Bede 30.1–2; Pintzuk 1991: 117)

Similarly in Latin there is a strong tendency to verb-final order (although Ledgeway 2012 argues that, despite this being the archaic order, Latin was already changing to VO as early as Plautus (200 BC); literary Classical Latin showed a strong tendency to OV order as an artificial stylistic device imitating the high-prestige archaic language):

(19) Latin:
      a.   Caesar Aeduos **frumentum flagitabat**
           Caesar Aedui   corn   was-demanding
           "Caesar kept demanding the corn of the Aedui"
           (Vincent 1988: 59)
      b.   ut .. ad ciuitatem gemitus popoli   omnis **auditus sit**
           that to city   groan   of-people all   heard   be
           "that the groans of all the people be heard (as far as) the town"
                            (*Peregr. Aeth.* 36, 3; Ernout and Thomas 1993: 229)

Compare the Latin examples in (19) with the corresponding sentences in Modern French:

(20) a.   César **exigeait**   **le blé** aux   Aeduis
           Caesar was-requiring the corn to-the A.
           "Caesar kept demanding the corn of the Aedui"
      b.   que les gémissements de tout le peuple **soient entendus** jusqu'en ville
           that the groans   of all the people be   heard   as-far-as town
           "that the groans of all the people be heard (as far as) the town"

Whatever the precise dating of the change, particularly its early stages, it is clear that between (early) Latin and Modern Romance there has been a general shift from head-initial to head-final patterns (see Ledgeway 2012: Ch. 5, for very detailed discussion and illustration).

Further, Li and Thompson (1974a; 1974b) assert that Mandarin word-order has been drifting from VO to OV for 2000 years (see also Huang 2013).

The "antisymmetric" approach to the relation between linear order and hierarchical structure introduced by Kayne (1994), which has the consequence that surface head-final orders are the result of leftward-movement of complements, allows us to think of word-order variation, and therefore word-order change, as due to parametric variation and change in leftward-movement options. For example, one way to derive OV and VAux orders would be as illustrated in (21) (the bracketed constituents are copies of moved elements):

(21) OV: [$_{vP}$ Obj [v [$_{VP}$ V (Obj)]]
      VAux: [$_{vP}$ VP [[$_v$ Aux] (VP)]]

Change from head-final to head-initial orders, then, involves the loss of leftward-movement. As already mentioned, Ledgeway (2012: Ch. 5) develops this approach in detail for the change from Latin to Romance, while Biberauer and Roberts (2005) illustrate it for the history of English. We can reduce this to the general characterisation of parameters given above if we assume that leftward-movement is triggered by a formal feature of functional heads (see Biberauer *et al.* (forthcoming) for a version of this idea).

4.3   Verb movement

A further kind of change, less readily documented in non-generative work on syntactic change, has to do with the loss or gain of various kinds of head-movement. The best-studied case of this kind involves the loss of verb-movement to T in Early Modern English, of the kind demonstrated to exist in Modern French but not (for main verbs) in Modern English by Pollock (1989).

In Early Modern English, until approximately 1600 or slightly later, main verbs were able to move to T (see Warner 1997: 381–386 for a very interesting discussion of the chronology of this change). We can see this from the fact that main verbs could be separated from their direct objects by negation and by adverbs, as in the following examples:

(22)   a.   if I **gave not** this accompt to you
             "if I didn't give this account to you"
             (1557: J. Cheke, Letter to Hoby; Görlach 1991: 223; Roberts 1999: 290)
       b.   The Turkes … **made anone redy** a grete ordonnaunce
             "The Turks … soon prepared a great ordnance."
             (c.1482: Kaye, *The Delectable Newsse of the Glorious Victorye of the Rhodyans agaynest the Turkes*; Gray 1985: 23; Roberts 1993: 253)

Examples such as these have a slightly familiar "Shakespearean" feel for many speakers of present-day English. Shakespeare lived from 1564 to 1616, and so in his English V-movement to T was possible; hence examples of the type in (22) can be found in his plays and poems. Despite this air of familiarity, the examples in (22) are ungrammatical in present-day English.

We take examples such as (22) to tell us that sixteenth-century English had the "French" value for V-to-T movement. If so, then if residual verb-second (e.g., in root interrogatives) involves T-to-C movement, as is widely assumed, we expect that main verbs were able to move to C in residual V2 environments at this time. This is correct, as (23) shows:

(23)   What **menythe this pryste**?
       What does this priest mean?
       (1466–7: Anon., from J. Gairdner (ed.), 1876, *The Historical Collections of a London Citizen*; Gray 1985: 11; Roberts 1993: 247)

(23) is ungrammatical for modern speakers. Here the main verb moves from V to T to C. V-to-T movement is allowed at this period of the language, as it is in Modern French.

Also, if it is correct to link Scandinavian-style object shift to V-to-T movement (Holmberg's Generalisation, see Holmberg 1986), we expect to find object shift in sixteenth-century English. Again, this expectation is borne out:

(24) a. if you **knew them** not

(1580, John Lyly; Roberts 1995: 274)

b. they **tell vs** not the worde of God

(1565, Thomas Stapleton; Roberts 1995: 274)

Here V has moved to T (we know this because it precedes *not*). The pronominal object (in fact it is an indirect object in (24b)) also precedes *not* and so we take this element, too, to have left VP. In (24b), the direct object presumably remains within VP.

Transitive expletive constructions are also found in earlier periods of English, up until approximately the sixteenth century, as (25) shows:

(25) a. Within my soul there doth conduce a fight

(Shakespeare; Jonas (1996: 151))

b. ... there had fifteene severall Armados assailed her

(1614, Ralegh Selections 151; Jonas 1996: 154)

So we witness the clustering of non-adjacency of the main verb and its direct object, main-verb movement to C in residual V2, transitive expletive constructions, and object-shift in sixteenth-century English. This cluster of properties in sixteenth-century English, and the absence of these properties in present-day English, may all be related to the loss of the V-to-T movement option – that is, a change in the movement-triggering property of finite T – at some point between the sixteenth century and the present.

It is possible, as originally suggested by Roberts (1985) (see also Rohrbacher 1997; Vikner 1995; 1997), that one causal factor involved in this change was the loss of verbal agreement marking in the sixteenth century, in particular the loss of plural agreement in present- and past-tense verbs (i.e., forms such as *we singen/sangen*). This idea, which has come to be known as the Rich Agreement Hypothesis, has proven somewhat controversial, in that it is difficult to identify exactly how much agreement is required for V-to-T movement; see Koeneman and Zeijlstra (2012) for a recent discussion. It is clear that the grammaticalisation of modals as T-elements, as discussed in §4.1, and the concomitant development of the apparently dummy auxiliary *do*, also played a role (see Roberts 1993; 2007).

4.4 Conclusion

Of course, the above examples do not exhaust the types of syntactic change, but they represent major instances of it. The very brief and oversimplified exposition given here illustrates how powerful the simple idea that syntactic change is change in the formal features of functional heads can be. Of course, the task is then to extend this to other types of syntactic change (see Roberts (2007) for discussion and illustration). But, having established the potential utility of the mechanism of parametric change, let us now look at its nature more closely.

In each case, we are dealing with syntactic change as defined in (7b). Owing to changes in the PLD, language contact, phonological and morphological changes, or perhaps earlier syntactic changes, a new system – new at least in relation to the system converged on by the preceding generation – is acquired.

The acquired systems stabilise after the critical period of language acquisition, and are typically associated with social and cultural value (see Weinreich *et al.* 1968) in an ultimately quite arbitrary way, as far as the system itself is concerned. It follows from this that language acquirers have the ability to acquire variation and have the capacity to "acquire" (perhaps more accurately "abduce") a new system. Interestingly, both of these conclusions depart from the usual idealisations in theoretical work on language acquisition.

So, an underspecified UG, allowing random variation in a few small areas, interacting with the PLD and the learning algorithm (which may itself impose certain preferences), gives rise to the phenomena of variation – both sociolinguistic and cross-linguistic – and change.

5 Parameter hierarchies and parameter change

Generally speaking, there has been a tendency in principles-and-parameters theory to think of all parameters as equal, at least in terms of their formal properties if not in terms of their effects on the outputs of the grammars they determine. A notable exception to this is Baker (2008), who distinguishes macro- and microparameters. In recent work, Biberauer and Roberts (2012) have developed this idea further, isolating four classes of parameter: **macro**, **meso**, **micro** and **nano**. They suggest the following rough taxonomy:

(26) For a given value v_i of a parametrically variant feature F:

    a. **Macroparameters**: all heads of the relevant type share v_i;
    b. **Mesoparameters**: all heads of a given naturally definable class, e.g. [+V], share v_i;
    c. **Microparameters**: a small, lexically definable subclass of functional heads (e.g. modal auxiliaries, pronouns) shows v_i;
    d. **Nanoparameters**: one or more individual lexical items is/are specified for v_i.

Following the general view of parametric change as involving abductive reanalysis of PLD through language acquisition, Biberauer and Roberts propose that **macroparameters** must be "easily" set; hence they resist reanalysis and are strongly conserved. **Meso-** and **microparameters** are correspondingly less salient in the PLD, and, subject to frequency considerations, **nanoparameters** are still more so; these are like irregular verbs, item-specific specifications which override the default specified by the Elsewhere Condition, and will be diachronically "regularised" unless sufficiently frequent.

In terms of Roberts' (2012) proposal for parameter hierarchies, the different kinds of parameters are hierarchically related to one another:

(27) *Hierarchy 1: Word order:*

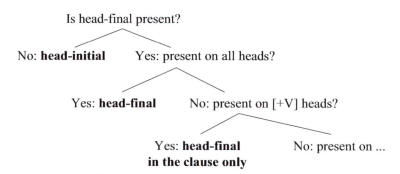

Here "head-final" can be reduced to a complement-movement feature, as described above in relation to the general approach in Kayne (1994). This hierarchy then really concerns the distribution of the feature triggering complement-movement. Roberts (2012) tentatively identifies four further hierarchies (concerning null arguments, word structure, A'-movement, and Case/Agree/A-movement). In terms of this conception of parameters, true macroparameters sit at the top of the network. As we move successively down, systems become more marked in relation to two third-factor induced markedness conditions, Input Generalization and Feature Economy (see below), parameters become meso then micro then nano (with the last of these effectively meaning "non-parametric"), and, most important for present purposes, systems become diachronically closer.

Once again, it is important to see that the hierarchies are *not* prespecified, but emerge from the interaction of the underspecified UG, the PLD, and the general markedness conditions, determining learning strategies and deriving from third-factor optimisation. The two conditions are Feature Economy (FE) (Roberts and Roussou 2003: 201), already mentioned briefly in the discussion of grammaticalisation above, and Input Generalisation (Roberts 2007: 274):

(28) a. Feature Economy:
          Given two structural representations R and R' for a substring of input text S, R is less marked than R' iff R contains fewer formal features than R';
      b. Input Generalisation (IG):
          If a functional head F sets parameter P_j to value v_i then there is a preference for similar functional heads to set P_j to value v_i.

Feature Economy implies, from the acquirer's perspective, that the minimum number of formal features consistent with the input should be postulated. Input Generalisation plausibly follows from the acquirer's initial "ignorance" of categorial distinctions (see Biberauer 2011; Branigan 2012); it is also possible that macroparameters may be set at a stage of acquisition at which categorial distinctions have yet to be acquired, and hence their nature may be due to the "ignorance" of the learner (Biberauer 2011; Branigan 2012). In this view, as categorial distinctions emerge, mesoparameters become available, refining the early acategorial, or categorially impoverished, system. Further, as functional categories emerge, microparameters become possible (see also Biberauer 2008: 12). This view can then explain how "superset" parameters can be set early without a "superset trap" arising; hence it is consistent with the Subset Principle (see Berwick 1985; Biberauer and Roberts 2009).

It follows from all of this that macroparameters are likely to be highly conserved diachronically. In relation to the word-order hierarchy given in (23), this implies that harmonically head-initial and head-final systems are likely to be stable. Certainly, several rigidly head-final systems are known to have been stably head-final for long periods: this is true of Dravidian (Steever 1998: 31) and of both Japanese and Korean, as far as we are aware, all three having at least a millennium of attestation and showing a consistent head-final ordering throughout that time. The same is true of radical pro-drop (the least marked null-argument option, according to Roberts 2012), attested throughout the recorded histories of Chinese and Japanese, for example, and of polysynthesis (perhaps the best-known example of a macroparameter, since Baker 1996): according to Branigan (2012), Proto-Algonquian was spoken 2000–3000 years ago. In that time numerous structural, lexical, and phonological features have changed, but polysynthesis has remained as a constant property of the family.

Ian Roberts

An example of a mesoparameter might be the classical null-subject or "pro-drop" parameter, as manifested in Latin and (most) Romance. Following Rizzi (1986), we can roughly characterise this as follows:

(29) T {has/lacks} the capacity to "license" *pro* in its Specifier.

This parameter has wide-ranging effects on the output, in that it affects all (finite) subjects, and there may be other associated effects involving "free" inversion and subject-extraction across complementisers (see Rizzi 1982). Diachronically, it has been stable from Latin through most of the recorded histories of Italian, Spanish, and Portuguese (except Brazilian since c.1900). North-West Romance varieties (French, some Northern Italian varieties, and Rhaeto-Romance) have, to varying degrees and in different ways, lost the fully productive null-subject option. This may have been due to Germanic influence.

6 The study of historical syntax

Against this general background, how should we go about studying syntactic change? To meet Niyogi's diachronic criterion of adequacy given at the end of §3 we must develop a greater understanding of each of the three elements which, according to Niyogi (2006), contribute to the dynamical system that is a language being spoken by a population. These are as follows:

(30) A. Learning and acquisition
      B. Language variation and population dynamics
      C. Language typology and UG.

To get a sense of the difficult nature of connecting acquisition and change, consider the fact that, between the ages of 2 and 3 years old, i.e. some time before linguistic maturity if this is characterised as the stable state, children know at least the following about the parameter values of the language they are in the process of acquiring (cf. Wexler (1998) on Very Early Parameter Setting):

(31) a. the value of the head direction parameter in their native language;
      b. the value of the V-to-T parameter in their native language;
      c. the value of the topic-drop and null-subject parameters;
      d. the value of the parameters governing question formation, the one governing overt movement or in-situ placement of the *wh*-element and the one regulating T-to-C movement (inversion).

                                                        (Guasti 2002: 148, 185, 242)

As we have seen, all of the parameters listed in (31) can be shown to be subject to diachronic change (see Roberts (2007: Ch. 1) for more detailed discussion). Hence change can be introduced at very early stages of acquisition, which are hard to directly study using standard methods. For further discussion of the relation between acquisition and change and the difficulties in documenting it, see Roberts (2007: Ch. 3).

Concerning the relation between language typology and UG, fruitful interaction is possible. A recent illustration of this comes from the Final-over-Final Constraint (FOFC), as discussed by Biberauer *et al.* (forthcoming a; henceforth BHR). FOFC can be stated informally as follows:

(32) A head-initial phrase cannot be immediately dominated by a head-final phrase in the same Extended Projection.

In other words, the configuration (33) is ruled out, where αP is dominated by a projection of β, γP is a sister of α, and α and β are heads in the same Extended Projection:

(33) *[$_{\beta P}$ ... [$_{\alpha P}$ ... α ... γP] ... β ...]

BHR show that FOFC accounts for the following cross-linguistically unattested orders (their (47), p. 42):

(34) *V-O-Aux   *[$_{AuxP}$ [$_{VP}$ V DP] Aux]
     *V-O-C   *[$_{CP}$ [$_{TP}$ T VP] C] or *[$_{CP}$ [$_{TP}$ [$_{VP}$ V O] T] C]
     *C-TP-V   *[$_{VP}$ [$_{CP}$ C TP] V]
     *N-O-P   *[$_{PP}$ [$_{DP/NP}$ D/N PP] P]
     *Num-NP-D(em)   *[$_{D(em)P}$ [$_{NumP}$ Num NP] D(em)]
     *Pol-TP-C   *[$_{CP}$ [$_{PolP}$ Pol TP] C]

FOFC has important implications for syntactic change. In the case of the verbal-sentential projections change from head-final to head-initial must proceed as follows:

(36) [[[O V] I] C] $\rightarrow$ [C [[O V] I]] $\rightarrow$ [C [I [O V]]] $\rightarrow$ [C [I [V O]]].

Any other route will violate FOFC. On the other hand, change from head-initial to head-final order will have to proceed 'bottom-up':

(37) [C [I [V O]]] $\rightarrow$ [C [I [O V]]] $\rightarrow$ [C [[O V] I]] $\rightarrow$ [[[O V] I] C].

Any other route will violate FOFC. There is in fact evidence from the history of English that the order in IP changed from head-final to head-initial before that in VP (see Biberauer *et al.* 2009: 8; Biberauer *et al.* 2010). Work on the history of Yiddish by Santorini (1992) and Wallenberg (2009) suggests that exactly the same thing happened in the history of Yiddish. Biberauer *et al.* (2010) also observe that OV to VO change from Latin to French appears to have followed the same pattern, with Ledgeway (2012: Ch. 5) showing in great detail that the same seems to hold true for ongoing word-order change in Latin to Romance, again a change from head-final to head-initial order.

Clearly, even approaching Niyogi's criterion of diachronic adequacy requires expertise in comparative and historical syntax, typology, acquisition, and population dynamics. But if "we are generalists in this way, then linguists can attain a level of explanation quite unlike what one finds in historical studies in other domains, such as the theory of biological species or political systems" (Lightfoot 2006: 166). This is certainly a goal to aspire to.

7 Conclusions

The variation and change that is prevalent in language finds its natural explanation within a Chomskyan linguistic paradigm. The existence of variation and change in language does not in any way argue against the generative approach to explaining language, contrary to what has often been asserted.

At this point in the development of the study of diachronic syntax we should "take advantage of the combined insights of the two major scientific revolutions in linguistics, those which gave rise respectively to the historical-comparative paradigm during the XIX century and the 'synchronic-cognitive' paradigm in the XX. It is such a combination that may yield substance to a good deal of the historical-explanatory program" (Longobardi 2003: 5).

Further reading

Lightfoot, D. 1979. *Principles of Diachronic Syntax*. Cambridge: Cambridge University Press.
Roberts, I. 2007. *Diachronic Syntax*. Oxford: Oxford University Press.
Weinreich, U., W. Labov, and W. Herzog. 1968. Empirical foundations for a theory of language change. In *Directions for Historical Linguistics*, ed. W. Lehmann and Y. Malkiel, 95–195. Austin: University of Texas Press.

References

Baker, M. 1996. *The Polysynthesis Parameter*. New York/Oxford: Oxford University Press.
Baker, M. 2001. *The Atoms of Language: The Mind's Hidden Rules of Grammar*. Oxford: Oxford University Press.
Baker, M. 2008. The macroparameter in a microparametric world. In *The Limits of Syntactic Variation*, ed. T. Biberauer, 351–74. Amsterdam: Benjamins.
Berwick, R. 1985. *The Acquisition of Syntactic Knowledge*. Cambridge, MA: MIT Press.
Berwick, Robert C., Paul Pietroski, Beracah Yankama, and Noam Chomsky. 2011. Poverty of the stimulus revisited. *Cognitive Science* 35(7):1207–1242.
Biberauer, T. (ed.). 2008. *The Limits of Syntactic Variation*. Amsterdam: Benjamins.
Biberauer, T. 2011. In defence of lexico-centric parametric variation: two 3rd factor-constrained case studies. Paper presented at the Workshop on Formal Grammar and Syntactic Variation: Rethinking Parameters (Madrid).
Biberauer, T., and P. Branigan. forthcoming. *Microparametric Expression of a Macroparameter: Afrikaans Verb Clusters and Algonquian Grammars*. Abstract: Universities of Cambridge/Stellenbosch and Memorial University, Newfoundland.
Biberauer, T., and I. Roberts. 2005. Changing EPP-parameters in the history of English: accounting for variation and change. *English Language and Linguistics* 9:5–46.
Biberauer, T., and I. Roberts. 2009. The return of the subset principle. In *Historical Linguistics and Linguistic Theory*, ed. P. Crisma and G. Longobardi, 58–74. Oxford: Oxford University Press.
Biberauer, T., and I. Roberts. 2012. The significance of what hasn't happened. Talk given at DiGS 14, Lisbon.
Biberauer, T., G. Newton, and M. Sheehan. 2009. Limiting synchronic and diachronic variation and change: the final-over-final constraint. *Language and Linguistics* 10(4):699–741.
Biberauer, T., M. Sheehan, and G. Newton. 2010. Impossible changes and impossible borrowings: the final-over-final constraint. In *Continuity and Change in Grammar*, ed. Anne Breitbarth, Christopher Lucas, Sheila Watts, and David Willis, 35–60. Amsterdam: John Benjamins.
Biberauer, T., A. Holmberg, and I. Roberts. forthcoming a. A syntactic universal and its consequences. To appear in *Linguistic Inquiry*.
Biberauer, T., A. Holmberg, I. Roberts, and M. Sheehan. forthcoming b. Complexity in comparative syntax: The view from modern parametric theory. In *Measuring Grammatical Complexity*, ed. F. Newmeyer and Laurel B. Preston. Oxford: Oxford University Press.
Branigan, Phil. 2012. Macroparameter learnability: an Algonquian case study. Ms. Memorial University of Newfoundland.
Campbell, L. 1998. *Historical Linguistics*. Edinburgh: University of Edinburgh Press.
Chomsky, N. 1965. *Aspects of the Theory of Syntax*. Cambridge, MA: MIT Press.
Chomsky, N. 1975. *Reflections on Language*. New York: Pantheon.

Chomsky, N. 1980. *Rules and Representations.* New York: Columbia University Press.

Chomsky, N. 1981. *Lectures on Government and Binding.* Dordrecht: Kluwer.

Chomsky, N. 1986. *Knowledge of Language: Its Nature, Origins and Use.* New York: Praeger.

Chomsky, N. 1995. *The Minimalist Program.* Cambridge, MA: MIT Press.

Chomsky, N. 2001. Derivation by phase. In *Ken Hale: A Life in Language*, ed. M. Kenstowicz, 1–52. Cambridge, MA: MIT Press.

Chomsky, N. 2005. Three factors in language design. *Linguistic Inquiry* 36:1–22.

Ernout, A., and F. Thomas. 1993. *Syntaxe Latine.* Paris: Klincksieck.

Görlach, M. 1991. *Introduction to Early Modern English.* Cambridge: Cambridge University Press.

Gray, D. 1985. *The Oxford Book of Late Medieval Prose and Verse.* Oxford: Oxford University Press.

Guasti, M.-T. 2002. *Language Acquisition: The Growth of Grammar.* Cambridge, MA: MIT Press.

Hauser, M., N. Chomsky, and W. Fitch. 2002. The faculty of language: What is it, who has it, and how did it evolve? *Science* 298:1569–1579.

Heine, B.. and T. Kuteva. 2002. *World Lexicon of Grammaticalization.* Cambridge: Cambridge University Press.

Heine, B., and M. Reh. 1984. *Grammaticalization and Reanalysis in African Languages.* Hamburg: Helmut Buske.

Holmberg, A. 1986. Word order and syntactic features in Scandinavian languages and English. PhD dissertation, University of Stockholm.

Huang, C.-T. J. 1982. Logical relations in Chinese and the theory of grammar. PhD dissertation, MIT.

Huang, C.-T. J. 2013. On syntactic analyticity and parametric Theory. To appear in *Handbook of Chinese Linguistics*, ed. C.-T. James Huang, Andrew Simpson, and Audrey Li. Oxford: Blackwell.

Jonas, D. 1996. Clause structure and verb syntax in Scandinavian and English. PhD dissertation, Harvard University.

Kayne, R. 1994. *The Antisymmetry of Syntax.* Cambridge, MA: MIT Press.

Keenan, E. 2002. Explaining the creation of reflexive pronouns in English. In *Studies in the History of English: A Millennial Perspective*, ed. D. Minkova and R. Stockwell, 325–355. Berlin: Mouton de Gruyter.

Koeneman, Olaf, and Hedde Zeijlstra. 2012. One law for the rich and another for the poor: The rich agreement hypothesis rehabilitated. Ms. University of Amsterdam.

Ledgeway, Adam. 2012. *From Latin to Romance: Morphosyntactic Typology and Change.* Oxford: Oxford University Press.

Li, C., and S.A. Thompson. 1975a. The semantic function of word order: A case study in Mandarin. In *Word Order and Word Order Change*, ed. C. Li, 163–195. Austin, TX: University of Texas Press.

Li, C., and S.A. Thompson. 1975b. An explanation of word-order change SVO>SOV. *Foundations of Language* 12:201–214.

Lightfoot, D. 1979. *Principles of Diachronic Syntax.* Cambridge: Cambridge University Press.

Lightfoot, D. 1991. *How to Set Parameters: Arguments from Language Change*, Cambridge, MA: MIT Press.

Lightfoot, D. 1999. *The Development of Language.* Oxford: Blackwell.

Lightfoot, D. 2006. *How New Languages Emerge.* Cambridge: Cambridge University Press.

Longobardi, G. 2001. Formal syntax, diachronic minimalism, and etymology: The history of French *Chez. Linguistic Inquiry* 32:275–302.

Longobardi, G. 2003. Methods in parametric linguistics and cognitive history. Ms. University of Trieste.

Meillet, A. 1912. L'évolution des formes grammaticales. Repr. in A. Meillet. 1958. *Linguistique Historique et Linguistique Générale*, Paris: Champion, 130–158.

Narrog, Heiko, and Bernd Heine. 2011. *The Oxford Handbook of Grammaticalization.* Oxford: Oxford University Press.

Niyogi, P. 2006. *The Computational Nature of Language Learning and Evolution.* Cambridge, MA: MIT Press.

Niyogi, P., and R. Berwick. 1995. The logical problem of language change. A.I. Memo No. 1516, MIT Artificial Intelligence Laboratory.

Niyogi, P., and R. Berwick. 1997. A dynamical systems model for language change. *Complex Systems* 11:161–204.

Pintzuk, S. 1991. Phrase structure in competition: Variation and change in Old English word order. PhD dissertation, University of Pennsylvania.

Pollock, J.Y. 1989. Verb movement, universal grammar, and the structure of IP. *Linguistic Inquiry* 20:365–424.

Rizzi, L. 1982. *Issues in Italian Syntax*. Dordrecht: Foris.

Rizzi, L. 1986. Null objects in Italian and the theory of *pro*. *Linguistic Inquiry* 17:501–557.

Roberts, I. 1985. Agreement parameters and the development of English modal auxiliaries. *Natural Language and Linguistic Theory* 3:21–58.

Roberts, I. 1993. *Verbs and Diachronic Syntax: A Comparative History of English and French*. Dordrecht: Kluwer.

Roberts, I. 1995. Object movement and verb movement in Early Modern English. In *Studies in Comparative Germanic Syntax*, ed. H. Haider, S. Olsen and S. Vikner, 269–284. Dordrecht: Kluwer.

Roberts, I. 1999. Verb movement and markedness. In *Language Creation and Language Change*, ed. M. DeGraff, 287–328. Cambridge, MA: MIT Press.

Roberts, I. 2007. *Diachronic Syntax*. Oxford: Oxford University Press.

Roberts, I. 2012. Macroparameters and minimalism: A programme for comparative research. In *Parameter Theory and Linguistic Change*, ed. C. Galves, S. Cyrino, R. Lopes, F. Sandalo, and J. Avelar, pp. 320–335. Oxford: Oxford University Press.

Roberts, I., and A. Roussou. 2003. *Syntactic Change: A Minimalist Approach to Grammaticalization*. Cambridge: Cambridge University Press.

Rohrbacher, B. 1997. *Morphology-driven Syntax*. Amsterdam: Benjamins.

Santorini, Beatrice. 1992. Variation and change in Yiddish subordinate clause word order. *Natural Language and Linguistic Theory* 10:595–640.

Steever, S. 1998. *The Dravidian Languages*. London: Routledge.

Sun, C. 1996. *Word-order Change and Grammaticalization in the History of Chinese*. Stanford, CA: Stanford University Press.

van Kemenade, A. 1987. *Syntactic Case and Morphological Case in the History of English*. Dordrecht: Foris.

Vikner, S. 1995. *Verb Movement and Expletive Subjects in the Germanic Languages*. Oxford: Oxford University Press.

Vikner, S. 1997. V-to-I movement and inflection for person in all tenses. In *The New Comparative Syntax*, ed. L. Haegeman, 189–213. London: Longman.

Vincent, N. 1988. Latin. In *The Romance Languages*, ed. M. Harris and N. Vincent, 26–78. London: Routledge.

Visser, F. 1963–73. *An Historical Syntax of the English Language*. Leiden: Brill.

Wallenberg, Joel. 2009. Antisymmetry and the conservation of c-command: scrambling and phrase structure in synchronic and diachronic perspective. PhD dissertation, University of Pennsylvania.

Warner, A. 1993. *English Auxiliaries: Structure and History*. Cambridge: Cambridge University Press.

Warner, A. 1997. The structure of parametric change, and V movement in the history of English. In *Parameters of Morphosyntactic Change*, ed. A. van Kemenade and N. Vincent, 380–393. Cambridge: Cambridge University Press.

Weinreich, U., W. Labov, and W. Herzog. 1968. Empirical foundations for a theory of language change. In *Directions for Historical Linguistics*, ed. W. Lehmann and Y. Malkiel, 95–195. Austin: University of Texas Press.

Wexler, K. 1998. Very early parameter setting and the unique checking constraint: A new explanation of the optional infinitive stage. *Lingua* 106:23–79.

20

Syntax in forward and in reverse

Form, memory, and language processing

Matthew W. Wagers

1   Introduction

The goal of this chapter is to explore the ways in which syntactic structure guides and, sometimes, confound language comprehension. We will ask how language users encode and navigate the abstract compositional structures that intervene between sound and meaning; and we will do so by focusing on the mnemonic properties and processes of syntactic structure. In other words, how does the language user know where they are in an expression, where they're going, and where they've been? To investigate these properties, evidence and case studies will be brought to bear from the areas of verbatim memory and short-term forgetting in dependency formation. The latter area corresponds to the 'forward' and 'reverse' of the title and encompasses the formation of both local and non-local dependencies. The first, however, is a somewhat unconventional focus and a topic often confined to research in applied linguistics; but, as I will try to argue, it provides an underappreciated, if nuanced, source of evidence for the existence of durably encoded partial syntactic descriptions.

Contemporary theories of grammar share a commitment to richly structured mental representations as necessary components of mature linguistic competence (Bresnan 2001; Chomsky 1981; 1995; Pollard and Sag 1994; Steedman 2000). They may differ in the particulars – number and kinds of representation – but they all posit abstract categories that can be combined in regular ways to form ordered, compositional objects. Many important generalizations about grammatical dependencies rely upon hierarchies of dominance and command, whether they be stated over phrase structures, grammatical functions, thematic roles, or related such scales. The explanatory benefit of abstraction over structured representations comes with computational challenges, however. The richness of the structure and its reliance on ordering relations present interesting constraints to the language processor. In the timescale of comprehension (tens and hundreds of milliseconds to seconds) the comprehender must apply knowledge about grammatical categories and relations to recognize and understand actual expressions. At the sentence level, pairings of words to structure must be recognized and encoded as part of the current, novel utterance. Because natural language expressions can be of considerable complexity and temporal extent, these novel structures must be encoded semi-durably so that they are accessible to later operations.

Consider the example in (1):

(1) (a) The bank account <u>from which</u> the investor <u>transferred</u> *(the funds) (*from)...
     (b) The bank account <u>from which</u> the investor asked that the teller <u>transfer</u>
             *(the funds) (*from) ...
         ... was overdrawn.

To successfully understand (1a) or (1b), both of which contain a movement dependency, it is necessary that the comprehender coordinate information presented by the verb, such as its subcategorization frames or thematic roles, with the information present in the relativized argument – namely, that it was pied-piped with its containing PP, and that the head of the PP is 'from' (and *not* 'to' or 'for'). (1b), an example of the unboundedness property of movement dependencies, suggests that the comprehender must be able to coordinate information that spans more than one clause. Although syntactically local dependencies may not span as many syntactic domains as non-local dependencies, some can nonetheless be as indefinitely extended in time as non-local dependencies. Consider (2):

(2) (a) <u>The bank account</u> <u>was</u>/*were seized by the SEC.
     (b) <u>The bank account</u> [in the overseas tax haven] <u>was</u>/*were seized by the SEC.
     (c) <u>The bank account</u> [that was opened by the canny investors in the overseas
             tax haven] <u>was</u>/*were seized by the SEC.
     (d) <u>The bank account</u>, after many delays in the courts, <u>was</u>/*were seized by the SEC.

Here establishing the agreement relation between the subject verb can be linearly interrupted by post-modification by PPs (2b), relative clauses of varying lengths and complexity (2c), and pre-verbal adjuncts (2d).

In the 1960s and 1970s there emerged a basic consensus that gross properties of the constituent structure assigned to an expression by the grammar were reflected in various perceptual and mnemonic measures (Fodor *et al.* 1974; Levelt 1974). Today the majority of the studies supporting this conclusion would be dubbed 'off-line': for example, asking experimental participants to recall the location of noise burst in a recorded stimulus (Bever *et al.* 1969) or to assign scores to pairs of words based on how related they were felt to be (Levelt 1974). They are informative, however, about what might be called the 'steady-state' encoding: the representation that persists once major comprehension processes have concluded at the sentence level. As experimental techniques matured, it became possible to use measures and designs that could probe ongoing processing on the time-scale of single words, morphemes and syllables – these include various reading and listening techniques, eye-tracking, electro- or magnetoencephalography, and hemodynamic brain imaging. It has become possible to ask not just which grammatical distinctions are reflected in the steady-state encoding but also whether the rapidly changing cognitive descriptions *in media res* are themselves syntactic descriptions that accurately reflect the operations or constraints of the grammar. In the past twenty years, using the finer measures and examining a broader collection of relationships, the facts of the matter are, perhaps unsurprisingly, mixed. Some kinds of real-time comprehension processes are tightly regulated by the grammar and never show evidence that anything but a grammatical analysis is entertained. Some processes, however, seem to entertain analyses of the expression which the grammar cannot generate or must exclude. We'll take up explanations for grammatical *fidelity*, on the one hand, and grammatical *fallibility*, on the other, in §3.

We must first ask: what is memory for linguistic structure like such that it supports the formation of the local and non-local dependencies that are subject to particular grammatical constraints? Of course, language users are not perfect – and both dependency types exhibited in (1) and (2) are ones that lead to errors in both comprehension and production, such as agreement attraction in subject–verb agreement (Bock and Miller 1991), or blindness to subcategorization restrictions in pied-piping (Wagers 2008). From these errors, we can hope to learn what stresses the real-time system and whether such stresses are related to memory mechanisms. First, however, I want to consider a more direct method of probing memory for syntactic structure: performance in recall and recognition.

As a point of departure, let us consider a classic finding from the literature on memory for lists: namely, that a string of words is more memorable if those words form a sentence, a fact dubbed the 'sentence superiority' effect. Miller and Isard (1964), among others, provided a dramatic demonstration of this fact in their study on center self-embedding. They taught participants very long sentences – twenty-two words in length – containing a series of relative clauses. Either the relative clauses were completely right-embedded, or between one and four of them were center self-embedded. Participants heard five repetitions of a test sentence and, following each repetition, tried to recall the sentence verbatim. In each item set, there was one condition in which the order of words was scrambled to create an ungrammatical 'word salad' list. Following sentences with zero or one self-embedded relatives, participants could recall around 80 percent of the words correctly on the first trial; and, by five repetitions, nearly 100 percent of the words could be recalled correctly. Unsurprisingly, sentences with center self-embeddings were much harder to recall at any given repetition: after the first trial, the percentage of correctly recalled words was only 60 percent; and, after five repetitions, it remained between 80–90 percent. By comparison, however, the word-salad condition only ever achieved 50 percent correct recall and only after five repetitions. In other words, even quadruple center self-embeddings – which are pathologically difficult to understand – are more memorable than a list containing the same words in a non-syntactically legal order. Despite the vintage of this finding (its fiftieth birthday approaches), the sentence superiority effect is something that theorists of human memory have continued to investigate (Baddeley *et al.* 2009).

For Miller and Isard (1964), the reason that linguistic structure should unburden memory is that it allows the perceiver to recode a stimulus from a level of analysis at which its constituent elements are numerous – such as a set of lexemes – to one at which its constituent elements are fewer – such as a set of clauses or other syntactic categories. This recoding, now ubiquitously referred to as 'chunking' in cognitive psychology (Miller 1956), is an appealing explanation for the sentence superiority effect because it directly relates memorability to the available compositional descriptions. The sentence superiority effect is thus thought to obtain because a syntactic level of description allows for ten to twenty labeled tokens (in the case of Miller and Isard 1964) to be replaced by maybe four or five. Chunking, thought of in these terms, has often been linked to the notion of short-term memory *capacity* (for a review, see Cowan (2001)). The term 'capacity' might suggest to us something like a claim about the *amount* of information that can be maintained or stored in memory. But it is important to recall that participants ultimately do recall an ordered list of words in these experiments – not a list of syntactic labels. As Fodor *et al.* (1974) observed, imposing a syntactic description on a sequence of words also *adds* considerable information: syntactic category labels, dominance relations, agreement features, and so on.

However, any apparent tension between storage capacity and the richness of syntactic representation can be dissolved if we abandon the idea that capacity is a claim about "amount of stuff that can be stored" (or the number of chunks that can happily inhabit short-term memory). And this indeed was exactly the point of Miller (1956), who observed that descriptions from a wide range of domains (letters, digits, words) run up against a relatively constant recoding limit, despite the varying amount of information required to represent a numeral versus a word versus a phrase.

What can we then say about the sentence superiority effect? A first attempt: the sentence superiority effect, as an instance of chunking, reflects an efficiency in memory management that the linguistic description affords. The problem with recalling twenty-two words in order, when those words do not form a sentence, is that the only solution to the problem is to remember each of the twenty-two words individually and to remember which word precedes the next. By adding information such as constituency or case or agreement, syntactic representations provide many more paths to recall individual nodes; the more routes to recalling an item, the more robust that item will be to forgetting (Anderson and Neely 1996). Words are no longer uniquely identified by their relative position in a chain, but rather they can be identified as the label of this complement or of that specifier, or the recipient of this thematic role or that grammatical function. By forcing representation at a complex but systematic level, the comprehender can take advantage of the regularity of syntactic structure to generate a set of cues rich enough and robust enough to reconstruct the string. A related possibility is that we routinely store whole or partial linguistic representations in a state that has virtually no capacity limitations, namely, in long-term memory. This claim may seem counterintuitive to some, but it is in fact a claim that many recent contemporary memory models force us into making – for example, Ericsson and Kintsch's long-term working memory model (1995) or content-addressable architectures with a commitment to stringent limitations on short-term memory (e.g., McElree 1998; McElree et al. 2003). We take up this possibility in greater depth in §3. The sentence superiority effect, in this case, would reflect a state of affairs in which short-term memory can contain sufficiently comprehensive cues or indexes to what has been stored in long-term memory. A simple view, but one compatible with a wide range of evidence, is that these indexes refer to large clause-like domains[1] (Glanzer et al. 1981; Roberts and Gibson 2002; Gilchrist et al. 2008). Additionally, there may be some additional welcome consequences to the idea that incidental syntactic representations are stored in a more or less durable long-term form – these include serving as input to processes of acquisition, learning, and adaptation involved in deriving form-based generalizations and in optimizing predictive behavior (see §3).

Before moving on to more evidence and case studies, it is worth returning to what is perhaps an underappreciated point in Miller and Isard (1964). Their experiment is often cited as an early experimentally controlled demonstration of the degradedness of center self-embedding. Yet, from another perspective, what is striking is not how much worse recall of words is from multiply center-embedded sentences, but how much better it is than the word salad conditions. Comprehenders must be imposing some description on the center self-embedded RCs that permit them to recall them with greater accuracy. The fact that self-embeddings can be difficult to interpret yet relatively memorable lends credence to the view that self-embeddings, in the course of parsing, give rise to accurate local syntactic descriptions that suffer either from lack of coherence at the global level (Tyler and Warren 1987; Ferreira et al. 2002; Tabor et al. 2004) or from an unwise allocation of computational resources for linking the chunks into a whole (Frazier and Fodor 1978).

At this point let us step back to see that the sentence superiority effect as a fact about daily mental life is not something we wanted to explain *per se*: we wanted to understand more generally the mnemonic properties of sentences because of what they might teach us about the way syntactic structure behaves in space and in time. I have alluded already to the idea that the syntactic descriptions of incidentally encountered sentences could be encoded as a matter of course into long-term memory, where those descriptions may not necessarily be linked together as a whole. In the remaining sections, we will consider in greater detail how whole sentences are retained in memory (§2); this will form an entrée into thinking about how, in mid-sentence, dependent elements from the past can be reliably recalled and the ways in which this impacts dependent elements to come in the future (§3).

2 Verbatim recall

On June 25, 1973, John Dean, who had until recently been White House counsel under President Nixon, appeared before the Senate Watergate Committee. Dean submitted an extensive opening statement in which he recounted the details of numerous meetings with Nixon and his inner circle. Senator Daniel Inouye was quite impressed: "Your 245-page statement is remarkable for the detail with which it recounts events and conversations occurring over a period of many months. It is particularly remarkable in view of the fact that you indicated that it was prepared without benefit of note or daily diary … Have you always had a facility for recalling the details of conversations which took place many months ago?" Dean's subsequent testimony seemed impressive enough that some in the press would dub him "the human tape recorder" (Neisser 1981). Of course, what is interesting about this situation is that there was in fact an actual tape recorder in the Nixon Oval Office faithfully logging all of these conversations. The White House later released some of the transcripts, in part motivated, it would seem, by a wish to discredit Dean's testimony. As Ulrich Neisser discovered in his 1981 *Cognition* study, there was almost nothing that Dean recounted which was exactly recorded by the tapes. For example, in his Senate testimony, Dean stated, "I can very vividly recall that the way [Nixon] … leaned over to Mr. Haldeman and said 'A million dollars is no problem.'" Though the transcript reveals repeated reference to a million dollars, the closest thing Nixon says to Dean's report is the following: "Now let me tell you. We could get the money. There is no problem in that …" (March 21, 1972). Neisser argued that Dean was in fact reasonably thematically accurate but only very rarely was he accurate verbatim. That is, he recounted a good *gist* version of the various Oval Office episodes, but he almost never got the exact language used correct. But Dean was, in a broad sense, vindicated by the Oval Office tapes because word-for-word verbatim recall is not the standard to which we hold accounts of conversations. The question is, why?

As we saw in the introduction, syntactic descriptions dramatically improve the recollection of long word lists, to near perfection for those sentences that can be fully parsed – so why couldn't Dean recall Nixon's words verbatim? This question might seem tendentiously framed, for surely the communicative function of utterances plays a dominant role in our storing what we store. And the exact form of sentences would seem to have minimal utility once all the intra-sentential grammatical relations are accounted for, all open dependencies satisfied, and its interpretation fixed (memorized verse is an important counter-example to this claim). But, as I will argue, it is probably not the case that we do not store the exact form of many of the utterances we heard; rather, we do so, but we also quickly lose access to those encodings by losing an effective index to them. Understanding *why* the exact form of sentences is degraded after other sentences intervene will crucially depend on us coming to an understanding not just about long-term memory but also about working memory in language comprehension. Information about syntactic form is constantly being shuttled from our immediate primary memory to secondary, or, long-term memory (Broadbent 1958; McElree 1998; McElree *et al.* 2003). And this happens on the time-scale of hundreds of milliseconds. That is, we are rearranging the contents of our memory very frequently during the understanding of even a simple sentence. For any linguistic expression, there is consequently no single encoding in memory. There is a constellation of encodings that have to be put back together in the right way. In the case of immediate recall, a blueprint for doing so plausibly remains in short-term memory; but it is quickly overwritten as the 'plans' for new, similar sentences take its place.

There were some early psycholinguistic demonstrations that whole sentence memory – in the form of verbatim recall – was quite labile. Sachs (1967) presented individuals with recorded passages that were interrupted at various points with a bell. She then asked them to say whether or not a probe sentence had occurred in the preceding passage: these probes were either identical to (i) some sentence in the passage, (ii) a syntactically altered but truth-conditionally equivalent version of the original, generated by applying a transformation such as extraposition, passivization, or dative shift, or (iii) a semantically altered version with permuted thematic roles. Only when the probe occurred immediately after the target sentence in the passage could experimental participants reliably discriminate the actual sentence from its altered versions. Just 80–160 syllables later, only discrimination of semantic alterations, and *not* syntactic alterations, remained substantially above chance. Similarly, Jarvella (1971) showed that verbatim recall was nearly perfect for sentences immediately following presentation but then plummeted to below 50 percent once another sentence was interposed. Interestingly, in his experimental design, participants read three clauses arranged under two root S nodes in one of two ways: either by grouping the middle clause with the first root S or with the second. The medial clause was recalled almost as well as the final clause if they were dominated by the same S, but not if the medial clause was dominated by the initial root S. Because the content of the three clauses was (largely) the same across conditions in terms of thematic roles, this finding suggested that surface syntactic organization played a key role in constraining recollection. Two such sets of relations could be recalled quite well if they co-occurred in the same sentence, but not if they straddled a sentence boundary.

A number of findings consistent with Sachs (1967) and Jarvella (1971) suggested that memory for exact form was fleeting (Bransford *et al.* 1972; Garrod and Trabasso 1973). As Clark and Clark (1977) summarized, "[people] 'study' speech by listening to it for its meaning and by discarding its word for word content quickly. They try to identify referents, draw inferences, get at indirect meaning, and in general build global representations of the situation being described." One notable empirical challenge to this view – at least, a refinement of its consequences – came from Bates *et al.* (1978), who discovered that truth-conditionally equivalent but pragmatically active distinctions in surface form could be retained quite well in a more enriched ("non-laboratory") context: in their study, participants watched a twenty-minute excerpt from the soap opera *Another World*. After the video excerpt, participants were asked whether certain utterances appeared in the program. The experimenters had selected a number of sentences that had either full names or pronouns and full clauses or elided ones. They were thus able to create positive probes by using those sentences verbatim; negative probes were created by switching full names with pronouns and full clauses with ellipses. Participants were significantly above chance at discriminating verbatim from non-verbatim versions of sentences in the program, with a slight advantage when the positive probe was not an anaphoric expression (i.e., when it was a name or a full clause). Bates and colleagues concluded that participants encoded form better in this setting because it was embedded in a richer interactional context, one in which pragmatic principles were active. Correctly assessing that a full clause was used, versus an elided one, could be aided by participants' ability to recall the conversational context in which the target sentence was uttered. On the basis of that context, Bates *et al.* argued, it would be possible to reconstruct the most felicitous expression to use based on various parameters of the discourse: for example, the topic of conversation, what had been previously mentioned, whose turn it was to speak, and so on. In other words, accurate verbatim recall might draw heavily upon reconstruction.

The idea that verbatim recall was, in effect, the re-production of a sentence in view of its interpretation and its constituent lexical items, was strengthened and refined by a series of experiments in the 1990s by Mary Potter and Linda Lombardi. Potter and Lombardi (1990) asked participants to (i) read a sentence (3a), then (ii) read a list of words (3b), (iii) perform a recognition task on the word list (3c), and (iv) recall that sentence (3d).

(3)   (a) *Sentence*:   "There stands the deserted **castle**, ready to explore."
       (b) *Word List*:   watch – **palace** – coffee – airplane – pen
       (c) *Recognition*:   RULER?   [i.e., did the word 'ruler' occur in (b)]
       (d′) *Recall*[correct]   "There stands the deserted castle, ready to explore."
       (d″) *Recall*[lure]   "There stands the deserted palace, ready to explore."

They found that participants could be lured into mis-recalling the sentence (3a) if the word list (3b) contained an item in the same semantic field as one of the words in the sentence. In this example, the word 'palace' is related by association to the word 'castle' – and, indeed, participants sometimes recalled (3d″), a near-verbatim version of (3a). This suggests that participants were not consulting some infallible 'transcript'-like encoding of (3a), but rather that recall involved a process in which the activated lexical item 'palace' could substitute for 'castle'. Lombardi and Potter (1992) showed that not only could words be substituted for one another but that such substitutions could force the constituent structure itself to be reformulated. For example, they considered ditransitive verbs, among which there are certain verbs, such as *give*, that allow their goal to be expressed both as a direct object ('V – DP_{GOAL} – DP_{THEME}') and as a prepositional object ('V – DP_{THEME} – PP_{GOAL}'). Other verbs, such as *donate*, allow only the latter frame. When non-alternating verbs such as *donate* were included as the lure in the word recognition task for a sentence that included an alternating verb such as *give*, participants not only substituted *donate* but adjusted the syntax to accommodate its subcategorization restrictions. Thus a target sentence like "The rich widow is going to give the university a million dollars," might be mis-recalled under luring conditions as "The rich widow is going to donate a million dollars to the university." While these results are reminiscent of Sachs (1967), who also showed that verbal alternations were quickly lost in a recognition task, note that verbatim recall was impaired even if no other sentences intervened – only words.

Lombardi and Potter (1992) argued that verbatim recall was not really recall in a strict sense – that is, one in which the contents of memory were read out as from a transcript – but rather that recall was an instance of highly constrained language production. Comprehenders, in their view, were possessed of a mental state in which there was a set of recently activated words and a salient conceptual representation. Verbatim recall, they reasoned, was what would occur most often if they sought to express that conceptual representation with those recently activated words. In this view, the fact that luring *give* with *donate* led to constituent structure adjustments is not surprising, since no syntactic structure independent of the lexemes was thought to be stored. Later work (Potter and Lombardi 1998) attempted to further assimilate verbatim recall to priming in sentence production (Bock 1986).

There is a strict version of Potter and Lombardi's theory according to which verbatim recall *is* sentence re-production and nothing else – that is, verbatim memory does not implicate stored compositional representations that were created in a recent event of sentence encoding. In other words, the mental record does not include *episodic compositional encodings* (to adapt a term-of-art from memory research). But there is a weaker interpretation: re-production of a sentence provides a powerful route to recollection of the sentence, but it is not the exclusive route. There are a few reasons for contemplating this view. One reason is the fact that intrusions were present but not overwhelming: in Lombardi and Potter (1992), for example, intrusion rates were low, ranging from 3 to 21 percent. However, in Potter and Lombardi (1990), which focused on synonym intrusion and not the intrusion of syntactically incompatible lexemes, rates ranged from 13 to 51 percent. This piece of evidence, if only a weak piece, suggests that the intrusion of lexemes incompatible with the previous syntactic structure was resisted. Moreover, recent research has demonstrated verbatim memory for expressions embedded in short texts, both in recognition and recall, that is less plausibly explained as reconstruction and can persist for some days (Gurevich *et al.* 2010). This research has brought a renewed emphasis on the functional role that exact memory for incidentally encountered language, at varying levels of analysis, might play in learning or in support of language comprehension (Arnon and Snider 2010). For the purposes of this chapter, we take the recent evidence, combined with studies such as Bates *et al.* (1978), to support the weaker interpretation of Lombardi and Potter (1992): at least under some circumstances, individuals durably store linguistic descriptions that are more than merely encodings of words, that is, episodic compositional encodings. Such descriptions may be only partial in nature; and it is perhaps a telling fact about almost all research in this arena that it has focused on whole sentence recall and recollection. One way of understanding the fragility of verbatim memory would be to link it to the non-unitary nature of linguistic encodings: if episodic compositional encodings do not necessarily span a whole sentence, then success at whole sentence recollection will depend on being able to access the *set* of encodings that exhaustively spans the sentence and linking them together. In other words, perhaps the theory of verbatim memory needs a theory of locality. In the next section, we will see that evidence from real-time sentence processing converges upon the conclusion that stored encodings of specific syntactic structures do exist and that those stored encodings may be fragmentary in nature: at least, they can be accessed without the mediation of the entire sentence to which they belong.

3 Backwards and forwards: remembering and forgetting in the short-term

In this section, we will consider the way in which intra-sentential syntactic dependencies are recognized or constructed in real-time processing. To do so, we will first focus intensively on subject-verb agreement and the phenomenon of agreement attraction. This will motivate the properties of a content-addressable memory architecture in which constituent encodings are stored and reactivated in working memory via skilled cue-based retrievals. We will then extend the discussion to other dependency types.

Language comprehenders are immediately sensitive to subject–verb agreement violations, as revealed (for example) by evoked response potentials on the verb (Hagoort *et al.* 1993; Osterhout *et al.* 1996; Münte *et al.* 1997, among others). For example, in sentence (4a), the agreement error would lead to higher reading times in a reading-time study or a larger evoked response potential (a LAN or a P600) on the auxiliary in EEG study (compared with the grammatical (4b)).

(4)   a.   *The *cat are* methodically stalking the squirrel.
      b.   The *cat is* methodically stalking the squirrel.

Interestingly, if (4a) were minimally modified to include a non-subject plural noun, then comprehenders become remarkably less sensitive to the violation (Pearlmutter *et al.* 1999; Wagers *et al.* 2009; Staub 2010; Dillon *et al.* 2013).

(5)   The *cat* in the bushes **are* methodically stalking the squirrel.

The lack of sensitivity, referred to as *agreement attraction*, is linked to the existence of the plural nominal embedded within the subject phrase. Agreement attraction has been amply documented in production: in the typical case, a singular subject modified by a prepositional phrase dominating a plural noun can elicit the erroneous production of a plural verb (Bock and Miller 1991; see Eberhard *et al.* (2005) for a comprehensive recent review). In comprehension, the behavioral and electrophysiological markers of subject–verb violations are substantially attenuated or sometimes completely abolished. We will use this fact to illustrate the ways that compositional encodings are created and accessed. First we consider, and ultimately dismiss, two promising candidate explanations.

The first explanation begins with the observation that there is a grammatically well-formed substring in sentences such as (5): "the bushes are methodically stalking the squirrel". Could the existence of this substring be responsible for reducing the comprehender's sensitivity to subject–verb agreement violations? The idea that comprehenders misidentify the embedded noun phrase as the subject, because it forms a grammatical sequence with the verb, would be congenial to the "local coherence" effects discussed by Tabor *et al.* (2004). It predicts that ungrammatical sentences such as (6) should also generate agreement attraction.

(6)   *The *cats* in the bush *is* methodically stalking the squirrel.

However, sentences such as (6) are rarely elicited in production (Eberhard *et al.* 2005); nor do they disguise the violation in comprehension (Pearlmutter *et al.* 1999; Wagers *et al.* 2009): only singular subjects can be "ignored" in agreement attraction configurations, a fact we will refer to as the *markedness property* of agreement attraction. A second argument against the substring explanation comes from syntactic structures that do not juxtapose the marked non-subject nominal and the verb. In (7), the relative clause head is plural and the relative clause subject is singular.

(7)   *The squirrels that the *cat are* methodically stalking …

Sentences such as (7) also give rise to agreement attraction, which is remarkable because the subject and verb are linearly adjacent (Kimball and Aissen 1971; Bock and Miller 1991;

Clifton *et al.* 1999; Wagers *et al.* 2009). We will refer to this as the *adjacency-independence property* of agreement attraction.

The existence of agreement attraction in (7) speaks to the second candidate explanation, according to which the subject of an agreement attraction configuration has been misvalued syntactically for number. This explanation, sometimes called the percolation or head-overwriting account (Pearlmutter *et al.* 1999; Eberhard *et al.* 2005), proposes that a plural number feature can percolate within the subject projection to overwrite a singular number feature (Eberhard 1997). This explanation makes sense of agreement attraction's markedness property, if features that are more marked are less likely to be overwritten (or, correspondingly, if unmarked features correspond to an absence). It also helps explain a relation observed in production whereby the syntactic distance between the subject head and the plural nominal (Franck *et al.* 2002) correlates with the likelihood of generating agreement attraction. However, the existence of the relative clause configuration in (7) is a challenge for the percolation explanation, since the subject does not contain the plural noun phrase. In other words, percolation fails if, as (7) suggests, agreement attraction has a *containment-independence* property (a sort of stronger version of adjacency-independence). A second challenge to the percolation explanation comes from more recent demonstrations that the grammatical versions of (5) and (7) are not any more difficult to process than versions with no plural (Wagers *et al.* 2009; Dillon *et al.* 2013). If feature percolation were an independent property of complex noun phrases, then grammatical strings should be rendered as illusorily ungrammatical in the same way that ungrammatical strings are rendered as illusorily grammatical. However, they are not, a property we will refer to as the *grammatical asymmetry* of agreement attraction. Finally, although comprehension and production of agreement align in many ways, it is interesting to note that the head-distance effect has not been compellingly demonstrated in comprehension (Pearlmutter 2000; cf. Dillon *et al.* 2013).

Wagers *et al.* (2009) and Dillon *et al.* (2013) propose that agreement attraction stems from the mechanism by which one dependent element causes the retrieval of another dependent element in working memory. A natural way to relate a verb and its subject is via the dominance relations provided by the phrase structure representation, since those are the relations that enter into calculation of agreement during a syntactic derivation. Dominance relations (or other syntactic prominence relations) could be used to guide the search for nodes in a hierarchical structure. For concreteness, suppose an inflected finite verb triggers a search for the person and number features of the subject in an attempt to unify its feature matrix with that of the subject. If this search considered only constituent encodings indexed by grammatical relations such as dominance, then the subject should be reliably retrieved and agreement attraction would be expected only if there was faulty percolation. But we argued against faulty percolation because it did not account for either the containment-independence or grammatical asymmetry of attraction. This suggests that the search considers constituent encodings that are not the subjects of the sentence. A search in which stored representations are not strictly or necessarily ordered during memory access is possible under a content-addressable theory of memory (McElree *et al.* 2003; Van Dyke and Lewis 2003; Lewis and Vasishth 2005; Van Dyke and McElree 2006). In a content-addressable theory, retrieval is essentially associative: features of a desired encoding, which are called cues, are compared against a set of encodings to find the best match. For example, a plural verb might indicate the features an appropriate subject phrase should have and then use those as cues. Examples include: nominative case, plural number, the syntactic category N, the phrase structural relation 'specifier', and so on. Given a set of cues, the likelihood of retrieving a target encoding depends on both the goodness-of-fit of those cues to that encoding and the distinctiveness of the cue-to-encoding match (Nairne 2006). The best-case scenario is one in which all cues are matched to a single encoding: that is, a case where both goodness-of-fit and distinctiveness are strong. Agreement attraction is a sort of worst-case scenario: as an ungrammatical string, neither goodness-of-fit nor distinctiveness-of-match is high for any encoding, and there is a partial match with the non-subject. Retrieval outcomes are correspondingly distributed between both the target subject encoding and the plural 'attractor' encoding (Wagers 2008; Dillon *et al.* 2013). The content-addressable approach is thus compatible with the key properties of agreement attraction: containment-/adjacency-independence, markedness, and grammatical asymmetry.

A situation in which a set of retrieval cues does not uniquely point to a single encoding but is compatible with multiple memories is one of high interference which gives rise to short-term forgetting (Anderson and Neely 1996). Agreement attraction is thus viewed as a kind of short-term forgetting, where 'forgetting' in this sense means losing effective access to a target memory. Are there other situations of interference in language processing? Most analogous to agreement attraction are examples of illusory case licensing in German: in instances where a dative argument is required – that is, by certain verbs – the absence of a dative in the grammatically licensed position goes relatively unnoticed (Bader *et al.* 2000). Just as in agreement attraction, however, the presence of a structurally inappropriate marked category – like a PP-embedded dative – can lead to the misperception of grammaticality (Sloggett 2013). However, interference extends beyond the licensing of visible morphosyntax to both phrase structural and thematic relations. Center self-embeddings have often been argued to reflect interference (Lewis 1996; cf. Miller and Chomsky 1963) because the similarity of multiple encodings prevents the effective access to a single target encoding. Van Dyke and Lewis (2003) and Van Dyke (2007) demonstrated that complex subjects, which themselves contain pronounced embedded subjects, can be especially difficult to integrate at the matrix verb – owing to the presence of either multiple clauses or multiple subjects. Arnett and Wagers (2012) extended this finding to demonstrate that complex subjects that embed event-denoting nominalizations with pronounced possessors likewise generate interference at the matrix verb.

Lewis and Vasishth (2005) embed a theory of language comprehension in the general ACT-R computational architecture ("Adaptive Control of Thought – Rational", Anderson and Lebiere 1998), which encompasses the potential for interference due to similarity. Interference due to retrieval is an especially acute problem in their language comprehension model because they posit that only a very small extent of a larger compositional representation is available for 'active' concurrent computation. As a hypothetical example, if a verb needs to be linked with its complement, a representation for the subject cannot simultaneously be actively maintained. If information is subsequently needed which is contained in the subject encoding, then it must be retrieved, possibly displacing the encoding of the object (or the verb). In the case of Lewis and Vasishth's (2005) model, the amount of information that is concurrently represented is roughly equivalent to an X-bar projection. The choice to represent large compositional structures in relatively small chunks is both a reflection of the ACT-R philosophy to align units of memory with units of learning and generalization as well as a response to the many empirical observations that working memory is highly capacity limited (Miller 1956; Broadbent 1958; McElree 1998; Cowan

2001; Öztekin *et al.* 2008; see Wagers and McElree (2013) for a linguistically oriented review). Although there is some disagreement about how to measure capacity, limitations of working memory capacity require the segmentation of large compositional representations into minimal units of some kind – a fact consistent with the conclusions reached about ver-batim memory skill in §2. It is the nature/size of these units that determines the frequency of retrieval: the smaller the unit, the more often retrieval will be necessary to integrate new incoming material with the syntactic context in language comprehension. And the more often it is necessary to retrieve, the more often interference can have its deleterious effects.

In sum, if a dependency needs to be formed from a retrospective vantage point – that is, when an input head requires information processed in a previous constituent – then the success or accuracy with which that information can be accessed and linked to the compu-tations in the 'present' is a joint product of (i) the way in which a compositional object has been segmented into encodings in memory; (ii) the accuracy of the cues used to identify the desired/candidate encoding; and (iii) the precision of those cues. We have discussed two broad situations in which (ii) or (iii) leads to poor outcomes: case and agreement attraction in ungrammatical strings (low accuracy) and subject identification in grammatical strings (low precision). Many other dependencies encompass a 'retrospective' vantage point: for example, calculation of scope and thematic roles in *wh*-dependency formation, antecedent search for pronouns, resolution of ellipsis, and so on. And, in those domains, researchers have uncovered evidence for varying degrees of processing difficulty when multiple similar encod-ings are present in memory (Gordon *et al.* 2001; Van Dyke and McElree 2006, English *wh*-dependencies; Xiang *et al.* 2013, Chinese *in-situ wh*-dependencies; Badecker and Straub 2002, for pronouns; Martin and McElree 2008; 2011, for VP ellipsis and sluicing).

Given how maladapted the memory architecture might seem to be for supporting struc-tured compositional representations, it is remarkable how robust language processing is in general. Phillips *et al.* (2012) observed that, while there are many cases in which language comprehenders overgenerate with respect to the grammar in real-time, there are also many cases in which language comprehenders hew very closely to the possibilities made availa-ble by the grammar. For example, comprehenders are sensitive to Principle C in the resolu-tion of cataphoric dependencies (Kazanina *et al.* 2007), to the appropriate locality conditions on the resolution of argument reflexive anaphora (Sturt 2003; Dillon *et al.* 2013), and to island boundaries in the resolution of *wh*-dependencies (Stowe 1986; Traxler and Pickering 1996; Phillips 2006). Identifying the causes of short-term forgetting, therefore, only paints half the picture – we can ask, analogously, why are certain aspects of the representation remembered so well?

Based on the foregoing cases of success, one generalization that Phillips *et al.* (2012) consider is that dependencies which are assembled predominantly 'left to right' are more accurate than those assembled 'right to left'. Examples that fit this generalization include cataphora and *wh*-dependencies formed via overt movement. In both those dependency types, the first element of the dependency (the expression-initial pronoun, the clause-pe-ripheral *wh*-phrase) signals the existence of the dependency to the comprehender more definitively than the second element (the name/description, the gap/resumptive pronoun). Why should order matter, though? One possibility is that positing a dependency based on its left element could affect subsequent actions to improve memory efficiency. For example, the processor could organize the component encodings of the representation to minimize the chance that the left dependent element will have to be retrieved (cf. Berwick and Wein-berg's (1984) computational argument for subjacency). Alternatively, it could adapt how it forms cues at the retrieval site to include not only the abstract grammatical features that inhere in the dependency itself but also contextual control cues that are encoded with incomplete dependencies so that incomplete dependencies *per se* can be more accurately targeted.

A final possibility for linking disparate linguistic events in a labile memory is to extend the mental representation beyond the input. Integration of the right dependent element can happen by hypothesis, so to speak, when it is triggered by the left context. For example, in the case of English *wh*-dependencies, encountering a *wh*-phrase would lead the comprehender to posit a subject phrase linked to the *wh*-phrase – for simplicity, suppose it is just a copy of that phrase. Further input serves to test this predicted extension of the representation (much as a scientist may attempt to test a hypothesis: cf. Chater *et al.* 1998), and correspondingly it need not trigger retrieval of candidate left context features. In our example, the presence of a phrase in subject position would be incompatible with the posited phrase structure, triggering a revision that links the copied phrase to another position. For many dependencies, retrieval might only ever be necessary in the parse when the predictions and the input do not match. The processing of overt *wh*-dependencies does seem to proceed essentially in this way: upon encountering an extracted phrase, the comprehender posits the next possible extraction site and assumes that is the correct representation until further input serves to disconfirm it (Stowe 1986; Phillips and Wagers 2007). The extent to which it is generally true that predictive processing elaborates an encoding in memory and renders it more accessible to future operations remains to be more fully explored; but, if so, it provides an important link between two major 'classes' of behavior in sentence processing: retrospective, or memory-dependent, behavior, in which information from the recent events must be retrieved in a skilled fashion; and prospective, or predictive, behavior, in which information about the future is projected forward. Predictive processing is apparent at all levels of language comprehension, and the greater the extent to which the linguistic context allows comprehenders to make stable guesses about the future, the more easily comprehension proceeds (Hale 2003; Levy 2008). The optimization of retrieval cues to reflect knowledge of language use – emphasizing not only its possible outcomes but also its likely ones – may be analogous to general strategies in the "long-term working memory" proposed by Ericsson and Kintsch (1995) to account for expert performance in many domains such as chess or mental arithmetic.

4 Closing

In this chapter, I have highlighted several research problems in which a characterization of memory is at the nexus of syntactic and psycholinguistic theory: the sentence superiority effect, verbatim memory, and short-term forgetting. Both relatively straightforward observation as well as sophisticated temporal dissections of language comprehension lead to the conclusion that language processing leaves in its wake a rich set of recently activated mental representations, ranging from simple features to episodic compositional encodings. This multiplicity of encodings provides many routes for the storage and recollection of previous linguistic events. In the moment, the language processor does an effective though not infallible job of maintaining the links between these smaller constituent representations to form what we think of as larger, sentence-/utterance-level, representations. As an utterance fades into the past, however, those smaller constituent representations become more difficult to link and reassemble. Similar encodings have displaced them and compete for processing in the new context – it is in this sense that larger compositional representations are forgotten. Against this backdrop we can see how the interaction of sentence processing with theories of memory is mediated by the content of syntactic representations. Theories of working memory, like theories of syntax, postulate domains of activity. Theories of syntax, like theories of working memory, postulate rules for linking domains via feature sharing. Whether these domains are the same – and whether the same features link the same kind of domains – remains a tantalizing question for future exploration.

Note

1 There has been persistent disagreement in the literature about what counts as 'clause-like' (e.g., Tanenhaus and Carroll 1975) and different researchers have used different working definitions in their experiments. It is an interesting question whether this disagreement might be resolved or better arbitrated if it were brought into contact with contemporary questions of locality – for example, what defines phase-hood (Chomsky 1999; 2005).

Further reading

Bates, E., W. Kintsch, and M. Masling. 1978. Recognition memory for aspects of dialogue. *Journal of Experimental Psychology: Human Learning and Memory* 4:187–197.

Bock, K., and C. Miller. 1991. Broken agreement. *Cognitive Psychology* 23:45–93.

Hale, J. 2003. The information conveyed by words in sentences. *Journal of Psycholinguistic Research* 32:101–123.

Kazanina, N., E.F. Lau, M. Lieberman, M. Yoshida, and C. Phillips. 2007. The effect of syntactic constraints on the processing of backwards anaphora. *Journal of Memory and Language* 56:384–409.

Lewis, R.L., and S. Vasishth. 2005. An activation-based model of sentence processing as skilled memory retrieval. *Cognitive Science* 29:375–419.

References

Anderson, J.R., and C. Lebiere. 1998. *The Atomic Components of Thought.* Mahwah, NJ: Erlbaum.

Anderson, M.C., and J.H. Neely. 1996. Interference and inhibition in memory retrieval. In *Handbook of Perception and Cognition: Memory*, ed. E.L. Bjork and R.A. Bjork, 237–313. San Diego: Academic Press.

Arnett, N.V., and M. Wagers. 2012. Subject encoding and retrieval interference. Paper given at CUNY Conference on Human Sentence Processing 2012.

Arnon, I., and N. Snider. 2010. More than words: Frequency effects for multi-word phrases. *Journal of Memory and Language* 62:67–82.

Baddeley, A.D., G.J. Hitch, and R.J. Allen. 2009. Working memory and binding in sentence recall. *Journal of Memory and Language* 61:438–456.

Badecker, W., and K. Straub. 2002. The processing role of structural constraints on the interpretation of pronouns and anaphors. *Journal of Experimental Psychology: Learning, Memory, and Cognition* 28:748–769.

Bader, M., M. Meng, and J. Bayer. 2000. Case and reanalysis. *Journal of Psycholinguistic Research* 29:37–52.

Bates, E., W. Kintsch, and M. Masling. 1978. Recognition memory for aspects of dialogue. *Journal of Experimental Psychology: Human Learning and Memory* 4:187–197.

Berwick R., and A. Weinberg. 1984. *The Grammatical Basis of Linguistic Performance: Language Use and Acquisition.* Cambridge, MA: MIT Press.

Bever, T.G., J.R. Lackner, and R. Kirk. 1969. The underlying structures of sentences are the primary units of immediate speech processing. *Perception & Psychophysics* 5:225–234.

Bock, J.K. 1986. Syntactic persistence in language production. *Cognitive Psychology* 18:355–387.

Bock, K., and C. Miller. 1991. Broken agreement. *Cognitive Psychology* 23:45–93.

Bransford, J.D., J.R. Barclay, and J.J. Franks. 1972. Sentence memory: A constructive versus interpretive approach. *Cognitive Psychology* 3:193–209.

Bresnan, J. 2001. *Lexical-Functional Syntax.* Oxford: Blackwell.

Broadbent, D.E. 1958. *Perception and Communication*. New York: Oxford University Press.

Chater, N., M. Crocker, and M. Pickering. 1998. The rational analysis of inquiry: The case of parsing. In *Rational Models of Cognition*, ed. N. Chater, M. Crocker, and M.J. Pickering, 441–468. Oxford: Oxford University Press.

Chomsky, N. 1981. *Lectures on Government and Binding*. Dordrecht: Foris.

Chomsky, N. 1995. *The Minimalist Program*. Cambridge, MA: MIT Press.

Chomsky, N. 1999. Derivation by phase. *MIT Occasional Papers in Linguistics, no 18*. Cambridge, MA: MIT Working Papers in Linguistics, Department of Linguistics and Philosophy.

Chomsky, N. 2005. On phases. In *Foundational Issues in Linguistic Theory: Essays in Honor of Jean-Roger Vergnaud*, ed. R. Freidin, C.P. Otero, and M.L. Zubizarreta, 133–166. Cambridge, MA: MIT Press.

Clark, H.H., and E.V. Clark. 1977. *Psychology and Language: An Introduction to Psycholinguistics*. New York: Harcourt Brace Jovanovich.

Clifton, C., L. Frazier, and P. Deevy. 1999. Feature manipulation in sentence comprehension. *Rivista di Linguistica* 11:11–39.

Cowan, N. 2001. The magical number 4 in short-term memory: a reconsideration of mental storage capacity. *Behavioral and Brain Sciences* 24:87–114.

Dillon, B., A. Mishler, S. Sloggett, and C. Phillips. 2013. Contrasting intrusion profiles for agreement and anaphora: Experimental and modeling evidence. *Journal of Memory and Language* 69:85–103.

Eberhard, K. 1997. The marked effect of number on subject–verb agreement. *Journal of Memory and Language* 36:147–164.

Eberhard, K., J. Cutting, and K. Bock. 2005. Making syntax of sense: Number agreement in sentence production. *Psychological Review* 112:531–559.

Ericsson, K. A., and W. Kintsch. 1995. Long-term working memory. *Psychological Review* 102: 211–245.

Ferreira, F., K.G.D. Bailey, and V. Ferraro. 2002. Good-enough representations in language comprehension. *Current Directions in Psychological Science* 11:11–15.

Fodor, J.A., T.G. Bever, and M.F. Garrett. 1974. *The Psychology of Language*. New York: McGraw-Hill.

Franck, J., G. Vigliocco, and J. Nicol. 2002. Attraction in sentence production: The role of syntactic structure. *Language and Cognitive Processes* 17:371–404.

Frazier, L., and J.D. Fodor. 1978. The sausage machine: A new two-stage parsing model. *Cognition* 6:291–325.

Garrod, S., and T. Trabasso. 1973. A dual-memory information processing interpretation of sentence comprehension. *Journal of Verbal Learning and Verbal Behavior* 12:155–167.

Gilchrist, A.L., N. Cowan, and M. Naveh-Benjamin. 2008. Working memory capacity for spoken sentences decreases with adult ageing: recall of fewer but not smaller chunks in older adults. *Memory* 16:773–787.

Glanzer, M., D. Dorfman, and B. Kaplan. 1981. Short-term storage in the processing of text. *Journal Of Verbal Learning And Verbal Behavior* 20:656–670.

Gordon, P.C., R. Hendrick, and M. Johnson. 2001. Memory interference during language processing. *Journal of Experimental Psychology: Learning, Memory, and Cognition* 27:1411–1423.

Gurevich, O., M.A. Johnson, and A.E. Goldberg. 2010. Incidental verbatim memory for language. *Language and Cognition* 2:45–78.

Hagoort, P., C. Brown, and J. Groothusen. 1993. The syntactic positive shift as an ERP measure of syntactic processing. *Language and Cognitive Processes* 18:439–583.

Hale, J. 2003. The information conveyed by words in sentences. *Journal of Psycholinguistic Research* 32:101–123.

Jarvella, R. 1971. Syntactic processing of connected speech. *Journal of Verbal Learning and Verbal Behavior* 10:409–416.

Kazanina, N., E.F. Lau, M. Lieberman, M. Yoshida, and C. Phillips. 2007. The effect of syntactic constraints on the processing of backwards anaphora. *Journal of Memory and Language* 56:384–409.

Kimball, J., and J. Aissen. 1971. I think, you think, he think. *Linguistic Inquiry* 2:241–246.

Levelt, W.J.M. 1974. *Formal Grammars in Linguistics and Psycholinguistics*. The Hague: Mouton.

Levy, R. 2008. Expectation-based syntactic comprehension. *Cognition* 106:1126–1177.

Lewis, R.L. 1996. Interference in short-term memory: The magical number two (or three) in sentence processing. *Journal of Psycholinguistic Research* 25:93–115.

Lewis, R.L., and S. Vasishth. 2005. An activation-based model of sentence processing as skilled memory retrieval. *Cognitive Science* 29:375–419.

Lombardi, L., and M. Potter. 1992. The regeneration of syntax in short term memory. *Journal of Memory and Language* 31:713–733.

McElree, B. 1998. Attended and non-attended states in working memory: Accessing categorized structures. *Journal of Memory and Language* 38:225–252.

McElree, B., S. Foraker, and L. Dyer. 2003. Memory and language memory structures that subserve sentence comprehension. *Journal of Memory and Language* 48:67–91.

Martin, A.E. and B. McElree. 2008. A content addressable pointer mechanism underlies comprehension of verb-phrase ellipsis. *Journal of Memory and Language* 58:879–906.

Martin, A.E. and B. McElree. 2011. Direct-access retrieval during sentence comprehension: Evidence from sluicing. *Journal of Memory and Language* 64:327–343.

Miller, G.A. 1956. The magical number seven, plus or minus two: Some limits on our capacity for processing information. *Psychological Review* 63:81–97.

Miller, G., and N. Chomsky. 1963. Finitary models of language users. In *Handbook of Mathematical Psychology*, vol. II, ed. R. Luce, R. Bush, and E. Galanter, 419–492. New York: Wiley.

Miller, G., and S. Isard. 1964. Free recall of self-embedded English sentences. *Information and Control* 7:292–303.

Münte, T.F., M. Matzke, and S. Johannes. 1997. Brain activity associated with syntactic incongruencies in words and pseudo-words. *Journal of Cognitive Neuroscience* 9:318–329.

Nairne, J.S. 2006. Modeling distinctiveness: Implications for general memory theory. In *Distinctiveness and Memory*, ed. R.R. Hunt and J.B. Worthen, 27–46, New York: Oxford University Press.

Neisser, U. 1981. John Dean's memory: a case study. *Cognition* 9:1–22.

Osterhout, L., R. McKinnon, M. Bersick, and V. Corey. 1996. On the language specificity of the brain response to syntactic anomalies: Is the syntactic positive shift a member of the P300 family? *Journal of Cognitive Neuroscience* 8:507–526.

Öztekin, I., B. McElree, B.P. Staresina, and L. Davachi. 2008. Working memory retrieval: Contributions of the left prefrontal cortex, the left posterior parietal cortex, and the hippocampus. *Journal of Cognitive Neuroscience* 21:581–593.

Parker, D., S. Lago, and C. Phillips. 2012. Retrieval interference in the resolution of anaphoric PRO. Conference paper presented at *Generative Linguistics in the Old World* 35.

Pearlmutter, N.J. 2000. Linear versus hierarchical agreement feature processing in comprehension. *Journal of Psycholinguistic Research* 29:89–98.

Pearlmutter, N.J., S.M. Garnsey, and K. Bock. 1999. Agreement processes in sentence comprehension. *Journal of Memory and Language* 41:427–456.

Phillips, C. 2006. The real-time status of island phenomena. *Language* 82:795–823.

Phillips, C., and M. Wagers. 2007. Relating structure and time in linguistics and psycholinguistics. In *Oxford Handbook of Psycholinguistics*, ed. G. Gaskell, 739–756. Oxford: Oxford University Press.

Phillips, C., M.W. Wagers, and E.F. Lau. 2012. Grammatical illusions and selective fallibility in real time language comprehension. In *Experiments at the Interfaces, Syntax and Semantics*, vol. 37, ed. J. Runner, 153–186. Bingley: Emerald Publications.

Pollard, C., and I.A. Sag. 1994. *Head-driven Phrase Structure Grammar*. Chicago, IL: University of Chicago Press.

Potter, M.C., and L. Lombardi. 1990. Regeneration in the short-term recall of sentences. *Journal of Memory and Language* 29:633–654.

Potter, M.C., and L. Lombardi. 1998. Syntactic priming in immediate recall of sentences. *Journal of Memory and Language* 38:265–282.

Roberts, R., and E. Gibson. 2002. Individual differences in sentence memory. *Journal of Psycholinguistic Research* 31:573–598.

Sachs, J.S. 1967. Recognition memory for syntactic and semantic aspects of connected discourse. *Perception & Psychophysics* 2:437–442.

Sloggett, S. 2013. Case licensing in processing: evidence from German. Poster presented at the 2013 CUNY Conference on Human Sentence Processing, Columbia, SC.

Staub, A. 2010. Response time distributional evidence for distinct varieties of number attraction. *Cognition* 114:447–454.

Steedman, M. 2000. *The Syntactic Process*. Cambridge, MA: MIT Press.

Stowe, L.A. 1986. Parsing *WH*-constructions: evidence for on-line gap location. *Language and Cognitive Processes* 1:227–245.

Sturt, P. 2003. The time-course of the application of binding constraints in reference resolution. *Journal of Memory and Language* 48:42–562.

Tabor, W., B. Galantucci, and D. Richardson. 2004. Effects of merely local coherence on sentence processing. *Journal of Memory and Language* 50:355–370.

Tanenhaus, M.K., and J.M. Carroll. 1975. The clausal processing hierarchy... and nouniness. In *Papers from the Parasession on Functionalism*, ed. R.E. Grossman, L.J. San, and T.J. Vance, 499–512. Chicago, IL: Chicago Linguistic Society.

Traxler, M.J., and M.J. Pickering. 1996. Plausibility and the processing of unbounded dependencies: An eye-tracking study. *Journal of Memory and Language* 35:454–475.

Tyler, L.K., and P. Warren. 1987. Local and global structure in spoken language comprehension. *Journal of Memory and Language* 26:638–657.

Van Dyke, J.A. 2007. Interference effects from grammatically unavailable constituents during sentence processing. *Journal of Experimental Psychology: Learning, Memory, and Cognition* 33:407–430.

Van Dyke, J., and R.L. Lewis. 2003. Distinguishing effects of structure and decay on attachment and repair: A cue-based parsing account of recovery from misanalyzed ambiguities. *Journal of Memory and Language* 49:285–316.

Van Dyke, J.A., and B. McElree. 2006. Retrieval interference in sentence comprehension. *Journal of Memory and Language* 55:157–166.

Wagers, M.W. 2008. The structure of memory meets memory for structure in linguistic cognition. Dissertation, University of Maryland, College Park, MD.

Wagers, M., and B. McElree. 2013. Working memory and language processing: Theory, data, and directions for future research. In *Cambridge Handbook of Biolinguistics*, ed. C. Boeckx and K. Grohmann, 203–231. Cambridge: Cambridge University Press.

Wagers, M.W., E.F. Lau, and C. Phillips. 2009. Agreement attraction in comprehension: Representations and processes. *Journal of Memory and Language* 61:206–237.

Xiang, M., B. Dillon, M. Wagers, F. Liu, and T. Guo. 2013. Processing covert dependencies: An SAT study on Mandarin *wh*-in-situ questions. *Journal of East Asian Linguistics*, doi: 10.1007/s10831-013-9115-1.

Major theories in acquisition of syntax research

Susannah Kirby

1   Why does acquisition matter?

Syntacticians working on adult languages are interested in representing *what* a speaker knows, when they know a language. Those who work in acquisition take this issue a step further, by addressing the question of *how* a speaker comes to have this knowledge.

Answering this question is complicated by two major factors, one methodological, and the other empirical. First, the generative syntactician's most basic tool has always been the metalinguistic judgment (Cowart 1997). Working with their own intuitions or with an experimental population's pool of judgments, the primary task has been to decide whether some sentence is acceptable in a given language. However, this type of metalinguistic ability may be late to develop in children, and thus may not be reliable for use with child speakers (but see McDaniel and Cairns 1996).

The second difficulty is that of hitting a moving target. Unlike adult speakers, who are thought to have stable mental grammars which do not change (much) from day to day, a child exists in a near-constant state of flux with regards to *what* they know about their language. The child is born with some minimal amount of linguistic knowledge—innately specified and/or attained via learning in utero (G_0)—and then progresses through a series of mental grammars until the point at which they attain the adultlike grammar (G_A), as represented in (1).

(1) $G_0, G_1, G_2, G_3,...,G_A$

This is a happy state of affairs for the learner, but it poses an extra challenge to researchers, who must not only document the state of the child's grammar at any given point, but also explain how the grammar moves from one state to the next.

Given these challenges, why should we take the trouble to study the acquisition of syntax? Because data from acquisition and theories of adult syntax crucially inform one another! Historically, the goal of syntax has been to account for syntactic phenomena in the simplest, most explanatory way, while also allowing for the variation attested crosslinguistically (Chomsky 1995). Many attempts to account for the constrained variation in adult languages have made crucial reference to the role of the learner, and often to the learner's innate knowledge about the limited ways in which languages may vary. To prove such theories, we must go directly to the source: to learners themselves.

On the other hand, the data that child language presents us with—specifically, the kinds of mistakes that children make on their way to adult competence—give us valuable information about the nature and organization of human grammars, as they are built from the ground up. This viewpoint gives syntacticians new insight into the full range of shapes that language can take, the true "building blocks" of the grammar, and the reasons why attested languages come to look the way they do. These are all elements which any comprehensive theory of adult syntax must specify.

A short chapter like this cannot possibly review the rich and varied literature on experimental methodologies or empirical data from children's language acquisition (L1A). Instead, this chapter aims to present the reader with an overview of two of the major theoretical camps in acquisition research (§2), and then to describe how each one accounts for two large tasks in acquisition: acquiring basic word order (BWO) (§3) and producing adult-like *wh*-questions (§4). The chapter concludes with a few final comparisons (§5) and suggestions for further reading.

2 Theories: nativism and emergentism

In the field of adult syntax, it is rare to find two researchers who espouse exactly the same model of the grammar, and the same holds true for those working with child language. Nevertheless, acquisitionists tend to fall into two main theoretical camps: nativist and emergentist. This section highlights the main differences between these two schools of thought.

2.1 Innate knowledge and modularity

To date, the predominant theory of L1A in generative syntax has been nativism: the idea that children come to the learning task with innately specified knowledge about the possible shapes a human language might take. This powerful hypothesis-formulating system, sometimes called "universal grammar" (UG), is thought to limit the logical hypothesis space, and thus to be responsible for the ease and rapidity that children show in learning their native languages (Chomsky 1959; Lightfoot 1982; Crain 1991).

One prominent version of nativism, the "principles and parameters" (P&P) approach (e.g. Chomsky 1986), proposes that UG consists of a number of principles universal to all languages, each of which has a limited number of parameters, which are set on a language-specific basis. On this view, syntactic acquisition is reduced to resolving which parameter setting each principle takes in the language being acquired. For example, a universal "null subject" principle (Rizzi 1982) might have as its possible parameters [+PRO-DROP] and [−PRO-DROP]. A child learning Italian must choose the former setting, while a child learning English should take the latter (Hyams 1986). The correct setting can be determined by attending to the positive evidence in the input—that is, the utterances that speakers produce.

One benefit to the P&P approach is that it easily accounts for "clustering effects", or syntactic contingencies: the fact that, crosslinguistically, certain phenomena tend to be correlated. For instance, a [+PRO-DROP] setting has been argued to account for why languages without expletives will also allow control into tensed clauses. Hyams (1986) claims that the optionality of subjects, lack of expletives, and absence of modals seen in child English all stem from an incorrect [+PRO-DROP] setting, and predicts that acquiring expletives could act as the "trigger" to reset the parameter, which in turn would cause an upsurge in lexical subject and modal use.

Early P&P views (including Hyams') suggested that the process of parameter-setting might be near-instantaneous, with the "triggering data" comprising perhaps a single exposure to the relevant form. More recent views have dropped this claim, to account for gradient effects. For instance, English—a non-pro-drop language—allows subject omission in imperatives and certain routinized or register-specific utterance types (2), while Italian—which is pro-drop—requires an expletive in certain contexts (3). Given the prevalence of such constructions, a parameter-setting process requiring only a single piece of data would fail, and multiple exposures are likely necessary in reaching adultlike competence (Kirby 2005; Kirby and Becker 2007).

(2)   a. Eat your peas.
      b. Time for bed.
      c. Great to see you!

(3)   **Ci** sono molte case bruciate
      "There are many houses burned"   (see Boeckx 1999)

The nativist approach initially arose as a response to the empiricist view that language is a learned behavior, completely driven by external stimuli (Skinner 1957). This "stimulus-response" view of language learning and adult use was overly simplistic, and since then a more nuanced emergentist view has gathered support. The primary claim made by proponents of the data-driven learning approach is that language "emerges" from other general cognitive faculties, the interactions between these faculties, and the child's experiences (O'Grady 2010). In this way, the human language system is a "new machine built out of old parts" (Bates and MacWhinney 1988, p. 147). Most emergentist researchers take a usage-based view (e.g. Langacker 1987), assuming that the characteristics of human language reflect *how* and *why* language is used. Instead of setting a few parameters, language learning is a more laborious process in which abstract syntactic generalizations are gradually constructed across individual exemplars. Such generalizations begin around specific lexical items (often verbs: Tomasello 1992; Goldberg 1999), and only slowly become more adultlike.

Emergentists do not have a simple explanation for why clustering effects appear in adult languages, but some would argue that the predictions the parameter-setting model makes for contingencies in L1A are not always borne out. In the case of the null subject parameter, the acquisition of expletive *it* by English-acquiring children does not appear to be correlated with consistent use of lexical subjects (Kirby 2005). Moreover, the expletives *it* and *there* are not always assimilated into the child's lexicon simultaneously (Kirby and Becker 2007). If a single parameter were responsible for these phenomena, they should appear together, or not at all.

Nativist and emergentist theories thus primarily differ in terms of their stance on the issue of whether language-specific knowledge is innate: nativists think it is, and emergentists think it is not. However, various instantiations of emergentism differ on their views of other types of innate knowledge. O'Grady's (1997) somewhat confusingly named "general nativism" assumes a handful of innate but generalized cognitive mechanisms (including perceptual, learning, conceptual, propositional, and computational modules) which aid not only in L1A, but also in a range of other cognitive functions. Other emergentist views hearken back to Piaget's (1923) view of language as a type of cultural knowledge, and stress the role of mechanisms like intention-reading, imitation (Tomasello *et al.* 1993), analogy (Childers and Tomasello 2001), and distributional analysis in acquisition, all of which are thought to be innately available. Importantly, emergentist theories explicitly compare language learning and use to *non-linguistic* cognitive and behavioral phenomena.

Claims about innateness therefore often overlap with the issue of modularity: the question of whether knowledge about language constitutes its own mental "module" (e.g. Fodor 1983). Nativists tend to believe that from the earliest point, language comprises a source of encapsulated knowledge: the "language faculty" (Hirschfeld and Gelman 1994). In contrast, the claim that language "emerges" from other mental faculties forces the conclusion that it does not *begin* as an autonomous module (even if other generalized modules do exist innately). However, emergentists might accept the proposal that the abstract linguistic knowledge that initially arises from generalized cognitive faculties eventually comes to comprise its own encapsulated core.

2.2   Words, rules, and the poverty of the stimulus

Any theory of syntax must account for the fact that speakers store unpredictable knowledge about words, including their phonological forms and meanings (the "lexicon": Chomsky 1986), as well as information about how to combine those words into phrases (the "grammar"). Theories of syntactic acquisition must additionally account for how children learn lexical items and the combinatorial processes through which phrases can be formed—how children come to have knowledge of "words and rules" (Pinker 2000).

Nativists tend to separate the work regarding "words and rules" intuitively between the lexicon and the grammar, with the lexicon being "learned" and the grammar being "acquired" (Carnie 2007). The argument from the poverty of the stimulus—the proposal that no amount of input could suffice to account for what speakers come to know about their native language—forms the basis for the nativist claim that a significant amount of linguistic knowledge is innate (Chomsky 1980). But children are not born knowing any *particular* language! At the very least, children must learn the lexical items of the language spoken around them; later, once they have partially stocked their lexicon, they can begin to combine these words given the (largely innately specified) rules that populate the grammar. Recently, more nuanced nativist accounts (e.g. Yang 2002, 2004, 2012) have begun to incorporate statistical/distributional learning models into their proposals about the acquisition of syntax. Such accounts are better able to handle gradient effects like those in (2)–(3).

In contrast with nativist views (especially earlier ones), emergentists do not believe that the stimulus is as impoverished as has been claimed, and argue that all of language learning can thus be data-driven (e.g. Pullum and Scholz 2002). Because emergentists do not espouse innate linguistic knowledge, they must account for how children learn not only the lexicon but also the abstract syntactic rules of the ambient language, and often, the processes entailed in learning the two are claimed to be similar. For example, Goldberg's (1995, 2006) construction grammar takes the stance that "words and rules" constitute a false dichotomy. Instead, speakers have knowledge of "constructions": learned form-meaning pairings at all levels—from morphemes, words, and idioms, up to phrase and sentence structures.

2.3 Continuity versus discontinuity

This difference in how the grammar is thought to become adultlike relates to a fundamental distinction in stance on the continuity/discontinuity debate. Nativists often fall on the side of continuity, claiming that child grammars differ from adult grammars only in the ways that adult grammars differ from each other (Pinker 1984), and that other apparent distinctions may be traced back to non-linguistic performance issues (Crain and Fodor 1993).

In contrast, emergentists often take the discontinuity view, arguing that child and adult grammars may differ radically. Emergentist researchers have argued for an extended period in development during which the child's grammar is unadultlike with regard to how multiword utterances are constructed. The lexical learning approach (Lieven *et al.* 1997) claims that children's earliest multiword utterances are completely unanalyzed frozen forms, like those in Step 1 (4). After memorizing several multiword chunks containing overlapping material, the child will eventually construct a slightly more abstract "slot-and-frame" pattern (Step 2), akin to the "pivot grammar" proposed by Braine (1963). Successive phases of internal reanalysis ultimately result in fully abstract, adultlike phrasal rules (Step 3). Note that the initial stages in learning a "word" and learning a "rule" are identical: namely, rote memorization of a phonological chunk.

(4)

Step 1	Step 2	Step 3
want+bottle want+teddy want+mama	want X	NP VP
have+it see+it want+it	X it	

These distinct nativist and emergentist views on how children construct multiword utterances are tied to the level of linguistic productivity hypothesized to be available to the child early in development. Adult language is thought to be partially characterized by an infinite creative ability (Hockett 1960), despite the fact that utterances are constructed from a limited number of morphemes and syntactic rules. The nativist view that children are born with much of what ultimately forms adultlike competence extends to the argument that children have access to adultlike productivity, limited only by "performance issues" like the size of their lexicon and working memory constraints (Crain and Fodor 1993). Creative, non-adultlike productions like the novel causatives in (5)—which cannot possibly be imitations—are often cited as support for productivity.

(5) a. I come it closer so it won't fall. [= "make it come closer", 2;3[1]]
b. Daddy go me around. [= "make me go around", 2;8]
c. I'm singing him. [= "making him sing", 3;1]   (from Bowerman 1974)

Emergentists take the opposite stance: because children do not initially have access to abstract rules, their language use is expected to be remarkably *unproductive*. As support for this claim, Lieven *et al.* (2003) examined a high-density corpus (30 hours over 6 weeks) from a child (2;1.11) acquiring English. They found that 63 percent of the child's 295 multiword utterances were predicted by previous utterances in the corpus, and that three-quarters of the remaining "novel" utterances differed only by a single word. Of course, the conclusions drawn from such data will depend on the particular researcher's definition of "productivity" (see Kowalski and Yang 2012).

It should be noted here that "data-driven" learning is not synonymous with learning that solely imitates things heard in the input (see Lieven 2010). The emergentist viewpoint, just like the nativist, holds that children actively construct a mental grammar over the course of development. The creative process of extracting the relevant abstract rules for the ambient language—and further, determining where certain rules may not apply—may occasionally take false turns, resulting in non-adultlike utterances like those in (5).

2.4 Summary

To recap, nativists and emergentists differ in how they answer the following questions:

- Is linguistic knowledge innate or learned?
- Is knowledge of language domain-specific/modular, or does it emerge from general cognitive abilities?
- Are "words" and "rules" learned via the same or different processes?
- Is there continuity or discontinuity between child and adult grammars?
- How productive is young children's language use?

Now that we have considered some of the major points of distinction between these views, let us examine their treatment of two key issues in syntactic development.

3 Basic word order

A defining feature of language is the ability to describe *who* did *what* to *whom*. Two major ways of distinguishing between the actors in a proposition are rigid word order (WO) and case assignment (O'Grady 1997). As a result, a major task for children learning the first type of language is acquiring the basic (i.e. most common; canonical; unmarked) WO of that language.

Evidence from comprehension studies suggests that children have some knowledge of BWO even before they begin to produce word combinations themselves, which occurs around 18–24 months (Brown 1973). Fernald (1992) played English sentences with normal and scrambled WOs to 14-month-olds, who showed a familiarity preference for the normal, unscrambled sentences.

More sophisticated sensitivity to BWO has been demonstrated with 16- and 19-month-old children (Hirsh-Pasek and Golinkoff 1996). In this study, children in the productive one-word stage (i.e. not yet producing word combinations) took part in a preferential look-ing task in which two videos differed only in the agent and patient of an action. For instance, children might be presented simultaneously with one video in which Elmo is tickling Grover, and another in which Grover is tickling Elmo. Then children would hear one of the prompts in (6). Notice that unlike the scrambled sentences used by Fernald, both these utterances are allowable in adult English. Thus, in order to succeed at the matching task, children must have a more subtle knowledge of constituent ordering.

(6) a. Look! Elmo is tickling Grover!
     b. Look! Grover is tickling Elmo!

Results indicated that children looked longer at the matching screen than the non-matching screen, suggesting their knowledge of SVO as the BWO in English.[2]

Children also show sensitivity to BWO in their first utterances in which "order" can be observed: two-word combinations. Brown (1973) reports data from the speech of 17 children (1;7–2;6) acquiring American English, Finnish, Swedish, Samoan, and Mexican Spanish. These children made only about 100 errors in many thousands of utterances. Pinker (1984) examined the productions from another 12 children acquiring five languages and concluded that WO was correct about 95 percent of the time in early speech. Examples of Adam's early productions appear in (7). Note that although the productions themselves are not adultlike, the relative ordering of the included elements is correct.

(7) Adultlike word order in Adam's two-word combinations (Brown 1973, p. 126, 141)

Example	Constituents
Adam write	Subject + Verb
Pillow dirty	Subject + Predicate
Play checkers	Verb + Object
Give doggie	Verb + Recipient
Put floor	Verb + Location
Adam hat	Possessor + Object

Even children learning "free word order" languages (which often depend on case-marking) have been found to show sensitivity to the canonical word order (and to respect restrictions on noncanonical WOs) at a young age—e.g. before 3;0 for Japanese (Sugisaki 2008).

However, children do occasionally make BWO errors in their productive speech. One notable type of mistake is represented in (8). In these utterances, children have used a verb-initial order which is not allowed in adult English.

(8) a. Came a man. (Eve, 1;6)
     b. Going it. (Naomi, 1;10)
     c. Fall pants. (Nina, 1;11)
     d. Broken the light. (Peter, 2;2)   (from Déprez and Pierce 1993)

Any account of the acquisition of BWO must explain not only children's early successes, but also the reasons they make the mistakes they do.

3.1 Nativist approaches to the acquisition of basic word order

Although WO is, on its surface, a temporal (in spoken or signed language) or linear (in written language) phenomenon, generative syntacticians working in GB/P&P and minimalism argue that BWO reflects underlying hierarchical relations and movement operations. Specifically, WO is derived as a result of whether each XP is head-initial or head-final, and whether feature-checking occurs through overt constituent movement (Chomsky 1986, 1995). In languages like English, in which verbs precede their object complements, phrases are (primarily) head-initial (9). In contrast, SOV languages like Turkish are head-final (10)

(Guasti 2002). Importantly, the head direction for languages like English and Turkish is highly consistent across XP types.

(9) English (SVO, head-initial)
    a. $XP \rightarrow Spec\ X'$
    b. $X' \rightarrow X^0\ YP$

(10) Turkish (SOV, head-final)
    a. $XP \rightarrow Spec\ X'$
    b. $X' \rightarrow YP\ X^0$

Recall that on the P&P view, L1A proceeds from determining (and setting) the appropriate parameter on a given principle, given positive evidence. Because head direction for a language may be consistent across XPs, seeing the ordering of elements in one XP could give a child information about the order in other XPs. For example, if the child notices that verbs come before objects, they may deduce that their language also has prepositions, that relative clauses follow heads, and so on (Pinker 1994). Thus, the relevant triggering data for setting the head-direction parameter could logically be any XP.

Because the input evidence which bears on head direction and BWO in languages like English is so rich and consistent, the nativist approach easily accounts for why children acquiring these languages show such early knowledge of BWO, as reviewed above. If any XP can serve as relevant data, then children receive ample positive evidence, and can set the relevant directionality parameters quite early (see also Gibson and Wexler 1994). However, such a proposal may not as easily extend to the acquisition of BWO in languages like Chinese, which are neither completely head-initial nor completely head-final (Huang 1982).

The remaining task for nativists is to explain why children occasionally make errors in which they produce WOs never encountered in the input, and which are inconsistent with the WO parameter they are thought to have set. Setting a parameter, at least on the strong view, is an "all-or-nothing" phenomenon; as a result, verb-initial utterances like those in (8) seem incompatible with early knowledge of BWO. Such utterances are rare, but why are they ever attested?

One proposal hinges on the fact that postverbal subjects in child English seem to occur overwhelmingly with unaccusative verbs: verbs whose syntactic subjects are semantic objects (Perlmutter 1978; Levin and Rappaport Hovav 1995; see also Baker 1988). Given this distribution, Déprez and Pierce (1993) argue that such productions provide support for the claim that children's linguistic *structures* are adultlike, even if their knowledge of the requisite post-D-structure *movements* is not. Specifically, these utterances suggest that children's S-structures correspond to adult D-structures. In light of this, Déprez and Pierce argue for continuity between child and adult grammars, and for adultlike competence of syntactic structure from the earliest points in development.

3.2 Emergentist approaches to the acquisition of basic word order

How do emergentist researchers explain the observations reviewed above? Recall that emergentists argue that syntactic generalizations are not innate but instead begin as lexically specific, learned patterns. Tomasello's (1992, 2003) "verb island hypothesis" suggests that at an early stage in acquisition, children learn item-based constructions in which a known verb is stored along with its participant roles in the correct order (11). At this point, there is no abstract generalization in the child's grammar. Later, the child will use similarities across participant roles and redundancies across argument structures to create more abstract, generalized rules.

(11)

Step 1	Step 2
KISSER + *kiss* + PERSON-KISSED	*NP V NP*
BREAKER + *break* + THING-BROKEN	*agent-action-patient*
DRINKER + *drink* + THING-DRUNK	

The claim that such generalizations begin as item-based constructions, not general semantic or syntactic descriptions, is supported by Tomasello's (1992) diary study of his daughter Travis (T). From 1;0–2;0, nearly all of T's multiword productions containing verbs were recorded and analyzed for the distinct sentence frames (i.e. the types and configurations of NPs/PPs) in which each verb appeared over time. The majority of T's non-repeated utterances were familiar frames with new NPs. T only slowly increased the number of frames in which she used a given verb, and there was often little overlap in frames across verbs. Tomasello concluded that T's use of a specific verb in a given frame on some day was best predicted not by her use of other verbs in that frame on that day, but her use of that verb in the frame on previous days (but see Ninio 2003 for a refutation of this claim). Lieven *et al.* (1997) similarly found that 12 English-acquiring children tended to use most of their verbs and predicates in only one construction type, and that 92 percent of these children's early utterances were predicted by 25 item-specific patterns.

Akhtar (1999) notes that when children produce adultlike WOs containing familiar verbs, it is impossible to determine whether they have formed a productive abstract rule (Step 2 of (11)) or simply internalized a verb-specific rule given patterns observed in the input (Step 1). The only way to test the nativist claim that young children have abstract knowledge of BWO is to test children on novel verbs, as in the famous "wug test" (Berko 1958). To this end, Akhtar taught 36 English-acquiring children (ages 2, 3, and 4) three novel verbs in varying WOs: SVO, *SOV, and *VSO. The verbs were modeled in utterances like those in (12) and presented along with scenes acted out with figurines, to provide contextual meanings.

(12) a. SVO: Elmo *dacking* the car!
   b. *SOV: Elmo the car *gopping*!
   c. *VSO: *Tamming* Elmo the car!

After the training period, children were prompted to produce the novel verbs, and the WO used with each verb was noted. On strong versions of the nativist approach, even the youngest children are expected to have already set their WO parameters to SVO; if so, they should correct non-SVO orders to SVO. In contrast, the data-driven approach predicts that children may recreate the non-SVO orders, since these have been encountered in the input.

At all ages, children were more likely to match the demonstrated WO when the verb was presented in SVO, and 4-year-olds consistently corrected the non-SVO orders to SVO, indicating that they had indeed established an abstract WO rule. However, 2- and 3-year-olds were as likely to use the non-English orders (*SOV, *VSO) as they were to correct them. A follow-up experiment, in which a known verb was produced in non-SVO order (e.g. *Elmo the car pushing!*) indicated that children were willing to correct sentences to SVO if they included familiar verbs. Thus, children's use of *SOV/*VSO was not just imitation or compliance.

Akhtar concludes that the parameter-setting approach is inconsistent with these facts, and that learning "SVO" is a gradual, data-driven process. Before age 4, children rely on verb-specific knowledge rather than any general understanding of BWO, which takes more time to appear. Similar results have been found with children acquiring French (Matthews *et al.*, 2007).

How do emergentist theories account for the non-adultlike data in (8)? Unlike generative theories of adult syntax, usage-based theories (e.g. Goldberg 1995, 2006) argue that there are no underlying levels of syntax (e.g. movement) or empty categories (trace). This theoretical stance results in a distinct idea about what the adultlike representation is for unaccusative verbs. Such verbs are not thought to involve movement of a semantic theme/object to syntactic subject position, and so emergentists must look elsewhere to explain children's postverbal subjects.

O'Grady (1997) suggests a semantic explanation which similarly hinges on the fact that the subjects of such verbs are themes. In English, themes overwhelmingly appear postverbally; as a result, children who make this particular mistake may have wrongly deduced that *all* semantic themes, regardless of their syntactic status, must appear after the verb.

Note that because nativist and emergentist approaches to postverbal subjects are attempting to account for the same small data set, this phenomenon does not conclusively provide support for one theory over the other.

4   *Wh*-questions

Crosslinguistically, adult languages differ with respect to where *wh*-elements appear. In languages like English,[3] Bulgarian, and Koromfe, a *wh*-word (or phrase) is fronted to a clause-initial position, a phenomenon often called "*wh*-movement". In contrast, languages like Mandarin and Japanese leave *wh*-words *in situ*, where the corresponding non-*wh*-element would appear (Tallerman 2011).

Along with *wh*-fronting, *wh*-questions in languages like English, Italian, and German require that a verbal element (a main verb or an auxiliary) appear in a position before the subject; this is "subject-auxiliary inversion" (SAI). As a result, *wh*-questions require that several elements appear in marked locations, compared to regular declarative utterances (13), and children must master these distinctions.

(13)   a.   Julia will eat lamb/what for dinner.
       b.   What will Julia — eat — for dinner?

The earliest *wh*-questions produced by children learning English tend to take the shape *Wh('s) NP*, in which a *wh*-word—usually *what* or *where*—is followed by an optional contracted copula and a noun phrase (Klima and Bellugi 1966; Brown 1968). Examples from children ages 17–20 months appear in (14).

(14)   a.   What's that?
       b.   Who that?
       c.   What's this?
       d.   What this?

    e. Where's helicopter?

    f. Where Mummy?   (from Radford, 1990)

Some researchers (e.g. O'Grady 1997) have argued that these are unanalyzed frozen forms not built on any productive *wh*-movement strategy, especially given that children at this age do not appear to comprehend *wh*-questions containing *what* and *where* (Klima and Bellugi 1966; Radford 1990), as illustrated in (15).

(15) a. Mother: What do you want me to do with his shoe?

         Child: Cromer shoe.

     b. Mother: What did you do?

         Child: Head.

     c. Mother: What are you doing?

         Child: No.

Children acquiring *wh*-movement languages continue to respect the adultlike positioning of *wh*-words in their productions. Guasti (2000) examined 2,809 *wh*-questions from four English-acquiring children (1;6–5;1) and found that most or all of the *wh-in situ* questions produced were echo questions. Early sensitivity to *wh*-fronting has been corroborated in a number of other *wh*-movement languages, including Dutch, German, Italian, and Swedish. Meanwhile, French-acquiring children produce moved and *in situ wh*-phrases, both of which are allowed in adult French (Guasti 2002).

Over the course of acquisition, children gradually increase their production and comprehension of *wh*-questions. In English, children begin to incorporate more of the *wh*-words, to produce adjunct questions (*where, when, why*), to lengthen and vary the questions asked, and to respond correctly to *wh*-questions, as shown in (16) (Klima and Bellugi 1966).

(16) a. Mother: What d'you need?

         Child: Need some chocolate.

     b. Mother: Who were you playing with?

         Child: Robin.

However, children do exhibit difficulties on the way to fully adultlike production of *wh*-questions, two of which I will highlight here. First, children acquiring English may go through a phase in which they use do-support and SAI with yes–no questions (17), but not with *wh*-questions (18) (Klima and Bellugi 1966).

(17) a. Can't you get it?

     b. Does the kitty stand up?

     c. Oh, did I caught it?

(18) a. What you had?

     b. How that opened?

     c. Why Paul caught it?

Second, after children have begun to consistently use SAI in positive *wh*-questions, they may continue to make inversion errors in negative *wh*-questions (Bellugi 1971). Stromswold

(1990) examined spontaneous production and found that children performed inversion correctly in 90.7 percent of positive questions, but in only 55.6 percent of negative ones. To explore this issue, Guasti *et al.* (1995) used an elicited production task and found that children aged 4–5 often produced one of three non-adultlike structures (19). In the "non-inverted" structure, the *wh*-word is correctly fronted, but the auxiliary is left in its lower position. In the "aux-doubling" structure, the auxiliary is produced twice: once in the (adultlike) higher position and once in the (non-adultlike) lower position. Finally, in the " *not*-structure", SAI is used but the negator is left uninverted.

(19) a. *Noninverted structure:* Where he couldn't eat the raisin? (4;0)
    b. *Aux-doubling:* What did he didn't wanna bring to school? (4;1)
    c. *Not-structure:* Why can you not eat chocolate? (4;1)

4.1   Nativist approaches to the acquisition of wh-questions

Nativists argue that the production of adultlike *wh*-questions involves correctly setting two parameters. First, a universal "*wh*-criterion" requires movement of a *wh*-phrase to Spec,CP to check a *wh*-feature in C (Rizzi 1996); crosslinguistic parameter-setting determines whether this *wh*-movement is overt (as in English) or covert (as in Mandarin). SAI is dictated by similar considerations: another parameter requires that an auxiliary raise from T to C to check an uninterpretable question feature (Adger 2003). These movements are illustrated in (20).

(20)

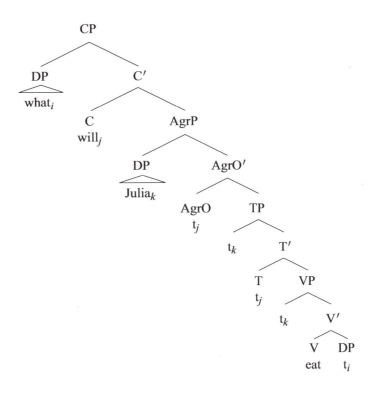

Children's early productions containing fronted *wh*-elements have been interpreted as evidence that an overt *wh*-movement parameter is set early, and that the *wh*-criterion is active in the earliest grammars (Guasti 2002), providing support for continuity. Early parameter-setting seems reasonable, since the evidence for *wh*-movement in the input is considerable; *wh*-questions (which involve *wh*-fronting) far outnumber echo questions (which do not). So why might children lag in their use of SAI?

The existence of a stage in which children perform SAI in yes–no questions but not *wh*-questions would be problematic for the notion that T-to-C movement is a result of parameter-setting (Ambridge *et al.* 2006). If the relevant parameter is set, why should children produce adultlike inversion in some contexts but not others? However, the existence of this stage is not uncontroversial. Some researchers have found evidence for it, others have not, and still others have found the opposite pattern to hold (i.e. children inverting more often in *wh*-questions). Stromswold (1990) suggests that variance in the application of SAI is due to extragrammatical (nonlinguistic) factors. Moreover, the presence of such a stage in child English may simply reflect the difficulty that children face in terms of setting a parameter correctly. The evidence for SAI in the input is fairly "noisy", since English auxiliaries undergo T-to-C, but lexical verbs do not. Such conflicting evidence may stall children as they sift through the data to determine the correct parameter setting (Guasti 1996).

The observation that children go through a stage in which SAI is adultlike in positive, but not negative, *wh*-questions is less controversial, and thus perhaps more problematic for the parameter-setting approach. To understand how nativists have accounted for this stage, consider how they have analyzed children's productions. In an adultlike negative *wh*-question, both the auxiliary and the negation should raise to C (21). In contrast, children in the Guasti *et al.* (1995) experiment produced non-inverted, aux-doubling, and *not*-structures (22).

(21) What$_i$ didn't$_j$ he t$_j$ want to bring t$_i$ to school?

(22) a. *Noninverted structure:* What he didn't want to bring to school?
      b. *Aux-doubling:* What did he didn't want to bring to school?
      c. *Not-structure:* What did he not want to bring to school?

Guasti (1996) notes that such productions are unlikely to result from processing limitations stemming from the use of negative elements, since Italian children at the same age (who are subject to the same age-specific cognitive limitations) do use SAI in negative *wh*-questions ((23)–(24)). Instead, the non-adultlike productions in child English must reflect grammatical constraints.

(23) Cosa non ta [sa] fare   il   bambino?
      what NEG can   do.INF the child?
      "What can't the child do?" (3;11)

(24) Perchè non vuole andare a   scuola la   bambina?
      why   NEG wants go.INF   to school the girl?
      "Why doesn't the girl want to go to school?" (4;7)

Notice that the non-adultlike productions illustrated in (22) share a common feature: in each case, the child avoids raising negation to C. Evidence from adult language indicates that this may reflect a crosslinguistic parameter specific to movement in negated structures: in adult Paduan (Italian), T-to-C movement occurs in positive *wh*-questions but is blocked in negative *wh*-questions (Poletto 1993). In short, movement in positive and negative contexts may be subject to distinct parameters. English-acquiring children who resist raising negation may have simply misset a parameter, and are thus "speaking Paduan"—hypothesizing that English has the same restriction on movement in negative *wh*-questions. (See Hiramatsu 2003 for more on aux-doubling structures.)

Moving out of this stage will eventually occur as a result of resetting the parameter correctly, after receiving enough positive evidence to deduce how negation works in adult-like SAI constructions (see also Thornton 2008).

4.2   Emergentist approaches to the acquisition of wh-questions

Emergentists argue that the acquisition of so-called "*wh*-movement" is driven by the data that children encounter in the input. Given the fact that the majority of *wh*-elements appear clause-initially in English, it is unsurprising that English-acquiring children should produce *wh*-words in fronted positions in their earliest *wh*-questions.

From this theoretical perspective, the use of routinized *Wh('s) NP* questions is important. The fact that such *wh*-questions appear to be unanalyzed forms with non-adultlike meanings (25) might provide a *wh*-parallel to the "verb islands" of BWO development: that is, they represent a period in which *wh*-questions are formed in a very limited way and built around specific lexical items, rather than on any productive *wh*-fronting strategy. This provides evidence for the discontinuity view.

(25)   What's+that?
       "I want to know the name of that thing"   (see Klima and Bellugi 1966)

For emergentist researchers, the observation that children may go through periods in which SAI is not consistently applied is unproblematic, given that emergentists do not believe SAI to reflect an inflexible parameter setting. Instead, the prediction is that children likely *will* show different levels of auxiliary fronting, based on the frequency with which they have encountered the auxiliary, or even the specific WH+AUX chunk, in initial position. For instance, this approach might provide the beginnings of an explanation for why some children make inversion errors with *why* after they have mastered other *wh*-words (including other adjunct wh's: Thornton 2008). A search of the COCA N-grams corpus (Davies 2011) indicates that *why* is much less frequent than other common *wh*-words (26).

(26)   Frequency of *Wh*-Words in the COCA N-Gram Corpus

Word	Tokens
what	1284606
who	1107784
when	1028347
where	443449
why	256693

Ambridge *et al.* (2006) provide experimental evidence that children learn SAI on a WH+AUX-specific basis. The authors tested 28 children (3;6–4;6) by eliciting non-subject *wh*-questions with *what, who, how*, or *why*; auxiliary *BE*, auxiliary *DO*, or modal *CAN*; and transitive verbs with 3sg or 3pl pronoun subjects. Twenty-four questions were elicited from each child, as in (27).

(27) Minnie is drinking something. I wonder what she is drinking. Ask the dog what she is drinking.

Children's errors were classified according to type: non-inversion (11 percent), auxiliary-doubling (6 percent), omitted auxiliary (2 percent), or other (5 percent). Results indicated that errors patterned not by *wh*-word, auxiliary, or subject number alone, but rather on the basis of specific WH+AUX chunks. For instance, children made significantly more non-inversion errors with *do* than with *does, am, are*, or *can*, and within utterances containing *do*, more errors were made with *who do* than with *what do*, which in turn showed higher error rates than *how do*. As the authors note, the generativist/nativist account—which views SAI as a process involving the category "aux", rather than specific lexical items or agreement forms—does not predict a performance distinction between *do* and *does*, nor among different *wh*-words paired with *do*. Instead, these findings support lexical learning predictions (e.g. Rowland and Pine 2000). Ambridge *et al.* 2006 suggest that what children initially learn is not a productive, abstract SAI rule, but rather lexically specific WH+AUX chunks (or even longer chunks, in the case of routinized questions). Errors reflect non-adultlike knowledge of the related combinations.

This explanation might extend to the observation that children master SAI in positive *wh*-questions earlier than in negative *wh*-questions. Another examination of the COCA N-grams corpus shows that the two question types differ sharply in their token frequency.[4]

(28) Frequency of Positive and Negative *Wh*-Questions in the COCA N-Gram Corpus

Positive		Negative	
Chunk	*Tokens*	*Chunk*	*Tokens*
what did	17014	*what didn't*	219
why did	14500	*why didn't*	4249
who did	12793	*who didn't*	4102
where did	3819	*where didn't*	—
when did	2927	*when didn't*	—

How frequency affects L1A is a matter of debate, but many researchers agree that the mechanism is much more complicated than simple token counts (Ambridge *et al.* 2006; Lieven 2010). For one thing, while frequency may affect the input to which children are exposed (thus acting as a "cause"), it also likely reflects pragmatic restrictions that both child and adult speakers are subject to ("effect"). In the case of *wh*-questions, there are far more contexts in which it is felicitous to ask a positive *wh*-question than a negative *wh*-question, since the latter often requires a special pragmatic context, like that in (29). In short, the lack of attested *when didn't* utterances in adult speech may reflect the fact that speakers do not often need them (30).

(29) You bought shoes, socks, pants, shirts, and hats... *What didn't you buy?*

(30) You went on Monday, Tuesday, Wednesday, and Thursday ... #*When didn't you go?*

As the combined result of low input frequency and pragmatic infelicity, children may have far fewer chances to practice negative *wh*-questions, resulting in a relative delay in their mastery.

5 Goals and parsimony in nativism and emergentism

As should be clear at this point, nativist and emergentist researchers approach problems in L1A from very different directions. This may arise from the fact that the two camps are trying to explain very different things (Carla Hudson Kam, personal communication). Nativist accounts of acquisition have their historical roots in generativist syntax. Crosslinguistic universals and limits on the attested variation in adult languages have been taken as evidence for an innate language faculty, and the nativist focus on L1A has thus largely been directed at highlighting the ways in which child grammars resemble possible adult grammars (even when they do not resemble the target grammar). In contrast, emergentist approaches take as their starting point the task of accounting for development, and are therefore fundamentally interested in the dimensions on which child language does *not* resemble the target (or any other) adult language.

This difference in objective results in different definitions of theoretical parsimony. Generative syntacticians have consistently aimed to provide an elegant, comprehensive account of the adult language faculty, which includes a nativist acquisition component. Meanwhile, emergentists seek theoretical parsimony in a catholic description of human cognition, and therefore attempt to account for the development of human language without reference to domain-specific ability.

Is it possible to reconcile these two theoretical camps? Perhaps. In his description of multiple domain-general processes which might circumvent the "logical problem" of L1A (namely, how it is acquired so quickly by children, without negative evidence; e.g. Lightfoot 1982), MacWhinney (2004) notes that in order to account for the correct setting of "parameters" which are dependent on multiple, complex cue patterns over time, nativist approaches (like Yang's, mentioned above) often build in a substantial (and sometimes domain-general) learning component—at which point these theories begin to resemble emergentist accounts. Thus, it may be the fate of the field that in the attempt to capitalize on their respective strengths in empirical coverage, emergentist and nativist theories ultimately converge.

Notes

1 Ages are presented in the format years;months[.days].
2 Because *subjects* in the test sentences were always *agents*, it is unclear whether children's behavior in the Hirsh-Pasek and Golinkoff (1996) experiment reflects an underlying generalization of "subject-verb-object" or instead "agent-action-patient". See Bever (1970), Pinker (1984), and Akhtar (1999).
3 Here I ignore so-called "echo questions" in English: e.g. *Julia will eat WHAT for dinner?!*
4 I thank a student in my Acquisition of Syntax class at Simon Fraser University for this idea.

Further reading

For more on empirical methodologies in syntactic acquisition, see the comprehensive discussions in McDaniel *et al.* (1996). For the acquisition of BWO, see O'Grady (1997, Ch. 4). For *wh*-questions, see O'Grady (1997, Ch. 7), Guasti (2002, Ch. 6), and Roeper and de Villiers (2011).

Contrasting nativist and emergentist proposals have been floated for many other phenomena not considered above, and I offer selected examples of these here. Wexler (Schütze and Wexler 1996;

Wexler 1998) offers a nativist proposal for the acquisition of tense/agreement morphology, and Pine *et al.* (2008) present an emergentist counterargument. Wexler has also presented nativist theories for the acquisition of the binding principles (Chien and Wexler 1990; Thornton and Wexler 1999); see Matthews *et al.* (2009) for more data, and challenges to both nativist *and* emergentist accounts. Becker (2006, 2009) and Kirby (2009) give nativist accounts for the acquisition of raising and control structures, but Becker's account includes a substantial learning component; Kirby (2012) offers an explicitly emergentist view for how these verbs are learned. O'Grady (2008) gives a concise survey of both nativist and emergentist approaches to the acquisition of *wanna*-contraction and scope interactions; see Crain and Thornton (1998) and Musolino (1998) respectively for nativist views on these issues.

References

Adger, D. 2003. *Core Syntax*. Oxford: Oxford University Press.

Akhtar, N. 1999. Acquiring basic word order: evidence for data-driven learning of syntactic structures. *Journal of Child Language* 26: 339–356.

Ambridge, B., C.F. Rowland, A.L. Theakston, and M. Tomasello. 2006. Comparing different accounts of inversion errors in children's non-subject *wh*-questions: 'What experimental data can tell us?' *Journal of Child Language* 33: 519–557.

Baker, M. 1988. *Incorporation: A Theory of Grammatical Function Changing*. Chicago: University of Chicago Press.

Bates, E., and B. MacWhinney. 1988. What is functionalism? *Papers and Reports on Child Language Development* 27: 137–152.

Becker, M. 2006. There began to be a learnability puzzle. *Linguistic Inquiry* 37: 441–456.

Becker, M. 2009. The role of NP animacy and expletives in verb learning. *Language Acquisition* 16: 283–296.

Bellugi, U. 1971. Simplification in children's language. In *Language Acquisition: Models and Methods*, ed. R. Huxley and D. Ingram. New York: Academic Press.

Berko, J. 1958. The child's learning of English morphology. *Word* 14: 150–177.

Bever, T. 1970. The cognitive basis for linguistic structures. In *Cognition and the Development of Language*, ed. J Hayes, 279–352. New York: Wiley.

Boeckx, C. 1999. Expletive split: Existentials and presentationals. In *Proceedings of the North East Linguistics Society*, Vol. 29, ed. P. Tamanji, M. Hirotani, and N. Hall, 57–69. Amherst, MA: GLSA.

Bowerman, M. 1974. Learning the structure of causative verbs: A study in the relationship of cognitive, semantic and syntactic development. *Papers and Reports on Child Language Development* 8: 142–178.

Braine, M. 1963. The ontogeny of English phrase structure: The first phase. *Language* 39: 1–13.

Brown, R. 1968. The development of *wh* questions in child speech. *Journal of Verbal Learning and Verbal Behavior* 7: 277–290.

Brown, R. 1973. *A First Language*. Cambridge, MA: Harvard University Press.

Carnie, A. 2007. *Syntax: A Generative Introduction*, 2nd edn. Malden, MA: Blackwell.

Chien, Y.-C., and K. Wexler. 1990. Children's knowledge of locality conditions in binding as evidence for the modularity of syntax and pragmatics. *Language Acquisition* 1: 225–295.

Childers, J. B., and M. Tomasello. 2001. The role of pronouns in young children's acquisition of the English transitive construction. *Developmental Psychology* 37: 739–748.

Chomsky, N. 1959. A review of B. F. Skinner's *Verbal Behaviour*. *Language* 35: 26–58.

Chomsky, N. 1980. *Rules and Representations*. Oxford: Oxford University Press.

Chomsky, N. 1986. *Knowledge of Language: Its Nature, Origin and Use*. New York: Praeger.

Chomsky, N. 1995. *The Minimalist Program*. Cambridge, MA: MIT Press.

Cowart, W. 1997. *Experimental Syntax: Applying Objective Methods to Sentence Judgments*. Thousand Oaks, CA: Sage Publications.

Crain, S. 1991. Language acquisition in the absence of experience. *Behavioral and Brain Sciences* 14: 597–650.

Crain, S., and J. Fodor. 1993. Competence and performance. In *Language and Cognition: A Developmental Perspective*, ed. E. Dromi, 141–171. Norwood, NJ: Ablex.

Crain, S., and R. Thornton. 1998. *Investigations in Universal Grammar.* Cambridge, MA: MIT Press.

Davies, M. 2011. N-grams data from the Corpus of Contemporary American English (COCA). See http://www.ngrams.info (accessed 31 January 2014).

Déprez, V., and A. Pierce. 1993. Negation and functional projections in early grammar. *Linguistic Inquiry* 24: 25–67.

Fernald, A. 1992. Human maternal vocalizations to infants as biologically relevant signals: An evolutionary perspective. In *The Adapted Mind: Evolutionary Psychology and the Generation of Culture*, ed. J. H. Barkow, L. Cosmides and J. Tooby. Oxford: Oxford University Press.

Fodor, J. A. 1983. *The Modularity of Mind.* Cambridge, MA: MIT Press.

Gibson, E., and K. Wexler. 1994. Triggers. *Linguistic Inquiry* 25: 407–454.

Goldberg, A. 1995. *Constructions: A Construction Grammar Approach to Argument Structure* Chicago: Chicago University Press.

Goldberg, A. 1999. The emergence of the semantics of argument structure constructions. In *The Emergence of Language*, ed. B. MacWhinney, 197–212. Mahwah, NJ: Lawrence Erlbaum Associates.

Goldberg, A. 2006. *Constructions at Work.* Oxford: Oxford University Press.

Guasti, M. T. 1996. The acquisition of Italian interrogatives. In *Generative Perspectives on Language Acquisition*, ed. H. Clahsen. Amsterdam: John Benjamins.

Guasti, M. T. 2000. An excursion into interrogatives in early English and Italian. In *The Acquisition of Syntax*, ed. M.-A. Friedemann and L. Rizzi. Harlow: Longman.

Guasti, M. T. 2002. *Language Acquisition: The Growth of Grammar.* Cambridge, MA: MIT Press.

Guasti, M. T., R. Thornton, and K. Wexler. 1995. Negation in children's questions: The case of English. In *Proceedings of the 19th Annual Boston University Conference on Language Development*, ed. D. MacLaughlin and S. McEwen. Somerville, MA: Cascadilla Press.

Hiramatsu, K. 2003. Children's judgments of negative questions. *Language Acquisition* 11: 99–126.

Hirschfeld, L. A., and S.A. Gelman. 1994. Toward a topography of mind: An introduction to domain specificity. In *Mapping the Mind: Domain Specificity in Cognition and Culture*, ed. L. A. Hirschfeld and S. A. Gelman, 3–35. Cambridge: Cambridge University Press.

Hirsh-Pasek, K., and R.M. Golinkoff. 1996. *The Origins of Grammar: Evidence from Early Language Comprehension.* Cambridge, MA: MIT Press.

Hockett, C. F. 1960. The origin of speech. *Scientific American* 203: 89–97.

Huang, J. 1982. Logical relations in Chinese and the theory of grammar. PhD thesis, MIT.

Hyams, N. 1986. *Language Acquisition and the Theory of Parameters.* Boston: Reidel.

Kirby, S. 2005. Semantics or Subcases? The Acquisition of Referential vs. Expletive *it*. Master's thesis, University of North Carolina at Chapel Hill, Chapel Hill, NC.

Kirby, S. 2009. Semantic scaffolding in first language acquisition: The acquisition of raising to-object and object control. PhD thesis, University of North Carolina at Chapel Hill.

Kirby, S. 2012. Raising is birds, control is penguins: Solving the learnability paradox. In *Proceedings of the 36th Annual Boston University Conference on Language Development*, ed. A. K. Biller, E. Y. Chung, and A. E. Kimball, Vol. 1, 269–280. Somerville, MA: Cascadilla Press.

Kirby, S., and M. Becker. 2007. Which *it* is it? The acquisition of referential and expletive *it*. *Journal of Child Language* 34: 571–599.

Klima, E. S., and U. Bellugi. 1966. Syntactic regularities in the speech of children. In *Psycholinguistic Papers*, ed. J. Lyons and R. J. Wales, 183–208. Edinburgh: Edinburgh University Press.

Kowalski, A., and C. Yang. 2012. Verb islands in child and adult grammar. In Proceedings of the 36th Annual Boston University Conference on Language Development, Vol. 1., ed. A. K. Biller, E. Y. Chung, and A. E. Kimball, 281–289. Somerville, MA: Cascadilla Press.

Langacker, R. 1987. *Foundations of Cognitive Grammar*, Vol. 1. Stanford, CA: Stanford University Press.

Levin, B., and M. Rappaport Hovav. 1995. *Unaccusativity at The Syntax-Lexical Semantics Interface.* Cambridge, MA: MIT Press.

Lieven, E. 2010. Input and first language acquisition: Evaluating the role of frequency. *Lingua* 120: 2546–2556.

Lieven, E., H. Behrens, J. Speares, and M. Tomasello. 2003. Early syntactic creativity: A usage based approach. *Journal of Child Language* 30: 333–370.

Lieven, E., J. Pine, and G. Baldwin. 1997. Lexically-based learning and early grammatical development. *Journal of Child Language* 24: 187–219.

Lightfoot, D. 1982. *The Language Lottery: Toward a Biology of Grammars*. Cambridge, MA: MIT Press.

MacWhinney, B. 2004. A multiple process solution to the logical problem of language acquisition. *Journal of Child Language* 31: 883–914.

Matthews, D., E. Lieven, A. Theakston, and M. Tomasello. 2007. French children's use and correction of weird word orders: A constructivist account. *Journal of Child Language* 34: 381–409.

Matthews, D., E. Lieven, A. Theakston, and M. Tomasello. 2009. Pronoun co-referencing errors: Challenges for generativist and usage-based accounts. *Cognitive Linguistics* 20: 599–626.

McDaniel, D., and H.S. Cairns. 1996. Eliciting judgments of grammaticality and reference. In *Methods for Assessing Children's Syntax*, ed. D. McDaniel, C. McKee, and H. S. Cairns, 233–254. Cambridge, MA: MIT Press.

McDaniel, D., C. McKee, and H.S. Cairns, eds. 1996. *Methods for Assessing Children's Syntax*. Cambridge, MA: MIT Press.

Musolino, J. 1998. Universal grammar and the acquisition of syntactic knowledge: An experimental investigation into the acquisition of quantifier-negation interaction in English. PhD thesis, University of Maryland.

Ninio, A. 2003. No verb is an island: Negative evidence on the verb island hypothesis. *Psychology of Language and Communication* 7: 3–21.

O'Grady, W. 1997. *Syntactic Development*. Chicago: University of Chicago Press.

O'Grady, W. 2008. Does emergentism have a chance? In *Proceedings of the 32nd Annual Boston University Conference on Language Development*, 16–35. Somerville, MA: Cascadilla Press.

O'Grady, W. 2010. Emergentism. In *The Cambridge Encyclopedia of the Language Sciences*, ed. P. C. Hogan, 274–276. Cambridge: Cambridge University Press.

Perlmutter, D. 1978. Impersonal passives and the unaccusative hypothesis. In *Proceedings of the 4th Annual Meeting of the Berkeley Linguistics Society*, 157–189. UC Berkeley.

Piaget, J. 1923. *The Language and Thought of the Child*. London: Routledge & Kegan Paul.

Pine, J., G. Conti-Ramsden, K.L. Joseph, E. Lieven, and L. Serratrice. 2008. Tense over time: testing the agreement/tense omission model as an account of the pattern of tense-marking provision in early child English. *Journal of Child Language* 35: 55–75.

Pinker, S. 1984. *Language Learnability and Language Development*. Cambridge, MA: Harvard University Press.

Pinker, S. 1994. *The Language Instinct*. New York: William Morrow.

Pinker, S. 2000. *Words and Rules: The Ingredients of Language*. Harper Perennial.

Poletto, C. 1993. Subject clitic-verb inversion in North Eastern Italian dialects. In *Syntactic Theory and the Dialects of Italy*, ed. A. Belletti. Turin: Rosenberg and Sellier.

Pullum, G. K., and B.C. Scholz. 2002. Empirical assessment of stimulus poverty arguments. *Linguistic Review* 19: 9–50.

Radford, A. 1990. *Syntactic Theory and the Acquisition of English Syntax: The Nature of Early Child Grammars of English*. Oxford: Blackwell.

Rizzi, L. 1982. *Issues in Italian Syntax*, Vol. 11 of Studies in Generative Grammar. Cinnaminson, NJ: Foris Publications.

Rizzi, L. 1996. Residual verb second and the *Wh* Criterion. In *Parameters and Functional Heads*, ed. A. Belletti, and L. Rizzi. Oxford: Oxford University Press.

Roeper, T., and J. de Villiers. 2011. The acquisition path for *wh*-questions. In *Handbook of Generative Approaches to Language Acquisition*, Vol. 41 of Studies in Theoretical Psycholinguistics, ed. J. de Villiers and T. Roeper, 189–246. Springer.

Rowland, C., and J. Pine. 2000. Subject-auxiliary inversion errors and *wh*-question acquisition: 'What children do know?' *Journal of Child Language* 27: 157–181.

Schütze, C., and K. Wexler. 1996. Subject case licensing and English root infinitives. In *Proceedings of the 20th Annual Boston University Conference on Language Development*, ed. A. Stringfellow, D. Cahma-Amitay, E. Hughes, and A. Zukowski, 670–681. Somerville, MA: Cascadilla Press.

Skinner, B. 1957. *Verbal Behavior*. London: Prentice Hall.

Stromswold, K. 1990. Learnability and the acquisition of auxiliaries. PhD thesis, MIT.

Sugisaki, K. 2008. Early acquisition of basic word order in Japanese. *Language Acquisition* 15: 183–191.

Tallerman, M. 2011. *Understanding Syntax*, 3rd edn. London: Hodder Education.

Thornton, R. 2008. Why continuity. *Natural Language and Linguistic Theory* 26: 107–146.

Thornton, R., and K. Wexler. 1999. *Principle B, VP Ellipsis and Interpretation in Child Grammar.* Cambridge, MA: MIT Press.

Tomasello, M. 1992. The social bases of language acquisition. *Social Development* 1: 67–87.

Tomasello, M. 2003. *Child Language Acquisition: A Usage-based Approach.* Cambridge, MA: Harvard University Press.

Tomasello, M., A.C. Kruger, and H.H. Ratner. 1993. Cultural learning. *Behavioral and Brain Sciences* 16: 495–552.

Wexler, K. 1998. Very early parameter setting and the unique checking constraint: A new explanation of the optional infinitive stage new explanation of the optional infinitive stage. *Lingua* 106: 23–79.

Yang, C. 2002. *Knowledge and Learning in Natural Language.* New York: Oxford University Press.

Yang, C. 2004. Universal grammar, statistics, or both? *TRENDS in Cognitive Sciences* 8: 451–456.

Yang, C. 2012. Computational models of syntactic acquisition. *WIREs Cognitive Science* 3: 205–213.

22

The evolutionary origins of syntax

Maggie Tallerman

1   Introduction: Syntactic phenomena and evolution

The only fact regarding the evolution of syntax of which we can be certain is that it has occurred in one species: *Homo sapiens*. We have no idea whether syntax preceded *sapiens*, and so may have existed in earlier hominin species – say, perhaps, *Homo heidelbergensis*, some half a million years ago – or whether syntax emerged, gradually or instantaneously, during the roughly 200,000 years of our existence. Equally, we have no idea whether any other recently extinct species in our lineage had any form of syntax, for instance our close relatives *Homo neanderthalensis*, a (sub)species that survived until around 30,000 years ago. Attempts to date syntax and to chart its origins are fraught with difficulty and will not be pursued here. Instead, I examine possible pathways of syntactic evolution and the evidence underpinning them.

I start with a brief review of the building blocks of syntax. Three formal devices give rise to open-ended and productive syntax: (a) semantic compositionality, whereby the meaning of a phrase is assembled from the meanings of its constituent parts; (b) the ordering of words and of phrases according to general and language-specific principles of linearization; (c) the formation of headed and hierarchically structured recursive phrases and clauses. All languages exploit these three principles; the first is definitional for language, but both linearization and constituency are employed to a greater or lesser extent in distinct language types. Stepping back a stage, before words can be combined syntactically they must come into existence and eventually become categorized into specific classes in language-specific ways.

All languages exploit various kinds of syntactic dependencies between elements. At the lowest level, indeed, the existence of local dependencies between words is what creates hierarchical structure. For instance, a transitive verb such as *procure* requires a direct object, specifically an object with the semantic property of being procurable; hence the oddness of *?Kim procured our sincerity*. Dependencies between non-adjacent elements in a clause occur extensively. These include agreement phenomena (e.g., *The books are falling over* vs. *The boy carrying the books is/*are falling over*); displacement phenomena of various kinds, such as *wh*-movement (*Who did you (say you would) send the book to ____ ?*);

and referential dependencies, including antecedent-anaphor relations and negative polarity dependencies (*No one/*everyone ever eats the biscuits*). As is clear from these examples, dependencies are often non-local and may range over several clauses; moreover, the *wh*-movement example also shows that not all elements in a dependency need be overtly realized: The link here is with a question word and a gap corresponding to the prepositional object. The extent to which individual languages exploit such dependencies also varies greatly. For instance, verb agreement may be entirely absent, as in Chinese and Japanese; *wh*-movement is also often absent, again shown by Chinese and Japanese.

How, though, did language acquire these devices? Do any of them – meaningful signal combinations, linearization principles, headed hierarchical structure with dependencies between elements – occur in other animal communication systems, in particular the communication of our closest primate relatives, the great apes? Essentially, the answer is no; considered surveys of animal communication can be found in Anderson (2004; 2008), Heine and Kuteva (2007: Ch. 3) and Hurford (2012). Both birdsong and whalesong exhibit minimal hierarchical structure and simple dependencies between song elements, and researchers in these fields recognize the occurrence of discrete phrases in the songs. None-theless, animal song can be formally described without context-free or phrase structure grammar (Hurford 2012: Ch. 1). Recursion is absent; no semantic dependencies occur; and even combinatoriality is minimally exploited. In primates, the call systems of some monkeys appear to show a very limited combinatorial system (e.g., Arnold and Zuberbühler 2008). However, there is no evidence of *semantic* compositionality in animal systems: The meanings of call sequences are not derived from the meanings of the individual parts. So far even this small degree of combination has not been reported in great ape communication.

Primate communication systems seem, then, to offer no insights into the evolution of syntax. There is, however, fairly widespread agreement that pre-human *cognitive* abilities give rise to fundamental properties that are subsequently exapted – taken over to fulfil a new function – for use in language. Modern primates may provide evidence of phylogenet-ically ancient capacities in this regard. Apes in the 'language lab' have no problem under-standing that arbitrary symbols for common nouns (say, a sign for 'banana') refer to types, not tokens (Savage-Rumbaugh *et al.* 1998), whereas a proper name given, say, to a human carer is not generalized to other humans of the same sex. Abilities of this type in our distant ancestors could ultimately have had functions in structuring language. However, questions surrounding which, if any, aspects of human cognition are domain-specific to language are highly controversial.

In the search for the origins of syntax there is clearly a paucity of direct evidence, and only tangential indirect evidence, for instance from investigations into the archaeological record. What, then, can linguists bring to the quest? As Jackendoff (2010: 65) notes: '[T]he most productive methodology seems to be to engage in reverse engineering.' Thus, we hope to discover the evolutionary origins of language by examining the modern language faculty. Evidence includes language acquisition, both in normal and pathological circum-stances, and instances of 'language genesis', such as pidgins/creoles, homesign, and emerg-ing sign languages. Some of these sources of evidence are drawn on in what follows. One note of caution should be sounded; processes occurring in modern ontogeny (the develop-ment of language in individuals) do not inevitably reflect those occurring in phylogeny (the development of language in the species). Study of the evolved language faculty in modern humans does not necessarily reveal much about the origins of the language faculty itself.

So far, I have taken for granted the interconnected notions that modern humans possess a language faculty, and that whatever underlies syntactic competence has in fact evolved, biologically, to a uniform state in modern humans. However, not all commentators agree with these twin premises. Before moving on, I briefly consider the question of whether there is in fact any 'evolution of syntax' to account for. Evans and Levinson have claimed that there is no language faculty: 'The diversity of language is, from a biological point of view, its most remarkable property' (2009: 446); under this view, the critical biological foundations for language are the vocal tract adaptations, rather than the capacity for syntax (or any other trait). The authors assert that languages display such radically different (surface) syntactic properties that there cannot be a domain-specific UG. Nonetheless, the accompanying peer commentaries demonstrate that, contra Evans and Levinson, it is not the case that anything goes in language; moreover, examining syntactic phenomena at an abstract rather than a superficial level reveals many underlying commonalities. The fact that all human infants – but no ape infants – can acquire any of the world's languages implies the presence of a language faculty: Thus, there is indeed a uniform syntactic competence in modern humans, sometimes known as I-language.

Intriguingly, though ('internal') I-language is invariant in modern populations, there are indications that languages themselves (E-languages, where E is 'external') are not all equally complex; chapters in Sampson *et al.* (2009) offer provocative discussion. Strong claims have also been made for syntactic simplicity in various languages. Well-known examples include Pirahã, which has been claimed to lack recursion (Everett 2005; but see Nevins *et al.* (2009) for counterarguments); Riau Indonesian (Gil 2009), which has been claimed to lack word classes (but see Yoder 2010); and creole languages in general (McWhorter 2005). Whatever the ultimate consensus concerning particular languages, it seems clear that not all aspects of syntax are exploited to the same degree in all languages. All languages form headed phrases, but so-called non-configurational languages (e.g., Warlpiri) frequently employ non-continuous constituents in their surface syntax. Such languages display extensive freedom of word order, with few linearization principles. A cross-linguistic noun/verb contrast appears to be invariant, but no other lexical or functional word classes are a prerequisite for syntax. Constructions such as passivization are frequently absent. It is clear, too, that emerging languages can function well without a full complement of syntactic constructions (e.g., Kegl *et al.* 1999; Sandler *et al.* forthcoming). We examine some of these issues below.

The remainder of the chapter is organized as follows. In Section 2, I briefly examine Minimalist views of the evolutionary origins of syntax. Here, it is taken as axiomatic that nothing precedes syntactic language. In contrast, Section 3 outlines various possible scenarios for pre-language, assuming a more gradual, 'layered' development of syntactic principles. Section 4 considers the evolution of movement processes. In Section 5, the processes of grammaticalization are examined, with a view to explaining the appearance of distinct word classes as well as various types of syntactic construction. Section 6 is a brief conclusion.

2 Syntax as a saltation

We cannot know whether syntax was a SALTATION – a biological trait with a sudden emergence – or whether it evolved gradually, in small incremental steps. Arguments are found on both sides of this debate, but current Minimalist work takes the former view: Biological changes that are critical for syntax appeared recently and suddenly. In this section I explore the Minimalist/'biolinguistic' perspective on the evolution of syntax.

Hauser *et al.* (2002) argue that investigations into the evolution of language must distinguish between the faculty of language in the broad sense (FLB) and in the narrow sense

(FLN). The idea is that FLB essentially contains properties shared with other animals (in cognition and/or communication): For example, vocal imitation and invention, which is rare in primates but occurs, say, in whalesong; or the capacity to understand and perhaps use referential vocal signals, which appears in a limited form in various vertebrates. Clearly, other animals do not employ these properties for language, so if such ancient non-linguistic traits also existed in our hominin ancestors they must at some point have taken on new, linguistic functions; this is exaptation. However, the real question for evolutionary linguistics concerns the content of FLN, which forms a subset of FLB and contains whatever aspects of the language faculty are uniquely human, and not adaptations/exaptations of ancient capacities that may also exist in other lineages.

What does FLN contain? Hauser *et al.* (2002) hypothesize that FLN's contents may be limited to what they term 'narrow syntax', most essentially the computational process which forms hierarchical structure, and which is generally known as Merge. 'Merge' is a recursive operation that forms a set from two existing elements, say A and B; the unit [AB] may itself be merged again with an element C, and so on: A + B→ [AB], [AB] + C → [[AB] C]. 'FLN takes a finite set of elements and yields a potentially infinite array of discrete expressions. This capacity of FLN yields discrete infinity …' (2002: 1571). In other words, repeated applications of Merge give rise to unlimited hierarchical structure. Interfaces with two linguistic systems are also required: firstly, the sensory-motor system (basically, concerned with phonetics/phonology); and, secondly, the conceptual-intentional system (concerned with semantics/pragmatics). These mappings must also be part of FLN.

In terms of the evolution of syntax, Hauser *et al.* (2002) suggest that if FLN is indeed so limited, there is little likelihood that it was an adaptation. The point here is that if the essence of syntax is something very simple, then it was probably not the result of a series of gradual, minor modifications (Berwick 2011). Merge is an all-or-nothing property – language has it, but no animal communication system does – and it does not seem to be decomposable into a set of interacting traits which could evolve gradually under the influence of natural selection. Contrast this, say, with the evolution of vision, in which small increments are both feasible and adaptive. Under this view, the genetic endowment for syntax is extremely minimal and could occur very abruptly: Berwick and Chomsky (2011) talk about Merge arising through 'some slight rewiring of the brain' or a 'minor mutation'. Evolution by natural selection would then play no part in the *emergence* of syntax, though it presumably perpetuated the language faculty itself, since this is clearly adaptive.

From this saltationary standpoint, there is little to discuss in terms of any putative pre-language:

> [T]here is no room in this picture for any precursors to language – say a language-like system with only short sentences.
>
> (Berwick and Chomsky 2011: 31)

> [T]here is no possibility of an intermediate language between a non-combinatorial syntax and full natural language syntax – one either has Merge in all its generative glory, or one has effectively no combinatorial syntax at all.
>
> (Berwick 2011: 99)

As Hurford (2012: 586) notes, though, the wording 'non-combinatorial syntax' is a contradiction in terms: 'Syntax is by definition combinatorial.' In any case, the Minimalist perspective cannot inherently rule out an earlier stage of language that had no syntax yet was *semantically* compositional: see §3 below.

What, though, of the lexical items available to undergo Merge? Before any syntax could develop, early hominins needed an innovation that did not occur in other primate species: Symbolic words, which are rightly regarded as a genuine evolutionary novelty (Deacon 1997). A critical step in any model of syntactic evolution must be the point at which basic concepts – which our pre-linguistic ancestors must have had – become, or become associated to, lexical items. The property turning concepts into true lexical items, crucially able to be combined by Merge, is termed their 'edge feature' by Chomsky (2008), or the 'lexical envelope' by Boeckx (2012). Chomsky points out that all combinable words (so, excluding the 'defective' items discussed in §3.1 below) have such features, which buy, for instance, the fact that a transitive verb must be merged with an appropriate object, as seen in §1. Thus, words and their features must also be part of the narrow language faculty; without lexicalized concepts there can be no syntax. However, as Bickerton (2009: Ch. 9) argues, it is logically problematic to assume that mergeable concepts appear first, then some mutation produces Merge itself, which combines these new lexical items. Why would mergeable concepts appear in the absence of Merge? Since the Chomskyan model assumes that the use of language for communication ('externalization') does not occur until after Merge evolves, what could drive the evolution of these specifically human concepts? In Bickerton's alternative outline, true symbols, the basis of lexical items, evolve gradually through the use of a pre-Merge protolanguage: Thus, language usage produces human concepts.

Ultimately, the language faculty certainly incorporated a structure-building 'Merge' operation; whether or not Minimalist tenets are adopted, all theories of language evolution must accept that there is a stage at which lexical items combine to form hierarchical structures. There are differing views, though, as to whether Merge was an early or late development, and indeed about whether or not a concatenative 'merge' operation in general cognition preceded language. From the Minimalist perspective, the Merge operation is considered recent, uniquely linguistic in origin, and not derived from any other capacity (Chomsky 2010: 53). Though Merge occurs elsewhere in human cognition (notably, in arithmetic), these other uses are derivative of language. Conversely, Jackendoff (2011) argues that Merge – and structural recursion in general – is not a recent development, and in fact is not domain-specific to language; Bickerton (2012) also proposes that Merge existed (as a cognitive operation) prior to language.

The idea that any kind of combination of concepts preceded the syntactic 'Merge' stage in language evolution is an anathema in current Minimalist thinking; under these views, there is no pre-syntactic stage in language evolution. However, this position is not generally adopted in language evolution studies: Most consider the idea that a system with the complexity of language emerged fully formed on the basis of a single mutation to be biologically implausible. As Jackendoff (2011) points out, the literature on birdsong contains no suggestions that it emerged in a single mutation from a non-songbird ancestor, yet song is considerably less complex than language. Contra the Minimalist view, then, most work in language evolution proposes that syntactic language emerged from some kind of pre-language, either by one or two major steps, or – an increasingly favoured view – by the gradual accretion of syntactic principles. Since each stage endows the speaker with greater expressive power, both for speaking and for thinking, it is reasonable to assume that all increments were adaptive. Section 3 examines the main views in the literature of what is typically known as PROTOLANGUAGE.

3 Concepts of protolanguage

3.1 The earliest words

Nothing word-like is produced by other animal species (Burling 2005). Non-linguists sometimes liken animal alarm calls – such as the leopard/eagle/snake calls of vervet monkeys – to words, but this is ill-conceived. Words have the property of displacement, whereas alarm calls are situation-specific; as Jackendoff (2002: 239) neatly remarks 'A leopard alarm call can report the sighting of a leopard, but cannot be used to ask if anyone has seen a leopard lately.' Crucially, full words are conventional, learned associations between a meaning, a sound (or gesture) pattern, and the 'edge features' regulating Merge; alarm calls are innately specified rather than learned.

What, then, could the very earliest (proto-)words have been like? It seems reasonable to suggest that at first, as in child language today, there was a one-word stage. Jackendoff (2002) proposes that this stage contained not referential items like true words, but proto-words similar to modern 'defective' lexical items, which include *yes/yep, no/nope, hi, hey, hello, goodbye, wow, hooray, yuck, oops, shh, psst, tsk-tsk, abracadabra*, and *cockadoodle-doo*; similar 'palaeo-lexical' items appear to occur in all languages. Notably, these linguistic fossils can be used alone as meaningful utterances, unlike full words; in fact, they *cannot* combine with other words, except when quoted, and, moreover, they have no word class. Thus, these words have phonology (interestingly, often outside of the normal phonology of the language, as is the case for *psst* and *tsk-tsk*) and semantics, but no syntax. Some, such as *ouch*, are largely involuntary and affective, a trait reminiscent of primate calls. However, unlike primate calls, they are culture-specific – like full lexical items. Since ancestral palaeo-lexical items could not be combined, they precede a stage with semantic compositionality. Nonetheless, they have word-like properties: Their form/meaning pairs are learned, conventional associations, which makes them appropriate models for the earliest stage in language evolution. Here, then, is another example of reverse engineering; if modern languages allow lexical items without syntax, there is good reason to think that the earliest stages of language evolution would too.

It would be difficult to over-emphasize the importance of the lexicon in the evolution of syntax, or the extent to which the lexicon is so distinctive from anything found in animal communication. Of course, the lexicon includes not just words, but also idioms and construction frames such as *the more S, the more S*, as in *The more they earned, the more they saved*. Our ability to learn, store, and retrieve bundles of meaning/sound/syntax is one of the critical novelties to be accounted for, though we have relatively little idea how this trait might have evolved.

3.2 Putative properties of early protolanguage

The concept of a pre-syntactic protolanguage (i.e., a pre-modern stage or series of stages in the evolution of language in hominins) is first outlined in Bickerton (1990) and further developed in subsequent work (e.g., Bickerton 2009; Calvin and Bickerton 2000). Bickerton adopts the Minimalist view that the crucial ingredients for syntax are lexical items plus Merge, but nonetheless argues for a pre-syntactic stage. Despite popularizing the protolanguage concept, Bickerton has consistently argued *against* a gradualist position on the evolution of true syntax; his early work suggests an abrupt transition from protolanguage to full language, though his more recent work (e.g., Bickerton 2012) outlines a more extended sequence of development stages, starting with the 'Merge' procedure for assembling words into hierarchical structures. Other authors, especially Jackendoff (2002; 2011), Hurford (2012), Heine and Kuteva (2007), and Progovac (2009), have suggested a gradual accretion of 'layers' of syntactic complexity (see §3.3). Not all authors adopt the term 'protolanguage', though I use it here as a convenient shorthand for the pre-language stages putatively used by early hominins.

Bickerton's protolanguage model starts, then, with proto-words; arbitrary symbols – Saussurean signs – either spoken or gestured. Presumably, such proto-words must represent a stage beyond the palaeo-lexical items discussed in the previous section, since they are referential under Bickerton's concept of protolanguage (e.g., Bickerton 2009). Proto-words are freely strung together in very short strings, constrained only by pragmatic/semantic context, with no ordering principles, no word classes, and no heads. Crucially, unlike animal calls, however, this protolanguage is semantically compositional, in the sense that proto-words combine to form meaningful utterances.

Bickerton argues that the protolanguage capacity is not lost in modern *Homo sapiens*, but, rather, occurs in various contexts where full language is not available. Child language before the age of about two years is typically cited, but evidence also comes from pidgins/creoles (McWhorter 2005); from some types of aphasia; from children such as 'Genie', prevented from acquiring language during the critical period (Curtiss 1977); from ad hoc 'homesign' systems used by deaf children with their hearing parents (Goldin-Meadow 2005); and from emerging sign languages such as Nicaraguan Sign Language (Kegl *et al.* 1999) and Al-Sayyid Bedouin Sign Language (ABSL; Aronoff *et al.* 2008; Sandler *et al.* forthcoming). Additionally, Bickerton maintains that the productions of trained apes, consisting of short, structureless sequences of signs or lexigram combinations on a keyboard, also represent protolanguage. Putative examples of modern 'protolanguage' are shown in (1) and (2):

(1)   Child language: Seth, 23 months (Bickerton 1995)
       Read story   Want dry off   Dry you
       Put on tight   Geese say   Take off
       Can talk?   Put your refrigerator Can put it

(2)   Koko, gorilla (Patterson 1978)
       More pour   Red berry   Catch me
       Koko purse   Go bed   You eat
       Me can't   Hurry gimme   More cereal

Any proposed 'modern' reflex of protolanguage is inevitably controversial as a putative proxy for ancestral protolanguage. Children and pidgin speakers, of course, have a fully modern language faculty, and children are at least receiving full target languages as input. Adults who lacked appropriate linguistic input, such as Genie, invariably display a wide range of developmental problems, obscuring whatever may be language-specific. And there is no real evidence that modern great apes reflect the cognitive abilities of our own ancestors, say, two million years ago; there is plenty of time for extensive modifications in the hominin lineage following our split from the *Pan* genus (modern chimpanzees and bonobos) some seven million years ago. Nonetheless, data from such sources probably represents our best chance of extrapolating to the properties of the earliest protolanguage. Apart, then, from its noted freedom in the ordering of elements, what properties of modern 'protolanguages' are presumed to be shared by ancestral protolanguage?

First, null elements occur without constraint in protolanguage (*Take off, Geese say, Put your refrigerator*), whereas in full languages the subcategorized arguments of verbs and other heads are normally overtly realized. Where null elements ('e' for 'empty') occur, they are required to be systematically linked to overt categories (e.g., *The book was found* [*e*] *under her bed*) and arguments are only null under restricted syntactic conditions (e.g., *Hungarian is hard* [*e*] *to learn* [*e*]). Discussing a modern 'protolanguage' context, Sandler *et al.* (forthcoming) note that in the early stages of the emergent sign language ABSL 'many predicates are not provided with explicit arguments, while for the younger signers, most of them are.' Often in full languages, arguments are null only if their feature content is realized by morphological agreement. Such (morpho)syntactic conditions are unlikely to have obtained in ancestral protolanguage. However, full languages do not all develop the same syntactic restrictions on the occurrence of empty categories; in Chinese, for example, any or all of the arguments of a verb can be null under the appropriate contextual conditions. The difference between languages such as Chinese and protolanguage is that specific discourse-pragmatic conditions regulate the appearance of null arguments in the former, but not in the latter.

Second, protolanguage has no hierarchical structure, and no syntactic relations occur between proto-words. Ancestral protolanguage putatively lacks the 'Merge' operation, consisting instead of short, unstructured word + word (+ word...) strings: A + B + C (Bickerton 2009: 187). Bickerton hypothesizes that words in protolanguage are transmitted separately to the organs of speech, rather than being hierarchically assembled in the brain prior to utterance, as in modern language. Ultimately, this 'beads-on-a-string' method of producing utterances is superseded by Merge, though it may remain the production method for modern kinds of 'protolanguage' illustrated above.

Third, as noted above, there are no word classes in protolanguage. Proto-words have no selectional restrictions, so cannot be divided into verbs and nouns. Though there is general agreement (with Bickerton 1990) that proto-verbs and proto-nouns were the earliest proto-word classes, there is debate about just which (semantic) proto-category might arise first. Jackendoff (2002: 259) suggests that at some point in language evolution 'words expressing situations' gained the special function that verbs have today, 'becoming grammatically essential to expressing an assertion'. That left a default class of other words, essentially nouns. So 'syntactic categories first emerged as a result of distinguishing verbs from everything else' (Jackendoff 2002: 259). Heine and Kuteva (2007), on the other hand, argue that nouns were the earliest categories (or rather, noun-like items – 'entities which served primarily the task of reference', Heine and Kuteva 2007: 59). Verbs appeared as the second layer in the development of word classes, either independently, or possibly emerging from nouns, though there is no direct evidence for this.

Crucially, there is no lexical/functional distinction in ancestral protolanguage; in fact, functional elements undoubtedly arose subsequent to the appearance of differentiated nouns and verbs. (Note, though, that child language consistently displays certain functional elements such as *no, more, some*, even at the two-word stage.) All other word classes, including all functional categories, are projected to develop from nouns and verbs (see §5). Heine and Kuteva (2007: 119) state that '[l]exical categories such as nouns and verbs are a prerequisite for other categories to arise.' What makes these accounts much more than Just-So stories is the fact that they have a secure empirical basis, drawing on well-attested cross-linguistic/historical pathways of development of word classes. Here, then, we have an excellent example of the kind of reverse engineering mentioned earlier.

In sum, in Bickerton's model of protolanguage, single-concept proto-words form the first stage; they are a prerequisite for the syntactic processes that follow. These early vocabulary items have, as yet, no lexical requirements, but can be concatenated loosely and asyntacti-cally. Other authors (e.g., Jackendoff 2002; Hurford 2012) more or less accept that such a stage existed, but propose a gradual, 'layered' development from protolanguage to full language, to which we now turn.

3.3 Emerging layers of grammar

Like Bickerton, Jackendoff (2002: Ch. 8; 2011) proposes that the concatenation of symbols occurred prior to the existence of hierarchical phrase structure. Unlike Bickerton, however, Jackendoff envisages a sequence of small, incremental steps in the evolution of syntax. Drawing on evidence from various proxies, such as pre-syntactic principles employed by naturalistic (adult) second language learners, Jackendoff proposes a set of protolinguistic 'fossil principles' matching linear order with semantic roles. For instance, in the potentially ambiguous *hit tree Fred*, 'Agent First' ensures that *tree* is the Agent. In *dog brown eat mouse*, 'Grouping' – the assumption that modifiers occur beside the word they modify – indicates that the dog is brown and not the mouse. 'Focus Last' produces orders like *In the room sat a bear*; its mirror image, Topic First, is typical of pidgins and of child language. Such principles are not yet syntactic; all depend solely on linear order. Sandler *et al.* (forth-coming) report that word order regularities often appear early on in emerging sign lan-guages too. Ancestral protolanguage putatively relied on purely semantically/pragmatically based principles of this kind to clarify the semantic roles of proto-words long before hier-archical structure – or any true syntax – existed. Summarizing his discussion of pre-syntax, Jackendoff notes: 'Whatever the particular details of [the] sorts of principle that map between semantic roles and pure linear order, they sharpen communication. They are therefore a plausible step between unregulated concatenation and full syntax' (2002: 250).

We find, too, that modern reflexes of these 'fossil principles' occur as syntactic lineariza-tion rules in full languages. Subjects are prototypically agents, and occur in initial (or pre-object) position in around 90 per cent of the world's languages. Many full languages, such as Japanese, employ a Topic First structure. And though non-configurational languages such as Warlpiri allow modifiers to be separated from their heads, contra a 'grouping' prin-ciple, this is made possible by extensive case-marking (almost certainly a late development in language evolution), which allows the syntactic constituency to be reconstructed.

In a similar vein, Hurford (2012: Ch. 9) suggests that the earliest 'protosentences' were Topic–Comment structures, 'two-element stand-alone clauses' (2012: 653), such as the child's *truck broke*. Hurford argues that these PROPOSITIONAL structures give rise to both the Noun–Verb distinction and also the Subject–Predicate distinction (a position also taken by Jackendoff 2002: 253). Initially, protolanguage speakers would follow pragmatic princi-ples: (1) Identify what you are talking about (Topic) and (2) give new information about what you are talking about (Comment). Certain word meanings are more likely to occur in the Topic slot; these are words for entities, such as *man, lion, tree*. Other meanings typically occur in the Comment slot; these denote actions or transient states, and include *run, stand, hungry*. Ultimately, these statistical preferences become conventionalized, so that a Noun (vs. predicate) category emerges.

Subjects appear to be derived from Topics too, probably significantly later (see also Jackendoff 2002: 260f). In fact, the 'subject' category itself is not always evident in full languages – for instance, those with ergative case; this also suggests a late emergence. Subjects and other grammatical relations are typically identified not just by their position but by relationships which they contract with other elements in the clause: We know we need to recognize grammatical relations because syntactic rules (such as agreement) refer to them. Crucially, then, grammatical relations such as subject are always conventionalized, fully syntactic categories, as evidenced by the fact that subjects coincide only sometimes with semantic categories such as 'agent' or 'topic'.

Where, though, do propositions themselves come from? Noting that predicates in natural language take up to three or four arguments as a maximum, Hurford (2007) argues that this limit corresponds to what humans (and indeed, other primates) can take in at a single glance. Thus 'There *is* a language-independent definition of a "single thought". It is derived from the limits of our ancient visual attention system, which only allows us to keep track of a maximum of four separate objects in a given scene' (Hurford 2007: 95, emphasis in original). As for the semantic roles of the arguments in a proposition, Bickerton (Calvin and Bickerton 2000) suggests that these too have ancient primate origins. Like modern primates living in complex social groups, our ancestors needed a 'social calculus' to keep track of reciprocity in their relationships, in terms of grooming, food sharing, defence in fights, and so on, thus avoiding the problem of free-loaders who don't reciprocate in kind. The calculus distinguishes various participants in an action (who did what for whom), and this, according to Bickerton, formed the basis for thematic roles such as AGENT, THEME, and GOAL. Of course, these are initially not at all syntactic. As words start to be combined, some principle must link the expression of participants to the action/event itself. At first, this linkage is neither syntactic nor obligatory. Ultimately, though, as the participants in the action of a predicate start to be regularly expressed, argument structure develops, associating specific grammatical functions with distinct predicates.

Modern languages display various vestiges of the 'layers' of syntactic evolution proposed by Hurford, Jackendoff, Heine and Kuteva, and others. Progovac (2009) argues that root small clauses such as those in (3) are syntactically simpler than full finite sentences; note, though, that again they constitute propositions. Often, they are verbless; even when they contain verbs, these lack tense/agreement (*Him retire/*retires?!*). Their pronominal subjects lack nominative case, but rather take the (English) default accusative. For Progovac, these properties are indicative of an earlier stage in the evolution of syntax, before the 'finite' layer of clause structure emerged. Even the noun phrases in such clauses typically lack determiners (3b). Extrapolating to ancestral protolanguage, we can posit smaller and earlier grammatical layers, before full DP/TP structure developed.

(3)   a. Him retire?! John a doctor?!
      b. Class in session. Problem solved. Case closed. Machine out of order.
      c. Me first! Everybody out!

Both Progovac and Jackendoff also suggest that compounding in the form of simple concatenation is a good candidate for a principle of protolanguage. Evidence that compounding may appear early in the evolution of syntax comes from its widespread use in pidgins and creoles (Plag 2006) and also in emerging sign languages such as ABSL (Sandler *et al.* forthcoming). In modern compounds, given two nouns, around twenty distinct semantic relationships can be conveyed (e.g., part-whole, as in *wheelchair*, or instrumental relations, as in *sunshade*). Meanings are pragmatically conveyed, with little restriction in form other than the position of the head (first/last).

Eventually, protolanguages need to signal relationships not just between words but between phrases. The principle that phrases are headed is vital in this process: One member of each constituent is the semantic/syntactic head (e.g., V within VP), and other elements in the phrase are its dependents (e.g., complements and adjuncts within VP). The word class of the head gives us the syntactic category of the whole phrase. Jackendoff (2011) argues that headedness was in no way an innovation in syntax, but rather is a pervasive principle in our general cognition. If this is correct, then the headedness principle probably predates language and was exapted for use in syntax, rather than being domain-specific. We can assume that the earliest heads in protolanguage were purely semantic, having no lexical requirements, and that these heads progressively accrue optional semantic dependents – at first, perhaps just typical collocations. As some dependents start to be used regularly, their properties are selected by the head they co-occur with. Distinct lexical classes (initially, noun vs. verb) do not exist until different semantic heads start to require semantically distinct types of dependents. Once a phrase consists of a head plus some specific and obligatory dependent, we have the beginnings of syntax. In this way, headed phrases emerge gradually; there is no need to propose a saltation to account for this aspect of syntax.

4 Merge and syntactic displacement

Syntactic displacement – a term which does not necessarily imply movement in a literal sense – is a sophisticated cognitive endowment, requiring the understanding that an expression appearing in one place in an utterance is semantically and syntactically linked to a (generally) null expression elsewhere. But this ability may stem from quite an early development in the evolution of syntax. Prior to the appearance of displacement itself, it seems likely that significant freedom in linear order characterized early languages and protolanguages (and indeed persists in some languages today, as mentioned above). As Jackendoff (2002: 255f) notes, both sentential adverbials and VP adverbials characteristically display much positional freedom in modern languages, and thus may constitute another 'linguistic fossil'. For instance, in (4) the phrases *probably* and *unbeknown to me* can occur at any of the points marked • (with appropriate intonation patterns):

(4) • The cat • would • devour my library ticket •

How, though, did movement rules arise? In Minimalist thinking, movement is considered merely part of the Merge operation, requiring no special developments in evolution: 'Crucially, the operation Merge yields the familiar *displacement* property of language: the fact that we pronounce phrases in one position, but interpret them somewhere else as well' (Berwick and Chomsky (2011: 31; their italics). The idea is that External Merge adds new material, while Internal Merge ('movement') takes a copy of an existing segment of the utterance and merges this with material already there, for instance deriving *who you will see who* from *you will see who*. The two instances of *who* are occurrences of a single item, rather than two distinct items. (Of course, only one of the copies is pronounced, but Berwick and Chomsky attribute this property to computational efficiency.) However, as McDaniel (2005) points out, under this account there is no logical reason why the copying operation itself should exist. Logically, it could easily be that items once selected could not be merged again; therefore, positing Internal Merge does after all add an extra syntactic layer to account for. This leaves, then, the question of why movement constructions such as *wh*-movement should exist at all, especially as many languages lack them.

A solution may lie in another characteristic property of protolanguage, seen for instance in the productions of 'language'-trained apes: Inconsistent ordering and much repetition. Utterances from the chimpanzee Nim Chimpsky (Terrace 1979) illustrate: for example,

Me banana you banana me you give. McDaniel suggests that movement has its origins in production in pre-syntactic protolanguage, where speakers, rather like Nim, found it 'advantageous to utter as many words as possible corresponding to a given thought' (McDaniel 2005: 160). For instance, if a leopard in a tree seems about to kill a baby, a speaker blurts out *baby tree leopard baby baby kill* – repeating the critical word *baby* several times. Thus, the 'copy' principle is already built into the system from the protolanguage stage, so that 'a [syntactic] system allowing movement … would have better accommodated the existing production mechanism' (McDaniel 2005: 162). Only much later would the system require that just one instance of a copied item is actually pronounced. Following McDaniel's proposals, Bickerton (2012: 467) suggests that, rather than being an innovation, movement rules in syntax may simply be a formalization from a protolanguage stage that freely allowed repetition of pragmatically salient constituents: 'There appears to be no evidence for hypothesizing a stage of language where word order was rigidly fixed and thus no constituent could be moved to a position of prominence.'

In sum, McDaniel's concept is a novel take on the emergence of syntactic displacement. Most researchers have assumed that pragmatic factors concerning the interpretation of language drove movement processes, in evolution as in modern language, thus using displacement to indicate topic, focus, scope, new/old information, questions of various kinds, and so on. In other words, movement emerges from a desire to manipulate information structure (Hurford 2012). However, McDaniel points out firstly that 'Interpretation … would work best if surface word order corresponded exactly to thematic structure' (2005: 155); movement is then inevitably a complication in the system. Secondly, movement is not invariably used for such pragmatic functions today: Consider *wh-in-situ*, preverbal or other dedicated focus positions, emphatic stress, and so on, where no movement is used.

This idea – copying a word or phrase for emphasis, and later on generally retaining just one of the copies – may also account for the ability to process non-local dependencies, a significant development in human linguistic capabilities. The moved item and its copy are dependent on each other, semantically linked but not adjacent: A plausible source for the earliest long-distance syntactic relationships.

5 Grammaticalization: Word classes, constructions, structure

As seen in §3 above, a sizable body of work suggests that, in the early stages of syntax, only two distinct word classes existed: Nouns and verbs. These are the earliest syntactic categories, and all other categories derive from them in a succession of 'layers' of grammatical evolution. This does not, incidentally, rule out the Minimalist characterization in which syntax comprises lexical items plus Merge. Ultimately, though, other lexical word classes (such as adjectives) plus the whole panoply of functional elements found in full language must originate somehow. Two major sources of evidence indicate how further word classes arose in language evolution. The first source is synchronic and diachronic change in attested languages (e.g. Heine and Kuteva 2007). The second is the study of 'emergent' languages, particularly pidgins/creoles and other restricted linguistic systems, and newly emerging sign languages, such as Nicaraguan Sign Language and Al-Sayyid Bedouin Sign Language (Kegl *et al.* 1999; Aronoff *et al.* 2008). All involve the group of unidirectional processes known as GRAMMATICALIZATION, where '[g]rammaticalization is defined as the development from lexical to grammatical forms, and from grammatical to even more grammatical forms' (Heine and Kuteva 2007: 32). Semantically based content words are, then, the ultimate source of functional elements such as determiners, adpositions, auxiliaries, complementizers, pronouns, negation markers, and the like; in turn, these closed-class free morphemes are the source of inflectional affixes such as tense, agreement, and case markers. Of course, new content words constantly enter both language and pre-language, and content words are not necessarily 'lost' as they grammaticalize. In fact, it is common for earlier meanings and lexical frames to be retained when grammaticalized forms develop alongside. English *keep* illustrates, retaining its lexical meaning, as in *Kim kept chickens*, despite the development of a semantically 'bleached', grammaticalized, aspectual auxiliary *keep*, as in *Kim kept shouting.*

Evidence for the primacy of nouns and verbs in evolution comes from the fact that only these categories are stable cross-linguistically, are generally open-class items (not true, however, of lexical verbs in some languages), and are putatively universal. To illustrate typical pathways of grammaticalization, here we see that both nouns and verbs often develop into adpositions:

(5)   N > P (Welsh) *mynydd* 'mountain' > *(i) fyny* 'up' (with initial consonantal mutation)
        maes 'field' > *mas* 'out'
        llawr 'floor' > *(i) lawr* 'down' (with initial consonantal mutation)

(6)   V > P (English)   *regarding, concerning, following, during*

In turn, prepositions may develop more functional uses, as is the case for the Welsh perfect aspect marker *wedi*, grammaticalized from the preposition *wedi* 'after'.

One effect of grammaticalization is to create markers of constituent boundaries in phrases and clauses. For instance, articles, demonstratives, and numerals typically mark the beginning or end of noun phrases; clause subordinators mark the start or end of clauses. Crucially, grammaticalization does not merely concern the creation of grammatical categories, it also leads to the formation of new syntactic constructions. These include recursive structures such as relativization, and, indeed, clausal embedding generally. The reverse engineering strategy – using evidence from observable language change in this case – clearly suggests that ancestral protolanguage initially had no clausal subordination. Rather, once whole propositions were formed, they were probably simply juxtaposed without one being embedded in the other. The history of English relative clauses, sketched in (7), illustrates; cross-linguistically, demonstratives are a typical source for markers of subordination (see Heine and Kuteva 2007: 226). The shift from Time 1 to Time 2 in such instances is never abrupt, but, rather, takes place gradually, and includes a transitional stage where the functional element is ambiguous between its two roles.

(7)   Time 1: Here is the fruit; **that** (one) I like.
        Time 2: Here is the fruit [**that** I like __].

In emerging languages (e.g., Aronoff *et al.* 2008; Sandler *et al.* forthcoming) we see the same phenomenon. Clauses in the early stages of ABSL, as represented by the utterances of older signers, have only one (animate) argument. A man throwing a ball to a girl would then be: GIRL STAND; MAN BALL THROW; GIRL CATCH (Sandler *et al.* forthcoming). Ambiguity over which argument bears which grammatical function does not arise, so the emerging language does not need argument structure marking. Moreover, there is no clausal embedding among older signers, whereas speakers from subsequent generations typically display prosodically marked dependent clauses, though these still lack syntactic markers of sentence complexity.

The development of functional elements via grammaticalization may even be critical in the formation of clausal subordination. Heine and Kuteva state that 'grammaticalization is a prerequisite for recursive structures to arise' (2007: 344). (8) illustrates the typical process, with a speech act verb 'say' in (a) being grammaticalized as a quotative marker in (b) and a complementizer in (c) (Heine and Kuteva 2007: 237):

(8)   Ewe (Kwa, Niger-Congo)

    a. e **bé?**
        2SG say
        'What are you saying? (Did I understand you correctly?)'
    b. é gblɔ **bé** "ma-á-vá etsɔ"
        3SG say BÉ 1SG-FUT-come tomorrow
        'He said "I'll come tomorrow".'
    c. me-nyá **bé** e-li
        1SG-know BÉ 2SG-exist
        'I know that you are there.'

Whereas relative clauses and other instances of clausal subordination appear to be more or less universal, other grammatical categories, such as case, tense, and agreement markers, are definitely more restricted in modern languages. The same applies to various constructions, such as the passive. Since they are optional, in the sense that many languages do not display them, these categories are argued to emerge late in language evolution (Heine and Kuteva 2007) via the usual kind of grammaticalization processes. For instance, nouns and verbs give rise to case markers, typically with an intermediate stage from N or V to P. Prepositions that once had more semantic content are frequently grammaticalized, with English *of* indicating possession, attribution, and so on (*the height of the desk*) and *to*, formerly used in a purely locative sense, now also indicating a semantic goal (*She spoke to Kim*). Free-standing pronouns frequently grammaticalize as affixes, a typical source of agreement morphology. Verbs often give rise to tense and aspectual auxiliaries, as illustrated by the grammaticalization of earlier English *will-an* (volitional 'will', still seen in *Do what you will*) to form a future auxiliary *will*; similarly, the motion verb *go to*, grammaticalized as *be going to*, forms another future (*I'm going to/gonna sit still*). Verbs are often the source of passive auxiliaries: English *get*, as in *My team got beaten*, illustrates. Passivization not only creates a new grammatical subject, it also forms a new syntactic construction. The same is true of the formation of relative clauses, illustrated in (7). *Wh*-question words – again, creating new constructions – also arise via grammaticalization; for instance, Welsh *beth* 'what' derives from the noun meaning 'thing', and Welsh *lle* 'where' derives from the noun meaning 'place'. Thus, it seems plausible that grammatical constructions themselves originate via processes of grammaticalization.

Another important strand involving grammaticalization is seen in work by John A. Hawkins (e.g., 2004). Hawkins proposes the Performance-Grammar Correspondence Hypothesis: 'Grammars have conventionalized syntactic structures in proportion to their degree of preference in performance' (2004: 3). What Hawkins shows is that language processing has shaped grammars, so that what appear to be principles of UG – such as the Head Parameter – can often be accounted for by performance pressures alone. So, in VO languages, not only do heads typically precede complements, 'light' constituents also precede 'heavy' ones. This can be seen, for example, in the contrast between *a yellow book* and *a book yellow with age*, where the post-modified AP must follow the head noun. Conversely, OV languages not only tend to have postpositions and head-final complementizers (e.g., Japanese), they also display a general heavy-before-light preference – the mirror image of VO languages. Hawkins' work indicates that many typological generalizations are 'bought' by functional considerations of this nature. For research into the evolution of syntax, this seems significant: If processing shapes grammars, as now seems indisputable, then we may begin to understand how the language faculty came to be the way it is.

Note, though, that functional and external explanations for aspects of language in no way invalidate the concept of a language faculty: '[T]o the extent certain properties recur in language across societies, it will be efficient for the learning process to incorporate those in the language faculty as predispositions' (Anderson 2008: 810).

6 Conclusion

We have seen in this chapter that although not all researchers accept the concept of a gradual emergence of syntax, there are good indications not only that it was possible for our ancestors to employ simpler pre-language stages – typically known as protolanguage – but also that plausible pathways from protolanguage to full language exist. Stages in the development of grammatical complexity are well attested in emerging languages of various kinds today, strongly suggesting that the evolution of syntax was probably also incremental for our ancestors. Despite the fact that all modern populations have the full language faculty, and therefore do not make perfect proxies for pre-linguistic hominins, the convergence of so many types of evidence from reverse engineering should give us confidence that proposals involving a gradual evolution of syntax are on the right track.

Further reading

Anderson, S.R. 2008. The logical structure of linguistic theory. *Language* 84:795–814.

> A stimulating discussion of the language faculty and its properties, and how they came to be the way they are through the mechanisms of evolution.

Bickerton, D. 2009. *Adam's tongue: How humans made language, how language made humans.* New York: Hill & Wang.

> A very readable popular overview of Bickerton's arguments concerning the origins of protolanguage and language, along with a feasible selective scenario.

Hurford, J.R. 2012. *The origins of grammar: Language in the light of evolution.* Oxford: Oxford University Press.

> An excellent, clear and fair-minded discussion of the kinds of issues outlined in this chapter, written for a general audience.

Jackendoff, R. 2011. What is the human language faculty? Two views. *Language* 87:586–624.

> A cogent critique of the Minimalist approach to the evolution of syntax and of language more generally, with alternative arguments clearly outlined.

Larson, R.K., V. Déprez, and H. Yamakido (eds). 2010. *The evolution of human language: Biolinguistic perspectives.* Cambridge: Cambridge University Press.

> Contains a reprint of the Hauser *et al.* 2002 paper, plus Jackendoff 2010 and other valuable chapters, written both from a Minimalist standpoint and from opposing perspectives.

References

Anderson, S.R. 2004. *Doctor Dolittle's delusion: animals and the uniqueness of human language.* New Haven, CT and London: Yale University Press.

Anderson, S.R. 2008. The logical structure of linguistic theory. *Language* 84:795–814.

Arnold, K., and K. Zuberbühler. 2008. Meaningful call combinations in a non-human primate. *Current Biology* 18:R202–R203.

Aronoff, M., I. Meir, C.A. Padden, and W. Sandler. 2008. The roots of linguistic organization in a new language. *Interaction Studies* 9:133–153.

Berwick, R.C. 2011. Syntax facit saltum redux: biolinguistics and the leap to syntax. In Di Sciullo and Boeckx (eds), 65–99.

Berwick, R.C., and N. Chomsky. 2011. The biolinguistic program: the current state of its development. In Di Sciullo and Boeckx (eds), 19–41.

Bickerton, D. 1990. *Language and species.* Chicago, IL: University of Chicago Press.

Bickerton, D. 1995. *Language and human behavior.* Seattle: University of Washington Press.

Bickerton, D. 2009. *Adam's tongue: How humans made language, how language made humans.* New York: Hill and Wang.

Bickerton, D. 2012. The origins of syntactic language. In Tallerman and Gibson (eds), 456–468.

Boeckx, C. 2012. The emergence of language, from a biolinguistic point of view. In Tallerman and Gibson (eds), 492–501.

Burling, R. 2005. *The talking ape: how language evolved.* Oxford: Oxford University Press.

Calvin, W.H., and D. Bickerton. 2000. *Lingua ex machina: reconciling Darwin and Chomsky with the human brain.* Cambridge, MA and London: MIT Press.

Chomsky, N. 2008. On phases. In *Foundational issues in linguistic theory*, ed. R. Freidin, C. Otero, and M.L Zubizarreta, 133–166. Cambridge, MA: MIT Press.

Chomsky, N. 2010. Some simple evo devo theses: how true might they be for language? In Larson et al. (eds), 45–62.

Curtiss, S. 1977. *Genie: A psycholinguistic study of a modern-day 'wild child'.* New York: Academic Press.

Deacon, T. 1997. *The symbolic species: the co-evolution of language and the human brain.* London: Allen Lane, The Penguin Press.

Di Sciullo, A.M., and C. Boeckx (eds). 2011. *The biolinguistic enterprise: New perspectives on the evolution and nature of the language faculty.* Oxford: Oxford University Press.

Evans, N., and S. Levinson. 2009. The myth of language universals: Language diversity and its importance for cognitive science. *Behavioral and Brain Sciences* 32:429–492.

Everett, D.L. 2005. Cultural constraints on grammar and cognition in Pirahã. Another look at the design features of human language. *Current Anthropology* 46:621–646.

Gil, D. 2009. How much grammar does it take to sail a boat? In Sampson et al. (eds), 19–33.

Goldin-Meadow, S. 2005. What language creation in the manual modality tells us about the foundations of language. *The Linguistic Review* 22:199–225.

Hauser, M., N. Chomsky, and W.T. Fitch. 2002. The faculty of language: what is it, who has it and how did it evolve? *Science* 298:1569–1579.

Hawkins, J.A. 2004. *Efficiency and complexity in grammars.* Oxford: Oxford University Press.

Heine, B., and T. Kuteva. 2007. *The genesis of grammar: a reconstruction.* Oxford: Oxford University Press.

Hurford, J.R. 2007. *The origins of meaning: language in the light of evolution.* Oxford: Oxford University Press.

Hurford, J.R. 2012. *The origins of grammar: language in the light of evolution.* Oxford: Oxford University Press.

Jackendoff, R. 2002. *Foundations of language: brain, meaning, grammar and evolution.* Oxford: Oxford University Press.

Jackendoff, R. 2010. Your theory of language evolution depends on your theory of language. In Larson et al. (eds), 63–72.

Jackendoff, R. 2011. What is the human language faculty? Two views. *Language* 87:586–624.

Kegl, J., A. Senghas, and M. Coppola. 1999. Creation through contact: Sign language emergence and sign language change. In *Language creation and language change: Creolization, diachrony and development*, ed. M. DeGraff, 179–237. Cambridge, MA: MIT Press.

Larson, R.K., V. Déprez, and H. Yamakido (eds). 2010. *The evolution of human language: Biolinguistic perspectives*. Cambridge: Cambridge University Press.

McDaniel, D. 2005. The potential role of production in the evolution of syntax. In *Language origins: Perspectives on evolution*, ed. M. Tallerman, 153–165. Oxford: Oxford University Press.

McWhorter, J. 2005. *Defining creole*. Oxford: Oxford University Press.

Nevins, A., D. Pesetsky, and C. Rodrigues. 2009. Pirahã exceptionality: A reassessment. *Language* 85:355–404.

Patterson, F.G. 1978. Language capacities of a lowland gorilla. In *Sign language and language acquisition in man and ape*, ed. F.C.C. Peng, 161–201. Boulder, CO: Westview Press.

Plag, I. 2006. Morphology in pidgins and creoles. In *The encyclopedia of language and linguistics*, ed. K. Brown, 305–308. Oxford: Elsevier.

Progovac, L. 2009. Layering of grammar: vestiges of protosyntax in present-day languages. In Sampson et al. (eds), 203–212.

Sampson, G., D. Gil, and P. Trudgill (eds). 2009. *Language complexity as an evolving variable*. Oxford: Oxford University Press.

Sandler, W., M. Aronoff, C. Padden, and I. Meir. forthcoming. Language emergence: Al-Sayyid Bedouin Sign Language. In *Cambridge handbook of linguistic anthropology*, ed. N. Enfield, P. Kockelman. and J. Sidnell. Cambridge: Cambridge University Press.

Savage-Rumbaugh, S., S.G. Shankar, and T. Taylor. 1998. *Apes, language and the human mind*. New York and Oxford: Oxford University Press.

Tallerman, M., and K.R. Gibson (eds). 2012. *The Oxford handbook of language evolution*. Oxford: Oxford University Press.

Terrace, H.S. 1979. *Nim*. New York: Knopf.

Yoder, B. 2010. Syntactic underspecification in Riau Indonesian. In *Work Papers of the Summer Institute of Linguistics, University of North Dakota Session*, vol. 50, ed. J. Baart. Downloadable from http://arts-sciences.und.edu/summer-institute-of-linguistics/work-papers/_files/docs/2010-yoder.pdf

Part V
Theoretical approaches to syntax

23
The history of syntax[1]

Peter W. Culicover

1 Introduction

The history of thinking about and describing syntax goes back thousands of years. But from the perspective of theorizing about syntax, which is our concern here, a critical point of departure is Chomsky's *Syntactic Structures* (Chomsky 1957; henceforth *SS*).[2] I begin with some general observations about the goals of contemporary syntactic theory. Then, after briefly summarizing the main ideas of *SS*, and discussing methodology, I review some of the more important extensions, with an eye towards understanding where we are today and how we got here.[3] I touch on some of the more prominent branch points later in the chapter, in order to preserve as much as possible a sense of the historical flow. For convenience, I refer to the direct line of development from *SS* as "mainstream" generative grammar (MGG). This term reflects the central role that the Chomskyan program has played in the field, in terms of the development of both his proposals and alternatives to them.

The contemporary history of syntax can be usefully understood in terms of a few fundamental questions. Answers to these questions have driven both the development of MGG and the development of alternative syntactic theories. Among the questions that have proven to be most central and continue to fuel research are these:

- What is the nature of syntactic structure?
- What is the status within syntactic theory of grammatical functions, thematic roles, syntactic categories, branching structure, and invisible constituents?
- What is the right way to account for linear order?
- What is the right way to capture generalizations about relatedness of constructions?
- What is the explanatory role of processing in accounting for acceptability judgments and thus the empirical basis for syntactic theorizing?

2 Grammars and grammaticality

A central assumption of MGG (and other theories) is that a language is a set of strings of words and morphemes that meet a set of well-formedness conditions. In MGG these are expressible as RULES. The rules constitute the grammar of the language and are part of the native speaker's linguistic knowledge. One task of the linguist is to formulate and test hypotheses about what the rules of a language are: that is, to determine the grammar. The linguist's hypothesis and the native speaker's knowledge are both called the GRAMMAR.

The evidence for a child learning a language consists minimally of examples of expressions of the language produced in context. It is assumed that on the basis of this evidence the learner arrives at a grammar. The grammar provides the basis for the speaker to produce and understand utterances of the language.

The descriptive problem for the linguist is to correctly determine the form and content of the speaker's grammar. Since *Aspects* (Chomsky 1965) it has been assumed in MGG that the grammar is only imperfectly reflected in what a speaker actually says. Absent from the CORPUS of utterances is a vast (in fact infinite) amount of data that the speaker could produce, but has not produced, and could comprehend if exposed to it. It contains a substantial number of utterances that contain errors such as slips of the tongue or are incomplete. Moreover, regular properties of the corpus such as the relative frequency of various expressions and constructions may not be relevant to the grammar itself (in either sense), but may be relevant to social and cognitive effects on the way in which the language defined by the grammar is used in communication.

The classical approach to the discovery of the grammar has been to take the judgments of a native speaker about the acceptability of an expression to be a reflection of the native speaker's knowledge: that is, the grammar. In simple cases such an approach is very reliable. For instance, if we misorder the words of a sentence in a language such as English, the judgment of unacceptability is very strong and reflects the knowledge of what the order should be. For example, (1b) is ungrammatical because the article *the* follows rather than precedes the head of its phrase.

(1) a. The police arrested Sandy.
     b. *Police the arrested Sandy.

Other cases are plausibly not a matter of grammar. Consider (2).

(2) a. Sandy divulged the answer, but I would never do it.
     b. *Sandy knew the answer, but I would never do it.

Intuitively, the difference between the two sentences is that *do it* can refer only to an action, *divulge* denotes an action, while *know* does not. Since (2b) is ill-formed for semantic reasons, the burden of explanation can be borne by the semantics.[4]

The distinction between grammaticality and acceptability was highlighted by Miller and Chomsky (1963), who observed that a sentence can be well-formed in the sense that it follows the rules of linear ordering, phrase structure, and morphological form, but is nevertheless unacceptable. Canonical cases involve center embedding (3).

(3) The patient that the doctor that the nurse called examined recovered.

The unacceptability of center embedding has been generally attributed to processing complexity and not to grammar (Gibson 1998; Lewis 1997).

The distinction between grammaticality and acceptability has not played a significant role in syntactic theorizing until recently, primarily because of the unavailability of theories of the mechanisms (e.g., processing) other than syntax itself that could explain the judgments (see §8.4). The theoretical developments traced below are primarily anchored in the assumption that acceptability that cannot be attributed to semantics or pragmatics reflects properties of the grammar itself.

3   Syntactic structures and the standard theory

3.1   Constituent structure

In *SS*, syntax is understood to be the theory of the structure of sentences in a language. This view has its direct antecedents in the theory of immediate constituents (IC), in which the function of syntax is to mediate between the observed form of a sentence and its meaning: "we could not understand the form of a language if we merely reduced all the complex forms to their ultimate constituents" (Bloomfield 1933: 161). Bloomfield argued that in order to account for the meaning of a sentence, it is necessary to recognize how individual constituents (e.g., words and morphemes), constitute more complex forms, which themselves constitute more complex forms.

In *SS*, basic or KERNEL sentences were derived by the successive application of rewrite rules such as those in (4).

(4) a. S   → NP VP
    b. VP   → V NP
    c. NP   → Art N
    d. V   → {arrested, ...}
    e. Art → {the, a, ...}
    f. N   → {police students, ...}

The application of such rules defines the IC structure of the sentence. For example:

(5)

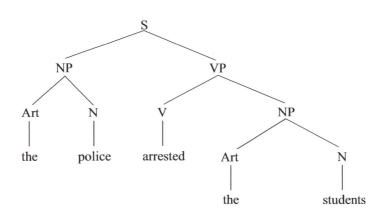

3.2 Transformations

The fundamental innovation of *SS* was to combine IC analysis with Harris' observation (e.g., Harris 1951) that sentences with (more or less) the same words and meaning are systematically related. For example, the active and the passive, exemplified in (6), are essentially synonymous and differ only by the arrangement of the words and a few individual forms (*be*, the inflection on the main verb, *by*).

(6) a. The police arrested the students.
  b. The students were arrested by the police.

For Harris, such relationships were captured through TRANSFORMATIONS of strings of words and morphemes.

In *SS*, such relationships among sentences are captured in terms of transformations of STRUCTURES. The passive transformation in *SS*, shown in (7), maps the structure of the active (e.g., (5)) into the structure of the passive. The object of the active, NP$_2$, occupies the subject position of the passive, and the subject of the active, NP$_1$, becomes the complement of the preposition *by*. A form of the verb *be* is inserted with the passive morpheme +*en*. A subsequent transformation attaches +*en* to the verb.

(7) (NP$_1$) V NP$_2$ $\Rightarrow$ NP$_2$ be + en V (by NP$_1$)

Chomsky notes in *SS* that the passive construction has distinctive properties: the passive participle goes with *be*, a transitive passive verb lacks a direct object,[5] the agentive *by*-phrase may appear in the passive but not in the active, the exact semantic restrictions imposed on the object of the active are imposed on the subject of the passive, and the semantic restrictions on the subject of the active are imposed on the *by*-phrase. The passive could be described independently of the active, but such a description would be redundant and would not explicitly capture the relationship between the two constructions. Chomsky concludes (p. 43): "This inelegant duplication, as well as the special restrictions involving the element *be*+*en*, can be avoided ONLY [my emphasis – PWC] if we deliberately exclude passives from the grammar of phrase structure, and reintroduce them by a rule … ." Much of MGG and alternatives follow from responses to this conclusion.

Deriving the passive from the active by a RULE captures not only their synonymy but also the distributional facts. Thus, Chomsky argued, phrase structure rules (PSRs) are not sufficient to characterize linguistic competence. A phrase structure characterization of the phenomena can capture the facts, but at the expense of generality and simplicity, as in the case of the English passive.

More complex sentences were derived in *SS* by the application of GENERALIZED TRANSFORMATIONS that applied to multiple simple sentences, as in (8).

(8) $\left[\begin{array}{l} \text{the police arrested the students} \\ \text{the students were protesting} \end{array}\right] \Rightarrow$

The police arrested the students who were protesting.

3.3 The shift to the Standard Theory

The shift from the *SS* theory to the Standard Theory (ST) in Chomsky (1965) was marked by three innovations: (i) since any order of application of the same rewrite rules produces the same structure, it is assumed in ST that PSRs such as (4a–c) specify a set of rooted trees as in (5) (Lasnik and Kupin 1977); (ii) since the full expressive power of generalized transformations is not needed, it was assumed in ST that complex structures are also specified by the PSRs, extended to allow for recursion, as in (9);

(9) S   → NP VP
     VP → V NP
     NP → Art N
     NP → Art N S

(iii) instead of rewrite rules, it was assumed that there is a LEXICON that specifies the properties of individual lexical items. A lexical item is inserted into a structure that is compatible with its properties – for example, a transitive verb is inserted into a structure such as (5) only if there is an NP in VP.

3.4 Levels of representation in the Standard Theory

Chomsky (1965) proposed that there are two levels of syntactic representation of a sentence, DEEP STRUCTURE and SURFACE STRUCTURE, related by sets of transformations. The meaning of a sentence, in particular the assignment of THEMATIC (θ-)ROLES (e.g., Agent, Patient) to the arguments, is determined by deep structure, while surface structure corresponds to the observed form, including linear order (now called PHONETIC FORM (PF)).

3.5 Constraining movement

A central consequence of the hypothesis that there are at least two transformationally related levels of syntactic representation is that constituents MOVE from their underlying positions to their observed positions in the structure. An example of movement is the derivation of the passive construction, in which the deep structure object moves to surface structure subject. Another is the movement of the English inflected auxiliary in subject Aux inversion (SAI) in (10b).

(10) a. Sandy will call.
      b. Will Sandy ___ call.

Yet another example is seen in English *wh*-questions, where the interrogative phrase appears in a position distinct from the position that determines its syntactic and semantic function in the sentence (marked in (11) with underscore).

(11) What are you looking at ___ ?

The question then arose: What kinds of movements are possible – how can they be constrained? Emonds (1970) observed that the passive transformation yields a structure that conforms to the general pattern of the language as characterized by the PSRs – that is, it is STRUCTURE PRESERVING. Emonds proposed that all transformations except those such as SAI that apply to the highest level of the structure (the ROOT) are necessarily structure preserving. (In later developments, all transformations are assumed to be structure preserving.)

3.6 Long distance dependencies and island constraints

English *wh*-questions such as (11) exemplify a class of FILLER-GAP or A′ CONSTRUCTIONS in natural language. The *wh*-phrase is in an A′ position – that is, a position where its syntactic or semantic function is not determined. A′ positions contrast with A positions such as subject and direct object.

The contemporary analysis of A′ constructions in MGG posits a CHAIN that links the constituent in A′ position to a gap in the A position that defines its grammatical and semantic function. In what follows, the gap is marked with *t* co-subscripted with the constituent in A′ position. Thus (11) is represented as *What$_i$ are you looking at t$_i$.*

A distinctive characteristic of such constructions in languages such as English is that there is no principled bound on the length of the chain. The *wh*-phrase may be linked to a gap in the complement, as in (12a), or in a more distant complement, as in (12b).

(12) a. Who$_i$ did you say [$_S$ you were looking at t$_i$]
    b. Who$_i$ did you say [$_S$ everyone thinks … [$_S$ you were looking at t$_i$]]

The chain containing *who$_i$* and *t$_i$* is thus called a LONG DISTANCE DEPENDENCY (LDD).

The broad theoretical significance for syntactic theory of LLDs was recognized as early as Chomsky (1964). He observed that extraction of a *wh*-phrase from certain syntactic contexts is less than fully acceptable. Chomsky showed that while (13) is ambiguous, extraction of an NP corresponding to *the boy*, as in (14), disambiguates – *walking to the railroad station* cannot be understood as a reduced relative modifying *the boy*. Chomsky concluded that extraction of *who* must be constrained in the structure (15).

(13) Mary saw the boy walking to the railroad station.

(14) Who did Mary see walking to the railroad station?
    a. 'Who did Mary see while she was walking to the railroad station?'
    b. Not: 'Who did Mary see who was walking to the railroad station?'

(15) Mary saw [$_{NP}$ [$_{NP}$ who] [$_S$ walking to the railroad station]

Chomsky's characterization of the configuration blocking extraction in (15) is that a phrase of category NP dominates another phrase of category NP, and the violation results from the extraction of the lower NP. He proposed "a hypothetical linguistic universal", subsequently referred to by Ross (1967: 13) as the A-OVER-A PRINCIPLE (16).

(16) If [a] phrase X of category A is embedded within a larger phrase ZXW which is also of category A, then no rule applying to the category A applies to X (but only to ZXW).

Ross (1967) showed that the A-over-A principle does not account for the full range of restrictions on A′ extractions in English.[6] The configurations that inhibit extraction are called ISLANDS, and they are ruled out in MGG by ISLAND CONSTRAINTS. The reason why these must be expressed as constraints on rules (and not as rules of grammar themselves) is that the unacceptable examples are otherwise well-formed. For example, in a violation of the COMPLEX NP CONSTRAINT, as in (17b), the form of the relative clause is not problematic, since the relative pronoun is in the proper position. The problem is the configuration of the chain.

(17) a. The police arrested the protesters who surrounded Sandy.

b. *The person [$_S$ **who**$_i$ the police arrested [$_{NP}$ the protesters [$_S$ who surrounded ***t***$_i$]]] was Sandy.

Moreover, the island constraints are arguably universal, and are thus not conditions on particular transformations.

Then the question arises how this knowledge could become part of a learner's grammar. Assuming that learners form grammars on the basis of the utterances they actually experience, it does not appear that there could be evidence that (17b) is ungrammatical, because it is well-formed from the perspective of structure (and rarely if ever produced). On the basis of such considerations, Chomsky (1965; 1973; 1981) argued that there are SYNTACTIC UNIVERSALS that constitute the human capacity for language. This is the ARGUMENT FROM THE POVERTY OF THE STIMULUS (APS), discussed further in §8.4.

4 Uniformity

At this point it is helpful to consider a methodology of MGG that is responsible for much of its historical development. This methodology is UNIFORMITY (Culicover and Jackendoff 2005), which aims at eliminating redundancy in grammatical formulations.

4.1 Interface uniformity

INTERFACE UNIFORMITY (IU) is the assumption that sentences with the same meaning share a syntactic representation. If meaning is determined by deep structure, as in ST, sentences with the same meaning have the same deep structure representation. For example, the active and the passive are derived from the same representation, and the passive transformation does not affect their meaning. This point was generalized in MGG to the assumption that transformations in general do not add or change meaning (the Katz–Postal Hypothesis: Katz and Postal 1964).

Broad application of IU in the form of the Katz–Postal Hypothesis in the 1960s and early 1970s led to the emergence of Generative Semantics (GS). Consistent with ST, GS assumed two levels of syntactic representation, DS and SS. If transformations do not change meaning, all meaning must be determined at DS. Without a distinct syntactic level to represent logical form, GS concluded that DS was equivalent to the meaning. The decline of GS by the mid-1970s was propelled by a number of factors, most notably a failure to properly distinguish between genuinely syntactic and non-syntactic phenomena. Failure to distinguish in the theory among syntactic ill-formedness, semantic anomaly, presupposition failure, pragmatic infelicity, and so on, made it impossible to construct an explanatory account (see §2 and Katz and Bever 1976).

4.2 Structural uniformity

STRUCTURAL UNIFORMITY (SU) requires that if two constituents in two different sentences have the same grammatical function, then they have the same underlying representation. The canonical application of SU is to English *wh*-questions (18a) and similar A$'$ constructions such as topicalization (18b) and relative clauses (18c).

(18) a. Who$_i$ did the police arrest t_i?

b. Sandy$_i$, the police finally arrested t_i!

c. I was introduced to the person [$_S$ who$_i$ the police arrested t_i].

Crucially, the filler has the same grammatical function as it (or a similar constituent) would have if it was in the position marked by the gap. SU thus REQUIRES that the filler occupy this position in deep structure. Classical MGG derivations apply MOVEMENT to map such a structure into one in which the filler is in the A′ position, forming a chain, as shown in (19).

(19) [the police finally arrested Sandy$_i$] → Sandy$_i$ [the police finally arrested t_i]

4.3 Derivational uniformity

Assuming that at least some structures are derived by transformations, sameness of structure is captured by assuming DERIVATIONAL UNIFORMITY (DU). A typical case is sluicing, exemplified in (20).

(20) The police arrested someone, but I don't know who.

The second clause means 'but I don't know *who the police arrested*'. By IU, the two questions must have the same syntactic representation. By DU, since the full question has *wh*-movement (an MGG assumption), so must the sluiced case. So the derivation of (20) involves at least *wh*-movement of *who* and deletion of *the police arrested*. Similar reasoning is applied in the analysis of a variety of ELLIPTICAL constructions (see Culicover and Jackendoff (2005; 2012) for discussion).

5 The Extended Standard Theory and the Revised Extended Standard Theory

The Extended Standard Theory (EST) and the Revised Extended Standard Theory (REST) are characterized by the recognition that some aspects of meaning are determined by derived structure (Jackendoff 1972), the introduction of the level of representation of LOGICAL FORM (LF), placing the burden of constraining the output of a transformation on general principles rather than the description of the transformation, constraining phrase structure through the X′ schema, and the introduction of TRACES.

5.1 S-structure and LF

In REST, deep and surface structure are renamed D- and S-STRUCTURE. D-structure determines the thematic component of interpretation, through the assignment of θ-roles to arguments in their underlying canonical position. LF is the representation of the logical properties of a sentence that depend on its syntactic structure – it is determined by transformations that apply to S-structure (May 1985). For example, scope ambiguities such as (21) are derived by applying movement to the quantifier phrases to yield different hierarchical LF structures, as shown in (22). The traces t in (22) mark the canonical positions of the extracted arguments (§5.4).[7]

(21) Everyone speaks two languages.
    a. 'There are two languages that everyone speaks' [wide scope of *two languages*]
    b. 'Everyone is bilingual' [narrow scope of *two languages*]

(22) a. [two languages]$_j$ [$_S$ everyone$_i$ speaks t_j][8]
    b. [everyone]$_i$ [$_S$ t_i speaks [two languages]$_j$]

Characteristic of EST/REST is the T-MODEL of derivation in (23).

(23)

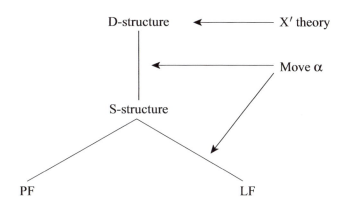

5.2 Move α

A transformation in ST was constrained by conditions stated in its formal description. Chomsky (1972) took a major step in shifting the burden of constraining transformations to general principles by decomposing the passive into simpler movement operations that otherwise apply freely. Central to this step was the analysis of English nominalization. It was assumed since Lees (1960) that nominalizations such as (24a) should be derived from sentences (24b) on the basis of IU. The θ-roles are essentially the same: *the enemy* is the Agent, and *the city* is the Patient.

(24) a. the enemy's destruction of the city
      b. The enemy destroyed the city.

Applying DU, Lakoff (1965) argued that the nominalization transformation should apply to the output of passive, on the basis of examples such as (25a–b).

(25) a. the city's destruction by the enemy
      b. The city was destroyed by the enemy.

However, Chomsky showed that passive can be decomposed into a structure preserving movement of the object to the subject position in both Ss and NPs, satisfying SU. (26) illustrates. ([$_{NP}$ e] denotes an empty NP position.)

(26) a. [$_{NP}$ e] destruction (of) the city (by the enemy) ⇒ [the city] *('s) destruction (*of) (by the enemy)
      b. [$_{NP}$ e] (be) destroyed (*of) the city (by the enemy) ⇒ [the city] (be) destroyed (*of) (by the enemy)

This analysis obviates the need for a nominalization transformation – the verb and its nominalization are lexically related. But, more importantly, in this analysis the transformations do not need to be stated in terms of the properties of the syntactic structures to which they apply. Crucially, the only structural condition that the movement in (26), called Move α, must satisfy is that it is structure preserving, a general principle.

5.3   X′ theory

Virtually all syntactic theorizing has proceeded from the assumption that languages have words, that a word is a member of at least one LEXICAL CATEGORY, and that at least some phrases are projections of lexical categories (the HEADS) and acquire their categories from them.[9] Applying SU, MGG generalized the observed relationship between the structure of S and the structure of NP. The result was X′ theory (Chomsky 1972; Jackendoff 1977).

In the strongest form of X′ theory, every phrase of every category in every language has the structure in (27). X^0 is the HEAD of the phrase, Spec is the SPECIFIER, and Comp is the COMPLEMENT. Both Spec and Comp may be empty, or may consist of more than one constituent, depending on the selectional properties of the head.

(27)

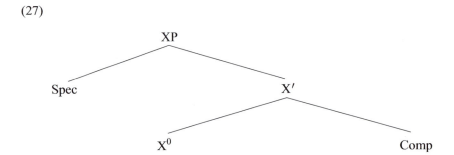

X′ theory makes it possible to formulate a more uniform and constrained account of movement, on the assumption that all movement is structure preserving. Extending this view to *wh*-questions and inversion means that a landing site has to be found for the *wh*-phrase and for the inflected auxiliary. The *wh*-phrase must move to an available phrasal position, while the inflected auxiliary must move to an available head position. Chomsky (1981) proposed that the inflection (INFL=I^0) is the head of S (the projection is IP) and the complementizer C^0 is the head of CP. The structure is given by the PSRs in (28)–(29).

(28)   IP → Spec I′
      I′ → I^0 VP

(29)   CP → Spec C′
      C′ → C^0 IP

The *wh*-phrase moves to the specifier of C^0 and I^0 moves to C^0 in SAI; both movements are structure preserving.

(30) $[_{CP} [_{SPEC} e] C^0 [_{IP} NP I^0_j ... \underline{wh\text{-}XP_i} ...]] \Rightarrow$
      $[_{CP} [_{SPEC} \underline{wh\text{-}XP_i}] I^0_j + C^0 [_{IP} NP t_j ... t_i ...]]$

5.4   Traces

Wasow (1972; 1979) proposed traces as a way to solve a puzzling binding fact noted by Postal (1971) – in (31b), who_i c-commands he_i but cannot bind it.

(31)   a.   *He_i thinks that Mary loves $John_i$.
       b.   *Who_i does he_i think that Mary loves t_i?

Wasow showed that (31b) can be ruled out by the same principle as (31a) if movement leaves a trace that is coindexed with the moved constituent; $John_i$ and the trace of who_i bear the same syntactic relationship to he_i.

Traces were ultimately extended in REST and GB to all movements, so that the underlying structure is reflected in the derived structure. With gaps linked to extracted elements, it became possible to interpret sentences fully on the basis of surface structure. This fact has played a central role in the development of non-movement accounts of A' constructions as early as Brame (1978) and Koster (1978), and was later given a comprehensive formal development in Head Driven Phrase Structure Grammar (HPSG) and Lexical Functional Grammar (LFG).

6   Government binding theory and principles and parameters theory

The shift to GB and PPT is characterized by the modularization of syntactic theory and by the introduction of the core–periphery distinction.

6.1   Modularity

MODULARITY is the idea that there are distinct components of the grammar, each of which obeys its own principles. Among the main components are: X' theory, θ theory, Case theory, binding theory, bounding theory, control theory, and government theory. θ THEORY concerns the correspondence between syntactic structure and the θ-roles governed by a head. CASE THEORY regulates the movement of arguments to positions where they can be case-marked. BINDING THEORY concerns the syntactic relationships between referentially dependent elements (such as pronouns) and their antecedents. BOUNDING THEORY is a reformulation of the island constraints. CONTROL THEORY concerns the interpretation of verbal complements lacking overt subjects. GOVERNMENT THEORY regulates the functions of these components – for example, θ-roles are assigned by a governor, Case is assigned by a governor, bounding constrains what a governor may govern, and the binding relation is constrained within a syntactic domain specified by a governor.

The core–periphery distinction holds that all languages share a common CORE GRAMMAR which is uniform up to parametric variation (e.g., the relative order of head and complement).

6.2   Extensions of X' theory

Space precludes a review in detail of the main features of each of the components of GB theory, which are complex in their own right and in their interactions. Many of these grew out of earlier proposals and remain influential. To take just one case, Pollock (1989), in a very influential article, observed that English and French differ systematically in a number of respects, most notably that:

- the constituent that undergoes inversion in English questions must be a tensed auxiliary verb, while in French it may be a tensed main verb;

(32) a. English: He will go ⇒ Will he go?; He goes ⇒ Does he go?/*Goes he?
    b. French: il va   ⇒ va-t-il
          he goes   goes-t-he
                    'Does he go?'

- *not* in English follows an auxiliary verb, while in French negative *pas* follows a tensed main verb;

(33) a. English: He will not go. *He goes not.
    b. French: Il (ne) va pas.
          he NE goes NEG
          'He doesn't go.'

- adverbs in French immediately follow a tensed transitive main verb, while in English they follow the VP, not the verb.[10]

(34) a. English: John (often) kisses (*often) Mary (often).
    b. French: Jean (*souvent) embrasse (souvent) Marie.
          John often kisses often Mary

Pollock proposed that the main difference between English and French, then, is that in English only auxiliary verbs attach to finite I^0, while in French main verbs do as well.

Analysis of additional details of verb–adverb ordering led Pollock to propose an "exploded" Infl, in which each feature is associated with a different head (AgrS, AgrO, and T(ense)).[11] Extending Pollock's analysis (again following DU), Chomsky (1991; 1993) proposed that all movements to Spec positions are motivated by FEATURE CHECKING. A feature on a head is CHECKED or DISCHARGED if there is a constituent in its Spec that agrees with it, as in (35). If a feature is not checked, the resulting derivation is ill-formed.[12]

(35)

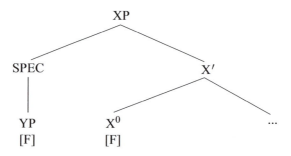

For example, in English a *wh*-phrase moves to Spec,CP in order to discharge the feature [WH] on C^0.

(36) $[_{CP} [_{SPEC} e] C^0[_{WH}] [_{IP} NP I^0 \ldots XP[_{WH}]_i \ldots]] \Rightarrow$
$[_{CP} [_{SPEC} XP[_{WH}]_i] C^0[_{WH}] [_{IP} NP I^0 \ldots t_i \ldots]]$

Abney (1987) extended the application of functional categories to the NP and the parallelism with IP, arguing that N^0 is head of NP and the determiner is head of DP (37). DP is currently the standard notation in MGG for what was called NP in ST and EST.

(37)

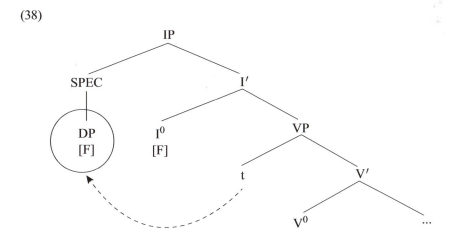

Abney also proposed that a possessive originates in Spec,NP and moves to Spec,DP to discharge a feature of D^0. This assumption allows all of the θ-roles of N^0 to be assigned within its maximal projection NP.

Extending this analysis to the sentence means that the subject DP originates as Spec,VP and moves to Spec,IP (see (38)).

(38)

This is the VP INTERNAL SUBJECT HYPOTHESIS. McCloskey (1997) argues that there is evidence for the internal subject positions predicted by the exploded Infl of Pollock, Chomsky, and others, as shown in (39).[13]

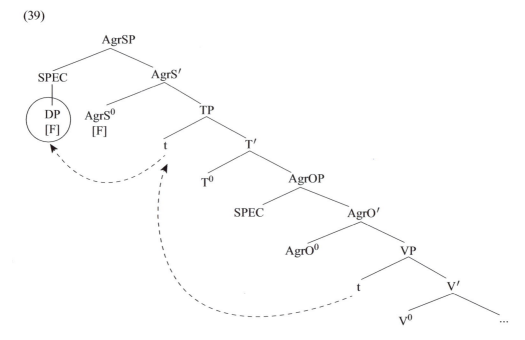

(39)

Applying DU, the exploded Infl/feature checking analysis was extended in GB to the derivation of the passive. AgrS was assumed to be associated with a Case feature (as is AgrO in the transitive sentence). In the passive, the Case feature on the direct object is discharged if the direct object moves to Spec,AgrS.

6.3 Binding and movement

A major innovation in GB was to propose a tight interaction between binding and movement. Chomsky (1980) proposed that the distribution of referentially dependent elements such as pronouns and anaphors (such as reflexives and reciprocals) is governed by principles that have essentially the following content. Assume that coindexing of two expressions in the syntactic representation marks the coreference. Assume also that a constituent α BINDS a constituent β if α and β are coindexed and α C-COMMANDS β (i.e., if the constituent immediately dominating α dominates β). Then these principles hold: (A) a reflexive must be locally bound, (B) a pronoun cannot be locally bound, (C) a pronoun cannot bind its antecedent. Locality here is defined in terms of X′ theory – it is essentially the XP headed by a governor, with some extensions and restrictions.

Constraining A movements was reconceived in GB in terms of conditions on the distribution of the trace in terms of binding theory. A movements are local, as is the binding of anaphors, suggesting that the trace of A movement is an anaphor. Non-local A movement violates Principle A of the binding theory since it is not locally bound.

6.4 Control

An important consequence of Uniformity is that it motivates abstract invisible constituents, which were introduced in REST and extended in GB/PPT. For example, the two sentences in (40) are synonymous.

(40) a. Susan$_i$ expects [$_S$ that she$_i$ will win].
 b. Susan expects to win.

If *she* is coreferential with *Susan* (marked with coindexing), and *she* bears the role Winner, IU and SU lead to the conclusion that the structure of (40b) is (41), where PRO is an invisible pronominal (Chomsky 1981).

(41) Susan$_i$ expects [$_S$ PRO$_i$ to win].

Control theory is concerned with the distribution of PRO. Case theory plays a role in accounting for this distribution – PRO cannot be Case-marked. Government theory determines Case assignment – Case is assigned to a constituent that is governed. Hence PRO cannot be governed.

6.5 Antisymmetry

In MGG, from *SS* onward, linear order is represented explicitly in the PSRs. An influential proposal at the end of the GB/PPT era is antisymmetry theory (Kayne 1994). Kayne proposed to remove observed linear order as a grammatical primitive and to treat it as dependent on configuration. In Kayne's proposal, linear order is determined by the structure in (27) and the Linear Correspondence Axiom (42).[14]

(42) **Linear Correspondence Axiom (LCA)**
 Let X, Y be non-terminals, and x, y terminals such that X dominates x and Y dominates y. Then if X asymmetrically c-commands Y, x precedes y. (Kayne 1994: 33)

(43) **C-Command**
 X c-commands Y iff X and Y are categories and X excludes Y and every category that dominates X dominates Y. (Kayne 1994: 16)
 Asymmetric C-Command
 X asymmetrically c-commands Y iff X c-commands Y and Y does not c-command X. (Kayne 1994: 4)

It follows from the LCA that underlying syntactic structure is uniformly binary branching and branches in the same direction (to the right, by stipulating "precedes" in (42)). Multiple branching precludes antisymmetry, and lack of antisymmetry results in no linear order by the LCA. Consider (44).

(44)

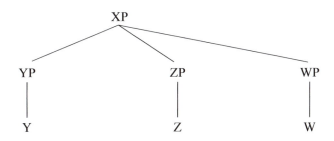

Since YP, ZP, and WP c-command one another, there is no asymmetric c-command. Then there is no linear ordering defined between y, z, and w. Hence XP is an impossible structure (according to the LCA).

Since observed linear order is often not of the form Spec-X^0-Comp, the LCA forces an account of many orders in terms of movement. For instance, in a verb-final language such as Japanese all complements and adjuncts of V must follow V and move to the left. On the additional assumption that all movement is structure preserving, there must be landing sites for all leftward movements. Moreover, there must be functional heads whose features guarantee derivation of the overt order, by feature checking. A typical derivation is given in (45). The derived order NP-V-I^0-C^0 is that found in Japanese. Moving IP to Spec,CP correctly blocks *wh*-movement, which does not occur in Japanese and similar V-final languages.

(45)

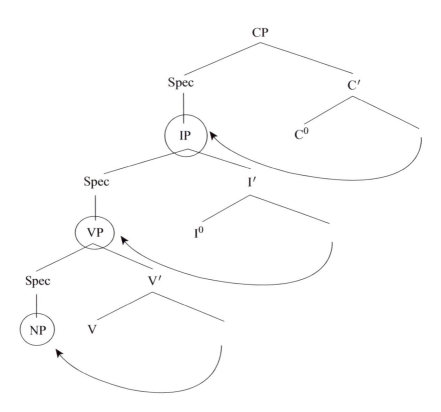

7 The Minimalist Program

Chomsky's goal in the Minimalist Program (MP) is to reduce GB/PPT as much as possible to general principles of economy, to reduce derivations to their most primitive components, and to eliminate as much as possible the formal devices that had developed around the MGG approach (as summarized in the preceding sections). An accompanying goal is to investigate the extent to which natural language syntax can be viewed as deviating minimally from an ideal computational system.

For instance, PSRs were eliminated in MP in favor of a primitive MERGE operation that combines two objects α and β, which are words or phrases, into a new object; this operation is "external" Merge. The label of the resulting object is standardly assumed to be either that of α or β (46).

(46)

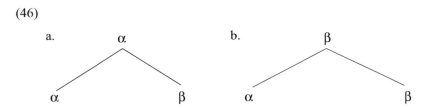

a. α / α β b. β / α β

Movement, or "internal Merge", is understood in MP as a combination of copying and deletion (47), an idea that has its roots in Chomsky's earliest work (Chomsky 1955).

(47)

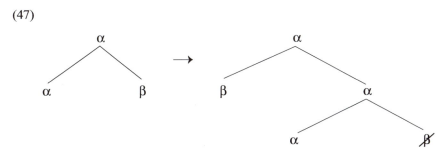

Movement is licensed when there is a feature of the merged constituent, the GOAL, that agrees with some feature of a head, the PROBE. The operation AGREE erases the feature of the goal if it matches that of the probe. Features that are not erased result in illegitimate derivations.

There are no island constraints in MP; rather, movement is constrained by DERIVATIONAL ECONOMY: each movement operation, or the length of each operation, or both, contributes to the complexity of a derivation (Chomsky 1995; Zwart 1996). Certain derivations can then be ruled out (in principle, at least) on the grounds that they are pre-empted by less complex derivations (see Johnson and Lappin (1997; 1999) for a critique). Suppose, for example, that α c-commands β, β commands γ, and both β and γ match the probe α. Since β is closer to α than γ, only β can Agree with α – this is the MINIMAL LINK CONDITION. For example, in (48) there are two *wh*-phrases but only the highest can undergo movement, as shown in (49).

(48) C^0[WH] [who[WH]$_i$ [$_{VP}$ was talking to whom[WH]$_j$]

(49) a.   (I wonder) who[WH]$_i$ C^0[WH] [t_i [$_{VP}$ was talking to whom[WH]]]
     b. *(I wonder) whom[WH]$_j$ C^0[WH] [who[WH]$_i$ [$_{VP}$ was talking to t_j]]

This data falls under the SUPERIORITY CONDITION of Chomsky (1973).

Another consequence of the reformulation of derivations in terms of Merge in MP and the elimination of PSRs is that there are no levels of representation such as D-structure and S-structure. The phonological form of a phrase is specified as it is constructed by Merge, by the operation SPELL-OUT, and its interpretation is also assumed to be constructed dynamically in the course of the derivation.[15] An extension of this idea is found in DISTRIBUTED

MORPHOLOGY, where a word is an abstract syntactic object, a complex word is derived by Merge, and the phonological form of a word is specified by Spell-out (Siddiqi 2010).

8 Some critical branch points

In this section I review briefly a number of theoretical developments that arose as a reaction to various aspects of MGG. A number of these have been taken up in the MP, resulting in some interesting convergences.

8.1 Derivations and representations

Head Driven Phrase Structure Grammar (HPSG; Pollard and Sag 1994) is one of the main alternatives to MGG. HPSG accounts for the derivation of sentences without assuming transformations. Since it assumes only one level of representation, HPSG is a MONOSTRATAL syntactic theory.

HPSG relaxes the assumption that phrase structure is a syntactic primitive whose properties are specified by a component of the grammar, leading to a major alternative to MGG.[16] In HPSG, phrase structure is implicit in the lexicon, hence it is a LEXICALIST theory. A typical lexical entry (for the verb *put*) is given in (50) (from Levine and Meurers (2006)).

(50)

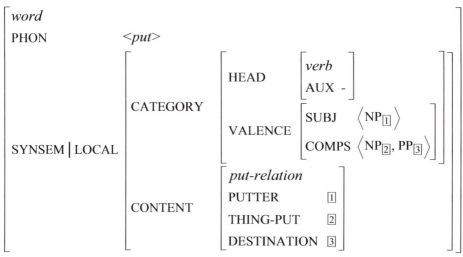

The hierarchical structure and linear ordering given by PSRs are expressed in HPSG by immediate dominance (ID) schemata and linear precedence (LP) statements. The features and the ID schema stipulate how to combine *put* with its complements (COMPS) and subject (SUBJ), and the semantic consequences. The structure emerges from this composition, as each VALENCE feature is satisfied by merging the current object with a phrase of a specified type according to the ID schemata. For example, *put* merges first with an NP, and the result is merged with a PP, to form the equivalent of a VP. (51) illustrates the derivation of the structure of *Sandy put the book on the table*.

(51)

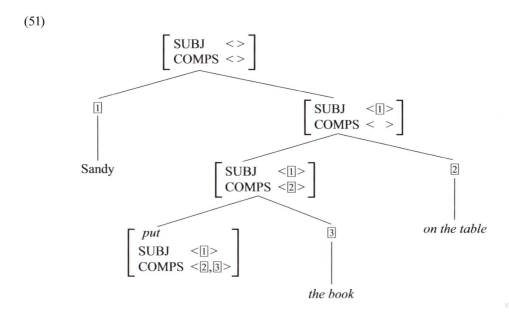

HPSG deals with sentential organization differently from MGG (as do other approaches), but there are important overlaps. In HPSG a phrase is a projection of its head, but there are no significant intermediate levels of syntactic representation and no abstract functional heads – hence HPSG observes the VP internal subject hypothesis by default. There is feature checking, but the valence features in question correspond directly to observable syntactic properties of heads such as SUBJ, COMPS, and so on. Failure to SATURATE a valence feature means that it is passed up through the structure and must be satisfied at a later point in the derivation of the sentence, producing the possibility of chains. The VALENCE PRINCIPLE requires that the feature values of a phrase be identical to those of its head. For instance, if there is no direct object adjacent to the verb, then the valence feature is saturated by adjoining an NP to the left edge of the structure, which yields a filler-gap construction.

To the extent that comparable features are assumed in HPSG and MGG to license the arguments and their overt forms, the MGG approach can be seen to be a notational variant of the HPSG approach, differing primarily in that it has a more abstract structure, motivated through the application of DU.

8.2   Grammatical functions

From the beginning, MGG has taken the position that grammatical functions (GFs) such as subject and object are not primitives, but are defined in terms of "epistemologically prior" properties of utterances such as linear precedence (Chomsky 1981: 10). However, GFs are actually defined configurationally in MGG (Chomsky 1965: 71): subject (of S) is an NP immediately dominated by S, object (of VP) is an NP immediately dominated by VP, predicate (of S) is a VP immediately dominated by S, and so on.

An important branch point in the development of syntactic theory is the assumption that the GFs are primitive. In LFG (Bresnan and Kaplan 1982) there is a level of F(UNCTIONAL)-STRUCTURE that corresponds in systematic ways to C(ONSTITUENT)-STRUCTURE. In a language such as English, the subject function corresponds to the configuration "NP immediately dominated by S", while in a case-marking language such as Russian it corresponds to "NP marked with nominative case".[17] LFG's c-structure is essentially equivalent to classical REST S-structure, and lacks functional heads except those that correspond to overt morphological forms.

In MGG, on the other hand, SU requires that the subject be represented uniformly – that is, configurationally – across languages. Hence, in an MGG analysis the subject in a case-marking language such as Russian is in the same configuration as it is in English. Furthermore, by DU, if a particular configuration leads to a particular case-marking in one language, then it must lead to the same case-marking in all languages. Hence the subject in English has nominative case, etc. However, in English and many other languages there is clearly no morphological case. The solution in MGG is to assume that there is abstract Case (Chomsky 1980; 1981). Whether Case is realized morphologically is a secondary matter of spelling out.

Non-transformational theories refer explicitly to GFs to characterize the relationship between active and passive. The MGG account accomplishes this result by assigning Patient to the object and then moving it to subject position. But in a non-transformational, or LEXICALIST, account, Patient is assigned directly to the subject in virtue of the verb being in the passive form. In LFG, for example, f-structure plays a direct role in the analysis of the passive. There is a lexical rule that derives the passive verb from the active form. This rule reassigns the correspondences between the GFs and the θ-roles governed by the verb (Bresnan 1982). The passive structure signals that the Agent role is not linked to the subject. Principles of mapping between syntactic structure and thematic representation then ensure that the Patient role is linked to the subject.

In HPSG a similar lexical rule rearranges the valence features of a verb and the θ-roles (Pollard and Sag 1987). Passive sentences are straightforward realizations of the basic structure of the language, similar to cases where the predicate is adjectival: cf. (52).

(52) a. Sandy was [$_{VP/AP}$ arrested by the police].
      b. Sandy was [$_{AP}$ asleep at the wheel].

There is a lexical rule that remaps the roles to the syntactic arguments when the verb is passive. The rule applies generally to all verbs.

Similar devices are found in other approaches. The crucial mediating factor is the lexicon, where the θ-roles are associated with individual lexical items (Gruber 1972; Jackendoff 1972; 1983; 1990).

Relational Grammar (Blake 1990; Perlmutter 1983) takes the grammatical relations Subject, Direct Object, and so on to be syntactic primitives, rather than constituent structure. The structure is represented in terms of the assignment of grammatical relations to phrases, and constructions such as the passive are derived by reassigning the grammatical relations (e.g., underlying Subject is assigned to Direct Object, and underlying Object is assigned to an Oblique grammatical relation). Linear order is defined over the final stage (or STRATUM) of grammatical relation assignments.

In Role and Reference Grammar (Van Valin and LaPolla 1997) the syntactic representation is expressed in terms not of the classical syntactic categories (§4.3) but of functional categories such as Clause, Referential Phrase, Predicate, and so on.[18] This shift is motivated in part by research on less well-studied languages, where it is less clear that the generalizations can be captured in terms of the classical syntactic categories.[19] There are no transformations in RRG; rather, there are rules that map directly between syntactic structure and semantic representations. Semantic arguments are ordered in a hierarchy according to their semantic role (Actor, Undergoer, etc.) and mapped to syntactic positions. An illustration is given in (53) (from Van Valin Jr. 2010: 736).

(53)

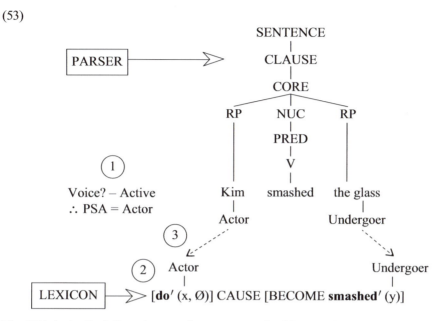

The PSA is the "privileged semantic argument", in this case the Actor, that gets mapped to the preverbal position – there is no mention of syntactic structure or grammatical functions such as Subject and Object.

In Simpler Syntax (Culicover and Jackendoff 2005) the Patient θ-role is linked to the Object GF. However, the passive is intransitive, so the Object cannot correspond to a syntactic constituent. It then corresponds by default to the Subject GF.

8.3   Constructions

MGG inherited the terminology CONSTRUCTION from traditional grammar; there is a "passive construction", a "*wh*-interrogative construction", and so on. By decomposing complex transformations such as the passive into the more primitive operation Move α, MGG gradually adopted the position that constructions as such are artifacts.

At the same time, many syntacticians have continued to treat constructions as grammatical primitives. Such a view has been explicitly formalized in Construction Grammar (Kay 2002), and has been widely adopted (see, e.g., Fillmore *et al.* 1988; Kay and Fillmore 1999; Goldberg 1995; 2006; Culicover and Jackendoff 2005; Sag 2012). The central empirical point is that some (if not all) syntactic structures have aspects of meaning associated with them that cannot be explained strictly in terms of the meanings of their constituents. In order to capture this part of the form-meaning relation, the construction *per se* must be part of the representation.

8.4   Explanation

While the Argument from the Poverty of the Stimulus (§1) is widely accepted, there are alternative views about where this type of knowledge could come from in the absence of direct experience. Processing accounts observe that there are well-formed examples with the same structure as the unacceptable examples, and attribute the judgment of ill-formedness to processing complexity (typically characterized in terms of memory limitations) (see Hofmeister *et al.* 2013f; Hofmeister 2011; Sag *et al.* 2007 and, for a critique, Phillips 2013). Fodor (1978) and Hawkins (2004) have argued that grammars evolve to incorporate dis-preferences for computationally complex structures. There are Bayesian approaches, which essentially argue that a structure can be judged unacceptable if there is an alternative structure that is significantly more likely, other things being equal (Pearl and Sprouse 2013).

9 Conclusion

The history of syntax shows a wide variety of theoretical alternatives, both internal to and external to MGG. Nevertheless, it is possible to see significant convergences: for example, the role of the lexicon in projecting syntactic structure and the dissociation of linear order and hierarchical structure. At the same time, there remain fundamental open questions, such as whether grammatical functions are primitives, the nature of syntactic categories, the relationship between syntactic structure and semantic interpretation, the status of syntactic constructions, the distinction between "core" and "peripheral" phenomena, the distinction between grammaticality and acceptability, and the origin and status of syntactic constraints. No doubt these issues will continue to animate the field, as they have since its inception.

Notes

1 I am grateful to Ray Jackendoff and Dan Siddiqi for comments on an earlier draft of this chapter and to the students and faculty of the 2012 Norwegian Summer School in Linguistics in Svolvaer for feedback and questions that have led to many significant improvements. All remaining errors are my responsibility.

2 For a survey of the work of the Sanskrit grammarians (around 1000 BC), see Staal (1967). According to Staal, the Sanskrit grammarians were concerned with grammatical relations but not word order (Sanskrit being a free word order language). For a comprehensive history of more recent syntactic thinking, see Graffi (2001). For extended social, political and intellectual histories of generative grammar, see Newmeyer (1980; 1986), Matthews (1993), and Tomalin (2006).

3 For a more extended review, see Culicover and Jackendoff (2005: Chs 1–3).

4 However, in the absence of a semantic theory in the 1960s, the distinction action/non-action had to be encoded syntactically. This was the approach taken by Generative Semantics (see §4.1), which assumed an abstract verb ACT only in (2a).

5 With caveats for examples such as *Sheila was sent flowers*. In this case, it is the indirect object that does not follow the verb.

6 Although Chomsky (1981: 212) continues to refer to A-over-A as a possible explanatory principle.

7 In GS the structures in (22) were taken to be the DS representations of sentence (21), which was derived by transformation (in this case, lowering of the quantifier phrase).

8 This is a simplification – it is assumed that both quantifier phrases undergo movement, and the scope is determined by which one is attached higher in the structure.

9 Role and Reference Grammar (RRG) appears to be an exception; see §8.2.

10 This statement is too strong, because an adverb can intervene between the verb and the direct object in English if the latter is "heavy" in some sense – for example:

    (i)   He ate quickly all of the fish on his plate.

    For discussion of the factors that contribute to heaviness, see Wasow (2009).

11 An extension of this approach appears in "cartographic" syntax, where the precise details of linear order are reduced to the hierarchical organization of functional categories both internal to the sentence and on the left periphery (Cinque 1999; Rizzi 2004).

12 A number of devices have been proposed to achieve this result: for example, unchecked syntactic features cause ill-formedness when mapped into PF and/or LF (Chomsky 1995).

13 The movement of the subject does not pass through Spec,Agr_O since it is presumably filled by the direct object.
14 The actual formulation of the LCA does not refer to a specific branching direction, but Kayne (1994: 33ff) argues that it reduces to precedence.
15 Thus the MP bears a close resemblance to Categorial Grammar.
16 For an extended review of phrase structure in generative grammar, see Carnie (2010), as well as Chapter 3.
17 This is an oversimplification, since categories other than NP can be subjects, and subject in Russian (and other languages) may have other than nominative case.
18 These are different than the "functional" categories Infl, C^0, D^0, and so on of GB. The GB categories should more accurately be termed "formal" categories, since they do not have to do with function. They have no meaning, but rather play a role in constraining the form of sentences.
19 For discussion of the issue in Salish and Tagalog, see Koch and Matthewson (2009) and references cited there.

Further reading

Culicover, P.W., and R. Jackendoff. 2005. *Simpler Syntax*. Oxford: Oxford University Press.
Matthews, P.H. 1993. *Grammatical Theory in the United States from Bloomfield to Chomsky*. Cambridge: Cambridge University Press.
Newmeyer, F. 1980. *Linguistic Theory in America*. New York: Academic Press.
Tomalin, M. 2006. *Linguistics and the Formal Sciences: the Origins of Generative Grammar*. Cambridge: Cambridge University Press.

References

Abney, S. 1987. *The Noun Phrase in its Sentential Aspect*. Cambridge, MA: MIT.
Blake, B.J. 1990. *Relational Grammar*. London: Routledge.
Bloomfield, L. 1933. *Language*. New York: Holt, Rinehart and Winston.
Brame, M. 1978. *Base Generated Syntax*. Seattle, WA: Noit Amrofer.
Bresnan, J. 1982. The passive in grammatical theory. In *The Mental Representation of Grammatical Relations*, ed. J. Bresnan, 3–86. Cambridge, MA: MIT Press.
Bresnan, J., and R. Kaplan. 1982. Lexical functional grammar: a formal system for grammatical representations. In *The Mental Representation of Grammatical Relations*, ed. J. Bresnan, 173–281. Cambridge, MA: MIT Press.
Carnie, A. 2010. *Constituent Structure*. Oxford: Oxford University Press.
Chomsky, N. 1955. *The Logical Structure of Linguistic Theory*. New York: Plenum.
Chomsky, N. 1957. *Syntactic Structures*. The Hague: Mouton.
Chomsky, N. 1964. *Current Issues in Linguistic Theory*. The Hague: Mouton.
Chomsky, N. 1965. *Aspects of the Theory of Syntax*. Cambridge, MA: MIT Press.
Chomsky, N. 1972. Remarks on nominalization. In *Readings in English Transformational Grammar*, ed. R. Jacobs and P. Rosenbaum, 184–221. Waltham, MA: Ginn and Co.
Chomsky, N. 1973. Conditions on transformations. In *Festschrift for Morris Halle*, ed. S. Anderson and P. Kiparsky, 232–286. New York: Holt, Rinehart and Winston.
Chomsky, N. 1980. On binding. *Linguistic Inquiry* 11:1–46.
Chomsky, N. 1981. *Lectures on Government and Binding*. Dordrecht: Foris.
Chomsky, N. 1991. Some notes on economy of derivation and representation. In *Principles and Parameters in Comparative Grammar*, ed. R. Freidin, 417–454. Cambridge, MA: MIT Press.
Chomsky, N. 1993. A minimalist program for linguistic theory. In *The View from Building 20*, ed. K. Hale and S.J. Keyser, 1–52. Cambridge, MA: MIT Press.
Chomsky, N. 1995. *The Minimalist Program*. Cambridge, MA: MIT Press.
Cinque, G. 1999. *Adverbs and Functional Heads: A Cross-linguistic Perspective*. Oxford: Oxford University Press.
Culicover, P.W., and R. Jackendoff. 2005. *Simpler Syntax*. Oxford: Oxford University Press.
Culicover, P.W., and R. Jackendoff. 2012. A domain-general cognitive relation and how language expresses it. *Language* 88:305–340.

Emonds, J. 1970. *Root and Structure Preserving Transformations.* Bloomington, IN: Indiana University Linguistics Club.

Fillmore, C.J., P. Kay, and M.C. O'Connor. 1988. Regularity and idiomaticity in grammatical constructions: the case of let alone. *Language* 64:501–539.

Fodor, J.D. 1978. Parsing strategies and constraints on transformations. *Linguistic Inquiry* 9:427–473.

Gibson, E. 1998. Linguistic complexity: Locality of syntactic dependencies. *Cognition* 68:1–76.

Goldberg, A.E. 1995. *Constructions: A Construction Grammar Approach to Argument Structure.* Chicago, IL: University of Chicago Press.

Goldberg, A.E. 2006. *Constructions at Work: Constructionist Approaches in Context.* Oxford: Oxford University Press.

Graffi, G. 2001. *200 Years of Syntax: a Critical Survey.* Amsterdam: John Benjamins.

Gruber, J.S. 1972. *Functions of the Lexicon in Formal Descriptive Grammars.* Bloomington, IN: Indiana University Linguistics Club.

Harris, Z. 1951. *Methods in Structural Linguistics.* Chicago, IL: University of Chicago Press.

Hawkins, J.A. 2004. *Complexity and Efficiency in Grammars.* Oxford: Oxford University Press.

Hofmeister, P. 2011. Representational complexity and memory retrieval in language comprehension. *Language and Cognitive Processes* 26:376–405.

Hofmeister, P., L. Staum Casasanto, and I.A. Sag. 2013. Islands in the grammar? Standards of evidence. In *Experimental Syntax and Island Effects*, ed. J. Sprouse and N. Hornstein, 42–63. Cambridge: Cambridge University Press.

Jackendoff, R. 1972. *Semantic Interpretation in Generative Grammar.* Cambridge, MA: MIT Press.

Jackendoff, R. 1977. *X-bar Syntax: A Study of Phrase Structure.* Cambridge, MA: MIT Press.

Jackendoff, R. 1983. *Semantics and Cognition.* Cambridge, MA: MIT Press.

Jackendoff, R. 1990. *Semantic Structures.* Cambridge, MA: MIT Press.

Johnson, D.E., and S. Lappin. 1997. A critique of the minimalist program. *Linguistics and Philosophy* 20:273–333.

Johnson, D.E., and S. Lappin. 1999. *Local Constraints vs. Economy.* Stanford, CA: CSLI.

Katz, J.J., and T.G. Bever. 1976. The rise and fall of empiricism. *An Integrated Theory of Linguistic Ability*, ed. T.G. Bever, J.J. Katz, and D.T. Langendoen, 11–64. New York: Crowell.

Katz, J.J., and P.M. Postal. 1964. *Toward an Integrated Theory of Linguistic Descriptions.* Cambridge, MA: MIT Press.

Kay, P. 2002. An informal sketch of a formal architecture for construction grammar. *Grammars* 5:1–19.

Kay, P., and C.J. Fillmore. 1999. Grammatical constructions and linguistic generalizations: The What's X doing Y? construction. *Language* 75:1–33.

Kayne, R.S. 1994. *The Antisymmetry of Syntax.* Cambridge, MA: MIT Press.

Koch, K., and L. Matthewson. 2009. The lexical category debate in Salish and its relevance for Tagalog. *Theoretical Linguistics* 35:125–137.

Koster, J. 1978. *Locality Principles in Syntax.* Dordrecht: Foris.

Lakoff, G. 1965. *Irregularity in Syntax.* New York: Holt, Rinehart and Winston.

Lasnik, H., and J.J. Kupin. 1977. A restrictive theory of transformational grammar. *Theoretical Linguistics* 4:173–196.

Lees, R.B. 1960. *The Grammar of English Nominalizations.* Bloomington, IN: Indiana University Research Center in Anthropology.

Levine, R.D., and W.D. Meurers. 2006. Head-driven phrase structure grammar: Linguistic approach, formal foundations, and computational realization. In *Encyclopedia of Language and Linguistics*, 2nd edn, ed. K. Brown, 237–252. Oxford: Elsevier.

Lewis, R.L. 1997. Specifying architectures for language processing: Process, control, and memory in parsing and interpretation. In *Architectures and Mechanisms for Language Processing*, ed. M. Pickering and C. Clifton, 56–89. Cambridge: Cambridge University Press.

McCloskey, J. 1997. Subjecthood and subject positions. In *Elements of Grammar*, ed. L. Haegeman, 198–235. Dordrecht: Kluwer Academic Publishers.

Matthews, P.H. 1993. *Grammatical Theory in the United States from Bloomfield to Chomsky.* Cambridge: Cambridge University Press.

May, R. 1985. *Logical Form.* Cambridge, MA: MIT Press.

Miller, G.A., and N. Chomsky. 1963. Finitary models of language users. In *Handbook of Mathematical Psychology*, vol. 2, ed. R.D. Luce, R.R. Bush, and E. Galanter, 419–491. New York: Wiley.

Newmeyer, F. 1980. *Linguistic Theory in America*. New York: Academic Press.

Newmeyer, F. 1986. *The Politics of Linguistics*. Chicago, IL: University of Chicago Press.

Pearl, L., and J. Sprouse. 2013. Computational models of acquisition for islands. In *Experimental Syntax and Island Effects*, ed. J. Sprouse and N. Hornstein, 109–131. Cambridge: Cambridge University Press.

Perlmutter, D.M. 1983. *Studies in Relational Grammar*. Chicago, IL: University of Chicago Press.

Phillips, C. 2013. Some arguments and non-arguments for reductionist accounts of syntactic phenomena. *Language and Cognitive Processes* 28:156–187.

Pollard, C., and I.A. Sag. 1987. *Information-based Syntax and Semantics Volume 1: Fundamentals*. Stanford, CA: CSLI.

Pollard, C., and I.A. Sag. 1994. *Head-driven Phrase Structure Grammar*. Chicago, IL: University of Chicago Press.

Pollock, J.-Y. 1989. Verb movement, universal grammar and the structure of IP. *Linguistic Inquiry* 20:365–424.

Postal, P.M. 1971. *Crossover Phenomena*. New York: Holt, Rinehart and Winston.

Rizzi, L. 2004. *The Structure of CP and IP*. New York: Oxford University Press.

Ross, J.R. 1967. *Constraints on Variables in Syntax*. Cambridge, MA: MIT.

Sag, I.A. 2012. Sign-based construction grammar: An informal synopsis. In *Sign-Based Construction Grammar*, ed. H.C. Boas and I.A. Sag, 69–202. Stanford, CA: CSLI.

Sag, I.A., P. Hofmeister, and N. Snider. 2007. Processing complexity in subjacency violations: The complex noun phrase constraint. *Proceedings of the 43rd Annual Meeting of the Chicago Linguistic Society*, 215–229. Chicago, IL: CLS.

Siddiqi, D. 2010. Distributed morphology. *Language and Linguistics Compass* 4:524–542.

Staal, J.F. 1967. *Word Order in Sanskrit and Universal Grammar*. Berlin: Springer.

Tomalin, M. 2006. *Linguistics and the Formal Sciences: the Origins of Generative Grammar*. Cambridge: Cambridge University Press.

Van Valin, J., D. Robert, and R.J. LaPolla. 1997. *Syntax. Structure, Meaning and Function*. Cambridge: Cambridge University Press.

Van Valin Jr., R. 2010. Role and reference grammar as a framework for linguistic analysis. In *The Oxford Handbook of Linguistic Analysis*, ed. B. Heine and H. Narrog, 703–738. Oxford: Oxford University Press.

Wasow, T. 1972. *Anaphoric Relations in English*. Cambridge, MA: MIT.

Wasow, T. 1979. *Anaphora in Generative Grammar*. Gent: E. Story-Scientia.

Wasow, T. 2009. Remarks on grammatical weight. *Language Variation and Change* 9:81–105.

Zwart, C.J.W. 1996. 'Shortest move' versus 'fewest steps'. In *Minimal ideas: Syntactic Studies in the Minimalist Framework*, ed. W. Abraham, S. Epstein, H. Thrainsson, and C.J.W. Zwart, 305–327. Amsterdam: John Benjamins.

24

Comparative syntax

Martin Haspelmath

1 Goals of comparative syntax

Not only elementary sound-meaning pairs (individual morphs) differ across languages but also the ways in which they are combined into complex units ('words', 'phrases', and 'clauses'). The comparative study of the similarities and differences between the combinatorial systems of languages is called *comparative syntax* or *syntactic typology*. Some initial examples of such differences between languages are given in (1)–(5), where the (a) and (b) examples show different types of languages.

(1) a. English
     Isabel shut the door.   (SVO)
     b. Japanese
     Taro   ga   to   o   shime-ta.   (SOV)
     Taro   NOM door ACC shut-PST
     'Taro shut the door.'

(2) a. Huallaga Quechua (Weber 1989: 15)   (accusative alignment)
     (i) *Hwan   puñu-yka-n.*
          Juan(NOM)   sleep-IMPFV-3.SBJ
          'Juan is sleeping.'
     (ii) *Hwan   Tumas-ta   maqa-n.*
          Juan(NOM)   Tomás-ACC hit-3.SBJ
          'Juan hits Tomás.'

     b. Lezgian (Haspelmath 1993)   (ergative alignment)
     (i) *Ali   ata-na.*
          Ali(ABS)   come-PST
          'Ali came.'
     (ii) *Ali-di   i   gaf-ar   luhu-zwa.*
          Ali-ERG   this   word-PL(ABS) say-IMPFV
          'Ali is saying these words.'

(3) a. Italian   (no independent subject pronouns)
         Quando viene   Diana, Ø mi chiama.
         when   comes Diana Ø me calls
         'When Diana comes, she calls me.'
     b. German   (independent subject pronouns)
         Wenn Diana kommt, ruft sie mich.
         when Diana comes calls she me
         'When Diana comes, she calls me.'

(4) a. Yoruba   (special reflexive pronoun)
         Màríà   rí   araa   rè   nínú   àwòrón.
         Mary   see   body   3.POSS inside picture
         'Mary saw herself in the picture.'
     b. Loniu (Hamel 1994: 54)   (no special reflexive pronoun)
         iy   itɛkɛni   iy   ilɛ   lɔ   tas
         3SG   3SG.throw   3SG   3SG.go in   sea
         'He threw him/himself into the sea.'

(5) a. Turkish   (question-word in situ)
         Zehra kim-i   gör-müş?
         Zehra who-ACC see-PST
         'Who did Zehra see?'
     b. Arabic   (question-word fronting)
         Maa ta-quulu?
         what 2SG-say
         'What are you saying?'

A further kind of difference that is often noted by linguists is the difference between morphological and phrasal expression: for example, the difference between case suffixes such as *-di* in Lezgian and postpositions such as *ga* and *o* in Japanese. However, it is probably impossible to make this distinction in a coherent way across languages (Haspelmath 2011a) and often the difference between morphological and phrasal expression is primarily an orthographic one (see, for instance, Spencer and Otoguro (2005) on the difficulty of deciding whether Japanese *ga* and *o* are suffixes or separate words). Thus, morphology is not a separate domain from syntax, and it would perhaps be better to call the entire combinatorial system of languages 'morphosyntax'. For simplicity, I just talk about syntax here, but it should be understood that morphology is included in it.

The syntactic patterns of different languages are often compared with the goal of reconstructing a common ancestral system or changes in a system over time, but this is possible only when we know that the languages are cognate – that is, genealogically related, going back to a common ancestor. This kind of syntactic comparison is more commonly called historical syntax (e.g., Harris and Campbell 1995), diachronic syntax (e.g., Roberts 2007), or historical-comparative syntax. The topic of the present chapter, by contrast, is the comparison of non-cognate languages, where similarities are not interpreted as inherited from a common ancestor.

The comparative study of syntactic patterns can have various goals:

(6) a. Studying languages contrastively, with the goal of facilitating foreign language learning (e.g., König and Gast 2007 on English–German contrasts).

b. Detecting areal patterns, with the goal of discovering ancient language contact influences (e.g., Muysken 2008).

c. Finding invariant patterns among the variation (i.e., syntactic universals, or universal syntactic principles).

d. Explaining why languages are the way they are (i.e., explaining the universals).

e. Explaining how language acquisition is possible despite the poverty of the stimulus.

f. Using universal principles (cf. 6c) to provide more elegant accounts of the systems of particular languages.

g. Using universal principles (cf. 6c) to explain regularities of syntactic change and of language acquisition.

Of these goals, (6a–c) are independent of each other, but (6d–g) all depend on (6c), the goal of finding invariant patterns (or universals), so this is the most prominent aspect of comparative syntax. For this reason, comparative syntax is also sometimes called *syntactic universals research* (cf. Croft 1990; 2003; Alexiadou 2002).[1]

2 Two research orientations in comparative syntax

There are two main research orientations that deal with comparative syntax, what I will call the *nonaprioristic approach* and the *restrictivist approach*. Although both compare the syntactic systems of diverse non-cognate languages, they differ substantially in their assumptions, goals, and research methods. Why they differ in this way is often not fully clear even to practitioners of both approaches, and it is one of the goals of this chapter to explicate the differences. More commonly, the nonaprioristic approach is called 'functional-typological' (or 'Greenbergian'), and the restrictivist approach is called 'generative' or 'formal' (or 'Chomskyan'), but these labels do not help us much to understand the differences, so I will not use them much.[2]

2.1 The nonaprioristic approach to comparative syntax

In the nonaprioristic approach, researchers compare languages with the goal of finding general properties shared by all or most languages, but they make no a priori assumptions about the kinds of categories and constructions that languages might have or about the kinds of explanations that might account for the generalizations.

The nonaprioristic approach is thus fully compatible with the anthropological tradition in linguistics that puts special emphasis on the ways in which languages differ. In particular, in this tradition linguists who analyze a language are urged to do justice to the language by describing it 'in its own terms' (Boas 1911), rather than by means of categories adopted from some other language (i.e., a priori categories). While it is certainly possible to describe all languages with the categories of medieval Latin school grammar (plus some ad hoc extensions), such descriptions are usually seen as lacking insight and as distorting the true picture of the languages. Of course, to the extent that languages truly are similar, these similarities can and should be reflected in the description (e.g., by choosing similar terms for similar categories), but this is a practical matter that does not constrain the description.

Comparison of languages is, then, based on the data provided by descriptivists, but not on the descriptive categories chosen by the language experts. Rather, a special set of universally applicable comparative concepts is developed that makes it possible to compare languages rigorously even though they have different categories and constructions (Haspelmath 2010a). The comparativist (typologist) need not have studied any language directly herself, as she bases her comparison entirely on the work of others. Thus, language description and language comparison are separate enterprises, often carried out by different groups of people (fieldworkers vs. armchair typologists), and by means of different sets of analytical tools (descriptive categories vs. comparative concepts).

When it comes to the interpretation of the results, nonaprioristic comparativists are open to all kinds of explanations, without an a priori preference for one of them: historical explanations in terms of language contact and geography, inheritance from a common ancestor in the very distant past, cultural influences on grammar, general processing constraints, considerations of efficiency of communication, general trends of diachronic change, cognitive constraints on acquisition, and others (see §5).

2.2 The restrictivist approach to comparative syntax

In the restrictivist approach, linguists also study the structures of non-cognate languages and compare them, but almost everything else is different from the nonaprioristic approach. In particular, they attempt to build a restrictive representational (or 'formal') framework by which all and only the possible languages can be described. Such a representational framework is often called a '(formal) theory',[3] and it is usually equated with what the child knows about language structure before being exposed to any language (the innate 'universal grammar' or 'the initial state of the language faculty'). The restrictivist approach has no interest in anthropological or cultural questions, but tends to situate itself within cognitive science or even biology (e.g., Anderson and Lightfoot 2004).

In the restrictivist approach, comparison of languages is expected to yield invariants which are due to universal grammar. As Baker and McCloskey (2007: 286–287) put it:

> [absolute universals] … must either be built into the design of the theory, or the theory must be developed in such a way that it guarantees their truth.

Comparative syntax is often portrayed as the best way to find out about the initial state of the language faculty. Even though the existence of rich innate structures is usually justified by the argument from the poverty of the stimulus, it is comparative syntax that is said to provide insight into what those innate structures might be (rather than, say, experiments with artificial languages to test the limits of what can be acquired).[4]

Universal grammar is generally thought to consist of universal substantive elements (features and categories) as well as universal formal patterns (architectures), so linguists who adopt this approach normally assume that a newly described language makes use of the same features and categories (and also operations such as movement) as have been used for other languages. They thus approach languages aprioristically, from a categorial universalist perspective (Haspelmath 2010a). This is clearly formulated by the principle in (7).

(7) Uniformity Principle
     In the absence of compelling evidence to the contrary, assume languages to be uniform, with variety restricted to easily detectable properties of utterances. (Chomsky 2001: 2)

Explanation of observed invariants is likewise aprioristic: Only explanation by innate structures is of interest to this approach. However, as clearly stated by Hoekstra and Kooij

(1988), explanation of universals (i.e., 6d) is not a primary goal of the Chomskyan approach. The primary explanandum in this research orientation is the possibility of language acquisition despite the poverty of the stimulus (6e), and the fact that languages exhibit certain regularities as a result of the innate structures is of only secondary interest.[5]

A very important aspect of the restrictivist approach is that language-particular analysis is said to be insightful when it can be shown to make use of features and operations that are assumed to be universal on the basis of other languages (6f). Language description and language comparison are thus not two separate enterprises:

> The in-depth, abstract analysis of a certain phenomenon ... and the study of what variation there is concerning that phenomenon ... are two sides of the same inquiry.
>
> (Cinque 2007: 93)

Thus, restrictivist linguists are engaged in language-particular analysis and cross-linguistic comparison simultaneously. There is just one set of concepts (universal features and categories) that is used both for description (analysis) and comparison. This also means that it is usually the same scholars who engage in analysis and comparison. Unlike in the nonaprioristic approach, restrictivists cannot easily mine the work of others for their comparative research, so the comparison rarely involves a large number of diverse languages (cf. Roberts (1997), where the discussion is mostly limited to Germanic and Romance languages, plus a bit of Celtic, Slavic, Japanese, and Chinese).

3 Identifying the comparanda

Before comparing languages, we need to identify elements that can be compared across languages. Clearly, what can be readily compared is meanings (or at least extralinguistic counterparts of linguistic forms) on the one hand, and sounds/gestures (acoustic/visual and articulatory patterns) on the other hand. How to compare more abstract patterns across languages is much less obvious. Consider again (1b), compared with its English counterpart *Taro shut the door*.

(1) b. Japanese
     Taro   ga   to   o   shime-ta.
     Taro   NOM   door   ACC   shut-PST
     'Taro shut the door.'

On the basis of the meanings of the parts of these two sentences, we can equate *Taro ga* with *Taro* ('Taro'), *to o* with *the door* ('door') and *shimeta* with *shut* ('shut'), and we can thus say that Japanese has 'Taro-door-shut' order, while English has 'Taro-shut-door' order in these particular sentences. But saying that Japanese generally has SOV order while English has SVO order is far more problematic, because it seems to presuppose that we can identify subjects, objects, and verbs (i.e. abstract syntactic categories) in both languages. But on what basis?

In the restrictivist approach, comparative syntacticians do not worry much about this issue and generally take comparability for granted, in the spirit of the Uniformity Principle in (7). Thus, it is generally assumed that Japanese has a subject in the same sense as English – that is, a noun phrase that occurs outside and higher than the verb phrase – as well as an object in the same sense as English – that is, a noun phrase that occurs inside the verb phrase as a sister of the verb.

In the nonaprioristic approach, comparability is a serious methodological concern and is typically discussed in textbooks (Croft 2003: 13–19; Dixon 2010–12: Vol. 1 Ch. 6), handbook articles (Stassen 2011), and in specialized articles (e.g., Lehmann 2005; Rijkhoff 2009; Haspelmath 2010a). The basic principle is, as stated above, that languages can be readily compared only with respect to meanings and sounds/gestures, but not with respect to their categories, because only meanings and sounds, but not categories, are universal. Thus, instead of saying that English has SVO order, while Japanese has SOV order, we must say that English has agent–action–patient order, while Japanese has agent–patient–action order. This is not the normal notation; for reasons of tradition, labels such as 'SVO' are widely used (e.g., by Dryer 2011a), but it has always been clear that this is what is meant ('in identifying such phenomena in languages of different structure, one is basically employing semantic criteria': Greenberg 1963: §1).

But in addition to semantic comparative concepts, comparative concepts can also have both formal and semantic components, in particular formal components referring to basic properties such as overt coding vs. zero, identity of coding vs. difference, or precede vs. follow. Thus, the comparative concepts *ergative* and *accusative* are defined with respect to identity of coding: A pattern is ergative if it treats the patient argument of a physical-effect verb (such as 'break', 'kill') in the same way as the single argument of a change-of-state verb such as 'die' or 'fall', and if both are different from the agent of a physical-effect verb (cf. Haspelmath 2011b).

What is crucial in the nonaprioristic approach is that the comparative concepts are universally applicable in the sense that the same criteria can be applied in all languages. This allows for rigorous objective comparison, with no arbitrary selection of criteria. The choice of comparative concepts is often based on the researchers' intuitions (Lazard 2005), but this is a methodological choice, not an assumption about the nature of language. Since the choice of semantic and formal comparative concepts is up to the individual linguist, one might ask in what sense this approach is nonaprioristic. The answer is that it is the claims about the nature of particular languages that make no a priori assumptions. Comparison is necessarily aprioristic, but it is separate from description/analysis.

In the restrictivist approach, by contrast, it is not necessary to apply the same criteria to identify categories across languages. The reason is that the comparison is done by means of categories which are assumed to be universal, despite the fact that they are manifested in diverse ways. For example, in English one normally identifies a VP by the rules of VP Preposing and VP Ellipsis. But since VP is assumed to be universal, the fact that such rules do not exist in other languages is not a problem. While some researchers may have doubts whether Japanese and Hungarian have a VP (cf. Sells 1991; É. Kiss 2002: 30–43), most generative linguists assume that these languages are like English in having a VP, on the basis of the Uniformity Principle in (7), plus perhaps some other kind of evidence for a combination of verb and object.[6] For the VSO language Welsh, for example, linguists often argue that the verb–object combination in non-finite structures shows the underlying order (e.g., Roberts 2005: 8). So even here, where one might think that evidence against a VP consisting of verb and object is compelling, one can claim that there is a VP if one takes movement operations into account. At least underlyingly, Welsh can be said to have a VP, but the verb is moved to pre-subject position to yield the observable VSO order (see also Baker 2010).

One price that the restrictivists thus have to pay is that they must make extensive a priori assumptions about the nature of universal grammar, and there is a serious danger that these assumptions will be coloured by the properties of familiar languages that happened to serve as the starting point of the investigation.[7] An even more serious problem is that there is quite a bit of subjectiveness in the choice of evidence that is taken as decisive for particular analyses (cf. Croft 2009). The nonaprioristic approach, by contrast, gets by with minimal assumptions about language, and the subjectiveness is limited to the methodological level (the selection of the comparative concepts).

4 Some syntactic universals

In (8), I list a few proposed (morpho)syntactic universals for illustration. These have different properties and different roles in the two research orientations, as will be discussed below.

(8) a. All languages have roots denoting things, roots denoting actions, and roots denoting properties (such as dimension, age, or value).

    b. All languages have morphemes denoting negation.

    c. No language has a rule that involves counting elements or features.

    d. If a language has dominant VSO order, then it has dominant adposition-noun order (Greenberg 1963, Universal 3).

    e. If a language has noun-possessor order, it tends to have preposition-NP order, and if it has possessor-noun order, it tends to have NP-postposition order (Dryer 2005; 2011b).

    f. If a language has OV order, then it tends to have no question-word fronting (Bach's generalization, Bach 1971; Roberts 2007: §1.5.1).[8]

    g. In almost all cases, the ergative case is overtly marked while the absolutive case is not overtly marked (Dixon 1979).[9]

    h. If a language with basic SV order has non-overt independent subject pronouns, it allows postverbal position of the overt subject (pro-drop parameter, Rizzi 1986, Holmberg 2010a).[10]

    i. Inflectional morphology occurs outside derivational morphology (Greenberg 1963, Universal 28).

    j. If a language allows question-word fronting from an adverbial clause, it also allows fronting from a complement clause.

    k. If a marker in a language expresses locative and dative roles, then it also expresses the allative role (Blansitt 1988).

    l. If the reflexive pronoun is distinct for the anaphoric pronoun for disjoint reference, it is longer than the anaphoric pronoun (often derived from it by an additional marker), or equally long (e.g., English *him-self* vs. *him-Ø*) (Haspelmath 2008c).[11]

    m. Lexicalist Hypothesis: The syntax neither manipulates nor has access to the internal structure of words (Anderson 1992: 84).

    n. Principle A of the Binding Theory: An anaphor must be bound in its governing category (Chomsky 1981).

On the one hand, syntactic universals can be divided into absolute universals and universal tendencies or preferences (also called 'statistical universals'). For example, while no exceptions to the general statements in (8a–c) are known, the statements in (8d–i) are generally true only as tendencies, and some of these statements are formulated in weaker terms ('almost all', 'tends to'). It may seem odd to call them 'universals' if they are not true of all languages, but the claim is that they represent general properties of human language, even if they are not manifested everywhere. What matters is that they represent skewed distributions – that is, deviations from the null hypothesis of random distribution. Dryer (1997), working in the nonaprioristic approach, argues that statistical universals are more valuable for comparative syntax than absolute universals, because if we do not limit ourselves to absolute universals we can characterize the nature of language much more precisely. There are simply far more generalizations that do not hold everywhere than absolute universals of the type (8a–c). Moreover, statistical tendencies can be tested by statistical methods on the basis of a world-wide sample, whereas absolute universals cannot be tested in this way (we can never examine all languages; see Bickel forthcoming).

Comparative syntacticians have again and again experienced the discovery of exceptions to seemingly exceptionless universals. For example, Universal 8d (if VSO, then prepositions) was thought to be exceptionless by Greenberg, but Dryer (2011a; 2011b) has documented six exceptions to this trend. This does not mean that there is no strong trend, because seventy-six VSO languages, the overwhelming majority, do have prepositions. But the trend should probably not make reference to VSO languages, because it is equally strong in SVO languages (303 SVO languages with prepositions, 33 SVO languages with postpositions). The fact that Universal 8d was exceptionless for Greenberg had to do with the relatively small size of his sample. And we need to keep in mind that all our samples are relatively small, when compared with the number of all languages ever spoken (according to Bickel's estimate (forthcoming), at least half a million languages have existed so far on earth). This means that only strong statistical trends can be demonstrated, whereas absolute universals can only be hypothesized. Thus, it is not clear that universals which are so far exceptionless (8a–c, perhaps also 8j–l) should have a special status.

In the restrictivist approach, only exceptionless (i.e., absolute) universals are relevant (Baker and McCloskey 2007: 287), because universal grammar is seen as an absolute limit on what kinds of languages can be acquired. Restrictivists thus have to dismiss universal trends as irrelevant to their enterprise, or alternatively explain away the exceptions by invoking specific interfering factors. This rigid limitation to absolute universals can hardly be justified by the appeal to innateness per se, but since the work in the restrictivist approach is not primarily comparative, but comparative and descriptive at the same time (§2.2), only the absolute interpretation of universal grammar has played a role. In most work on concrete grammatical problems, linguists have appealed to universal grammar to provide an elegant account of particular languages (6f): Language-particular analyses are said to be insightful insofar as they make ample use of universal grammar, keeping language-particular stipulation to a minimum. In this research context, universal preferences are useless – if a generalization amounts to no more than a tendency, speakers still have to learn that their language follows the tendency. But the goal of restrictivist work has been to minimize what is learned. In the nonaprioristic approach, by contrast, description and comparison are two distinct enterprises: Descriptivists are happy to stipulate large numbers of facts that are general across languages (because minimizing the task of acquisition is not seen as important), and comparativists try to find cross-linguistic generalizations with various degrees of strength.

Another subdivision of universals is into unrestricted universals (8a–c, g, i, m–n) and implicational universals (8d–h, j–l). Implicational universals are far more numerous than unrestricted universals, and they are more interesting because they tell us something about relationships between properties. Thus, in practice most cross-linguistic research on universals has centred on implicational universals.

The nonaprioristic approach is interested only in universals that are formulated in terms of universally applicable comparative concepts and can thus be tested. Universals such as (8m) (the Lexicalist Hypothesis) and (8n) (Principle A of the Binding Theory) are not of interest, because the terms that they make use of ('syntax', 'word', 'anaphor', 'governing category') are not defined in such a way that they can be identified objectively across languages. In the restrictivist approach, they have been very widely discussed because they seem to allow elegant accounts for particular phenomena in particular (prominent) languages. But how such universal claims can be tested is quite unclear. In practice, most linguists have applied these principles across languages on the basis of uniformity assumptions – for example, they simply assumed that elements that are written between spaces are words (for 8m), and that expressions in other languages which are similar to English *himself* are anaphors (and are thus relevant for Principle A, 8n).

5 Explanation of universals in the nonaprioristic approach

As mentioned earlier, nonapriorists appeal to a variety of explanatory factors to account for universals of morphosyntax, without excluding or preferring any factor a priori.

Cognitive constraints on learnability are not prominent in cross-linguistic work of this sort, but of course not any kind of language is learnable, so it is clear that the cognitive makeup of humans and its genetic basis play a role in understanding universals. For example, that grammatical patterns apparently never involve counting elements or features (e.g., 'delete the fourth syllable', 'place the clitic after the third last constituent'; Universal 8c) may well be due to the 'cognitive code' (i.e., constraints on internalizing mental grammars). However, just as most of the explanation of biological phenotypes appeals not to the genetic code (i.e., constraints on forming genotypes) but to evolution and adaptation, most of the explanation of linguistic phenotypes (i.e., languages) comes from diachrony and efficiency of processing and communication (see Haspelmath (2004) for this analogy between biology and linguistics). The remainder of this section gives just a few examples of plausible explanations (see also Moravcsik (2011) for a recent survey, as well as Hawkins (1988)).

5.1. Diachrony

Some important regularities seem to be due to macro-trends of diachronic change, in particular grammaticalization:

(9) Grammaticalization: Roots with concrete meanings develop into supporting elements with more abstract, grammatical meanings (e.g. Lehmann 1995; Narrog and Heine 2011)

This macro-trend is not very well understood (cf. Haspelmath (1999b); Roberts and Roussou (2003) for very divergent accounts), but it explains why preposition-NP order is generally found in languages with noun-possessor order and with verb-object order (universals 8d–e): Adpositions generally arise by grammaticalization from relational nouns with a possessor, or from verbs combined with an object (e.g. Bybee 1988; Aristar 1991). Even though we may not understand well why adpositions hardly ever develop in other ways, we can take this macro-trend as an explanation of the word-order correlation. The same explanation holds for the correlation between verb-object order and auxiliary-verb order (Dryer 1992: 100–101), but it does not extend readily to the link between verb-object and noun-possessor order (see §5.2 below).

Another grammatical regularity with a plausible diachronic explanation is the fact that grammatical meanings are usually expressed by affixes or function words and only rarely by stem changes (e.g., plurals such as *book-s*, which are cross-linguistically far more frequent than plurals such as *foot/feet*). Bybee and Newman (1995) have found that stem changes are just as easy to learn as affixes, so they propose that stem changes are rarely found in languages not because of learnability constraints but because new affixes arise all the time via grammaticalization. There is thus a rich, inexhaustible source of new affixes, whereas productive stem changes do not arise and spread as easily in diachronic change.

Quite a few generalizations of coexpression ('semantic-map universals', cf. Haspelmath 2003), such as universal (8k) above, are due to general tendencies of semantic change, such as the tendency for abstract meanings to develop from concrete meanings (e.g., Heine *et al.* 1991). Thus, the fact that allative markers which are coexpressed with patient markers are also coexpressed with dative markers has to do with the general tendency that allative markers tend to be extended to mark recipients and recipient markers tend to be extended to mark patients. Allative markers cannot extend to mark patients directly (see Cristofaro (2010) for the general argument that semantic-map universals are due to diachronic tendencies).

5.2. Ease of processing

In language production, it is clear that speakers prefer word orders that make it easier for hearers to recognize constituents quickly. Thus, relative clause extraposition is often used in English when the relative clause is long and when the modified NP is not the last constituent in the clause:

(10) *She put* [*the book*]$_{NP}$ *on the shelf* [*that she borrowed from the university library lastweek*]$_{NP}$.

If the relative clause is not extraposed here, the hearer has to wait for a long time before all constituents are recognized – that is, the constituent recognition domain is very long. According to Hawkins (1990; 2004), the same preference for short constituent recognition domains also accounts for quite a few word order regularities across languages. In particular, heads tend to be adjacent because this leads to shorter constituent recognition domains. Compare the four hypothetical language types in (11a–d).

(11) a. VO & N-Possessor: *found* [*house* [*of* our new teacher]]
      b. VO & Possessor-N: *found* [[*of our new teacher*] *house*]
      c. OV & N-Possessor: [*house* [*of our new teacher*]] *found*
      d. OV & Possessor-N: [[of our new *teacher*] *house*] *found*

In these examples, the words in the constituent recognition domain are printed in italics. We see that in (11a) and (11d), where the heads are adjacent, the constituent recognition domain is just three words long, whereas it is six words long in (11b–c). Thus, the languages of type (11a and d) are easier to parse, and Hawkins proposes that this explains why they are found much more widely across the world's languages than languages with nonharmonic orders. According to Hawkins (1999; 2004: Ch. 7), similar considerations of processing efficiency explain universals such as (8j) about extractions (filler-gap dependencies).

5.3. Communicative efficiency

The simplest way in which syntactic patterns can be user-friendly is by being only as long as needed. Efficient communication systems are expected to have more robust signals for information that cannot be predicted, whereas information that is predictable is coded by short, inexpensive signals. The syntactic patterns of languages are full of examples of this general regularity. For example, in many languages highly predictable (topical) referents can simply be omitted, and in most other languages they are expressed by anaphoric pronouns, which are much shorter than full noun phrases. Another example is ellipsis, which is often restricted to information that is highly predictable from the context.

But the link between predictability and shortness of coding can be more subtle and less obvious. In particular, coding asymmetries are often correlated with predictability differences due to frequency (cf. Haspelmath 2008a). Thus, the fact that the ergative case is usually overtly marked (universal 8g), in contrast to the absolutive case, and likewise the accusative case is generally overtly marked, in contrast to the nominative, is due to their frequency: Absolutive and nominative are necessarily more frequent, as they occur in both intransitive and transitive clauses (see Greenberg (1966: 37–38) for the original observation). Similarly, anaphoric pronouns with disjoint reference show a strong tendency to be shorter than anaphoric pronouns with coreference (reflexive pronouns, 'anaphors') (universal 8l). There are quite a few further form asymmetries that correlate with frequency asymmetries (this is called 'typological markedness' by Croft (2003: Ch. 4)), such as those in (12).

(12) singular/plural, present/future, 3rd person/2nd person, active/passive, affirmative/negative, declarative/interrogative, masculine/feminine, attributive adjective/predicative adjective (including copula), positive/comparative, predicative verb/nominalized verb, action word/agent noun

Thus, communicative efficiency explains a host of regularities that linguists often discuss in terms of semantic or purely structural generalizations. But once the factor of language use and the possibility of diachronic adaptation (Haspelmath 1999a; Givón 2010) is taken into account, many universal patterns cease to be mysterious.

Communicative efficiency is often discussed under the labels of 'economy' and 'iconicity', and the resulting patterns have occasionally also been modeled within Optimality Theory (see, most notably, Aissen (2003)). Optimality Theory makes use of functional notions but constructs a restrictive framework by turning these notions into constraints, which are technical elements of the framework. It is thus an interesting intermediate approach between the nonaprioristic approach and the restrictivist approach, to which we now turn.

6 Explanation of universals in the restrictivist approach

Even though the explanation of observed cross-linguistic generalizations has not been the primary research goal for generative linguistics as a whole, over the last few decades many comparative linguists have adopted the restrictivist perspective and have attempted to derive cross-linguistic invariants from a restricted formal representational framework. As noted above, the formal framework is not just the metalanguage that is used by linguists to analyze particular languages, but is assumed to be identical to the tools that language learners have available for formulating an internal grammar. The basic idea is thus that, out of the large set of logically possible languages, only a small subset is actually attested because only these language types are acquirable. At the same time, the formal framework is said to allow insightful analysis of particular languages, where 'insightful' often means that it is shown that the language falls within a restricted range of permitted variation. Linguists often say that the observed variation 'falls out' from the proposed formal framework.

Let us consider two examples of this sort of explanation. First, consider Anderson's (1992) explanation of Universal (8i) (derivation occurs outside derivation). Anderson assumes that grammatical generalizations are distributed over two separate components, the Syntax and the Lexicon. Derivational morphology is part of the Lexicon and inflectional morphology is part of the Syntax. While the Lexicon feeds the Syntax, the Syntax cannot be the input to the Lexicon. These restrictive assumptions about innate structures (expressed by the representational framework) explain the observation that languages generally do not show derivational affixes outside inflectional affixes.

Second, Kayne (1994: 54) explains something similar to Universal (8f) (the lack of question-word fronting in OV languages) on the basis of his influential antisymmetry proposal, which (in effect) says that heads always precede complements in underlying structure – that is, that verb-object and initial-complementizer orders are always basic. Other orders, such as object-verb order and final-complementizer order, must be derived from these orders by movement, but movement has to be to the left (on the basis of another widely made uniformity assumption). Thus, a subordinate clause with final complementizer such as (13) from Japanese must be derived from a basic order with initial complementizer (much like English) by a movement rule that moves the clause to the pre-complementizer position.

(13) [*Yooko-wa Masa-o aisite iru*]$_S$ [[*to*]$_{COMP}$ [*t*]$_S$]
     Yoko-TOP Masa-ACC loving is   COMP
     'that Yoko loves Masa'

But the pre-complementizer position ('specifier of complementizer') is usually assumed to be the position to which question-words are fronted. If this position is filled by the clause itself, not only in subordinate clauses with an overt complementizer but in all clauses, then question-word fronting is blocked because no landing site is available for a moving question-word. Thus, the restrictive framework, which only allows head-initial order, manages to explain a gap in attested logically possible language types.[12]

But restrictivists have been even more ambitious. Since the early 1980s, they have often argued that the formal framework should be much more general than is suggested by the language-particular rules and constructions that fill the pages of descriptive grammars. Instead, observable grammatical patterns should be derived from the interaction of a restricted number of highly general principles and a restricted number of parametric choices. This approach thus came to be known as 'Principles and Parameters' (e.g., Chomsky and Lasnik 1993; Fukui 1995). The idea was that a single abstract parameter could be responsible for a whole range of observable properties, and the hope was that the problem of language acquisition would be solved by restricting the child's task to that of setting such parameters on the basis of limited evidence. So suppose that there is an innate principle such as (14a) with an associated parameter such as (14b):

(14) a. phrases consist of lexical heads and phrasal complements
     b. the head may (a) precede or (b) follow the complement

This parameter ('the head-directionality parameter', Chomsky and Lasnik 1993: 518; Roberts 2007: 92–108) captures the association between verb-object and adposition-complement order (cf. universal 8d), as well as some of the other Greenbergian word-order correlations. At the same time, it simplifies the child's task of language acquisition: Observing a single head-complement order will allow the child to set this parameter – that is, the child can correctly produce novel combinations that she has never heard before. Reducing observed variation between languages to highly general parameters would thus 'show that the apparent richness and diversity of linguistic phenomena is illusory and epiphenomenal, the result of interaction of fixed principles under slightly varying conditions' (Chomsky 1995: 8). We could say that the children's acquisition task is manageable because they 'are not acquiring dozens or hundreds of rules; they are just setting a few mental switches' (Pinker 1994: 112). The most accessible and engaging account of this vision of a small set of abstract parameters ('macroparameters') that predict a clustering of observed properties is provided by Baker (2001), and the best recent introduction for readers who are also interested in some technical details is Roberts (2007). The latter is not by accident a work on diachronic syntax: The parametric approach has been particularly influential in diachronic work on typological change, where linguists have sometimes argued that certain changes happened simultaneously with other changes because both are manifestations of a single macroparametric change (cf. 6g).

However, even though the parametric approach was very prominent in generative syntax throughout the 1980s and 1990s, it has not been an unequivocal success. The head-directionality parameter has not been defended widely because it is very clear that it is only a statistical tendency. Much more research has gone into the null-subject parameter, which asserts that if null-subjects are possible, then free subject inversion and subject extraction to a higher clause are also possible (universal 8h, Rizzi 1986; Roberts 2007: 24–40). The reason for the extraordinary attention to this particular phenomenon was that this was easy to investigate for Western linguists: the claim is that French and English have one setting of the parameter, while Spanish and Italian have the other setting. However, even though some linguists still regard it as a valid parameter (Holmberg 2010a), most seem to have concluded that this parameter has failed (Haider 1994; Newmeyer 1998: 357–359; Croft 2003: 80–83). As in quite a few other cases, a clustering of properties that seemed to hold in a few languages has dissolved once more and more languages were taken into account.

More generally, since the late 1990s, parameters have become less and less prominent in generative syntax. Some linguists have emphasized the importance of microparameters over macroparameters (Black and Motapanyane 1996; Kayne 2000), but this is not much more than different terminology for abandoning the search for clustering of properties in the world's languages. A number of influential linguists have been more explicit: Pica (2001: v–vi) found that 'twenty years of intensive descriptive and thoretical research has shown … that such meta-parameters do not exist', Newmeyer (2004; 2005) has argued against the parametric approach, and Boeckx (2014) actually declares the parametric approach incompatible with the biolinguistic program (see also Haspelmath (2008b), where it is argued that the search for macro-types has been unsuccessful not only within generative linguistics but also among nonapriorists, who had succumbed to the same temptation earlier). Some generative syntacticians are still pursuing the parametric program (Cinque 2007; Baker 2010; Biberauer et al. 2010), but even Baker (2008) admits that the expectations have not been fulfilled, and the approach has clearly lost some of its earlier attractiveness. And, perhaps tellingly, Holmberg's (2010b) recent defense of the parametric program limits itself to the discussion of two language types within the Scandinavian languages, which can hardly provide evidence for universally relevant innate parameters.

The main difficulty faced by the parametric approach is that it is committed to explaining language invariants and the acquisition of particular systems at the same time. This means that exceptions cannot be tolerated. It is not possible, for example, to retreat to the position that the head-directionality parameter explains the general tendency for head-complement orders to correlate across categories, because it is claimed that macroparameters help the child to acquire the language. But the child does not know whether her language is well-behaved or belongs to the minority of nonconforming languages, and there is no evidence that children produce incorrect typologically normal orders (Newmeyer 2005: 100). In the case of head directionality, the acquisitional advantage does not seem to be particularly important, because there is ample evidence for the correct order. But where children have little evidence for the right patterns, linguists too tend to have a hard time finding the cross-linguistic evidence. So it is difficult to produce a convincing example of a link between restrictions on cross-linguistic patterns and the poverty of the stimulus in acquisition.

7 Concluding remarks

After some promising starts in the early part of the twentieth century (Schmidt 1926), comparative syntax began to flourish with the Greenbergian program in the 1960s and 1970s (Greenberg 1963; 1978; Comrie 1981; Croft 1990), and in the generative tradition, it began to flourish with the principles-and-parameters program (Chomsky 1981; Baker 1988; Haegeman 1997a; Cinque 1999).

However, over the last decade, as more and more research has shown the enormous difficulties faced by both research programs, it seems that a more sober attitude has come to prevail. The easy generalizations that were formulated on the basis of a few languages often look less neat when further evidence is adduced. But, on the whole, where generalizations have been based on a world-wide sample from the start (as in the work of Schmidt (1926) and Greenberg (1963)), and where they have been formulated as statistical claims, they have stood the test of time better than where they have been based on just two or a few (related or contiguous) languages and have been claimed to be absolute universals. So, as statistical generalizations, we still have quite a few very interesting invariants (e.g., those in 8a–g, i–k above) that seem to reflect something deeper about human language.

Still, the general trend in recent years has been towards the particularist pole of the universalist–particularist spectrum (see Bossong (1992) for an interesting historical account of the pendulum-like movement between both poles in the history of Western linguistics). The documentation of endangered languages has acquired enormous prestige, and fieldworkers tend to emphasize the individual character of 'their' language over the general properties of human cognition and culture. Historical explanations in terms of language contact have become prominent as a result of research on linguistic areas (Muysken 2008) and as a result of the increasing availability of maps that show the geographical distribution of linguistic features (Haspelmath *et al.* 2005; Michaelis *et al.* 2013). Bickel (2007: 239) notes that typology has recently been moving away from the question of what is a possible language to questions about the historical and geographical factors that influence cross-linguistic distributions. And Evans and Levinson (2009) have gone so far as to say that language universals are a 'myth'.

The challenge is thus to find a way of accounting for very widespread properties of languages such as the universals in (8a–g, i–k), while at the same time allowing for unforeseen differences between languages in the kinds of features and categories that they exhibit, as well as the kinds of meanings that they express (Wierzbicka 1998; Levinson and Meira 2003; Davis *et al.* 2014). It seems to me that the answer has to lie in a separation of language-particular analysis and cross-linguistic generalization (Haspelmath 2010a; 2010b). If speakers are relatively free to generalize in different directions and to internalize grammars with the most diverse categories and features, we can account for the diversity that we observe throughout the world. And if we compare languages on the basis of universally applicable comparative concepts which are not identical to the categories used by individual languages, we can formulate testable statistical universals and propose general explanations for them that are at least in part rooted in cognition (but also in communication). Our explanations may not be as uniform and as all-encompassing as has often been thought, but a universalist perspective on human languages is not incompatible with a particularist attention to the details of individual languages.

Notes

1 The term *syntactic typology* is perhaps used more widely than *comparative syntax* (cf. Lehmann 1978; Croft 1995), but 'typology' is a curious nineteenth-century term (going back to a time when comparative syntacticians wanted to find idealized macro-types of languages) that has no analogy in other fields. Comparative syntax is completely parallel to comparative psychology or comparative zoology, so we need no idiosyncratic term for it.

2 Note that there are some linguists who see themselves in the generative tradition, but do not adopt a restrictivist approach (in particular in sign-based construction grammar, Boas and Sag (2012); but these do not work much on comparative syntax).

3 See Haspelmath (2010b) for problems with the term 'theory', which is used in confusingly different ways. I generally try to avoid the term. (Likewise, I try to avoid the term 'formal', which has no clear definition in current linguistics.)

4 Haegeman (1997b:1) writes: 'The comparative approach in the generative tradition addresses the following questions: (i) what is knowledge of language? (ii) how is this knowledge acquired? ... In order to answer these questions we have to identify which linguistic properties can vary across languages and which are constant.'

5 Not accidentally, the issue of acquisition despite the poverty of the stimulus was called 'Plato's Problem' in Chomsky (1986), a label that indicates the depth of the problem. 'Greenberg's problem', as (6d) could be called, has not been remotely as prominent in the philosophical literature of the Chomskyan tradition.

6 Over the last two decades, the question whether a language has a VP has not often been even asked in mainstream generative syntax, probably because it has been widely assumed that all phrasal patterns are binary, and ternary branching (NP – V – NP) is impossible (this is another application of the Uniformity Principle).

7 Three examples: (i) since European languages are written with spaces between words, linguists often assume that all languages distinguish between words and phrases (Haspelmath 2011a); (ii) linguists often assume that all languages have nouns, verbs, and adjectives (Haspelmath 2012); (iii) since English, German, and French have obligatory subject pronouns, linguists often assume that languages where subject pronouns may be absent actually have null subject pronouns (cf. Kibrik 2011: 76–77; Haspelmath 2013).

8 Cf. Turkish in (5a).

9 Cf. Lezgian in (2b).

10 Cf. Italian in (3a).

11 Cf. also Yoruba in ex. (4a).

12 Actually, Kayne explains not Universal (8f), but another, related universal, namely the association between question-word fronting and complementizer order. It is actually quite doubtful whether such an association exists. In Dryer's (2012) sample, 61 out of 169 complementizer-initial languages, but only 4 out of 27 complementizer-final languages have question-word fronting. So question-word fronting seems to be more frequent in complementizer-initial languages, but there are not very many complementizer-final languages to begin with.

Further reading

Baker, Mark. 2001. *The atoms of language*. New York: Basic Books.
Roberts, Ian G. 2007. *Diachronic syntax*. Oxford: Oxford University Press.

Croft, William. 2003. *Typology and universals*, 2nd edn. Cambridge: Cambridge University Press.
Comrie, Bernard. 1981. *Language universals and linguistic typology: Syntax and morphology*. Oxford: Blackwell (2nd edn 1989).
Dixon, R.M.W. 2010–12. *Basic linguistic theory* (3 vols). Oxford: Oxford University Press.
Shopen, Timothy (ed.). 2007. *Language typology and syntactic description*, 3 vols. Cambridge: Cambridge University Press.

References

Aissen, Judith L. 2003. Differential object marking: Iconicity vs. economy. *Natural Language and Linguistic Theory* 21(3):435–483.
Alexiadou, Artemis (ed.). 2002. *Theoretical approaches to universals*. Amsterdam: Benjamins.
Anderson, Stephen R. 1992. *A-morphous morphology*. Cambridge: Cambridge University Press.
Anderson, Stephen R., and David W. Lightfoot. 2004. *The language organ: Linguistics as cognitive physiology*. Cambridge: Cambridge University Press.
Aristar, Anthony R. 1991. On diachronic sources and synchronic pattern: An investigation into the origin of linguistic universals. *Language*:1–33.
Bach, Emmon. 1971. Questions. *Linguistic Inquiry* 2:153–166.
Baker, Mark C. 1988. *Incorporation: A theory of grammatical function changing*. Chicago, IL: University of Chicago Press.
Baker, Mark. 2001. *The atoms of language*. New York: Basic Books.
Baker, Mark. 2008. The macroparameter in a microparametric world. In *The limits of syntactic variation*, ed. Theresa Biberauer, 351–373. Amsterdam: Benjamins.
Baker, Mark. 2010. Formal generative typology. In *The Oxford handbook of linguistic analysis*, ed. Bernd Heine and Heiko Narrog, 285–312. Oxford: Oxford University Press.
Baker, Mark C., and Jim McCloskey. 2007. On the relationship of typology to theoretical syntax. *Linguistic Typology* 11(1):285–296.
Biberauer, Theresa, Anders Holmberg, Ian G. Roberts, and Michelle Sheehan (eds). 2010. *Parametric variation: Null subjects in minimalist theory*. Cambridge: Cambridge University Press.
Bickel, Balthasar. 2007. Typology in the 21st century: Major current developments. *Linguistic Typology* 11(1):239–251.
Bickel, Balthasar. forthcoming. Linguistic diversity and universals. In *Cambridge handbook of linguistic anthropology*, ed. Nick J. Enfield, Paul Kockelman, and Jack Sidnell. Cambridge: Cambridge University Press.
Black, James R., and Virginia Motapanyane. 1996. *Microparametric syntax and dialect variation*. Amsterdam: Benjamins.
Blansitt, Edward L., Jr. 1988. Datives and allatives. In *Studies in syntactic typology*, ed. Michael Hammond, Edith A. Moravcsik, and Jessica R. Wirth, 173–191. Typological Studies in Language, 17. Amsterdam: Benjamins.
Boas, Franz. 1911. Introduction. In *Handbook of American Indian languages*, ed. Franz Boas, 1–83. Washington, DC: Bureau of American Ethnology.
Boas, Hans Christian, and Ivan A. Sag (eds). 2012. *Sign-based construction grammar*. Stanford, CA: CSLI Publications.
Boeckx, Cedric. 2014. What principles and parameters got wrong. In *Linguistic variation in the minimalist framework*, ed. Carme Picallo. Oxford: Oxford University Press.
Bossong, Georg. 1992. Reflections on the history of the study of universals: The example of the partes orationis. In *Meaning and grammar: Cross-linguistic perspectives*, ed. Michel Kefer and Johan van der Auwera, 3–16. Berlin: Mouton de Gruyter.
Bybee, Joan L. 1988. The diachronic dimension in explanation. In *Explaining language universals*, ed. John A. Hawkins, 350–379. Oxford: Blackwell.
Bybee, Joan L., and Jean E. Newman. 1995. Are stem changes as natural as affixes? *Linguistics* 33(4):633–654.
Chomsky, Noam A. 1981. *Lectures on government and binding*. Dordrecht: Foris.
Chomsky, Noam A. 1986. *Knowledge of language: Its nature, origin, and use*. New York: Praeger.
Chomsky, Noam A. 1995. *The minimalist program*. Cambridge, MA: MIT Press.
Chomsky, Noam A. 2001. Derivation by phase. In *Ken Hale: A life in language*, ed. Michael Kenstowicz, 1–52. Cambridge, MA: MIT Press.

Chomsky, Noam, and Howard Lasnik. 1993. The theory of principles and parameters. In *Syntax*, vol. 1, ed. Joachim Jacobs, Arnim von Stechow, Wolfgang Sternefeld, and Theo Vennemann, 506–569. Berlin: Walter de Gruyter.

Cinque, Guglielmo. 1999. *Adverbs and functional heads: A cross-linguistic approach*. New York: Oxford University Press.

Cinque, Guglielmo. 2007. A note on linguistic theory and typology. *Linguistic Typology* 11(1): 93–106.

Comrie, Bernard. 1981. *Language universals and linguistic typology: Syntax and morphology*. Oxford: Blackwell (2nd edn 1989).

Cristofaro, Sonia. 2010. Semantic maps and mental representation. *Linguistic Discovery* 8(1):35–52.

Croft, William. 1990. *Typology and universals*. Cambridge: Cambridge University Press.

Croft, William. 1995. Modern syntactic typology. In *Approaches to language typology*, ed. Masayoshi Shibatani and Theodora Bynon, 85–144. Oxford: Oxford University Press.

Croft, William. 2003. *Typology and universals*, 2nd edn. Cambridge: Cambridge University Press.

Croft, William. 2009. Methods for finding language universals in syntax. In *Universals of language today*, ed. Sergio Scalise, Elisabetta Magni, and Antonietta Bisetto, 145–164. Berlin: Springer.

Davis, Henry & Gillon, Carrie & Matthewson, Lisa. 2014. How to investigate linguistic diversity: Lessons from the Pacific Northwest. *Language* 90: 000–000.

Dixon, R.M.W. 1979. Ergativity. *Language* 55:59–138.

Dixon, R.M.W. 2010–12. *Basic linguistic theory* (3 vols). Oxford: Oxford University Press.

Dryer, Matthew S. 1992. The Greenbergian word order correlations. *Language* 68(1):81–138.

Dryer, Matthew S. 1997. Why statistical universals are better than absolute universals. *Chicago Linguistic Society* 33:123–145.

Dryer, Matthew S. 2005. Order of genitive and noun. In Haspelmath et al. (eds), 350–353.

Dryer, Matthew S. 2011a. Order of subject, object and verb. In *The world atlas of language structures online*, ed. Matthew S. Dryer and Martin Haspelmath. Munich: Max Planck Digital Library, chapter 81. Available online at http://wals.info/chapter/81 (accessed 31 January 2014).

Dryer, Matthew S. 2011b. Order of adposition and noun phrase. In *The world atlas of language structures online*, ed. Matthew S. Dryer and Martin Haspelmath. Munich: Max Planck Digital Library, chapter 85. Available online at http://wals.info/chapter/85 (accessed 31 January 2014).

Dryer, Matthew S. 2012. On the position of interrogative phrases and the order of complementizer and clause. In *Theories of everything: In honor of Edward Keenan*, ed. Thomas Graf, Denis Paperno, Anna Szabolcsi, and Jos Tellings, 72–79. UCLA Working Papers in Linguistics 17. Los Angeles, CA: UCLA.

É. Kiss, Katalin. 2002. *The syntax of Hungarian*. Cambridge: Cambridge University Press.

Evans, Nicholas, and Stephen C. Levinson. 2009. The myth of language universals: Language diversity and its importance for cognitive science. *Behavioral and Brain Sciences* 32(05):429–448.

Fukui, Naoki. 1995. The principles-and-parameters approach: A comparative syntax of English and Japanese. In *Approaches to language typology*, ed. Masayoshi Shibatani and Theodora Bynon, 327–372. Oxford: Clarendon Press.

Givón, T. 2010. The adaptive approach to grammar. In *The Oxford handbook of linguistic analysis*, ed. Bernd Heine and Heiko Narrog, 27–49. Oxford: Oxford University Press.

Greenberg, Joseph H. 1963. Some universals of grammar with particular reference to the order of meaningful elements. In *Universals of language*, ed. Joseph H. Greenberg, 73–113. Cambridge, MA: MIT Press.

Greenberg, Joseph H. 1966. *Language universals: With special reference to feature hierarchies*. The Hague: Mouton.

Greenberg, Joseph H. (ed.). 1978. *Universals of human language*. 4 vols. Stanford, CA: Stanford University Press.

Haegeman, Liliane M.V. (ed.). 1997a. *The new comparative syntax*. London: Longman.

Haegeman, Liliane. 1997b. Introduction: On the interaction of theory and description in syntax. In *The new comparative syntax*, ed. Haegeman, Liliane, 1–32. London: Longman.

Haider, Hubert. 1994. (Un-)heimliche Subjekte — Anmerkungen zur pro-drop Causa, im Anschluß an die Lektüre von Osvaldo Jaeggli and Kenneth J. Safir, eds, *The null subject parameter*. *Linguistische Berichte* 153:372–385.

Hamel, Patricia J. 1994. *A grammar and lexicon of Loniu, Papua New Guinea*. Pacific Linguistics, Series C-103. Canberra: Australian National University.

Harris, Alice C., and Lyle Campbell. 1995. *Historical syntax in cross-linguistic perspective.* Cambridge: Cambridge University Press.

Haspelmath, Martin. 1993. *A grammar of Lezgian.* Berlin: Mouton de Gruyter.

Haspelmath, Martin. 1999a. Optimality and diachronic adaptation. *Zeitschrift für Sprachwissenschaft* 18(2):180–205.

Haspelmath, Martin. 1999b. Why is grammaticalization irreversible? *Linguistics* 37(6):1043–1068.

Haspelmath, Martin. 2003. The geometry of grammatical meaning: Semantic maps and crosslinguistic comparison. In *The new psychology of language*, vol. 2, ed. Michael Tomasello, 211–243. New York: Lawrence Erlbaum.

Haspelmath, Martin. 2004. Does linguistic explanation presuppose linguistic description? *Studies in Language* 28:554–579.

Haspelmath, Martin. 2008a. Frequency vs. iconicity in explaining grammatical asymmetries. *Cognitive Linguistics* 19(1):1–33.

Haspelmath, Martin. 2008b. Parametric versus functional explanations of syntactic universals. In *The limits of syntactic variation*, ed. Theresa Biberauer, 75–107. Amsterdam: Benjamins.

Haspelmath, Martin. 2008c. A frequentist explanation of some universals of reflexive marking. *Linguistic Discovery* 6(1):40–63.

Haspelmath, Martin. 2010a. Comparative concepts and descriptive categories in cross-linguistic studies. *Language* 86(3):663–687.

Haspelmath, Martin. 2010b. Framework-free grammatical theory. In *The Oxford handbook of linguistic analysis*, ed. Bernd Heine and Heiko Narrog, 341–365. Oxford: Oxford University Press.

Haspelmath, Martin. 2011a. The indeterminacy of word segmentation and the nature of morphology and syntax. *Folia Linguistica* 45(2):31–80.

Haspelmath, Martin. 2011b. On S, A, P, T, and R as comparative concepts for alignment typology. *Linguistic Typology* 15(3):535–567.

Haspelmath, Martin. 2012. How to compare major word-classes across the world's languages. In *Theories of everything: In honor of Edward Keenan*, ed. Thomas Graf, Denis Paperno, Anna Szabolcsi and Jos Tellings, 109–130. UCLA Working Papers in Linguistics 17. Los Angeles, CA: UCLA.

Haspelmath, Martin. 2013. Argument indexing: A conceptual framework for the syntax of bound person forms. In *Languages across boundaries: Studies in memory of Anna Siewierska*, ed. Dik Bakker and Martin Haspelmath, 197–226. Berlin: De Gruyter Mouton.

Haspelmath, Martin, Matthew S. Dryer, David Gil, and Bernard Comrie (eds). 2005. *The world atlas of language structures.* Oxford: Oxford University Press.

Hawkins, John A. (ed.). 1988. *Explaining language universals.* Oxford: Blackwell.

Hawkins, John A. 1990. A parsing theory of word order universals. *Linguistic Inquiry* 21(2):223–261.

Hawkins, John A. 1999. Processing complexity and filler-gap dependencies across grammars. *Language* 75:244–285.

Hawkins, John A. 2004. *Efficiency and complexity in grammars.* Oxford: Oxford University Press.

Heine, Bernd, Ulrike Claudi, and Friederike Hünnemeyer. 1991. *Grammaticalization: A conceptual framework.* Chicago, IL: University of Chicago Press.

Hoekstra, Teun, and Jan G. Kooij. 1988. The innateness hypothesis. In *Explaining language universals*, ed. Hawkins, John A., 31–55. Oxford: Blackwell.

Holmberg, Anders. 2010a. Null subject parameters. In *Parametric variation: Null subjects in minimalist theory*, ed. Theresa Biberauer, Ian G. Roberts, Anders Holmberg, and Michelle Sheehan, 88–124. Cambridge: Cambridge University Press.

Holmberg, Anders. 2010b. Parameters in minimalist theory: The case of Scandinavian. *Theoretical Linguistics* 36(1):1–48.

Kayne, Richard S. 1994. *The antisymmetry of syntax.* Cambridge, MA: MIT Press.

Kayne, Richard. 1996. Microparametric syntax: Some introductory remarks. In *Microparametric syntax and dialect variation*, ed. James R. Black and Virginia Montapanyane, ix–xvii Amsterdam: John Benjamins. (Reprinted in Kayne 2000: 3–9).

Kayne, Richard S. 2000. *Parameters and universals.* New York: Oxford University Press.

Kibrik, Andrej A. 2011. *Reference in discourse.* Oxford: Oxford University Press.

König, Ekkehard, and Volker Gast. 2007. *Understanding English-German contrasts.* Berlin: Erich Schmidt Verlag.

Lazard, Gilbert. 2005. What are we typologists doing? In *Linguistic diversity and language theories*, ed. Zygmunt Frajzyngier, Adam Hodges, and David S. Rood, 1–23. Amsterdam: Benjamins.

Lehmann, Christian. 1995. *Thoughts on grammaticalization*. Munich: Lincom Europa.

Lehmann, Christian. 2005. Zum Tertium comparationis im typologischen Sprachvergleich. In *Beitrage zum romanisch-deutschen und innerromanischen Sprachvergleich. Akten der gleichnamigen internationalen Arbeitstagung (Leipzig, 4.10.-6.10.2003)*, vol. 1, ed. Christian Schmitt and Barbara Wotjak, 157–168. Bonn: Romanistischer Verlag.

Lehmann, Winfred P. (ed.). 1978. *Syntactic typology: Studies in the phenomenology of language*. Austin, TX: University of Texas Press.

Levinson, Stephen C., and Sergio Meira. 2003. 'Natural concepts' in the spatial topological domain—adpositional meanings in crosslinguistic perspective: an exercise in semantic typology. *Language* 79(3):485–516.

Michaelis, Susanne Maria, Philippe Maurer, Martin Haspelmath, and Magnus Huber (eds). 2013. *The atlas of Pidgin and Creole language structures*. Oxford: Oxford University Press.

Moravcsik, Edith A. 2011. Explaining language universals. In *The Oxford handbook of language typology*, ed. Jae Jung Song, 69–89. Oxford: Oxford University Press.

Muysken, Pieter (ed.). 2008. *From linguistic areas to areal linguistics*. Amsterdam: Benjamins.

Narrog, Heiko, and Bernd Heine (eds). 2011. *The Oxford handbook of grammaticalization*. Oxford: Oxford University Press.

Newmeyer, Frederick J. 1998. *Language form and language function*. Cambridge, MA: MIT Press.

Newmeyer, Frederick J. 2004. Against a parameter-setting approach to language variation. *Linguistic Variation Yearbook* 4:181–234.

Newmeyer, Frederick J. 2005. *Possible and probable languages: A generative perspective on linguistic typology*. Oxford: Oxford University Press.

Pica, Pierre. 2001. Introduction. *Linguistic Variation Yearbook* 1:v–xii.

Pinker, Steven. 1994. *The language instinct*. New York: W. Morrow and Co.

Rijkhoff, Jan. 2009. On the (un) suitability of semantic categories. *Linguistic Typology* 13(1):95–104.

Rizzi, Luigi. 1986. Null objects in Italian and the theory of pro. *Linguistic Inquiry* 17(3):501–557.

Roberts, Ian G. 1997. *Comparative syntax*. London: Arnold.

Roberts, Ian G. 2005. *Principles and parameters in a VSO language: A case study in Welsh*. Oxford: Oxford University Press.

Roberts, Ian G. 2007. *Diachronic syntax*. Oxford: Oxford University Press.

Roberts, Ian G., and Anna Roussou. 2003. *Syntactic change: A minimalist approach to grammaticalization*. Cambridge: Cambridge University Press.

Schmidt, Wilhelm. 1926. *Die Sprachfamilien und Sprachenkreise der Erde*. Heidelberg: Winter.

Sells, Peter. 1991. VP in Japanese: evidence from *-te* complements. In *Japanese/Korean Linguistics*, ed. Hajime Hoji, 319–334. Stanford, CA: CSLI.

Shopen, Timothy (ed.). 2007. *Language typology and syntactic description*, 3 vols. Cambridge: Cambridge University Press.

Spencer, Andrew, and R. Otoguro. 2005. Limits to case – a critical survey of the notion. In *Competition and variation in natural languages: The case for case*, ed. Mengistu Amberber and Helen de Hoop, 119–145. Dordrecht: Elsevier Publishers.

Stassen, Leon. 2011. The problem of cross-linguistic identification. In *The Oxford handbook of language typology*, ed. Jae Jung Song, 90–99. Oxford: Oxford University Press.

Weber, David John. 1989. *A grammar of Huallaga (Huánaco) Quechua*. Berkeley, CA: University of California Press.

Wierzbicka, Anna. 1998. Anchoring linguistic typology in universal semantic primes. *Linguistic Typology* 2(2):141–194.

25

Principles and Parameters/Minimalism

Terje Lohndal and Juan Uriagereka

1 Introduction[1]

The Minimalist Program (MP) grew out of the theory of Government and Binding (GB), the first instantiation of a theory of Principles and Parameters (P&P) as developed in Chomsky (1981). So both GB and MP are part of the P&P approach to the study of the Faculty of Language (Freidin and Vergnaud 2001; Hornstein *et al.* 2005; Lasnik and Uriagereka 2005; Boeckx and Uriagereka 2006; Freidin 2012; Lasnik and Lohndal 2013). Rather than conceptualizing them as different frameworks, we view the MP as an attempt to rationalize the principles of GB.

In what follows we focus on the distinction between minimalism conceived as applying principles of science and as making a substantial claim about the architecture of the Faculty of Language. The chapter organizes this general thesis as follows. In Section 2 we provide some background for the MP, describing how it evolved. Section 3 is the substantial part of the chapter, where we discuss the consequences of the different views one may have of the MP. In Section 4 we discuss some prospects and challenges for minimalism, relating them to the notion of a program. Section 5 concludes the chapter.

2 Background

The first explicitly minimalist paper, Chomsky (1993), was concerned with unifying a certain set of data and theories that had become prominent in the 1980s. What we may think of as "early minimalism" took what was known from GB for granted and attempted to unify/eliminate relevant conditions. A good example of this approach is the suggestion that Case checking happens in functional agreement projections.[2] Consider the data in (1).

(1) a. John likes **him**.
     b. **She** chased the cat.
     c. Mary proved [$_{IP}$ **him** wrong].

In (1a) we have an object that gets accusative Case, in (1b) a subject that gets nominative Case, and in (1c) an exceptionally Case-marked subject that gets accusative Case (all relevant items in bold). Within GB, the phrasal configurations for these three Cases are different, although attempts were made to make government account for all of them (see Uriagereka (1988; 2012) for discussion). Accusative Case is assigned to the complement of the verb, nominative Case to the specifier of TP, and exceptionally Case marked subjects in SpecIP of the embedded sentence somehow get their Case from the main verb.[3] Chomsky (1993) reanalyzes these cases and argues that all Case checking happens in specifier–head relationships. This is made possible by invoking abstract agreement projections for objects: Chomsky argues that Case checking happens in the agreement projection for objects in both (1a) and (1c). Of course, it is not obvious that **him** in either instance occupies a specifier position in overt syntax. However, the possibility emerges that the checking takes place in the covert component of LF, where the specifier–head relationship instantiates Case checking.[4]

This example illustrates the overall logic: (i) The basic tenets of the GB theory are assumed to be correct: that lexical items get Case, what the Case-bearing heads are, the positions in which lexical items that get Case occupy; (ii) However, the lack of unification in the domains in which lexical items get Case is suspect; therefore (iii) The new theory rationalizes what a Case checking domain is by suggesting the specifier-head relation, independently needed for subject–verb agreement, as the locus for all checking operations – even if abstract moves are thereby invoked (e.g., Case checking happens at LF).[5] In this way the MP attempts to rationalize GB and provide a more principled theory by eliminating overlapping conditions (Freidin and Vergnaud 2001: 642).

Chomsky also argues in the same paper that it is desirable to and possible to dispense with two grammar-internal components assumed within GB:

(2)

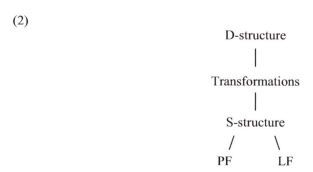

This is the "T," or "inverted Y", model: The grammar takes lexical items from the lexicon and constructs a D-structure, the locus for theta roles and the Theta Criterion. Transformations map this structure into an S-structure representation (as is patent in the case of a passive or a *wh*-structure). This is the point at which the structure is simultaneously transferred to the sound and the meaning interfaces. Clearly S-structure, and arguably D-structure, are grammar-internal representations. Chomsky then explores whether they can be dispensed with, while maintaining empirical coverage:

> Each derivation determines a linguistic expression, an SD, which contains a pair (π, λ) meeting the interface conditions. Ideally, that would be the end of the story: each linguistic expression is an optimal realization of interface conditions expressed in

elementary terms (chain link, local X-bar-theoretic relations), a pair (π, λ) satisfying these conditions and generated in the most economical way. Any additional structure or assumptions require empirical justification.

(Chomsky 1993/1995: 186–187)

Chomsky notes that the Projection Principle and the Theta Criterion (see Chomsky 1981) argue for D-structure only if their empirical properties must be captured at that level of representation. Work on the configurational properties of theta roles (Hale and Keyser 1993; 2002) and the treatment of theta roles as features (Hornstein 1999) challenges this view (though see Uriagereka 2008). Chomsky (1993: 21) furthermore recalls the problem posed by complex adjectival ("*tough*") constructions such as (3a). These are assumed to have the S-structure representation in (3b), where *t* represents the trace of an empty operator *Op*.

(3)   a. John is easy to please.
      b. John is easy [$_{CP}$ Op [$_{IP}$ PRO to please *t*]]
      c. it is easy [$_{CP}$ [$_{IP}$ PRO to please John]]

(3c) shows that the matrix subject is not a theta-position; therefore, *John* in (3b) has no theta-role at D-structure. Chomsky (1981) liberalizes lexical insertion so as to allow *John* to be inserted in the course of the derivation, thereby being assigned a theta-role at LF. However, as Howard Lasnik observed, this technical solution does not work: a subject of arbitrary complexity may be inserted in place of *John*:

(4)   [That Mary is easy to please] is easy to discover.

Literally inserting an entirely formed sentence (which contains the very structure we are analyzing) is of course senseless. Instead, the system is then driven to a version of "generalized transformations" in the sense of Chomsky (1955). That, however, indicates that there is no D-structure *level of representation* that (4) could start from, given all that we have said so far.[6]

Typical arguments for S-structure involve differences between languages. Some move *wh*-items overtly, others covertly (Huang 1982; Lasnik and Uriagereka 1988). A language may move V to T overtly or covertly (Pollock 1989). The question is whether S-structure is required to account for such differences. Chomsky (1993) argues that it is not, and that languages differ in terms of which features they make use of and whether those features require overt or covert movement for their appropriate checking (see Hornstein *et al.* (2005) for perspective).[7]

The elimination of D- and S-structure paved the way for a perspective on parametric variation that dates back to Borer (1984):

> [P]arametric differences must be reduced to morphological properties if the Minimalist Program is framed in the terms so far assumed. There are strong reasons to suspect that LF conditions are not relevant. We expect languages to be very similar at the LF level, differing only as a reflex of properties detectable at PF; the reasons basically reduce to conditions of learnability. Thus, we expect that at the LF level there will be no relevant difference between languages with phrases overtly raised or in situ (e.g., *wh*-phrases or verbs). Hence, we are led to seek morphological properties that are reflected at PF.

(Chomsky 1993/1995: 192)

We will briefly return to features, which essentially trigger and drive derivations, in §4 (see Adger 2010; Adger and Svenonius 2011; Boeckx 2010).

An important difference between GB and the MP stems from the focus on *interfaces* and the role they play in a theory. Freidin and Vergnaud (2001: 640–641) see three assumptions that are unique to the MP: (1) the interface levels LF and PF are the only relevant linguistic levels, (2) all conditions are interface conditions, and (3) a linguistic expression is the *optimal* realization of these conditions.[8] Together these assumptions constitute the Strong Minimalist Thesis (Chomsky 2000), which is a conjecture about the organization of the Faculty of Language. The thesis, as such, could of course be right or wrong – but it serves as a working hypothesis to guide theorizing.

That said, in our view there is no paradigm change here: The focus on interfaces is a natural continuation of the approach initiated by Chomsky and Lasnik (1977) with the idea of representational *filters*. Lasnik and Saito's (1984; 1992) very broad *Affect Alpha* transformation takes this idea to its extreme: There are no constraints on whether a category alpha can be affected; only output constraints or filters that apply after the representation has been generated. In our view, directly or indirectly current work tries to rationalize the filters (witness Case conditions) in order to understand why the interfaces are structured the way they are (for some work on this see Uriagereka (2008); Lohndal (2012); Samuels (2012)).

Needless to say, in order to understand the interfaces it is pertinent to seek conditions outside of the internal properties of the linguistic system, which poses a difficult question: How do language-internal properties interact with the rest of the mind? Boeckx and Uriagereka (2006: 542) take such concerns to "have become all the more relevant within the MP, especially because this system explores the rational conjecture that some fundamental properties of the language faculty are the way they are precisely *because of* the system's interaction with the rest of the mind". They mention language acquisition (e.g., Crain and Thornton 1998), language change (e.g., Lightfoot 1999), and language use (e.g., Berwick and Weinberg 1984) as examples of cases where linguists have looked at the relevant interactions between the internal system and external properties.

Now, there is a further difference between GB and the MP that runs deeper than the focus on interfaces. We consider this matter in the next section.

3 What is Minimalism?

There are various ways to characterize the MP. So far we have discussed how the program largely focuses on *eliminating* theoretical primitives that GB postulated, while hopefully maintaining the same empirical coverage. Following Martin and Uriagereka (2000), we can call this approach *methodological minimalism*:

> What one might call a "weak minimalist thesis" is nothing new. The drive for simple and nonredundant theories of the world (or Occam's razor) is taken for granted in the core sciences. Even within the more specialized science of linguistics, this working methodology has brought undeniable success. From such a perspective, minimalism is just a new way to refer to what many people have been doing for a long time: seeking the best way to theorize about a particular domain of inquiry. We think of this thesis as *methodological minimalism*.
>
> (Martin and Uriagereka 2000: 1)

We can contrast the methodological view with what the same authors call *ontological minimalism*. This is another name for the Strong Minimalist Thesis, discussed above. Chomsky (2000: 92) states things as follows:

> Suppose that a super-engineer were given design specifications for language: "Here are the conditions that FL must satisfy; your task is to design a device that satisfies these conditions in some optimal manner (the solution might not be unique)." The question is, how close does language come to such optimal design?

From this perspective, the question is not how good our theory of the Faculty of Language is but, rather, how good the Faculty itself is (see Chomsky 2000: 141, n. 12). Put differently, we are asking whether the faculty of language is optimally designed. Related to this question is why the computational system of human language is organized the way it is. *Why* do certain principles hold and not others? (Chomsky 2000: 92; 2004).

It is important to be aware of the immediate problems related to asking such *why*-questions. Chomsky is rather clear on this, as the following quote illustrates:

> Questions of this kind are not often studied and might not be appropriate at the current level of understanding, which is, after all, still quite thin in a young and rapidly changing approach to the study of a central component of the human brain, perhaps the most complex object in the world, and not well understood beyond its most elementary properties.
>
> (Chomsky 2000: 93)

The difficulty in providing substantial answers in this domain is not empirical. Rather, it is a question of design: Why is one design preferred to a number of other ones that anyone could easily imagine? Even though such a question is central to Minimalism, it is not totally novel (see Freidin and Lasnik (2011) for some roots of Minimalism). Berwick and Weinberg put it like this:

> ... if the "language faculty" is even roughly analogous to other organs of the body (like the heart), then we might reasonably expect, just as in the case of other systems of the body, that it has been "well designed" according to some as yet undetermined criteria of efficiency. This scenario clearly takes for granted the usual backdrop of natural selection. Since one of the evolutionary "design criteria" could well have been ease of language processing, it is certainly conceivable that efficient parsability has played a role in the shaping of the language faculty.
>
> (Berwick and Weinberg 1982: 167)

Aside from explicitly raising design questions, this quote foreshadows concerns about the evolution of language. Berwick and Weinberg mention natural selection, though today we know that there are other ways in which good design can arise in nature (see Kaufmann (1993) and Gould (2002), among many others).

Because the questions raised by ontological minimalism are extremely challenging, most minimalists have focused on the methodological aspects of Minimalism, though in actual practice it is hard to differentiate between methodological minimalism and ontological minimalism, since the latter by necessity contains elements of the former. Let us briefly consider the development from X-bar theory to Bare Phrase Structure as an example.

3.1   From X-bar theory to Bare Phrase Structure

Chomsky (1986a, henceforth *Barriers*) provides a generalization of X-bar structure (Chomsky 1970; Jackendoff 1977), though systematic attempts had already been made by Chomsky (1981), Stowell (1981), den Besten (1983), and Thiersch (1985), to mention some important works.[9] Prior to *Barriers*, the maximal projections were taken to be VP, NP, AP, and PP. In addition, there was S (rewritten as NP Infl VP) and Se (rewritten as Comp S). Comp includes at least C and *wh*-expressions. The immediate problem is that S does not conform to X-bar theory: It is not endocentric since it has no head, which means that there is no projection from a head to a maximal projection. S′ is also not uniformly endocentric since when Comp is filled by complex phrasal material, it cannot be the *head* of S′, by definition (a head is not a complex phrase). Because of these problems, Stowell (1981: Ch 6) suggests that the head of S is Infl, as illustrated in (5). This is very similar to the proposal made by Williams (1981: 251), which suggests that S is headed by Tense, and also by Pesetsky (1982), which presents similar considerations:

(5)

```
          IP
         / \
      ...   I'
           / \
          I   VP
```

Once IP replaces S, a natural step is to reconsider S′. Stowell (1981: Ch 6) proposes that C is the head of S′. The optional specifier then becomes the target of *wh*-movement (see Thiersch (1985) for a detailed elaboration). We then have the structure in (6) (see also Chomsky (1986a)).

(6)

```
          CP
         / \
      ...   C'
           / \
          C   IP
```

With this in place, it is possible to formulate restrictions on movement based on what can appear in a head position and what can appear in a specifier position (see Travis (1984) and Rizzi (1990), among many others).

The reanalysis of S and S′ paves the way for a generalization of X-bar theory. Chomsky (1986a:3) proposes that X-bar is a structure, as in (7), where X* stands for zero or more occurrences of some maximal projection and $X = X^0$.[10]

(7)   a. $X' = X \ X''*$
       b. $X'' = X''* \ X'$

(7) does not force binarity (a node may have more than two daughters). One can either restrict X-bar theory so that it does observe binarity – assuming that it is empirically correct – by

"hard-wiring" that condition into the X-bar theory, or else follow proposals such as those in Kayne (1984; 1994) to the effect that independent grammatical constraints require all relations of immediate dominance to be binary. (See also Fukui and Speas (1986); Fukui (2006); Speas (1990) for very relevant discussion.)

For reasons that we cannot go into now, Kayne's theory forces the elimination of the distinction between X′ and XP. Chomsky (1995a; 1995b) goes further, arguing that X-bar levels should be eliminated altogether. This is an essential feature of the theory of Bare Phrase Structure (BPS). The gist of this theory is summarized as follows: "Minimal and maximal projections must be determined from the structure in which they appear without any specific marking; as proposed by Muysken (1982) they are relational properties of categories, not inherent to them" (Chomsky 1995a:61).[11] Chomsky (1995b:242) ties the ban on marking such properties and maximal and minimal projections to the Inclusiveness Condition:[12]

(8) *Inclusiveness Condition*
     Any structure formed by the computation is constituted of elements already present in the lexical items. No new objects are added in the course of computation apart from rearrangements of lexical properties.

                                                        (Chomsky 1995b: 228)

Another way to look at BPS is to say that phrase structure consists solely of lexical items. This effectively means that, instead of being represented as in (9), phrases would more accurately be represented as in (10) (setting aside how verbs get their inflection and where the arguments ultimately belong in the structure):

(9)
```
                    VP
                   /  \
                 DP    V′
                 |    / \
               John  V   DP
                     |   |
                   chews gum
```

(10)
```
                  chews
                  /  \
               John   chews
                      / \
                  chews  gum
```

These lexical items are accessed at the LF interface, and no units apart from the lexical items can be part of the computation. Thus bar-levels, as such, have no ontological status within BPS. For a critical discussion of BPS see Starke (2004), Jayaseelan (2008), and Lohndal (2012).

The change from X-bar theory to BPS showcases several aspects of minimalism. It shows the methodological part, since BPS makes use of fewer theoretical primitives than

X-bar theory. It also shows the ontological part, since BPS makes a different claim about the phrase structure component: There are only lexical items and these, together with constraints on Merge, generate hierarchical phrase structures. We also see how the methodological aspect, by pushing it to some appropriate limit, actually leads to the ontological aspect: (10) involves less information than (9), and the information that it does involve is linguistically more relevant.

Let us now move on to discuss the emphasis on economy conditions that has become a characteristic of minimalism.

3.2 Minimalism and economy

Lappin *et al.* (2000) claim that economy conditions are new to the MP. However, Freidin and Vergnaud (2001) and Freidin and Lasnik (2011) show that this is not the case. Chomsky has been explicit regarding this as well:

> In early work, economy considerations entered as part of the evaluation metric, which, it was assumed, selected a particular instantiation of the permitted format for rule systems, given PLD. … it seems that economy principles of the kind explored in early work play a significant role in accounting for properties of language. With a proper formulation of such principles, it may be possible to move toward the minimalist design: a theory of language that takes a linguistic expression to be nothing other than a formal object that satisfies the interface conditions in the optimal way. A still further step would be to show that the basic principles of language are formulated in terms of notions drawn from the domain of (virtual) conceptual necessity.
>
> (Chomsky 1993/1995: 171)

Freidin and Vergnaud (2001: 642) offer the Case Filter as one example, and we will use their discussion as an illustration.

In its original formulation, the Case Filter prohibits a phonetically realized nominal expression that has not been marked for abstract Case in the syntax. The Filter is a stipulation added in order to account for the facts. Within the MP there is no Case Filter as such. Rather, a more general principle is assumed: Full Interpretation, originally suggested in Chomsky (1986b). Full Interpretation can be seen as an economy condition: derivations that adhere to it are taken to be better than derivations that do not. The principle requires that all features in a derivation be legible at the relevant interfaces. Thus the principle bans superfluous symbols in general, ruling out vacuous quantification and features that have no values at the interfaces. Case is an instance of the latter, since an uninterpretable Case feature will cause a crash at the LF interface. The underlying assumption is that all features need an interpretable value in order to be legible at the interfaces. While Full Interpretation can be argued to subsume the Case Filter, the converse is not the case.[13]

Freidin and Vergnaud argue that the same logic extends to another example, involving a standard case of an Empty Category Principle (ECP) violation,[14] as in (11), where *t* is the trace of *John* and T is the category Tense.

(11) *John T is believed [that *t* T is happy]

Within GB the ungrammaticality of this example was taken to follow from the fact that the trace *t* was not properly licensed (see note 13). Freidin and Vergnaud (2001: 642–643) propose to subsume the ungrammaticality of (11) under Full Interpretation. They assume that the nominative Case feature of *John* is checked in the embedded clause by T_2, as is the nominative Case feature of T_2. When *John* moves to the subject position of the matrix clause, the nominative Case feature of *John* has already been checked. This means that the nominative Case feature on T_1 cannot be checked. An unchecked feature causes the derivation to crash. Thus Full Interpretation accounts for data that previously were accounted for using the Case Filter and the ECP. This is a good example of the eliminativist angle of minimalism at work: Two apparently unrelated conditions are reduced to a single one at a different level of abstraction.

Freidin and Vergnaud (2001: 643) welcome the use of Full Interpretation instead of the Case Filter and the ECP:

> … this analysis, which explains deviance on the basis of legibility conditions imposed by cognitive systems that interface with C_{HL} [the computational system of human languages], strikes us as a more promising explanatory account than the postulation of various constraints internal to C_{HL} that basically reflect the complexity of the phenomena in an essentially descriptive fashion.

As an interface condition, Full Interpretation demands that all elements introduced in a derivation be legible at the interfaces. This has an interface filtering effect: derivations that do not fulfill this requirement do not converge. Surely Full Interpretation is more fundamental than the more ad-hoc Case Filter or ECP.

The discussion above has provided a concrete example of how minimalism focuses on interface conditions. The current hypothesis is actually that there are multiple points at which the derivation transfers to the interfaces (Uriagereka 1999, building on Bresnan 1971; Chomsky 2000; 2001). These transfer points are usually called "phases", and there has been much work regarding their structure and nature. See Gallego (2012) for a comprehensive discussion that considerations of space prevent us from undertaking.

Another example of economy comes from what Rizzi (1990) calls Relativized Minimality.[15] Rizzi proposes a unified account of the following cases:

(12) a. *[$_\alpha$ Fix] John [$_\beta$ can] t(α) the car
b. *[$_\alpha$ John] seems [$_\beta$ it] is certain t(α) to be here.
c. *[$_\alpha$ how] did John wonder [$_{CP}$ [$_\beta$ what] Mary fixed t(β) t(α)]

In (12a) the Head Movement Constraint is violated, (12b) is an instance of superraising, and in (12c) the *wh*-island constraint is violated. Contrary to the traditional picture we just outlined, Rizzi argues that the same violation obtains in these cases. He proposes Relativized Minimality, given in (13).

(13) *Relativized Minimality*
α cannot cross (= move to a position c-commanding) β if β c-commands α, and β is the same type as α.

The relevant types are characterized as follows (Rizzi 1990).

(14) a. *Head positions*
If α adjoins to a head, β is a head.

b. *A-positions*
If α adjoins to an A-position, β is an A-specifier.

c. *A-bar positions*
If α adjoins to an A-bar specifier, β is an A-bar specifier.

The account is that in (12a), the head α moves across another head β, in (12b) α crosses the embedded A-specifier β, and in (12c) α crosses the embedded A-bar specifier β.

Rizzi's Relativized Minimality is a representational principle – it applies to the entire representation that has been generated in the transformational component. Chomsky and Lasnik (1993), in contrast, interpret the principle in terms of "least effort", an economy consideration. We can illustrate by considering the following data.

(15) a.   Guess who bought what?
      b.   *Guess what who bought?

This is a 'superiority effect', which Chomsky and Lasnik analyze in terms of Relativized Minimality. There might seem to exist two derivational options in (12), as one ought to be able to front either *who* or *what*. As the contrast shows, however, that is not the case, and only *who* can be fronted. Studying the relevant paradigms, the generalization appears to be that one always has to involve the question word that is "closest to the position where it ends up moving", as first observed by Chomsky (1973). Another way to put this is that the distance "traveled" by the moving element has to be minimized. This account can be generalized to the cases in (12) as well. The minimalist approach is to take this as an instance of economy in the derivation and not as a condition on representations. (See also Richards (2001) for interesting extensions.)

More generally, conditions arising with respect to movement operations have been captured in terms of Relativized Minimality (see Starke (2001) for a comprehensive discussion), when combined with considerations about phases (Uriagereka 1998; Chomsky 2001, 2008; Müller 2011). Space considerations prevent us from discussing this here.

For more discussion of economy, see, for example, Collins (1997), Kitahara (1997), Reinhart (2006), and Lasnik and Lohndal (2013).

3.3   The programmatic nature of minimalism

Since Chomsky (1993), Chomsky and other scholars have consistently insisted that minimalism is a program, not a theory. The following quote makes this clear:

> [t]here are minimalist questions, but no minimalist answers, apart from those found in pursuing the program: perhaps that it makes no sense, or that it makes sense but is premature.
>
> (Chomsky 2000: 92)

One answer to a question is not a priori more or less minimalist than another answer. Minimalism as such does not provide the means to decide on a specific theory. Rather, it is a framework within which one can pursue a multitude of perspectives. Thus many practitioners call it a program. The most comprehensive attempt at justifying the programmatic nature of minimalism can be found in Boeckx (2006), which we now rely on.

Programs are by nature abstract. Boeckx uses Hilbert's Program as an illustration. David Hilbert proposed this program in the early 1920s as a call for a formalization of all of mathematics in axiomatic form, together with a proof that this axiomatization of mathematics is consistent (Boeckx 2006: 86). He understood programs as a set of guidelines and proposed boundary conditions that could be used to determine whether the program was successful. Although Kurt Gödel proved that Hilbert's program cannot be carried out to completion, it has had an important influence not just on mathematics but also in logic, computer science, and beyond.

As Boeckx points out, physicists rarely use programs. However, he quotes Feyerabend to illustrate that the notion can be applied to physics (Boeckx 2006: 86):

> There may not exist a single theory, one 'quantum theory', that is used in the same way by all physicists. The difference between Bohr, Dirac, Feynman and von Neumann suggests that this is more than a distant possibility ...
>
> (Feyerabend 1993: 191)

Lakatos (1970) narrows programs down to *research* programs, identifying properties that characterize these: programs have a core, are slow to mature, and their rigor may not be stellar at first – but they present an openness and flexibility that may lead to theoretical insight. For the MP, the core is arguably the optimal connection with interfaces: All research within the MP is to create a theory of syntax that mediates sound and meaning.[16] Beyond this core, there is a lot of variation, which Boeckx (2006: 94–95) contextualizes:

> As Lakatos stressed, programs are more than a core. They consist of auxiliary hypotheses that may vary from one researcher to the next, and they have a heuristic, a plan for addressing problems ... Different auxiliary hypotheses, or different arrangement of the elements of a program's core, may lead to radically different questions, empirical problems, solutions, etc.

In the programmatic perspective, the object of study has to be approached with an open mind and different ways of answering a question may need to be entertained – or there will be unanswered questions. Freidin and Vergnaud (2001: 647) provide the following quote from Chomsky (1980: 9–10) regarding the consequences of implementing what is typically called the Galilean style:

> [it entails a] readiness to tolerate unexplained phenomena or even as yet unexplained counterevidence to theoretical constructions that have achieved a certain degree of explanatory depth in some limited domain, much as Galileo did not abandon his enterprise because he was unable to give a coherent explanation for the fact that objects do not fly off the earth's surface.

Evidently, the challenge for a research program is to determine whether it is 'progressive' or 'degenerative', to use Lakatos's terms: Whether it produces results that move the program forward (e.g., unexpected predictions), or whether assumptions are just made in order to accommodate the facts. Although we have our own opinions, we will not take a position on that matter here with regards to MP, since it is too early to make predictions.

4 Prospects and challenges

Empirical progress within MP is evident to us in various areas, such as the theory of ellipsis (see, e.g., Merchant 2001; Lasnik 2001). The framework is also able to analyze scores of different languages, continuing in the tradition of its predecessor. Most work adopts a rich number of features, since features are seen as the "driving force" of a derivation; see Adger (2010) and Adger and Svenonius (2011) for comprehensive discussion, and Boeckx (2010) for some problems. These features and their flexibility make it generally possible to achieve cross-linguistic coverage. Together with categorical assumptions made in the cartographic approach (Rizzi 1997; Cinque 1999, and many others), features have made it possible to achieve a great deal of descriptive adequacy. However, questions remain about their explanatory adequacy, both in terms of how a child acquires the relevant subsets of projections and features, and more generally in terms of the nature of the features themselves and how they relate to one another.

Some scholars have argued that it is time to produce theories that can be evaluated and falsified (see, e.g., Hornstein 2009). Soon after the MP was initiated, Lasnik (1999: 6) stated that "there is not yet anything close to a Minimalist theory of language". Differences in the underlying philosophy of science will in part determine whether a scholar regards programs as sufficient or whether theories are required for genuine progress. The basic question here is related to whether an approach has to be falsified. Lakatos (1968; 1970) argues that it should not be easy to refute a program; rather, one sticks to the core assumptions and tries to develop it in various ways.

In many ways this is exactly what has happened within the MP. It has generated new work on the interfaces and their relationship to syntax, a sign that the program is still progressive (see, e.g., Hauser *et al.* (2002) and the various reactions it provoked, or the array of authors in Di Sciullo *et al.* (2010); Piattelli-Palmarini *et al.* (2009); or Di Sciullo and Boeckx (2011), most of whom would term their approach as both "minimalist" and "interdisciplinary"). However, that does not mean that practitioners can avoid addressing fundamental questions such as why the system has the features it does, or why the interfaces are structured the way they are. Issues along these lines, surrounding features and connections between the narrow and broad perspectives of the Faculty of Language (in the sense in Hauser *et al.* (2002)), will likely be at the forefront of much forthcoming research.

5 Conclusions

This chapter has surveyed some core issues within the Principles and Parameters approach to the study of language. We have focused on the transition from GB to the MP, and have tried to explain the rationale behind the change. We have argued that the MP is an attempt to rationalize GB and to move beyond explanatory adequacy. We then discussed the nature of minimalism and presented two approaches: methodological and ontological minimalism. We also used the change from X-bar theory to Bare Phrase Structure to illustrate these conceptions. Then we discussed why Minimalism is a program and what that label entails, focusing on Lakatos's work. Lastly, we discussed a few challenges for minimalism and suggested that whether Minimalism should be seen as a program or a theory by and large depends on one's view of the philosophy of science.

Notes

1 We are grateful to the editors for feedback on this chapter.
2 The capital 'c' denotes abstract case, following Vergnaud (1977) and Chomsky (1981).

3 There is a substantial difference between Case *assignment* and Case *checking*, which we set aside here. See Lasnik (2008: 24) for discussion and a historical overview of Case considerations.

4 The other logical possibility, pursued by Lasnik and Saito (1991) and Koizumi (1995), based on Postal (1974), is that the object in each instance is in fact displaced to a specifier position – but the verb has displaced to an even higher position.

5 The other presupposition is that conditions obtaining overtly in one language may obtain covertly in others. At the time a variety of studies analyzed object agreement in such languages as Basque, Hindi, or Navajo, and the observation was generalized to languages without overt object agreement.

6 Curiously, it is not clear how to analyze "tough"-movement in minimalist terms, given the strange nature of the null operator. See Hicks (2009) for a review and a recent analysis.

7 Chomsky (1995b: 197) asserts: "the Minimalist Program permits only one solution to the problem: PF conditions reflecting morphological properties must force V-raising in French but not in English".

8 Optimal realization is another way of saying that the syntax is perfectly organized for the purposes of satisfying the requirements that the interfaces set. Freidin and Vergnaud (2001: 649) provide a useful clarification of the notion of 'perfection':

> … the notion of 'perfection' often invoked within the MP is *ultimately* a mathematical notion, calling for a higher level of mathematical formalization of syntax [footnote left out]. The Minimalist conjecture that C_{HL} [the computational system of human language] is a 'perfect system' is a tentative claim about the form and the complexity of each computation. The claim is (i) that each computation can be represented as an abstract mathematical structure completely defined by interface (output) conditions and (ii) that this structure is an extremum in some mathematical space.

9 We will not be concerned here with the historical development of phrase structure. For a comprehensive review, see Freidin (2007; 2012), Lasnik and Lohndal (2013).

10 This is what Chomsky said, but it cannot be exactly what he meant. (7a) should read $X' = X\ Y''*$ because otherwise a verb, for example, could only take a VP complement, and similarly for (7b) and specifiers.

11 Muysken's (1982) proposal is "that bar level is not a primitive of the grammar at all, rather 'maximal projection' and 'minimal projection' are defined terms, and intermediate projections are simply the elsewhere case" (Muysken 1982). This proposal is closely related to Speas (1990: 35).

12 This condition could be seen as one extension of an idea in Katz and Postal (1964: 44–45), developed in Chomsky (1965: 132), where transformations are taken not to introduce meaning-bearing elements.

13 This discussion also presupposes that the Case Filter is an interface condition, see Chomsky (1995b: 197), and of course poses the question of what Case features ultimately are or why they are part of the computation (see Pesetsky and Torrego 2001; Uriagereka 2002: Ch 8; 2009).

14 The ECP presents conditions under which traces (of movement) are allowed to exist within given configurations, relating to whether such configurations are directly associated to lexical verbs or similar elements, or whether their antecedent is in some definable sense local to the trace.

15 The following summary is based on Kitahara (1997), to which we refer the reader for a more comprehensive discussion.

16 Boeckx himself argues in (2006) that the core of minimalism consists of a focus on (i) economy, (ii) virtual conceptual necessity, and (iii) symmetry.

Further reading

Boeckx, Cedric (ed.). 2011. *The Oxford Handbook of Linguistic Minimalism*. Oxford: Oxford University Press.

Overview chapters on minimalism written by its leading practitioners.

Bošković, Željko, and Howard Lasnik (eds). 2007. *Minimalist Syntax: The Essential Readings*. Malden: Blackwell.

A collection of important papers on minimalism.

Freidin, Robert, and Jean-Roger Vergnaud. 2001. Exquisite connections: Some remarks on the evolution of linguistic theory. *Lingua* 111:639–666.

An important paper discussing the development of modern generative grammar.

Hornstein, Norbert, Jairo Nunes, and Kleanthes K. Grohmann. 2005. *Understanding Minimalism*. Cambridge: Cambridge University Press.

An introduction to the Minimalist Program based on a comparison with Government and Binding.

Ramchand, Gillian, and Charles Reiss (eds). 2007. *The Oxford Handbook of Linguistic Interfaces*. Oxford: Oxford University Press.

Overview chapters on linguistic interfaces written by its leading practitioners.

References

Adger, David. 2010. A minimalist theory of feature structure. In *Features: Perspectives on a Key Notion in Linguistics*, ed. Anna Kibort and Greville G. Corbett, 185–218. Oxford: Oxford University Press.

Adger, David, and Peter Svenonius. 2011. Features in minimalist syntax. In *The Oxford Handbook of Linguistic Minimalism*, ed. Cedric Boeckx, 27–51. Oxford: Oxford University Press.

Berwick, Robert C., and Amy S. Weinberg. 1982. Parsing efficiency, computational complexity, and the evaluation of grammatical theories. *Linguistic Inquiry* 13:165–191.

Berwick, Robert C., and Amy S. Weinberg. 1984. *The Grammatical Basis of Linguistic Performance*. Cambridge, MA: MIT Press.

Boeckx, Cedric. 2006. *Linguistic Minimalism*. Oxford: Oxford University Press.

Boeckx, Cedric. 2010. A tale of two minimalisms – Reflections on the plausibility of crash-proof syntax and its free merge alternative. In *Derivational Simplicity in Minimalist Syntax*, ed. Michael Putnam, 105–124. Amsterdam: John Benjamins.

Boeckx, Cedric, and Juan Uriagereka. 2006. Minimalism. In *The Oxford Handbook of Linguistic Minimalism*, ed. Gillian Ramchand and Charles Reiss, 541–573. Oxford: Oxford University Press.

Borer, Hagit. 1984. *Parametric Syntax*. Dordrecht: Foris.

Bresnan, Joan. 1971. Sentence stress and syntactic transformations. *Language* 47:257–281.

Chomsky, Noam. 1955. The logical structure of linguistic theory. Ms. Harvard University.

Chomsky, Noam. 1965. *Aspects of the Theory of Syntax*. Cambridge, MA: MIT Press.

Chomsky, Noam. 1970. Remarks on nominalization. In *Readings in English Transformational Grammar*, ed. Roderick A. Jacobs and Peter S. Rosenbaum, 184–221. Waltham, MA: Ginn.

Chomsky, Noam. 1973. Conditions on transformations. In *A Festschrift for Morris Halle*, ed. Stephen R. Anderson and Paul Kiparsky, 232–286. New York: Holt, Rinehart and Winston.

Chomsky, Noam. 1980. On binding. *Linguistic Inquiry* 11:1–46.

Chomsky, Noam. 1981. *Lectures on Government and Binding*. Dordrecht: Foris.

Chomsky, Noam. 1986a. *Barriers*. Cambridge, MA: MIT Press.

Chomsky, Noam. 1986b. *Knowledge of Language*. New York: Praeger.

Chomsky, Noam. 1993. A minimalist program for linguistic theory. In *The View from Building 20*, ed. Kenneth Hale and Samuel Jay Keyser, 1–52. Cambridge, MA: MIT Press [reprinted as chapter 3 in Chomsky 1995b].

Chomsky, Noam. 1995a. Bare phrase structure. *Evolution and Revolution in Linguistic Theory: A Festschrift in Honor of Carlos Otero*, ed. Héctor Campos and Paula Kempchinsky, 51–109. Washington D.C.: Georgetown University Press.

Chomsky, Noam. 1995b. *The Minimalist Program*. Cambridge, MA: MIT Press.

Chomsky, Noam. 2000. Minimalist inquiries: The framework. In *Step by Step: Essays on Minimalist Syntax in Honor of Howard Lasnik*, ed. Roger Martin, David Michaels, and Juan Uriagereka, 89–155. Cambridge, MA: MIT Press.

Chomsky, Noam. 2001. Derivation by phase. In *Ken Hale: A Life in Language*, ed. Michael Kenstowicz, 1–50. Cambridge, MA: MIT Press.

Chomsky, Noam. 2004. Beyond explanatory adequacy. In *Structure and Beyond: The Cartography of Syntactic Structures*, ed. Adriana Belletti, 104–131. Oxford: Oxford University Press.

Chomsky, Noam. 2008. On phases. *Foundational Issues in Linguistic Theory: Essays in Honor of Jean-Roger Vergnaud*, ed. Carlos Otero, Robert Freidin and María-Luísa Zubizarreta, 133–166. Cambridge, MA: MIT Press.

Chomsky, Noam, and Howard Lasnik. 1977. Filters and control. *Linguistic Inquiry* 8:425–504.

Chomsky, Noam, and Howard Lasnik. 1993. The theory of principles and parameters. In *Syntax: An International Handbook of Contemporary Research*, ed. Joachim Jacobs, Arnim von Stechow, Wolfgang Sternefeld, and Theo Venneman, 506–569. New York: Walter de Gruyter.

Cinque, Guglielmo. 1999. *Adverbs and Functional Heads: A Cross-linguistic Perspective*. Oxford: Oxford University Press.

Collins, Chris. 1997. *Local Economy*. Cambridge, MA: MIT Press.

Crain, Stephen, and Rosalind Thornton. 1998. *Investigations in Universal Grammar*. Cambridge, MA: MIT Press.

den Besten, Hans. 1983. On the interaction of root transformations and lexical deletive rules. In *On the Formal Syntax of the Westgermania*, ed. Werner Abraham, 47–131. Amsterdam: John Benjamins.

Di Sciullo, Anna Maria, and Cedric Boeckx (eds). 2011. *The Biolinguistic Enterprise: New Perspectives on the Evolution and Nature of the Human Language Faculty*. Oxford: Oxford University Press.

Di Sciullo, Anna Maria, Massimo Piattelli-Palmarini, Kenneth Wexler, Robert Berwick, Lyle Jenkins, Juan Uriagereka, Karin Stromsvold, Lisa Cheng, Heidi Harley, Andrew Wedel, James McGilvray, Elly van Gelderen, and Thomas Bever. 2010. The biological nature of human language. *Biolinguistics* 4:4–34.

Feyerabend, Paul. 1993. *Against Method*. New York: Verso.

Freidin, Robert. 2007. *Generative Grammar: Theory and its History*. London: Routledge.

Freidin, Robert. 2012. A brief history of generative grammar. In *The Routledge Handbook of the Philosophy of Language*, ed. Delia Fara Graf and Gillian Russell, 895–916. London: Routledge.

Freidin, Robert, and Howard Lasnik. 2011. Some roots of minimalism. In *The Oxford Handbook of Linguistic Minimalism*, ed. Cedric Boeckx, 1–26. Oxford: Oxford University Press.

Freidin, Robert, and Jean-Roger Vergnaud. 2001. Exquisite connections: Some remarks on the evolution of linguistic theory. *Lingua* 111:639–666.

Fukui, Naoki. 2006. *Theoretical Comparative Syntax*. London: Routledge.

Fukui, Naoki, and Margaret Speas. 1986. Specifiers and projection. *MIT Working Papers in Linguistics: Papers in Theoretical Linguistics* 8:128–172.

Gallego, Ángel J. (ed.). 2012. *Phases: Developing the Framework*. Berlin: Mouton de Gruyter.

Gould, Stephen Jay. 2002. *The Structure of Evolutionary Theory*. Cambridge, MA: Harvard University Press.

Hale, Kenneth, and Samuel Jay Keyser. 1993. On argument structure and the lexical expression of grammatical relations. In *The View from Building 20*, ed. Kenneth Hale and Samuel Jay Keyser, 53–110. Cambridge, MA: MIT Press.

Hale, Kenneth, and Samuel Jay Keyser. 2002. *Prolegomenon to a Theory of Argument Structure*. Cambridge, MA: MIT Press.

Hauser, Marc D., Noam Chomsky, and W. Tecumseh Fitch. 2002. The faculty of language: What is it, who has it, and how did it evolve? *Science* 298:1569–1579.

Hicks, Glyn. 2009. *Tough*-constructions and their derivation. *Linguistic Inquiry* 40:535–566.

Hornstein, Norbert. 1999. Movement and control. *Linguistic Inquiry* 30:69–96.

Hornstein, Norbert. 2009. *A Theory of Syntax*. Cambridge: Cambridge University Press.

Hornstein, Norbert, Jairo Nunes, and Kleanthes K. Grohmann. 2005. *Understanding Minimalism*. Cambridge: Cambridge University Press.

Huang, C.T. James. 1982. Logical relations in Chinese and the theory of grammar. Doctoral dissertation, MIT.

Jackendoff, Ray. 1977. *X-bar Syntax: A Study of Phrase Structure*. Cambridge, MA: MIT Press.

Jayaseelan, K.A. 2008. Bare phrase structure and specifier-less syntax. *Biolinguistics* 2:87–106.

Jenkins, Lyle. 2000. *Biolinguistics*. Cambridge: Cambridge University Press.

Katz, Jerrold J., and Paul Postal. 1964. *An Integrated Theory of Linguistic Descriptions*. Cambridge, MA: MIT Press.

Kaufmann, Stuart. 1993. *Origins of Order: Self-organization and Selection in Evolution*. Oxford: Oxford University Press.

Kayne, Richard S. 1984. *Connectedness and Binary Branching*. Dordrecht: Foris.

Kayne, Richard S. 1994. *The Antisymmetry of Syntax*. Cambridge, MA: MIT Press.

Kitahara, Hisatsugu. 1997. *Elementary Operations and Optimal Derivations*. Cambridge, MA: MIT Press.

Koizumi, Masatoshi. 1995. Phrase structure in minimalist syntax. Doctoral dissertation, MIT.

Lakatos, Imre. 1968. Criticism and the methodology of scientific research programmes. *Proceedings of the Aristotelian Society* 69:149–186.

Lakatos, Imre. 1970. Falsifications and the methodology of scientific research programs. In *Criticism and the Growth of Knowledge*, ed. Imre Lakatos and Alan Musgrave, 91–195. Cambridge: Cambridge University Press.

Lappin, Shalom, Robert Levine, and David Johnson. 2000. The structure of unscientific revolutions. *Natural Language and Linguistic Theory* 18:665–671.

Lasnik, Howard. 1999. *Minimalist Analysis*. Oxford: Blackwell.

Lasnik, Howard. 2001. When can you save a structure by destroying it? *Proceedings of NELS* 31:301–320.

Lasnik, Howard. 2008. On the development of case theory: Triumphs and challenges. In *Foundational Issues in Linguistic Theory: Essays in Honor of Jean-Roger Vergnaud*, ed. Carlos Otero, Robert Freidin and María-Luísa Zubizarreta, 17–41. Cambridge, MA: MIT Press.

Lasnik, Howard, and Mamoru Saito. 1984. On the nature of proper government. *Linguistic Inquiry* 15:235–289.

Lasnik, Howard, and Mamoru Saito. 1991. On the subject of infinitives. In *Papers from the 27th Regional Meeting of the Chicago Linguistic Society*, ed. Lise M. Dobrin, Lynn Nichols, and Rosa M. Rodgriuez, 324–343. Chicago, IL: Chicago Linguistic Society.

Lasnik, Howard, and Mamoru Saito. 1992. *Move α: Conditions on its Application and Output*. Cambridge, MA: MIT Press.

Lasnik, Howard, and Juan Uriagereka. 1988. *A Course in GB Syntax*. Cambridge, MA: MIT Press.

Lasnik, Howard, and Juan Uriagereka. 2005. *A Course in Minimalist Syntax*. Malden: Blackwell.

Lasnik, Howard, and Terje Lohndal. 2013. Brief overview of the history of generative syntax. In *The Cambridge Handbook of Generative Syntax*, ed. Marcel den Dikken, 26–60. Cambridge: Cambridge University Press.

Lightfoot, David W. 1999. *The Development of Language*. Malden: Blackwell.

Lohndal, Terje. 2012. Without specifiers: Phrase structure and events. Doctoral dissertation, University of Maryland.

Lohndal, Terje, and Juan Uriagereka. forthcoming. Third factor explanations and universal grammar. In *The Oxford Handbook of Universal Grammar*, ed. Ian Roberts. Oxford: Oxford University Press.

Martin, Roger, and Juan Uriagereka. 2000. Introduction: Some possible foundations of the minimalist program. In *Step by Step: Essays on Minimalist Syntax in Honor of Howard Lasnik*, ed. Roger Martin, David Michaels, and Juan Uriagereka, 1–29. Cambridge, MA: MIT Press.

Merchant, Jason. 2001. *The Syntax of Silence*. Oxford: Oxford University Press.

Müller, Gereon. 2011. *Constraints on Displacement. A Phase-based Approach*. Amsterdam: John Benjamins.

Muysken, Pieter. 1982. Parametrizing the notion "Head". *Journal of Linguistic Research* 2:57–75.

Pesetsky, David. 1982. Paths and categories. Doctoral dissertation, MIT.

Pesetsky, David, and Esther Torrego. 2001. T-to-C movement: Causes and consequences. In *Ken Hale: A Life in Language*, ed. Michael Kenstowicz, 355–426. Cambridge, MA: MIT Press.

Piattelli-Palmarini, Massimo, Juan Uriagereka, and Pello Salaburu (eds), 2009. *Of Minds and Language: A Dialogue with Noam Chomsky in the Basque Country*. Oxford: Oxford University Press.

Pollock, Jean-Yves. 1989. Verb movement, universal grammar, and the structure of IP. *Linguistic Inquiry* 20:365–424.

Popper, Karl. 1959. *The Logic of Scientific Discovery*. London: Hutchinson.

Postal, Paul M. 1974. *On Raising*. Cambridge, MA: MIT Press.

Reinhart, Tanya. 2006. *Interface Strategies*. Cambridge, MA: MIT Press.

Richards, Norvin. 2001. *Movement in Language*. Oxford: Oxford University Press.

Rizzi, Luigi. 1990. *Relativized Minimality*. Cambridge, MA: MIT Press.

Rizzi, Luigi. 1997. The fine structure of the left periphery. In *Elements of Grammar: A Handbook of Generative Syntax*, ed. Liliane Haegeman, 281–337. Dordrecht: Kluwer.

Samuels, Bridget. 2012. *Phonological Architecture: A Biolinguistic Perspective*. Oxford: Oxford University Press.

Speas, Margaret J. 1990. *Phrase Structure in Natural Language*. Dordrecht: Kluwer.

Starke, Michal. 2001. Move reduces to merge: A theory of locality. Doctoral dissertation, University of Geneva.

Starke, Michal. 2004. On the inexistence of specifiers and the nature of heads. In *Structure and Beyond: The Cartography of Syntactic Structures*, ed. Adriana Belletti, 252–268. Oxford: Oxford University Press.

Stowell, Tim. 1981. Origins of phrase structure. Doctoral dissertation, MIT.

Thiersch, Craig. 1985. VP and scrambling in the German Mittelfeld. Ms. University of Tilburg.

Travis, Lisa. 1984. Parameters and effects of word order variation. Doctoral dissertation, MIT.

Uriagereka, Juan. 1988. On government. Doctoral dissertation, University of Connecticut.

Uriagereka, Juan. 1998. *Rhyme and Reason*. Cambridge, MA: MIT Press.

Uriagereka, Juan. 1999. Multiple spell-out. *Working Minimalism*, ed. Samuel David Epstein and Norbert Hornstein, 251–282. Cambridge, MA: MIT Press.

Uriagereka, Juan. 2002. *Derivations*. London: Routledge.

Uriagereka, Juan. 2008. *Syntactic Anchors*. Cambridge: Cambridge University Press.

Uriagereka, Juan. 2009. Uninterpretable features in syntactic evolution. In *Of Minds and Language: A Dialogue with Noam Chomsky in the Basque Country*, ed. Massimo Piattelli-Palmarini, Juan Uriagereka, and Pello Salaburu, 169–183. Oxford: Oxford University Press.

Uriagereka, Juan. 2012. *Spell-out and the Minimalist Program*. Oxford: Oxford University Press.

Vergnaud, Jean-Roger. 1977. Letter to Noam Chomsky and Howard Lasnik on "Filters and Control", April 17, 1977. Printed in *Foundational Issues in Linguistic Theory*, 2008, ed. Robert Freidin, Carlos P. Otero, and Maria Luisa Zubizarreta, 4–15. Cambridge, MA: MIT Press.

Williams, Edwin. 1981. On the notions "lexically related" and "head of a word". *Linguistic Inquiry* 12:245–274.

26

Head-driven Phrase Structure Grammar

Felix Bildhauer

1 Introduction

Head-driven Phrase Structure Grammar (HPSG) is a constraint-based grammar framework. An HPSG grammar consists of a signature, which specifies an ontology of linguistic objects, plus a set of descriptions or constraints imposed on those objects (the so-called principles, which together make up the "theory" of the grammar). In all but the earliest versions, HPSG adopts a model theoretic view on syntax. Constraints are formulated in a logical description language, and those (and only those) objects that satisfy all constraints are well formed according to the grammar. There is no formal difference between lexical entries, syntactic phrases and grammar rules, all of them being descriptions of linguistic entities. Generalizations about such entities are expressed through inheritance hierarchies and, in the case of lexical items, also by means of lexical rules.

The basic building block of linguistic structure in HPSG is the Saussurean sign, that is, a compound of form and meaning (and syntactic properties). HPSG thus posits multiple levels of linguistic structure (e.g., phonological, syntactic, semantic) and represents them in parallel, but it is surface-oriented in the sense that it does not relate several representations of the same level via transformations. Moreover, HPSG grammars restrict the use of empty elements to a minimum or avoid them altogether. Since descriptions/constraints typically relate different levels of structure to each other, there is no such thing as "autonomy of syntax" in HPSG. Rather, if one accepts the notion of "interface" between different dimensions of linguistic description in constraint-based grammar (see Kuhn (2007) for discussion), then most constraints in HPSG can be thought of as interface constraints (Pollard 1999). HPSG was initially conceived as a lexicalist theory of grammar, with most of the information that shapes the structure of phrases and sentences being located in word structures, whereas grammar rules were highly schematic. However, as HPSG analyses started to cover linguistic phenomena beyond classical textbook examples, numerous phrasal templates have been proposed that are more richly specified syntactically and, notably, also in terms of semantics. Tree-configurational notions, such as c-command, do not have a theoretical status in HPSG. Phrase structure and linear realization of constituents are modeled independently of each other via distinct sets of constraints (immediate dominance constraints and linear precedence constraints, respectively).

HPSG grammars are standardly thought of as competence grammars, accounting for the linguistic object types shared by speakers of a speech community, and have been argued to be fully compatible with theories of language performance (Sag and Wasow 2011). Various mathematically rigorous formalizations have been proposed for HPSG grammars of the kind of Pollard and Sag (1994) (King 1989, 1994, 1999; Pollard 1999; Richter 2004b, 2007). The current state of the art is Richter's (2004b; 2007) *Relational Speciate Re-entrant Language* (RSRL), an extension of King's (1999) description language. In actual grammar writing, though, the constraints of a grammar are stated not as formulae of one of these description languages, but rather informally as attribute-value-matrices (AVMs). However, if AVMs follow certain conventions, they can be unambiguously mapped to RSRL formulae and are thus an alternative form of notation.

2 Historical perspectives

Building on work in *Generalized Phrase Structure Grammar* (Gazdar *et al.* 1985), HPSG was developed by Carl Pollard and Ivan A. Sag in the mid-1980s at Stanford and at the Hewlett-Packard laboratories in Palo Alto. It is situated among other non-derivational approaches to grammar such as Categorial Grammar, Lexical-Functional Grammar and Tree Adjoining Grammar. Pollard and Sag's 1987 work is the first comprehensive presentation of the framework, but by 1994 fundamental aspects had undergone a major revision, to the extent that Pollard and Sag's 1994 monograph is generally cited as the standard reference. The most important change concerns the philosophical and formal underpinnings of the framework: The 1987 predecessor used "feature structures" as representations of partial information about linguistic entities, whereas the 1994 version adopts a model-theoretic view in which "feature structures" are understood as total models of linguistic entities, with underspecification occurring only in descriptions of those feature structures (see Pullum (2007) for a brief introduction to model theoretic syntax). Much subsequent work in HPSG is based on a further revised version of the framework sketched in Chapter 9 of the 1994 monograph. However, HPSG is not a monolithic framework. While most analyses of individual phenomena and larger grammar fragments share a core of their ontologies and constraints, the need for formal explicitness in the analysis of linguistic phenomena has led to a number of adaptations of HPSG that differ with respect to the inventory of feature structures and constraints.

3 Descriptive devices

This section briefly introduces the technical machinery of HPSG, along with notational conventions as used in much published work in HPSG. Readers primarily interested in how HPSG handles specific grammatical phenomena may skip this section and refer back to it as needed.

3.1 Feature structures

Pollard and Sag (1994) use "feature structures" as a formal device for modeling linguistic entities, as they did in the 1987 predecessor framework. From a technical perspective, however, the kind of object referred to as a "feature structure" is not the same in these two versions, and the structures underlying current HPSG are again formally different from both of these (see Richter 2004b). Nevertheless, the structures currently assumed are still

Felix Bildhauer

widely referred to as "feature structures", and for convenience this term will be used in the remainder of this article.

Feature structures serve as total models of linguistic objects, and every feature structure is assigned a type (or a sort; both terms are used interchangeably in the literature). Informally, a feature structure can be depicted as a labeled directed graph, where the node labels are types and the arc labels are attributes (or features; both terms are used interchangeably). The node that an arc points to is interpreted as the value of the corresponding attribute. A value can be complex, that is, it can itself have attributes (outgoing arcs). Arcs originating from different nodes may point to the same node, indicating structure sharing (token identity of values), one of HPSG's main explanatory mechanisms. Figure 26.1 illustrates a feature structure as a labeled directed graph.

3.2 Types

In HPSG, each linguistic entity is of a certain type. The existence of each type must be stated explicitly in an HPSG grammar's signature, along with a declaration of appropriate attributes for each type and, for each attribute, a statement about the type of its value. In linguistic grammar writing, type names often match the name of the attribute for which they are an appropriate value, but this is not a formal requirement. Types are organized in a hierarchy that expresses subtype and supertype relations. A subtype inherits all the attributes from its supertype and is subject to all constraints imposed on its supertype. It is also possible for a subtype to have more than one supertype, in which case the subtype

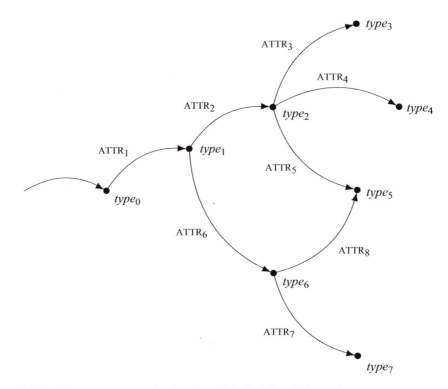

Figure 26.1   A feature structure depicted as a labeled directed graph

inherits the attributes from all supertypes, and is subject to the constraints imposed on all of its supertypes (multiple inheritance). Types without any subtypes, i.e., the "leaves" of an inheritance hierarchy, are maximal types. The assumption is that the maximal types exhaustively partition the universe of linguistic objects ("closed-world-assumption"). The purpose of arranging types in an inheritance hierarchy is to express "vertical" generalizations about linguistic objects. Originally, inheritance was monotonic in HPSG; that is, every constraint imposed on a supertype must also be satisfied by all subtypes of that type. However, there are also variants of HPSG that make use of non-monotonic inheritance (e.g., Ginzburg and Sag 2000), such that constraints imposed on a supertype can be overwritten by constraints imposed on a subtype. Figure 26.2 illustrates a type hierarchy that includes a case of multiple inheritance.

3.3   Constraints

There is a crucial distinction between feature structures and descriptions of feature structures. In HPSG, feature structures are total models of linguistic objects, that is, they encode all the relevant information about the linguistic objects of which they are models. Descriptions, on the other hand, need not be complete in this sense. A description can be partial, in which case one or more attributes appropriate for a type are omitted, or their values are not maximally specific, or type labels are missing altogether. HPSG uses such partial descriptions to express generalizations about classes of linguistic objects (a "constraint", as in "constraint-based", is simply a description of feature structures). Accordingly, descriptions/constraints are also called the "principles" of the grammar. Examples include the "Head Feature Principle", diverse immediate dominance schemata (templates that constrain the structure of syntactic phrases), and linear precedence constraints (which describe constituent order). Constraints are stated as implications, where the left-hand side is a type on which a constraint is imposed, and the right-hand side is a description that any feature structure belonging to this type must satisfy. Alternatively, a description of a feature structure can serve as the antecedent, in which case any feature structure satisfying that description must also satisfy the description on the right-hand side. Technically, descriptions are formulae of a logical description language, but they are usually presented in the form of AVMs in actual grammar writing.

In an AVM, a type and its attributes are enclosed in square brackets. The type name may be indicated in the upper or lower left corner. Types and attributes are conventionally typeset in italics and small caps, respectively. Structure sharing (two different arcs of a graph pointing to the same node) is indicated using small indexed boxes such as $\boxed{1}$, $\boxed{2}$, etc. The constraint shown in 26.3(a) is a complete description of the feature structure in Figure 26.1. The constraint in 26.3(b) is a partial description of that feature structure because it does not

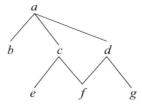

Figure 26.2   A type hierarchy with multiple inheritance: Type f is a subtype of type c and type d

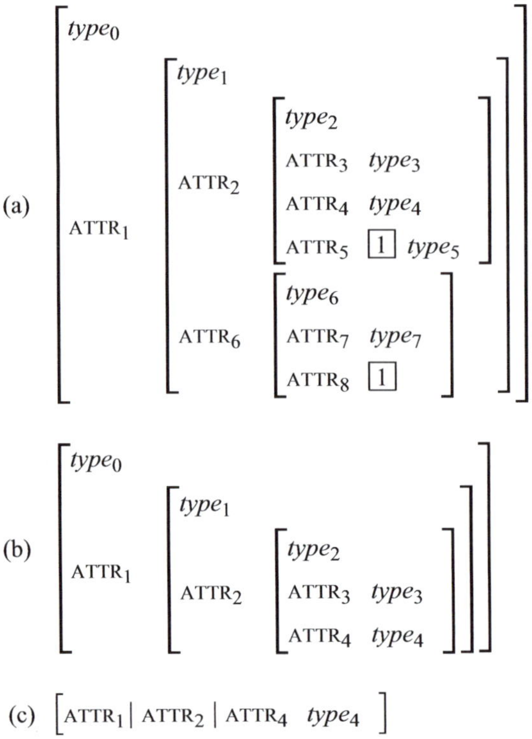

$$
\text{(a)} \quad
\begin{bmatrix}
type_0 \\
\text{ATTR}_1
\begin{bmatrix}
type_1 \\
\text{ATTR}_2
\begin{bmatrix}
type_2 \\
\text{ATTR}_3 \quad type_3 \\
\text{ATTR}_4 \quad type_4 \\
\text{ATTR}_5 \quad \boxed{1} \; type_5
\end{bmatrix} \\
\text{ATTR}_6
\begin{bmatrix}
type_6 \\
\text{ATTR}_7 \quad type_7 \\
\text{ATTR}_8 \quad \boxed{1}
\end{bmatrix}
\end{bmatrix}
\end{bmatrix}
$$

$$
\text{(b)} \quad
\begin{bmatrix}
type_0 \\
\text{ATTR}_1
\begin{bmatrix}
type_1 \\
\text{ATTR}_2
\begin{bmatrix}
type_2 \\
\text{ATTR}_3 \quad type_3 \\
\text{ATTR}_4 \quad type_4
\end{bmatrix}
\end{bmatrix}
\end{bmatrix}
$$

$$
\text{(c)} \quad
\begin{bmatrix}
\text{ATTR}_1 \mid \text{ATTR}_2 \mid \text{ATTR}_4 \quad type_4
\end{bmatrix}
$$

Figure 26.3 AVMs as complete descriptions (a) and partial descriptions (b) and (c) of the feature structure given in Figure 26.1

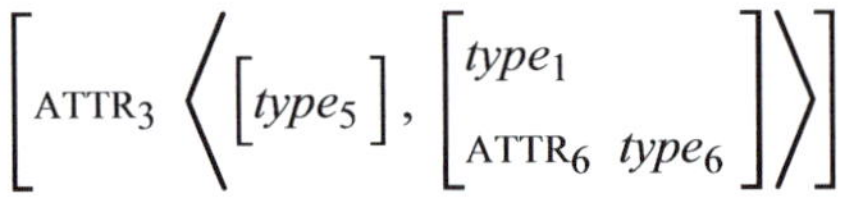

$$
\begin{bmatrix}
\text{ATTR}_3 \quad \left\langle \begin{bmatrix} type_5 \end{bmatrix}, \begin{bmatrix} type_1 \\ \text{ATTR}_6 \quad type_6 \end{bmatrix} \right\rangle
\end{bmatrix}
$$

Figure 26.4 List notation in AVMs using angle brackets: In this example, the list is the value of ATTR_3 and has exactly two elements

specify the values of ATTR_5 and ATTR_6. This AVM therefore describes the feature structure in Figure 26.1, but in addition it also describes all feature structures that differ from it in the values of ATTR_5 or ATTR_6, or both.

If a description makes reference to only a single attribute of a type, the type name and the square brackets surrounding that type are often omitted in AVMs, yielding a sequence of attributes. The AVM in Figure 26.3(c) illustrates this notation of paths which is very common in the HPSG literature.

Some attributes take a list as their value. In AVMs, list elements (which can be arbitrarily complex objects) are enclosed in angle brackets, as illustrated in Figure 26.4. Similarly, sets are written using curly brackets.

AVM notation of constraints is illustrated in Figure 26.5, showing both a type antecedent constraint and a complex antecedent constraint. The constraint in 26.5(a) states that in any feature structure of type $type_0$, the values of the paths $\text{ATTR}_1|\text{ATTR}_2|\text{ATTR}_5$ and $\text{ATTR}_1|\text{ATTR}_6|\text{ATTR}_8$ are identical. The constraint in 26.5(b) also enforces identity of these values, but only for

$$(a) \quad type_0 \quad \Rightarrow \quad \left[ATTR_1 \left[\begin{array}{l} ATTR_2 \mid ATTR_5 \; \boxed{1} \\ ATTR_6 \mid ATTR_8 \; \boxed{1} \end{array} \right] \right]$$

$$(b) \quad \left[\begin{array}{l} type_0 \\ ATTR_1 \mid ATTR_2 \mid ATTR_3 \; type_9 \end{array} \right] \Rightarrow \left[ATTR_1 \left[\begin{array}{l} ATTR_2 \mid ATTR_5 \; \boxed{1} \\ ATTR_6 \mid ATTR_8 \; \boxed{1} \end{array} \right] \right]$$

Figure 26.5 A type antecedent constraint and a complex antecedent constraint

$$\left[\begin{array}{l} word \\ LEX\text{-}DTR \quad stem \end{array} \right] \qquad\qquad \left[stem \right] \longmapsto \left[word \right]$$

(a) Representation as a   (b) Alternative representation
(complex) word

Figure 26.6 Schematic representation of a lexical rule. In this example, the rule maps stems to words. Any particular lexical rule would specify further information for the "input" and "output"

those instances of $type_0$ that have a $ATTR_1 \mid ATTR_2 \mid ATTR_3$ value of $type_9$. Note that the constraint in Figure 26.5(a) applies to the feature structure in Figure 26.1, whereas the constraint in 26.5(b) does not because the feature structure in Figure 26.1 does not satisfy the description on the left-hand side (unless the type hierarchy defines $type_3$ as a subtype of $type_9$).

3.4 Lexical rules

While inheritance hierarchies express vertical generalizations, lexical rules capture horizontal generalizations about lexical items. Simplifying somewhat, a lexical rule expresses a relation between two words (or between a word and a stem, or between two stems). Lexical rules constitute a key mechanism in HPSG and provide the basis for non-transformational accounts of a range of phenomena, including passives and long-distance dependencies (see Section 4.9 for an example). Lexical rules are themselves descriptions of words (or stems) and relate one set of words (or stems) to another set of words (or stems) via a special attribute, called LEX-DTR in Figure 26.6(a). A popular alternative notation is shown in Figure 26.6(b). Intuitively, the left-hand side of 26.6(b) describes the "input" of the rule, the right-hand side describes the "output" and, as a convention, information that is not explicitly mentioned is assumed to be identical on the "input" and "output". The representation in Figure 26.6(a) makes it clear, though, that there is nothing procedural about lexical rules: They are just subtypes of *word* (or, in some cases, *stem*).

Although Pollard and Sag include lexical rules in their 1994 presentation of the framework, their logical status was settled only later. In fact, there exist two different formal conceptualizations of lexical rules. In addition to the "description-level" view on lexical rules presented here (Meurers and Minnen 1997), "meta-level" lexical rules have been proposed (Calcagno 1995). These are not themselves *word* or *stem* objects, but rather a device external to the grammar (see Meurers (2001) for discussion).

$$\begin{bmatrix} \text{ATTR}_{10} & \boxed{3} \\ \text{ATTR}_{11} & \boxed{1} \\ \text{ATTR}_{12} & \boxed{2} \end{bmatrix} \wedge \text{ append}(\boxed{1},\boxed{2},\boxed{3})$$

(a) Adjoined to the AVM

$$\begin{bmatrix} \text{ATTR}_{10} & \text{append}(\boxed{1},\boxed{2}) \\ \text{ATTR}_{11} & \boxed{1} \\ \text{ATTR}_{12} & \boxed{2} \end{bmatrix}$$

(b) Function inside the AVM

$$\begin{bmatrix} \text{ATTR}_{10} & \boxed{1} \oplus \boxed{2} \\ \text{ATTR}_{11} & \boxed{1} \\ \text{ATTR}_{12} & \boxed{2} \end{bmatrix}$$

(c) Function using the append symbol "$\oplus$"

Figure 26.7 Notation of relational constraints

3.4.1 Relational constraints

Pollard and Sag's (1994) HPSG fragment of English uses relation symbols in some of its descriptions. With Richter's (2004b) extension of the underlying mathematical formalism (King 1999), such relations between components of linguistic entities have become part of the description language. Relational symbols are specified in the signature of a grammar. The intended meaning of a relation is defined as a description, i.e., as part of the theory of a grammar. The relation can then be used in formulating descriptions that express linguistic generalizations. For example, the append relation relates three lists, where the third list is the concatenation of the first two lists. It is used in the formal statement of a number of grammatical principles. In the AVM notation, there are two ways of including a relation in a description: The relational expression is either adjoined to an AVM, and some or all of its arguments are structure-shared with components of that AVM; or a functional notation is used, in which case the relational expression is lacking one of its arguments and appears inside the AVM, where it represents the value of the missing argument. Moreover, a few relations that occur over and over again in descriptions, such as the append relation, have a dedicated functional symbol which can be used as a shorthand. Thus, the three descriptions in Figure 26.7 are equivalent: The tags $\boxed{1}$, $\boxed{2}$, and $\boxed{3}$ represent lists, and each of the descriptions states that the value of ATTR$_{10}$ is a list which is the concatenation of the lists $\boxed{1}$ and $\boxed{2}$.

4 Modeling linguistic structures in HPSG

4.1 The overall feature architecture

Both words and syntactic phrases are modeled as signs in a Saussurean sense and thus are a representation of form and meaning. This view is reflected in the type hierarchy, where the type *sign* has *word* and *phrase* as its subtypes, as illustrated in Figure 26.8.

The AVM in Figure 26.9 shows the (partial) description of feature structures that represent linguistic signs and illustrates the feature architecture commonly assumed in HPSG. Some attribute names are regularly abbreviated in the HPSG literature, but they are given in their full form here for ease of readability. This section is intended as a brief overview, and later sections will deal with individual attributes in more detail.

Phonological properties of a sign are represented under the attribute PHONOLOGY (abbr. PHON). Its value is a list of phonemes, but more complex structures such as metrical trees or metrical grids have been used as well (e.g., Bird and Klein 1994; Bildhauer 2008; Bonami and Delais-Roussarie 2006). However, in much of the HPSG literature, it is common to use the orthographic form as the value of PHONOLOGY if a detailed account of phonology is not

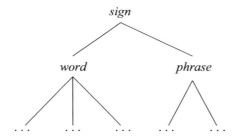

Figure 26.8 Subtypes of *sign*: *word* and *phrase*. Both have their own subtypes

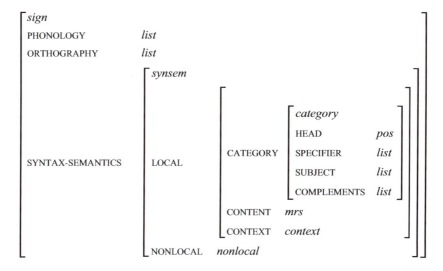

Figure 26.9 Description of a linguistic sign in HPSG

required for a given analysis. Sometimes, the PHONOLOGY attribute is replaced by ORTHOGRAPHY altogether. The SYNTAX-SEMANTICS attribute of a sign (abbr. SYNSEM) bundles the information that a head selecting for this sign can access. Under the NONLOCAL attribute, information is stored about a sign's nonlocal dependencies (extracted constituents, relative- and *wh*-phrases). The attribute LOCAL (abbr. LOC) models a sign's local properties, where syntactic, semantic, and context-related information is distinguished. The details of the sign's semantic representation under the CONTENT attribute (abbr. CONT) depend on the particular semantic formalism used; a common choice is Minimal Recursion Semantics (Copestake *et al.* 2005), in which case the value of the CONTENT attribute is an object of type *mrs*. The attribute CATEGORY (abbr. CAT) stores information that is relevant in local syntactic contexts. The HEAD attribute bundles information that is "projected" to the dominating phrase when the sign acts as the head of this phrase ("head" will be used loosely here and throughout to denote both a lexical head and an immediate constituent of a phrase that contains the lexical head). The value of the HEAD attribute is a type representing the sign's part-of-speech. Each of these *pos* types may introduce its own set of attributes, allowing for different parts of speech to project different sorts of information. The three list-valued attributes SPECIFIER, SUBJECT, and COMPLEMENTS (abbr. SPR, SUBJ, and COMPS, respectively)

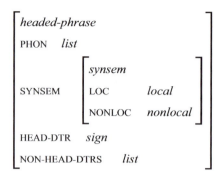

Figure 26.10 Partial description of a headed phrase

specify the sign's valency and contain descriptions of arguments that must be realized in local syntactic contexts (see Section 4.3).

In addition, there are attributes that are appropriate only for certain subtypes of *sign*. One such attribute is ARGUMENT-STRUCTURE (abbr. ARG-ST), which is located under CATEGORY and is appropriate for words but not for phrases. Technically, this involves introducing two subtypes of *category*; to avoid this additional complication, some analyses have introduced ARG-ST as an attribute appropriate of *word* objects, not *category*. The purpose of ARG-ST is to represent on a single list all the arguments subcategorized by a head. A relational constraint, the Argument Realization Principle, maps the elements on ARG-ST (via structure sharing) to the valence lists, and languages may differ as to the details of this mapping. For example, depending on the language, a verb may not always require a subject, i.e., the grammar may allow verbs with an empty SUBJ list. The elements on the ARG-ST list are ordered by increasing obliqueness, as illustrated in Figure 26.13. This list plays a key role in linking syntactic arguments with semantic roles as well as in the HPSG account of binding, and it has also been used in analyses of phenomena that affect a head's local subcategorization requirements (for instance, cliticization in Romance languages).

On the other hand, signs representing phrases (i.e., the type *phrase* and all its subtypes) bear the additional attribute NON-HEAD-DTRS ("non-head daughters"), whose value is a list of the signs that are immediate constituents of the phrase. Note that the NON-HEAD-DTRS list represents only immediate dominance relations and not the linear ordering of immediate constituents. Moreover, phrases that have a syntactic head are of type *headed-phrase* and bear the additional attribute HEAD-DTR ("head daughter"), which takes a *sign* object as its value (Figure 26.10). By virtue of inheritance, subtypes of *headed-phrase* also have the HEAD-DTR attribute. When talking about immediate dominance relations, the dominating phrase is frequently referred to as the "mother", and the information encoded under the attributes NON-HEAD-DTRS and HEAD-DTR is often represented graphically as a tree structure to enhance readability. Thus, diagrams such as those in Figures 26.11(a) and (b) are used interchangeably.

4.2 The lexicon

A lexical entry in HPSG is a description of a feature structure of type *word*, and some versions of HPSG also include descriptions of stems in the lexicon. As an illustration, Figure 26.12 shows part of the structure of the German noun "Umschlag" ("envelope"). A lexical description specifies phonological information under the PHON attribute. Moreover,

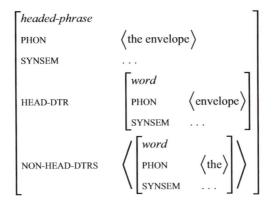

(a) AVM representation of immediate dominance

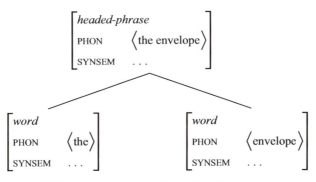

(b) Tree representation of immediate dominance

Figure 26.11   Representation of phrase structure

it contains information about the word's subcategorization frame. In this example, the SPR list contains the description of a determiner (shaded in gray), indicating that the noun "Umschlag" must locally combine with a determiner to yield a saturated phrase. Agreement is generally modeled as structure sharing, and the requirement for two constituents to agree in certain feature values is stated as part of a lexical description. In the German example, the noun and the determiner must share their case values ([2]) as well as their NUMBER and GENDER values ([4] and [5], respectively). Note that number and gender information is located in the noun's semantic description (in the form of dedicated attributes on the noun's index; see Section 4.5).

Contrary to what Figure 26.12 may suggest, individual lexical entries do not actually specify a rich amount of information. Lexical items usually have a considerable number of properties in common, and instead of representing the shared information redundantly in individual lexical entries, it is encoded by constraints on classes of lexical items. Lexical classes can be captured in an appropriate type hierarchy for subtypes of *word* and *stem*. Ideally, an individual lexical entry only specifies idiosyncratic properties of a particular lexical item, such as its meaning and its phonological form. This is called the hierarchical organization of the lexicon. For instance, while a lexical entry specifies the ARG-ST list, it would not actually include a specification of the valence lists because the mapping from

ARG-ST to the valence lists is taken care of by a more general constraint applying to all words (the Argument Realization Principle). Similarly, agreement between the noun "Umschlag" and its determiner would not be stated at the level of the individual lexical entry, but would instead be expressed as a constraint on, e.g., the class of common nouns. Depictions of lexical entries such as Figure 26.12 thus contain information from various sources and serve didactic purposes.

For a more detailed introduction to the structure of the lexicon, see Flickinger (1987) and Koenig (1999). HPSG approaches to morphology can be found in Bonami and Boyé (2002), Crysmann and Bonami (2012), Koenig (1999), and Miller and Sag (1997), among others. Van Eynde (2006) proposes an in-depth analysis of NP structure that differs from the one sketched here.

4.3 Valence

In HPSG, every *sign* object specifies the arguments it has to combine with in order to satisfy local subcategorization requirements. In the original proposal of Pollard and Sag (1994), a single list-valued attribute (SUBCAT) was used for this purpose, but it was soon abandoned in favor of a structurally more complex representation of valence via three

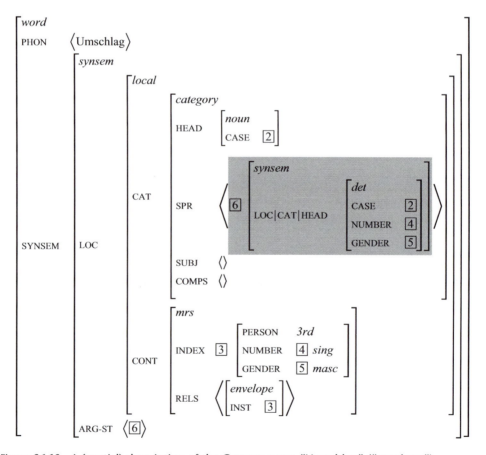

Figure 26.12 A (partial) description of the German noun "Umschlag" ("envelope")

different list-valued attributes (SPECIFIER, SUBJECT, and COMPLEMENTS). Not all HPSG analyses actually use all three of them because, depending on the object language, less than three lists may be sufficient. In any case, these lists do not contain descriptions of subcategorized constituents (which are of type *sign*), but rather descriptions of the SYNSEM values of subcategorized constituents (which are of type *synsem*). The motivation for this is to constrain the kind of information a head may select for. For example, since immediate constituency is encoded via the DTRS attribute, subcategorization is blind with respect to an argument's phrase structure because the DTRS list is not a component of *synsem* objects. The feature geometry of standard HPSG thus encodes a strong assumption about the locality of subcategorization. A sign that has empty valence lists is said to be saturated. Figure 26.13 illustrates the valence lists of various lexical items. The valence specifications (as opposed to ARG-ST) would not be part of the descriptions as listed in the lexicon, but rather follow from the Argument Realization Principle. Note also the notation used for the elements on the valence lists in Figure 26.13: "NP [CASE *nom*]" is actually shorthand for the description in Figure 26.14. Similarly, abbreviations such as DET, VP, S are often used within AVMs for better readability, sometimes with additional attributes as in the present case. It is important to keep in mind that such symbols are merely a shorthand notation for descriptions of feature structures and do not have a theoretical status in HPSG.

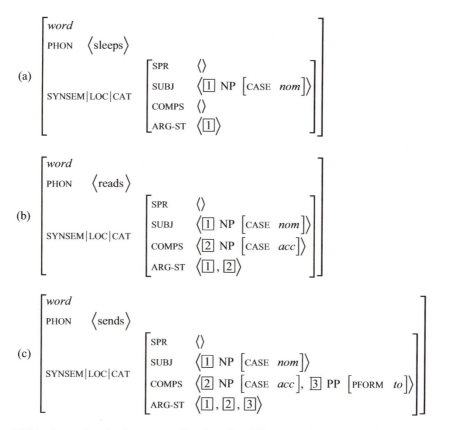

Figure 26.13 Example of valence specifications for different verbs. The Argument Realization Principle maps the elements from ARG-ST to the valence lists SUBJ and COMPS

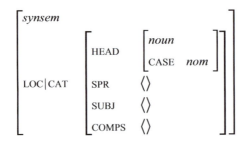

Figure 26.14 Expressions such as "NP[CASE nom]" are shorthand for a feature structure description (in this example, a saturated nominal projection)

The valence specification on a sign interacts with partial descriptions of phrases in licensing phrase structure, as sketched in the next section.

4.4 Phrase structure

Despite its name, HPSG does not have phrase structure rules in the traditional sense. Rather, as any other structure in HPSG, a phrase is well-formed if and only if it satisfies the constraints of the grammar. Some of these constraints are the so-called immediate dominance schemata (or ID schemata, for short), which are partial descriptions of phrases and take over some of the work that phrase structure rules accomplish in traditional phrase structure grammars. The term "grammar rules" is also sometimes used to refer to ID schemata.

Phrases come in different types which are arranged in an inheritance hierarchy. A handful of these phrasal types are very general and serve to model different ways in which a head can combine with a dependent, for example, a head combining with a complement, or a head combining with its specifier, or a head combining with a modifier. Additional, more specific phrasal types (not discussed here) are necessary to model sub-regularities or idiosyncratic structures, which often do not have a recognizable syntactic head (see, e.g., Jackendoff (2008) and Jacobs (2008) for examples of such configurations). Figure 26.15 shows a number of phrasal types commonly assumed in much work in HPSG. The various subtypes of *headed-phrase* interact in particular ways with the specifications of their daughters, as will be explained below.

4.4.1 Subjects

The type *head-subject-phrase* describes the combination of a head with its subject. It makes reference to its head daughter's SUBJ list and ensures that its non-head daughter satisfies the description listed there. Moreover, the type *head-subject-phrase* makes sure that the phrase resulting from the combination of a head with its subject does not itself subcategorize for a subject constituent. Technically, this is modeled via structure sharing, as shown in the constraint on *head-subject-phrase* given in Figure 26.16. The *synsem* object on the head daughter's SUBJ list is structure-shared with the SYNSEM value of the head daughter. The SUBJ list of *head-subject-phrase* itself is empty, indicating that it no longer needs to combine with a subject constituent. The values of the other two valence attributes SPR and COMPS are identical on the mother and on the head daughter in a *head-subject-phrase*, whatever these values are. Thus combining a head with its subject does not affect any other subcategorization requirements of that head.

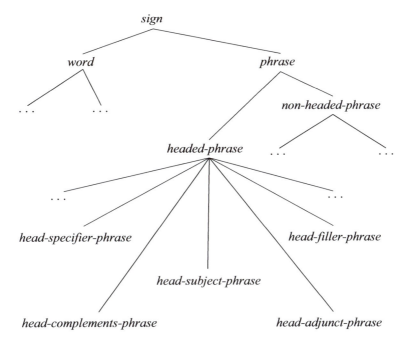

Figure 26.15   Type hierarchy showing subtypes of *sign*

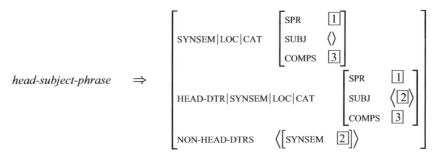

Figure 26.16   An immediate dominance schema for *head-subject-phrase*: A partial description of a phrase

4.4.2   Complements

The syntactic combination of a head with its complements works similarly and is modeled with the type *head-complements-phrase*. As one would expect, the head daughter in a *head-complements-phrase* forms a phrase with constituents whose SYNSEM values are described by elements on its COMPS list rather than the SUBJ list. Moreover, *head-complements-phrase* in principle allows for more than one argument to combine with the head daughter in a single phrase, yielding a DTRS list with more than two signs on it and thus a "flat", *n*-ary branching syntactic structure (as opposed to the binary branching *head-subject-phrase*). Technically, this is achieved by relating the mother's COMPS list, the mother's NON-HD-DTRS list, and the head daughter's COMPS list via the append relation. (Actually, things are slightly more complicated, for it is not the NON-HD-DTRS list that is involved in the append relation, but rather the list of *synsem* objects of its members (see Section 4.3). The relation signs-to-synsems

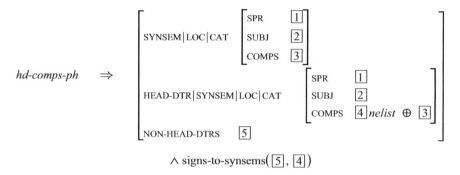

$$hd\text{-}comps\text{-}ph \quad \Rightarrow \quad \begin{bmatrix} \text{SYNSEM}\,|\,\text{LOC}\,|\,\text{CAT} & \begin{bmatrix} \text{SPR} & \boxed{1} \\ \text{SUBJ} & \boxed{2} \\ \text{COMPS} & \boxed{3} \end{bmatrix} \\ \\ \text{HEAD-DTR}\,|\,\text{SYNSEM}\,|\,\text{LOC}\,|\,\text{CAT} & \begin{bmatrix} \text{SPR} & \boxed{1} \\ \text{SUBJ} & \boxed{2} \\ \text{COMPS} & \boxed{4}\,nelist \oplus \boxed{3} \end{bmatrix} \\ \\ \text{NON-HEAD-DTRS} & \boxed{5} \end{bmatrix}$$

$$\wedge \text{ signs-to-synsems}(\boxed{5}, \boxed{4})$$

Figure 26.17 Immediate dominance schema for *head-complements-phrase*. The head daughter's COMPS list is split into two parts: The list $\boxed{4}$ is a non-empty list (*nelist*) of *synsem* objects corresponding to the non-head daughters, and the list $\boxed{3}$ contains the *synsem* objects of any remaining complements. List $\boxed{3}$ is "passed up" to the mother, and if it is not empty, the mother will combine with the remaining complement(s) in another instance(s) of *head-complements-phrase*

in Figure 26.17 serves to "extract" the *synsem* objects out of a list of signs: $\boxed{5}$ is a list of signs, and $\boxed{4}$ is the list of the *synsem* objects corresponding to these signs.)

Figure 26.18 illustrates the combination of a head with its complements. In Figure 26.18(a), all complements combine with the verb "gives" in a single instance of *head-complements-phrase*. By contrast, in Figure 26.18(b) one complement combines with the head daughter, and the resulting *head-complements-phrase* acts as the head daughter in another instance of *head-complements-phrase*, where it combines with the remaining complement. HPSG does not assume either of these structures to be universally appropriate for describing natural language. Both of them have been widely used in the HPSG literature, and in addition to the object language under discussion, the choice also depends to some degree on issues of the interaction of these structures with other constraints in a given grammar. In any case, on grounds of linguistic or other considerations, *head-complements-phrase* can easily be further constrained in a way that excludes either the flat or the binary branching structure.

More complex patterns of complementation have received considerable attention in HPSG. Since the pioneering work by Hinrichs and Nakazawa (1994), complex predicates have been modeled as instances of "argument attraction". Via structure sharing, a head attracts elements from its complement's ARG-ST list into its own ARG-ST list. Analyses in terms of argument attraction include Abeillé and Godard (1996, 2002), Monachesi (1998), and Müller (2002), to name just a few.

4.4.3 Adjuncts

Following Pollard and Sag (1994), standard HPSG analyzes adjuncts as selecting for the head they modify. There are alternative proposals that treat particular classes of adjuncts like complements (e.g., Bouma *et al.* 2001). Such adjuncts-as-complements approaches have been criticized for not correctly predicting adjunct scope in certain configurations (see Levine 2003), and will not be further discussed in this section.

A modifier selects a head via the MODIFIED attribute (MOD, for short), the value of which is a description of (the SYNSEM value of) the constituent it adjoins to. Signs that are not modifiers are specified as [MOD *none*]. Since adjuncts are often phrases, MOD is a head

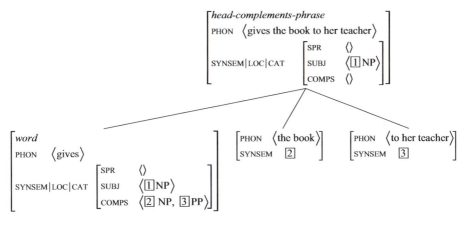

(a) Ternary branching ("flat") *head-complements-phrase*

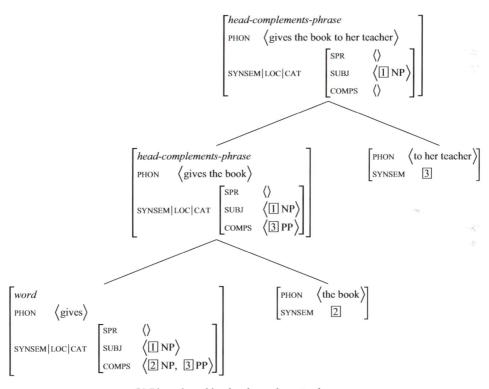

(b) Binary branching *head-complements-phrase*

Figure 26.18   Different realizations of *head-complements-phrase*: Flat versus binary branching

feature, which ensures that the MOD value of a phrase is identical to the MOD value of its lexical head. An adjunct syntactically combines with the modified constituent in an instance of *head-adjunct-phrase*, a dedicated ID schema that makes reference to the MOD attribute. The constraint on *head-adjunct-phrase*, shown in Figure 26.19, states that the non-head daughter's MOD value is identical to the head daughter's SYNSEM value, thus guaranteeing

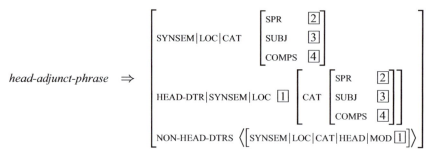

Figure 26.19 Immediate dominance schema for *head-adjunct-phrase*

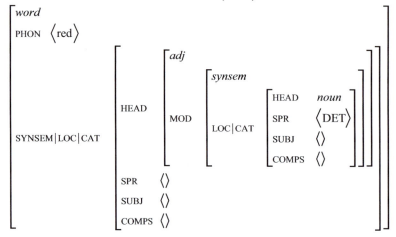

(a) (Partial) description of the attributive adjective "red"

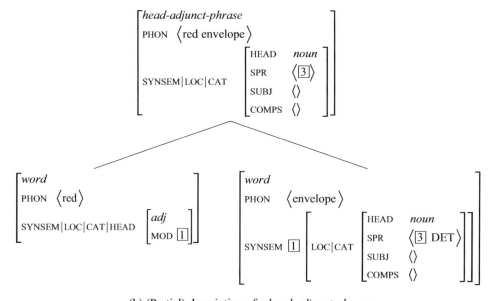

(b) (Partial) description of a *head-adjunct-phrase*

Figure 26.20 Analysis of adjunction

that an adjunct can only combine with a constituent that is compatible with its MOD value. Furthermore, the valence specifications of the mother are identical to that of the head daughter, thus adjunction has no impact on subcategorization. Figure 26.20(a) shows a partial description of the attributive adjective "red", and Figure 26.20(b) gives an example of an adjunction structure.

4.4.4 Projection of head values

The main characteristic of a headed phrase is the sharing of certain properties between the head daughter and the mother ("projection"). Exactly which properties are involved depends on the head daughter's part-of-speech. For example, in a saturated nominal projection (i.e., an NP), the CASE value is shared between the NP and the lexical head noun because it must be visible to heads that subcategorize for the NP. For the same reason, verbal projections must share the VFORM value ("verb form") of the head verb, and prepositions must project information about the particular form of the preposition, etc. HPSG deals with this by bundling under the HEAD attribute all and only the information that is shared between a head and its projections. The Head Feature Principle is a constraint on the type *headed-phrase* which ensures the required structure sharing (cf. the AVM in Figure 26.21):

> **Head Feature Principle**: The HEAD value of any headed phrase is structure-shared with the HEAD value of the head daughter.

Figure 26.22 illustrates the effect of the Head Feature Principle on a head complement structure. Note how the HEAD value of the verb "gives" is identical to the HEAD value of the verb phrase "gives the book to her teacher".

$$
\textit{headed-phrase} \quad \Rightarrow \quad \begin{bmatrix} \text{SYNSEM} \mid \text{LOC} \mid \text{CAT} \mid \text{HEAD} \quad \boxed{1} \\ \text{HEAD-DTR} \mid \text{SYNSEM} \mid \text{LOC} \mid \text{CAT} \mid \text{HEAD} \quad \boxed{1} \end{bmatrix}
$$

Figure 26.21 The Head Feature Principle (Pollard and Sag 1994: 34)

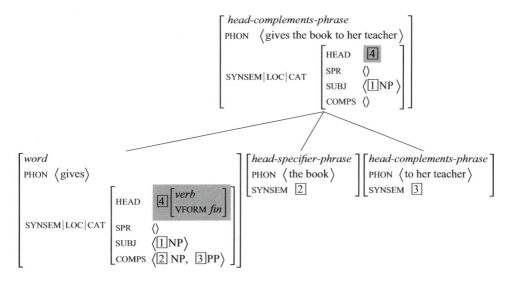

Figure 26.22 Structure sharing of HEAD values in a *head-complements-phrase*

4.5 Semantics

In parallel to phonological and syntactic properties, every *sign* object includes a representation of its meaning. This means that a semantic representation is computed at every level of syntactic composition. It is the rule rather than the exception in the HPSG literature to also address semantics when proposing a syntactic analysis of a phenomenon.

While Pollard and Sag's (1994) original proposal was couched in Situation Semantics (Barwise and Perry 1983), a number of different semantic frameworks have been used in HPSG grammars since then, including underspecification formalisms such as Minimal Recursion Semantics ("MRS", Copestake *et al.* 2005) and Lexical Resource Semantics (Richter 2004a). The following sketch of the treatment of semantics in HPSG will be based on MRS, which is probably the most widely used formalism in the HPSG community today.

The semantic representation of a sign is located under SYNSEM|LOC|CONT and is of type *mrs*. Simplifying somewhat, *mrs* has the attributes INDEX and RELS ("relations"). The value of INDEX is of type *index*, which has several subtypes. For example, the index used in describing nominal objects is of type *referential*. It can be thought of as a discourse referent and bears additional attributes that play a role in modeling person, number, and gender agreement. A sign's semantics in the proper sense is expressed in terms of a number of elementary predications. Maximal subtypes of *elementary-predication* represent particular predicates such as *give*, *probably*, and *envelope*. These subtypes have attributes which encode semantic roles. The inventory of such attributes varies considerably in the HPSG literature, ranging from very specific roles (such as GIVER, GIFT, GIVEE) to very schematic ones (such as ACTOR, THEME, GOAL). Elementary predications of nominal objects have an INST ("instance") attribute, and those representing events bear an EVENT attribute, both of which share their value with the CONT|INDEX value in the lexical entry of the word. Figure 26.23 shows (simplified) semantic descriptions of the words "envelope" and "sends".

The semantics of a phrase are calculated on the basis of the semantics of its daughters and the semantics of the ID schema that licenses it. The last point is especially important: While a very general ID schema such as *head-complements-phrase* is not normally thought of as adding semantic content, there may be other, more specific ID schemata which might very well contribute to the overall meaning. HPSG allows in principle for such constructional meaning by introducing the attribute C-CONT on phrases. The value of C-CONT is an *mrs* object, the RELS list of which will be non-empty if an ID-schema has semantic content. The Semantics Principle ensures that the meaning of phrases is composed in the way just described. Technically, another relational constraint is required to refer to the RELS lists of

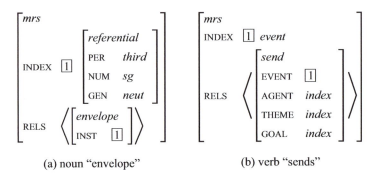

(a) noun "envelope"   (b) verb "sends"

Figure 26.23 Semantic description using MRS (simplified)

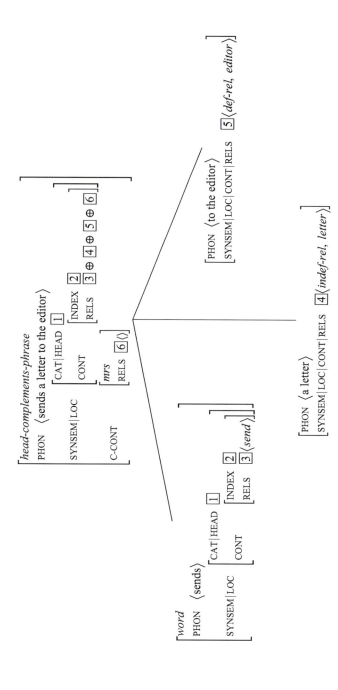

Figure 26.24 Semantic composition in a phrase

any number of daughters (cf. the explanation in the section on *head-complements-phrase* above), so the Semantics Principle will only be given in prose here:

> **Semantics Principle**: In a headed phrase, the CONT|INDEX value is structure-shared with the CONT|INDEX value of the head daughter, and the CONT|RELS list is the concatenation of the CONT|RELS lists of all the daughters and the C-CONT|RELS list of the mother.

Figure 26.24 illustrates the effect of the Semantics Principle, assuming that *head-complements-phrase* has no constructional content (i.e., the ID schema in Figure 26.17 should be extended such that the phrase has an empty C-CONT list). For details of how elementary predications are plugged into each other to yield well formed formulae, see Copestake *et al.* (2005).

4.6   Linking

Linking of syntactic arguments with semantic roles is specified in the lexical entry of the head that selects for the arguments. To this end, the referential index of each argument listed on the head's ARG-ST list is identified with a semantic role in the head's elementary predication. Figure 26.25 illustrates this with a lexical entry for the verb "sends".

4.7   Binding

Pollard and Sag (1994) formulate a binding theory based on obliqueness relations among arguments ("o-command"), thereby avoiding a number of problems that arise when binding principles are defined on the basis of syntactic tree configurations. HPSG's binding principles are stated with respect to the elements on the ARG-ST list, for these are ordered by obliqueness. Nevertheless, some questions remain with respect to the HPSG account of binding (see Müller (1999: Chapter 20.4) for discussion).

4.8   Case assignment

The CASE values of a head's arguments are not always maximally specific in the lexicon. (In the lexical entries illustrated above, CASE values are indeed most specific for the sake of exposition.) Some of them are underspecified as [CASE *str*] ("structural"), and their specific CASE value depends on the syntactic environment in which they occur. In HPSG, the assignment of structural case is constrained by the Case Principle (Meurers 1999, 2000; Przepiórkowski 1999), which is reminiscent of the one proposed in Yip *et al.* (1987).

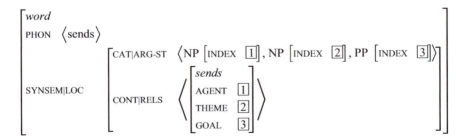

Figure 26.25   Argument linking

The Case Principle refers to the list that contains all the arguments of a head (ARG-ST) and states the following (for nominative–accusative languages):

- In a verbal context, the least oblique argument with structural case is assigned nominative case, unless it is raised by another head.
- In a verbal context, all remaining arguments (if any) with structural case are assigned accusative case.
- In a nominal context, an argument with structural case is assigned genitive case.

4.9 Passives

Following Bresnan (1982), the HPSG approach to passives is lexicon based. A lexical rule takes a verb stem as its "input" and licenses the passive participle of that verb. Figure 26.26 shows a simplified version of the Passive Lexical Rule (for a detailed account, see, e.g., Müller and Ørsnes (forthcoming)).

The left-hand side of the Passive Lexical Rule in Figure 26.26 states that the first element on the ARG-ST list of the input verb stem is a nominal phrase bearing structural case. The right-hand side describes a passive participle whose ARG-ST list is like the ARG-ST list of the input stem, except that the first element is missing. Since a word's valency lists are "filled" by the Argument Realization Principle, the Passive Lexical Rule does not have to mention the participle's SUBJ or COMPS lists.

For instance, the grammar of English requires a subject to be present, and hence the first element of the ARG-ST list is mapped to SUBJ. If the input to the Passive Lexical Rule is an intransitive verb, the Argument Realization Principle for English cannot map any element to the subject valence feature, which explains why no impersonal passives exist in English. German, on the other hand, is a language that admits subjectless sentences, and hence impersonal passives are not ruled out. The CASE value of the members of the ARG-ST list is determined by the Case Principle. For instance, the direct object of an active transitive verb will be the first element on the ARG-ST list of the passive participle and thus will be assigned nominative case in the passive. The PHON value of the passive participle is calculated by a function on the basis of the verb stem's PHON value. As a notational convention, specifications that are not explicitly mentioned in the lexical rule are assumed to be identical on the input and output. Thus, the linking of syntactic arguments to semantic roles is not affected by the Passive Lexical Rule.

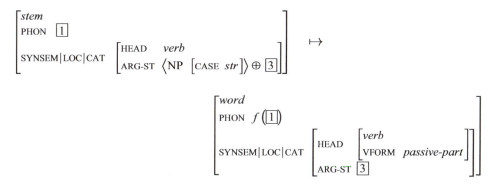

Figure 26.26 The Passive Lexical Rule

Felix Bildhauer

4.10   Extraction

Information about nonlocal dependencies of a sign is represented under SYNSEM|NONLOCAL, where the two attributes INHERITED and TO-BIND are located. Each of them has the three attributes SLASH, QUE, and REL, that play a role in accounting for extraction phenomena, *wh*-elements, and relative clauses, respectively. This section illustrates the mechanism used in describing nonlocal dependencies and concentrates on the SLASH list. For a treatment of *wh*-elements and relative clauses in HPSG, see Ginzburg and Sag (2000) and Pollard and Sag (1994: Chapters 4 and 5). Nonlocal attributes take a set as their value in standard HPSG, but for simplicity, we will assume here that they are list-valued. For a formal treatment of set descriptions, see Pollard and Moshier (1990).

HPSG models the extraction of constituents from other constituents (i.e., the nonlocal realization of a head's dependents) without reference to syntactic movement. Instead, it adapts the GPSG analysis of extraction. The NONLOC|INHER|SLASH attribute encodes information about extracted dependents locally on the phrases from which they are missing. There exist several variants of how this is achieved technically, but all of these only involve constraints on local syntactic configurations. The original proposal by Pollard and Sag (1994) uses a phonetically empty element (a "trace") that occurs in the place of the missing dependent. The lexical entry of the trace is given in Figure 26.27.

A trace syntactically combines with a head in exactly the same way that regular arguments or adjuncts do, e.g., in an instance of *head-complements-phrase* or *head-adjunct-phrase*. However, while a trace does not make any phonological contribution, its LOCAL value is identified with the single element on its NONLOC|INHER|SLASH list. A trace's LOCAL value is not specified in the lexical entry, but when the trace acts as the complement of, say, a verb, its LOCAL value is automatically structure-shared with the LOCAL value of the corresponding item on the verb's COMPS list. Thus, any restrictions that the verb imposes on (the LOCAL value of) that complement are also represented as the trace's LOCAL value and, by structure sharing, on the trace's NONLOC|INHER|SLASH list. The Nonlocal Feature Principle ensures that information about a missing constituent is made available on dominating phrases. This can be thought of as "passing up" the information successively to mother nodes, although strictly speaking, there is no "succession" or "passing up", but only structure sharing. The Nonlocal Feature Principle formulated below is a simplified version that focuses on the SLASH value and omits the nonlocal attributes QUE and REL.

Nonlocal Feature Principle: The value of INHERITED|SLASH on a phrasal sign is the concatenation of the INHERITED|SLASH values on the daughters minus the TO-BIND|SLASH value on the head daughter.

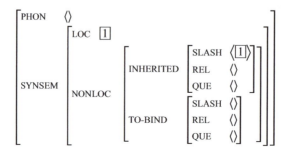

Figure 26.27   Lexical entry of a trace

The third component in the analysis of extraction is an additional immediate dominance schema that licenses the combination of a constituent (the "filler") with the phrase from which it is missing (the head daughter). Such *head-filler-phrase*s are constrained as shown in Figure 26.28 (again using list-valued NONLOC attributes instead of set-valued ones).

The HPSG analysis of extraction is illustrated in Figure 26.29 with a topicalization construction. The direct object of the verb "hates" is locally realized as a trace. Via structure sharing, a description of the missing complement is "passed up" to successively larger phrases. The NP "Kim" is an appropriate filler, i.e., its LOCAL value is compatible with the item on the INHER|SLASH list of the upper *head-subject-phrase*. The long distance dependency is then bound off in an instance of *head-filler-phrase*. As the INHER|SLASH list of the *head-filler-phrase* is empty, no additional filler can attach to it.

In the classical HPSG analysis of extraction sketched so far, one of the subcategorization requirements of a head is satisfied with a kind of "dummy" (the trace). An alternative approach that does not make use of empty elements was proposed in Sag (1997). On this account, the valency of a head is in fact locally reduced by a combination of a lexical rule and a relational constraint on argument realization (mapping from ARG-ST to the valence lists). Bouma *et al.* (2001) elaborate on this approach to include the extraction of adjuncts. However, modeling extraction in the lexicon is problematic for the semantic description of certain coordination structures (see Levine and Hukari (2006) for discussion and a full account of extraction).

4.11 Constituent order

The linear order of immediate constituents in a phrase is described by a separate set of constraints, so called LP (linear precedence) rules. Technically, these rules constrain the PHON value of the mother as a function of certain properties of the daughters, but they are often stated informally as in Figure 26.30, where "<" means "precedes". In this example, taken from Abeillé and Godard's (2002) analysis of French, the LP rule states that the head-daughter precedes any non-head daughter in a *head-complements-phrase*. Similar rules can be formulated for other phrasal types such as *head-subject-phrase*, *head-filler-phrase*, and so on.

LP rules are usually local in the sense that they only constrain the order of sister constituents. An alternative approach to constituent order in HPSG uses so-called ordering

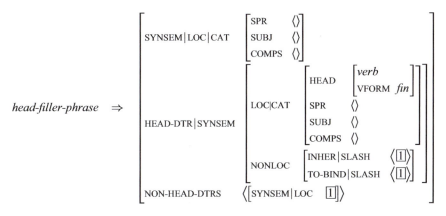

Figure 26.28   Immediate dominance schema for *head-filler-phrase*

Felix Bildhauer

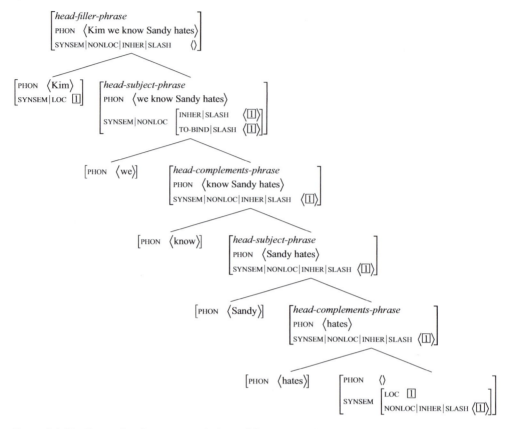

Figure 26.29 Example of extraction (adapted from Pollard and Sag 1994)

$$head\text{-}complements\text{-}phrase \quad \Rightarrow \quad \text{HEAD-DTR} < \text{X}$$

Figure 26.30 A linear precedence constraint specifying the order of immediate constituents in a *head-complements-phrase*

domains (Reape 1994) and allows immediate constituents of different phrases to occur interleaved in linear order. In this setting, LP rules may be formulated which constrain the order among constituents that are not syntactic sisters. Analyses on the basis of such domains have been proposed, e.g., for the linearization of constituents in the German *Mittelfeld* (e.g., Kathol 2001; Müller 1999, 2002). For a discussion of the adequacy of this approach see Müller (2005, 2013b).

4.12 Sentence types and discourse

Finally, there are several proposals within HPSG for modeling a sign's discourse-related properties. For instance, Ginzburg and Sag (2000) offer a fine-grained account of sentence types, and a number of studies integrate aspects of information structure into the HPSG framework (e.g., Bildhauer 2008; De Kuthy 2002; Engdahl and Vallduví 1996). Due to limitations of space, these aspects can merely be mentioned here.

5 Current developments

In the last one and a half decades, the idea that idiosyncratic or semi-transparent constructions make up for a large part of language has gained much ground in the linguistic community (see also Culicover (1999), Ginzburg and Sag (2000: 5), Jackendoff (1997: Chapter 7), and Kuhn (2007: 619) on the arbitrariness of the "core vs. periphery" distinction). Grammar has come to be seen by many as a continuum ranging from highly schematic constructions to very specific ones, and an adequate theory of grammar should be able to deal with the whole range in a principled way. In this connection, the role of head-drivenness has been subject to some discussion (e.g., Jackendoff 2008; Jacobs 2008). Despite its name, and although the grammar originally outlined in Pollard and Sag (1994) is head-driven, the architecture of HPSG is well suited to modeling a constructionist view of grammar, as there is no formal difference between words, phrases, and grammar rules. Nothing in the formalism prevents the grammar writer from postulating phrasal types that are more richly specified syntactically and/or semantically than, e.g., *head-subject-phrase* or *head-adjunct-phrase*, in order to account for sub-regularities or even total idiosyncrasies. Starting with Sag's (1997) analysis of English relative clauses, HPSG has seen a number of proposals along these lines (see, e.g., Haugereid (2009) for a constructionist approach to argument linking in HPSG; Ginzburg and Sag (2000) on the syntax and semantics of questions; Webelhuth (2012) on English that-clauses), but discussion continues about whether particular phenomena are better analyzed in terms of lexical or phrasal constructions (see Müller 2006; Müller and Wechsler 2013). Pushing the idea of constructionist HPSG even further, *Sign-Based Construction Grammar* (Sag 2012) has recently emerged as a framework that aims at bringing HPSG even closer to Berkeley Construction Grammar (see Fillmore *et al.* (1988); Kay and Fillmore (1999) among others).

6 Computer implementations of HPSG grammars

Given HPSG's strict formalization and the explicitness of its analyses, computer implementations of grammar fragments have gained some popularity among practitioners of HPSG (see Müller (2013a: 193–194) for a list of implemented HPSG fragments in a variety of languages). Such implementations can be used in computer applications, and they serve as a check of consistency for hand-crafted HPSG grammars. Even moderately sized grammar fragments usually reach a degree of complexity that makes "manual" evaluation a very hard task (Abney 1996: 20; Bierwisch 1963: 163). Any broad coverage HPSG fragment (often called a "resource grammar") is probably impossible to test using pencil and paper, and the same is true in a setting where multiple grammar fragments of different languages are built around a common core of constraints. It should be noted, though, that computer implementations are not a requirement and in fact most researchers working in HPSG do not implement their theories.

At the time of writing, there are two larger groups of researchers working on grammar implementations: DELPH-IN (Deep Linguistic Processing with HPSG; http://www.delph-in.net) and the CoreGram project (http://hpsg.fu-berlin.de/Projects/CoreGram.html). The respective groups in these projects use the two major implementation platforms: The LKB system (Copestake 2002) and the TRALE platform (Meurers *et al.* 2002; Müller 2007;

Penn 2004). A comparison between these two can be found in Melnik (2005). In the context of the LKB, the Grammar Matrix (Bender *et al.* 2002) is a popular tool for speeding up the development of new HPSG grammars in the initial phase.

Further reading

- The paper by Hinrichs and Nakazawa (1994) pioneers the HPSG analysis of complex predicates in terms of argument attraction. This approach has been highly influential and is used in the analyses of a host of different phenomena.
- Although most HPSG analyses of particular phenomena include a section on semantics, the present chapter sketches semantic composition only in very rough terms. Copestake *et al.* (2005) is a detailed introduction to Minimal Recursion Semantics and its implementation with typed feature structures.
- Sag *et al.* (2003) is an introduction to syntactic theory that is compatible with many assumptions in HPSG. Since it simplifies various aspects for didactic purposes, it should be seen neither as an introduction to HPSG, nor to Sign-Based Construction Grammar.
- An exhaustive bibliography of HPSG-related literature is hosted at http://hpsg.fu-berlin.de/ HPSG-Bib.

References

Abeillé, A. and Godard, D. 1996. La complémentation des auxiliaires en français. *Langages*, 122: 32–61.

_____ 2002. The Syntactic Structure of French Auxiliaries. *Language*, 78(3): 404–452.

Abney, S. P. 1996. Statistical Methods and Linguistics. In Klavans, J. L. and Resnik, P. (eds), *The Balancing Act: Combining Symbolic and Statistical Approaches to Language, Language, Speech, and Communication*, pages 1–26. London; Cambridge, MA: MIT Press.

Barwise, J. and Perry, J. 1983. *Situations and Attitudes*. Cambridge, MA: MIT Press.

Bender, E. M., Flickinger, D. P., and Oepen, S. 2002. The Grammar Matrix: An Open-source Starter-kit for the Rapid Development of Cross-linguistically Consistent Broad-coverage Precision Grammars. In Carroll, J., Oostdijk, N., and Sutcliffe, R. (eds), *Proceedings of the Workshop on Grammar Engineering and Evaluation at the 19th International Conference on Computational Linguistics*, pages 8–14.

Bierwisch, M. 1963. *Studia Grammatica 2: Grammatik des deutschen Verbs*. Berlin: Akademie Verlag.

Bildhauer, F. 2008. *Representing Information Structure in an HPSG Grammar of Spanish*. PhD thesis, Universität Bremen. Retrieved from http://www.hpsg.fu-berlin.de/~fbildhau/diss/ felix-bildhauer-diss.pdf. (accessed 31 January 2014).

Bird, S. and Klein, E. 1994. Phonological Analysis in Typed Feature Systems. *Computational Linguistics*, 20(3): 455–491.

Bonami, O. and Boyé, G. 2002. Suppletion and Dependency in Inflectional Morphology. In Van Eynde, F., Hellan, L., and Beermann, D. (eds), *The Proceedings of the 8th International Conference on Head-Driven Phrase Structure Grammar*, pages 51–70. Stanford, CA: CSLI Publications.

Bonami, O. and Delais-Roussarie, E. 2006. Metrical Phonology in HPSG. In Müller, S. (ed.), *Proceedings of the 13th International Conference on Head-driven Phrase Structure Grammar*, pages 39–59. Stanford, CA: CSLI Publications.

Bouma, G., Malouf, R., and Sag, I. A. 2001. Satisfying Constraints on Extraction and Adjunction. *Natural Language and Linguistic Theory*, 1(19): 1–65.

Bresnan, J. 1982. The Passive in Lexical Theory. In Bresnan, J. (ed.), *The Mental Representation of Grammatical Relations*, MIT Press Series on Cognitive Theory and Mental Representation, pages 3–86. Cambridge, MA; London: MIT Press.

Calcagno, M. 1995. Interpreting Lexical Rules. In Morrill, G. V. and Oehrle, R. T. (eds), *Proceedings of the Formal Grammar Conference*.

Copestake, A. 2002. *Implementing Typed Feature Structure Grammars*, Vol. 110 in CSLI Lecture Notes. Stanford, CA: CSLI Publications.

Copestake, A., Flickinger, D., Pollard, C., and Sag, I. 2005. Minimal Recursion Semantics. An Introduction. *Research on Language and Computation*, 3: 281–332. Retrieved from http://lingo.
stanford.edu/sag/papers/copestake.pdf. (accessed 31 January 2014).

Crysmann, B. and Bonami, O. 2012. Establishing Order in Type-based Realisational Morphology. In
Müller, S. (ed.), *Proceedings of the 19th International Conference on Head-Driven Phrase Structure Grammar*, pages 123–143.

Culicover, P. W. 1999. *Syntactic Nuts: Hard Cases, Syntactic Theory, and Language Acquisition*,
Vol. 1 of *Foundations of Syntax*. Oxford: Oxford University Press.

De Kuthy, K. 2002. *Discontinuous NPs in German*. Stanford, CA: CSLI Publications.

Engdahl, E. and Vallduví, E. 1996. Information Packaging in HPSG. In Grover, C. and Vallduví, E.
(eds), *Studies in HPSG*, Vol. 12 in Edinburgh Working Papers in Cognitive Science, pages 1–31.
Edinburgh: Centre for Cognitive Science, University of Edinburgh.

Fillmore, C. J., Kay, P., and O'Connor, M. C. 1988. Regularity and Idiomaticity in Grammatical
Constructions: The Case of Let Alone. *Language*, 64: 501–538.

Flickinger, D. P. 1987. *Lexical Rules in the Hierarchical Lexicon*. PhD thesis, Stanford University.

Gazdar, G., Klein, E., Pullum, G. K., and Sag, I. A. 1985. *Generalized Phrase Structure Grammar*.
Cambridge, MA: Harvard University Press.

Ginzburg, J. and Sag, I. A. 2000. *Interrogative Investigations: The Form, Meaning, and Use of
English Interrogatives*. Stanford, CA: CSLI Publications.

Haugereid, P. 2009. *Phrasal Subconstructions: A Constructionalist Grammar Design, Exemplified
with Norwegian and English*. PhD thesis, Norwegian University of Science and Technology.

Hinrichs, E. W. and Nakazawa, T. 1994. Linearizing AUXs in German Verbal Complexes. In
Nerbonne, J., Netter, K., and Pollard, C. J. (eds), *German in Head-driven Phrase Structure
Grammar*, Vol. 46 in CSLI Lecture Notes, pages 11–38. Stanford, CA: CSLI Publications.

Jackendoff, R. S. 1997. *The Architecture of the Language Faculty*, Vol. 28 of *Linguistic Inquiry
Monographs*. Cambridge, MA; London: MIT Press.

——— 2008. Construction after Construction and Its Theoretical Challanges. *Language*, 84(1):
8–28.

Jacobs, J. 2008. Wozu Konstruktionen? *Linguistische Berichte*, 213: 3–44.

Kathol, A. 2001. Positional Effects in a Monostratal Grammar of German. *Journal of Linguistics*,
37(1): 35–66.

Kay, P. and Fillmore, C. 1999. Grammatical Constructions and Linguistic Generalizations: The
What's X Doing Y? Construction. *Language*, 75(1): 1–33.

King, P. 1989. *A Logical Formalism for Head-driven Phrase Structure Grammar*. PhD thesis,
University of Manchester.

——— 1994. An Expanded Logical Formalism for Head-driven Phrase Structure Grammar.
Arbeitspapiere des SFB 340, University of Tübingen.

——— 1999. Towards Truth in Head-driven Phrase Structure Grammar. In Kordoni, V. (ed.), *Tübingen
Studies in Head-driven Phrase Structure Grammar*, Vol. 132 in Arbeitspapiere des SFB 340,
pages 301–352. Stuttgart, Germany: Univ., Sonderforschungsbereich 340.

Koenig, J.-P. 1999. *Lexical Relations*, Stanford Monographs in Linguistics. Stanford, CA: CSLI Publications.

Kuhn, J. 2007. Interfaces in Constraint-based Theories of Grammar. In Ramchand, G. and Reiss, C.
(eds), *The Oxford Handbook of Linguistic Interfaces*, pages 613–649. Oxford: Oxford University
Press.

Levine, R. D. 2003. Adjunct Valents: Cumulative Scoping Adverbial Constructions and
Impossible Descriptions. In Kim, J. and Wechsler, S. (eds), *Proceedings of the 9th International
Conference on Head-driven Phrase Structure Grammar*, pages 209–232. Stanford, CA: CSLI
Publications.

Levine, R. D. and Hukari, T. E. 2006. *The Unity of Unbounded Dependency Constructions*, Vol. 166
in CSLI Lecture Notes. Stanford, CA: CSLI Publications.

Melnik, N. 2005. From "Hand-Written" to Computationally Implemented HPSG Theories. In
Müller, S. (ed.), *The Proceedings of the 12th International Conference on Head-Driven Phrase
Structure Grammar*, pages 311–321. Stanford, CA: CSLI Publications. Retrieved from http://
cslipublications.stanford.edu/HPSG/6/. (accessed 31 January 2014).

Meurers, W. D. 1999. Raising Spirits (and Assigning Them Case). *Groninger Arbeiten zur German-
istischen Linguistik (GAGL)*, 43: 173–226.

_____ 2000. Lexical Generalizations in the Syntax of German Non-finite Constructions. Arbeitspapiere des SFB 340 145, Eberhard-Karls-Universität, Tübingen. Retrieved from http://www.ling.ohio-state.edu/~dm/papers/diss.html. (accessed 31 January 2014).

_____ 2001. On Expressing Lexical Generalizations in HPSG. *Nordic Journal of Linguistics*, 24(2).

Meurers, W. D. and Minnen, G. 1997. A Computational Treatment of Lexical Rules in HPSG as Covariation in Lexical Entries. *Computational Linguistics*, 2(4): 543–568.

Meurers, W. D., Penn, G., and Richter, F. 2002. A Web-based Instructional Platform for Constraint-based Grammar Formalisms and Parsing. In Radev, D. and Brew, C. (eds), *Effective Tools and Methodologies for Teaching NLP and CL*, pages 18–25. New Brunswick, NJ: Association for Computational Linguistics. Retrieved from http://www.sfs.uni-tuebingen.de/~dm/papers/diss.html.

Miller, P. H. and Sag, I. A. 1997. French Clitic Movement without Clitics or Movement. *Natural Language and Linguistic Theory*, 15(3): 573–639.

Monachesi, P. 1998. Italian Restructuring Verbs: A Lexical Analysis. In Hinrichs, E., Kathol, A., and Nakazawa, T. (eds), *Complex Predicates in Nonderivational Syntax*, Vol. 30 of *Syntax and Semantics*, pages 313–368. San Diego, CA: Academic Press.

Müller, S. 1999. *Deutsche Syntax deklarativ. Head-driven Phrase Structure Grammar für das Deutsche*, Vol. 394 in Linguistische Arbeiten. Tübingen: Max Niemeyer Verlag. Retrieved from http://hpsg.fu-berlin.de/~stefan/Pub/hpsg.html. (accessed 31 January 2014).

_____ 2002. *Complex Predicates: Verbal Complexes, Resultative Constructions, and Particle Verbs in German*, Vol. 13 in Studies in Constraint-based Lexicalism. Stanford, CA: CSLI Publications. Retrieved from http://hpsg.fu-berlin.de/~stefan/Pub/complex.html. (accessed 31 January 2014).

_____ 2005. Zur Analyse der deutschen Satzstruktur. *Linguistische Berichte*. Retrieved from http://hpsg.fu-berlin.de/~stefan/Pub/satz-lb.html. (accessed 31 January 2014).

_____ 2006. Phrasal or Lexical Constructions? *Language*, 82(4): 850–883. Retrieved from http://hpsg.fu-berlin.de/~stefan/Pub/phrasal.html. (accessed 31 January 2014).

_____ 2007. The Grammix CD Rom. A Software Collection for Developing Typed Feature Structure Grammars. In Holloway King, T. and Bender, E. (eds), *Grammar Engineering across Frameworks 2007*, Studies in Computational Linguistics Online. Stanford, CA: CSLI Publications.

_____ 2013a. *Grammatiktheorie*. Vol. 20 in Stauffenburg Einführungen. Tübingen: Stauffenburg Verlag, 2nd edition. Retrieved from http://hpsg.fu-berlin.de/~stefan/Pub/grammatiktheorie.html. (accessed 31 January 2014).

_____ 2013b. *Head-driven Phrase Structure Grammar: Eine Einführung*. Vol. 17 in Stauffenburg Einführungen. Tübingen: Stauffenburg Verlag, 3rd edition. Retrieved from http://hpsg.fu-berlin.de/~stefan/Pub/hpsg-lehrbuch.html. (accessed 31 January 2014).

Müller, S. and Wechsler, S. M. 2013. Lexical Approaches to Argument Structure. Ms. Freie Universität Berlin. Retrieved from http://hpsg.fu-berlin.de/~stefan/Pub/arg-st.html. (accessed 31 January 2014).

Müller, S. and Ørsnes, B. forthcoming. Danish in Head-driven Phrase Structure Grammar. Ms. Freie Universität Berlin. Retrieved from http://hpsg.fu-berlin.de/~stefan/Pub/danish.html. (accessed 31 January 2014).

Nerbonne, J., Netter, K., and Pollard, C. J. (eds) 1994. *German in Head-driven Phrase Structure Grammar*. Vol. 46 in CSLI Lecture Notes. Stanford, CA: CSLI Publications.

Penn, G. 2004. Balancing Clarity and Efficiency in Typed Feature Logic Through Delaying. In *Proceedings of the 42nd Meeting of the Association for Computational Linguistics*, pages 239–246.

Pollard, C. J. 1999. Strong Generative Capacity in HPSG. In Kathol, A., Koenig, J.-P., and Webelhuth, G. (eds), *Lexical and Constructional Aspects of Linguistic Explanation*, Vol. 1 in Studies in Constraint-Based Lexicalism, pages 281–298. Stanford, CA: CSLI Publications.

Pollard, C. J. and Moshier, A. M. 1990. Unifying Partial Descriptions of Sets. In Hanson, P. (ed.), *Information, Language and Cognition, Vancouver Studies in Cognitive Science I*, pages 285–322. Vancouver: University of British Columbia Press.

Pollard, C. J. and Sag, I. A. 1987. *Information-based Syntax and Semantics*. Stanford, CA: CSLI Publications.

Pollard, C. J. and Sag I. A. 1994. *Head-driven Phrase Structure Grammar*. Chicago, IL; London: University of Chicago Press.

Przepiórkowski, A. 1999. On Case Assignment and "Adjuncts as Complements". In Webelhuth, G., Koenig, J.-P., and Kathol, A. (eds), *Lexical and Constructional Aspects of Linguistic Explanation*, Vol. 1 in Studies in Constraint-Based Lexicalism, pages 231–245. Stanford, CA: CSLI Publications.

Pullum, G. K. 2007. The Evolution of Model-theoretic Frameworks in Linguistics. In Rogers, J. and Kepser, S. (eds), *Workshop Proceedings of Model-theoretic Syntax at 10*, pages 1–10.

Reape, M. 1994. Domain Union and Word Order Variation in German. In Nerbonne, J., Netter, K., and Pollard, C. J. (eds), *German in Head-driven Phrase Structure Grammar*, Vol. 46 in CSLI Lecture Notes, pages 151–198. Stanford, CA: CSLI Publications.

Richter, F. 2004a. *Foundations of Lexical Resource Semantics*. Habilitationsschrift, Seminar für Sprachwissenschaft, Eberhard-Karls-Universität Tübingen.

_____ 2004b. *A Mathematical Formalism for Linguistic Theories with an Application in Head-driven Phrase Structure Grammar*. Phil. dissertation (2000), Eberhard-Karls-Universität Tübingen.

_____ 2007. Closer to the Truth: A New Model Theory for HPSG. In Rogers, J. and Kepser, S. (eds), *Workshop Proceedings of Model-theoretic Syntax at 10*, pages 101–110.

Rogers, J. and Kepser, S. (eds) 2007. *Workshop Proceedings of Model-theoretic Syntax at 10*.

Sag, I. A. 1997. English Relative Clause Constructions. *Journal of Linguistics*, 33(2): 431–484. Retrieved from http://lingo.stanford.edu/sag/papers/rel-pap.pdf.

_____ 2012. Sign-based Construction Grammar: An Informal Synopsis. In Boas, H. C. and Sag, I. A. (eds), *Sign-based Construction Grammar*, pages 69–202. Stanford, CA: CSLI Publications.

Sag, I. A., Wasow, T., and Bender, E. M. 2003. *Syntactic Theory: A Formal Introduction*. Stanford, CA: CSLI Publications, 2nd edition.

Sag, I. A. and Wasow, T. 2011. Performance-compatible Competence Grammar. In Borsley, R. and Börjars, K. (eds), *Non-Transformational Syntax: Formal and Explicit Models of Grammar: A Guide to Current Models*, pages 359–377. Oxford; Cambridge, MA: Blackwell.

Van Eynde, F. 2006. NP-internal Agreement and the Structure of the Noun Phrase. *Journal of Linguistics*, 42(1): 139–186.

Webelhuth, G. 2012. The Distribution of That-Clauses in English: An SBCG Account. In Boas, H. C. and Sag, I. A. (eds), *Sign-based Construction Grammar*, pages 203–228. Chicago, IL: The University of Chicago Press.

Yip, M., Maling, J., and Jackendoff, R. S. 1987. Case in Tiers. *Language*, 63(2): 217–250.

27

Lexical-Functional Grammar

George Aaron Broadwell

1 Introduction

Lexical-Functional Grammar (LFG) is a syntactic theory first developed by Joan Bresnan and Ron Kaplan in the mid to late 1970s. Kaplan and Bresnan (1982) is a foundational source that lays out most of the basic elements of the theory. Though LFG has changed and evolved in numerous ways since its first development, many of its fundamental properties were established in these early papers and have remained relatively constant since then. Since Falk (2001), Bresnan (2001b), and Dalrymple (2001) all provide detailed book-length descriptions of current work in LFG, this chapter is oriented toward providing an overview of basic ideas of the theory for those who are unfamiliar with it. It is also focused on syntactic representations in LFG, though a fuller account would include semantic, prosodic, informational, and other representations. The last section of this chapter will talk about recent developments and changes in the theory.

2 Some fundamental ideas of LFG

I take the following ideas to be fundamental to LFG: **(a) Multiple syntactic representation:** Syntactic objects (words, phrases, sentences) have more than one representation; the different representations capture different properties of the objects in question. The different representations have different structural properties; some representations are expressed as syntactic trees and others are feature structures. **(b) Constituent structure** (c-str) shows word order and constituency. This representation uses traditional syntactic trees. Order is a crucial property of c-structure. The terminal nodes of such trees are words, not inflectional or derivational morphemes. Use of null elements in c-structure is kept to a minimum, and in many LFG analyses there are no empty categories at all. **(c) Functional structure** (f-str) captures information about grammatical functions, such as SUBJECT and OBJECT, as well as morphosyntactic information such as CASE, NUMBER, PERSON, TENSE and so on.[1] Linear order is irrelevant to f-structure. Features are formally represented as attribute value matrices (AVMs), where an attribute can take a symbol, a semantic form, a set, or another f-structure as its value. Identical symbols, sets, or f-structures can appear as values of more than one attribute in an f-structure, but the semantic forms are unique. Null elements are frequent in f-structure. Featural information at f-structure can come from multiple sources, including the lexicon, morphology, and c-structure. **(d) Variable correspondence:** While c-structure and f-structure are universal, the correspondence between the representations is cross-linguistically variable. The grammar for any individual language needs to include a specification of how word order and constituency correspond to grammatical functions in the language. Formally this involves working out the correspondence rules between c-structure and f-structure.

It is easiest to understand these fundamentals by looking at a comparison of similar sentences in two languages, Warlpiri and English, along with their c-structure and f-structure representations:[2]

(1)

    a.   Kurdu-ngku   wita-ngku   ka   wajilipi-nyi.   *Warlpiri*
          Child-ERG   small-ERG   ASP   chase-PRES
          'The small child is chasing it.' (Simpson 1991: 265–267)

    b.

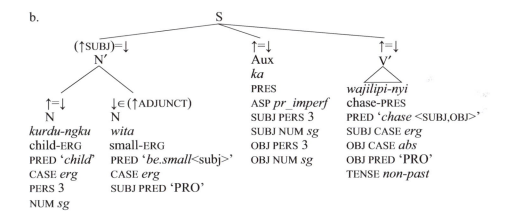

c.

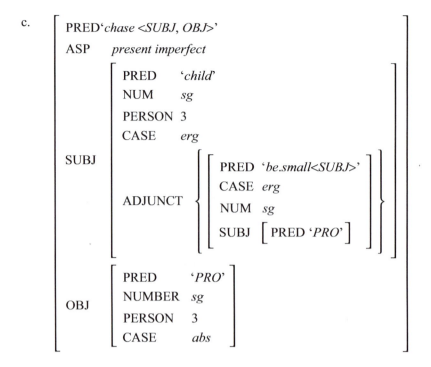

(2)

a. The small child is chasing it.   *English*

b.

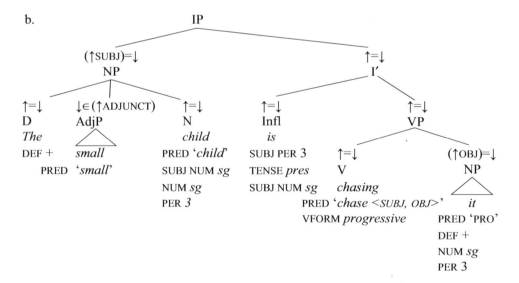

c.
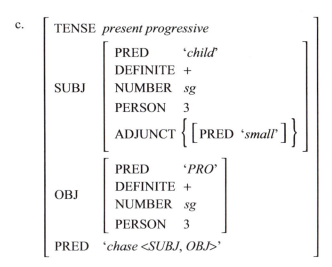

$$
\left[
\begin{array}{ll}
\text{TENSE} & \textit{present progressive} \\
\text{SUBJ} & \left[
\begin{array}{ll}
\text{PRED} & \textit{'child'} \\
\text{DEFINITE} & + \\
\text{NUMBER} & \textit{sg} \\
\text{PERSON} & 3 \\
\text{ADJUNCT} & \left\{ \left[\text{PRED} \;\; \textit{'small'} \right] \right\}
\end{array}
\right] \\
\text{OBJ} & \left[
\begin{array}{ll}
\text{PRED} & \textit{'PRO'} \\
\text{DEFINITE} & + \\
\text{NUMBER} & \textit{sg} \\
\text{PERSON} & 3
\end{array}
\right] \\
\text{PRED} & \textit{'chase <SUBJ, OBJ>'}
\end{array}
\right]
$$

Let us see how these representations illustrate the fundamental ideas listed above.

1. **Multiple representations**. As these examples show, each sentence in Warlpiri and English has a distinct c-structure and f-structure. The c-structures are expressed as tree diagrams; the f-structures are AVMs.
2. **C-structure properties**. Each c-structure shows the linear order and constituency of the sentence. The terminal nodes in the c-structure trees are words, not inflectional or derivational morphemes. Note in particular that *kurdu-ngku* 'child-erg' is a single node in the Warlpiri c-structure (1b), as is the word *chased* in the English tree (2b). Some languages have separate words or clitics which express case or tense, and in those languages it would be appropriate to posit Case and Tense as functional heads. There are no empty elements in the c-structures. In particular, there is no null pronoun corresponding to the object of the verb 'chased' in the c-structure representation of the Warlpiri sentence.
3. **F-structure properties**. Because feature structures are less familiar to many readers than tree structures, it is worth spending a little time on the details of an f-structure in order to make its interpretation clear. Each group of elements enclosed by brackets gives us information about some linguistic element (for example, a sentence or a noun phrase.) The order of features in a feature structure is irrelevant. PRED features, which represent the semantic form and subcategorization of the f-structure heads, are conventionally listed first in f-structures, but nothing bears on this. So the fact that the PRED feature appears first in the Warlpiri f-structure and last in the English f-structure does not mean anything. The PRED will in general show the semantics of the head of the linguistic object that is being described.

If we consider the f-structure in (2c), the largest set of brackets contains the PRED attribute whose value is *'chase<SUBJ, obj>'*. In other words, the linguistic object (or clause) being described is headed by the word that means 'chase'. F-structures conventionally include a shorthand representation of the predicate's subcategorization as well, so we know that 'chase' is transitive. We also know that the clause described has the *present progressive* value for the feature TENSE.

Within the clause, there are two other subsidiary feature structures, one headed by *child*, and one headed by a pronominal. (We list its PRED value as 'PRO', since the actual referent of the pronominal will be established by the discourse.) The f-structures associated with *child* and the pronoun each have their own PERSON and NUMBER features. When we look at the range of the kinds of attribute value pairs that are needed in f-structures we see that some attributes, such as TENSE, take an atomic value, while other attributes, such as SUBJ, take other feature structures as a value. Yet other attributes, such as PRED, take a semantic form as a value. Finally, the attribute ADJUNCT has a set as its value; in our example the set has only one member, but adjunct elements may be multiply instantiated in a sentence.

We also see that, while the c-structure does not contain null elements, the f-structure of the Warlpiri sentence does contain a null element 'PRO' as the value of the OBJ PRED. We also see that features at f-structure come from multiple sources – some lexical, some morphological, and some due to annotations on the c-structure.

In the English f-structure (2c), the word *child* has at least the following features specified in the lexicon: [PRED '*child*'; NUM *sg*; PER 3]. The words *is* and *chasing* have at least the features [PRED '*chase* <SUBJ, OBJ>', SUBJ NUM *sg*; SUBJ PER 3; TENSE *present*; VFORM *progressive*]. The fact that *the small child* serves as subject of the sentence comes from the annotation ($\uparrow$SUBJ)=$\downarrow$ on the c-structure node which dominates it.

In the Warlpiri f-structure (1c), the word *kurdu-ngku* 'child-erg' contains two morphemes. The first morpheme, *kurdu*, has the features [PRED '*child*'; NUM *sg*; PER 3] in its lexical entry, and the case suffix *-ngku* adds the feature [CASE *erg*].

The language-specific rules that regulate the correspondence between the c-structure and f-structure are expressed by PS-rules, annotated to show information about the correct correspondence. For English, the relevant PS rules for this subset of the grammar are:

(3) a. IP $\rightarrow$ NP   I'
              ($\uparrow$SUBJ)=$\downarrow$ $\uparrow$=$\downarrow$
     b. I' $\rightarrow$ Infl   VP
              $\uparrow$=$\downarrow$ $\uparrow$=$\downarrow$
     c. VP $\rightarrow$ V   (NP)   (NP)   (PP)
              $\uparrow$=$\downarrow$ ($\uparrow$OBJ)=$\downarrow$ ($\uparrow$OBJ$_\theta$)=$\downarrow$ ($\uparrow$OBL$_\theta$)=$\downarrow$
     d. NP $\rightarrow$ (Det)   AdjP* N
              $\uparrow$=$\downarrow$ $\downarrow$$\in$($\uparrow$ADJUNCT) $\uparrow$=$\downarrow$

For Warlpiri, the relevant PS rules for this subset of the grammar are:

(4) a. S $\rightarrow$ (AUX) α α*
              α = N', V', Particle
              Assign $\uparrow$=$\downarrow$ or (GF$\uparrow$)=$\downarrow$ freely, where GF is any grammatical function.
     b. N' $\rightarrow$ N^{-1}* N*
              Assign $\uparrow$=$\downarrow$ or $\downarrow$ $\in$($\uparrow$ADJUNCT) freely

The issue of variable correspondence between these levels of representation is a major area of research within LFG to which I turn in the following section.

3   Correspondence and annotation

The annotated PS-rules for a language show the same order and constituency relationships as conventional PS-rules, along with information about how each element in the PS-rule corresponds to f-structure.

The English and Warlpiri PS-rules express two different ways in which c-structures and f-structures may be related to each other. The Warlpiri system is of the non-configurational type, with a very free mapping between the two structures. English, in contrast, has a tightly constrained mapping between c-structure and f-structure.

It is easiest to understand the way annotation works if we look again at the English c-structure and f-structure pair for the sentence *The small child is chasing it* (repeated here as 5).[3] The root of the c-structure tree will correspond to the outermost attribute-value matrix in the f-structure.

(5)

   a. The small child is chasing it. *English*

   b.

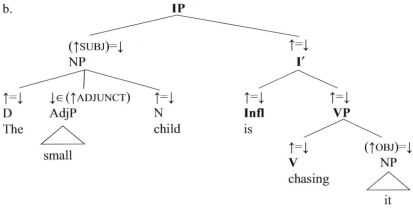

   c.

$$\begin{bmatrix} \text{TENSE} & \textit{present progressive} \\[4pt] \text{SUBJ} & \begin{bmatrix} \text{PRED} & \textit{`child'} \\ \text{DEFINITE} & + \\ \text{NUMBER} & \textit{sg} \\ \text{PERSON} & 3 \\ \text{ADJUNCT} & \left\{ \begin{bmatrix} \text{PRED `small'} \end{bmatrix} \right\} \end{bmatrix} \\[4pt] \text{OBJ} & \begin{bmatrix} \text{PRED} & \textit{`PRO'} \\ \text{DEFINITE} & + \\ \text{NUMBER} & \textit{sg} \\ \text{PERSON} & 3 \end{bmatrix} \\[4pt] \text{PRED} & \textit{`chase <SUBJ,OBJ>'} \end{bmatrix}$$

Any node under the root with the annotation ↑=↓ will contribute its featural information to this AVM, and of the daughters of the nodes with the ↑=↓ annotation, any daughter with the ↑=↓ annotation will also contribute its featural information. In the tree shown here, all the nodes in boldface are connected by a series of ↑=↓ annotations to the root, and all of the information from all these nodes goes into the AVM, which corresponds to the root.

Thus, in this AVM, the information about the tense and predicate of the sentence are contributed by the Infl and the verb to the AVM which corresponds to the root.

We now examine the daughters of the root node which do not have the ↑=↓ annotation. The [NP, IP] node has the annotation (↑SUBJ)=↓ which means that this node (↓) plays the role of (=) SUBJ in its mother's f-structure (↑SUBJ). Within the NP, both the Det and the N have the ↑=↓ annotation, showing that both contribute to the SUBJ f-structure. In this example, *the* contributes the [DEFINITE +] feature and *child* contributes the features [PRED *'child'*; PERSON 3; NUMBER *sg*].

Also among the daughters of NP is an AdjP annotated ↓ ∈ (↑ADJUNCT), read as 'this node is a subset of the mother's ADJUNCTS'. Because ADJUNCT is a set-valued attribute, multiple sister nodes might have this annotation, and they would all go into a set.

4 Variable analyses: A strength and potential weakness

The analysis of the sentence shown here uses a NP structure, where N serves as the head of NP. However, since Det is also annotated ↑=↓, this has the effect of making it a kind of co-head at f-structure.

Some LFG analyses of English instead use a DP analysis of English. It would also be possible to have the AdjP adjoined to the complement of the Det, rather than a sister to the Det. If we implemented both these changes to the analysis, we could instead have a c-structure tree like the following:

(6)

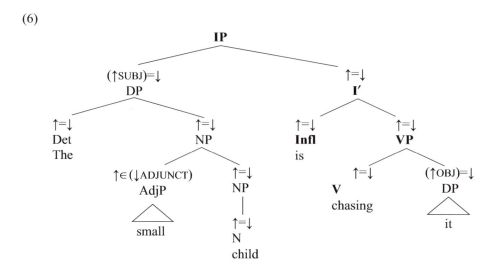

Given the annotations on this c-structure, it will map to exactly the same f-structure as the previous c-structure.

Depending on one's ideas about the relationship between theory and description, this flexibility in c-structure analyses might be considered either a strength or a weakness. From the LFG point of view, it is entirely possible that some languages have NPs with Det co-heads, while others have DPs. It might also be the case that a language has evolved historically from one structure to the other.

Since c-structure in LFG encodes only order and constituency, facts about agreement or predication relations would not be good arguments for the right c-structure. This usually makes it necessary to find some facts about word order in order to decide on the correct c-structure analysis.

While this flexibility of analysis allows the theory to model descriptive generalizations very closely, it is also true that LFG predicts a wider range of possible syntactic trees than some other syntactic theories. This might be regarded as a weakness if one views the aim of syntax as constraining possible structures as tightly as possible; on the other hand, if syntactic structures are rather variable cross-linguistically one might view the LFG flexibility of analysis as a virtue, since it does not require the use of a small set of structures in cases where they are not well-motivated.

5 F-structure well-formedness constraints

While c-structures can be rather variable in LFG analyses, f-structures are much more uniform cross-linguistically, and constraints on f-structures play a key role in explaining many phenomena related to agreement, case, subcategorization, and anaphora.

To see the role of f-structure in accounting for agreement, let us consider again the subject NP in the previous English example *The small child is chasing it*. If instead, we had ungrammatical string **These small child is chasing it*:

(7)

a.

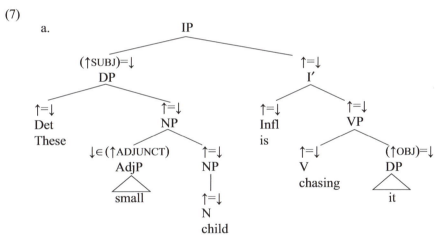

b.

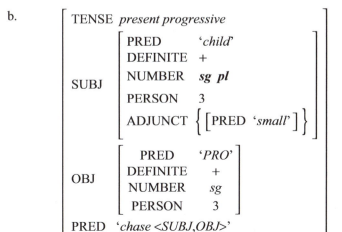

There is nothing wrong with this c-structure (7a), but when the corresponding f-structure (7b) is constructed, we see the following feature clash: The word *these* contributes the features [DEFINITE +; DEIXIS *distal*; NUMBER *pl*], while the word *child* contributes the features [PRED 'child'; PERSON 3; NUMBER *sg*]. Because the annotations on the Det and the N cause both sets of information to go to the same f-structure, the resulting f-structure has conflicting values for NUMBER. This f-structure violates one of the basic well-formedness conditions for f-structures, *Consistency* (8), which can be stated as follows:[4]

(8)   *Consistency*: In any f-structure, every attribute has exactly one value.

Because NUMBER has two values in the f-structure corresponding to the subject, the sentence is predicted to be ungrammatical.

In this example, the Det and N serve as co-heads of the corresponding f-structure, so their features must be compatible with each other. We can also account for agreement at a longer distance, such as between subject and object, by allowing an auxiliary or verb to specify features for its arguments. Consider the c-structure (9a) and f-structure (9b) of the ungrammatical string *The small child are chasing it*:

(9)

a.

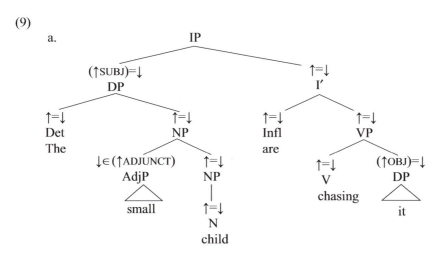

b.

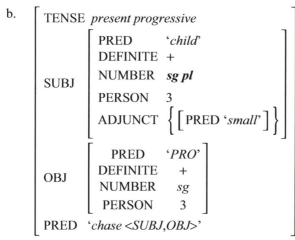

The same clashing f-structure results – in this case, because the word *are* has the features [TENSE *present progressive*; SUBJ NUM *pl*]. Here we see that *are* specifies not only its own features but also the number feature for the subject.[5] The lexically specified features of *are* will put the feature [NUM *pl*] in the f-structure for the SUBJ, but the features of *child* will put the feature [NUM *sg*] in the same f-structure.

Two other important features are *completeness* and *coherence*, which together ensure that predicates have neither too many nor too few arguments. To understand these principles, we first need to understand the grammatical functions that LFG assumes and the ways in which they are classified.

(10)

Grammatical Function	Definition	Examples
SUBJECT (SUBJ)	Subject	*John likes hummus.*
OBJECT (OBJ)	Primary/first object	*The senator sponsored <u>the bill</u>.* *The senator sent his constituents <u>a newsletter</u>.*
OBJECT$_\theta$ (OBJ$_\theta$)	Secondary, thematically restricted object	*The senator sent his constituents a newsletter.*
OBLIQUE$_\theta$ (OBL$_\theta$)	A complement which is a PP or has oblique case	*The senator sent a newsletter <u>to his constituents</u>.*
COMPLEMENT (COMP)	Clausal complement which contains its subject	*The Times reported <u>that the senator had resigned</u>.*
OPEN COMPLEMENT (XCOMP)	Clausal complement which does not contain its subject	*I told John <u>to go</u>.*
ADJUNCT (ADJ)	Modifer, non-argument	*John likes <u>spicy</u> hummus.*
OPEN ADJUNCT (XADJ)	Adjunct missing its subject	*<u>Finding Paris too expensive</u>, Mary left for Sofia a day early.*
POSSESSIVE (POSS)[6]	Possessor	*<u>Margaret's</u> contribution*
TOPIC (TOP)	Grammaticalized discourse function for old information. Must be linked to another grammatical function.	*Hummus$_i$, I love it$_i$.* *A student <u>whose GPA</u> __ is below 2.0 for three semesters faces suspension.*
FOCUS (FOC)	Grammaticalized discourse function for new information. Must be linked to another grammatical function.	*<u>Which books</u> do you recommend __?*

Of these functions, the governable functions are:

(11) *Governable functions*: SUBJ, OBJ, OBJ$_\theta$, OBL$_\theta$, COMP, XCOMP

By governable, we essentially mean the functions that appear in the subcategorizations of the verbs of a language. Given this definition of governable functions, *Completeness* and *Coherence* can be defined as follows:

(12) *Completeness*
An f-structure is complete if and only if it contains all the governable grammatical functions listed in the subcategorization of its predicate.

(13) *Coherence*

An f-structure is coherent if and only if all the governable grammatical functions it contains are listed in the subcategorization of its predicate.

Completeness and Coherence play a role in LFG comparable to the Theta Criterion in Government Binding Theory, Full Interpretation in Principles and Parameters, or the Valence Principle in HPSG.

We can see how these principles work by considering the ungrammatical strings *The small child is chasing the dog the cat* and *The small child is chasing*. The c-structure (14a) and f-structure (14b) are shown below:

(14)

a.

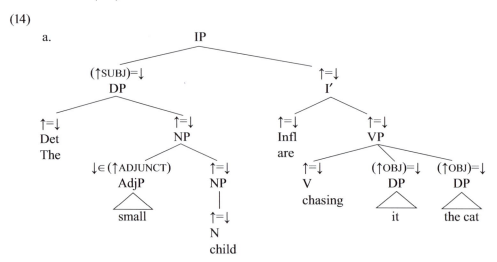

b

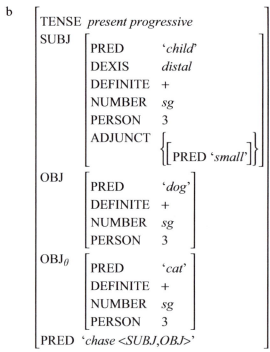

The f-structure for *The small child is chasing the dog the cat* violates Coherence because the governable grammatical function OBJ_θ appears in the f-structure but does not appear in the subcategorization *chase<SUBJ, OBJ>*.

Turning from a sentence with too many arguments to a sentence with too few, we can consider the sentence *The small child is chasing*, which violates Completeness. The c-structure is shown in (15a) and the f-structure is shown in (15b). This sentence violates Completeness because the subcategorization for *chase <SUBJ, OBJ>* calls for both a SUBJ and OBJ, but this f-structure does not contain an OBJ.

(15)

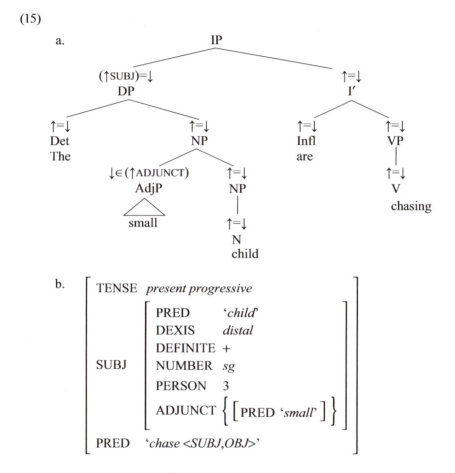

Another implication of the Coherence which is perhaps not as immediately obvious is that, with few exceptions, nearly every f-structure contains a PRED.[7] If it did not, then the string *The small child the dog* would be allowed. Since the SUBJ and OBJ functions are governable, the fact that they do not appear in the subcategorization of any predicate means that this sentence will violate Coherence.

6 Endocentric and non-endocentric structures

The flexibility of c-structure analyses in LFG, discussed above for the English NP or DP, is also shown by comparing the English and Warlpiri sentences. Warlpiri is a non-configurational language with extremely free word order. Hale (1983) and Simpson (1991) have given a number of arguments against the existence of a VP constituent in Warlpiri and, if we examine the PS-rule for the Warlpiri S (repeated below), we see that there is no VP rule.

(16) S → (AUX) α α*
α = N′, V′, Particle
Assign ↑=↓ or (GF↑) =↓ freely, where GF is any grammatical function.

A brief clarification on the position of auxiliaries is necessary to understand this rule. Simpson (1991) argues that auxiliaries are generated in initial position. If an auxiliary is monosyllabic, it obligatorily appears in second position after the initial α; if composed of more than one syllable, the encliticization process is optional. This repositioning of the auxiliary is the result of a late-level rule of sentence phonology, which Simpson (1991: 63) formulates as follows:

(17) *Warlpiri encliticization rule*:]AUX [α] [α]* → [α+AUX] [α]*

This example also shows something about the LFG conception of the relationship between c-structure and phonology. C-structure is thought of as being very close to the phonological realization of the sentence, but cliticization processes are also allowed to reorder the string before pronunciation. However, more extensive kinds of stylistic rules, which reorder phrases, are banned.

Returning to the question of the Warlpiri PS-rule, Simpson's rule accounts for both nominal and verbal sentences, so there is no obligatory V node under S. Assignment of annotations to the nodes is also free. This PS-rule will therefore massively over-generate structures, but the well-formedness conditions on f-structures can successfully rule out most of the bad results.

Consider, first, sentences that contain a verb. If we generate more than one verb, we will have a situation that can be schematically depicted as follows:

(18)

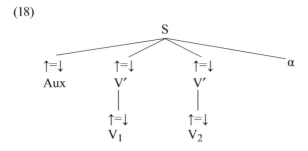

This c-structure would lead to an f-structure such as (19), where the AVM associated with the root of the tree has a PRED attribute with two values: one associated with the first verb and the other associated with the second verb. PRED may have only a single value, so this is a Consistency violation.

(19)

$$\begin{bmatrix} Other\ Attributes & Other\ Values \\ \text{PRED} & verb_1 \quad verb_2 \end{bmatrix}$$

Suppose we insert a V′ into the structure along with one or more N′ structures. Then if we insert more or fewer N's than are listed in the subcategorization of the predicate or if we assign these N's functions other than those called for in the subcategorization, we will violate Coherence, Completeness, or both.

Simpson also assumes that the lexical entries of verbs specify the case of the arguments associated with them. For intransitive verbs, this will be absolutive case for the subject, and for transitive verbs absolutive on the object and ergative on the subjects. Other cases will be associated with particular semantic roles.

The verb *wajilipi* 'chase' requires ergative case for its subject. If we instead use absolutive case on the subject, the sentence will be ungrammatical with the indicated sense:

(20) *Kurdu wita   ka   wajilipi-nyi.
     Child small ASP chase-PRES
     'The small child is chasing it.'

(Simpson 1991: 265–267)

The ungrammaticality of this example will follow from the Consistency requirement, since lexical entry for the verb *wajilipi* includes at least [PRED 'chase'<SUBJ, OBJ>; SUBJ CASE *erg*, OBJ CASE *abs*]. Since the initial NP has been assigned the grammatical function SUBJECT, the [CASE *abs*] feature from *kurdu* and *wita* will also go into the f-structure corresponding to the SUBJ. There it will conflict with the information coming from the verb, as shown in (21):

(21)

$$
\begin{bmatrix}
\text{PRED} & \text{'chase<SUBJ,OBJ>'} \\
\text{TENSE} & \text{present imperfect} \\
\text{SUBJ} & \begin{bmatrix}
\text{PRED} & \text{'child'} \\
\text{DEFINITE} & + \\
\text{NUMBER} & sg \\
\text{PERSON} & 3 \\
\text{CASE} & \textbf{abs erg} \\
\text{ADJUNCT} & \left\{ \begin{bmatrix}
\text{PRED 'small'} \\
\text{CASE } abs \\
\text{NUM } sg \\
\text{SUBJ } [\text{PRED 'PRO'}]
\end{bmatrix} \right\}
\end{bmatrix} \\
\text{OBJ} & \begin{bmatrix}
\text{PRED} & \text{'PRO'} \\
\text{DEFINITE} & + \\
\text{NUMBER} & sg \\
\text{PERSON} & 3
\end{bmatrix}
\end{bmatrix}
$$

Thus the basic well-formedness conditions for f-structure, along with free assignment of functions to the c-structure, gives a good account of the non-configurationality of Warlpiri syntax.

7 Pro-drop via lexical rule

If we examine the Warlpiri c-structure/f-structure correspondence more closely, another question arises. How is it that the requirement for an object in the subcategorization of *chase* <SUBJ, OBJ> is met?

The most basic lexical entry for *wajilipi* ought to contain the features [PRED 'chase' <SUBJ, OBJ>; SUBJ CASE *erg*, OBJ CASE *abs*]. Simpson (1991: 148) argues for a lexical rule that optionally introduces PRO as an argument of a verb, stated as follows:

(22) *PRO-introduction rule*
   If an argument-taking predicate selects a grammatical function G, it may optionally introduce a null pronominal to represent G by introducing a PRED feature equation (↑G PRED) = 'PRO'.

Thus the form of the lexical entry that is relevant for this particular Warlpiri sentence is ['chase<SUBJ, OBJ>'; SUBJ CASE *erg*, OBJ CASE ABS, OBJ PRED '*PRO*'].

Because the PRO introduction rule is optional, we can use the version of the lexical entry without [OBJ PRED 'PRO'] when a nominal object is present and the version of the lexical entry with [OBJ PRED 'PRO'] when the nominal object is not present.

What would happen if the rule of PRO introduction were obligatory? Andrews (1990) argues that this is the situation with Irish synthetic agreement. Some inflected forms in the Irish verbal paradigm preclude the use of a pronoun, as in the following examples (McCloskey and Hale 1984: 489–490):

(23) a. Chuirfinn   isteach   ar   an   phost   sin
        put.CONDIT.1SG   into   on   the   job   that
        'I would apply for that job.'
     b. *Chuirfinn   mé   isteach   ar   an   phost   sin
        put.CONDIT.1SG   I   into   on   the   job   that

Andrews argues that the synthetic form of the lexical entry for the verb 'put' contains at least the following information [PRED '*apply*<SUBJ, OBL$_\theta$>'; SUBJ NUM *sg*; SUBJ PER 1; SUBJ PRED 'PRO']. If we construct the f-structure for the ungrammatical Irish sentence, the relevant portion of the f-structure will be as follows (24):

(24)

$$\begin{bmatrix} \text{ASPECT} & \textit{conditional} & \\ \text{SUBJ} & \begin{bmatrix} \text{PRED} & PRO_1 \ PRO_2 \\ \text{NUM} & \textit{sg} \\ \text{PER} & 1 \end{bmatrix} \\ \text{OBL}_\theta & [...] \\ \text{PRED} & \textit{'apply<SUBJ,OBJ>'} \end{bmatrix}$$

This will violate Consistency, since the SUBJ PRED feature will have two values, '*PRO$_1$*' and '*PRO$_2$*'. Recall from above that all semantic forms are uniquely instantiated, so, although both are pronominals, they count as distinct for the purposes of the Consistency requirement.

8 Rank at f-structure and the relational hierarchy

Despite the flat c-structure of the Warlpiri sentence, there are nevertheless a number of subject/object asymmetries in the language, including familiar ones such as the following:

(25) a. Ngarrka-ngku   ka-nyanu   nya-nyi.
      Man-ERG   PRES-REFLEX   see-PRES
      'The man sees himself.'
   b. *Ngarrka   ka-nyanu   nya-nyi.
      Man   PRES-REFLEX   see-PRES
      (Himself sees the man.)

(Hale 1983; Simpson 1991: 14–15)

These will have very similar c-structure representations, but rather different f-structures.[8] The grammatical c-structure/f-structure pair are shown as (26); the ungrammatical pair is (27). Since the c-structure representations do not include any null pronouns, we obviously cannot rely on these representations to distinguish the two sentences from each other.

(26)

a.

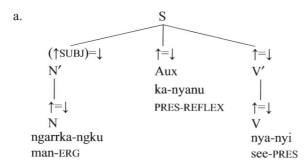

b.

$$\begin{bmatrix} \text{PRED} & \text{'see<SUBJ,OBJ>'} \\ \text{TENSE} & \text{present imperfect} \\ \text{SUBJ} & \begin{bmatrix} \text{PRED} & \text{'man'} \\ \text{NUMBER} & \text{sg} \\ \text{PERSON} & 3 \\ \text{INDEX} & i \end{bmatrix} \\ \text{OBJ} & \begin{bmatrix} \text{PRED} & \text{'PRO'} \\ \text{NUMBER} & \text{sg} \\ \text{PERSON} & 3 \\ \text{INDEX} & i \end{bmatrix} \end{bmatrix}$$

(27) a.

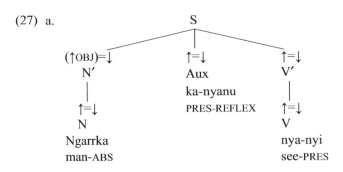

b.

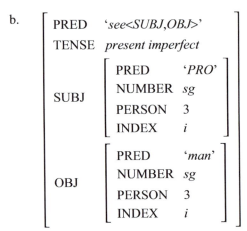

However, the reflexive affix on the auxiliary indicates that there is PRO argument of the main predicate that is coreferential with another argument, and we can use this information to construct the correct f-structure for the sentence. F-structure representations do include the pronouns, so they are a more appropriate representation for capturing the contrast. Here LFG uses two related notions. The first notion is that there is a hierarchy of grammatical functions, as follows:

(28) *Relational Hierarchy*: SUBJ > OBJ > OBJ$_\theta$ > OBL$_\theta$ > COMP > ADJ

The second notion is one of containment at f-structure. The two may be combined into a single definition of rank and a definition of binding that includes outranking.

(29) *Syntactic Rank*:
A locally outranks B if A and B belong to the same f-structure and A is more prominent than B on the relational hierarchy. A outranks B if A locally outranks some C which contains B. (Bresnan 2001b:213)

(30) *Binding*: A binds B if A outranks B and A and B are coindexed.

A general condition on reflexive pronouns in most languages is that they must be bound in some domain (see Truswell, this volume). Warlpiri is like other languages in that it requires the element associated with the reflexive to be bound.

In the f-structure for 'The man sees himself', the object PRO is bound because its antecedent outranks it. The antecedent is a SUBJ and the reflexive is an OBJ. In the f-structure for 'Himself sees the man', the antecedent fails to bind the pronoun since it fails to outrank it.

This portion of the LFG theory of anaphor is thus rather similar in conception to a theory of anaphor in terms of asymmetrical c-command. However, note that c-command is a notion defined over tree structures, so if a language has a flat structure with subject and object as sisters, c-command does not work correctly to predict the possible coreference relations. Since the LFG approach to anaphor also uses the relational hierarchy, it can distinguish f-structure coarguments from each other based on grammatical function.

Another advantage to a theory of anaphora that includes grammatical functions is that it is quite natural to express constraints on the grammatical function of an anaphor or antecedent. So if an anaphor requires a subject antecedent, this is an easily expressed generalization within LFG.

It is also possible that the correct formulation of the constraints on anaphora in some languages may refer to c-structure or a combination of c-structure and f-structure constraints. K.P. Mohanan (1982; 1983) argues, for example, that an overt pronoun may not precede a quantificational binder (e.g., *each child*), a generalization which refers to c-structure precedence. Bresnan's (1995; 2001b) approach to Weak Crossover also uses a combination of f-structural and c-structural constraints to account for typological variation in the phenomenon.

9 LFG approaches to movement and empty categories

Most LFG approaches to long-distance dependency do not posit empty elements in the c-structure representation (but see Falk (2001); Bresnan (2001b) for an alternative view). However, all would posit an element that plays multiple roles in f-structure. In general one of these roles is a grammatical function (SUBJ, OBJ, NUM, etc) while the other role is a discourse function (TOPIC, FOCUS). Thus Dalrymple (2001: 397) gives the following c-structure and f-structure pair for the sentence *Chris, we think that David likes*:[9]

(31) a.

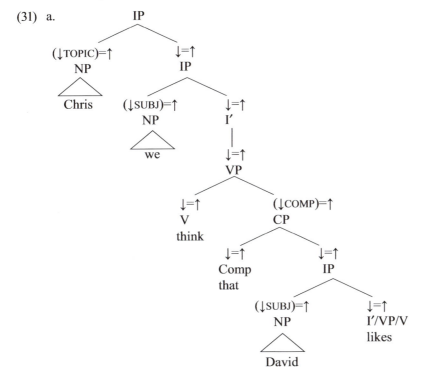

b.
$$
\begin{bmatrix}
\text{PRED} & \textit{'think<SUBJ,COMP>'} \\
\text{TOPIC} & \begin{bmatrix} \text{PRED} & \textit{'Chris'} \end{bmatrix} \; \boxed{1} \\
\text{SUBJ} & \begin{bmatrix} \text{PRED} & \textit{'PRO'} \\ \text{NUM} & \textit{pl} \\ \text{PER} & 1 \end{bmatrix} \\
\text{COMP} & \begin{bmatrix} \text{PRED} & \textit{'like<SUBJ,OBJ>'} \\ \text{SUBJ} & \begin{bmatrix} \text{PRED} & \textit{'David'} \end{bmatrix} \\ \text{OBJ} & \boxed{1} \end{bmatrix}
\end{bmatrix}
$$

In the f-structure for this sentence (31b), we see that the NP *Chris* is both the TOPIC of the main clause and the OBJECT of the subordinate clause. This is shown here in the f-structure by the tag $\boxed{1}$, which identifies this f-structure as the value of two different attributes.[10]

Constraints on long-distance dependencies within LFG would be stated over the path between the shared positions within the f-structure. The outermost part of such a path is typically a discourse function such as TOPIC or FOCUS and the innermost part is a grammatical function. In the example given here, the path between the TOPIC and the OBJECT must pass through the f-structure labeled COMP, and this is a licit path. The general LFG approach to such constructions, outlined in more detail in Dalrymple (2001) and Falk (2001), is to look at restrictions on the outermost function, the innermost function, and various portions of the path of a long-distance dependency path through an f-structure. It thus shares with other forms of generative grammar a goal of accounting for such constructions in grammar.

A possible advantage for an approach based in f-structures is that they are rich in featural information that seems relevant to long-distance dependencies, such as the distinctions between COMPLEMENTS and ADJUNCTS and featural information about tense.

In the LFG approach to long-distance dependencies, the f-structure contains a shared element which is comparable to trace in other theories. In the LFG treatment of passives, however, there is no comparable element. Instead, LFG posits distinct lexical entries for the active and passive verbs in sentences such as the following:

(32) a. John captured the prisoner. *'capture<SUBJ,OBJ>'*
      b. The prisoner was captured. *'(be) captured<SUBJ>'*

How does one capture the generalization about the relationship between the two lexical entries? In early forms of LFG, there were lexical rules that directly mapped one lexical entry into another lexical entry. However, in current LFG practice, the generalization is captured through another level of representation, **argument-structure**, plus a set of linking rules, known as Lexical Mapping Theory (Bresnan and Kanerva 1989; Alsina 1996), which link arguments with particular thematic roles to preferred grammatical functions.

To take the very simple case of the verb under discussion, we can assume the active form of *capture* has the following thematic roles, and that they are classified by Lexical Mapping Theory with two features [± Object] and [± Restricted] as follows:

(33) *capture* <   Agent,   Patient>
                 [-Object]   [-Restricted]

The Lexical Mapping Rules then apply to link the thematically highest ranking argument to the SUBJ grammatical function.

Passive morphology has the effect of making the Agent of the verb unavailable for linking. We can represent this with the null symbol in our argument-structure representation of the passive:

(34) *(be) captured* < Agent, Patient>
                  Ø   [-Restricted]

Because the Patient is now the highest thematic argument available for linking, the Lexical Mapping Rules will link it with the SUBJ grammatical function.

There is still a lexical rule for passive in English in current LFG, but it is far less powerful than its earlier incarnation. An approximate version of the rule would be as follows:

(35) V <θ, ...> ⇒ V < θ, ...>
              [VFORM *past participle*] Ø

We can interpret this rule as follows: 'Take a verb with subcategorization that selects for an initial thematic argument θ plus some number of other arguments. Make the verb form past participle and make the initial argument θ unavailable for linking.'

Lexical Mapping Theory has been applied to the English passive and also to the analysis of Romance causatives (Alsina 1996), complex predication (Butt 1995), and Chicheŵa locative inversion (Bresnan and Kanerva 1989).

10 Other areas of research in LFG

This chapter has surveyed some basic ideas in LFG, but many areas of productive research in LFG have gone unmentioned. In addition to the two primary syntactic representations, c-structure and f-structure, LFG also assumes representations of other parts of the grammar which interact in important ways with the syntax.

Phrasal semantics is represented in an s-structure representation, and the theory of *glue semantics* (Dalrymple 1999; Asudeh 2012) has in recent years developed an account of the mapping function between syntax and semantics, where the primary syntactic representation providing input to the mapping is the f-structure, not the c-structure.

I(nformation)-structure is a representation that shows the informational status of constituents as old, new, prominent, or neutral. Some such information is conveyed by the grammaticalized discourse functions TOPIC and FOCUS, but i-structure may also be determined by c-structure, morphology, and prosody. King (1995), Butt and King (1996), and Dalrymple and Mycock (2011) are influential works on i-structure and its interaction with prosody. See Dalrymple and Nikolaeva (2011) for a more recent application of i-structure to the analysis of differential object marking.

Apart from the exploration of the different kinds of representations that are necessary and the mapping relationships between them, this chapter should also mention that Optimality-Theoretic approaches to LFG have been an important line of research in recent years. Major sources include Bresnan (2000; 2001a), Sells (2001), and Kuhn (2003).

Finally, LFG continues to be one of the leading approaches to computational linguistics. Since the early days of the theory, there has been an emphasis on the mathematical and computational foundations of the formalism. This has led to the successful industrial development of implemented versions of computational grammars, including the PowerSet search engine (now incorporated into the Microsoft Bing Search). Much recent work on computational research has focused on the automatic induction of LFG grammars from treebanks. Major sources on computation within LFG include Butt *et al.* (1999), Crouch (2005), Cahill *et al.* (2005), and Cahill *et al.* (2008).

Notes

1 A list of the grammatical functions assumed is listed below in §5.
2 I have provided here a slightly simplified version of the c-structures and f-structures for Warlpiri proposed by Simpson (1991). See Austin and Bresnan (1996) for an alternative LFG account of Warlpiri, which places the material before the auxiliary in a [Spec, IP] position.
3 For expositional purposes, I present here an informal method of understanding related c-structure/ f-structure pairs. For a more rigorous procedure, see Kaplan and Bresnan (1982) or Dalrymple (2001).
4 This statement oversimplifies for expository purposes. Although most attributes take a single value, there are a few attributes, such as ADJUNCT, which take sets as their values. See Dalrymple (2001) for a more careful formulation.
5 The correct features for *are* are, of course, somewhat more complicated than this account recognizes. One problem is the use of *are* with singular *you*; a second problem is the use of *are* as a default in some tags (*I'm convincing you, aren't I?*); a third problem is variability of singular/ plural agreement in examples such as *The parliament is/are in session*. For discussion of LFG and LFG-compatible approaches to some of these issues see Bresnan (2001b) and Wechsler (2011).
6 In some work (e.g., Asudeh and Toivenen 2009), this function is instead called SPECIFIER and includes both possessors and quantifiers.
7 Expletive elements such as *it* and *there* in English would constitute exceptions.
8 For presentational purposes, I have slightly revised the f-structures from Simpson (1991) and included a feature INDEX, used in a number of LFG works, such as Bresnan (2001b) and Falk (2001). It is likely that in a more sophisticated account of anaphora, information about the reference of noun phrases ought not to be present in the f-structures, but should be present in the semantic structures of the sentences, as in Dalrymple (1993; 2001).
9 For reasons of compactness, the c-structure tree abbreviates the non-branching I', VP, V structure dominating *likes* at the bottom of the tree.
10 In many LFG publications, a line is drawn between the two positions in the f-structure to show the relationship.

Further reading

The annual proceedings of the LFG conference are available online at http://cslipublications. stanford.edu/LFG/.
Asudeh, Ash. 2012. *The Logic of Pronominal Resumption*. Oxford: Oxford University Press.
Dalrymple, Mary, and Mycock, Louise. 2011. The Prosody-Semantics Interface. In *Proceedings of LFG2011*. Stanford, CA: CSLI Publications.
Dalrymple, Mary, and Irina Nikolaeva. 2011. *Objects and Information Structure*. Cambridge: Cambridge University Press.

References

Alsina, Alex. 1996. *The Role of Argument Structure in Grammar*. Stanford, CA: CSLI Publications.
Andrews, Avery. 1990. Unification and Morphological Blocking. *Natural Language and Linguistic Theory* 8(4):507–557.
Asudeh, Ash. 2012. *The Logic of Pronominal Resumption*. Oxford: Oxford University Press.

Asudeh, Ash, and Ida Toivonen. 2009. Lexical-Functional Grammar. In *The Oxford Handbook of Linguistic Analysis*, ed. Bernd Heine and Heiko Narrog, 392–432. Oxford: Oxford University Press.

Austin, Peter, and Joan Bresnan. 1996. Non-configurationality in Australian Aboriginal languages. *Natural Language and Linguistic Theory* 14:215–268.

Bresnan, Joan (ed.). 1982. *The Mental Representation of Grammatical Relations*. Cambridge, MA: MIT Press.

Bresnan, Joan. 1995. Linear Order, Syntactic Rank, and Empty Categories: On Weak Crossover. In Dalrymple et al. (eds), 241–274.

Bresnan, Joan. 2000. Optimal Syntax. In *Optimality Theory: Phonology, Syntax, and Acquisition*, ed. Joost Dekkers, Frank van der Leeuw, and Jeroen van de Weijer, 334–385. Oxford: Oxford University Press.

Bresnan, Joan. 2001a. The Emergence of the Unmarked Pronoun. *Optimality-theoretic Syntax*, ed. Geraldine Legendre, Stem Vikner, and Jane Grimshaw, 113–142. Cambridge, MA: MIT Press.

Bresnan, Joan. 2001b. *Lexical-Functional Syntax*. Oxford: Blackwell.

Bresnan, Joan, and Jonni M. Kanerva. 1989. Locative Inversion in Chicheŵa: A Case Study of Factorization in Grammar. *Linguistic Inquiry* 20:1–50.

Butt, Miriam. 1995. *The Structure of Complex Predicates in Urdu*. Stanford, CA: CSLI Publications.

Butt, Miriam, and Tracy Holloway King. 1996. Structural Topic and Focus without Movement. In *Online Proceedings of the First LFG Conference*, ed. M. Butt and T.H. King. Downloadable from http://csli-publications.stanford.edu/LFG/2/lfg97.html (accessed 31 January 2014).

Butt, Miriam, Tracy Holloway King, María-Eugenia Niño, and Frédérique Segond. 1999. *A Grammar Writer's Cookbook*. Stanford, CA: CSLI Publications.

Cahill, Aoife, Martin Forst, Michael Burke, Mairéad McCarthy, Ruth O'Donovan, Christian Rohrer, Josef van Genabith, and Andy Way. 2005. Treebank-based Acquisition of Multilingual Unification Grammar Resources. *Research on Language and Computation* 3(2):247–279.

Cahill, Aoife, Michael Burke, Ruth O'Donovan, Stefan Riezler, Josef van Genabith, and Andy Way. 2008. Wide-coverage Deep Statistical Parsing Using Automatic Dependency Structure Annotation. *Computational Linguistics* 34(1):81–124.

Crouch, Richard. 2005. Packed Rewriting for Mapping Text to Semantics and KR. In *Proceedings of the Sixth International Workshop on Computational Semantics*. http://citeseerx.ist.psu.edu/viewdoc/download?doi=10.1.1.94.7085&rep=rep1&type=pdf

Dalrymple, Mary. 1993. *The Syntax of Anaphoric Binding*. Stanford, CA: CSLI Publications.

Dalrymple, Mary (ed.). 1999. *Semantics and Syntax in Lexical Functional Grammar: The Resource Logic Approach*. Cambridge, MA: MIT Press.

Dalrymple, Mary. 2001. *Lexical Functional Grammar*. San Diego, CA: Academic Press.

Dalrymple, Mary, and Mycock, Louise. 2011. The Prosody-Semantics Interface. In *Proceedings of LFG2011*, Stanford, CA: CSLI Publications.

Dalrymple, Mary, and Irina Nikolaeva. 2011. *Objects and Information Structure*. Cambridge: Cambridge University Press.

Dalrymple, Mary, Ronald M. Kaplan, John T. Maxwell III, and Annie Zaenen (eds). 1995. *Formal Issues in Lexical-Functional Grammar*. Stanford, CA: CSLI Publications.

Falk, Yehuda. 2001. *Lexical-Functional Grammar: An Introduction to Parallel Constraint-based Syntax*. Stanford, CA: CSLI Publications.

Hale, Kenneth. 1983. Warlpiri and the Grammar of Non-configurational Languages. *Natural Language and Linguistic Theory* 1:5–47.

Kaplan, Ronald M., and Joan Bresnan. 1982. Lexical-Functional Grammar: A Formal System for Grammatical Representation. In Bresnan (ed.), 173–281. Reprinted in Dalrymple et al. (1995: 29–135).

Keenan, Edward O., and Bernard Comrie. 1977. Noun Phrase Accessibility and Universal Grammar. *Linguistic Inquiry* 8:63–99.

King, Tracy Holloway. 1995. *Configuring Topic and Focus in Russian*. Stanford, CA: CSLI Publications.

Kuhn, Jonas. 2003. *Optimality-Theoretic Syntax: A Declarative Approach*. Stanford, CA: CSLI Publications.

McCloskey, James, and Kenneth Hale. 1984. On the Syntax of Person-Number Inflection in Modern Irish. *Natural Language and Linguistic Theory* 1(4):487–533.

Mohanan, K.P. 1982. Grammatical Relations and Clause Structure in Malayalam. In Bresnan (ed.), 504–589.

Mohanan, K.P. 1983. Functional and Anaphor Control. *Linguistic Inquiry* 14:641–674.

Perlmutter, David (ed.). 1983. *Studies in Relational Grammar I*. Chicago, IL: University of Chicago Press.

Sells, Peter (ed.). 2001. *Formal and Empirical Issues in Optimality-Theoretic Syntax*. Stanford, CA: CSLI Publications.

Simpson, Jane. 1991. *Warlpiri Morpho-syntax: A Lexicalist Approach*. Dordrecht: Kluwer.

Wechsler, Stephen. 2011. Mixed Agreement, the Person Feature, and the Index/Concord Distinction. *Natural Language and Linguistic Theory* 29:999–1031.

28

Role and Reference Grammar

Robert D. Van Valin, Jr.

1 Introduction

Every linguistic theory is motivated by a particular set of issues, the consequences of which set it apart from other theories. The broad questions – such as What is a possible human language? How is language acquired? – are shared by most approaches. The initial motivating questions for Role and Reference Grammar [RRG] were 'What would a linguistic theory look like if it were based on the analysis of languages with diverse structures, such as Lakhota, Tagalog, Dyirbal, and Barai (Papua New Guinea), rather than on the analysis of English and similar languages?' and 'How can the interaction of syntax, semantics and pragmatics in different grammatical systems best be captured and explained?' The two questions emphasize the importance of taking account of typologically diverse languages in the formulation of a linguistic theory, and they indicate that the resulting theory will be one in which semantics and pragmatics play significant roles. In other words, RRG is a theory of the syntax–semantics–pragmatics interface.

Because linguistics is an integral part of cognitive science, most theories seek to contribute to the understanding of language acquisition and language processing. RRG asks 'can language acquisition be accounted for without recourse to an autonomous Language Acquisition Device?', and 'can a model of grammar that answers the typological and theoretical questions posed above provide any insights into the neurocognitive processing of language?' The last chapter of Van Valin and LaPolla (1997) [VVLP] addresses the first question, and the tentative conclusion is that the acquisition of a variety of core grammatical phenomena can be explained in RRG terms, including some for which it has been argued that there is no evidence available to the child regarding them, such as subjacency.[1] In the last few years there has been research on applying RRG to language processing, both in computational and neurolinguistic terms. Computational implementation of RRG is in its infancy, but the results so far are very promising.[2] With regard to sentence processing, one of the distinctive attributes of RRG, to be discussed in more detail below, is the bidirectionality of the linking between syntax and semantics. The RRG linking algorithm maps from semantics to syntax and from syntax to semantics, as will be shown in §3. This is an idealization of what a speaker does (semantics to syntax) and what a hearer does (syntax to semantics). Hence the design of the theory makes it readily amenable to psycho- and neurolinguistic sentence processing models, as argued in Van Valin (2006).[3]

2 The architecture of RRG

RRG belongs to the group of parallel architecture theories (Culicover and Jackendoff 2005). The organization of RRG is given in Figure 28.1.

There is a direct mapping between the semantic and syntactic representations of a sentence, unmediated by any kind of abstract syntactic representations; this excludes not only derivational representations but also the use of abstract functional- or relational-structures. The theory specifies only a single syntactic representation for a sentence (§2.1), and it corresponds to the actual form of the sentence (morphophonemics aside). RRG does not allow any phonologically null elements in the syntax.[4] RRG thus posits a very concrete syntactic representation, and this constrains the theory considerably. The syntactic representation is linked via the linking algorithm (§3) to the semantic representation (§2.2). The remaining component in Figure 28.1 is labeled 'discourse-pragmatics', and it is parallel to the linking algorithm. This signals that discourse-pragmatics, primarily as realized in information structure (§2.4), plays a role in the linking between syntax and semantics. Crucially, however, exactly what role it plays can vary across languages, and this variation is the source of important cross-linguistic differences among languages.

2.1 The syntactic representation of a sentence

Clause structure is not analyzed in RRG in terms of X-bar syntax or even traditional immediate constituency structure; rather, it is formulated in a semantically based model known as the 'layered structure of the clause'. It is based on two fundamental oppositions, which are found in all languages: an opposition between predicating elements and non-predicating elements, on the one hand, and, among the non-predicating elements, an opposition between those which are semantically related to the predicate and those which are not. In other words, all languages distinguish predicates, arguments, and modifying adjuncts, and this follows from the nature of language as a system of communication. Much of what is communicated is information about states of affairs in the world, and this involves reference and predication; consequently languages have syntactic categories specialized for referring and predicating. The essential units in this model of the clause are (i) the *nucleus*, which contains the predicate, (ii) the *core*, which contains the nucleus plus the arguments of the predicate in the nucleus, and (iii) a *periphery* for each layer, which contains adjunct modifiers, both phrasal (e.g., PPs) and non-phrasal (e.g., adverbs). The structure of a simple English clause is given in Figure 28.2; this is the constituent projection of the clause.[5]

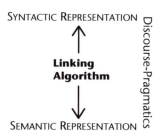

SYNTACTIC REPRESENTATION

**Linking
Algorithm**

SEMANTIC REPRESENTATION

Discourse-Pragmatics

Figure 28.1 The organization of RRG

There is no verb phrase in the layered structure, because it is not universal.[6]

The predicate in the nucleus need not be a head, nor is it restricted to a particular lexical category. While the most common category for the predicate in the nucleus is undoubtedly verb, adjectives, as in *Pat is tall* (*be* is analyzed as a tense-carrying auxiliary, not as a predicate), nominal phrases, as in ***Mary is a very good lawyer***, and adpositional phrases, as in ***Sam is at the office***, can all serve as the predicate in the nucleus. Hence the notion of nucleus in the RRG theory of constituent structure is not the projection of a lexical head, and therefore the core and clause are non-endocentric.[7]

Some languages have a 'pre-core slot', which is the position of *wh*-words in languages such as English and German, and a 'left-detached position', which is the position of the pre-clausal element in a left-dislocation construction. In addition, some verb-final languages have a 'post-core slot' (e.g., Japanese; Shimojo 1995), and some languages also have a 'right-detached position', which is the position of the post-clausal element in a right-dislocation construction. These are not universal and must be motivated on language-specific grounds.

The second major component of the RRG theory of clause structure is the theory of OPERATORS. Operators are closed-class grammatical categories such as aspect, negation, tense, and illocutionary force. An important property of operators is that they modify specific layers of the clause. The most important operators are presented in Table 28.1.

Languages do not necessarily have all operators as grammatical categories; English, for example, lacks evidentials as a grammatical category. The absolutely universal ones are

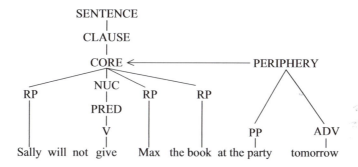

Figure 28.2 The layered structure of the clause in English

Table 28.1 Operators

Nuclear operators:
  Aspect
  Negation
Core operators:
  Modality (root modals, e.g. ability, permission, obligation)
  Internal (narrow scope) negation
Clausal operators:
  Status (epistemic modals, external negation)
  Tense
  Evidentials
  Illocutionary Force

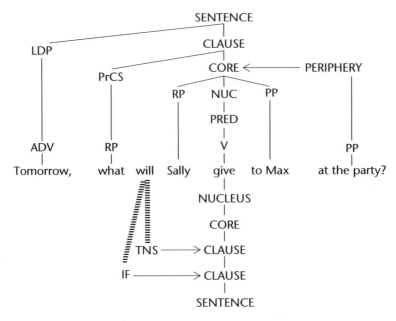

Figure 28.3 An English sentence with both constituent and operator projections

illocutionary force and negation. Operators are depicted in an additional projection of the clause, which is the mirror image of the constituent projection. The structure of an English sentence with constituent and operator projections is given in Figure 28.3.

In this example, *will* is connected to both 'tense' and 'IF' in the operator projection, because it signals these two operator categories, and, furthermore, the fact that they are both clausal operators is explicit. This representation will be relevant to the analysis of complex sentences, where the scope of operators over the linked units is very important (see §2.5).

The sentence in Figure 28.3 involves a left-detached position as well as a pre-core slot with a *wh*-expression. Note the lack of an empty argument position in the core corresponding to the *wh*-word in the PrCS; see note 4. *Sally* is a direct core argument, while *Max* is an oblique core argument.

A typologically significant claim made in Foley and Van Valin (1984) was that the linear order of the morphemes expressing the operators is a function of their scope. That is, morphemes expressing nuclear operators occur closer to the nucleus than morphemes expressing core operators, and these in turn appear closer to the nucleus than morphemes expressing clausal operators, when an ordering relationship among them can be adduced – that is, they all occur on the same side of the nucleus.

In Figures 28.2 and 28.3 the nominal phrases are labeled 'RP' instead of 'NP'. 'RP' stands for 'reference phrase' and, unlike 'NP' but like the nucleus, it is not necessarily the projection of a lexical head; it is non-endocentric. The nucleus of an RP is not restricted to nominals; see Van Valin (2008b) for detailed discussion. RPs have both constituent and operator projections, with the operator projection containing categories such as definiteness, deixis, quantification, and number. Examples of RPs and their layered structure are given in Figure 28.4 (from Van Valin 2005: 25).

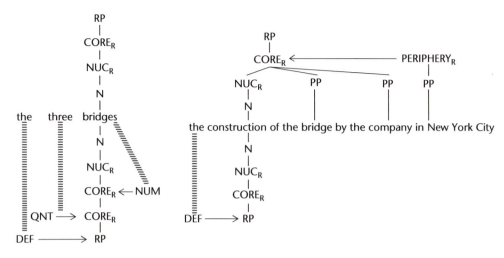

Figure 28.4 The layered structure of the RP with operator projection

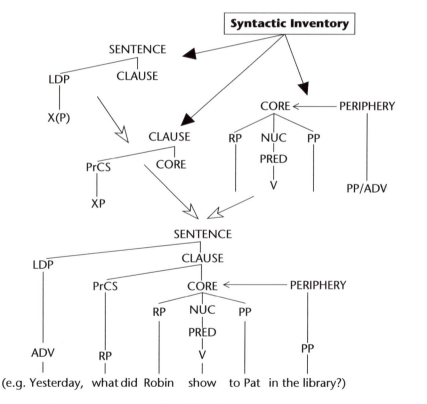

Figure 28.5 Combining syntactic templates from the syntactic inventory

The final point to mention with respect to syntactic representation is that tree structures are stored as syntactic templates, which are then combined to form the structure of a sentence. Syntactic templates are stored in what is called the *syntactic inventory*; an example of combining templates is given in Figure 28.5 (Van Valin 2005: 15).

Robert D. Van Valin, Jr.

2.2 The semantic representation of a sentence

The semantic representation of a sentence is built on the lexical representation of the verb or predicating element. It is a decompositional representation inspired by Vendler's (1967) theory of *Aktionsart*. The four basic classes (state, achievement, accomplishment, and activity) are supplemented by two additional classes, semelfactives (punctual events; Smith 1997) and active accomplishments (telic uses of activity verbs such as *devour, run to the store*); in addition, there are causative versions of each. Examples of the six classes are in (1), and sentences illustrating them plus their causative counterparts are in (2).

(1) a. States: *be sick, be tall, be dead, love, know, believe, have*
  b. Activities: *march, swim, walk* (– goal PP); *think, eat* (+ mass noun/bare plural RP)
  c. Semelfactives: *flash, tap, burst* (the intransitive versions), *glimpse*
  d. Achievements: *pop, explode, shatter* (all intransitive)
  e. Accomplishments: *melt, freeze, dry* (the intransitive versions), *learn*
  f. Active accomplishments: *walk* (+ goal PP), *eat* (+ quantified RP), *devour*

(2) a. State: The girl is afraid of the lion.
  a′. Causative state: The lion frightens/scares the girl.
  b. Achievement: The balloon popped.
  b′. Causative achievement: The cat popped the balloon.
  c. Semelfactive The light flashed.
  c′. Causative semelfactive The conductor flashed the light.
  d. Accomplishment: The snow melted.
  d′. Causative accomplishment: The hot water melted the snow.
  e. Activity: The dog walked in the park.
  e′. Causative activity: The boy walked the dog in the park.
  f. Active accomplishment The dog walked to the park.
  f′. Causative active accomplishment: The boy walked the dog to the park.

Syntactic and semantic tests determine *Aktionsart* (see VVLP:§3.2.1; Van Valin 2005: §2.1.1). As the examples in (2e–f′) show, a single verb, such as *walk*, can have more than one *Aktionsart* interpretation. This verb would be listed in the lexicon as an activity verb, and lexical rules would derive the other uses from the basic activity use (see VVLP:§4.6; Van Valin 2013).

The system of lexical decomposition builds on Dowty (1979). The lexical representation of a verb or other predicate is termed its *logical structure* [LS]. State predicates are represented simply as **predicate′**, while all activity predicates contain **do′**. Accomplishments, which are durative, are distinguished from achievements, which are punctual. Accomplishment LSs contain BECOME, while achievement LSs contain INGR, which is short for 'ingressive'. Semelfactives contain SEML. In addition, causation is treated as an independent parameter which crosscuts the six *Aktionsart* classes, hence the twelve classes in (3). It is represented by CAUSE in LSs. The lexical representations are given in Table 28.2 (Van Valin 2005).

Examples of simple English sentences with the LS of the predicate are presented in (3).

(3) a. STATES
    The vase is shattered. **shattered′** (vase)
    The Queen saw the portrait. **see′** (Queen, portrait)

b. ACTIVITIES
The door squeaks.   **do'** (door, [**squeak'** (door)])
Chris ate pizza.   **do'** (Carl, [**eat'** (Carl, pizza)])

c. SEMELFACTIVES
The light flashed.   SEML **do'** (light, [**flash'** (light)])
Sam glimpsed Sally.   SEML **see'** (Sam, Sally)

d. ACHIEVEMENTS
The balloon popped.   INGR **popped'** (balloon)

e. ACCOMPLISHMENTS
The snow melted.   BECOME **melted'** (snow)
Bill learned karate.   BECOME **know'** (Bill, karate)

f. ACTIVE ACCOMPLISHMENTS
Carl ate the pizza.   **do'** (Carl, [**eat'** (Carl, pizza)]) & INGR **eaten'** (pizza)
Paul ran to the store.   **do'** (Paul, [**run'** (Paul)]) & INGR **be-at'** (store, Paul)

g. CAUSATIVES
The sun melted the snow.   [**do'** (sun, Ø)] CAUSE [BECOME **broken'** (snow)]
The cat popped the balloon.   [**do'** (cat, Ø)] CAUSE [INGR **popped'** (balloon)]
Fred rolled the ball.   [**do'** (Fred, Ø)] CAUSE [**do'** (ball, [**roll'** (ball)])]

Full semantic representations of sentences also contain lexical representations of the RPs, adjuncts, and grammatical operators such as tense and aspect; see VVLP: §4.4, 4.7; Van Valin 2005: §2.2–2.3.

2.2.1 Semantic macroroles

The semantic role of an argument is determined by its position in the LS of the predicate, and the linking system refers to an element's LS position. The traditional thematic role labels are used only as mnemonics for the LS argument positions; for example, 'theme' is the mnemonic for the second position (y) in a two-place locational LS such as **be-at'** (x, y). RRG postulates two generalized semantic roles, or *semantic macroroles*, which play a critical role in the linking system. They are *actor* and *undergoer*, the two primary arguments of a transitive predication; the single argument of an intransitive predicate can be either actor

Table 28.2 Lexical representations for Aktionsart classes

Verb Class	Logical Structure
STATE	**predicate'** (x) or (x,y)
ACTIVITY	**do'** (x, [**predicate'** (x) or (x, y)])
ACHIEVEMENT	INGR **predicate'** (x) or (x,y), or INGR **do'** (x, [**predicate'** (x) or (x, y)])
SEMELFACTIVE	SEML **predicate'** (x) or (x,y), or SEML **do'** (x, [**predicate'** (x) or (x, y)])
ACCOMPLISHMENT	BECOME **predicate'** (x) or (x,y), or BECOME **do'** (x, [**predicate'** (x) or (x, y)])
ACTIVE ACCOMPLISHMENT	**do'** (x, [**predicate$_1$'** (x, (y))]) & BECOME/INGR **predicate$_2$'** (z, x) or (y)
CAUSATIVE	α CAUSE β, where α, β are LSs of any type

or undergoer, depending upon the semantic properties of the predicate. The basic distinction is illustrated in the following German examples.

(4) a. Der Hund [SUBJ, ACTOR] hat das Fleisch [OBJ, UNDERGOER] aufgegessen.
        'The dog ate the meat.'
     b. Der Hund [SUBJ, ACTOR] ist um das Haus herumgelaufen.
        'The dog [SUBJ, ACTOR] ran around the house.'
     c. Der Hund [SUBJ, UNDERGOER] ist gestorben.
        'The dog [SUBJ, UNDERGOER] died.'
     d. Das Fleisch [SUBJ, UNDERGOER] wurde vom Hund [ACTOR] aufgegessen.
        'The meat [SUBJ, UNDERGOER] was eaten by the dog [ACTOR].'

In an English clause with an active voice transitive verb, the actor is the initial RP in the core (the traditional subject), and the undergoer is always the direct RP immediately following the nucleus.

The relationship between LS argument positions and macroroles is expressed in the Actor–Undergoer Hierarchy [AUH] in Figure 28.6. There is a fundamental asymmetry in the AUH: the leftmost argument in a LS (in terms of the AUH) is always the actor, but the rightmost argument is only the default choice for undergoer (with some verbs in some languages, not universally). This possible variation in the selection of the undergoer is the basis of the RRG analysis of dative shift and related phenomena (see §3).[8]

2.2.2 Transitivity and lexical entries for verbs

Transitivity in RRG is defined semantically in terms of the number of macroroles a predicate takes. This is known as 'M-transitivity' (Narasimhan 1998), in order to differentiate it from the number of syntactic arguments a predicate takes, its 'S-transitivity'. The three M-transitivity possibilities are: transitive (2 macroroles), intransitive (1 macrorole), and atransitive (0 macroroles). It is necessary to point out in the context of this discussion of three-place predicates that there is no third macrorole. From theoretical and empirical perspectives, there are no grounds for positing a third macrorole (see Van Valin (2004) and (2005: 64–66) for detailed discussion). The theoretical term for the third argument in a ditransitive predication, such as *the picture* in the English sentence *Sam showed Sally the picture*, is 'non-macrorole direct core argument'.

The principles determining the M-transitivity of verbs are given in (5).

(5) Default Macrorole Assignment Principles
     a. Number: the number of macroroles a verb takes is less than or equal to the number of arguments in its LS.
         1. If a verb has two or more arguments in its LS, it will take two macroroles.
         2. If a verb has one argument in its LS, it will take one macrorole.

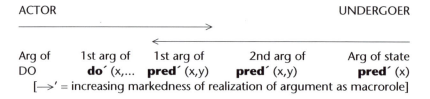

Figure 28.6 The Actor–Undergoer Hierarchy

b. Nature: for predicates which have one macrorole.
  1. If the verb LS contains an activity predicate, the macrorole is actor.
  2. If the verb LS has no activity predicate in it the macrorole is undergoer.

If a verb is irregular and has exceptional transitivity, this will be indicated in its lexical entry by '[MRα]', where 'α' is a variable for the number of macroroles. Examples of lexical entries for some English verbs are given in (6).

(6) a. *kill*   [**do'** (x, Ø)] CAUSE [BECOME **dead'** (y)]
  b. *own*   **have'** (x, y)
  c. *belong (to)*   **have'** (x, y) [MR1]
  d. *see*   **see'** (x, y)
  e. *watch*   **do'** (x, [**see'** (x, y)])
  f. *show*   [**do'** (w, Ø)] CAUSE [BECOME **see'** (x, y)]
  g. *run*   **do'** (x, [**run'** (x)])

A major claim in RRG is that no syntactic subcategorization information of any kind needs to be specified in the lexical entries for verbs. For regular verbs, all that is necessary is the LS and nothing more, as in all except (7c). For most irregular verbs, only the macro-role number is required to be specified. The prepositions that mark oblique arguments with verbs such as *show* are predictable from general principles and need not be listed in the lexical entry (see below; also Jolly 1993; VVLP:§7.3.2). All of the major morphosyntactic properties of verbs and other predicates follow from their LS together with the linking system.

2.3 Grammatical relations

In the earliest work on RRG (e.g., Foley and Van Valin 1977; Van Valin 1977; 1981) it was argued that grammatical relations such as subject and direct object are not universal and cannot be taken as the basis for adequate grammatical theories. In place of them, RRG employs the notion of 'privileged syntactic argument' [PSA], which is a construction-specific relation defined as a restricted neutralization of semantic roles and pragmatic functions for syntactic purposes in a grammatical construction. The other core arguments in a clause are characterized as direct or oblique core arguments; there is nothing in RRG corresponding to direct or indirect object (see Van Valin 2005: Ch 4).

Languages have selection principles to determine the PSA; the main ones are given in (7) and (8).

(7) Privileged syntactic argument selection hierarchy:
  Arg of DO > 1st arg of **do'** > 1st arg of **pred'** (x,y) > 2nd arg of **pred'** (x,y) > **pred'** (x)

(8) Privileged Syntactic Argument Selection Principles
  a. Accusative construction: Highest ranking direct core argument in terms of (7)-default
  b. Ergative constructions: Lowest ranking direct core argument in terms of (7)-default

   c. Restrictions on PSA in terms of macrorole status:
     1. Languages in which only macrorole arguments can be PSA: German, Italian, Dyirbal, Jakaltek, Sama, ...
     2. Languages in which non-macrorole direct core arguments can be PSA: Icelandic, Georgian, Japanese, Korean, Kinyarwanda, ...

The PSA selection hierarchy in (7) is the actor part of the AUH. For a language such as English, (8a) captures the fact that, in an active voice clause with a transitive verb, the actor is the PSA, whereas, for a language such as Dyirbal, in an active voice clause with a transitive verb the undergoer is the PSA, following (8b). These are the default choices; it is possible for an undergoer to serve as PSA in a passive construction in accusative languages, and it is possible for an actor to function as PSA in an antipassive construction in syntactically ergative languages. Languages also differ with respect to whether the PSA has to be a macrorole: German, Italian, Dyirbal, and Sama (Philippines; Walton 1986) limit PSA selection to actors and undergoers only, while Icelandic, Georgian, and Kinyarwanda permit non-macrorole direct core arguments to function as PSA (see VVLP: §7.3.1.1; Van Valin 1981; 2005: §4.2).

An aspect of (8a–b) with considerable typological implications is whether it is a default rule, as in English, German, Dyirbal, and many other languages, or whether it is an absolute rule, as in Lakhota, Warlpiri, and many other languages. In Lakhota the highest ranking argument in the LS is always the PSA; there is no other choice, as the language lacks a voice opposition. Thus, with a transitive or other multi-argument verb, the grammar allows the speaker no options as to which argument is selected as the PSA. The contrast between PSAs in English-type languages and Lakhota-type languages can be captured in a distinction between 'variable PSAs' [most English constructions] vs. 'invariable PSAs' [all Lakhota constructions].[9] In languages with variable PSAs, in particular constructions, such as those like (9) below, one of the factors affecting which argument may be selected as PSA is information structure. It has long been recognized that there is a strong tendency for the RP selected as PSA to be the most topical in the particular context. In RRG variable PSAs in such constructions are analyzed as 'pragmatically influenced PSAs'; it should be noted that not all variable PSAa are pragmatically influenced. There is no pragmatic influence on PSA selection with invariable PSAs.[10]

PSAs may be categorized functionally as controllers or pivots, as illustrated in (9) and (10).

(9) a. The angry woman$_i$ slapped Sam$_j$ and then ____$_{i/*j}$ left.
     CONTROLLER   PIVOT
  b. Sam$_j$ was slapped by the angry woman$_i$ and then ____$_{*i/j}$ left.
     CONTROLLER   PIVOT

(10) a. Helen$_i$ convinced the angry woman$_j$ [____$_{*i/j}$ to slap Sam].
                CONTROLLER PIVOT
  b. The angry woman$_j$ was convinced by Helen$_i$ [____$_{*i/j}$ to slap Sam].
     CONTROLLER   PIVOT

Pivots are canonically the missing argument in a construction, as in (9) and (10), while controllers prototypically supply the interpretation for a pivot. It should be noted that there can be pivots without controllers (e.g., the extracted element in an extraction construction) and controllers without pivots (e.g., reflexive controllers). An additional distinction, the contrast between syntactic and semantic pivots and controllers, is exemplified in these examples. In the construction in (9), the controller is the first RP in the core, the traditional 'subject', regardless of its semantic function, whereas in the construction in (10), the controller is the undergoer argument, regardless of its syntactic status. Hence the controller in (9) is a syntactic controller (variable and potentially pragmatically influenced), while the controller in (10) is an invariable semantic controller. The types of pivots and controllers that the constructions of a language have are typologically very significant.

2.4   The information structure representation of a sentence

The morphosyntactic means for expressing the discourse-pragmatic status of elements in a sentence is called 'information structure'(also 'focus structure'), and the approach to information structure in RRG is based on Lambrecht (1994). He proposes that there are recurring patterns of the organization of information across languages, which he calls 'focus types'. The three main types are presented in (11), with data from English and Italian; focal stress is indicated by small caps.

(11)   Focus structure in English and Italian (Lambrecht 1994; Bentley 2008)
　　　a. Q: What happened to your car?　　　　**Predicate Focus**
　　　　　A:　i. My car/It broke DOWN.　　　　　English
　　　　　　　ii. (La mia macchina) si è ROTTA.　Italian
　　　b. Q: What happened?　　　　　　　　　　**Sentence Focus**
　　　　　A:　i. My CAR broke down.　　　　　　English
　　　　　　　ii. Mi si è rotta la MACCHINA.　　　Italian
　　　c. Q: I heard your motorcycle broke down.　**Narrow Focus**
　　　　　A:　i. My CAR broke down./　　　　　　English
　　　　　　　It was my CAR that broke down.
　　　　　　　ii. Si è rotta la mia MACCHINA./　Italian (Lit: 'broke down my car'/
　　　　　　　È la mia MACCHINA che si è rotta.)　'it's my car that broke down'

Information structure is formally represented by an additional projection of the clause, the focus structure projection, illustrated in Figure 28.7 for narrow focus in English (Van Valin 2005: 80). It has three main components. *Basic information units* [IU] correspond to the information content captured by a simple *wh*-word such as *who*, *what* or *where*. In simple sentences this notion may seem redundant with the syntactic phrases of the constituent projection, but it plays an important role in the analysis of information structure in complex sentences. The second component is the *actual focus domain*, which is what is actually in focus in a given context; the elements in small caps in (11) are in the actual focus domain in those examples; in Figure 28.7 it is represented by the triangle. The third component, which was introduced in RRG and is not part of Lambrecht's original theory, is the *potential focus domain*. Languages differ with respect to constraints on where the actual focus domain can be in a clause. In some, such as English, it can fall on any word or phrase. In others, such as Italian, it is precluded from the preverbal core position and can only include the nucleus and what follows, hence the inverted subjects and cleft in (11b–c) (see VVLP: §5.4, Van Valin (1999); Bentley (2008) for detailed discussion). The potential focus domain is a property of the grammar of the language, while the actual focus domain is contextually determined; it is represented by the dotted lines in Figure 28.7.

It is possible to represent all three projections in a single tree, as in Figure 28.7 (Van Valin 2005: 80). It must be emphasized that these are not three distinct representations of the sentence; rather, they are representations of three types of information which are simultaneously present in the sentence, and the grammar can refer to any of the three or combinations thereof.

In Van Valin (2005) formal representations of context based on Discourse Representation Theory (Kamp and Reyle 1993; Heusinger 1999) are incorporated into the theory, in order to derive the different focus types. They can also play an important role in linking in some languages (see Van Valin 2005: §5.4.1; Shimojo 2008; 2009). A new development in the theory is an explicit representation of prosody (O'Connor 2008), which is represented in an independent prosodic projection.

2.5 The structure of complex sentences

The three central components of the LSC are also the fundamental building blocks of complex sentences. The unmarked pattern for complex sentences involves combining nuclei with nuclei, cores with cores, clauses with clauses, or sentences with sentences. These are termed levels of 'juncture'. Sentential junctures are complex constructions made up of multiple sentences, while clausal junctures involve sentences containing multiple clauses. Examples of nuclear junctures from French, English, and Mandarin are given in (12). Justifications for these structures can be found in Van Valin (2005).

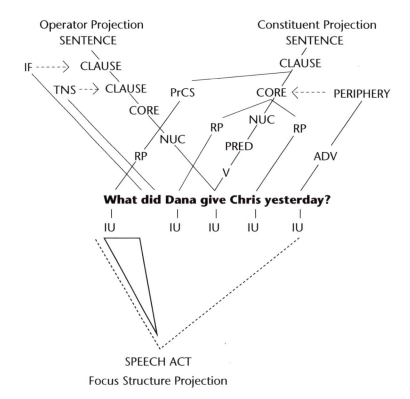

Figure 28.7 English sentence with all three projections represented

(12) a. Je ferai   manger   les gâteaux   à   Jean.
      1sg make.FUT   eat   the cakes   to   John
      'I will make John eat the cakes.'
      [two nuclei, *faire* and *manger*, in a single core]
   b. John forced open the door.
      [two nuclei, *force* and *open*, in a single core]
   c. Tā   qiāo   pò   le   yí   ge   fànwǎn.
      3sg hit   break PRFV   one   CL   bowl
      'He broke (by hitting) a ricebowl.'
      [two nuclei, *qiāo* 'hit' and *pò* 'break', in a single core]   (Hansell 1993)

Core junctures involve two or more cores (which may themselves be internally complex) in a clause. Examples from French, English, and Mandarin are given in (13). In this type of core juncture, the two cores share a core argument.

(13) a. Je laisserai   Jean   manger   les gâteaux.
      1sg let.FUT   John   eat   the cakes
      'I will let John eat the cakes.'
   b. I ordered Fred to force the door open.
   c. Tā   jiāo   wǒ   xiě   zì.
      3sg teach 1sg write characters
      'She teaches me to write characters.'

Of equal importance in the theory of complex sentences is the set of possible syntactic and semantic relations between the units in a juncture. The syntactic relations between units are called 'nexus' relations. Traditionally, only two basic nexus relations are recognized: Coordination and subordination. Subordination is divided into two subtypes, daughter subordination and peripheral subordination. They are illustrated in Figure 28.8.

The embedded clause in the first sentence is a daughter of the core node, while in the second the embedded clause is an adjunct in the periphery modifying the core.

In addition to distinguishing two types of subordination, RRG, following Olson's (1981) analysis of clause linkage in Barai (a Papuan language), posits a third nexus type: 'Cosubordination', which is essentially a tight, dependent coordination. The dependence is operator

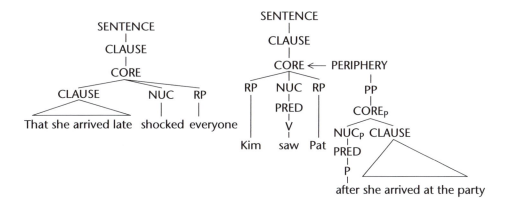

Figure 28.8   Daughter and peripheral subordination at the core level in English

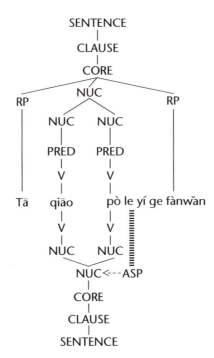

Figure 28.9 Nuclear cosubordination in Mandarin in (12c)

dependence: that is, in cosubordination, the units obligatorily share one or more operators at the level of juncture. In the Mandarin example in (12c), aspect obligatorily has scope over both nuclei: that is, both are interpreted as having perfective aspect and therefore the nexus is cosubordination. This is represented in Figure 28.9.

The following examples from Turkish (Watters 1993) illustrate obligatory operator sharing and the lack of it in Turkish core cosubordination and coordination, respectively. The deontic modal, a core operator (see Table 28.1), has scope over both cores in (14a) but only over the second core in (14b).[11]

(14)   a.   Core cosubordination
       Gid-ip   gör-meli-yiz.
       go-CNV   see-MODAL-1pl
       'We ought to go and see.'
       b.   Core coordination
       Müzik   dinle-yerek,   uyu-yabil-ir-im.
       music   listen-CNV   sleep-MODAL-AOR-1sg
       'While listening to music, I can sleep.'
       (Not 'while I am able to listen to music, I am able to sleep.')

The following sentences from Kewa (Franklin 1971) are a minimal triple for the three nexus types at the clause level.

(15)   a.   Nipú   ípu-la   pare   ní   paalá   na-pía.   Coordination
       3sg   come-3sgPRES   but   1sg   afraid   NEG-be.1sgPRES
       'He is coming, but I am not afraid.'

    b. (Ní) Épo   lá-ri   épa-wa.   Cosubordination
       (1sg) whistle say-SIM.SS come-1sgPAST
       'I whistled while I came,' or 'I came whistling.'
    c. (Ní) Épo   lá-lo-pulu   irikai épa-lia.   Subordination (peripheral)
       (1sg) whistle say-1sgPRES-CAUSAL dog   come-3sgFUT
       'Because I am whistling, the dog will come.'

The RRG analysis of complex sentences distinguishes dependence from embedding, and this has important consequences for the analysis of familiar structures. How does one establish that a unit is embedded? The canonical instance of daughter subordination is the use of a phrase or clause as a core argument of a predicate, and these phrases have certain syntactic properties: they can become the PSA of a passive construction, if functioning as undergoer, and they can be *it*-clefted. This is illustrated in (16)–(18).

(16) a. Tom bought the new book by Sally Smith.
    b. The new book by Sally Smith was bought by Tom.
    c. It was the new book by Sally Smith that Tom bought.

Clausal arguments and gerunds have this property as well.

(17) a. Max believed that John highjacked the meeting.
    b. That John highjacked the meeting was believed by Max.
    c. It was that John highjacked the meeting that Max believed.

(18) a. Marsha regretted kissing Roger the most.
    b. Kissing Roger was regretted by Marsha the most.
    c. It was kissing Roger that Marsha regretted the most.

Thus clausal complements and gerunds have the same distributional properties as simple NP phrasal core arguments, which are unequivocally embedded, and accordingly they exemplify daughter subordination.

What about infinitival complements? The standard analysis of sentences such as (19a) is that the infinitive is the embedded object of the verb, just like the simple NP in (19a'), yet it does not have the distributional properties of simple NPs.

(19) a.   Sam tried to open the door.
    a'. Sam tried the door.
    b.   *To open the door was tried by Sam.
    b'. The door was tried by Sam.
    c.   *It was to open the door that Sam tried.
    c'. It was the door that Sam tried.

The contrast between (18) and (19) is striking: in both the linked unit is subjectless, non-finite, and sub-clausal, but the gerund shows the same properties as a simple NP object, whereas the infinitive does not. The infinitive can be neither passivized nor *it*-clefted. Hence the infinitive *to open the door* cannot be analyzed as the 'direct object' of *try* and therefore not as daughter-subordinate in (19a). This is an instance of a syntax–semantics mismatch: at the semantic level, *x to open the door* is the second argument of *try*, whereas

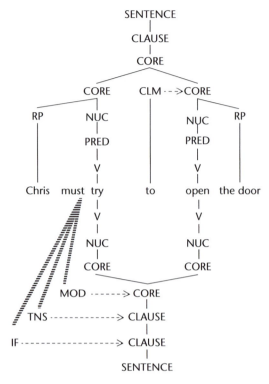

Figure 28.10 The core cosubordinate structure of (20b)

in the syntax it does not occupy a syntactic core argument position, unlike a simple NP, as in (16) and (19a′), the gerund in (18), or the *that*-clause in (17). If one adds a deontic modal operator to (18) and (19), there is a clear contrast.

(20) a. Marsha should regret kissing Roger the most.
      b. Sam must try to open the door.

Marsha's obligation in (20a) is to regret something; she is not obliged to kiss Roger. In (20b), in contrast, Sam is obliged not just to try anything but rather to try to open the door; in other words, the scope of the modal operator obligatorily extends over both cores, just as in (14a) in Turkish. The structure of (20b) is given in Figure 28.10. Tense and IF are necessarily shared as well, but for a different reason: they are clausal operators and therefore have scope over the whole clause, which entails scope over the constituent cores in the clause.

While the infinitive is dependent on the finite unit with respect to the interpretation of deontic modality, it is not embedded as a core argument in it: that is, it is a flat structure, core cosubordination (see also Roberts 2012). Thus, dependence does not necessarily entail (daughter) subordination.

The four levels of juncture combine with the three nexus types to generate eleven possible complex sentence types; there is no sentential cosubordination because there are no sentence-level operators, hence no possible operator sharing. In addition, both subtypes of subordination are possible at the clause, core, and nuclear levels. Not all of them are instantiated in every language. The juncture–nexus types found in a language may be realized by more than one formal construction type: for example, both *Mary sat playing the guitar* and *Robin tried to open the door* instantiate core cosubordination, while both *For Sam to leave now would be a mistake* and *Lisa's losing her job shocked everyone* instantiate core subordination in English. The juncture–nexus types may be ordered into a hierarchy in terms of the tightness of the syntactic link between the units: that is, in terms of how integrated the units are into a single unit or whether they are coded as distinct units.

These syntactic clause-linkage relations are used to express semantic relations between the units in the linkage – for example causation, purpose, psych-action, direct and indirect perception, cognition, propositional attitude, direct and indirect discourse, circumstances, conditionals, and temporal sequence (Van Valin 2005: 206–207). These relations may be formalized in terms of the same decomposition used for verbs (see Van Valin 2005: 207–208; also Ohori 2001; 2005).

The semantic relations form a continuum expressing the degree of semantic cohesion between the propositional units linked in the complex structure – that is, the degree to which they express facets of a single action or event or discrete actions or events. The syntactic linkage relations are ranked hierarchically in terms of the strength of the syntactic bond between the units. The interaction of the two hierarchies yields important generalizations about the syntax–semantics interface in complex sentences (see Van Valin and Wilkins 1993; VVLP; Van Valin 2005; Kockelman 2003; Good 2003; Guerrero 2006).

3 Linking between syntax and semantics

All of the components of the RRG linking system have been introduced. The linking between syntax and semantics is governed by a very general principle called the 'Completeness Constraint' (Van Valin 2005: 129–130); it states simply that all of the specified arguments in the semantic representation of a sentence must be realized in the syntax in some way, and conversely that all of the expressions in the syntax must be linked to something in the semantic representation of a sentence, in order to be interpreted.

An important part of the linking involves finite verb agreement, case assignment, and preposition assignment. The finite verb agreement rule for accusative languages such as English, German, and Croatian is given in (21).

(21) Finite verb agreement in Croatian, German and Icelandic:
The controller of finite verb agreement is the highest ranking core macrorole argument (in terms of (7)).

The rule is not formulated with respect to any syntactic position or function, or with respect to any case. Case assignment rules are formulated in a similar way. The basic rules for direct core arguments in accusative languages are given in (22) and for ergative languages in (23); these do not pertain to case assigned by adpositions.

(22) Case marking rules for accusative languages:
    a. Highest ranking core macrorole (in terms of (8)) takes nominative case.
    b. Other core macrorole takes accusative case.

(23) Case marking rules for ergative languages:
    a. Lowest ranking core macrorole (in terms of (8)) takes absolutive case.
    b. Other core macrorole takes ergative case.

In addition, there is a rule for dative case assignment, which applies to both systems:

(24) Assign dative case to non-macrorole direct core arguments (default).

Dative case is assigned only when the rules for the other cases cannot apply.[12] In a language such as English, without RP case marking, there are rules for preposition assignment (Jolly 1993). The rules for *to* and *from* are given in (25).[13]

(25) Preposition assignment rules for English
    a. Assign *to* to NMR *x* argument in LS segment: ...BECOME/INGR **pred′** (x, y)
    b. Assign *from* to NMR *x* argument in LS segment:...BECOME/INGR NOT **pred′**(x, y)

The rule in (25a) is particularly important for the 'dative shift' verbs in English, such as *give*, *send*, *show*, and so on. The alternation in (26) is handled in terms of variable undergoer selection; both sentences would have the same LS, given in (26c).

(26) a. Mary handed a letter to Sally.
    b. Mary handed Sally a letter.
    c. [**do′** (Mary, Ø)] CAUSE [INGR **have′** (Sally, letter)]

In (26a) undergoer selection reflects the default choice in terms of the AUH in Figure 28.6: that is, the rightmost argument in LS is chosen to function as undergoer. In (26b), on the other hand, the second lowest ranking argument (which is also the second highest ranking), *Sally*, is selected as undergoer. In (26a) the conditions for (25a) are met, and therefore *Sally* is marked by *to*. In (26b), however, it is not met, and therefore it does not apply. Alternations with verbs such as English *present*, German *schenken* vs. *beschenken* 'give as a gift', Croatian *darovati* 'give as a gift', and Dyirbal *wugal* 'give' are all analyzed as instances of variable undergoer selection (see Van Valin 2005: §4.4; Van Valin 2007).

Most of what counts as 'syntax' in many theories is handled in RRG in terms of constraints on the semantic representation, in terms of information structure, or in the syntactic phase of the linking. The analysis of reflexivization in RRG follows the approach in Jackendoff (1992) and states the hierarchical constraints for core-internal ('clause-bound' in other theories) reflexivization at the LS level, not with respect to the syntactic representation. The principles affecting the scope and interpretation of quantifiers are related to information-structure contrasts, not phrase structure. RRG treats constructions as an important part of syntax, and they are represented in terms of constructional schemas. Cross-constructional and cross-linguistic generalizations are captured in terms of the general principles and constraints that constitute the linking algorithms – for example, the AUH, the LSC, the PSA selection hierarchy. Only the idiosyncratic, language-specific features of constructions are represented in constructional schemas, which may include syntactic, morphological, semantic, and pragmatic (focus structure) information.

A simple example from English illustrating the operation of the semantics-to-syntax linking algorithm is given in Figure 28.11. The numbers refer to the general steps of the algorithm: (1) constructing the semantic representation of the sentence in the lexicon; (2) assigning actor and undergoer; (3) determining PSA selection, case and adposition assignment, and agreement; (4) selecting the appropriate syntactic template from the syntactic inventory; and (5) linking the elements from the semantic representation into the appropriate positions in the syntactic representation.[14] The numbers in the diagram, especially 2–3, should not be interpreted as indicating steps in a derivation. Rather, they signal steps in the linking which involve adding morphosyntactic information to the semantic representation. The output of step 3 could equally well be represented as '... [**do'** (Sandy[Actor, *by*-ACC], Ø)] CAUSE [INGR **have'**[passive, 3pl] (Chris[NMR, *to*-ACC], flowers[Und, PSA, NOM])]...'.

Because this sentence is a passive, the undergoer appears as the 'subject', with the actor appearing in a peripheral PP marked with *by*. These language-specific details would be represented in the constructional schema for the English passive, given in Table 28.3.

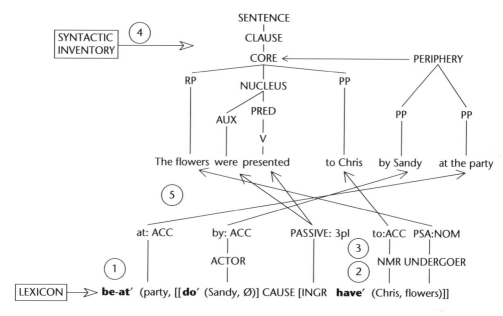

Figure 28.11 Linking from semantics to syntax in a simple sentence in English

Table 28.3 Constructional schema for English passive (plain)

CONSTRUCTION: English passive (plain)
SYNTAX: Template(s): (following template selection principles; not given above) PSA: (8a,c2), Variable [± pragmatic influence] Linking: Undergoer to PSA; Actor omitted or in peripheral *by*-PP
MORPHOLOGY: Verb: past participle Auxiliary: *be*
SEMANTICS: PSA is not instigator of state of affairs but is affected by it (default)
PRAGMATICS: Illocutionary force: Not imperative Focus structure: No restrictions; PSA = topic (default)

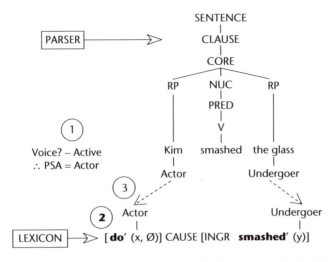

Figure 28.12 Linking from syntax to semantics in a simple sentence in English

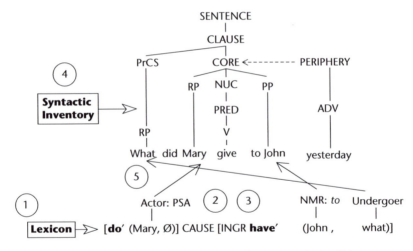

Figure 28.13 Linking from semantics to syntax in a *wh*-question in English

The information in the constructional schema is a combination of general principles (template selection principles, PSA selection principles, general characterization of non-default PSA selection) and language-specific information, such as the form of the verb and the choice of auxiliary. See Van Valin (2005) for detailed discussion and explication of all of these points.

A simple example of the linking from syntax to semantics is given in Figure 28.12. Here, again, the numbers refer to the general steps in the algorithm: (1) extract all of the information possible from the overt morphosyntactic form of the sentence, including the voice of the verb (if the language has voice), case marking, word order, and adpositions; (2) retrieve the LS of the predicate in the nucleus from the lexicon and assign macroroles to the extent

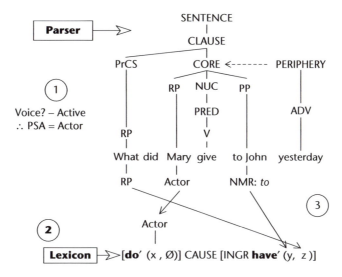

Figure 28.14 Linking from syntax to semantics in a *wh*-question in English

possible; and (3) link the information derived from steps (1) and (2). The syntactic representation is produced by the parser, which turns the acoustic input into a labeled syntactic representation.

The linking in a *wh*-question in English, in both directions, is illustrated in Figures 28.13 and 28.14; the linking of the peripheral adjunct *yesterday* is not represented. In the linking from semantics to syntax in Figure 28.13, the undergoer *what* is linked directly to the PrCS; there is no empty argument position in the core – that is, no trace. The rule in (25a) applies to assign *John* the preposition *to*.

There are two important complications in the syntax-to-semantics linking with this sentence, as shown in Figure 28.14. First, no conclusion can be drawn from the morphosyntax regarding the function of *what*; hence in step 1 it is simply labeled 'RP'. Second, because *give* is a variable undergoer selection verb it is not possible to assign undergoer to an argument in the LS in step 2, unlike in Figure 28.13. So the linking of *John* is determined by using the inverse of (25a) as a linking principle: since *John* is marked by *to*, it must be the first argument of **have'**. After *Mary* is linked to the x argument and *John* to y, the Completeness Constraint forces the linking of *what* to the z argument, which yields the correct interpretation. Constraints on *wh*-question formation and other 'extraction' constructions are explained in terms of the interaction of information structure and syntax, in particular in terms of restrictions on the potential focus domain (Van Valin 1995; 1998; 2005).

4 Conclusion

The more complete picture of RRG that emerges from this discussion is given in Figure 28.15.

In the linking from semantics to syntax, the source of the syntactic representation is the templates of the syntactic inventory. In the syntax to semantics linking, the source is the parser. The lexicon plays an important role in both. Discourse-pragmatics – that is, information structure – interacts with the linking algorithm in significant ways at various steps.

Robert D. Van Valin, Jr.

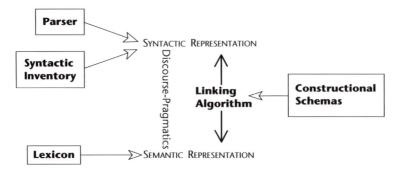

Figure 28.15 Organization of Role and Reference Grammar (final)

Constructional schemas provide the language-specific morphosyntactic information that complements the general, cross-linguistically valid principles of the theory.

Notes

1 In addition to the references in VVLP (1997) see also Van Valin (1998; 2001; 2002), Weist (2002), Weist *et al.* (2004).

2 See Kailuweit *et al.* (2003), Butler (2007), Nolan (2004b), Guest (2008), Guest and Brown (2007).

3 See also Bornkessel *et al.* (2004), Bornkessel and Schlesewsky (2006a; 2006b), Bornkessel-Schlesewsky and Schlesewsky (2008; 2009).

4 RRG does allow zero morphemes in morphological paradigms; what is excluded is phonologically null pronouns (*pro*, PRO), noun phrases (traces), light verbs, adpositions, etc., in syntactic representations.

5 Abbreviations: ABS 'absolutive', ADV 'adverb', AUH 'Actor-Undergoer Hierarchy', CNV 'converb marker', DET 'determiner', ERG 'ergative', IF 'illocutionary force', LDP 'left-detached position', LOC 'locative', LS 'logical structure', NMR 'non-macrorole', NUC 'nucleus', PERF 'perfect', PrCS 'pre-core slot', PRED 'predicate', PRO 'pronoun', PROG 'progressive', PSA 'privileged syntactic argument', RP 'reference phrase', TNS 'tense'.

6 In languages which have VPs, such as English, the VP-like units are derived from a number of different constructional sources; a particularly important one is the interaction of the constituent projection of the clause with the focus structure projection; see Van Valin (2005: §3.5). See also the structure of the linked core in Figure 28.10. What is crucial from an RRG perspective is that VPs are derived units in clause structure, not basic ones; hence they are not an inherent part of the constituent projection.

7 See Everett (2008) for a discussion of intentional state constructions in Wari', an Amazonian language, in which whole clauses can serve as the nucleus of a sentence.

8 RRG treats the notion of 'agent' rather differently from other theories. The basic notion is 'effector', which is the first argument of **do'** and is unspecified for agentivity. With many verbs, a human effector may be interpreted as an agent in certain contexts. If the verb lexicalizes agentivity, as with *murder*, then the logical structure contains 'DO', which indicates that the argument must be interpreted as an agent. See Holisky (1987), Van Valin and Wilkins (1996), VVLP, §3.2.3.2, for detailed discussion. Also, primary-object languages patterns require a modified undergoer selection principle, namely that the undergoer is the second-highest ranking argument in the LS; see Guerrero and Van Valin (2004), Van Valin (2005: 123–127).

9 While it is normally the case that languages with variable PSAs have a voice opposition, it is not always the case. See Van Valin (2009) for discussion of two languages, Liangshan Nuoso and Barai, which have variable PSAs but lack a formal voice opposition.

10 The name of the theory stems from its origin as a theory of grammatical relations: cross-linguistically, different grammatical relations are constituted by varying grammaticalization of semantic *role* and discourse-pragmatic – that is, *reference* – relations. In Lakhota, semantic role

considerations are primary, whereas in English, Tagalog, and Dyirbal, discourse-pragmatic properties such as topicality can influence PSA selection in some cases.

11 The term 'coordination' here is being used for an abstract linkage relation referring to a relationship of equivalence and operator independence at the level of juncture. It is distinct from conjunction, which is a construction type of the general form 'X *conj* Y', which may be one of the formal instantiations of coordinate nexus.

12 There is also a rule for assigning instrumental case, but it is complex and not necessary for this discussion. See Van Valin (2005: §4.4).

13 There is also a rule for assigning *with*, which is very similar to the rule for instrumental case.

14 There are general principles governing the selection of the syntactic templates to be combined, which are not given here. Also, step 5 is language-specific, since every language has its own linearization principles, which is not to deny the existence of cross-linguistic ordering generalizations.

Further reading

Guerrero, L., S. Ibáñez Cerda, and V. Belloro (eds). 2009. *Studies in role and reference grammar*. México City: UNAM.
Kailuweit, R., B. Wiemer, E. Staudiger, and R. Matosović (eds). 2008. *New applications of role and reference grammar*. Newcastle: Cambridge Scholars Publishing.
Nakamura, W. (ed.). 2011. *New perspectives in role and reference grammar*. Newcastle: Cambridge Scholars Publishing.
Van Valin, R.D., Jr. 2005. *Exploring the syntax-semantics interface*. Cambridge: Cambridge University Press.
Van Valin, R.D., Jr (ed.). 2008. *Investigations of the syntax-semantics-pragmatics interface*. Amsterdam: John Benjamins.

References

Bentley, Delia. 2008. The interplay of focus structure and syntax: evidence from two sister languages. In Van Valin (ed.), 263–284.
Bornkessel, I., and M. Schlesewsky. 2006a. The extended argument dependency model: A neurocognitive approach to sentence comprehension across languages. *Psychological Review* 113:787–821.
Bornkessel, I., and M. Schlesewsky. 2006b. Generalised semantic roles and syntactic templates: A new framework for language comprehension. In Bornkessel et al. (eds), 327–353.
Bornkessel, I., M. Schlesewsky, and R.D. Van Valin Jr. 2004. Syntactic templates and linking mechanisms: A new approach to grammatical function asymmetries. Poster presented at 17th CUNY Conference on Human Sentence Processing. Downloadable from http://linguistics.buffalo.edu/people/faculty/vanvalin/rrg/vanvalin_papers/rrg_adm_CUNY04.pdf (accessed 31 January 2014).
Bornkessel, I., M. Schlesewsky, B. Comrie, and A. Friederici. (eds). 2006. *Semantic role universals and argument linking: Theoretical, typological and psycholinguistic perspectives*. Berlin: Mouton de Gruyter.
Bornkessel-Schlesewsky, I., and M. Schlesewsky. 2008. Unmarked transitivity: A processing constraint on linking. In Van Valin (ed.), 413–434.
Bornkessel-Schlesewsky, I., and M. Schlesewsky. 2009. *Processing syntax and morphology*. Oxford: Oxford University Press.
Butler, C. 2007. Notes towards an incremental implementation of the role and reference grammar semantics-to-syntax mapping rules for English. In *Structural-functional studies in English grammar. In honour of Lachlan Mackenzie*, Studies in Language Companion Series 83, 275–307. Amsterdam and Philadelphia: John Benjamins.
Culicover, P. and R. Jackendoff. 2005. *Simpler syntax*. Oxford: Oxford University Press.
Dixon, R.M.W. 1972. *The Dyirbal language of north Queensland*. Cambridge: Cambridge University Press.
Dowty, D. 1979. *Word meaning and Montague grammar*. Dordrecht: Reidel.
Everett, D. 2008. Wari' intentional state constructions. In Van Valin (ed.), 381–412.
Foley, W., and R.D. Van Valin Jr. 1977. On the viability of the notion of 'subject' in universal grammar. *BLS* 3:293–320.

Foley, W., and R.D. Van Valin Jr. 1984. *Functional syntax and universal grammar*. Cambridge: Cambridge University Press.

Franklin, K. 1971. *A grammar of Kewa, New Guinea*. (=*Pacific Linguistics C-16*). Canberra: Australian National University.

Givón, T. 1980. The binding hierarchy and the typology of complements. *Studies in Language* 4:333–377.

Good, Jeff. 2003. Clause combining in Chechen. *Studies in Language* 27:113–170.

Guerrero, L. 2006. *The structure and function of Yaqui complementation*. Munich: Lincom.

Guerrero, L., and R.D. Van Valin Jr. 2004. Yaqui and the analysis of primary object languages. *IJAL* 70:290–319.

Guerrero, L., S. Ibáñez, and V. Belloro (eds). 2009. *Studies in role and reference grammar*. México City: UNAM.

Guest, Elizabeth, Lena Moburg, John Etchells, Rolf Kailuweit, Tobias Bender, Matthias Hartung, Eva Staudinger, and Alexander Valet. 2003. Parsing English, Swedish and French using the RRG paradigm. Paper presented at the 2003 International Conference on Role and Reference Grammar, UNESP São José do Rio Preto, Brazil.

Guest, E. 2008. Parsing for role and reference grammar. In Van Valin (ed.), 435–454.

Guest, E., and S. Brown. 2007. Using role and reference grammar to support computer-assisted assessment of free text answers. Unpublished ms. Leeds Metropolitan University.

Hansell, M. 1993. Serial verbs and complement constructions in Mandarin: A clause linkage analysis. In Van Valin (ed.), 197–233.

Heusinger, K. von. 1999. Intonation and information structure. Habilitationschrift, University of Konstanz.

Holisky, D. 1987. The case of the intransitive subject in Tsova-Tush (Batsbi). *Lingua* 71:103–132.

Jackendoff, R. 1992. Mme. Tussaud meets the binding theory. *Natural Language and Linguistic Theory* 10:1–31.

Jolly, J. 1993. Preposition assignment in English. In Van Valin (ed.), 275–310.

Kamp, Hans. and Uwe Reyle. 1993. *From discourse to logic*. Hingham, MA: Kluwer.

Kockelman, P. 2003. The interclausal relations hierarchy in Q'eqchi' Maya. *IJAL* 69:25–48.

Lambrecht, K. 1994. *Information structure and sentence form*. Cambridge: Cambridge University Press.

Narasimhan, B. 1998. A lexical semantic explanation for 'quirky' case marking in Hindi. *Studia Linguistica* 52:48–76.

Nolan, B. (ed.). 2004a. *RRG 2004 book of proceedings*. Downloadable from http://linguistics.buffalo. edu/people/faculty/vanvalin/rrg/RRG2004%20Book%20of%20Proceedings.pdf (accessed 31 January 2014).

Nolan, B. 2004b. First steps toward a computational RRG. In Nolan (ed.), 196–223.

O'Connor, Rob. 2008. A prosodic projection for role and reference grammar. In Van Valin (ed.), 227–244.

Ohori, T. 2001. Some thoughts on a new systematization of interclausal semantic relations. Paper presented at 2001 Role and Reference Grammar Conference, University of California, Santa Barbara.

Ohori, T. 2005. More thoughts on the semantic representation in RRG: Event types and the semantics of clause linkage. Paper presented at the 2005 International RRG Conference, Taiwan. Downloadable from http://wings.buffalo.edu/linguistics//people/faculty/vanvalin/rrg/vanvalin_papers/OHORI.pdf (accessed 31 January 2014).

Olson, M. 1981. Barai clause junctures: toward a functional theory of interclausal relations. PhD dissertation, Australian National University.

Roberts, J.R. 2012. Serial verbs in English: An RRG analysis of catenative verb constructions. *Functions of language* 19:201–234.

Shimojo, M. 1995. Focus structure and morphosyntax in Japanese: *Wa* and *ga*, and word order flexibility. PhD dissertation, SUNY at Buffalo. Downloadable from http://wings.buffalo.edu/linguistics//people/faculty/vanvalin/rrg/shimojo/MitsuDis.pdf (accessed 31 January 2014).

Shimojo, M. 2008. How missing is the missing verb? The verb-less numeral quantifier construction in Japanese. In Van Valin (ed.), 285–304.

Shimojo, M. 2009. Focus structure and beyond: Discourse-pragmatics in RRG. In Guerrero et al. (eds), 113–142.

Silverstein, M. 1976. Hierarchy of features and ergativity. In *Grammatical categories in Australian languages*, ed. R. Dixon, 112–171. Canberra: Australian Institute of Aboriginal Studies.

Smith, C. 1997. *The parameter of aspect*, 2nd edn. Dordrecht: Reidel.

Van Valin, R.D. Jr. 1977. Ergativity and the universality of subjects. *CLS* 13:689–706.

Van Valin, R.D. Jr. 1981. Grammatical relations in ergative languages. *Studies in Language* 5: 361–394.

Van Valin, R.D. Jr (ed.). 1993. *Advances in role and reference grammar*. Amsterdam/Philadelphia: John Benjamin.

Van Valin, R.D. Jr. 1994. Extraction restrictions, competing theories and the argument from the poverty of the stimulus. In *The reality of linguistic rules*, ed. Susan D. Lima, Roberta Corrigan, and Gregory K. Iverson, 243–259. Amsterdam/Philadelphia: John Benjamin.

Van Valin, R.D. Jr. 1995. Toward a functionalist account of so-called 'extraction constraints'. In *Complex structures: A functionalist perspective*, ed. Betty Devriendt, Louis Goossens, and Johan van der Auwera, 29–60. Berlin: Mouton de Gruyter.

Van Valin, R.D. Jr. 1998. The acquisition of *wh*-questions and the mechanisms of language acquisition. In *The new psychology of language: Cognitive and functional approaches to language structure*, ed. M. Tomasello, 221–249. Mahwah, NJ: LEA.

Van Valin, R.D. Jr. 1999. Generalized semantic roles and the syntax-semantics interface. In *Empirical issues in formal syntax and semantics 2*, ed. F. Corblin, C. Dobrovie-Sorin, and J.-M. Marandin, 373–389. The Hague: Thesus.

Van Valin, R.D. Jr. 2001. The acquisition of complex sentences: a case study in the role of theory in the study of language development. *CLS* 36–2:511–531.

Van Valin, R.D. Jr. 2002. The development of subject-auxiliary inversion in English *wh*-questions: an alternative analysis. *Journal of Child Language* 29:161–175.

Van Valin, R.D. Jr. 2004. Semantic macroroles in role and reference grammar. In *Semantische Rollen*, ed. R. Kailuweit and M. Hummel, 62–82. Tübingen: Narr.

Van Valin, R.D. Jr. 2005. *Exploring the syntax-semantics interface*. Cambridge: Cambridge University Press.

Van Valin, R.D. Jr. 2006. Semantic macroroles and language processing. In I. Bornkessel et al. (eds), 263–302.

Van Valin, R.D. Jr. 2007. The role and reference grammar analysis of three-place predicates. *Suvremena Lingvistika* 33(63):31–64.

Van Valin, R.D. Jr (ed.). 2008a. *Investigations of the syntax-semantics-pragmatics interface*. Amsterdam: John Benjamins.

Van Valin, R.D. Jr. 2008b. RPs and the nature of lexical and syntactic categories in role and reference grammar. In Van Valin (ed.), 161–178.

Van Valin, R.D. Jr. 2009. Privileged syntactic arguments, pivots, and controllers. In Guerrero et al. (eds), 45–68.

Van Valin, R.D. Jr. 2013. Lexical representation, co-composition, and linking syntax and semantics. In *Advances in generative lexicon theory*, ed. James Pustejovsky, Pierrette Bouillon, Hitoshi Isahara, Kyoko Kanzaki, and Chungmin Lee, 67–107. Dordrecht: Kluwer.

Van Valin, R.D. Jr, and R.J. LaPolla. 1997. *Syntax: structure, meaning and function*. Cambridge: Cambridge University Press.

Van Valin R.D. Jr, and D. Wilkins. 1993. Predicting syntactic structure from semantic representations: *remember* in English and its equivalents in Mparntwe Arrernte. In Van Valin (ed.), 499–534.

Van Valin R.D. Jr, and D. Wilkins. 1996. The case for 'effector': Case roles, agents and agency revisited. In *Grammatical constructions*, ed. M. Shibatani and S. Thompson, 289–322. Oxford: Oxford University Press.

Vendler, Z. 1967. *Linguistics in philosophy*. Ithaca, NY: Cornell University Press.

Walton, C. 1986. *Sama verbal semantics: classification, derivation and inflection*. Manila: Linguistic Society of the Philippines.

Watters, J. 1993. An investigation of Turkish clause linkage. In Van Valin (ed.), 535–560.

Weist, R.M. 2002. The first language acquisition of tense and aspect: A review. In *Tense-aspect morphology in L2 acquisition*, ed. R. Salaberry and Y. Shirai, 21–78. Amsterdam: John Benjamins.

Weist, R., A. Pawlak, and J. Carapella. 2004. Syntactic-semantic interface in the acquisition of verb morphology. *Journal of Child Language* 31:31–60.

29

Dependency Grammar

Timothy Osborne

1 Introduction

When one begins to construct a theory of syntax, a fundamental decision is to be made: Will the theory be based on the principle of dependency or on the principle of constituency? If dependency is chosen, the theory will be a dependency grammar (DG), whereas if constituency is chosen, it will be a constituency grammar (= phrase structure grammar). Both grammar types are well represented. Examples of prominent DGs are Word Grammar, Meaning-Text Theory, Lexicase, and Functional Generative Description. Examples of prominent constituency grammars are Categorial Grammar, Lexical Functional Grammar, Government and Binding Theory, Head-Driven Phrase Structure Grammar, and Minimalist Program. From a historical perspective, each grammar type is associated above all with the seminal work(s) of a single linguist. DGs are associated most with the seminal work of Lucien Tesnière, *Éléments de syntaxe structurale*, posthumously published in 1959, and constituency grammars with the seminal works of Noam Chomsky (e.g., 1957; 1965).

DGs see syntactic structure consisting of elements (e.g., words) and the dependencies that connect these elements into hierarchical structures. Constituency grammars also acknowledge dependencies, but these dependencies are indirect, since they are mediated by higher nodes. The dependency relation is a strict mother–daughter relation, whereas the constituency relation is a part–whole relation. While the dependency vs. constituency distinction is crucial to the overall theory of syntax, both relations accomplish the same thing. They are both grouping words (and other syntactic units) in such a manner that syntactic structure can be acknowledged. The two are not, however, notational variants of the same thing, which means that the one type of grammar can do things that the other cannot, and vice versa.

The dependency vs. constituency distinction is understood best in terms of the tree structures associated with each – for example:

(1)

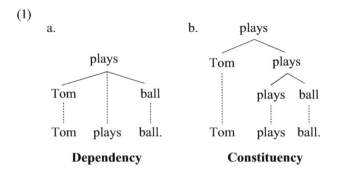

a. **Dependency**

b. **Constituency**

The words themselves are used as the labels in the tree structures, a convention that is employed consistently throughout this chapter. The dependencies between words in (1a) are direct; the words are connected to each other directly. These same dependencies are also present in the constituency tree (1b), although they are no longer direct, but, rather, are mediated by higher nodes. The strict mother–daughter dependency relation is visible in (1a) insofar as the head word *plays* dominates its dependents *Tom* and *ball*. And the part–whole relation of constituency is present in (1b) insofar as the parts combine with each other in such a manner that a greater unit is the result. The words *plays* and *ball* combine to create the greater unit *plays ball*, and *Tom* and *plays ball* combine to create the greatest unit *Tom plays ball*.

This contribution considers the theory of syntax and grammar that arises when one chooses dependency over constituency. It calls attention to aspects of dependency that distinguish DGs from constituency grammars. Some key aspects of DGs are surveyed, whereby a couple of widespread misconceptions about DG are corrected.

2 Historical notes

While the history of dependency in the study of grammar reaches back to the earliest recorded grammars – that is, back to Pānini – and has been identified in the grammars of Ibn Mada (1120–1196, Cordoba) and Thomas von Erfurt (around 1300, Erfurt), most modern DGs are traced to the works of Lucien Tesnière (1893–1954). Tesnière was a Frenchman, a polyglot, and a professor of linguistics at the universities in Strasbourg and Montpellier. Tesnière's seminal work, his *Éléments de syntaxe structurale*, appeared posthumously in 1959. The *Éléments* laid down a comprehensive theory of syntax and grammar that builds on the dependency concept. Interestingly, Tesnière himself did not employ the term *dependency grammar*; that choice of terminology may be attributable to Hays (1964).

Dependency grammar has until recently been on the periphery of mainstream syntax in Anglo-American linguistics. However, in mainland Europe, interest in DG was and is stronger, especially in Germany and Eastern Europe. This fact is likely due in part to the perception that a dependency-based system is better suited as the basis for the analysis of languages with freer word order than English. In Germany, both East and West, a number of prominent dependency grammars began appearing in the 1970s and the tradition extends up to this day. Examples include Heringer (1970), Baum (1976), Kunze (1975), Engel (1994), Heringer (1996), and Eroms (2000). Ágel *et al.*'s (2003/6) massive two-volume collection of essays on DG and valency theory, with well over 100 authors contributing to the collection, is especially worth noting. In Prague the works of Sgall *et al.* (e.g., 1986) in the framework of Functional Generative Description and in Moscow and later Montreal the works of Mel'čuk (e.g., 1988) in the framework of Meaning-Text Theory have significantly influenced the development of DG. The works of Starosta (e.g., 1988) in Hawaii in the Lexicase framework are worth noting and, in London, the works of Hudson (e.g. 1984; 1990; 2007) in the Word Grammar framework have had a major impact on the field.

Much of the recent interest in DG is not coming from the theoretical works just mentioned, however, but rather is coming from the field of computational linguistics. Dependency-based systems are increasingly being used for computational applications, such as for tagging, parsing, and generating tree banks (see Nivre 2010; 2011). Dependency-based computational systems have been around since the 1960s (e.g., Hays 1964; Gaifman 1965), but they too have remained on the periphery until relatively recently.

3 Dependencies

The following three sections introduce central aspects of syntactic dependencies: some of the various conventions for representing dependencies are illustrated; the key trait that distinguishes dependency, a one-to-one ratio, from constituency, a one-to-one-or-more ratio, is emphasized; and the diagnostics that help identify the presence and direction of dependencies – that is, constituency tests – are illustrated.

3.1   Representing dependencies

A dependency between two elements is a binary, asymmetric relation. In other words, a dependency connects two elements, whereby one element is taken to be the head over the other. Dependencies are therefore directed; they always point from head down to dependent. A number of varying conventions are employed to represent dependencies. For example:

(2)

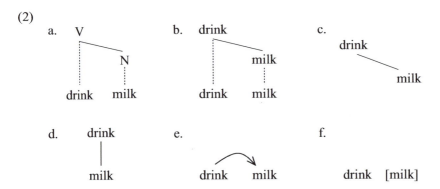

These six structures illustrate the main conventions employed to represent dependencies. In each case, a dependency connects the two words, whereby the verb *drink* is taken to be head over the dependent noun *milk*. Although the conventions vary, the analysis is consistent; the asymmetric dependency relation between the two words is clearly indicated.

Structure (2a) employs the categories of the words as labels in the tree, whereas (2b) uses the words themselves to label the nodes in the tree. Both (2a) and (2b) include the further convention whereby the string of words is placed below and attached with dotted vertical projection lines to the nodes in the tree. This convention is beneficial for the examination of discontinuities. The convention in (2c) judges the string below and the dotted projection lines to be unnecessary; it simplifies the tree down to the words/nodes and the dependencies that connect them into a structure. The convention shown in (2d) abstracts away from linear order, focusing only on hierarchical order. The arrow in (2e) illustrates another widely employed convention whereby arcs point from heads to their dependents. And, finally, (2f) uses a rare bracketing convention: dependents are enclosed in more brackets than their head. While all six of these conventions are employed in the literature on DG, the convention shown in (2b) is employed throughout this paper, mainly because it renders dependencies arguably in the most transparent manner possible.

3.2 One-to-one

The dependency principle is a one-to-one ratio: each element in a sentence corresponds to one and only one node in the syntactic structure of that sentence. This strict one-to-one correspondence stands in contrast to the constituency relation, which is a one-to-one-or-more ratio: a given sentence element corresponds to one or more nodes in the structure. Dependency structures are therefore minimal compared to their constituency grammar counterparts, as the following, more extensive, trees illustrate:

(3)

a.

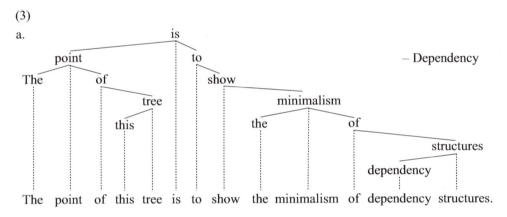

b.

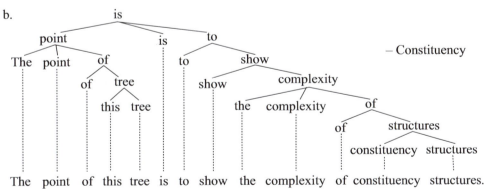

The sentence contains thirteen words, so there are exactly thirteen nodes in the dependency tree; the one-to-one ratio is clear. The constituency tree, in contrast, contains twenty-two nodes; the one-to-one-or-more ratio is also clear. The constituency tree is the direct translation of the dependency tree, which means that it is unlike most constituency trees mainly because it lacks a finite VP constituent.[1] By its very nature, dependency is hardly capable of acknowledging a finite VP constituent (although it readily acknowledges non-finite VP constituents).[2]

The strict one-to-one relation of dependency places a great restriction on the amount of syntactic structure that one can posit. The layered (= tall) trees associated with many constituency grammars – for instance, those that build on the X-bar schema – are not possible. While dependency does not prohibit the analysis of syntactic structure from positing empty nodes, most DGs avoid empty units (in non-coordinate and non-elliptical structures).

3.3   Identifying dependencies

Dependency-based structures are identified using the same diagnostics that most any grammar is likely to employ to discern the grouping of elements into syntactic units. Constituency tests are primary tools in the toolkit to this end. The manner in which words are grouped into subtrees (= constituents) in DGs is supported by the units that constituency tests identify (see Osborne 2005: 254ff.; 2006: 53ff.; 2008: 1126ff.; Osborne *et al.* 2011: 322ff.). Subject and object NPs, for instance, are depicted as constituents. For example:

(4)

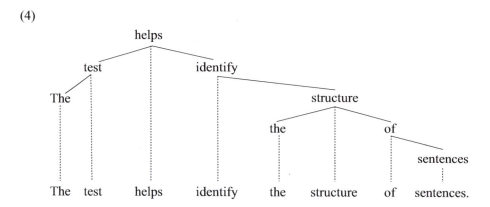

The subject NP *the test* and the object NP *the structure of sentences* appear as constituents (= subtrees), which is consistent with the results of standard constituency tests (topicalization, clefting, pseudoclefting, proform substitution, answer fragments, etc.). The non-finite VP *identify the structure of sentences* is shown as a constituent, too, which is also consistent with the results of constituency tests.

The determiners *the* and *the* are depicted as constituents as well, although they are not identified as constituents by constituency tests. That determiners and attributive adjectives (= pre-noun modifiers) fail many constituency tests is addressed in terms of Ross' (1967) Left Branch Condition. Constituents that appear on left branches under nouns fail many constituency tests. The final two constituents in the tree – that is, *of sentences* and *sentences* – can at least marginally be identified as constituents using the tests: for example, *?What do the tests identify the structure of?*.

The finite VP unit is of particular interest when considering what constituency tests reveal about the nature of sentence structure. As stated above, a core difference between dependency- and constituency-based grammars concerns the status of finite VP. Constituency grammars almost unanimously assume the existence of such a constituent for English (and many other languages), whereas DGs are hardly capable of acknowledging the existence of such a constituent. The results from constituency tests do not deliver a clear judgment in this area, although they tend to support the DG stance that finite VP is not a constituent. For example:

(5)   The test <u>helps identify the structure of sentences</u>.

a. *…and <u>helps identify the structure of sentences,</u> the test.   – Topicalization
b. *It is <u>helps identify the structure of sentences</u> that the test (does).   – Clefting
c. *What the test (does) is <u>helps identify the structure of sentences</u>.   – Pseudoclefting
d. The test <u>does so/that</u>.   – Proform
                                                                                            substitution
e. What does the test do? - <u>?Helps identify the structure of sentences</u>. – Answer fragment

The topicalization, clefting, and pseudoclefting tests suggest that the finite VP *helps identify the structure of sentences* is not a constituent. The proform substitution test using *does so/that*, in contrast, does seem to identify the finite VP as a constituent. However, it may be the case that *so/that* is the only proform in (5d), since the verb *does* can be interpreted as a full verb in such a case, which means it is a full verb just like *helps* is a full verb. The answer fragment test does not deliver a clear result, although I prefer to repeat the subject in the answer: - *It helps identify the structure of sentences*.

The one constituency test that indisputably suggests that finite VP is a constituent is coordination. For example:

(5)   f. The test [helps identify the structure of sentences] and [is widely employed].

The finite VP has clearly been coordinated in (5f). Therefore, the constituency grammar approach, which takes finite VP to be a constituent and builds on this core assumption, appears to be empirically justified. There is a difficulty with coordination as a constituency test, however. Coordination suggests, namely, that many strings are constituents that no grammar – regardless of whether it is dependency- or constituency-based – takes to be a constituent. For example:

(6)   a. [The boys bathed] and [the girls dried] the dog.
       b. [Why does he] and [when does she] want to do that?
       c. He [drops off the boys before] and [picks them up after] school.
       d. Sam sent [me flowers] and [you chocolates] last week.

For most theories of sentence structure, the strings enclosed in brackets in these sentences do not qualify as constituents. The validity of coordination as a diagnostic for constituent structure is therefore in doubt.[3]

In sum, constituency tests do not deliver solid evidence for the existence of a finite VP constituent, which means the DG rejection of the binary division of the clause is not indefensible. In fact, the results of most standard constituency tests support the DG view of sentence structure, since they identify far fewer constituents than constituency grammars posit.

4 Types of dependencies

Some DGs distinguish between types of dependencies (e.g., Mel'čuk 1988: 106ff.; Nichols 1986; Jung 1995: 3ff.). In addition to syntactic dependencies, one also acknowledges semantic and/or morphological dependencies. Semantic dependencies are in some sense more basic and closer to thought than syntactic and morphological dependencies. They are characterized in terms of *predicate–argument structures*. Morphological dependencies, in contrast, are surface manifestations that are distinct and separate from syntactic dependencies; they are characterized in terms of *form determination*. Syntactic dependencies are seen as mediating between these two other types of dependencies. They are characterized in terms of *distribution*. These three dependency types are summarized as follows:

1. Semantic dependencies → Predicate–argument structures
2. Morphological dependencies → Form determination
3. Syntactic dependencies → Distribution

Beyond these three, one can also acknowledge prosodic and phonological dependencies, although these additional types of dependencies are not considered below. Failure to distinguish between types of dependencies results in confusion. Semantic and/or morphological dependencies are misinterpreted as syntactic dependencies. The result is an inconsistent and unprincipled analysis of sentence structure.

4.1   Predicates and their arguments

Semantic dependencies concern predicates and their arguments, a given predicate selecting its arguments. If we assume that the arguments of a given predicate semantically depend on their predicate, then a situation often results where a semantic dependency points in the opposite direction to a syntactic dependency; semantic dependencies can point up or across the syntactic hierarchy. For example:

(7)

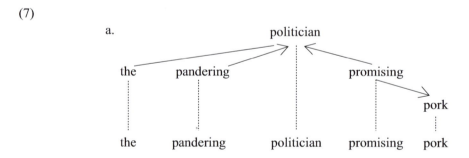

The participles *pandering* and *promising* are forms of content verbs and, as such, they are predicates; and, like all predicates, they select their arguments. The predicate *pandering* selects *the … politician* as its argument, and the predicate *promising* selects *the … politician* and *pork* as its arguments. The arrows indicate the direction of these semantic dependencies; two of the semantic dependencies run in the opposite direction to the syntactic dependencies – that is, they point up the tree. From a syntactic point of view, the two participles *pandering* and *promising* clearly modify the noun *politician* and are therefore syntactically dependent on the noun, but, from a semantic point of view, the noun is dependent on the participles because it is (part of) an argument of the participle predicates.

(7) illustrates the manner in which semantic dependencies can run counter to syntactic dependencies. It also occurs frequently that a given semantic dependency exists between two units that are not connected by a syntactic dependency at all. For example:

(8)

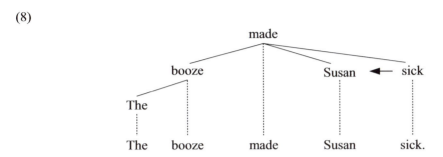

The predicative adjective *sick* is a predication over the object argument *Susan*, yet there is no syntactic dependency that connects the two words. What this means is that the semantic dependency is completely independent of the syntactic hierarchy. Failure to distinguish between semantic and syntactic dependencies might motivate the incorrect assumption that *Susan* is a syntactic dependent of *sick*, since it is an argument of *sick*.

Meaning-Text Theory (Mel'čuk 1988) acknowledges and accommodates semantic dependencies in terms of a separate level of representation. The semantic level is one of seven in the stratified model, and it is the "deepest" of the seven. On this level, only the semantic dependencies are present. The MTT semantic level for the noun phrase in (7) might look something like this – for examples of semantic representations like the one here, see Kahane (2003: 549) and Mel'čuk (2003: 189):

(9)

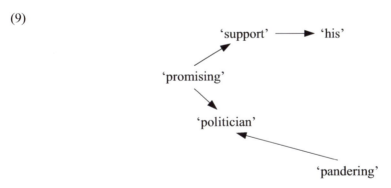

Function words such as *the* are absent. The arrows point from predicates to their arguments. The structure should be read as though no hierarchy of units is present. A given semantic unit can often serve as the argument of more than one predicate, as is the case here with '*politician*'.

4.2 Form determination

Form determination is the basis for morphological dependencies, which are manifest as agreement and concord. When a word or part of a word influences the form of some other word, the latter morphologically depends on the former. Like semantic dependencies,

Timothy Osborne

morphological dependencies can be entirely independent of syntactic dependencies. That is, many morphological dependencies exist between words that are not directly connected to each other by syntactic dependencies.

First, however, consider how the morphological dependency of subject–verb agreement in English points up the syntactic hierarchy and the morphological dependency of determiner–noun agreement points down the syntactic hierarchy:

(10)

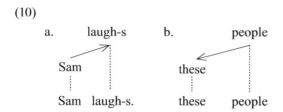

The trees shown are again according to syntactic dependencies, but the arrows show the direction of the morphological dependencies. The first person singular subject *Sam* in (10a) determines the form of the finite verb *laugh-s*; it requires the appearance of the third person singular present tense inflectional suffix *-s*, which means the morphological dependency points up the syntactic hierarchy. The opposite situation obtains in (10b), where the plural noun *people* requires the plural form of the demonstrative determiner *these* (not *this*).

English has relatively little inflectional morphology and so there are few morphological dependencies. Examples from related languages, however, demonstrate that morphological dependencies can also point across the syntactic hierarchy, as the following examples from German and French illustrate:

(11)

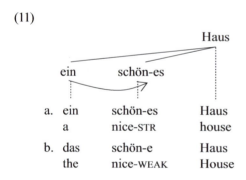

(12)

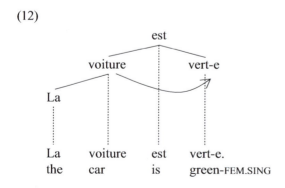

The choice of determiner in the German noun phrases on the left influences the ending on the adjective. The indefinite article *ein* in (11a) lacks an ending for gender (and case), which means the ending of the attributive adjective *schön* must be strong. The definite article *das* in (11b), however, shows gender and number (neuter singular), which means the adjective ending on *schön* is the weak -*e*. Thus a morphological dependency points from the determiner to the adjective, the former influencing the ending that appears on the latter.[4] There is, however, no syntactic dependency that connects the two words. A similar situation obtains in (12). The gender and number of the noun *voiture* (feminine singular) determines the ending on the predicative adjective *vert-e*. Hence the morphological dependency points across the syntactic hierarchy from the noun to the adjective.

The acknowledgement of morphological dependencies such as the ones just illustrated – especially those illustrated with examples (10a–b) – motivated Nichols (1986) to distinguish between head-marking and dependent-marking languages. Languages that contain numerous morphological dependencies that point up the syntactic hierarchy from dependents to their heads are known as *head-marking languages*, whereas languages that contain numerous morphological dependencies that point from heads to their dependents are known as *dependent-marking languages*. Of course many languages have a mix of head-marking and dependent-marking structures, and it is likely that purely head- or dependent-marking languages do not exist. This distinction, which has become a mainstay for language typology, is possible by acknowledging both syntactic and morphological dependencies.

4.3   Distribution

While syntactic dependencies are the focus of most work in DG, coming up with a solid criterion that reliably identifies the presence and direction of every syntactic dependency has proven difficult and, to my knowledge, no single criterion or operational test has been identified that delivers certainty in every case. The prominent head debate between Zwicky (1985) and Hudson (1987) provides the best illustration of the difficulty. Zwicky's and Hudson's goal was to identify one or more criteria that could reliably identify the heads of phrases. They examined concepts such as argumenthood, concord, distribution, government, and subcategorization. Of these concepts, distribution seems to be the notion that provides the best foundation for the concept of syntactic dependencies (see Owens 1984: 36; Schubert 1988: 40; Mel'čuk 2003: 200). The word in a given phrase that is most responsible for determining the environments in which that phrase can appear is the root of that phrase.[5]

But even if there is some measure of agreement that distribution is the basis for syntactic dependencies, no single operational test has demonstrated the ability to identify heads reliably. While the constituency tests mentioned and illustrated above (topicalization, clefting, pseudoclefting, proform substitution, answer fragments) are certainly helpful diagnostics in this area, there are cases where they do not deliver certainty about constituent structure, which means that they do not always succeed at discerning head from dependent.[6] Furthermore, the applicability and utility of constituency tests can vary greatly depending on the language at hand. Given these difficulties, the preferred methods for identifying heads are heuristic. One generalizes across related structures and even across distinct languages to reach decisions about the presence and direction of syntactic dependencies.

One diagnostic that was not mentioned or illustrated above but that is useful in many cases and is easy to employ should be mentioned here: *omission*. A given constituent that can be omitted from a phrase without rendering the resulting greater structure unacceptable or altering the meaning significantly is NOT the root of that phrase. For example:

(13) a. The milk is good.
       b. Milk is good. – Omission identifies *milk* as the root of the noun phrase *the milk*.

(14) a. You stop!
       b. Stop! – Omission identifies *stop* as the root of the clause *You stop!*.

(15) a. That is very good.
       b. That is good. – Omission identifies *good* as the root of the adjective phrase *very good*.

Of course, omission as a diagnostic for identifying the roots of phrases is limited in its applicability. Often both words of a two-word phrase appear obligatorily, meaning that neither word can be omitted. Confronted with this difficulty, one must reach to other methods for discerning head from dependent.

Two frequently occurring structures where omission does not help distinguish head from dependent are subject–verb and preposition–noun combinations. For example:

(16) a. Sam   slept.
       b. across town

Omission does not deliver a verdict about the direction of the syntactic dependency because both words appear obligatorily. That a dependency connects the two words is not disputed, but certainty about which word is head over the other is not easy to establish. Noteworthy in this respect is the fact that these combinations were the ones Bloomfield (1933) judged to be exocentric: that is, he deemed them to lack heads entirely. Bloomfield's understanding of syntax was, however, constituency-based. The possibility of an exocentric analysis is not available for dependency-based grammars because dependency by its very nature sees all structure as endocentric.

A variety of considerations can deliver a verdict about head and dependent in such cases. The existence of subject-less clauses in many languages suggests that the subject depends on the verb – for example, German *Nun wird gearbeitet* 'Now is worked → One is working now' – and even in English, the imperative is usually formed without expressing the 2nd person subject, as illustrated in example (14b). Furthermore, in many so-called *pro-drop languages* definite subject pronouns are usually omitted in everyday speech. Facts such as these strongly support the conclusion that the finite verb is head over the subject nominal. Concerning preposition–noun combinations, as in (16b), the fact that in certain limited cases the preposition can appear without its complement suggests that the preposition is head over the nominal – for example, *She walked across the street toward us → She walked across toward us*. Furthermore, prepositions are more restricted in their distribution than nominals. For instance, a prepositional phrase cannot appear in subject position, whereas noun phrases can. This fact points to the preposition as head, since it is determining the distribution of the entire phrase in which it appears.

To conclude the discussion of the three dependency types, it must be emphasized that failure to distinguish between semantic, morphological, and syntactic dependencies has been a source of confusion. At times semantic or morphological criteria are taken to determine syntactic dependencies. Morphological dependencies especially can generate confusion in this area, since there is much variation in the direction of these dependencies cross-linguistically. These difficulties are overcome if one distinguishes between the three types of dependencies just sketched.

5 Word order

The following three subsections examine some aspects of the DG approach to word order.

5.1 Two ordering dimensions

Tesnière (1959; 1969: 16ff.) emphasized that syntactic units are organized along two dimensions, the precedence dimension (linear order) and the dominance dimension (hierarchical order). The influence of the precedence dimension is obvious, since the words of utterances precede and follow each other. They appear on a time line that extends from the start to the end of the utterance. A speaker cannot speak more than one word at a time, nor can more than one word be written at a time. The influence of the dominance dimension is less obvious, but it too is clearly present. Words are grouped in such a manner that meaning-bearing units can be acknowledged. Dominance is the organizational principle that groups words into syntactic units. How a theory approaches these two ordering dimensions has a big impact on the underlying nature of the grammar. In particular, whether or not the theory separates the two dimensions and addresses each in isolation is telling.

Following a practice employed extensively by Tesnière (1959), dependency grammars have traditionally separated the two ordering dimensions. The dominance dimension is deemed more "basic" in a sense than the precedence dimension. For Tesnière, syntactic units are organized first along the dominance dimension in the mind of a speaker. When a speaker utters a sentence, the words that make up that sentence are ordered hierarchically first. The actual act of uttering the words requires the change-over to linear order – that is, the hierarchical order of the words is changed over to the linear order of sequence as the words are enunciated. In contrast to the speaker, Tesnière emphasized that the listener perceives the linear order of the words as they are uttered and then adds hierarchical order to them, grouping the words of the sequence in such a manner that meaning can be assigned to these groups. This separation of the ordering dimensions influenced the later development of DG greatly, since many traditional dependency hierarchies lack linear order entirely.

The sentence *That idea works* illustrates these concepts:

(17)

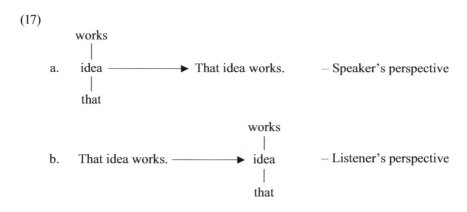

The speaker, in order to express an idea, adds linear order to hierarchical order, whereas the listener adds hierarchical order to linear order.[7] It should be apparent that this understanding of how meaning is conveyed relies heavily on a separation of the ordering dimensions. This separation has had a major impact of the development of DG in general, since the traditional approach focuses more on hierarchical order than on linear order. The focus on hierarchical order is evident in the numerous dependency trees from early works; these trees tend to convey hierarchical order only, sometimes even ignoring actual word order almost entirely.

The emphasis on hierarchical order has had both a positive and a negative impact on the development of DG. It has been positive because it has helped motivate the insight that DG is well suited to explore the syntax of free word order languages. Dependency structures are, in fact, more capable than constituency structures of separating the ordering dimensions and examining the hierarchical dimension in isolation. Consider the following trees in this regard:

(18)

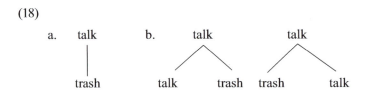

The dependency tree (18a) ignores linear order entirely; it says nothing about whether *trash* precedes or follows *talk* in an actual utterance. The constituency trees in (18b), in contrast, must position *talk* in front of *trash* or *trash* in front of *talk* because the two words are sisters in the hierarchy. The necessity to place the one in front of the other means that constituency cannot produce tree structures that abstract away from linear order.[8] Dependency is hence more capable of focusing on the one ordering dimension in isolation (on the vertical dimension). The discontinuities associated with free word order become less problematic because fewer crossing lines appear in the trees.

The DG focus on hierarchical order has been negative, however, insofar as it has also generated the inaccurate impression that DG has little to say about actual word order phenomena. This impression is supported by the dearth of detailed DG analyses of many word order altering mechanisms. Systematic and detailed DG accounts of phenomena such as extrapostion, *wh*-fronting, scrambling, and topicalization are rare. Despite this impression, one should note that dependency-based structures are fully capable of exploring word order phenomena in a principled fashion, a fact that will become evident shortly.

5.2 Projectivity and discontinuities

The principle by which DGs explore actual word order phenomena is called *projectivity* (see, for instance, Hays 1964; Gaifman 1965; Robinson 1970; Mel'čuk 1988: 35ff.; Heringer 1996: 259ff.; Groß 1999: 174ff.; Eroms 2000: 311ff.). This principle refers to concrete syntax trees and the dependencies that they contain. Dependency hierarchies where every dependent is adjacent to its head or to a sister constituent are said to be *projective*, whereas projectivity is violated if a given dependent is adjacent to a word that separates it from and dominates its head. Projectivity violations, when they occur, are clearly visible in syntax trees:

(19)

a.

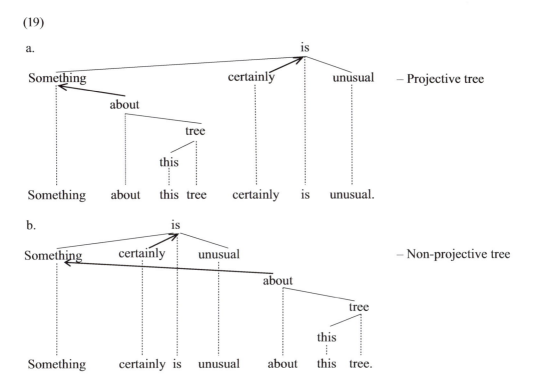

– Projective tree

Something   about   this tree   certainly   is   unusual.

b.

– Non-projective tree

Something   certainly is   unusual   about   this   tree.

The arrow dependency edge marks an adjunct. The arrow points away from the adjunct, indicating that semantic selection runs opposite to the direction of the syntactic dependency – see (7a). Trees such as (19a), in which there are no crossing lines, are projective; every constituent is adjacent to its head or to a sister constituent. In (19b), in contrast, the constituent *about this tree* is not adjacent to its head nor to a sister constituent (it has no sister constituent). In such cases, crossing lines obtain in the tree. These crossing lines identify a projectivity violation, which in this case is due to extraposition. The extraposed constituent *about this tree* is separated from its head by a word that dominates its head (*is*). A more common term to denote projectivity violations is *discontinuity*. When projectivity is violated in the manner illustrated here, a discontinuity is present. Constituency grammars often call discontinuities *long-distance dependencies*.

The following trees illustrate discontinuities further. A *wh*-fronting discontinuity from English, a clitic climbing discontinuity from French, and a scrambling discontinuity from German are given:

(20)

a.

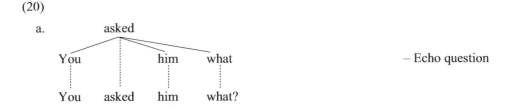

– Echo question

You   asked   him   what?

Timothy Osborne

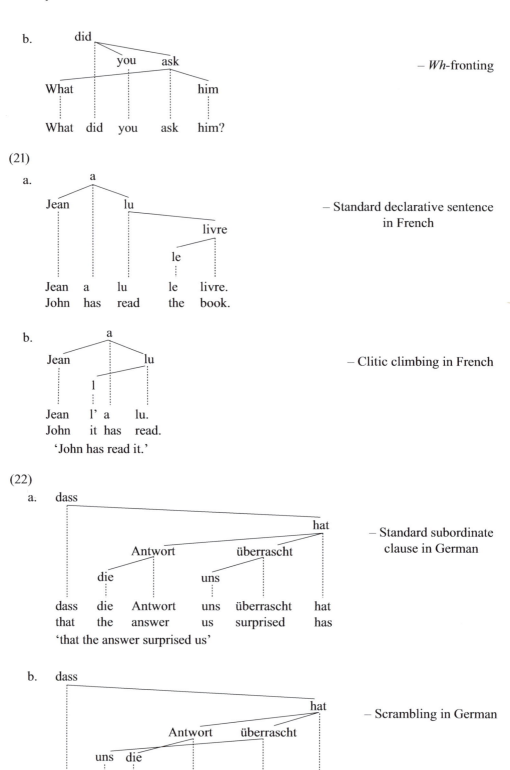

b.

– *Wh*-fronting

What did you ask him?

(21)

a.

– Standard declarative sentence
in French

| Jean | a | lu | le | livre. |
| John | has | read | the | book. |

b.

– Clitic climbing in French

| Jean | l' | a | lu. |
| John | it | has | read. |

'John has read it.'

(22)

a.

– Standard subordinate
clause in German

| dass | die | Antwort | uns | überrascht | hat |
| that | the | answer | us | surprised | has |

'that the answer surprised us'

b.

– Scrambling in German

| dass | uns | die | Antwort | überrascht | hat |

618

The a-sentences show (what can be considered) canonical word order where the structures are all projective. The crossing lines in the b-sentences, however, illustrate various types of discontinuities. Owing to the *wh*-fronting, clitic climbing, and scrambling mechanisms, crossing lines obtain, which means that discontinuities are present. The manner in which dependency grammars address these discontinuities can vary. As discussed above, the traditional DG approach to word order might not be overly concerned about such projectivity violations, since the hierarchical structures across the a- and b-sentences remain largely consistent. Some more modern DGs, however, strive to produce a principled account of such discontinuities. The discussion now turns to one of these accounts.

5.3 Rising

Some DGs address discontinuities like the ones just illustrated in terms of a flattening of structure (see, for instance, Duchier and Debusmann 2001; Hudson 2000: 32; Gerdes and Kahane 2001; Eroms and Heringer 2003: 26; Groß and Osborne 2009). The discontinuity is "overcome" by allowing the displaced constituent to take on a word as its head that is not its governor. That is, the displaced constituent climbs up the structure in a sense, attaching to a word that dominates its governor. The discussion here follows Groß and Osborne (2009) in calling this mechanism *rising*. Dashed dependency edges and a g subscript are used to indicate the presence of rising. The rising analyses of the b-examples from the previous section are as follows:

(23)

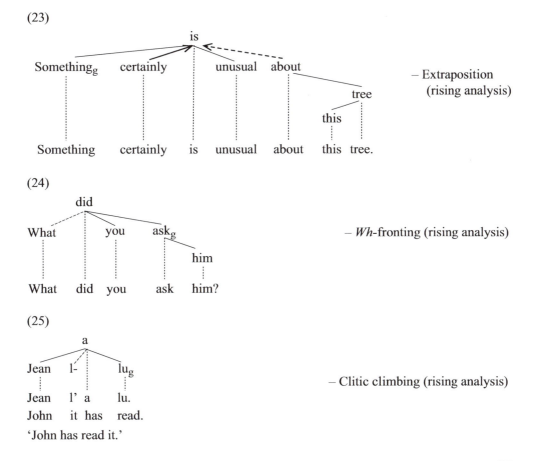

– Extraposition (rising analysis)

(24)

– *Wh*-fronting (rising analysis)

(25)

– Clitic climbing (rising analysis)

(26)

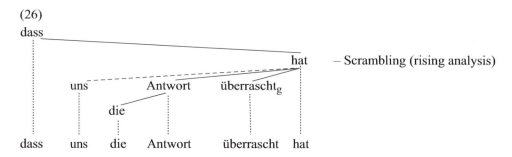

– Scrambling (rising analysis)

dass   uns   die   Antwort   überrascht   hat

Each of these sentences contains an instance of rising. The displaced constituent "rises" up the structure to attach to a word that dominates its governor. The dashed dependency edge indicates that the head of the risen constituent is not its governor, and the g-subscript identifies the governor of the risen constituent. An important aspect of the rising analysis of discontinuities is that the DGs that posit the flatter structures for discontinuities are non-derivational in the syntax. What this means is that the term *rising* must be understood as a metaphor. Rising in the literal sense does not occur; the displaced constituent is in no way understood to have been attached to its governor at a deep level of syntax.

By acknowledging rising in the manner shown, one can argue that true discontinuities never actually occur. What is perceived as a discontinuity is actually just an instance where a displaced constituent has taken on a word as its head that is not its governor. The nature of the various discontinuity types can be explored by examining the minimal chain of words (= catena) that extends from the root of the displaced constituent to the governor of that constituent.

6 Catenae

A recent development within DG is the *catena* unit (see O'Grady 1998; Osborne 2005; Osborne and Groß 2012; Osborne *et al.* 2012). The next two sections examine catenae.

6.1 Four syntactic units

Any element (word or morph) or any combination of elements that is continuous in the vertical dimension (i.e., with respect to dominance) is a catena. The catena unit is much more flexible than the constituent, and the argument has therefore been put forward that the catena is better suited to serve as the basic unit of syntactic (and morphosyntactic) analysis than the constituent. The definitions of the catena and three similarly defined units are now presented together. The intent is to build understanding of the catena by way of comparison with the three similarly defined units:

String
A word or a combination of words that is continuous with respect to precedence.

Catena
A word or a combination of words that is continuous with respect to dominance.

Component
A word or a combination of words that is continuous with respect to both precedence and dominance: that is, it is both a string and a catena.

Constituent
A component that is complete.

A given component is *complete* if it includes all the words that its root word dominates. This definition of the constituent is equivalent in the relevant sense to the definition of the constituent in phrase structure grammars (= A NODE PLUS ALL THE NODES THAT THAT NODE DOMINATES).

These units are illustrated using the following dependency tree:

(27)

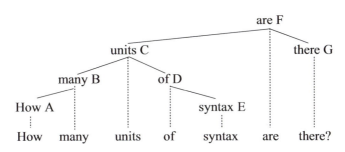

The capital letters serve to abbreviate the words. All of the words and word combinations that qualify as one or more of the four units are listed next:

28 distinct strings in (27)
A, B, C, D, E, F, G, AB, BC, CD, DE, EF, FG, ABC, BCD, CDE, DEF, EFG, ABCD, BCDE, CDEF, DEFG, ABCDE, BCDEF, CDEFG, ABCDEF, BCDEFG, and ABCDEFG.

35 distinct catenae in (27)
A, B, C, D, E, F, G, AB, BC, CD, CF, DE, FG, ABC, BCD, BCF, CDE, CFG, ABCD, ABCF, BCDE, BCDF, BCFG, CDEF, CDFG, ABCDE, ABCDF, ABCFG, BCDEF, BCDFG, CDEFG, ABCDEF, ABCDFG, BCDEFG, and ABCDEFG.

24 distinct components in (27)
A, B, C, D, E, F, G, AB, BC, CD, DE, FG, ABC, BCD, CDE, ABCD, BCDE, CDEF, ABCDE, BCDEF, CDEFG, ABCDEF, BCDEFG, and ABCDEFG.

7 distinct constituents in (27)
A, E, G, ABB, DE, ABCDE, and ABCDEFG

The word combinations that qualify as strings are continuous in the horizontal dimension – that is, with respect to precedence – whereas the word combinations that qualify as catenae are continuous in the vertical dimensions. A word combination that is continuous in both dimensions is a component, and any word combination that forms a subtree is a constituent.

The number of distinct catenae in the tree, 35, is comparatively large. The corresponding constituency grammar tree of sentence (27) could contain at most 13 overt constituents ($= 2n - 1$, where n = number of words). Thus there are almost three times more catenae in sentence (27) than there can be constituents. One must note in this regard, however, that there are many more word combinations in (27) that fail to qualify as catenae than there are that qualify as catenae. The total number of distinct word combinations in (27) is 127 ($= 2^7 - 1$, where 7 = number of words), which means that there are 92 ($= 127 - 35$) word combinations in (27) that fail to qualify as catenae, including AC, BF, EG, ABD, CDG, ABDE, ACEG, ABDEF, ABCDEG, etc.

Timothy Osborne

The numbers are instructive because they demonstrate that while the catena is a much more flexible and inclusive unit than the constituent, it is also quite restricted. Any mechanism of syntax that requires the relevant unit to be a catena has therefore excluded a large number of word combinations as potential candidates under consideration for that rule. The argument that has been put forth in this regard (Osborne and Groß 2012; Osborne *et al.* 2012) is that the catena is flexible enough to acknowledge those word combinations that behave as syntactic units with respect to a wide variety of phenomena, whereas at the same time it is also limited enough to exclude those word combinations that do not behave as syntactic units with respect to the same phenomena.

The validity of the catena concept has been established empirically in two broad areas: with respect to form-meaning correspondences and with respect to specific mechanisms of syntax, such as those associated with ellipsis and discontinuities. Owing to space limitations, however, only the first of these two areas – that is, form-meaning correspondences – is discussed and illustrated in this contribution.

6.2 Lexical items

Units of meaning are matched to units of form, whereby these units of form are catenae, but often not constituents. This point is now established with examples from four types of constructions: prepositional verbs, particle verbs, idioms more broadly construed, and periphrastic verb combinations. The words that build these constructions usually form catenae in the syntax and can therefore be stored as catenae in the lexicon.

Prepositional verb constructions consist of a verb plus a specific preposition. The two words constitute a single semantic unit owing to their non-compositionality of meaning. That is, the meaning of a given prepositional verb construction does not derive directly from the combination of the meanings of the verb and the preposition as each is understood in isolation. The catena unit overcomes the difficulties associated with this non-compositional meaning. The verb and its preposition form a catena. For example:

(28)

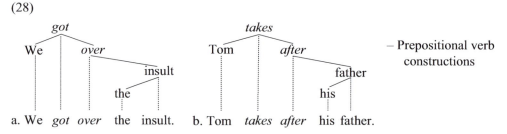

a. We *got over* the insult.   b. Tom *takes after* his father.   – Prepositional verb constructions

The two words of the prepositional verb constructions are in italics; these two words form a catena each time, and these catenae are stored in the lexicon as single units. Particle verb constructions are similar:

(29)

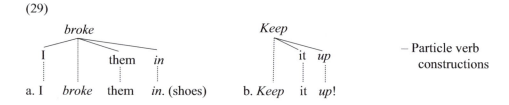

a. I *broke* them *in*. (shoes)   b. *Keep* it *up*!   – Particle verb constructions

622

The verb and particle together (italics) form a catena and can therefore be stored in the lexicon as concrete syntactic units. Light verb constructions consist of a light verb and (usually) a noun. The light verb is semantically poor, the main content being provided by the noun. For example:

(30)

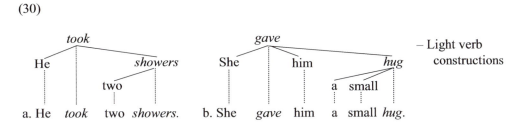

- Light verb constructions

a. He *took* two *showers*.   b. She *gave* him a small *hug*.

The light verb and its noun together (in italics) constitute the main clause predicate. Together they form a catena and can thus be stored in the lexicon as single units.

The next examples illustrate that the same insight is true of multi-word idioms:

(31)

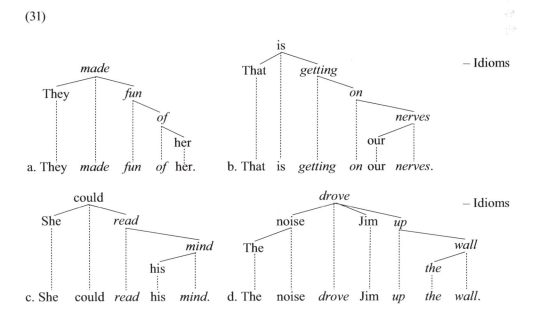

- Idioms

a. They *made* *fun* *of* her.   b. That *is* *getting* *on* our *nerves*.

- Idioms

c. She could *read* his *mind*.   d. The noise *drove* Jim *up* the *wall*.

The fixed words of each idiom (in italics) form a catena, and this catena is the core of the main clause predicate. For instance, the idiom *X drives X up the wall* is a predicate that takes the two arguments marked by the Xs, which in this case are filled by *the noise* and *Jim*. It should be apparent that the fixed words of these idioms cannot be construed as forming constituents in any sense.

Periphrastic verb constructions of all types are the matrix predicate of their clauses. These predicates are catenae in syntax. For example:

(32)

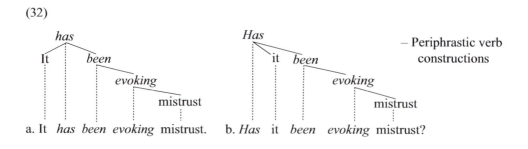

a. It *has been evoking* mistrust.	b. *Has* it *been evoking* mistrust?

(33)

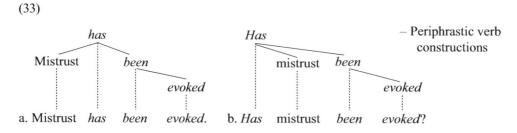

a. Mistrust *has been evoked.*	b. *Has* mistrust *been evoked?*

The periphrastic verb constructions (in italics) express functional content of perfect and progressive aspect, and active or passive voice. Each time, the italicized catena is the matrix predicate. These predicates remain catenae when subject–auxiliary inversion occurs. What this means is that the predicates (and arguments) of predicate–argument structures are manifest in syntax as concrete units – that is, as catenae.

The examples (28)–(33) have demonstrated that lexical items (units of meaning) are stored as catenae. The building blocks of meaning are catenae. Frege's principle of compositionality is in fact defensible, but not in the expected sense – that is, not in terms of constituents, but in terms of catenae. Units of meaning are assigned to catenae, be these units of meaning predicates, arguments, or combinations of function words.

7   Conclusion

This contribution has provided an introduction to and some discussion of some of the central concepts of and recent developments in dependency-based theories of syntax. Instead of recapping the discussion, however, one central trait of DG is emphasized in conclusion. This trait is the parsimony of dependency-based systems. The number of nodes in dependency-based structures tends to be approximately half that of constituency-based structures. The greatly reduced number of nodes means a greatly reduced amount of syntactic structure in general. The minimalism of these reduced structures then permeates the entire theoretical apparatus. Most DGs draw attention to this fact, and, in so doing, they are appealing to Occam's Razor: the simpler theory is the better theory, other things being equal.

Notes

1   The dependency tree (3a) lacks a finite VP constituent because there is no node/word that exhaustively dominates *is to show the minimalism of dependency structures*, this string being the one that constituency grammars almost unanimously judge to be a constituent in line with the traditional binary division of the clause into a subject NP and a predicate VP.

2 The constituent is not traditionally considered to be a unit of dependency structures. If one adopts a theory-neutral definition of the constituent, however, constituents can be acknowledged in both constituency- and dependency-based systems. In a tree, a constituent consists of any node/word and all the nodes/words that that node/word dominates.

3 Constituency grammars might object here that sentences (6a–c) involve the so-called *right node raising* mechanism (RNR), and they therefore do not constitute an argument against the validity of the coordination diagnostic. This objection is without merit because it requires one to augment the theoretical apparatus in a theory-specific manner in order to save the coordination test. To settle a dispute between theories, only theory-neutral empirical considerations should count.

4 There is another morphological dependency not shown in (11). This morphological dependency points from *Haus* down the hierarchy to *schön-es*. The ending *-es* reflects the fact that *Haus* is neuter singular.

5 The current discussion draws a distinction between the *head* and the *root* of a given constituent. The root of a constituent is the one word within that constituent that is not dominated by any other word in that constituent. In contrast, the head of a given constituent is the one word outside of that constituent that immediately dominates that constituent. Failure to distinguish between these two notions has led to confusion. The term *head* is often employed for both concepts in many dependency grammars.

6 See the discussion surrounding (5–6) above for an example of the contradictory results delivered by constituency tests.

7 Tesnière did not discuss how the linearization procedure works – that is, he did not discuss how the language faculty converts the hierarchy to the sequence in (17a). Presumably, linearization rules convert dependencies to sequences. For example, in English a determiner–noun dependency is linearized to a determiner–noun sequence – that is, a linearization rule requires that a dependent determiner be positioned in front of its head noun; a preposition–noun dependency is linearized to a preposition–noun sequence – that is, a linearization rule requires that a dependent noun be positioned after its head preposition. Flexibility in word order arises mainly when sister dependents are linearized, discourse factors influencing the order of the sisters in relation to each other.

8 The problem occurs for dependency structures as well when sister dependents are present. The point, however, is that the problem occurs much less often in dependency structures.

Further reading

Hays, D. 1964. Dependency theory: A formalism and some observations. *Language* 40:511–525.

Hudson, R. 2007. *Language networks: The new word grammar.* Oxford: Oxford University Press.

Mel'čuk, I. 1988. *Dependency syntax: Theory and practice.* Albany, NY: State University of New York Press.

Osborne, T., M. Putnam, and T. Groß. 2012. Catenae: Introducing a novel unit of syntactic analysis. *Syntax* 15(4):354–396.

Tesnière, L. 1959. *Éléments de syntaxe structural.* Paris: Klincksieck.

References

Ágel, V., L. Eichinger, H.-W. Eroms, P. Hellwig, H. Heringer, and H. Lobin (eds). 2003/6. *Dependency and valency: An international handbook of contemporary research.* Berlin: Walter de Gruyter.

Baum, R. 1976. *Dependenzgrammatik.* Tübingen: Niemeyer.

Bloomfield, L. 1933. *Language.* New York: Henry Holt.

Chomsky, N. 1957. *Syntactic structures.* The Hague/Paris: Mouton.

Chomsky, N. 1965. *Aspects of the theory of syntax.* Cambridge, MA: MIT Press.

Duchier, D., and R. Debusmann. 2001. Topology dependency trees: A constraint based account of linear precedence. In *Proceedings from the 39th annual meeting of the Association Computational Linguistics (ACL) 2001,* 180–187. Toulouse.

Engel, U. 1994. *Syntax der deutschen Sprache,* 3rd edn. Berlin: Walter de Gruyter.

Eroms, H.-W. 2000. *Syntax der deutschen Sprache.* Berlin: Walter de Gruyter.

Eroms, H.-W., and H. Heringer. 2003. Dependenz und lineare Ordnung. In *Dependency and valency: An international handbook of contemporary research,* ed. V. Ágel et al., 247–262. Berlin: Walter de Gruyter.

Gaifman, C. 1965. Dependency systems and phrase-structure systems. *Information and Control* 8:304–337.

Gerdes, K., and S. Kahane. 2001. Word order in German: A formal dependency grammar using a topology model. In *Proceedings from the 39th annual meeting of the Association Computational Linguistics (ACL) 2001*, 220–227. Toulouse.

Groß, T. 1999. *Theoretical foundations of dependency syntax*. Munich: Iudicium.

Groß, T. and T. Osborne 2009. Toward a practical dependency grammar theory of discontinuities. *SKY Journal of Linguistics* 22: 43–90.

Hays, D. 1964. Dependency theory: A formalism and some observations. *Language* 40:511–525.

Heringer, H. 1970. *Theorie der deutschen Syntax*. München: Hueber Verlag.

Heringer, H. 1996. *Deutsche Syntax dependentiell*. Tübingen: Stauffenberg.

Hudson, R. 1984. *Word grammar*. Oxford: Blackwell.

Hudson, R. 1987. Zwicky on heads. *Journal of Linguistics* 23:109–132.

Hudson, R. 1990. *An English word grammar*. Oxford: Basil Blackwell.

Hudson, R. 2000. Discontinuities. In *Les grammaires de dépendance (Dependency grammars), Traitement automatique des langues* 41, ed. Sylvaine Kahane, 7–56. Paris: Hermes.

Hudson, R. 2007. *Language networks: The new word grammar*. Oxford: Oxford University Press.

Jung, W.-Y. 1995. *Syntaktische Relationen im Rahmen der Dependenzgrammatik*. Series Beiträge zur germinastischen Sprachwissenschaft 9. Hamburg: Helmut Buske Verlag.

Kahane, S. 2003. The meaning-text theory. In *Dependency and valency: An international handbook of contemporary research*, ed. V. Ágel et al., 546–569. Berlin: Walter de Gruyter.

Kunze, J. 1975. *Abhängigkeitsgrammatik*. Studia Grammatika XII. Berlin: Akademie-Verlag.

Mel'čuk, I. 1988. *Dependency syntax: Theory and practice*. Albany, NY: State University of New York Press.

Mel'čuk, I. 2003. Levels of dependency description: Concepts and problems. In *Dependency and valency: An international handbook of contemporary research*, ed. V. Ágel et al., 188–229. Berlin: Walter de Gruyter.

Nichols, J. 1986. Head-marking and dependent-marking grammar. *Language* 62:56–119.

Nivre, J. 2010. Dependency parsing. *Language and Linguistics Compass* 4(3):138–152.

Nivre, J. 2011. Bare-bones dependency parsing. In *Security and intelligent information systems. Lecture notes in computer science*, Volume 7053, ed. Pascal Bouvry, Mieczysław A. Kłopetek, Franck Leprévost, Małgorzata Marciniak, Agnieszka Mykowiecka, and Henryk Rybiński, 20–32. Springer.

O'Grady, W. 1998. The syntax of idioms. *Natural Language and Linguistic Theory* 16:79–312.

Osborne, T. 2005. Beyond the constituent: A dependency grammar analysis of chains. *Folia Linguistica* 39(3–4):251–297.

Osborne, T. 2006. Shared material and grammar: A dependency grammar theory of non-gapping coordination. *Zeitschrift für Sprachwissenschaft* 25:39–93.

Osborne, T. 2008. Major constituents: And two dependency grammar constraints on sharing in coordination. *Linguistics* 46(6):1109–1165.

Osborne, T., and T. Groß. 2012. Constructions are catenae: Construction grammar meets dependency grammar. *Cognitive Linguistics* 23(1):163–214.

Osborne, T., M. Putnam, and T. Groß. 2011. Bare phrase structure, label-less trees, and specifier-less syntax: Is minimalism becoming a dependency grammar? *The Linguistic Review* 28:315–364.

Osborne, T., M. Putnam and T. Groß. 2012. Catenae: Introducing a novel unit of syntactic analysis. *Syntax* 15:354–396.

Owens, J. 1984. On getting a head: A problem in dependency grammar. *Lingua* 66:25–42.

Robinson, J. 1970. Dependency structures and transformational rules. *Language* 46:259–285.

Ross, J. 1967. Constraints on variables in syntax. Doctoral dissertation, MIT.

Schubert, K. 1988. *Metataxis: Contrastive dependency syntax for machine translation*. Dordrecht: Foris.

Sgall, P., E. Hajičová, and J. Panevová. 1986. *The meaning of the sentence in its semantic and pragmatic aspects*. Dordrecht: D. Reidel Publishing Company.

Starosta, S. 1988. *The case for lexicase: An outline of lexicase grammatical theory*. New York: Pinter Publishers.

Tesnière, L. 1959. *Éléments de syntaxe structural*. Paris: Klincksieck.

Tesnière, L. 1969. *Éléments de syntaxe structural*, 2nd edn. Paris: Klincksieck.

Zwicky, A. 1985. Heads. *Journal of Linguistics* 21:1–29.

30

Morphosyntax in Functional Discourse Grammar

J. Lachlan Mackenzie

1   Introduction to Functional Discourse Grammar

Functional Discourse Grammar (FDG; Hengeveld and Mackenzie 2008) arose in the first decade of this century as a functionally and typologically oriented theory of the organization of natural languages.[1] 'Functional' here means that the theory seeks to elucidate how the forms of language reflect the multiple functions that they serve in human interaction.[2] 'Typological' refers to the theory's desire to draw on and contribute to language typology, the study of variation across the languages of the world. And the word 'discourse' in the name of the theory alludes to the fact that human communication, both monologue and dialogue, takes the form of coherent discourse. Discourse is an activity and breaks down into a succession of Discourse Acts; the focus of FDG is on the analysis of these Discourse Acts and their morphosyntactic and phonological expression.

Whereas many theories of syntax assume the complete Clause as the basic unit of description, FDG observes that the Discourse Act may correspond to various morphosyntactic forms, from a single Word to a Clause (or more). In the following example from English, FDG recognizes three Discourse Acts, expressed by a single word, a Clause, and a sequence of two Phrases respectively:

(1)   Mother, it's surely time for lunch, isn't it?

Taking the Discourse Act as its starting point allows FDG to give equal coverage to all morphosyntactic forms, without privileging the Clause and without regarding units that are less than Clauses – for example the first and third Discourse Acts in (1) – as truncated Clauses.

Discourse Acts are the smallest building blocks of discourse and group into Moves. A Move is defined as either provoking a reaction or being a reaction. So (1) is a Move and Mother's answer to (1) will also be a Move. The Move is the highest layer of analysis in FDG, since there appear to be no grammatical processes triggered by larger units of discourse.

J. Lachlan Mackenzie

Let us now put these introductory remarks in a broader framework by considering the overall architecture of Functional Discourse Grammar as presented in Hengeveld and Mackenzie (2008) (see Figure 30.1).

The first thing that Figure 30.1 makes clear is that the expression 'FDG' is really *pars pro toto*, because the grammar is only one of four components of an overall theory of verbal interaction. In addition to the Grammatical Component, on which the present chapter will concentrate, there is a Conceptual Component that develops the speaker's communicative intention, a Contextual Component that contains all the perceptual information and social awareness that is relevant for the language under analysis as well as short-term memory for linguistic phenomena, and an Output Component which converts the phonological analysis to spoken, written, or gestural form. Alongside the model presented in Figure 30.1, which mimics speech production, a complementary model is assumed that mimics speech comprehension (see Giomi forthcoming).

Let us now focus on the Grammatical Component, which is the FDG proper. Figure 30.1 makes it clear that syntax does not play a central role in the architecture of FDG. Rather,

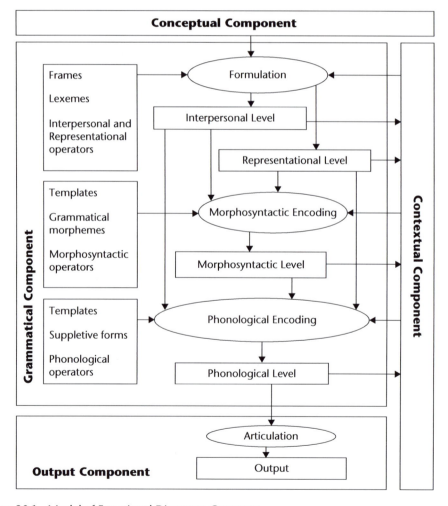

Figure 30.1 Model of Functional Discourse Grammar

628

FDG is built around two major operations, Formulation and Encoding. Formulation is concerned with how each language organizes the intentions and content coming in from the Conceptual Component into Discourse Acts, while Encoding deals with how each Discourse Act, as it emerges from Formulation, is expressed. As Figure 30.1 shows, Formulation leads to two levels of analysis: the Interpersonal Level, which is so called because it provides an analysis of all the aspects of a Discourse Act that reflect its role in the interaction between the Speaker and the Addressee, and the Representational Level, which is so called because it provides an analysis of how the Speaker represents the content that is being communicated. Consider (2):

(2)   Hey you, get your bloody bike out of my garden!

Here the Interpersonal Level (IL) will provide analyses for the existence of two Discourse Acts in this Move (*hey you* and the rest) as well as the presence of an Imperative Illocution in the second Discourse Act, the deictic references to the first and second person (*my*; *you*, *your*), the imprecation *bloody* and the so-called Subacts of Reference and Ascription (see below for an explanation). The Representational Level (RL) will cover the presence of the lexical items *get, bike, out* and *garden* (representing the 'world' being talked about) as well as the relationship that links *get* to its three 'arguments' (the implicit Agent *you*, the Undergoer *your bike* and the Location *out of my garden*); in addition, the RL will display the internal semantic structuring of the two explicit arguments *your ... bike* and *out of my garden* and indeed *my garden* itself. What we see, then, is that in the analysis of linguistic data the two Formulation Levels share the work. From the perspective of the IL, *out of my garden* allows the Speaker to refer the Addressee to something; from the perspective of the RL, *out of my garden* provides the content, as a Location. Not everything is present at both levels, however: *bloody* is absent at RL, since it is purely about how the Speaker wants to affect the Addressee and is not part of how s/he represents the world; similarly, the entire Discourse Act *hey you* is purely interpersonal and accordingly, as shown in Figure 30.1, can be sent straight from the IL to the Phonological Level, bypassing the Representational and Morphosyntactic Levels.

Encoding also has two Levels, the Morphosyntactic Level (ML) and the Phonological Level (PL). Their task is to convert the twofold analysis in Formulation (the IL and the RL) into, first, an ordered sequence of morphosyntactic units (ML) and then an ordered sequence of phonological units (PL). A major difference between the Formulation and Encoding Levels is that the former are essentially unordered, since they are analyses of pragmatics and semantics respectively, not of form. As an example of the ordering task of the ML, consider *your bloody bike* from (2) above: the ML, using the dual input from the IL and RL, must ensure that the IL element *bloody* is placed in the Adjective Phrase position that is available before the RL element *bike*.[3] This is typical of the FDG approach to morphosyntax as involving a continual interleaving of the expression of interpersonal and representational elements.

All four Levels involve internal layering. As we already saw, Discourse Acts, which by their nature are distinguished at the IL, group into Moves. This is shown in (3), which states that the Move M_1 consists of Discourse Acts A_1, A_2, etc.; Π is a position for operators (see below):

(3) $(\Pi M_1: [(\Pi A_1), (\Pi A_2), ...] (M_1))$

The layering principle entails that each category consists of smaller units (until the lowest layer of analysis is reached). Thus Discourse Acts also consist of smaller units, four at most: the Illocution (F_1), the two Speech Participants (P_1 and P_2), and the Communicated Content (C_1):

(4) (ΠA_1: [(ΠF_1) (ΠP_1) (ΠP_2) (ΠC_1)] (A_1))

Notice that the four components of (A_1) are grouped together within square brackets; these symbolize that the relationship among them is configurational, FDG parlance for units that are at the same layer. Where units are not at the same layer, the relationship is said to be hierarchical, with the higher unit taking the lower one in its scope. The distinction between configuration and hierarchy is crucial to understanding how morphosyntax works in FDG (see §4 below).

The Communicated Content ((ΠC_1) in (4)) breaks the Discourse Act down into its component mini-activities, known as Subacts. When a Speaker performs a Discourse Act, she is typically carrying out two kinds of Subact: she can refer (i.e., draw the Addressee's attention to something) or she can predicate (i.e., ascribe some property). Correspondingly, FDG recognizes Subacts of Reference (R_1) and Subacts of Ascription (T_1), which stand in a configurational relationship with one another:

(5) (ΠC_1 : [(ΠT_1) ... (ΠR_1) ...] (C_1))

In the Discourse Act *get your bloody bike out of my garden* in (2), for example, the Communicated Content contains one Subact of Ascription, corresponding to *get*, and two Subacts of Reference, corresponding to *your bloody bike* and *out of my garden*.[4] Notice that in (2) the Speaker does not refer to the Actor (here, the owner of the bike); at the RL, however, the Actor will be present as being semantically relevant.

Any of the units of the Interpersonal Level may be expanded by one or more modifiers. At the IL, these are lexical elements that have a pragmatic rather than semantic role to play. Thus *bloody* in (2) will be analysed as a modifier of a Subact of Reference; similarly, *please* can serve to mitigate an Imperative and thus is a modifier of an Illocution, and *however* usually modifies a Move, indicating how it contrasts with other Moves in the preceding discourse. Modifiers are represented after a colon, as in (6):

(6) (ΠR_1: ... (R_1): bloody$_{Adj}$ (R_1))

The essential difference between modifiers (symbolized in (7) below as Σ) and operators (Π) is that the former involve a lexical item while the latter form a closed class in each language and correspond to grammatical rather than lexical elements at the ML. Here is a summary of the structure of the Interpersonal Level (in practice, representations are run together on a single line, but here for purposes of exposition each layer is placed on its own line); notice that the variables (M_1, A_1, etc.), operators (Π) and modifiers (Σ) are all indicated in upper case:

(7) (ΠM₁: [Move

      (ΠA₁: [Discourse Act

          (ΠF₁: ILL (F₁): Σ (F₁))   Illocution

          (ΠP₁: ... (P₁): Σ (P₁))   Speaker

          (ΠP₂: ... (P₂): Σ (P₂))   Addressee

          (ΠC₁: [Communicated Content

              (ΠT₁: [. . .] (T₁): Σ (T₁))   Subact of Ascription

              (ΠR₁: [. . .] (R₁): Σ (R₁))   Subact of Reference

          ] (C₁): Σ (C₁))   Communicated Content

      ] (A₁): Σ (A₁))   Discourse Act

  ] (M₁): Σ (M₁))   Move

All the other three Levels are layered in a similar way. The RL is organized as follows:

(8) (π p₁: Propositional Content

      (π ep₁: Episode

         (π e₁: State-of-Affairs

            [(π f₁: [Configurational Property

              (π f₂: ♦ (f₂): [σ (f₂)])   Lexical Property

              (π x₁: ♦ (x₁): [σ (x₁)])   Individual

              ...

            ] (f₁):   [σ (f₁)])   Configurational Property

         (e₁)]: [σ (e₁)])   State-of-Affairs

      (ep₁): [σ (ep₁)])   Episode

    (p₁): [σ (p₁)])   Propositional Content

As will be clear, the variables, operators and modifiers at the RL are indicated in lower case. ♦ symbolizes a lexical head. To see an application of (8), consider the somewhat simplified example of an RL analysis in (9), in the standard horizontal presentation, which corresponds to the Discourse Act expressed in (10):

(9) (p₁: (Pres ep₁: (Neg e₁: (Prog f₁: [(f₁: heed_V (f₁)) (1x₁: child_N (x₁): lazy_Adj (x₁))_A
    (mx_j: teacher_N (x_j))_U] (f₁)) (e₁)) (ep₁)) (p₁))

(10) The lazy child is not heeding the teachers.

In this analysis,[5] there are no operators at the Propositional Content layer (p_i), but there is the absolute-tense operator Present on the Episode layer (ep_i), the polarity operator Negative on the State-of-Affairs layer (e_i), the aspect operator Progressive on the Configurational Property layer (f_i), and the number operators '1' and 'm' (singular and plural respectively) on the Individual layer (x_i and x_j respectively). Each will have an effect on the non-lexical material in morphosyntactic encoding: Pres is encoded as the present tense (cf. *is*); Neg is encoded as the grammatical morpheme *not*; Prog is encoded as the suffix *-ing*; 1 is encoded as the lack of any marking on *child* and m as the plural marking in *teachers*. Notice also that the various layers are related hierarchically but that the content of the Configurational Property (f_i) consists of three units that are in a configurational relationship (and therefore enclosed in square brackets). The example contains one modifier, 'lazy', applied to (x_i).

The remainder of the chapter will consider how the dual result of the operation of the Interpersonal and Representational Levels is expressed morphosyntactically. Section 2 will introduce the basics of the Morphosyntactic Level. Section 3 will discuss the relationship between Formulation and Encoding, setting out the major mapping principles and the notion of transparency. Section 4 introduces the notion of absolute and relative positions at the Clause, Phrase, and Word layers and Section 5 goes on to talk about two phenomena that are distinctive to the Morphosyntactic Level, dummies and agreement. In Section 6, there is a brief discussion of the relation between the Morphosyntactic and Phonological Levels, and the chapter closes with an overview of current and recent FDG work on morphosyntax.

2   The Morphosyntactic Level

One major component of formulating conceptual material in language is the choice of lexical items, and it will be apparent from the examples given above that lexical properties are already introduced in Formulation. The task of the Morphosyntactic Level (ML) is to merge the information given at the IL and the RL in such a way that these lexical items are appropriately ordered within a hierarchical morphosyntactic structure and are supported by appropriately ordered grammatical morphemes. Which morphemes are applied is to a very large extent dependent upon the operators and functions present in the IL and RL representations. The Morphosyntactic Level of FDG recognizes four layers – in bottom-up order, Word (Xw_1), Phrase (Xp_1), Clause (Cl_1), and Linguistic Expression (Le_1) – where X indicates the type of Word or Phrase, e.g., (Vw_1) 'Verb word' or (Np_1) 'Noun phrase'. (Note that the variables at ML always take the form of an upper-case and one or more lower-case letters.) FDG does not recognize the sentence as a layer, since sentencehood is a property of (some) written languages. A Linguistic Expression is any combination of Clauses, Phrases, and Words; thus (1) above is a Linguistic Expression. The layers relevant to the ML are the following:

(11)   (Le_1 :   Linguistic Expression

        (Cl_1:   Clause

            (Xp_1 :   Phrase

                (Xw_1 :   Word

                    (Xs_1)   Stem

                    (Aff_1)   Affix

                (Xw_1))   Word

            (Xp_1))   Phrase

        (Cl_1))   Clause

    (Le_1))   Linguistic Expression

In keeping with the generally recognized rank scale, Words make up Phrases and Phrases make up Clauses. However, where the language under analysis has recursive structure, Phrases may also contain Phrases or Clauses, and Clauses may contain Clauses. In addition, FDG allows for Clauses to contain Words (e.g., *not* in (10) above) and permits Words to contain not only Morphemes but also Words, Phrases, and even Clauses. In Bininj Gun-Wok (Evans 2003: 536), for example, we find examples of Words such as the following:

(12) Ga-[ganj-ngu-nihmi]-re.
       3-meat-eat-GER-go.PST.PFV
       'He goes along eating meat.'

Here the Phrase *ganj* 'meat' is clearly an argument of the incorporated verb *-ngu-*, not of the incorporating verb *-re*. The embedded clausal nature of the incorporated unit is furthermore reflected in the gerundial ending *-nihmi* with which the incorporated verb is provided. The extent to which recursion applies is an empirical question to be examined per language. The possible existence of languages without recursivity has been extensively discussed of late (Everett 2005; Nevins *et al.* 2009); FDG is set up to recognize languages with any degree of recursivity, from none to the maximum.

It is clear from (11) that FDG takes the position that there is no essential difference between syntax and morphology, hence the name of the Morphosyntactic Level and the title of this chapter. As we shall see in §4, the template structure that is characteristic of FDG's approach to clausal syntax also applies within the Phrase and within the Word, and phenomena such as dummies and agreement are equally prevalent among the constituent parts of the Word. This is the basis for not positing a separate Morphological Level.

It should be emphasized that the categories applied at the ML (Word, Phrase, …) apply at that Level only and relate to formal, strictly morphosyntactic categories. The lexical properties that are introduced at the IL and RL are provided with a subscript indicating the lexeme class to which they belong; see (9) above. In English, which has the lexeme classes Verb (functioning as head of a Subact of Ascription), Noun (head of a Subact of Reference), Adjective (modifier in a Subact of Reference), and Adverb (modifier in a Subact of Ascription), there is generally a good correspondence between these lexeme classes and the Word classes (Nw_1), (Vw_1), $(Adjw_1)$, and $(Advw_1)$. In the isolate Warao, however, the same lexical item may be used in the second, third, and fourth functions, as seen in the data from Romero-Figueroa (1997: 49, 50, 119) in (13); this is a manifestation of a more general observation about Warao that only the lexeme classes Verb and Nonverb need to be distinguished:

(13) a. yakera
          goodness
          'goodness'
      b. Hiaka   yakera   auka   saba   tai   nisa-n-a-e.
          garment goodness daughter for   3SG.F buy-SG-PUNCT-PST
          'She bought a beautiful dress for her daughter.'
      c. Oko   kuana   yaota-te   arone   yakera   nahoro-te, …
          1PL   hardness work-NONPST   although goodness eat-NONPST
          'Although we work hard and eat well, … .'

It is clear that the syntactic context in which *yakera* occurs – after the Verb word in (13b) and before the Verb word in (13c) – is an a priori justification for analysing it as an Adjective word in the first context and as an Adverb word in the second. To give another example, Dutch clearly distinguishes (Manner) Adverb words from Adjective words (for example, in terms of their positional distribution in syntax and the fact that the former cannot be inflected but the latter can), but in the lexicon of Dutch only one lexeme class is needed: all members of the lexeme class Modifier can correspond to either an Adjective or an Adverb at the ML.

3 Mapping principles

Although language is a symbolic construct and thus could tolerate a maximally arbitrary relation between function and form, in actual languages we observe a range of phenomena that betray a large degree of homology of function and form: this is indeed the observation that justifies all functional grammars. Encoding is therefore assumed not to be autonomous from Formulation. On the contrary, the relation between the ML and the Formulation levels is governed by three principles, each of which contributes to maximizing the parallelism between the levels, thereby enhancing the transparency of the relationship. These three principles are known in FDG as Iconicity, Domain Integrity, and Functional Stability. These have recently been subsumed by Hengeveld (2011) under a more general principle of Transparency.

Iconicity can be illustrated by the correspondence between the order in which Moves and Discourse Acts (at the IL) and Propositions and Episodes (at the RL) are represented and the order in which they are expressed. The possibility of adding modifiers that indicate the position of a unit in a sequence (*firstly, secondly,* …) or the role of a proposition in an argument (*therefore, however,* …), as well as operators on States-of-Affairs that allude to relative positioning in a temporal sequence (Anterior, Simultaneous, Posterior, …), all indicate that the ordering in physical reality and mental experience should be reflected at the higher layers of the IL and RL. For this reason (14a) is more natural than (14b):

(14) a. The game began at 7.30 and ended in a draw.
 b. ?The game ended in a draw and began at 7.30.

As with all three principles to be discussed here, Iconicity can be overridden by other communicative factors. Consider the following examples:

(15) a. The game, which began at 7.30, ended in a draw.
 b. The game, which ended in a draw, began at 7.30.

FDG analyses non-restrictive relative clauses of the type shown in (15) as Discourse Acts (unlike restrictive relatives, which belong to the same Discourse Act as the antecedent). In (15a), Iconicity is respected, because the beginning of the game is mentioned before its conclusion; (15b), despite being anti-iconic, is also an acceptable form because Iconicity is overridden by the speaker's focus on the starting time of the game.

The principle of Domain Integrity refers to the cross-linguistic preference for the units that belong together at the IL and RL also to be juxtaposed at the ML. In other words, modifiers should ideally be placed in expression next to the heads that they modify; and functions and operators should be expressed by elements that are close to the morphosyntactic units to which they apply; and the realization of one Subact of Reference, for example, should not be interrupted by that of another Subact of Reference.

Again, this principle applies as a default, but many languages show instances where Domain Integrity is overridden by other communicative strategies. Here are some simple examples from English:

(16) a. Are you going into town?
     b. What are you looking at?

(17) I am now going into town.

(18) The guy has arrived who's going to fix my lock.

In (16a) the integrity of the Verb phrase (Vp) *are going* (notice in passing that Vp in FDG covers the totality of verbs in a Clause, but nothing more) is violated by the placement of *are* in clause-initial position to signal an Interrogative Illocution. In (16b) there is in addition to the non-integrity of the Vp a violation of the integrity of the Adposition phrase (Adp) *at what*, given the clause-initial placement of the question-word in English, which is justified by its Focus status. In (17) the Vp *am going* loses integrity by being interrupted by an Adverb phrase (Advp) *now*. And in (18) the integrity of the Np *the guy who's going to fix my lock* is broken by the placement of the modifying relative clause in clause-final position.

(16a) and (16b) involve the clause-initial position (P^I; see §4), whose special functionality frequently causes domain integrity violations. (17) shows another common source of such violations, the placement of modifiers: as we shall see in §4, a peculiarity of FDG is that modifiers get their positions before their heads do. (18), finally, shows the role of the clause-final position (P^F) as a placement option for bulky modifiers.

The principle of Functional Stability requires that constituents with the same specification, be it interpersonal or representational, must be placed in the same position relative to other categories. In Turkish, for example, a Focus-bearing constituent is placed in immediately pre-verbal position, with the tense-bearing verb position also being fixed, namely as P^F. Although this is generally backed up by prosodic means, immediately preverbal position is a sufficient indication of Focus status. Within the Word layer (i.e., in morphology), the principle of Functional Stability is of particular importance in the sense that in complex words the relative order of meaning-bearing elements will strongly tend to be fixed. This is important in the analysis of words such as the following from Turkish (Lewis 1967: 124), in which the suffix *-miş* occurs twice in succession, once as a resultative and once as an evidential suffix:

(19) Gel-miş-miş-Ø.
     come-RES-NONVIS.PST-3SG
     'S/he is said to have come.'

It is the position closer to the stem that marks off the first occurrence of the suffix as 'resultative' and the position further from the stem that indicates the evidentiality status of the second occurrence.

The three principles taken together are understood within FDG as part of a more general theory of Transparency, which is designed to examine how and why languages (fail to) display a one-to-one mapping between meaning and form. Given that FDG recognizes four Levels, all of which are related (see Figure 30.1), the number of mutual relations among the Levels is $(4 \times (4 - 1))/2 = 6$; of these six, this chapter focuses on two, the relation between the IL and ML and that between the RL and ML.

Languages are seen to have varying degrees of transparency, with some displaying relations between levels which are relatively opaque. For example, the presence of expletive elements adds to opacity: where English adds the expletive *there* and introduces a copula to express an existential State-of-Affairs (see §5 below), Tagalog uses no expletives in such contexts and thus is in this regard more transparent:

(20) Marami-ng   pera.
     lot-LNK   money
     'There is a lot of money.'

Tense-copying in reported speech is another example of opacity, since the tense used by the original speaker has to be reconstructed. A language such as Russian is thus transparent in this respect, see:

(21) Tanja skaza-l-a,   čto   ona   tancu-et.   (Leufkens 2013: 193)
     Tanja say-PST-F   that 3SG   dance.PRS-3SG
     'Tanja said that she was (lit. is) dancing.'

The construction known in transformationalist circles as 'raising' also involves opacity, since the domain integrity of the embedded verb and its argument is violated. Thus a language that lacks raising is in that regard more transparent – for example, Persian (Taleghani 2008: 6):

(22) Be nazar mi-y-âd   (ke) bačče-hâ in film-o   dide   bâ-š-an.
     to view DUR-come-3SG COMP child-PL this movie-ACC see.PTCP SBJ-be-3PL
     'The children seem to have seen this movie', lit. 'It comes to view that the children have seen this movie.'

Among many morphological properties that contribute to opacity, we may here mention cumulation, where one affix is in a one-to-many relationship with meaning elements: cf. *-ó* in Spanish:

(23) Lleg-ó.
     arrive-IND.PST.PFV.3SG
     'S/he arrived.'

Here one affix contains information about mood, tense, aspect, person, and number.

4 Four positions

One of the major tasks of the Morphosyntactic Level involves determining the left-to-right ordering of the elements of the Clause, the Phrase, and the Word. This, crucially, involves templates, which contain one to four absolute positions. FDG research conducted to date (see Hengeveld 2013) has revealed that the initial (P^I), second (P^2), middle (P^M), and final (P^F) positions are potential starting points for the construction of templates. These four are thus cross-linguistically relevant, but do not all apply in every language. Which absolute positions are relevant for a specific language has to be determined empirically, on the methodological assumption that the fewest possible should be applied and that different absolute positions may be required at the layer of the Clause, the Phrase, and the Word. For reasons of space, we will concentrate here on the ordering of the elements of the Clause.

Once an absolute position has been occupied, the template is expanded with further relative positions. This is illustrated in (24):

(24) P^I P^{I+1} P^{I+2} ...
  P^2 P^{2+1} P^{2+2} ...
    ... P^{M-2} P^{M-1} P^M P^{M+1} P^{M+2} ...
      ... P^{F-2} P^{F-1} P^F

We see here that if we find evidence for a position P^I, it may be expanded to the right by further positions (P^{I+1}) etc. P^F may only be expanded to the left, while P^M may be expanded in either direction. P^2, finally, can only be expanded to the right and its presence logically excludes the possibility of P^I being expanded to the right. Each row of absolute and relative positions is known as a domain (Connolly 2012).

We can see the system in action in Dutch, the morphosyntax of which requires a template that contains P^I, P^2, P^M, and P^F:

(25) Ik (P^I) heb (P^2) gisteren (P^M) ge-faal-d (P^F).
  1SG AUX.1SG yesterday PTCP-fail-PTCP
  'I failed yesterday.'

The justification for recognizing a P^2 in Dutch comes from the fact that Dutch declarative main clauses reserve this position for finite verbs (in this case a finite auxiliary). This entails, given that P^2 cannot expand leftwards, that *ik* is in P^I. *Gefaald*, like non-finite verbal elements generally, goes to the clause-final position.[6] *Gisteren*, introduced as a modifier at the Episode layer of the RL, is in P^M (we shall see presently that elements that correspond to the hierarchical part of structure in Formulation are placed first and have prior access to absolute positions). The access of *heb* to an absolute position is also justified by its role as a tense marker, corresponding to an operator at the same Episode layer. Notice that whatever word order variations on (25) occur, *heb* remains in the P^2 position. Consider the following alternatives:

(26) a. Gisteren (P^I) heb (P^2) ik (P^{2+1}) gefaald (P^F).
  b. Gefaald (P^I) heb (P^2) ik (P^{2+1}) gisteren (P^F).

Our discussion of (25) has used dynamic vocabulary such as 'are placed first', 'goes to', 'pushes back'. This is justified by FDG's 'dynamic' approach to constituent order, in which the various operations that lead to morphosyntactic structure are ordered in sequence. This order does not run parallel to the incremental processing of the utterance (indeed, given the leftwards expansion of P^M and P^F, this would not be thinkable). Rather, the order of the so-called 'dynamic implementation' indicates 'the sequence of steps that the analyst must take in understanding and laying bare the nature of a particular phenomenon' (Hengeveld and Mackenzie 2008: 2).

Within that dynamic implementation, a strict distinction is made between 'hierarchical ordering' and 'configurational ordering'. In FDG, unlike most if not all other approaches to morphosyntax, elements that derive from the configurationally structured parts of the

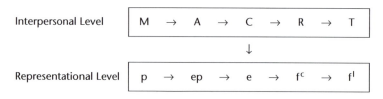

Figure 30.2 Ordering of expression of hierarchical elements in FDG

underlying representations (at both the IL and RL) are not ordered until all the elements of the hierarchically structured parts have been placed in the template. This means that elements corresponding to modifiers, operators, and functions are placed first, while configurationally organized elements go to the remaining places. Not only that, but the hierarchical ordering within the IL and the RL is respected in a downwards direction, and IL layers are all dealt with before the RL layers. The downward progression through the hierarchies is shown in Figure 30.2.

Figure 30.2 should be understood as entailing that, in hierarchical ordering, modifiers, operators, and functions at the Move layer of the IL are first to be placed, and last to be placed are modifiers, operators, and functions at the Configurational Property and Lexical Property layers within the RL.

This procedure is justified by, for example, the observation that 'discourse markers' typically occupy a peripheral position in the syntax of the clause, and thus are immediately taken to occupy P^I or P^F, inevitably relegating any elements placed later to a slightly less peripheral position, namely P^{I+n} (if available) or P^{F-n}. In (27), for example, the discourse marker *so* can only precede the Discourse Act-modifying adverb *unfortunately*, which in turn can only precede the Episode-modifying *today*:

(27) So (P^I) unfortunately (P^{I+1}) today (P^{I+2}) I have a terrible hangover.

As exemplified in (27), the languages of the world typically give a syntactically more peripheral position to interpersonal than to representational modifiers (this is also a possible interpretation of Cinque's (1999) proposals for a universal hierarchy of 'clausal functional projections'), which justifies giving IL modifiers priority over RL ones. The procedure sketched here is thus another manifestation of the principle of Iconicity discussed in §3: scope correlates with relative position.

As for the medial position, FDG does not take the usual position that adverbs are squeezed into the interstices of a fundamental structure predefined, for example, by subject, verb, and object, but rather that these configurational elements go to positions that are determined by a medial adverb, if present. Let us compare the following translational equivalents in English (28a), French (28b) and Portuguese (28c–d):

(28) a. John often writes letters.
　　　b. Jean écrit souvent des lettres.
　　　c. O João muitas vezes escreve cartas.
　　　d. O João escreve muitas vezes cartas.

In all these examples the State-of-Affairs modifier (*often*, *souvent*, *muitas vezes*) will be placed in advance of the configurational elements – the verbal predicate 'write' and its arguments 'John' and 'letters'. In English, with *often* in P^M, the verb goes to P^{M+1} position, which associates it closely with the object *letters* which is forced into P^{M+2}, cf. * ... *writes often letters*. In French *souvent* is in P^M, which forces the verb *écrit* back to P^{M-1} and the Undergoer *des lettres* occupies P^{M+1}. In Portuguese, *muitas vezes* 'lit. many times' also occupies P^M, with the verb *escreve* 'writes' going into either P^{M-1} or P^{M+1}. Superficially similar 'SVO' languages thus differ in how they react to the presence of a medially placed modifier. For the argument that a typology of languages based on S, V, and O is insufficient to deal with these differences, see Hengeveld (2013).

The approach sketched here also accounts for the relative peripherality of Topic and Focus positions in relevant languages. Topic and Focus are pragmatic functions of Subacts of Reference and Ascription and thus are dealt with after the highest layers of the IL but before any RL matters. In Tzotzil (Aissen 1992), if a Topic and a Focus constituent are both present the Topic occurs in the initial position and the Focus in the post-initial position. The language is otherwise predicate-initial, so that the verb now ends up in the third position, P^{I+2}:

(29) A   ti   prove   tzeb-e (P^I) sovra (P^{I+1}) ch'ak'bat (P^{I+2}).
      TOP   DEF   poor   girl-TOP   leftovers   was.given
      'It was leftovers that the poor girl was given.'

If there is only a Topic or a Focus the predicate is in post-initial position, and if there is neither a Topic nor a Focus it is in initial position. Notice that the final position of the verb in (29) should not mislead us into assuming that it is in P^F. What we see is in fact a post-poned initial constituent.

The placement of constituents with respect to their semantic functions is illustrated for Turkish in (30) (Kornfilt 1997: 90):

(30) Hasan   kitab-ı (P^{F-2}) Ali-ye (P^{F-1}) ver-di (P^F).
      Hasan.NOM   book-ACC   Ali-DAT   give-PST.3SG
      'Hasan gave the book to Ali.'

In Turkish, the placement of the accusative and dative Nps – unlike the nominative Np, which is a Subject – is determined by their semantic functions (as stated at the RL). The order shown in (30) may be changed as a result of pragmatic function assignment (which, coming from the IL, takes precedence over RL matters), but in neutral contexts the Recipient precedes the predicate and is itself preceded by the Undergoer in positions relative to the absolute final position of the predicate.

To conclude this section, let us consider two examples of the application of FDG's top-down, centripetal approach within the Phrase and within the Word respectively. (31), from the Siouan language Hidatsa (Matthews 1965), contains the Vp *apaari ki stao ski*:

(31) Wira i   apaari ki   stao   ski.
      tree it   grow   INCH   REM.PST   CERT
      'The tree must have begun to grow a long time ago.'

First to be placed in this Vp will be the highest operator, the certainty operator from the Propositional Content layer at the RL; then the Episode operator 'remote past' is positioned, and finally the Lexical Property operator 'inchoative'. Within the Vp, then, *ski* occupies P^F, *stao* P^{F-1}, and *ki* P^{F-2}, with the verb being in P^{F-3}. In the following example from the

Barbacoan language Tsafiki (Ecuador; Dickinson (2002: 7), cited in Aikhenvald (2004)), we see the same kind of principles determining the order of morphemes at the Word layer in the word *finutie*:

(32) Manuel ano   fi-nu-ti-e.
     Manuel food   eat-PERC-REP-DECL
     'It is said Manuel must have eaten.'

The affixes in this word reflect elements of both the IL and the RL. From the IL we have a Declarative Illocution at the (F)-layer within the Discourse Act and a hierarchically lower Reportative operator at the Communicated Content layer (C). From the RL we have an evidential operator at the Propositional Content layer. It is the illocution-marking affix *-e* that is placed first in the word, in P^F position; then the affix *-ti* at P^{F-1}; then the affix *-nu* at P^{F-2}; and finally the stem *fi* at P^{F-3}.

The placement of affixes before stems, of specifiers before heads, and of adverbial modifiers before the 'core constituents' may seem counter-intuitive, but the result is a consistent approach to ordering at three different layers of morphosyntax which does justice to the high degree of iconicity that characterizes the relation between meaning and form.

5   Dummies and agreement

In the dynamic implementation of the construction of the Morphosyntactic Level it may occur that certain positions at the Clause, Phrase, or Word layer remain unfilled despite the language in question normally requiring those positions to be occupied. In such cases, the languages have recourse to dummies, morphosyntactic elements to which nothing corresponds at the IL or RL. The existence of dummies, and of agreement, also to be treated in this section, shows that morphosyntax in FDG does not involve simply a one-to-one mapping from the Formulation levels.

Among the dummy elements recognized in FDG are the italicized elements in the following examples:

(33) a. *It* is snowing.
     b. *There are* various reasons for that.
     c. *It* is a pity that you are retiring.

In (33a) the IL does not contain a Referential Subact corresponding to *it*, nor is there an Individual at the RL, but simply a lexical property 'snow'. Nevertheless, the syntax of English requires a Subject to be present in a complete Clause, and the morphosyntax provides the 'dummy' element *it* for this purpose. In (33b) the English existential construction is non-lexical (in the sense that no lexical verb of existence is required, cf. Portuguese *Existem várias razões por isso* 'exist-PRS.3PL various reasons for that'). Non-lexical existentials (cf. (20) above) are the expression of a single Referential Subact at the IL, in this case expressed as 'various reasons for that'. In the absence of an Ascriptive Subact, a dummy *there* is inserted, which, being non-verbal in nature, subsequently requires the verbal support of a copula. Thus neither existential *there* nor the copula corresponds to anything in Formulation. Example (33c) involves an embedded Subject Clause corresponding to a subordinated Propositional Content at RL, which, because of its relative morphosyntactic weight, is postponed to P^F position. As with (33a), the Subject position is necessarily filled by the dummy *it*.

In English, the Subject takes a position preceding the finite verb, which by virtue of expressing the Episode operator 'absolute tense', occupies P^M. The dummy position occupied by *it* in (33a) and (33c), and by *there* in (33b) is P^{M-1}; this is also the default position for Subjects in English, which can of course be pushed back to earlier positions (P^{M-n}) by any intervening modifiers.

In FDG, copulas are always analysed as 'dummy elements', in the sense that they are inserted at the ML and correspond to nothing at the IL or RL; after all, they neither refer nor ascribe, and have no semantic content. The copula in examples such as the following, from Spanish, can be seen as mitigating a mismatch between form and function:

(34) a. Este   hombre   es   carpintero.
PROX   man   COP.PRS.3SG   carpenter
'This man is a carpenter.'
b. Esta   mesa   es   de   madera.
PROX   table   COP.PRS.3SG   of   wood
'This table is made of wood.'

If a non-verb, such as a Noun, Adjective, or Adpositional Phrase, is used as the main predicate in a predication, the result is a mismatch between the definitional function of the non-verb and its actual use. Certain languages tolerate this match; others, by inserting a verbal copula, make it explicit that the non-verb is being used in predicative function (see Hengeveld (1992) for extensive discussion).

The copula in (34) is the bearer of the absolute present tense, which corresponds to an operator at the Episode layer at the RL, and of the indicative mood, which corresponds to a DECL Illocution at the IL. These facts together lead to the information pres.ind being positioned in P^M position. Present tense in Spanish requires a verb to which to attach, and there are basically two to choose from, *ser* and *estar*; which is chosen depends on the presence (> *estar*) or absence (> *ser*) of the Progressive operator at the Configurational Property layer. What is positioned in P^M of (34) is thus a placeholder (see §6 for more detail), which contains the information pres.ind.

Languages can also differ at the Phrase layer in whether they require copula insertion. Compare in this regard English with Hungarian:

(35) a. the boy in the garden
b. a   kert-ben   levő   fiú
ART   garden-INESS   COP.PTCP.SIM   boy
'lit. the in the garden being boy'

Within the Np, Hungarian requires that modifying Phrases are accompanied by a copula, whereas English disallows copulas with that function.

Another phenomenon that involves morphosyntactic material for which there is no correspondence in Formulation is agreement. True syntactic agreement is quite rare across the languages of the world (Siewierska 2004: 268). Consider the following example from French:

(36) Nous   chant-ons.
1PL   sing-1PL
'We are singing.'

J. Lachlan Mackenzie

Here there is agreement since the pronoun *nous* cannot be dropped without changing the Illocution (to hortative). The result of the copying is the introduction of a placeholder <1Pl> in morphosyntactic structure, as shown in (37):

(37) (Cl$_i$: [(Np$_i$: (Nw$_i$: /nu/ (Nw$_i$)) (Np$_i$))$_{Subj}$ (Vp$_i$: (Vw$_i$: /ʃãt/-pres<1Pl> (Vw$_i$)) (Vp$_i$)] (Cl$_i$))

French differs in this respect from other Romance languages in which the verbal suffix carries the meaning, as in Spanish (38a):

(38) a. Esta-mos   canta-ndo.
          AUX-1PL   sing-GER
       b. Nosotros   esta-mos   canta-ndo.
          1PL   AUX-1PL   sing-GER
       c. Esta-mos   canta-ndo   nosotros.
          AUX-1PL   sing-GER   1PL
          'We are singing.'

In (38b) and (38c) the finite verb does not agree with the Subject *nosotros*. Rather, there is a relation of cross-reference between the first person plural verb and the pronoun, which has been introduced into P^I (in 38b) or P^F (in 38c) by virtue of its Focus or Contrast function. (See also Hengeveld (2012) for the argument that in examples such as (38a) appeal is made to the Contextual Component.) This cross-reference is a matter for the IL, where in marked forms such as (38b) and (38c) the same referent is unusually referred to with two Subacts. One of these introduces the pronominal form directly, either as a set of abstract features to be spelled out at the ML or, quite plausibly for Spanish *nosotros*, as a lexical item. This Subact will in any case bear a pragmatic function. The other Subact has no pragmatic function and corresponds to the argument of the predicate at the RL.

Agreement within the Phrase takes many forms across the languages of the world. One issue that has attracted attention within FDG is the contrast between 'grammatical' and 'semantic' agreement (Dikker and Van Lier 2005). The former, covering, for example, the concord between the number and gender of nouns in Spanish and any modifying adjectives, can be handled entirely within the ML by means of a copying mechanism similar to that shown in (37) above. The latter is more complex and can be exemplified with the following Phrase from Swahili:

(39) ki-faru   m-kubwa
      CL7-rhinoceros CL1-big
      'a big rhinoceros'

where the class-7 lexeme *faru* basically covers inanimates (Ashton 1944: 14), yet the adjective bears the class-1 marker, which covers animates. Agreement is thus with the natural class of the referent and not with the grammatical class of the noun. Dikker and Van Lier's (2005) proposal is that examples such as this require that not just Formulation (as is assumed in the standard model) but also Encoding should be accessible to the Conceptual Component of the overarching theory of verbal interaction.

Agreement within the Word, finally, is illustrated by the following example from the Kiowa-Tanoan language Southern Tiwa (New Mexico and Texas; Allen *et al.* 1984: 293):

(40) Te-shut-pe-ban.
      1.SG.SBJ>PL.OBJ-shirt-make-PST
      'I made (the) shirts.'

The selection of the portmanteau morpheme *te-* shows that the incorporated Undergoer is treated as a regular argument, triggering agreement on the incorporating verb.

6 Relationship with the Phonological Level

The task of Encoding is shared between the Morphological and Phonological Levels. Languages differ in whether a particular distinction in Formulation corresponds to effects at the ML or PL. There appears to be a certain trade-off between the two Encoding levels, such that a distinction that is encoded at one level need not also be encoded at the other. English, for example, has no morphosyntactic way of indicating the Contrast status of the capitalized Nps in the following example:

(41) I didn't eat the BREAD, I ate the RICE.

Rather, the phonological structure compensates by using a combination of intonation and stress. In the Niger-Congo language Wolof (Senegal, Gambia, Mauritania), by contrast, as Rialland and Robert (2001) have shown, there is no intonational marking of Contrast. Here, the Contrast element is placed in Clause-initial position, followed by a marker (in this case *laa*) inflected in agreement with the Subject of the following Vp, as in (42):

(42) Lekkuma   mburu   mi,   ceeb   bi   laa   lekk.
      eat.NEG.1SG bread   DEF   rice   DEF CONTR.1SG eat
      'I didn't eat the BREAD, I ate the RICE.'

This 'focus', as the authors call it, 'has no effect on the melodic contour of the sentences' (Rialland and Robert 2001: 899).

One important function of the PL is to provide phonemic form for the above-mentioned placeholders introduced at the ML. In Spanish, for instance, with reference to an example such as (23) above, the placeholder "indpastpf3sg" (corresponding to the interpersonal and representational operators Decl, Past, Perf, and a "3sg" argument) appears at the PL as /o/ in a stressed syllable after verbs of the class to which /λeg-/ 'arrive' belongs.

7 Recent and current FDG work on morphosyntax

It has been implicit in the preceding presentation of the ML that FDG recognizes placement rules but not displacement (i.e., structure-changing) rules. In languages in which Domain Integrity is violable, FDG cannot have recourse to rules which move elements out of an originally integrated syntactic structure. The problem of discontinuity in syntax is tackled by Van de Velde (2012), who considers examples like the following:

(43) We have [several important books]$_{Np}$ in stock [about global warming]$_{Adp}$.

He argues that the connection between *several important books* and *about global warming* is established at the RL while they are separate units at the ML. Focusing on data from

Dutch, he shows that while the factors triggering discontinuity may originate in the IL (e.g., Focus assignment), it is purely morphosyntactic features that determine which discontinuities are possible and which not.

FDG, in keeping with an increasing groundswell of opinion in typological linguistics, does not assume Subject and Object to be universal categories. These syntactic functions are applied only when a language has 'morphosyntactic alignment' – that is, where the form of a language neutralizes interpersonal and representational distinctions. English is held to have Subject because active clauses neutralize the distinction between Actor and Undergoer in the subjective case and because the Undergoer of passive clauses also adopts the subjective case; it has Object where the distinction between Recipient and Undergoer is not made. Other languages do not have Subject or Object in this sense and have either interpersonal or representational alignment; those with Subject but no Object may have a mixed system. As Butler (2012) points out, in some languages the identification of a 'privileged syntactic argument' may even be construction-specific.

Current work on the ML is concerned with testing the system on various languages. Mackenzie (2009) applies it to aspects of Scottish Gaelic syntax and Wolvengrey (2011) to the syntax of Plains Cree; neither language has syntactic functions. Wolvengrey illumines Plains Cree syntax by identifying P^M as the position for the predicate, showing the necessity of assuming a P^2 and stressing the functionality of P^I as a location for Focus, Topic, and Contrast constituents. Another important stream is the further exploration of the notion of transparency as a typological parameter (Hengeveld 2011): one hypothesis is that 'young' languages (e.g., creoles and new sign languages) show relative transparency, develop greater opacity as they grow 'older', and then revert to relative transparency in situations of extreme language contact. Since transparency is distinct from simplicity and can be tested very precisely, this work is likely to contribute to current debates on the relation between cognition and language.

Abbreviations used in glosses

ACC	accusative	NOM	nominative
ART	article	NONPAST	non-past
AUX	auxiliary	NONVIS	non-visual sensory evidence
CERT	certain	OBJ	object
CL	class	PERC	perceived
COMP	complementizer	PFV	perfective
CONTR	contrast	PL	plural
COP	copula	PROX	proximate
DAT	dative	PRS	present tense
DECL	declarative	PST	past tense
DUR	durative	PUNCT	punctual
F	feminine	REM	remote
GER	gerund	REP	reportative
INCH	inchoative	RES	resultative
IND	indicative	SBJ	subject
INESS	inessive	SG	singular
LNK	linker	SIM	simultaneous
NEG	negative	TOP	topic

Notes

1 I wish to thank Kees Hengeveld for his very useful comments on an earlier version of this chapter. I gratefully acknowledge financial support from the grants INCITE09 204 155PR (XUGA) and FFI2010-19380 (MINECO).

2 Another justification for the term 'functional' is that FDG recognizes pragmatic, semantic, and syntactic functions; syntactic functions are similar to the 'grammatical functions' found in the f-structure of Lexical-Functional Grammar (Asudeh and Toivonen 2010: 431).

3 There is no space here to do more than mention the role of the Phonological Level in the placement of *bloody* in *your un-bloody-sightly bike*, where *bloody* appears before the stressed syllable within the Phonological Word /ʌnˈsaɪtlɪ/.

4 There are further Subacts of Ascription, corresponding to *bike* and *garden*, within these two Subacts of Reference.

5 Note that in the analysis of a specific example (an 'instantiation'), the numerical subscripts are replaced by alphabetical subscripts, starting with 'i'.

6 More precisely, it goes to the clause-final domain, since there is an alternative to (25), namely *Ik heb gefaald gisteren*, where *gisteren* goes to P^F and pushes *gefaald* one position back to P^{F-1}.

Further reading

García Velasco, Daniel, and Gerry Wanders. 2012. Introduction: The morphosyntactic level in Functional Discourse Grammar. *Language Sciences* 34:384–399.

Raises a number of additional issues, such as the absence of movement rules, the treatment of discontinuity, and the introduction of syntactic functions such as Subject and Object.

Hengeveld, Kees, and J. Lachlan Mackenzie. 2008. *Functional Discourse Grammar: A typologically-based theory of language structure*. Oxford: Oxford University Press.

Gives a fuller account of the Morphosyntactic Level on pp. 282–419.

References

Aikhenvald, Alexandra Y. 2004. *Evidentiality*. Oxford: Oxford University Press.

Aissen, Judith. 1992. Topic and focus in Mayan. *Language* 51:43–80.

Allen, Barbara J., Donna B. Gardiner, and Donald G. Frantz. 1984. Noun incorporation in Southern Tiwa. *International Journal of American Linguistics* 50:292–311.

Ashton, Ethel O. 1944. *Swahili grammar (including intonation)*. London: Longman.

Asudeh, Ash, and Isa Toivonen. 2010. Lexical-Functional Grammar. In *The Oxford handbook of linguistic analysis*, ed. Bernd Heine and Heiko Narrog, 425–458. Oxford: Oxford University Press.

Butler, Christopher S. 2012. Syntactic functions in Functional Discourse Grammar and Role and Reference Grammar: an evaluative comparison. *Language Sciences* 34:480–490.

Cinque, Guglielmo. 1999. *Adverbs and functional heads: A cross-linguistic perspective*. Oxford: Oxford University Press.

Connolly, John H. 2012. The constituent ordering process in functional discourse grammar. *Language Sciences* 34:455–467.

Dickinson, Connie. 2002. Complex predicates in Tsafiki. Doctoral dissertation, University of Oregon.

Dikker, Suzanne, and Eva van Lier. 2005. The interplay between syntactic and conceptual information: Agreement domains in FDG. In *Studies in functional discourse grammar*, ed. J. Lachlan Mackenzie and María de los Ángeles Gómez-González, 83–108. Berne: Peter Lang.

Evans, Nicolas D. 2003. *Bininj Gun-Wok: A pan-dialectal grammar of Mayali, Kunwinjku and Kune*, 2 vols. Canberra: Australian National University.

Everett, Daniel L. 2005. Cultural constraints on grammar and cognition in Pirahã: Another look at the design features of human language. *Current Anthropology* 46:621–646.

Giomi, Riccardo. forthcoming. Grammar, context and the hearer: A proposal for a hearer-oriented model of functional discourse grammar. *Pragmatics* 24.

Hengeveld, Kees. 1992. *Non-verbal predication: Theory, typology, diachrony*. Functional grammar series 15. Berlin and New York: Mouton de Gruyter.

Hengeveld, Kees (ed.). 2011. Transparency in functional discourse grammar. *Linguistics in Amsterdam* 4. Downloadable from http://www.linguisticsinamsterdam.nl/. (accessed 31 January 2014).

Hengeveld, Kees. 2012. Referential markers and agreement markers in functional discourse grammar. *Language Sciences* 34:468–479.

Hengeveld, Kees. 2013. A new approach to clausal constituent order. In *Casebook in functional discourse grammar*, ed. J. Lachlan Mackenzie and Hella Olbertz, 15–38. Amsterdam and Philadelphia, PA: Benjamins.

Hengeveld, Kees, and J. Lachlan Mackenzie. 2008. *Functional discourse grammar: A typologically-based theory of language structure*. Oxford: Oxford University Press.

Kornfilt, Jaklin. 1997. *Turkish*. Descriptive grammars series. London: Routledge.

Leufkens, Sterre. 2013. Time reference in English indirect speech. In *Casebook in functional discourse grammar*, ed. J. Lachlan Mackenzie and Hella Olbertz, 189–212. Amsterdam and Philadelphia, PA: Benjamins.

Lewis, G.L. 1967. *Turkish grammar*. Oxford: Clarendon.

Mackenzie, J. Lachlan. 2009. Aspects of the interpersonal grammar of Gaelic. *Linguistics* 47: 885–911.

Matthews, George Hubert. 1965. *Hidatsa syntax*. The Hague: Mouton.

Nevins, Andrew, David Pesetsky, and Cilene Rodrigues. 2009. Pirahã exceptionality: A reassessment. *Language* 85:355–404.

Rialland, Annie, and Stéphane Robert. 2001. The intonational system of Wolof. *Linguistics* 39: 893–939.

Romero-Figueroa, Andrés. 1997. *A reference grammar of Warao*. LINCOM Studies in Native American Linguistics 6. Munich and Newcastle: Lincom Europa.

Siewierska, Anna. 2004. *Person*. Cambridge: Cambridge University Press.

Taleghani, Azita Hojatollah. 2008. *Modality, aspect and negation in Persian*. Amsterdam and Philadelphia, PA: Benjamins.

Van de Velde, Freek 2012. PP extraction and extraposition in functional discourse grammar. *Language Sciences* 34:433–454.

Wolvengrey, Arok E. 2011. *Semantic and pragmatic functions in Plains Cree syntax*. Utrecht: LOT Publications.

31

Construction Grammar

Seizi Iwata

1 Introduction

Goldberg's (1995) constructional account attracts attention precisely because it offers a radically new way to account for syntactic expression of arguments, and her essential claim is unchanged in her subsequent works (Goldberg and Jackendoff 2004; Goldberg 2006, 2009). Therefore, this chapter focuses on this aspect of Construction Grammar.[1] After briefly reviewing Goldberg's account (Section 2), we will see how the several issues that crop up in relation to her theory have been addressed by other scholars committed to Construction Grammar: how to account for "overriding" cases (Section 3); the interaction between verbs and constructions (Section 4); and levels of abstraction (Section 5). The chapter ends with a brief discussion of the current shift of attention among practitioners of Construction Grammar (Section 6).

2 From verbs to constructions

2.1 Goldberg (1995)

Since Chomsky (1965), subcategorisation properties, along with selectional restrictions, have been taken to be specified in the verb's lexical entry. Rivière (1982) points out, however, that resultatives pose a challenging problem to this widely held view. First, selectional restrictions are violated in (1): Namely, the post-verbal NPs express human beings, which cannot possibly be the object of a drinking activity.

(1) a. They drank him under the table.
     b. He drank himself senseless.

(Rivière 1982: 686)

Second, subcategorisation restrictions are violated in (2): *Laugh* is an intransitive verb and should not be followed by direct objects, but NPs appear after the verb.

(2) a. He laughed himself *sick*.
     b. The audience laughed the actors *out/off the stage*.

(Rivière 1982: 686)

What is more puzzling is that these post-verbal NPs cannot stand alone. In the absence of the result AP or PP, the sentences are ill-formed.

(3) a. *He laughed himself.
     b. *The audience laughed the actors.

(Rivière 1982: 686)

For these reasons, resultatives pose a challenging problem to projectionist accounts (e.g., Levin and Rappaport Hovav 1995), which are based on the assumption that the lexical properties of each verb are fixed and that the phrasal patterns are projections thereof. One conceivable solution might be to posit a lexical rule which changes the lexical property of the base verb (Randall 1983; also Rappaport and Levin 1988; Pinker 1989, among others). But this does not look very attractive, because it would lead to rampant polysemy.

While scholars committed to the projectionist assumption were struggling to explain why resultatives may violate the selectional and subcategorisational restrictions of the base verb, an entirely different solution was proposed outside of the generative camp. Specifically, Goldberg (1995) argues that the observed syntax and semantics are due to constructions, rather than verbs:

> On a constructional approach to argument structure, systematic differences in meaning between the same verb in different constructions are attributed directly to the particular constructions.

(Goldberg 1995: 4)

Thus Goldberg (1995) posits a transitive resultative construction as described in Figure 31.1.

The resultative expressions are claimed to be obtained by fusing individual verbs with this construction. Thus the verb *wipe* has a lexical entry involving two participant roles: a wiper (a person who does the wiping) and a wiped (a thing that is wiped), as shown in (4a), while the verb *talk* has a lexical entry containing only a talker role (a person who talks), as shown in (4b).

(4) a. wipe <**wiper wiped**>
         He wiped the table clean.
     b. talk <**talker**>
         He talked himself blue in the face.

(Goldberg 1995: 189)

It is then posited that these participant roles fuse with the argument roles of the construction: <agent patient result-goal>. In the case of *wipe*, wiper and wiped roles are fused with agent and patient roles, and the result-goal role is contributed by the construction, as shown in Figure 31.2.

By contrast, in the case of *talk*, the talker role is fused with the agent role, while patient and result-goal roles are contributed by the construction, as shown in Figure 31.3.

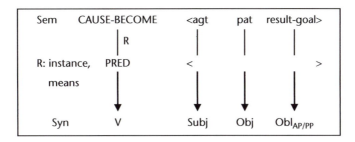

Figure 31.1 Transitive resultative construction (Goldberg 1995: 189)

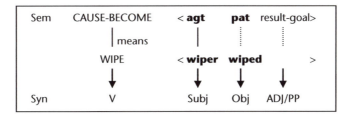

Figure 31.2 Composite structure: Resultative + *wipe* (Goldberg 1995: 190)

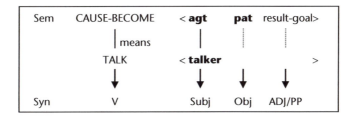

Figure 31.3 Composite structure: Resultative + *talk* (Goldberg 1995: 190)

The fusion of participant roles and argument roles is regulated by the following two principles:

The Semantic Coherence Principle: Only roles which are semantically compatible can be fused.

The Correspondence Principle: Each participant role that is lexically profiled and expressed must be fused with a profiled argument role of the construction.

(Goldberg 1995: 50)

In Goldberg's constructional approach, then, the verb remains the same. It is the construction that is responsible for the syntax and semantics of the resulting expression. Thus we can avoid positing an implausible verb sense every time the phrasal pattern cannot be attributed to the lexical verb.

Furthermore, given that constructions are a pairing of form and meaning, we can account for why the post-verbal NP cannot stand alone in (3).

(2) a. He laughed himself *sick*.
    b. The audience laughed the actors *out/off the stage*.

(Rivière 1982: 686)

(3) a. *He laughed himself.
     b. *The audience laughed the actors.

(Rivière 1982: 686)

Because the resultative semantics is associated with the fixed syntax [Subj V Obj Obl], it is no wonder that both (3a) and (3b), failing to be of the required syntax, cannot be licensed by the resultative construction.

Thus Goldberg's constructional account looks very attractive for dealing with phenomena in which the phrasal pattern cannot be attributed to the verb meaning. Significantly, such "non-compositional" phenomena are not limited to resultatives: caused-motion expressions as in (5a), ditransitive expressions as in (5b), and *way* expressions as in (5c), all of which are rather difficult to handle in projectionist accounts, can be easily accommodated in Goldberg's constructional approach.

(5) a. He sneezed the napkin off the table.
     b. She baked him a cake.
     c. Pat fought her way into the room.

2.2   Basic tenets of Construction Grammar

At this point, let us have a brief look at some of the fundamental assumptions on which Goldberg's account is based, and which seem to be of relevance in this handbook. First and foremost, Construction Grammar is a non-derivational theory, taking a monostratal approach to syntax. Syntactic and semantic commonalities shared between different expressions are captured by multiple inheritance, rather than by derivation. Thus (6a), (6b), and (6c) all inherit from the caused-motion construction. (6b) and (6c) are understood to additionally inherit from the passive construction and the *it*-cleft construction, respectively, as in Figure 31.4, rather than undergoing further syntactic transformations.

(6) a. John put the box on the table.
     b. The box was put onto the table.
     c. It was John who put the box on the table.

Second, constructions are defined as pairings of form and meaning. And third, lexicon and grammar form a continuum, rather than being separate modules. When these two assumptions

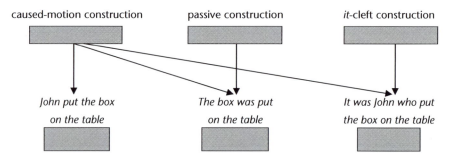

Figure 31.4 Multiple inheritance

are put together, it follows that not only phrasal expressions such as (1), (2), and (5) but also words and even morphemes count as constructions. In other words, constructions are necessarily symbolic in the sense of Cognitive Grammar (Langacker 1987), irrespective of the size of the linguistic expression in question.

Significantly, herein lies a fundamental difference between Generative Grammar and Construction Grammar, which is made explicit by Croft (2001) (rather than by Goldberg herself). Namely, in Generative Grammar the syntax, the semantics, and the phonology are represented in different components, each of which consists of rules operating over primitive elements of the relevant types. The lexicon is the only place where information from different components meets together. Correspondence at higher levels could be accommodated only by resorting to linking rules that link complex syntactic structures to their semantic interpretation or to their phonological realisation (Jackendoff 1997b; 2002; Culicover and Jackendoff 2005). Thus the syntactic structure of *Heather sings* is represented on its own as in Figure 31.5(a). In Construction Grammar, by contrast, the syntactic structure and the semantic structure are always paired with each other, as can be seen in the representation of the same sentence in Figure 31.5(b).

In Construction Grammar, then, a grammar consists of constructions and constructions alone.

2.3 Non-compositionality is not really an issue

There is one more thing to be said here. As seen in §2.1, the biggest appeal of Goldberg's account is that it offers a way to handle non-compositional cases. In fact, Goldberg (1995) gives an explicit definition to the effect that constructions are necessarily non-compositional:

> C is a construction iff$_{def}$ C is a form-meaning pair $<F_i, S_i>$ such that some aspect of F_i or some aspect of S_i is not strictly predictable from C's component parts or from other previously established constructions.
>
> (Goldberg 1995: 4)

Accordingly, many scholars seem to feel that constructions are special mechanisms that come to rescue non-compositional cases, and non-compositional cases alone.

In practice, however, Goldberg is ambivalent on this point. Quite often she uses the term "construction" without bothering about the (non)compositionality of the target phenomenon

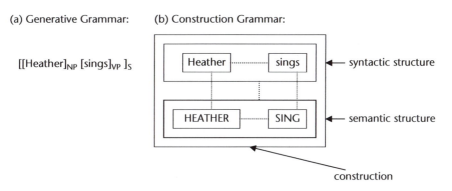

(a) Generative Grammar: (b) Construction Grammar:

[[Heather]$_{NP}$ [sings]$_{VP}$]$_S$

Figure 31.5 Simplified representations of *Heather sings*

in question. As a matter of fact, in her later works (Goldberg and Jackendoff 2004; Goldberg 2006; 2009) she switches to a different definition:

> Construction grammar defines constructions to be any stored pairings of form and function; … In addition, stored (typically highly frequent) regularities between form and meaning are considered constructions *even if they are fully compositional.*
>
> (Goldberg and Jackendoff 2004: 533, fn.1, emphasis mine)

> Any linguistic pattern is recognised as a construction as long as some aspect of its form or function is not strictly predictable from its component parts or from other constructions recognised to exist. In addition, patterns are stored as constructions *even if they are fully predictable* as long as they occur with sufficient frequency.
>
> (Goldberg 2006: 5, emphasis mine)

Thus while it is true that Goldberg's account can handle non-compositional cases, not all constructions are non-compositional. Goldberg's following remark makes sense only against this later version of her definition of constructions.

> … the idea that the network of constructions captures our grammatical knowledge of language *in toto*, i.e. *it's constructions all the way down.*
>
> (Goldberg 2006: 18, emphasis mine)

In fact, constructions are intended by construction grammarians to capture both compositional and non-compositional cases, which can be appreciated by considering the dichotomy proposed by Michaelis (2003; 2004). Michaelis divides constructions into two types, *concord* constructions and *shift* constructions, as defined in (7a) and (7b), respectively.

(7) a. *Concord construction.* A construction which denotes the same kind of entity or event as the lexical expression with which it is combined.
  b. *Shift construction.* A construction which denotes a different kind of entity or event from the lexical expression with which it is combined.

(Michaelis 2004: 28–29)

Michaelis argues that in the case of shift constructions the overriding principle in (8) is at work.

(8) The overriding principle: If a lexical item is semantically compatible with its morphosyntactic context, the meaning of the lexical item conforms to the meaning of the structure in which it is embedded.

(Michaelis 2004: 25)

Clearly, this amounts to the same thing as what Goldberg claims when she says that constructions superimpose their syntax and semantics on those of lexical verbs. It should be kept in mind, therefore, that while Goldberg's account can handle "overriding" cases, this is only one aspect of constructional approaches.

This being said, the fact remains that Goldberg's theory attracts attention precisely because of its ability to handle overriding cases. In what follows, therefore, let us see in turn how this aspect of Goldberg's account has been treated in subsequent studies by scholars committed to Construction Grammar.

3   How to account for "overriding" cases

3.1   Boas (2003)

Taken literally, Goldberg's statement is too strong: It might appear as if constructions could freely superimpose their syntax and semantics on any verb. Boas (2003) draws attention to this potential problem by pointing out that the sentences in (9) are not acceptable,[2] despite the fact that the lexical entries of the verbs in (10) are not that different from those in (4a) and (4b).

(9)   a.   ?He wiped the table dirty.
      b.   *He spoke himself blue in the face.
      c.   *He whispered himself blue in the face.
      d.   *He grumbled himself blue in the face.
      e.   *He grouched himself blue in the face.

(Boas 2003: 105)

(10)   a.   wipe **<wiper wiped>**
      b.   speak **<speaker>**
      c.   whisper **<whisperer>**
      d.   grumble **<grumbler>**
      e.   grouch **<groucher>**

(Boas 2003: 106)

This "overgeneration" problem arises precisely because in Goldberg's theory the fusion of verbs and constructions amounts to nothing more than a matching of role labels (e.g., agent and wiper), despite Goldberg's remark that verb meanings "must include reference to a background frame rich with world and cultural knowledge" (Goldberg 1995: 27).

Instead, Boas (2003) opts for a more lexically based account of resultatives, by giving substance to the claim that verb meanings are to be characterised in terms of Fillmorean "scenes".

> A word's meaning can be understood only with reference to a structured background of experience, beliefs, or practices, constituting a kind of conceptual prerequisite for understanding the meaning. Speakers can be said to know the meaning of the word only by first understanding the background frames that motivate the concept that the word encodes.
>
> (Fillmore and Atkins 1992: 76–77)

Specifically, Boas (2003) defines "verb meaning" somewhat broadly, according to which there are two components:

'on-stage' information
conceptually relevant information about an event that is immediately linguistically relevant for the interpretation of the meaning denoted by an event-frame.

(Boas 2003: 173)

'off-stage' information
… although one is subconsciously aware of the off-stage information associated with a word when encountering it in discourse it does not bear mention because it is by default associated with the word by the rest of the speech community.

(Boas 2003: 173–174)

Given this broader notion of verb meaning, Boas argues that resultatives are characterised by the fact that the result phrase specifies the outcome of the verbal event.

Boas (2003) divides resultatives into conventionalised ones, as exemplified in (11) and (12), and non-conventionalised ones, as in (13).

(11) a. Jack painted the house red.
      b. Dave hammered the metal flat.

(12) a. Pam ran her feet sore.
      b. Flora talked herself hoarse.

(13) He sneezed the napkin off the table.

Conventionalised resultatives are further divided into two subtypes, according to whether the post-verbal NP is selected by the verb, as in (11), or not, as in (12). So let us see in turn how the three types are analysed.

First, in analysing (11a), a conventionalised resultative with a verb-selected object, Boas represents the verb meaning of *paint* as in (14).

(14) Simplified event-based frame semantic representation of prototypical *paint*

SOURCE	Path	Path	Path	GOAL
Ag	Ag	Ag	Ag	Ag (W p2)
Pt	Pt	Pt	Pt	Pt (p3)

(adapted from Boas 2003: 178 and 191)

The boxes from left to right are intended to represent the several stages in temporal order, with the left-most SOURCE box being the initial stage, and the right-most GOAL box the final stage. The arrow stands for a force-dynamic relation between an Agent and a Patient. Overall, then, these boxes express that an Agent acts on a Patient, and this acting-on continues until the final stage represented by the GOAL box.

Given that resultatives are obtained by focusing on the outcome of the verbal event, the resultative *paint – red* is represented as in (15).

(15) Linking to syntax from the event-frame of prototypical *paint*

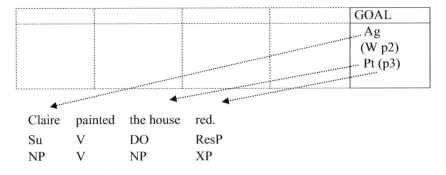

(adapted from Boas 2003: 192)

As noted above, the right-most GOAL box expresses the final stage, which contains Ag (person covering a surface with paint), W (world knowledge), Pt (surface), and p3 (property associated with the prototypical intended end result of applying paint to a surface). Ag and Pt are on-stage information, while those in parentheses are off-stage information. So the subject and the direct object correspond to the two participants in the on-stage information, whereas the result phrase corresponds to the outcome of painting as contained in the off-stage information.

Conventionalised resultatives with a non-verb-selected object are accounted for in essentially the same way.

(16)   fake object resultatives with *run*

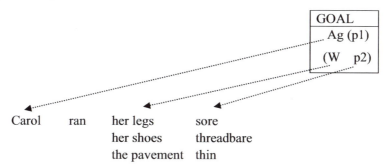

(adapted from Boas 2003: 251)

Unlike *paint*, *run* involves a single participant in its on-stage information, which is linked to subject position. But our world knowledge tells us that, after running, the runner's legs may become sore, her shoes may become threadbare, or the pavement may become thin. All this information is recruited from the off-stage information of *run*, and is eligible for being linked to syntactic positions.

Thus, with conventionalised resultatives, participants and result states are included in the verb meaning, be it on-stage or off-stage, as defined above. Whether the post-verbal NP is a verb-selected object or not is a matter of whether perspectivising a prototypical patient (as contained in the on-stage information) or a non-prototypical patient (as contained in the off-stage information).

The natural question that arises is, of course, how to deal with "overriding" cases of resultatives, as in (17), which are cited by Goldberg as support for her constructional account of caused-motion and resultative constructions.

(17)   a. He sneezed the napkin off the table.
       b. Dan talked himself blue in the face.
       c. She drank him under the table.

Boas excludes (17c) and (17b) from his account of resultatives on the grounds that (17c) is an idiomatic expression and (17b) is a special construction with the meaning of "to overdo an activity".

Now only (17a) remains. It is a little too far-fetched to claim that our world knowledge tells us that, as a result of sneezing, the napkin flies off the table. Rather, Boas (2003) characterises (17a) as a non-conventionalised resultative, arguing that (18a) is actually created as an analogy of (18b).

(18) a. Tom blew the napkin off the table.
      b. Tom sneezed the napkin off the table.

(Boas 2003: 269)

To recapitulate, in Boas' account participants and result states that appear in resultatives are due to verb meanings as broadly defined (on-stage + off-stage). In this sense, the pendulum has been swung back once again to verb meanings. Non-conventionalised resultatives such as *He sneezed the napkin off the table*, which apparently support Goldberg's account, are handled as a case of analogy.

2.2 Kay (2005)

Kay (2005) calls into question the possibility of a caused-motion construction. Apparently, Goldberg is justified in positing a caused-motion construction to handle expressions such as (19a) and (20a) because the path PPs cannot be omitted, as shown in (19b) and (20b).

(19) a. They laughed him off the stage.
      b. *They laughed him.

(20) a. Frank sneezed the tissue off the table.
      b. *Frank sneezed the tissue.

(Kay 2005: 88)

This is certainly in line with the claim noted in §2.1 that a given form is paired with its associated semantics.

Kay points out, however, that Goldberg extends her caused-motion construction even to cases such as (21a) and (22a), whose path PPs can be omitted, as in (21b) and (22b).

(21) a. They chased the poor guy out of the room.
      b. They chased the poor guy.

(22) a. Frank threw the key on the table.
      b. Frank threw the key.

(Kay 2005: 88)

Clearly, in these cases the sense of caused-motion is inherent in the verb meanings, rather than being superimposed by the putative construction.

Kay further observes that, if there is indeed a caused-motion construction, it should license expressions such as (23).

(23) a. *She screamed him out of her apartment.
      b. *He bragged her to sleep.
      c. *The bomb went off/detonated the desk through the window.

(Kay 2005: 89)

For these reasons, Kay rejects the existence of a caused-motion construction, rather arguing that what is at work here is *a pattern of coinage* and likening the putative caused-motion phenomenon to the implicit formula behind the 'A as NP' expressions in (24).

(24) a. light as a feather
      b. heavy as lead
      c. quick as a wink

(Kay 2005: 90)

These 'A as NP' expressions denote an extreme degree of a scalar adjective, and new members may be created on the analogy of already existing ones, but the productivity is not very high. Similarly, Kay argues that "the relatively small number of attested caused-motion expressions … may represent a pattern of coinage reflected in a rich maze of lexicalisations." (Kay 2005: 90–91) According to Kay, (19a) and (20a) are nonce applications of the pattern. Thus *sneeze – off the table* is once again claimed to be a case of analogical extension.

4 The role of verb meaning

One reason for the apparent plausibility of Goldberg's claim that constructions superimpose their syntax and semantics on lexical verbs comes from the treatment of verb meanings: The verb meaning is represented simply in terms of an array of participant roles, on which an array of argument roles (of the construction) is superimposed. Yet, by conducting a more detailed analysis of verb meanings, an entirely different picture emerges.

4.1 Nemoto (1998)

According to Goldberg (1995), ditransitive expressions are obtained by fusing the argument roles with the participant roles of each verb. But in the case of ditransitive *save* this tactic does not appear sufficient. After all, ditransitive *save* has the following (at least) four versions.

(25) a. John saved his boss the business letters.
      b. The director saved the section chief the trouble of sacking Bill.
      c. Steve saved Mary cooking time.
      d. If you buy the family-size box it will save you £1.

(Nemoto 1998: 219)

In (25a) John's boss is expected to receive the business letters at some future point in time. In (25b) the section chief is released from the unpleasant task of sacking Bill. In (25c) Steve's action brings about a situation in which Mary need not use her time as originally planned. In (25d), if the addressee meets the specified condition, he may cut the spending in question by £1.

Obviously, these four versions cannot be properly distinguished from each other by fusing the argument roles <agent, recipient, patient> with, say, <saver, saved>.

The verb meaning of *save* involves far more than can be captured by <saver, saved>. Following the spirit of Fillmore (1982) and Fillmore and Atkins (1992), Nemoto (1998) thus uncovers three background frames for *save*: Rescue, Storage, and Waste-Prevention Frames. Of the three, the Storage and Waste-Prevention Frames are directly relevant to an account of the four versions of ditransitive *save* in (25), so let us see them in turn.

The Storage Frame contains two elements, a keeper and a commodity, with the former keeping the latter:

The Storage Frame

Categories:
>   keeper: the person engaged in storing
>   commodity: something valued by the keeper and expected to be needed later.
Relation: A keeper keeps a commodity for the future.

(Nemoto 1998: 227)

Save as characterised against this frame thus has the two frame elements in (26a), which are syntactically realised as subject and direct object in (26b).

(26) a. [keeper, commodity]
     b. I decided I'd save the wine for later. (COBUILD)

Next, the Waste-Prevention Frame has many more elements: resources, preventer, resource-possessor, trouble, and part of the resources, with two relations holding among these elements.

The Waste-Prevention Frame

Categories:
>   resources: resources intended for a certain purpose
>   preventer: someone or something preventing the resources from being wasted
>   resource-possessor: the person who possesses the resources
>   trouble: the activity involving the waste of the resources
>   part of the resources: that part of the resources which turns into the one that need
>   not be used as originally planned

Relations: (i) A preventer causes a resource-possessor not to have trouble
              (ii) A preventer causes a resource-possessor to have part of the resources at
                   his/her disposal.

Nemoto (1998: 228)

Of these frame elements, the preventer role is realised as the subject, while the trouble role, resources role, or part of the resources role may appear as the direct object. Thus in (27a) the subject expresses a preventer role and a resource-possessor role, and the direct object a trouble role; in (27b) the subject expresses a preventer role and the direct object a trouble role.

(27) a. Mary saved a lot of trouble.
     b. Using a computer saved a lot of trouble.

In (28a) the subject is a preventer and a resource-possessor, and the direct object a resource; in (28b) the subject is a preventer and the direct object a resource. And so on.

(28) a. You can save fuel if you drive at a regular speed.
　　 b. Plastics are easier to handle than the vulcanized rubber formerly used, and they save time and money.

Given these two frames, Nemoto argues that (29a) is a ditransitive sentence with storage *save*, and (29b–c) are ditransitive sentences with waste-prevention *save*.

(29) a. John saved his boss the business letters.
　　 b. The director saved the section chief the trouble of sacking Bill.
　　 c. Steve saved Mary cooking time.
　　 d. If you buy the family-size box it will save you £1.

In (29a) the subject is a keeper and the direct object a commodity, so the two roles as defined in the Storage Frame are fused with the argument roles of the construction, while the indirect object is contributed by the construction. Accordingly, the fusion of argument roles and participant roles is as described in Figure 31.6.

By contrast, in (29b) the subject is a preventer, the indirect object a resource-possessor, and the direct object a trouble, all of which are available in the Waste-Prevention Frame. This means that all three of the roles in the Waste-Prevention Frame are fused with the argument roles of the construction. Thus the fusion in (29b) is as shown in Figure 31.7.

In (29c) the subject is a preventer, the indirect object a resource-possessor, and the direct object a resource, whereas in (29d) the subject is a preventer, the indirect object a resource-possessor, and the direct object a part of the resources. Again, therefore, in both cases all three of the participant roles in the Waste-Prevention Frame are syntactically realised.

Nemoto's study is significant not only in demonstrating that a detailed investigation into verb meaning is essential to an adequate account of the observed syntax and semantics but also in showing that most of the arguments apparently contributed by constructions are actually present in the Storage Frame and the Waste-Prevention Frame in the case of *save*. In fact, for ditransitive sentences with waste-prevention *save*, all three roles are actually present in the frame from the start. That is, the verb meaning is not overridden here.

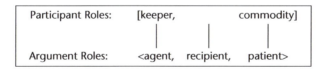

Figure 31.6　Fusion of roles for storage *save* (Nemoto 1998: 230)

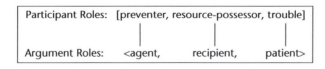

Figure 31.7　Fusion of roles for waste-prevention *save* (Nemoto 1998: 231)

4.2　Iwata (2006)

Certain negative verbs such as *refuse* and *deny* are known to occur ditransitively.

(30) a. Joe refused Bob a raise in salary.
     b. His mother denied Billy a birthday cake.

(Goldberg 1995: 33)

According to Goldberg (1995), these ditransitive expressions are instances of class C in the constructional network. The constructional meaning of this class is claimed to be "X causes Y not to receive Z" (Goldberg 1995: 39).

Since the sense of transfer does not seem to be inherent in the meanings of *refuse* and *deny*, Goldberg's constructional analysis appears to be on the right track. However, not all negative verbs can appear ditransitively, as Goldberg herself is aware.

(31) Sally {refused/denied/*prevented/*disallowed/*forbade} him a kiss.

(Goldberg 1995: 130)

Goldberg's theory has nothing to say about why this should be the case, for all these negative verbs should have basically the same lexical entries, as in (32).

(32) a. refuse <**refuser refused**>
     b. deny <**denier denied**>
     c. prevent <**preventer prevented**>
     d. disallow <**disallower disallowed**>
     e. forbid <**forbidder forbidden**>

Iwata (2006) shows that this apparent puzzle can be resolved by carefully examining the compatibility between the verbs and the construction. First, following Wierzbicka (1988), Iwata regards ditransitive *deny* and ditransitive *refuse* as being closely related to ditransitive *allow*.

(33) a. John denied Mary access to the children.
     b. The Dean refused John permission to go to an overseas conference in the middle of the term.
     c. Dr Brown allowed John two cigarettes a day.

(Wierzbicka 1988: 381)

This is further supported by the fact that with all three of these verbs the direct object tends not to stand for a specific, tangible object.

(34) a. *John denied Mary the flower.
     b. *Father refused John the ball.
     c. *Mother allowed Mary the doll.

(Wierzbicka 1988: 382)

Iwata (2006) thus concludes that the relevant constructional meaning is "X does not allow Y to receive Z," rather than "X causes Y not to receive Z."

Next, Iwata demonstrates that both *refuse* and *deny* are actually semantically compatible with this constructional meaning. First, the verb meaning of *refuse* is taken to be "to say that he/she will not do something." By substituting "allow somebody to receive something" for the "do something" component of this verb meaning, we get "to say that he/she will not *refuse*: to say that he/she will not *do something*.

↓

"to say that he/she will not *allow sb. to receive sth.*" =
"to not allow sb. to receive sth."

Figure 31.8   From *refuse* to the ditransitive semantics

deny: to say that *something* is not the case.

"to say that it is not the case *that he/she allows sb. to receive sth.*" =
"to not allow sb. to receive sth."

Figure 31.9   From *deny* to the ditransitive semantics

allow somebody to receive something," which essentially amounts to "to not allow somebody to receive something." This is exactly what has been identified above as the semantics of the relevant construction: "X does not allow Y to receive Z." Thus the meaning of ditransitive-*refuse* is arrived at by elaborating the semantics of *refuse*, as shown in Figure 31.8.

Next, the verb meaning of *deny* seems to be something like "to say that something is not the case." Again, by substituting "that he/she allows somebody to receive something" for the "something" component, we get "to say that it is not the case that somebody can receive something," which once again amounts to "to not allow somebody to receive something," as summarised in Figure 31.9.

Now, recall that Goldberg (1995) excludes *forbid* from the class of negative verbs that ditransitivise, as in (31) above. However, ditransitive *forbid* is actually attested in the BNC (= British National Corpus), as in (35), though in a much smaller number than ditransitive *refuse* and ditransitive *deny*.

(35) a. … if he should continue to molest his wife and daughter the law allows an injunction to be brought against him, *forbidding him access* to the marital home.
   b. Irenius insists that any social contact between English and Irish be suppressed and expressly advocates *forbidding the English the opportunity* of learning Gaelic.

(BNC)

Remarkably, the availability of ditransitive *forbid* can be similarly accounted for. By taking the verb meaning of *forbid* to be "to state that something is not allowed," we can easily arrive at the semantics of the relevant construction: By substituting "somebody's receiving something" for "something (not to be allowed)," we get "to not allow somebody to receive something," as shown in Figure 31.10.

Again, therefore, the fact that *forbid* may appear ditransitively is motivated by the verb meaning, as with *refuse* and *deny*.

Things are different with *disallow* and *prevent*. Thus *disallow* basically means "to not accept something as valid," as instantiated in (36).

(36) a. England scored again, but the whistle had gone and the goal was disallowed.
   b. It was a shock to hear him rule that my testimony would be disallowed.

(COBUILD)

> *forbid*: to state that *something* is not allowed.
>
> $\downarrow$
>
> "to state that *sb's receiving sth* is not allowed by him/her" =
> "to not allow sb. to receive sth."

Figure 31.10 From *forbid* to the ditransitive semantics

This is entirely different from the ditransitive version of *refuse, deny,* or *forbid,* where the subject entity is in a position to allow somebody to do something, but chooses not to do so. It is no wonder, then, that *disallow* does not appear ditransitively.

Similarly with *prevent*: while *prevent* is apparently very similar to *forbid,* the notion of "to not allow" is lacking. Thus in several dictionaries the definition of *prevent* reads as follows: "to stop something from happening" (Macmillan), "to stop (something) happening or (someone) doing something" (CIDE), or "to ensure that something does not happen" (COBUILD). Clearly, whichever definition is chosen, it cannot be elaborated into "to not allow somebody to receive something." Again, therefore, it is quite natural that *prevent* cannot appear ditransitively.

Thus, even with apparently "overriding" cases, only semantically compatible verbs may appear ditransitively. Iwata (2006) thus convincingly demonstrates that constructions are not as powerful as Goldberg's exposition will have us believe, along with Boas (2003) and Nemoto (1998). However, unlike Boas and Nemoto, Iwata (2006) also shows that the very practice of representing the verb meaning by means of a list of participant roles does not always work. After all, the relationship between *refuse, deny,* and *forbid,* on the one hand, and their ditransitive counterparts on the other, as summarised in Figures 31.8–31.10, cannot be captured if one sticks to Goldberg's way of representation (For further discussion of the role that verb meanings play, see Iwata (2005); Nemoto (2005); Croft (2009)).

5 Generalisations at lower levels

5.1 Croft (2003)

In Goldberg (1995) English ditransitive expressions are claimed to constitute a constructional polysemy, involving the following six classes.

(37) A. Central sense: Agent successfully causes recipient to receive patient.
      1. Verbs that inherently signify acts of giving: *give, pass, hand, serve, feed,* …
      2. Verbs of instantaneous causation of ballistic motion: *throw, toss, slap, kick, poke, fling, shoot,* …
      3. Verbs of continuous causation in a deictically specified direction: *bring, take…*
   B. Conditions of satisfaction imply that agent causes recipient to receive patient
      1. Verbs of giving with associated satisfaction conditions: *guarantee, promise, owe,* …
   C. Agent causes recipient not to receive patient
      1. Verbs of refusal: *refuse, deny*
   D. Agent acts to cause recipient to receive patient at some future point in time
      1. Verbs of future transfer: *leave, bequeath, allocate, reserve, grant,* …
   E. Agent enables recipient to receive patient
      1. Verbs of permission: *permit, allow*

F. Agent intends to cause recipient to receive patient
    1. Verbs involved in scenes of creation: *bake, make, build, cook, sew, knit, …*
    2. Verbs of obtaining: *get, grab, win, earn, …*

Croft (2003) argues, however, that this is not strictly a case of polysemy. Polysemy is a phenomenon by which a single form is associated with more than one meaning, as shown in Figure 31.11.

Accordingly, the "constructional polysemy" thesis is tantamount to claiming that a single form [SBJ VERB OBJ1 OBJ2] is associated with six different "senses," as shown in Figure 31.12.

But if the English ditransitive construction were polysemous in this way, one would expect that one and the same verb would appear with more than one sense. Thus the verb *bring* would be found not only with sense A but also with sense F, with the meaning "X brings Z with the intention of causing Y to receive Z"; *kick* could occur not only with sense A but also with sense C, with the meaning "X kicks Z, causing Y not to receive Z"; and so on.

This is not the case, however. Actually, only those verbs in a certain verb class may appear in a given class: Only creation and obtaining verbs (*bake, get*) appear in class F; only negative verbs (*refuse, deny*) appear in class C; and so on.

Croft (2003) points out that in order to specify which verb classes occur with each "sense", the polysemous representation along the lines of Figure 31.12 will not do. Instead, there is a distinct construction for each "sense" specifying the verb classes found with each meaning, as shown in Figure 31.13.

Here the verbal slot for each construction is written as FUTURE.GIVING.VERB or PERMIT.VERB, rather than simply as VERB, so as to capture the fact that only verbs of future giving may appear in class D or only verbs of permission in class E, and so on. Croft

Figure 31.11   Polysemous form-meaning correspondence

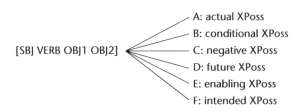

Figure 31.12   Putative constructional polysemy of the ditransitive construction

A: [SBJ GIVING.VERB OBJ1 OBJ2] ———— [actual XPoss]
B: [SBJ COND.GIVING.VEB OBJ1 OBJ2] —— [conditional XPoss]
C. [SBJ REFUSE.VERB OBJ1 OBJ2] ———— [negative XPoss]
D. [SBJ FUT.GIVING.VERB OBJ1 OBJ2] —— [future XPoss]
E. [SBJ PERMIT.VERB OBJ OBJ2] ———— [enabling XPoss]
F. [SBJ CREATE.VERB OBJ1 OBJ2] ———— [intended XPoss after creation]

Figure 31.13   Verb-class-specific constructions (adapted from Croft 2003: 57)

E. [SBJ *permit* OBJ1 OBJ2] —————— [enabling XPoss by permitting]

   [SBJ *allow* OBJ1 OBJ2] —————— [enabling XPoss by allowing]

F. [SBJ *refuse* OBJ1 OBJ2] —————— [negative XPoss by refusing]

   [SBJ *deny* OBJ1 OBJ2] —————— [negative XPoss by denying]

Figure 31.14   Verb-specific constructions (adapted from Croft 2003: 58)

calls these form–meaning pairings *verb-class-specific constructions*, which capture generalisations at the level of verb classes.

But this is not the end of the story. While the verb-class-specific constructions, as in Figure 31.13, may ensure that only verbs of a given verb class occur in the construction at hand, not every member of the verb class can always do so. Thus not every permission verb may appear ditransitively, as in (38a), and not every negative verb may appear in the ditransitive construction, as in (38b).

(38) a. Sally permitted/allowed/*let/*enabled Bob a kiss.
      b. Sally refused/denied/*prevented/*disallowed/*forbade him a kiss.

It is thus necessary to specify each verb that occurs in the ditransitive construction, as in Figure 31.14. Croft calls these constructions *verb-specific constructions*.

Croft (2003) has thus introduced more concrete constructions than those envisaged in Goldberg (1995). Verb-specific constructions are constructions with specific lexical content for the verb, and they essentially capture the subcategorisation property and the selectional restriction. Verb-class-specific constructions are slightly more abstract, but still much more specific than Goldberg's (1995) abstract constructions. Croft argues that since the existence of verb-specific constructions and verb-class-specific constructions does not preclude the existence of a more schematic construction, his proposed levels of constructions may well co-exist with Goldberg's abstract constructions.

5.2   Iwata (2008) and Boas (2010)

Inspired by Croft (2003), Iwata (2008) develops a hierarchical organisation of constructions in which verb-specific constructions, verb-class-specific constructions, and abstract constructions co-exist. According to Iwata (2008), introduction of lower-level constructions is an automatic consequence of the usage-based view: Constructions are nothing other than schemas in the sense of Cognitive Grammar (Langacker 1987; 1991; 1999; Taylor 2002). Schemas are available at various degrees of abstraction. Therefore, constructions should be available at various degrees of abstraction, too.

Significantly, such lower-level constructions are more useful for describing linguistic facts. Iwata (2008) argues that the locative alternation, as in (39), is better accounted for at the level of verb-class-specific constructions, rather than at the level of abstract constructions.

(39) a. He sprayed paint onto the wall. (locatum-as-object variant)
      b. He sprayed the wall with paint. (location-as-object variant)

Boas (2010) also explicitly incorporates the notion "levels of abstraction" into his theory. Thus Boas admits four levels of abstraction for the construction that deals with communication verbs (e.g., *tell, inform, advise*), as summarised in Table 31.1.

Table 31.1 Increasing levels of semantic abstraction (Boas 2010: 69)

Level of abstraction	Type of construction (Pairing of a specific FEC with one valence pattern)		Number of LUs	Example
Frame-level 3	Even more abstract	[speaker, addressee, topic] ↓ ↓ ↓ [NP, NP, PP[about]]	Multiple LUs evoking higher level frames in the same domain	Communication
Frame-level 2	More abstract	[speaker, addressee, topic] ↓ ↓ ↓ [NP, NP, PP[about]]	Multiple LUs evoking higher level frames in the same domain	Statement/ Questioning
Frame-level 1	Frame specific construction	[speaker, addressee, topic] ↓ ↓ ↓ [NP, NP, PP[about]]	Multiple LUs evoking the same frame share this mapping	TELLING
LU-level	Mini-construction	[speaker, addressee, topic] ↓ ↓ ↓ [NP, NP, PP[about]]	Only one LU	tell inform advise

Already Boas (2003) argues for *mini-constructions*, which pair a single syntactic valence pattern with a specific set of frame elements so as to capture the intricate syntactic and semantic differences exhibited by verbs closely related in meaning. His mini-constructions are now located at the bottom level of this hierarchy.

Although the details of implementation are different between Iwata (2008) and Boas (2009; 2010), it is significant that the two scholars, who have been working on how to overcome the problems with Goldberg's (1995) account (as amply demonstrated in the previous sections), have arrived at basically the same view of constructions. This is certainly not a coincidence. In fact, the intricate interaction between verbs and constructions is far easier to capture by means of lower-level constructions.

6 Constructions as tools for describing language

When Goldberg's (1995) constructional account was first presented, it attracted attention mainly because of its putative ability to handle non-compositional phenomena such as resultatives. The subsequent constructional research by other scholars, however, has not necessarily taken for granted "overriding" cases. If anything, the seemingly overriding cases are accorded a rather secondary place (§3), or some of them are shown to be not exactly overriding cases because they are semantically compatible with verbs (§4). Thus constructions are not as powerful as initially proposed by Goldberg (1995).

Seen in this light, then, what is most essential to constructions is that they are symbolic in the sense of Cognitive Grammar, rather than that they have the putative ability to handle overriding cases. But this invites the following question: What is the difference between Construction Grammar and Cognitive Grammar? In Cognitive Grammar there are only three structures: semantic, phonological, and symbolic (= association between semantic and phonological structures). Langacker (2005a; 2005b) states that his use of the term

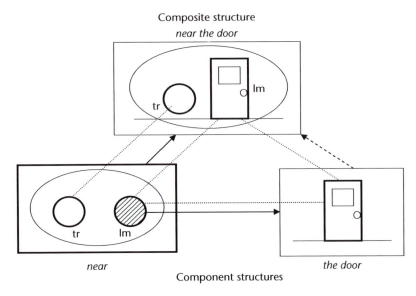

Composite structure
near the door

near

Component structures

the door

Figure 31.15   Minimal construction in Cognitive Grammar (Langacker 2005a: 169)

"construction" is broader than in Construction Grammar, in that any *symbolically complex expression* – be it fixed or novel, regular or irregular – constitutes a construction. Thus, canonically, a minimal construction consists of two *component structures* which are integrated to form a *composite structure*, as in Figure 31.15.

In Cognitive Grammar, by constructions are meant complex expressions (also see Taylor 2002: 561–562). Accordingly, (plain) words and morphemes do *not* count as constructions. Apart from this terminological difference, however, the distance between Cognitive Grammar and Construction Grammar is far smaller than Langacker claims.[3] After all, all "symbolic constructions" in Cognitive Grammar count as constructions in Construction Grammar, as should be clear by now.

As a matter of fact, more and more cognitively oriented scholars are using constructions (particularly lower-level constructions) to describe linguistic facts: Barðdal (2006; 2008), Höche (2009), Traugott (2003; 2007), Trousdale (2008), and van Bogaert (2010; 2011), to name just a few. Particularly noteworthy is the move to use constructions to account for historical changes, led by Traugott and Trousdale (see also Fried 2009).

That is, constructions serve as very convenient tools for describing linguistic facts as they are, without separating form from meaning (or function).

Notes

1   In Goldberg (2006: 213–226), her version of Construction Grammar is referred to as Cognitive Construction Grammar, to be distinguished from Unification Construction Grammar (Fillmore *et al.* 1988; Kay and Fillmore 1999), Radical Construction Grammar (Croft 2001), or Cognitive Grammar (Langacker 1987; 1991; 1999; Taylor 2002). But in this chapter what is meant by Construction Grammar is virtually the totality of the three versions (Cognitive Construction Grammar, Radical Construction Grammar, and Cognitive Grammar), as will become clear at the end of this chapter. As for the "Unification Construction Grammar," it is currently called Sign-based Construction Grammar (see Chapter 25 in this volume).

2 The asterisked examples might sound better if they are understood by analogy with the acceptable ones. The same is true of (23).
3 But not nil. One crucial difference between Cognitive Grammar and Construction Grammar (and Radical Construction Grammar) is that Cognitive Grammar does not allow for the existence of syntactic categories (e.g., VP or NP).

Dictionaries

CIDE = *Cambridge International Dictionary of English* 1995.
COBUILD = *Collins COBUILD English Dictionary*, 2nd edn 1995.
Macmillan = *Macmillan English Dictionary* 2002.

Further reading

- For both pros and cons of Goldberg's theory see *Cognitive Linguistics* 20–21. 2009.
- For a compendium of discussions surrounding argument structure constructions see Chapter 9 in Croft, William. 2012. *Verbs*. Oxford: Oxford University Press.
- For the definition and general discussion of constructions see Croft, William, and Alan Cruse. 2004. *Cognitive Linguistics*. Cambridge: Cambridge University Press.
- For a critique of Goldberg's account see van der Leek, Frederike. 2000. Caused-motion and the 'bottom-up' role of grammar. In *Constructions in Cognitive Linguistics*, ed. A. Foolen and F. van der Leek, 301–331. Amsterdam and Philadelphia, PA: John Benjamins.

References

Barðdal, Jóhanna. 2006. Construction-specific properties of syntactic subjects in Icelandic and German. *Cognitive Linguistics* 17:39–106.
Barðdal, Jóhanna. 2008. *Productivity: Evidence from Case and Argument Structure in Icelandic*. Amsterdam and Philadelphia, PA: John Benjamins.
Boas, Hans Christian. 2003. *A Constructional Approach to Resultatives*. Stanford, CA: CSLI Publications.
Boas, Hans Christian. 2009. Verb meanings at the crossroads between higher-level and lower-level constructions. *Lingua* 120:22–34.
Boas, Hans Christian. 2010. The syntax-lexicon continuum in construction grammar: A case study of English communication verbs. *Belgian Journal of Linguistics* 24, 54–82.
Chomsky, Noam. 1965. *Aspects of the Theory of Syntax*. Cambridge, MA: MIT Press.
Croft, William. 2001. *Radical Construction Grammar: Syntactic Theory in Typological Perspective*. Oxford: Oxford University Press.
Croft, William. 2003. Lexical rules vs. constructions: A false dichotomy. In *Motivation in Language*, ed. H. Cuyckens, T. Berg, R. Dirven, and K.-U. Panther, 49–68. Amsterdam and Philadelphia, PA: John Benjamins.
Croft, William. 2009. Connecting frames and constructions: A case study of *eat* and *feed*. *Constructions and Frames* 1:7–28.
Culicover, Peter W., and Ray Jackendoff. 2005. *Simpler Syntax*. Oxford: Oxford University Press.
Fillmore, Charles J. 1982. Frame semantics. In *Linguistics in the Morning Calm*, ed. Linguistic Society of Korea, 111–137. Seoul: Hanshin Publishing Co.
Fillmore, Charles J., and Beryl T. Atkins. 1992. Toward a frame-based lexicon: The semantics of RISK and its neighbours. In *Frames, Fields, and Contrasts: New Essays in Semantic and Lexical Organisation*, ed. Adrienne Lehrer and Eva Feder Kittay, 75–102. Hillsdale, NJ: Lawrence Erlbaum Associates.
Fillmore, Charles J., Paul Kay, and Mary Catherine O'Connor. 1988. Regularity and idiomaticity in grammatical constructions: The case of *let alone*. *Language* 64:501–538.
Fried, Mirjam. 2009. Construction grammar as a tool for diachronic analysis. *Constructions and Frames* 1:261–290.
Goldberg, Adele. 1995. *Constructions: A Construction Grammar Approach to Argument Structure*. Chicago, IL: University of Chicago Press.

Goldberg, Adele. 2006. *Constructions at Work: The Nature of Generalisation in Language*. Oxford: Oxford University Press.

Goldberg, Adele. 2009. The nature of generalisation in language. *Cognitive Linguistics* 20:93–127.

Goldberg, Adele, and Ray Jackendoff. 2004. The English resultative as a family of constructions. *Language* 80:532–568.

Höche, Silke. 2009. *Cognate Object Constructions in English: A Cognitive-Linguistic Account*. Tübingen: Gunter Narr Verlag.

Iwata, Seizi. 2005. The role of verb meaning in locative alternations. In *Grammatical Constructions: Back to the Roots*, ed. M. Fried and H.C. Boas, 101–118. Amsterdam and Philadelphia, PA: John Benjamins.

Iwata, Seizi. 2006. Where do constructions come from? *English Linguistics* 23:493–533.

Iwata, Seizi. 2008. *Locative Alternation: A Lexical-Constructional Approach*. Amsterdam and Philadelphia, PA: John Benjamins.

Jackendoff, Ray. 1997a. Twistin' the night away. *Language* 73:534–539.

Jackendoff, Ray. 1997b. *The Architecture of the Language Faculty*. Cambridge, MA: MIT Press.

Jackendoff, Ray. 2002. *Foundations of Language*. Oxford: Oxford University Press.

Jackendoff, Ray. 2008. Construction after construction and its theoretical challenges. *Language* 84:8–28.

Kay, Paul. 2005. Argument structure constructions and the argument-adjunct distinction. In *Grammatical Constructions: Back to the Roots*, ed. M. Fried and H.C. Boas, 71–98. Amsterdam/Philadelphia, PA: John Benjamins.

Kay, Paul, and Charles J. Fillmore. 1999. Grammatical constructions and linguistic generalisations: The *What's X doing Y?* construction. *Language* 75:1–33.

Langacker, Ronald. 1987. *Foundations of Cognitive Grammar, Vol. 1: Theoretical Prerequisites*. Stanford: Stanford University Press.

Langacker, Ronald. 1991. *Foundations of Cognitive Grammar, Vol. 2: Descriptive Applications*. Stanford: Stanford University Press.

Langacker, Ronald. 1999. *Grammar and Conceptualisation*. Berlin: Mouton de Gruyter.

Langacker, Ronald. 2005a. Integration, grammaticisation, and constructional meaning. In *Grammatical Constructions: Back to the Roots*, ed. M. Fried and H.C. Boas, 157–189. Amsterdam and Philadelphia, PA: John Benjamins.

Langacker, Ronald. 2005b. Construction grammars: Cognitive, radical, and less so. In *Cognitive Linguistics: Internal Dynamics and Interdisciplinary Interaction*, ed. F. Ruiz de Mendoza Ibanez and M. Sandra Pena Cervel, 101–159. Berlin and New York: Mouton de Gruyter.

Levin, Beth, and Malka Rappaport Hovav. 1995. *Unaccusativity: At the Syntax-Lexical Semantics Interface*. Cambridge, MA: MIT Press.

Michaelis, Laura. 2003. Word meaning, sentence meaning, and syntactic meaning. In *Cognitive Approaches to Lexical Semantics*, ed. Hubert Cuyckens, Renè Dirven, and John R. Taylor, 163–209. Berlin and New York: Mouton de Gruyter.

Michaelis, Laura. 2004. Type shifting in construction grammar: An integrated approach to aspectual coercion. *Cognitive Linguistics* 15:1–67.

Nemoto, Noriko. 1998. On the polysemy of ditransitive *save*: The role of frame semantics in construction grammar. *English Linguistics* 15:219–242.

Nemoto, Noriko. 2005. Verbal polysemy and frame semantics in construction grammar: Some observations on the locative alternation. In *Grammatical Constructions: Back to the Roots*, ed. M. Fried and H. C. Boas, 119–136. Amsterdam and Philadelphia, PA: John Benjamins.

Pinker, Steven. 1989. *Learnability and Cognition: The Acquisition of Argument Structure*. Cambridge, MA: MIT Press.

Randall, Janet. 1983. A lexical approach to causatives. *Journal of Linguistic Research* 2:73–105.

Rappaport, Malka, and Beth Levin. 1988. What to do with theta-roles. In *Syntax and Semantics* 21: *Thematic Relations*, ed. W. Wilkins, 7–36. New York: Academic Press.

Rivière, Claude. 1982. Objectionable objects. *Linguistic Inquiry* 13:685–689.

Taylor, John. 2002. *Cognitive Grammar*. Oxford: Oxford University Press.

Traugott, Elizabeth Closs. 2003. Constructions in grammaticalisation. In *The Handbook of Historical Linguistics*, ed. B.D. Joseph and R.D. Janda, 624–647. Oxford: Blackwell.

Traugott, Elizabeth Closs. 2007. The concepts of constructional mismatch and type-shifting from the perspective of grammaticalisation. *Cognitive Linguistics* 18:523–557.

Trousdale, Graeme. 2008. Constructions in grammaticalisation and lexicalisation: Evidence from the history of a composite predicate construction in English. In *Constructional Approaches to English Grammar*, ed. Graeme Trousdale and Nikolas Gisborne, 33–67. Berlin and New York: Mouton de Gruyter.

Van Bogaert, Julie. 2010. A constructional taxonomy of *I think* and related expressions: Accounting for the variability of complement-taking mental predicates. *English Language and Linguistics* 14:399–427.

Van Bogaert, Julie. 2011. *I think* and other complement-taking mental predicates: A case of and for constructional grammaticalisation. *Linguistics* 49:295–332.

Wierzbicka, Anna. 1988. *The Semantics of Grammar*. Amsterdam: John Benjamins.

32

Categorial Grammar

Mark Steedman

1 Introduction

Categorial Grammar (CG) is a "strictly" lexicalized theory of natural language grammar, in which the linear order of constituents and their interpretation in the sentences of a language are entirely defined by the lexical entries for the words that compose them, while a language-independent universal set of rules projects the lexicon onto the strings and corresponding meanings of the language. Many of the key features of categorial grammar have over the years been assimilated by other theoretical syntactic frameworks. In particular, there are recent signs of convergence from the Minimalist program within the transformational generative tradition (Chomsky 1995; Berwick and Epstein 1995; Cormack and Smith 2005; Boeckx 2008: 250).

Categorial grammars are widely used in various slightly different forms discussed below by linguists interested in the relation between semantics and syntactic derivation. Among them are computational linguists who for reasons of efficiency in practical applications wish to keep that coupling as simple and direct as possible. Categorial grammars have been applied to the syntactic and semantic analysis of a wide variety of constructions, including those involving unbounded dependencies, in a wide variety of languages (e.g. Moortgat 1988b; Steele 1990; Whitelock 1991; Morrill and Solias 1993; Hoffman 1995; Nishida 1996; Kang 1995, 2002; Bozşahin 1998, 2002; Komagata 1999; Baldridge 1998, 2002; Trechsel 2000; Cha and Lee 2000; Park and Cho 2000; Çakıcı 2005, 2009; Ruangrajitpakorn *et al.* 2009; Bittner 2011, 2014; Kubota 2010; Lee and Tonhauser 2010; Bekki 2010; Tse and Curran 2010).

CG is generally regarded as having its origin in Frege's (1879) remarkable *Begriffsschrift*, which proposed and formalized the language that we now know as first-order predicate logic (FOPL) as a Leibnizian calculus in terms of the combination of functions and arguments, thereby laying the foundations for all modern logics and programming languages, and opening up the possibility that natural language grammar could be thought of in the same way. This possibility was investigated in its syntactic and computational aspect for small fragments of natural language by Ajdukiewicz (1935) (who provided the basis for the modern notations), Bar-Hillel (1953) and Bar-Hillel *et al.* (1964) (who gave categorial grammar its name), and Lambek (1958) (who initiated the type-logical interpretation of CG).

It was soon recognized that these original categorial grammars were context-free (Lyons 1968), and therefore unlikely to be adequately expressive for natural languages (Chomsky 1957), because of the existence of unbounded or otherwise "long range" syntactic and semantic dependencies between elements such as those italicized in the following examples:[1]

(1)   a. These are *the songs* they say that the Sirens *sang*.
        b. The Sirens *sang* and say that they wrote *these songs*.
        c. *Some Siren* said that she had written *each song*.   ($\exists\forall/\forall\exists$)
        d. *Every Siren* thinks that the sailors heard *her*.

Frege's challenge was taken up in categorial terms by Geach (1970) (initiating the combinatory generalization of CG), and Montague (1970b) (initiating direct compositionality, both discussed below). In particular, Montague (1973) influentially developed the first substantial categorial fragment of English combining syntactic analysis (using a version of Ajdukiewicz's notation) with semantic composition in the tradition of Frege (using Church's λ-calculus as a "glue language" to formalize the compositional process).

In the latter paper, Montague used a non-monotonic operation expressed in terms of structural change to accommodate long range dependencies involved in quantifier scope alternation and pronoun-binding, illustrated in (1c,d). However, in the earlier paper (Montague, 1970b) he had laid out a more ambitious program, according to which the relation between syntax and semantics in all natural languages would be strictly homomorphic, like the syntax and semantics in the model theory for a mathematical, logical, or programming language, in the spirit of Frege's original program.

For example, the standard model theory for the language of FOPL has a small context-free set of syntactic rules, recursively defining the structure of negated, conjunctive, quantified, etc. clauses in terms of operators $\neg$, $\wedge$, $\forall x$, etc. and their arguments. The semantic component then consists of a set of rules paired one-to-one with the syntactic rules, compositionally defining truth of an expression of that syntactic type solely in terms of truth of the arguments of the operator in question (see Robinson 1974).

Two observations are in order when seeking to generalize such Fregean systems as FOPL to human language. One is that the mechanism whereby an operator such as $\forall x$ "binds" a variable x in a term of the form $\forall x[P]$ is not usually considered part of the syntax of the logic. If it is treated syntactically, as has on occasion been proposed for programming languages (Aho 1968), then the syntax is in general no longer context-free.[2]

The second observation is that the syntactic structures of FOPL can be thought of in two distinct ways. One is as the *syntax of the logic* itself, and the other is as a *derivational structure* describing a process by which an interpretation has been constructed. The most obvious context-free derivational structures are isomorphic to the logical syntax, such as those which apply its rules directly to the analysis of the string, either bottom-up or top-down. However, even for a context-free grammar, derivation structure may be determined by a different "covering" syntax, such as a "normal form" grammar. (Such covering grammars are sometimes used for compiling programming languages, for reasons such as memory efficiency.) Such covering derivations are irrelevant to interpretation, and do not count as a representational level of the language itself. In considering different notions of structure involved in theories of natural language grammar, it is important to be clear whether one is talking about logical syntax or derivational structure.

Recent work in categorial grammar has built on the Frego-Montagovian foundation in two distinct directions, neither of which is entirely true to its origins. One group of researchers has made its main priority capturing the semantics of diverse constructions in natural languages using standard logics, often replacing Montague's structurally non-monotone "quantifying in" operation by more obviously compositional rules or memory storage devices. Its members have tended to either remain agnostic as to the syntactic operations involved or assume some linguistically-endorsed syntactic theory such as transformational grammar or GPSG (e.g. Partee 1975; Cooper 1983; Szabolcsi 1997; Jacobson 1999; Heim and Kratzer 1998), sometimes using extended notions of scope within otherwise standard logics (e.g. Kamp and Reyle 1993; Groenendijk and Stokhof 1991; Ciardelli and Roelofsen 2011), or tolerating a certain increase in complexity in the form of otherwise syntactically or semantically unmotivated surface-compositional syntactic operators or type-changing rules on the syntactic side (e.g. Bach 1979; Dowty 1982; Hoeksema and Janda 1988; Jacobson 1992; Hendriks 1993; Barker 2002) and the Lambek tradition (e.g. Lambek 1958, 2001; van Benthem 1983, 1986; Moortgat 1988a; Oehrle 1988; Morrill 1994; Carpenter 1995; Bernardi 2002; Casadio 2001; Moot 2002; Grefenstette *et al.* 2011).

Other post-Montagovian approaches have sought to reduce syntactic complexity, at the expense of expelling some apparently semantic phenomena from the logical language entirely, particularly quantifier scope alternation and pronominal binding, relegating them to offline specification of scopally underspecified logical forms (e.g. Kempson and Cormack 1981; Reyle 1993; Poesio 1995; Koller and Thater 2006; Pollard 1984), or extragrammatical discourse reference (e.g. Webber 1978; Bosch 1983).

One reason for this diversity and divergence within the broad church of categorial grammar is that the long-range and/or unbounded dependencies exemplified in (1) above, which provide the central challenge for any theory of grammar and for the Fregean approach in particular, fall into three distinct groups. Relativization, topicalization, and right node-raising are clearly unbounded and clearly syntactic, being subject to strong island constraints, such as the "fixed subject constraint", as in (2a).

(2) a. #This is *the Siren* they wonder whether *sang* a song.
    b. *Some Siren* claimed that *each song* was the best.   ($\exists\forall/\#\forall\exists$)
    c. *Every Siren* claimed that *some song* was the best.   ($\forall\exists/\exists\forall$)
    d. *Every Siren* thinks that *her* song is the best.

On the other hand, the binding of pronouns and other nominals as dependents of quantifiers is equally clearly completely insensitive to islands, as in (2d), while quantifier scope inversion is a mixed phenomenon, with the universals *every and each* apparently unable to invert scope out of embedded subject positions, as in (2b), while the existentials can do so (2c).

The linguistic literature in general is conflicted on the precise details of what species of dependency and scope is allowed where. However, there is general agreement that while syntactic long-range dependencies are mostly nested, and the occasions when crossing dependencies are allowed are very narrowly specified syntactically, intrasentential binding of pronouns and dependent existentials is essentially free within the scope of the operator. For example, crossing and nesting binding dependencies in the following seem equally good:

(3) Every sailor$_i$ knows that every Siren$_j$ thinks she$_j$ /he$_i$ saw him$_i$ /her$_j$.

It follows that those researchers whose primary concern is with pronoun binding in semantics tend to define their Fregean theory of grammar in terms of different sets of combinatory operators from those researchers whose primary concern is syntactic dependency. Thus, not all categorial theories discussed below are commensurable.

2 Pure Categorial Grammars

In all CG varieties, elements like verbs are associated with a syntactic "category" which identifies them as Fregean *functions*, and specifies the type and directionality of their arguments and the type of their result. We here use the "result leftmost" notation in which a rightward-combining functor over a domain β into a range α is written α/β, while the corresponding leftward-combining functor is written $\alpha\backslash\beta$.[3]

α and β may themselves be function categories. For example, a transitive verb is a function from (object) NPs into predicates—that is, into functions from (subject) NPs into S:

(4) likes := $(S\backslash NP)/NP$

All varieties of Categorial Grammar also include the following rules for combining forward- and backward-looking functions with their arguments:

(5) *Forward application:* $(>)$
  $X/Y\ Y\ \Rightarrow\ X$

(6) *Backward application:* $(<)$
  $Y\ X\backslash Y\ \Rightarrow\ X$

These rules have the form of very general binary phrase-structure rule schemata. In fact, pure categorial grammar is just context-free grammar written in the accepting, rather than the producing, direction, with a consequent transfer of the major burden of specifying particular grammars from the PS rules to the lexicon. While it is now convenient to write derivations as in (7a), they are equivalent to conventional phrase structure derivations (7b):

(7) a.
```
     Mary      likes       bureaucracy        b.  Mary  likes  bureaucracy
     ----     --------      -----------            NP     V       NP
      NP      (S\NP)/NP        NP                    \      \     /
              ------------------------>               \      \ VP
                     S\NP                              \      /
              --------------------<                      S
                     S
```

It is important to note that such tree structures are simply a representation of the process of derivation. They do not necessarily constitute a level of representation in the formal grammar.

CG categories can be regarded as encoding the semantic type of their translation, and this translation can be made explicit in the following expanded notation, which associates a logical form with the entire syntactic category, via the colon operator, which is assumed to have lower precedence than the categorial slash operators. (Agreement features are also included in the syntactic category, represented as subscripts, much as in the work of Bach (1983). The feature 3s is "underspecified" for gender and can combine with the more specified 3sm by a standard unification mechanism that we will pass over here—cf. Shieber (1986).)[4]

(8) likes := $(S\backslash NP_{3s})/NP:\lambda x\lambda y.likes'xy$

We must also expand the rules of functional application in the same way:

(9) *Forward application: (>)*
 $X/Y : f \quad Y : a \quad \Rightarrow \quad X : fa$

(10) *Backward application: (<)*
 $Y : a \quad X \backslash Y : f \quad \Rightarrow \quad X : fa$

They yield derivations like the following:

(11)

$$
\frac{\dfrac{\text{Mary}}{NP_{3sm} : mary'} \quad \dfrac{\dfrac{\text{likes}}{(S \backslash NP_{3s})/NP : likes'} \quad \dfrac{\text{bureaucracy}}{NP : bureaucracy'}}{S \backslash NP_{3s} : likes'\ bureaucracy'} >}{S : likes'\ bureaucracy'\ mary} <
$$

The derivation yields an S with a compositional interpretation, equivalent under a convention of left associativity to (*likes' bureaucracy'*) *mary'*.

Coordination can be included in CG via the following category, allowing constituents of like type to conjoin to yield a single constituent of the same type:[5]

(12) and $:= (X \backslash X)/X$

Since X is a variable over any type, and all three Xs must unify with the *same* type, it allows derivations like the following.

(13)

$$
\frac{\dfrac{\text{I}}{NP} \quad \dfrac{\dfrac{\text{detest}}{(S \backslash NP)/NP} \quad \dfrac{\dfrac{\text{and}}{(X \backslash X)/X} \quad \dfrac{\text{oppose}}{(S \backslash NP)/NP}}{\dfrac{((S \backslash NP)/NP) \backslash ((S \backslash NP)/NP)}{(S \backslash NP)/NP}}}{S \backslash NP} \quad \dfrac{\text{bureaucracy}}{NP}}{S}
$$

3 Combinatory Categorial Grammar

In order to allow coordination of contiguous strings that do not constitute constituents, Combinatory Categorial Grammar (CCG) allows certain further operations on functions and arguments related to Curry's combinators **B**, **T**, and **S** (Curry and Feys 1958).

3.1 *Function composition* B

Functions may not only apply to arguments, but also *compose* with other functions, under the following rule, first proposed in modern terms in the work of Ades and Steedman (1982) but with antecedents in the work of Geach (1970) and as a theorem of Lambek (1958):

(14) *Forward composition: (> B)*
 $X/Y \quad Y/Z \quad \Rightarrow \quad X/Z$

The most important single property of combinatory rules like this is that their semantics is completely determined under the following principle:

(15) *The principle of combinatory transparency:* The semantic interpretation of the category resulting from a combinatory rule is uniquely determined by the interpretation of the slash in a category as a mapping between two sets.

In the above case, the category X/Y is a mapping of Y into X and the category Y/Z is that of a mapping from Z into Y. Since the two occurrences of Y identify the *same* set, the result category X/Z is that mapping from Z to X which constitutes the composition of the input functions. It follows that the only semantics that we are allowed to assign, when the rule is written in full, is as follows:

(16) *Forward composition:* ($>$**B**)
$$X/Y : f \quad Y/Z : g \quad \Rightarrow \quad X/Z : \lambda x.f(gx)$$

No other interpretation is allowed.[6]

The operation of this rightward composition rule in derivations is indicated by an underline indexed $>$**B** (because Curry called his composition combinatory **B**). Its effect can be seen in the derivation of sentences like *I detest, and will oppose, bureaucracy,* which crucially involves the composition of two verbs to yield a composite of the same category as a transitive verb (the rest of the derivation is given in the simpler notation). It is important to observe that composition also yields an appropriate interpretation for the composite verb *will oppose,* as $\lambda x.\lambda y.will'(oppose' x) y$, a category which if applied to an object *bureaucracy* and a subject *I* yields the proposition $will'(oppose' bureaucracy') me'$. The coordination will therefore yield an appropriate semantic interpretation.[7]

(17)

I	detest	and	will	oppose	bureaucracy
NP	$(S\backslash NP)/NP$	$(X\backslash X)/X$	$(S\backslash NP)/VP : will'$	$VP/NP : oppose'$	NP

$$(S\backslash NP)/NP : \lambda x.\lambda y.will'(oppose'x)y \quad {}^{>\mathbf{B}}$$
$$(S\backslash NP)/NP \quad {}^{<\Phi>}$$
$$S\backslash NP \quad {}^{>}$$
$$S \quad {}^{<}$$

3.2 Type-raising T

Combinatory grammars also include type-raising rules, originally proposed in the study by Steedman (1985) but with antecedents in generalized quantifier theory, which turn arguments into functions over functions-over-such-arguments. These rules allow arguments to compose, and thereby take part in coordinations like *I detest, and Mary likes, bureaucracy.* For example, the following rule allows the conjuncts to form as below (again, the remainder of the derivation is given in the briefer notation):

(18) *Subject type-raising:* ($>$T)
$$NP : a \quad \Rightarrow \quad S/S(S\backslash NP) : \lambda f.fa$$

(19)

I	detest	and	Mary	likes	bureaucracy
NP	$(S\backslash NP)/NP$	$(X\backslash X)/X$	NP	$(S\backslash NP)/NP$	NP

$$\frac{I}{NP} \quad \frac{detest}{(S\backslash NP)/NP} \quad \frac{and}{(X\backslash X)/X} \quad \frac{Mary}{NP} : mary' \quad \frac{likes}{(S\backslash NP)/NP} : \lambda x.\lambda y.likes'xy \quad \frac{bureaucracy}{NP}$$

$$\frac{}{S/(S\backslash NP)} >\mathbf{T} \qquad \frac{}{S/(S\backslash NP)} >\mathbf{T}$$
$$: \lambda f.f\,mary'$$

$$\frac{\qquad\qquad\qquad}{S/NP} >\mathbf{B} \qquad \frac{\qquad\qquad\qquad}{S/NP} >\mathbf{B}$$
$$: \lambda x.likes'\,x\,mary'$$

$$\frac{\qquad\qquad\qquad\qquad\qquad}{S/NP} <\Phi>$$

$$\frac{\qquad\qquad\qquad\qquad\qquad\qquad\qquad}{S} >$$

Rule (18) has an "order-preserving" property. That is, it turns the NP into a *rightward* looking function over *leftward* function, and therefore preserves the linear order of subjects and predicates specified in the lexicon for the language.

Like composition, type-raising rules are required by the principle of combinatory transparency (15) to be transparent to semantics. This fact ensures that the raised subject NP has an appropriate interpretation, and can compose with the verb to produce a function that can either coordinate with another nonstandard constituent of the same type or reduce with an object *bureaucracy* to yield *likes' bureaucracy' mary'* via a nonstandard left-branching alternative derivation to (11), delivering the same logical form.

The latter alternative derivational structures are sometimes misleadingly referred to as "spuriously" ambiguous (Karttunen 1989), and deprecated as exacerbating the search problem for the parser. However, any theory of grammar that covers the same range of coordination phenomena will engender the same degree of nondeterminism in derivation. We return to this question in Section 7.

While other solutions to the problem of getting subjects to combine with the transitive verb can readily be imagined, the inclusion of order-preserving type-raising is essential to the account of coordination afforded by CCG, because it allows *sequences of arguments* to compose. We defer discussion of this question until Section 3.6, where we will see that type-raising should be constrained as an essentially lexical operation, identifiable with the traditional notion of *case*, whether morphologically marked, as in Latin and Japanese, or positionally marked or "structural", as in English.

3.3 Substitution S

For reasons that we will come to directly, the following rule of a type closely related to composition, first proposed by Szabolcsi (1983, 1992) under the name "connection", and discussed at length by Steedman (1987), is required for the analysis of the parasitic gap construction, illustrated in (21):

(20) *Backward crossed substitution:* ($<\mathbf{S}$)
$$Y/Z : g \quad (X\backslash Y)/Z : f \quad \Rightarrow \quad X/Y : \lambda x.(fx)(gx)$$

(21) I will [[burn]$_{VP/NP}$ [without reading] $_{(VP\backslash VP)/NP}$] $_{VP/NP}$ [any report longer than 100 pages]$_{NP}$

3.4 The space of possible combinatory rules in CCG

Rule (20) is of interest for exploiting all and only the degrees of freedom that are available under the following universal syntactic projection principles (the term "principal functor" refers to the input functor whose range is the same as the range of the output—in the notation used above, the functor whose range is X):

(22) *The principle of directional consistency*
The inputs to a combinatory rule must be directionally consistent with the principal functor—if the latter applies to the result of the subordinate fuctor to the left, it must be rightmost of the inputs, and vice versa.

(23) *The principle of directional inheritance*
The argument(s) in a function that is the output of a combinatory rule must be directionally consistent with the corresponding argument(s) in the input functors—if an argument of the output bears a slash of a given directionality, all occurrences of that argument in the inputs must bear a slash of the *same* directionality.

These rules are perfectly illustrated by Szabolcsi's rule (20): although the inputs bear different "crossing" directionality (which is allowed), the principal functor $(X\backslash Y)/Z$ is looking for the result Y of the subordinate functor Y/Z to its left, so it is rightmost (*consistency*), and the argument Z of the output X/Z bears a rightward slash in both inputs (*inheritance*).

The lexical type-raising rules are limited by these principles to the order preserving cases (30) and (31): raised categories which change word order, such as topics and the relative pronouns discussed in the next section, have to change the result type.

3.5   Extraction

Since complement-taking verbs like *think*, VP/S, can in turn compose with fragments like *Mary likes*, S/NP, we correctly predict that right-node raising is unbounded, as in (24a) and (25a), below, and also provide the basis for an analysis of the similarly unbounded character of leftward extraction, as in (24b) and (25b):[8]

(24) a. [[I detest] $_{S/NP}$ and [you think Mary likes] $_{S/NP}$] $_{S/NP}$ [bureaucracy.] $_{NP}$
   b. The bureaucracy $_N$ [[that] $_{(N\backslash N)/(S/NP)}$ [you think Mary likes] $_{S/NP}$] $_{N\backslash N}$

(25) a. I will [[sieze] $_{VP/NP}$ and [burn without reading] $_{VP/NP}$] $_{VP/NP}$ [any report longer than 100 pages.] $_{NP}$
   b. The reports $_N$ [[that] $_{(N\backslash N)/(S/NP)}$ [I will burn without reading] $_{S/NP}$] $_{N\backslash N}$

3.6   Coordination

This apparatus has been applied to a wide variety of coordination phenomena, including "argument-cluster coordination", "backward gapping" and "verb-raising" constructions in a variety of languages by the authors listed in the introduction. The first of these is relevant to the present discussion, and is illustrated by the following analysis, from Dowty (1988, cf. Steedman 1985):[9]

(26)
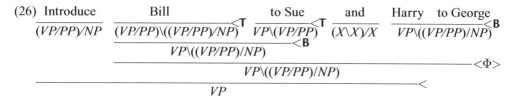

The important feature of this analysis is that it uses "backward" rules of type-raising $<$T and composition $<$**B** that are the exact mirror-image of the two "forward" versions introduced as examples (14) and (18), which similarly guarantee that the semantics of nonstandard constituents like *Bill to Sue* is such as to reduce appropriately with a ditransitive verb like *give*. It is in fact a prediction of the theory that such a construction can exist in English, and its inclusion in the grammar requires no additional mechanism whatsoever.

The earlier papers show that no *other* non-constituent coordinations of dative-accusative NP sequences are allowed in any language with the English verb categories, given the assumptions of CCG. Thus the following are ruled out in principle, rather than by stipulation:

(27) a. *Bill to Sue and introduce Harry to George
      b. *Introduce to Sue Bill and to George Harry

In English the phenomenon shows up in all constructions that can be assumed to involve multiple arguments of the same functor:[10]

(28) a. I introduced Bob to Carol, and Ted to Alice.
      b. I saw Thelma yesterday, and Louise the day before.
      c. Will Gilbert arrive and George leave?
      d. I persuaded Warren to take a bath and Dexter to wash his socks.
      e. I promised Mutt to go to the movies and Jeff to go to the play.
      f. I told Shem I lived in Edinburgh and Shaun I lived in Philadelphia.
      g. I bet Sammy sixpence he would win and Rosie a dollar she would lose.
      h. I like Ike and you, Adlai.

A number of related well-known cross-linguistic generalizations first noted by Ross (1970) concerning the dependency of so-called "gapping" upon lexical word order are also captured (see Dowty (1988) and Steedman (1985, 1990, 2000b)). The pattern is that in languages whose basic clause constituent order subject-verb-object (SVO), the verb or verb group that goes missing is the one in the right conjunct, and not the one in the left conjunct. The same asymmetry holds for VSO languages like Irish. However, SOV languages like Japanese show the opposite asymmetry: the missing verb is in the *left* conjunct.[11] The pattern can be summarized as follows for the three dominant constituent orders (asterisks indicate the excluded cases):[12]

(29) SVO: *SO and SVO   SVO and SO
      VSO: *SO and VSO   VSO and SO
      SOV: SO and SOV *SOV and SO

This observation can be generalized to individual constructions within a language: just about any construction in which an element apparently goes missing preserves canonical word order in an analogous fashion: (26) above is an example of this generalization holding of a verb-initial construction in English.

Phenomena like the above immediately suggest that all complements of verbs bear type-raised categories. However, we do not want anything *else* to type-raise. In particular, we do not want raised categories to raise again, or we risk infinite regress in our rules. One way to deal with this problem is to explicitly restrict the two type-raising rules to the relevant arguments of verbs, as follows, a restriction that is a natural expression of the resemblance of type-raising to some generalized form of (nominative, accusative, etc., morphological or structural) grammatical *case*—cf. Steedman (1985, 1990).

(30) *Forward type-raising:* ($>$ **T**)
$X : a \implies T/(T \backslash X) : \lambda f . fa$

(31) *Backward type-raising:* ($<$ **T**)
$X : a \implies T \backslash (T/X) : \lambda f . fa$

The other solution is to simply expand the lexicon by incorporating the raised categories that these rules define, so that categories like NP have raised categories, and all functions into such categories, like determiners, have the category of functions into raised categories.

These two tactics are essentially equivalent, because in some cases we need both raised and unraised categories for complements. (The argument depends upon the observation that any category that is not a barrier to extraction must bear an unraised category, and any argument that can take part in argument-cluster coordination must be raised—cf. Dowty 2003.) The correct solution from a linguistic point of view, inasmuch as it captures the fact that some languages appear to lack certain unraised categories (notably *PP* and *S'*), is probably the lexical solution. However, the restricted rule-based solution makes derivations easier to read and allows them to take up less space.

Since categories like NP can be raised over a number of different functor categories, such as predicate, transitive verb, ditransitive verb etc, and since the resulting raised categories $S \backslash (S/NP)$, $(S \backslash NP) \backslash ((S \backslash NP)/PP)$, etc. of NPs, PPs, etc are quite hard to read, it is sometimes convenient to abbreviate the raised categories as a schema written $NP^{\uparrow}$, $PP^{\uparrow}$, etc.[13]

3.7 Generalizing combinatory rules

A number of generalized forms of the combinatory rules are allowed. We have already noted the need for crossed directionality in rules. Thus for composition we have the following rule allowed under principles (22) and (23)

(32) *Backward crossed composition:* ($>$ **B**$_x$)
$Y/Z : g \quad X \backslash Y : f \implies X/Z : \lambda x . f(gx)$

This rule allows "heavy NP-shifted" examples like the following:

(33) I will [[go]$_{VP/PP}$ [next Sunday] $_{VP \backslash VP}$]$_{VP/PP}$ [to London]$_{PP}$

We also generalize all composition rules to higher valency in the subordinate input function, to a small bound equal to the highest valency specified in the lexicon, say ≤ 4, thus:[14]

(34) *Backward crossed second-order composition:* ($<$ **B**$_x^2$)
$(Y/Z)/W : g \quad X \backslash Y : f \implies (X/Z)/W : \lambda w \lambda z . f(gwz)$

Such rules allow examples like the following, related to (33):

(35) I shall [[present]$_{(VP/PP)/NP}$ [next Sunday]$_{VP \backslash VP}$]$_{VP \backslash VP}$ [a prize]$_{PP}$ [to each winner]$_{PP}$

The inclusion of crossed second order composition in the theory of grammar allows unbounded crossing dependency of the kind investigated in Dutch and Zurich German by Huybregts and Shieber, and is the specific source of greater than context-free power in CCG.

The inclusion of crossed combinatory rules means that lexical items must be restricted to avoid overgeneration in fixed word-order languages like English. For example, while adverbial adjuncts can combine with verbs by crossed combination as above, adnominal adjuncts cannot:

(36) *An $[old]_{N/N}$ $[with\ a\ limp]_{N\backslash N}$ man

Accordingly, we follow Hepple (1990), Morrill (1994), Moortgat (1997), and more specifically Baldridge and Kruijff (2003) in lexically distinguishing the slash-type of English adnominals and their specifiers as only allowed to combine by non-crossed rules, writing them as follows:

(37) with $:= N\backslash_\Diamond N$

Similarly, the coordination category (12) must be rewritten as follows, where the *modality limits it to only combining via the application rules:

(38) and $:= (X\backslash_* X)/_* X$

This is managed using a simple type-lattice of features on slashes in categories and rules due to Baldridge, whose details we pass over here (see Steedman and Baldridge 2011).

3.8   Free word order

When dealing with the phenomenon of free order, it may be convenient for some languages to represent some group of arguments of a head as combining in any order to yield the same semantic result. Following Hoffman (1995) and Baldridge (2002), if three arguments A, B, C are completely free-order with respect to a head yielding S, we might write its category as in (a) below. If it requires all three to the left (or right) in any order, we might write the category as in (b) (or (c)). If the head requires A to the left and the other arguments in any order to the right, we might write the category as in (d):

(39) a. $S\{|A,|B,|C\}$
      b. $S\{\backslash A,\backslash B,\backslash C\}$
      c. $S\{/A,/B,/C\}$
      d. $S\{\backslash A,/B,/C\}$

Braces $\{\ldots\}$ enclose multisets of arguments that can be found in any order in the specified direction. The question then arises of how multisets behave under combinatory rules such as composition.

Baldridge points out that, to preserve the near context-free expressive power of CCG, it is crucial to interpret the multiset notation as merely an abbreviation for exhaustive listing of all the ordered categories that would be required to support the specified orders. (For example, $S\{\backslash A, \backslash B, \backslash C\}$ abbreviates the set $\{((S\backslash A)\backslash B\backslash C, ((S\backslash A)\backslash C)\backslash B, ((S\backslash B)\backslash A)\backslash C, ((S\backslash B)\backslash C)\backslash A, ((S\backslash C)\backslash A)\backslash B, ((S\backslash C)\backslash B)\backslash A\}$.)

The combinatory rules, such as the various forms of composition, must then be defined so that they preserve this interpretation, crucially involving the same limit of $n \leq 4$ on the degree of generalized composition. Again, we pass over the details here, but if this constraint is not observed, then the expressive power of the grammar explodes to that of full indexed grammars (cf. note 14).

Hoyt and Baldridge (2008) use composition as a unary rule to define certain further linguistically motivated combinatory species, notably those corresponding to Curry's **D** combinator (Wittenburg 1987). All of these rules obey the principles (22) and (23).

3.9 Combinators and the theory of grammar

It is important for any theory to keep its intrinsic degrees of freedom as low as possible with respect to the degrees of freedom in the data it seeks to explain. In the case of the theory of grammar, this means limiting the set of languages covered or generated to the smallest "natural family of languages" that includes all and only the possible human languages. That set is known to lie somewhere between the context-free and context-sensitive levels of the Chomsky hierarchy. Since most phenomena of natural language look context-free, the lower end of that vast range is the region to aim for.

Quite simple systems of combinators, including the typed **BTS** system that underlies CCG, are, in the absence of further restriction, equivalent to the simply typed λ-calculus—that is, to unconstrained recursively enumerable systems. It is the universal restrictive "projection principles" (22) and (23), together with the restriction of generalized composition **B**^{n} and X in the coordination category schema $(X \backslash X)/X$ in (12) to a bound on valency tentatively set at $n \leq 4$, that crucially restricts the (weak) expressive power of CCG to the same low level as tree-adjoining grammars (TAG, Joshi 1988) and linear indexed grammars (LIG, Gazdar 1988). This level is the least more expressive natural family of languages that is known than context-free grammars (Vijay-Shanker and Weir 1994).

This "nearly context-free" class is very much less expressive than the very properly sub-context-sensitive" classes such as full indexed grammars (IG, Aho 1968, 1969), which can express "non-constant growth" languages like a^{2^n}, and full linear context-free rewriting systems (LCFRS, Weir 1988), also known as multiple context free grammars (MCFG). The latter are shown by Kanazawa and Salvati (2012) to include the total scrambling language MIX, and have been argued by Stabler (2011) to characterize Chomskian minimalist grammars.

A word is in order on the relation of the "nearly context-free" formalisms CCG, TAG, and LIG. While weakly equivalent, they belong to different branches of the (extended) Chomsky hierarchy. Weir showed that the natural generalization of TAG is to full LCFRS/MCFG, while the natural generalization of CCG is to full IG. LCFRS and IG do not stand in an inclusion relation, although both are very properly contained in—that is, very much less expressive than—full context sensitive grammars, which for practical purposes are essentially as expressive as recursively enumerable systems (Savitch 1987).

This low expressive power brings a proof of polynomial parsability (Vijay-Shanker and Weir 1994), the significance of which is that standard "divide and conquer" context-free parsing algorithms readily generalize to CCG and the related formalisms. This fact, together with its semantic transparency, is the key to the widespread uptake of CCG in computational linguistic applications, particularly those which require semantic interpretation and/or accuracy with long-range dependencies, such as semantic parsing, question answering, and text entailment (see below).

In considering the rival merits and attractions of some of the alternative forms of CG considered below, it is worth keeping in mind the question of whether they are comparably constrained in expressive power and complexity.

4 Categorial grammars with WRAP combinatory rules

Categories like (8) exhibit a pleasing transparency between the syntactic type $(S\backslash NP)/NP$ and the logical form $\lambda x\lambda y.likes'\ xy$: both functions want the object as first argument and the subject as last argument, reflecting the binding asymmetry below in the fact that the subject commands (is attached higher than) the object:

(40) a.   John$_i$ likes himself$_i$.
     b.   #Himself$_i$ likes John$_i$.

(Indeed, in such cases the λ-binding in the logical form is redundant: we could just write it as *likes'*.)

However, similar binding asymmetries like the following are not so simple:

(41) a.   I introduced John$_i$ to himself$_i$.
     b.   #I introduced himself$_i$ to John$_i$.

If we want to continue to capture the binding possibilities in terms of command, then we need to make a choice. If we want to retain the simple surface compositional account of extraction and coordination proposed earlier in Sections 3.5 and 3.6 we will need a category like the following for the ditransitive, in which derivational command and logical form command are no longer homomorphic:

(42) introduced := $((S\backslash NP)/PP)/NP : \lambda n\lambda p\lambda y.introduced'pny$

This category captures the asymmetry in (41) in the fact that the first NP argument n lf-commands the second PP argument p in the logical form *introduced'pny*, despite the fact that the former commands the latter in the derivation according to the syntactic type. As a consequence, we can no longer eliminate the explicit λ-binding logical form, and if binding theory asymmetries like (41) are to be explained in terms of command, it cannot be derivational command, but must be command at the level of logical form.

This use of logical form should not been seen as proliferating levels of representation in the theory of grammar, as Dowty has suggested. In such versions of CG, logical form is the *only* structural level of representation: no rule of syntax or semantics is defined in terms of derivation structure.

If on the other hand we wish to continue to account for such binding asymmetries in terms of derivational command, maintaining strict isomorphism between syntactic and semantic types in ditransitive categories like (42), and eliminating any distinction between derivational structure and logical form, as Bach, Dowty, and Jacobson, among others, have argued, we need a different category for *introduced*, taking the PP as its first most oblique argument, and the NP as its second.

(43) introduced := $((S\backslash NP)/_{\otimes}NP)/PP : \lambda p\lambda n\lambda y.introduced''\ pny$

We must also introduce a further combinatory family of "wrapping" rules that "infix" the second string argument as first argument, as in (44), marking the second argument of the syntactic type of English polytransitive verbs for combination by such a rule, as in (43):[15]

(44) *Right wrap:* $(>_{\mathscr{RW}})$
      $(X/_{\mathscr{RW}}Y)/Z : f \quad Y : a \quad Z : b \quad => \quad X : fba$

Bach (1979), Jacobson (1992), and Dowty (1997) have strongly advocated the inclusion of wrap rules and categories in CG, both empirically on the basis of a wide variety of constructions in a number of languages, and on grounds of theoretical parsimony, based on the fact that all logical forms in categories and rules like (43) and (44) are eliminable, and derivation structure is the only level of representation in the theory.

There can be no doubt of the empirical strength of the generalization that the linear order of arguments in verb-initial constructions is typically the inverse of that required for the command theory of binding. However, the argument from parsimony is less conclusive. Dowty's claim seems to be that the naive category (42) makes an intrinsic use of logical form to switch the order of application to the arguments. However, this operation is entirely local to the lexicon, and therefore seems entirely equivalent to including the same information in syntax via the wrapping slash. The inclusion of wrap categories like (43) in place of (42), together with wrap rules like (44), engenders considerable complication in the syntactic theory. In particular, the simple and elegant account of constituent cluster coordination as a necessary corollary prediction in the **BTS** system including type-raising and composition alone, exemplified earlier by (26), is no longer available in a combinatory grammar including rule (44) (see Dowty 1997 for a very clear exposition of the difficulty).

Dowty has proposed a number of solutions to this problem, including an "ID/LP" version of categorial grammar (Dowty 1996), following Zwicky (1986), in which combination (immediate domination, ID) is discontinuous, and is filtered by constraints on order (linear precedence, LP). Dowty (1997) shows how a multimodal categorial grammar of a kind discussed in the next section can be extended with uninterpreted structural rules of permutation triggered by typed string concatenation operators, (The latter are reminiscent of the product operator used by Pickering and Barry (1993) as an alternative to composition and type-raising for making argument clusters like "Bill to Sue" into constituents.) Dowty's grammar captures the full range of constructions addressed in standard CCG, including crossed dependency and argument cluster coordination. However, the theoretical difficulties are considerable, and the details must be passed over here. It remains unclear whether structural rules and product operators can be made to force Ross's generalization (29) in the straightforward way that CCG restricted to **BTS** combinatory rules does.

5 Lambek grammars

Despite a superficially similar categorial slash notation, Lambek grammars constitute a quite different approach to the extension of the pure categorial grammar of Ajdukiewicz (1935) and Bar-Hillel (1953), building on the view of categorial grammar *as a logic* initiated by Lambek (1958, 1961). This approach treats the categorial slash as a form of (linear) logical implication, for which the antecedent-canceling application rules perform the role of modus ponens.[16]

Lambek's contribution was to add further logical axioms of associativity, product-formation, and division, from which harmonic composition and order-preserving type raising emerge as theorems (although crossing composition and the S combinator do not). The resulting calculus was widely assumed to be weakly equivalent to context-free grammar, although the involvement of an axiom schema in its definition meant that the actual proof of the equivalence was not forthcoming until the work of Pentus (1993). (In fact, the original Lambek calculus supports essentially the same analysis of unbounded dependency as context-free GPSG, but with the advantage of semantic isomorphism.) Paradoxically, despite context-free equivalence, the original context-free calculus lacks a polynomial-time recognition algorithm, because the mapping to equivalent context-free grammars that would afford such an algorithm is not itself polynomial, a result that was also widely anticipated (e.g. Hepple (1999)) but hard to prove, until Pentus (2003) proved that as well.

5.1 Pregroup grammars

Partly in response, Lambek (2001) has recently proposed pregroup grammar as a simpler base for type-based grammars. Like LG, pregroup grammars (PG) are context-free (Buszkowski 2001), but they have a polynomial conversion to CFG (Buszkowski and Moroz 2008). They inherit the associative property of LG of combining the English subject and transitive verb as a single operation, rather than tediously requiring two successive operations of type raising and composition. While pregroup grammar thereby obscures the relation between type raising and grammatical case, the associativity operator obeys the principles of adjacency, consistency, and inheritance defined above, and is definable in terms of the combinators B and T. It could therefore be consistently incorporated in CCG grammar or parser, if so desired, without losing the advantages of the latter's mildly trans-context-free expressive power.

Pregroup grammars are so called because of the involvement of free pregroups as a mathematical structure in their definition. Kobele and Kracht (2005) show that one natural generalization of pregroup grammars defined in terms of *all* pregroups and allowing the empty string symbol generates all recursively enumerable languages—that is, is equivalent to the universal Turing machine. Tupled pregroup grammars, a more constrained generalization of context-free pregroup grammars by Stabler (2004a,b), have been shown to be weakly equivalent to set-local MC-TAG, the multiple context-free grammars (MCFGs) of Seki *et al.* (1991), and the minimalist grammars of Stabler and Keenan (2003). Such calculi are, as noted earlier, much more expressive than CCG and TAG, being equivalent to full LCFRS. Their learnability is investigated by Béchet and Foret (2007).

Other generalizations of the original Lambek calculi include abstract categorial grammar (de Groote 2001; de Groote and Pogodalla 2004), lambda grammar (Muskens 2007), convergent grammar (CVG) (de Groote *et al.*, forthcoming), and the Lambek–Grishin calculus or symmetric categorial grammar (Moortgat 2007, 2009). The expressive power of these systems seems likely to be also that of full LCFRS.

5.2 Categorial type logic

In a separate development from the original Lambek calculi, Moortgat (1988a) and van Benthem (1988) importantly showed that simply adding further axioms such as permutation or crossing composition to the Lambek calculus causes it (unlike CCG) to collapse into permutation completeness. Instead, they and Oehrle (1988) proposed to extend the Lambek calculus using "structural rules" and typed slashes of the kind originated by Hepple (1990) and discussed in Section 3.7, to control associativity and permutativity. Specific proposals of this kind include hybrid logical grammar (Hepple 1990, 1995), type-logical grammars (Morrill 1994, 2011; Carpenter 1997), term-labeled categorial type systems (Oehrle 1994), type-theoretical grammars (Ranta 1994), and multimodal categorial grammar (Moortgat 1997; Carpenter 1995; Moot and Puite 2002; Moot and Retoré 2012; cf. Baldridge 2002).

Carpenter and Baldridge showed that the type-logical categorial grammars were potentially very expressive indeed. TLG thus provides the general framework for comparing categorial systems of all kinds, including CCG (Baldridge and Kruijff 2003).

6 Semantics in categorial grammars

Although the primary appeal of categorial grammars since Montague derives from the aforementioned close relation between categorial derivation and semantic interpretation, there is a similar diversity in theories of the exact nature of the mapping from categorial syntax and semantics to that concerning the exact nature of the syntactic operations themselves. The main focus of disagreement is on the question of whether a representational level of logical form distinct from syntactic derivational structure is involved or not.[17]

Montague himself was somewhat divided on this question. Montague (1970a,b) argued that there was no logical reason why natural languages, any more than formal logical languages, should have more than one representational level. However, later (Montague 1973), he included operations such as "quantifying in" that made apparently essential use of logical form via operations with no surface syntactic reflex. The literature since Montague has similarly followed two diverging paths, which I will distinguish as "sacred" and "profane".[18]

The sacred path usually adhered to by Partee, Dowty, Jacobson, Hendriks, and Szabolci follows the Montague of 1970 in assuming a standard logic such as first-order (modal) predicate logic (FOPL) as the language of thought or logical form, and seeking to eliminate 1973-style intrinsic use of logical form by elaborating the notion of syntactic derivation via various additional combinators, such as wrapping, type-lowering, and specialized binding combinators. The official name for this sacred approach is "direct surface compositionality": it seeks to eliminate logical form and make derivation the sole structural level of representation.[19]

Because phenomena like the dependency of bound variable pronouns in (1d) tend to be much less restricted than strictly syntactic dependencies like relativization, the sacred approach has in practice shown itself quite willing to abandon the search for low expressive power in surface syntax characteristic of GPSG and CCG. There is a natural affinity between the sacred approach to semantics and the more expressive forms of Lambek and type-logical grammars, although Carpenter (1997) combines Morrill's type logical syntax with an essentially profane semantics.

The profane approach follows the opposite strategy. If the chosen representation for logical form appears to require non-monotonic structure-changing operations such as quantifier-raising and quantifying-in (or extraneous equivalent type-changing derivational operations), then there must just be something wrong in the choice of logical representation. The logical language itself should be changed, perhaps by eliminating quantifiers and introducing discourse referents (Kamp and Reyle 1993) and referring expressions (Fodor and Sag 1982), or Skolem terms (Kratzer 1998; Steedman 1999, 2012; Schlenker 2006) in their place. If pronoun binding obeys none of the same generalizations as syntactic derivation, do it non-derivationally (Steedman 2012). It is surface derivation that should be eliminated as a representational level. In fact there may be very many derivation structures yielding the same logical form. There is a close affinity between the profane approach to semantics and computational linguistics.

In the end, the difference between these two approaches may not be very important, since they agree on the principle that there should be only one level of structural representation, and differ only on its relation to surface derivation. Nevertheless, they have in practice led to radically different semantic theories. We will consider them briefly in turn.

6.1   The sacred approach: direct surface compositionality

The sacred approach to semantics differs from the profane in making the following assumptions:

1. Surface derivational structure is the *only* representational level in the theory of grammar corresponding to logical form and supporting a model-theoretic semantics.
2. No other representation of logical form is necessary to the theory of grammar, and any use of logical formulae to represent meanings distinct from derivation structures is a mere notational convenience.

Dowty (1979), Partee and Rooth (1983), Szabolcsi (1989), Chierchia (1988), Hendriks (1993), Jacobson (1999), Barker (2002), Jäger (2005), and colleagues follow Montague in seeking to extend categorial grammar to the problem of operator semantics, including pronoun-binding by quantifiers, exemplified in the following:

(45)   a.   Every sailor$_i$ believes every Siren$_j$ knows he$_i$ heard her$_j$
       b.   Every sailor$_i$ believes every Siren$_j$ knows she$_j$ saw him$_i$

As noted in the introduction, such examples show that bound variable pronouns are free to nest or cross dependencies with quantificational binders. Such dependencies are also immune to the island boundaries that block relativization, of which the fixed subject condition on extraction illustrated in (46) provides one of the strongest examples.

(46)   a.   Every sailor$_i$ believes that he$_i$ won.
       b.   #A Siren who(m) every sailor$_i$ believes that won$_i$

Following Szabolcsi (1989), these authors seek to bring pronoun binding within the same system of combinatory projection from the lexicon as syntactic dependency. Jacobson (1999; 2007: 203–4) assigns pronouns the category of a nominal syntactic and semantic identity function, with which the verb can compose. However, instead of writing something like $NP|NP : \lambda x.x$ as the category for "him" she writes $NP^{\{NP\}}: \lambda x.x$.[20] Constituents of the type of verbs can be subject to a unary form of composition or "division", which she calls the Geach rule.[21]

For example, intransitive "won" $S\backslash NP$ can acquire a further category $S^{\{NP\}}\backslash NP^{\{NP\}}$: $\lambda i \lambda y.won'y$. Such Geach types can combine with a pronoun (or any NP $NP^{\{NP\}}$ containing a pronoun, such as "his mother" or "a man he knows") by function composition, so that "he won" yields the category $S^{\{NP\}}$: $\lambda y.won'y$ rather than the standard category S: $won'him'$.[22]

Constituents of the same type as verbs can also undergo a unary combinatory rule which Jacobson calls **z**. For example, "believes" $(S \backslash NP)/S : \lambda s \lambda y.believes'sy$, can become $(S \backslash NP)/S^{\{NP\}} : \lambda p \lambda y.believes'(py)y$, which on application to "he won", $S^{\{NP\}} : \lambda y.won'y$, yields "believes he won", $S \backslash NP : \lambda y. believes'(won'y)y$. This predicate can combine as the argument of the standard generalized quantifier category for "Every sailor", $S/(S \backslash NP) : \lambda p.\forall y[sailor'y \Rightarrow believes'(py)y]$, to yield:

(47) Every sailor believes he won $S : \forall y [sailor'y \Rightarrow believes'(won'y)y]$

However, the freedom of multiple pronouns to either nest or intercalate bindings to scoping quantifiers, as in (45), coupled with the fact that binding may be into and out of strong islands such as English subject position, as in (46a), means that Jacobson's binding categories $X^{\{Y...\}}$ have to form a separate parallel combinatory categorial system. It is not easy to see how to combine these two combinatory systems in a single grammar without exploding the category type system. Jacobson (1999: 105, n.19) in fact proposes to give up the CCG account of extraction entirely, and to revert to something like the GPSG account (the latter is known to be incomplete—see Gazdar (1988)).

Similar problems attend attempts to treat quantifier scope via surface syntactic derivation. There is a temptation to think that the "object wide scope" reading of the following scope-ambiguous sentence (a) arises from a derivation in which a type-raised object $S \backslash (S/NP) : \lambda p.\exists x[woman \ x \wedge p \ x]$ derivationally commands the nonstandard constituent $S/NP : \lambda y.\forall z[man \ z \Rightarrow loves \ yz]$ to yield $S : \exists x \ [woman \ x \wedge \forall z[man \ z \Rightarrow loves \ xz]]$ (eg. Bernardi 2002: 22).

(48) a. Every man loves a woman.
      b. Every man loves and every boy fears a woman.

However, (48b) has *only* the object c-command derivation. Yet it undoubtedly has a narrow scope reading involving possibly different women. If scope is to be handled by derivational command we therefore have to follow Hendriks (1993) in introducing otherwise syntactically unmotivated type-*lowering* operations, with attendant restrictions to ensure that they do not then raise again to yield unattested mixed-scope readings, such as the one in which men love possibly different narrow scope women, and boys all fear the same wide scope woman.

Solutions to all of these problems have been proposed by Hendriks, Jacobson, and Jäger, and in the continuation-based combinatory theory of Barker (2001) and Shan and Barker (2006), but it is not yet clear whether they can be overcome without compromising the purely syntactic advantages of CG with respect to, for example, extraction. If not, there is some temptation to consider binding and scope as distinctively anaphoric properties of logical form that are orthogonal to syntactic derivation, as is standard in logic proper and in programming language theory.

6.2   The profane approach: natural semantics

The profane approach to semantics has been called "natural semantics", in homage to Lakoff's 1970 proposal for a natural logic underlying the generative semantics approach to the theory of grammar in the early 1970s, of which Partee (1970) was an early categorial exponent. The proposal was influentially taken up by Sánchez Valencia (1991, 1995) and Dowty

(1994) within categorial frameworks, and extended elsewhere by MacCartney and Manning (2007). Natural semantics departs from the sacred approach, and from other proposals within generative semantics of that period, in three important respects.

1. Logical form is the *only* representational level in the theory of grammar supporting a model-theoretic semantics.
2. Surface-syntactic derivation is *not* a level of representation in the theory of grammar, and does not require or support a model theory distinct from that of logical form. It is merely a description of the computation by which a language processor builds (or expresses) a logical form from (or as) a string of a particular language, and is entirely redundant with respect to interpretation or realization of meaning.
3. The language of natural logical form should not be expected to be anything like traditional logics such as FOPL, invented by logicians and mathematicians for very different purposes. The sole source of information we have as to the nature of this "hidden" language of thought is linguistic form, under the strong assumption of syntactic/semantic homomorphism shared by all categorial grammarians.

The profane natural approach to semantics therefore questions the core assumption of Lambek and type-logical approaches that surface syntax is itself a *logic*. By the same token, natural semantics questions the core assumption of direct surface compositionality concerning the redundancy of logical form. It is derivational structure that is semantically redundant, not logical form. If keeping derivation simple requires lexical logical forms to wrap derivational arguments, as in (42), then let them do so (Carpenter 1997: 437). If the attested possibilities for quantifier scope alternation do not seem to be compatible with any simple account of derivation, then replace generalized quantifiers with devices that simplify derivations, such as referring expressions or Skolem terms (Steedman 2012).

There have been recent signs of a rapprochement between these views. Jacobson (2002: 60) points out that the use of WRAP rules in some combinatory versions of CG demands structural information that is exactly equivalent to that in the profane λ-binding category (42) and Dowty's 1997 concatenation modalities. Dowty (1996, drafted around 1991; 2007) has drawn a distinction following Curry (1961) between a level of "tectogrammatics", defining the direct compositional interpretation of the equivalent of logical form, and one of "phenogrammatics", equivalent to surface derivation. (Dowty 2007: 58–60) regards the responsibility for defining the ways phenogrammatical syntax can "encode" tectogrammatical structure as a question for psycholinguistics, as concerning a processor which he seems to view as approximate and essentially related to what used to be called performance. These are clear and welcome signs of convergence between these extremes. Perhaps, as is often the case in human affairs, the sacred and the profane are quite close at heart.

7 Computational and psycholinguistic applications

It is unfashionable nowadays for linguistic theories to concern themselves with performance. Moreover, most contemporary psychological and computational models of natural language processing return the compliment by remaining ostentatiously agnostic concerning linguistic theories of competence.

Nevertheless, one should never forget that linguistic competence and performance must come into existence together, as a package deal in evolutionary and developmental terms. The theory of syntactic competence should therefore ultimately be transparent to the theory of the processor. One of the attractions of categorial grammars is that they support a very direct relation between competence grammars and performance parsers.

The central problems for practical language processing by humans or by machine are twofold. First, natural language grammars are very large, involving thousands of constructions. (The lexicon derived from section 02-21 of the categorial CCGbank version of the 1M-word Penn Wall Street journal corpus (Hockenmaier and Steedman 2007) contains 1224 distinct category types, of which 417 only appear once, and is known to be incomplete.)

Second, natural grammars are hugely ambiguous. As a result, quite unremarkable sentences of the kind routinely encountered in an even moderately serious newspaper have thousands of syntactically well-formed analyses. (The reason why human beings are rarely aware that a sentence has more than a single analysis is that nearly all of the other analyses are semantically anomalous, especially when the context of discourse is taken into account.)

The past few years have shown that ambiguity of this degree can be handled practically in parsers of comparable coverage and robustness to humans, by the use of statistical models, and in particular those that approximate semantics by modeling semantically relevant head-dependency probabilities such as those between verbs and the nouns that head their (subject, object, etc.) arguments (Hindle and Rooth 1993; Magerman 1995; Collins 1997). Head-word dependencies compile into the model a powerful mixture of syntactic, semantic, and world-dependent regularities that can be amazingly effective in reducing search.[23]

Categorial grammars of the kinds discussed here were initially expected to be poorly adapted to practical parsing, because of the additional derivational ambiguity introduced by the nonstandard constituency discussed at the end of Section 3.2. However, a number of algorithmic solutions minimizing redundant combinatory derivation have been discovered (König 1994; Eisner 1996; Hockenmaier and Bisk 2010).

Doran and Srinivas (2000), Hockenmaier and Steedman 2002, Hockenmaier (2003, 2006), Clark and Curran (2004), and Auli and Lopez (2011a,b,c) have shown that CCG can be applied to wide-coverage, robust parsing with state-of-the-art performance. Granroth-Wilding (2013) has successfully applied CCG and related statistical parsing methods to the analysis of musical harmonic progression. Birch *et al.* (2007), Hassan *et al.* (2009), and Mehay and Brew (2012) have used CCG categories and parsers as models for statistical machine translation.

Prevost (1995) applied the nonstandard surface structures of CCG to the control of prosody and intonation in synthesis of spoken English from information-structured semantics. White (2006) extended this to efficient sentence realization for CCG, while Kruijff-Korbayová *et al.* (2003) have applied CCG in dialog generation. Gildea and Hockenmaier (2003) and Boxwell *et al.* (2009, 2010) have applied CCG to and with semantic role labeling.

Briscoe (2000), Buszkowski and Penn (1990) and Kanazawa (1998) discuss learnability of categorial grammars, while Villavicencio (2002, 2011), Buttery (2004, 2006), McConville (2006), Zettlemoyer and Collins (2005, 2007), Kwiatkowski *et al.* (2010, 2011, 2012), and Krishnamurthy and Mitchell (2012) have exploited the semantic transparency of CCG to model semantic parsing and grammar induction from pairs of strings and logical forms, as a model of child language acquisition in humans. Piantadosi *et al.* (2008) have used CCG to model acquisition of quantifier semantics.

Pereira (1990) applied a unification-based version of Lambek grammar to the derivation of quantifier scope alternation. Bos and Markert (2005a,b, 2006) and Zamansky *et al.* (2006) have applied DRT-semantic CCG and Lambek grammars to text entailment, while Harrington and Clark (2007, 2009) have used a CCG parser to build semantic networks for large-scale question answering, using spreading activation to limit search and update.

Indeed, the main current obstacle to further progress in computational applications is the lack of labeled data for inducing bigger lexicons and models for stronger parsers, a problem to which unsupervised or semisupervised learning methods appear to offer the only realistic chance of an affordable solution. The latter methods have been applied to categorial grammars by Watkinson and Manandhar (1999), Thomforde (2013) and Boonkwan (2013).

Grefenstette *et al.* (2011), Grefenstette and Zadrzadeh (2011), and Kartsaklis *et al.* (2013) propose an application of pregroup grammars to compositional assembly of vector-based distributional semantic interpretations (cf. Mitchell and Lapata 2008). Lewis and Steedman (2013) propose a different form of distributional semantics for open-class words in CCG based on paraphrase clustering, and apply it to question answering and text entailment tasks.

Multimodal and type-logical categorial grammars support the notion of "proof nets" (Moortgat 1997; Moot and Puite 2002), related to an earlier idea of "count invariance", which has been applied in wide coverage parsing in the Grail system by Moot (2010), Moot and Retoré (2012). Morrill (2000, 2011) seeks to model "garden-path" phenomena and other aspects of human psycholinguistic performance algorithmically using proof nets, exploiting the potential of generalized categorial grammars to deliver incremental predominantly left-branching analyses supporting semantic interpretation.

8 Conclusion

Categorial grammars of all kinds have attractive properties for theoretical and descriptive linguists, psycholinguists, and computational linguists, because of their strict lexicalization of all language-specific information, and the consequent simplicity of the interface that they offer between syntactic derivation and compositional semantics on the one hand, and parsing algorithms and the statistical and head dependency-based parsing models that support robust wide-coverage natural language processing on the other. The non-standard notion of surface derivational structure that they offer is particularly beneficial in the cross-linguistic analysis of coordination, extraction, and intonation structure.

Acknowledgements

I am grateful to Polly Jacobson for answering a number of questions during the preparation of this chaapter, which was supported by EU ERC Advanced Fellowship 249520 GRAMPLUS and EU IP EC-FP7-270273 Xperience.

Notes

1 These constructions in English were shown by Gazdar (1981) to be coverable with only context-free resources in generalized phrase structure grammar (GPSG), whose "slash" notation for capturing such dependencies is derived from but not equivalent to the categorial notation developed below. However, Huybregts (1984) and Shieber (1985) proved Chomsky's widely accepted conjecture that in general such dependencies require greater than context-free expressive power.

2 This observation might be relevant to the analysis of "bound variable" pronouns like that in (1d).

3 There is an alternative "result on top" notation due to Lambek (1958), according to which the latter category is written $\beta\backslash\alpha$. Lambek's notation has advantages of readability in the context-free case, because all application is adjacent cancellation. However, this advantage does not hold for trans-context-free theories which include non-Lambek operators such as crossed composition. For such grammars, and for any analysis in which the semantics has to be kept track of, the Lambek notation is confusing, because it does not assign a consistent left-right position to the result α vs. the argument β.

4 Another notation, more in the spirit of Prolog-style unification-based formalisms like lexical functional grammar and head-driven phrase structure grammar associates a unifiable logical form with each primitive category, so that the same transitive verb might appear as follows (cf. Uszkoreit 1986; Karttunen 1989; Bouma and van Noord 1994; Zeevat 1988):

(i) likes := $(S : likes' \, y \, x \backslash NP_{3s} : x)/NP : y$

The advantage is that the predicate-argument structure is built directly by unification with X and Y in rules like (5) and (6), which need no further modification to apply (cf. Pereira and Shieber 1987). Otherwise, the choice is largely a matter of notational convenience.

5 The semantics of this category, or rather category schema, is given by Partee and Rooth (1983), and is omitted here as a distraction. We will come to certain restrictions on the combinatory potential of this category below.

6 This principle would follow automatically if we were using the alternative unification-based notation discussed in note 4 and the composition rule as as it is given in (14).

7 The analysis compresses two applications into a single coordination step labeled $<\phi>$, and begs some syntactic and semantic questions about the interpretation of modals.

8 See the earlier papers and Steedman (1996, 2000a) for details, including fixed subject effects and other extraction asymmetries, and the involvement of similar apparently nonconstituent fragments in intonational phrasing.

9 In more recent work, Dowty has disowned this analysis, on the ground that it makes an "intrinsic" use of logical form to account for binding phenomena. This issue is discussed further in the works of Dowty (1997) and Steedman (1996), and more briefly below.

10 This assumption precludes a small clause analysis of the basic constructions.

11 A number of apparent exceptions to Ross's generalization have been noted in the literature and are discussed by Steedman (2000b). Ross's constraint is there stated in terms of overall order properties of languages and constructions rather than any notion of "underlying" word order.

12 Languages that order object before subject are sufficiently rare as to apparently preclude a comparable data set, although any result of this kind would be of immense interest.

13 In computational implementations English type-raised categories are usually schematized in this way, because its word order is sufficiently rigid to allow the statistical parsing model to resolve the ambiguity locally.

14 If there is no bound on n, the expressive power of the system jumps to that of full indexed grammar (Srinivas 1997).

15 Such rules correspond to the Curry and Feys (1958) combinatory **C**. There are actually a number of ways that wrap might be written as a combinatory rule, and it is not always clear from the literature which is assumed. I follow the categorial notation of Bach (1979) and Jacobson (1992).

16 The attraction of viewing grammars as logics rather than combinatory algebras or calculi seems to be that they then support a model theory that can be used as a basis for proofs of soundness and completeness of the syntax. It should be noticed that such a logic and model theory is distinct from the standard logic implicit in the applicative semantics for the categorial grammar itself or the corresponding set of standard context-free productions.

17 However, Montague's stern use of the word "proper" in his 1973 title may have reflected the fact that his treatment of quantified terms like *Every Siren* and *a song* assigned them the type of proper nouns like *John* and *she* under the description theory of of Russell and Frege. Any implication that other treatments were somehow *im*proper may have been a donnish pun. This possibility is not always appreciated by those who proliferate titles in semantics of the form "The proper treatment of X".

18 Of course, I am exaggerating the differences for mnemonic reasons. Most of us combine both traits.

19 If all one wants to do with a logic is prove truth in a model, then structural representation itself can technically be eliminated entirely, in favor of direct computation over models. But if you want to do more general inference, then in practice you need *some* structural representation.

20 Jacobson does not usually include set-delimiting braces {...} in her notation for categories including bindable pronouns, but sentences like (45) show that in general these superscripts are composable (multi)sets.

21 The unary Geach rule is implicitly schematized as unary $\mathbf{B}^n$ along lines exemplified for (34).

22 Jacobson η-reduces the redundant abstraction in terms like $\lambda y.won'y$ to e.g. *won'*, but in the absence of explicit types (as in $won'_{<e,t>}$) I let it stand as more intelligible.

23 The two main varieties of statistical model, the probabilistic/generative and the weighted/discriminative, are discussed by Smith and Johnson (2007).

Further reading

Lyons (1968) includes an early and far-seeing introduction to pure categorial grammar and its potential role in theoretical linguistics. Wood (1993) provides a balanced survey of historical and early modern approaches. Buszkowski *et al.* (1988), Oehrle *et al.* (1988), and Casadio and Lambek (2008) provide useful collections of research articles, the former reprinting a number of historically significant earlier papers. Moortgat (1997), Steedman and Baldridge (2011), Lambek (2008), Morrill (2011), Moot and Retoré (2012), and Bozşahin (2012) are more specialized survey articles and monographs on some of the contemporary varieties of categorial grammar discussed above, often with comparisons across approaches. Partee (1976), Dowty (1979), and Barker and Jacobson (2007) represent (mostly) sacred approaches to semantics within categorial grammar, while Carpenter (1997) and Steedman (2012) represent the unabashedly profane.

A number of open-source computational linguistic tools for CCG applications are available at http://groups.inf.ed.ac.uk/ccg/software.html and via SourceForge at http://openccg.sourceforge.net The categorial CCGbank version of the Penn WSJ treebank is available from the Linguistic Data Consortium (Hockenmaier and Steedman 2005) and has been improved by Vadas and Curran (2007) and Honnibal *et al.* (2010). Hockenmaier has developed a German CCGbank (Hockenmaier 2006). The Grail type-logical parser and related resources are available at http://www.labri.fr/perso/moot/grail3.html.

References

Ades, Anthony and Steedman, Mark. 1982. On the order of words. *Linguistics and Philosophy* 4: 517–558.

Aho, Alfred. 1968. Indexed grammars—an extension of context-free grammars. *Communications of the Association for Computing Machinery* 15: 647–671.

———. 1969. Nested stack automata. *Communications of the Association for Computing Machinery* 16: 383–406.

Ajdukiewicz, Kazimierz. 1935. Die syntaktische Konnexität. In Storrs McCall (ed.), *Polish Logic 1920–1939*, 207–231. Oxford: Oxford University Press. Trans. from *Studia Philosophica* 1: 1–27.

Auli, Michael and Lopez, Adam. 2011a. A comparison of loopy belief propagation and dual decomposition for integrated CCG supertagging and parsing. In *Proceedings of the 49th Annual Meeting of the Association for Computational Linguistics: Human Language Technologies*, Portland, OR, 470–480. Stroudsberg, PA: ACL.

———. 2011b. Efficient CCG parsing: A* versus adaptive supertagging. In *Proceedings of the 49th Annual Meeting of the Association for Computational Linguistics: Human Language Technologies*, Portland, OR, 1577–1585. Stroudsberg, PA: ACL.

———. 2011c. Training a log-linear parser with loss functions via softmax-margin. In *Proceedings of the Conference on Empirical Methods in Natural Language Processing*, Edinburgh, 333–343. Stroudsberg, PA: ACL.

Bach, Emmon. 1979. Control in Montague grammar. *Linguistic Inquiry* 10: 513–531.

———. 1983. Generalized categorial grammars and the English auxiliary. In Frank Heny and Barry Richards (eds), *Linguistic Categories: Auxiliaries and Related Puzzles*, II, 101–120. Dordrecht: Reidel.

Baldridge, Jason. 1998. Local scrambling and syntactic asymmetries in Tagalog. Master's thesis, University of Pennsylvania.

———. 2002. Lexically specified derivational control in combinatory categorial grammar. PhD thesis, University of Edinburgh.

Baldridge, Jason and Kruijff, Geert-Jan. 2003. Multi-modal combinatory categorial grammar. In *Proceedings of 11th Annual Meeting of the European Association for Computational Linguistics*, 211–218. Budapest.

Bar-Hillel, Yehoshua. 1953. A quasi-arithmetical notation for syntactic description. *Language* 29: 47–58.

Bar-Hillel, Yehoshua, Gaifman, Chaim, and Shamir, Eliyahu. 1964. On categorial and phrase structure grammars. In Yehoshua Bar-Hillel (ed.), *Language and Information*, 99–115. Reading, MA: Addison-Wesley.

Barker, Chris. 2001. Integrity: A syntactic constraint on quantifier scoping. In *Proceedings of the 20th West Coast Conference on Formal Linguistics*, 101–114. Somerville, MA: Cascadilla.

_____. 2002. Continuations and the nature of quantification. *Natural Language Semantics* 10: 211–242.

Barker, Chris and Jacobson, Pauline (eds). 2007. *Direct Compositionality*. Oxford: Oxford University Press.

Béchet, Denis, Foret, Annie, and Tellier, Isabelle. 2007. Learnability of pregroup grammars. *Studia Logica* 87: 225–252.

Bekki, Daisuke. 2010. *Nihongo Bunpoo no Keesiki Riron: Katsuyoo Taikee, Toogo Koozoo, Imi Goosee [Formal Theory of Japanese Grammar: The System of Conjugation, Syntactic Structure, and Semantic Composition]*. Nihongo Kenkyuu Soosyo [Japanese Frontier Series] 24. Tokyo: Kurosio Publishers.

Bernardi, Raffaella. 2002. Reasoning with polarity in categorial type-logic. PhD thesis, Universiteit Utrecht.

Berwick, Robert and Epstein, Samuel. 1995. Computational minimalism: The convergence of 'minimalist' syntax and categorial grammar. In A. Nijholt, G. Scollo, and R. Steetkamp (eds), *Algebraic Methods in Language Processing 1995: Proceedings of the Twente Workshop on Language Technology 10, jointly held with the First Algebraic Methodology and Software Technology (AMAST) Workshop on Language Processing*. Enschede, The Netherlands: Faculty of Computer Science, Universiteit Twente.

Birch, Alexandra, Osborne, Miles, and Koehn, Philipp. 2007. CCG supertags in factored translation models. In *Proceedings of the 2nd Workshop on Statistical Machine Translation*, Prague, 9–16. Stroudsberg, PA: ACL.

Bittner, Maria. 2011. Time and modality without tenses or modals. In Renate Musan and Monika Rathert (eds), *Tense across Language*, 147–188. Tübingen: Niemeyer.

Bittner, Maria. 2014. *Temporality: Universals and Variation*. Malden, MA: Wiley-Blackwell.

Boeckx, Cedric. 2008. *Bare Syntax*. Oxford: Oxford University Press.

Boonkwan, Prachya. 2013. Scalable semi-supervised grammar induction using cross-linguistically parameterized syntactic prototypes. PhD thesis, Edinburgh.

Bos, Johan and Markert, Katja. 2005a. Combining shallow and deep NLP methods for recognizing textual entailment. In *Proceedings of the First PASCAL Challenge Workshop on Recognizing Textual Entailment*, 65–68. http://www.pascal-network.org/Challenges/RTE/: Pascal. (accessed 31 January 2014).

_____. 2005b. Recognising textual entailment with logical inference. In *Proceedings of the 2005 Conference on Empirical Methods in Natural Language Processing (EMNLP 2005)*, 628–635.

_____. 2006. When logical inference helps determining textual entailment (and when it doesn't). In *Proceedings of the Second PASCAL Challenge Workshop on Recognizing Textual Entailment*. Pascal.

Bosch, Peter. 1983. *Agreement and Anaphora*. New York: Academic Press.

Bouma, Gosse and van Noord, Gertjan. 1994. Constraint-based categorial grammar. In *Proceedings of the 32nd Annual Meeting of the Association for Computational Linguistics*, Las Cruces, NM. Stroudsberg, PA: ACL.

Boxwell, Stephen, Mehay, Dennis, and Brew, Chris. 2009. Brutus: A semantic role labeling system incorporating CCG, CFG, and dependency features. In *Proceedings of the Joint Conference of the 47th Annual Meeting of the ACL and the 4th International Joint Conference on Natural Language Processing of the AFNLP*, Suntec, Singapore, 37–45. Stroudsberg, PA: ACL.

_____. 2010. What a parser can learn from a semantic role labeler and vice versa. In *Proceedings of the 2010 Conference on Empirical Methods in Natural Language Processing*, 736–744. Stroudsberg, PA: ACL.

Bozşahin, Cem. 1998. Deriving predicate-argument structure for a free word order language. In *Proceedings of International Conference on Computational Linguistics*, Montreal, 167–173. Stroudsberg, PA: ACL.

_____. 2002. The combinatory morphemic lexicon. *Computational Linguistics* 28: 145–186.

_____. 2012. *Combinatory Linguistics*. Berlin: de Gruyter.

Briscoe, Ted. 2000. Grammatical acquisition: Inductive bias and coevolution of language and the language acquisition device. *Language* 76: 245–296.

Buszkowski, Wojciech. 2001. Lambek grammars based on pregroups. In *Proceedings of Logical Aspects of Computational Linguistics*, 95–109.

Buszkowski, Wojciech, Marciszewski, Witold, and van Benthem, Johan. 1988. *Categorial Grammar*. Amsterdam: John Benjamins.

Buszkowski, Wojciech and Moroz, Katarzyna. 2008. Pregroup grammars and context-free grammars. In Claudia Casadio and Joachim Lambek (eds), *Computational Algebraic Approaches to Natural Language*, 1–21. Monzah: Polimetrica.

Buszkowski, Wojciech and Penn, Gerald. 1990. Categorial grammars determined from linguistic data by unification. *Studia Logica* 49: 431–454.

Buttery, Paula, 2004. A quantitative evaluation of naturalistic models of language acquisition; the efficiency of the triggering learning algorithm compared to a categorial grammar learner. In *Proceedings of the Workshop on Psycho-Computational Models of Human Language Acquisition*, 3–10. Geneva: COLING.

Buttery, Paula. 2006. Computational models for first language acquisition. PhD thesis, University of Cambridge.

Carpenter, Bob. 1995. The Turing-completeness of multimodal categorial grammars. In Jelle Gerbrandy, Maarten Marx, Maarten de Rijke, and Yde Venema (eds.), *Papers Presented to Johan van Benthem in Honor of His 50th Birthday. European Summer School in Logic, Language and Information, Utrecht, 1999*. Amsterdam: ILLC, University of Amsterdam.

_____. 1997. *Type-Logical Semantics*. Cambridge, MA: MIT Press.

Casadio, Claudia. 2001. Non-commutative linear logic in linguistics. *Grammars* 4: 167–185.

Casadio, Claudia and Lambek, Joachim (eds). 2008. *Computational Algebraic Approaches to Natural Language*. Polimetrica.

Çakıcı, Ruket. 2005. Automatic induction of a CCG grammar for Turkish. In *Proceedings of the Student Workshop, 43rd Annual Meeting of the ACL, Ann Arbor, MI*, 73–78. Stroudsberg, PA: ACL.

_____. 2009. Parser models for a highly inflected language. PhD thesis, University of Edinburgh.

Cha, Jeongwon and Lee, Geunbae. 2000. Structural disambiguation of morpho-syntactic categorial parsing for Korean. In *Proceedings of the 18th International Conference on Computational Linguistics*, Saarbrücken, 1002–1006. Stroudsberg, PA: ACL.

Chierchia, Gennaro. 1988. Aspects of a categorial theory of binding. In Richard Oehrle, Emmon Bach, and Deirdre Wheeler (eds), *Categorial Grammars and Natural Language Structures*, 125–151. Dordrecht: Reidel.

Chomsky, Noam. 1957. *Syntactic Structures*. The Hague: Mouton.

_____. 1995. Bare phrase structure. In Gert Webelhuth (ed.), *Government and Binding Theory and the Minimalist Program*, 383–439. Oxford: Blackwell.

Ciardelli, Ivano and Roelofsen, Floris. 2011. Inquisitive logic. *Journal of Philosophical Logic* 40: 55–94.

Clark, Stephen and Curran, James R. 2004. Parsing the WSJ using CCG and log-linear models. In *Proceedings of the 42nd Annual Meeting of the Association for Computational Linguistics*, Barcelona, 104–111. Stroudsberg, PA: ACL.

Collins, Michael. 1997. Three generative lexicalized models for statistical parsing. In *Proceedings of the 35th Annual Meeting of the Association for Computational Linguistics*, Madrid, 16–23. Stroudsberg, PA: ACL.

Cooper, Robin. 1983. *Quantification and Syntactic Theory*. Dordrecht: Reidel.

Cormack, Annabel and Smith, Neil. 2005. What is coordination? *Lingua* 115: 395–418.

Curry, Haskell B. 1961. Some logical aspects of grammatical structure. In Roman Jakobson (ed.), *Structure of Language and its Mathematical Aspects: Proceedings of the Symposium in Applied Mathematics*, vol. 12, 56–68. Providence, RI: American Mathematical Society.

Curry, Haskell B. and Feys, Robert. 1958. *Combinatory Logic: Vol. I*. Amsterdam: North-Holland.

Davidson, Donald and Harman, Gilbert (eds). 1972. *Semantics of Natural Language*. Dordrecht: Reidel.

de Groote, Philippe. 2001. Towards abstract categorial grammars. In *Proceedings of the 39th Annual Meeting of the Association for Computational Linguistics*, Toulouse, 148–155. Stroudsberg, PA: ACL.

de Groote, Philippe and Pogodalla, Sylvain. 2004. On the expressive power of abstract categorial grammars: Representing context-free formalisms. *Journal of Logic, Language and Information* 13: 421–438.

de Groote, Philippe, Pogodalla, Sylvain, and Pollard, Carl. forthcoming. About parallel and syntactocentric formalisms: What the encoding of convergent grammar into abstract categorial grammar tells us. *Fundamenta Informaticae*.

Doran, Christy and B. Srinivas, 2000. A wide coverage CCG parser. In Anne Abeille and Owen Rambow (eds), *Proceedings of the 3rd TAG+ workshop, Jussieu, March 1994*, 405–426. Stanford, CA: CSLI Publications.

Dowty, David. 1979. *Word Meaning in Montague Grammar*, 1st edn. Dordrecht: Reidel.

_____. 1982. Grammatical relations and Montague grammar. In Pauline Jacobson and Geoffrey K. Pullum (eds.), *The Nature of Syntactic Representation*, 79–130. Dordrecht: Reidel.

_____. 1988. Type-raising, functional composition, and nonconstituent coordination. In Richard Oehrle, Emmon Bach, and Deirdre Wheeler (eds), *Categorial Grammars and Natural Language Structures*, 153–198. Dordrecht: Reidel.

_____. 1994. The role of negative polarity and concord marking in natural language reasoning. In *Proceedings of the 4th Conference on Semantics and Theoretical Linguistics*. Rochester, NY: CLC Publications, Cornell University.

_____. 1996. Towards a minimalist theory of syntactic structure. In Harry Bunt and Arthur van Horck (eds), *Discontinuous Constituency*, 11–62. The Hague: Mouton de Gruyter.

_____. 1997. Nonconstituent coordination, wrapping, and multimodal categorial grammars: Syntactic form as logical form. In Maria Luisa Dalla Chiara (ed.), *Structures and Norms in Science*, 347–368. Berlin: Springer. Extended version at http://www.ling.ohio-state.edu/~dowty/. (accessed 31 January 2014).

_____. 2003. The dual analysis of adjuncts/complements in categorial grammar. In Ewald Lang, Claudia Maienborn, and Cathry Fabricius-Hansen (eds), *Modifying Adjuncts*, 33–66. Berlin: Mouton de Gruyter.

_____. 2007. Compositionality as an empirical problem. In Chris Barker and Pauline Jacobson (eds), *Direct Compositionality*, 23–101. Oxford: Oxford University Press.

Eisner, Jason. 1996. Efficient normal-form parsing for combinatory categorial grammar. In *Proceedings of the 34th Annual Meeting of the Association for Computational Linguistics, Santa Cruz, CA*, 79–86. San Francisco: Morgan Kaufmann.

Fodor, Janet Dean and Sag, Ivan. 1982. Referential and quantificational indefinites. *Linguistics and Philosophy* 5: 355–398.

Frege, Gottlob. 1879. Begriffsschrift, eine der arithmetischen nachgebildete Formelsprache des reinen Denkens. Halle: Louis Nebert. Translated with commentary and corrections as "*Begriffsschrift*, a formula language, modeled upon that of arithmetic, for pure thought", in van Heijenoort (1967: 1–82).

Gazdar, Gerald. 1981. Unbounded dependencies and coordinate structure. *Linguistic Inquiry* 12: 155–184.

_____. 1988. Applicability of indexed grammars to natural languages. In Uwe Reyle and Christian Rohrer (eds), *Natural Language Parsing and Linguistic Theories*, 69–94. Dordrecht: Reidel.

Geach, Peter. 1970. A program for syntax. *Synthèse* 22: 3–17. Reprinted as Davidson and Harman (1972: 483–497).

Gildea, Dan and Hockenmaier, Julia. 2003. Identifying semantic roles using combinatory categorial grammar. In *Proceedings of the 2003 Conference on Empirical Methods in Natural Language Processing*, 57–64. Sapporo, Japan.

Granroth-Wilding, Mark. 2013. Harmonic analysis of music using combinatory categorial grammar. PhD thesis, University of Edinburgh.

Grefenstette, Edward and Sadrzadeh, Mehrnoosh. 2011. Experimental support for a categorical compositional distributional model of meaning. In *Proceedings of the 2011 Conference on Empirical Methods in Natural Language Processing*, Edinburgh, 1394–1404. Stroudsberg, PA: ACL.

Grefenstette, Edward, Sadrzadeh, Mehrnoosh, Clark, Stephen, Coeke, Bob, and Pulman, Stephen. 2011. Concrete sentence spaces for compositional distributional models of meaning. In *Proceedings of the 9th International Conference on Computational Semantics*, 125–134. Oxford: IWCS.

Groenendijk, Jeroen and Stokhof, Martin. 1991. Dynamic predicate logic. *Linguistics and Philosophy* 14: 39–100.

Harrington, Brian and Clark, Stephen. 2007. Asknet: Automated semantic knowledge network. In *Proceedings of the 22nd National Conference on Artificial Intelligence (AAAI'07)*, 889–894. AAAI Press.

_____. 2009. ASKNet: Creating and evaluating large scale integrated semantic networks. *International Journal of Semantic Computing* 2: 343–364.

Hassan, Hany, Sima'an, Khalil, and Way, Andy. 2009. A syntactified direct translation model with linear-time decoding. In *Proceedings of the 2009 Conference on Empirical Methods in Natural Language Processing*, Singapore, 1182–1191. Stroudsberg, PA: ACL.

Heim, Irene and Kratzer, Angelika. 1998. *Semantics in Generative Grammar*. Oxford: Blackwell.

Hendriks, Herman. 1993. Studied flexibility: categories and types in syntax and semantics. PhD thesis, Universiteit van Amsterdam.

Hepple, Mark. 1990. The grammar and processing of order and dependency: A categorial approach. PhD thesis, University of Edinburgh.

_____. 1995. Hybrid categorial logics. *Logic Journal of IGPL* 3: 343–355.

_____. 1999. An Earley-style predictive chart parsing method for Lambek grammars. In *Proceedings of the 37th Annual Meeting of the Association for Computational Linguistics*, College Park, MD, 465–472. Stroudsberg, PA: ACL.

Hindle, Donald and Rooth, Mats. 1993. Structural ambiguity and lexical relations. *Computational Linguistics* 19: 103–120.

Hockenmaier, Julia. 2003. Parsing with generative models of predicate-argument structure. In *Proceedings of the 41st Meeting of the Association for Computational Linguistics, Sapporo*, 359–366. San Francisco: Morgan-Kaufmann.

_____. 2006. Creating a CCGbank and a wide-coverage CCG lexicon for German. In *Proceedings of the 44th Annual Meeting of the Association for Computational Linguistics*, Sydney, 505–512. Stroudsberg, PA: ACL.

Hockenmaier, Julia and Bisk, Yonatan. 2010. Normal-form parsing for combinatory categorial grammars with generalized composition and type-raising. In *Proceedings of the 23nd International Conference on Computational Linguistics*, 465–473. Beijing.

Hockenmaier, Julia and Steedman, Mark. 2002. Generative models for statistical parsing with combinatory categorial grammar. In *Proceedings of the 40th Meeting of the Association for Computational Linguistics*, 335–342. Philadelphia.

_____. 2005. *CCGbank*. LDC2005T13. ISBN 1-58563-340-2.

_____. 2007. CCGbank: a corpus of CCG derivations and dependency structures extracted from the Penn Treebank. *Computational Linguistics* 33: 355–396.

Hoeksema, Jack and Janda, R. 1988. Implications of process morphology for categorial grammar. In Richard Oehrle, Emmon Bach, and Deirdre Wheeler (eds), *Categorial Grammars and Natural Language Structures*, 199–248. Dordrecht: Reidel.

Hoffman, Beryl. 1995. Computational analysis of the syntax and interpretation of "Free" word-order in Turkish. PhD thesis, University of Pennsylvania. Publ. as IRCS Report 95–17. Philadelphia: University of Pennsylvania.

Honnibal, Matthew, Curran, James and Bos, Johan. 2010. Rebanking CCGbank for improved NP interpretation, In *Proceedings of the 48th Annual Meeting of the Association for Computational Linguistics*, Uppsala, Sweden, 207–215. Stroudsberg, PA: ACL.

Hoyt, Frederick and Baldridge, Jason. 2008. A logical basis for the D combinator and normal form in CCG. In *Proceedings of Association for Computational Linguistics-08: HLT*, Columbus, OH, 326–334. Stroudsberg, PA: ACL.

Huybregts, Riny. 1984. The weak inadequacy of context-free phrase-structure grammars. In Ger de Haan, Mieke Trommelen, and Wim Zonneveld (eds), *Van Periferie naar Kern*, 81–99. Dordrecht: Foris.

Jacobson, Pauline. 1992. The lexical entailment theory of control and the tough construction. Ivan Sag and Anna Szabolcsi (eds), *Lexical Matters*, 269–300. Stanford, CA: CSLI Publications.

_____. 1999. Towards a variable-free semantics. *Linguistics and Philosophy* 22: 117–184.

_____. 2002. The (dis)organization of the grammar. *Linguistics and Philosophy* 25: 601–626.

_____. 2007. Direct compositionality and variable-free semantics: The case of "Principle B" effects. In Chris Barker and Pauline Jacobson (eds), *Direct Compositionality*, 191–236. Oxford: Oxford University Press.

Jäger, Gerhard. 2005. *Anaphora and Type-logical Grammar*. Dordrecht: Springer.

Joshi, Aravind. 1988. Tree-adjoining grammars. In David Dowty, Lauri Karttunen, and Arnold Zwicky (eds), *Natural Language Parsing*, 206–250. Cambridge: Cambridge University Press.

Kamp, Hans and Reyle, Uwe. 1993. *From Discourse to Logic*. Dordrecht: Kluwer.

Kanazawa, Makoto. 1998. *Learnable Classes of Categorial Grammars*. Stanford, CA: CSLI/folli.

Kanazawa, Makoto and Salvati, Sylvain. 2012. MIX is not a tree-adjoining language. In *Proceedings of the 50th Annual Meeting of the Association for Computational Linguistics (Volume 1: Long Papers)*, Jeju Island, Korea, 666–674. Stroudsberg, PA: ACL.

Kang, Beom-Mo. 1995. On the treatment of complex predicates in categorial grammar. *Linguistics and Philosophy* 18: 61–81.

_____. 2002. Categories and meanings of Korean floating quantifiers—with some reference to Japanese. *Journal of East Asian Linguistics* 11: 485–534.

Kartsaklis, Dimitri, Sadrzadeh, Mehrnoosh, and Pulman, Stephen. 2013. "Separating Disambiguation from Composition in Distributional Semantics." In *Proceedings of the Conference on Natural Language Learning*, 114–123. Sofia: ACL.

Karttunen, Lauri. 1989. Radical lexicalism. In Mark Baltin and Anthony Kroch (eds), *Alternative Conceptions of Phrase Structure*, 43–65. Chicago: University of Chicago Press.

Kempson, Ruth and Cormack, Annabel. 1981. Ambiguity and quantification. *Linguistics and Philosophy* 4: 259–309.

Kobele, Gregory and Kracht, Marcus. 2005. On pregroups, freedom, and (virtual) conceptual necessity. In *Proceedings of the 28th Annual Penn Linguistics Colloquium*, University of Pennsylvania Working Papers in Linguistics, Philadelphia.

Koller, Alexander and Thater, Stefan. 2006. An improved redundancy elimination algorithm for underspecified descriptions. In *Proceedings of the International Conference on Computational Linguistics/Association for Computational Linguistics*, Sydney, 409–416. Stroudsberg, PA: Coling/ACL.

Komagata, Nobo. 1999. Information structure in texts: A computational analysis of contextual appropriateness in English and Japanese. PhD thesis, University of Pennsylvania.

König, Esther. 1994. A hypothetical reasoning algorithm for linguistic analysis. *Journal of Logic and Computation* 4: 1–19.

Kratzer, Angelika. 1998. Scope or pseudo-scope: Are there wide-scope indefinites? In Susan Rothstein (ed.), *Events in Grammar*, 163–196. Dordrecht: Kluwer.

Krishnamurthy, Jayant and Mitchell, Tom. 2012. Weakly supervised training of semantic parsers. In *Proceedings of Joint Conference on Empirical Methods in Natural Language Processing and Computational Natural Language Learning*, Jeju Island, Korea, 754–765. Stroudsberg, PA: ACL.

Kruijff-Korbayová, Ivana, Ericsson, Stina, Rodríguez, Kepa Joseba, and Karagrjosova, Elena. 2003. Producing contextually appropriate intonation in an information-state based dialogue system. In *Proceedings of the 10th Conference of the European Chapter of the Association for Computational Linguistics (EACL)*, Budapest, 227–234. Stroudsberg, PA: ACL.

Kubota, Yusuke. 2010. (In)flexibility of constituency in Japanese in multi-modal categorial grammars with structured phonology. PhD thesis, Ohio State University.

Kwiatkowski, Tom, Goldwater, Sharon, Zettlemoyer, Luke, and Steedman, Mark. 2012. A probabilistic model of syntactic and semantic acquisition from child-directed utterances and their meanings. In *Proceedings of the 13th Conference of the European Chapter of the ACL (EACL 2012)*, Avignon, 234–244. Stroudsberg, PA: ACL.

Kwiatkowski, Tom, Zettlemoyer, Luke, Goldwater, Sharon, and Steedman, Mark. 2010. Inducing probabilistic CCG grammars from logical form with higher-order unification. In *Proceedings of the Conference on Empirical Methods in Natural Language Processing*, Cambridge, MA, 1223–1233. Stroudsberg, PA: ACL.

_____. 2011. Lexical generalization in CCG grammar induction for semantic parsing. In *Proceedings of the Conference on Empirical Methods in Natural Language Processing*, Edinburgh, 1512–1523. Stroudsberg, PA: ACL.

Lakoff, George. 1970. Linguistics and natural logic. *Synthèse* 22: 151–271. Reprinted in Davidson and Harman (1972: 545–665).

Lambek, Joachim. 1958. The mathematics of sentence structure. *American Mathematical Monthly* 65: 154–170.

_____. 1961. On the calculus of syntactic types. In Roman Jakobson (ed.), *Structure of Language and Its Mathematical Aspects: Proceedings of the Symposium in Applied Mathematics*, vol. 12, 166–178. Providence, RI: American Mathematical Society.

_____. 2001. Type grammars as pregroups. *Grammars* 4: 21–39.

_____. 2008. *From Word to Sentence*. Milan: Polimetrica.

Lee, Jungmee and Tonhauser, Judith. 2010. Temporal interpretation without tense: Korean and Japanese coordination constructions. *Journal of Semantics* 27: 307–341.

Lewis, Michael and Steedman, Mark. 2013. Combined distributional and logical semantics. *Transactions of the Association for Computational Linguistics* 1: 179–192.

Lyons, John. 1968. *Introduction to Theoretical Linguistics*. Cambridge: Cambridge University Press.

MacCartney, Bill and Manning, Christopher D. 2007. Natural logic for textual inference. In *Proceedings of the ACL-PASCAL Workshop on Textual Entailment and Paraphrasing*, Prague, 193–200. Stroudsberg, PA: ACL.

Magerman, David. 1995. Statistical decision tree models for parsing. In *Proceedings of the 33rd Annual Meeting of the Association for Computational Linguistics*, Cambridge, MA, 276–283. Stroudsberg, PA: ACL.

McConville, Mark. 2006. Inheritance and the CCG Lexicon. In *Proceedings of the 11th Conference of the European Chapter of the Association for Computational Linguistics*, 1–8. Stroudsberg, PA: ACL.

Mehay, Denis and Brew, Chris. 2012. CCG syntactic reordering models for phrase-based machine translation. In *Proceedings of the Seventh Workshop on Statistical Machine Translation*, Montreal. Stroudsberg, PA: ACL.

Mitchell, Jeff and Lapata, Mirella. 2008. Vector-based models of semantic composition. In *Proceedings of the Annual Meeting of the Association for Computational Linguistics*, Columbus, OH, 236–244. Stroudsberg, PA: ACL.

Montague, Richard. 1970a. English as a formal language. In Bruno Visentini (ed.), *Linguaggi nella Società e nella Technica*, 189–224. Milan: Edizioni di Communità. Reprinted as Thomason (1974: 188–221).

_____. 1970b. Universal grammar. *Theoria* 36: 373–398. Reprinted as Thomason (1974: 222–246).

_____. 1973. The proper treatment of quantification in ordinary English. In Jaakko Hintikka, J. M. E. Moravcsik, and Patrick Suppes (eds), *Approaches to Natural Language: Proceedings of the 1970 Stanford Workshop on Grammar and Semantics*, 221–242. Dordrecht: Reidel. Reprinted as Thomason (1974: 247–279).

Moortgat, Michael. 1988a. Categorial investigations. PhD thesis, Universiteit van Amsterdam. Published by Foris, Dordrecht, 1989.

_____. 1988b. Mixed composition and discontinuous dependencies. In Richard Oehrle, Emmon Bach, and Deirdre Wheeler (eds), *Categorial Grammars and Natural Language Structures*, 319–348. Dordrecht: Reidel.

_____. 1997. Categorial type logics. Johan van Benthem and Alice ter Meulen (eds), *Handbook of Logic and Language*, 93–177. Amsterdam: North-Holland.

_____. 2007. Symmetries in natural language syntax and semantics: The Lambek-Grishin calculus. In *Proceedings of Workshop on Logic, Language, Information, and Computation (WoLLIC)*, Lecture Notes in Computer Science 4576, 264–284. Berlin: Springer.

_____. 2009. Symmetric categorial grammar. *Journal of Philosophical Logic* 38: 681–710.

Moot, Richard. 2002. Proof Nets for Linguistic Analysis. Ph.D. thesis, University of Utrecht.

_____. 2010. Automated extraction of type-logical supertags from the spoken Dutch corpus. In Srinivas Bangalore and Aravind Joshi (eds), *Complexity of Lexical Descriptions and its Relevance to Natural Language Processing: A Supertagging Approach*. Cambridge, MA: MIT Press.

Moot, Richard and Puite, Quintijn. 2002. Proof nets for the multimodal Lambek calculus. *Studia Logica* 71: 415–442.

Moot, Richard and Retoré, Christian. 2012. *The Logic of Categorial Grammars*, Lecture Notes in Computer Science 6850. Berlin: Springer.

Morrill, Glyn. 1994. *Type-logical Grammar*. Dordrecht: Kluwer.

_____. 2000. Incremental processing and acceptability. *Computational Linguistics* 26: 319–338.

_____. 2011. *Categorial Grammar: Logical Syntax, Semantics, and Processing.* Oxford: Oxford University Press.

Morrill, Glynn and Solias, Teresa. 1993. Tuples, discontinuity, and gapping. In *Proceedings of 6th Conference of the European Chapter of the Association for Computational Linguistics*, Utrecht, 287–297. Stroudsberg, PA: ACL.

Muskens, Reinhard. 2007. Separating syntax and combinatorics in categorial grammar. *Research on Language & Computation* 5: 267–285.

Nishida, Chiyo. 1996. Second position clitics in Old Spanish and categorial grammar. In Aaron Halpern and Arnold Zwicky (eds), *Approaching Second: Second-position Clitics and Related Phenomena*, 33–373. Stanford, CA: CSLI Publications.

Oehrle, Richard. 1988. Multidimensional compositional functions as a basis for grammatical analysis. In Richard Oehrle, Emmon Bach, and Deirdre Wheeler (eds), *Categorial Grammars and Natural Language Structures*, 349–390. Dordrecht: Reidel.

_____. 1994. Term-labelled categorial type systems. *Linguistics and Philosophy* 17: 633–678.

Oehrle, Richard, Bach, Emmon, and Wheeler, Deirdre (eds). 1988. *Categorial Grammars and Natural Language Structures.* Dordrecht: Reidel.

Park, Jong and Cho, Hyung-Joon. 2000. Informed parsing for coordination with combinatory categorial grammar. In *Proceedings of the 18th International Conference on Computational Linguistics*, Saarbrücken, 593–599. Stroudsberg, PA: Coling/ACL.

Partee, Barbara. 1970. Negation, conjunction, and quantifiers: Syntax vs. semantics. *Foundations of Language* 6: 153–165.

_____. 1975. Montague grammar and transformational grammar. *Linguistic Inquiry* 6: 203–300.

Partee, Barbara (ed.). 1976. *Montague Grammar.* New York: Academic Press.

Partee, Barbara and Rooth, Mats. 1983. Generalised conjunction and type ambiguity. In Rainer Bäu erle, Christoph Schwarze, and Arnim von Stechow (eds), *Meaning, Use, and Interpretation of Language*, 361–383. Berlin: de Gruyter.

Pentus, Mati. 1993. Lambek grammars are context-free. In *Proceedings of the IEEE Symposium on Logic in Computer Science, Montreal*, 429–433.

_____. 2003. Lambek calculus is NP-complete. Tech. Rep. TR-2003005, Graduate Center, City University of New York, New York.

Pereira, Fernando. 1990. Categorial semantics and scoping. *Computational Linguistics* 16: 1–10.

Pereira, Fernando and Shieber, Stuart. 1987. *Prolog and Natural Language Analysis.* Stanford, CA: CSLI Publications.

Piantadosi, Steven, Goodman, Noah, Ellis, Benjamin, and Tenenbaum, Joshua. 2008. A Bayesian model of the acquisition of compositional semantics. In *Proceedings of the 30th Annual Meeting of the Cognitive Science Society*, 1620–1625. Washington, DC.

Pickering, Martin and Barry, Guy. 1993. Dependency categorial grammar and coordination. *Linguistics* 31: 855–902.

Poesio, Massimo. 1995. Disambiguation as (defeasible) reasoning about underspecified representations. In *Papers from the Tenth Amsterdam Colloquium*. Amsterdam: ILLC, Universiteit van Amsterdam.

Pollard, Carl. 1984. Generalized context free grammars, head grammars, and natural languages. PhD thesis, Stanford University.

Prevost, Scott. 1995. A semantics of contrast and information structure for specifying intonation in spoken language generation. PhD thesis, University of Pennsylvania.

Ranta, Aarne. 1994. *Type-theoretical Grammar.* Oxford: Oxford University Press.

Reyle, Uwe. 1993. Dealing with ambiguities by underspecification. *Journal of Semantics* 10: 123–179.

Robinson, Abraham. 1974. *Introduction to Model Theory and to the Metamathematics of Algebra*, 2nd ed. Amsterdam: North-Holland.

Ross, John Robert. 1970. Gapping and the order of constituents. In Manfred Bierwisch and Karl Heidolph (eds), *Progress in Linguistics*, 249–259. The Hague: Mouton.

Ruangrajitpakorn, Taneth, Trakultaweekoon, Kanokorn, and Supnithi, Thepchai. 2009. A syntactic resource for Thai: CG treebank. In *Proceedings of the 7th Workshop on Asian Language Resources*, Suntec, Singapore, 96–102. Stroudsberg, PA: ACL.

Sánchez Valencia, Víctor. 1991. Studies on natural logic and categorial grammar. PhD thesis, Universiteit van Amsterdam.

———. 1995. Parsing-driven inference: Natural logic. *Linguistic Analysis* 25: 258–285.

Savitch, Walter. 1987. Context-sensitive grammar and natural language syntax. In Walter Savitch, Emmon Bach, William Marsh, and Gila Safran-Naveh (eds), *The Formal Complexity of Natural Language*, 358–368. Dordrecht: Reidel.

Schlenker, Philippe. 2006. Scopal independence: A note on branching and wide scope readings of indefinites and disjunctions. *Journal of Semantics* 23: 281–314.

Seki, Hiroyuki, Matsumura, Takashi, Fujii, Mamoru, and Kasami, Tadao. 1991. On multiple context-free grammars. *Theoretical Computer Science* 88: 191–229.

Shan, Chung-Chieh and Barker, Chris. 2006. Explaining crossover and superiority as left-to-right evaluation. *Linguistics and Philosophy* 29: 91–134.

Shieber, Stuart. 1985. Evidence against the context-freeness of natural language. *Linguistics and Philosophy* 8: 333–343.

———. 1986. *An Introduction to Unification-Based Approaches to Grammar*. Stanford, CA: CSLI Publications.

Smith, Noah and Johnson, Mark. 2007. Weighted and probabilistic context-free grammars are equally expressive. *Computational Linguistics* 33: 477–491.

Srinivas, Bangalore. 1997. Complexity of lexical descriptions and its relevance to partial parsing. PhD thesis, University of Pennsylvania, Philadelphia. Published as IRCS Report 97-10.

Stabler, Edward. 2004a. Tupled pregroup grammars. In Claudia Casadio and Joachim Lambek (eds), *Computational Algebraic Approaches to Morphology and Syntax*, 23–52. Milan: Polimetrica.

———. 2004b. Varieties of crossing dependencies: Structure-dependence and mild context sensitivity. *Cognitive Science* 28: 699–720.

———. 2011. Computational perspectives on minimalism. In Cedric Boeckx (ed.), *Oxford Handbook of Linguistic Minimalism*, 617–641. Oxford University Press.

Stabler, Edward and Keenan, Edward. 2003. Structural similarity. *Theoretical Computer Science* 293: 345–363.

Steedman, Mark. 1985. Dependency and coordination in the grammar of Dutch and English. *Language* 61: 523–568.

———. 1987. Combinatory grammars and parasitic gaps. *Natural Language and Linguistic Theory* 5: 403–439.

———. 1990. Gapping as constituent coordination. *Linguistics and Philosophy* 13: 207–263.

———. 1996. *Surface Structure and Interpretation*, Linguistic Inquiry Monograph 30. Cambridge, MA: MIT Press.

———. 1999. Quantifier scope alternation in CCG. In *Proceedings of the 37th Annual Meeting of the Association for Computational Linguistics*, College Park, MD, 301–308. Stroudsberg, PA: ACL.

———. 2000a. Information structure and the syntax-phonology interface. *Linguistic Inquiry* 34: 649–689.

———. 2000b. *The Syntactic Process*. Cambridge, MA: MIT Press.

———. 2012. *Taking Scope: The Natural Semantics of Quantifiers*. Cambridge, MA: MIT Press.

Steedman, Mark and Baldridge, Jason. 2011. Combinatory categorial grammar. In Robert Boyer and Kirsti Börjars (eds), *Non-transformational Syntax: A Guide to Current Models*, 181–224. Oxford: Blackwell.

Steele, Susan. 1990. *Agreement and Anti-Agreement: A Syntax of Luiseño*. Dordrecht: Reidel.

Szabolcsi, Anna. 1983. ECP in categorial grammar. Manuscript, Max Planck Institute, Nijmegen, The Netherlands.

———. 1989. Bound variables in syntax: Are there any? In Renate Bartsch, Johan van Benthem, and Peter van Emde Boas (eds), *Semantics and Contextual Expression*, 295–318. Dordrecht: Foris.

———. 1992. On combinatory grammar and projection from the lexicon. In Ivan Sag and Anna Szabolcsi (eds), *Lexical Matters*, 241–268. Stanford, CA: CSLI Publications.

Szabolcsi, Anna (ed.). 1997. *Ways of Scope-taking*. Dordrecht: Kluwer.

Thomason, Richmond (ed.). 1974. *Formal Philosophy: Papers of Richard Montague*. New Haven, CT: Yale University Press.

Thomforde, Emily. 2013. Semi-supervised lexical acquisition for wide-coverage parsing. PhD thesis, University of Edinburgh.

Trechsel, Frank. 2000. A CCG account of Tzotzil pied piping. *Natural Language and Linguistic Theory* 18: 611–663.

Tse, Daniel and Curran, James R. 2010. Chinese CCGbank: Extracting CCG derivations from the Penn Chinese Treebank. In *Proceedings of the 23rd International Conference on Computational Linguistics*, 1083–1091. Beijing: Coling/ACL.

Uszkoreit, Hans. 1986. Categorial unification grammars. In *Proceedings of the International Conference on Computational Linguistics*, Bonn, 187–194. Stroudsberg, PA: Coling/ACL.

Vadas, David and Curran, James. 2007. Adding noun phrase structure to the Penn Treebank, In *Proceedings of the 45th Annual Meeting of the Association of Computational Linguistics*, Prague, 240–247. Stroudsberg, PA: ACL.

van Benthem, Johan. 1983. Five easy pieces. In Alice ter Meulen (ed.), *Studies in Model-Theoretic Semantics*, 1–17. Dordrecht: Foris.

———. 1986. *Essays in Logical Semantics*. Dordrecht: Reidel.

———. 1988. The semantics of variety in categorial grammar. In Wojciech Buszkowski, Witold Marciszewski, and Johan van Benthem (eds), *Categorial Grammar*, 37–55. Amsterdam: John Benjamins.

van Heijenoort, Jean (ed.). 1967. *From Frege to Gödel: A Source Book in Mathematical Logic*, 1879–1931. Cambridge, MA: Harvard University Press.

Vijay-Shanker, K. and Weir, David. 1994. The equivalence of four extensions of context-free grammar. *Mathematical Systems Theory* 27: 511–546.

Villavicencio, Aline. 2002. The acquisition of a unification-based generalised categorial grammar. PhD thesis, University of Cambridge.

———. 2011. Language acquisition with feature-based grammars. In Robert Boyer and Kirsti Börjars (eds), *Non-transformational Syntax: A Guide to Current Models*, 404–442. Blackwell.

Watkinson, Stephen and Manandhar, Suresh. 1999. Unsupervised lexical learning with categorial grammars. In *Proceedings of the Workshop on Unsupervised Learning in Natural Language Processing, ACL-99, College Park, MA, 59–66*. Stroudsberg, PA: ACL.

Webber, Bonnie. 1978. A formal approach to discourse anaphora. PhD thesis, Harvard University. Published by Garland, New York, 1979.

Weir, David. 1988. Characterizing mildly context-sensitive grammar formalisms. PhD thesis, University of Pennsylvania, Philadelphia. Published as Technical Report CIS-88-74.

White, Michael. 2006. Efficient realization of coordinate structures in combinatory categorial grammar. *Research on Language and Computation* 4: 39–75.

Whitelock, Pete. 1991. What sort of trees do we speak? A computational model of the syntax-prosody interface in Tokyo Japanese. In *Proceedings of the Fifth Conference of the European Chapter of the Association for Computational Linguistics*, Berlin, 75–82. Stroudsberg, PA: ACL.

Wittenburg, Kent. 1987. Predictive combinators: A method for efficient processing of combinatory grammars. In *Proceedings of the 25th Annual Conference of the Association for Computational Linguistics, Stanford*, Stanford, CA, 73–80. Stroudsberg, PA: ACL.

Wood, Mary McGee. 1993. *Categorial Grammars*. London: Routledge.

Zamansky, Anna, Francez, Nissim, and Winter, Yoad. 2006. A "natural logic" inference system using the Lambek calculus. *Journal of Logic, Language, and Information* 15: 273–295.

Zeevat, Henk. 1988. Combining categorial grammar and unification. In Uwe Reyle and Christian Rohrer (eds), *Natural Language Parsing and Linguistic Theories*, 202–229. Dordrecht: Reidel.

Zettlemoyer, Luke and Collins, Michael. 2005. Learning to map sentences to logical form: Structured classification with probabilistic categorial grammars. In *Proceedings of the 21st Conference on Uncertainty in AI (UAI)*, 658–666. Edinburgh: AAAI.

———. 2007. Online learning of relaxed CCG grammars for parsing to logical form. In *Proceedings of the Joint Conference on Empirical Methods in Natural Language Processing and Computational Natural Language Learning (EMNLP/CoNLL)*, Prague, 678–687. Stroudsberg, PA: ACL.

Zwicky, Arnold. 1986. Concatenation and liberation. In *C LS 22: Papers from the General Session*, 65–74. Chicago Linguistic Society, University of Chicago.

Index

A-bar movement: and Case 162; and CED 179–80; and CSC 180–1; cross-linguistic variation 171–5; distinctions from A-movement 167–9; and ellipsis 200; and ergative languages 182–3; failure of 177–85; and improper movement 183–4; and landing sites 171–4, 176–7; multiple *wh*-movement 174–6; and 'pied-piping' 169–70; and relative clauses 170–1; and *wh*-interactions 177–8; and *wh*-phrases 170–8, 181, 183

A-movement: and control 241–2, 243, 254, 258; distinctions from A-bar movement 167–9; and scrambling 265, 276–7; and syntax–lexicon interface 340

A'-movement 232–3, 265, 276–8

Abeillé, A. 549

Abels, Klaus 84

Abney, Steven 46–7, 48, 58, 66–9, 80, 95, 477

ABSL (Al-Sayyid Bedouin Sign Language) 452–3, 455, 457, 458–9

absolute adjectives 93

absolute universals 493, 496–7, 503

abstract case 150, 152–6, 162–3, 484, 516

Ackema, Peter 312, 329, 339

acquisition of syntax: and basic word order 431–5; and continuity/discontinuity 430–1; cross-linguistic variation 435–6, 438–9; emergentism 427–31, 433–5, 439–41; nativism 427–31, 432–3, 437–9, 441; and poverty of the stimulus 429; study of 4; and *wh*-questions 435–41

Activation Condition 242

ACT-R (Adaptive Control of Thought–Rational) 419

Adger, David 310

adjectives: categorical status of 95–6; and Cinque 102–5; critical discussion topics 92–8; current issues/research 98–105; defining 89–90; historical perspectives 90–2; and intersectivity 91, 96–8; and 'linkers' 105; and modification 94, 96–7, 98–100, 102–5; and N-movement 92–3, 95, 98, 101–2; placement of 92–5; uses of 90

adjunction: and adjunct control 245–51; and adverbs 108, 118, 120, 122, 123, 125; future research directions 20–1; and head movement 138–9; and HPSG 540–3, 548, 549, 551; and Merge theory 20; and transformational grammar 4

adverbs: and adjunction 108, 118, 120, 122, 123, 125; cartographic approach 108, 117–20, 126; cross-linguistic variation 116, 125–6; domain expressions 114, 122; functional 112–14, 115, 122; generalizations 114–16; and head movement 117; and linear order 108, 109, 118–19, 123; modern study of 108; and modification 109, 112, 114–15, 120–1; and morphology 120–1; participant 112, 114, 119–20, 122; and *Pesetsky's Paradox* 124–5; and phrase structure 109, 120, 124; predicational 109–12, 115–16, 122–3; and 'roll-up' movements 118–20; 'scopal' approach 108, 120–4, 125–6; and Spec position 117–18; theoretical issues 124–7; types of 109–16; and UG 108, 117, 119; and Weight Theory 121; and word order 108, 109, 115, 116, 118–19, 123, 125–6

agent-oriented adverbs 111

'agreement attraction' 416–19

Akhtar, N. 434–5

Aktionsart theory 584, 585

Aldridge, Edith 162

Alexiadou, Artemis 81–2, 84, 98

allative markers 499

alternations 25, 29

Ambridge, B. 439–40

anaphoric relations 214–15, 216–18, 219, 231

Anderson, Stephen 350–1, 359, 501

Andrews, Avery 570

Anti-Lexicalism 356–60

antisymmetry 17, 174, 479–80

Antisymmetry theory 174

aphasia 133, 145–6, 147

Argument Realization Principle 534, 536, 547

Lieber (1992). However, this is not the dominant view among contemporary morphologists. For an opposed view, see Anderson (1992), reviewed by Carstairs-McCarthy (1993).

A classic discussion of secondary compounds is Lieber (1983). See also section 4.4 in Carstairs-McCarthy (1992).

	Language Engineer	Accountant
Salary:	$87K-$130K	$88K - $128K
Years of school:	1-5 yrs	2 yrs
Where would I move?	Brandeis, UW	Anywhere, unless considering actuarial science
Job growth:	Amazon → Apple LE → DS (might need PhD)	CFO for NGO Fin. Advisor @ Vanguard
Private practice:	No	HR Block → private practice (can WFH)
Reskilling:	Self-taught	Continuing ed to maintain certification
Work style:	Collaborative, lots of uncertainty	lots of authoring, solitary work
technical skills:	Python, R	Excel

7 A word and its structure

7.1 Meaning and structure

In Chapter 2 it was pointed out that many words have meanings that are predictable, more or less, on the basis of their components. Some words are so predictable, indeed, that they do not have to be listed as lexical items. This predictability of meaning depends on how the structure of complex word forms guides their interpretation. Even with words that are lexically listed, unless their meaning is entirely different from what one might expect, such guidance is relevant. This chapter is about how it operates, and also (in Section 7.5) about circumstances under which meaning and structure appear to diverge.

In some words, structure is straightforward. For example, the lexeme HELPFUL, already discussed in Chapter 5, is derived from the noun base HELP by means of the adjective-forming suffix -*ful*. Because there are only two elements in this word form, it may seem there is not much to say about its structure. Even with just these two components, however, there is clearly a distinction between the actual word form *helpful* and the ill-formed one *-ful-help* – a distinction that will be discussed in Section 7.2. Sections 7.3 and 7.4 deal with affixed words and compounds that have more than two components, such as *unhelpfulness* and *car insurance premium*. Finally, in Section 7.5, we will confront a dilemma posed by items like *French history teacher* in its two interpretations ('French teacher of history' and 'teacher of French history').

7.2 Affixes as heads

Chapter 5 showed how, in English derivational morphology, suffixes heavily outnumber prefixes. In Chapter 6 we saw that most compounds are headed, with the head on the right. Superficially these two facts are unconnected. Consider, however, the role played by the head *house* of a compound such as *greenhouse*. As head, *house* determines the compound's

71

argument roles (in Construction Grammar) 648–9

Argument Selection Principle 27

argument structure: and alternations 25, 29; and HPSG 534; and lexical decomposition 28–33; and lexicon-syntax interface 26–33; and LFG 574; neo-constructionist approach 34–6; perspectives on 24–6, 36; and syntax–lexicon interface 323, 329–41; and syntax–semantics interface 310–11, 315; and thematic proto-roles 26–8; and theta-roles 329–41

'argument structure extension' 36

Aristotle 3

Arnett, N. V. 419

Aronoff, Mark 348, 354–5

Aspects of the Theory of Syntax (book) 42–3, 466

Assembly Problem 374

asymmetric coordination 180

ATB (Across-the-Board) movement 206–7

AUH (Actor–Undergoer Hierarchy) 586, 588, 596

Austin, P. 292

Autolexical Syntax theory 287–8, 297

AVMs (attribute value matrices) 527, 529–30, 532, 557, 561–2, 568

Baayan, Harald 355

Bach, Emmon 673, 683

backward application (in Categorial Grammar) 673–4

Bailyn, John 275

Baker, Mark 30, 49, 52, 78, 90, 136, 137, 285, 286–7, 291, 296–7, 298, 327, 349, 358, 392, 402, 493, 502

Baldridge, Jason 680, 681, 685

Bantu (language) 371–2, 374, 380

Barker, Chris 219–20, 687

Barrie, M. 287

Barriers (book) 514

Barss–Lasnik effects 119, 123, 124, 125

Barwise, Jon 79, 81

basic word order 264, 265–70, 431–5

Bates, E. 414–15

Béchet, Denis 684

Beck, D. 89

Begriffsschrift (book) 670

Belletti, Adriana 137, 333

Bernstein, J. 95

Berwick, Robert 393, 394, 449, 513

Biberauer, T. 400, 402

Bickel, Balthasar 497

Bickerton, D. 450, 451–2, 453–4, 455, 457

binding domains 216–18, 224–8

binding theory: and anaphoric relations 214–15, 216–18, 219, 231; and blocking principle 226;

complementarity/noncomplementarity 226–30; and connectivity 230–4, 235; and coreference 219–21; distinctions within 224–6; and functional categories 50; future research directions 234–5; GB theory *see* GB (Government and Binding) theory; and locality effects 215; and obviation 215, 221–4

Bittner, Maria 159

blocking 353, 358

blocking principle 226

Bloomfield, L. 468, 614

BNC (British National Corpus) 661

Boas, F. 293

Boas, Hans Christian 653–6, 662, 664–5

Bobaljik, Jonathan 120, 139–40, 159–60

Boeckx, Cedric 141, 243, 450, 502, 512, 518–19

Bolinger, D. 94

Booij, Geert 351

Borer, Hagit 51, 328

Bošković, Zeljko 76, 77–8, 252, 274–5

Bouma, G. 549

BPS (bare phrase structure): framework development 5; future research directions 17–20; and head movement 133, 139–40, 146; and LA 14–15; and linearization 16–17; and Merge theory 13; and minimalism 515–16

Bresnan, Joan 292, 556

Brody, M. 142

Brown, R. 432

Brown, S. 139–40

Bruening, B. 290

Büring, D. 225, 231

Butler, Christopher 644

Bybee, Joan 499

Cable, Seth 170

Caha, P. 55–6

Campbell, L. 397–8

Cann, Ronnie 312

Carpenter, Bob 685

cartographic approaches 54–5, 66, 70–1, 108, 117–20, 126

Case: abstract 150, 153–6; and agreement 157–60; configurational approach 160–1; and control 244–5, 255; cross-linguistic variation 151–2, 155; defining 150; and development of DP-hypothesis 67; and DP 154–5, 160, 162; and ellipsis 194, 197, 204; in ergative languages 151, 161–2; and functional categories 55–7; and functional structure 83–4; and grammatical functions 484; head-centered approach 160; and head movement 143–4; and HPSG 546–7; and minimalism 158–9, 509–10, 516–17; morphological 151–3, 161; and nonconfigurationality 292; and noun

incorporation 286; and RRG 595–6; structural
determination of 160–1; versions of 150–1
Case assigners 156–7
Case Filters 153–5, 158–9, 516–17
Case licensing 153
Case Principle 546–7
Case Uniqueness Principle 153
catenae 620–4
causative–inchoative alternation 336–7
caused-motion construction 656–7
CCG (Combinatory Categorial Grammar)
    674–82, 689–90
CED (condition on extraction domain) 179–80,
    246–7, 249–50
CG (Categorial Grammar): application of 670;
    and categorial type logic 684–5;
    combinatory 674–82, 689–90; and
    combinators 681; computational/
    psychological models 688–90; and
    coordination 677–9; cross-linguistic
    generalizations 678–9; development of
    670–2; and extraction 677; and free word
    order 680–1; and function composition
    674–5; generalizing combinatory rules
    679–80; and Lambek grammars 683–5; and
    logical form 682–3, 685–6, 688; and
    long-range dependencies 672; 'profane
    approach' 685–6, 687–8; pure 673–4;
    'sacred approach' 685–7; and semantics
    670–2, 673, 675, 685–8; and substitution
    676; and theories of grammar 681–2; and
    type-raising 675–6, 678–9; and 'wrap' rules
    682–3, 688
chains 309
Chierchia, Gennaro 72, 73, 78, 311
Chingoni (language) 338
Chomsky, Noam: and A-bar movement 167,
    169, 175–6; and binding theory 215, 216, 218,
    234–5; and Case 156; and chains 309; and
    constituency grammar 604; and
    contemporary linguistic research 3–4, 5, 7,
    8, 10, 11–13, 14–15, 18–20; and control
    241–2, 247, 255, 256–7; and copy theory 230;
    and DP-hypothesis 66, 70–1, 85; and
    featuring checking 476; and functional
    categories 42–3, 57–9; and GB theory 478;
    and LDD 469; and lexicalism 346–7, 350,
    355; and Merge theory 450; and MGG 465;
    and minimalism/Minimalist Program 139,
    140, 158–9, 481, 509–16, 518, 519; and
    standard theory 468–9, 473–4; and
    syntax–phonology interface 366; and
    syntax–semantics/pragmatics interface
    313; and transformations 468, 473;
    and UG 391–2, 396; and Uniformity
    Principle 493–4
'chunking' 411–12

Cinque, Guglielmo 54–5, 70, 84, 95, 98–9,
    102–5, 108, 117, 119–20, 310, 638
Clark, E. V. 414
Clark, H. H. 414
clausal adverbs 109, 111, 115–16
clause-internal scrambling 275–6, 277–8
clefting strategy 173–4
clitics 359, 368, 617–19
cognitive constructionism 34
Cognitive Grammar 316, 651, 664, 665–6
coherence (in Lexical-Functional Grammar)
    565–7
Collins, C. 372–3
combinatory transparency principle 675
communicative efficiency 499–500
Comorovski, Ileana 312
comparative syntax: and generalizations 492,
    496–7, 500–1, 503–4; goals of 490–2;
    identifying comparanda 494–6; and
    morphology 490–1, 501; nonaprioristic
    approach 492–3, 495–6, 497–500;
    restrictivist approach 493–4, 495–6, 497–8,
    500–3; syntactic universals 496–8; and UG
    493, 495–6, 497
competition-based theory 226, 227, 229–30,
    234
complementarity 226–30
complementary distribution 155, 215–16, 227
complementizer-trace phenomena 181–2
completeness (in Lexical-Functional Grammar)
    565–7
Completeness Constraint 595
compositionality (in syntax–semantics/
    pragmatics interface) 308–9
comprehending language structure: and
    agreement attraction 416–19; and
    dependency formation 409–10, 416, 418–21;
    future research directions 420–1; and
    sentence superiority' effect 411–13; and
    short-term forgetting 409, 419; and verbatim
    recall 409, 413–16
computational linguistics 575–6
concentric phenomena 114–15
Conceptual Component (in Functional
    Discourse Grammar) 628–9
Conceptual Semantics 314, 316, 335
concord constructions 652
configurational approach 26, 160–1
configurational languages 265–6
Configurationality Parameter 289
Conflation mechanism 142
connectivity 230–4, 235
consistency (in Lexical-Functional Grammar)
    564, 569, 570
constituency grammar 604–5, 607, 608–9, 617,
    621–2
constituent structure 467

Construction Grammar: argument roles 648–9; basic tenets of 650–1; and Boas 653–6, 664–5; and Cognitive Grammar 651, 664, 665–6; and Croft 663–4; and Generative Grammar 651; and Goldberg 34, 647–50, 651–2, 653, 655–7, 660–1, 662, 664–5; and Iwata 659–62, 664–5; and Kay 656–7; lower-level generalisation 662–5; and Nemoto 657–9; and non-compositionality 651–2; and 'overriding' cases 653–7, 665; and participant roles 648–9; and polysemy 662–3; and resultative constructions 648–50, 653–6; and Storage Frames 657–9; and subcategorisation 647–8; and verb meaning 657–62; and Waste-Prevention Frames 657–9

constructionism 34–6

constructions (in MGG) 485

Contextual Component (in Functional Discourse Grammar) 628

control: and A-movement 241–2, 243, 254, 258; adjunct control 245–51; and Case 244–5, 255; and CED 246–7, 249–50; and cross-linguistic variation 241–2, 245–6, 252–3; and D-Structure elimination 255–7, 259; and Duck Principle 240, 241, 243, 244, 245, 250, 251, 253–4, 257; and minimalism 239, 241–2, 244–5, 247, 251, 253, 255–6, 257–9; and MTC 239, 242–5, 246, 251–7, 258–9; and NOC 239, 245–6, 254; and OC 239, 240, 241–3, 245–6, 250–4, 254–5, 257, 258–9; and phonetic realization 251–4; PRO-based approaches 239, 240–1, 242–4, 245, 249–51, 254–5, 257–9; theory requirements 239–40, 254

control theory 478–9

'controllers' 588–9

conventional implicatures 312

conventionalised resultatives 654–6

Coon, Jessica 318

Cooper, Robin 79, 81

coordination (in Categorial Grammar) 677–9

Coppock, Elizabeth 207

Copy Theory 197, 230, 232–3, 247–9, 251, 252–3, 279

coreference 219–21

Correspondence Principle 377–8, 649

CPR (Canonical Precedence Relation) 273

cran morphs 354–5

Croft, William 89, 90, 663–4

cross-linguistic variation: in A-bar movement 171–5; in acquisition of syntax 435–6, 438–9; in adverbs 116, 125–6; in Case 151–2, 155; in control 241–2, 245–6, 252–3; in dependency grammar 617–20; in determiner phrase 71–8; in Functional Discourse Grammar 633–4, 636, 637–40, 641–4; in functional categories 73; in functional

structure 71–9; in Left Branch Extraction 75–6, 78; in lexical categories 73; in Lexical-Functional Grammar 557–61, 567–72; in morphology–syntax interface 350–1, 358–9; in nominal phrase 71–9; in Role and Reference Grammar 588–96; in syntactic change 391–2, 397–8, 399; in syntax–lexicon interface 331–2, 338–41; in syntax–phonology interface 366, 368–9, 371–2, 374, 380–1; *see also* comparative syntax

CSC (Coordinate Structure Constraint) 180–1

Dalrymple, Mary 315, 573–4

Davis, H. 290

de Reuse, W. J. 294

Dean, John 413

Deep Structure 308, 313, 314

degree/measure adverbs 113

Delsing, H. 96

demonstratives 81–2

dependent elements 228

Déprez, V. 433

derivational morphology 501

derivational structures 671

Descartes, René 3

Determiner Spreading 99–100

DG (dependency grammar): and catenae 620–4; and constituency grammar 604–5, 607, 608–9, 617, 621–2; cross-linguistic variation 617–20; and distribution 613–15; and form determination 611–13; history of 605–6; identifying dependencies 608–9; lexical items 622–4; and morphology 610, 611–13, 614–15; and one-to-one correspondence 607–8; and predicate–argument structures 610–11; representing dependencies 606–7; types of dependencies 609–15; and word order 615–20

Di Domenico, Elisa 84

Di Sciullo, Anna-Maria 287, 322–3, 351, 352, 355, 358

diachronic syntax 393, 395–8, 402–6, 457, 498–500, 502

Dikken, Den 105

Dikker, Suzanne 642

Dillon, B. 418–19

direct modification 98, 103–5

direct reference 366, 370, 380, 381–2

'direct surface compositionality' 685–7

directional consistency principle 677

directional inheritance principle 677

discontinuities 430–1, 617–19

Discourse Acts 627, 629–30, 634, 638

discourse-oriented adverbs 109–10, 111, 114, 122

discourse-pragmatics 580, 589, 599–600

'discourse transparency' 284–5
discrete infinity 3, 7–8, 12–13, 18, 20, 449
Distributed Morphology 136, 287–8, 297, 308, 348, 349, 360
ditransitive expressions 659–62, 663–4
Dixon, R. 89
Dobashi, Y. 373, 379–80
domain adverbs 114, 122
Domain Integrity principle (in Functional Discourse Grammar) 634–5
domain juncture 365
domain limit 365
'domain of the word' 357–8
domain span 365
dominance dimension 615–16
dominance relations 418
Dowty, David 26–8, 584, 682–3, 688
Drossard, W. 294, 295
DRT (Discourse Representation Theory) 316, 590
Dryer, Matthew 497
DU (derivational uniformity) 472, 473, 478, 483, 484
Duck Principle 240, 241, 243, 244, 245, 250, 251, 253–4, 257
dummy elements (in Functional Discourse Grammar) 640–2
durativity 310
Dynamic Syntax 312

ECM (Exceptional Case Marking) 156, 216–17, 227, 228–30
ECP (Empty Category Principle) 286, 516–17
Éléments de syntaxe structural (book) 604, 605
ellipsis: and A-bar movement 200; and antecedents 192, 193, 200–2; and Case 194, 197, 204; controversial cases 203–8; and empty object 208; and Gapping 205–7; and identity 198–203; and interpretive analysis 195–6; interpretation of 192–3; island-repair effects 198–9; and PGs 199–200; and size mismatch 201–3; and sluicing 193–6, 197–8, 199, 203–4; and stripping 196–8, 203–5; and structural mismatch 193, 198; study of 192–3; syntactic analysis 193–5, 196–8, 200–1, 203–4; and voice mismatch 200–1; and wh-phrase 193–5, 196
EM (External Merge) 12–13, 481
emergentism 427–31, 433–5, 439–41
Emonds, J. 469
empty objects 208
Encoding (in Functional Discourse Grammar) 629, 632, 634, 642, 643
End-based Theory 369–70
endocentric projections 10
ergative languages 151, 161–2, 182–3, 331–2
Ericsson, K. 412

Ernst, Thomas 120, 121
EST (Extended Standard Theory) 215, 308, 472–3
Evans, Nicholas 296, 448, 503–4
eventhood 310
evolution of syntax: formal devices of syntax 446; and grammaticalization 457–60; and layers of grammar 454–6; and Merge theory 449–50, 456–7; and minimalism 448–50; protolanguage concepts 451–6; and saltation 448–50; and syntactic phenomena 446–8
exclamatives 312
exempt anaphora 231
exocentric projections 10
extended projections 47–9, 52, 55, 60
Extension Condition 139–40, 175–6, 247, 249–50, 251
external arguments 333–7, 339
extraction (in Categorial Grammar) 677
extraction (in HPSG) 548–9

Faculty of Language 448–9, 509, 513
Falk, Yehuda 574
FDG (Functional Discourse Grammar): and agreement 640, 642–3; components of 628; cross-linguistic variation 633–4, 636, 637–40, 641–4; current research 643–4; and Discourse Acts 627, 629–30, 634, 638; and dummy elements 640–2; and Encoding 629, 632, 634, 642, 643; and Formulation 629, 632, 634, 637, 640, 641, 642–3; four positions of 636–40; internal layering 629–32; mapping principles 634–6; Morphosyntactic Level 629, 632–4, 636–43
FE (Feature Economy) 403
'feature structures' 527–8
featuring checking 476–7
Fernald, A. 431
Feyerabend, Paul 519
Figure role (in argument structure) 32
finite agreement 157–8
Finkel, L. 145
Fitzpatrick, Justin 169
FLB (faculty of language in the broad sense) 448–9
FLN (faculty of language in the narrow sense) 448–9
focus movement 197, 203, 205
Fodor, J. 317, 411, 486
FOFC (Final-over-Final Constraint) 404–5
Foley, W. 582
FOPL (first-order predicate logic) 670, 671, 685, 688
Foret, Annie 684
Formulation (in Functional Discourse Grammar) 629, 632, 634, 637, 640, 641, 642–3

forward application (in Categorial Grammar) 673–4
'fossil principles' 454
Frascarelli, M. 382
Frege, Gottlob 670, 671–2
Freidin, Robert 512, 516, 517, 519
Frey, Werner 108
Friedmann, N. 146
fronting 4
Fujii, Tomohiro 252–33
Fukui, Naoki 17, 49, 52, 273–4
Full Interpretation 329, 517
function composition (in Categorial Grammar) 674–5
functional adverbs 112–14, 115, 122
functional categories: and cartographic syntax 54–5; and Chomsky 57–9; cross-linguistic variation 73; as distinct class 49–52; expansion of 57–60; and extended projections 47–9, 52, 55, 60; and head movement 46–7, 49–50, 52–3, 54, 55; integration of 44–9; and Marantz 59–60; and Minimalist Program 57–8; as 'minor categories' 42–4; and morphology 52, 53, 55–6; and movement 49–51; and nano-syntax 55–7; and nominal system 46–7; and parallel structures 47–9; and parameters 51–2; and projection 49; proliferation of 52–7; and X'-theory 45–6, 60
Functional Stability principle (in Functional Discourse Grammar) 635
functional structure: cross-linguistic variation 71–9; defining 65; and development of DP-hypothesis 65, 66–71; non-D functional items 79–85

'gapping' 205–7, 677–8
GB (Government and Binding) theory: and adverbs 126, 127; and binding domains 216–18, 228; and Case 157, 159; and connectivity 230, 232; and control 246–7; and DP-hypothesis 67–8; distinctions within 224; and functional categories 47; and functional structure 84; and head movement 133–4, 135, 138, 139; and history of syntax 475–80; and Minimalist Program 509, 510–12, 520; and scrambling 264; and syntax–semantics/pragmatics interface 309, 314
gender 84
Generalized Alignment Theory 370–2
Generalized Quantifier Theory 311
generalized transformations 7, 256, 468–9, 511
generative constructionism 34–5
generative grammar: and adjectives 90; and Case 150; and Construction Grammar 651; and contemporary linguistic research 3, 5, 7, 11, 13; and control 257–8; and functional

structure 65; and head movement 136; and history of lexicalism 346–9; and history of syntax 465, 483–5; and Lexical-Functional Grammar 574; and syntax–phonology interface 366; and syntax–semantics/pragmatics interface 308, 313–14, 316–17; and UG 391–2; see also MGG
Ghini, M. 382
'glue semantics' 314–15, 575
Godard, D. 549
Gödel, Kurt 519
Goldberg, Adele 34, 647–50, 651–2, 653, 655–7, 660–1, 662, 664–5
Government and Binding Theory see GB (Government and Binding) theory
GPSG (Generalized Phrase Structure Grammar) 315, 348, 548, 672, 684, 685, 687
Grammatical Component (in Functional Discourse Grammar) 628
grammaticality 465–7
grammaticalization 396–8, 457–60, 498
Greenberg, Joseph 84, 497, 503,
Grice, H. Paul 312, 317
Grimshaw, Jane 48, 57, 310, 323, 332
Grodzinsky, Y. 145
Groß, T. 619
Ground role (argument structure) 32
Guasti, M. T. 437, 438

H Tone Plateau 378
Haddad, Youssef 251–2, 254
Haider, Hubert 121, 122, 125
Hale, Kenneth 30–3, 36, 47, 48, 58, 142, 159, 264, 265–6, 288–9, 290–1, 298, 327
Halle, Morris 347–8, 366
Hankamer, Jorge 358
Harley, H. 136, 142
Haugen, J. D. 288
Hauser, M. 393, 448–9
Hawkins, John A. 459–60, 486, 499
Hays, D. 605
Head Feature Principle 543
head movement (HM): and adjunction 138–9; and adverbs 117; and aphasia 133, 145–6, 147; and BPS 133, 139–40, 146; current status of 133, 143–5; development of 133, 136–9; and functional categories 46–7, 49–50, 52–3, 54, 55; and Government and Binding Theory 133–4; and HMC 134–5, 145, 146; inception of 133–5; and LHM 135; and Merge 139–40, 142, 144–5; and Minimalist Program 133, 139–43, 146; and noun incorporation 286–7; and Relativized Minimality 517–18; and substitution 138–9; and syntactic change 400, 403; and word formation 136–8; and XP movement 134, 138, 139, 140, 141, 145–6

Heck, Fabian 170
Heim, Irene 315–16
Heine, B. 453
Hendriks, Herman 687
Hengeveld, Kees 628, 634
Higginbotham, J. 91
Higgins, F. 232
Hilbert, David 519
Hinrichs, E. 540
history of syntax: and GB theory 475–80; and grammatical functions 483–4; and grammaticality 465–7; and HPSG 475, 482–3; and Minimalist Program 480–2; and P&P framework 475, 478–80; and poverty of the stimulus 485–6; and standard theory 468–9, 472–5; and syntactic structures 467–71; and uniformity 471–2
HMC (Head Movement Constraint) 134–5, 145, 146
Hoekstra, Teun 493–4
Hoffman, Beryl 680
Hoji, Hajime 268–9, 270, 277
Hornstein, Norbert 250, 330
Horvath, Julia 335
Hoyt, Frederick 681
HPSG (Head Driven Phrase Structure Grammar): and adjunction 540–3, 548, 549, 551; and argument structure 534; and AVMs 527, 529–30, 532; and binding 546; and Case 546–7; computer implementations of 551–2; constituent order 549–50; and constraints 529–31; current developments 551; defining 526–7; descriptive devices 527–32; development of 527; and discourse 550–1; and extraction 548–9; feature architecture 532–4; and 'feature structures' 527–8; and head movement 133; and head-complements-phrase 539–40, 546, 548; and head-subject-phrase 538–9, 549, 551; and history of syntax 475, 482–3; and interface constraints 526; lexical rules 531, 534–6; and Passive Lexical Rule 547; and phrase structure 538; projection of head values 543; and relational constraints 532; and semantics 544–6; and syntax–semantics/pragmatics interface 314, 315; and types 528–9; and valence 536–8
HTA (High Tone Anticipation) 380–1
Huang, C.-T. 179, 227, 391
Hudson, R. 606, 613
Hulk, Aafke 313
Hurford, J. R. 449–50, 454, 455
Hyams, N. 427–8

IC (immediate constituents) 467
Iconicity principle 634
ID (immediate dominance) schemata 482–3
identity 198–203

idioms 171, 322, 334–5, 355, 357, 451, 623
IG (Input Generalisation) 403
Iggesen, Oliver 152
IL (Interpersonal Level) 629–30, 632, 633–4, 638, 640, 641–2
IM (Internal Merge) 12–13, 18, 481
implicational universals 497
improper movement 183–4
inclusiveness condition 515
Incremental Theme role (argument structure) 32
independent elements 228
Index of Synthesis 350
indirect modification 98–100, 103–5
indirect reference 366, 370, 378, 382
Inertia Principle 394
infinitival clauses 154–6, 246
inflectional morphology 501
influential antisymmetry 501
'information structure' representation 589–90
inherent case 161–2
innate knowledge 428–9
Inouye, Daniel 413
interface categories 367
interfaces: *see under* morphology–syntax interface; syntax–lexicon interface; syntax–phonology interface; syntax–semantics/pragmatics interface
internal arguments 334–5, 339
Internal Subject Hypothesis 169
International Journal of American Linguistics 298
interpretation (in syntax–semantics/pragmatics interface) 308–9
interrogative clauses 270–2, 274
intersectivity 91, 96–8
intervention effects 181
invariant patterns 492
Isard, S. 411, 412
Ito, J. 367, 375–6
IU (interface uniformity) 471, 473
Iwata, Seizi 659–62, 664–5

Jackendoff, R. 44, 57, 66–7, 69, 80, 108, 227, 229, 309, 325, 447, 450, 451, 453–6
Jacobson, Pauline 683, 686–7, 688
Jarvella, R. 414
Jelinek, Eloise 78, 289–90, 291, 292
Jiwarli (language) 292
Johns, A. 285, 287
Johnson, Kyle 206

K(ase)P 83–4
Kabardian (language) 173–4
Kaisse, E. M. 370
Kamp, Hans 90, 97, 316
Kanazawa, Makoto 681

Kaplan, Ronald 357, 556
Kay, Paul 656–7
Kayne, Richard 17, 21, 108, 174, 372, 399, 403, 479, 501
Keenan, Edward 394, 684
Keyser, Samuel 30–3, 36, 58, 142, 327
Kimatuumbi (language) 371–2, 374
Kintsch, W. 412
Kiss, K. E. 291
Kitahara, Hisatsugu 178
Klein, Ewan 308–9
Klima, E. 216
Kobele, Gregory 684
Koenig, J.-P. 297
Kooij, Jan 493–4
Koopman, H. 134
Kracht, Marcus 684
Kratzer, Angelika 315–16
Krifka, Manfred 309
Kruijff, Geert-Jan 680
Kuno, S. 233
Kuroda, Shige-Yuki 208, 269
Kuteva, T. 453

LA (labeling algorithm) 14–15, 17, 18–19
Laka, Itziar 162
Lakatos, Imre 519, 520
Lakoff, George 473, 687–8
Lamarche, J. 91–2, 101, 102
Lambek, Joachim 683–5
Lambrecht, K. 590
Lamontagne, Greg 55, 83–4
Landau, Idan 242–3, 244, 246, 255, 258
landing sites 171–4, 176–7
language acquisition 8, 10
language faculty 447–8
'language genesis' 447
LaPolla, R. J. 579
Lappin, Shalom 516
Larson, R. 57, 58, 94, 97–8
Lasnik, Howard 141, 153, 205, 229, 255, 512, 518, 520
'Last-Resort' view 18, 274
Late-Insertion framework 360–1
layered clause structure 580–1, 583
LBE (Left Branch Extraction) 75–6, 78, 196, 198–9, 207
LCA (Linear Correspondence Axiom) 108, 118–19, 287, 479–80
LDD (long distance dependency) 469
'least effort' principle 518
Lebeaux, David 20, 232–4, 235
Ledgeway, A. 400
Lees, R. 216, 473
Left Branch Condition 608
Legate, Julie 162, 291
LeSourd, P. S. 290

Levin, Beth 28–9, 35, 310–11
Levinson, Stephen 448, 503–4
Lewis, R. L. 419
lexical categories: cross-linguistic variation 73; and 'minor' functional categories 42, 43–4; and expansion of functional categories 57, 58, 59–60; and functional categories as distinct class 49, 51; and proliferation of functional categories 55, 57
Lexical Conceptual Structure 325–6
lexical decomposition 28–33
Lexical Integrity Principle 348, 357, 360
lexical processes 286, 287
Lexical Resource Semantics 544
lexicalism: and Anti-Lexicalism 356–60; history of 346–9; Strong 346, 348, 352–6; Weak 346, 348, 349–52
Lexicalist Hypothesis 133, 136
lexicon-syntax interface 26–33
LF (logical form): and Categorial Grammar 682–3, 685–6, 688; and ellipsis 194; and standard theory 472; and syntax–phonology interface 372; and syntax–semantics/pragmatics interface 313
LFG (Lexical-Functional Grammar): and annotation 561, 562; and argument structure 574; and AVMs 557, 561–2, 568; and coherence 565–7; and completeness 565–7; and consistency 564, 569, 570; and constituent structure 556, 557–63, 568–71, 573, 575; cross-linguistic variation 557–61, 567–72; development of 556; and empty categories 573; endocentric/non-endocentric structures 567–9; and functional structure 556–67, 568–74, 575; fundamental ideas of 556–60; further research areas 575–6; and generalization 573–4; and history of syntax 475, 483–4; and Lexical Mapping Theory 574–5; and long-distance dependency 573–4; and multiple syntactic representation 556, 559–60; and nonconfigurationality 291–3, 297; and PRO introduction rule 570; relational hierarchy 571–3; and syntax–lexicon interface 340; and syntax–semantics/pragmatics interface 314–15; and variable correspondence 557, 560–2; variable analyses 562–3; well-formedness constraints 563–7
LHM (Long Head Movement) 135
LIs (lexical items) 11, 15, 19
Li, C. 399
Li, Y. 49–51, 52
Lieber, Rochelle 326, 352, 358–60
Lieven, E. 434
Lightfoot, D. 396
linear order 108, 109, 118–19, 123, 373–4, 615–16

linearization 16–17, 18, 372–4, 380–1, 446–7, 448, 454
'linkers' 105
listedness 355
LMT (Lexical Mapping Theory) 314, 574–5
locality 179, 215
logophoricity 234
Lombardi, Linda 415–16
long-distance dependencies 352, 531, 573–4, 617
long-distance scrambling 275–6, 278, 279–80
Longobardi, Giuseppe 73–4
long-range dependencies 672, 681
Lorenzo, G. 296
lower-level generalisation (in Construction Grammar) 662–5
LP (linear precedence) 482–3, 549–50
LS (logical structure) 584–6, 596, 598–9
LTD (Low Tone Deletion) 380–1
Lyons, John 8, 10

Mackenzie, J. Lachlan 628, 644
macroparameters 402–3
MacWhinney, B. 441
Mada, Ibn 605
Mandarin (language) 98–9, 391–2, 397, 399, 591–2
manner adverbs 109–12, 115–16
Marantz, Alec 34, 59–60, 161, 331, 334–5, 349, 357
Marelj, Marijana 329
Martin, Roger 244, 512
Massam, D. 286, 287
Match Theory 376–9, 382
Mathieu, E. 287
Matsuoka, Mikinari 270
Matthewson, L. 290
Mattissen, J. 293, 294–5
Matushansky, O. 140, 142
maximal projections 12
McCloskey, James 169, 176–7, 477, 493
McDaniel, D. 456–7
Meaning-Text Theory 606, 611
Medeiros, David 84–5
Meillet, A. 396
memory: and agreement attraction 416–19; capacity of 419–20; and dependency formation 410–11, 416, 418–21; future research directions 420–1; and 'sentence superiority' effect 411–13; and short-term forgetting 409, 419–21; and verbatim recall 409, 413–16
Merchant, Jason 196, 198–9, 200–2
Merge: and adjunction 20; and BPS 13; and control 247–9, 256–7; development of 5, 11–13; and EM 12–13; and evolution of syntax 449–50, 456–7; future research

17–18, 19–20; and head movement 139–40, 142, 144–5; and history of syntax 480–2; and IM 12–13, 18; and LA 14–15; and linearization 16; and Move-α 13; and P&P framework 11; and phrase-markers 12; and projections 12; and PSRs 11; and scrambling 279; and SOs 11–13; and UG 11; and X-bar theory 13
mesoparameters 402–4
Mester, A. 367, 375–6
methodological minimalism 512–13
MGG (mainstream generative grammar): and antisymmetry 479; and constructions 485; and grammatical functions 483–5; and grammaticality 465–7; and HPSG 482–3; and island constraints 469–70; and LDD 469; and transformations 468; and uniformity 471–2; and X'-theory 474, 477
Michaelis, Laura 652
Michelson, K. 297
microparameters 402
middle formation 337–8, 339–40
Miller, G. 411, 412, 466
Minimal Link Condition 178
minimal projections 12
minimalism: background to 509–12; and BPS 515–16; and Case 509–10, 516–17; characteristics of 512–19; and control 239, 241–2, 244–5, 247, 251, 253, 255–6, 257–9; and economy 516–18; and evolution of syntax 448–50; future research directions 520; and morphology–syntax interface 346, 348–9, 352; and noun incorporation 287; programmatic nature of 518–19; and scrambling 264; and syntax–phonology interface 372–4, 379–82; and syntax–semantics/pragmatics interface 316; and X-bar theory 514–16
Minimalist Program (MP): and Case 158–9; characteristics of 512–19; and control 251, 255–6, 257, 259; and functional categories 57–8; future research directions 520; and GB theory 509, 510–12, 520; and head movement 133, 139–43, 146; and history of lexicalism 349; and history of syntax 480–2; and interfaces 512, 517; and nonconfigurationality 291; and P&P framework 509; and phrase structure evolution 13; programmatic nature of 518–19; and scrambling 264; and syntax–phonology interface 365, 379; and syntax–semantics/pragmatics interface 313
Mirror Principle 136, 142, 349
Mithun, M. 284, 285
Miyagawa, Shigeru 268, 270, 272

ML (Morphosyntactic Level) 629, 632–4, 636–43

modals 396–7

modification 94, 96–7, 98–100, 102–5, 109, 112, 114–15, 120–1

modifiers (in Functional Discourse Grammar) 630–1, 638

modularity 429, 475

Mohanan, K.P. 573

Mohawk (language) 284, 290, 291, 296

Montague Grammar 308

Montague, Richard 671–2, 685

Moortgat, Michael 684–5

Moravcsik, Edith 159

morphemes: and FDG 632; and functional categories 52, 53, 55; and morphology–syntax interface 353–4; and polysynthesis 293–5, 298; and RRG 582

morphological case 151–3, 161

morphology: and adverbs 120–1; and binding theory 225; and comparative syntax 490–1, 501; and DG 610, 611–13, 614–15; defining 322; and functional categories 52, 53, 55–6; and grammatical functions 484; and head movement 140; and LFG 575; and Nominal Mapping Parameter 72; and noun incorporation 284, 287–8; and syntax–semantics/pragmatics interface 308; *see also* ML (Morphosyntactic Level)

morphology–syntax interface: and Anti-Lexicalism 356–60; contentiousness surrounding 345–6; cross-linguistic variation 350–1, 358–9; future research directions 360–1; and history of lexicalism 346–9; and minimalism 346, 348–9, 352; and Strong Lexicalism 346, 348, 352–6; and Weak Lexicalism 346, 348, 349–52

morphosemantic operations 29

morphosyntactic operations 29

Move-α 10, 13, 264–5, 473–4

MRS (Minimal Recursion Semantics) 533, 544

MTC (Movement Theory of Control) 239, 242–5, 246, 251–7, 258–9

Müller, Natascha 313

multiple sluicing 203–4

Multiple Spell-Out Theory 372–3, 378, 380

Muskens, Reinhard 308

Muysken, Pieter 12

MVC (Morphological Visibility Condition) 296

Nakazawa, T. 540

nanoparameters 402

nano-syntax 55–7, 348, 349, 360

nativism 427–31, 432–3, 437–9, 441

natural selection 513

'natural semantics' 687–8

'nearly context-free' formalisms 681

Neeleman, Ad 84

Neisser, Ulrich 413

Nemoto, Noriko 657–9, 662

neo-constructionism 34–6

Nespor, M. 365, 368–9, 382

'neutral' case systems 151–2

Newman, Jean 499

'nexus' relations 591

NI (noun incorporation) 283–8, 297, 298

Nichols, J. 613

Nilsen, Øystein 122

Nishigauchi, Taisuke 172

Nixon, Richard 413

Niyogi, P. 393, 394–5, 404–5

NOC (non-obligatory control) 239, 245–6, 254

Nominal Mapping Parameter 72–3

nominal phrase: cross-linguistic variation 71–9; defining 65; and development of DP-hypothesis 65, 66–71; non-D functional items 79–85

nominal system 46–7

nominalization 7, 473

non-absolute adjectives 93

non-aprioristic approach (in comparative syntax) 492–3, 495–6, 497–500

non-complementarity 226–30

non-compositionality 651–2

non-configurational languages 265–6

non-configurationality 288–93, 297, 298

non-conventionalised resultatives 654, 656

non-D functional items 79–85

non-intersective adjectives 97–8

Nonlocal Feature Principle 548

Nordlinger, R. 292–3

null morphemes 353–4

number 82–3

Obligatory Case Parameter 161

obviation 215, 221–4

OC (obligatory control) 239, 240, 241–3, 245–6, 250–5, 257, 258–9

Occam's Razor 245, 250, 355, 356–7, 624

Oehrle, Richard 684–5

'off-stage' information 653, 655

Olson, M. 591

'omission' 613–14

'on-stage' information 653, 655

On the Definition of Word (book) 358

ontological minimalism 513

operators (in Functional Discourse Grammar) 630–1

operators (in Role and Reference Grammar) 581–3, 591–2

Optimality Theory 370–2, 500, 575

optional movement 264, 273–4

Originator role (argument structure) 32

Origins of Phrase Structure (thesis) 45

orthography 533
Osborne, T. 619
Otani, Kazuyo 208
Ouhalla, J. 51–2
Output Component (in Functional Discourse
    Grammar) 628
'overgeneration' 653
'overriding' cases (in Construction Grammar)
    653–7, 665

P&P (Principles-and-Parameters) framework:
    and acquisition of syntax 427–8, 433; and
    adverbs 117, 126; and comparative syntax
    501; and head movement 133; and language
    acquisition 8, 10; and nonconfigurationality
    289, 291–2, 297; and polysynthesis 296; and
    history of syntax 475, 478–80; and Merge
    theory 11; and Minimalist Program 509; and
    syntactic change 391–2, 402; and syntax–
    semantics/pragmatics interface 308, 314; and
    UG 391–2
PA (Pronominal Argument) language 290
PAH (Pronominal Argument Hypothesis) 290,
    292
Pak, M. 380–1
parallel structures 47–9
Parallelism Requirement 242
parametric approach (in comparative syntax)
    502–3
Partee, Barbara 81, 97, 311, 687
'partial control' effects 243
participant roles (in argument structure) 34
participant roles (in Construction Grammar)
    648–9
particle verbs 359–60
Passamaquoddy (language) 290
Passive Lexical Rule 547
passive transformational relation 4
passivization 169, 337–8, 339–40, 349, 448, 459
Pentus, Mati 684
'percolation' 418
perfect projection 48
Performance-Grammar Correspondence
    Hypothesis 459–60
Pesetsky, David 178, 333
Pesetsky's Paradox 124–5
PF (Phonetic Form) 141–2, 146, 194, 196, 199,
    205, 313, 372
PGs (parasitic gaps) 183, 199–200
Phillips, C. 420
phonetic realization 251–4
phonology 532–3, 568
phrasal compounds 359–60
phrasal nodes 9
phrasal semantics 575
phrase structure: and adverbs 109, 120, 124;
    components 6; and expansion of functional

categories 57–60; and generative research 5;
    and HPSG 538; and integration of functional
    categories 44–8; and MP 13; and
    nonconfigurationality 289, 298; and
    proliferation of functional categories 52;
    rules *see* PSRs; and syntax–semantics/
    pragmatics interface 315–16
phrase-markers 5–7, 9, 12, 16, 19
Pica, P. 225–6
'pied-piping' 169–70
Pierce, A. 433
Pinker, S. 432
Pittner, Karin 108
'pivots' 588–9
PL (Phonological Level) 629, 643
Plank, Frank 353
'Plato's problem' 8
PLD (Primary Linguistic Data) 393, 397,
    401–2, 403
PLs (projection lines) 142, 606
PNC (productive noninflectional concatenation)
    294
Pollard, Carl 231, 527, 531–2, 540, 544, 546,
    548
polypersonalism 294
polysemy 662–3
polysynthesis 290, 291, 293–7, 298
Portner, Paul 312
Potsdam, Eric 251–2, 254
Potter, Mary 415–16
poverty of the stimulus 393–4, 429, 485–6
PPPs (participant adverbials) 112, 114, 119–20,
    122
pragmatics 312–13, 316–17
precedence dimension 615
predicate–argument structures 610–11
predicational adverbs 109–12, 115–16,
    122–3
predicative adjectives 91, 98, 99, 106, 154, 611,
    613
primates 447–8, 449, 452, 456–7
Principle of Minimal Distance 255
PRO-based approaches 239, 240–1, 242–4, 245,
    249–51, 254–5, 257–9, 479
probe sentences 414–15
processing, ease of 499
productivity 355–6
'profane approach' (in Categorial Grammar)
    685–6, 687–8
Progovac, Ljiljana 77, 455
Projection Principle 25, 289, 511
projection-free syntax 14–15
projectivity 616–19
Proper Binding Condition (PBC) effect 265,
    278–9

prosodic domains 365–6, 36–89, 372–4, 380–2
Prosodic Hierarchy Theory 367–8, 375–9
PRO-theorem 218
proto-agent role 27–8
protolanguage concepts 451–6
proto-patient role 27
PSA (privileged syntactic argument) 587–8, 593, 596, 598
pseudoclefts/pseudoclefting 173, 231–2, 608–9, 613
PSR (Phrase Structure Rules): and development of DP-hypothesis 66; and head movement 142; historical overview 5–8; and HPSG 482; and linearization 16; and Merge theory 11; and phrase-markers 5–7; and standard theory 469; and transformations 468; and X-bar theory 8–10
psych-verbs 332–3
PTI (Phrasal Tone Insertion) 371
PVP (Parameter Value Preservation) 273

quantifiers 79–81, 267, 311
quantity-related adverbs 113
'quirky' subjects 159, 160–1

Rackowski, Andrea 179
Rainer, Franz 353
'raising' 636
Ramchand, Gillian 35–6, 309, 310
Rappaport Hovav, Malka 28–9, 35, 310–11
reciprocals 214
reductionism approach (in adjective use) 90–1
Reed, Sylvia 318
reflexives 214, 219, 223
reflexivization 337–8, 340–1
Reinhart, Tanya 16, 221, 222, 227–30, 232, 234, 328–9, 335, 339, 340
Relational Grammar 484
Relation-based Theory 368–9
Relative Clause Formation 7
relative clauses (in A-bar movement) 170–1
Relativized Minimality 517–18
Relevance Theory 312, 317
remnant movement approach 143
'reprojection' analyses 140–1
REST (Revised Extended Standard Theory) 472–3, 475, 478
restrictivist approach (in comparative syntax) 493–4, 495–6, 497–8, 500–3
resumptive pronouns 185
retrieval outcomes 418–19
Reuland, E. 227–30, 232, 234
rhythmic categories 367
Rich Agreement Hypothesis 401
Richards, Norvin 179
Richter, F. 527, 532

Riemsdijk, Henk van 195–6
right adjunction (adverbs) 108, 118, 120, 122, 123, 125
'rising' 619–20
Ritter, Elizabeth 82–3, 84
Rivière, Claude 647
Rizzi, Luigi 70, 333, 404, 517–18
RL (Representational Level) 629, 631–2, 633–4, 637–42
Roberts, Ian 138–9, 143–5, 396–7, 401, 402–3, 400, 402, 502
Rodrigues, Cliene 243, 245, 246
'roll-up' movements 118–20
Rooryck, J. 230
Rosen, C. 287
Rosenbaum, P. S.255
Ross, John Robert 177, 180, 184, 194, 264, 469, 608, 678
Rothman, Jason 313
Roussou, A. 396–7
RRG (Role and Reference Grammar): and Case 595–6; and complex sentence structure 590–5; cross-linguistic variation 588–96; and discourse-pragmatics 580, 589, 599–600; and grammatical relations 587–9; and head movement 133; and history of syntax 484–5; 'information structure' representation 589–90; and layered clause structure 580–1, 583; and logical structure 584–6; and operators 581–3, 591–2; and semantic macroroles 585–6; and semantic representation 580, 584–5, 595–9; and syntactic representation 580–3, 595–9; theoretical basis 579–80; and transitivity 586–7
RSRL (Relational Speciate Re-entrant Language) 527
Rudin, Catherine 174
'ruleless grammar' 10
Russell, Bertrand 356
Ruys, Eddie 180–1

Sachs, J. S. 414, 415
'sacred approach' (in Categorial Grammar) 685–7
Sadler, Louise 29
Sadock, J. M. 285, 287–8
Safir, K. 226, 229–30, 234
Sag, Ivan 231, 308–9, 527, 531–2, 540, 544, 546, 548
SAI (subject-auxiliary inversion) 435, 436–40
Saito, Mamoru 266–8, 270, 278–80, 512
saltation 448–50
Salvati, Sylvain 681
Samuels, B. D. 380
Sandler, W. 453, 454
Sapir, Edward 285, 353

Saussurean signs 452, 526, 532
scalar implicatures 311
Schoorlemmer, Maaike 312, 339
'scopal' approach 108, 120–4, 125–6
scope ambiguity 269–70
scrambling: and basic word order 264, 265–70; and dependency grammar 617–20; defining 264–5; empirical puzzles 278–80; and free word order 265; and GB theory 264; and minimalism 264; and Move-α 264–5; and nature of syntactic movement 270–2; and optional movement 264, 273; syntactic properties of 265, 275–8; triggering 265, 273–5; and *wh*-phrases 270–2, 274
Seki, Hiroyuki 684
Selkirk, E. 369–70, 376–8
semantic approach/perspectives: and adjectives 89–90, 95, 96–8; and adverbs 108–9, 115, 117, 119–24; and argument structure 24–6, 28–30, 32, 36; and binding theory 222–3, 227–9; and Categorial Grammar 670–2, 673, 675, 685–8; and CED 179–80; and dependency grammar 610–11; and ellipsis 193, 201–2; and functional categories 48–9, 57, 58, 60; and functional structure 71–5, 78–9; and HPSG 544–6; and noun incorporation 284–5, 287–8; and RRG 579–80, 584–6, 591, 593–4, 595–9; and scrambling 270–2; and syntax–lexicon interface 323, 325–8, 332, 334–5, 339; *see also* syntax–semantics/pragmatics interface
Semantic Coherence Principle 649
semantic compositionality 446–7
Semantics Principle 544–6
'sentence superiority' effect 411–13
separationism approach (adjective use) 90, 91
Shakespeare, William 400
Shan, Chung-Chieh 687
shift constructions 652
Shih, C. 93, 98
short extraction structures 199–200
short-term forgetting 409, 419–21
Siegel, M. 98
sign language 452–3, 455, 457, 458–9
Siloni, Tal 329, 335, 340
Simpson, Jane 568, 569
Single Event Condition 180
singulary transformations 7
Situation Semantics 544
SLH (Strict Layer Hypothesis) 367–8, 369, 371, 375
sluice stripping 203–5
sluicing 193–6, 197–8, 199, 203–4
SOs (syntactic objects) 11–13, 15–16, 18–19
speaker-oriented adverbs 110–11, 122
Speas, M. 290, 291
Spec-head relations 10, 14, 17, 158

Spell-Out 95–6, 141, 313, 372–4, 378, 380, 481–2
Spencer, Andrew 29, 359
Split Morphology Hypothesis 351–2, 356
Split VP Hypothesis 157
Sproat, R. 93, 98
Sprouting 202
Stabler, Edward 681, 684
Standard Theory 133–4, 308, 313, 468–9, 472–5
Starke, M. 55, 57
Starosta, S. 606
'statue readings' 229–30
'steady-state' encoding 410
Steedman, Mark 675–6
Steinbach, Markus 312
stem allomorphy 352–3
Stepanov, Artur 180
Stjepanovic, S. 141
Storage Frames 657–9
Stowell, Tim 10, 45–6, 514
stripping 196–8, 203–5
Stromswold, K. 436–7, 438
Strong Lexicalism 346, 348, 352–6
Strong Minimalist Thesis 512, 513
structural mismatch 193, 198
SU (structural uniformity) 471–2, 474
subject-oriented adverbs 110–11
sublexical co-reference 360
Subset Principle 403
substitution 138–9, 676
successive-cyclic movement 176–7, 179
'superiority effect' 518
Surface Structure 308, 313
Svenonius, Peter 96, 101, 310
Swiping 202
syntactic change: and cross-linguistic variation 391–2, 397–8, 399; dynamical-systems approach 394–5; examples of 395–402; and grammaticalisation 396–8; and P&P framework 391–2, 402; parameter hierarchies/change 402–4; and study of historical syntax 404–5; and UG 391–5, 397, 401–2; and verb movement 400–1; and word-order change 398–400
syntactic displacement 456–7
syntactic perspective (in argument structure) 24–33, 36
Syntactic Structures (book) 346, 465, 467, 468
syntax–lexicon interface: and argument structure 323, 329–41; cross-linguistic variation 331–2, 338–41; defining the lexicon 322–3; and external arguments 333–7; and Theta Criterion 329–31; and theta-roles 324–9
syntax–phonology interface: cross-linguistic variation 366, 368–9, 371–2, 374, 380–1; and End-based Theory 369–70; and Generalized Alignment Theory 370–2; and minimalism 372–4, 379–82; and prosodic domains

365–6, 368–9, 372–4, 380–2; and Prosodic Hierarchy Theory 367–8, 375–9; and Relation-based Theory 368–9; research into 365–6; and SLH 367–8, 369, 371, 375; standard theories of 366–70
syntax–semantics/pragmatics interface: future research directions 18–19, 318; interface issues 307–13; and linearization 16; models of 313–17
Szabolcsi, Anna 676–7, 686

Tagalog (language) 173
Takahashi, Diako 77, 179, 271–2, 274–5
Takano, Yuji 17, 269–70
Tenny, Carol 311
Tesnière, Lucien 604, 605, 615
The English Noun Phrase in its Sentential Aspect (thesis) 46
thematic proto-roles 26–8
Theta Criterion 25, 35, 309, 329–31, 510–11, 566
theta-roles: and argument structure 329–41; and syntax–lexicon interface 324–9
Theta System 328–9, 332
Theta Theory 25, 26–7, 35, 309
third-factor principles 19, 20
Thompson, S. A. 399
time-related adverbs 112–13
Tomasello, M. 433–4
topicalization 4
Toyoshima, T. 140
traces 475
transformational grammar 3–4, 6–7, 42, 346–7, 349
transformational rules 5–8, 11
transitivity 77, 586–7
Transparency principle (in Functional Discourse Grammar) 634–6
Travis, Lisa 55, 83–4, 146
'tripartite' case systems 152
Truckenbrodt, Hubert 371
Truswell, Robert 179, 180
type assignment 310–11
type-raising (in Categorial Grammar) 675–6, 678–9

UG (Universal Grammar): and acquisition of syntax 427–8; and adverbs 108, 117, 119; and comparative syntax 493, 495–6, 497; and contemporary linguistic research 4; and control 239; dynamical-systems approach 394–5; and generative grammar 391–2; and grammaticalisation 397; and LA 15; and language acquisition 8, 10; and Merge theory 11; and nonconfigurationality 298; and P&P framework 391–2; and PLD 393, 397, 401–2, 403; and poverty of the stimulus 393–4
unaccusative verbs 31–3

unaccusativity 310–11
unergative verbs 31–3
uniformity 471–2
Uniformity of Theta Assignment Hypothesis 286, 339
Uniformity Principle 493–4, 495
universal endocentricity 19–20
universal tendencies 496–7
unrestricted universals 497
Uriagereka, Juan 372, 512

valence 536–8
Van Benthem, Johan 684–5
Van de Velde, Freek 643–4
Van der Meulen, A. C. 145, 146
Van Dyke, J. 419
Van Geenhoven, V. 288
Van Lier, Eva 642
Van Riemsdijk, H. 233
Van Urk, Coppe 179
Van Valin, R. D. 579, 580, 582, 590, 598
Vanden Wyngaerd, G. 230
variable binding 219–21, 223
Vasishth, S. 419
Vendler, Z. 584
'verb island hypothesis' 433–4
verbatim recall 409, 413–16
verb-class-specific constructions 663–4
verb-oriented/modifying adverbs 109, 112, 114–15, 121
Vergnaud, Jean-Roger 153, 512, 516, 517, 519
Verkuyl, Henk 309
Vogel, I. 365, 368–9, 382
voice mismatch 200–1
von Erfurt, Thomas 605
VPE (VP-ellipsis) 193, 200–1

Wagers, M. 418–19
Warlpiri (language) 288–9, 290, 291, 292, 557–61, 567–72
Wasow, T. 475
Waste-Prevention Frames 657–9
Watanabe, Akira 172
Watergate scandal 413
Weak Lexicalism 346, 348, 349–52
weak minimalist thesis 512
Weight Theory 121
Weinberg, Amy 513
WFRs (word-formation rules) 347–8
wh-dependencies 420–1
Whitman, John 208
wh-phrases: and A-bar movement 170–8, 181, 183; and ellipsis 193–5, 196; and scrambling 270–2, 274
wh-questions 170, 173, 435–41, 459, 469–71, 474, 598–9
Wilder, C. 98

Williams, Edwin 233, 287, 322–3, 333, 334, 339, 351, 352, 355, 358
Willim, Ewa 76
Wilson, Deirdre 317
Wolvengrey, Arok E. 644
Word-based Hypothesis 348, 354
'wrap' rules 682–3, 688

X'-Theory 45–6, 60, 66–7, 69, 474, 475–8
X-Bar Theory: future research directions 19; and head movement 134, 135, 139, 140; and labeling by projection 10; and linearization 16–17; and Merge theory 13; and minimalism 514–16; and phrase-markers 9; and PSRs 8–10; and Spec-head relations 10; and syntax–phonology interface 369–70

Yoshida, Masaya 199, 203, 207

Zanuttini, Raffaella 312
Zwicky, A. 613

Made in the USA
Las Vegas, NV
18 December 2021

38694830R00402